Zeynep Sonbeler

FINANCIAL

As one of our valued rental customers, you're already familiar with the top-notch level of vehicles and service Enterprise gives you. Did you know that Enterprise Car Sales could also offer you the same level of quality and service with your next car purchase?

Our friendly staff understands how important a used vehicle purchase can be and will help make your next vehicle purchase more convenient and enjoyable than you ever imagined. At Enterprise Car Sales, you'll get the service you want and deserve. That means shopping a wide selection of the best hand-picked cars, without the pressures of negotiating. And, when you find that perfect vehicle, we'll go above and beyond to make sure that you're completely satisfied. It's a car-buying experience so unique, Enterprise Car Sales customers couldn't be happier with their purchase.

The Perfect Used Car Package – The way buying a used vehicle should be.

Haggle-Free Buying

- **One-Price System** – Fair and competitive no-haggle pricing was pioneered by Enterprise 40 years ago.
- **Vehicle Certification** – Rigorous testing with ASE-certified inspections ensures a worry-free vehicle for you.
- **Trade-Ins and Financing** – We can accommodate and assist you with your trade-in.

Worry-Free Ownership

FINANCIAL ACCOUNTING A·N·D REPORTING

Second Edition

Mark E. Haskins
University of Virginia

Kenneth R. Ferris
Thunderbird, American Graduate School of International Management

Robert J. Sack
University of Virginia

Brandt R. Allen
University of Virginia

IRWIN
Chicago ■ Bogotá ■ Boston ■ Buenos Aires ■ Caracas
London ■ Madrid ■ Mexico City ■ Sydney ■ Toronto

Irwin Book Team

Publisher: Michael W. Junior
Associate editor, Accounting: George Werthman
Developmental assistant: Kelly Lee
Editorial coordinator: Martin Quinn
Marketing manager: Heather L. Woods
Project editor: Karen J. Nelson
Production supervisor: Pat Frederickson
Interior designer: Michael Warrell
Cover designer: Stuart Patterson, Image House Design
Cover photo: Peter Dazely, Tony Stone Images
Prepress buyer: Charlene R. Perez
Compositor: Shepard Poorman Communications Corporation
Typeface: 10/12 Times Roman
Printer: Von Hoffmann Press, Inc.

Times Mirror
Higher Education Group

Library of Congress Cataloging-in-Publication Data

Financial accounting and reporting / Mark E. Haskins . . . [et al.]. —
2nd ed.
p. cm.
Includes index.
ISBN 0-256-16713-3
1. Financial statements. 2. Corporations — Accounting.
I. Haskins, Mark E.
HF5681.B2F456 1997
657'.3 — dc20 96-3743

Printed in the United States of America
1 2 3 4 5 6 7 8 9 0 VH 3 2 1 0 9 8 7 6

To our students, who have sought to know more
and in doing so have challenged us to find
better ways to teach.

ABOUT THE AUTHORS

Mark E. Haskins Mr. Haskins is Professor of Business Administration at the Darden Graduate School of Business Administration at the University of Virginia. He received his Bachelor of Business Administration from the University of Cincinnati and his Master of Business Administration from Ohio University. He received his Doctor of Philosophy in Accounting from Pennsylvania State University.

Mr. Haskins has worked as an auditor for the international accounting firm Arthur Young & Co. He has provided executive education programs for a number of major U.S. corporations domestically and abroad.

Mr. Haskins is coauthor of two other Irwin texts titled *Corporate Financial Reporting: Text and Cases*, by Brownlee, Ferris, and Haskins, and *International Financial Reporting and Analysis: A Contextual Emphasis*, by Haskins, Ferris, and Selling.

Kenneth R. Ferris Kenneth R. Ferris is a Distinguished Professor of World Business at the American Graduate School of International Management (Glendale, Arizona). He received a B.B.A. and an M.B.A. from George Washington University and earned an M.A. and a Ph.D. from Ohio State University. He previously served on the faculties of Northwestern University and Southern Methodist University and has taught at numerous academic institutions in Australia, Japan, and New Zealand. Professor Ferris is the author of *Financial Accounting* and *Corporate Reporting: A Casebook* and is also a co-author of *Corporate Financial Reporting* by Brownlee, Ferris, and Haskins, and *International Financial Reporting and Analysis: A Contextual Emphasis*, by Haskins, Ferris, and Selling, all published by Irwin.

Robert J. Sack Mr. Sack is a Professor of Business Administration at the Darden School, the University of Virginia. He joined the Darden School after three years as the chief accountant of the SEC's Enforcement Division and 25 years in public practice as a partner of Touche Ross & Co. where he held a number of positions, including those of National Director of Accounting and Auditing Practice and Director of Professional Standards for Touche Ross International. Mr. Sack is a graduate of Miami University (Ohio).

Mr. Sack has written extensively on the subject of ethics in accounting. For three years he served as managing co-editor of *Accounting Horizons*.

Brandt R. Allen Brandt R. Allen is the James C. Wheat Professor of Business Administration and Associate Dean for International Affairs at the Darden Graduate Business School, University of Virginia. Before joining the Virginia faculty in 1970, he taught at the Harvard Business School and before that he was a research engineer with the Boeing Company.

He is a well-known author, consultant, and lecturer in both the United States and Europe on the subject of information systems management. His current research focus is on how companies formulate and implement information systems strategy. He is a member of the Conference Board's Council of Information Management Executives. Professor Allen holds a B.S. in mathematics, an M.B.A. from the University of Washington, and a doctorate from Harvard University in control and information systems.

PREFACE

STATEMENT OF PURPOSE

In a past issue of the *Saturday Review*, an article titled "18,000,000 Books Nobody Reads" cited corporate annual reports as very low in interest, clarity, and understandability. This text's primary objective is, to a large extent, to confront this problem by developing future business leaders' financial statement literacy and to do so in a way that incorporates the abilities to (1) understand the nature of business transactions, (2) identify relevant economic events for reporting, (3) determine the most appropriate financial measures for those events, and (4) analyze the effects of those events in firm performance and financial condition. To this end, an underlying theme of the text is that accounting is not divorced from the world it describes or from the behaviors it measures and influences.

Philosophically, we believe that an introductory accounting text, whether used at the undergraduate or MBA level, does not need to explore every nuance of accounting practice and thought. Rather, the most important and predominant contemporary and classical accounting conventions are our foci. In this regard, the goal is to expose and discuss the underlying rationales of those practices and evaluate their effectiveness in providing useful information for decision making. Foremost among the practices investigated are those that purport to portray corporate financial position, operating results, cash flows, manager performance, and financial strength.

Even though the rule orientation of accounting practice cannot be ignored, both the classroom and the boardroom are appropriate places for questioning and debating those rules and conventions. Such scrutiny is crucial because it is important for students to develop an understanding of the management choices that must be made regarding what information to report, how best to report it, when to do so, and where controls are needed to assure reliable and relevant reporting. A critical aspect of these choices, dealt with in this text, is a concern for (1) the characteristics of information that make it most useful for decision making; (2) the characteristics of decision makers that also influence the usefulness of information; and (3) the subsequent behavior of managers, subordinates, and external constituencies that can be expected as a result of implementing certain reporting choices.

There are two reasons for our management/user approach. First, it allows us to deal comprehensively with a complex topic. Second, it helps the student retain a focus on concepts and ideas rather than on procedures. This approach requires considerable discipline on the part of the student, to mentally delegate his or her time to an understanding of business issues and a mastery of the basic financial reporting concepts without becoming too preoccupied with accounting mechanics. Thus, this text is designed primarily for those courses and student groups where the focus is on a balance between the understanding and use of accounting information and its preparation. Provided with a backdrop of contemporary management and financial concerns, students will see that accounting is a significant part of the world it purports to portray rather than an end in itself. On the contrary, students are provided the perspective that accounting information is a critical instrument in presenting a corporation's financial picture to important external constituencies. The raising of issues and concerns springing from this orientation facilitates a focus on substance and also frames students' learning because they have the comfort of a more familiar general business context for thinking about the accounting issue at hand.

KEY FEATURES

Real world based. The authors view accounting as an integral part of corporate decision making and financial analysis. Thus, accounting is not an end but a means to achieving relevant and reliable insights about business conditions, results, and opportunities. Like the first edition, the second edition repeatedly grounds the discussion of accounting issues and methods in contexts of management decision making, financial analysis, management judgments and estimates, behavioral consequences, and/or the political arena, whichever context is most germane. Such an approach poses accounting as a vital, dynamic phenomenon rather than a sterile, procedural set of mechanics. To this end, the text contains *nearly 100* excerpts from recent annual reports that serve to highlight the realities of the issue at hand and to exemplify the fact that the financial reporting issues presented are pertinent to the day-to-day information concerns faced by real-world managers, lenders, investors, and financial statement users in general.

Holistic business approach. The book's managerial orientation frequently leverages the discussion of a particular topic via linkages with strategic and other functional area concerns typically encountered by managers. For example, receivables issues involve credit and collection policies in addition to the accounting issues. Inventory topics include operations concerns such as JIT and standard costing. In addition, the second edition discusses the international aspects germane to many of the financial reporting issues covered in the chapters.

Opportunities for student involvement. The end-of-chapter materials provide opportunities for a well-rounded student experience. Discussion questions provide issues for thought and debate where "solutions" are well-reasoned, integrated views as opposed to looking up the chapter paragraph that provides the answer. Problems are structured to provide ample opportunities for polishing one's procedural skills as well as for developing a feel for the differences in results when different methods, assumptions, and/or judgments are invoked. The cases provide real-world settings for exploring the usefulness of accounting information to decision makers who have different perspectives and purposes, come from different environments, and value different outcomes.

Group work and communication skills. Many of the cases lend themselves to group assignments and/or classroom presentation and write-up. Instructors are presented with materials that provide lots of degrees of freedom in this regard.

Ethics and international. Haskins and Sack have been actively engaged in the development and teaching of ethics materials and courses. Such a perspective is imbedded throughout the text. Haskins and Ferris teach international financial reporting courses and provide a chapter dedicated to that topic, a chapter that has also benefited from the many years of international work experience of Sack and Allen.

Key terms. The language involved in financial reporting encompasses many new terms. Each time a new key term is used in the text, it appears in blue type. In addition, a listing of key terms appears at the end of each chapter, and an extensive glossary appears at the end of the text.

Appendixes. In order to provide instructors a number of degrees of freedom regarding the depth with which to explore a topic, many chapters contain appendixes that provide opportunities for exploring a particular topic in a more detailed manner. It is important to note, however, that a comprehensive, powerful course can be constructed without having to use the appendixes.

ORGANIZATION

This text consists of four major parts and is organized not unlike other texts in its basic sequencing. Do not, however, conclude that it is just like other texts. As has already been pointed out, the orientation taken toward topics, the emphasis placed on certain facets of the topics, and the integration with a larger context make this text distinctive.

Part I. These introductory chapters provide the background for the entire text. In particular, the first chapter's presentation of the PepsiCo annual report sets the financial reporting agenda and "creates the need to know." During its discussion, students realize that accounting quickly transcends the necessary but mundane concerns of a green-eye-shaded bookkeeper to encompass those of key managers interested, among other things, in knowing what has been achieved, identifying what remains to be done, monitoring and motivating people better, and efficiently, effectively, and inexpensively raising capital from external sources.

Using generally familiar business contexts, a variety of basic skills are then developed in the remaining Part I chapters. Paramount among the skills developed are (1) the double-entry method of recording transactions; (2) preparation of basic balance sheets and statements of income and owners' equity; (3) familiarity with the language of accounting; and (4) an understanding of some of the fundamental concepts of accounting (e.g., accrual vs. cash, matching, historical costs, materiality) and of the process by which accounting standards are set.

The objective of these three chapters is for students to become comfortable defining a users' information needs, report the most pertinent information in the most useful way, interpret the story reflected by the information, identify the key assumptions underlying the information being reported, and consider the alternative interpretations that would arise with certain changes in some of the key assumptions. Establishing such a dialectical process at a text's outset is important because students must continually consider such an array of issues in order to appreciate and understand the evolutionary nature of contemporary accounting practice.

Part II. The four chapters in this section of the text introduce in more detail the three basic financial statements — the balance sheet, income statement, and statement of cash flows — and provide students with some classical financial analysis tools. All four chapters draw heavily on the concepts, language, and concerns raised in Part I. Moreover, all four chapters integrate the PepsiCo annual report presented in Chapter 1 into their discussions as well as utilizing other corporate annual report examples.

An explicit premise running through these chapters is that management has a great deal of influence over the results presented. That is, the financial statements are discussed in such a way as to highlight the fact that they are a part of management's thinking as they make decisions throughout the years. We believe such an orientation not only is valid but also ascribes a great deal of vitality to the statements: They are not merely a sterile codification of numerous transactions whose total implications and results are not known until year-end.

The purpose of dealing so intensely with these financial statements and their analysis at this point in the text is that subsequent chapter topics can then be discussed and debated as to their impact on the three financial statements. Such an objective parallels the manager concerns raised in the chapters and poses very effective learning opportunities for students' recognition of both the key accounting *and* managerial concerns.

Part III. The chapters in this part are centered on the theme of measuring, reporting, interpreting, and using financial information pertaining to assets, liabilities, and owners' equity. In these chapters students really begin to see clearly and powerfully that accounting simply describes events and circumstances, and those descriptions are a joint product of certain official guidelines, and, more importantly, of the assumptions, actions, and judgments of managers. These chapters consider the financial reporting issues surrounding some of the daily and strategic concerns of managing assets, liabilities, and owners' equity. Moreover, they explore the tension between reporting the "most favorable" versus the "most realistic" picture.

As an example, the text and some of the end-of-chapter materials pertaining to marketable securities bring to light the issues of (1) distinguishing the relative merits of reporting historical costs versus current market values and (2) dealing with the prescriptive nature of FASB rules. Both issues underlie much of financial reporting. In particular, the first issue is often viewed by the uninformed as a shortcoming of financial reporting. We believe students should be sensitive to the pros and cons of reporting costs *and* current values and should be able to identify situations where one or the other may be more appropriate. In regard to the second issue, students become acutely aware of the volatility that is possible in reported earnings if how things are to be reported is simply left to the discretion of management. They thus realize a need for constraining the discretion available to managers in reporting their companies' financial position and results of operations. This is not to say that the need for management judgments and the consequences of such decisions become less important; on the contrary, a thorough knowledge of official guidelines (constraints) is merely an important prerequisite to identifying viable reporting options, structuring business transactions compatibly with the most desirable ways of reporting them, and factoring into one's decisions the information needs of the interested constituencies.

Besides grounding an accounting issue in the context of a business decision or users' information needs, the chapters also leverage students' understanding of other topics to help in their learning of particular financial reporting topics that may be new to them. For example, anticipating the potentially overwhelming nature of the bonds, leases, and pension topics, the text builds on a thread common to all three topics and familiar to most business students at this point in their education — the present value of a stream of future cash flows. As each of these three topics is introduced via this touchstone, the awesomeness of dealing with the technical aspects of their financial reporting requirements fades. In fact, for most students, the literacy threshold for these three topics, which at the outset seems unachievably distant, becomes reachable with the use of the present value perspective building block already familiar and mastered by most.

Part IV. This final section of the book provides students with an opportunity to consider some of the specific challenges involved in understanding the financial reporting practices of non-U.S. companies as well as some of the nuances inherent in communicating the more qualitative aspects of a company's financial well-being. To these ends, Chapter 15 provides a brief overview of the financial reporting environment and practices in two other countries — Japan and the United Kingdom. This chapter contains recent annual reports from Kawasaki Steel Corporation and Rolls-Royce Plc. We view this chapter as integral to a first course in financial reporting because it provides one more opportunity for students to digest the details of an annual report and to then articulate (1) their understanding of the company, (2) the key accounting conventions used, and (3) how those conventions might have been different for that particular company and how they differ, if at all, from U.S.-based practices. Pedagogically, stark contrasts in settings (i.e., foreign versus U.S.) are used to highlight the financial reporting concerns that transcend borders and those that do not. The PepsiCo annual report can also be revisited to provide a basis for review and compare/contrast with the Kawasaki and Rolls-Royce reports.

The final chapter focuses on some of the interesting challenges and opportunities chief financial officers are likely to encounter as they seek to provide the financial markets with the disclosures that are perceived to be of vital importance in portraying the real depth and breadth of a company's financial health and prospects. Many of the issues are outside the purview of current GAAP but are in many ways tied to efforts to complement, enhance, or clarify the presently required GAAP disclosures.

SUPPLEMENTAL MATERIALS

An *Instructor's Manual* is available to accompany the text. The manual provides "solutions" and suggestions for class discussion. In addition, the manual provides several possible course outlines with pertinent assignments.

Two other supplements are available. Some instructors may find the companion *Test Bank,* both printed and computerized, a useful resource. Finally, PowerPoint software, called *ReadyShows,* has been created to facilitate classroom lectures; the software provides instructors with an interactive alternative to traditional teaching transparencies. For a small fee, students may purchase a printed notebook (called *ReadyNotes*) that follows the PowerPoint presentations to help them in their notetaking.

ACKNOWLEDGMENTS

We gratefully acknowledge the following individuals for the helpful insights they provided us:

Professor Paul K. Chaney
Vanderbilt University

Professor Roger H. Chope
University of Oregon

Professor Richard G. File
University of Nebraska

Professor Albert A. Schepanski
University of Iowa

Professor Philip M. J. Reckers
Arizona State University

Professor Peter Wilson
Duke University

Professor Marshall K. Pittman
University of Texas/San Antonio

Professor Joseph H. Bylinski
University of North Carolina

Professor Dennis Murray
University of Colorado

Professor Janet I. Kimbrell
Oklahoma State University

Professor Robert Kneckel
University of Florida.

Over the years we have benefitted from the ideas and contributions of our colleagues E. R. Brownlee II, C. Ray Smith, and numerous research assistants. Their help has been invaluable. Invaluable too has been the help of several people at Irwin — Karen Nelson, Michael Warrell, George Werthman, and Martin Quinn. Their support has been indispensable.

Mark E. Haskins
Kenneth R. Ferris
Robert J. Sack
Brandt R. Allen

CONTENTS IN BRIEF

PART I

Overview of Financial Statements 1

PART II

Using and Understanding the Basic Financial Statements 153

PART III

Measuring and Reporting Assets and Equities Using Generally Accepted Accounting Principles 355

PART IV

Special Considerations in Preparing and Using Accounting Data 733

CONTENTS

PART II

Using and Understanding the Basic Financial Statements 153

CHAPTER 4

The Balance Sheet 154

CHAPTER 5

The Income Statement 205

CHAPTER 6

The Statement of Cash Flows 262

CHAPTER 10

Active Investments and Business Combinations 442

CHAPTER 11

Noncurrent Assets: Fixed Assets, Intangible Assets, and Natural Resources 491

CHAPTER 12

Accounting for Liabilities: Basic Concepts, Payables, Accruals, and Interest-Bearing Debt 544

CHAPTER 13

Leases, Retirement Benefits, and Deferred Income Taxes 600

CHAPTER 14

Owners' Equity 676

PART IV

Special Considerations in Preparing and Using Accounting Data 733

CHAPTER 15

Financial Reporting in Two Other Countries 734

CHAPTER 16

Communicating Corporate Value 826

Glossary G1

Index I1

PART I

Overview of Accounting and Financial Statements

CHAPTER 1

Accounting as the Language of Business

Accounting is a language that people within a firm can use to discuss its projects and progress with one another, and that they can use to tell outsiders what's happening in the firm without giving too many of its secrets to competitors. . . . Natural languages develop grammar and vocabulary without the intervention of standard-setting bodies (with few exceptions, like French). Artificial languages like computer programming languages and the language of accounting seem to benefit from official standards. Standards can be effective even when they are not mandatory: People usually follow a standard because it reduces the cost of communicating with others.[1]

Key Chapter Issues

- Just what is accounting? Is it numbers? Is it words? Is it some combination of the two? When the president of a company reports to shareholders, what is the role of the accounting language and what part of the report is ordinary business language?
- The idea that accounting is a language suggests an art form rather than a science. What implications does that perspective suggest for management?
- What is the difference between an internal management accounting system and an external financial reporting system?
- Accounting communicates information to help people make decisions. What kinds of decisions are at issue?
- What is GAAP? Why is it important? Where does it come from?

[1]F. Black, "Choosing Accounting Rules," *Accounting Horizons,* December 1993, p. 1.

Accounting is a language used by businesspeople to communicate the financial health of their enterprise. Like any language, accounting adheres to certain conventions and concepts that users of financial statements must understand to appreciate the story being told. The primary objective of this book is to help you understand those concepts and conventions and consequently become literate and conversant in the language of accounting.

ACCOUNTING AS A LANGUAGE

Businesspeople use accounting to communicate the results of their company's operations to interested stakeholders both inside and outside the company. It is not enough for a manager to say, at the end of a particular quarter, "We did pretty well." Everyone who has an interest in the company — the management team, the employees, the creditors, the stockholders — will ask for more concrete information. They will want to know, "How were sales? Did margins hold up? What was the bottom line?" Answering such questions requires the use of the language of accounting.

It is important that we explain right at the outset what we mean when we use the word **accounting.** When we talk about accounting, as in the sentence "Accounting is the language of business," we mean the numbers that measure the results of the business *and* the explanatory text that provides perspective on the numbers. For example, it may be important to know that sales for the quarter just ended were $653,908, but it is more useful to also know that sales in the same quarter last year were $632,685 and that the increase in sales was due to a 6 percent increase in unit prices offset by a 3 percent decrease in unit volume. Accounting reports typically include raw data (sales for the current quarter), comparative data (sales during a preceding period, or budgeted sales), and explanatory text (**footnotes** or similar commentary). The amount of accounting information — and the mix of data and text — to be included in an accounting report will depend on the kinds of decisions to be made by the users of the report. Accounting information is not generated for its own sake: The cost of an accounting and reporting system is justified only when the reports help people make better decisions.

People inside and outside the company have decisions to make. Senior managers use accounting information to evaluate the operations of the company and its people and to make decisions about the company. The decisions addressed range from the longest term to the most immediate, including concerns about the company's strategic direction (which business units offer the most potential), resource allocation (which products warrant more advertising dollars), and compensation (which employee teams deserve a fiscal pat on the back). But operating managers use accounting information also: to articulate their business plans (if we can increase market penetration by 3 percent we will need $1,500,000 in additional capital) and to identify emerging opportunities and problems that need attention and action (overhead costs for May were $45,000 over plan even though production was right on plan).

People outside the company also have decisions to make, and managers use accounting information to communicate with a variety of interested external stakeholders, including the following:

- Stockholders, who will decide whether to keep their stock or sell it; and, if they keep it, whether they will vote for incumbent management. Obviously, accounting information is also of interest to potential stockholders, who will decide whether to buy the stock and, if so, at what price.

- Creditors and suppliers, who will decide whether to extend credit and, if they decide to extend credit, the interest rate they will charge.
- Employees and unions, who will evaluate the company's performance as they consider whether they can argue for increased wages and benefits.

As you reflect on this notion of accounting as a medium of communication that provides information to people to help them make decisions, let us direct your thoughts to several implications for managers that flow from that understanding:

1. The complexity and sophistication of the accounting used will vary directly with the nature of the audience addressed. In the same way that couples married for a long time develop a shorthand way of talking to each other, two people operating a partnership can get along quite nicely with a rudimentary accounting system. To manage the company they will need key data on operations, but they will be so close to the business that little interpretive text will be necessary. When their business grows to the point that they need outside financing from a bank or a group of stockholders, the managers will find that those outsiders expect a fairly complete accounting for their investment. Going much further, a multinational company with complex internal operations and a wide range of outside stakeholders will find it necessary to maintain a very comprehensive accounting system to satisfy the needs of the company's diverse constituency. The cost of that increasingly complex accounting and reporting system is part of the price a company pays as it grows in the larger business community.
2. Users of accounting information are interested in both the company's past performance and its future prospects. For example, stockholders want to know what management did with the resources they have been given: Were those resources employed profitably, and have they been preserved? But stockholders also want to know what the company is likely to do in the future: Will the company's earnings increase enough to justify an increase in the stock price? Because of user needs for **stewardship information** and for **prospective information,** accounting tries to communicate both the past and the future. The difficulty inherent in that dual duty complicates the language of accounting. Assume that a company purchased a piece of property when it began operations 25 years ago. Should the accounting reports show that property at its original purchase price to demonstrate that management has maintained that original asset for the benefit of the owners? Or should the accounting reports show the property at its current market value so as to indicate the future cash flows the company might earn from the property? Today's accounting conventions in the U.S., for example report assets at their historic cost as an acknowledgment of the importance of management's stewardship function. However, there is continued pressure in the financial community to provide more future-oriented information. Managers understand that readers of a financial report use that report to measure their stewardship, but they also understand that readers use the reported results from the past periods as the base point for projections about the future of the company. The fact that both of those expectations must be met explains much of the complexity of current financial reporting.
3. Businesspeople spend a large part of their working day talking or writing about the business. Some part of that communication is in the form of accounting, and some is in the form of a more generalized business vocabulary. There really isn't any clear dividing line between accounting-as-a-language and the larger business communication system, and it probably isn't important that the dividing line is

illusive. It is enough to acknowledge that accounting is a specialized segment of the overall business vocabulary — a specialized segment that has evolved to help businesspeople communicate their companies' financial results.

4. As in any language, the symbols of accounting carry meaning from one person to another only because those people agree on the meaning of the symbols. The symbols and their meaning change over time, when all parties in the communication process agree that the changes make sense. Some of those changes come from usage, as they do with normal language. Unlike public speech, however, the accounting language has several authorities who worry about its effectiveness and have the power to police it and to amend it when necessary. To use the accounting language effectively, all parties to the communication process need to understand the basic conventions and symbols and to stay current as the language evolves. Users of financial reports, such as bankers or stockholders, are interested in the published company information they receive and generally prefer more rather than less financial data from companies. Corporate managers carry the primary burden of telling the company's story. To tell that story most effectively, managers must know how to make the best use of the available accounting conventions and, where necessary, develop supplemental communication techniques.
5. Finally, managers often have a vested interest in the decisions that will be made regarding their company. That vested interest has the potential to be a conflict of interest when the decisions turn on the financial story presented by the managers. Every manager has an ethical obligation to be alert to the potential for a conflict of interest and to use accounting in such a way as to describe business results objectively and fairly — regardless of the effect that fair presentation may have on his or her personal well-being.

No language created by humanity has ever been able to claim perfect communication effectiveness. In the following chapters we will focus on the ways accounting is used in the business world, but we will also try to identify the areas in which accounting conventions remain inadequate.

GENERALLY ACCEPTED ACCOUNTING PRINCIPLES

For intracompany communications, managers can, and usually do, establish accounting rules and conventions to use solely in the company's *internal* reporting system. As a consequence, the reports produced by the internal reporting system can be tailored to the specific informational needs of individual managers. For example, a production manager might need accounting information about the number and cost of units in production, and a sales manager might need information focusing on the selling price and quantities available for sale. Thus the internal reporting system may produce a diverse set of accounting reports, each prepared to satisfy a particular informational need of its internal user. The rules and conventions that guide the internal reporting system can be designed by the managers themselves to suit their specific informational needs. This internal reporting system is commonly called **managerial accounting.**

Although internal accounting reports may vary between companies, *external* accounting reports are more standardized. Because external reports are distributed to a diverse user group, with no naturally common frame of reference, it would be very difficult for the managers of any one company to establish, on their own, a set of reporting conventions for that company's external reports that would automatically ensure understanding by all of those users. It could be argued that the users ought to make the effort to understand each company's individualized accounting approach. The managers could argue that their company is unique and, therefore, they ought to be able to develop an approach to accounting and reporting that is best suited to their circumstances. That approach would require individual users to spend the time to understand the company, its industry, *and* its accounting. The financial community has concluded that it is better for society as a whole if we have one approach to external accounting that all users can understand reasonably well, even if that means that some reporting companies have to alter their preferred approach to fit into the common mold. Although some unique "dialects" are used in highly specialized industries, by and large, external financial reporting adheres to a common body of communication practices mutually accepted and established by the financial community. The rules and conventions that guide the public communication of financial results are referred to as **generally accepted accounting principles** or **GAAP,** and the process is commonly called **financial accounting.**

Most of us encounter financial accounting in the annual and quarterly reports that companies distribute to their external constituencies. Some of those public reports provide a great deal of company-specific information, while others are comparatively Spartan. However, all public financial reports provide a set of accounting-based **financial statements** and the related explanatory text, and that financial presentation is of interest to us in this text.

Companies say that their financial statements (and the supporting text) are "prepared in accordance with generally accepted accounting principles" or GAAP. This means that the financial statements meet the standards that the larger community has come to expect for such financial reports. But compliance with GAAP goes beyond meeting a generalized expectation; it also means that the statements meet the requirements of the law. The federal securities laws in the U.S., for example, specify that every company that has publicly traded debt or equity must provide financial reports, on a regular basis, to the securities holders, and the courts have determined that those financial reports must be presented in accordance with GAAP. Because of the pervasiveness and the power of the securities marketplace, the GAAP standard that applies to public companies has also become the standard for privately owned companies that issue financial statements to outside parties.

But what is this thing called GAAP? A formal definition describes it as

> a technical term that encompasses the conventions, rules, and procedures necessary to define accepted accounting practice at a particular time. It includes not only broad guidelines of general application but also detailed practices and procedures. Those conventions, rules and procedures provide a standard by which to measure financial presentations.[2]

GAAP is a collection of broad concepts and narrow practices that are generally accepted at a point in time. Together, those concepts and practices become the benchmark for managers as they prepare their company's financial reports. The understanding that GAAP is composed of practices that have become generally accepted is important because it reminds us that the resultant financial statements are to communi-

[2]*Codification of Statements on Auditing Statements,* Section 411.02, The American Institute of CPAs (New York, New York, 1994).

cate to a diverse, public audience. The notion that the ideas in GAAP are accepted at a point in time is important because it reminds us that GAAP evolves, over time, as new transactions require new accounting thinking. The statement that GAAP is a collection of concepts and practices is important because it will help us see that accounting is not a codified set of rules that can be memorized but is more a body of common law that needs to be studied as a hierarchy. That GAAP hierarchy includes

- Overall concepts that can be adopted. (For example, because the financial markets do not like surprises, financial reporting tends to be conservative.)
- More specific practices that have been established by standard setters and that can be understood in the context of the overall concepts. (For example, even though we expect great things from our research department, the payoff from such efforts has proven to be uncertain, so we have a specific accounting standard that dictates that research expenditures are charged to expense in the period when they are incurred rather than carried forward into a future period as an asset.)
- Generally accepted but unwritten procedures and practices that can be analogized from more formally established standards. (We expect great things from our advertising expenditures, too, but because that payoff is also uncertain those expenditures are also charged to expense when incurred rather than deferred until the expected sales are realized.)

While it is important to emphasize the idea that GAAP is a collection of generally accepted practices, it is also important to point out that a number of organizations work hard at molding GAAP according to the public interest. Three institutions in the United States are in the forefront of the effort to push the development of GAAP:

- Under the direction of Congress, the **Securities and Exchange Commission** (SEC) administers the laws that regulate U.S. securities markets. Because an efficient capital market requires timely and useful information, the SEC also has the responsibility to establish the form and content of the information that companies are to provide to their public constituencies. The SEC has chosen to specify the required general business disclosures (description of business risks and opportunities, details of management compensation, and so on) but, for a number of reasons, has delegated to the private sector the establishment of specific accounting standards.
- The **Financial Accounting Standards Board** (FASB) was established in 1973 as the private sector's most recent effort to respond to the SEC's delegation of its standard-setting authority. The FASB is supported by contributions from the major accounting firms and associations, by large corporations, and by the securities industry. Seven independent expert accountants sit on the board, and their efforts are supported by over 100 staff people. The FASB issues Statements on Financial Accounting, Technical Bulletins, and Interpretations, all of which establish (or document) provisions of GAAP. The topics on the board's agenda typically include long-standing controversies as well as new, emerging issues.
- The **American Institute of Certified Public Accountants** (AICPA) represents the CPAs who work as independent auditors in public accounting firms as well as the CPAs who work as the accounting officers of large and small companies. The AICPA has a number of committees that consider accounting issues and publish position papers. Those position papers stand as part of GAAP, at least

until the FASB is able to consider the subject and issue a more formal, authoritative pronouncement.

In Chapter 2 we will say more about the process of establishing accounting standards and the organizations involved.

The principal focus of this text is financial accounting and the most important provisions of GAAP. It should be noted, however, that most companies maintain multiple reporting systems — an internal system for management communications and an external system for communication with outside constituencies. And because some outside constituencies may have special interests (and the power to demand special responses), a company may actually maintain multiple external reporting systems. For example, a company may use a GAAP reporting system for its shareholders and bankers, a separate system following the Internal Revenue Service Code for its income tax filings, and a third system to present financial information required by applicable regulatory agencies, such as the Office of Thrift Supervision (for savings and loan institutions) or the Federal Energy Regulatory Commission (for public utilities).

The internationalization of our economy has added another dimension to the accounting communications required of most companies. If, for example, a company has debt or equity securities traded on the public exchanges of other countries, it will probably be required to prepare financial reports according to the GAAP rules of those countries as well as in its home country. Each major country has developed its own approach to creating financial accounting standards. Thus, although there is some uniformity, there are also some significant differences in these standards from one country to another. For example, in Germany it has been understood that a company has a larger responsibility to its employees and the community than it does to its stockholders. As a consequence, German accounting standards tend to smooth out the peaks and valleys in income so as to present a longer-term, more stable view of company performance. In the United States the stockholders have a more dominant say in the running of the company, and so U.S. accounting standards require more immediate recognition of business events, resulting in more extreme swings in reported results. Such differences are embedded in each country's GAAP and also in their tax and commercial law.

Participants in the international financial markets, however, have become impatient with philosophic arguments that seek to justify GAAP differences across countries and have insisted that the accounting rules be harmonized. They claim that the nationalistic differences in accounting confuse investors and therefore inhibit the flow of international capital. In response to that pressure, the **International Accounting Standards Committee** (IASC) was created, and of late, has stepped up its efforts to harmonize the diverse practices used around the world. The committee was formed by the accounting professions in the major capitalistic countries but has historically been largely ineffective because each country's committee representative has been inclined to argue in favor of that country's practices. Now, however, the IASC has instituted a major effort to establish, by 1999, a set of GAAP that will be acceptable to securities markets around the world. There is a great deal of enthusiasm for the project, but no one underestimates the philosophical, political, and practical challenges that lie ahead.

Before we leave this introduction to GAAP, one final observation is in order: The flexibility in GAAP is sometimes frustrating to those who expect it to be categorical and rule oriented. It is true that some basic conventions and rules have been established through common usage or pronouncement and must be accepted as they are; however, as with any language, the application of GAAP provides for a surprising amount of latitude in the preparation of financial statements. That flexibility arises as a result of three factors. First, for some transactions, widely diverse accounting approaches had become entrenched as alternative GAAP long before the SEC or the FASB was established, and those equally acceptable alternative approaches remain in the "language." Second, the financial community continues to develop new business transactions, and, until new standards are established, different ways of approaching the accounting for those creative transactions will become accepted in practice. And, third, business transactions are complex and unique, and very often managers will develop different interpretations of broadly written financial reporting standards as they try to apply those generalized standards to their specific circumstances. This flexibility in GAAP means that there may be more than one acceptable answer to a question. Indeed, it provides an exciting challenge for managers to make the best use of the potential power of the accounting language in communicating the essence of the business they have created.

THE FINANCIAL REPORTING PROCESS: AN OVERVIEW

While it is true that GAAP is important to our thinking because it is the standard by which management measures its financial reporting, it is not the end objective of our study in this text. The real objective of our study is the financial reporting process — the process management uses to accumulate all of the business transactions during a period, put a dollar value on them, sort them and evaluate them, and produce a GAAP-based financial report. That process is illustrated in Exhibit 1.1. The process of preparing the financial statements really flows through the center of the diagram, subject to the control of management and the influence of the independent auditor. We can see from this illustration that financial statements are fundamentally a summary of all of a company's business transactions tempered by a wide variety of financial judgments made by management. Those transactions and judgments are in turn subject to a company's **internal control structure,** which assures that all transactions and all necessary judgments have been recognized and that they are classified and correctly described in the company's records. A company's accounting system sorts all of the transactions and judgments into similar or related groupings and then aggregates that input in accounts so that the summarized financial statements can be prepared.

As suggested by the top portion of the diagram, the design and maintenance of the internal control structure and the preparation of financial statements are the direct responsibility of corporate management. The control structure typically includes checks and balances such that no one employee is responsible for all aspects of a transaction or any single aspect of the reporting process. The control structure also includes written policies and procedures for the accounting staff, including such things as diverse as a chart of accounts that sets out which transactions are to be recorded in which accounts, as well as a code of conduct, which helps the accounting people remember that the users of the financial reports expect those reports to be objective and fair. The control structure will also include an internal audit function to monitor the performance of the accounting system and the fairness of the financial reports.

At the culmination of the accounting process, management evaluates the resulting financial statements to be sure that the end result makes good business sense. That financial statement review begins with the financial management team but should also

EXHIBIT 1.1

Overview of the Accounting Communication Process

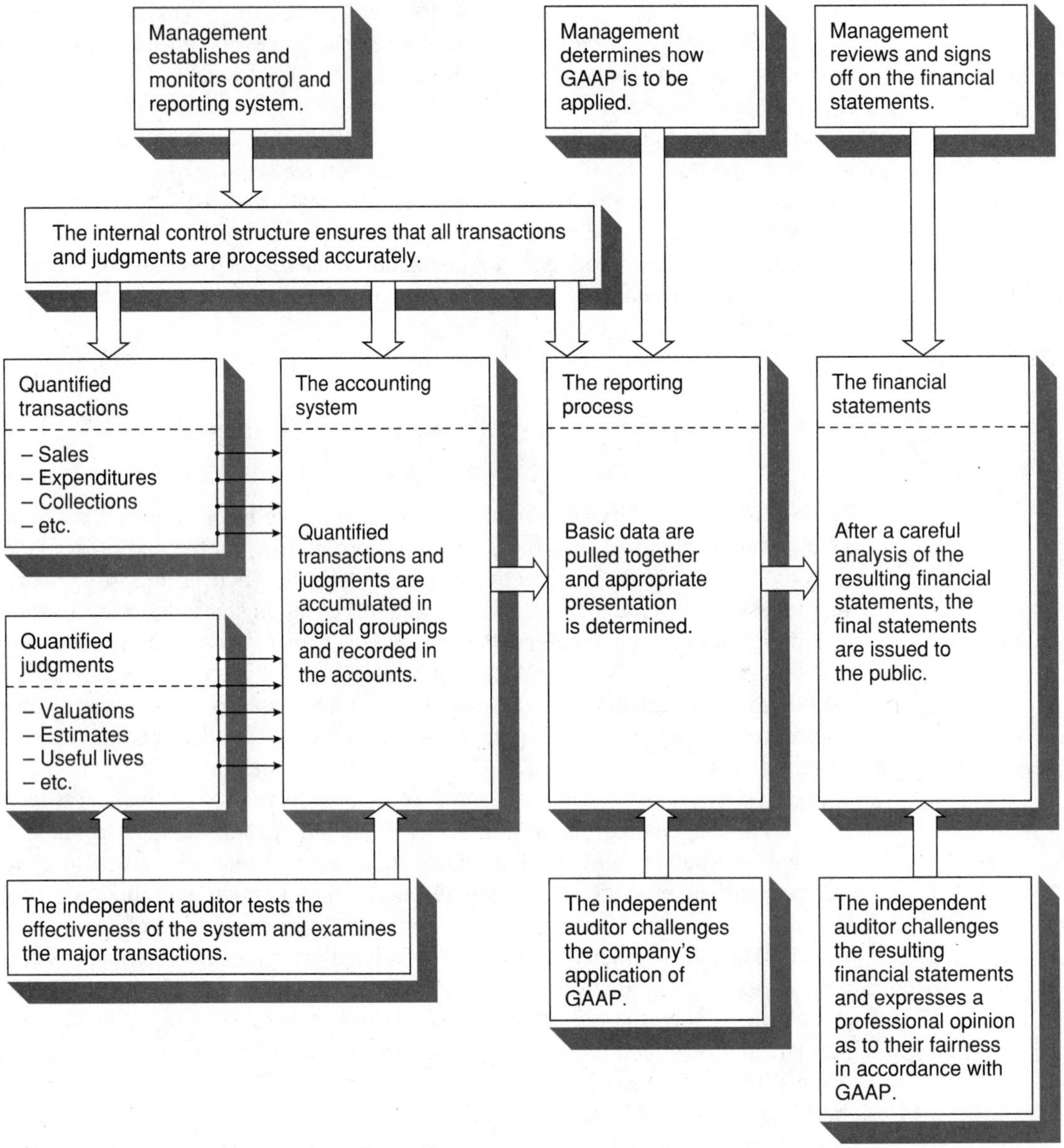

include operating management (because they know the business best) and top management and the board of directors (because they are ultimately responsible to the stockholders and creditors). To emphasize that responsibility, for example, the New York Stock Exchange insists that all of its listed companies include in their annual reports a report from top management and the board of directors, in which they acknowledge their responsibility for the fairness of the company's financial statements and assert their discharge of those responsibilities. As more managements see that responsibility more clearly, the reporting practice is spreading to other companies listed on other exchanges.

Although corporate management is responsible for preparing the financial statements and ensuring their overall fairness, the independent external auditor is responsible for testing the underlying accounting data and expressing an opinion as to the fairness of the resulting financial statements. As we noted earlier, for a number of reasons, management might have a vested interest in the financial picture that the statements portray, and, because of the potential for a serious conflict of interest, the financial community has determined that it is useful to have an independent opinion as to the fairness of those statements. Almost every company, therefore, engages an **independent auditor** to review its financial statements for fairness and consistency with GAAP.

An auditor's examination of a set of financial statements (typically referred to as an **audit**) is conducted according to a set of professional standards referred to as **generally accepted auditing standards** (GAAS). Those standards require the auditor to test the way the system processes routine transactions, to consider the appropriateness of the accounting methods used, and to evaluate the application of GAAP in the company's financial statements. Because an audit relies on test samples of the company's transactions and financial statement accounts, an auditor is typically not held responsible for immaterial errors in the financial statements or for small frauds. But most courts have said that an auditor is responsible for finding material misstatements, whether they result from accounting errors or from management fraud.

Based on their examination, independent auditors issue a report presenting an opinion as to the fairness of the financial statements prepared by management. We will review the content of that report in more detail when we look at the PepsiCo financial statements in the next section of this chapter. The most important element of the auditor's report is the **auditor's opinion.** If all goes well, the auditor expresses the opinion that the financial statements fairly present the company's financial condition and results of operations in accordance with generally accepted accounting principles. Obviously, the financial community expects to see such a positive opinion (sometimes referred to as a *clean opinion*) in every company's financial statements. Occasionally, for one reason or another, an auditor finds it necessary to issue an opinion indicating that the financial statements *do not* fairly present the company's financial condition and results of operations in accordance with GAAP. However, the power of the public's expectations is typically so great that most managers work diligently to avoid a financial reporting dispute with their independent auditors.

PEPSICO, INC. — AN ILLUSTRATION

To focus our discussion, and to illustrate how the ideas we have been discussing are applied in practice, we have included at the end of this chapter the "financial review" section from the 1994 annual report to shareholders issued by PepsiCo, Inc. As do many companies, PepsiCo provides a wide range of information in its annual reports, including an overview of the business by the chairman and detailed discussion of operations by management. That commentary is interesting and important, but we want to narrow our focus and look at the way PepsiCo manages its financial reporting responsibility. With that objective in mind, we have reproduced here only the financial review section of the company's annual report.

PepsiCo's financial review for 1994 includes the following elements:

1. *The management analysis*, which provides insight on the company and comments on the results reported for the year, considering the company as a whole. For example, management comments on the major economic issues facing the company and explains how they manage those issues. They also outline some of the key factors that influenced the changes in reported results from one year to another. All of this discussion is designed to help readers understand the numbers reported in the financial statements that follow.
2. *Business segments*, which take the management analysis down to the level of PepsiCo's three operating segments — beverages, snack foods, and restaurants. In addition to the text, which describes the company's products, and comments on the segment results, management also provides key accounting numbers for the domestic and international operations of the three segments. In a complex company such as PepsiCo, that segment information is very important; it tells us, for example, that total sales have grown 13.6 percent during the last five years, but that the biggest growth has been in snack foods, at 15.5 percent. Perhaps more important, the most profitable segment, as a percentage of sales, is still the beverage business, the slowest-growing segment. Happily, the most profitable in terms of assets employed is the snack food business, although it is interesting that the company has been putting most of its new capital investment in restaurants and beverages. All of that data could be important to you, as a potential investor, because you can use it, together with your own assessment of where the markets might be heading, as you make your own projections for the future of PepsiCo. You will be interested in the historical development presented in these numbers, but you will also want to make an estimate of the company's earnings five years from now. The trends in this segment data can be used as the base point for your projections.
3. *The consolidated statement of income* and its management analysis, which tell us that sales are up 13 percent and that net income is up 12 percent over 1993. Those results are likely to be important to you as a potential investor, especially when you consider that Coca-Cola's sales grew 15.8 percent and its net income grew 17.4 percent in 1994. The detail in the income statement — the various expenses and costs — could help you understand how those results were achieved and what they might mean for the future.
4. *The consolidated balance sheet* and its management analysis, which explain that cash and investments are down slightly but that assets overall are up 5 percent. The balance sheet also explains that the company shifted its debt structure, reducing short-term borrowings and increasing long-term borrowings. Finally, the balance sheet tells the shareholders that their equity in the company grew 8 percent as a result of earnings that the company retained and reinvested in the business.
5. *The consolidated statement of cash flows* and its management analysis, which tell us that the company's operations produced $3.7 billion of cash and that the company invested $2.3 billion of that cash flow back into the business, used a good bit more to retire debt, and paid $540 million to the shareholders as dividends.
6. *The consolidated statement of shareholders' equity*, which details all of the significant transactions affecting the shareholders' accounts during the past three years. Perhaps the most important of these transactions are the earnings retained each year and the charge for the dividends paid out. In 1994 the company paid to its shareholders about 35 percent of the prior year's earnings. As a shareholder you

might expect a similar payout this year, and because earnings increased by 12 percent, you might expect a similar increase in your dividends.

7. *Notes to the consolidated financial statements*, which explain the more interesting accounting decisions management made in preparing the financial statements, and which expand on the financial presentation in the basic statements.

   For example, in the fourth paragraph of Note 1, management explains that they are studying their accounting policy for promotional discounts. The company has been following two different policies for these discounts, treating them as marketing expenses in the snack food business and as a sales reduction in the beverage business. Both policies have support in GAAP, but the company has begun to wonder whether one approach may really be better than the other. The note tells us what the company has been doing, and rightly warns us that the presentation next year might be different.

   The notes also provide us with supplementary detail. Because the basic statements are intended as a general-purpose presentation for a large and diverse audience, they are summarized to a significant degree. Management understands that some readers will be interested in more detail in certain areas and provides those details in the notes. For example, the two largest assets are presented on the balance sheet as single line items: Note 7 provides more detail of the property, plant, and equipment account, and Note 8 provides more detail on the makeup of the intangible assets.

   Finally, the notes also put words around important issues that cannot be quantified. The basic statements are, of course, expressed in concrete numbers, but a company may have a number of transactions in process that are not yet precisely measurable. For example, PepsiCo's Note 19, Contingencies, explains that the company has directly and indirectly guaranteed obligations aggregating $187 million. PepsiCo obviously hopes that it will not be called upon to make good on any of those guarantees; and, until a future event happens to force the company to act on any one guarantee, the exact dollar amount that it will have to expend cannot be determined. Because the future cost of fulfilling those guarantees cannot be currently measured with any degree of precision, that contingent obligation is not reflected in the basic financial statements, and the company's exposure is simply noted for the reader's information.

8. *Reports from management and the independent auditors*, which are intended to support the financial statements and enhance their credibility. The statement of "Management's Responsibility for Financial Statements" is a public acknowledgment of this responsibility by PepsiCo's management; it is an assertion that the company's system of internal control is adequate and offers a pledge by top management that the presented data are reliable and in accordance with GAAP.

   The "Report of Independent Auditors" follows the standardized format that the AICPA recommends and that the financial community has come to expect. The first paragraph of the report is a statement of the scope of the audit examination and a brief statement differentiating management's responsibilities for the financial statements from those of the independent auditor. The second paragraph states whether the audit was performed in accordance with generally accepted auditing standards. It also briefly explains what an audit entails and emphasizes the auditor's role in investigating possible material misstatements of the financial statements. The third paragraph is a statement of opinion as to whether the company's financial condition and results of operations have been reported "fairly, in all material respects . . . in conformity with generally accepted accounting principles." The opinion expressed by PepsiCo's independent public accountant, KPMG Peat Marwick, is the standard "clean" or **unqualified opinion.** The fourth paragraph calls our attention to a number of changes that PepsiCo made in its accounting policies during the three years covered by the report.

9. *Selected financial data*, which provide the information we need if we are interested in the trend of results quarter by quarter during the last two years or the trend of results year by year during the last 10 years.

Overall, the annual accounting report contains an enormous quantity of financial information about a company and its operations. We suggest that you take a few moments to familiarize yourself with the general content of the annual financial report of PepsiCo, Inc., presented in the following pages.

PEPSICO, INC. 1994 FINANCIAL REVIEW

Management's Analysis – Overview

To enhance understanding of PepsiCo's financial performance, the various components of Management's Analysis are presented near the pertinent financial statements. Accordingly, in addition to this overview, separate analyses of the results of operations, financial condition and cash flows appear on pages 31, 33 and 35, respectively. Also, the analysis of each industry segment's net sales and operating profit performance begins on pages 5, 11 and 17.

Marketplace Actions

PepsiCo's domestic and international businesses operate in markets that are highly competitive and subject to global and local economic conditions including inflation, commodity price and currency fluctuations and governmental actions. In Mexico, for example, our businesses have benefited in past years from improving conditions. Conversely, the significant devaluation of the Mexican peso at the end of 1994 and continuing into 1995 will not only negatively impact reported earnings from Mexico due to translation, but is expected to create a much less favorable economic climate in the country. Other examples include risks associated with political instability and its related dislocations in countries where PepsiCo operates and possible employee benefit or minimum wage legislation in the U.S. and elsewhere, increasing the cost of providing benefits and compensation to employees. PepsiCo's operating and investing strategies are designed, where possible, to mitigate these factors through aggressive actions on several fronts including: (a) enhancing the appeal and value of its products through brand promotion, product innovation, quality improvement and prudent pricing actions; (b) providing better service to customers; (c) increasing worldwide availability of its products; (d) acquiring businesses and forming alliances to increase market presence and utilize resources more efficiently; and (e) containing costs through efficient and effective purchasing, manufacturing, distribution and administrative processes.

Restructurings

Restructuring actions realign resources for more efficient and effective execution of operating strategies. As a result, PepsiCo continually considers and executes restructuring actions that vary in size and impact, for example, from a minor sales force reorganization at a local facility to a significant organizational and process redesign affecting an entire operating division. The resulting cost savings or profits from increased sales are reinvested in the business to increase PepsiCo's shareholder value. Major restructuring actions announced in 1992 and now underway or completed in the beverage and international snack food segments resulted in charges totaling $193.5 million ($128.5 million after-tax or $0.16 per share). In 1994, $28.3 million ($17.4 million after-tax or $0.02 per share) of the 1992 restructuring accruals were reversed into income, primarily reflecting refinements of the original domestic beverage accrual estimate and management's decision to reduce the scope of the domestic beverage restructuring. The majority of the amount reversed into income was offset by additional charges in 1994 for new actions. The remaining accruals for the 1992 restructuring actions of $39 million outstanding at year-end 1994 represent expected cash payments of which $25 million, $11 million and $3 million are expected to be paid in 1995, 1996 and 1997, respectively.

Annual cost savings from the 1992 restructuring actions, when fully implemented, are expected to be approximately $75 million primarily from reduced employee and facility costs. In addition, while difficult to measure, the domestic beverage segment is also expected to benefit by an estimated $90 million annually from centralization of purchasing activities and incremental volume and pricing from improvements in administrative and business processes. The combined gross benefits realized in 1994 from the 1992 restructuring actions are estimated to be approximately $50 million. These benefits are expected to increase annually until fully realized in 1998. See Notes 2 and 16 for additional detail related to the 1992 restructuring charges. See Management's Analysis of beverage and snack food performance on pages 5 and 11, respectively, for a discussion of the 1992 restructuring charges and related anticipated benefits.

Derivatives

PepsiCo uses derivative instruments primarily to reduce borrowing costs and hedge future purchases of certain commodities. PepsiCo's policy is to not use derivative instruments for speculative purposes and has procedures in place to monitor and control their use. PepsiCo's credit risk related to derivatives is considered low. Financing-related derivative contracts are only entered into with strong creditworthy counterparties and are generally of relatively short duration. Purchases of commodities are hedged with commodity futures contracts traded on national exchanges.

Reduce Borrowing Costs: PepsiCo enters into interest rate and foreign currency swaps to effectively change the interest rate and currency of specific debt issuances with the objective of reducing borrowing costs. These swaps are generally entered into concurrently with the issuance of the debt they are intended to modify. The notional value, payment and maturity dates of the swaps match the principal, interest payment dates and maturity dates of the related debt. Accordingly, any market impact (risk or opportunity) associated with these swaps is fully offset by the opposite market impact on the related debt. See Notes 9 and 10 for additional details regarding interest rate and currency swaps.

Hedge Commodity Costs: PepsiCo hedges future commodity purchases when we believe it will result in lower net costs. The futures contracts entered into do not exceed expected usage nor do they generally extend beyond one year. While PepsiCo expects to generate lower commodity costs over time by entering into these futures contracts, it is possible that the commodity costs will be higher than if futures contracts were not entered into. PepsiCo believes it has the ability to raise prices if commodity prices increase; however, it expects to do so only if the increase is other than temporary and it would not place PepsiCo at a competitive disadvantage. Open contracts at year-end 1994 and gains and losses realized in 1994 or deferred at year-end were not significant.

PEPSICO, INC. 1994 FINANCIAL REVIEW

Currency Exchange Effects

In 1994, 1993 and 1992, international businesses represented 18.6%, 18.0% and 17.7%, respectively, of PepsiCo's total segment operating profits. Operating in international markets sometimes involves volatile movements in currency exchange rates. The economic impact of currency exchange rate movements on PepsiCo is complex because such changes are often linked to variability in real growth, inflation, interest rates, governmental actions and other factors. In addition, these changes, if material, can cause PepsiCo to adjust its financing and operating strategies, for example, pricing, promotion and product strategies and decisions concerning sourcing of raw materials and packaging. Because PepsiCo operates in a mix of businesses and numerous countries, management believes currency exposures are fairly well diversified. Moreover, management believes that currency exposures are not a significant factor in competition at the local market operating level. When economically appropriate, however, PepsiCo enters into foreign currency hedges to minimize specific cash flow transaction exposures. The following paragraphs describe the effects of currency exchange rate movements on PepsiCo's reported results. See Other Factors Expected to Impact 1995 Results on page 26.

As currency exchange rates change, translation of the income statements of international businesses into U.S. dollars affects year-over-year comparability of operating results. In 1994 and 1993, sales and operating profit growth rates for our consolidated international businesses were not materially impacted by the translation effects of changes in currency exchange rates. The effects on comparability of sales and operating profits arising from translation of the income statements of international businesses are identified, where material, in Management's Analysis of segment operating results. These translation effects exclude the impact of businesses in highly inflationary countries, where the functional currency is the U.S. dollar.

Changes in currency exchange rates also result in reported foreign exchange gains and losses which are included as a component of unallocated expenses, net (see page 28). PepsiCo reported a net foreign exchange gain of $4.5 million in 1994 compared to net foreign exchange losses of $41.2 million and $17.4 million in 1993 and 1992, respectively. These reported amounts include translation gains and losses arising from remeasurement into U.S. dollars of the net monetary assets of businesses in highly inflationary countries as well as transaction gains and losses. Transaction gains and losses arise from monetary assets such as receivables and short-term investments as well as payables (including debt) denominated in currencies other than a business unit's functional currency. In implementing strategies to minimize after-tax financing costs, the effects of expected currency exchange rate movements on debt and short-term investments are considered along with related interest rates in measuring effective net financing costs.

Beginning in 1993, Mexico was no longer categorized as highly inflationary. PepsiCo did not calculate the net foreign exchange gain or loss that would have been reported in 1993 had businesses in Mexico been accounted for as highly inflationary; however, translation gains and losses for businesses in Mexico were not a significant component of the above 1992 amount.

Certain Factors Affecting Comparability

Accounting Changes

PepsiCo's financial statements reflect the noncash impact of accounting changes adopted in 1994 and 1992. In 1994, PepsiCo was required to adopt Statement of Financial Accounting Standards No. 112, "Employers' Accounting for Postemployment Benefits" (SFAS 112). The cumulative effect of adopting SFAS 112, an $84.6 million charge ($55.3 million after-tax or $0.07 per share), principally represented estimated future severance costs related to services provided by employees prior to 1994. As compared to the previous accounting method, the current year impact of adopting SFAS 112 was immaterial to 1994 operating profits. See Note 14 for additional details.

Also in 1994, PepsiCo adopted a preferred method for calculating the market-related value of plan assets used in determining the return-on-asset component of annual pension expense and the cumulative net unrecognized gain or loss subject to amortization. The cumulative effect of adopting this change, which related to years prior to 1994, was a benefit of $37.8 million ($23.3 million after-tax or $0.03 per share). As compared to the previous accounting method, the change reduced 1994 pension expense by $35.1 million ($21.6 million after-tax or $0.03 per share). See Note 13 for additional details.

Effective the beginning of 1992, PepsiCo early adopted Statements of Financial Accounting Standards No. 106, "Employers' Accounting for Postretirement Benefits Other Than Pensions" (SFAS 106), and No. 109, "Accounting for Income Taxes" (SFAS 109). The cumulative effect of adopting SFAS 106, a $575.3 million charge ($356.7 million after-tax or $0.44 per share), represented estimated future retiree health benefit costs related to services provided by employees prior to 1992. The cumulative effect of adopting SFAS 109, a $570.7 million tax charge ($0.71 per share), primarily represented the recognition of additional deferred tax liabilities related to acquired identifiable intangible assets as of the beginning of 1992. See Notes 12 and 17 for additional details regarding the adoption of SFAS 106 and SFAS 109, respectively.

Other Factors

Comparisons of 1994 to 1993 are affected by an additional week of results in the 1994 reporting period. Because PepsiCo's fiscal year ends on the last Saturday in December, a fifty-third week is added every 5 or 6 years. The fifty-third week increased 1994 earnings by an estimated $54.0 million ($34.9 million after-tax or $0.04 per share). See Items Affecting Comparability, Fiscal Year, on page 27 for the impact on PepsiCo's business segments.

PepsiCo recorded a one-time, noncash gain of $17.8 million ($16.8 million after-tax or $0.02 per share) resulting from a public share offering by BAESA, a bottling joint venture in South America. See Note 4 for additional details.

PEPSICO, INC. 1994 FINANCIAL REVIEW

Significant U.S. Tax Changes Affecting Historical and Future Results

U.S. federal income tax legislation enacted in August 1993 included a provision for a 1% statutory income tax rate increase effective for the full year. As required under SFAS 109, the increase in the tax rate resulted in a noncash charge of $29.9 million ($0.04 per share) for the adjustment of net deferred tax liabilities as of the beginning of 1993.

The 1993 tax legislation also included a provision to reduce the tax credit associated with beverage concentrate operations in Puerto Rico. This change limited the tax credit on income earned in Puerto Rico in the first year to 60% of the amount allowed under the previous tax law, with the limit further reduced ratably over the following four years to 40%. The provision, which became effective for PepsiCo's operations on December 1, 1994, had an immaterial impact on 1994 earnings. Had the provision become effective at the beginning of 1994, earnings for the year would have been reduced by approximately $60 million or $0.07 per share. Similarly, had the 40% credit limit been effective in 1994, earnings would have been reduced by an additional $30 million or $0.04 per share over the 60% credit limit.

In 1994, the U.S. Department of the Treasury proposed a change to a current regulation (known as Q&A 12), which would further reduce the tax incentives associated with the beverage concentrate operations in Puerto Rico. This proposal applies to PepsiCo's sales of concentrate from its operations in Puerto Rico to its related bottlers in the U.S. If it had been adopted as proposed in 1994, the change would have become effective for PepsiCo on December 1, 1994 with an immaterial impact on 1994 earnings. However, had the 60% credit limit (discussed above) and the currently proposed Q&A 12 been in effect at the beginning of 1994, earnings for the year would have been reduced by an estimated $112 million or $0.14 per share. Had the 40% credit limit and proposed Q&A 12 both been effective in 1994, the impact would have reduced 1994 earnings for the year by an additional $30 million or $0.04 per share over the 60% credit limit. The estimated impacts are subject to change depending upon the final provisions of Q&A 12, if enacted. PepsiCo and others are vigorously opposing the proposed change.

PepsiCo's full year 1995 tax rate is not expected to exceed 35%. The expected tax rate reflects PepsiCo's forecasted 1995 mix of U.S. and generally lower taxed foreign earnings, the reduction in the tax credit on income earned in Puerto Rico resulting from the 1993 U.S. tax legislation and the assumed enactment in 1995 of Q&A 12, as currently proposed, partially offset by significant adjustments reflecting the anticipated resolution in 1995 of audit issues related to prior years.

The unfavorable effect of Q&A 12 will not be included in the 1995 effective tax rate unless it is enacted. The benefits due to the adjustments will be included in the 1995 tax rate when the audit issues related to prior years have been resolved. Accordingly, the potential exists for volatility in PepsiCo's 1995 quarterly effective tax rates depending on the timing of these events, as well as other factors.

Other Factors Expected to Impact 1995 Results

In late 1994 and early 1995, the Mexican peso devalued significantly relative to the U.S. dollar. The primary impact of the devaluation on 1994 financial results was an estimated $275 million unfavorable change in the currency translation adjustment account in Shareholders' Equity, representing the reduced book value of PepsiCo's Mexican peso-denominated net assets. The impact on 1994 earnings was immaterial. Quantifying the adverse impact of the devaluation on 1995 operating results, financial condition and cash flows is difficult because, in addition to the translation impact, the devaluation is likely to result in many changes to the business environment including government actions, accelerated inflation and its impact on prices and costs, reduced consumer demand and the impact of higher interest rates on our trade customers and bottlers. Although PepsiCo expects to report lower earnings in 1995 from its operations in Mexico than it otherwise would have because of the devaluation and its related effects, PepsiCo has begun to take actions in Mexico and in other parts of the world to mitigate the effects of the devaluation. PepsiCo's operations in Mexico, primarily related to snack foods, constituted about 5% and 7% of PepsiCo's 1994 consolidated net assets and cash flows from operations, respectively, and contributed 7% and 8% of PepsiCo's 1994 net sales and segment operating profits, respectively. See Management's Analysis of each industry segment for additional discussion regarding the impact of the devaluation of the Mexican peso. In addition, PepsiCo anticipates that earnings from its affiliates in Mexico accounted for by the equity method, primarily related to beverages, will also be unfavorably impacted. Equity results reported in 1994 from affiliates in Mexico were not material.

As quantified in Other Factors on page 25, comparisons of 1995 to 1994 will be adversely affected by the additional week's results in the 1994 fiscal year.

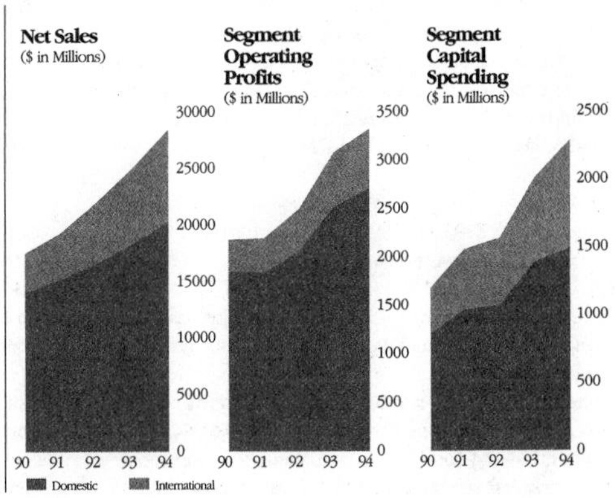

PEPSICO, INC. 1994 FINANCIAL REVIEW

Business Segments

This information constitutes Note 2 to the Consolidated Financial Statements. (dollars in millions)

PepsiCo operates on a worldwide basis within three industry segments: beverages, snack foods and restaurants. The beverage segment primarily markets its Pepsi, Diet Pepsi, Mountain Dew and other brands worldwide and 7UP internationally, and manufactures concentrates for its brands for sale to franchised bottlers worldwide. The segment also operates bottling plants and distribution facilities located in the U.S. and in various international markets, and manufactures and distributes ready-to-drink Lipton tea products in North America. In addition, under separate distribution and joint venture agreements, the segment distributes certain previously existing, as well as manufactures and distributes new jointly-developed, Ocean Spray juice products in the U.S. and Canada. The snack food segment manufactures, distributes and markets chips and other snacks worldwide, with Frito-Lay representing the domestic business. The international snack food business includes major operations in Mexico, the U.K. and Canada. The restaurant segment consists primarily of the operations of the worldwide Pizza Hut, Taco Bell and KFC chains. PFS, PepsiCo's restaurant distribution operation, supplies company-owned and franchised restaurants, principally in the U.S. Net sales and operating profits of PFS' franchisee operations have been allocated to each restaurant chain.

Unallocated Expenses, net includes corporate headquarters expenses, minority interests, primarily in the Gamesa (Mexico) and Wedel (Poland) snack food businesses, foreign exchange translation and transaction gains and losses and other corporate items not allocated to the business segments. Corporate Identifiable Assets consist principally of short-term investments held outside the U.S. and investments in affiliates.

PepsiCo has invested in about 75 joint ventures, principally international and all within PepsiCo's three industry segments, in which it exercises significant influence but not control. Equity in net income of these affiliates was $37.8, $30.1, and $40.1 in 1994, 1993 and 1992, respectively. The increase in 1994 primarily reflected increased profits at Snack Ventures Europe (SVE). The decline in 1993 primarily reflected the expansion costs in a beverage affiliate in India and lower profits at SVE. International snack food affiliates, which represented the largest component of equity in net income of affiliates, contributed $34.3, $24.1 and $23.2 in 1994, 1993 and 1992, respectively. Dividends received from affiliates totaled $33.1, $16.4 and $29.6 in 1994, 1993 and 1992, respectively.

PepsiCo's year-end investments in affiliates totaled $1.3 billion in 1994, $1.1 billion in 1993 and $904.9 in 1992. The increase in 1994 reflected advances to California Pizza Kitchen (CPK), a domestic casual dining restaurant chain, and investments in international franchised bottling operations in Thailand and China, partially offset by the translation impact of the late 1994 devaluation of the Mexican peso. Significant investments in affiliates at year-end 1994 included $234.3 in General Bottlers, a U.S. franchised bottler, $162.9 in CPK, $160.2 in a KFC Japan joint venture, $123.2 in BAESA, a franchised bottler with operations in South America, and $80.9 in SVE.

Items Affecting Comparability

Fiscal Year

1994 consisted of 53 weeks and the years 1989 through 1993 consisted of 52 weeks. The estimated favorable impact on net sales of the fifty-third week was $433.5, increasing beverage, snack food and restaurant net sales by $118.9, $142.6 and $172.0, respectively. The estimated favorable impact on operating profits of the fifty-third week was $64.5, increasing beverage, snack food and restaurant operating profits by $16.8, $26.0 and $22.9, respectively, and increasing unallocated expenses, net by $1.2.

Unusual Items

Unusual charges totaled $193.5 in 1992, $170.0 in 1991 and $83.0 in 1990. These unusual items were as follows:

Beverages - 1992 included $145.0 in charges consisting of $115.4 and $29.6 to reorganize and streamline domestic and international operations, respectively. 1990 included a $10.5 domestic charge for trade receivables exposures.

Snack Foods - 1992 included a $40.3 charge principally to consolidate the Walkers businesses in the U.K. 1991 included $127.0 in charges consisting of $91.4 and $23.6 to streamline domestic and U.K. operations, respectively, and $12.0 to dispose of all or part of a small unprofitable business in Japan. 1990 included a $10.6 domestic charge for trade receivables exposures.

Restaurants - 1991 included $43.0 in charges at KFC consisting of $34.0 to streamline operations and $9.0 related to a delay in the U.S. roll-out of a new product. 1990 included $28.0 in charges consisting of $17.6 for closure of certain underperforming restaurants (Pizza Hut - $9.0, Taco Bell - $4.0 and KFC - $4.6) and $10.4 for reorganization charges for Pizza Hut.

Unallocated Expenses, net - 1992 included an $8.2 charge to streamline operations of the SVE joint venture. 1990 included $33.9 in charges consisting of $18.0 for accelerated contributions to the PepsiCo Foundation and $15.9 to reduce the carrying amount of an international Pizza Hut affiliate.

See Note 16 and Management's Analysis of beverage and snack food performance on pages 5 and 11, respectively, for additional information on restructurings.

Accounting Changes

In 1994, PepsiCo adopted a preferred method for calculating the market-related value of plan assets used in determining annual pension expense (see Note 13) and extended the depreciable lives on certain domestic Pizza Hut delivery assets. As compared to the previous accounting methods, these changes increased 1994 operating profit by $49.1, increasing beverage, snack food and restaurant profits by $12.4, $15.5 and $19.6 (almost all domestic), respectively, and decreasing 1994 unallocated expenses, net by $1.6.

In 1992, PepsiCo adopted Statements of Financial Accounting Standards No. 106 and 109, "Employers' Accounting for Postretirement Benefits Other Than Pensions" and "Accounting for Income Taxes," respectively. As compared to the previous accounting methods, these changes reduced 1992 operating profit by $72.8, decreasing beverage, snack food and restaurant profits by $22.4, $30.8 and $15.4, respectively, and increasing 1992 unallocated expenses, net by $4.2. See Notes 12 and 17, respectively.

PEPSICO, INC. 1994 FINANCIAL REVIEW

Industry Segments

(dollars in millions)

		Growth Rate [a] 1989 - 1994	**1994**	1993	1992	1991	1990
Net Sales							
Beverages:	Domestic	7.2%	**$ 6,541.2**	$ 5,918.1	$ 5,485.2	$ 5,171.5	$ 5,034.5
	International	22.2%	**3,146.3**	2,720.1	2,120.4	1,743.7	1,488.5
		10.9%	**9,687.5**	8,638.2	7,605.6	6,915.2	6,523.0
Snack Foods:	Domestic	9.3%	**5,011.3**	4,365.3	3,950.4	3,737.9	3,471.5
	International	32.0%	**3,253.1**	2,661.5	2,181.7	1,512.2	1,295.3
		15.5%	**8,264.4**	7,026.8	6,132.1	5,250.1	4,766.8
Restaurants:	Domestic	13.2%	**8,693.9**	8,025.7	7,115.4	6,258.4	5,540.9
	International	26.4%	**1,826.6**	1,330.0	1,116.9	868.5	684.8
		14.9%	**10,520.5**	9,355.7	8,232.3	7,126.9	6,225.7
Combined Segments							
	Domestic	10.1%	**20,246.4**	18,309.1	16,551.0	15,167.8	14,046.9
	International	26.6%	**8,226.0**	6,711.6	5,419.0	4,124.4	3,468.6
		13.6%	**$28,472.4**	$25,020.7	$21,970.0	$19,292.2	$17,515.5
By Restaurant Chain							
	Pizza Hut	12.8%	**$ 4,474.4**	$ 4,128.7	$ 3,603.5	$ 3,258.3	$ 2,949.9
	Taco Bell	18.3%	**3,401.4**	2,901.3	2,460.0	2,038.1	1,745.5
	KFC	14.7%	**2,644.7**	2,325.7	2,168.8	1,830.5	1,530.3
		14.9%	**$10,520.5**	$ 9,355.7	$ 8,232.3	$ 7,126.9	$ 6,225.7
Operating Profits							
Beverages:	Domestic	12.1%	**$ 1,022.3**	$ 936.9	$ 686.3	$ 746.2	$ 673.8
	International	20.0%	**194.7**	172.1	112.3	117.1	93.8
		13.2%	**1,217.0**	1,109.0	798.6	863.3	767.6
Snack Foods:	Domestic	8.9%	**1,025.1**	900.7	775.5	616.6	732.3
	International	27.1%	**351.8**	288.9	209.2	140.1	160.3
		12.2%	**1,376.9**	1,189.6	984.7	756.7	892.6
Restaurants:	Domestic	12.2%	**658.8**	685.1	597.8	479.4	447.2
	International	4.3%	**71.5**	92.9	120.7	96.2	75.2
		11.3%	**730.3**	778.0	718.5	575.6	522.4
Combined Segments							
	Domestic	11.1%	**2,706.2**	2,522.7	2,059.6	1,842.2	1,853.3
	International	20.6%	**618.0**	553.9	442.2	353.4	329.3
		12.3%	**3,324.2**	3,076.6	2,501.8	2,195.6	2,182.6
Equity Income			**37.8**	30.1	40.1	32.2	30.1
Unallocated Expenses, net			**(160.8)**	(200.2)	(170.7)	(116.0)	(170.6)
Operating Profit		12.6%	**$ 3,201.2**	$ 2,906.5	$ 2,371.2	$ 2,111.8	$ 2,042.1
By Restaurant Chain							
	Pizza Hut	7.5%	**$ 294.8**	$ 372.1	$ 335.4	$ 314.5	$ 245.9
	Taco Bell	18.7%	**270.3**	253.1	214.3	180.6	149.6
	KFC	9.0%	**165.2**	152.8	168.8	80.5	126.9
		11.3%	**$ 730.3**	$ 778.0	$ 718.5	$ 575.6	$ 522.4

Geographic Areas [b]

	Net Sales			Segment Operating Profits			Identifiable Assets		
	1994	1993	1992	**1994**	1993	1992	**1994**	1993	1992
United States	**$20,246.4**	$18,309.1	$16,551.0	**$2,706.2**	$2,522.7	$2,059.6	**$14,218.4**	$13,589.5	$11,957.0
Europe	**2,177.1**	1,819.0	1,349.0	**16.7**	47.4	52.6	**3,062.0**	2,666.1	1,948.4
Mexico	**2,022.8**	1,613.4	1,234.6	**261.4**	223.1	172.1	**994.7**	1,217.1	1,054.6
Canada	**1,244.3**	1,206.1	979.6	**81.6**	101.7	78.9	**1,342.1**	1,364.0	1,340.6
Other	**2,781.8**	2,073.1	1,855.8	**258.3**	181.7	138.6	**2,195.6**	1,675.1	1,282.0
Combined Segments	**$28,472.4**	$25,020.7	$21,970.0	**$3,324.2**	$3,076.6	$2,501.8	**21,812.8**	20,511.8	17,582.6
Corporate							**2,979.2**	3,194.0	3,368.6
							$24,792.0	$23,705.8	$20,951.2

(a) Five-year compounded annual growth rate. Operating profit growth rates exclude the impact of previously disclosed 1989 unusual items affecting international beverages and domestic Taco Bell and KFC. There were no unusual items in 1994.

PEPSICO, INC. 1994 FINANCIAL REVIEW

Amortization of Intangible Assets

	Growth Rate (a) 1989 - 1994	**1994**	1993	1992
Beverages	7.6%	$ **164.8**	$ 157.4	$ 137.6
Snack Foods	17.8%	**42.0**	40.9	40.5
Restaurants	28.9%	**105.4**	105.4	87.8
	14.0%	$ **312.2**	$ 303.7	$ 265.9

	Growth Rate (a) 1989 - 1994	**1994**	1993	1992
By Restaurant Chain:				
Pizza Hut	31.6%	$ **41.5**	$ 44.7	$ 33.3
Taco Bell	22.9%	**26.9**	23.0	16.4
KFC	31.2%	**37.0**	37.7	38.1
	28.9%	$ **105.4**	$ 105.4	$ 87.8

Depreciation Expense

	Growth Rate (a) 1989 - 1994	**1994**	1993	1992
Beverages	14.9%	$ **385.4**	$ 358.5	$ 290.6
Snack Foods	11.7%	**297.0**	279.2	251.2
Restaurants	17.5%	**538.8**	457.2	374.3
Corporate		**7.0**	6.6	6.9
	15.0%	$ **1,228.2**	$ 1,101.5	$ 923.0

	Growth Rate (a) 1989 - 1994	**1994**	1993	1992
By Restaurant Chain:				
Pizza Hut	17.8%	$ **218.6**	$ 193.4	$ 150.5
Taco Bell	18.1%	**156.0**	124.6	101.5
KFC	16.7%	**164.2**	139.2	122.3
	17.5%	$ **538.8**	$ 457.2	$ 374.3

Identifiable Assets

	Growth Rate (a) 1989 - 1994	**1994**	1993	1992
Beverages	9.1%	$ **9,566.0**	$ 9,105.2	$ 7,857.5
Snack Foods	8.8%	**5,043.9**	4,994.5	4,628.0
Restaurants	18.6%	**7,202.9**	6,412.1	5,097.1
Corporate		**2,979.2**	3,194.0	3,368.6
	10.4%	**$24,792.0**	$23,705.8	$20,951.2

	Growth Rate (a) 1989 - 1994	**1994**	1993	1992
By Restaurant Chain:				
Pizza Hut	20.9%	**$2,536.4**	$2,232.9	$1,676.8
Taco Bell	21.1%	**2,390.7**	2,075.9	1,523.7
KFC	14.2%	**2,275.8**	2,103.3	1,896.6
	18.6%	**$7,202.9**	$6,412.1	$5,097.1

Capital Spending (c)

	Growth Rate (a) 1989 - 1994	**1994**	1993	1992
Beverages	20.4%	$ **677.1**	$ 491.3	$ 343.7
Snack Foods	15.6%	**532.1**	491.4	446.2
Restaurants	20.3%	**1,072.0**	1,004.4	757.2
Corporate		**7.2**	20.8	18.0
	19.0%	$ **2,288.4**	$ 2,007.9	$ 1,565.1
Domestic	13.7%	$ **1,492.6**	$ 1,388.0	$ 1,069.0
International	35.7%	**795.8**	619.9	496.1
	19.0%	$ **2,288.4**	$ 2,007.9	$ 1,565.1

	Growth Rate (a) 1989 - 1994	**1994**	1993	1992
By Restaurant Chain:				
Pizza Hut	19.3%	$ **389.0**	$ 295.0	$ 212.8
Taco Bell	35.4%	**473.4**	459.4	339.0
KFC	5.6%	**209.6**	250.0	205.4
	20.3%	**$1,072.0**	$1,004.4	$ 757.2

Acquisitions and Investments in Affiliates (d)

	1994	1993	1992
Beverages	$ **195.0**	$ 711.5	$ 717.5
Snack Foods	**11.8**	75.5	201.3
Restaurants	**147.8**	588.7	480.4
	$ **354.6**	$ 1,375.7	$ 1,399.2
Domestic	$ **87.8**	$ 757.3	$ 549.5
International	**266.8**	618.4	849.7
	$ **354.6**	$ 1,375.7	$ 1,399.2

	1994	1993	1992
By Restaurant Chain:			
Pizza Hut	$ **94.6**	$ 312.9	$ 247.7
Taco Bell	**32.3**	186.8	72.4
KFC	**20.9**	89.0	160.3
	$ **147.8**	$ 588.7	$ 480.4

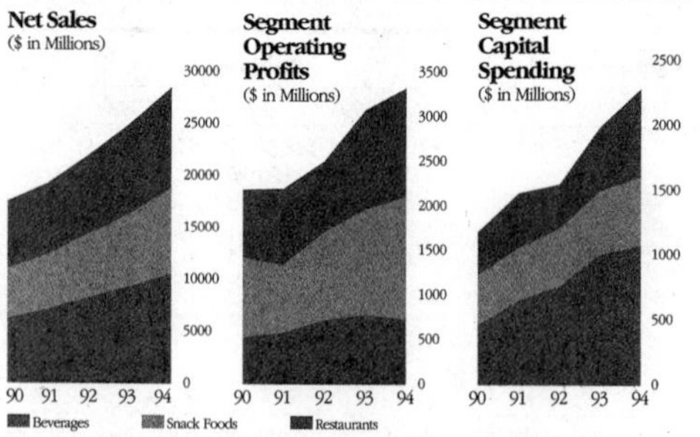

(b) The results of centralized concentrate manufacturing operations in Puerto Rico and Ireland have been allocated based upon sales to the respective areas.

(c) Included noncash amounts related to capital leases, largely in the restaurant segment, of $35.2 in 1994, $26.3 in 1993 and $15.5 in 1992.

(d) Included noncash amounts related to treasury stock and debt issued in domestic transactions of $38.8 in 1994, $364.5 in 1993 and $189.5 in 1992. Of these noncash amounts, 14%, 65% and 58%, respectively, related to the beverage segment and the balance related to the restaurant segment.

PEPSICO, INC. 1994 FINANCIAL REVIEW

Consolidated Statement of Income

(in millions except per share amounts)
PepsiCo, Inc. and Subsidiaries
Fifty-three weeks ended December 31, 1994 and fifty-two weeks ended December 25, 1993 and December 26, 1992

	1994	1993	1992
Net Sales	**$28,472.4**	$25,020.7	$21,970.0
Costs and Expenses, net			
Cost of sales	**13,715.4**	11,946.1	10,611.7
Selling, general and administrative expenses	**11,243.6**	9,864.4	8,721.2
Amortization of intangible assets	**312.2**	303.7	265.9
Operating Profit	**3,201.2**	2,906.5	2,371.2
Gain on joint venture stock offering	**17.8**	–	–
Interest expense	**(645.0)**	(572.7)	(586.1)
Interest income	**90.4**	88.7	113.7
Income Before Income Taxes and Cumulative Effect of Accounting Changes	**2,664.4**	2,422.5	1,898.8
Provision for Income Taxes	**880.4**	834.6	597.1
Income Before Cumulative Effect of Accounting Changes	**1,784.0**	1,587.9	1,301.7
Cumulative Effect of Accounting Changes			
Postemployment benefits (net of income tax benefit of $29.3)	**(55.3)**	–	–
Pension assets (net of income tax expense of $14.5)	**23.3**	–	–
Postretirement benefits other than pensions (net of income tax benefit of $218.6)	**–**	–	(356.7)
Income taxes	**–**	–	(570.7)
Net Income	**$ 1,752.0**	$ 1,587.9	$ 374.3
Income (Charge) Per Share			
Before cumulative effect of accounting changes	**$ 2.22**	$ 1.96	$ 1.61
Cumulative effect of accounting changes			
Postemployment benefits	**(0.07)**	–	–
Pension assets	**0.03**	–	–
Postretirement benefits other than pensions	**–**	–	(0.44)
Income taxes	**–**	–	(0.71)
Net Income Per Share	**$ 2.18**	$ 1.96	$ 0.46
Average shares outstanding used to calculate income (charge) per share	**803.6**	810.1	806.7

See accompanying Notes to Consolidated Financial Statements.

Allocation of 1994 Net Sales

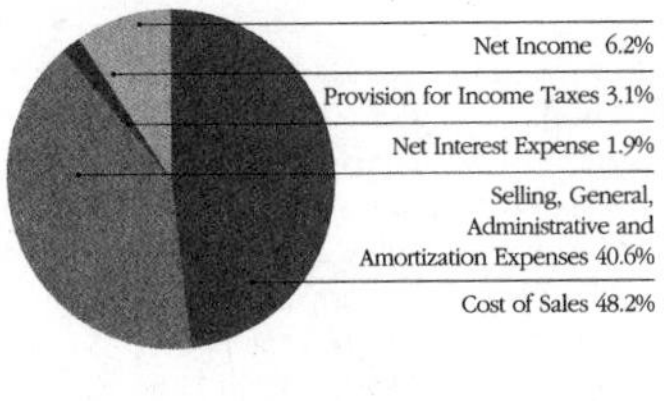

PEPSICO, INC. 1994 FINANCIAL REVIEW

Management's Analysis – Results of Operations

(See Management's Analysis – Overview on page 24 for background information and Business Segments on page 27 for detail of segment results.)

To improve comparability, Management's Analysis includes analytical data to indicate the impact of beverage and snack food acquisitions, net of operations sold or contributed to joint ventures (collectively, "net acquisitions"). Acquisition impacts represent the results of the acquired businesses for periods in the current year corresponding to the prior year periods that did not include the results of the businesses. Restaurant units acquired, principally from franchisees, and constructed units are treated the same for purposes of this analysis and are collectively referred to as "additional restaurant units." Also, the analysis indicates, as applicable, the impact of the ongoing effects of the 1994 accounting changes (see Notes 13 and 14), the 1994 BAESA gain (see Note 4), the 1993 deferred tax charge due to U.S. tax legislation (see Note 17) and the 1992 restructuring charges (see Note 16), collectively referred to as "the Unusual Items."

Comparisons of 1994 to 1993 were impacted by an additional week's results in 1994 which contributed about $433.5 million or 2 points to growth in Net Sales and increased earnings by about $54.0 million ($34.9 million after-tax or $0.04 per share).

Net Sales rose $3.5 billion or 14% in 1994 of which $215 million or 1 point was contributed by net acquisitions. The balance of the increase reflected volume gains of $2.2 billion and $934 million due to additional restaurant units. Sales grew $3.1 billion or 14% in 1993. Net acquisitions contributed $1.1 billion or 5 points to sales growth. The balance of the increase reflected $913 million from additional restaurant units, volume gains that contributed $850 million and higher pricing. International sales grew 23% in 1994 and 24% in 1993 with net acquisitions contributing 1 point and 16 points, respectively. International sales represented 29%, 27% and 25% of total sales in 1994, 1993 and 1992, respectively. The long-term trend of an increasing international component of sales may be interrupted in the near term as a result of the unfavorable impact of the devaluation of the Mexican peso in late 1994 and early 1995 and its related effects.

Cost of sales as a percentage of Net Sales was 48.2%, 47.7% and 48.3% in 1994, 1993 and 1992, respectively. The decline in the 1994 gross margin reflected a mix shift to lower-margin businesses in international beverages and worldwide restaurants and lower net pricing in domestic beverages, partially offset by a mix shift to higher-margin packages and products in international snack foods and manufacturing efficiencies in domestic snack foods. The 1993 gross margin improvement was driven by lower product costs (packaging and ingredients) in domestic beverages.

Selling, general and administrative expenses rose 14% in 1994 and 13% in 1993, reflecting base business growth. Excluding the Unusual Items, Selling, general and administrative expenses rose 14% in 1994 and 16% in 1993, and as a percentage of Net Sales were 39.6%, 39.4% and 38.8% in 1994, 1993 and 1992, respectively. In 1994, Selling, general and administrative expenses grew at the same rate as sales. In 1993, selling and distribution expenses grew at a faster rate than sales, but marketing expenditures grew at a slower rate. These changes reflect the impact of worldwide bottling acquisitions and flat marketing expenditures in domestic beverages.

Amortization of intangible assets rose 3% in 1994 and 14% in 1993. This noncash expense reduced Net Income Per Share by $0.29, $0.28 and $0.24 in 1994, 1993 and 1992, respectively.

Operating Profit increased 10% in 1994 and 23% in 1993. Excluding the Unusual Items, operating profit increased $262 million or 9% in 1994 and $342 million or 13% in 1993, driven by combined segment operating profit growth of 7% in 1994 and 14% in 1993. The 1994 increase reflected $850 million from higher volumes and $73 million from additional restaurant units, partially offset by higher operating expenses. Growth in 1993 reflected $425 million from higher volumes and $89 million from additional restaurant units, partially offset by increased operating expenses. International segment profits grew 12% in 1994 and 8% in 1993, reflecting double-digit increases in snack foods and beverages, partially offset by a double-digit decline in restaurants. International profits represented 19%, 18% and 19% of combined segment operating profits in 1994, 1993 and 1992, respectively. This percentage may be affected in the near term due to the devaluation of the Mexican peso and its related effects. Small foreign exchange gains in 1994 compared to 1993's foreign exchange losses, and increased equity in net income of affiliates, which are not included in segment profits, aided 1994 total operating profit growth.

Gain on Joint Venture Stock Offering of $17.8 million ($16.8 million after-tax or $0.02 per share) related to the public offering of shares by the BAESA joint venture. See Note 4.

Interest expense, net of Interest income, increased 15% in 1994 and 2% in 1993. The 1994 increase reflected higher average borrowings partially offset by higher interest rates on investment balances. The change in 1993 reflected higher average borrowings and lower average short-term investment balances partially offset by lower interest rates. Excluding the impact of net acquisitions, net interest expense increased 10% in 1994 and declined 9% in 1993.

Provision for Income Taxes as a percentage of pretax income was 33.0%, 34.5% and 31.4% in 1994, 1993 and 1992, respectively. The 1993 effective tax rate, excluding the Unusual Item, was 33.3%. The slight decline in 1994 reflected reversal of valuation allowances related to deferred tax assets and an increase in the proportion of income taxed at lower foreign rates offset by the absence of 1993's favorable adjustment of certain prior year foreign accruals. The 1993 increase of 1.9 points reflected higher U.S. and foreign effective tax rates, an increase in the proportion of income taxed at the higher U.S. tax rate and higher state taxes, partially offset by the favorable adjustment of prior year accruals.

Income and Income Per Share Before Cumulative Effect of Accounting Changes ("income" and "income per share") in 1994 increased 12% to $1.8 billion and 13% to $2.22, respectively, and in 1993 increased 22% to $1.6 billion and 22% to $1.96, respectively. Excluding the Unusual Items, income and income per share rose 8% and 9%, respectively, in 1994 and 13% and 12%, respectively, in 1993. Growth in income per share was depressed by estimated dilution from acquisitions of $0.03 or 1 point in 1994 and $0.05 or 3 points in 1993, primarily due to international beverage acquisitions in both years.

The Mexican peso devaluation may unfavorably impact Net Sales and Net Income in 1995; however, due to many uncertainties in Mexico, we are unable to quantify the impacts. See Management's Analysis – Overview on page 26 and pages 8, 13 and 17 for each industry segment for discussion regarding the impacts.

PEPSICO, INC. 1994 FINANCIAL REVIEW

Consolidated Balance Sheet

(in millions except per share amount)
PepsiCo, Inc. and Subsidiaries
December 31, 1994 and December 25, 1993

	1994	1993
ASSETS		
Current Assets		
Cash and cash equivalents	$ 330.7	$ 226.9
Short-term investments, at cost	1,157.4	1,573.8
	1,488.1	1,800.7
Accounts and notes receivable, less allowance: $150.6 in 1994 and $128.3 in 1993	2,050.9	1,883.4
Inventories	970.0	924.7
Prepaid expenses, taxes and other current assets	563.2	499.8
Total Current Assets	5,072.2	5,108.6
Investments in Affiliates	1,295.2	1,090.5
Property, Plant and Equipment, net	9,882.8	8,855.6
Intangible Assets, net	7,842.1	7,929.5
Other Assets	699.7	721.6
Total Assets	$24,792.0	$23,705.8
LIABILITIES AND SHAREHOLDERS' EQUITY		
Current Liabilities		
Accounts payable	$ 1,451.6	$ 1,390.0
Accrued compensation and benefits	753.5	726.0
Short-term borrowings	678.5	2,191.2
Income taxes payable	671.7	823.7
Accrued marketing	546.2	400.9
Other current liabilities	1,168.9	1,043.1
Total Current Liabilities	5,270.4	6,574.9
Long-term Debt	8,840.5	7,442.6
Other Liabilities	1,852.1	1,342.0
Deferred Income Taxes	1,972.9	2,007.6
Shareholders' Equity		
Capital stock, par value 1⅔¢ per share: authorized 1,800.0 shares, issued 863.1 shares	14.4	14.4
Capital in excess of par value	934.4	879.5
Retained earnings	7,739.1	6,541.9
Currency translation adjustment and other	(470.6)	(183.9)
	8,217.3	7,251.9
Less: Treasury stock, at cost: 73.2 shares and 64.3 shares in 1994 and 1993, respectively	(1,361.2)	(913.2)
Total Shareholders' Equity	6,856.1	6,338.7
Total Liabilities and Shareholders' Equity	$24,792.0	$23,705.8

See accompanying Notes to Consolidated Financial Statements.

PEPSICO, INC. 1994 FINANCIAL REVIEW

Management's Analysis – Financial Condition

(See Management's Analysis – Overview on page 24 for background information.)

Assets increased $1.1 billion or 5% over 1993. Short-term investments largely represent high-grade marketable securities portfolios held outside the U.S. The portfolio in Puerto Rico, which totaled $853 million at year-end 1994 and $1.3 billion at year-end 1993, arises from the operating cash flows of the centralized concentrate manufacturing facility that operates under a tax incentive grant. The grant provides that the portfolio funds may be remitted to the U.S. without any additional tax. PepsiCo remitted $380 million of the portfolio to the U.S. in 1994 and $564 million in 1993. PepsiCo continually reassesses its alternatives to redeploy its maturing investments in this and other portfolios held outside the U.S., considering other investment opportunities and risks, tax consequences and overall financing strategies.

Liabilities rose $569 million or 3% over 1993. Income taxes payable decreased $152 million or 18%, reflecting the prepayment of taxes in 1994 related to a federal tax audit. Other liabilities increased $510 million or 38%, reflecting a reclassification of amounts from Other current liabilities, normal growth in long-term liabilities and recognition of a liability for postemployment benefits under SFAS 112.

At year-end 1994 and 1993, $4.5 billion and $3.5 billion, respectively, of short-term borrowings were classified as long-term, reflecting PepsiCo's intent and ability, through the existence of its unused revolving credit facilities, to refinance these borrowings. PepsiCo's unused credit facilities with lending institutions, which exist largely to support the issuances of short-term borrowings, were $3.5 billion at year-end 1994 and 1993. Effective January 3, 1995, PepsiCo replaced its existing credit facilities with new credit facilities aggregating $4.5 billion, of which $1.0 billion expire in 1996 and $3.5 billion expire in 2000. Annually, these facilities can be extended an additional year upon the mutual consent of PepsiCo and the lending institutions.

Financial Leverage is measured by PepsiCo on both a market value and historical cost basis. PepsiCo believes that the most meaningful measure of debt is on a net basis, which takes into account its large investment portfolios held outside the U.S. These portfolios are managed as part of PepsiCo's overall financing strategy and are not required to support day-to-day operations. Net debt reflects the pro forma remittance of the portfolios (net of related taxes) as a reduction of total debt. Total debt includes the present value of operating lease commitments.

PepsiCo believes that market leverage (defined as net debt as a percent of net debt plus the market value of equity, based on the year-end stock price) is an appropriate measure of PepsiCo's financial leverage. Unlike historical cost measures, the market value of equity primarily reflects the estimated net present value of expected future cash flows that will both support debt and provide returns to shareholders. The market net debt ratio was 26% at year-end 1994 and 22% at year-end 1993. The increase was due to a 13% decrease in PepsiCo's stock price as well as an 8% increase in net debt. PepsiCo has established a long-term target range of 20-25% for its market net debt ratio to optimize its cost of capital.

As measured on an historical cost basis, the ratio of net debt to net capital employed (defined as net debt, other liabilities, deferred income taxes and shareholders' equity) was 49% at year-end 1994 and 50% at year-end 1993. The decline was due to a 9% increase in net capital employed, partially offset by the increase in net debt.

Because of PepsiCo's strong cash generating capability and its strong financial condition, PepsiCo has continued access to capital markets throughout the world.

At year-end 1994, about 60% of PepsiCo's net debt portfolio was exposed to variable interest rates, up from about 55% in 1993. In addition to variable rate debt, all net debt with maturities of less than one year is categorized as variable. PepsiCo prefers funding its operations with variable rate debt because it believes that, over the long-term, variable rate debt provides more cost effective financing than fixed rate debt. PepsiCo will issue fixed rate debt if advantageous market opportunities arise. A 1 point change in interest rates on variable rate net debt would impact annual interest expense, net of interest income, by approximately $38 million ($21 million after-tax or $0.03 per share) assuming the level and mix of the December 31, 1994 net debt portfolio was maintained.

PepsiCo's negative operating working capital position, which principally reflects the cash sales nature of its restaurant operations, effectively provides additional capital for investment. Operating working capital, which excludes short-term investments and short-term borrowings, was a negative $677 million and $849 million at year-end 1994 and 1993, respectively. The $172 million decline in negative working capital primarily reflected reclassification of amounts from Other current liabilities to Other Liabilities and base business growth in the more working capital intensive bottling and snack food operations exceeding the growth in restaurant operations.

Shareholders' Equity increased $517 million or 8% from 1993. This change reflected an 18% increase in retained earnings due to $1.8 billion in net income less dividends declared of $555 million. This growth was offset by a $448 million increase in treasury stock that reflected share repurchases, net of shares used for stock option exercises and acquisitions, and a $287 million unfavorable change in the currency translation adjustment account (CTA). The CTA change primarily reflected the impact of the devaluation of the Mexican peso in late 1994 on the translation of our peso denominated net assets.

Based on income before cumulative effect of accounting changes, PepsiCo's return on average shareholders' equity (ROAE) was 27.0% in 1994 and 27.2% in 1993. The ROAE was 26.5% in 1994 and 25.3% in 1993, excluding from both income and shareholders' equity the effect of the accounting changes and BAESA gain in 1994 as well as the $29.9 million charge in 1993 due to 1993 U.S. tax legislation.

PEPSICO, INC. 1994 FINANCIAL REVIEW

Consolidated Statement of Cash Flows

(in millions)
PepsiCo, Inc. and Subsidiaries
Fifty-three weeks ended December 31, 1994 and fifty-two weeks ended December 25, 1993 and December 26, 1992

	1994	1993	1992
Cash Flows – Operating Activities			
Income before cumulative effect of accounting changes	**$ 1,784.0**	$ 1,587.9	$ 1,301.7
Adjustments to reconcile income before cumulative effect of accounting changes to net cash provided by operating activities:			
Depreciation and amortization	**1,576.5**	1,444.2	1,214.9
Deferred income taxes	**(66.9)**	83.3	(52.0)
Other noncash charges and credits, net	**391.1**	344.8	315.6
Changes in operating working capital, excluding effects of acquisitions:			
Accounts and notes receivable	**(111.8)**	(161.0)	(45.7)
Inventories	**(101.6)**	(89.5)	(11.8)
Prepaid expenses, taxes and other current assets	**1.2**	3.3	(27.4)
Accounts payable	**30.4**	143.2	(102.0)
Income taxes payable	**54.4**	(125.1)	(16.9)
Other current liabilities	**158.7**	(96.7)	135.2
Net change in operating working capital	**31.3**	(325.8)	(68.6)
Net Cash Provided by Operating Activities	**3,716.0**	3,134.4	2,711.6
Cash Flows – Investing Activities			
Acquisitions and investments in affiliates	**(315.8)**	(1,011.2)	(1,209.7)
Capital spending	**(2,253.2)**	(1,981.6)	(1,549.6)
Proceeds from sales of property, plant and equipment	**55.3**	72.5	89.0
Short-term investments, by original maturity:			
More than three months-purchases	**(218.6)**	(578.7)	(1,174.8)
More than three months-maturities	**649.5**	846.0	1,371.8
Three months or less, net	**(9.9)**	(8.3)	(249.4)
Other, net	**(268.3)**	(109.4)	(30.8)
Net Cash Used for Investing Activities	**(2,361.0)**	(2,770.7)	(2,753.5)
Cash Flows – Financing Activities			
Proceeds from issuances of long-term debt	**1,285.2**	710.8	1,092.7
Payments of long-term debt	**(1,179.5)**	(1,201.9)	(616.3)
Short-term borrowings, by original maturity:			
More than three months-proceeds	**1,303.8**	3,033.6	911.2
More than three months-payments	**(1,727.7)**	(2,791.6)	(2,062.6)
Three months or less, net	**113.8**	839.0	1,075.3
Cash dividends paid	**(540.2)**	(461.6)	(395.5)
Purchases of treasury stock	**(549.1)**	(463.5)	(32.0)
Proceeds from exercises of stock options	**97.4**	68.6	82.8
Other, net	**(43.5)**	(36.7)	(30.9)
Net Cash (Used for) Provided by Financing Activities	**(1,239.8)**	(303.3)	24.7
Effect of Exchange Rate Changes on Cash and Cash Equivalents	**(11.4)**	(3.4)	0.4
Net Increase (Decrease) in Cash and Cash Equivalents	**103.8**	57.0	(16.8)
Cash and Cash Equivalents – Beginning of Year	**226.9**	169.9	186.7
Cash and Cash Equivalents – End of Year	**$ 330.7**	$ 226.9	$ 169.9
Supplemental Cash Flow Information			
Cash Flow Data			
Interest paid	**$ 591.1**	549.5	574.7
Income taxes paid	**$ 663.1**	675.6	519.7
Schedule of Noncash Investing and Financing Activities			
Liabilities assumed in connection with acquisitions	**$ 223.5**	897.0	383.8
Issuance of treasury stock and debt for acquisitions	**$ 38.8**	364.5	189.5
Book value of net assets exchanged for investment in affiliates	**$ –**	60.8	86.7

See accompanying Notes to Consolidated Financial Statements.

PEPSICO, INC. 1994 FINANCIAL REVIEW

Management's Analysis – Cash Flows

(See Management's Analysis – Overview on page 24 for background information.)

Cash flow activity in 1994 reflected strong cash flows from operations of $3.7 billion and $421 million in net proceeds from short-term investment activities. These amounts were used to fund capital spending of $2.3 billion, purchases of treasury stock totaling $549 million, dividend payments of $540 million, acquisition activity of $316 million and net debt repayments of $204 million.

One of PepsiCo's most significant financial strengths is its internal cash generation capability. In fact, after capital spending and acquisitions, each industry segment generated positive cash flows in 1994, with particularly strong results from beverages and snack foods. Net cash flows from PepsiCo's domestic businesses were partially offset by international uses of cash, reflecting strategies to accelerate growth of international operations.

The significant devaluation of the Mexican peso in late 1994 and early 1995 did not materially impact 1994 consolidated cash flows. However, because PepsiCo's operations in Mexico represented approximately 7% of consolidated cash flows from operations in 1994, the devaluation and its related effects are expected to have an unfavorable impact on 1995 cash flows from operations. In addition to the actions taken to mitigate the unfavorable impact on operating profits, the operations in Mexico will defer a portion of their capital spending. Nonetheless, significant uncertainties remain in Mexico and, as a result, it is not possible to quantify the impact on 1995 cash flows. In addition, actions are being taken in other parts of the world intended to mitigate the impact. See Management's Analysis – Overview on page 26 for additional discussion.

Net Cash Provided by Operating Activities in 1994 rose $582 million or 19% over 1993, and in 1993 grew $423 million or 16% over 1992. Income before noncash charges and credits rose 6% in 1994 and 24% in 1993. The increases in depreciation and amortization noncash charges of $132 million in 1994 and $229 million in 1993 reflected capital spending and in 1993, acquisitions. The 1994 decrease of $150 million in the deferred income tax provision was primarily due to the effect in 1994 of converting from premium based casualty insurance to self-insurance for most of these risks and adopting SFAS 112 for accounting for postemployment benefits. The 1993 increase of $135 million in the deferred income tax provision was primarily due to the lapping of 1992 effects related to restructuring accruals and prefunded employee benefit expenses and the impact of 1993 U.S. tax legislation. The cash provided in 1994 from working capital was $357 million better than 1993, reflecting normal increases in accrued liabilities across all of our businesses, lapping the effect of higher income tax payments and a lower provision in 1993 and improved trade receivable collections, partially offset by the impact on accounts payable of the timing of a large year-end payment to prefund employee benefits. The 1993 over 1992 net increase of $257 million in cash used for operating working capital reflected slower collections of domestic accounts receivable, advance domestic purchases of product ingredients, the higher payments of income taxes and the lapping of 1992 and 1991 effects related to restructuring accruals, partially offset by the payment to prefund employee benefits.

Investing Activities over the past three years reflected strategic spending in all three industry segments through capital spending, acquisitions and investments in affiliates. PepsiCo seeks investments that generate cash returns in excess of its long-term cost of capital, which is estimated to be approximately 11% at year-end 1994. See Note 5 for a discussion of acquisition activity. About 75% of the total acquisition activity in 1994 represented international transactions, compared to 45% in 1993 and 60% in 1992. PepsiCo continues to seek opportunities to strengthen its position in its domestic and international industry segments through such strategic acquisitions.

Increased capital spending in 1994 was driven by beverages reflecting investments in equipment for new packaging and new products in the U.S. and emerging international markets, primarily Eastern Europe. Capital spending increases in 1993 and 1992 were driven by restaurants, primarily for new units. Restaurants represented about half of the total capital spending in all three years. Restaurants, beverages and snack foods represent 40%, 30% and 30%, respectively, of the estimated $2.4 billion spending in 1995. This reflects a shift primarily from restaurants to snack foods. Beverages and snack foods 1995 capital spending reflects production capacity expansion and equipment replacements, while restaurants is primarily for new units. Restaurant capital spending in 1995 may be further reduced depending upon future decisions as described beginning on page 17. Approximately one-third of the planned 1995 capital spending relates to international businesses, about the same as the prior three years. Cash provided by operations is expected to be sufficient to fund the expected capital spending.

Investment activity in PepsiCo's short-term portfolios, primarily held outside the U.S., provided $421 million in 1994 and $259 million in 1993, respectively, compared to the increased net investment of $52 million in 1992.

Financing Activities. The 1994 over 1993 change in cash flows from net financing activities was a use of $937 million, primarily reflecting net repayments of short and long-term debt of $204 million compared to net proceeds of $590 million in 1993. The 1993 over 1992 change in cash flows from financing activities was a use of $328 million, primarily due to increased purchases of treasury stock.

At year-end 1994, PepsiCo had authority to issue $3.4 billion of long-term debt and had facilities in place in the U.S., Europe and Japan to take advantage of marketplace opportunities. The principal purposes of these shelf registrations are for financing growth activities and refinancing borrowings.

Cash dividends declared were $555 million in 1994 and $486 million in 1993. PepsiCo targets a dividend payout of about one-third of the prior year's income from ongoing operations, thus retaining sufficient earnings to provide financial resources for growth opportunities.

Share repurchase decisions are evaluated considering management's target capital structure and other investment opportunities. In 1994, PepsiCo repurchased 15.0 million shares at a cost of $549 million. Subsequent to year-end, PepsiCo repurchased 3.4 million shares through February 7, 1995 at a cost of $121 million. Including these repurchases, 18.8 million shares have been repurchased under the 50 million share repurchase authority granted by PepsiCo's Board of Directors on July 22, 1993.

PEPSICO, INC. 1994 FINANCIAL REVIEW

Consolidated Statement of Shareholders' Equity

(in millions except per share amounts)
PepsiCo, Inc. and Subsidiaries
Fifty-three weeks ended December 31, 1994 and fifty-two weeks ended December 25, 1993 and December 26, 1992

	Capital Stock						Currency	
	Issued		Treasury		Capital in Excess	Retained	Translation Adjustment	
	Shares	Amount	Shares	Amount	of Par Value	Earnings	and Other	Total
Shareholders' Equity, December 28, 1991 ...	863.1	$ 14.4	(74.0)	$ (745.9)	$ 476.6	$ 5,470.0	$ 330.3	$ 5,545.4
1992 Net income	–	–	–	–	–	374.3	–	374.3
Cash dividends declared (per share-$0.51)	–	–	–	–	–	(404.6)	–	(404.6)
Currency translation adjustment	–	–	–	–	–	–	(429.3)	(429.3)
Shares issued in connection with acquisitions	–	–	4.3	44.2	115.3	–	–	159.5
Stock option exercises, including tax benefits of $57.5	–	–	6.3	65.3	74.9	–	–	140.2
Purchases of treasury stock	–	–	(1.0)	(32.0)	–	–	–	(32.0)
Other	–	–	0.1	1.4	0.8	–	–	2.2
Shareholders' Equity, December 26, 1992 ...	863.1	$ 14.4	(64.3)	$ (667.0)	$ 667.6	$ 5,439.7	$ (99.0)	$ 5,355.7
1993 Net income	–	–	–	–	–	1,587.9	–	1,587.9
Cash dividends declared (per share-$0.61)	–	–	–	–	–	(485.7)	–	(485.7)
Currency translation adjustment	–	–	–	–	–	–	(77.0)	(77.0)
Purchases of treasury stock	–	–	(12.4)	(463.5)	–	–	–	(463.5)
Shares issued in connection with acquisitions	–	–	8.9	170.2	164.6	–	–	334.8
Stock option exercises, including tax benefits of $23.4	–	–	3.4	46.0	46.1	–	–	92.1
Pension liability adjustment, net of deferred taxes of $5.1	–	–	–	–	–	–	(7.9)	(7.9)
Other	–	–	0.1	1.1	1.2	–	–	2.3
Shareholders' Equity, December 25, 1993 ...	863.1	$ 14.4	(64.3)	$ (913.2)	$ 879.5	$ 6,541.9	$ (183.9)	$ 6,338.7
1994 Net income	**–**	**–**	**–**	**–**	**–**	**1,752.0**	**–**	**1,752.0**
Cash dividends declared (per share-$0.70)	**–**	**–**	**–**	**–**	**–**	**(554.8)**	**–**	**(554.8)**
Currency translation adjustment	**–**	**–**	**–**	**–**	**–**	**–**	**(294.6)**	**(294.6)**
Purchases of treasury stock	**–**	**–**	**(15.0)**	**(549.1)**	**–**	**–**	**–**	**(549.1)**
Stock option exercises, including tax benefits of $27.1	**–**	**–**	**4.9**	**80.8**	**44.5**	**–**	**–**	**125.3**
Shares issued in connection with acquisitions	**–**	**–**	**0.9**	**15.1**	**13.7**	**–**	**–**	**28.8**
Pension liability adjustment, net of deferred taxes of $5.1	**–**	**–**	**–**	**–**	**–**	**–**	**7.9**	**7.9**
Other	**–**	**–**	**0.3**	**5.2**	**(3.3)**	**–**	**–**	**1.9**
Shareholders' Equity, December 31, 1994	**863.1**	**$14.4**	**(73.2)**	**$(1,361.2)**	**$934.4**	**$7,739.1**	**$(470.6)**	**$6,856.1**

See accompanying Notes to Consolidated Financial Statements.

PEPSICO, INC. 1994 FINANCIAL REVIEW

Notes to Consolidated Financial Statements

(tabular dollars in millions except per share amounts)

Note 1 - Summary of Significant Accounting Policies
The preparation of the Consolidated Financial Statements requires estimates and assumptions that affect amounts reported and disclosed in the financial statements and related notes. Actual results could differ from those estimates. Certain reclassifications were made to prior year amounts to conform with the 1994 presentation. Significant accounting policies are discussed below, or where applicable, in the Notes that follow.

Principles of Consolidation. The financial statements reflect the consolidated accounts of PepsiCo, Inc. and its controlled affiliates. Intercompany accounts and transactions have been eliminated. Investments in affiliates in which PepsiCo exercises significant influence but not control are accounted for by the equity method and the equity in net income is included in Selling, general and administrative expenses.

Marketing Costs. Marketing costs are reported in Selling, general and administrative expenses and include costs of advertising, marketing and promotional programs. Promotional discounts are expensed as incurred and other marketing costs not deferred at year-end are charged to expense ratably in relation to sales over the year in which incurred. Marketing costs deferred at year-end consist of media and personal service advertising prepayments, promotional materials in inventory and production costs of future media advertising; these assets are expensed in the year first used.

Promotional discounts to retailers in the beverage segment are classified as a reduction of sales; in the snack food segment, such discounts are generally classified as marketing costs. The difference in classification reflects our historical view that promotional discounts had become so pervasive in the beverage industry, compared to the snack food industry, that they were effectively price discounts and should be classified accordingly. This differing accounting classification was also supported by a survey of the accounting practice of others in the beverage and snack food industries. PepsiCo plans to review its accounting policy in 1995 to determine whether the different accounting classification for beverages and snack foods still reflects the substance of the activity and whether it continues to be consistent with others in our industries. Depending on the outcome of the review, PepsiCo may change its accounting classification of beverage or snack food promotional discounts. Any change will not impact reported earnings as it would only result in a reclassification of the cost of promotional discounts between Net Sales and Selling, general and administrative expenses.

Cash Equivalents. Cash equivalents represent funds temporarily invested (with original maturities not exceeding three months) as part of PepsiCo's management of day-to-day operating cash receipts and disbursements. All other investment portfolios, largely held outside the U.S., are primarily classified as short-term investments.

Net Income Per Share. Net income per share is computed by dividing net income by the weighted average number of shares and share equivalents outstanding during each year.

Research and Development Expenses. Research and development expenses, which are expensed as incurred, were $152 million, $113 million and $102 million in 1994, 1993 and 1992, respectively.

Fiscal Year. PepsiCo's fiscal year ends on the last Saturday in December and, as a result, a fifty-third week is added every 5 or 6 years. The fiscal year ending December 31, 1994 consisted of 53 weeks.

Note 2 - Business Segments
Information regarding industry segments and geographic areas of operations is provided on pages 27 through 29.

Note 3 - Items Affecting Comparability
The fifty-third week, as described in Note 1, increased earnings in 1994 by approximately $54.0 million ($34.9 million after-tax or $0.04 per share). See Items Affecting Comparability on page 27 for the estimated impact of the fifty-third week on comparability of net sales and operating profits.

The effects of unusual items, primarily restructuring charges, and accounting changes on comparability of operating profits are provided in Items Affecting Comparability on page 27.

Information regarding the 1994 gain from a public share offering by PepsiCo's BAESA joint venture and a 1993 charge to increase net deferred tax liabilities as of the beginning of 1993 for a 1% statutory income tax rate increase due to 1993 U.S. tax legislation are provided in Notes 4 and 17, respectively.

Note 4 - Joint Venture Stock Offering
In 1993, PepsiCo entered into an arrangement with the principal shareholders of Buenos Aires Embotelladora S.A. (BAESA), a franchised bottler with operations in Argentina and Costa Rica. PepsiCo contributed certain assets, primarily bottling operations in Chile and Uruguay, while the shareholders contributed all of their outstanding shares in BAESA, representing 72.8% of the voting control and 42.5% of the ownership interest. Through this arrangement, PepsiCo's ownership in BAESA, which is accounted for by the equity method, was 25.9%.

On March 24, 1994, BAESA completed a public offering of 2.9 million American Depositary Shares (ADS) at $34.50 per ADS, which are traded on the New York Stock Exchange. In conjunction with the offering, PepsiCo and certain other shareholders exercised options for the equivalent of 1.6 million ADS. As a result of these transactions, PepsiCo's ownership in BAESA declined to 23.8%. The transactions generated cash proceeds for BAESA of $136.4 million. The resulting one-time, noncash gain to PepsiCo was $17.8 million ($16.8 million after-tax or $0.02 per share).

Note 5 - Acquisitions and Investments in Affiliates
During 1994, PepsiCo completed acquisitions and affiliate investments aggregating $355 million, principally for cash. In addition, approximately $41 million of debt was assumed in these transactions, most of which was subsequently retired. This activity included equity investments in international franchised bottling operations, primarily in Thailand and China, and acquisitions of international and domestic franchised restaurant operations and franchised and independent bottling operations, primarily in India and Mexico.

During 1993, PepsiCo completed acquisitions and affiliate investments aggregating $1.4 billion, principally comprised of $1.0 billion in cash and $335 million in PepsiCo Capital Stock.

PEPSICO, INC. 1994 FINANCIAL REVIEW

Approximately $307 million of debt was assumed in these transactions, more than half of which was subsequently retired. This activity included acquisitions of domestic and international franchised restaurant operations, the buyout of PepsiCo's joint venture partners in a franchised bottling operation in Spain and the related acquisition of their fruit-flavored beverage concentrate operation, the acquisition of the remaining 85% interest in a large franchised bottling operation in the Northwestern U.S., the acquisition of a regional Mexican-style casual dining restaurant chain in the U.S. and equity investments in certain franchised bottling operations in Argentina and Mexico.

During 1992, acquisitions and affiliate investment activity aggregated $1.4 billion, principally for cash. In addition, approximately $218 million of debt was assumed in these transactions, most of which was subsequently retired. This activity included acquisitions of international (primarily Canada) and domestic franchised bottling operations and a number of domestic and international franchised restaurant operations, the buyout of PepsiCo's joint venture partner in a Canadian snack food business and an equity investment in a domestic casual dining restaurant chain featuring gourmet pizza. In addition, PepsiCo exchanged certain previously consolidated snack food operations in Europe with a net book value of $87 million for a 60% equity interest in an international snack food joint venture with General Mills, Inc. PepsiCo secured a controlling interest in its Mexican cookie affiliate, Gamesa, through an exchange of certain non-cookie operations of Gamesa for its joint venture partner's interest.

The acquisitions have been accounted for by the purchase method; accordingly, their results are included in the Consolidated Financial Statements from their respective dates of acquisition. The aggregate impact of acquisitions was not material to PepsiCo's net sales, net income or net income per share; accordingly, no related pro forma information is provided.

Note 6 - Inventories

Inventories are valued at the lower of cost (computed on the average, first-in, first-out or last-in, first-out [LIFO] method) or net realizable value. The cost of 38% of 1994 inventories and 41% of 1993 inventories was computed using the LIFO method. Use of the LIFO method increased the total 1994 and 1993 year-end inventory amounts below by $5.5 million and $8.9 million, respectively.

	1994	1993
Raw materials and supplies	**$454.8**	$463.9
Finished goods	**515.2**	460.8
	$970.0	$924.7

See page 24 of Management's Analysis – Overview, for a discussion of PepsiCo's use of futures contracts to hedge its exposure to market price fluctuations for certain raw materials. Gains and losses on these contracts are deferred and included in the related cost of raw materials when purchased. Gains and losses realized in 1994 or deferred at year-end were not significant. As of December 31, 1994, PepsiCo had various open contracts, generally expiring by December 1995, which were not material.

Note 7 - Property, Plant and Equipment

Property, plant and equipment are stated at cost. Depreciation is calculated principally on a straight-line basis over the estimated useful lives of the assets. Depreciation expense in 1994, 1993 and 1992 was $1.2 billion, $1.1 billion and $923 million, respectively.

	1994	1993
Land	**$ 1,321.6**	$ 1,186.4
Buildings and improvements	**5,664.1**	5,017.6
Capital leases, primarily buildings	**451.2**	402.6
Machinery and equipment	**8,208.1**	7,175.0
Construction in progress	**485.1**	468.4
	16,130.1	14,250.0
Accumulated depreciation	**(6,247.3)**	(5,394.4)
	$ 9,882.8	$ 8,855.6

Note 8 - Intangible Assets

Identifiable intangible assets arose from the allocation of purchase prices of businesses acquired and consist principally of reacquired franchise rights and trademarks. Reacquired franchise rights relate to acquisitions of franchised bottling and restaurant operations and trademarks principally relate to acquisitions of international snack food and beverage trademarks. Amounts assigned to such identifiable intangibles were based on independent appraisals or internal estimates. Goodwill represents the residual purchase price after allocation to all identifiable net assets.

Intangible assets are amortized on a straight-line basis over appropriate periods generally ranging from 20 to 40 years. Accumulated amortization, included in the amounts below, was $1.6 billion and $1.3 billion at year-end 1994 and 1993, respectively.

	1994	1993
Reacquired franchise rights	**$3,974.0**	$3,959.7
Trademarks	**768.5**	849.1
Other identifiable intangibles	**249.7**	204.1
Goodwill	**2,849.9**	2,916.6
	$7,842.1	$7,929.5

The recoverability of carrying amounts of intangible assets is evaluated on a recurring basis. The primary indicators of recoverability are current or forecasted profitability over the estimated remaining life of the intangible assets, measured as the combined operating profit of the acquired business (including amortization of the intangible assets) and existing businesses that are directly related to the acquired business. Consideration is also given to the estimated disposal values of certain identifiable intangible assets compared to their carrying amounts. If recoverability of an intangible asset is unlikely based on the evaluation, the carrying amount is reduced by the amount it exceeds the forecasted operating profits and any disposal value. For the three-year period ended December 31, 1994, there were no significant adjustments to the carrying amounts of the intangible assets resulting from these evaluations.

PEPSICO, INC. 1994 FINANCIAL REVIEW

Note 9 - Short-term Borrowings and Long-term Debt

	1994	1993
Short-term Borrowings		
Commercial paper (5.4% and 3.3%) **(A)**	**$ 2,254.4**	$ 3,535.0
Current maturities of long-term debt issuances **(A)**	**987.5**	1,183.1
Notes (5.4% and 3.5%) **(A)**	**1,492.4**	394.0
Other borrowings (6.5% and 6.3%)	**444.2**	529.1
Amount reclassified to long-term debt **(B)**	**(4,500.0)**	(3,450.0)
	$ 678.5	$ 2,191.2
Long-term Debt		
Short-term borrowings, reclassified **(B)**	**$ 4,500.0**	$ 3,450.0
Notes due 1995 through 2008 (6.6% and 6.5%) **(A)**	**3,724.7**	3,873.8
Euro notes, 8% due 1997	**250.0**	–
Zero coupon notes, $795 million due 1995-2012 (14.6% and 14.4% annual yield to maturity)	**219.2**	327.2
Japanese yen 3.3% bonds due 1997 **(D)**	**200.8**	–
Swiss franc perpetual Foreign Interest Payment bonds **(C)**	**213.0**	212.2
Swiss franc 5¼% bearer bonds due 1995 **(D)**	**99.7**	90.1
Swiss franc 7⅛% notes due 1994 **(D)**	**–**	69.8
Capital lease obligations (See Note 11)	**298.2**	291.4
Other, due 1995-2015 (8.1% and 6.6%)	**322.4**	311.2
	9,828.0	8,625.7
Less current maturities of long-term debt issuances	**(987.5)**	(1,183.1)
	$ 8,840.5	$ 7,442.6

The interest rates in the above table indicate, where applicable, the weighted average rates at year-end 1994 and 1993, respectively.

The carrying amount of long-term debt includes any related discount or premium and unamortized debt issuance costs. The debt agreements include various restrictions, none of which are presently significant to PepsiCo. Subsequent to year-end 1994, PepsiCo issued $150 million of Notes through February 7, 1995.

The annual maturities of long-term debt through 1999, excluding capital lease obligations and the reclassified short-term borrowings, are: 1995-$1.0 billion, 1996-$1.1 billion, 1997-$1.0 billion, 1998-$1.2 billion and 1999-$280 million.

See Management's Analysis – Overview on page 24 for a discussion of PepsiCo's use of interest rate swaps and currency exchange agreements and its management of the inherent credit risk and Note 10.

(A) The following table indicates the notional amount and weighted average interest rates, by category, of interest rate swaps outstanding at year-end 1994 and 1993, respectively. The weighted average variable interest rates that PepsiCo pays, which are indexed primarily to either commercial paper or LIBOR rates, are based on rates as of the respective balance sheet date and are subject to change. Terms of interest rate swap agreements match the debt they modify and terminate in 1995 through 2008. The differential to be paid or received on interest rate swaps is accrued as interest rates change and is charged or credited to interest expense over the life of the agreements. The carrying amount of each interest rate swap is reflected in the Consolidated Balance Sheet as a receivable or payable under the appropriate current asset or liability caption.

	1994	1993
Receive fixed-pay variable:		
Notional amount	**$1,557.0**	$ 570.0
Weighted average receive rate	**5.89%**	5.96%
Weighted average pay rate	**6.12%**	3.28%
Receive variable-pay variable:		
Notional amount	**$1,008.5**	$ 465.0
Weighted average receive rate	**4.90%**	3.81%
Weighted average pay rate	**5.99%**	3.17%
Receive variable-pay fixed:		
Notional amount	**$ 215.0**	$ 265.0
Weighted average receive rate	**6.56%**	3.84%
Weighted average pay rate	**8.22%**	7.46%

The following table identifies the composition of total debt (excluding capital lease obligations and the effect of the reclassified amounts from short-term borrowings) after giving effect to the impact of interest rate swaps. All short-term borrowings are considered variable interest rate debt for purposes of this table.

	1994		1993	
	Carrying Amount	**Weighted Average Interest Rate**	Carrying Amount	Weighted Average Interest Rate
Variable interest rate debt:				
Short-term borrowings	**$5,178.5**	**6.19%**	$5,641.2	4.11%
Long-term debt	**1,102.5**	**6.25%**	567.6	4.75%
	6,281.0	**6.20%**	6,208.8	4.17%
Fixed interest rate debt	**2,939.8**	**6.96%**	3,133.6	6.95%
	$9,220.8	**6.44%**	$9,342.4	5.10%

(B) At year-end 1994 and 1993, PepsiCo had unused revolving credit facilities covering potential borrowings aggregating $3.5 billion. Effective January 3, 1995, PepsiCo replaced its existing credit facilities with new revolving credit facilities aggregating $4.5 billion, of which $1.0 billion expire in 1996 and $3.5 billion expire in 2000. At year-end 1994 and 1993, $4.5 billion and $3.5 billion, respectively, of short-term borrowings were classified as long-term debt, reflecting PepsiCo's intent and ability, through the existence of the unused credit facilities, to refinance these borrowings. These credit facilities exist largely to support the issuances of short-term borrowings and are available for acquisitions and other general corporate purposes.

(C) The coupon rate of the Swiss franc 400 million perpetual Foreign Interest Payment bonds issued in 1986 is 7½% through 1996. The bonds have no stated maturity date. At the end of each 10-year period after the issuance of the bonds, PepsiCo and the bondholders each have the right to cause redemption of the bonds. If not redeemed, the coupon rate will be adjusted based on the prevailing yield of 10-year U.S. Treasury Securities. The principal of the bonds is denominated in Swiss francs. PepsiCo can, and intends to, limit the ultimate redemption amount to the U.S. dollar proceeds at issuance, which is the basis of the carrying amount. Interest payments are made in U.S. dollars and are calculated by applying the coupon rate to the original U.S. dollar principal proceeds of $214 million.

(D) PepsiCo has entered into currency exchange agreements to hedge its foreign currency exposure on these issues of non-U.S. dollar-denominated debt. At year-end 1994, the carrying amount of this debt aggregated $301 million and the receivables and payables under related currency exchange agreements aggregated $50 million and $2 million, respectively, resulting in a net effective U.S. dollar liability of $253 million with a weighted average interest rate of 6.6%. At year-end 1993, the aggregate carrying amount of the debt and the receivables under related currency exchange agreements were $160 million and $41 million, respectively, resulting in a net effective U.S. dollar liability of $119 million with a weighted average fixed interest rate of 6.5%. The carrying amount of each currency exchange agreement is reflected in the Consolidated Balance Sheet as a receivable or payable under the appropriate current and noncurrent asset and liability captions. Changes in the carrying amount of a currency exchange agreement resulting from exchange rate movements are offset by changes in the carrying amount of the related non-U.S. dollar-denominated debt, as both amounts are based on current exchange rates.

Note 10 - Fair Value of Financial Instruments

The carrying amounts in the following table are included in the Consolidated Balance Sheet under the indicated captions, except for debt-related derivative instruments (interest rate swaps and currency exchange agreements), which are included in the appropriate current or noncurrent asset or liability caption. Investments consist primarily of debt securities and have been classified as held-to-maturity. Noncurrent investments mature at various dates through 2000.

Because of the short maturity of cash equivalents and short-term investments, the carrying amount approximates fair value. The fair value of noncurrent investments is based upon market quotes. The fair value of debt, debt-related derivative instruments and guarantees is estimated using market quotes, valuation models and calculations based on market rates.

See Management's Analysis – Overview on page 24 and Note 9 for more information regarding PepsiCo's use of interest rate swaps and currency exchange agreements and its management of the inherent credit risk.

	1994		1993	
	Carrying Amount	**Fair Value**	Carrying Amount	Fair Value
Assets				
Cash and cash equivalents . . .	**$ 330.7**	**$ 330.7**	$ 226.9	$ 226.9
Short-term investments	**$1,157.4**	**$1,157.4**	$1,573.8	$1,573.8
Other assets (noncurrent investments)	**$ 48.0**	**$ 47.5**	$ 55.5	$ 55.4
Liabilities				
Debt:				
Short-term borrowings and long-term debt, net of capital leases .	**$9,220.8**	**$9,265.4**	$9,342.4	$9,626.0
Debt-related derivative instruments:				
Open contracts in asset position . .	**(51.3)**	**(51.4)**	(42.4)	(72.7)
Open contracts in liability position .	**7.9**	**54.1**	1.2	32.8
Net debt	**$9,177.4**	**$9,268.1**	$9,301.2	$9,586.1
Guarantees	**–**	**$ 2.7**	–	$ 1.7

Note 11 - Leases

PepsiCo has noncancelable commitments under both capital and long-term operating leases, primarily for restaurant units. Certain of these units have been subleased to restaurant franchisees. In addition, PepsiCo is lessee under noncancelable leases covering vehicles, equipment and nonrestaurant real estate. Capital and operating lease commitments expire at various dates through 2088 and, in many cases, provide for rent escalations and renewal options. Most leases require payment of related executory costs which include property taxes, maintenance and insurance.

Future minimum commitments and sublease receivables under noncancelable leases are as follows:

	Commitments		Sublease Receivables	
	Capital	Operating	Direct Financing	Operating
1995	$ 58.9	$ 313.0	$ 3.2	$ 9.6
1996	53.9	276.4	3.0	8.8
1997	46.7	247.3	2.7	7.7
1998	65.2	228.7	2.3	6.7
1999	34.4	203.3	2.0	6.0
Later years . .	279.0	1,072.1	7.1	24.2
	$538.1	$2,340.8	$20.3	$63.0

At year-end 1994, the present value of minimum payments under capital leases was $298 million, after deducting $1 million for estimated executory costs and $239 million representing imputed interest. The present value of minimum receivables under direct financing subleases was $13 million after deducting $7 million of unearned interest income.

PEPSICO, INC. 1994 FINANCIAL REVIEW

Rental expense and income were as follows:

	1994	1993	1992
Rental expense			
Minimum	**$433.5**	$392.3	$351.5
Contingent	**31.7**	27.5	27.5
	$465.2	$419.8	$379.0
Rental income			
Minimum	**$ 11.7**	$ 12.2	$ 10.2
Contingent	**3.5**	4.4	4.5
	$ 15.2	$ 16.6	$ 14.7

Contingent rentals are based on sales by restaurants in excess of levels stipulated in the lease agreements.

Note 12 - Postretirement Benefits Other Than Pensions

PepsiCo provides postretirement health care benefits to eligible retired employees and their dependents, principally in the U.S. Retirees who have 10 years of service and attain age 55 while in service with PepsiCo are eligible to participate in the postretirement benefit plans. The plans are not funded and were largely noncontributory through 1993.

In 1992, PepsiCo adopted Statement of Financial Accounting Standards No. 106, "Employers' Accounting for Postretirement Benefits Other Than Pensions." The cumulative effect of this change in accounting for years prior to 1992 resulted in a noncash charge of $575.3 million pretax ($356.7 million after-tax or $0.44 per share).

Effective in 1993 and 1994, PepsiCo implemented programs intended to stem rising costs and introduced retiree cost-sharing, including adopting a provision which limits its future obligation to absorb health care cost inflation. These amendments resulted in an unrecognized prior service gain of $191 million, which is being amortized on a straight-line basis over the average remaining employee service period of 10 years as a reduction in postretirement benefit expense beginning in 1993.

The postretirement benefit expense for 1994, 1993 and 1992 included the following components:

	1994	1993	1992
Service cost of benefits earned	**$ 18.6**	$ 14.7	$25.5
Interest cost on accumulated postretirement benefit obligation	**41.4**	40.6	50.8
Amortization of prior service (gain) cost	**(19.6)**	(19.6)	0.1
Amortization of net loss	**5.6**	0.5	–
	$ 46.0	$ 36.2	$76.4

The decline in the 1993 expense was primarily due to the plan amendments, reflecting reductions in service and interest costs as well as the amortization of the unrecognized prior service gain.

The 1994 and 1993 postretirement benefit liability included the following components:

	1994	1993
Actuarial present value of postretirement benefit obligation:		
Retirees	**$(288.6)**	$(313.8)
Fully eligible active plan participants	**(88.1)**	(107.3)
Other active plan participants	**(148.0)**	(206.9)
Accumulated postretirement benefit obligation	**(524.7)**	(628.0)
Unrecognized prior service gain	**(151.9)**	(171.5)
Unrecognized net loss	**11.5**	148.6
	$(665.1)	$(650.9)

The discount rate assumptions used in computing the information above were as follows:

	1994	1993	1992
Postretirement benefit expense	**6.8%**	8.2	8.9
Accumulated postretirement benefit obligation	**9.1%**	6.8	8.2

The year-to-year fluctuations in the discount rate assumptions primarily reflect changes in U.S. interest rates. The discount rate represents the expected yield on a portfolio of high-grade (AA rated or equivalent) fixed-income investments with cash flow streams sufficient to satisfy benefit obligations under the plans when due.

As a result of the plan amendments discussed above, separate assumed health care cost trend rates are used for employees who retire before and after the effective date of the amendments. The assumed health care cost trend rate for employees who retired before the effective date is 9.5% for 1995, declining gradually to 5.5% in 2005 and thereafter. For employees retiring after the effective date, the trend rate is 8.0% for 1995, declining gradually to 0% in 2005 and thereafter. A 1 point increase in the assumed health care cost trend rate would have increased the 1994 postretirement benefit expense by $2.0 million and would have increased the 1994 accumulated postretirement benefit obligation by $20.6 million.

Note 13 - Pension Plans

PepsiCo sponsors noncontributory defined benefit pension plans covering substantially all full-time domestic employees as well as contributory and noncontributory defined benefit pension plans covering certain international employees. Benefits generally are based on years of service and compensation or stated amounts for each year of service. PepsiCo funds the domestic plans in amounts not less than minimum statutory funding requirements nor more than the maximum amount that can be deducted for federal income tax purposes. International plans are funded in amounts sufficient to comply with local statutory requirements. The plans' assets consist principally of equity securities, government and corporate debt securities and other fixed income obligations. For 1994 and 1993, the domestic plan assets included 6.9 million shares of PepsiCo Capital Stock, with a market value of $227.2 million and

PEPSICO, INC. 1994 FINANCIAL REVIEW

$265.7 million, respectively. Dividends on PepsiCo Capital Stock of $4.7 million and $4.0 million were received by the domestic plans in 1994 and 1993, respectively.

The international plans presented below are primarily comprised of those in the U.K. and Canada for all three years as well as those in Mexico and Japan for 1994 and 1993. Information for 1992 has not been restated, since complete information for plans in Mexico and Japan was not available. Inclusion of the plans in Mexico and Japan increased the 1994 and 1993 pension expense by $7.9 million and $5.5 million, respectively.

The net pension expense (income) for company-sponsored plans included the following components:

	Domestic Plans			International Plans		
	1994	1993	1992	**1994**	1993	1992
Service cost of benefits earned	**$ 69.8**	$ 57.1	$ 52.3	**$ 15.0**	$ 12.4	$ 8.6
Interest cost on projected benefit obligation	**84.0**	75.6	72.0	**15.4**	15.0	10.9
Return on plan assets:						
Actual loss (gain)	**19.7**	(161.5)	(61.3)	**8.1**	(40.8)	(36.0)
Deferred (loss) gain	**(130.5)**	70.9	(26.2)	**(32.5)**	20.4	18.6
	(110.8)	(90.6)	(87.5)	**(24.4)**	(20.4)	(17.4)
Amortization of net transition (gain) loss	**(19.0)**	(19.0)	(19.0)	**(0.2)**	0.3	–
Net other amortization	**9.1**	8.8	8.2	**1.7**	1.7	(6.5)
	$ 33.1	$ 31.9	$ 26.0	**$ 7.5**	$ 9.0	$ (4.4)

Reconciliations of the funded status of the plans to the pension liability are as follows:

	Domestic Plans				International Plans			
	Assets Exceed Accumulated Benefits		Accumulated Benefits Exceed Assets		Assets Exceed Accumulated Benefits		Accumulated Benefits Exceed Assets	
	1994	1993	**1994**	1993	**1994**	1993	**1994**	1993
Actuarial present value of benefit obligation:								
Vested benefits	**$ (774.0)**	$ (726.0)	**$(21.6)**	$(192.8)	**$(124.4)**	$(138.8)	**$(22.8)**	$(28.0)
Nonvested benefits	**(97.4)**	(99.0)	**(1.6)**	(28.3)	**(2.3)**	(3.4)	**(7.4)**	(5.4)
Accumulated benefit obligation	**(871.4)**	(825.0)	**(23.2)**	(221.1)	**(126.7)**	(142.2)	**(30.2)**	(33.4)
Effect of projected compensation increases	**(111.1)**	(131.6)	**(47.6)**	(41.7)	**(24.1)**	(22.9)	**(10.1)**	(18.4)
Projected benefit obligation	**(982.5)**	(956.6)	**(70.8)**	(262.8)	**(150.8)**	(165.1)	**(40.3)**	(51.8)
Plan assets at fair value	**1,133.0**	1,018.7	**2.8**	185.2	**213.4**	221.7	**15.5**	17.3
Plan assets in excess of (less than) projected benefit obligation	**150.5**	62.1	**(68.0)**	(77.6)	**62.6**	56.6	**(24.8)**	(34.5)
Unrecognized prior service cost	**30.6**	11.7	**30.0**	49.9	**3.5**	3.2	**0.3**	0.5
Unrecognized net (gain) loss	**(71.3)**	16.0	**3.7**	26.1	**14.0**	11.9	**(3.1)**	7.7
Unrecognized net transition (gain) loss	**(73.1)**	(89.0)	**0.3**	(2.8)	**(1.8)**	(2.6)	**4.9**	8.1
Adjustment required to recognize minimum liability	**–**	–	**–**	(33.0)	**–**	–	**–**	(4.3)
Prepaid (accrued) pension liability	**$ 36.7**	$ 0.8	**$(34.0)**	$ (37.4)	**$ 78.3**	$ 69.1	**$(22.7)**	$(22.5)

The assumptions used to compute the information above were as follows:

	Domestic Plans			International Plans		
	1994	1993	1992	**1994**	1993	1992
Discount rate – pension expense	**7.0%**	8.2	8.4	**7.3%**	9.0	9.5
Expected long-term rate of return on plan assets	**10.0%**	10.0	10.0	**11.3%**	10.8	10.8
Discount rate – projected benefit obligation	**9.0%**	7.0	8.2	**9.3%**	7.4	9.0
Future compensation growth rate	**3.3%-7.0%**	3.3-7.0	3.3-7.0	**3.0%-8.5%**	3.5-8.5	5.0-7.0

The discount rates and rates of return for the international plans represent weighted averages.

The year-to-year fluctuations in the discount rate assumptions primarily reflect changes in interest rates. The discount rates represent the expected yield on a portfolio of high-grade (AA rated or equivalent) fixed-income investments with cash flow streams sufficient to satisfy benefit obligations under the plans when due. The higher assumed discount rates used to measure the 1994 projected benefit obligation compared to the assumed discount rate used to measure the 1993 projected benefit obligation changed the funded status of certain plans from underfunded to overfunded.

PEPSICO, INC. 1994 FINANCIAL REVIEW

In 1994, PepsiCo changed the method for calculating the market-related value of plan assets used in determining the return-on-asset component of annual pension expense and the cumulative net unrecognized gain or loss subject to amortization. Under the previous accounting method, the calculation of the market-related value of assets reflected amortization of the actual capital return on assets on a straight-line basis over a five-year period. Under the new method, the calculation of the market-related value of assets reflects the long-term rate of return expected by PepsiCo and amortization of the difference between the actual return (including capital, dividends and interest) and the expected return over a five-year period. PepsiCo believes the new method is widely used in practice and preferable because it results in calculated plan asset values that more closely approximate fair value, while still mitigating the effect of annual market-value fluctuations. Under both methods, only the cumulative net unrecognized gain or loss which exceeds 10% of the greater of the projected benefit obligation or the market-related value of plan assets is subject to amortization. This change resulted in a noncash benefit in 1994 of $37.8 million ($23.3 million after-tax or $0.03 per share) representing the cumulative effect of the change related to years prior to 1994 and $35.1 million in lower pension expense ($21.6 million after-tax or $0.03 per share) related to 1994 as compared to the previous accounting method. Had this change been applied retroactively, pension expense would have been reduced by $16.4 million ($10.7 million after-tax or $0.01 per share) and $9.5 million ($6.5 million after-tax or $0.01 per share) in 1993 and 1992, respectively.

Note 14 - Postemployment Benefits Other Than to Retirees
Effective the beginning of 1994, PepsiCo adopted Statement of Financial Accounting Standards No. 112 (SFAS 112), "Employers' Accounting for Postemployment Benefits." SFAS 112 requires PepsiCo to accrue the cost of certain postemployment benefits to be paid to terminated or inactive employees other than retirees. The principal effect to PepsiCo results from accruing severance benefits to be provided to employees of certain business units who are terminated in the ordinary course of business over the expected service lives of the employees. Previously, these benefits were accrued upon the occurrence of an event. Severance benefits resulting from actions not in the ordinary course of business will continue to be accrued when those actions occur. The cumulative effect charge upon adoption of SFAS 112, which relates to years prior to 1994, was $84.6 million ($55.3 million after-tax or $0.07 per share). As compared to the previous accounting method, the current year impact of adopting SFAS 112 was immaterial to 1994 operating profits. PepsiCo's cash flows have been unaffected by this accounting change as PepsiCo continues to largely fund postemployment benefit costs as incurred.

Note 15 - Franchise Arrangements
Franchise arrangements with restaurant franchisees generally provide for initial fees and continuing royalty payments to PepsiCo based upon a percentage of sales. The arrangements are intended to assist franchisees through, among other things, product development and marketing programs initiated by PepsiCo for both its company-owned and franchised operations. On a limited basis, franchisees have also entered into leases of restaurant properties leased or owned by PepsiCo (see Note 11). Royalty revenues, initial fees and rental payments from franchisees, which are included in Net Sales, aggregated $407 million, $357 million and $344 million in 1994, 1993 and 1992, respectively. Franchise royalty revenues, which represent the majority of these amounts, are recognized when earned. PepsiCo also has franchise arrangements with beverage bottlers, which do not provide for royalty payments.

Note 16 - Restructurings
PepsiCo recorded restructuring charges of $193.5 million in 1992 ($128.5 million after-tax or $0.16 per share) and $149.0 million in 1991 ($102.3 million after-tax or $0.13 per share). The 1992 charge related principally to streamlining and reorganizing the domestic beverage business, consolidating the snack food businesses in the U.K. and streamlining an acquired beverage bottling business in Spain. The 1991 charge related to streamlining snack food operations in the U.S. and U.K. and operations at KFC. These charges were classified in Selling, general and administrative expenses and were primarily for costs requiring future cash outlays. The annual accrual activity, including asset valuation allowances, and the related components were as follows:

	1994	1993	1992
Annual Accrual Activity			
Balance – Beginning of year	**$121.7**	$ 253.2	$112.6
New restructuring charges	–	–	193.5
New restructuring accruals - purchase price adjustments **(A)**	–	–	41.5
Accretion of interest on net present value of severance	**2.8**	6.9	–
Cash payments	**(50.6)**	(122.8)	(83.5)
Asset write-offs	**(4.0)**	(9.1)	(10.3)
Change in estimates	**(28.7)**	(6.5)	(0.6)
Balance – End of year	**$ 41.2**	$ 121.7	$253.2
Accrual Components			
Facility closings/fixed asset disposals	**$ 3.0**	$ 13.9	$ 35.3
Employee terminations **(A)**	**36.1**	103.2	153.9
Relocation of employees and equipment	**0.7**	2.2	29.1
Nonrecurring costs of redesigning core business processes **(B)**	–	0.7	25.3
Other	**1.4**	1.7	9.6
Balance – End of year **(C)**	**$ 41.2**	$ 121.7	$253.2

(A) Included amounts for termination of employees of an acquired beverage bottling business in Spain accounted for as a purchase. The acquired business was formerly accounted for as a 30% owned equity investment. Upon acquisition of the remaining 70%, 30% of the restructuring charge was included in income and 70% was a purchase price adjustment.

(B) Included only specific nonrecurring incremental and direct costs for activities clearly identifiable with the redesign of the domestic beverages' core business processes.

(C) The 1994 year-end balance of $41 million, which was primarily included in Other current liabilities, represented estimated future cash payments of $26 million, $12 million and $3 million in 1995, 1996 and 1997, respectively.

PEPSICO, INC. 1994 FINANCIAL REVIEW

Note 17 - Income Taxes

In 1992, PepsiCo adopted Statement of Financial Accounting Standards No. 109 (SFAS 109), "Accounting for Income Taxes." PepsiCo elected to adopt SFAS 109 on a prospective basis, resulting in a noncash tax charge in 1992 of $570.7 million ($0.71 per share) for the cumulative effect of the change related to years prior to 1992. The cumulative effect primarily represented the recording of additional deferred tax liabilities related to identifiable intangible assets, principally acquired trademarks and reacquired franchise rights, that have no tax bases. These deferred tax liabilities would be paid only in the unlikely event the related intangible assets were sold in taxable transactions.

Detail of the provision for income taxes on income before cumulative effect of accounting changes was as follows:

		1994	1993	1992
Current	Federal	**$642.0**	$466.8	$413.0
	Foreign	**174.1**	195.5	170.4
	State	**131.2**	89.0	65.7
		947.3	751.3	649.1
Deferred	Federal	**(63.9)**	78.2	(18.8)
	Foreign	**(1.8)**	(12.5)	(33.5)
	State	**(1.2)**	17.6	0.3
		(66.9)	83.3	(52.0)
		$880.4	$834.6	$597.1

In 1993, a charge of $29.9 million ($0.04 per share) was recorded to increase net deferred tax liabilities as of the beginning of 1993 for a 1% statutory income tax rate increase under 1993 U.S. tax legislation. The effect of the higher rate on the 1993 increase in net deferred tax liabilities through the enactment date of the legislation was immaterial.

U.S. and foreign income before income taxes and cumulative effect of accounting changes were as follows:

	1994	1993	1992
U.S.	**$1,762.4**	$1,633.0	$1,196.8
Foreign	**902.0**	789.5	702.0
	$2,664.4	$2,422.5	$1,898.8

PepsiCo operates centralized concentrate manufacturing facilities in Puerto Rico and Ireland under long-term tax incentives. The foreign amount in the above table includes approximately 50% (consistent with the allocation for tax purposes) of the income from U.S. sales of concentrate manufactured in Puerto Rico. See Management's Analysis – Overview on page 26 for a discussion of the reduction of the U.S. tax credit associated with beverage concentrate operations in Puerto Rico.

Reconciliation of the U.S. federal statutory tax rate to PepsiCo's effective tax rate on pretax income, based on the dollar impact of these major components on the provision for income taxes, was as follows:

	1994	1993	1992
U.S. federal statutory tax rate	**35.0%**	35.0%	34.0%
State income tax, net of federal tax benefit	**3.2**	2.9	2.3
Effect of lower taxes on foreign income (including Puerto Rico and Ireland)	**(5.4)**	(3.3)	(5.0)
Adjustment to the beginning-of-the-year deferred tax assets valuation allowance	**(1.3)**	–	–
Reduction of prior year foreign accruals	–	(2.0)	–
Effect of 1993 tax legislation on deferred income taxes	–	1.1	–
Nondeductible amortization of domestic goodwill	**0.8**	0.8	0.9
Other, net	**0.7**	–	(0.8)
Effective tax rate	**33.0%**	34.5%	31.4%

Detail of the 1994 and 1993 deferred tax liabilities (assets) was as follows:

	1994	1993
Intangible assets other than nondeductible goodwill	**$ 1,627.8**	$ 1,551.0
Property, plant and equipment	**506.4**	552.3
Safe harbor leases	**171.2**	177.5
Zero coupon notes	**110.6**	103.5
Other	**336.7**	549.0
Gross deferred tax liabilities	**2,752.7**	2,933.3
Net operating loss carryforwards	**(306.0)**	(241.5)
Postretirement benefits	**(248.3)**	(268.0)
Self-insurance reserves	**(71.2)**	(10.8)
Deferred state income taxes	**(69.1)**	(39.9)
Restructuring accruals	**(15.8)**	(42.0)
Various accrued liabilities and other	**(551.2)**	(686.8)
Gross deferred tax assets	**(1,261.6)**	(1,289.0)
Deferred tax assets valuation allowance	**319.3**	249.0
Net deferred tax liability	**$ 1,810.4**	$ 1,893.3
Included in:		
Prepaid expenses, taxes and other current assets	**$ (166.9)**	$ (138.2)
Other current liabilities	**4.4**	23.9
Deferred income taxes	**1,972.9**	2,007.6
	$ 1,810.4	$ 1,893.3

The valuation allowance related to deferred tax assets increased by $70.3 million in 1994 primarily resulting from additions related to current year net operating losses, partially offset by reversals related to prior year net operating losses. The net operating loss carryforwards largely related to a number of state and foreign jurisdictions and generally expire over a range of dates.

Deferred tax liabilities have not been recognized for bases differences related to investments in foreign subsidiaries and joint ventures. These differences, which consist primarily of unremitted earnings intended to be indefinitely reinvested, aggregated approximately $3.8 billion at year-end 1994 and $3.2 billion at year-end 1993, exclusive of amounts that if remitted in the future would result in little or no tax under current tax laws and the Puerto Rico tax incentive grant. Determination of the amount of unrecognized deferred tax liabilities is not practicable.

Tax benefits associated with exercises of stock options of $27.1 million in 1994, $23.4 million in 1993 and $57.5 million in 1992 were credited to shareholders' equity. A change in the functional currency of operations in Mexico from the U.S. dollar to local currency in 1993 resulted in a $19.3 million decrease in the net deferred foreign tax liability that was credited to shareholders' equity.

Note 18 - Employee Incentive Plans

PepsiCo has established certain employee incentive plans under which stock options are granted. A stock option allows an employee to purchase a share of PepsiCo Capital Stock (Stock) in the future at a price equal to the fair market value on the date of the grant.

Under the PepsiCo SharePower Stock Option Plan, approved by the Board of Directors and effective in 1989, essentially all employees other than executive officers, part-time and short-service employees may be granted stock options annually. The number of options granted is based on each employee's annual earnings. The options generally become exercisable ratably over five years from the grant date and must be exercised within 10 years of the grant date. SharePower options were granted to approximately 128,000 employees in 1994, 118,000 employees in 1993 and 114,000 employees in 1992.

The shareholder-approved 1987 Long-Term Incentive Plan (the 1987 Plan), which has provisions similar to prior plans, provides incentives to eligible senior and middle management employees. In addition to grants of stock options, which are generally exercisable between 1 and 15 years from the grant date, the 1987 Plan allows for grants of performance share units (PSUs) to eligible senior management employees. A PSU is equivalent in value to a share of Stock at the grant date and vests for payment four years from the grant date, contingent upon attainment of prescribed Corporate performance goals. PSUs are not directly granted, as certain stock options granted may be surrendered by employees for a specified number of PSUs within 60 days of the option grant date. During 1994, 1,541,187 stock options were surrendered for 513,729 PSUs. At year-end 1994, 1993 and 1992, there were 629,202, 491,200 and 484,698 outstanding PSUs, respectively.

Grants under the 1987 Plan are approved by the Compensation Committee of the Board of Directors (the Committee), which is composed of outside directors. Payment of awards other than stock options is made in cash and/or Stock as approved by the Committee, and amounts expensed for such awards were $7 million, $5 million and $11 million in 1994, 1993 and 1992, respectively. Under the 1987 Plan, a maximum of 54 million shares of Stock can be purchased or paid pursuant to grants. There were 7 million, 20 million, 22 million and 32 million shares available for future grants at year-end 1994, 1993, 1992 and 1991, respectively. The Committee does not intend to grant future awards under the 1987 Plan.

On May 4, 1994, PepsiCo's shareholders approved the 1994 Long-Term Incentive Plan (the 1994 Plan). The 1994 Plan continues the principal features of the 1987 Plan and authorizes a maximum of 75 million shares of Stock which may be purchased or paid pursuant to grants by the Committee. The first awards under the 1994 Plan were made as of January 1, 1995.

1994, 1993 and 1992 activity for the stock option plans included:

(options in thousands)	SharePower	Long-Term Incentive
Outstanding at December 28, 1991	23,801	27,834
Granted	8,477	12,653
Exercised	(1,155)	(5,155)
Surrendered for PSUs	–	(503)
Canceled	(2,327)	(1,839)
Outstanding at December 26, 1992	28,796	32,990
Granted	9,121	2,834
Exercised	(1,958)	(1,412)
Surrendered for PSUs	–	(96)
Canceled	(2,524)	(966)
Outstanding at December 25, 1993	33,435	33,350
Granted	**11,633**	**16,237**
Exercised	**(1,820)**	**(3,052)**
Surrendered for PSUs	**–**	**(1,541)**
Canceled	**(3,443)**	**(2,218)**
Outstanding at December 31, 1994	**39,805**	**42,776**
Exercisable at December 31, 1994	**16,115**	**18,439**
Option prices per share:		
Exercised during 1994	$17.58 to $36.75	$4.11 to $38.75
Exercised during 1993	$17.58 to $36.75	$4.11 to $36.31
Exercised during 1992	$17.58 to $35.25	$4.11 to $29.88
Outstanding at year-end 1994	$17.58 to $36.75	$7.69 to $42.81

Note 19 - Contingencies

PepsiCo is subject to various claims and contingencies related to lawsuits, taxes, environmental and other matters arising out of the normal course of business. Management believes that the ultimate liability, if any, in excess of amounts already provided arising from such claims or contingencies is not likely to have a material adverse effect on PepsiCo's annual results of operations or financial condition. At year-end 1994 and 1993, PepsiCo was contingently liable under guarantees aggregating $187 million and $276 million, respectively. The guarantees are primarily issued to support financial arrangements of certain PepsiCo joint ventures, and bottling and restaurant franchisees. PepsiCo manages the risk associated with these guarantees by performing appropriate credit reviews in addition to retaining certain rights as a joint venture partner or franchisor. See Note 10 for information related to the fair value of the guarantees.

PEPSICO, INC. 1994 FINANCIAL REVIEW

Management's Responsibility for Financial Statements

To Our Shareholders:

Management is responsible for the reliability of the consolidated financial statements and related notes, which have been prepared in conformity with generally accepted accounting principles and include amounts based upon our estimates and judgments, as required. The financial statements have been audited and reported on by our independent auditors, KPMG Peat Marwick LLP, who were given free access to all financial records and related data, including minutes of the meetings of the Board of Directors and Committees of the Board. We believe that the representations made to the independent auditors were valid and appropriate.

PepsiCo maintains a system of internal control over financial reporting designed to provide reasonable assurance as to the reliability of the financial statements. The system is supported by formal policies and procedures, including an active Code of Conduct program intended to ensure employees adhere to the highest standards of personal and professional integrity. PepsiCo's internal audit function monitors and reports on the adequacy of and compliance with the internal control system, and appropriate actions are taken to address significant control deficiencies and other opportunities for improving the system as they are identified. The Audit Committee of the Board of Directors, which is composed solely of outside directors, provides oversight to the financial reporting process through periodic meetings with our independent auditors, internal auditors and management. Both our independent auditors and internal auditors have free access to the Audit Committee.

Although no cost effective internal control system will preclude all errors and irregularities, we believe our controls as of December 31, 1994 provide reasonable assurance that the financial statements are reliable.

Wayne Calloway

Wayne Calloway
Chairman of the Board and Chief Executive Officer

Robert H. Dettmer

Robert G. Dettmer
Executive Vice President and Chief Financial Officer

Robert L. Carleton

Robert L. Carleton
Senior Vice President and Controller

February 7, 1995

Report of Independent Auditors

Board of Directors and Shareholders
PepsiCo, Inc.

We have audited the accompanying consolidated balance sheet of PepsiCo, Inc. and Subsidiaries as of December 31, 1994 and December 25, 1993, and the related consolidated statements of income, cash flows and shareholders' equity for each of the years in the three-year period ended December 31, 1994, appearing on pages 27, 28, 29, 30, 32, 34 and 36 through 45. These consolidated financial statements are the responsibility of PepsiCo, Inc.'s management. Our responsibility is to express an opinion on these consolidated financial statements based on our audits.

We conducted our audits in accordance with generally accepted auditing standards. Those standards require that we plan and perform the audit to obtain reasonable assurance about whether the financial statements are free of material misstatement. An audit includes examining, on a test basis, evidence supporting the amounts and disclosures in the financial statements. An audit also includes assessing the accounting principles used and significant estimates made by management, as well as evaluating the overall financial statement presentation. We believe that our audits provide a reasonable basis for our opinion.

In our opinion, the consolidated financial statements referred to above present fairly, in all material respects, the financial position of PepsiCo, Inc. and Subsidiaries as of December 31, 1994 and December 25, 1993, and the results of its operations and its cash flows for each of the years in the three-year period ended December 31, 1994, in conformity with generally accepted accounting principles.

As discussed in Notes 14 and 13 to the consolidated financial statements, PepsiCo, Inc. in 1994 adopted the provisions of the Financial Accounting Standards Board's Statement of Financial Accounting Standards No. 112, "Employers' Accounting for Postemployment Benefits," and changed its method for calculating the market-related value of pension plan assets used in the determination of pension expense, respectively. As discussed in Notes 12 and 17 to the consolidated financial statements, PepsiCo, Inc. in 1992 adopted the provisions of the Financial Accounting Standards Board's Statements of Financial Accounting Standards No. 106, "Employers' Accounting for Postretirement Benefits Other Than Pensions," and No. 109, "Accounting for Income Taxes," respectively.

KPMG Peat Marwick LLP

KPMG Peat Marwick LLP
New York, New York
February 7, 1995

PEPSICO, INC. 1994 FINANCIAL REVIEW

Selected Quarterly Financial Data

(in millions except per share amounts, unaudited)
PepsiCo, Inc. and Subsidiaries

	First Quarter (12 Weeks) 1994[(a)]	1993	Second Quarter (12 Weeks) 1994[(a)(c)]	1993	Third Quarter (12 Weeks) 1994[(a)]	1993[(d)]	Fourth Quarter (17/16 Weeks)[(e)] 1994[(a)]	1993	Full Year (53/52 Weeks)[(e)] 1994[(a)(c)]	1993[(d)]
Net sales	**$5,728.9**	5,091.6	**6,557.0**	5,890.3	**7,064.0**	6,316.4	**9,122.5**	7,722.4	**28,472.4**	25,020.7
Gross profit	**$2,944.4**	2,641.4	**3,419.5**	3,102.8	**3,684.0**	3,322.1	**4,709.1**	4,008.3	**14,757.0**	13,074.6
Operating profit	**$ 550.5**	506.0	**785.0**	750.4	**961.7**	851.6	**904.0**	798.5	**3,201.2**	2,906.5
Income before income taxes and cumulative effect of accounting changes	**$ 438.4**	391.6	**672.2**	635.7	**830.3**	736.5	**723.5**	658.7	**2,664.4**	2,422.5
Provision for income taxes	**$ 155.6**	131.2	**225.7**	208.9	**288.9**	278.3	**210.2**	216.2	**880.4**	834.6
Income before cumulative effect of accounting changes	**$ 282.8**	260.4	**446.5**	426.8	**541.4**	458.2	**513.3**	442.5	**1,784.0**	1,587.9
Cumulative effect of accounting changes [(b)]	**$ (32.0)**	–	**–**	–	**–**	–	**–**	–	**(32.0)**	–
Net income	**$ 250.8**	260.4	**446.5**	426.8	**541.4**	458.2	**513.3**	442.5	**1,752.0**	1,587.9
Income (charge) per share:										
Income before cumulative effect of accounting changes	**$ 0.35**	0.32	**0.55**	0.53	**0.68**	0.56	**0.64**	0.55	**2.22**	1.96
Cumulative effect of accounting changes [(b)]	**$ (0.04)**	–	**–**	–	**–**	–	**–**	–	**(0.04)**	–
Net income per share	**$ 0.31**	0.32	**0.55**	0.53	**0.68**	0.56	**0.64**	0.55	**2.18**	1.96

(a) Included the current year benefit of changing the method for calculating the market-related value of plan assets used in determining the return-on-asset component of annual pension expense and the cumulative net unrecognized gain or loss subject to amortization, which reduced full-year pension expense by $35.1 ($21.6 after-tax or $0.03 per share). This benefit was prorated over each of the four quarters. See Note 13.

(b) Represented the cumulative net effect related to years prior to 1994 of adopting SFAS 112, "Employers' Accounting for Postemployment Benefits," and the change in the method for calculating the market-related value of pension plan assets. See Notes 14 and 13, respectively.

(c) Included a $17.8 gain ($16.8 after-tax or $0.02 per share) arising from a public share offering by PepsiCo's BAESA joint venture in South America. See Note 4.

(d) Included a $29.9 charge ($0.04 per share) to increase net deferred tax liabilities as of the beginning of 1993 for a 1% statutory income tax rate increase due to 1993 U.S. tax legislation. See Note 17.

(e) Fiscal years 1994 and 1993 consisted of 53 and 52 weeks, respectively. The estimated favorable impact of the 53rd week on 1994 fourth quarter and full-year earnings was $54.0 ($34.9 after-tax or $0.04 per share).

Cumulative Earnings Growth vs. Change in Stock Price in 1994

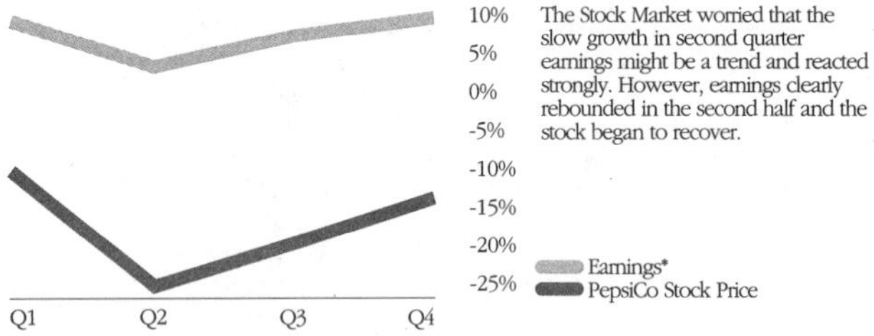

* Excludes unusual items noted above in notes (c) and (d).

PEPSICO, INC. 1994 FINANCIAL REVIEW

Selected Financial Data

(in millions except per share and employee amounts, unaudited)
PepsiCo, Inc. and Subsidiaries

	Growth Rates				
	Compounded		Annual		
	10-Year 1984-94	5-Year 1989-94	1-Year 1993-94	1994(a)(b)	1993(c)
Summary of Operations					
Net sales	15.0%	13.6%	13.8%	**$28,472.4**	25,020.7
Cost of sales and operating expenses				**25,271.2**	22,114.2
Operating profit	18.6%	12.5%	10.1%	**3,201.2**	2,906.5
Gain on joint venture stock offering (h)				**17.8**	–
Interest expense				**(645.0)**	(572.7)
Interest income				**90.4**	88.7
Income from continuing operations before income taxes and cumulative effect of accounting changes	19.2%	14.7%	10.0%	**2,664.4**	2,422.5
Provision for income taxes				**880.4**	834.6
Income from continuing operations before cumulative effect of accounting changes	20.3%	14.6%	12.3%	**$ 1,784.0**	1,587.9
Cumulative effect of accounting changes (i)				**$ (32.0)**	–
Net income (j)	23.5%	14.2%	10.3%	**$ 1,752.0**	1,587.9
Per Share Data					
Income from continuing operations before cumulative effect of accounting changes	21.0%	14.5%	13.3%	**$ 2.22**	1.96
Cumulative effect of accounting changes (i)				**$ (0.04)**	–
Net income (j)	24.2%	14.0%	11.2%	**$ 2.18**	1.96
Cash dividends declared	14.2%	16.9%	14.8%	**$ 0.700**	0.610
Average shares and equivalents outstanding				**803.6**	810.1
Cash Flow Data (k)					
Net cash provided by continuing operations	14.2%	14.5%	18.6%	**$ 3,716.0**	3,134.4
Cash acquisitions and investments in affiliates				**$ 315.8**	1,011.2
Cash capital spending	15.0%	19.0%	13.7%	**$ 2,253.2**	1,981.6
Cash dividends paid	13.3%	17.4%	17.0%	**$ 540.2**	461.6
Year-End Position					
Total assets	17.7%	10.4%	4.6%	**$24,792.0**	23,705.8
Long-term debt	29.5%	7.8%	18.8%	**$ 8,840.5**	7,442.6
Total debt (l)	25.9%	6.5%	(1.2)%	**$ 9,519.0**	9,633.8
Shareholders' equity				**$ 6,856.1**	6,338.7
Per share	14.8%	12.0%	9.3%	**$ 8.68**	7.94
Market price per share	22.9%	11.1%	(13.4)%	**$ 36¼**	41⅞
Shares outstanding				**789.9**	798.8
Employees	12.1%	12.1%	11.3%	**471,000**	423,000
Statistics					
Return on average shareholders' equity (m)				**27.0%**	27.2
Market net debt ratio (n)				**26%**	22
Historical cost net debt ratio (o)				**49%**	50

All share and per share amounts reflect three-for-one stock splits in 1990 and 1986. Additionally, PepsiCo made numerous acquisitions in most years presented and a few divestitures in certain years. Such transactions did not materially affect the comparability of PepsiCo's operating results for the periods presented, except for certain large acquisitions made in 1986, 1988 and 1989, and the divestitures discussed in Notes (g) and (j).

(a) Included the current year benefit of changing the method for calculating the market-related value of plan assets, which reduced full-year pension expense by $35.1 ($21.6 after-tax or $0.03 per share). See Note 13.
(b) Fiscal years 1994 and 1988 each consisted of 53 weeks. Normally, fiscal years consist of 52 weeks; however, because the fiscal year ends on the last Saturday in December, a week is added every 5 or 6 years. The 53rd week increased 1994 earnings by approximately $54.0 ($34.9 after-tax or $0.04 per share) and 1988 earnings by approximately $23.2 ($15.7 after-tax or $0.02 per share).
(c) Included a $29.9 charge ($0.04 per share) to increase net deferred tax liabilities as of the beginning of 1993 for a 1% statutory income tax rate increase due to 1993 U.S. tax legislation. See Note 17.
(d) Included $193.5 in unusual charges for restructuring ($128.5 after-tax or $0.16 per share). See Note 2 on page 27 and Note 16.
(e) Included $170.0 in unusual charges ($119.8 after-tax or $0.15 per share). See Note 2 on page 27.
(f) Included $83.0 in unusual charges ($48.8 after-tax or $0.06 per share). See Note 2 on page 27.
(g) Included a $156.0 unusual charge ($62.0 after-tax or $0.07 per share) related to a program to sell several international bottling operations.
(h) The $17.8 gain ($16.8 after-tax or $0.02 per share) in 1994 arose from a public share offering by PepsiCo's BAESA joint venture in South America. See Note 4. The $118.2 gain ($53.0 after-tax or $0.07 per share) in 1990 arose from an initial public offering of new shares by a KFC joint venture in Japan and a sale by PepsiCo of a portion of its shares.

Net Sales
($ in Millions)

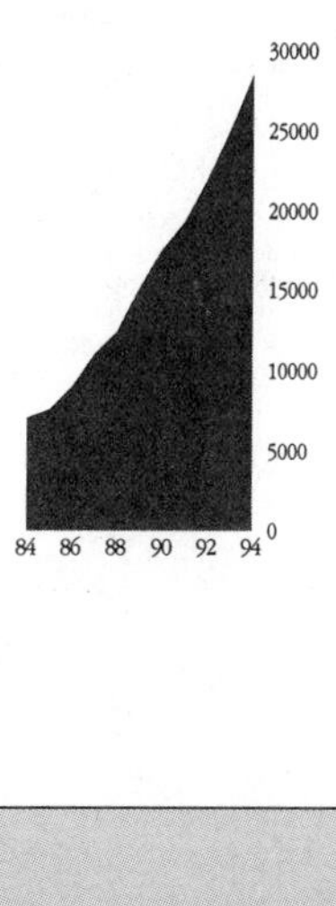

PEPSICO, INC. 1994 FINANCIAL REVIEW

1992(d)	1991(e)	1990(f)	1989	1988(b)	1987	1986	1985	1984(g)
21,970.0	19,292.2	17,515.5	15,049.2	12,381.4	11,018.1	9,017.1	7,584.5	7,058.6
19,598.8	17,180.4	15,473.4	13,276.6	11,039.6	9,890.5	8,187.9	6,802.4	6,479.3
2,371.2	2,111.8	2,042.1	1,772.6	1,341.8	1,127.6	829.2	782.1	579.3
–	–	118.2	–	–	–	–	–	–
(586.1)	(613.7)	(686.0)	(607.9)	(342.4)	(294.6)	(261.4)	(195.2)	(204.9)
113.7	161.6	179.5	175.3	120.5	112.6	122.7	96.4	86.1
1,898.8	1,659.7	1,653.8	1,340.0	1,119.9	945.6	690.5	683.3	460.5
597.1	579.5	563.2	438.6	357.7	340.5	226.7	256.7	180.5
1,301.7	1,080.2	1,090.6	901.4	762.2	605.1	463.8	426.6	280.0
(927.4)	–	–	–	–	–	–	–	–
374.3	1,080.2	1,076.9	901.4	762.2	594.8	457.8	543.7	212.5
1.61	1.35	1.37	1.13	0.97	0.77	0.59	0.51	0.33
(1.15)	–	–	–	–	–	–	–	–
0.46	1.35	1.35	1.13	0.97	0.76	0.58	0.65	0.25
0.510	0.460	0.383	0.320	0.267	0.223	0.209	0.195	0.185
806.7	802.5	798.7	796.0	790.4	789.3	786.5	842.1	862.4
2,711.6	2,430.3	2,110.0	1,885.9	1,894.5	1,334.5	1,212.2	817.3	981.5
1,209.7	640.9	630.6	3,296.6	1,415.5	371.5	1,679.9	160.0	–
1,549.6	1,457.8	1,180.1	943.8	725.8	770.5	858.5	770.3	555.8
395.5	343.2	293.9	241.9	199.0	172.0	160.4	161.1	154.6
20,951.2	18,775.1	17,143.4	15,126.7	11,135.3	9,022.7	8,027.1	5,889.3	4,876.9
7,964.8	7,806.2	5,899.6	6,076.5	2,656.0	2,579.2	2,632.6	1,162.0	668.1
8,671.6	8,034.4	7,526.1	6,942.8	4,107.0	3,225.1	2,865.3	1,506.1	948.9
5,355.7	5,545.4	4,904.2	3,891.1	3,161.0	2,508.6	2,059.1	1,837.7	1,853.4
6.70	7.03	6.22	4.92	4.01	3.21	2.64	2.33	2.19
42¼	33¾	25¾	21⅜	13⅛	11¼	8¾	7⅞	4⅝
798.8	789.1	788.4	791.1	788.4	781.2	781.0	789.4	845.2
372,000	338,000	308,000	266,000	235,000	225,000	214,000	150,000	150,000
23.9	20.7	24.8	25.6	26.9	26.5	23.8	23.1	15.4
19	21	24	26	24	22	28	15	12
49	51	51	54	43	41	46	30	17

(i) Represents the cumulative effect of adopting in 1994 SFAS 112, "Employers' Accounting for Postemployment Benefits," and changing the method for calculating the market-related value of plan assets used in determining the return-on-asset component of annual pension expense and the cumulative net unrecognized gain or loss subject to amortization (see Notes 14 and 13, respectively) and adopting in 1992 SFAS 106, "Employers' Accounting for Postretirement Benefits Other Than Pensions," and SFAS 109, "Accounting for Income Taxes" (see Notes 12 and 17, respectively). Prior years were not restated for these changes in accounting.

(j) Included impacts of discontinued operations, the most significant of which were in 1985 and 1984. 1985 included income of $123.6 after-tax ($0.15 per share) and 1984 included charges of $62.5 after-tax ($0.07 per share) resulting from PepsiCo disposing of its sporting goods and transportation segments.

(k) Cash flows from other investing and financing activities, which are not presented, are an integral part of total cash flow activity.

(l) Total debt includes short-term borrowings and long-term debt, which for 1987 through 1990 included a nonrecourse obligation.

(m) The return on average shareholders' equity is calculated using income from continuing operations before cumulative effect of accounting changes.

(n) The market net debt ratio represents net debt as a percent of net debt plus the market value of equity, based on the year-end stock price. Net debt is total debt, which for this purpose includes the present value of long-term operating lease commitments, reduced by the pro forma remittance of investment portfolios held outside the U.S. For 1987 through 1990, total debt was also reduced by the nonrecourse obligation in the calculation of net debt.

(o) The historical cost net debt ratio represents net debt (see Note n) as a percent of capital employed (net debt, other liabilities, deferred income taxes and shareholders' equity).

Income Per Share From Continuing Operations*
(In Dollars)

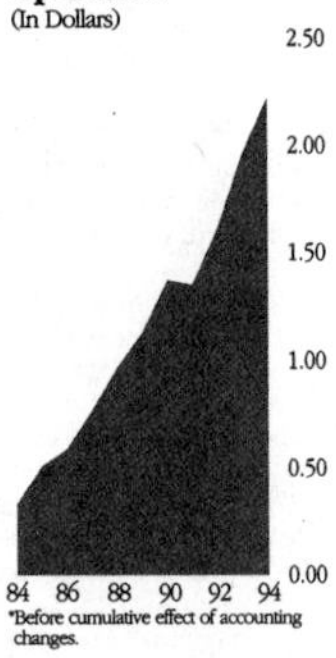

*Before cumulative effect of accounting changes.

SUMMARY

Accounting is the language of business. Accounting reports are used to convey information about the financial health and performance of companies to various external constituencies such as creditors, lenders, shareholders, public interest groups, employees, and various governmental agencies, all of whom have decisions to make.

The focus of this text is on financial accounting and the generally accepted accounting principles used in preparing quarterly and annual accounting reports. Our goal is to help you become financial statement literate and to be conversant in the language of accounting.

NEW CONCEPTS AND TERMS

Accounting (p. 3)
American Institute of Certified Public Accountants (p. 7)
Audit (p. 11)
Auditor's opinion (p. 11)
Financial accounting (p. 6)
Financial Accounting Standards Board (p. 7)
Financial statements (p. 6)
Footnotes (p. 3)
Generally accepted accounting principles (GAAP) (p. 6)
Generally accepted auditing standards (p. 11)
Independent auditor (p. 11)
Internal control structure (p. 9)
International Accounting Standards Committee (p. 8)
Managerial accounting (p. 5)
Prospective information (p. 4)
Securities and Exchange Commission (p. 7)
Stewardship information (p. 4)
Unqualified opinion (p. 14)

ISSUES FOR DISCUSSION

D1.1 Identify five different users of accounting information and discuss briefly the kinds of decisions they must make and the kinds of accounting information they should have in making those decisions.

Assume that the PepsiCo, Inc., financial statements are typical of the statements provided by U.S. companies to their public stockholders. Do those statements meet the information needs you outlined above? To the extent that they do not, why might that be so? Where might users go to find the information needed?

D1.2 Assume that you are the chief accounting officer of a major manufacturing company. Identify and describe five principal differences that might exist between your company's managerial accounting reports and its financial accounting reports. Why might those differences exist?

D1.3 Assume that you are a member of Congress and that it is the early 1930s. The Depression is a very painful reality for everyone. The financial reporting systems in our country have been allocated part of the blame for the financial collapse, and new answers are being sought for old questions. A number of different voices are arguing their positions. Some believe that we ought to have a government-mandated financial reporting system to which every company that wants to sell stock to the public must adhere. Others, who believe that the marketplace will reward companies that provide useful information and will penalize those that do not, argue that we should have no standardized financial reporting requirement. They argue that each company should be allowed to devise its own report to shareholders. In the middle ground are those who argue for some standardization of financial reports disseminated to the public but at the same time insist that the standardized format be developed by private sector initiative.

a. Outline the advantages and disadvantages of each of the above three alternatives from the standpoint of the financial community as a whole.

b. Assume that each of the three alternatives is offered in legislation. Which alternative would you vote for, and why?

D1.4 In your own words, explain what is meant by an internal control structure. You may find it helpful to couch your explanation in the context of a hypothetical company, for example, a rapidly growing manufacturer of electronic components.

D1.5 Chapter 1 briefly describes the role of the Financial Accounting Standards Board and notes that Board members are experienced professionals, independent of their former employers. Why would you think those two requirements might be important?

D1.6 It has been suggested by both businesspeople and politicians that we change the rules that now require all publicly held companies to issue quarterly reports. They suggest that we follow the practice of some other countries and require only semiannual reports. Outline the advantages and disadvantages of that proposal from as many different perspectives as you think might be relevant.

D1.7 Based on your reading of the report of PepsiCo management and the report from the independent auditor, both presented in the chapter, describe in your own words the responsibilities of management and of the auditors for the preparation of the PepsiCo financial statements. How are they similar? How are they different? This division of responsibilities has evolved over time. Why might it have evolved as it did?

D1.8 In Note 1 PepsiCo describes its policies with regard to marketing costs. What other approach could management have taken with regard to those costs? How might PepsiCo's financial statements have been different if an alternative approach had been adopted?

D1.9 Based on your reading of the PepsiCo financial statements, identify five measures of performance that you believe to be important and explain why you selected those five. Also identify five measures of PepsiCo performance that you believe might be important to a decision to buy PepsiCo shares but are not available to you from these financial statements. Why might those measures not be reported in a public financial statement?

D1.10 Assume that you will have dinner tomorrow night with an old college friend who is now a successful CPA. Based on your reading of the PepsiCo financial statements, identify the 10 most important questions about accounting and the financial reporting process that you would like to pose to your friend. (Try to make those questions as complete as possible. At the conclusion of this course, you ought to go back and see how many of those questions you can answer for yourself.)

CHAPTER 2

There Is More to Accounting Than Meets the Eye

What advantages a merchant derives from double entry bookeeping! It is among the finest inventions of the human mind; and every good householder should introduce it into his economy.[1]

Key Chapter Issues

- I'm ready to wade into this thing called accounting, but before I set out on this journey, can I get a general road map to help establish a perspective?
- What is the significance of the accounting equation A = L + OE? What is the logic behind that algebraic expression?
- What are these tools called the balance sheet, the income statement, and the statement of cash flow? How do we use them? How are they different? How do they relate to each other?
- GAAP is an acronym for Generally Accepted Accounting Principles; where does that general acceptance come from? How would we know when we had achieved it? Who is entitled to proclaim it and interpret it?

[1]A quote attributed to J. Wolfgang von Goethe (1749–1832) contained in S. James and R. Parker, *A Dictionary of Business Quotations*, (NY, NY: Simon & Schuster), p. 1.

In Chapter 1 we set forth the idea that accounting is essentially a communications vehicle and could be compared to a language. We also introduced generally accepted accounting principles (GAAP) as the set of conventions that makes it possible for accounting to communicate to a diverse audience. That discussion pointed out that the word *accounting* means both the numbers included in financial reports and the text that explains and expands on those numerical measures. We looked briefly at the process of preparing financial reports, and we introduced a real-life example we will use throughout the book — the 1994 financial report published by PepsiCo, Inc.

In this chapter we move beyond that introductory discussion to a second level of inquiry. In the first segment of this chapter we look more deeply into some of the important principles that underlie GAAP, and we consider several institutions that guide the development of the principles, practices, and procedures included within GAAP. In the second segment we explore the basic financial statements in more depth and look at the way those financial statements interrelate. In the final segment, we look at the way PepsiCo applied some of the fundamental accounting principles using the company's 1994 financial statements as the vehicle for that discussion.

SOME FUNDAMENTAL QUESTIONS IN ACCOUNTING

The discussion in the introductory chapter was, necessarily, somewhat abstract. However, the process of preparing financial statements for a particular company is never an abstract exercise. Preparing financial statements requires a real person to find specific answers to specific questions. These questions have energized financial people for many years, and the answers that have emerged form the backbone of our present set of generally accepted accounting principles. It will be useful at this stage of our inquiry to consider those questions and the answers that are outlined for us in GAAP.

To pursue these questions and their answers, let us create a context. As you think through the following discussion, assume that you have formed a new company to borrow some money to buy an apartment building. Let us assume that you have invested $20,000 of your own money in the company. Let us also assume that the company used your $20,000, borrowed an additional $80,000 from a bank, and then paid $100,000 to buy an existing apartment building. The company's business will be to collect rent from the tenants, pay for maintenance and utilities, pay the principal and interest on the debt, and pay you any profits that may result from the company's operations. As you periodically prepare financial statements to report the status of the company and its success or failure, you will be forced to address a number of questions.

What Is the Entity Whose Operations Are to Be Covered by This Report?

You could elect to prepare statements that reflected only the assets and the activities of the real estate company by itself; alternatively, you could prepare financial statements that reported all of your personal assets and activities, which would of course include the assets and activities of the real estate venture you just created. What assets and activities should be included in the financial statements you will prepare, and what should be left out? To make that decision you might ask, "What information does the expected reader of these statements need to know? What information does the reader of these statements have a right to know?" For example, if the bank is entitled to look at only the real estate business to satisfy the $80,000 loan, the financial statements you prepare for it should cover only the business' activities. However, if the bank has the right to look at the real estate business *and* your personal activities to satisfy the bank loan, it might ask for combined financial statements that cover your own personal activities as well as those of the business.

Following that line of thought, you might also argue that the company's financial statements should include the assets and the activities of your building's tenants — after all, their financial well-being will be crucial to your success and to the bank's ability to collect on its loan. However, the relationship you have with your company is not the same as the relationship you or your company has with the building's tenants. You control your company, and you can pretty well dictate its activities. However, neither you nor your company controls the building's tenants, and they are under no obligation to you or your company except to comply with the terms of the lease. Their assets are not available to you except for the rent they owe. That same thinking directs GAAP. Under GAAP, financial statements include or encompass all of the activities of a particular entity and any other entities that it controls. For example, for various legal reasons, you might want your real estate company to create a subsidiary company and to assign to that subsidiary all of the maintenance work on your building. Regardless of the legal separation of the two companies, the consolidated financial statements of the parent real estate company would include all of its own activities and the activities of the maintenance company. If that maintenance work was instead subcontracted to an independent janitorial firm, your real estate company would not include the activities of that entity. Under GAAP, **consolidated financial statements** typically include the activities of the legal parent company and the activities of all of those other entities that the parent controls. This convention is known as the **entity principle.**

What Measurement Basis Should Be Used in Preparing These Financial Statements?

The simplest measurement basis for the preparation of financial statements is the **cash basis.** The cash basis determines success by comparing the amount of cash on hand at the end of a period against the amount of cash on hand at the beginning of the period. More cash is good; less cash is bad.

Cash-basis accounting is used by some very small companies when there is little difference between a long-range and a short-range view of the business. Cash-basis accounting focuses on cash today and ignores the future cash-generating potential of any other form of asset. For example, in the hypothetical case we are using as our model, a balance sheet prepared on a cash basis of accounting would show no assets (or liabilities) for your company after its purchase of the building; worse, the income statement for the first period would show a loss of $20,000 because of the cash expended for the down payment. The cash basis of accounting is concerned only with *current* cash effects and ignores the possibility of *future* cash effects. Cash-basis accounting, for example, ignores the fact that your company purchased the building because you expected it to earn more cash (in the future) than you initially paid for it, as well as the fact that the building retains that future cash-generating ability. Cash-basis accounting is not considered to be GAAP.

This is not to imply, however, that cash flow information is not useful. It would be very useful to the readers of your company's financial statements to know that all of the company's cash was used for the down payment on the building and that the company would have to borrow money to meet emergency needs. Cash flow information is important to financial statement readers who want a near-term perspective on a company. The financial community has indicated that it wants cash flow information for its near-term decisions, but there has also been a demand for more sophisticated measures of financial status and of operating results.

At the other extreme, you could prepare the financial statements for your real estate business using **fair value accounting.** Under fair value accounting, assets and liabilities are included on a balance sheet at the value of their expected future cash flows, which is, of course, their current market value. If it is not immediately apparent to you why the market value of an asset should be the present value of its future cash flows, stop a minute and consider the thought process you might follow in a decision to purchase 100 shares of PepsiCo stock. You would most likely estimate the dividends you would receive in the future and the increase in share price that might develop during the period you expect to hold the stock. You would then reduce those expected future cash flows back to today's equivalent dollar value, using a discount rate equal to the percentage return you expect on a common stock such as PepsiCo. If the expected future cash flows, discounted at the rate of return you demand, are more than the current market price of the PepsiCo stock, you would buy the stock; alternatively, if the present value of those expected cash flows is less than the current price of the PepsiCo stock, you would look for another investment. That same process describes almost every asset purchase (and sale) decision — including your decision to have your company buy an apartment building for $100,000.

Under fair value accounting, the building you purchased in our example would, at the outset, be valued at $100,000 (assuming you paid fair value for your purchase). If its market value increased to $110,000 by the end of the next accounting period, the balance sheet would reflect that new value, and the $10,000 gain would be included with all of the company's other transactions in the determination of the business's net income for the period. Under this accounting, owners' equity is simply the difference between the aggregate fair value of the assets and that of the debt. Similarly, income (or loss) is simply the difference in the owners' equity at the beginning and at the end of an accounting period. The fair value method has intuitive appeal — it is logical to see the equity of the company as the net fair value of all of its assets and liabilities. However, it is difficult to implement because it is often difficult to obtain fair and accurate values for assets and liabilities. Fair value accounting is not yet accepted under GAAP.

GAAP requires a middle ground, the **accrual method** of accounting. Accrual accounting assumes that assets *will* generate future cash flows, but because the future is uncertain, a conservative assumption is made that those future cash flows *will be no more* than the assets' original cost. Seldom is a value in excess of the assets' cost ever recognized in the financial statements under U.S. GAAP. This convention is called the **historical cost principle.** However, sometimes we know just enough about the future to be worried. If we know enough about the future to be concerned that the assets might not generate enough cash flow to cover their cost, the original cost values are reduced to the lower, expected future cash flow. Financial people reduce this idea to a shorthand expression: "Assets are carried at the **lower of cost or market.**" This pragmatic modification of the historical cost principle illustrates another accounting axiom: "Never anticipate gains but always anticipate losses."

Accrual accounting is more sophisticated than cash-basis accounting because it assumes that your expenditure to buy the building was made with the reasonable expectation that you would realize a future cash flow benefit from your purchase. But the accrual method is more practical than the fair value method because it ignores "what if" value changes. In fact, under accrual accounting, assets are valued at their *future* cash flows only when the amounts of those future flows are validated by a transaction with a third party. Going back to our model, the building you purchased would continue to be carried at its historical cost of $100,000 even though a number of qualified appraisers assured you that it *could* be sold for $110,000. Only when the building is actually sold to a third party — when that third party takes on the risks of ownership — will that increase in value be recognized in your company's financial statements.

Assuming that your company adopts accrual accounting, the future benefit inherent in the building would be recorded as an asset with a value of $100,000. A floor buffing machine, purchased today to help keep the halls clean, would also be recorded as an asset — at its purchase price — because you expect the machine to be usable over a period of years. If you purchased a fire insurance policy that provided coverage for the next three years, that policy would also be an asset because you expect that the benefit you will get from that current expenditure will extend out over the life of the policy. All of those assets are expected to provide the company with a future value. As we will see later, costs that have been deferred as assets this period will be allocated as expenses against the operations of the periods that will benefit from their use. Under accrual accounting, an expenditure that benefits the future is recorded as an asset today but will be recognized as an expense in the future when that benefit is realized. Conversely, the money you pay to the janitors to clean the building is a current expense charged against operations of the current period. That expenditure is not an asset because that current cleaning provides no future benefit — the building will have to be cleaned again tomorrow.

Accrual accounting also recognizes the reality of credit in the business world. It measures the cash consequences of a promise given or received when the promise is exchanged, not when the cash actually changes hands. If you sell the building for $110,000 and a third party buys it, promising to pay $110,000 12 months from today, your company would record that promise as an asset (referred to as a *receivable*) at the expected cash flow of $110,000. Similarly, you would remove the building from your balance sheet because it is no longer yours. The liability to the bank remains because you can't pay off the bank loan with a promise — you have to wait until the buyer actually gives you the cash before you can pay off the debt. The difference between the asset value ($110,000) and the debt ($80,000) is the owners' equity. The difference between that equity balance ($30,000) at the end of the period and the equity balance at the beginning ($20,000) is the company's income for the year. That gain on the sale is income in that year, even though the cash will not be received until the following year. Accrual accounting assumes that credit transactions will be completed in the ordinary course of business.

Should Your Company's Financial Statements Forecast the Future or Should They Report Only the Past?

Most people who read a financial report are primarily interested in the company's future and are only secondarily interested in its past. Investors and lenders are interested to know what management did with the assets entrusted to its care during the last year, but, more importantly, they want to know whether their investment in the company will bear fruit in the future. With that reader interest in mind, some companies — especially relatively new ones — have prepared financial statements on a prospective basis, outlining the financial results they *expect* to have in the next several years. All projections are by definition uncertain, and most companies have been reluctant to expose themselves to the criticism that would inevitably follow a missed projection. Although prospective-oriented financial statements have a logical appeal, they have not been widely used and are not considered part of GAAP.

GAAP financial statements report a company's historical results based on completed transactions with third parties. Some have described this focus on the past as the **transaction principle.** Under our present financial system, companies publicly report their historical results and usually keep private their expectations about the future. Individual financial statement readers use that historical information and, factoring in their feelings about the future, make their own personal estimates of the company's future results. In effect, the historical financial statements become the basis for those individual's projections of the company's future results. Some people will make that extrapolation more successfully than others — some people are more successful investors than others.

How Should the Company's Ongoing Operations Be Allocated over Time to Prepare Reports for a Specific Period?

Measuring a company's success would be simple if we had only to summarize its operations at the end of its life. The owner's original cash investment would have been fully exploited and converted back to cash. Success would be measured by comparing the amount of cash on hand at the end with the amount of cash that was on hand at the beginning of the company's life. Your company purchased the building because you thought it would produce future cash flows for you. If we could wait 30 years until you were ready to retire, we might accumulate all of the company's cash receipts, including rentals and the proceeds from the final sale of the property; in addition, we would accumulate all of the company's disbursements, including payments to the maintenance people and to the bank for the retirement of the loan. If the receipts exceeded the disbursements by more than $20,000 (your original investment), you could say that the company was successful. If not, the investment was a bad deal. It will be obvious that neither you nor the bank will want to wait 30 years to determine whether the venture was successful. And, consequently, GAAP attempts to deal with the problem of measuring results in those intervening years through a convention known as the **periodic measurement principle.**

Under GAAP, individual business transactions are assessed to determine whether the underlying activities impact the current measurement period, a future measurement period, or a series of future periods. Then, all of the financial effects of that transaction are accumulated in the accounts as assets or liabilities and, in turn, recognized as income or expense in the appropriate measurement period. In a manufacturing example, if a company produced goods in June and sold them in September, the financial statements for June, July, and August would recognize the cost of those manufactured items as an asset that we call *inventory.* In September the financial statements would recognize the revenue from the sale, the costs to make the items sold, and an estimate of the future cost of possible warranty work on the merchandise — all in the measurement of income for that month.

But let us return to our real estate example. Assume that a tenant signed a three-year lease on a suite in your building and that the lease is cancelable with 60 days' notice. The leasing agent who found the tenant for you earned a $15,000 commission, payable immediately. Under GAAP you would recognize the rent income monthly, as the lease runs its course. Thus, the rental income is allocated to the periods when it is earned, a convention known as the **allocation principle.** But what should the company do about the commission paid? Under GAAP you would treat that payment as an asset when paid and then allocate it as an expense over the periods when the rent is received. The logic behind this is that the rent would not have been received without that payment to the agent; thus, GAAP requires that the cost of earning the income be matched with the recognition of the income itself, a convention known as the **matching principle.** It is also true that the largest asset involved in earning the rent is the building. Under GAAP, *all* costs involved in earning revenue must be matched against that revenue, including the cost of long-lived assets such as buildings. GAAP requires you to allocate the $100,000 cost of the building over its expected revenue-earning life of, say, 30 years — another illustration of the allocation principle. That application of the allocation principle is called **depreciation.** Allocation and matching are important requisites to the notion of measuring company results period by period.

How Conservative (Aggressive) Should I Be When Making the Estimates Required by the Financial Statements?

As you read the preceding discussion, you may have asked what would happen if the building has a longer (or shorter) life than 30 years. If it actually has a life of 50 years, you will have allocated too much of the building's cost to the early years and as a result will have reported too little net income in those years. You also may have wondered what would happen if the tenant occupying your suite on a three-year lease moved after the first year. In that case you would have misestimated the life of the commission asset, and you would have allocated too little commission expense to that first year, overstating net income. Estimates are involved in almost every allocation decision that managers make as they prepare GAAP-based financial statements. Because no one (especially investors and lenders) likes unpleasant surprises, most managers adopt a conservative posture as they make those estimates. The logic is that it is better to be conservative about the future so that surprises, if any, are good surprises. This convention is known as the **conservatism principle.**

It should be apparent from the real estate example we discussed that the application of conservatism can create a conflict between future and current results: Protecting against unpleasant future surprises may distort current results. Consider the following example from the retailing world. An expenditure for employee training that precedes the opening of a new store could justifiably be accounted for as an asset when the expenditure is made and then allocated to expense over some future period after the store is open and generating sales. In effect, those training costs would be matched with the revenues they are expected to generate. An alternative, more conservative view would be to treat those training expenditures as expenses immediately when they are incurred. That posture could be justified by arguing that future sales from the store are uncertain and, until they are realized, the benefits expected from the training are unrealized as well. The store manager must make that allocation decision — future period expense versus current period expense — based on the likelihood that future sales will be sufficient to recover the current training expenditures. This decision requires careful, informed judgment and a sense of balance: An ultraconservative policy may result in an unrealistically bleak financial picture for the current period, whereas an ultraliberal policy may result in an unrealistically positive picture for the current period followed by disproportionately high expenses in future periods.

Do All Assets of My Company Still Have the Potential to Earn Cash Equal to Their Carrying Value Today?

GAAP provides for the fact that allocation estimates will sometimes prove to be wrong and that now and then, an expenditure that was treated as an asset in one period will subsequently be seen as having no future cash-earning benefit. When that happens, GAAP requires the remaining asset value to be charged off as an expense in the period when that discovery is made. (This is another application of the shorthand expression we referred to earlier — assets are carried at the lower-of-cost-or-market value.) Well-managed companies have programs in place to challenge periodically the carrying value of all of their assets to make sure that any declines in estimates of future benefits are recognized as soon as they become apparent. (Incidentally, GAAP does not permit companies to go back and restate prior years' financial statements for incorrect estimates. If hindsight shows that you were too conservative or too liberal, the effect of the adjustment required is to be recognized only in the financial statements for the period when you realize that your estimate was faulty.)

May I (Must I) Change My Estimates or My Accounting Principles?

Companies occasionally find that — while their assets continue to have value — the future period of benefit that they originally estimated is now seen to be different. Suppose that after 10 years your company decided that the useful economic life of its building was really 50 years rather than 30 years. No accounting would be required at that time because you would simply spread the remaining cost over the remaining (now 40) years. If you concluded that the building life was really only 20 years instead of 30 years, the remaining cost would be allocated over the remaining 10 years. The financial community assumes that financial statements are prepared consistently from one period to the next so that a series of income statements covering a period of years fairly reports the trend in income. The fundamental estimates are not changed year to year but only when required by the facts — a convention we call the **consistency principle.** If significant estimates are changed, GAAP requires that a footnote be included in the financial statements to explain the change and the dollar effect of the change on the future years' income statements.

For many types of economic transactions, a number of alternative accounting methods are available, each producing a very different result. When alternative reporting approaches exist, GAAP requires that a company disclose in the footnotes accompanying its financial reports the accounting method that has been selected. Should circumstances change, warranting the use of a different accounting principle, the effect of the change on reported income must be disclosed in the footnotes to permit financial statement users to compare current period results with results from the prior period, which were determined using the prior accounting method — again reflecting the consistency principle.

How Much Detail Must I (May I) Include in These Financial Statements?

The ideal accounting report includes all material (that is, significant) information but excludes all trivial or irrelevant details. The financial community (and the courts) have said that financial statements must include all "material information." *Material information* has been defined as information that might influence the decisions of a reasonable person. Managers must ask themselves whether details about their company's financial status would influence the decisions of a potential investor; if so, the information must be included in the basic financial statements themselves or in the related footnotes.

It follows from that understanding about the content of the financial statements themselves that management will, when making accounting estimate decisions, focus its attention principally on those items that might have a material effect on the accounting reports. Immaterial items are given less attention or are ignored. Clearly, careful judgments are required in preparing a set of financial statements, and the responsible manager will exercise that judgment, thinking all the while about the potential readers of the financial statements: investors, creditors, and the public. This convention is known as the **materiality principle.**

THE STANDARD-SETTING PROCESS

The principles outlined in the above set of questions and answers form the basis of GAAP in the United States. As we suggested in Chapter 1, however, GAAP is more than a set of principles; GAAP includes a large body of practice and procedure that builds on these principles and enables people to apply the broad principles to specific transactions.

The idea that the principles (and practices and procedures) in GAAP are "generally accepted" suggests that these accounting guidelines emerge from practice as a consensus, and that assessment of GAAP is partly true. Today, however, financial transactions are complex, and the need for timely information from companies is acute. The financial community has decided that it would be inappropriate to wait for a consensus to emerge about a new accounting question and has agreed that the consensus should be led by an authorized standard-setting body. The following discussion outlines the movement toward an institutional approach to the setting of accounting guidelines and the protagonists in that evolution.

At the turn of the century the financial community in the U.S. was relatively small. When local businesses borrowed strictly from local banks, personal reputations were more important than financial status in the granting of a loan. Stocks and bonds were investment vehicles only for a small, wealthy, well-acquainted group. To the extent that investments were made outside that group, they were based on personal recommendations of investment bankers. Because communication between creditor and borrower, or between investor and investee, could be direct and personal, financial reporting tended to be tailored and unique, even informal. That informal financial reporting system served the community well for a number of years, but as the community grew and became more diverse, the need for a more rigorous reporting system became apparent.

The need for more formal regulation of the form and content of financial reporting became dramatically apparent with the stock market crash of 1929. The widespread impact of the crash made it clear that a reporting system that relied on personal contact was no longer appropriate. Because the *public* was now seen to be affected by the country's financial system, and more particularly by the financial reporting system, Congress passed the Securities Acts of 1933 and 1934 and created the Securities and Exchange Commission (SEC).

The SEC has the responsibility to regulate the various stock exchanges, the broker-dealers who buy and sell on those exchanges, and mutual funds. The commission also has the authority to establish the "form and content" of the financial disclosures required of publicly held companies. Under the commission's rules, any company that sells stocks or bonds to the public must prepare a financial disclosure package (referred to as a **prospectus**) to give potential investors the information they need to decide whether to buy a company's securities. Every company that has sold securities to the public in the past must, on an ongoing basis, prepare an annual disclosure package (referred to as **Form 10-K**) and quarterly reports (referred to as **Form 10-Q**). Those annual and quarterly reports are designed to help existing investors decide whether they want to retain their investment or to sell, and to help potential investors decide whether they want to buy a company's securities.

Although the SEC has the statutory authority to establish the requirements for corporate reporting, it has chosen to exercise its authority very sparingly. The commission has established some requirements for disclosure of basic business information, but, almost from the beginning, it has elected to delegate the development of accounting standards to the private sector. There are probably a number of reasons for that delegation policy. First, the original SEC commissioners concluded that the best accounting rules for the nation's complex financial community would be developed by practitioners with field experience rather than by government employees. Second, the commissioners also concluded that the financial community was more likely to follow rules that it had established for itself than rules that had been set by outsiders, especially a governmental agency. Finally, it became apparent to the commission that enormous pressure was likely to be brought to bear on whoever was responsible for accounting standards. The SEC chose to stand behind the private sector and prod it on rather than face the pressure groups directly.

In response to this prodding, the major certified public accounting (CPA) firms, under the auspices of the American Institute of Certified Public Accountants, began the process of establishing written, standardized, generally accepted accounting principles in 1936. Until 1959, that effort was staffed by senior executives of the leading CPA firms. They were enormously productive at the start, but eventually their deliberations on matters of principle bogged down in debates over firm preference. Apparently, it was difficult for such strongly motivated, visible people to compromise ardently held firm positions. To focus those deliberations on the issues, a new standard-setting body was established in 1959 and staffed with technical experts from each of the large CPA firms. This group, the Accounting Principles Board (APB), was again effective in its early years but was overwhelmed by the "go-go" financial years of the late 1960s. Some people argued that the APB became too technical, too restrictive, and not sufficiently practical. Others argued that the APB had been too willing to compromise in the interest of producing timely new standards. In any event, the criticism from the financial community became so strong that the APB lost its standard-setting effectiveness. It was abolished in 1973, and the Financial Accounting Standards Board (FASB) was created to take its place.

Recognizing that the prior standards-setting efforts, relying as they did on the major CPA firms, suffered from a narrow power base, the FASB was designed to appeal to the financial community as a whole. The board is funded by voluntary contributions from four different accounting organizations, from The Securities Industry Association, from The Financial Analysts Association, and from several large corporations. Board members are selected on the basis of their general reputation in the field without regard to their prior affiliation.

The board's procedures require extensive due process. It solicits community advice as it considers its agenda. When a new issue is added to the board's agenda, the staff researches the issue and prepares a discussion memorandum that outlines all of the important points of view that have been expressed. The board solicits written comments in response to every discussion memorandum and very often holds public hearings. Based on community input and the board's own deliberations, an exposure draft of a new standard is prepared and circulated for additional comments. After considering public responses to the exposure draft, the board makes final refinements and issues a **statement of financial accounting standards.**

The pronouncements of the board have considerable authority. The SEC considers them to be GAAP for purposes of complying with U.S. securities laws, and CPA firms consider the board's statements to be GAAP for the general-purpose financial statements issued by private companies outside the SEC's jurisdiction.

The board was quite successful in its early years, and in its 20-year history has issued more than 120 standards as well as a wide variety of interpretative releases. In more recent years, the board has been subject to increased criticism. Some members of the business community argue that the board has become too concerned with technical accounting questions, and they claim that the cost of complying with the FASB's standards exceeds the benefits to the financial community. That critical assessment is partly true. But it is also true that several of the board's standards have forced companies to recognize liabilities and expenses that were not previously reflected in their financial statements. Part of the criticism of the board is the reaction one might expect whenever more rigorous standards are imposed. Time will tell whether the financial community will continue to support a self-regulated standard-setting process or whether the SEC will be forced to assume that responsibility.

In addition to the pronouncements of the FASB and its predecessors, U.S. GAAP is also established by prevailing accounting practice. In the past, as much as 75 percent of GAAP may have been unwritten precedent. Today, as a result of the work of the FASB, the reverse is true, and probably less than 25 percent of GAAP is based solely on informal, unwritten precedent. Because business is a dynamic process with new financial transactions always being created, no standard-setting agency could ever hope to keep up with the rapid evolution of finance and accounting. When no formal accounting pronouncements exist, new GAAP will continue to be inferred from practices developed by accounting practitioners drawing on the fundamental principles that have historically formed the basis for all GAAP.

THE BASIC FINANCIAL STATEMENTS: AN EXPLORATION

Under generally accepted accounting principles, companies report their financial activities using four basic financial statements:

- The **balance sheet,** also referred to as the **statement of financial position,** presents in summary form the assets a company owned at a particular date, the liabilities the company owed to its lenders and suppliers, and the funds that the owners of the company have invested or left in the company as of that same date.
- The **income statement,** also referred to as the **statement of earnings** or operations, summarizes those transactions that produced revenue for a company as a result of selling products or services during a specific period and those transactions that resulted in expenses for the company during that same period. The difference between the aggregate revenues and aggregate expenses is the net income (or loss) for the company.

- The **statement of owners' equity** summarizes the major transactions that affected the owners' investment in a company, including the company's net income (or loss) and the amount of those earnings that were distributed to the owners during a given period.
- The **statement of cash flows** summarizes the sources of a company's cash funds available for use during a given period and the uses that the company made of those funds.

Under U.S. GAAP, all companies are required to provide a balance sheet, an income statement, and a statement of cash flows as part of their annual report. A statement of owners' equity is also frequently provided, although that information may be presented as part of a company's financial statement footnotes rather than as a separate financial statement. Together, these statements form the nucleus of most accounting reports. We will briefly overview the contents and purpose of each statement now and will consider each one in detail in subsequent chapters.

But before we consider these financial statements, a brief word on the international setting is appropriate. In a previous section, "Some Fundamental Questions in Accounting," we considered the various postulates and principles that underlie much of what is called GAAP. These same issues exist all over the world, and hence the accounting standard setting body in each country faces these same fundamental questions — and their answers are often the same as those reached in the United States. On occasion, however, a different answer is reached, and we will point out these differences in the chapters that follow.

Balance Sheet

The purpose of the balance sheet is to present, as of a particular point in time, the various resources available for use by a company and the sources the company called upon to fund the acquisition of those resources. These resources are generally referred to as the company's **assets,** and the sources of funding for those resources are either its **liabilities** or its **owners' equity.** As you might surmise, equity is a source of funding provided by its owners. Liabilities, on the other hand, are the sources of funding provided by a company's creditors. In more formal terms:

- *Assets* are tangible or intangible resources, such as cash, property, or patents, that can be measured in dollars, are owned or controlled by a company, and are expected to provide future economic benefit to the company. The building your real estate company purchased, in our earlier discussions in this chapter, is a classic example of an asset.
- *Liabilities* are the company's obligations to repay money loaned to it, to pay for goods or services it has received, or to fulfill its warranty obligations, all stated in dollars. Again, the bank debt your real estate company incurred to purchase its building is a good example of a liability.
- *Owners' equity* measures the owners' investment in a company, which may be either in the form of direct investment through the purchase of shares of stock, or indirectly through the retention of the company's earnings. The initial investment you made in your real estate company ($20,000) is an example of direct investment equity. The cash you put in was paid out as the down payment, but your equity remains. If you choose to leave the company's earnings in the company rather than have them distributed to you, those retained earnings are also an example of owners' equity.

The relationship between the assets (A), liabilities (L), and owners' equity (OE) of a company represents the foundation of accounting. This fundamental relationship may be expressed as

$$A = L + OE$$

In words, the assets of a company at any one time always equal the sum of its liabilities and its owners' equity. In more abstract terms, every resource has a source. Not only does this relationship represent the cornerstone of accounting, but also it is the basis of the balance sheet. The balance sheet is like a snapshot presenting the assets of a company juxtaposed against its liabilities and owners' equity as of a particular moment. Over the course of a company's life, a great many transactions will impact the balance sheet accounts. The balance sheet shows the net result of all of those transactions at any one date — the net balances in those asset, liability, and owners' equity accounts.

Pictorially, the balance sheet looks like this:

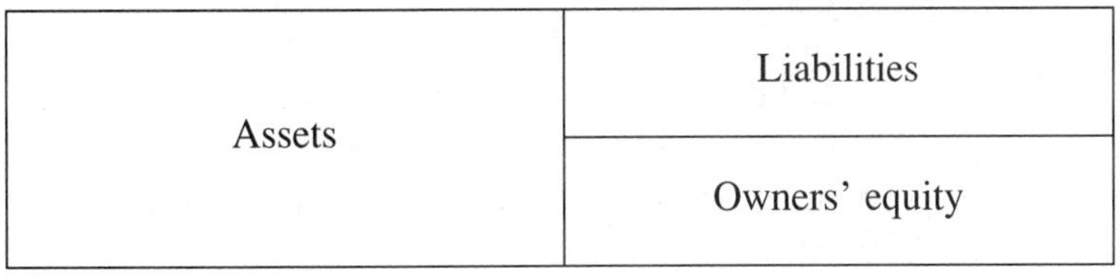

Note that the right and left sides of this box must always be equal. The composition or relative proportions of the right side will vary, however, depending on the sources a company calls upon to fund the acquisition of its assets. In our earlier real estate example, the $100,000 asset equaled the sum of the $80,000 in debt and the $20,000 in equity. If you had put only $10,000 into the company and had borrowed $90,000, the right and left sides of the box would still have been equal, although the relative size of the right-hand boxes would have been different.

Income Statement

Although the balance sheet presents the status of a company's assets, liabilities, and owners' equity *as of* a particular point in time, the income statement presents the results of a series of income-generating transactions *over* a period of time. The income statement reports the revenues earned and the expenses incurred by the company during a given period of operations:

- **Revenues** are the actual or expected cash inflows arising from a company's **sales** of products or services during a specific period.
- **Expenses** are the **costs** a company incurred in its efforts to generate revenues during that same period.
- **Net income** (or loss) is the excess (or insufficiency) of revenues over expenses; it represents a summary measure of the overall performance of a company for a given period.

The income statement tells us whether the stockholders are better off as a result of this year's activities, and it helps them understand why they are better off. Did the company sell enough product at the right price? Did management keep expenses under control and in line with the volume of business? What kinds of expenses did we incur this year — were they product related, selling related, or administrative costs?

The relationship between the revenues (R), expenses (E), and net income (NI) of a company may be expressed as

$$NI = R - E$$

and this expression forms the basis of the income statement.

Statement of Owners' Equity

The statement of owners' equity measures both the period-end balance of the owners' investment in a company and the changes in that investment over a period of time. The owners' investment in a company may take several forms: direct investment through the purchase of shares of stock or indirect investment through the retention of some (or all) of the company's earnings for a period.

- **Capital stock** represents the proceeds a company received from the sale of stock to its shareholders. Sales of stock *between* shareholders do not impact the company's financial statements because those transactions have no direct financial effect on the company.
- **Earnings** (or net income) are the net result of the company's operations for a period — its revenues and expenses. Accounting theory assumes that the company is operated for the benefit of the shareholders, and so the net results of operations (earnings or loss) for a period are added to (or subtracted from) the owners' equity account, pending a decision to distribute some of those earnings to the individual shareholders.
- **Dividends** are the earnings of a company that are paid out to the owners. In a corporation, the owners are not automatically entitled to receive a distribution of the company's earnings; instead, the earnings are paid out to shareholders only when the board of directors believes it will be safe (for the company) to do so. Because the payment of dividends is at the company's discretion, that expenditure of funds is not considered an expense but simply a reduction in equity. Dividends are understood legally to be a distribution of the earnings of the company, and accounting policy follows that understanding.
- **Retained earnings** are the aggregate of the company's earnings that are retained in the enterprise for future corporate use — that is, those earnings of the company that have not been paid out to its owners as dividends.

The relationship between owners' equity (OE), capital stock (CS), and retained earnings (RE) can be expressed as

$$OE = CS + RE$$

Substituting the net income (NI) and dividends (D) buildup of the retained earnings account for its end-of-period net balance, the statement of owners' equity can be expressed as

OE	=	CS	+	NI	−	D
at the report date		at the report date		for all periods from day 1		for all periods from day 1

Combining this equation for the statement of owners' equity with the overall equation we developed earlier for the balance sheet (A = L + OE), we have

A	=	L	+	CS	+	NI	−	D
at the report date		at the report date		at the report date		for all periods from day 1		for all periods from day 1

And, finally, combining this equation with the one developed for the income statement (NI = R − E), gives us the following comprehensive set of relationships

A	=	L	+	CS	+	R	−	E	−	D
at the report date		at the report date		at the report date		for all periods from day 1		for all periods from day 1		for all periods from day 1

The Interrelationship of the Basic Financial Statements

It is important at this point to stop and consider an important implication of our discussion so far: From an accounting standpoint, the balance sheet is the senior, or the primary, financial statement because all business transactions impact the balance sheet in some way. The income statement is a junior or secondary financial statement because it is only affected by the revenue and expense transactions that flow through the retained earnings account in the balance sheet. The retained earnings account in the balance sheet reflects the sum of all of the revenue and expense transactions since the company's beginning, while the income statement presents the revenue and expense transactions for a particular period. To say that the balance sheet is the senior financial statement does not mean that the balance sheet provides more important information to the reader; it simply means that the balance sheet deals with all of the company's transactions, while the income statement deals with only those transactions that affect one aspect of the balance sheet — the retained earnings account.

A balance sheet is a summary of all transactions affecting the company as of a point in time. In theory, we could prepare a balance sheet for this year-end without regard to the balance sheet we prepared at last year-end. But in reality, this year's balance sheet will be an update of the balances from last year: Last year's balance sheet provides the foundation for the construction of this year's balance sheet, and we simply add or subtract from those foundation numbers the effect of transactions during this year. Every balance sheet account will have been affected by some transactions during the year, which will increase or decrease the balance in the account. Shareholders don't care about the detailed transactions that increased or decreased most balance sheet accounts, but they do care about the transactions that affected their equity accounts, in particular the retained earnings account. The income statement is designed to meet that need. With only a few exceptions, an income statement summarizes all of the revenue and expense transactions that increased or decreased the balance in the retained earnings account from last year to this year.

Let's go back to our earlier discussion of your real estate company. You began the company by contributing $20,000 in exchange for all of the company's stock. As a result of that original transaction, the company increased its owners' equity by $20,000 and increased its cash asset by an equal amount. When the company bought the building, making a cash down payment of $20,000 and borrowing the rest of the $100,000 purchase price, the company reduced its cash asset, increased its building asset, and increased its debt liability. In both of those transactions, the accounting equation, A = L + OE, was satisfied, and the balance sheet remained in balance. At the completion of the purchase, the $100,000 building asset is equal to the sum of the $20,000 equity and the $80,000 bank loan.

That building purchase has no income effect because the transaction did not result in revenue or expense. But now let's suppose that a tenant rents first floor retail space for $500 a month. When the tenant makes a payment on the lease at the end of the month, the company receives cash of $500 and records rent revenue in an equal amount. Let us also assume that your company employed a janitorial service to keep the retail area clean, spending $100 to have that work performed. As a result of the activities for the month the cash asset account will be increased by $500 and decreased by $100; the same increase and decrease will impact the owners' equity account — retained earnings — because all revenue and expenses accumulate for the benefit (or detriment) of the owners. The balance sheet stays in balance, with a net increase in cash of $400 and an equal net increase in retained earnings. The income statement for that first month will summarize the transactions in the retained earnings account and will show revenue of $500 and expense of $100, for a net income of $400. Both the rent receipt and the payment to the janitorial service affected both sides of the balance sheet. The rent revenue aspect of the cash receipt and the maintenance expense aspect of the cash disbursement affected only the income statement.

Use our simple real estate example to solidify several important ideas about accounting transactions:

1. *All* of a company's business transactions affect its balance sheet, but only those that have to do with revenue or expense are *also* reflected in the income statement.
2. All revenue and expense transactions impact owners' equity (the retained earnings account), and they also impact some other balance sheet account. That will be so because the balance sheet must always be in balance: Any transaction that impacts the owners' equity account must have an equal impact somewhere else in the balance sheet.
3. A balance sheet as of a current date is connected to an earlier balance sheet as of a prior date by the intervening transactions. The income statement is a summary of the intervening transactions that affected the retained earnings account. The income statement acts as a bridge between a current and an earlier balance sheet. (Accountants describe this connection by saying that the financial statements *articulate* — they work together.)
4. The income statement for a period is a summary — or a recap — of the revenue and expense transactions that flowed through the retained earnings account during that period. Looking at the balance in the retained earnings account at the end of an accounting period will tell us how much of the company's earnings (if any) have been retained for the use of the business; looking at the change in the retained earnings account from one year to the next would tell us whether the company added anything to the owners' investment during the year. But neither of those numbers will tell us anything about the operations of the company during the current period. The income statement analyzes all of the revenue and expense transactions during one period and not only summarizes them so that we can determine *whether* the owners are better off as a result of the operations for that period, but also provides the detail so that we know *why* (or why not) they are better off.

In the final equation we developed during our earlier discussion, we had

A	=	L	+	CS	+	R	−	E	−	D
at the report date		at the report date		at the report date		for all periods from day 1		for all periods from day 1		for all periods from day 1

We can use this formula to see how the income statement connects the balance sheet for one period with the balance sheet for the next. Let's go back to the real estate company we have been using as our model. At the end of its first month of operations, the company had purchased a building and rented one store. It had received one month's rent of $500 and paid cleaning costs of $100. Let us now assume that we are in the second month of operations and that another retail store has opened, paying additional rent of $600 a month. The maintenance people agree to charge an additional $100 to clean that store, in addition to their charge for the first store. We could present the above formulas for the end of the first month (End of Period 1) and the end of the subsequent month (End of Period 2) as follows:

A	=	L	+	CS	+	R	−	E	−	D
EOP1		EOP1		EOP1		from day 1 to EOP1		from day 1 to EOP1		from day 1 to EOP1

and

A	=	L	+	CS	+	R	−	E	−	D
EOP2		EOP2		EOP2		from day 1 to EOP2		from day 1 to EOP2		from day 1 to EOP2

The cumulative income statement for the company, for the period from its beginning, would be

R	−	E	= NI
from day 1 to EOP2		from day 1 to EOP2	

or

$$\$1{,}600 - \$300 = \$1{,}300$$

But a cumulative income statement doesn't tell much about current operations. The income statement for the most current period, the company's second month, would be

R	−	R	−	E	−	E	= NI
from day 1 to EOP2		from day 1 to EOP1		from day 1 to EOP2		from day 1 to EOP1	

or

$$\$1{,}100 \quad - \quad \$200 \quad = \$900$$

The income statement for that second month will reflect only those transactions that increased the balance in the retained earnings account — in the owners' equity portion of the balance sheet — between the end of month 1 and the end of month 2.

This articulation idea we have been discussing can be shown graphically as in Exhibit 2.1. The relationship between the income statement, the statement of owners' equity, and the balance sheet can also be shown in a schematic, as in Exhibit 2.2.

EXHIBIT 2.1

Diagrammatic Relationship of the Income Statement and Balance Sheet

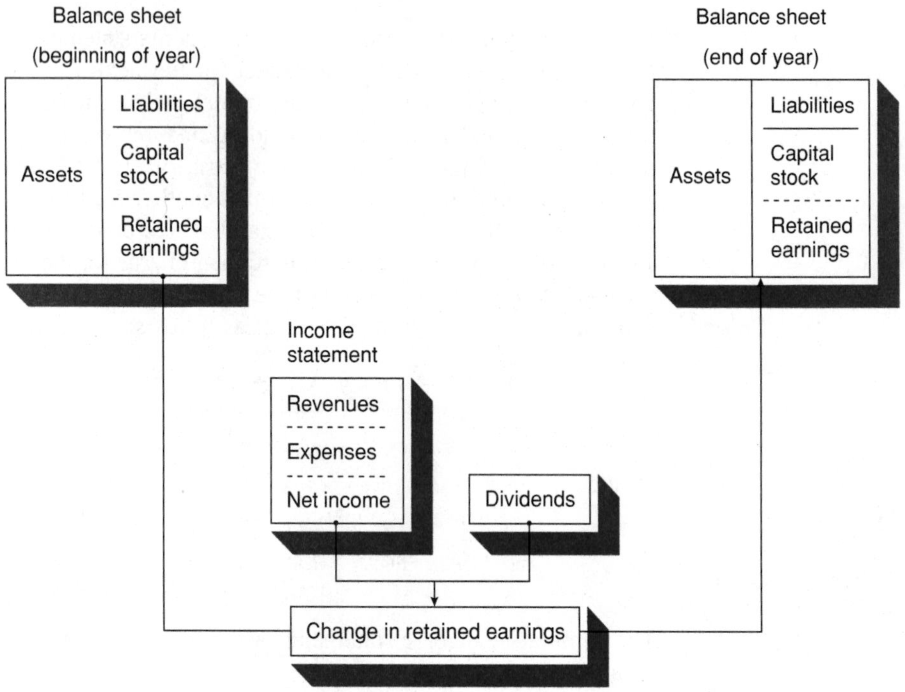

Statement of Cash Flows

The purpose of the statement of cash flows is to explain the change in cash occurring between two successive accounting periods. The cash flows of a company may be conveniently segmented into three principal categories of interest to financial statement users: cash flows from operations, from investing, and from financing.

Cash flows from operations refers to the net cash flows resulting from the company's principal business operations. In essence, the operating cash flow measures the net income of the company on a cash basis. **Cash flows from investing** refers to buying and selling long-lived assets (e.g., buildings and equipment), making and collecting loans, and acquiring and disposing of another company's debt or equity instruments. Finally, **cash flows from financing** refers to the activities of a company to obtain funds from existing and new shareholders, provide them a return *on* and a return *of* their investment, and borrow and repay amounts borrowed.

The statement of cash flows is analogous to the income statement: They both summarize the transactions in a balance sheet account during one period of time. The income statement summarizes the transactions that increased or decreased the retained earnings account, while the statement of cash flows summarizes the transactions that increased or decreased the cash account. Integrating the statement of cash flows into our picture of the financial reporting process yields Exhibit 2.3.

EXHIBIT 2.2

Diagrammatic Relationship of the Balance Sheet, the Income Statement, and the Statement of Owners' Equity

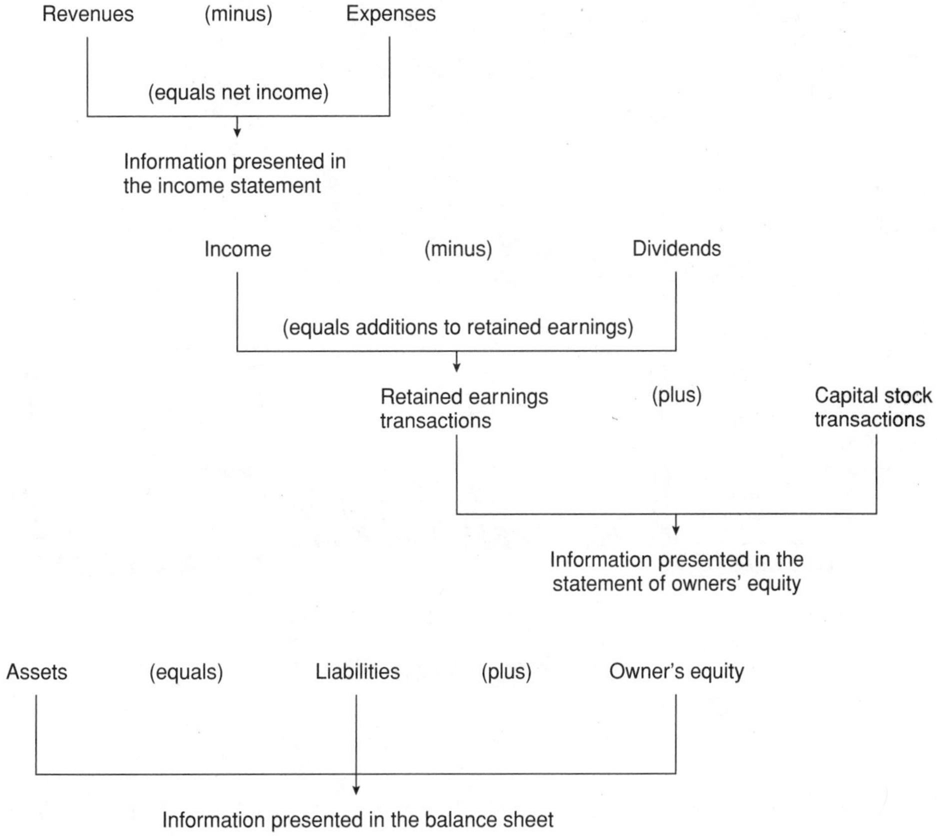

Earlier we described the difference between cash-basis accounting and accrual accounting, but it is worth restating briefly now: The income statement is prepared assuming accrual accounting, while the statement of cash flows is prepared assuming cash-basis accounting. Net income will not be equal to the net change in cash because there are some transactions that impact net income but not cash (for example, sales on credit) and some transactions that impact cash but not income (for example, the purchase of a truck). The two statements measure different things and can (must) be used for different purposes:

- The income statement measures results of operations assuming a credit society and an orderly, normal use of assets — such as equipment and inventory — over time. It helps a reader evaluate the company's performance during the period and make projections about future performance.
- The statement of cash flows outlines the sources and use of cash during a period. It helps a reader see the company's business strategy and make projections of the company's cash needs in future periods.

EXHIBIT 2.3

Diagrammatic Relationship of the Basic Financial Statements

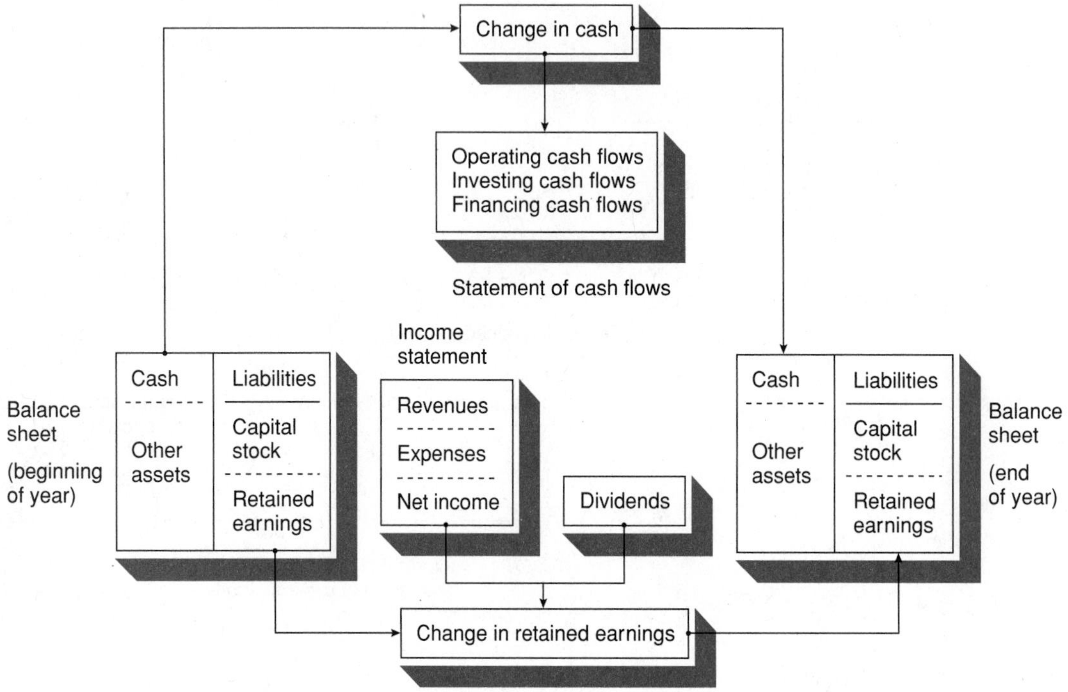

In this chapter we have talked about some very important material. To demonstrate the relevance of the ideas we have been discussing, and to put them into a more specific context, we would like to refer you back to the PepsiCo financial review that was included at the end of Chapter 1.

First, note that PepsiCo's financial statements articulate; that is, the three statements are interrelated. Looking at the balance sheet (page 23), we can see that the retained earnings at December 31, 1993, were equal to $6,541.9 million. The statement of shareholders' equity (page 27) shows us that the balance at the end of 1993 was increased by the 1994 income of $1,752.0 and was decreased by dividends paid during the year of $554.8 million. That series of transactions created a new balance in the retained earnings account of $7,739.1, which is included in shareholders' equity in the balance sheet at December 31, 1994. The income added to retained earnings in 1994 is, of course, the income that is reported in the income statement (page 21). The income for 1994, reported in the income statement, connects the balance sheet at the end of 1993 and the balance sheet at the end of 1994.

Also notice that the 1993 balance sheet reports cash of $226.9 million and the 1994 balance sheet reports cash of $330.7 million. The statement of cash flows (page 25) depicts a $103.8 million increase in cash as the net of cash provided by operations, cash used for investments, cash used for financing activities, and a small charge to recognize the effect of changes in exchange rates. The change in cash, as analyzed in the statement of cash flow, provides another connection between the balance sheet at December 31, 1993, with the balance sheet at the end of December 31, 1994.

PepsiCo's 1994 balance sheet illustrates several other principles we have been discussing. For example, look at the 1994 amount for accounts receivable. You will see that PepsiCo reports more than $2 billion in amounts due from customers and others. That asset represents cash the company expects to receive in the future as a result of past transactions. Because the company prepares its financial reports on an accrual basis rather than on a cash basis, those transactions were recorded when the parties agreed to the transaction, and it is not necessary for PepsiCo to wait until the cash changes hands to recognize the impact of those transactions. The total amount the company should receive from its customers is $2,201.5 million, but management knows that some of those customers will fall on hard times and will be unable to pay. PepsiCo adheres to the principles of conservatism and periodic measurement and recognizes, at December 31, 1994, an estimate of the loss that they will incur as they work to collect those accounts receivable. Management has reduced the total amount due by a $150.6 million allowance for those accounts that will subsequently prove to be uncollectible. Experience says that there *will* be some credit losses as the company works at collecting its accounts receivable, and conservatism and the matching principle says that those losses should be anticipated now. Experience says that even as we made sales on credit in 1994, we knew that there would be some losses associated with the collection of the receivables. The periodic measurement principle says that those losses should be recorded as part of the activity of the period when the company first knew that the losses were coming.

Some of the other accounting principles we have been discussing are illustrated in the footnotes to the PepsiCo financial statements. For example, in Note 1, "Summary of Significant Accounting Policies":

- The comments under "Principles of Consolidation" explain PepsiCo's application of the entity principle. The company includes, in its consolidated financial statements, all of the activities of the parent company, PepsiCo, "and its controlled affiliates." In other words, if there is a PepsiCo subsidiary in Canada that operates a soft drink bottling plant, and if PepsiCo owns enough of that affiliate's stock to control that business, all of that company's assets and liabilities are added together with those of other controlled companies and those of the parent to form the consolidated balance sheet. Also, that company's sales and expenses would be combined with those of all the other commonly controlled companies to form the consolidated income statement.
- On the other hand, those companies in which PepsiCo "exercises significant influence but not control" are accounted for under the equity method. PepsiCo does not include, in its consolidated financial statements, the assets, liabilities, sales, and expenses of those affiliates where it does not have the ability to control the entities; instead, in those situations, PepsiCo recognizes in its financial statements only its share of the equity of those ventures (reported as investments in affiliates in the balance sheet) and its share of the ventures' earnings (included as a reduction in selling and administrative expenses in the income statement). The company does not tell us what the financial statements would look like if the affiliates were consolidated, but we can be sure that both assets and liabilities (and sales and expenses) would increase.
- The comments under "Marketing Costs" describe the company's application of accrual accounting and illustrate the use of the allocation and matching

principles. PepsiCo has concluded that expenditures for marketing and promotional activities do not meet the definition of an asset in that the benefit to a future period of a current period's advertising campaign is too uncertain. Instead, those expenditures are charged to expense in the year the service is purchased. Selling and administrative expenses increased 14 percent in 1994, and a large part of that increase must have been for advertising; obviously, net income for 1994 would have been higher if the company could have deferred recognition of those costs until a later year. To justify that deferral, management would have to have determined that some of the 1994 advertising would generate revenues in a future year. They could then have recorded those current expenditures as assets this year and carried them forward to allocate them as expenses of that future year. But there is no assurance of any such payoff, and so the advertising expenditures are treated as expenses in this year.

- Note that the company does treat promotional materials on hand as an asset as well as expenditures for production costs for future media campaigns. Those expenditures are carried as assets until management decides to use the promotional material (or the media campaign) in an advertising campaign. When the materials are used, however, those costs will be expensed.
- Comments further down in the "Marketing Costs" segment demonstrate the consistency principle. Management explains that they have been treating promotional discounts different ways in different businesses: In the beverage segment, discounts are treated as reductions in sales, while in snack foods they have been treated as marketing costs. Management explains that they are reviewing their accounting policies in this area and may make changes next year. If they do make a change next year, the footnotes will describe the change and the effect on the reported results so that the reader will understand how trends in sales and expenses were affected by this accounting change.

In Note 6, "Inventories," and Note 7, "Property, Plant, and Equipment," PepsiCo illustrates the historical cost principle, the transaction principle, and the principles of matching and allocation. The company's expenditures for raw materials are not charged to expense immediately but are carried forward as assets in the inventory account until the product is manufactured and sold to the wholesale distributor. That is true for the resulting finished goods, too. Those ready-to-deliver products are carried at their aggregate manufacturing cost even though it is a pretty sure thing that they will be sold and that the sales prices will be realized. Until there is a transaction with a third party, the value implied in those finished goods is not recognized in the financial statements.

The costs associated with the inventory are carried as assets until the products are sold; when the products are sold, those related costs are recognized as expenses and matched against the related revenue. Those costs are allocated to an accounting period based on the timing of the related transaction. PepsiCo's property, plant, and equipment costs are also carried at original cost, but those costs are expensed to future accounting periods based not on related transactions but on the passage of time. The costs of those assets are expensed over time, pro rata, based on management's estimate of the number of periods that will benefit from having those assets at work. The company has $14.3 billion in assets that will be used up over time (buildings, lease rights, and machinery and equipment). Depreciation expense for 1994 was $1.2 billion, which says that the costs of those assets are being expensed over — allocated to — an average life of about 12 years.

In Note 8, "Intangible Assets," PepsiCo management illustrates the lower-of-cost-or-market principle. They explain that they have a number of intangible assets, including franchise rights, trademarks, and goodwill, and that the company evaluates those assets on a recurring basis to make sure that their investment in those assets will be recovered from the benefits generated from ongoing operations. If it seems likely that the cost of any asset will not be recovered, the carrying value (usually the cost of acquiring the asset) is reduced to its approximate market value. Any such write-down would be an expense in the period when the decline in value is determined.

Note 10, "Fair Value of Financial Instruments," illustrates an interesting compromise with the historical cost principle: All assets and liabilities are reported in the financial statements at their original cost values, but everyone knows that some assets (and some liabilities) have very measurable market values. To help the reader understand more fully the cash flow–producing potential of the balance sheet and the interest rate exposure implied in the company's financial position, U.S. GAAP requires a supplementary disclosure of the fair value of all financial assets and liabilities — referred to as *financial instruments*. As we might expect, PepsiCo has more financial debts than it has financial assets; the company tells us that the market value of that net debt was much higher than its carrying value in 1993, but that difference has moderated in 1994. Because the company's debt was worth more on the market than its recorded value, we can assume that the interest rates required by those debt instruments were high compared to the then current market rates. By swapping interest obligations and making other changes, PepsiCo management was able to bring its interest rates closer to the market rates in 1994.

Finally, Note 19, "Contingencies," illustrates both the conservatism and the transaction principles. As we noted in Chapter 1, the company has guaranteed the liabilities of some of its affiliates, probably to help them borrow for expansion. The company does not expect to have to make good on those guarantees, and so long as there has been no such transaction there is no need to record any such obligation. However, conservatism does require the company to warn the reader that there is a degree of exposure for $187 million of others' debts.

SUMMARY

Under U.S. GAAP, companies are required to report their financial activities using the basic financial statements: the balance sheet, the income statement, the statement of owners' equity, and the statement of cash flows. Because those statements will be read by a large and diverse group of users, the financial community has said that the financial statements will be prepared in accordance with a set of standards we call GAAP. Those "generally accepted accounting principles" do indeed follow a set of overarching principles, but they are also established in more articulate form by the FASB, an independent standard-setting body supported by the financial community and backed by the SEC.

NEW CONCEPTS AND TERMS

Accrual method (p. 46)
Allocation principle (p. 49)
Assets (p. 54)
Balance sheet (p. 53)
Capital stock (p. 56)
Cash basis (p. 45)
Cash-basis accounting (p. 45)
Cash flows from operations (p. 60)
Cash flows from investing (p. 60)
Cash flows from financing (p. 60)
Conservatism principle (p. 49)
Consistency principle (p. 50)

Consolidated financial statements (p. 45)
Costs (p. 55)
Dividends (p. 56)
Depreciation (p. 49)
Earnings (p. 56)
Entity principle (p. 45)
Expenses (p. 55)
Fair value accounting (p. 46)
Form 10-K (p. 52)
Form 10-Q (p. 52)
Historical cost principle (p. 46)
Income statement (p. 53)
Liabilities (p. 54)
Lower-of-cost-or-market value (p. 46)
Matching principle (p. 49)
Materiality principle (p. 51)
Net income (loss) (p. 55)
Owners' equity (p. 54)
Periodic measurement principle (p. 48)
Prospectus (p. 52)
Retained earnings (p. 56)
Revenues (p. 55)
Sales (p. 55)
Statement of cash flows (p. 54)
Statement of earnings (p. 53)
Statement of financial position (p. 53)
Statement of financial accounting standards (p. 53)
Statement of owners' equity (p. 54)
Transaction principle (p. 48)

ISSUES FOR DISCUSSION

D2.1 Two attributes of an asset are its cost and its value. What role do these attributes play in financial statements?

D2.2 We have all heard companies state that their employees are their most important assets. Where do those assets appear on published balance sheets? Why should that be so?

D2.3 You just inherited a company whose accounting records depict owners' equity totalling $400,000. You don't want the company. Would you accept an offer for $400,000 for the company? Explain. If you sell the company for $600,000 will the buyer's balance sheet report the company at $400,000 or $600,000? Explain. If you thought the company could be sold for $800,000 and therefore rejected the $600,000 offer, at what amount will the newly acquired company be reported on your balance sheet? Explain.

D2.4 Consider yourself a prospective investor. Explain briefly how you might use the three basic financial statements (the balance sheet, the income statement, and the statement of cash flows) in your investment decision. What different insights would you expect those three different statements to provide for your investment decision?

D2.5 In 1994 PepsiCo reported net income for the year of $1,752 million (as reported in the statement of net income) and a net increase in cash and cash equivalent of $103.8 million (as reported in the statement of cash flows). What do those two numbers mean to you as a potential investor in PepsiCo?

D2.6 We say that the accounting equation forces the right side of the balance sheet to always be in balance with the left side, or alternatively that every resource has a source. A company's earnings for the year, retained for use in the business, represent a source. Where might that source have been invested? Where would we find the equivalent of that source on the left side of the balance sheet?

D2.7 A number of sources of funds are available to a company, and those different sources are compensated in different ways. A supplier might sell steel to a company on a credit basis, asking for payment in full by 90 days. A bank would be willing to lend money to a company for periods of from 90 days to any number of years. A shareholder, thinking that the shares can always be sold to someone else if need be, is willing to invest funds in a company. Where do these sources appear in the balance sheet? Where does the compensation required by the sources for the uses of their funds appear in the income statement?

D2.8 A college friend has been quite successful with a computer software company she began shortly after graduation. The company now needs more money for expansion, and your friend is about to sell stock to a select group of investors. She has been preparing financial statements for her company for her own use but will now have to prepare financial reports for outsiders. Explain for your friend the advantages and disadvantages of adopting aggressive accounting policies or conservative accounting policies. Give as many examples as you can, together with your overall explanation.

D2.9 You are the president of a small computer company that led the market in the introduction of a low-priced laptop computer. With a manufacturing cost of $1,500 and a retail price of $3,000, the company did quite well. In the last several years, the major companies in the industry have surpassed your original product by introducing a few technical refinements. You are now ready to introduce Version 2 of your product, which will be a dramatic leap over the competition. However, you still have about 5,000 units of the earlier model. Your salespeople tell you that you have only two alternatives. The salespeople are confident that the units can be sold to college students at a discounted price of $500 each. Alternatively, it may be possible to sell those units at full retail price in some of the less developed countries. How (and why) should this choice be reflected in your company's financial statements?

D2.10 Since you won $100,000 in the state lottery, you have been besieged with proposals to invest your gains. Most recently, Harry Schultz, president of Schultz Corporation, has suggested that you invest $50,000 in the common stock of his company's manufacturing subsidiary. He has shown you the financial statements of the subsidiary and they look promising. On the balance sheet, you see that the assets are mostly raw material inventory and production equipment. The liabilities are quite small and consist mostly of ordinary trade payables to creditors. The income statements show a steady growth in sales and a very satisfactory return. You understand that Schultz Corporation as a whole has not been doing well recently because of price-cutting competition. The president assures you that the manufacturing side of the business is quite healthy and urges your investment.

Would you buy an equity interest in the manufacturing subsidiary? Why or why not? If you are uncertain about making the investment at this time, outline the additional information you would like to have before making that investment, and explain why that information might be important to you.

PROBLEMS

P2.1 Using the accounting equation. Applying the basic accounting equation to the Northfield Corporation at two successive year-ends yields the following results:

Year End	Assets	=	Liabilities	+	Equity
1993	$40,000	=	$30,000	+	$10,000
1994	$35,000	=	$20,000	+	$15,000

Required:

Assuming that no dividends were declared and that no additional capital was invested by the owners, what amount would Northfield have reported as its net income or loss for the 1994 year? Please explain your answer in the context of the facts here.

P2.2 Accounting concepts. Think about each of the situations described below in the context of the chapter section, "Some Fundamental Questions in Accounting":

a. Disneyland in Anaheim, California, sells coupon books of 20-, 30-, and 40-ride tickets that can be used anytime that the park is open. Assume that in January 1994 the amusement park sold $15 million worth of these coupon books. The proceeds were recorded initially as a liability, not as revenue.

b. Disneyland reports on its balance sheet the Anaheim, California, property on which the amusement park is located at its 1955 purchase price.

c. Sky Rider, Inc., specializes in the design and construction of roller coaster rides for amusement parks around the world. Each custom ride takes about two and one-half years to design and build, and the firm typically works on only three or four rides at a time. Nevertheless, the company publishes an annual report with a full income statement detailing its revenues and expenses for each year.

d. Taco Bell, a division of PepsiCo, Inc., owns numerous "taco ranches." The costs to develop each ranch are deferred and reported on the balance sheet as an asset to be written off over the estimated commercially productive lives of the "taco trees."

e. Mac Donald purchased 800 shares of capital stock in PepsiCo, Inc., in January 1993 for $40 per share on the advice of his stockbroker, Ham Berger. Mac then sold one-half of the purchased shares at $38 per share in August of that same year. PepsiCo's annual report, however, reveals that 863.1 million shares have been outstanding for the last three years. The average book value of the outstanding shares has been $8.30 per share in 1994.

Required:

For each of the above situations, describe the accounting concept or principle that applies as the basis for the accounting followed.

P2.3 PepsiCo and the accounting equation. Think about the PepsiCo financial statements we studied in Chapter 1 and Chapter 2. Assume that the company entered into the transactions listed below.

Required:

Using the three-part box described in this chapter,

<table>
<tr><td rowspan="2">Assets</td><td>Liabilities</td></tr>
<tr><td>Owners' equity</td></tr>
</table>

describe in your own words how the following six transactions might affect PepsiCo's financial statements:

a. The sale of common stock to a group of investors for $1 million.

b. The sale of a new issue of bonds to investors in the amount of $5 million.

c. Use of the proceeds of the stock sale and the bond sale to retire a $6 million bank debt.

d. The purchase of $100,000 worth of sausage for the production of pizza, paid in cash as demanded by the sausage maker.

e. The purchase of $250,000 worth of cans and bottles for bottling Pepsi, to be paid for within 30 days.

f. Results for the month of January indicating the aggregate net income from all the units of $25 million.

P2.4 Projections from historic financials. PepsiCo does not publish earnings projections, but the company does provide historical detailed segment information, multiyear income statements, and cash flow statements, and they also provide text commentary (i.e., "Management's Analysis"). Study PepsiCo's business segment data, its income statement, its cash flow statement, and the related management commentaries, and prepare the following:

Required:

a. Based solely on the data in the statements and the related commentaries, what would *you* project PepsiCo's 1995 net income to be? Explain the factors that influenced your judgment.

b. Identify five pieces of information you would like to have that make your projection more reliable. Where would you go to get that information? Do you think you could convince the FASB of the importance of that information so that it would be provided to public stockholders in future financial statements? Why or why not?

P2.5 Accrual versus cash basis accounting. Meredith, Miller, and Associates, Inc., is a management consulting group that was organized for business on August 1, 1994. Greg Meredith and Kate Miller each contributed $20,000 cash for shares of capital stock in the new company. The firm also borrowed $15,000 from a local bank on September 1, 1994; the loan was to be paid in full on August 30, 1995, with interest at the rate of 12 percent annually.

The new company rented office space on September 1, paying two months' rent in advance. The regular monthly rental fees of $600 per month were to be made on the first day of each month beginning on November 1. The company purchased a word-processing system and a fax machine in early August at a total cost of $3,600 cash. The owners estimated that the useful life of the office equipment was three years.

For the five months ended December 31, 1994, the company had rendered $31,000 in consulting services. Of this amount, $19,000 had been collected by year-end. Other costs incurred and paid in cash by year-end included the following:

Utilities	$ 550
Part-time typist	6,000
Miscellaneous office supplies	325

Unpaid bills at year-end included a telephone bill for $75 and wages for the typist of $600.

Required:

You have been retained by the firm of Meredith, Miller, and Associates, Inc., to prepare a set of accounting statements as of December 31, 1994. Using the above information, prepare a balance sheet, an income statement, and a statement of cash flows using the accrual basis of accounting; also prepare an income statement using the cash basis of accounting. On the basis of your findings, be prepared to comment on the performance of the company during its first five months of operation.

P2.6 Accounting data attributes. As a part of its effort to develop a conceptual basis for accounting, the FASB prepared the accompanying chart. The board felt that its rule-making program would proceed on a more solid foundation if it could outline conceptually the most important qualities that accounting data should have. It was understood that proposed accounting standards would then be judged against these qualities to see if the new standard would produce accounting information that would achieve these qualities at an acceptable cost. This chart has become a benchmark for the board and other accounting thinkers.

Required:

For each quality identified by the FASB, describe in your own words what that quality means and how it might be manifested in a set of accounting data.

CHART FOR PROBLEM P2.6

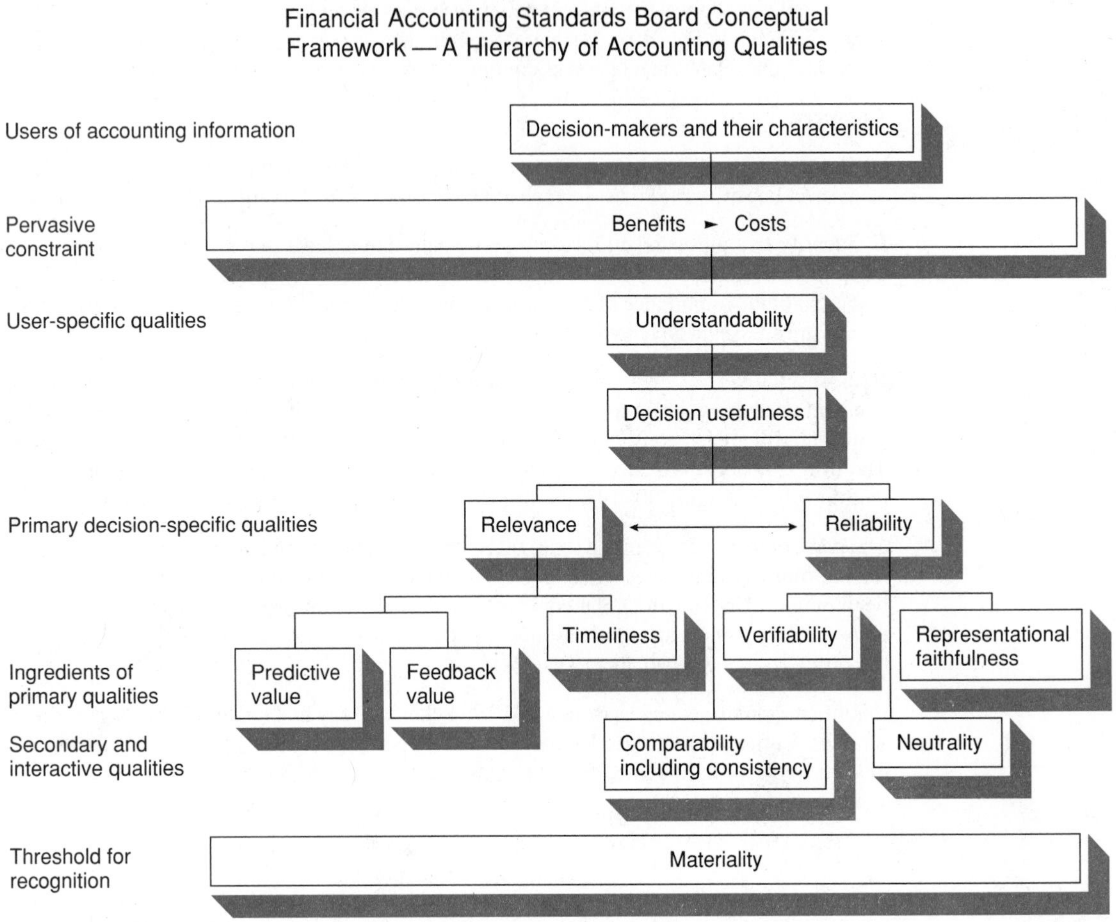

FASB Concepts Statement No. 2, *Qualitative Characteristics of Accounting Information,* is copyrighted by the Financial Accounting Standards Board, 401 Merritt 7, P.O. Box 5116, Norwalk, CT 06856-5116, U.S.A. Portions are reprinted with permission. Copies of the complete document are available from the Financial Accounting Standards Board.

P2.7 Focusing on the users of accounting information. Look again at the chart in P2.6. When the FASB outlined that Hierarchy of Accounting Qualities, they had in mind a general-purpose use of the resulting accounting data. But, of course, there are many users of accounting information, including current stockholders, future stockholders, creditors, employees, and so on. Each user group will have different uses for accounting data, and so different attributes of accounting will be more or less important to each.

Required:

Identify three different user groups that might have an interest in accounting data, and prepare a single-page paper on each, discussing which of the accounting qualities outlined in the chart in P2.6 might be most important to them, and why.

P2.8 Annual report information. The following list identifies a number of items that might tell you something about a company. Study this list from the standpoint of a potential investor.

(1) Brief history of business
(2) Financial statements for last five years (audited if possible)
  (a) Balance sheets
  (b) Income statements

(3) Evaluation of labor relations and terms of union contracts
(4) Description, age, and general evaluation of plants, manufacturing equipment, warehouses, branches, and delivery equipment, owned or leased
(5) Trend of sales of each of principal products for five years
(6) Description of corporate structure
(7) Number of employees
(8) Explanation of unusual items on financial statements
(9) List of officers and directors, their affiliations and background
(10) Principal competitors — comparative share of market
(11) Stock distribution, number of stockholders, principal stockholders
(12) Description of marketing and distribution methods and areas
(13) Details of debt
(14) Status of income tax audit and liability
(15) Percentage ownership of stock available for acquisition
(16) Description and cost of fringe benefits (insurance, medical, pensions)
(17) Details of unrecorded and contingent liabilities
(18) Description of any option, incentive, or profit-sharing plans
(19) Organization, functions of principal executives, ages
(20) Description of principal customers — share of business
(21) Projection of sales and earnings over next five years
(22) Willingness of management to continue in business
(23) Terms of principal contracts and leases
(24) Extent of export sales
(25) Major capital expenditures presently authorized
(26) Status of litigation and any other claims or suits against the company
(27) Extent of advertising
(28) Estimate of major capital expenditures required over next five years
(29) Copies of annual reports to shareholders
(30) Copy of charter and bylaws
(31) Cost of capital
(32) Social responsibility activities
(33) Major subsidiaries and affiliates

Required:

Prepare a brief paper identifying the top 10 items from the list that you would want to be able to study and review. Why did you select those items? Which would you expect to find in the company's annual report to stockholders?

P2.9 Prolific FASB. Since its inception in 1973, the FASB had issued 125 Financial Accounting Statements (FAS) as of June 1, 1994, as well as numerous interpretations and concepts releases. Listed below are the titles of the first 100 FASs. Study the list from the standpoint of a user of financial statements, from the standpoint of a corporate executive, or from the standpoint of a preparer of financial statements.

FASB Statements (FAS)

No.	Title
1	Disclosure of Foreign Currency Translation Information
2	Accounting for Research and Development Costs
3	Reporting Accounting Changes in Interim Financial Statements (an amendment of APB Opinion No. 28)
4	Reporting Gains and Losses from Extinguishment of Debt (an amendment of APB Opinion No. 30)
5	Accounting for Contingencies

No.	Title
6	Classification of Short-Term Obligations Expected to Be Refinanced (an amendment of ARB No. 43, Chapter 3A)
7	Accounting and Reporting by Development Stage Enterprises
8	Accounting for the Translation of Foreign Currency Transactions and Foreign Currency Financial Statements
9	Accounting for Income Taxes — Oil and Gas Producing Companies (an amendment of APB Opinions No. 11 and 23)
10	Extension of "Grandfather" Provisions for Business Combinations (an amendment of APB Opinion No. 16)
11	Accounting for Contingencies — Transition Method (an amendment of FASB Statement No. 5)
12	Accounting for Certain Marketable Securities
13	Accounting for Leases
14	Financial Reporting for Segments of a Business Enterprise
15	Accounting by Debtors and Creditors for Troubled Debt Restructurings
16	Prior Period Adjustments
17	Accounting for Leases — Initial Direct Costs (an amendment of FASB Statement No. 13)
18	Financial Reporting for Segments of a Business Enterprise — Interim Financial Statements (an amendment of FASB Statement No. 14)
19	Financial Accounting and Reporting by Oil and Gas Producing Companies
20	Accounting for Forward Exchange Contracts (an amendment of FASB Statement No. 8)
21	Suspension of the Reporting of Earnings per Share and Segment Information by Nonpublic Enterprises (an amendment of APB Opinion No. 15 and FASB Statement No. 14)
22	Changes in the Provisions of Lease Agreements Resulting from Refundings of Tax-Exempt Debt (an amendment of FASB Statement No. 13)
23	Inception of the Lease (an amendment of FASB Statement No. 13)
24	Reporting Segment Information in Financial Statements that are Presented in Another Enterprise's Financial Report (an amendment of FASB Statement No. 14)
25	Suspension of Certain Accounting Requirements for Oil and Gas Producing Companies (an amendment of FASB Statement No. 19)
26	Profit Recognition on Sales-Type Leases of Real Estate (an amendment of FASB Statement No. 13)
27	Classification of Renewals or Extensions of Existing Sales-Type or Direct Financing Leases (an amendment of FASB Statement No. 13)
28	Accounting for Sales with Leasebacks (an amendment of FASB Statement No. 13)
29	Determining Contingent Rentals (an amendment of FASB Statement No. 13)
30	Disclosure of Information about Major Customers (an amendment of FASB Statement No. 14)
31	Accounting for Tax Benefits Related to U.K. Tax Legislation Concerning Stock Relief
32	Specialized Accounting and Reporting Principles and Practices in AICPA Statements of Position and Guides on Accounting and Auditing Matters (an amendment of APB Opinion No. 20)
33	Financial Reporting and Changing Prices
34	Capitalization of Interest Cost
35	Accounting and Reporting by Defined Benefit Pension Plans
36	Disclosure of Pension Information (an amendment of APB Opinion No. 8)
37	Balance Sheet Classification of Deferred Income Taxes (an amendment of APB Opinion No. 11)
38	Accounting for Preacquisition Contingencies of Purchased Enterprises (an amendment of APB Opinion No. 16)
39	Financial Reporting and Changing Prices: Specialized Assets — Mining and Oil and Gas (a supplement to FASB Statement No. 33)
40	Financial Reporting and Changing Prices: Specialized Assets — Timberlands and Growing Timber (a supplement to FASB Statement No. 33)
41	Financial Reporting and Changing Prices: Specialized Assets — Income-Producing Real Estate (a supplement to FASB Statement No. 33)
42	Determining Materiality for Capitalization of Interest Cost (an amendment of FASB Statement No. 34)
43	Accounting for Compensated Absences
44	Accounting for Intangible Assets of Motor Carriers (an amendment of Chapter 5 of ARB 43 and an interpretation of APB Opinions 17 and 30)
45	Accounting for Franchise Fee Revenue
46	Financial Reporting and Changing Prices: Motion Picture Films (a supplement to FASB Statement No. 33)

No.	Title
47	Disclosure of Long-Term Obligations
48	Revenue Recognition When Right of Return Exists
49	Accounting for Product Financing Arrangements
50	Financial Reporting in the Record and Music Industry
51	Financial Reporting by Cable Television Companies
52	Foreign Currency Translation
53	Financial Reporting by Producers and Distributors of Motion Picture Films
54	Financial Reporting and Changing Prices: Investment Companies (an amendment of FASB Statement No. 33)
55	Determining whether a Convertible Security Is a Common Stock Equivalent (an amendment of APB Opinion No. 15)
56	Designation of AICPA Guide and Statement of Position (SOP) 81-1 on Contractor Accounting and SOP 81-2 concerning Hospital-Related Organizations as Preferable for Purposes of Applying APB Opinion 20 (an amendment of FASB Statement No. 32)
57	Related Party Disclosures
58	Capitalization of Interest Cost in Financial Statements That Include Investments Accounted for by the Equity Method (an amendment of FASB Statement No. 34)
59	Deferral of the Effective Date of Certain Accounting Requirements for Pension Plans of State and Local Governmental Units (an amendment of FASB Statement No. 35)
60	Accounting and Reporting by Insurance Enterprises
61	Accounting for Title Plant
62	Capitalization of Interest Cost in Situations Involving Certain Tax-Exempt Borrowings and Certain Gifts and Grants (an amendment of FASB Statement No. 34)
63	Financial Reporting by Broadcasters
64	Extinguishments of Debt Made to Satisfy Sinking-Fund Requirements (an amendment of FASB Statement No. 4)
65	Accounting for Certain Mortgage Banking Activities
66	Accounting for Sales of Real Estate
67	Accounting for Costs and Initial Rental Operations of Real Estate Projects
68	Research and Development Arrangements
69	Disclosures about Oil and Gas Producing Activities (an amendment of FASB Statements No. 19, 25, 33, and 39)
70	Financial Reporting and Changing Prices: Foreign Currency Translation (an amendment of FASB Statement No. 33)
71	Accounting for the Effects of Certain Types of Regulation
72	Accounting for Certain Acquisitions of Banking or Thrift Institutions (an amendment of APB Opinion No. 17, an interpretation of APB Opinions 16 and 17, and an amendment of FASB Interpretation No. 9)
73	Reporting a Change in Accounting for Railroad Track Structures (an amendment of APB Opinion No. 20)
74	Accounting for Special Termination Benefits Paid to Employees
75	Deferral of the Effective Date of Certain Accounting Requirements for Pension Plans of State and Local Governmental Units (an amendment of FASB Statement No. 35)
76	Extinguishment of Debt (an amendment of APB Opinion No. 26)
77	Reporting by Transferors for Transfers of Receivables with Recourse
78	Classification of Obligations that are Callable by the Creditor (an amendment of ARB No. 43, Chapter 3A)
79	Elimination of Certain Disclosures for Business Combinations by Nonpublic Enterprises (an amendment of APB Opinion No. 16)
80	Accounting for Futures Contracts
81	Disclosure of Postretirement Health Care and Life Insurance Benefits
82	Financial Reporting and Changing Prices: Elimination of Certain Disclosures (an amendment of FASB Statement No. 33)
83	Designation of AICPA Guides and Statement of Position on Accounting by Brokers and Dealers in Securities, by Employee Benefit Plans, and by Banks as Preferable for Purposes of Applying APB Opinion 20 (an amendment of FASB Statement No. 32 and APB Opinion No. 30 and a rescission of FASB Interpretation No. 10)
84	Induced Conversions of Convertible Debt (an amendment of APB Opinion No. 26)
85	Yield Test for Determining whether a Convertible Security Is a Common Stock Equivalent (an amendment of APB Opinion No. 15)
86	Accounting for the Costs of Computer Software to Be Sold, Leased, or Otherwise Marketed
87	Employers' Accounting for Pensions
88	Employers' Accounting for Settlements and Curtailments of Defined Benefit Pension Plans and for Termination Benefits

No.	Title
89	Financial Reporting and Changing Prices
90	Regulated Enterprises — Accounting for Abandonments and Disallowances of Plant Costs (an amendment of FASB Statement No. 71)
91	Accounting for Nonrefundable Fees and Costs Associated with Originating or Acquiring Loans and Initial Direct Costs of Leases (an amendment of FASB Statements No. 13, 60, and 65 and a rescission of FASB Statement No. 17)
92	Regulated Enterprises — Accounting for Phase-in Plans (an amendment of FASB Statement No. 71)
93	Recognition of Depreciation by Not-for-Profit Organizations
94	Consolidation of All Majority-Owned Subsidiaries (an amendment of ARB No. 51, with related amendments of APB Opinion No. 18 and ARB No. 43, Chapter 12)
95	Statement of Cash Flows
96	Accounting for Income Taxes
97	Accounting and Reporting by Insurance Enterprises for Certain Long-Duration Contracts and for Realized Gains and Losses from the Sale of Investments
98	Accounting for Leases: • Sale-Leaseback Transactions Involving Real Estate • Sales-Type Leases of Real Estate • Definition of the Lease Term • Initial Direct Costs of Direct Financing Leases (an amendment of FASB Statements No. 13, 66, and 91 and a rescission of FASB Statement No. 26 and Technical Bulletin No. 79-11)
99	Deferral of the Effective Date of Recognition of Depreciation by Not-for-Profit Organizations (an amendment of FASB Statement No. 93)
100	Accounting for Income Taxes — Deferral of the Effective Date of FASB Statement No. 96 (an amendment of FASB Statement No. 96)

Required:

Prepare a one-page essay discussing the attributes of this list from the perspective of either a user or a preparer. (Hint: you might look for patterns of certain types, general vs. specific statements, numbers of revisions, and so on.)

P2.10 Accounting politics. Consider the following statements that have been made about accounting and accounting standards:

> "The numbers that accountants report have, or at least are widely thought to have, a *significant* impact on *economic behavior.* Accounting rules therefore affect human behavior. Hence, the process by which they are made is said to be political. It is then only a short step to the assertion that such rules are properly to be made in the political arena, by counting heads and deciding accounting issues by some voting mechanism."[1]

> "The process of setting accounting standards can be described as democratic because like all rule-making bodies the board's right to make rules depends ultimately on the consent of the ruled."[2]

> "The [FASB's] objective must be responsive to many more considerations than accounting theory or our notions of economically useful data. . . . Corporate reporting standards should result in data that are useful for economic decisions *provided that*

[1,4,5]D. Solomons, "The Politicization of Accounting," *The Journal of Accountancy* (November 1978), pp. 65–72.

[2]*The Structure of Establishing Financial Accounting Standards* (Stanford, Conn.: FAF, April 1977), p. 19.

the standard is consistent with the national macroeconomic objectives and the economic programs designed to reach these goals."[3]

"Information cannot be neutral — it cannot therefore be reliable — if it is selected or presented for the purpose of producing some chosen effect on human behavior. It is this quality of neutrality which makes a map reliable; and the essential nature of accounting, I believe, is cartographic. Accounting is financial mapmaking."[4]

"Some [would say that] the financial phenomena which accountants must report are not independent of the reporting methods selected."[5]

Required:

Prepare a one-page essay explaining your views on the debate described in the above quotes. Your analysis should consider the implications of both sides of the argument, both for the external users of financial statements and for the preparers of that data.

P2.11 The cost today of future benefits. The CEO of JJ Corp., JoAnn Jones, was visibly upset. The regular Monday morning meeting of the Executive Committee had gone reasonably well (sales were up, costs were under control), but it had come to a very disturbing conclusion. The chief financial officer had offered some concluding comments describing a new ruling from some organization called the Financial Accounting Standards Board, which threatened to wipe out the company's net worth (i.e., OE). The JJ Corp. contract with the union required, among other things, that the company pay the Blue Cross/Blue Shield bills for retirees and their spouses. In the past, those insurance premiums had been charged to expense in the period when they were paid: That accounting process was simple and straightforward, although the expenses had gone up dramatically in recent years. Under this new accounting rule, JJ Corp. would be required to estimate, as the employees worked, how much the insurance premiums would be after they retired. A pro rata portion of that future payment was to be allocated as an expense to the periods when the employees were working. The current charge for that future payment was sure to depress current net income materially. Worse, the new rule required the company to record a liability now for the payments to be due to those employees currently retired. To record that liability, the company would have to record a reduction in shareholder's equity. The preliminary estimate of that liability was greater than the company's net worth as of the most recent year-end.

Jones had been concerned about the impact of the rising cost of health insurance and had joined with other executives in the state to "do something about health care costs." This move from the FASB was not what she had in mind, however. She argued with her CFO, saying, "How can we possibly estimate what those future premiums might be? How can we predict how many employees will stay with us until retirement or how long they will live after retirement? And health care costs cannot stay this high — we *will* find a way to reduce them. If we base our estimates of future payments on the premiums we are paying today, we will seriously overcharge current earnings. It may be that the company will be forced to drop health insurance coverage as a benefit. Then what will we do with those accrued charges?"

Required:

Based on the discussion above and your reading of Chapter 2, prepare a two-page commentary on this issue, arguing in your own words Jones's point of view and then the probable basis of the FASB requirement. State your own conclusion, making sure that it is well justified.

---

[3]David M. Hawkins, "Financial Accounting, the Standards Board and Economic Development," one of the 1973–74 Emanuel Saxe Distinguished Lectures in Accounting, published by the Bernard M. Baruch College, City University of New York, April 1975, pp. 7–8.

P2.12 Regulation without representation. After an extended discussion between Jones and her CFO regarding the requirements of the FASB's new accounting standard "Other Post-Employment Benefits" (the initial phase of that discussion was outlined in Problem 2.11 above), Jones finally accepted the idea that the new statement was GAAP and was a fact of life. The impact of that standard on her company's financial statements made her angry, nonetheless. She said that she was putting her health care cost campaign on the back burner, and she resolved to do something about the accounting profession instead. She asked how it was possible that the FASB could make such an important ruling without some check on its authority. She made some reference to the Boston Tea Party. She asked the company's attorney and the CFO to look into the authority and the standing of the FASB. A little later they reported back to her, explaining that the Securities Laws had given statutory authority for accounting rule making to the Securities and Exchange Commission, which had delegated that authority to the FASB. They explained the board's independent status and its funding basis. Jones immediately picked up her dictaphone and composed a letter to her congressperson, arguing that accounting was too important to be left to the accountants, and demanding that the SEC take back its rule-making position. She explained to her associates that she was sure that the business community would have a stronger voice in accounting matters if they could speak through their congressional representatives, and through them to the SEC.

Required:

Prepare a one-page memorandum to Jones, explaining why she should not send that letter. You may also suggest some other courses of action for her, as long as you can develop strong logic for your alternatives.

P2.13 Current value reporting. The managers of Property Developments, Inc., were concerned about the depressed price at which the company's stock was trading. It had not gotten much above the $5 range, suggesting that Wall Street thought the company was worth about $5,000,000. The company's net worth (net worth = A − L), according to the most recent financial statements, was about $4,500,000, but everyone knew that the historical cost financial statements seriously understated the value of the company's portfolio of shopping plazas and apartment complexes. It was suggested that the market price of the stock might go up if the value of the company's properties was better understood by a wider audience. PDI management discussed together the pros and cons of preparing and publishing current value financial statements for the company. Eventually they agreed that the potential benefit was worth the cost, and the discussion turned to implementation of the idea. An interesting and heated argument ensued as to the definition of *current value* as the term might be used in connection with the preparation of current value financial statements.

The operations manager argued that the properties should be valued at eight times their cash flow, inasmuch as that is the way the company looked at properties they were considering buying.

The construction manager argued that the current value of the properties was the current cost of replacing them, given the inflation that had swept through the construction industry.

The chief financial officer argued that the properties ought to be valued at the price obtained in the sale of comparable properties, inasmuch as that is the way a potential corporate raider would look at the individual properties in a campaign to liquidate the company.

Required:

Assume that the company is going to prepare current value basis financial statements as a supplement to its GAAP-based, historical cost statements. How should the current values be determined? On the basis of some multiple of current cash flow? On the basis of replacement cost? On the basis of comparable properties' sale prices? Present the rationale for your position.

P2.14 Fortunate Corporation finally finds a buyer. Fortunate Corporation had been through very difficult times. Its principal product had been left behind in a consumer style shift, and the company had been forced to get along by manufacturing and selling accessory products. New management had resolved to reduce excess capacity (and operating costs) to maintain the viability of at least some aspects of the company. They put the company's original facility, old Plant #1, on the market, but there were very few inquiries from potential buyers. Then one day, close to the end of the fiscal year, the realtor called to tell them disturbing news: the State Highway Department had announced plans to build a bypass around town and was planning to route the new road right through the center of old Plant #1. The plant and its land were on the books at $10,000,000. Based on the realtor's advice, the company was asking $11,500,000 in its current campaign to dispose of the property. The attorney was able to get a firm commitment from the state that it would buy the property from the company, paying $12,000,000 three years from today in accordance with eminent domain procedures.

Required:

Discuss the application of the notion of lower of cost or market in this situation. How should this situation be reflected in the current year's company financial statements? Why?

P2.15 Applications of materiality concept. Consider the application of the idea of materiality in each of the following situations. Assume that for the year ended December 31, 1994, the company has total assets of $10,000,000 and net worth (net worth = A – L) of $3,000,000; sales were $10,000,000 two years ago, $11,000,000 last year, and $12,000,000 this year; net income was $400,000 two years ago, $550,000 last year, and $650,000 this year.

a. Research and development had never been a major expense for the company but had been growing about 5 percent a year. In 1994, it had grown to $500,000. The company had always disclosed in a footnote the amount of R&D expense it had incurred each year but had never included it as a separate line item in the income statement. R&D expenses had always been included in the line item "General and Administrative Expenses."

b. The company's subsidiary in Australia had a fire in its accounting department in mid-December and will not be able to get its financial reports to the home office in accordance with the original schedule for the preparation of the annual report to stockholders. Waiting until the data can be reconstructed and delivered to the home office will mean postponing the usual shareholder meeting for at least a month. In its report to the home office for the 11 months ended November 30, 1994, the subsidiary reported assets of $1,000,000, owners' equity of $300,000, and earnings-to-date of $25,000.

c. Each year the company counted all of the products-in-inventory on hand at all of its locations, priced out those inventory count sheets, and adjusted the balance sheet inventory amount to equal the values indicated by the priced count sheets. That process had been completed in early January, and the inventory account had been adjusted up to $3,000,000. The rest of the work required to pull together the financial statements was almost done, and that was good because the final statements had been promised to the bank early next week. Unfortunately, the inventory control manager called to report an error in the inventory pricing process. It seems that the computer program used to price the count sheets had slipped a decimal point: A product that should have had a value of $5 had been priced at $50. As a result the total inventory was overvalued by $250,000. That error overstated inventory by 8.3 percent, total assets by 2.5 percent, and after-tax income for the year by 19 percent.

d. The financial statements were completed and delivered to the bank and mailed to the shareholders. The manager of the Tucson plant called to say that an accounting employee had disappeared yesterday, and that when people had checked around they found that $10,000 in cash was gone from the plant vault. The employee had been responsible for the plant's payroll and vendor payment system. The plant had processed about $4,000,000 in payroll and $7,000,000 in vendor purchases last year.

Required:

For each of the situations outlined above, explain what you think the company ought to do, giving particular consideration to the concept of materiality. How should the notion of materiality impact the decisions suggested by the above situations?

General Motors
Consolidated Balance Sheet
For the Years Ended December 31, 1994 and 1993

Assets	**December 31,**	
(Dollars in millions)	**1994**	**1993**
Cash and cash equivalents	**$ 10,939.0**	$ 13,790.5
Other marketable securities	**5,136.6**	4,172.2
Total cash and marketable securities	**16,075.6**	17,962.7
Finance receivables — net	**54,077.3**	53,874.7
Accounts and notes receivable (less allowances)	**8,977.8**	6,389.2
Inventories (less allowances)	**10,127.8**	8,615.1
Contracts in process (less advances and progress payments of $2,311.2 and $2,739.2)	**2,265.4**	2,376.8
Net equipment on operating leases (less accumulated depreciation of $5,374.7 and $4,579.6)	**20,061.6**	13,095.3
Deferred income taxes	**19,693.3**	20,798.1
Other assets (less allowances)	**20,625.5**	17,757.3
Property		
Real estate, plants, and equipment — at cost	**69,807.9**	67,966.4
Less accumulated depreciation	**42,586.4**	41,725.5
Net real estate, plants, and equipment	**27,221.5**	26,240.9
Special tools — at cost (less amortization)	**7,559.1**	7,983.9
Total property	**34,780.6**	34,224.8
Intangible assets — at cost (less amortization)	**11,913.8**	13,106.9
Total Assets	**$198,598.7**	$188,200.9
Liabilities and Stockholders' Equity		
Liabilities		
Accounts payable (principally trade)	**$ 11,635.0**	$ 10,276.5
Notes and loans payable	**73,730.2**	70,441.2
United States, foreign, and other income taxes — deferred and payable	**2,721.0**	2,409.3
Postretirement benefits other than pensions	**40,018.2**	37,920.0
Pensions	**14,353.2**	22,631.6
Other liabilities and deferred credits	**42,867.3**	38,474.8
Total Liabilities	**185,324.9**	182,153.4
Stocks Subject to Repurchase	**450.0**	450.0
Stockholders' Equity		
Preference stocks	**2.4**	4.2
Common stocks		
$1-2/3 par value (issued, 754,345,782 and 720,105,471 shares)	**1,257.2**	1,200.2
Class E (issued, 268,125,255 and 263,089,320 shares)	**26.8**	26.3
Class H (issued, 78,720,022 and 75,705,433 shares)	**7.9**	7.6
Capital surplus (principally additional paid-in capital)	**13,149.4**	12,003.4
Net income retained for use in the business (accumulated deficit)	**1,785.8**	(2,002.9)
Subtotal	**16,229.5**	11,238.8
Minimum pension liability adjustment	**(3,548.4)**	(5,311.2)
Accumulated foreign currency translation adjustments	**(100.4)**	(494.4)
Net unrealized gains on investments in certain debt and equity securities	**243.1**	164.3
Total Stockholders' Equity	**12,823.8**	5,597.5
Total Liabilities and Stockholders' Equity	**$198,598.7**	$188,200.9

Reference should be made to the Notes to Financial Statements.

General Motors Operations with GMAC on an Equity Basis
Consolidated Balance Sheet
For the Years Ended December 31, 1994 and 1993

Assets *(Dollars in millions)*	December 31, 1994	December 31, 1993
Current Assets		
Cash and cash equivalents	$ 9,731.4	$ 9,762.5
Other marketable securities	1,245.0	722.5
Total cash and marketable securities	10,976.4	10,485.0
Accounts and notes receivable		
Trade	7,873.1	5,563.1
Nonconsolidated affiliates	2,080.4	2,955.2
Inventories	10,127.8	8,615.1
Contracts in process	2,265.4	2,376.8
Prepaid expenses and deferred income taxes	6,455.6	8,036.3
Total Current Assets	39,778.7	38,031.5
Equity in Net Assets of Nonconsolidated Affiliates	9,204.3	8,638.5
Deferred Income Taxes	16,318.6	14,874.1
Other Investments and Miscellaneous Assets	14,835.5	12,586.4
Property — Net	34,661.4	34,103.9
Intangible Assets	11,536.4	12,746.1
Total Assets	$126,334.9	$120,980.5
Liabilities and Stockholders' Equity		
Current Liabilities		
Accounts payable	$ 10,905.0	$ 9,546.5
Loans payable	993.7	1,449.6
Income taxes payable	144.7	389.9
Accrued liabilities and deferred income taxes (including current portion of postretirement benefits other than pensions)	26,584.4	23,823.3
Stocks subject to repurchase	450.0	—
Total Current Liabilities	39,077.8	35,209.3
Long-Term Debt	6,082.3	6,218.4
Payable to GMAC	1,212.5	1,355.5
Capitalized Leases	136.4	165.2
Postretirement Benefits Other Than Pensions	37,348.0	35,423.6
Pensions	11,223.1	20,583.3
Other Liabilities and Deferred Income Taxes	16,752.2	14,739.7
Deferred Credits	1,678.8	1,238.0
Stocks Subject to Repurchase	—	450.0
Stockholders' Equity	12,823.8	5,597.5
Total Liabilities and Stockholders' Equity	$126,334.9	$120,980.5

P2.16 Consolidating the entire entity. The preceding exhibit presents the balance sheet of General Motors Corporation on a fully consolidated basis, including all of the accounts of General Motors Acceptance Corporation. The next exhibit presents General Motors treating GMAC as though it was just a single investment. (Note that the shareholders' equity is the same in both presentations. You should also know that GMAC's total assets are $85.5 billion, its liabilities are $77.6 billion, and its shareholders' equity is $7.9 billion. GM owns 100 percent of GMAC and so its $7.9 billion investment in GMAC is included in the line "Equity in Net Assets of Unconsolidated Affiliates" in the second exhibit.)

Required:

Both exhibits present the balance sheet of General Motors, but they rely on different underlying assumptions. Which presentation seems best to you, and why?

P2.17 Articulated financial statements. Under GAAP, the net earnings for the year less dividends accrued must be equal to the change in net assets (A–L) from the end of last year to the end of the current year, *ceterus paribus*. Some have suggested that balance sheets ought to be prepared on a current value basis so as to present a better measure of the shareholders' equity. That idea has been difficult to sell to the financial community because it implies that the income statement would reflect year-to-year changes in value, and those value-driven fluctuations would make it appear that management was not in control of the company. To deal with that concern, it has been suggested that the balance sheet be prepared on a current cost basis and that the income statements ought to be prepared on a historical cost basis. In effect, those commentators are willing to do away with the idea that the balance sheet and the income statement are inextricably linked — that is, they need not be articulated.

Required:

Prepare two short memos, each addressed to the president of Property Developments, Inc. (P 2.13 above). One memo should argue that the company's balance sheet and income statement could be prepared on different bases, and that they do not need to articulate. The other memo should argue that the statements should be prepared on the same basis and that it is important to preserve the GAAP requirement of articulation.

P2.18 Standards for the MD&A. The Securities and Exchange Commission requires (among other things) that companies provide full financial statements to their shareholders every year, as well as a text presentation called "Management Discussion and Analysis" (the MD&A). The financial statements must be prepared in accordance with GAAP, but there are no standards for the preparation of the MD&A. The SEC's rules for the MD&A simply require management to explain the changes in results from one year to the next, comment on the company's liquidity, and highlight any factor that might make the current statements an inappropriate basis for predicting future trends for the company. Compliance with this requirement has been uneven; some companies have presented quite detailed analytical comparisons of results between years, and some have confined their presentations to simple statements explaining, for instance, that unit sales are up while unit prices have declined. There has been some debate as to whether the SEC (or the FASB) should set more specific standards for the MD&A presentations: more specific standards would obviously enhance the comparability of information between companies, but more specific standards could inhibit the presentation of what is essentially qualitative information.

Required:

Visit your school's library, and select three annual reports from three different companies in the same industry. Read the president's letter and make your own analysis of the companies' results, as reflected in the financial statements. With that general background, study the MD&A presentation in those reports. Based on your assessment of the quality of those MD&A presentations, prepare a one-page letter addressed to the Securities and Exchange Commission, arguing for either greater specificity in the MD&A requirements or continued flexibility in the rules. Your letter should flow logically from the results of your study of the three examples.

CASES

C2.1 An Accounting Game: The Sheepherders (Part One).* In the high mountains of Chatele, two sheepherders, Deyonne and Batonne, sit arguing their relative positions in life — an argument that has been going on for years. Deyonne says that he has 400 sheep, while Batonne has only 360 sheep. Therefore, Deyonne is much better off. Batonne, on the other hand, argues that he has 30 acres of land while Deyonne has only 20 acres; then too, Deyonne's

*M. Carlson and J. W. Higgins, "A Games Approach to Introducing Accounting," *Accounting Education: Problems and Prospects* (Sarasota, Fla.: American Accounting Association, 1974). Reproduced with permission of the American Accounting Association.

land was inherited while Batonne had given 35 sheep for 20 acres of land 10 years ago. This year he gave 40 sheep for 10 additional acres of land. Batonne also makes the observation that of Deyonne's sheep 35 belong to another man, and he merely keeps them.

Deyonne counters that he has a large one-room cabin that he built himself. He claims that he has been offered three acres of land for the cabin. Besides these things, he has a plow, which was a gift from a friend and is worth a couple of goats; two carts that were given him in trade for a poor acre of land; and an ox that he acquired for five sheep.

Batonne goes on to say that his wife has orders for five coats to be made of homespun wool and that she will receive 25 goats for them. His wife has 10 goats already, three of which have been received in exchange for one sheep just last year. She has an ox that she acquired in a trade for three sheep. She also has one cart that cost her two sheep. Batonne's two-room cabin, even though smaller in dimension than Deyonne's, should bring him two choice acres of land in trade. Deyonne is reminded by Batonne that he owes Tyrone three sheep for bringing up his lunch each day last year.

Required:

In your opinion, who is wealthier — Deyonne or Batonne?

C2.2 An Accounting Game: The Sheepherders (Part Two).† A year has elapsed since you solved Part One of the Sheepherders Game. After studying your solution to Part One, Deyonne and Batonne grudgingly accepted your opinion as to their relative wealths at the end of last year. The passage of time has not diminished their penchant for argument, however. Now they're arguing about who had the largest income for the year just ended.

Deyonne points out that the number of sheep that he personally owns at year-end exceeds his personal holdings at the beginning of the year by 80, whereas Batonne's increase was only 20. Batonne replies that his increase would have been 60 had he not traded 40 sheep during the year for 10 acres of additional land. Besides, Batonne points out that he exchanged 18 sheep during the year for food and clothing items, whereas Deyonne exchanged only seven for such purposes. The food and clothing have been pretty much used up by the end of the year.

Batonne is happy because his wife made five coats during the year (fulfilling the orders she had at the beginning of the year) and received 25 goats for them. She managed to obtain orders for another five coats (again for 25 goats) — orders on which she has not yet begun to work. Deyonne points out that he took to making his own lunches this year; therefore, he does not owe Tyrone anything now. Deyonne was very unhappy one day last year when he discovered that his ox had died of a mysterious illness. Both men are thankful, however, that none of the other animals died or was lost.

Except for the matters reported above, Deyonne's and Batonne's holdings at the end of the current year are the same as their holdings at the end of last year.

Required:

How would you, as an outside observer to this argument, define "income?" Given your definition, whose income — Deyonne's or Batonne's — was greater for the past year?

C2.3 Accrual versus cash basis accounting. Apex Machine Tool found itself with an exciting opportunity. A valued customer ordered a special tool and promised to pay $10,000 a year in rent, over a 10-year period, for the use of the tool. Apex ran some numbers and estimated that the tool could be built for $60,000 ($25,000 in material, $10,000 in design cost, and

†M. Carlson and J. W. Higgins, "A Games Approach to Introducing Accounting," *Accounting Education: Problems and Prospects* (Sarasota, Fla.: American Accounting Association, 1974). Reproduced with permission of the American Accounting Association.

$25,000 in labor and other factory costs), although it was clear that fabrication of the tool would take the better part of a year to complete.

On November 1, 1993, Apex's board of directors approved the project. During the next two months all of the engineering was completed; during January 1994 the steel was ordered and received; the fabrication was completed during the rest of 1994, and the tool was delivered to the customer in December 1994. To finance the purchase of the steel and pay for the cost of the engineering and fabrication, Apex borrowed $60,000 using the rental agreement from the customer as collateral. The bank insisted that the principal on the loan ($60,000) be repaid in equal annual installments of $10,000 beginning December 31, 1995. The bank also insisted on annual interest payments, due December 31 each year, at 10 percent of the average amount of the loan outstanding during the year.

The customer is very happy with the tool but does not expect to have any use for it after the 10-year rental period. Apex plans to take the tool back at the end of the rental period and is sure that it will be good for many more years of useful service. At this time, however, Apex has no other customers in mind for the tool.

Required:

a. Create a time line for the 12 years beginning in 1993 (as illustrated below) and indicate in words where — in which period — the events described above will fall for both a cash basis and an accrual basis.

Cash basis
Accrual basis |——— 1993 ———|——— 1994 ———|——— 1995 ———|

b. Put a label on each of those events, on each side of the line; for example, using the cash basis of accounting, what is the nature of the steel purchase in the early part of 1994? What is the nature of that purchase, using the accrual basis of accounting?

c. Create two sets of income statements for this project, for each of the years 1993, 1994, 1995, 1999, and 2004. One set of statements should use the cash basis of accounting and one set should use the accrual basis.

d. Describe in your own words how the management of Apex might have applied the matching principle and the allocation principle to the above situation, and how its judgments might have been affected by the notion of conservatism.

CHAPTER 3

The Accounting Process

Nowadays, you hear a lot about fancy accounting methods, like LIFO and FIFO, but back then we were using the ESP method, which really sped things along when it came time to close those books. It's a pretty basic method: If you can't make your books balance, you take however much they're off by and enter it under the heading ESP, which stands for Error Some Place.[1]

Key Chapter Issues

- I recognize the importance of the accounting equation, but with all of a business's daily transactions, how do we keep the equation in balance?
- How do we get a business event into the accounting system, and how do we get that business event through the system and into the financial statements?
- What kinds of business events are recorded in the accounting system and what kinds of events are not? How do we decide which events are recorded and which are not?
- When I was younger, I took a clock apart to see what made it tick. Can we do the same thing with the accounting process?
- How does the relationship between the balance sheet, the income statement, and the statement of cash flows play out in real life? Can you show me an example?

[1]S. Walton and J Huey, *Sam Walton, Made in America: My Story* (NY: Doubleday Books, 1992), p. 53.

In the discussion in the first two chapters we compared accounting to a language, and we outlined some of the overarching principles that language depends upon for its effectiveness as a communications vehicle. In this chapter we want to focus on the accounting process, which gathers the information to be reported and which actually carries the communication to the user. If you were responsible for the six o'clock news you would continually polish your vocabulary and your syntax, but you would also work hard to be sure that your news gathering and your analytical skills were at their best. In the news business, what you have to say really is more important than the way you say it. And so it is with accounting. Managers are concerned that their companies' financial statements comply with GAAP and that the resulting reports communicate effectively. But they also pay a great deal of attention to the underlying accounting process so that what they say in their accounting reports is comprehensive, accurate, and truthful.

The accounting process involves four steps: *measuring* the company's business events; *recording* and storing the quantified measures; sorting through those accumulated, quantified business events and *reporting* the results; and *analyzing* and interpreting those reports. In this chapter we touch briefly on the process of measuring, reporting, and analyzing. We will have more to say about the measurement aspect of the process in subsequent chapters as we discuss the accounting for individual assets and liabilities, and we will have more to say about reporting and analyzing specifically in the next two chapters and again in the individual asset and liability chapters. The principal focus of this chapter, however, is on the recording process. We have elected to devote considerable attention to the recording process in this early chapter because we believe that a good understanding of that recording process facilitates the subsequent effective use and interpretation of the financial information generated by those processes.

ACCOUNTING INFORMATION SYSTEMS

Measuring

A wide variety of information about an enterprise might be useful to investors and other third parties. However, accounting systems measure, record, and report only those events and transactions that can be objectively measured. For example, it may be quite significant that the president of a company resigned or that a new president has been hired, and a press release describing those events may be given wide distribution. However, because it is difficult to quantify the loss the company has realized as a result of the resignation of a valued leader, or the gain the company will realize as a result of bringing on a new, energetic CEO, neither event would be recorded in the accounting records of the company or reported in the company's financial statements. At the other extreme, severance pay due to the departing CEO or the hiring bonus paid to the new CEO *can* be measured objectively and *will* be recorded in the company's accounts and reflected in its financial statements.

Measurement questions are frequently difficult. Although most economic events and transactions (for example, sales of merchandise for cash, purchases of equipment, payment of salaries) can be measured relatively easily. More complex events and transactions (for example, sales on credit terms, expenditures for research and development, the purchase of another business) present more serious measurement problems, as we will see in later chapters.

Imagine the spectrum of possible transactions, and their impact on the financial statements, on a continuum that looks like this:

Impact is apparent and measurable	Impact is likely and estimable	Impact is uncertain and unmeasurable

Accounting attempts to deal with all of those events and transactions that are objectively measurable and those that are at least reasonably estimable. For example, at the far left side of the spectrum, the purchase of merchandise is quite routinely recorded at the amount to be paid to a vendor. In the middle of the spectrum, a product recall is probably recognized in the financial statements, assuming that the cost of the recall can be estimated with a reasonable degree of certainty. Other events and transactions, the financial effects of which cannot be reasonably foreseen or quantified, cannot be recorded in the financial statements and must be explained to those third parties who have an interest in the company via other communication techniques. As an example of an event at the far right side of the spectrum, think about a pharmaceutical company that has just received regulatory permission to market a new, potentially powerful drug; that event will almost certainly be described in press reports and in the president's letter in the annual report to stockholders. But because the financial success of the new product is not known and because its impact cannot be measured until the market reacts, the event of the new product approval is not recognized in the financial statements. As you can imagine, management depends on its accounting systems to deal with events and transactions on the left side of the continuum and devotes most of its attention to events that fall at the center or the far right side of the spectrum. As management people think about their reporting responsibility, they work hard at making the best estimate they can for the items in the center of the spectrum — which will be recorded in the financial statements based on management's estimated amounts. And management people work hard looking for other ways besides the financial reporting process (using press releases, speeches, analyst presentations, and so forth) to communicate the effect of those events at the right of the spectrum.

Recording

Accounts and the information system. The accounting system of any enterprise is effectively an **information system.** That is, it is a system in which the financial aspects of events and transactions are evaluated, processed, and then reported to various information users. Like all information systems, an accounting system contains files in which the basic data can be stored for future use or processing. In accounting systems, these files are known as **accounts.**

When a business event occurs, the monetary effects of the event are evaluated; if those effects can be measured with a fair degree of accuracy, they are recorded and stored in the appropriate accounts. The accounts are used as storehouses to accumulate the monetary effects of all of the events affecting the entity. Some events will result in increases to an account, others will result in decreases. For example, if we maintained an account for inventory, purchases from suppliers would add to the Inventory account, whereas sales to customers would decrease the Inventory account. At any time, management can look at an account and see how much activity has taken place and can see what the current **balance** in the account is. Going back to our inventory example, management can look on the shelves to see how much product is physically on hand: but to report to our banker or another third party how much inventory is on hand, it is more effective to report the cost of that inventory on the shelves. The cost of the inventory on hand will be available in the accounting system, as the balance in the Inventory account.

Each account represents some kind of asset, or some type of liability, or a component of owners' equity. In theory, a company could maintain only three accounts: a single asset account, a single liability account, and one owners' equity account. Most companies, however, have many more accounts; the number of accounts needed depends on the complexity of the business and the amount of detail to be presented in the accounting reports. For example, a company may maintain one account labeled "Cash" and accumulate in that account all of the financial effects of events and transactions that impact its cash. On the other hand, many companies maintain individual accounts for different kinds of property and equipment — a separate account for trucks, another for tools, and a third for the factory building. Again, the number of accounts maintained depends on the complexity of the business and on the amount of detail that is to be presented in the basic financial statements.

In manual accounting systems, the accounts are known as **T-accounts,** principally because their format depicts a large "T." The vertical trunk of the "T" divides the account into a left side and a right side. One side is used to accumulate the effects of those transactions that increase the account balance; the other side is used to accumulate the effects of those transactions that decrease the account balance. As we shall see in a later discussion, whether the right side or the left side is used to accumulate increases or decreases depends on the nature of the account. The balance in the account at any time is simply the difference between the total of the increases and the total of the decreases. To prepare a financial report at any particular time, management need only use the balances in each account. A balance sheet is a display of all of the balances in the balance sheet accounts; an income statement is a display of all of the account balances in the income statement accounts.

Computer-based accounting systems also depend on the concept of accounts. The fundamentals of the recording process are the same whether the system is manual or computer based. The monetary amount of each measurable event or transaction is ascribed to the particular account affected; the processing system aggregates all those transactions that affect particular accounts and determines a new balance after each transaction is entered. When the processing for a period is complete, the balances in the accounts are displayed in a financial report. In a computerized system, the accounts no longer have a left side and a right side, rather the increases and decreases are simply entered into the account chronologically. The accounts still act as the repository for the aggregation of transactions, however, and still produce a balance, which is the net result of all of the transactions affecting that account.

It may be helpful to visualize an account as a discrete place where the financial effects of economic events and transactions are accumulated. For example, a simple hypothetical asset account might appear as follows under a manual system and a computerized system:

Manual Accounting System

Asset Account

Beginning balance	$10,000		
Entry #1	1,000	Entry #2	$ 500
Entry #3	2,000	Entry #4	1,500
Entry #6	3,000	Entry #5	2,000
Ending balance	$12,000		

Computerized Accounting System

Asset Account

Beginning balance	$10,000
Entry #1	$ 1,000
Entry #2	(500)
Entry #3	2,000
Entry #4	(1,500)
Entry #5	(2,000)
Entry #6	3,000
Ending balance	$12,000

The double-entry system. Understanding that accounts are the repositories where we accumulate and store information, we need to look at the process that actually enters the information into the accounts. But to understand the logic of that entry process, we ought to go back to some basics from the earlier chapters. You will remember that we said that every resource available to the company has a source, and because of that truism, the company's assets always had to be equal to the sum of its liabilities and owners' equity. We stated that basic relationship as

$$A = L + OE$$

An Italian mathematician, Luca Pacioli, developed that equation several centuries ago and invented the double-entry accounting system we use today. His equation holds each business responsible for its assets, and asks, "Where did the funding come from to provide the company's assets?" And perhaps more importantly, it asks, "To whom is management accountable for the protection and employment of those assets?" Going to the accounting process, he reasoned that the best way to be sure that the accounting equation was always in balance was to use a **double-entry accounting system.** Under Pacioli's double-entry system, every time a change was made in one of the accounts represented in the equation, an equal change had to be made in some other account in the equation.

Think of a company's balance sheet as being a delicate balance beam, with a fulcrum at its equal sign and its assets equal to the sum of its liabilities and its equity. If you then think of a business event you would like to enter on that balance beam, you will see that the event must either have an equal effect on each side of the balance beam or have an equal on-and-off effect on one side. To keep the balance beam level, an entered event must either impact both sides equally or have a self-canceling effect on one side. That balance beam is an accounting system. In accounting every event is understood to have a double implication because every new resource must have a source, and vice versa. Every accounting event will have two aspects to it: The event will either add equal amounts to both sides of the equation or have a self-canceling effect on one side. In a double-entry accounting system, both aspects of the event are recorded at the same time to be sure that the equation is always in balance. Some accounting events result in an increase in an asset and in a liability; some result in the reverse. Some events result in an increase in an asset and an increase in owners' equity; some result in the reverse. Some events result in an increase in one asset and a decrease in another asset, while others result in an increase in a liability and a decrease in owners' equity.

Consider, for example, a retailer's purchase of $30,000 of merchandise inventory for cash. One asset (inventory) will be increased by $30,000 while another asset (cash) will be decreased by an equal amount. If, however, the retailer purchased the inventory on credit, an asset (inventory) would be increased by $30,000, as would a liability (accounts payable to suppliers). When the retailer pays its suppliers, its liabilities (accounts payable) decrease by $30,000 as do its assets (cash). *All* of the many transactions of even the most complex company are expressed in exactly this manner; an increase or a decrease in one account must, of necessity, result in an equal change in another account. Regardless of the transaction, the basic accounting equation must always remain in balance.

In a double-entry system, the two aspects of an event are formally entered into the accounts using an **entry.** You can't just say to the system, "Please increase an asset and a liability"; being a system, it will expect something more systematic. Going back to the retailer example we just cited, the entry to purchase the inventory for cash would be written to look something like this:

Inventory (A)	increase $30,000
Cash (A)	decrease $30,000

We will have more to say later about the actual form of the entry used by most businesspeople.

Accounts represent repositories (that is, the physical place) where the financial effects of a company's economic events and transactions are accumulated; *entries* represent the monetary expression of those events — that is, the physical input to those accounts. As management thinks through the accounting impact of any business transaction, it usually visualizes the transaction in the form of an entry — which accounts are affected, which accounts are increased, and which are decreased. It is almost always easy to visualize one half of an entry, but sometimes the other half of the entry is more problematic. For example, paying a $10,000 bill for advertising clearly reduces cash, but what should the other side of the entry be? Should another asset, perhaps customer awareness, be increased? Or should owners' equity be decreased because the advertising is simply a business expense? As you confront accounting questions, you will find it helpful to think through the two sides of each entry in this way. Remember that the accounting equation (again, A = L + OE) must remain in balance. That discipline is the principal advantage of Pacioli's double-entry system.

Thinking through a debit and a credit. As we noted earlier, manual systems use accounts that are physically divided into a left side and a right side. For reasons that are now lost in time, the left side of those accounts is referred to as the *debit side* and the right side is referred to as the *credit side*. The words *debit* and *credit* are, unfortunately, used in a variety of ways in the business world, as with credit memo or a debit memo. When they are used in an accounting record-keeping context, **debit** and **credit** are simply shorthand ways to refer to the part of an accounting entry that affects the left (debit) side of an account and the right (credit) side of an account, respectively. (Incidentally, when those terms are written, the shorthand is often carried further — debit is usually abbreviated "dr." and credit is usually abbreviated "cr.")

The use of the words *debit* and *credit* gained wide acceptance during the period when manual accounting systems were in place. They continue to be used in accounting discussions today — even in these days of computerized systems when accounts do not have a left or right side but are simply a collection of electronic impulses. Some additional background on the use of these words and some expansion on the way the words are used in the electronic age may be helpful.

Custom has determined that, at least in the United States, balance sheets are prepared with assets on the left side of the balance sheet and the liabilities and owners' equity on the right side. From that convention, it followed that the monetary effect of an event that increased an asset was entered on the left side of the asset T-account. The monetary effect of an event that increased a liability or a component of owners' equity account was entered on the right side of the liability and owners' equity T-accounts. We were just considering a retailer's purchase of merchandise inventory by paying cash or by buying on credit; the cash purchase would result in a $30,000 entry to the left side of the inventory account (an increase in that asset) and a $30,000 entry to the right side of the cash account (a decrease in that asset). The purchase on credit would result in a $30,000 entry to the left side of the inventory account (an increase in that asset) and an equal entry to the right side of the accounts payable account (an increase in that liability account).

Building on our earlier discussion of debits and credits, it follows that the entry to the left side of the inventory account is a debit (left-side) entry and the entry to the right side of the cash account or the accounts payable account is a credit (right-side) entry. It will always be so: Increases in assets are left-side entries (debits) while a decrease in an asset account is a right-side entry (a credit). Conversely, an increase in a liability account is a right-side entry (credit) while decreases in liabilities and owners' equity are left-side entries (debits). Finally, because revenues and expenses accrue to the benefit or detriment of the owners, an increase in a revenue account is always a credit entry, while an increase to an expense is always a debit entry. The logic of this system of maintaining accounts — that is, the use of debits and credits — can be more readily seen in the following illustration:

Account Title	
Left Debit	*Right* Credit

The balance sheet accounts can be depicted as follows — think about the way our retailer's purchases impact these accounts and the accounting equation:

Assets		=	**Liabilities**		+	**Owners' Equity**	
Dr. increase	Cr. decrease		Dr. decrease	Cr. increase		Dr. decrease	Cr. increase

Income statement accounts can be depicted in this way:

Revenues		–	**Expenses**		=	**Net Income (an addition to or subtraction from retained earnings)**	
Dr. decrease	Cr. increase		Dr. increase	Cr. decrease		Dr. decrease (Loss)	Cr. increase (Income)

The words *debit* and *credit* are used in the same way in companies in which the accounting system is computerized — the debit entry means an increase in an asset or expense account or a decrease in a liability or owners' equity account, while a credit entry means an increase in a liability or revenue account or an owners' equity account but a decrease in an asset account. The day may come when an increase is referred to simply as an *increase* and a decrease is referred to simply as a *decrease*. Until that day comes, however, it is easier for accountants and businesspeople to adapt to existing conventions and refer to entries with the terms *debits* and *credits*.

Let us summarize what we have been discussing. We have said that every accounting transaction must affect at least two accounts and that the debit side of the transaction must always equal the credit side. We have also stated that accountants and businesspeople analyze a transaction by considering which accounts are affected, in what amounts, and then by thinking through the various debit and credit entries that are required. To record a business event in the company's accounts, an entry is required. Management people follow these steps in the development of that required entry:

1. Is the transaction (or event) complete, and is its effect objectively measurable?
2. What kind of account (for example, asset, liability, or owners' equity) is affected? What specific accounts are affected?
3. Are the affected accounts increased or decreased, and by how much?
4. What are the debit (left-side) and credit (right-side) effects of the transaction according to the rules of double-entry accounting for entering data in the accounts?

When that thinking process is complete, the transaction can be reduced to a written entry so that the information can be processed by the accounting system. A typical entry format looks like this:

Debit (Dr.) Account Name (A, L, or OE)	(inc./dec.) Amount	
Credit (Cr.) Account Name (A, L, or OE)		(inc./dec.) Amount

Most accounting information systems require a standardized format for their accounting entries to ensure that the system processes all entries properly. Throughout the remainder of this text, we will follow these widely accepted recording rules:

1. The left-side (debit) portion of an entry will be presented first, followed by the right-side (credit) portion which is also slightly indented.
2. The Dr. and Cr. designations will be included, as will the increase (inc.) and decrease (dec.) designation.
3. The full name of the affected account will be used, as will the account classification — asset (A), liability (L), owners' equity (OE), revenue (R), or expense (E).

To illustrate this analytical approach, consider the earlier example in which a retailer purchased merchandise inventory on credit for $30,000. Your responses to the above four questions might appear as follows:

Question	Answer
1. Status of the transaction:	Complete and measurable.
2. Accounts affected:	Asset — Merchandise Inventory (A). Liability — Accounts Payable (L).
3. Amounts involved:	Merchandise Inventory increased by $30,000. Accounts Payable increased by $30,000.
4. Left-side/right-side effects:	Enter $30,000 on left side of Merchandise Inventory account (a debit) and $30,000 on right side of Accounts Payable account (a credit).

Reduced to entry format, this transaction (and the answers to the four questions) can be summarized as follows:

	Left Side	Right Side
Dr. Merchandise Inventory (A)	**(inc.) 30,000**	
Cr. Accounts Payable (L)		**(inc.) 30,000**

As a second illustration, consider a transaction involving the payment of $30,000 by the retailer for the merchandise previously purchased. Following the four steps outlined earlier, this event can be stated as an entry as follows:

Dr. Accounts Payable (L)	(dec.) 30,000	
Cr. Cash (A)		(dec.) 30,000

These two transactions would be reflected in the retailer's T-accounts as follows:

Cash (A)

Beginning bal.	XXX		
		Entry	30,000

Inventory (A)

Beginning bal.	XXX	
Entry	30,000	

Accounts Payable (L)

		Beginning bal.	XXX
Entry	30,000	Entry	30,000

Pictorially, these transactions affect the accounting equation as follows:

- The purchase of inventory:

Assets	*Liabilities*
Inventory + 30,000	Accounts Payable + 30,000
	Owners' Equity

- The payment of the invoice for previously purchased merchandise:

Assets	*Liabilities*
Cash – 30,000	Accounts Payable – 30,000
	Owners' Equity

The size of the two halves of the box (depicting the balance sheet) may increase or decrease as transactions are recorded, but the two sides must always remain in balance. Before continuing, think about other transactions that might affect the company and visualize how they would affect the parts of the box.

Processing and Preparing the Financial Statements

After the financial effects of business transactions have been stated as entries for the accounting information system, those entries are then entered into the accounts. This entering process is called **posting**, because the individual entries are posted to the affected accounts.

The process of analyzing business transactions, recognizing the financial effects as entries, and then posting the entries to the ledger T-accounts continues on a day-to-day basis in most companies. At some regular interval (weekly, monthly, quarterly, or annually), the net effect of the individual transactions posted to each account (that is, the balance resulting from the increases and decreases) is determined, and the account balances are drawn together into a set of accounting reports. To produce the accounting reports, a number of end-of-period activities must be undertaken, principally to ensure that the accounting information is reliable.

In addition to the entries that have been developed on an ongoing day-to-day basis, some **adjusting entries** may be required as of the end of the period. Company management frequently uses the end of the period as a stimulus to objectively challenge its financial position and ask some of the fundamental questions we discussed in Chapter 2. For example,

- You will remember that in Chapter 2 we said that a fundamental question had to do with the allocation of the effects of a company's operations over time. More specifically, a chief financial officer (CFO) might ask whether the product development expenses that have been accumulated in an expense account should really be treated as an expense this year or whether there is enough evidence of future payback from that product to justify treating the development expenditures as an asset and allocating the costs over the future years in which the payback will be realized.
- Another question raised in Chapter 2 asked whether all of the company's assets were likely to produce future cash flows in excess of their carrying values. More specifically, management might ask about the value of inventory reflected in the inventory account. The CFO might ask the operations and marketing people to challenge whether there might be a product obsolescence problem or a lower-of-cost-or-market problem that requires a reduction in the balance sheet amount for inventory.
- And, following up on another question posed in Chapter 2, management might challenge its perception of the lawsuit recently filed against the company. Although an aggressive, defensive posture may be appropriate for the courtroom, management must ask for a conservative estimate of the cost of losing that suit and then consider whether that estimate of loss needs to be recognized in the accounts and in the financial statements.

Depending on the answers to such introspective questions, additional entries may be required to adjust the balances in the accounts before the accounting process can be brought to a close for the period.

Another end-of-period activity is the preparation of a **trial balance.** The trial balance is a list of the balances in all of the company's accounts. The trial balance has two uses: (1) It provides an opportunity to examine the aggregated results of the individual entries to see whether the resulting balances make sense as compared to what management expected them to be; and (2) it provides an opportunity to see whether the sum of the accounts with ending debit balances equals the sum of the accounts with ending credit balances. In effect, the trial balance tells us whether our individual entries were in balance and whether we posted the debits and credits correctly. If that review of the trial balance identifies any errors or omissions, they are corrected with further adjusting entries. Depending on the extent of those final corrections, an adjusted trial balance may be prepared to prove that the system is now ready to produce the financial statements. Although the trial balance does not provide any guarantee that we posted the entries to the right accounts, it does provide assurance that the fundamental accounting equation remains in balance.

The next step in the accounting process is the **closing.** There isn't much judgment involved in an accounting closing, and while you ought to have a pretty good idea of how the closing fits into the overall scheme of things, you need not pursue it in any depth. In real life, companies maintain individual accounts for all of their revenue accounts and all of their expense accounts, as well as their asset, liability, and owners' equity accounts. At the end of an accounting period, management "closes" the revenue and expense accounts by transferring their balances to the retained earnings account, in effect increasing the retained earnings balance by the net income for the period.

The hardware store example we will work through at the end of this chapter will follow that approach, and when you get there you will see that the final entry for the year is the closing entry. If that full-blown process makes sense to you, feel free to follow it through. However, it is clear that the closing process adds several steps to the overall process and you may find it easier to ignore the individual revenue and expense accounts and to think of all revenue transactions as direct additions to retained earnings and all expense transactions as direct deductions from retained earnings. Net income then will be the net result of those additions and deductions from retained earnings *during this current period.* If that approach makes sense to you, you can avoid not only the revenue and expense accounts but also the closing of those accounts to retained earnings. That shortcut approach will be more efficient and should work just as well, given the simplified examples we will be using. But more importantly, it may be easier for you to see how to apply the accounting equation if you visualize every revenue transaction as a direct addition to retained earnings rather than an indirect addition through a subordinate revenue account. Similarly, the impact on the basic equation of an expense transaction may be more clear if you visualize every expense as a direct reduction from retained earnings rather than as an indirect reduction through a subordinate expense account.

To illustrate that idea, consider the following entry, which records cash sales of $50,000 for the month.

Dr. Cash (A)	(inc.) 50,000	
Cr. Product Sales (R/*RE*)		(inc.) 50,000

Note that we have expanded the account classification for the sales side of the entry to indicate that it affects a revenue account (R) and that revenue is really an addition to retained earnings, (*RE*). Throughout the rest of this chapter we will use that double classification scheme for all entries that affect either revenue or expense. In the rest of the book we will classify income statement accounts as either an R or an E; we expect you to know that revenues are additions to retained earnings and expenses are deductions from retained earnings.

If you follow the shorthand approach outlined above, you will enter all revenue and expense transactions directly into retained earnings and prepare the income statement for the year as an analysis of the transactions flowing through that account during that year. In contrast to this shorthand approach, the following discussion illustrates how the closing process works and how that process produces an income statement and a retained earnings balance.

At the end of an accounting period, after all of the necessary adjusting entries have been posted, the income statement is prepared using the period-end balances in the revenue and expense accounts. Once that statement is prepared and net income for the period is determined, the revenue and expense accounts are "closed" using an overall entry that zeroes out the balances in the individual revenue and expense accounts and transfers those balances to the retained earnings account. Remembering that a revenue account typically has a right-side balance (a credit balance) and that expense accounts typically have left-side balances (debit balances), a simple company might make the following **closing entry** at the end of a month:

Dr. Sales (R)	(dec.) 14,812	
Cr. Cost of Product Sold (E)		(dec.) 8,914
Cr. Selling and Administrative Expenses (E)		(dec.) 2,414
Cr. Retained Earnings (OE)		(inc.) 3,484

Of course, the net amount transferred to retained earnings ($3,484) is the net income for that period. The revenue and expense accounts are closed out because they are **temporary accounts:** They serve as repositories for transactions that impacted that accounting period, but they do not (and should not) reflect events that occurred in any prior period. The balance sheet accounts, including the retained earnings account, carry their balances forward to the next period; because they carry a balance forward from year to year and are not closed out at the end of each period, they are called **permanent accounts.** For example, the balance in the inventory account at the end of one accounting period is the beginning balance in that account for the next accounting period. Revenue and expense accounts do not carry their balances over to the next period. Because of the closing entry, the balance in the revenue and expense accounts at the beginning of the next period will have a zero balance and will be ready to begin the accumulation of revenue and expense transactions of that next period.

Let's go back to PepsiCo as our reference point. The balance in PepsiCo's cash account at December 31, 1994, is $330.7 million. That balance reflects the balance on hand at the beginning of 1994, plus or minus the effects of all of the transactions that affected cash during the year. But the balance in the net sales account at December 31, 1994, was $28,472.4 million, reflecting only those sales that occurred during the year. The accounting system knows to treat the cash account as a carryover account and the net sales account as a this-year-only account because the net sales account at December 31, 1993, was closed to retained earnings. The beginning balance in the net sales account at January 1, 1994, was zero; at December 31, 1994, *before* the closing entry for 1994, it was $28,472.4 million; at December 31, 1994, *after* the closing entry for 1994, it was again zero. The ending balance in the retained earnings account at December 31, 1994, was $7,739.1 million; the beginning balance in retained earnings, for the year that will end on December 31, 1995, is exactly the same.

Whether the shorthand approach or the more complete approach is adopted, an income statement is prepared to summarize all of the revenue and expense transactions

EXHIBIT 3.1

The Accounting Cycle

Phase	Information Activity	Time Frame
1. Measuring and recording	Analyze economic transactions. State transactions in accounting language with entries. Post entries to ledger accounts.	During the accounting period
2. Processing: Summarizing, verifying, and aggregating	Prepare trial balance. Prepare adjusting entries. Prepare closing entries.	End of period
3. Reporting	Prepare financial statements.	End of period

that affected the retained earnings account during the year. Similarly, a statement of cash flows is prepared to summarize all of the transactions that affected the cash account during the year. Finally, the balance sheet is prepared, drawing on the balances in the various balance sheet accounts.

To prepare the statements, management uses the basic data from the trial balance and presents that data in a way that most meaningfully communicates the company's results. During the preparation of the financial statements, some accounts may be aggregated, but other balances may have to be disaggregated. In addition, management may decide that for a fair presentation of the company's results, supplemental footnotes are required. In the end, management must satisfy itself that the resulting financial presentation is fair and in accordance with GAAP. This entire process is called the **accounting cycle** and is outlined in Exhibit 3.1.

Before considering an illustration of the accounting cycle, a final word is appropriate. The double-entry accounting system is used throughout the world. While specific account labels may differ, every country has essentially adopted this approach to the recording of financial data. Hence, as you work through this text and encounter financial data from other countries, the differences you may observe will be unrelated to how the data was recorded; thus the differences are likely to be due to differing accounting paradigms or principles.

THE ACCOUNTING PROCESS ILLUSTRATED: BLUE RIDGE HARDWARE CO.

To illustrate the accounting process and the preparation of the basic financial statements, we will trace the business activities of a hypothetical company, Blue Ridge Hardware Co., from its first transaction through the end of its first year of operations. This illustration assumes a manual accounting system because it is easier to see the development of the entries and the flow of those entries through the accounts into the final financial statements.

First Year of Operations

The following pages present the basic business transactions that a small retailer might encounter during its first year of operations. The illustration describes the events affecting the business and then outlines the entries required as a result of those transactions.

Finally, the accounting process is completed with the preparation of a trial balance and the formal financial statements. For simplicity in this illustration, all similar transactions that occurred throughout the year have been grouped and only the yearly totals are recorded. For example, transaction no. 5 in the following illustration reflects the total merchandise purchased by the business on account throughout the entire year. On the company's books, however, each purchase of merchandise inventory made throughout the year would have been recorded separately and chronologically.

Transaction no. 1. On April 1, 1994, two friends formed the Blue Ridge Hardware Co. and filed for a corporate charter from the state. Each invested $5,000 cash in the new company and received 5,000 shares of stock for the investment. Following the four-step approach outlined on page 90, the effect of the transaction is estimable. The accounts affected are the cash account and the owners' equity account; both will be increased by the amount of cash contributed to the company, and the entry will look like this:

Dr. Cash (A)	(inc.) 10,000	
Cr. Capital Stock (OE)		(inc.) 10,000

GAAP says that a company may not generate income as a result of transactions with its owners. This receipt of cash increases owners' equity but not retained earnings. It impacts the balance sheet but not the income statement.

Transaction no. 2. Also on April 1, 1994, a three-year lease was signed for the building in which the hardware store is located. The lease called for a monthly rental of $300 and was cancelable by either the lessor or the lessee (Blue Ridge Hardware) with at least 60 days' advance notice.

No entry is needed. This business transaction does not affect the financial resources or obligations of Blue Ridge Hardware. Even though the business signed the lease, the contract is an **executory agreement** that will be consummated over time. Because the lease is readily cancelable by either party, its impact cannot be reasonably estimated and so it will not be recorded in the accounts. As the business uses the building, the monthly lease payments are recorded (see transaction no. 11).

Transaction no. 3. A total of $7,500 was borrowed from a local bank on April 1, 1994. Repayment is to be made over a five-year period, and interest at 12 percent per year is due annually on March 31 on the unpaid balance:

Dr. Cash (A)	(inc.) 7,500	
Cr. Bank Loan Payable (L)		(inc.) 7,500

This receipt of cash is not a revenue item because it must be paid back sometime in the future. Note that the loan carries with it an obligation to pay interest on the borrowed funds. That commitment is not recorded when the loan proceeds are received because (like the lease payments in transaction no. 2) interest accrues over time and is recorded only as time elapses — usually at the end of each accounting period during the adjusting entry process.

Transaction no. 4. During the month of April, store equipment was purchased for $10,000 cash:

Dr. Store Equipment (A)	(inc.) 10,000	
Cr. Cash (A)		(dec.) 10,000

Transaction no. 5. During the year, merchandise inventory in the amount of $57,400 was purchased on credit. Payment was usually due within 30 days of the purchase date:

Dr. Merchandise Inventory (A)	(inc.) 57,400	
Cr. Accounts Payable (L)		(inc.) 57,400

The purchase of equipment in transaction no. 4 is simply an exchange of one asset for another. Similarly, the purchase of inventory in transaction no. 5 is also treated as the acquisition of an asset even though the various suppliers have not yet been paid. The inventory purchase transaction recognizes the payment promise that Blue Ridge Hardware made when it ordered and received the merchandise. The fulfillment of that promise is recognized as a separate, subsequent transaction (see transaction no. 10). The equipment and the inventory are both considered to be assets because they both have continuing value and because both will help the store produce future cash flows from future operations. Because the expense associated with these cash payments will benefit future operations and because we want to match that expense with the related future benefit, we treat the expenditures as assets today and charge them to expense in future transactions (see transactions no. 8 and 15).

Transaction no. 6. During the year, cash sales amounted to $29,800:

Dr. Cash (A)	(inc.) 29,800	
Cr. Sales Revenue (R/*RE*)		(inc.) 29,800

Transaction no. 7. During the year, credit sales amounted to $44,700:

Dr. Accounts Receivable (A)	(inc.) 44,700	
Cr. Sales Revenue (R/*RE*)		(inc.) 44,700

Both cash sales and credit sales (transactions no. 6 and no. 7) can be considered as revenues for the company because they result from consummated transactions with third-party customers. Note that the credit sales are treated as revenues just as though they had been collected in cash. In both entries, an asset account is increased, as is the revenue (retained earnings) account. The collection of those accounts receivable is treated as a separate transaction affecting only the balance sheet (see transaction no. 9).

Transaction no. 8. The cost of merchandise sold during the year totaled $44,700:

Dr. Cost of Merchandise Sold (E/*RE*)	(inc.) 44,700	
Cr. Merchandise Inventory (A)		(dec.) 44,700

This entry matches the cost of the merchandise sold with the revenue generated by its sale: The difference between the total sales and the cost of merchandise sold is the gross profit from the sales, sometimes called the gross margin. The amount of the original purchase price of the merchandise that is to be allocated to the sale transaction is typically the subject of considerable study and analysis by financial managers and will be covered in detail in later chapters of this book.

Transaction no. 9. Collections of cash from accounts receivable totaled $40,500:

Dr. Cash (A)	(inc.) 40,500	
Cr. Accounts Receivable (A)		(dec.) 40,500

Transaction no. 10. Payments for merchandise inventory previously purchased on credit amounted to $53,600:

Dr. Accounts Payable (L)	(dec.) 53,600	
Cr. Cash (A)		(dec.) 53,600

Transactions no. 9 and 10 are examples of transactions that affect only asset and liability accounts. They represent an exchange of one asset for another or a settlement of a liability using an asset. The revenue or expense aspect of these transactions was recognized earlier when the basic sales and purchase events were consummated. Accrual accounting looks at business events and separates their economic effects from their cash effects.

Transaction no. 11. Cash paid for building rent for the year totaled $3,600:

Dr. Rent Expense (E/*RE*)	(inc.) 3,600	
Cr. Cash (A)		(dec.) 3,600

Transaction no. 12. Cash wages paid to employees totaled $14,600. As of March 31, 1995, wages earned by employees but not yet paid were $700:

Dr. Wage Expense (E/*RE*).	(inc.) 15,300	
Cr. Cash (A)		(dec.) 14,600
Cr. Wages Payable (L)		(inc.) 700

Transaction no. 13. Cash paid for utilities amounted to $450. Blue Ridge Hardware estimated that when the March bills were all processed, the company would owe an additional $200 as of March 31, 1995:

Dr. Utilities Expense (E/*RE*).	(inc.) 650	
Cr. Cash (A)		(dec.) 450
Cr. Utilities Payable (L)		(inc.) 200

Transaction no. 14. On March 31, 1995, the interest on the bank loan for the first year was paid:

Dr. Interest Expense (E/*RE*)	(inc.) 900	
Cr. Cash (A)		(dec.) 900

Transactions no. 13, 14, and 15 recognize various operating expenses for the current period. These transactions are charged to expenses — that is, they are *not* added to an asset — because they create no measurable future benefit for the store.

Transaction no. 15. At year-end the owners estimated that the store equipment had a 10-year life and that one year had passed. Therefore, an adjusting entry was made to allocate $1,000 of the original cost (see transaction no. 4) of the equipment to expense in this first period:

Dr. Depreciation Expense (E/*RE*)	(inc.) 1,000	
Cr. Accumulated Depreciation (CA)		(inc.) 1,000

Some portion of the original cost of the store equipment was used to produce the revenues earned in this period. Under GAAP, the cost of long-lived assets must be allocated to specific accounting periods; the usual way to accomplish this allocation is to estimate the useful life of the asset and to charge a pro rata portion of the cost of that asset to expense each elapsed year. This process of allocation is called depreciation. At times it will be useful to know the original cost of a company's plant and equipment. Therefore, rather than reduce the asset account directly, the annual depreciation allocation is credited to a **contra asset** (CA) account called *Accumulated Depreciation.* This contra account is reported on the balance sheet as a deduction from the store equipment account, thereby preserving the original cost of the equipment and also reporting its net *undepreciated cost.* The undepreciated cost is often referred to as its **book value.**

Transaction no. 16. Estimated federal and state income taxes paid during the year amounted to $600. At fiscal year-end an additional $2,300 in taxes were due on the income actually earned during the year:

Dr. Income Tax Expense (E/*RE*)	(inc.) 2,900	
Cr. Cash (A)		(dec.) 600
Cr. Income Taxes Payable (L)		(inc.) 2,300

Transaction no. 17. Cash dividends of $2,000 were declared and paid:

Dr. Dividends Declared (COE)	(inc.) 2,000	
Cr. Cash (A)		(dec.) 2,000

Repeating an earlier observation, **dividends** are not considered to be an expense of the business but are understood to be distributions of profits to owners. As such, a dividend declaration affects only the balance sheet — a distribution of the income that is added to retained earnings for the year. The Dividends Declared account is a **contra owners' equity** (COE) account, and when the accounts for the year are closed, it is netted to the Retained Earnings account as a partial offset to the earnings for the year.

We can now derive the individual account balances for Blue Ridge Hardware as of March 31, 1995. We will have established a separate account for each specific asset, liability, owners' equity, revenue, and expense account. Together, these accounts form the **chart of accounts** for Blue Ridge Hardware. Because April 1, 1994, was the first day of operations, the beginning balance in each account is $0. Second, we post each entry in the appropriate account and then determine the fiscal year-end balance of each account. The resulting preclosing account balances are shown in Exhibit 3.2.

To verify that the company's accounts are in balance, we can prepare a trial balance using the ledger account balances in Exhibit 3.2. As Exhibit 3.3 reveals, the trial balance for Blue Ridge Hardware is in balance, which tells us that equivalent amounts of debits and credits were posted to the accounts.

The next step in the accounting process involves preparing the income statement, which is followed by preparing the closing entries for the temporary accounts. Finally, we will prepare a balance sheet, a statement of owners' equity, and a statement of cash flows. These final steps in the accounting cycle are illustrated sequentially in Exhibit 3.4 through Exhibit 3.8. Visualize the management of Blue Ridge Hardware as they study the account balances in the trial balance, as they think about the kinds of transactions summarized in each account, and as they decide how the accounts should be displayed in the financial statements. On one level, the process is relatively easy: The income statement is prepared from the revenue and expense accounts or from an analysis of the entries flowing through the retained earnings account during the year. (And the revenue and expense accounts are closed out, ready to start another year.) The balance sheet is prepared using the balances in the asset, liability, and owners' equity accounts at the end of the year. The statement of cash flows is prepared from an analysis of the entries flowing through the cash account during the year. At a mechanical level, the preparation of the financial statements follows easily from the accounting system.

At a PepsiCo level, the process of preparing financial statements from a trial balance is more difficult. Management must decide which accounts can be combined, which should be presented as separate line items on the statements, and which accounts must be broken down into more detail. The objective of this process is to be sure that the financial statements include enough information to present a fair picture of the company without obscuring reality and without too much detail.

EXHIBIT 3.2

Blue Ridge Hardware Co.
Ledger Accounts
For the Fiscal Year Ended March 31, 1995

Balance Sheet Accounts:

Assets = Liabilities + Owners' Equity

Assets

Cash

4-1-94	0		
(1)	10,000	(4)	10,000
(3)	7,500	(10)	53,600
(6)	29,800	(11)	3,600
(9)	40,500	(12)	14,600
		(13)	450
		(14)	900
		(16)	600
		(17)	2,000
	87,800		85,750
3-31-95	2,050		

Accounts Receivable

4-1-94	0		
(7)	44,700	(9)	40,500
	44,700		40,500
3-31-95	4,200		

Merchandise Inventory

4-1-94	0		
(5)	57,400	(8)	44,700
3-31-95	12,700		

Store Equipment

4-1-94			
(4)	10,000		
3-31-95	10,000		

Accumulated Depreciation: Store Equipment

		4-1-94	0
		(15)	1,000
		3-31-95	1,000

Liabilities

Accounts Payable

		4-1-94	0
(10)	53,600	(5)	57,000
		3-31-95	3,800

Wages Payable

		4-1-94	0
		(12)	700
		3-31-95	700

Utilities Payable

		4-1-94	0
		(13)	200
		3-31-95	200

Income Taxes Payable

		4-1-94	0
		(16)	2,300
		3-31-95	2,300

Bank Loan Payable

		4-1-94	0
		(3)	7,500
		3-31-95	7,500

Owners' Equity

Capital Stock

		4-1-94	0
		(1)	10,000
		3-31-95	10,000

Retained Earnings

		4-1-94	0

Dividends Declared

4-1-94	0		
(17)	2,000		
3-31-95	2,000		

Income State Accounts:

Sales Revenue

Debit	Credit	
	4-1-94	0
	(6)	29,800
	(7)	44,700
		74,500

Cost of Merchandise Sold

Debit		Credit
4-1-94	0	
(8)	44,700	
	44,700	

Wage Expense

Debit		Credit
4-1-94	0	
(12)	15,300	
	15,300	

Income Tax Expense

Debit		Credit
4-1-94	0	
(16)	2,900	
	2,900	

Interest Expense

Debit		Credit
4-1-94	0	
(14)	900	
	900	

Rent Expense

Debit		Credit
4-1-94	0	
(11)	3,600	
	3,600	

Utilities Expense

Debit		Credit
4-1-94	0	
(13)	650	
	650	

Depreciation Expense

Debit		Credit
4-1-94	0	
(15)	1,000	
	1,000	

EXHIBIT 3.3

Blue Ridge Hardware Co.
Trial Balance as of
March 31, 1995

Account Title	Debit Balance	Credit Balance
Cash	$ 2,050	
Accounts Receivable	4,200	
Merchandise Inventory	12,700	
Store Equipment	10,000	
Accumulated Depreciation		$ 1,000
Accounts Payable		3,800
Wages Payable		700
Utilities Payable		200
Income Taxes Payable		2,300
Bank Loan Payable		7,500
Capital Stock		10,000
Retained Earnings		0
Dividends Declared	2,000	
Sales		74,500
Cost of Merchandise Sold	44,700	
Rent Expense	3,600	
Wage Expense	15,300	
Utilities Expense	650	
Income Tax Expense	2,900	
Interest Expense	900	
Depreciation Expense	1,000	
Total	$100,000	$100,000

EXHIBIT 3.4

Blue Ridge Hardware Co.
Income Statement
For the Year Ended March 31, 1995

Net revenues		$74,500
Less: Cost of merchandise sold		(44,700)
Gross margin		29,800
Less: Operating expenses		
Rent expense	$ 3,600	
Wage expense	15,300	
Utilities expense	650	
Depreciation expense	1,000	
		(20,550)
Income from operations		9,250
Less: Interest expense		(900)
Income before taxes		8,350
Less: Federal and state income taxes		(2,900)
Net income		$5,450
Net income per share (10,000 shares outstanding)		$0.545

EXHIBIT 3.5

Blue Ridge Hardware Co.
Closing Entries as of
March 31, 1995

To close the revenue accounts:				
Dr. Sales Revenue (R/*RE*) . . . . (dec.)	74,500			
Cr. Retained Earnings (OE)			(inc.)	74,500
To close the expense accounts:				
Dr. Retained Earnings (OE) . . . . (dec.)	69,050			
Cr. Cost of Merchandise Sold (E/*RE*)			(dec.)	44,700
Cr. Rent Expense (E/*RE*)			(dec.)	3,600
Cr. Wage Expense (E/*RE*)			(dec.)	15,300
Cr. Utilities Expense (E/*RE*)			(dec.)	650
Cr. Interest Expense (E/*RE*)			(dec.)	900
Cr. Depreciation Expense (E/*RE*)			(dec.)	1,000
Cr. Income Tax Expense (E/*RE*)			(dec.)	2,900
To close the Dividends Declared account:				
Dr. Retained Earnings (OE) . . . . (dec.)	2,000			
Cr. Dividends Declared (COE)			(dec.)	2,000

EXHIBIT 3.6

Blue Ridge Hardware Co.
Balance Sheet
As of March 31, 1995

Assets		**Equities**	
Current assets:		Current liabilities:	
Cash	$ 2,050	Accounts payable	$ 3,800
Accounts receivable	4,200	Wages payable	700
Merchandise inventory	12,700	Utilities payable	200
Total current assets	$18,950	Income tax payable	2,300
		Total current liabilities	$ 7,000
Noncurrent assets:			
Store equipment	10,000	Noncurrent liabilities:	
Less:		Bank loan payable	7,500
Accumulated depreciation	(1,000)	Total liabilities	$14,500
Total noncurrent assets	$ 9,000		
		Owners' equity:	
Total assets	$27,950	Capital stock	10,000
		Retained earnings	3,450
			13,450
		Total liabilities and owners' equity	$27,950

EXHIBIT 3.7

Blue Ridge Hardware Co.
Statement of Owners' Equity
As of March 31, 1995

	Capital Stock		
	Shares	**Dollars**	**Retained Earnings**
At April 1, 1994	0	0	0
Stock sales	10,000	$10,000	
Net income for the year			$5,450
Dividends declared			(2,000)
At March 31, 1995	10,000	$10,000	$3,450

EXHIBIT 3.8

Blue Ridge Hardware Co.
Statement of Cash flows
For the year Ended March 31, 1995

Operating activities:	
Net income	$ 5,450
Add: Depreciation on store equipment	1,000
	$ 6,450
Adjustments for:	
Accounts receivable	$ (4,200)
Merchandise inventory	(12,700)
Accounts payable	3,800
Wages payable	700
Utilities payable	200
Income tax payable	2,300
Cash flow from operating activities	$ (3,450)
Investing activities	
Purchase of store equipment	$(10,000)
Cash flow from investing activities	$(10,000)
Financing activities	
Cash dividends paid	$ (2,000)
Proceeds from bank loan	7,500
Sale of capital stock	10,000
Cash flow from financing activities	$ 15,500
Increase in cash	$ 2,050
Cash, beginning of year	0
Cash, end of year	$ 2,050

To put you in the mind of the Blue Ridge Hardware owners, study the trial balance and the accounts (Exhibits 3.2 and 3.3) and see how those data were used in creating the financial statements in Exhibits 3.4, 3.6, 3.7, and 3.8. Think about the presentation of these statements, and ask yourself whether you might have made different decisions. (Should we have reported sales in two segments — as cash sales and credit sales? Should we describe our inventory in different categories, such as household items, hardware items, and so forth? Was it necessary to spell out all of the changes in the balance sheet accounts in the determination of cash flow from operations?) And then think about what those financial statements tell you about the operations. To take the process further and ensure that you understand the closing entry process and the linkage between net income and retained earnings, we suggest that you post the journal entries from Exhibit 3.5 to the ledger accounts in Exhibit 3.2. After this posting, all temporary accounts should have a zero ending balance, and the net income of Blue Ridge Hardware will have been transferred to Retained Earnings.

Analysis of Blue Ridge Hardware Co.

Now that the accounting process is complete and the financial reports of Blue Ridge Hardware prepared, let us briefly consider what these reports reveal about the enterprise. First, Exhibit 3.4, the income statement, indicates that for the year ended March 31, 1995, Blue Ridge Hardware earned net income of $5,450 on net revenues of $74,500. Because most companies have more expenses than can be justified by the volume of sales during their initial building years, they often lose money during their first year (or years) of operations; with that perspective, it is encouraging that Blue Ridge Hardware achieved a positive net income — its sales volume exceeded its cost of operations. Exhibit 3.7 reveals that, on the basis of these earnings, the enterprise also declared and paid a dividend in the amount of $2,000. And because the full amount of net income for the period was not distributed as a dividend, the owners' investment in the enterprise grew by $3,450. Several important points merit noting. First, the net increase in retained earnings is matched by an equal net increase in the aggregate asset accounts, although it is impossible to find the exact, complementary matching increases. Second, dividends are not reported as an expense of the business on the income statement but instead are a distribution of the company's income to its stockholders. Third, to the extent that the income for the period is not distributed as dividends, it has the same effect as if the owners had invested that amount of new funds in the enterprise.

With respect to the financial condition of the enterprise, Exhibit 3.6, the balance sheet, reveals that at year-end Blue Ridge Hardware has the following:

- Total assets (and aggregate liabilities and equity) of $27,950.
- Total liabilities of $14,500.
- Owners' equity of $13,450.

The owners' equity, or the company's **net worth,** is the value that would remain *if* all assets could be converted to cash at their balance sheet values and then used to satisfy all existing liabilities. The liquidation of a company, however, is a rare event, and it is also unlikely that the cash liquidation values of the assets would exactly equal their book value. Consequently, an alternative description of owner's equity or net worth is to say that it is the **net book value** of all assets minus the book value of all liabilities.

The balance sheet also reveals that Blue Ridge Hardware has current assets totaling $18,950, which exceeds not only its total current liabilities of $7,000 but also the sum of current and noncurrent liabilities (that is, $14,500). This indicates that the enterprise is relatively secure in terms of its ability to pay off its outstanding obligations. Finally, Exhibit 3.8, the statement of cash flows, reveals that the enterprise generated a net cash inflow from financing activities in the amount of $15,500 and spent $10,000 in cash on investing activities. An additional $3,450 was spent in support of the company's operations, leaving a net cash balance of $2,050 at year end. To ensure the continued success of the enterprise, it is important for Blue Ridge Hardware to become a net positive generator of cash flows from operations. Clearly, the company will be viable only if the cash flows from operating activities are consistently positive.

SUMMARY

The purpose of this chapter has been to discuss and illustrate the accounting process used in preparing accounting reports. This process involves several distinct activities: analyzing business transactions to assess their financial effect on the assets, liabilities, and owners' equity of an enterprise; recording this analysis in various data files; verifying the accuracy of the recording process; and, finally, preparing and analyzing the financial statements.

Although it is important for you to understand how accounting reports are prepared and how the accounting system operates, our principal goal is to ensure that you understand fully how accounting reports communicate and what they reveal about the operations and financial condition of the enterprise. With that objective in mind, in the chapters that follow we focus not on the process of financial statement preparation but on analyzing important business transactions for the purpose of understanding what information the accounting statements convey.

NEW CONCEPTS AND TERMS

Accounts (p. 85)
Accounting cycle (p. 95)
Accounting information system (p. 85)
Adjusting entries (p. 92)
Balance (p. 86)
Book value (p. 98)
Chart of accounts (p. 99)
Closing (p. 93)
Closing entries (p. 94)
Contra asset account (p. 98)
Contra owners' equity (p. 99)
Credit (p. 88)
Debit (p. 88)
Dividends (p. 99)
Double-entry accounting system (p. 87)
Entry (p. 88)
Executory agreement (p. 96)
Information system (p. 85)
Net book value (p. 105)
Net worth (p. 105)
Permanent accounts (p. 94)
Posting (p. 92)
T-accounts (p. 86)
Temporary accounts (p. 94)
Trial balance (p. 93)

ISSUES FOR DISCUSSION

D3.1 Describe at least five events that a company is likely to experience that would not be measured, recorded, and reported in the company's financial statements.

D3.2 A number of accounting educators have likened the accounting process of recording transactions to that of the typical filing system found in most offices. Explain the parallels as you see them.

D3.3 Visualize the millions of transactions that a Fortune 500 company would engage in throughout a year with a variety of other parties, for differing monetary amounts, and for different purposes. Identify some of the ways in which errors might enter the accounting cycle, and suggest mechanisms to minimize the likelihood of those errors occurring and/or going undetected.

D3.4 What purposes are served by the preparation of a trial balance, balance sheet, and income statement? How frequently should they be prepared?

D3.5 The accounting cycle described in this chapter is a standard approach employed by most companies, who will then often modify it to better suit their needs. Discuss some of the unique circumstances of particular companies that would possibly lead to slight modifications and/or customizations of the accounting cycle.

D3.6 The income statements prepared by Atlantic Coast Manufacturing Company detail the company's results of operations for the year ended December 31, 1994. Some of the line items from that income statement appear below. For each of those items, describe in your own words what the source of the numbers might have been.

a. Sales — $500,000

b. Payroll Expense — $250,000

c. Bad Debt Expense — $25,000

d. Computer Depreciation — $30,000

e. Selling Expense — $75,000

D3.7 Atlantic Coast Manufacturing maintains cash in a box at the reception desk and in the plant for buying stamps and paying for other small expenses; each box usually contains $250. The company maintains three different bank accounts with a local bank. One is its general corporate account with an average balance of $1 million, another is the factory payroll account with an average balance of $250,000, and the third is the executive payroll account with an average balance of $50,000. The company usually has between $100,000 and $200,000 of excess cash invested in U.S. Treasury bills. Atlantic has total assets of $10 million and a net worth (net worth = A – L) of $4 million.

How many accounts should the company maintain to collect the transactions affecting its cash and its cash-equivalent items? How many line items should the company present on its balance sheet to describe its cash and cash-equivalent items? Please explain the reasoning behind your answers.

D3.8 Describe each of the following in your own words. Explain how each enters into recording and processing financial data and into preparing and presenting financial statements.

a. Permanent and temporary accounts.

b. Adjusting entries and closing entries.

c. The trial balance.

D3.9 As you worked through the accounting process illustrated by the Blue Ridge Hardware example, you learned something about the accounting process and enhanced your understanding of accounting concepts. That understanding will be developed further in subsequent chapters, but it will be useful to articulate your developing understanding as it grows. In that context, describe the following in your own words:

a. The difference between an asset and an expense.

b. The impact of accrual accounting on the measurement of operating results.

c. The notion of depreciation.

D3.10 You are the president of a small paint manufacturer located in the Pacific Northwest. Your paint products are sold throughout a three-state area. Because the economy has been flat, your business has been hurt. Nonetheless, sales for 1994 were about $25 million and net income was about $3 million. It is now February 1995, and as you begin to draw together the data you need for your company's 1994 report to shareholders, the production people bring you distressing news. It appears that one lot of paint that was shipped late last year is defective. If it is applied when the weather is at all humid, the paint blisters and peels badly. They have already notified the distributors and begun a recall, but it appears that some of that batch has gotten into the retail distribution network and in fact has been sold to contractors and homeowners. Production people estimate the cost of recalling the entire lot at $300,000. However, if anyone has actually used the paint on a job site, the paint will have to be scraped off carefully and thoroughly. There obviously is no way to know how much of the paint might have been sold to end users and how much of it might have been applied on specific jobs.

How should this event be reflected in the company's financial statements for 1994?

PROBLEMS

P3.1 Statement preparation. Prill Corporation's December 31, 1995, trial balance contained the following account balances. Prepare an income statement, a balance sheet, and a statement of stockholders' equity for the Prill Corporation as of December 31, 1995.

Accounts Payable: $27,900
Advertising Expense: $5,000
Cash: $1,800
Dividends Paid: $1,000
Income Tax Expense: $6,000
Interest Expense: $2,000
Building (net): $29,700
Depreciation Expense: $1,200
Notes Payable: $6,500
Office Salaries Expense: $19,000
Office Supplies Used: $2,000
Salaries Payable: $500

Accounts Receivable: $19,000
Capital Stock: $60,000
Cost of Goods Sold: $243,000
Sales: $292,000
Income Tax Payable: $3,000
Land: $44,000
Merchandise Inventory: $29,000
Long-Term Debt: $11,000
Notes Receivable: $5,200
Office Supplies Inventory: $1,000
Retained Earnings, 1/1/95: $8,000

P3.2 Transaction analysis. Describe the effect of each of the following events on a company's assets, liabilities, and owners' equity:

a. Selling a surplus warehouse.

b. Signing a three-year employment contract with a new CEO.

c. Paying for next quarter's TV ad time.

d. Purchasing raw materials for cash.

e. Financing the purchase of a car through GMAC.

f. Purchasing raw materials on account.

g. Another month passes on our outstanding loan.

h. Paying salaries.

i. Selling inventory on account.

j. Purchasing some shares of stock.

k. Paying dividends.

P3.3 Transaction analysis. For each of the following events note what account should be debited or credited and whether the account is increased or decreased.

Events	Debit	Credit
a. Sold additional shares of capital stock.		
b. Signed a loan to buy delivery truck.		
c. Purchased supplies for cash.		
d. Rendered services and collected cash for those services.		
e. Rendered services to customers who agreed to pay for those services later.		
f. Purchased supplies on account.		
g. Paid utility bill.		
h. Paid office rent.		
i. Collected cash from customers for whom services were previously performed.		
j. Paid interest on the loan.		
k. Used supplies in connection with performing services.		
l. Repaid part of the bank loan principal.		
m. Paid cash dividends to stockholders.		

P3.4 Transaction analysis and T-accounts. The following are *selected* accounts and account balances of the TAP Company on June 30, 1994:

Account	Balance Debit (Credit)
Cash	$ 125,230
Accounts Receivable	230,520
Office Equipment	358,600
Accumulated Depreciation	(105,400)
Notes Payable	(34,000)
Accounts Payable	(35,000)
Sales Revenue	(478,720)
Sales Discounts	24,000
Gain on Sale of Office Equipment	(4,000)
Inventory	219,340
Purchase Discounts	(2,220)
Cost of Sales	287,232

In addition, the TAP Company entered into the following transactions during the month of July 1994.

July 6 Sold for $7,000 some office equipment that had originally cost $20,000; accumulated depreciation taken to date on the equipment totaled $15,000.
July 7 Sales transactions in the amount of $20,000 were completed, on account, with terms of 2/10, net 30.
July 10 Purchased $10,000 worth of merchandise inventory for cash.
July 15 Purchased a new word processing system costing $40,000, paying $15,000 down and signing a 90-day note, with interest at 10 percent for the balance.
July 16 Received payment of $19,600 for the July 7 sales transactions.
July 19 Completed sales transactions for cash in the amount of $42,000.
July 20 Purchased $26,000 worth of merchandise inventory on account with terms of 2/10, net 30.
July 22 Returned $2,000 worth of defective merchandise from the July 20 purchase for a credit to TAP's account.
July 27 Paid the remaining balance of July 20 purchase less an appropriate discount.

Required:

Analyze and record the above transactions in journal entry form and then determine the July 31 account balances using T-accounts.

P3.5 Account analysis. Up-n-Down Corporation has published annual financial statements since it first sold stock to a group of nonfamily investors. The company's balance sheets at December 31, 1993 and 1994, were as follows:

	December 31, 1993	December 31, 1994
Cash	$ 222	$ 17
Accounts receivable	7,523	8,003
Less: Allowance for doubtful accounts	(116)	(170)*
Inventories	6,745	5,848
Prepaid insurance	805	632 *
Deferred catalog costs	1,519	2,483 *
Land and buildings	4,344	4,344 *
Equipment	2,858	3,268 *
Less: Accumulated depreciation	(1,682)	(2,457)*
Total assets	$22,218	$21,968
Accounts payable	$ 8,022	$ 6,801
Bank borrowings	7,445	6,925 *
Salaries payable	453	585
Taxes payable	1,111	1,298
Capital stock	3,110	3,110 *
Retained earnings	2,077	3,249 *
Total liabilities and equity	$22,218	$21,968

Required:

For each of the accounts starred above, describe the transactions that might have accounted for the changes in the balances between the two years. Your descriptions should indicate whether the entry used to record the transaction(s) increased or decreased the account and what other accounts might have been affected by the other side of the entry.

P3.6 Account analysis. The T-account here depicts a number of transactions that increased and decreased the cash account of Cassidy, Inc., during 1995.

Cash (A)

1-1-95	Balance	–0–	(E)	Paid for store equip.	9,000
(A)	From capital stock	12,500	(F)	Cash sales returned	1,000
(B)	Bank loan	11,500	(G)	Paid mdse. suppliers	55,000
(C)	Cash sales	32,800	(H)	Paid rent	4,800
(D)	Collections of receiv.	43,000	(I)	Paid employees	16,000
			(J)	Paid utilities	600
			(K)	Paid est. income tax	1,000
			(L)	Paid other expenses	900
			(M)	Paid on bank loan — On principal $2,000 interest $600	2,600
			(N)	Paid dividends	2,000
12-31-95	Balance	6,900			

Required:

For each of the identified entries (A through N), prepare a one- or two-sentence explanation of the event that caused the transaction. Be sure that your explanation describes the other account that would have been affected by the entry.

P3.7 Resources and sources. Resourceful Products Incorporated includes the following asset accounts in its balance sheet:

a. Cash

b. Land

c. Merchandise inventory

d. Accounts receivable

e. Delivery truck

f. Factory building

g. Investments

Required:

Thinking about the basic accounting equation, where every resource has a source, list the most likely source or sources for each of the resources just identified.

P3.8 Events and the affected accounts. Consider the following events, which were part of the activities of the Springtime Sales Company during 1994:

a. Sales of merchandise on account.

b. Purchase of merchandise on account.

c. Purchase of a delivery truck with a 10 percent down payment.

d. Sale of common stock for cash.

e. Purchase of a certificate of deposit with a bank transfer.

f. Purchase of a three-year insurance policy for cash.

g. Amortization of one year's coverage of the insurance policy.

h. Payment of wages to hourly employees.

i. Payment of a dividend to shareholders.

Required:

For each of these events, describe the nature of the accounts that would be affected (asset, liability, owners' equity, revenue or expense) and, in the context of the basic accounting equation, explain the rationale for your answer.

P3.9 Event analysis. The accounting records of the Floyd Corporation include the following entries:

(a)	Dr. Accounts Receivable (A)	(inc.) 70,400	
	Cr. Revenue (R)		(inc.) 70,400
(b)	Dr. Cash (A)	(inc.) 78,960	
	Cr. Accounts Receivable (A)		(dec.) 78,960
(c)	Dr. Operating Expenses (E)	(inc.) 720	
	Cr. Supplies on Hand (A)		(dec.) 720
(d)	Dr. Equipment (A)	(inc.) 2,720	
	Cr. Cash (A)		(dec.) 2,720
(e)	Dr. Accounts Payable (L)	(dec.) 2,560	
	Cr. Cash (A)		(dec.) 2,560
(f)	Dr. Notes Payable (L)	(dec.) 20,000	
	Dr. Interest Expense (E)	(inc.) 160	
	Cr. Cash (A)		(dec.) 20,160
(g)	Dr. Dividends (COE)	(inc.) 12,800	
	Cr. Cash (A)		(dec.) 12,800

Required:

For each entry, prepare a one-sentence description of the underlying event.

P3.10 Event analysis. The accounting records of Cecil, Inc., include the following entries:

(a)	Dr. Rent Expense (E)	(inc.) 4,500	
	Cr. Prepaid Rent (A)		(dec.) 4,500
(b)	Dr. Unearned Passenger Revenue (L)	(dec.) 27,000	
	Cr. Passenger Revenue (R)		(inc.) 27,000
(c)	Dr. Salaries Expense (E)	(inc.) 4,950	
	Cr. Salaries Payable (L)		(inc.) 4,950
(d)	Dr. Repairs and Maintenance Expense (E)	(inc.) 7,800	
	Cr. Accounts Payable (L)		(inc.) 7,800
(e)	Dr. Repairs and Maintenance Expense (E)	(inc.) 5,550	
	Cr. Spare Parts on Hand (A)		(dec.) 5,550
(f)	Dr. Accounts Receivable (A)	(inc.) 3,800	
	Cr. Office Equipment (A)		(dec.) 3,800
(g)	Dr. Land (A)	(inc.) 24,500	
	Cr. Cash (A)		(dec.) 2,450
	Cr. Notes Payable (L)		(inc.) 22,050
(h)	Dr. Cash (A)	(inc.) 6,900	
	Cr. Accounts Receivable (A)		(dec.) 6,900
(i)	Dr. Cash (A)	(inc.) 12,000	
	Cr. Capital Stock (OE)		(inc.) 12,000

Required:

For each entry, prepare a one-sentence description of the underlying event.

P3.11 Account balances. The Holding Corporation, Inc., is a regional distributor of containers. Some of the accounts the company maintains are the following:

(1) Cash in Bank

(2) Insurance Expense — Warehouse

(3) Inventory

(4) Factory Overhead Crane

(5) Accumulated Depreciation — Truck Fleet

(6) Sales

(7) Legal Fees

(8) Interest Expense — Bank Loan

(9) Unearned Revenue

Required:

a. For each of these accounts, is the normal account balance a debit or credit? Explain.

b. For each of these accounts, describe the nature of the events that affect each. Note one illustrative entry affecting the right side of the account and one affecting the left side of the account.

P3.12 More complex events and the affected accounts. Consider the following series of events that were part of the activities of the OnTime Manufacturing Company during 1994:

a. On June 30, 1994, the treasurer called the company's banker and asked her to buy a Treasury bill, debiting the company's account. The bill cost $100,000 and carried an interest rate of 10 percent, the interest to be paid at maturity. At December 31, 1994, the company still had the investment.

b. On March 31, 1994, the company bought a lift truck to help move material around in the factory. The truck cost $25,000, but the dealer agreed to finance $20,000 of the purchase price. The company signed a five-year note for $20,000, at 10 percent interest, with interest payable quarterly and principal payable in five equal annual installments.

c. To prepare for a substantial expansion, the company sold $10,000,000 of 10-year, 8 percent bonds on October 1, 1994. An investment banker helped put together the offering document, and an attorney researched the legal aspects of the offering. The total of the professional fees paid to these two firms was $75,000. The bonds require semiannual interest payments and require that the principal be paid in full at maturity.

d. The company owned a piece of land next to its main plant, which they intended to use for the expansion discussed in point (c). During December 1994 the company paid an engineering company $50,000 to make soil tests on the land and paid an architect $50,000 for a preliminary drawing of the anticipated new plant expansion. By the time December 31, 1994, had come, however, the economy had softened substantially, and there was now considerable question as to whether the market was really ready to buy more of the company's products. The expansion plans were put on the back burner for at least a year.

Required:

For each of these events, describe the nature of the accounts that would be affected (asset, liability, owners' equity, revenue or expense) at the date of the event and as of December 31, 1994. In the context of the basic accounting equation, explain the rationale for each answer.

P3.13 Some unusual applications of accrual accounting

a. The 1994 annual report from CPC International, a large food company, includes the following footnote (dollars in millions):

Restructuring charge

In June 1994 the company recorded a charge of $227 million, $137 million after taxes or $0.92 per common share, to recognize the cost of restructuring. This program compresses into a period from mid-1994 to mid-1996 restructuring activities needed to meet the competitive challenge of increasingly unifying markets throughout the world.

The majority of the charge relates to the company's European and North American consumer foods business. The restructuring charge and its utilization are summarized below:

$ Millions	Total Charge	Utilized in 1994	To Be Utilized in Future Periods
Employee severance	$102	$ 12	$ 90
Plant and support facilities	114	114	—
Other	11	—	11
Total	$227	$126	$101

> The charge is designed to cover the cost of a phased reduction of about 2,600 employees worldwide and the cost of realignment of manufacturing capacity. The realignment will be achieved through a combination of plant closures, specializations, and relocations of production. In total, 24 consumer foods plants and four corn refining plants will be affected by the restructuring.
>
> The time period for completion of the restructuring is from a few months at some sites to two years in instances where alternative production facilities are to be constructed.
>
> At December 31, 1994, $57 million was included in current liabilities and $44 million was included in noncurrent liabilities.

Required:

How would this restructuring program have been recognized in the company's accounts in 1994? What entries might have been made, and what accounts would have been affected? In what ways was the restructuring program not reflected in the 1994 accounts? Explain the rationale the company might have used to support its combination of accounting and disclosure.

b. IBM Corporation describes its exposure for environmental problems with the following footnote in its 1994 annual report (dollars in millions):

> In addition, the company continues to participate in environmental assessments and cleanups at a number of locations, including operating facilities, previously owned facilities, and Superfund sites. The company accrues for all known environmental liabilities for remediation cost when a cleanup program becomes probable and costs can be reasonably estimated. Estimated environmental costs associated with postclosure activities, such as the removal and restoration of chemical storage facilities and monitoring, are accrued when the decision is made to close a facility. The amounts accrued, which are undiscounted and do not reflect any insurance recoveries, were $179 million and $77 million at December 31, 1994 and 1993, respectively. The increase in the accrual relates to expected costs of postclosure activities, reassessment of remediation activities at operating facilities, and participation at additional Superfund sites.
>
> The amounts accrued do not cover sites that are in the preliminary stages of investigation where neither the company's percentage of responsibility nor the extent of cleanup required have been identified. Also excluded is the cost of internal environmental protection programs that are primarily preventive in nature. Estimated environmental costs are not expected to materially impact the financial position or results of the company's operations in future periods. However, environmental cleanup periods are protracted in length, and earnings in future periods are subject to changes in environmental remediation regulations.

Required:

How would this environmental exposure have been recognized in the company's accounts in 1994? What entries might have been made, and what accounts would have been affected? In what ways was the environmental exposure not reflected in the 1994 accounts? Explain the rationale the company might have used to support its combination of accounting and disclosure.

P3.14 Aggregation and disaggregation. The annual report to shareholders published by Procter & Gamble for the year ended June 30, 1994, includes a balance sheet as shown in Exhibit 1 and footnotes, one of which is shown in Exhibit 2.

EXHIBIT 1

Procter & Gamble
Consolidated Balance Sheet
(millions of dollars)

	June 30 1994	June 30 1993
ASSETS		
Current Assets		
Cash and cash equivalents	**$ 2,373**	$ 2,322
Marketable securities	**283**	306
Accounts receivable	**3,115**	3,111
Inventories	**2,877**	2,903
Deferred income taxes	**716**	740
Prepaid expenses and other current assets	**624**	593
	9,988	9,975
Property, Plant, and Equipment	**10,024**	9,485
Goodwill and Other Intangible Assets	**3,754**	3,762
Other Assets	**1,769**	1,713
Total	**$25,535**	$24,935
LIABILITIES AND SHAREHOLDERS' EQUITY		
Current Liabilities		
Accounts payable — trade	**$ 2,604**	$ 2,269
Accounts payable — other	**660**	642
Accrued liabilities	**2,961**	2,838
Taxes payable	**440**	726
Debt due within one year	**1,375**	1,812
	8,040	8,287
Long-Term Debt	**4,980**	5,174
Other Liabilities	**3,336**	3,850
Deferred Income Taxes	**347**	183
	16,703	17,494
Shareholders' Equity		
Convertible Class A preferred stock	**1,942**	1,969
Common stock — shares outstanding: 1994 — 684,348,359; 1993 — 681,754,226	**684**	682
Additional paid-in capital	**560**	477
Currency translation adjustments	**(63)**	(99)
Reserve for employee stock ownership plan debt retirement	**(1,787)**	(1,836)
Retained earnings	**7,496**	6,248
	8,832	7,441
Total	**$25,535**	$24,935

Required:

a. Management presumably thought that the balance sheet was appropriate and presented in accordance with GAAP. Why was it then necessary to add the detail provided in the footnote? What information does that footnote information provide to you, as a prospective investor? Pick three of the footnoted items and explain the importance of the information provided.

b. Why might the company have presented property, plant, and equipment as one number on the balance sheet, providing the detail in a footnote, whereas all of the current assets and current liabilities are detailed separately on the balance sheet? If it was important to provide the detail of the current assets and current liabilities, why did the company elect to provide only one number on the balance sheet for inventory, providing the detail in a footnote?

EXHIBIT 2

Procter & Gamble
Selected Footnotes

4. BALANCE SHEET INFORMATION

June 30	1994	1993
Inventories		
Raw materials and supplies	**$ 1,087**	$ 1,154
Work in process	**213**	196
Finished products	**1,577**	1,553
	2,877	2,903
Replacement cost of LIFO inventories	**663**	1,097
Stated value of LIFO inventories	**462**	1,013
Excess of replacement cost over the stated value	**201**	84
Property, Plant, and Equipment		
Buildings	**3,027**	2,703
Machinery and equipment	**12,249**	11,607
Land	**550**	494
Timberlands, less depletion	**70**	73
	15,896	14,877
Less accumulated depreciation	**5,872**	5,392
	10,024	9,485
Goodwill and Other Intangible Assets		
Goodwill	**$ 3,564**	$ 3,472
Trademarks and other intangible assets	**946**	957
	4,510	4,429
Less accumulated amortization	**756**	667
	3,754	3,762
Accrued Liabilities		
Marketing expenses	**842**	753
Compensation expenses	**393**	395
Restructuring reserves	**870**	817
Other	**856**	873
	2,961	2,838
Other Liabilities		
Postretirement health care and life insurance benefits	**1,432**	1,410
Restructuring reserves	**1,035**	1,810
Other	**869**	630
	3,336	3,850

5. LONG-TERM DEBT

The following presents the carrying value of outstanding long-term debt:

June 30	1994	1993
9½% notes due 1998	**$ 200**	200
6¼% notes due 1995	**200**	200
8% notes due 2003	**200**	200
7.1% notes due 1994	**200**	200
6.85% notes due 1997	**200**	200
7⅜% debentures due 2023	**175**	175
8.7% notes due 2001	**175**	175
5.2% notes due 1995	**150**	150
9⅝% notes due 2001	**150**	150
8½% notes due 2009	**149**	149
10⅞% Canadian dollar bonds due 2001	**145**	157
Commercial paper	**765**	423
9.36% ESOP debentures, Series A, due 2021, guaranteed by the company	**1,000**	1,000
8.08%–8.33% serial ESOP notes, due 1994–2004, guaranteed by the company	**787**	836
Other, due in varying amounts through 2036	**978**	1,609
	5,474	5,824
Less amounts included in debt due within one year	**494**	650
Total long-term debt	**4,980**	5,174

The following payments are required during the next five fiscal years: 1995 — $494; 1996 — $468; 1997 — $416; 1998 — $322; and 1999 — $293.

P3.15 Industry-specific accounts. The following account titles were selected from 1994 annual reports published by various major companies:

a. "Amortization of Special Tools"

b. "Dealer Deposits"

c. "Accrued Marketing"

d. "Timber and Timberlands, Net of Timber Depletion"

e. "Leasehold Costs, Improvements, Store Fixtures, and Equipment"

f. "Exploration Expense"

g. "Charge for Discontinuing Automatic Blanket Operations"

h. "Operating Revenues:
Local Service
Interstate Access
Intrastate Access
Toll
Other"

Required:

For each of these account titles, indicate whether the account is a balance sheet account or an income statement account. And for each caption describe the kinds of event(s) that might be reflected in the account.

P3.16 Transaction analysis: The Bash Company.* The Bash Company, a Charlottesville, Virginia, retailer, was formed on July 1, 1994. During the month of July, the corporation experienced 11 different business transactions. At the end of the month, Bash prepared the following trial balance:

Bash Company
Trial Balance
July 31, 1994

Account	Debit (Left)	Credit (Right)
Cash	$103,000	
Accounts Receivable	6,500	
Allowance for Doubtful Accounts		$ 600
Inventory	10,000	
Equipment (net of $500 depreciation taken to date)	119,500	
Accounts Payable		50,000
Loan Payable (10 annual payments)		120,000
Interest Payable		1,000
Salaries Payable		8,000
Capital Stock		50,000
Retained Earnings		?
	$239,000	$?

Transaction Number	Accounts Affected	Dollar Effect: Debit (Left)	Dollar Effect: Credit (Right)
1			
2			
3			
4			
5			
6			
7			
8			
9			
10			
11			

Required:

Based on the data contained in the trial balance:

a. Fill in the spaces with question marks with the appropriate amounts.

b. Use the preceding chart to prepare the accounting entries for the 11 transactions that occurred during July. The transactions may be recorded in any order.

Note the following:

1. All sales were on account.
2. All asset purchases were on credit, and no payments were made against these liabilities during the month.
3. No cash was paid for any of the expenses incurred during the month.
4. Because of an unexpected occurrence, one account receivable (totaling $500) was written off during the month.

P3.17 Transaction analysis: Denver Wholesale Sporting Goods, Inc.* Below is a partial list of business events entered into by Denver Wholesale Sporting Goods, Inc., during the first fiscal quarter of 1994. Determine how each event, as of the date it occurred, would be recognized, if at all, in the 1994 financial statements. If the event should not be recognized, write NOT RECOGNIZED. If the event should be recognized now for financial-reporting purposes, indicate how (e.g., + or –) and by what dollar amount each of the following financial statement components would be affected (if there is no change in a particular column, leave that space blank): Cash, Net Current Assets (current assets minus current liabilities), Total Assets, Net Assets (total assets minus total liabilities), and Net Income.

	M = Million (Enter + or – and dollar amount or NOT RECOGNIZED)				
	Cash	Net Current Assets	Total Assets	Net Assets	Net Income
Sold capital stock for $3M.	+3M	+3M	+3M	+3M	
a. Purchased $8M of merchandise on account.					
b. Sold merchandise for $5M cash (entry for sales only).					
c. Recognized $4M cost of merchandise just sold (entry for cost only).					
d. Borrowed $4M cash, issuing a 90-day, 10% note.					
e. Repaid $4M loan (**d** above) plus $0.1M interest (for 90 days).					
f. Received an order for $3M of merchandise to be shipped next quarter.					
g. Collected a $0.5M account receivable.					
h. Bought equipment for $1M cash.					

i. Signed a year's rental agreement for office space for $0.1M a month. ________ ________ ________ ________ ________

j. Sold for $0.4M cash a long-term stock investment that had cost $0.5M (in prior years, the investment's market value fluctuated between $0.6M and $0.7M). ________ ________ ________ ________ ________

k. Paid cash dividends of $0.2M. ________ ________ ________ ________ ________

l. The company has been told that its warehouse and material-handling equipment shown at $10M net would cost $15M if replaced today. ________ ________ ________ ________ ________

m. Paid a $0.3M account payable. ________ ________ ________ ________ ________

n. Recognized $0.4M annual depreciation on equipment. ________ ________ ________ ________ ________

o. Bought a $6M machine, paying $2M in cash and signing a 10-year note for the balance. ________ ________ ________ ________ ________

p. The board of directors authorized $10M for capital expenditures to be made next year. ________ ________ ________ ________ ________

q. Received notice of a lawsuit against the company for $1M. ________ ________ ________ ________ ________

r. Sold a machine that had a book value of $1.5M for $2.0M cash. ________ ________ ________ ________ ________

s. Discovered that, because of obsolescence, inventory that cost $0.8M was estimated to have a net realizable value of only $0.5M. ________ ________ ________ ________ ________

t. An account receivable of $0.2M from a sale made during 1993 was determined to be uncollectible. ________ ________ ________ ________ ________

P3.18 Transaction analysis: Computer Corner, Inc. In the fall of 1993, Gary Reed inherited $100,000. He promptly quit his job, and he and his wife Connie decided to take $75,000 of the inheritance and start their own business. In January 1994, the Reeds opened Computer Corner, Inc., a small retail computer store. At the end of 1994 the trial balance of Computer Corner, Inc. appeared as follows:

Computer Corner, Inc.
Trial Balance
December 31, 1994

	Balance	
Account	**Debit (left)**	**Credit (right)**
Cash	$ 23,700	
Accounts Receivable	39,300	
Allowance for Uncollectible Accounts		$ 4,000
Inventory	65,000	
Prepaid Rent	4,000	
Property and Equipment (Net)	22,500	
Accounts Payable		25,000
Salaries Payable		3,500
Interest Payable		3,000
Loan Payable		30,000
Common Stock		75,000
Retained Earnings		14,000
	$154,500	$154,500

The following information pertains to the business during its first year of operation:

1. Signed a five-year lease in January that stipulated a monthly rent of $4,000.
2. Borrowed $30,000 in January from a local bank. The term of the loan was five years and the interest rate was 10 percent.
3. Cash sales for the year totaled $200,000. Credit sales for the year totaled $180,000.
4. One account receivable in the amount of $500 was written off in November as uncollectible.
5. Inventory purchased during the year totaled $280,000. All inventory purchases were on an accounts payable basis.
6. Purchases of property and equipment for the year totaled $25,000 and were paid in cash.
7. Operating expenses for the year included the following:

Supplies	$ 3,500
Utilities	3,000
Insurance	2,000
Salaries	70,000
Advertising	6,500
	$85,000

Included in the Salaries figure was $50,000 attributable to Gary and Connie Reed.

8. The Reeds withdrew $8,000 during the year that was not salary related.

Required:

Based on the information presented in items 1–8 and on the December 31, 1994, trial balance, prepare the journal entries to record the activities of Computer Corner, Inc., for 1994, *including* the initial investment by the owners. Your entries do not need to be recorded in any particular sequence.

P3.19 Transaction analysis — The Eastside Bank and Trust Co. The trial balances for the Eastside Bank and Trust Co., as of June 30, 1994, and July 31, 1994, were as follows (000s omitted):

At June 30			At July 31	
Debit (left)	Credit (right)		Debit (left)	Credit (right)
1,200		Cash on hand	1,040	
3,000		Short-term investments	3,000	
300		Interest receivable	325	
20,000		Mortgage loans	19,800	
	2,000	Allowance for credit losses		2,000
8,000		Bank equipment	8,200	
	2,000	Accumulated depreciation on bank equipment		2,045
5,000		Long-term investments	5,000	
	15,000	Deposits		15,675
	12,000	8%, 10-year bonds, dated 1/1/94		12,000
	480	Interest payable		80
	500	Accrued dividends		–0–
	3,020	Retained earnings		3,020
	2,500	Capital stock		2,500
	–0–	Dividend income		50
	–0–	Interest income		225
	–0–	Interest expense	155	
	–0–	Bad debts expense	–0–	
	–0–	Rent expense	10	
	–0–	Payroll expense	15	
	–0–	Other expense	50	

The bank follows the practice of charging a borrower's mortgage with the interest due each month and crediting a depositor's account with the interest paid each month. The short-term investment portfolio consists of municipal bonds, which pay interest at different dates during the year, mostly during the spring and fall months. The long-term investments consist of common stocks, which pay dividends whenever they are declared, usually in the month following a quarter-end.

Required:

Prepare the entries that would have been required to recognize the bank's activities in July, up to the point as reflected in the trial balance. There will be 14 entries; these 14 entries treat all similar transactions as having been summarized in one transaction, so that, for example, interest on all mortgages should be recognized in one entry.

P3.20 Preparation of financial statements — The Eastside Bank and Trust Co. Assume the following additional facts about the Eastside Bank and Trust Company, discussed in P3.19:

(1) Assume that the market value of the short-term investments (municipal bonds) is about equal to the cost.

(2) Assume that the market value of the long-term investments (common stocks) is $2,000, well below the recorded cost. The dramatic drop was reportedly due to unsettling developments in the investment company's foreign markets which were not expected to improve.

(3) Assume that most of the mortgages are fixed-term mortgages and that they carry an average interest rate of 12 percent.

(4) Assume that in early July a large, out-of-town bank announced that it was opening a branch office down the street from Eastside's office and that it was going to offer 6.5 percent on its deposits as long as they were left on deposit for at least one year. Eastside has been paying only 6 percent on its deposits.

(5) Assume that the economy in Eastside's community had been reasonably healthy, but one of the major industries in town has announced that it has lost a defense contract; that contract loss could translate into a 4 percent jump in the area's unemployment rate.

(6) Assume that Eastside's normal income tax rate is 40 percent.

Required:

a. Using the data from the trial balances in P3.19 and the information from the assumptions here, make any adjusting entries you think might be required for the bank's accounts as of July 31, 1994; prepare the closing entries for the bank as of the end of July; and prepare the bank's July financial statements.

b. Based on those financial statements and the understanding about the bank's operations you have gained as a result of preparing those statements, outline and briefly discuss the five most important recommendations you would present to the bank's executive committee when they meet next week to review the financial statements for July and to consider plans for the second half of 1994.

CASES

C3.1 Transaction analysis: Garland Creations, Inc.* Sandy Lawson had been determined to own her own company after completing her MBA. As an accomplished seamstress, she had always had a little business on the side making clothes for friends and specialty stores. The success of the Cabbage Patch dolls convinced her that there was money in stuffed toys. She decided that there was an unexploited niche for a family of animals, each having its own personality.

She took the savings of $7,044 that she had accumulated over the year and, with $263 worth of materials, set out to realize her dreams. Her family was very supportive and lent her $6,000 on a short-term note. She used $3,000 of this to purchase the specialized sewing equipment that she needed to make the animals.

From her years in the clothing business, she managed to find a supplier willing to let her have 90 days credit and invested in an additional $7,364 of materials on 90-day credit terms. Her own car was on its last legs, so she purchased a good secondhand pickup truck for $6,600 that she financed through a bank with a $1,600 deposit. A member of the family had an unused garage where she could set up her equipment. Installation of the equipment cost her $1,053. A year's insurance to cover the equipment cost an additional $1,000. A variety of different supplies necessary to get her operations off the ground absorbed another $963.

---

*This case was prepared by Michael F. van Breda. Copyright 1988 by Michael F. van Breda. Reprinted with permission.

By the end of the first six months she had made a substantial payment to her supplier, leaving a balance owed of $3,726 in the account. Sales had gone well and brought in a very welcome and reassuring inflow of cash totaling $12,325. She attributed these sales partly to the advertisement that she had run in a trade magazine, which had cost her $2,442.

Although she had not been able to repay her family or the bank any of the capital that they had lent her, she had paid the family $360 in interest. Wages had totaled $10,697.

While everyone else headed off for New Year's Eve parties, Sandy Lawson sat down at her desk to determine how well her business had done in the first six months of its life. She had worked extremely hard making stuffed toy animals and was proud of the different personalities that she had been able to create. They surrounded her on all sides as she pored over the numbers.

The results, as she figured them, were very pleasing to her. They appear below.

Garland Creations
Income Statement
For the Six Months Just Ended

Revenue		$12,325
Opening inventory	$ 263	
Purchases	7,364	
Wages	10,697	
Prepaid expenses	2,053	
Supplies	963	
Total	21,340	
Less: Closing inventory	16,005	
Cost of goods sold		5,335
Gross margin		6,990
Advertising expenses		2,442
Interest expense		360
Net income		$ 4,188

Garland Creations
Balance Sheet
As of the End of the Six Months Just Ended

Cash	$ 616
Inventory	16,005
Current assets	$16,621
Equipment	3,000
Truck	6,600
Total assets	$26,221
Accounts payable	$ 3,726
Notes payable	6,000
Current liabilities	$ 9,726
Bank loan	5,000
Capital	7,307
Retained earnings	4,188
Total equities	$26,221

Required:

a. Using the description of events in the case and the financial statements provided, replicate the journal entries and the T-accounts Sandy prepared to record the first six months of her business.

b. Where you believe it appropriate, adjust her accounting to better reflect the events. Revise her statements accordingly.

c. Comment on how well the business has done.

C3.2 Overview of the accounting cycle: Photovoltaics, Inc.* Photovoltaics, Inc., is a Texas-based manufacturer and distributor of photovoltaic solar energy units. The company was founded in 1990 by Arthur Manelas and Harry Linn. Manelas, formerly a research scientist with NASA, had been operating a small photovoltaic manufacturing company in Massachusetts when Linn, a marketing consultant to industry and himself an owner of a solar energy company in Oregon, proposed the joint venture.

The founders planned to take advantage of a major shift in consumer attitudes from fossil fuel energy production to cleaner, cheaper energy generation using wind, water, or sun. The joint venture would merge Linn's marketing experience and access to capital with Manelas' prior manufacturing knowledge and government patent on the photovoltaic unit.

The development of photovoltaic technology had begun in 1954 when scientists at the Bell Laboratories found that crystals of silicon could turn sunlight into electricity. The scientists observed that an electric current was produced when photons, or light energy, would strike silicon atoms, thereby causing electrons to be released. The first application of this technology involved the U.S. space program; NASA used photovoltaic solar cells to power the Vanguard I satellite in 1958.

Today photovoltaic cells are used to power buoys in shipping channels, transmitters on mountain tops, and communication equipment on offshore drilling platforms. In remote locations in Indonesia, Africa, and Australia, where electrical service neither exists nor is cost justified, photovoltaic arrays are used to generate electricity to power such life-sustaining equipment as water pumps and medical refrigerators storing vaccines.

Compared with power generated from such traditional sources as hydroelectric-, coal-, or oil-fueled plants, early photovoltaic arrays were prohibitively expensive (e.g., $2,000 per peak watt). Recent technological advances, however, made the cells so efficient and economical (i.e., $0.185 per peak watt) that they were now competitive with existing alternative energy sources. Elmer B. Kaelin, president of the Potomac Edison Company, warned utility executives that the day was quickly approaching when "homeowners will have every incentive to install solar collectors and pull the plug on the electric company."

Convinced that excellent market opportunities for the solar arrays existed, Linn began preparing a prospectus that could be used to help raise capital to significantly expand Manelas's current operations. The two founders had located a manufacturing facility in Lowell, Massachusetts, that would cost approximately $8 million to acquire and equip with updated production equipment. Based on his prior experience, Linn knew that prospective investors would expect to see the following:

- A statement of financial position classifying the company's assets and equities as they would appear at the preproduction stage.
- A pro forma earnings statement for the first year of operations.
- A pro forma balance sheet as it would appear at the end of the first year of operations.
- A pro forma cash flow statement for the first year of operations.

*This case was prepared by Kenneth R. Ferris. Copyright 1990 by Kenneth R. Ferris.

In anticipation of preparing these reports, Linn collected the following information and arrived at the following projections:

Data related to preproduction transactions

1. Ten million shares of common stock (par value $1) were authorized for sale by the charter of incorporation. Manelas received 500,000 shares in exchange for rights to the photovoltaic patent, and Linn received an equal number of shares after capitalizing the firm with $500,000 in personal funds.
2. Incorporation and attorney's fees amounted to $27,000.
3. The $8 million purchase price of the manufacturing facility and equipment was to be allocated as follows: building — $4.5 million, land — $750,000, and equipment — $2.75 million. In addition, raw materials and partially completed solar units had been purchased on credit from Manelas's original manufacturing company at a cost of $1.3 million. A note, secured by the inventory itself and accruing interest at a rate of 10 percent per annum on the unpaid balance, was issued to Manelas.

Projected data

4. Sales of common stock to independent investors and venture capitalists would total 2.5 million shares. A selling price of $3.25 per share was set, and transaction costs of 1.5 percent of the stock proceeds were projected.
5. Revenues from the sale of solar arrays for the first year were projected to be $480,000, with one-fifth of this amount estimated to be uncollected by year-end. The company had decided to follow a particularly rigid credit policy until operations were well established; hence, no provision for bad debts would be established because no uncollectible accounts were anticipated.
6. Cash purchases of raw materials were estimated at $70,000; the cost of units sold was projected at $215,000.
7. Insurance on the building, equipment, and inventory was expected to cost $2,700 per year.
8. Labor costs were estimated at $72,000; selling and administrative costs were projected at 2 percent of gross sales.
9. The useful life of the acquired assets were estimated as follows:

Building:	20 years
Equipment:	10 years

Linn decided to write the patent off over its legal life of 17 years and the organizational costs (i.e., incorporation and attorney fees) over five years.

10. Salaries to Linn and Manelas were set at $20,000 each for the first year.
11. No principal repayments would be made on the 10 percent notes issued to Manelas during the first year of operations.
12. Income taxes would be calculated as follows:

Income Level	Tax Rate
$0–50,000	15%
50,001–75,000	25
75,001–100,000	34
100,001–335,000	39
335,001–above	34

The company would be required to pay 80 percent of its taxes by year-end.

13. Fifty percent of net income after taxes would be distributed to investors as dividends.

Required:

a. Consider the informational needs of a developing company. Design an efficient accounting system for Photovoltaics, Inc. What accounts would be needed?

b. Prepare the three accounting statements needed for the prospectus.

c. As a prospective investor in the company, what factors would you look for in the accounting statements to help you decide whether to invest in the venture?

C3.3 Accounting cycle: Skyler Pharmacy.* From its beginning in 1980 through February 28, 1993, Skyler Pharmacy operated as a sole proprietorship with Mr. Bennett Skyler as owner. On March 1, 1993, the business was incorporated as Skyler Pharmacy, Inc., and the business changed its fiscal year from the calendar year to the 12 months ended February 28th. For federal income tax purposes, the corporation qualified as a Subchapter S small business corporation, whose income, whether distributed or not, was taxed directly to the individual stockholder(s).

When Mr. Skyler began the store in 1980, he planned to emphasize his prescription service and to sell prescription and standard drug items only. The character of the store he planned permitted the use of modest quarters (627 square feet store area). The original quarters leased in 1980 were still being used despite a sizable increase in sales volume. The increase in annual sales volume and the large proportion of sales represented by prescriptions are indicated in the following fifteen-year history:

Year	Total Sales	Prescription Sales	Number of Prescriptions
1980	56,549	23,456	18,888
1981	67,631	27,147	20,742
1982	72,661	29,936	21,985
1983	77,315	34,186	22,697
1984	83,371	38,950	22,410
1985	86,186	42,156	23,656
1986	78,994	37,519	20,223
1987	83,220	44,716	20,349
1988	95,268	58,006	22,955
1989	104,782	67,037	24,399
1990	120,614	74,715	25,782
1991	123,174	77,620	25,078
1992	129,507	85,328	27,586
12 mos. ended 2/28/93	129,334	84,009	26,570
12 mos. ended 2/28/94	126,715	85,681	26,699

In 1993–94 the store's employees were:

Mr. Bennett Skyler, manager and pharmacist
Mr. Samuel R. Rison, pharmacist (resigned during year)
Mr. Heartwell B. James, pharmacist (replaced Mr. Rison)
Ms. Irene Gowen, store clerk
Ms. Lois West, store clerk
Ms. Eva Mae Boulware, store clerk
Mr. John Randolph Hart, delivery man and janitor

*This case is based on Jameson's Pharmacy (K), prepared by Billy T. O'Brien under the supervision of Almand R. Coleman, Professor Business Administration. Names and figures have been disguised.

Because his employees used exceptional tact and courtesy in dealing with customers, Mr. Skyler maintained a salary scale above the "going rate" in the community. The store was not operated at nights or on Sundays. Mr. Skyler, however, utilized a telephone call service that enabled customers to reach either him or his other pharmacist at all hours for emergency prescription needs.

Credit and Collection

Mr. Skyler commented on his receivable problems as follows:

"Aside from prescriptions, I spend more of my time on credit and collections than on anything else. That and getting my accounting records to balance take up a good part of my time. In this community we have monthly payrolls for the most part. This means that I have to wait at least a month to collect for my charge sales, so I have a pretty heavy investment in receivables. But I've gotten a number of good accounts from other stores who have found it necessary to reduce their receivables investment.

"My credit procedure is fairly informal. I know the people of this community, so when customers ask for credit, I either know or can find out pretty quickly what their credit reputation is. If they don't meet my requirements, I sell to them for cash only. Of course, I make some mistakes in extending credit. My mistakes are usually 'slow pay' customers who are able to pay me but pay somebody else instead. Occasionally a 'slow pay' customer turns into a 'no pay' one, and I have to write the account off, but I don't have many like this.

"The way I bill, at the end of each month, I always have at least one month's sales in my month-end receivables. At the end of February I sent out bills for $15,720, of which $6,928 represented February sales being billed for the first time. Before we send out the bills, Ms. West puts on my desk the ledger sheets of 'slow pay' customers, and I go over these to see which ones seem to be so because of unusual circumstances I know about. For the others on the list, I indicate the ones to receive one of my special collection letters. One of the letters I use reads as follows:

> We are sorry that we must again remind you of your account, now past due, as shown on the enclosed photostatic copy of your ledger sheet.
>
> This merchandise was charged to you with the understanding that we would receive payment within 30 days — it has been much longer.
>
> We cannot afford to give terms longer than this because our employees are paid twice a month, and our purchases are on a strict 30-day basis.
>
> Our credit standing is important to us, just as yours is to you. We can't settle our accounts unless you pay us — and so it is all down the line. This business of paying bills is simply a 'round robin' affair, and each of us is dependent on the other fellow.
>
> So, please send us a check before you lay this letter aside. We really can use the money, and will appreciate your cooperation.
>
> Sincerely yours,
> SKYLER PHARMACY
> Bennett Skyler

"From time to time I've wondered how far I should go in extending credit, whether I'm being too tight, and what it would mean if I took on more marginal customers."

Record Keeping

Mr. Skyler attempted to maintain his record keeping at a minimum:

X 1. *He deposited all receipts in the bank each day, and made all disbursements by check.* He established a "change fund" of $225, which was kept in the cash register at all times. Since he deposited the exact amount of his daily receipts in the bank (on the following morning), he made the bank become a sort of second bookkeeper and proof for him with respect to cash receipts and cash disbursements.

2. *He eliminated the usual merchandise purchases journal and accounts payable account.* After the end of each month when he received statements from his suppliers and other creditors, he held his check disbursement record open, drew checks to the suppliers and others for the discounted amounts of their bills, and entered the checks in the check disbursement record in the month when the purchases were made or expenses incurred. He held the checks he drew in this fashion until their respective discount dates when he mailed them to the suppliers.

3. *He had one of his store clerks keep the customers' charge accounts and send out monthly statements.* Each morning the clerk spent about an hour at the bookkeeping machine, posting to the customers' ledger accounts and monthly statements the charge sales tickets and "received on account" tickets for the previous day.

Mr. Skyler's primary records were: (a) his cash register, (b) his sales and cash receipts record, and (c) his check disbursement record.

Mr. Skyler's sales and cash receipts record was a record of the store's daily totals for

1. Cash sales (including excise taxes).

2. Charge sales (including excise taxes).

3. Bank deposits.

4. Cash received on account.

5. Excise taxes collected (memo record).

To obtain daily totals for these five items, Mr. Skyler utilized his daily cash register tape (giving totals for cash sales, cash received on account, and excise taxes collected), together with (a) tickets for charge sales to be charged to individual customers' accounts and (b) tickets for cash "received on account" showing the individual customers' accounts to be posted. He made an adding machine run of the charge sales tickets to get the day's total to be entered in the sales and cash receipts record. He proved:

1. The total of each day's "received on account" tickets against his cash register total.

2. The total of the bank deposit (made the following morning) against the sum of the day's totals for cash sales and cash received on account.

He entered the day's total for the five items in the five columns of his sales and cash receipts record, which he totaled for each month. At the end of the year, he summarized the monthly figures.

Mr. Skyler's check disbursement record was a chronological record of disbursements by check as recorded from check stubs. This record showed the date, check number, and payee, and entry of the amount of the check in columns for:

1. Merchandise paid for

2. Salaries and wages

3. Other store expenses

4. Other payments

He totaled these columns monthly, and at the end of the year summarized the monthly figures. Mr. Skyler made it a practice to take every discount available to him, so the amounts in the merchandise-paid-for column represented the discounted amounts. As a matter of personal interest, Mr. Skyler maintained a memo record of the discounts he took each month and for the year as a whole.

Mr. Skyler kept the sales and cash receipts and check disbursements records himself for the information it afforded him. At the end of each year, he supplied the year's totals and other information to a local certified public accountant as a basis for the preparation of the corporation's income tax return.

In March 1994 the following information was available with respect to the corporation's fiscal year ended February 28, 1994:

1. *Balance sheet as of beginning of fiscal year, March 1, 1993:*

Assets	
Cash in store (change fund)	$ 225
Cash in bank	11,964
Trade receivables	14,852
Merchandise inventory	15,884
Store equipment and other fixed assets (net)	2,346
Organization costs	236
	$ 45,507
Liabilities	
Accounts payable	$ 4,614
Accrued taxes	1,059
Bonus payable to S. R. Rison	2,274
Capital stock	34,000
Retained earnings	3,560
	$ 45,507

2. *Twelve months' summary of sales and cash receipts record:*

Cash sales (including $78 excise tax)	$ 46,697
Charge sales (including $118 excise tax)	80,018
Bank deposits	125,462
Cash received on account from customers	78,765

3. *Twelve months' summary of check disbursement record:*

Merchandise paid for (net of $2,049 discounts)	$ 69,738
Salaries and wages (including $11,750 for B. Skyler)	33,697
Other store expenses	12,184
	$115,619
Other payments	30,609
Total check disbursements	$146,228

4. *Analysis of "other payments":*

Payments on accounts payable outstanding at 3/1/93		$ 4,614
Payments on accrued taxes outstanding at 3/1/93		1,059
Payment on bonus payable (S. R. Rison) outstanding at 3/1/93		2,274
Donations to United Fund, T.B. Association, Chamber of Commerce*		125
Excise tax paid		196
Refunds to customers for sales returned		100
Capital items:		
Freezer	$ 1,300	
Stamp machine	121	
Store sign	490	
Leasehold improvements	537	
Office chair	58	2,506
Paid to B. Skyler:		
Advance to B. Skyler	$ 7,972	
Dividend on capital stock	11,763	19,735
Total (as per #3 above)		$ 30,609

*Mr. Skyler continued, in the corporation's records, his former practice of keeping donations separately recorded from other store expenses. The local C.P.A. considered these donations as other store expenses of the corporation.

5. *Unrecorded borrowing from bank:*

On February 9, 1994, Mr. Skyler had arranged for a $5,000, 5 percent 60-day loan from the bank. The interest of $42 was deducted from the proceeds, and the pharmacy's account was credited with $4,958 on February 9, 1994. An entry needs to be made to record this transaction with care being taken to allocate the $42 interest, one-third to retained earnings and two-thirds to prepaid interest.

6. *A reconciliation of the bank account at February 28, 1994, showed as follows:*

Balance as per bank statement 2/28/94	$ 3,211
Add: Deposits of 2/26, 2/27, and 2/28 receipts in transit to bank	846
	$ 4,057
Deduct: Outstanding checks	7,897
Adjusted overdraft per books 2/28/94	$(3,840)

The difference between the "adjusted overdraft per books" of $(3,840), shown above, and the balance of $(3,844) shown by the pharmacy's records was $4. It was decided that it would not be worthwhile to try to trace this difference, so an adjustment of $4 is to be made to the bank balance and other store expenses.

Included among the "outstanding checks" were 43 checks totaling $7,347, which had actually been drawn after February 28, 1994, and which had been entered in the February check disbursement record, held "open."

These checks had been drawn for merchandise purchased in February and for other store expenses incurred in February. An entry is to be made to restore the total of these checks, $7,347, to cash in bank and to accounts payable at February 28, 1994.

7. *Mr. Skyler's summary of trade receivables from customers showed as follows:*

Total amount of customers' accounts at March 1, 1993	$14,852
Charge sales during year	80,018
	$94,870
Received on account during year	78,765
Total amount of customers' accounts unpaid at February 28, 1994	$16,105

Note: The total of the balances of individual customer's statements mailed at February 28, 1994, was $15,720. The difference of $385 represented accounts determined to be worthless and written off.

8. Mr. Skyler and his employees listed and counted the merchandise stock on hand at February 28, 1994. Those items of merchandise that had become obsolete were shown at no value or at a nominal value, while all currently salable items were valued at the price that the store had paid for them. The inventory sheets were then totaled. The total inventory for the prescription department was $8,661 and for other merchandise in the store, $7,672. The final figure for the entire inventory at February 28, 1994, was therefore $16,333.

Mr. Skyler observed that through experience, and as a result of keeping his own records, he had a feel for how much inventory he had on hand at any one time. He noted that the $16,333 physical inventory figure was pretty close to his preliminary estimate of $16,000 for stock on hand at February 28, 1994.

9. The local C.P.A. prepared a depreciation schedule for the fiscal year ended February 28, 1994, as follows:

Kind of Property	Original Cost	Undepreciated Cost Remaining @ 3/1/93	Depr. Life	Year's Depr.
Blower, etc.	$ 164	$ 14	15	$ 11
Typewriter and cabinet	315	15*	10	–0–
Cash register	390	25*	10	–0–
Ledger tray	47	5*	10	–0–
Safe	363	187	20	18
Pricing machine	197	86	10	20
Air conditioners	780	177	7	111
Stenorette	246	16	5	49
Various office equipment	866	529	10	87
Copier	342	251	10	34
1980 truck (salvage $100)	1,722	1,041	5	323
	$5,432	$2,346		$653
Additions during 1993–94:				
Stamp machine	121	—	10	6
Freezer	1,300	—	5	130
Office chair	58	—	10	3
Leasehold improvements	537	—	6	45
Store sign	490	—	10	25
	$2,506	$2,346		$862
Add: Cost of additions during 1993–94		2,506		
		$4,852		
Deduct: Depreciation for year		862		
Cost remaining at 2/28/94		$3,990		

*Estimated salvage value

An entry should be made for depreciation for the year.

10. The local C.P.A. noted also:

a. That employer Social Security taxes for January and February 1994, in the amount of $194, had been incurred and needed to be shown as a liability at 2/28/94.

b. That, similarly, the corporation had incurred state income taxes in the amount of $432 for the fiscal year ended 2/28/94.

He thought it would be all right to combine these two items into one total and so make only one entry.

11. The local C.P.A. observed that, for income tax purposes, the corporation had elected to amortize organization costs of $295 over a 60-month period. An entry for $59 amortization should be made.

12. Mr. Skyler had entered into profit-sharing arrangements with both Mr. Rison and Mr. James, the terms of which provided for an annual bonus based upon the corporation's net profit before bonus but after providing for their regular salaries and for a salary of $11,750 to Mr. Skyler. These salaries are included in the $33,697 total for Salaries and Wages (#3 above). On the basis of the information developed by him, the local C.P.A. determined the bonuses to be $367 for Mr. Rison and $612 for Mr. James, no part of which had been paid at 2/28/94.

Required:

a. Prepare accounting entries for 1994 events in usual form:

(1) In analyzing transactions for the information contained in Items 2, 3, and 4, it is suggested you break it up as follows:

(a) One entry, designated *A*, for cash sales.
(b) Another entry, designated *B*, for charge sales.
(c) Another entry, designated *C*, for collections on customer accounts.
(d) One entry, *D*, for merchandise paid for, for salaries and wages, and for other store expenses.
(e) Another entry, *E*, for "other payments" (Item 4).

(2) Make entries, designated *F, G, H*, and so on, as and, if appropriate, for the remainder of the information given.

b. Enter your entries in the T-accounts below.

c. Prepare a trial balance.

d. Prepare a combined statement of income and retained earnings by filling in blanks appropriately on the form provided.

e. Prepare a comparative balance sheet by filling in blanks on the form provided.

f. Prepare a simple summary of cash receipts and disbursements for 1993–94 by filling in blanks appropriately below:

Beginning balance	$ ______
ADD: Cash receipts	______
	$ ______
DEDUCT: Cash disbursements	______
Ending balance	$ ______

g. How would you explain to the inquisitive Mr. Skyler:

(1) Why "cash receipts" in (f) are not the same as "sales" income on the income statement?
(2) Why "cash disbursements' in (f) are not the same as "cost of goods sold" and "expenses" on the income statement?

Cash on hand — Change fund (asset)

3/1/93 Balance	225	

Cash in bank (asset)

3/1/93 Balance	11,964	

Trade receivables (asset)

3/1/93 Balance	14,852	

Merchandise inventory (asset)

3/1/93 Balance	15,884		

Store equipment and other fixed assets (asset)

3/1/93 Balance	2,346		

Prepaid interest (asset)

3/1/93 Balance	–0–		

Organization costs (asset)

3/1/93 Balance	236		

Advances to B. Skyler (asset)

3/1/93 Balance	–0–		

Notes payable — bank (liability)

		3/1/93 Balance	–0–

Accounts payable (liability)

		3/1/93 Balance	4,614

Accrued taxes (liability)

		3/1/93 Balance	1,059

Bonus payable — S. R. Rison (liability)

		3/1/93 Balance	2,274

Bonus payable — H. B. James (liability)

		3/1/93 Balance	–0–

Capital stock (owner's equity)

		3/1/93 Balance	34,000

Retained earnings (owners' equity)

		3/1/93 Balance	3,560

Skyler Pharmacy, Inc.
Combined Statement of Income and Retained Earnings
For Fiscal Year Ended February 28, 1994

		Amount
Sales (less discounts, returns, and allowances)		$
Cost of goods sold:		
Inventory — beginning of year	$	
Add merchandise purchases		
	$	
Deduct inventory — end of year		
Total cost of goods sold		
Gross margin		$
Expenses:		
Proprietor's salary	$	
Employees' compensation		
Depreciation		
Debts charged off		
All other store expenses		
Total expenses		
Net profit for year		$
Retained earnings balance, 3/1/93		
		$
Deduct dividends		
Retained earnings, 2/28/94		$

Skyler Pharmacy, Inc.
Comparative Balance Sheets
February 28, 1994 and March 1, 1993

	2/28/94	3/1/93	Increase (Decrease)
Assets			
Cash in store and in bank	$	$12,189	$
Trade receivables		14,852	
Merchandise inventory		15,884	
Store equipment and other fixed assets (net)		2,346	
Prepaid interest		–0–	
Organization costs		236	
Advances to B. Skyler		–0–	
Total assets	$	$45,507	$
Liabilities and Owners' Equity			
Notes payable — bank	$	$ –0–	$
Accounts payable		4,614	
Accrued taxes		1,059	
Bonus payable — S. R. Rison		2,274	
Bonus payable — H. B. James		–0–	
Capital stock		34,000	
Retained earnings		3,560	
Total liabilities and owners' equity	$	$45,507	$

C3.4 Projected financial statements: The Law Brothers.* In the summer of 1959, John and Harry Law were considering a proposal by Tom Johnson that the three men form a new corporation for the packing and distribution of oysters.

Background

In 1939 John Law, graduate of an eastern business school, and Harry Law, law school graduate, bought a farm on the Rappahannock River in Virginia and operated it as a partnership. They retained as manager Tom Johnson, who had served in the same capacity for the previous owner.

Two years later, in 1941, they decided to go into the oyster planting business and accordingly purchased a lease on approximately 200 acres of planting grounds in the river along the farm's shore line.[1] They also had a 42-foot oyster boat built for "dredging" and made Mr. Johnson boat captain and manager of the planting operations.

Mr. Johnson managed both businesses until 1954 when he retired as manager of the farm. To augment his income from the planting operation, he purchased a truck, hired a driver, and began distributing oysters from several packing houses in the area to hotels, restaurants, and food stores around the state.

Thus by 1959, all three men had 18 years of experience in planting oysters and a good understanding of the packing operation through association with it. Since 1954 Mr. Johnson had also developed contacts with a number of distribution outlets.

The Planting Operation

Oysters in the Rappahannock River were rarely known to "strike" (reproduce) but they did grow large and fat. On the other hand, in the lower James River they struck annually but did not grow to a sufficient size for harvesting. It was the practice, therefore, for the Rappahannock planters to buy the young "seed oysters" from the lower James River and plant them in the Rappahannock, where they were allowed to mature.

The seed oysters were planted in the fall and left for three years before they were harvested. During this time the death rate was high. For example, seed oysters ran about 1,000 to 1,200 per bushel, while mature oysters averaged from 250 to 300 per bushel. The harvest, however, was usually on a one-for-one basis; that is, one bushel recovered for one bushel planted. Thus about three-fourths of the oysters died during the three-year period.

Sometimes unusual factors such as blight, fungus attacks, and weather conditions caused even higher losses. In 1955 Hurricane Hazel destroyed about 70 percent of the oyster crop in the Rappahannock River because the heavy rainfall brought too much fresh water and silting into the oyster growing areas.

Two further risks that had been of concern to those in the oyster business were the possible increases (1) in river pollution by industrial plants and city sewage operations and (2) in silting caused by clearing and cultivating the lands along the river banks.

The mature oysters were harvested from September through March by "dredging."[2] They were usually thin in the early fall after the warm summer months, but grew fatter during the winter. The demand for oysters, however, began in late August and early September, notwithstanding their poorer condition then.

---

*Case prepared by H. Lee Boatwright, Jr., 1960, under the supervision of Almand R. Coleman, Professor Business Administration. Case revised in 1966. Names, places, and figures have been disguised.

[1]The Commonwealth of Virginia authorized 20-year leases on private planting grounds. These leases were salable and renewable.

[2]A "dredge" is a very large rake trailing a net that catches the oysters as they are raked off the bottom. The dredge is dragged along the oyster bed until the net is full, then winched in and dumped on deck.

Operations of the Public Rocks

The Commonwealth of Virginia maintained public oyster grounds for the many local water men who made their living oystering in the winter and crabbing or fishing in the summer. The "tongers," as these men were called, had small boats and brought up the oysters by hand with tongs, since no dredging was permitted on the public rocks. A good tonger could generally get about 10 to 12 bushels on a favorable day, but during bad weather, when the river was rough, they could not go out at all because of the small size of their boats. The public rocks were open only from October 1 to March 31.

The tongers usually sold their catch to local packing houses, but at times when the demand was high, they sold some oysters to "buy boats" that came out in the river from packers who wanted to fill out their capacity. These buy boats generally offered a slightly better price than the tongers could get from the local packers.

The Packing Operation

The packing house bought oysters from both private planters and tongers as needed to fill capacity or meet customer orders. Generally the house bought that amount on one day which it expected to pack the next. The price fluctuated considerably with the supply and demand.

Two different methods of purchase were used. The tonger was paid by the bushel when he unloaded his catch. The price per bushel had ranged in 1957 and 1958 from \$2.75 to \$3.75. For the private planters, on the other hand, "buying them on the meats" was most common. The planter was paid by the gallon according to how much his oysters shucked out. Here, of course, a great deal depended on how fat the oysters were, but over the course of a season one bushel would generally average out about 5½ pints of "meat." The price paid to the planter was the going price for bulk oysters at the plant site (\$4.50 to \$5.50 per gallon in the preceding two years) less the labor cost of shucking (\$1.00 per gallon) and a charge (20¢ per bushel) for overhead and handling. The packer made his profit on the increase from blowing (which will be explained below) and the value of the shells.[3] Exhibit 1 shows a sample calculation of "buying on the meats."

The oysters were carried from the large bins in which they were stored into the shucking room where they were shucked (opened) by hand. The shuckers were paid strictly on piece-rate, one dollar per gallon, and could open on the average about twelve gallons per day.

The shuckers also performed the grading function. Oysters were sold in two sizes, selects and standards. Selects were large oysters and measured about 250 per gallon. All of the smaller oysters were classified as standards. In the fall, when the oysters were thin, there were more standards than selects, but during the winter there were more selects, so that over the course of a season they averaged out about even.

After being shucked, the oysters went to the blowing room where they were put into large vats of fresh water for washing. Air was blown in from the bottom to agitate and wash the oysters. Since during this operation the oysters took on some water and air, they actually increased in size. For example, five gallons before blowing produced about six afterward.

Next the oysters were packed in cans and put on ice until they were sold. The packer usually had regular customers who picked up the oysters at the plant on the same or following day. Because the produce was perishable,[4] the packing house tried to process only enough to meet a known demand. For this reason the inventory rarely exceeded one day's "shell stock" and one day's

[3]One bushel of oysters produced a bushel of shells, which could be sold for 13¢ per bushel.

[4]Oysters would stay fresh about a week to 10 days if properly iced.

EXHIBIT 1

THE LAW BROTHERS
Sample Calculation of Buying on the Meats

Purchase	176 bushels		
Production (5½ pts./bu.)	121 gallons		
Payment due planters:			
Gross ($5.00/gal.)			$605.00
Less:			
Wages paid to shuckers ($1.00/gal.)		$121.00	
Overhead and handling charge ($0.20/bu.)		35.20	156.20
Net to planter			$448.80

packed oysters.[5] Customers paid their bills fairly promptly, so that accounts receivable averaged about seven days' sales.

Some packers had their own trucks for distribution to wholesalers, restaurants, hotels, and independent grocers who required delivery.

In 1957 and 1958, the packers' selling price had fluctuated between $4.50 and $5.50 for standards and $5.50 and $6.50 for selects.

See Exhibit 2 for further information on the oyster industry.

The Proposal

In the spring of 1959, Johnson came to the Law brothers with a proposal that they start a packing business. He had done much of the preliminary planning since he intended to go into the venture anyway, but he wanted them in to ensure a supply of oysters. He offered to put up one-half or one-third of the capital required in order to get the business under way.

Johnson had already selected a plant site that was well located in a protected cove with plenty of water for the boats to come in very close to the bank. This meant that not only did the site have an advantage over many houses that were located in unprotected areas and thus could not unload oysters in bad weather, but it was not necessary to build a long and expensive unloading dock. There was also an advantage in handling efficiency since the oysters could be unloaded very near the storage bins. The two and a half acres of land would cost $1,420, and Johnson estimated that improvements, including the dock, would run about $1,500.

In the next few months, Johnson and the Laws visited other packing houses to determine the size of the building, the layout, and the equipment required. The packers with whom they talked were somewhat discouraging, saying that business had not been good in recent years. John Law commented on this, "Yes, they were discouraging, but we saw that they were all driving Buicks, so we didn't pay too much attention to it."

The three men decided that a plant providing room for 25 shuckers would be the most efficient because there would be a minimum of indirect labor. With 25 or fewer shuckers, only one man would be needed to distribute oysters in the shucking room and only one to run the blowing and packing operations. Harry Law observed, "We found that the oyster house, to be most economical, had to be built for 25 shuckers or multiples of 25."

[5]Some of the large packers froze oysters for year-round distribution, and for such an operation a much larger investment in inventory and equipment was required. A small local packer had also experimented unsuccessfully with freezing oysters.

EXHIBIT 2

THE LAW BROTHERS
Additional Technical Note on Oyster Industry Consisting of:
(1) News Articles in the *Richmond Times-Dispatch* about the Time of the Case and (2) Additional Information on Packing Cans and Oyster Shells

Richmond Times-Dispatch
January 18, 1960, Issue

RAPPAHANNOCK OYSTERS ACCLAIMED FOR QUALITY
by Christine Hall

Urbanna, January 17

" 'The Rappahannock accounts for about one-third of Virginia's total oyster production, which in turn is one-half of the United States' total,' Ryland said."

" 'Until a few years ago,' he added, 'Virginia contributed only about a third of the total. But Delaware, New Jersey, and New York oyster grounds have suffered a 90 percent loss in their annual crop.' "

"Oyster harvesting is big business. With a total production of approximately 10,500,000 gallons — or 75 million pounds — the United States supplies five-eighths of all market oysters produced in the world."

"The two methods permitted for harvesting oysters from the Rappahannock River are known as patent tonging and shaft tonging. The use of patent tongs, a mechanical grappling device operated by a motor, is restricted to the lower river in water depths of 20 to 30 feet."

First Three Months

"Virginia law allows the use of patent tongs only during the first three months of each oyster season — October through December — on the Rappahannock, but in the Chesapeake Bay the legal period is extended through February."

"Shaft tonging begins with the opening of oyster season on the public grounds or 'Rock,' October 1, and continues until the season closes at the end of April."

"Oystermen operate shaft, or hand tongs, from open boats. The shafts or handles range in length from 24 to 32 feet, and are attached to long-toothed, pincer-line tongs hinged together. With this device the oysters are located on the bottom and brought to the surface, where they are dumped on the culling board in the boat."

"Most boat crews consist of two tongers and a third man who culls the catch by throwing back all oysters under the legal size of three inches in length. A few watermen prefer to work alone, tonging and culling their catch in turn."*

Public and Private Grounds

"Virginia's annual oyster harvest is taken from both public and private grounds. The public rock is maintained by the Commission of Fisheries at state expense for the benefit of the public. A $3.50 license, an oyster boat, and know-how are the only items required to get into the business of tonging oysters from public grounds, which contain some 300,000 acres of the state's river and bay bottoms."

"Private grounds, which account for an additional 125,000 acres, are leased from the state by the planters at a present annual rate of $1 per acre in the rivers, and 50 cents an acre in Chesapeake and part of Mobjack Bay,' Ryland explained."

"Ryland and 55 other inspectors patrol the public oyster grounds in 16 police boats to enforce the state's oystering laws."

March 14, 1960, Issue

MIDDLESEX OYSTERMEN HARD HIT BY WEATHER
by Christine Hall

Urbanna, March 13

"Bad weather has cost Middlesex County oystermen an estimated $350,000 in lost income in the past two weeks."

"The estimate was furnished by J. W. Ferguson, the largest seafood packer in this area. He said, 'I normally buy about 4,200 bushels of oysters a week, but since March 1, I have only been able to buy 275 bushels — 200 week before last and only 75 bushels last week.' "

"Ferguson, who owns two of approximately 35 oyster packing houses on the Rappahannock River, estimated that he buys 12 percent of the 8,500 bushels of oysters tonged daily from the river's public oyster grounds."

"Boats and oystermen on both sides of the river have been kept ashore for nearly three weeks by the extreme cold, high winds, ice, and snow. The limited number of boats that ventured into the river on calm days were soon forced back to shore by the cold. 'You just can't hold onto an icicle but so long, and that is what the tongs would be after a few dips into the water,' Ferguson said."

*The requirement that tongers throw back "all oysters under the legal size of three inches in length" accounts for the fact that oysters bought from tongers will usually be "cleaner" than those acquired from planters. This accounts for the difference between the price per bushel paid tongers and the "net" per bushel paid to the planter in "buying them on the meats."

EXHIBIT 2 continued

"The lack of activity on the public rocks has thrown at least 600 people out of work temporarily. The tongers were being paid $3.50 per bushel for the oysters."

"Seafood packing houses in the area have been forced to either close down or resort to dredging from their private oyster grounds. Mechanically operated dredge boats are not hampered by cold weather unless the creeks are completely locked in by ice."

" 'We have been operating our packing houses with oysters dredged from our private beds,' Ferguson said. 'Our main problem, however, has been the heavy snow preventing our employees from getting to work.' The Ferguson Seafood Packing Company employs 94 people — 60 of them oyster shuckers."

"Oystermen and packers alike are looking forward to the return of normal operations, possibly this week, because the seafood business is Middlesex County's biggest industry."

October 1, 1960, Issue

OYSTER SEASON OPENS TODAY

Urbanna, September 30

"Despite the rumors of high oyster mortalities in the Rappahannock River, oyster boats from Tangier Island, Mathews, and Gloucester began arriving in Middlesex County creeks Friday in preparation for the opening of the season Saturday."

"The Rappahannock's most productive grounds, a 40-mile stretch that extends along the entire shoreline length of Middlesex County, is the working area for some 1,000 boats. This area produces one-third of Virginia's oysters. A normal day's catch from the Rappahannock, in a good season, is approximately 15,000 bushels."

"Oyster buyers and packers were uncertain Friday just what they would pay per bushel for the Saturday catch. Estimates ranged from $3.50 to $4.25. B. B. Newman, an Urbanna buyer, said the first day would be more or less a guess. 'We really won't know what to pay until after a load has been bought, shucked out, and the condition of the oysters determined,' he said."

"Thirty to thirty-five buy boats operate on the river, some coming from as far away as the Eastern Shore and Maryland. These large boats buy oysters from the smaller tonger boats and deliver to the packing houses."

"Speculation as to the condition of the oysters that will be tonged Saturday was the topic of conversation along the waterfront Friday. . . . "

"Regardless of the reports that oysters will be scarce this season, oystermen by the hundred will be out on the Rappahannock when day breaks Saturday morning. 'We will wait and see for ourselves,' is the consensus of the watermen."

October 23, 1960, Issue

TO PLANT OR NOT TO PLANT? — OYSTER THREAT FACED WITH MIXED EMOTIONS

Urbanna, October 22

" 'The next generation won't even remember it,' one oysterman said here this week."

"Said another: 'We can work, we can sell, and we can be sure we are in the market this winter at least.' Then he added, 'as for next winter and the future . . . ' He shrugged and spread his hands."

"Oystermen all along the Rappahannock and elsewhere in Virginia face a deadly threat to their livelihood. It is the mysterious MSX that has been blamed for destroying Delaware's oyster industry and heavily damaging Maryland's."

"The oyster killer was discovered in Virginia last year, and already it has caused widespread mortalities — up to 80 percent in some state waters. Last week a marine scientist said evidence of the deadly microorganism has been found in the Rappahannock River and the valuable seed beds in the James River."

Trace Noted

"In both places, only a trace of MSX was noted. The scientists cautioned against alarm. They noted that although it is fatal to oysters, the tiny organism has no effect on humans."

"Fat and tasty Rappahannock River oysters are famous throughout the world. Almost all taken from the river are produced in a 40-mile stretch of the river extending from the mouth at Chesapeake Bay."

"The annual catch from this area represents about one-third of the total oyster production in Virginia. Watermen working the beds in the river tong approximately 15,000 bushels of oysters from the Rappahannock each day of the oyster season. The entire economy of the area is tied in with the oyster industry, and an oyster killer would seriously affect the income of a large number of workers."

Certain Beds Favored

"Tiny oysters — or spats — are born and grow initially at their best in certain beds, as in the lower James. But later, the small oyster — the seed — is transplanted and thrives in other beds. The Rappahannock is usually a highly favorable environment."

"Oysters require three years to mature. Those planted this year will be tonged and sold in 1963, if they are still alive."

"There's the gamble. The oysterman now is faced with the decision of whether it is worth the risk to plant for a crop he may not harvest."

EXHIBIT 2 concluded

"Last March, two Norfolk oyster firms — the two largest in Virginia — stopped buying and planting seed oysters."

"And while many Rappahannock River watermen are optimistic about the future of the oyster industry, some have followed the Norfolk firm's example."

"J. W. Ferguson of Remlik, an oysterman who also operates one of the largest packing firms on the Rappahannock, said, 'I'm being cautious this year. I've only planted about 4,000 bushels of seed so far this year.' In a normal year, Ferguson said he plants about 50,000 bushels."

"Ferguson said he felt the quantity of seed oysters planted by Virginia oystermen this season will depend to a large extent on prices demanded for seed by James River tongers."

"Under the present risk, 60 cents a bushel is the top price which planters can afford to pay, he said."

"This is almost bottom price. The tongers want $1 or more per bushel, and the James River Tongers Association is considering asking the Virginia Commission of Fisheries to relax the law prohibiting the sale of seed oysters outside the state in order to boost the seed market price."

"The Rappahannock oyster planters argue that the tongers should bear some of the risk, too. R. H. Woodward of Middlesex County, president of the Virginia Oyster Planters Association, said 'I think most planters will agree that 60 cents is the top price which can be paid for seed under present conditions.' "

"Woodward said he felt that most planters would agree to a suggested plan of paying the tongers 40 cents a bushel and putting an additional 60 cents per bushel into a bank fund. If the planter made a profit from the seed, the extra 60 cents would be paid to the tongers, said Woodward, and if the seed died, the extra money would help the planter cover his loss."

"Ferguson said he believes firmly that the oyster industry will survive the MSX crisis."

" 'The next generation won't ever remember this thing we call MSX,' he said. 'And my guess is that oysters will soon build an immunity to it and which will make it run out long before we begin to run out of oysters.' "

"Other Rappahannock River oystermen also continue planting."

" 'We'll just take the chance on MSX,' said F. S. Garret, Jr., of Bowlers Wharf in Essex County, one of the river's largest planters. 'We can't say we were not warned, but in this business you have to keep re-planting or get out.' "

Answers to Specific Questions on Cans and Shells (as of the time of the case)

I. Do the oyster houses buy enough cans for a season at one clip, or do they buy little by little through the season?

Packers do not generally order enough cans for a season but do give the supplier an estimate of the need. In some cases the cans have to be lithographed to show the brand and in all instances the packer's number has to appear on the lid. For this reason the packer must keep the supplier informed well in advance of his needs. The majority would not have adequate storage place for a season's supply.

II. Will a bushel of shells bring 13 cents? Are the shells a salable item, or are they hard to move?

Shells are readily salable on the shellpile at some 12–14 cents per bushel, the variance in the price being largely dependent upon where the purchaser proposes to use them. The majority of the shells are purchased by the state and are put on the public oyster bottom, that is to say, bottom within the Baylor survey. It costs the planter an additional 6 cents per bushel to load and plant the shells so that the cost to the planter on the bottom is approximately 20 cents per bushel. These are planted for the purpose of making available material on which the spat can catch, thereby creating the strike.

The second reason for choosing this size was that the Laws' oyster grounds would provide about 20,000 bushels of the estimated practical capacity of 35,000 bushels per season. If the plant were larger, they would have to rely more heavily on the tongers to fill out capacity. On this subject, Harry Law commented, "We don't want to get too large, because we want to use our oysters when we can't get rock oysters."

A local contractor estimated that the building would cost about $18,000. The equipment required would run about $4,000.

Consideration was given to taking over Johnson's trucking business to provide some initial customers. If so, the company would pay Johnson $3,100 for his truck and hire his driver to make deliveries and serve as a general handyman around the plant.

Next, the three estimated the operating costs and expenses that would be incurred, based on their experience and the information they had been able to gather. They knew that cans would cost 25¢ per gallon but had to estimate the other expenses for such things as electricity, telephone, gas and oil, and so on. These, they thought, would run about $150 per week for the seven-month, 30-week season.[6]

The salaries, to be paid only during the season, would be as follows:

Manager (Johnson)	$80.00 per week
Truck driver	$80.00 per week
Blowing room operator	$60.00 per week
Oyster carrier	$50.00 per week

The Laws made no provision for paying themselves salaries, although they thought that each would have to put in at least one day per week at the plant on business matters, plus some time on day-to-day operating decisions.

Finally, the Law brothers and Johnson discussed how they would set up and finance the business if it looked like a good venture. They decided that if they went into the venture they would incorporate and elect to be taxed as a partnership under Subchapter S of the Internal Revenue Code. Harry Law pointed out, "We would incorporate for two reasons: limited liability and divisibility in the case of death."[7] Since they would draw virtually all of the earnings out of the business, the tax election would avoid double taxation on the profits.

To finance the business they intended to borrow as much as possible from the local bank. John Law said, "We're pretty sure we can get a 10-year mortgage on the fixed assets[8] for about 50 percent of their value. We would have to put up the rest."

Other Considerations

In speaking of his views on the proposal, Harry Law said that he had been thinking for a number of years that such a move would be advantageous. "We will be paid the same amount for our shell stock and anything the packing business makes will be just gravy. John and I have discussed the matter from time to time, but neither of us has wanted to take the supervision job nor, up to now, had we found anyone we felt we could rely on to do a good job for us. The manager's job requires a lot of knowledge of the business, long hours, and the ability to deal effectively with the tongers, shuckers, and buyers. Without Johnson's interest, we probably would not now be seriously considering the plan."

John Law said he had two main thoughts on the matter. "Since he (Johnson) has been here for 20 years, I would be doubly interested in any business proposition that would help him as well as us. He has done a splendid job operating our boat and managing the planting and harvesting of our oysters. We would be willing to assume new business risks with Johnson that we wouldn't assume with others because of our past successful relationship. We hope we can work out something with him. We don't want him to go in with someone else.

"Secondly, since there is no exact market for shell stock (a bushel of shell stock is inexact because it shucks out differently and therefore brings a different price), the one way that buyer and seller can know best what they are doing is to sell 'em on the meats. To do this,

[6]As was customary, they would also have to operate a small store for the shuckers who bought their lunches at the plant. This store would carry bread, canned meats, beans, cigarettes, candy, and so on, but the Laws did not expect it to have a substantial effect on profit.

[7]All three men were in their fifties.

[8]Except the truck.

each jag (boatload) has to be separated. Then you are dependent on your shucking house to be honest with you. Also, a shucker who shucks on a piece-rate basis might push aside the small oysters. There is less pressure on the shucking house to be efficient in keeping jags separated and in preventing the shuckers from passing over the small ones when it is buying on the meats.

"When you sell this way, you are subject to such errors. By selling to ourselves, I feel we could eliminate some of these errors.

"Another thing. Seafood prices change rather rapidly according to supply and demand. There is no quoted price in the paper or anything. When an Indian summer comes along, the price of a gallon may drop 50 cents or a dollar.[9] As a planter you don't keep up with the market as well. I think sometimes the shucking houses don't reflect a rising market in their buying prices as quickly as they do when prices are off. At any rate I think we can eliminate this uncertainty."

There were some deterrent factors that the Laws considered. The most important of these was the serious blight that had hit the Delaware Bay area, cutting production there in half from 1957 to 1958. There were indications that the 1959 crop in the Delaware Bay would be almost completely destroyed. This blight had not as yet been found in the Chesapeake Bay growing areas, but it had made its appearance on the ocean side of the Eastern Shore. There was a possibility that if the blight got into the Chesapeake, the whole industry would be out of business indefinitely.

Secondly, a branch of the AFL-CIO had been attempting to organize the fishing industry in the area. Indications were that attempts would be made to organize the shuckers also. The latter had not had a raise in pay for seven or eight years in spite of the large increase in retail prices over the same period.

Lastly, the Laws knew that competition in the area for the public rock catch would be strong, particularly when the demand was high.

Required:

a. Let us suppose the two Law brothers forecast that the minimum volume the business would handle in the first year would be the 20,000 bushels from themselves plus 5,000 bushels from tongers. Does this seem a reasonable assumption? Let's suppose further that they projected transactions as noted below. Do these seem reasonable? If you think any are questionable, note and supply alternatives.

[9]Unseasonably warm weather brought a marked decrease in the demand for oysters.

		Prior to 10/1/59		10/1/59 to 4/15/60, incl.
Stockholders pay in cash for capital stock	(A)	26,500		—
Receive cash from bank for $12,500 6% 10-year mortgage	(B)	12,500		—
Pay cash for property, plant, and equipment	(C)	30,000		—
Pay cash for oysters bought from John and Harry Law:				
4,000 bu. @ $2.75,	(D)	11,000		
and 16,000 @ $2.75		—	(N)	44,000
Pay cash for oysters bought from tongers: 5,000 bu. @ $3.25		—	(O)	16,250
Pay shuckers @ $1 per gallon:				
3,700 bu. @ 70% equals 2,590 gals.	(E)	2,590		
16,300 bu. @ 70% equals 11,410 gals.		—	(P)	15,160
5,000 bu. @ 75% equals 3,750 gals.				
Pay salaries @ $270 a week	(F)	1,080	(Q)	7,020
Pay for cans @ 25¢, 8,000 and 13,300, respectively	(G)	2,000	(R)	3,325
Pay for elec., tel., gas & oil, etc.	(H)	600	(S)	3,900
Sell oysters @ $5.50 average price:				
In Sept., 2,590 gals. @ 120% = 3,108 gals. less 308 unsold at Sept. 30	(I)	15,400		—
After Sept., 15,160 gals. @ 120% = 18,192 gals. plus 308 unsold at Sept. 30		—	(T)	101,750
Cost of oysters sold:				
2,800 gals @ 4.357	(J)	12,200		—
18,500 gals.		—	(U)	82,125
Receive on account	(K)	9,400	(V)	107,750
Shell pile developed: 3,700 @ 13¢	(L)	481		
21,300 @ 13¢		—	(W)	2,769
Sell shells for cash		—	(X)	3,250
Pay semi-annual installment on mortgage (12,500 ÷ 14.87747486 = 840.20)				
Interest $375, on principal, $465		—	(Y)	840
Recognize depreciation on buildings and equipment	(M)	150	(Z)	900
Pay dividends to stockholders		—		—

b. Pick out of the transactions above those that involve receiving or paying cash, and prepare a projected summary of cash receipts and disbursements with three columns headed:

1st column — "Prior to 10/1/59"
2nd column — "10/1/59 to 4/15/60"
3rd column — "Total"

What conclusions can you draw from this statement?

c. Prepare the entries for transactions *A* through *M* occurring in the period prior to 10/1/59. (Note: Enter all costs of oysters, shucking, and cans in the inventories account.)

d. Enter the transactions into T-accounts:

Cash on hand and in bank
Accounts receivable
Inventories of oysters in shells, shucked oysters, canned oysters, cans, and oyster shells
Property, plant, and equipment
Mortgage payable
Capital stock
Retained earnings

e. Determine the balance of each T-account.

f. Prepare entries for transactions *N* through *Z,* for the period of 10/1/59 to 4/15/60, and post to the T-accounts.

g. Prepare a trial balance of the T-accounts as of 4/15/60.

h. Prepare a projected income statement for the period from the beginning of business through April 15, 1960.

i. What does the projected income statement show that the projected cash receipts and disbursements summary does not? And vice versa?

j. Let's suppose now that the two Law brothers forecast that the business might buy 10,000 more bushels from tongers in the first year. How much would revenue change? How much would expenses change? How much net profit?

k. Should the two Law brothers go into the venture? What risks would they be taking? What problems are they likely to have?

C3.5(A) Starting a new business: Garden Center, Inc.* In January of 1990 Mary Jane Bowers was reviewing her plans for the April 1 opening of a garden center in Lynchburg, Virginia. She and her husband John had selected Lynchburg as their new home after they decided to leave the large northern city where they had both worked for the prior 10 years. Mary Jane had a degree in horticulture and had worked for a large chemical company in its agricultural herbicide division. Consistent with the decision to change their locale, Mary Jane decided to change her work status as well. She decided that she would devote her working day to her real love and go into business for herself with a retail garden store selling plants, trees, and shrubs.

Mary Jane accumulated information on retail garden stores from a number of sources, talked to suppliers, looked at potential locations, and established a banking relationship with the Campbell National Bank. Mary Jane wanted to make sure that she had enough money to get the business off to a good start. She had heard that many small businesses failed because they were undercapitalized.

After careful study and analysis, Mary Jane made the following projections for the first year of operations of The Garden Center, Inc.:

1. April 1, 1990 — The business would be incorporated and Mary Jane and John would buy $30,000 of capital stock.
2. April 1, 1990 — The Campbell National Bank would loan the Garden Center, Inc., $16,000 to be repaid in equal principal payments over four years. The interest rate was 13 percent, payable at the end of each year when the principal payment was made.
3. April 1, 1990 — A pickup truck would be purchased for $6,000, $5,000 of which was to be financed by the Campbell National Bank. The loan would be repaid over three years at the rate of $168 per month for a total of $6,050.
4. April 1, 1990 — Purchase display equipment for $3,000 cash.
5. April 1, 1990 — Purchase a rototiller for $200 cash.
6. April 1, 1990 — Purchase a cash register for $1,800 cash.
7. April 1, 1990 — Purchase inventory of plants, trees, and shrubs for $30,000 cash.

---

*This material was prepared by C. Ray Smith, Professor of Business Administration. Rev. 9/93.

8. The following transactions were projected between April 1, 1990, and March 31, 1991:

Cash sales	$170,000
Sales on account	30,000

9. Additional purchases of plants, trees, and shrubs for $100,000. Mary Jane planned to price all items to give her a 40 percent gross margin; that is, if an item cost $6.00, it would sell for $10.00.

10. Advertising expenses were projected at 5 percent of sales or $10,000 for the year.

11. Mary Jane categorized a group of expenses as ongoing. They were projected as follows:

Rent	$3,600 ($300 per month)
Telephone	$600 ($50 per month)
Utilities	$2,400 ($200 per month)
Payroll	$56,000 ($20,000 for Mary Jane and $36,000 for three regular and four part time employees)

12. Monthly payments of $168 were to be made on the truck loan described in item 3.

13. Principal payment of $4,000 was to be made on the bank loan described in item 2 with interest of $2,080.

Required:

a. Prepare entries for items 1–13.

b. Post to T-accounts.

c. Prepare a projected balance sheet as of the end of the day on April 1, 1990.

d. Prepare a summary of projected cash receipts and disbursements for the period April 1, 1990, to March 31, 1991.

e. How much profit (approximately) do you think Mary Jane will make in her first year of business if things go as planned?

f. Make a list of the additional information you think you need to prepare a projected income statement for the year ending March 31, 1991, and a balance sheet as of March 31, 1991. Why do you need the information?

g. What will be the break-even point in sales dollars for The Garden Center, Inc.?

C3.5(B) Starting a new business: Garden Center, Inc. — one year later.* Mary Jane Bowers opened The Garden Center, Inc., as planned on April 1, 1990. She believed the first year had been good, and in mid-April 1991 she was considering expanding her product line to include fertilizer, tools, and other garden accessories. She thought she might need an additional loan, however, if she decided to expand. With that idea in mind, she decided to prepare an income statement and balance sheet for the year just completed in order to get a clear picture of her actual progress and to show to the bank if she had to seek additional financing.

Certain events presented in the C3.5(A) Garden Center case did, in fact, come to pass as forecast — those numbered 1, 3, 4, 5, and 6. These transactions have been posted to the T-accounts in Exhibit 1. In addition, the following information had been accumulated as of April 15, 1991, from the company's checkbook, sales records, purchase records, payroll records, and notes Mary Jane had written to herself as the year had progressed:

*Case prepared by Mark E. Haskins and C. Ray Smith. Rev. 9/93.

1. Sales for the year were $210,000, broken down as follows:

Cash sales	$100,000
Sales on account	$30,000
Multibank charge card	$80,000

(The bank deducted 2% from the charge card sales; Mary Jane had received $78,400 deposited to her bank account.)

2. The $16,000 bank loan was not received until July 1.

3. She purchased a pocket calculator for $72 cash.

4. A total of $158,000 of plants, shrubs, and trees was purchased during the year. Mary Jane took an inventory on March 31, 1991, and figured that the salable merchandise still on hand had cost $32,000. During the year, she had to throw away items that cost her $6,000 because they died.

5. Advertising expenses were $11,000, paid in cash.

6. Ongoing expenses paid in cash turned out to be as follows:

Rent	$ 3,600
Telephone	500
Utilities	3,000
Payroll	$54,000 (including $20,000 for Mary Jane)

The employees had actually been paid $46,000; $8,000 had been withheld for income and Social Security taxes. Of the $8,000 withheld, $7,200 had been paid, and $800 was still owed to the U.S. government.

In addition, Mary Jane discovered certain payroll-related expenses. The company paid $2,815 in Social Security taxes and $785 in unemployment taxes.

7. Twelve monthly payments of $168 each had been made on the truck loan. According to information from the bank, the interest was $577 for the first year, $350 the second year, and $123 the third year.

8. Mary Jane figured that her equipment would have a life as follows:

   a. Rototiller, 2 years

   b. Truck, 4 years

   c. Display cases, 10 years

   d. Cash register, 10 years

The following events were noted by Mary Jane. She wasn't sure how to handle them.

9. She would have to make the principal payment of $4,000 and interest of $2,080 on June 30, 1991, rather than March 31, 1991, as originally planned.

10. She had purchased a three-year liability insurance policy on April 2, 1990, for $330.

11. She still owed $10,000 to suppliers for plants and other materials that had been purchased.

12. $10,000 of the sales on account had not been collected. One landscape contractor who owed her $800 had gone bankrupt. (Assume the $800 is included in the $10,000 that remains uncollected at 3/31/91.)

13. On September 30, 1990, she had entered into a purchase contract with one of her suppliers to purchase $30,000 of small house plants during the following year. By making this commitment, she was guaranteed one-day delivery, top-quality plants, and a reduced price.

14. On March 31, 1991, she signed a five-year lease agreement for the building space that she rented. The annual rent would be $3,600.

15. One of her large contractor customers had paid her $1,800 in advance on March 1 for azaleas to be delivered in June.

16. On February 1, 1991, Mary Jane had purchased a $10,000-face-value U.S. Treasury bill that would mature on May 1. She had paid $9,850 for the Treasury bill.

17. The Garden Center guaranteed its trees and shrubs for one year if properly planted. To date, no items had been replaced.

18. Federal income taxes were 17 percent on the first $25,000 of income and (assume) 46 percent on all income over $25,000. State income taxes were 5 percent of the income reported on the federal tax return.

Required:

a. Prepare entries for items 1–18.

b. Post the entries to the T-accounts in Exhibit 1.

c. Prepare the trial balance in Exhibit 2.

d. Prepare a summary of cash receipts and disbursements in Exhibit 3.

e. Prepare the income statement for the fiscal year through March 31, 1991, in Exhibit 4.

f. Prepare the balance sheet for March 31, 1991, in Exhibit 5.

g. Explain the differences between the income statement and the statement of cash receipts and disbursements.

h. How well did Mary Jane do in her first year of operations? What advice do you have for her as she enters her second year?

EXHIBIT 1

The Garden Center, Inc. — One Year Later

T-Accounts

Cash (A)

(a)	30,000*	(b)	1,000*
		(c)	3,000*
		(c)	200*
		(c)	1,800*

Inventory (A)

Treasury Bill (A)

Accounts Receivable (A)

Interest Receivable (A)

Prepaid Insurance (A)

Equipment (Net) (A)

(b)	6,000*		
(c)	3,000*		
(c)	200*		
(c)	1,800*		

Customer Advance (L)

Accounts Payable (L)

Interest Payable (L)

Payroll Taxes Withheld (L)

Income Taxes Payable (L)

Loan Payable (Truck) (L)

		(b)	5,000*

Loan Payable (4 year) (L)

Capital Stock (OE)

		(a)	30,000*

Retained Earnings (OE)**

*As presented in the previous case.

**Because there are so few entries, record all of the Garden Center's revenue and expense transactions in the Retained Earnings account, providing appropriate descriptive labels.

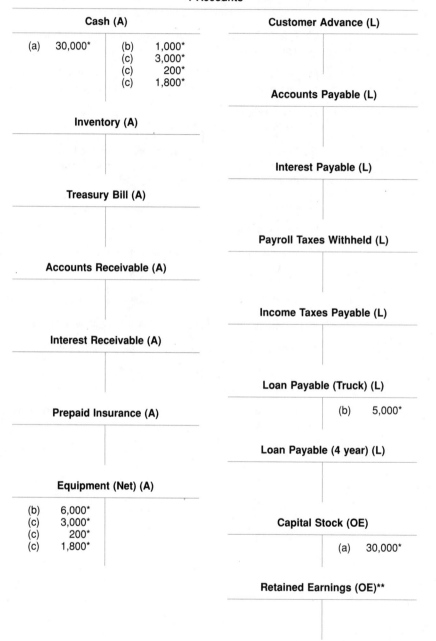

EXHIBIT 2

The Garden Center, Inc. — One Year Later

Trial Balance
(March 31, 1991)

	Debit (Left-Side)	Credit (Right-Side)
Cash		
Treasury bill		
Accounts receivable		
Inventory		
Prepaid insurance		
Interest receivable		
Equipment (net)		
Customer advance		
Accounts payable		
Interest payable		
Payroll taxes withheld		
Income taxes payable		
Loan payable (truck)		
Loan payable (4 year)		
Capital stock		
Retained earnings		
Total		

EXHIBIT 3

The Garden Center, Inc. — One Year Later

Summary of Cash Receipts and Disbursements
(for the year ending March 31, 1991)

Beginning cash balance	–0–
Plus cash receipts	
Less cash disbursements	
Ending cash balance	

EXHIBIT 4

The Garden Center, Inc. — One Year Later

Income Statement
(for the year ended March 31, 1991)

Sales	
Interest income	
Total revenue	
Cost of Goods Sold	
Gross margin	
Credit card charges	
Interest	
Depreciation	
Advertising	
Rent	
Telephone	
Utilities	
Wages and salaries	
Payroll taxes	
Insurance	
Uncollectible accounts	
Miscellaneous	
Total expenses	
Income before income taxes	
Income taxes	
Net Income	

EXHIBIT 5

The Garden Center, Inc. — One Year Later

Balance Sheet
(March 31, 1991)

Assets		
Current assets		
Cash		
Treasury bills		
Accounts receivable		
Inventory		
Prepaid insurance		
Interest receivable		
Total current assets		
Other assets		
Equipment (net)		
Total Assets		
Liabilities and Owners' Equity		
Current liabilities		
Customer advance		
Accounts payable		
Interest payable		
Payroll taxes withheld		
Income taxes payable		
Loans payable		
Total current liabilities		
Other liabilities		
Loan payable		
Total liabilities		
Owners' Equity		
Capital stock		
Retained earnings		
Total owners' equity		
Total Liabilities and Owners' Equity		

PART II

Using and Understanding the Basic Financial Statements

CHAPTER 4

The Balance Sheet

The importance of the contents of a company's balance sheet cannot be overemphasized. One of the key characteristics that I look for in a potential acquisition is a company whose stock price does not fully reflect the underlying economic value of its operating assets.[1]

Key Chapter Issues

- What is the balance sheet, and what are its principal elements?
- What are the key accounting concepts and conventions underlying the balance sheet?
- What are the principal methods of valuing a company's assets, liabilities, and shareholders' equity?
- What information does a balance sheet convey about a company's financial health?

[1]Harold C. Simmons, President and CEO, Valhi, Inc.

As defined in Chapter 2, the **balance sheet,** or statement of financial position, is an accounting report that summarizes the assets a company owned, the liabilities it owed, and the owners' investment — their original investment and that share of prior years' earnings that have been left with the company. The balance sheet may be thought of as a photograph of the financial status and condition of a company. The balance sheet, like a photograph, depicts the assets and the equities of a company *as of* a particular date. To appreciate fully the photograph's color, texture, and tone — that is, to understand the complete image in that picture — the financial statement user must understand the specific elements that compose the balance sheet and how these elements are related. That understanding is the focus of this chapter.

THE ELEMENTS OF THE BALANCE SHEET

The principal elements of a company's balance sheet are its assets, liabilities, and shareholders' (or owners') equity. To provide a context for the discussion of these elements, we will refer to Exhibit 4.1, which presents PepsiCo's consolidated statement of financial condition for 1994 with comparative data for 1993. This statement details the year-end balances for each of PepsiCo's principal asset accounts, as well as the principal creditor and owner claims on those assets.

We have said that a balance sheet presents a picture of a company's financial status at a given point in time. Theoretically, a balance sheet could be prepared as of any day of the year. Most companies monitor individual elements of their balance sheet on a daily or weekly basis, but normally the complete financial picture is taken only as of a month-end, a quarter-end, or a year-end. Most companies use a calendar year for their accounting reports, but they are not required to do so. In fact, it is often more logical to use a different 12-month period, referred to as a **fiscal year,** ending after a business peak. Many retail companies, for example, use a fiscal year that ends in February or March because December and January are significant trade periods. As an example, Circuit City Stores, Inc., the largest consumer electronics retail chain in the United States, uses a fiscal year ending on the last day of February. PepsiCo, on the other hand, divides its fiscal year into 13 four-week periods, and so, of course, every so often the company must have a 53-week year.

Assets: A Company's Resources

A company's assets are the resources that it owns and that provide future economic benefit to the company (that is, can be deployed to generate a profit). Exhibit 4.1 reveals that PepsiCo had more than $24,792.0 million in assets as of December 31, 1994, placing it 21st in the Fortune 500 asset rankings. PepsiCo's five principal asset categories are:

- Current assets
- Investment in affiliates
- Property, plant, and equipment, net
- Intangible assets, net
- Other assets

PepsiCo's **current assets** include the assets that the company expects to sell or consume as part of its operations during the next year. These assets include cash and cash equivalents, short-term investments, accounts and notes receivable, inventories, prepaid expenses, taxes, and any miscellaneous current assets. The order of

EXHIBIT 4.1

PepsiCo, Inc.
Consolidated Balance Sheet
December 31, 1994, and December 25, 1993
(in millions except per share amount)

	1994	1993
ASSETS		
Current Assets		
Cash and cash equivalents	$ 330.7	$ 226.9
Short-term investments, at cost	1,157.4	1,573.8
	1,488.1	1,800.7
Accounts and notes receivable, less allowance: $150.6 in 1994 and $128.3 in 1993	2,050.9	1,883.4
Inventories	970.0	924.7
Prepaid expenses, taxes, and other current assets	563.2	499.8
Total Current Assets	5,072.2	5,108.6
Investments in Affiliates	1,295.2	1,090.5
Property, Plant, and Equipment, net	9,882.8	8,855.6
Intangible Assets, net	7,842.1	7,929.5
Other Assets	699.7	721.6
Total Assets	$24,792.0	$23,705.8
LIABILITIES AND SHAREHOLDERS' EQUITY		
Current Liabilities		
Accounts payable	$ 1,451.6	$ 1,390.0
Accrued compensation and benefits	753.5	726.0
Short-term borrowings	678.5	2,191.2
Income taxes payable	671.7	823.7
Accrued marketing	546.2	400.9
Other current liabilities	1,168.9	1,043.1
Total Current Liabilities	5,270.4	6,574.9
Long-Term Debt	8,840.5	7,442.6
Other Liabilities	1,852.1	1,342.0
Deferred Income Taxes	1,972.9	2,007.6
Shareholders' Equity		
Capital stock, par value 1⅔¢ per share: authorized 1,800.0 shares, issued 863.1 shares	14.4	14.4
Capital in excess of par value	934.4	879.5
Retained earnings	7,739.1	6,541.9
Currency translation adjustment and other	(470.6)	(183.9)
	8,217.3	7,251.9
Less: Treasury stock, at cost: 73.2 shares and 64.3 shares in 1994 and 1993, respectively	(1,361.2)	(913.2)
Total Shareholders' Equity	6,856.1	6,338.7
Total Liabilities and Shareholders' Equity	$24,792.0	$23,705.8

presentation of the current assets is intended to inform the reader of the relative liquidity of the assets. Thus, the most liquid current asset is cash, whereas the least liquid is the prepaid expenses. In the U.S. this format of most-to-least liquid is also followed for the asset category as a whole. Thus, the most liquid assets are listed first with the least liquid assets listed last. Just the reverse order is sometimes used in other countries (for example, Germany).

The item **cash and cash equivalents** refers to funds held in corporate bank accounts, cash on hand at various company locations, and cash invested in short-term financial instruments, such as certificates of deposit. **Short-term investments,** on the other hand, are temporary, highly marketable investments that PepsiCo has in stocks and/or bonds of other companies, such as IBM or AT&T. When a company has a temporary surplus of cash on hand, it may invest these funds in short-term investments to maximize the return on those funds until they are again needed for operations. Because these short-term investments are readily converted to cash, they are frequently aggregated with cash and cash equivalents and called the **liquid assets** of a company. (PepsiCo subtotals its liquid assets — $1,488.1 million in 1994 — but does not label them as such.) These liquid assets include cash and other assets that can be readily converted to cash.

The item **accounts and notes receivable** represents the amounts owed to PepsiCo by its customers who purchased the company's products on credit but had not, as of year-end, paid for those purchases. Accounts receivable are also frequently called **trade receivables** and usually represent sales whose payments are expected in 30, 60, or 90 days after the customer has received the goods and been billed for them. Notes receivable, on the other hand, represent credit sales whose payments are usually not expected within 90 days; because of the large amount of money involved, the amount owed is formally stated in a contractual agreement to pay (that is, a "note"). Under GAAP, sales involving accounts or notes receivable are recognized as revenues earned that period following the **accrual method;** that is, the sale is recorded because the selling company has completed its part of the sale transaction and expects to be paid. The asset received in exchange for the goods delivered is a promise to be paid, and thus a receivable is recorded by the selling company. In accounting entry form the application of this concept can be illustrated as follows:

Dr. Accounts Receivable (A)	(inc.) $10,000	
Cr. Sales (R)		(inc.) $10,000

At the time of sale, the receivables are recorded at the cash equivalency that PepsiCo expects to receive from the credit sale. When companies make an individual sale on credit, they fully expect to collect the cash. Realistically, however, management also knows that some part of the total receivables yet to be collected will prove to be uncollectible. Therefore, an amount reflecting this estimated uncollectible portion, called the **allowance for uncollectible accounts,** is recorded as a contra asset and deducted from the receivable balance reported on the balance sheet. Because management knows that the uncollectible accounts estimate pertains to credit sales already recorded as revenue, the **matching principle** requires that the current period's operating results include an estimate of the cost of that loss, called the **bad debts expense.** Together, these two important concepts can be illustrated with the following single entry:

Dr. Bad Debts Expense (E)	(inc.) $2,000	
Cr. Allowance for Uncollectible Accounts (CA)		(inc.) $2,000

Looking at the current asset section of PepsiCo's balance sheet, we can see how the effects of these concepts are disclosed on the balance sheet:

	1994	1993
Current Assets		
Cash and cash equivalents	$ 303.7	$ 226.9
Short-term investments, at cost	1,157.4	1,573.8
	1,488.1	1,800.7
Accounts and notes receivable, less allowance: $150.6 in 1994 and $128.3 in 1993	2,050.9	1,883.4
Inventories	970.0	924.7
Prepaid expenses, taxes, and other current assets	563.2	499.8
Total Current Assets	5,072.2	5,108.6

Note that the allowance account is netted against the outstanding balance of accounts and notes receivable — a common financial disclosure practice.

The item **inventories** refers to the aggregate cost of the salable merchandise owned by PepsiCo that is available to meet customer demands. PepsiCo's footnotes reveal that the Inventory account includes amounts for raw materials (such as sugar) and supplies (such as cartons) as well as finished goods (such as Pepsi concentrate in barrels ready to ship to bottlers). Inventory is recorded on the company's books at its cost, namely the price paid to suppliers plus any additional costs incurred to date to convert the inventory materials or supplies into a final salable condition (or its net realizable value, if lower). The difference between the aggregate cost of the finished goods available for sale and the expected sales price represents PepsiCo's potential profit, which under GAAP is not recorded in the financial statements until the merchandise has actually been sold.

The final item in the current assets section of the balance sheet is **prepaid expenses.** These assets involve expenditures for the prepayment of such items as rent, insurance, or taxes. Some contractual arrangements (such as rent and insurance) often require payment in advance; in other arrangements, prepayments may earn certain price discounts from suppliers and therefore simply make good business sense. In either case, prepaid expenses represent past cash outflows for which the company expects to receive some future benefit. Following the allocation principle, which we discussed in Chapter 2, that prepayment will be removed from the asset account and charged to an expense account over time as the future benefits are realized.

Although a portion of PepsiCo's assets are clearly identified as *current,* by inference the remaining assets are considered *noncurrent.* Because of the delineation between current and noncurrent assets (and liabilities), PepsiCo's balance sheet can be said to be a **classified balance sheet.** That delineation, however, is not required in all cases, and when no delineation of current and noncurrent assets (or liabilities) exists, the balance sheet is considered to be an **unclassified balance sheet.** The decision to present a classified balance sheet or an unclassified balance sheet is usually tied to the company's **operating cycle.** If the company's operating cycle — that is, the period of time between beginning production of a product and collecting the proceeds from the sale of a finished product — is less than one year, a classified balance sheet is prepared. An unclassified balance sheet is often used by companies whose operating cycle is longer than one year (for example, a winery, a timber company, a real estate development company, or an insurance company).

Noncurrent assets are a company's long-lived resources whose consumption or use will take place over more than one accounting period. These assets are frequently segmented into tangible and intangible assets. **Tangible assets,** like property, plant, and equipment, possess identifiable physical characteristics, whereas intangible assets, like goodwill, do not. Nonetheless, both tangible and intangible assets possess revenue-producing characteristics that make them valuable to a company over future periods.

Among PepsiCo's noncurrent assets are investments in affiliates; property, plant, and equipment; intangible assets; and other assets. From Exhibit 4.1, these noncurrent assets are disclosed as follows:

	1994	1993
Investments in Affiliates	$1,295.2	$1,090.5
Property, Plant, and Equipment, net	9,882.8	8,855.6
Intangible Assets, net	7,842.1	7,929.5
Other Assets	699.7	721.6

Long-term investments involve investments in other companies' stocks or bonds that will be maintained for longer than just the coming year. For example, PepsiCo's footnotes reveal that in 1993 it entered into a joint venture with the shareholders of Buenos Aires Embotelladora S.A., a franchised Pepsi bottler with operations in Argentina and Costa Rica. This investment, along with others made in 1994 in companies operating in China, India, Mexico, and Thailand, is summarized in the Investments in Affiliates. PepsiCo considers an "affiliate" to be any company in which it holds a sufficiently large long-term investment to be able to influence the affiliate's decision making, but not so large as to represent a controlling interest (that is, greater than 50 percent of the outstanding voting shares). **Property, plant, and equipment,** on the other hand, are those long-lived, tangible assets necessary to conduct a company's basic business operations. For a company such as PepsiCo, this category includes its manufacturing equipment and facilities, storage equipment, and vehicles. These assets are often called the **fixed assets** of a company. Like inventory, a company's fixed assets are an integral part of its basic operations, but they differ from inventory in two important respects. First, property, plant, and equipment are not owned for the purpose of being sold to customers. Second, these assets are expected to benefit PepsiCo's operations for many years. Because of the extended productive life of these assets, the company's cost of property, plant, and equipment is expensed over the assets' expected useful lives rather than totally in the year of acquisition.

The process of allocating a fixed asset's cost over various years is called **depreciation** and is based on the allocation principle discussed in Chapter 2. When an asset is depreciated, a portion of its original cost is charged to expense, and the other side of the entry increases a contra asset account. As you will remember from the discussion of Blue Ridge Hardware in Chapter 3, many financial statement users want to know the original cost of plant and equipment; hence, the annual depreciation charge is not deducted from the asset account directly but rather is accumulated in a contra asset (CA) account. The contra asset account is presented on the asset side of the balance sheet but usually carries a credit balance.

The actual accounting entry for depreciation expense appears as follows:

Dr. Depreciation Expense (E)	(inc.) 30,000	
Cr. Accumulated Depreciation (CA)		(inc.) 30,000

As reported on the balance sheet, **accumulated depreciation** includes not only the current period's charge to expense but also that portion of the asset's cost that has been allocated (that is, expensed) in prior accounting periods. The Accumulated Depreciation account balance is deducted from the Property, Plant, and Equipment account balance in reporting the net fixed assets in the balance sheet. The original cost of an asset less the balance in the Accumulated Depreciation account is called the **net book value** or carrying value of the asset. A review of PepsiCo's footnotes reveals that the acquisition cost of its property, plant, and equipment was $16,130.1 million as of December 31, 1994, and the accumulated depreciation as of that date was $6,247.3 million. Only the net book value of these assets (that is, $9,882.8 million) is included in the company's total assets.

We will have more to say about the accounting for property, plant, and equipment and about the process of depreciation in Chapter 11. At this point, however, it is perhaps helpful to emphasize that accounting for depreciation is intended *only* as a process to allocate prior expenditures to future periods. From an economic standpoint, plant and equipment lose *and* gain value over time as a result of a wide variety of factors. As we noted in our discussion of the historical cost principle in Chapter 2, U.S. GAAP accounting is based on original costs and thus does not deal with day-to-day, year-to-year changes in *market values*.[2] Hence, the financial statements do not reflect the impact that economic effects such as new technologies or increased market demand might have on the values of a company's plant and equipment. Again, depreciation is simply the process of allocating the original cost of an asset over the future periods expected to benefit from that earlier investment.

Intangible assets refer to a group of economic resources, usually lacking identifiable physical characteristics but possessing significant revenue-producing characteristics. PepsiCo's footnotes indicate that this asset category includes reacquired franchise rights, trademarks and tradenames, and goodwill. In the context of accounting, *goodwill* does *not* refer to a company's favorable or positive consumer image or to the costs PepsiCo incurred for constructive environmental or societal projects. Instead, **goodwill** indicates that PepsiCo previously acquired one or more companies for a purchase price in excess of the *fair market value* of the acquired company's net assets (that is, its total assets minus total liabilities). Thinking about PepsiCo's acquisition program, we can see how the company might have purchased a substantial amount of goodwill by paying a premium for its acquisition of the well-established, successful Kentucky Fried Chicken and Pizza Hut franchises. Like property, plant, and equipment, the cost of goodwill and other intangible assets is normally allocated over the expected useful life of these assets. The process of allocating the cost of an intangible asset over its useful life is called **amortization.**

The final noncurrent asset category is **other assets,** which represent an aggregation of miscellaneous assets that are, individually, immaterial in amount.

Liabilities: A Company's Obligations

As defined in Chapter 2, the liabilities of a company are the dollar measures of its obligations to repay money loaned to it, to pay for goods or services it has received, or to fulfill commitments it has made. In essence, a company's liabilities represent claims

[2]In Chapter 11 we will learn that in some countries, like the United Kingdom, the balance sheet value of property, plant, and equipment may be adjusted upward to reflect its current market value.

on its assets. As with assets, it is convenient to aggregate liabilities into current and noncurrent categories, which delineate the expected repayment period for the liability. Thus, a **current liability** is an obligation due during the next operating cycle or the next year, whichever is longer. A **noncurrent liability** is one that will be paid at some future point in time beyond the next operating cycle or year.

PepsiCo's balance sheet shows that the company has four principal liability categories:

- Current Liabilities
- Long-Term Debt
- Other Liabilities
- Deferred Income Taxes

Within the current liabilities category, PepsiCo discloses six different items: accounts payable, accrued compensation and benefits, short-term borrowings, income taxes payable, accrued marketing, and other current liabilities. The basis for the sequencing of these accounts is not as clear-cut as it is on the asset side of the balance sheet. The sequencing within the current liability section and on the entire right side (that is, the equity side) of the balance sheet is primarily intended to reflect the priority standing of the various creditors (i.e., accounts payable are listed before accrued compensation and benefits). That priority ranking, however, is tempered by the expected order of repayment of the various current liabilities (that is, current liabilities followed by long-term debt, accounts payable followed by taxes payable). The disclosure of these accounts (see Exhibit 4.1) on PepsiCo's balance sheet appears as follows:

	1994	1993
Current Liabilities		
Accounts payable	$1,451.6	$1,390.0
Accrued compensation and benefits	753.5	726.0
Short-term borrowings	678.5	2,191.2
Income taxes payable	671.7	823.7
Accrued marketing	546.2	400.9
Other current liabilities	1,168.9	1,043.1
Total Current Liabilities	5,270.4	6,574.9

Accounts payable or **trade payables** represent the amounts owed to various suppliers for goods and services purchased on credit but not yet paid. The common business practice of giving a purchaser 30 days to pay results in an account receivable for the seller/supplier and an account payable for the buyer/user. **Accrued compensation and benefits** refers to the wages and related employee benefits, such as dental and health care, that PepsiCo's employees have earned but that the company has not yet paid. **Short-term borrowings,** on the other hand, may refer to either short-term bank borrowings, current maturities of long-term debt, or trade notes payable. **Trade notes** represent amounts owed to suppliers for goods or services purchased on credit. Short-term bank (or other financial institution) borrowings refer to cash loans that are usually due in 90 to 180 days. **Current maturities of long-term debt** represent the portion of long-term bank or other borrowings that are due to be paid within the next operating cycle or year. As an example, the principal portion of a 20-year mortgage that is due to be paid in the next 12 months is classified in the current liabilities section of the balance sheet.

Income taxes payable represent PepsiCo's estimate of the income taxes that will be owed to federal, state, local, and foreign authorities when the tax returns for the period are completed sometime in 1995. Under accrual accounting, the balance sheet must reflect all obligations owed as of the date of the statement, even if the exact amounts due are not immediately determinable. Thus, the preparation of the 1994 balance sheet may require that some liabilities, such as the 1994 deferred income taxes, be estimated. **Accrued marketing** refers to PepsiCo's advertising, promotional, and selling costs that have already been deducted as an expense on the company's 1994 income statement but that have not yet been paid for. Finally, **other current liabilities** represent those miscellaneous obligations of the company, which individually are immaterial in amount and thus are aggregated. Examples of this might include various accrued expenses such as interest owed on borrowed funds or utilities payable for electricity already used.

PepsiCo's noncurrent liabilities fall into three principal categories: long-term debt, other liabilities, and deferred income taxes. According to PepsiCo's footnotes, the **long-term debt** includes amounts borrowed from financial institutions, various bonds sold in the United States and in other countries, certain types of long-term lease obligations, and certain short-term borrowings reclassified as long term. A **bond** is a financial instrument carrying a specified rate of interest (the **coupon rate**) and a specified repayment date (the **maturity date**), which is normally sold to investors as a way to raise funds for a company. PepsiCo's footnotes reveal that the company has sold bonds denominated in U.S. dollars, Swiss francs, and Japanese yen. The lease obligations refer to noncancelable lease arrangements involving the use of various leased assets, such as Pizza Hut or Taco Bell restaurants and equipment. The short-term borrowings reclassified as long term reflect PepsiCo's intent (and ability) to refinance these borrowings on a long-term basis, either by the issuance of new long-term debt or by a "rollover" of the existing short-term borrowing (usually through a revolving credit agreement). From Exhibit 4.1, these noncurrent obligations are disclosed as follows:

	1994	1993
Long-term debt	$8,840.5	$7,442.6
Other liabilities	1,852.1	1,342.0
Deferred income taxes	1,972.9	2,007.6

Other liabilities is an aggregation of miscellaneous long-term liabilities (for example, pension and postretirement benefit obligations) and various accounts having a credit balance. Finally, **deferred income taxes** refers to U.S. and foreign income taxes that are not currently being paid but will be paid at some future date. The topic of deferred income taxes is covered in detail in Chapter 13.

Shareholders' Equity: The Owners' Investment in a Company

Shareholders' equity refers to the owners' or shareholders' investment in a company. As noted in Chapter 2, the shareholders' investment usually takes two primary forms: the shareholders' purchase of shares of stock from the company and the company's retention of a portion of its earnings.

When a company sells shares of stock, the proceeds are reflected in the **Capital Stock** account. The securities laws of some states permit companies to sell **no-par**

value stock, and companies incorporated in those states may include the entire proceeds from a stock sale in a single account designated simply as Capital Stock or **Common Stock.** However, most states in the United States require that a company's capital stock carry a **par value** or **stated value.** The par or stated value of a stock is the **legal value** of a single share of stock and is, in theory, the portion of shareholders' equity that may not legally be paid out as a dividend. That distinction is only theoretical, however, because the par or stated value is established (and can be changed by) the board of directors. Normally, there is no relationship between par value and the fair market value of a stock. For example, although PepsiCo issued capital stock with a par value of $0.0167, its shares traded on the New York Stock Exchange during 1994 in the range of $28 to $40.

From Exhibit 4.1, PepsiCo's owners' equity section on the balance sheet appears as follows:

	1994	1993
Shareholders' Equity		
Capital stock, par value 1 2/3 ¢ per share: authorized 1,800.0 shares, issued 863.1 shares	$ 14.4	$ 14.4
Capital in excess of par value	934.4	879.5
Retained earnings	7,739.1	6,541.9
Currency translation adjustment	(470.6)	(183.9)
	8,217.3	7,251.9
Less: Treasury stock, at cost: 73.2 shares in 1994, 64.3 shares in 1993	(1,361.2)	(913.2)
Total Shareholders' Equity	$6,856.1	$6,338.7

Because most companies intentionally set a relatively low par or stated value, shares of stock are normally sold at a price in excess of their par or stated value. When this occurs, the excess is reflected in the **Paid-in Capital in Excess of Par (or Stated) Value** account. Thus, the combination of the par value and the capital in excess of par value represents the total contributed capital of a company.

It is instructive to pause here and put this discussion of shareholders' capital in perspective. The distinction between the par value of a stock and the total proceeds received on the sale of the stock is important only for some very narrow legal purposes and is of no consequence to company's management. In fact, some companies organized in "par value" states have decided to ignore the distinction in preparing their financial statements and simply present a combined total for capital stock. That aggregate common stock amount represents the amount that the shareholders have paid the company for the stock purchased directly from the company. The discussion of the entity principle in Chapter 2 pointed out that the financial statements reflect only the transactions of the entity, not the transactions of the owners on their own behalf. Therefore, the financial statements reflect purchases of shares by the shareholders directly from the company as well as sales of shares back to the company. However, the company's financial statements do *not* reflect purchases and sales of shares between shareholders and other outsiders.

A company's **charter of incorporation** specifies, among other things, the maximum number of shares of capital stock that can be issued; these are often referred to as the **authorized shares.** When authorized shares are sold to investors, they become **issued shares.** In the United States, companies may repurchase some of their issued shares and retire them or hold them as **treasury stock. Outstanding shares** represent the company's issued shares less any shares held in the treasury. Treasury stock is usually repurchased with the intent to reissue it at some future date, perhaps to the company's employees or to facilitate a merger with another company. Because treasury stock is no longer on the open market but is expected to be reissued, it is accounted for as a contra shareholders' equity account.[3]

Remember that capital stock is recorded at the price that the purchasing shareholders paid when they bought the stock directly from the company. Logically, treasury stock is also recorded at the price that the company paid when it reacquired the shares on the open market. Because stock markets tend to fluctuate in response to many factors, there is almost always a difference between the original issue price and the price at which treasury shares are repurchased. Because the GAAP accounting model does not reflect changes in the value of a company's stock from year to year, a company's repurchase of any significant number of shares can result in an anomalous presentation of its owners' equity. For example, note that as of December 31, 1994, PepsiCo held $1,361.2 million in treasury stock, which exceeds the total proceeds that it received from the original sale of the stock (that is, $948.8 million) by $412.4 million. A number of companies purchased substantial amounts of their own stock during major restructurings in the 1980s, and, as a result, their aggregate owners' equity is a nominal balance or even a negative number. It is worth repeating that owners' equity, or net worth, is the difference between the company's assets stated at their book values and the company's liabilities stated at their book values. Owners' equity would be a measure of the fair value of a company *only* if the book value of the assets and the liabilities were also equal to their market values — a coincidence that rarely happens, and so the owners' equity number must be understood to be no more (or less) than a balancing number that forces a company to discipline its accounting process and maintain the A = L + OE equation.

The second principal form of shareholders' equity is the earned capital or **retained earnings.** The retained earnings of a company represent the historical, cumulative portion of net income that has been retained in the company to support ongoing operations and has not been paid out to shareholders as dividends. PepsiCo's financial statements reveal that of the $1,752.0 million in net income earned in 1994, $554.8 million (see p. 27) was paid as dividends to capital stock shareholders, leaving $1,197.2 million as an addition to retained earnings.

Finally, PepsiCo, like many large companies, conducts a significant portion of its operations in foreign countries. The "Business Segments" section of PepsiCo's financial statements (see Chapter 1) reveals that in 1994 foreign operations generated approximately 19 percent of the company's operating profits. Many of these operations are conducted by wholly owned foreign subsidiary corporations. To prepare the *consolidated* financial statements presented in PepsiCo's annual reports, the financial results of these foreign subsidiaries must be combined with the results of the domestic (U.S.) operations.

As you are probably aware, many factors cause fluctuations in the relative exchange rate of the U.S. dollar with foreign currencies, making it difficult to combine the financial data of foreign subsidiaries with those of domestic subsidiaries. Much of the effect of foreign currency exchange rate fluctuation is captured in the current income

[3]In some countries, such as France, treasury stock may be accounted for as an asset, usually under the heading "noncurrent investments."

statement, but special financial reporting issues (to be discussed in Chapter 10) arise involving assets and liabilities acquired in periods prior to the current period. In essence, PepsiCo's foreign assets and liabilities held in 1993 were consolidated at the exchange rate that existed in 1993; yet in 1994, those assets and liabilities must be consolidated at 1994's exchange rate. A **currency translation adjustment** is needed to capture the effect of any exchange rate fluctuations between the two periods and the cumulative adjustment amount is reported in a separate shareholders' equity account. In 1994, PepsiCo's Currency Translation Adjustment account decreased by $286.7 million, reflecting a substantial increase in the value of the U.S. dollar relative to the foreign currencies in countries where PepsiCo operates.

CONCEPTS AND CONVENTIONS UNDERLYING THE BALANCE SHEET

The measurement and valuation of the various asset and equity accounts on the balance sheet reflect a diverse set of GAAP concepts subject to a variety of management estimates, judgments, and preferences. In chapters 8–14 we will discuss these issues at length; however, for the moment, let us simply overview the core set of concepts and conventions.

An Overall Balance Sheet Focus

As noted in Chapter 2, the fundamental measurement system used to prepare the balance sheet is the accrual method. Under the accrual method, the financial effects of a transaction are recognized when it occurs without regard to the timing of its cash effects. Thus, the amounts due from customers for product sales that have not yet been paid for (that is, accounts and notes receivable) may be recognized as assets. In addition, the amounts owed for purchases of inventories or other assets (that is, accounts and notes payable) may be reported as liabilities on the balance sheet. Thus, whether or not cash has been received or paid is irrelevant. Assets are recognized on the balance sheet when a company takes possession of or receives title to an asset, and liabilities are recorded when it has incurred an obligation.

Assets

As noted earlier in this chapter as we discussed PepsiCo's various asset accounts, the initial value assigned to each asset on the balance sheet is its acquisition cost, which is assumed to be the fair market value at the time of acquisition. For accounting purposes, *acquisition cost* is defined to encompass more than just the invoice price of an asset. All costs incurred in bringing an asset to its intended, usable condition are considered to be part of its cost. Thus, transportation costs or legal fees associated with acquiring an asset are a part of its cost in addition to the purchase price.

The value of most assets, however, fluctuates over time. In some cases, as with land, the value may increase, whereas with other assets, such as a car, the value will probably fall. Under the historical cost principle, however, the original acquisition cost of an asset is preserved on the balance sheet. There are a number of reasons for this rigidly observed convention. Most importantly, original cost values represent objective evidence as to the value of an asset at least at one point in time. Experience has demonstrated that it is often quite difficult (and expensive) to obtain similarly objective, reliable measures at points in time after the original purchase date. An estimated market value established by management for its own company's assets often proves to be optimistic — and is, of course, subject to manipulation. In the United States, corporate management has generally been reluctant to estimate market values for assets in part because those estimates have so often proven to be wrong and the management involved has lost credibility. Interestingly, users have also been reluctant to give much credence to estimated values and so there has been no market demand for that information. As a result, GAAP-based financial statements in the United States recognize value changes only when they are validated by a sale in an arm's length transaction to a third party.

That fear of estimated values is a fact in the United States but is not necessarily present in other countries. In many other countries (especially Australia, Canada, and the United Kingdom), periodically appraising the fixed assets of a company and reflecting those appraised values in the company's balance sheet is perfectly acceptable. That asset write-up process has the advantage of quantifying, for the reader of the financial statements, the effect of changes in value on a company. For example, the write-up of assets logically results in an increase in owners' equity; that increase in asset value and that increase in owners' equity could mitigate the anomaly that results when a company buys back its own stock at an aggregate amount greater than the original proceeds received when it was issued. Also, the depreciation of those appraised values increases the company's operating costs and provides a clearer measure of the company's ability to increase its own sales prices in concert with changes in the purchasing value of the local currency. Because those value changes are not reflected in the financial statements of U.S. companies, statement users must (and usually do) make their own adjustments, mentally, as they consider the meaning of those historical cost–based numbers.

What is true for increases in an asset's value, however, is not the case if the value of an asset declines over time. In such a case, the diminishment in value should be recognized in the financial statements in one of several ways. Consider, for example, the current assets. Because current assets are considered to be available for use in current operations and for the repayment of current liabilities, an attempt is made to value these assets at their **net realizable value.** Thus, as we see in the case of PepsiCo, when a portion of the outstanding accounts or notes receivables is *not* expected to be collected, an estimate of the uncollectible amount is created and is deducted from the gross receivable balance. As a consequence, only the net realizable value (that is, the net collectible value) of the receivables is included in the total current asset balance.

Similarly, if the market value of an investment in trading securities has fallen below the investment's original cost, the value of the investment should be reduced (written down) to the lower market value using a convention called the mark-to-market method. Under this method, an Allowance for Decline in Value of Trading Investments — a contra asset account — is created and deducted from the original cost of the investment, thereby reflecting only the net realizable value of the investment in the current asset total. As might be expected, inventories are also valued at market but only when market is less than cost. Inventory cost is usually substantially less than its normal sales price, but occasionally product obsolescence or physical damage reduces the net realizable value of inventory below its carrying cost. Companies typically make periodic analyses of their inventories, and when cost/market problems appear, that decline in value is recognized as an expense during the period when the decline occurs. An entry for that write-down might look like this:

Dr. Cost of Obsolete Inventory (E)	(inc.) $10,000	
Cr. Allowance for Obsolete Inventory (CA)		(inc.) $10,000

In the case of noncurrent assets, the downward revaluation process may occur in several forms. In general, if the value of any asset becomes permanently impaired so that the future revenue-producing capacity of the asset is materially diminished, the value of the asset should be written down. If, for example, PepsiCo held stock in another company for speculative investment purposes and the value of the stock fell permanently, perhaps because the company lost a major lawsuit involving its principal business activity, PepsiCo's balance sheet valuation of the investment would be written down. That write-down would be recorded as a reduction to the balance sheet account Available-for-Sale Securities and as a loss in the current period's income statement.

The value of some assets, however, declines over time due to their use in operations. Property, plant, and equipment, for example, are consumed (or used up) in the process of producing goods and services for sale by a company. This kind of value diminishment is recognized under the matching principle. Each period a portion of the original cost of property, plant, and equipment is removed from the balance sheet and assigned to the income statement as depreciation expense. Although this allocation process is designed to reflect the consumption of property, plant, and equipment due to operations, it does not necessarily ensure that the balance sheet value of these assets will be equivalent to their current market value. Indeed, other market factors may cause the value of property, plant, and equipment to be greater than, or less than, their reported net book value. As noted above, if a decrement in value due to other than normal wear and tear is judged to be permanent, the value of the asset should be written down. In no case, however, would an appreciation in value be recognized unless and until the asset is sold.

To summarize, then, assets are initially recorded at their acquisition cost. When such values decline due to market externalities or to internal use, the asset values are reduced. When such values increase, with few exceptions (see Chapter 8), no recognition is given in the financial statements. Thus, it may be said that asset values are rarely overstated but may indeed be understated relative to their current fair market value.

Liabilities

The valuation of liabilities on the balance sheet is substantially less complex than the valuation of assets. Theoretically *all* liabilities are valued at the **present value** of the future cash outflows (or other equivalent asset flows) required to satisfy the obligation. The present value of a liability is determined by **discounting** the required future cash outflows using a given rate of interest called the *discount rate* (see Chapter 12). In a word, the discounting process recognizes the time value of money and the fact that a dollar due tomorrow is less costly than a dollar due today. For example, $1,000 due one year from today discounted at 8 percent has a present value of only $925.93.

Although present value is the fundamental valuation approach used for all liabilities, as a practical matter it is rarely used to value short-term liabilities. By definition, short-term liabilities are expected to be satisfied or paid off in the coming year, and there is little difference between the *maturity value* of a short-term liability and its present value. Thus, current liabilities are normally reported on the balance sheet at their maturity value or the amount of cash (or other equivalent assets) required to satisfy the obligation at its maturity or due date. Long-term liabilities are also usually stated at their present values because they carry an (unrecorded) interest obligation. (It is noteworthy that in some countries, such as Japan, long-term liabilities are valued not at their present value but rather at their maturity or settlement value.) So long as the required interest on an obligation is equal to the market rate of interest on the date when the debt is incurred, the debt can be considered to be stated at its present value. The present value of a liability is determined only once — when the obligation is initially incurred. Unlike assets, liabilities are never revalued on the balance sheet to reflect changes in their underlying market values.

Shareholders' Equity

Although the valuation of assets and liabilities may be defined or explained with reference to specific valuation concepts or methods, the valuation of shareholder or owners' equity is generally not. The valuation of owners' equity on the balance sheet is not an independent process but is the residual valuation that results from subtracting the liabilities from the assets. Capital stock is valued at the amount of assets received in exchange for the stock; treasury stock is valued at its acquisition cost. However, the reported value of retained earnings — the residual earnings after dividends have been paid — depends on the revenues and expenses reflected in the income statement. As you learned from your work in Chapter 3, every revenue and expense decision impacts an asset or a liability, and so the residual of those asset-liability/revenue-expense accounting decisions comes to rest in retained earnings.

The Balance Sheet: International Considerations

Thus far, our discussion of the balance sheet has focused on the format and presentation characteristic of U.S. companies. Not all nations, however, follow the same conventions, concepts, or presentation style. For example, Exhibit 4.2 presents the 1994 consolidated balance sheet of Glaxo Plc, a British pharmaceutical company. A cursory review of this exhibit quickly reveals a number of notable differences:

- The order of asset presentation is reversed — fixed assets appear before current assets, thus running from low liquidity to high liquidity.
- The assets and liabilities are comingled, with current liabilities subtracted from current assets to yield net current assets, and then subtracted from total assets; long-term liabilities are then deducted to arrive at the company's net asset position (or "net worth").
- A presentation format of A – L = OE is used, rather than A = L + OE.
- Many terminology differences exist:

U.S.	British
Inventory	Stocks
Accounts receivable	Debtors
Liabilities	Creditors
Capital stock	Called up share capital
Capital in excess of par value	Share premium account
Retained earnings	Profit and loss reserve

EXHIBIT 4.2

Glaxo Plc

Consolidated Balance Sheet

	Audited as at 30.6.94 £m
Fixed Assets	
Tangible assets	3,184
Investments	55
	3,239
Current Assets	
Stocks	575
Debtors	1,310
Investments	2,708
Cash at bank	55
	4,648
Creditors: Amounts falling due within one year	2,130
Net Current Assets	2,518
Total Assets Less Current Liabilities	5,757
Creditors: Amounts falling due after more than one year	169
Convertible Bonds	129
Provisions for Liabilities and Charges	293
Net Assets	5,166
Capital and Reserves	
Called up share capital	762
Share premium account	229
Other reserves	4,052
Equity Shareholders' Funds	5,043
Equity Minority Interests	123
Capital Employed	5,166

These and other differences may confuse or mislead unwary users of foreign financial statements. They also illustrate the very obvious conclusion that generally accepted accounting practices can and do differ around the world. Throughout the remaining chapters, we will attempt to point out some of these differences. And, in Chapter 15, the financial reporting practices of two countries, Japan and the United Kingdom, will be considered in more detail.

ANALYZING FINANCIAL STATEMENTS

As we observed in Chapter 1, accounting is a language, a communication device, and therefore not an end in itself. Thus, the presentation of accounting information in a stylized format such as the balance sheet is merely the beginning of the communication process. The recipient of the balance sheet and the other basic financial statements must then use the presented financial data to draw inferences and conclusions about the financial status of a company. Hence, we now focus on the question of how to analyze, evaluate, and interpret balance sheet data.

The analysis of the balance sheet, and of the basic financial statements in general, can occur at various levels of sophistication. At the most fundamental level, an analyst or other financial statement user can review and identify the absolute level of various important account balances. For example, it may be important to note the absolute level of cash on hand. If the level of cash on hand is sufficient to meet a company's most urgent needs (for example, to pay employee salaries and replenish sold inventory), it is unlikely that the company will need to borrow money in the current period to support operations.

In most cases, however, merely identifying the absolute level of various account balances does not provide sufficient information to analyze fully a company's financial position. The absolute level of inventory on hand, for example, informs us only that a company does have some inventory on hand to begin operations in the next period; the absolute level does not tell us, however, whether the available inventory will be sufficient to sustain sales or whether the company will need to purchase or manufacture additional units and, if so, how soon.

To address these more sophisticated questions, it is often useful to construct ratios of various related account balances. For example, to assess the adequacy of existing inventory levels, it might be instructive to compare the level of inventory on hand to the level of cost of goods sold in the prior period. This ratio would then indicate whether the existing inventory was sufficient to cover expected sales, assuming that they are approximately equivalent to the prior period sales.

Ratio analysis is frequently used to gain a more complete understanding of a company's financial stature and condition. Ratios may be investigated both within a given accounting period and across a number of accounting periods. When ratios (or absolute balances) are compared across time periods, particular trends in a company's financial condition or operations may be identified. Not surprisingly, this type of across-period analysis is called **trend analysis.** To facilitate the analysis of financial trends, most companies provide accounting data for at least the current period and the prior period. Moreover, some companies, such as PepsiCo, provide summary financial data for as many as 10 years in the annual report. Later in this chapter we will consider some ratio trend data for PepsiCo.

Trend analysis is also often aided by the use of **common-size financial statements,** in which all amounts are expressed as a percentage of some base financial statement item. For example, a common-size balance sheet might express all asset accounts as a percentage of total assets and all equity accounts as a percentage of total equities. Trend analysis of common-size statements permits the analyst to determine, for example, how the relative composition of total assets or total equities is changing over time.

In addition to comparing a company's performance from one year to the next, it is also instructive to compare the financial results of a given company with those of other companies within the same industry or with industry averages. For example, by comparing the financial results of PepsiCo with those of other soft drink and/or restaurant companies, an investor may be able to identify which firm presents the best investment opportunity within the industry. Similarly, Standard and Poor's and Moody's investor services, among others, provide industry data to permit comparisons of one company against the average of all companies within a given industry. Use of such data may enable an investor to determine whether a company is outperforming or underperforming the average for that industry. Later in this chapter we will compare PepsiCo's balance sheet information to that of the overall beverage industry and to a variety of industry averages.

Perhaps the most advanced level of financial analysis involves predicting the future financial performance of a company. Most companies prepare projections or **pro forma financial statements** based on assumptions about the future for their own internal planning purposes, but very few companies issue those financial statements publicly. The policy of publishing historic financial statements rather than pro formas is based on two factors. First, actual results almost always turn out differently than the original projections, and few executives have been willing to subject their credibility to the inevitable criticism when actual results are different than the projections. The second factor is economic; if the results are materially different from the pro forma, someone is sure to sue. Even if the projections were prepared in good faith, the company and its management will be forced to devote significant efforts to defend the projections.

Nonetheless, investments should always be made on the basis of expectations about the future, not on the results of the past. Under our present financial structure, companies do not publish projections, but independent financial analysts do. They prepare and analyze their own pro forma financial statements for publicly traded companies based on published history and carefully developed assumptions about the company's future environment. Building on that history and assumptions about the future, financial analysts develop pro forma financial statements and then commit themselves to estimates of the analyzed company's future earnings. We will return to this topic in Chapters 5 and 6, where the preparation of pro forma cash flow and income statements will be illustrated.

ANALYZING THE BALANCE SHEET

Ratio analysis is typically utilized to gain an understanding of a company's liquidity, solvency, profitability, and asset management effectiveness. **Liquidity** refers to the likelihood or ability of a company to satisfy its short-term obligations; **solvency** refers to a company's ability to satisfy its long-term obligations. **Profitability,** on the other hand, refers to a company's overall income-generating ability, and **asset management effectiveness** refers to the ability of a company's managers to utilize its assets effectively to produce a return for the company's creditors and owners.

Most profitability ratios are based on income statement accounts; consequently, this topic will be deferred until Chapter 5. The balance sheet, however, is a good source of information regarding a company's liquidity, solvency, and asset management effectiveness. We now turn to some widely accepted indicators of these financial characteristics.

Liquidity

Liquidity is frequently evaluated on the basis of four indicators: (1) the level of cash on hand, (2) the quick ratio, (3) the level of working capital, and (4) the current ratio.

The level of cash (and cash equivalents) on hand is a precise indication of the level of highly liquid resources available for a company's debt repayment or other operating needs. Cash on hand is very measurable and therefore quite certain, but it is also a very conservative measure of liquidity. Only in the most extreme circumstances would a company have to pay all of its bills using only its cash on hand. Hence, a more realistic measure of liquidity is the **quick ratio,** which is calculated as follows:

$$\text{Quick ratio} = \frac{\text{Cash} + \text{Marketable securities} + \text{Accounts receivable}}{\text{Current liabilities}}$$

The quick ratio examines only the liability coverage provided by the **quick assets**—highly liquid current assets such as cash, cash equivalents, short-term investments, and receivables. Accounts and notes receivables are considered to be quick assets because they can usually be sold to a financial institution or a financial corporation that buys receivables from other companies at a discount (that is, at a price less than the amount to be collected) and earns a profit when the receivables are collected.

A somewhat more general indicator of liquidity that is broader in scope is the level of working capital. Working capital is measured as current assets minus current liabilities. Thus **working capital** is a measure of the net current assets that would be available to support a company's continuing operations *if* all of its current assets could be converted to cash at their balance sheet values and the proceeds used to satisfy its current liabilities. The equation is as follows:

$$\text{Working capital} = \text{Current assets} - \text{Current liabilities}$$

A ratio based on the concept of working capital is the **current ratio,** which is calculated by dividing current assets by current liabilities:

$$\text{Current ratio} = \frac{\text{Current assets}}{\text{Current liabilities}}$$

Both working capital and the current ratio are "coverage" indicators; the former indicates the extent to which current assets cover current liabilities in an *absolute* sense, and the latter indicates the extent of coverage in a *relative* sense. A high current ratio (that is, a substantial amount of working capital) indicates good liquidity, suggesting that a company's currently maturing obligations are likely to be paid on time. A ratio that is too high, however, may suggest an unproductive use of resources because the current assets might be used more effectively by converting them to cash and purchasing, for example, high-yield stocks or bonds.

To illustrate these liquidity measures, let us consider PepsiCo's balance sheet for 1994 (see Exhibit 4.1). This balance sheet reveals that, as of December 31, 1994, PepsiCo had cash and cash equivalents of $1,488.1 million on hand, working capital of $(198.2) million, a current ratio of 0.96:1, and a quick ratio of 0.67:1. The current and quick ratios reveal that for every dollar of current liabilities, PepsiCo held $0.96 of current assets and $0.67 of quick assets.

To determine whether these measures indicate high, low, or average liquidity, one can compare them to existing industry averages, to those of a competitor (see Exhibit 4.3), and to the results of prior years. Because PepsiCo's balance sheet contains comparative data for 1993, a trend analysis can be easily undertaken.

	1994	1993
Cash and cash equivalents	$1,488.1 million	$1,800.7 million
Working capital	(198.2) million	(1,466.3) million
Current ratio	0.96:1	0.78:1
Quick ratio	0.67:1	0.56:1

A comparison indicates that PepsiCo's liquidity in 1994 improved somewhat from that in 1993. Although the level of cash and cash equivalents decreased by more than $312.6 million, the level of working capital increased by more than $1,268.1 million. The increase in working capital is also depicted in the improvement in both the current and quick ratios. PepsiCo's liquidity position appears to be superior to

EXHIBIT 4.3

Financial Ratios for 1994 for Selected Industries, The Coca-Cola Company, and PepsiCo, Inc.

Industry	Current Ratio	Quick Ratio	Total Debt to Total Assets	Long-Term Debt to Owners' Equity	Times Interest Earned	Inventory Turnover	Receivable Turnover
Panel A: Industry Data							
Air transportation	1.7:1	1.2:1	51 percent	0.48:1	2.4 times	23.2 times	10.4 times
Beverages	2.1:1	1.2:1	52 percent	0.46:1	2.9 times	20.2 times	12.9 times
Chemicals	1.9:1	1.3:1	53 percent	0.20:1	2.4 times	16.0 times	8.0 times
Retail	4.3:1	1.1:1	38 percent	0.25:1	2.0 times	4.4 times	18.1 times
Steel	2.0:1	1.2:1	56 percent	0.51:1	3.8 times	13.8 times	8.0 times
Panel B: Coca-Cola and PepsiCo							
Coca-Cola	0.84:1	0.49:1	62 percent	0.47:1	19.7 times	5.9 times	12.1 times
PepsiCo	0.96:1	0.67:1	72 percent	1.29:1	5.1 times	14.1 times	13.9 times

Source: Dun & Bradstreet's *Industry Norms & Key Business Ratios.*

that of Coca-Cola in 1994 (see Exhibit 4.3); both the current ratio (0.96 versus 0.84) and the quick ratio (0.67 versus 0.49) are somewhat higher for PepsiCo. In Chapter 6 we will see that there are additional ways to assess a company's liquidity, namely in terms of its operating cash flow.

Solvency

Solvency refers to a company's long-term debt repayment ability and is frequently evaluated on the basis of three indicators: (1) the total debt-to-total assets ratio, (2) the long-term debt-to-owners' equity ratio, and (3) the times-interest-earned ratio. The first two ratios measure the relative *amount* of long-term debt outstanding; the third ratio is a *coverage* ratio of the extent to which current debt interest charges are being covered by current earnings.

The concept of solvency and the thrust of these debt-level ratios suggest a negative connotation, as though debt is to be avoided and reduced whenever possible. Debt is not always bad; in fact, it is sometimes healthy. A more positive way to describe a company's debt level is to say that the stockholders' equity is **leveraged;** in effect, a leveraged company supplements its owners' funds with funds from other sources to "lever up" (or "gear up" as they would say in the U.K.) the return to the owners. Before we explore these debt-level ratios, it is appropriate to consider debt at a conceptual level.

The level of debt a company carries — its leverage — is a strategic decision, and that decision is based on the degree of certainty associated with its future cash flows. If the future cash flows are relatively predictable, the company may be able to borrow funds with bank loans or bond issuances at relatively low rates of interest. If a company can borrow money at an after-tax cost that is lower than the cost of its owners' equity funds, that borrowing enables the company to increase its return to its owners. (It may very well be possible to use borrowed funds less expensively than owners' equity funds because interest expense is tax deductible whereas dividends are not.) For example, assume that a company is considering a plant expansion project that is expected to cost $1 million and is expected to earn $100,000 after taxes. If the company is now earning a 10 percent return for its stockholders, that expansion project will not make the company (or its stockholders) any better off. But if the company can borrow 80 percent of those funds at an after-tax cost of 8 percent, the return on the shareholders' investment in this project will grow to 18 percent, as follows:

	Project Funded with Owners' Equity Funds	Project Funded with Borrowed Funds
Cost	$1,000,000	$1,000,000
Borrowed funds	0	800,000
Stockholder funds invested	1,000,000	200,000
Expected return	100,000	100,000
Interest cost	–0–	64,000
Net return to stockholders	100,000	36,000
Rate of return to stockholders	10%	18%

Leverage is powerful, but it has the power to hurt as well as help. If the project in our example is not as successful as was planned and earns only $50,000 a year, the company will lose money on the $200,000 investment of owners' equity funds. The decision to lever up or lever down is, perhaps, the ultimate expression of management balance. Too much leverage cheats the stockholders of their maximum return. PepsiCo explains its strategy in its annual report with these words:

> In managing its capital structure, PepsiCo utilizes financial leverage to optimize the overall cost of capital, considering the favorable tax treatment of debt, while maintaining operating and financial flexibility.

The ratios that follow describe a company's debt exposure, but they should be looked at from two perspectives: Creditors obviously want to maximize their protection, but stockholders look for the best balance of debt and equity to ensure the highest return at the least level of risk.

The **total debt-to-total assets ratio** is a measure of the extent to which a company's assets are financed by creditors and is calculated as follows:

$$\text{Total debt-to-total assets ratio} = \frac{\text{Total debt}}{\text{Total assets}}$$

In general, the lower the ratio, the more solvent a company is thought to be. The higher the ratio, the less solvent and the more leveraged (or "geared") a company is considered to be.

A related equation is leverage, generally expressed as a whole number:

$$\text{Leverage} = \frac{\text{Total assets}}{\text{Total owners' equity}}$$

The lower the leverage number is, the more the company has used equity to finance its assets and the lower its exposure to downturns in its business. The higher the number is, the more the company is relying on its creditors for financing, and the more benefits the shareholders derive from those borrowed funds — and the more exposed they are to the risks of the company's business.

The **long-term debt-to-equity ratio** measures the relative composition of a company's long-term capital structure, and is calculated as follows:

$$\text{Long-term debt-to-equity ratio} = \frac{\text{Long-term debt}}{\text{Owners' equity}}$$

In general, the lower this ratio, the higher the proportion of long-term financing provided by the owners and the more solvent a company is thought to be. Alternatively, the higher this ratio, the more leveraged a company is and the less solvent it is thought to be. In general, creditors like a lower debt-to-equity ratio because they have a prior claim on a company's assets and prefer to have a larger equity cushion beneath them.

A final index of a company's ability to manage its long-term debt is given by the **times-interest-earned ratio**, also known as the interest coverage ratio:

$$\text{Times-interest-earned ratio} = \frac{\text{Net income before income tax + Interest expense}}{\text{Interest expense}}$$

Note that this ratio is calculated using pretax net income because interest is a tax-deductible expense; hence, the numerator is a measure of a company's pretax, pre-interest income. This ratio measures the extent to which a company's earnings during a period cover its interest payments for the same period. In general, the higher the ratio the better, although a high ratio may indicate either high pretax profits or low debt levels. In either case, a high ratio is generally associated with greater solvency and the ability to add new borrowings (that is, increased leverage) in the future. A very low ratio may indicate that the company may be missing an opportunity to generate positive marginal returns by not sufficiently leveraging its assets. The times-interest-earned ratio is an income statement–based indicator of solvency.

To illustrate these solvency ratios, consider again information drawn from PepsiCo's 1994 financial statements:

	1994	1993
Total debt-to-total assets ratio	72.3%	73.3%
Long-term debt-to-equity ratio	1.29:1	1.17:1
Times-interest-earned ratio	5.1 times	5.2 times

As compared to that in 1993, PepsiCo's solvency in 1994 declined somewhat. While the percentage of assets financed by external borrowings declined from 73.3 percent to 72.3 percent, the ratio of long-term debt to equity increased from 1.17 times to 1.29 times. (Stated alternatively, the level of long-term debt as a percentage of equity increased from 117 percent to 129 percent.) The times-interest-earned ratio declined from 5.2 times to 5.1 times. As compared to Coca-Cola (see Exhibit 4.3), all of PepsiCo's solvency indicators appear less favorable. Both PepsiCo's total debt-to-total assets ratio (72 percent versus 62 percent) and its long-term debt-to-owners' equity ratio (1.29 versus 0.47) are higher than those of Coca-Cola. In addition, PepsiCo's times-interest-earned ratio of 5.1 is substantially below that of Coca-Cola (19.7). These solvency measures reflect PepsiCo's increased borrowings associated with its recent acquisitions, as well as Coca-Cola's decision to decentralize its bottling operations debt to its 49 percent owned subsidiary, Coca-Cola Enterprises, Inc.

Asset Management

Asset management refers to how efficiently a company utilizes its assets. A company with superior asset management usually experiences superior earnings and profitability relative to competitors within its industry. Asset management effectiveness is usually investigated with respect to a company's inventory, receivables, and noncurrent assets. Five such indicators are (1) the inventory turnover ratio, (2) the number of days of inventory on hand, (3) the accounts receivable turnover ratio, (4) the average receivable collection period, and (5) the noncurrent asset turnover ratio.

The quality of a company's inventory management is often revealed by the inventory turnover ratio and the number of days of inventory on hand. The **inventory turnover ratio** measures the number of times that the average level of inventory on hand was sold, or turned, during an accounting period and is calculated as follows:

$$\text{Inventory turnover ratio} = \frac{\text{Cost of goods sold for the period}}{\text{Average inventory held during the period}}$$

In general, the higher the inventory turnover ratio, the more profitable a company is and the more effective the inventory management is thought to be. A high turnover rate also helps to reduce the potential of loss due to product obsolescence or deterioration. If the turnover ratio is too high, however, it may indicate that the company is losing sales opportunities because inventory levels are inadequate. Unfortunately, there is no ideal turnover rate, and to judge the effectiveness of inventory management, it is important to compare this ratio to that of prior periods, to industry averages, or to competitor ratios (see Exhibit 4.3).

An instructive derivative of the inventory turnover ratio is the **number of days' inventory-on-hand ratio.** This ratio highlights whether inventory levels are appropriate for the current level of sales volume and is calculated as follows:

$$\text{Number of days' inventory on hand} = \frac{\text{365 days}}{\text{Inventory turnover ratio}}$$

This indicator measures the average number of days required to liquidate the existing stock of inventory based on current sales volume. A high number of day's inventory-on-hand ratio usually reflects an excessive quantity of inventory on hand, suggesting that current production should be curtailed. Alternatively, a very low number of days' inventory-on-hand ratio may also be problematic, indicating an inadequate quantity of inventory on hand and the potential for lost sales or customer complaints. Like the inventory turnover ratio, the number of day's inventory-on-hand ratio has no ideal number.

The quality of receivable management is usually evaluated in the context of the accounts (notes) receivable turnover ratio and the average receivable collection period. The **receivable turnover ratio** is a measure of the rate at which a company's accounts and notes receivable are converted to cash. In general, a high ratio indicates excellent receivables management. A low ratio, on the other hand, may indicate serious problems in the sales-receivables-collection cycle. The ratio is calculated as follows:

$$\text{Receivable turnover ratio} = \frac{\text{Net credit sales for the period}}{\text{Average receivable balance for the period}}$$

A derivative of the receivable turnover ratio is the **average receivable collection period,** which measures the average number of days that a receivable is outstanding before the amount is collected. This ratio provides a good indication of the quality of the cash collection policies a company followed relative to the credit terms granted and is calculated like this:

$$\text{Average receivable collection period} = \frac{\text{365 days}}{\text{Receivable turnover ratio}}$$

A low collection period (in days) not only indicates effective asset management but also provides evidence as to the liquidity of a company's accounts and notes receivable.

These ratios are abstractions, but the impact of the underlying numbers is quite real. It is generally understood that inventory carrying costs are annually at least 20 percent of the value of the inventory. These carrying costs include the cost of the funds invested, the cost of storage and insurance, and the cost of spoilage, which occurs simply because the inventory is on hand. Management must trade off that inventory carrying cost against its need for customer service as it evaluates its inventory turn statistics. The trade-off may not have to be all that painful, however: One major manufacturer found that it was carrying 10 different variations of the same part, each minutely different from the other, because these parts were used on 10 different finished products. The company found that it was able to maintain its customer service levels *and* reduce its inventory levels by redesigning the basic part so that it could be used on all of the finished products, regardless of their variation.

Similarly, accounts receivable have a real cost to the seller, including the cost of the funds invested, the service costs, and the cost of bad debt losses. Typically, bank credit card companies charge the merchant 3–4 percent of the amount of a charge sale to cover credit operations costs and provide some measure of profit. Again, management must weigh the cost of its own credit operations against the profit potential of the sale, which might be lost should the customer go somewhere with easier credit policies.

A final indicator of the quality or effectiveness of a company's asset management is given by the **noncurrent asset turnover ratio.** Unlike the previous four ratios that focus on the current assets, this ratio examines a company's utilization of its long-term revenue-producing assets. The ratio is calculated as follows:

$$\text{Noncurrent asset turnover ratio} = \frac{\text{Net sales for the period}}{\text{Average noncurrent asset balance for the period}}$$

In general, the higher the ratio the better. A high turnover ratio indicates that management is effective in generating revenues from the noncurrent assets that it has at its disposal. A high turnover rate can also be problematic, however, if the reason for the high turnover is the liquidation of the company's noncurrent assets. Similarly, a decreasing ratio may not necessarily indicate poor noncurrent asset utilization if the decline is a result of an increased investment in noncurrent assets.

To illustrate the asset management ratios, consider again PepsiCo's 1994 financial statements:

	1994	1993
Inventory turnover ratio	14.1 times	12.9 times
Number of days' inventory on hand	25.9 days	28.3 days
Receivable turnover ratio	13.9 times	13.3 times
Average receivable collection period	26.3 days	27.7 days
Noncurrent asset turnover ratio	1.61 times	1.49 times

PepsiCo's asset management position in 1994 compares very favorably to that in 1993. Both the inventory turnover and the receivable turnover ratios have improved (remember — a higher turnover is usually preferred to a lower one), causing corresponding decreases in the days' inventory-on-hand ratio and the receivable collection period ratio. The noncurrent asset turnover ratio also improved. As compared to Coca-Cola (see Exhibit 4.3), PepsiCo's inventory turnover occurs 14.1 times per year versus only 5.9 times for Coca-Cola, and its receivable turnover is 13.9 times versus 12.1 times for Coca-Cola. Both of these turnover ratios indicate PepsiCo's superior asset management.

Management Issues

The balance sheet is a powerful analytical tool not only for financial analysts and investors but also for a company's management. In essence, the balance sheet helps managers reach a variety of decisions. Liquidity measures generated from balance sheet data inform management whether the company has sufficient cash (or cash equivalents) on hand to meet the company's operating needs for the coming period. If the decision is that more liquid resources are needed, solvency measures help management determine the best way to raise the needed funds — by the sale of long-term bonds or stock, by bank borrowing, or by some other means. Asset management indicators, on the other hand, help managers assess the extent to which a firm is operating according to previously established goals or plans. These evaluations are part of what is commonly called the "control function" of management — evaluating the extent to which a company is performing according to strategic plans or budgets. For example, if management has determined that the desired number of days' inventory on hand is 45 (that is, the quantity of inventory on hand is sufficient to cover the next 45 days of sales), then a days' inventory-on-hand ratio of 60 indicates that there is excess inventory and the production of new inventory should be slowed. Similarly, if the days' inventory-on-hand ratio falls to 10, management will be alerted that the company may be unable to give prompt, timely service to all of its customers, suggesting that production schedules probably need to be accelerated. Finally, the balance sheet is also an important evaluation instrument for management themselves. By considering such ratios as the noncurrent asset turnover ratio, the board of directors can assess just how effective the top management of a company was at using the company's resources to produce sales. This information can help the directors decide whether management deserves a bonus or, more importantly, whether the current management team should be replaced.

SUMMARY

The balance sheet is one of the basic financial statements prepared to communicate a company's financial status and condition. The balance sheet summarizes the assets a company owned, the liabilities it owed, and the accumulated funds that its owners have invested in or left with the company to cover its operating needs.

The balance sheet may be used to investigate a company's liquidity, solvency, leverage, and asset management effectiveness. By itself, the balance sheet reveals very little about the profitability of a company's operations. Hence, the development of a complete understanding of a company's financial health requires considerations beyond the balance sheet, such as an analysis of the income statement, which is the focus of the following chapter.

NEW CONCEPTS AND TERMS

Accounts payable (p. 161)
Accounts and notes receivable (p. 157)
Accrual method (p. 157)
Accrued compensation and benefits (p. 161)
Accrued marketing (p. 162)
Accumulated depreciation (p. 160)
Allowance for uncollectible accounts (p. 157)
Amortization (p. 160)
Asset management effectiveness (p. 171)
Authorized shares (p. 163)
Average receivable collection period (p. 176)
Bad debts expense (p. 157)

Balance sheet (p. 155)
Bond (p. 162)
Capital stock (p. 162)
Cash and cash equivalents (p. 157)
Charter of incorporation (p. 163)
Classified balance sheet (p. 158)
Common-size financial statements (p. 170)
Common stock (p. 163)
Coupon rate (p. 162)
Currency translation adjustment (p. 165)
Current assets (p. 155)
Current liability (p. 161)
Current maturities of long-term debt (p. 161)
Current ratio (p. 172)
Deferred income taxes (p. 162)
Depreciation (p. 159)
Discounting (p. 167)
Fiscal year (p. 155)
Fixed assets (p. 159)
Goodwill (p. 160)
Income taxes payable (p. 162)
Intangible assets (p. 160)
Inventory (p. 158)
Inventory turnover ratio (p. 176)
Issued shares (p. 163)
Legal value (p. 163)
Leverage (p. 173)
Liquid assets (p. 157)
Liquidity (p. 171)
Long-term debt (p. 162)
Long-term debt-to-equity ratio (p. 174)
Long-term investments (p. 159)
Matching principle (p. 157)
Maturity date (p. 162)
Net book value (p. 160)
Net realizable value (p. 166)
No-par value stock (p. 162)
Noncurrent assets (p. 159)
Noncurrent asset turnover ratio (p. 177)
Noncurrent liability (p. 161)
Number of day's inventory-on-hand ratio (p. 176)
Operating cycle (p. 158)
Other assets (p. 160)
Other current liabilities (p. 162)
Other liabilities (p. 162)
Outstanding shares (p. 164)
Paid-in capital in excess of par (stated) value (p. 163)
Par value (p. 163)
Prepaid expenses (p. 158)
Present value (p. 167)
Profitability (p. 171)
Pro forma financial statements (p. 171)
Property, plant, and equipment (p. 159)
Quick assets (p. 172)
Quick ratio (p. 171)
Ratio analysis (p. 170)
Receivable turnover ratio (p. 176)
Retained earnings (p. 164)
Short-term borrowings (p. 161)
Short-term investments (p. 157)
Solvency (p. 171)
Stated value (p. 163)
Tangible assets (p. 159)
Times-interest-earned ratio (p. 175)
Total debt-to-total assets ratio (p. 174)
Trade notes (p. 161)
Trade payables (p. 161)
Trade receivables (p. 157)
Treasury stock (p. 164)
Trend analysis (p. 170)
Unclassified balance sheet (p. 158)
Working capital (p. 172)

ISSUES FOR DISCUSSION

D4.1 Most companies present a classified balance sheet; that is, they divide both assets and liabilities into long-term and short-term items. Banks (and some other types of businesses) do not do that but instead present an unclassified balance sheet that makes no distinction between current and long-term items. See the following asset presentation from Synovus Financial Corporation. Why might an unclassified balance sheet be appropriate for a bank?

Consolidated Statements of Condition
Synovus Financial Corp.
(in thousands)

	December 31	
	19X2	**19X1**
Assets:		
Cash and due from banks, including cash deposits at the Federal Reserve in order to meet reserve requirements of $24,356 and $15,869 for 19X2 and 19X1, respectively	$ 162,425	$ 137,212
Short-term, interest-earning deposits with banks	6,237	3,613
Federal funds sold	77,795	46,717
Investment securities (approximate market value of $438,623 and $341,795 for 19X2 and 19X1, respectively) (note 2)	435,348	347,916
Loans (note 3)	1,615,345	1,341,892
Less:		
Unearned income	(22,471)	(19,912)
Reserve for possible loan losses (note 3)	(26,628)	(21,372)
Loans, net	1,566,246	1,300,608
Premises and equipment (note 5)	75,319	61,098
Other assets	87,045	59,777
Total assets	$2,410,415	$1,956,941

D4.2 The current liability section of most balance sheets includes an item called *current payments on long-term debt.* If that item represents payments due on long-term debt, why is it included in current liabilities? Does the current asset section of those balance sheets include an item called *current depreciation on long-term assets?* Why or why not?

D4.3 The current assets and liabilities from The Mead Corporation's balance sheet are as follows (all dollar amounts in millions):

December 31	19X5	19X4
Current assets:		
Cash and cash equivalents	$ 21.1	$ 21.1
Accounts receivable, less allowance for doubtful accounts of $24.0 in 19X5 and $25.6 in 19X4	528.9	536.1
Inventories (Note B)	394.6	381.0
Prepaid expenses	37.4	42.4
Total current assets	$982.0	$980.6

December 31	19X5	19X4
Current liabilities:		
Accounts payable:		
Trade	$261.4	$290.1
Affiliated companies	28.1	64.7
Outstanding checks	102.6	57.7
Accrued wages	83.3	84.1
Taxes, other than income	52.8	50.1
Other current liabilities	152.7	132.7
Current maturities of long-term debt	12.7	12.6
Total current liabilities	$693.6	$692.0

How would you explain the fact that the company has a current liability titled "outstanding checks"? How might that fact affect your perceptions of the company's liquidity? How would it affect the company's current ratio? Its working capital? Its quick ratio?

D4.4 Monsanto describes its credit standing with the following words (from the management discussion and analysis segment reviewing the balance sheet):

> **Monsanto Maintains Strong Financial Position**
> Monsanto's financial position remained strong this year, as evidenced by Monsanto's current "A" or better debt rating. Financial resources were adequate to support existing businesses and to fund new business opportunities.
>
> Working capital at year-end was at the same level as that of the prior year-end. Receivables increased primarily as a result of higher fourth quarter sales versus the prior year's fourth quarter sales. The increase in current liabilities principally related to the Agricultural Products restructuring that increased short-term debt. . . .
>
> Total short- and long-term debt at year-end was $258 million higher than that of the prior year-end. The additional long-term debt was used principally for capacity expansions. To maintain adequate financial flexibility and access to debt markets worldwide, Monsanto management intends to maintain an "A" debt rating. Important factors in establishing that rating are the ratio of total debt to total capitalization, which was 35 percent, and the interest coverage ratio, which was 4.8. . . .
>
> Monsanto uses financial markets around the world for its financing needs and has available various short- and medium-term bank credit facilities, which are discussed in the notes to financial statements. These credit facilities provide the financing flexibility to take advantage of investment opportunities that may arise and to satisfy future funding requirements.

In your own words, describe Monsanto's interest in maintaining its "A" rating. Why might they be interested in that rating? What would you expect the company to do to preserve that rating?

D4.5 The balance sheet presents a picture of a company's assets, liabilities, and owners' equity as of a point in time. In general, the balance sheet reports items at their historical cost. Consider the typical line items reported in a balance sheet. As the manager of the company publishing the balance sheet, which items would you prefer to report at current market values? As a potential investor in the company, on which ones would you like to have information regarding market values? Discuss how the demand for market value information may or may not be consistent with the reporting notions of relevance and reliability.

D4.6 The value of ratio analysis depends to a great extent on one's ability to interpret the ratios in the context of a company's particular environment. In this regard, discuss how the quick and current ratios for companies in the following industries may or may not differ:

- Defense contractor
- Distillery
- Hotel chain
- Sports franchise

D4.7 The 1980s and the start of the 1990s were periods of major change in the way companies were organized and financed. Elaborate on how corporate balance sheets would be impacted by such phenomena as corporate acquisitions, junk bonds, downsizing, outsourcing of production/assembly, and just-in-time inventory techniques.

D4.8 Consider the PepsiCo balance sheet presented at the end of Chapter 1. Identify all the line items in that balance sheet that you believe are based on certain subjective judgments and/or estimates of PepsiCo management. What is the nature of each of those subjective decisions?

Identify several such areas of judgment and discuss whether the judgmental discretion now allowed should be reduced via additional standard setting.

D4.9 In PepsiCo's "Selected Financial Data" section of its annual report, presented in Chapter 1, it is reported that the 1994 historical cost net debt ratio is 49.0 percent and its market net debt ratio is 26.0 percent. Fully explain and interpret these two items.

D4.10 Consider the following phrases:

a. Realizable value — Present value
b. Fixed assets — Intangible assets
c. Liabilities — Owners' equity
d. Market value — Historical cost

Prepare a commentary on each of the above pairings, explaining how they are alike and how they are different in the context of a company's balance sheet.

PROBLEMS

P4.1 Account identification. With Sears Roebuck and Co. in mind, classify each of the following accounts as either assets, liabilities, or owners' equity:

a. Accounts Payable
b. Prepaid Rent
c. Cash
d. Common Stock
e. Inventory
f. Taxes Payable
g. Land
h. Customer Deposit
i. Patent
j. Accounts Receivable
k. Retained Earnings
l. Pension Obligation
m. Securities Investment

P4.2 Comparisons of asset mix. Different companies will have different assets available for their use, largely because of the characteristics of their industry as well as various company-specific factors. Individual companies will fund their assets from different sources as well, depending on the cost and availability of capital to the industry and to the specific company.

Required:

a. Select five different companies — three in the same industry and two in completely different industries — and for each company determine the percentage of assets represented by cash and cash equivalents, receivables, inventory, plant and equipment, and long-term investments and other assets. Comment on the similarities and the differences you may have noticed.

b. Calculate the current ratio for each of the five companies you selected. Compare the ratios for each of the companies, and explain what the ratio tells you about that company and about the group of companies in your sample.

P4.3 Current and noncurrent assets and liabilities. Consider the following account titles from a recent balance sheet of Fast Foods Inc.:

a. Accrued Wages

b. Inventories

c. Machinery and Equipment

d. Investment in Affiliated Companies

e. Deferred Income Taxes

f. Other Liabilities

g. Treasury Stock

h. Mortgage Payable

i. Accumulated Depreciation

j. Prepaid Advertising

k. Unfunded Pension Benefits Obligation

l. Goodwill

m. Customer Deposit

Required:

Classify each account as either a current asset or a current liability, or a noncurrent asset or a noncurrent liability. Explain any assumptions you found necessary to make.

P4.4 Financial analysis. Collins Cutlery has a current ratio, based on its June 30, 1995, balance sheet, of 2:1. During the following six months, these independent events took place:

1. Sold an old truck for cash.
2. Declared a cash dividend on common stock.
3. Sold inventory on account (at a profit).
4. Paid off mortgage five years early.
5. Paid cash for a customer list.
6. Temporarily invested cash in government bonds.
7. Purchased inventory for cash.
8. Wrote off an account receivable as uncollectible.
9. Paid the declared cash dividend.
10. Purchased a computer with a two-year promissory note.
11. Collected accounts receivable.
12. Borrowed from bank on a 90-day note.

Required:

For each of the above events, indicate the effect of that event on Collins's working capital and current ratio and its ratio of total debt to equity. Make whatever assumptions you believe necessary to complete this exercise.

P4.5 Balance sheet preparation. Presented below are the balance sheet accounts of Global Communications, Inc., as of December 31, 1995:

Accounts payable	$ 4,200	Capital stock, $1 par	$30,000
Accounts receivable	3,000	Discount on bonds payable	1,000
Accumulated depreciation — buildings	5,000	Equipment	18,000
Accumulated depreciation — equipment	3,000	Income taxes payable	3,100
Allowance for uncollectible accounts	500	Inventory — raw material	2,100
Bonds payable (due 2008)	10,000	Inventory — finished goods	5,000
Buildings	20,000	Land	19,000
Cash	4,500	Marketable securities (current asset)	2,000
		Paid-in capital in excess of par value	16,000
		Patent	20,000
		Retained earnings	?
		Wages payable	1,000

Required:

Prepare the December 31, 1995, balance sheet of Global Communications.

P4.6 Balance sheet accounts: assets. The Dow Jones Company presents the following items in the asset side of its balance sheet. Explain why the items with asterisks might be considered assets for Dow Jones. Comment on the source of the numbers attributed to those assets.

Dow Jones & Company, Inc.
Consolidated Balance Sheets
December 31, 19X5 and 19X4
(in thousands)

	19X5	19X4
Assets		
Current assets:		
Cash and cash equivalents	$ 46,197	$ 60,791
Accounts receivable — trade, net of allowance for doubtful accounts of $14,151 in 19X5 and $13,221 in 19X4	160,843	138,964
Newsprint inventory	18,439	21,026
Deferred income taxes	9,483	
Other current assets	33,805	44,703
Total current assets	268,767	265,484
Investments in associated companies at equity	71,896	83,414
Other investments	82,736	103,205
Plant and property, at cost:		
Land	21,661	21,661
Buildings and improvements	306,387	269,688
Equipment	1,000,679	889,218
Construction in progress	41,498	44,053
	1,370,225	1,224,620
Less, allowance for depreciation	652,468	539,528
	717,757	685,092
Excess of cost over net assets of businesses acquired, less accumulated amortization of $82,236 in 19X5 and $54,880 in 19X4	1,510,120	963,939
Other assets	37,060	10,647
Total assets	$2,688,336	$2,111,781

P4.7 Balance sheet accounts: liabilities. Contel Corporation lists the following items in the current liabilities section of the balance sheet. Explain what these items are and why they have to be recorded by Contel as a liability. Why are they current liabilities? Comment on the source of the numbers attributed to those liabilities.

Contel Corporation
Balance Sheet
As of December 31
(in thousands)

	19X4	19X3
Liabilities and Stockholders' Equity		
Current liabilities:		
Current maturities of long-term obligations and preferred stock redemptions	$ 194,419	$ 93,640
Interim borrowings	173,073	26,279
Accounts payable	478,579	404,029
Accrued taxes	67,088	166,929
Accrued interest	33,345	35,520
Accrued benefits	53,178	74,444
Advance billings and customer deposits	63,294	77,058
Other	169,429	100,972
	$1,232,405	$978,871

P4.8 Short-term and long-term debt. Snap-On Tools Corporation includes a footnote in a recent Annual Report, describing its debt situation as follows:

> At December 29, 19X5, the company had bank lines of credit totaling $101.3 million available for short-term borrowing, including support of commercial paper issuance. Of this amount, $100 million required compensating balances of 2 percent. Notes payable to banks totaled $11.5 million as of December 29, 19X5, and $6.0 million as of December 30, 19X4. Commercial notes payable totaled $65.0 million as of December 29, 19X5, and $31.0 million as of December 30, 19X4. There were no short-term borrowings during 19X3.
>
> Maximum short-term borrowings outstanding at the end of any month in 19X5 and 19X4 were $77.0 million and $37.0 million, respectively. The average outstanding borrowings were $56.7 million in 19X5 and $16.6 million in 19X4. The weighted average daily interest rates for 19X5 and 19X4 were 8.1 percent and 9.3 percent, respectively. The weighted average interest rates on outstanding borrowings at December 29, 19X5, and December 30, 19X4, were 8.1 percent and 8.7 percent, respectively.
>
> Interest payments approximated $7.3 million and $3.8 million for 19X5 and 19X4, respectively. For 19X3, interest expense approximated interest payments.
>
> The company's annual maturities on its long-term debt due in the next five years are $0.4 million for years 19X6 through 19X9 and $0.2 million thereafter.
>
> The company's long-term debt consisted of the following for fiscal years ended (amounts in thousands):

	19X5	19X4
6.6% revenue bonds payable in varying annual installments through 2009	**$6,400**	$6,500
Other	**1,300**	1,625
	7,700	8,125
Less: Current maturities	**(425)**	(425)
Total long-term debt	**$7,275**	$7,700

Required:

a. What amounts will Snap-On Tools report in its December 29, 19X5, balance sheet as its short-term and long-term debt balances?

b. In your own words, what other interesting information did you gather from the footnote? Why might the management of Snap-On Tools have decided to make that information available to us?

P4.9 Working with ratios. At lunch one day in the First National Bank's executive dining room, you notice a coworker lunching by himself and studying a set of financial statements. He seems frustrated and is talking to himself. You hear him say, as he picks up his briefcase and leaves, "I do not understand what is going on with this borrower — none of this makes any sense to me." You start to follow him out, when you notice that he has left a scratch sheet behind covered with figures and notes. The bulk of his scratching appears to be a set of ratios. The scratch sheet is as follows:

	This Year	Last Year
Return on owners' equity (net income divided by avg. OE)	22%	19%
Working capital	20,000	5,000
Current ratio	1.25	1.07
Quick ratio	0.5	0.5
Trade receivables, days' sales outstanding	73.00	81.11
Inventory turnover	1.25	1.69
Interest coverage	3.75	4.17
Long-term debt to owners' equity	0.8	0.6
% dividends to owners' equity	22%	19%

Required:

Identify five important issues regarding this borrower this year, which might explain the ratios developed by your frustrated friend.

P4.10 Balance sheets in the United States and abroad. In the United States, GAAP requires companies to present their balance sheets in descending order of liquidity; for example, the asset side begins with cash and concludes with intangible assets. In many other countries the balance sheets focus on the productivity of the assets, and so they begin with property, plant, and equipment, add net current assets, deduct long-term liabilities, and end with owners' equity. As an illustration of that different perspective, the following exhibit presents the balance sheet of an English music and film rental company, Thorne EMI. The next exhibit presents the balance sheet of Time Warner, a U.S. publishing and entertainment company.

Required:

Prepare a one-page paper outlining the results of your review of the exhibits. Your paper should explain which presentation might be preferred by which type of financial statement user, and why. You should express your own preference and justify your position logically. Based on your knowledge of U.S. business history and your thinking about the thrust of the U.S. approach to balance sheet presentation, comment on why that presentation might have evolved here.

Thorne EMI
Balance Sheet
(at March 31)

	19X6 £m	19X5 £m
Fixed assets		
Music publishing copyrights	**269.7**	216.8
Tangible fixed assets	**1,192.0**	1,126.3
Investments	**119.6**	109.6
Net assets of retail financing subsidiaries	**—**	19.2
	1,581.3	1,471.9
Current assets		
Stocks	**354.0**	363.5
Debtors	**816.4**	693.7
Investments: cash equivalents	**48.9**	45.3
Cash at bank and in hand	**95.5**	83.6
	1,314.8	1,186.1
Creditors: amounts falling due within one year		
Borrowings	**(185.1)**	(125.6)
Other creditors	**(1,200.3)**	(1,137.9)
	(1,385.4)	(1,263.5)
Net current liabilities	**(70.6)**	(77.4)
Total assets less current liabilities	**1,510.7**	1,394.5
Creditors: amounts falling due after more than one year		
Borrowings	**(353.5)**	(319.4)
Other creditors	**(47.3)**	(16.2)
	(400.8)	(335.6)
Provisions for liabilities and charges		
Deferred taxation	**(36.6)**	(36.2)
Other provisions	**(175.7)**	(146.6)
	(212.3)	(182.8)
	897.6	876.1
Capital and reserves		
Called-up share capital	**77.5**	96.6
Share premium account	**159.8**	55.6
Other reserves	**627.2**	646.1
Goodwill	**(710.6)**	(653.6)
Profit and loss reserve	**503.5**	498.6
Shareholders' funds	**657.4**	643.3
Minority interests	**240.2**	232.8
	897.6	876.1

Time Warner
Balance Sheet
(at December 31, in millions of dollars)

	19X5	19X4
Assets		
Current assets		
Cash and equivalents	$ 172	$ 234
Receivables, less allowances for doubtful receivables and returns of $761 and $766	2,071	2,005
Inventories	1,239	1,006
Other current assets	464	589
Total current assets	3,946	3,834
Receivables due after one year	552	435
Noncurrent inventories	1,759	1,876
Investments	1,874	1,455
Land and buildings	776	701
Cable television equipment	2,585	2,362
Furniture, fixtures, and other equipment	1,180	975
	4,541	4,038
Less accumulated depreciation and amortization	(1,415)	(1,094)
Property, plant, and equipment, net	3,126	2,944
Excess of cost over net assets acquired	9,073	9,044
Cable television franchises	3,097	3,281
Music copyrights, record catalogs, and other assets	1,910	1,922
Total assets	**$25,337**	**$24,791**
Liabilities and Shareholders' Equity		
Current liabilities		
Accounts payable and accrued expenses	$ 3,601	$ 3,137
Debt due within one year	31	54
Accrued income taxes	19	79
Total current liabilities	3,651	3,270
Long-term debt	11,184	10,838
Deferred income taxes	2,637	2,546
Unearned portion of paid subscriptions	521	449
Other liabilities	1,030	932
Shareholders' equity		
Preferred stock, $1 par value, 250 million shares authorized, 117.9 and 111.7 million shares issued, $5.954 and $5.584 billion liquidation preference	118	112
Common stock, $1 par value, 750 million shares authorized, 70.4 million shares issued	70	70
Paid-in capital	6,919	6,537
Retained earnings	499	1,299
Treasury stock, at cost, 12.9 million common shares and 0.7 million preferred shares in 19X5, and 13 million common shares in 19X4	(1,292)	(1,262)
Total shareholders' equity	6,314	6,756
Total liabilities and shareholders' equity	**$25,337**	**$24,791**

P4.11 Assets at cost or at current value. Pacific Dunlop is an Australian manufacturer of latex products, clothes, and electrical equipment. The company follows normal Australian accounting for its plant and equipment, providing regular revaluations by independent appraisers and by the company officers. The results of that accounting are detailed in the following footnote from its recent financial statements. (The Australian-GAAP based balance sheet reports total property, plant, and equipment of $1,008,197.)

Property, Plant, and Equipment

		Consolidated 1990 ($000)	1989 ($000)
(a) Freehold land	Independent valuations 31/12/1988	**82,874**	91,383
	Officers' valuations 31/12/1988	**608**	804
	At cost	**15,498**	16,537
		98,980	108,724
(b) Freehold buildings	Independent valuations 31/12/1988	**110,452**	116,660
	Officers' valuations 31/12/1988	**964**	992
	At cost	**54,011**	52,282
		165,427	169,934
	Less provision for depreciation	**16,535**	12,005
		148,892	157,929
(c) Leasehold land and buildings	Independent valuations 31/12/1988	**9,661**	12,381
	Officers' valuations 31/12/1988	**1,107**	1,192
	At cost	**17,685**	9,963
		28,453	23,536
	Less provision for amortisation	**4,484**	3,445
		23,969	20,091
(d) Plant and equipment	Independent valuations 1965–1985		77
	Officers' valuations 1970–1983	**4,915**	4,915
	Deemed value 1962	**47**	990
	At cost	**959,018**	902,218
		963,980	908,200
	Less provision for depreciation	**427,430**	375,464
		536,550	532,736
(e) Leased plant and equipment	At cost	**89,664**	45,863
	Less provision for amortisation	**14,776**	14,072
		74,888	31,791
(f) Buildings and plant under construction	At cost	**124,918**	83,489
		1,008,197	934,760

Required:

Comment on the Australian accounting policy, as exemplified in the Pacific Dunlop footnote. Should the accounting profession in the United States permit a similar policy for fixed assets? What would the advantages and disadvantages be for such a policy for U.S. companies? For their financial statement presentation? For their internal management? For their public policy position?

P4.12 Foreign currency adjustments. Monsanto, Procter & Gamble, Seagrams, and Snap-On Tools all made the same general statement in their footnotes regarding their policies for the translation of financial statements of subsidiaries that conduct business in currencies other than the U.S. dollar. Monsanto's statement is typical: "Most of Monsanto's non-U.S. entities' financial statements are translated into U.S. dollars using current exchange rates. Unrealized currency adjustments in the Statement of Consolidated Financial Position are accumulated in shareholders' equity."

The accumulated currency adjustment accounts in shareholders' equity for the four companies, at year-end 19X5 and 19X4, were as follows (in millions of dollars):

	Balance in the Account	
	19X5	19X4
Monsanto	188	24
Procter & Gamble	44	(63)
Snap-On Tools	(152)	(103)
Seagrams	(13)	(158)

Required:

Assume that the underlying balance sheets of the companies' non-U.S. subsidiaries have not changed significantly. Explain what has happened to cause the changes in the accumulated currency adjustments in each case.

P4.13 Leverage. A condensed balance sheet and a condensed income statement for the Lever-Up Corporation for 1995 are as follows:

Condensed Balance Sheet (000 omitted)

	12/31/95
Current assets	$ 4,500
Fixed assets (net)	9,000
Goodwill	2,500
Total assets	$16,000
Current liabilities	$ 3,000
8% bonds payable	8,000
Owners' equity	5,000
Liabilities and equity	$16,000

Condensed Income Statement (000 omitted)

	for the year ended 12/31/95
Sales	$25,000
Cost of sales	16,250
Administrative and selling expenses	6,200
Interest expense	640
Pre-tax income	2,010
Income tax	804
Net income	$ 1,206

Lever-Up's sales have been as high as $30,000,000 and as low as $20,000,000 during the last five years, but its interest coverage (profit before taxes and interest divided by interest) has always been in excess of 4.5 during all of those years. The company has maintained an open line of credit with its bank, which would allow it to borrow up to $5,000,000 for a five-year term at 10 percent.

Required:

a. Using the exhibits as a base, prepare at least four different sets of pro forma financial statements to demonstrate the effect of an increase in leverage on the company's return on equity ratio (net income divided by average owners' equity). Two of your pro forma presentations should assume the same sales and operating expenses but different levels of borrowing. As the debt is increased, reduce the level of owners' equity. The other pro forma presentations should assume an increase in debt and increased and decreased levels of sales (assume that cost of sales vary in proportion with sales and that other expenses are fixed).

b. Prepare a letter to the chairman of the board of Lever-Up, outlining some of the things she might think about as she considers a change in the company's debt/equity structure.

P4.14 Treasury stock. The H. J. Heinz Company has 287,400,000 common shares outstanding, and that has been the case for the last several years. The company reported that it had 59,900 shares of its convertible preferred stock outstanding and that it has 33,881,804 shares in its treasury at May 2, 19X5, and that it had 30,437,230 shares in its treasury at May 3, 19X4. The shareholder's equity balance sheet accounts for the company were as follows (thousands of dollars):

	19X5	19X4
Convertible preferred stock	$ 599	$ 757
Common stock	71,850	71,850
Additional capital	152,158	109,665
Retained earnings	2,560,780	2,263,829
Translation adjustments	(73,910)	(89,205)
Total	2,711,477	2,356,896
Treasury shares	(777,548)	(579,658)

Required:

Calculate the per-share values of the preferred stock, the common stock, the total outstanding stock, and the treasury shares, for each year. Why are some values the same each year? Why are some different? Why should there be a difference in the per-share value of the outstanding stock and the treasury stock?

P4.15 3M versus Philip Morris Companies, Inc. Philip Morris is a global consumer products company, manufacturing and marketing tobacco (such as Marlboro), food (such as Kraft) and beer (such as Miller) brands around the world. 3M is a global leader not only in consumer markets (for example, Scotch tape) but also in industrial, commercial, and health care markets. Their balance sheets are presented in the following exhibits.

Required:

Calculate all pertinent ratios as well as common-size balance sheets for both companies. Note the key differences and similarities. Comment on the relative positions of each one, year-to-year and to each other, from the perspective of a potential investor in the companies' common stock.

Philip Morris Companies, Inc.
Consolidated Balance Sheets
(in millions of dollars)

	19X5	19X4
Assets		
Consumer products		
Cash and cash equivalents	$ 146	$ 118
Receivables, net	4,101	2,956
Inventories:		
Leaf tobacco	2,458	2,202
Other raw materials	1,934	1,521
Finished product	2,761	2,028
	7,153	5,751
Other current assets	967	555
Total current assets	12,367	9,380
Property, plant, and equipment, at cost:		
Land and land improvements	664	611
Buildings and building equipment	4,004	3,554
Machinery and equipment	8,480	7,305
Construction in progress	1,133	887
	14,281	12,357
Less accumulated depreciation	4,677	3,900
	9,604	8,457
Goodwill and other intangible assets (less accumulated amortization of $1,178 and $745)	19,037	15,682
Other assets	1,675	1,569
Total consumer products assets	42,683	35,088
Financial services and real estate		
Finance assets, net	3,220	2,845
Real estate held for development and sale	418	383
Other assets	248	212
Total financial services and real estate assets	3,886	3,440
Total assets	$46,569	$38,528

Philip Morris Companies, Inc.
Consolidated Balance Sheets
(in millions of dollars)
continued

	19X5	19X4
Liabilities		
Consumer products		
Short-term borrowings	**$ 1,034**	$ 489
Current portion of long-term debt	**863**	752
Accounts payable	**2,462**	1,917
Accrued liabilities:		
Taxes, except income taxes	**851**	596
Employment costs	**832**	805
Other	**3,553**	2,876
Income taxes	**1,366**	1,190
Dividends payable	**399**	318
Total current liabilities	**11,360**	8,943
Long-term debt	**15,285**	13,646
Deferred income taxes	**1,316**	897
Other liabilities	**3,499**	2,622
Total consumer products liabilities	**31,460**	26,108
Financial services and real estate		
Short-term borrowings	**724**	633
Long-term debt	**836**	905
Deferred income taxes	**1,382**	1,111
Other liabilities	**220**	200
Total financial services and real estate liabilities	**3,162**	2,849
Total liabilities	**34,622**	28,957
Contingencies (Note 13)		
Stockholders' Equity		
Common stock, par value $1.00 per share (935,320,439 shares issued)	**935**	935
Earnings reinvested in the business	**10,960**	9,079
Currency translation adjustments	**561**	143
	12,456	10,157
Less cost of treasury stock (9,101,348 and 6,790,848 shares)	**509**	586
Total stockholders' equity	**11,947**	9,571
Total liabilities and stockholders' equity	**$46,569**	$38,528

Minnesota Mining and Manufacturing (3M) Company and Subsidiaries
As of December 31
(dollars in millions)

	19X5	19X4
Assets		
Current assets		
Cash and cash equivalents	$ 294	$ 413
Other securities	297	339
Accounts receivable — net	2,367	2,075
Inventories	2,355	2,120
Other current assets	416	349
Total current assets	5,729	5,296
Investments	471	342
Property, plant, and equipment — net	4,389	3,707
Other assets	490	396
Total	$11,079	$9,741
Liabilities and Stockholders' Equity		
Current liabilities		
Accounts payable	$ 811	$ 689
Payroll	377	332
Income taxes	342	305
Short-term debt	736	455
Other current liabilities	1,073	905
Total current liabilities	3,339	2,686
Deferred income taxes	160	200
Other liabilities	710	592
Long-term debt	760	885
Stockholders' equity — net	6,110	5,378
Shares outstanding — 19X5: 219,833,403; 19X4: 222,663,756		
Total	$11,079	$9,741

P4.16 Mobil versus Amoco. Mobil Corporation and Amoco Corporation are two of the world's leading oil exploration and production companies. The exhibits contain three-year comparative balance sheets for both companies.

Required:

Calculate the ratios you believe are most pertinent as well as common-size balance sheets, and then comment on the relative positions of each company. Based on just this balance sheet analysis, which company do you believe to be in the strongest financial position? Does it appear that they have similar attitudes toward leverage and liquidity? Why might their approach be the same? Why not? Why might they have taken the approach to liquidity and leverage that they did?

Amoco Corporation
Consolidated Statement of Financial Position
At December 31, in millions of dollars

	19X5	19X4	19X3
Assets			
Current assets			
Cash	**268**	231	233
Marketable securities	**2,131**	949	294
Accounts and notes receivable (net)	**4,226**	3,606	3,341
Inventories			
Crude oil and petroleum products	**361**	379	385
Chemical products	**412**	379	364
Other products and merchandise	**43**	47	39
Materials and supplies	**317**	307	277
Prepaid expenses and income taxes	**458**	530	460
	8,216	6,428	5,393
Investments and other assets			
Investments and related advances	**483**	503	725
Long-term receivables and other assets	**804**	852	706
	1,287	1,355	1,431
Properties			
At cost	**43,818**	42,430	41,509
Less — Accumulated depreciation, depletion, etc.	**21,112**	19,783	18,414
Net	**22,706**	22,647	23,095
Total assets	**32,209**	30,430	29,919
Liabilities and Shareholders' Equity			
Current liabilities			
Current installments of long-term obligations	**215**	257	225
Short-term obligations	**492**	483	444
Accounts payable	**3,697**	3,114	2,909
Accrued liabilities	**1,216**	1,162	984
Taxes payable (including income taxes)	**1,179**	872	906
	6,799	5,888	5,468
Long-term debt			
United States dollars	**4,946**	5,326	5,512
Foreign currencies	**66**	68	247
	5,012	5,394	5,759
Capitalized lease obligations	**237**	264	290
Deferred credits and other noncurrent liabilities			
Income taxes	**4,716**	4,394	4,342
Other	**1,363**	793	712
Minority interest in subsidiary companies	**14**	13	6
Shareholders' equity			
Common stock	**2,138**	2,178	2,208
Earnings retained and invested in the business	**11,925**	11,536	11,172
Foreign currency translation adjustment	**5**	(30)	(38)
	14,068	13,684	13,342
Less — Common stock held in treasury at cost	**—**	—	—
Total shareholders' equity	**14,068**	13,684	13,342
Total liabilities and shareholders' equity	**32,209**	30,430	29,919

Mobil Corporation
Balance Sheet
At December 31 in millions

	19X3	19X4	19X5
Assets			
Current assets			
Cash and cash equivalents	$ 889	$ 1,485	**$ 1,138**
Accounts and notes receivable	5,113	5,706	**7,134**
Inventories			
Crude oil and petroleum products	3,270	2,993	**3,064**
Chemical products	389	381	**434**
Other, including materials and supplies	822	824	**805**
Total inventories	4,481	4,198	**4,303**
Prepaid expenses and other current assets	695	531	**656**
Total current assets	11,178	11,920	**13,231**
Investments and long-term receivables	2,939	2,787	**3,054**
Properties, plants, and equipment, at cost	43,493	44,575	**47,568**
Less accumulated depreciation, depletion, and amortization	19,645	21,129	**23,087**
Net properties, plants, and equipment	23,848	23,446	**24,481**
Deferred charges and other assets	855	927	**899**
Total assets	$38,820	$39,080	**$41,665**
Liabilities and Shareholders' Equity			
Current liabilities			
Short-term debt	$ 902	$ 1,645	**$ 3,016**
Accounts payable and accrued liabilities	6,043	6,156	**7,132**
Income, excise, state gasoline, and other taxes payable	2,379	2,495	**2,755**
Deferred income taxes	931	920	**750**
Total current liabilities	10,255	11,216	**13,653**
Long-term debt	6,498	5,317	**4,298**
Reserves for employee benefits	514	707	**768**
Deferred credits and other noncurrent obligations	1,448	1,173	**1,197**
Accrued restoration and removal costs	526	595	**665**
Deferred income taxes	3,848	3,751	**3,947**
Minority interest in subsidiary companies	45	47	**65**
Shareholders' equity	15,686	16,274	**17,072**
Total liabilities and shareholders' equity	$38,820	$39,080	**$41,665**

P4.17 Spring's Industries, Inc. The following exhibit includes some excerpts from Spring's Industries, Inc.'s "Selected Financial Data" section of their 1990 annual report. Spring's manufactures and markets home furnishings, finished fabrics, and industrial textiles. Some of their major brand names are Springmaid, Bali, and Ultima.

Required:

Review the data and comment on the financial condition of Spring's over the 10-year period presented. In particular: *(a)* What is Spring's average accounts receivable collection period and days' sales in inventory? *(b)* Asset turnover? *(c)* Long-term debt-to-equity ratio? *(d)* Total debt-to-assets ratio? What do those ratios indicate to you as a potential investor? Finally, what might explain the fluctuating current ratio?

Spring's Industries, Inc.
Selected Financial Data

	1990	1989	1988	1987	1986	1985	1984	1983	1982	1981
Class A stock price range:										
High	**39½**	45¼	38¾	38¼	28¹⁄₁₆	23	20⅛	22⅜	20⅛	13³⁄₁₆
Low	**16⅞**	30½	27	20¾	20½	15⅝	15¼	17³⁄₁₆	10	8½
Capital Expenditures and Depreciation *(in millions)*:										
Capital expenditures	**$ 117.8**	$ 108.3	$ 77.1	$ 69.9	$ 57.0	$ 37.4	$ 50.9	$ 67.1	$ 39.9	$ 37.1
Depreciation	**72.6**	67.5	62.1	57.8	55.6	37.6	31.9	27.6	23.5	21.5
Shareholders and Employees:										
Approximate number of shareholders	**3,400**	3,500	3,700	3,400	3,300	3,400	3,500	3,500	3,800	4,500
Average number of employees	**23,200**	24,100	23,400	23,100	23,500	17,000	16,800	18,000	19,400	20,200
Statistical Data:										
Income to net sales	**(0.4)%**	3.4%	2.9%	3.4%	2.2%	1.3%	3.8%	4.1%	4.3%	4.4%
Net income (loss) to average shareholders' equity	**(1.2)%**	11.6%	10.2%	11.5%	7.3%	3.0%	8.4%	9.2%	11.3%	11.4%
Operating return on assets employed *(e)*	**7.7%**	11.2%	12.0%	12.3%	8.8%	4.4%	9.7%	10.7%	12.5%	16.4%
Inventory turnover *(f)*	**5.6**	5.8	6.2	5.8	5.0	5.7	5.8	5.8	5.1	5.4
Accounts receivable turnover *(g)*	**6.2**	6.4	6.4	6.5	6.3	6.2	6.2	6.3	6.2	6.3
Net sales divided by average assets *(h)*	**1.6**	1.7	1.7	1.6	1.5	1.5	1.5	1.5	1.6	1.9
Current ratio	**2.5**	2.4	2.7	3.0	3.3	3.1	4.8	4.4	5.2	3.9
Selected Balance Sheet Data *(in millions)*:										
Working capital	**$ 356.5**	$ 354.9	$ 389.8	$ 428.1	$ 402.2	$ 381.1	$ 279.8	$ 270.5	$ 283.7	$ 255.9
Property:										
Cost	**1,087.9**	978.0	872.5	803.6	749.3	710.3	561.7	536.1	484.9	452.2
Accumulated depreciation	**(563.7)**	(503.0)	(448.0)	(410.5)	(366.0)	(324.6)	(311.2)	(296.9)	(285.7)	(267.2)
Net	**524.2**	475.0	424.5	393.1	383.3	385.7	250.5	239.2	199.2	185.0
Total assets	**1,201.1**	1,188.4	1,118.3	1,083.7	1,010.4	1,013.1	615.0	602.2	561.1	543.3
Long-term debt	**260.4**	227.5	238.5	256.8	271.0	308.1	39.1	46.4	50.4	54.4
Shareholders' equity	**560.9**	585.1	541.6	505.0	464.6	442.2	441.2	419.0	395.8	364.7

(e) Pretax income before restructuring costs and interest expense divided by average of month-end total assets used in continuing operations.

(f) Cost of goods sold divided by average of month-end inventories.

(g) Net sales divided by average of month-end receivables.

(h) Net sales divided by average of month-end total assets used in continuing operations.

Note: Selected financial data includes M. Lowenstein Corporation, Uniglass, and Carey-McFall from their dates of acquisition in November 1985, February 1988, and March 1989, respectively.

CASES

C4.1 Analyzing the balance sheet: United Foods. The comparative balance sheets of United Foods, as of February 28, 19X5 and 19X4, are presented below. Perform a ratio analysis on the company and comment on its solvency, its liquidity, and its return on assets. What advice would you have for United Foods management? (Note that the company earned $5.8 million in 19X5 on sales of $170 million. The company's gross margin was $38.2 million. Note also that in 19X5 the item "other assets" includes an insurance claim receivable for $6.6 million, which is the estimated replacement cost of a processing plant destroyed in a fire. Filing and recording that claim resulted in an after-tax gain of $4.0 million, which is included in net income for 19X5.)

United Foods
Comparative Balance Sheet
As of February 28

	19X5	19X4
Assets		
Cash and cash equivalents	$ 1,367,000	$ 1,103,000
Accounts and notes receivable, less allowance of $212,000 and $286,000 for possible losses	16,320,000	15,108,000
Inventories	54,363,000	40,159,000
Prepaid expenses and miscellaneous	3,047,000	2,536,000
Total current assets	75,097,000	58,906,000
Property and equipment		
Land and land improvements	8,185,000	6,693,000
Buildings and leasehold improvements	19,177,000	18,755,000
Machinery, equipment, and improvements	63,929,000	57,902,000
	91,291,000	83,350,000
Less accumulated depreciation and amortization	(37,102,000)	(32,480,000)
Net property and equipment	54,189,000	50,870,000
Other assets	10,887,000	2,164,000
	$140,173,000	$111,940,000

United Foods
Comparative Balance Sheet
As of February 28
(continued)

	19X5	19X4
Liabilities and Stockholders' Equity		
Current liabilities:		
Accounts payable	$ 12,715,000	$ 6,996,000
Accruals:		
Compensation and related taxes	3,533,000	2,744,000
Pension contributions	876,000	1,455,000
Income taxes	128,000	853,000
Workers compensation insurance	1,074,000	870,000
Miscellaneous	1,263,000	1,730,000
Current maturities of long-term debt	1,034,000	881,000
Total current liabilities	20,623,000	15,529,000
Long-term debt, less current maturities	60,199,000	43,186,000
Deferred income taxes	2,934,000	—
Total liabilities	83,756,000	58,715,000
Commitments and contingencies		
Stockholders' equity		
Preferred stock, $1 par — shares authorized, 10,000,000		
Common stock, Class A, $1 par — shares authorized, 25,000,000; issued 7,642,650 and 7,635,732	7,643,000	7,636,000
Common stock, Class B, $1 par — shares authorized, 10,000,000; issued 7,102,987 and 7,109,905	7,103,000	7,110,000
Additional paid-in capital	8,720,000	8,901,000
Retained earnings	38,335,000	35,269,000
	61,801,000	58,916,000
Treasury stock, at cost, 1,890,004 and 1,991,004 shares	(5,384,000)	(5,691,000)
Total stockholders' equity	56,417,000	53,225,000
	$140,173,000	$111,940,000

C4.2 Analyzing the balance sheet: Tyson Foods, Inc. The comparative balance sheets of Tyson Foods at September 30, 19X5 and 19X4, are presented next. Perform a ratio analysis on the company and comment on its liquidity, solvency, and return on assets. Compare the results of your work on the Tyson balance sheet with the results of your work on the United Foods balance sheet (see C4.1) and comment on the circumstances of the two companies and their apparent strategies. (Note that Tyson earned $120 million in 19X5 on sales of $3.825 billion. Gross margin was $748.5 million.)

Tyson Foods, Inc.
Comparative Balance Sheets
For the Years Ending December 31
(in thousands)

	19X5	19X4
Assets		
Current assets:		
Cash and cash equivalents	$ 16,943	$ 56,490
Accounts receivable	90,839	247,979
Inventories	472,264	408,663
Other current assets	5,812	6,124
Net assets held for sale	—	30,396
Total current assets	585,858	749,652
Property, plant, and equipment, at cost:		
Land	36,945	24,492
Buildings and leasehold improvements	480,691	435,075
Machinery and equipment	876,555	796,166
Land improvements and other	54,057	55,238
Buildings and equipment under construction	50,020	44,291
	1,498,268	1,355,262
Less: Accumulated depreciation	427,152	334,506
Net property, plant, and equipment	1,071,116	1,020,756
Excess of investments over net assets acquired	784,209	745,778
Investments and other assets	59,879	69,894
Total assets	$2,501,062	$2,586,080
Liabilities and Shareholders' Equity		
Current liabilities:		
Current portion of long-term debt	$ 70,058	$ 55,048
Trade accounts payable	203,915	212,001
Accrued salaries and wages	118,947	98,020
Federal and state income taxes payable	8,489	16,714
Accrued interest payable	17,029	6,618
Other current liabilities	64,723	75,747
Current deferred income taxes		5,564
Total current liabilities	483,161	469,712
Long-term debt	950,407	1,319,385
Deferred income taxes	404,506	349,263
Shareholders' equity:		
Common stock ($0.10 par value):		
Class A — Authorized 60,000,000 shares; issued 34,734,131 shares in 19X5 and 31,574,473 shares in 19X4	3,473	3,157
Class B — Authorized 40,000,000 shares; issued 34,241,259 shares in 19X5 and 34,244,499 shares in 19X4	3,424	3,425
Capital in excess of par value	171,021	75,306
Retained earnings	500,268	382,661
	678,186	464,549
Treasury stock — 668,587 shares in 19X5 and 1,162,986 shares in 19X4, at cost	9,343	10,041
Unamortized deferred compensation	5,855	6,788
Total shareholders' equity	662,988	447,720
Total liabilities and shareholders' equity	$2,501,062	$2,586,080

C4.3 Balance sheets tell a story.* Presented below are six balance sheets. The balance sheet amounts are expressed as percentages of total assets in order to reflect relative amounts for each account. Each balance sheet represents a different company from a different industry. The industries and companies represented are:

Commercial bank (Sovran Financial Corp.)
Supermarket chain (Albertson's Inc.)
Advertising agency (Interpublic Group)
Discount store chain (Wal-Mart Stores, Inc.)
Electric utility (Pacific Gas & Electric Co.)
Chemical co. (Dow Chemical Co.)

Match the industry with the appropriate column based on your understanding of some of the financial implications of operating in that industry. The identifications often require two or more distinguishing features.

	Year Ended					
	(1) 12/31	(2) 2/2	(3) 12/31	(4) 12/31	(5) 11/31	(6) 12/31
Assets						
Cash and equivalents	11.3	5.1	.3	.5	.2	5.1
Accounts receivable	65.5	2.7	6.9	12.4	2.0	66.0
Inventory	—	27.2	3.1	12.8	52.7	—
Other current assets	—	2.2	3.9	7.4	2.2	7.7
Total current assets	76.8	37.2	14.2	33.1	57.1	78.8
Net plant and equipment	2.2	60.3	74.8	34.5	41.9	7.6
Other assets	21.0	2.5	11.0	32.4	1.0	13.6
Total assets	100%	100%	100%	100%	100%	100%
Liabilities						
Notes payable	15.9	.7	2.9	10.3	.6	3.1
Accounts payable	73.5	23.6	3.8	10.3	21.9	56.3
Accrued taxes	—	1.5	.1	1.2	1.9	2.4
Other current liabilities	.6	4.9	4.3	7.5	8.1	7.7
Total current liabilities	90.0	30.7	11.1	29.3	32.5	69.5
Long-term debt	1.9	11.1	36.6	17.4	18.8	2.1
Other liabilities	1.7	7.9	12.0	7.9	1.4	6.5
Total liabilities	93.6	49.7	59.7	54.6	52.7	78.1
Equity						
Preferred stock	—	—	5.4	—	—	—
Common stock and surplus	1.6	6.5	24.7	12.6	3.6	8.6
Retained earnings	4.8	43.8	10.2	41.5	43.7	18.1
Treasury stock	—	—	—	(8.7)	—	(3.8)
Total equity	6.4	50.3	40.3	45.4	47.3	22.9
Total liabilities and equity	100%	100%	100%	100%	100%	100%

C4.4 Balance sheet reviews. Reproduced on the following pages are three balance sheets from companies in very different industries. After a careful reading of each, hypothesize as to what industries are represented. Be prepared to explain your choice by highlighting specific attributes of each balance sheet.

Company A	Dollars in millions 19X5	19X4
Assets		
Cash and due from banks	$ 2,222	$ 2,344
Interest-bearing deposits with banks	1,696	3,518
Federal funds sold and securities purchased under resale agreements	1,410	2,464
Trading account assets	3,211	2,975
Investment securities (market value $8,559 and $6,555)	8,556	6,546
Loans	40,554	39,001
Reserve for possible credit losses	(2,139)	(2,677)
Premises and equipment	880	808
Customers' liability on acceptances	1,178	970
Accrued interest receivable	710	895
Other assets	3,252	3,635
Total assets	$61,530	$60,479
Liabilities		
Demand deposits in domestic offices	$ 6,367	$ 6,653
Time deposits in domestic offices	18,049	18,498
Deposits in foreign offices	15,780	16,483
Total deposits	40,196	41,994
Federal funds purchased and securities sold under repurchase agreements	7,203	4,813
Long-term debt	2,531	3,400
Other borrowings	3,866	3,526
Acceptances outstanding	1,187	982
Accrued taxes and other expenses	1,019	1,084
Other liabilities	2,100	1,299
Total liabilities	58,102	57,098
Shareholders' Equity		
Nonredeemable preferred stock	579	479
Common stock (outstanding 73,161,618 and 69,935,708 shares)	73	70
Surplus	2,171	2,089
Undivided profits	605	743
Total shareholders' equity	3,428	3,381
Total liabilities and shareholders' equity	$61,530	$60,479

Company B	19X5 (thousands)	19X4 (thousands)
Assets		
Electric utility plant		
Production	$1,382,758	$1,388,061
Transmission	325,310	318,758
Distribution	542,840	518,208
General	147,321	133,443
Construction work in progress	30,218	23,748
	2,428,447	**2,382,218**
Less — Accumulated depreciation	741,856	674,678
	1,686,591	1,707,540
Current Assets		
Cash and temporary cash investments	661	628
Accounts receivable	32,974	33,762
Materials and supplies, at average cost	22,319	3,408
Fuel inventory, at average cost	97,530	108,349
Prepayments and other	14,195	15,612
	167,679	161,759
Deferred charges and other assets	**15,419**	**10,801**
	$1,869,689	**$1,880,100**
Capitalization and Liabilities		
Capitalization		
Common stock, $18 par value, authorized 7,600,000 shares, issued and outstanding 7,536,640 shares	$ 135,660	$ 135,660
Paid-in capital	245,000	245,000
Retained earnings	260,894	259,509
Total common stock equity	**641,554**	**640,169**
Preferred stock		
Not subject to mandatory redemption	14,358	14,309
Subject to mandatory redemption	36,422	36,095
Long-term debt	576,095	595,988
Total capitalization	**1,268,429**	**1,286,561**
Current liabilities		
Long-term debt due within 12 months	2,769	2,564
Advances from affiliates	14,320	13,584
Accounts payable	22,658	45,012
Customer deposits	12,605	12,513
Accrued taxes	24,990	15,675
Accrued interest	19,083	19,217
Other	19,617	17,569
	116,042	**126,134**
Deferred credits		
Income taxes	361,141	357,367
Investment tax credits	102,295	107,229
Other	21,782	2,809
	485,218	**467,405**
	$1,869,689	**$1,880,100**

Company C	19X5 (in thousands)	19X4 (in thousands)
Assets		
Current Assets		
Cash and cash equivalents	**$ 2,008,983**	$ 1,655,264
Accounts receivable, net of allowance of $87,632 and $74,345	**3,206,765**	2,965,408
Inventories		
Raw materials	**352,976**	360,135
Work in process	**479,472**	570,064
Finished goods	**705,810**	707,802
Total inventories	**1,538,258**	1,638,001
Prepaid expenses	**345,797**	255,195
Net deferred federal and foreign income tax charges	**521,809**	381,140
Total Current Assets	**7,621,612**	6,895,008
Property, Plant, and Equipment, at Cost		
Land	**352,296**	300,540
Buildings	**1,712,204**	1,599,673
Leasehold improvements	**569,885**	530,773
Machinery and equipment	**4,392,609**	3,817,587
Total property, plant, and equipment, at cost	**7,026,994**	6,248,573
Less accumulated depreciation	**3,158,902**	2,602,677
Net property, plant, and equipment	**3,868,092**	3,645,896
Other assets, net	**165,117**	126,875
Total Assets	**$11,654,821**	$10,667,779
Liabilities and Stockholders' Equity		
Bank loans and current portion of long-term debt	**$ 12,538**	$ 29,755
Accounts payable	**660,819**	553,818
Federal, foreign, and state income taxes	**453,997**	445,977
Salaries, wages, and related items	**472,153**	300,393
Deferred revenues and customer advances	**903,038**	833,831
Other current liabilities	**787,224**	230,265
Total Current Liabilities	**3,289,769**	2,394,039
Net deferred federal and foreign income tax credits	**33,137**	102,048
Long-term debt	**150,001**	136,019
Total Liabilities	**3,472,907**	2,632,106
Stockholders' Equity		
Common stock, $1.00 par value; authorized 450,000,000 shares; issued 130,008,231 shares	**130,008**	130,008
Additional paid-in capital	**2,565,487**	2,469,711
Retained earnings	**6,257,199**	6,366,418
Treasury stock at cost; 7,453,501 shares and 8,471,655 shares	**(770,780)**	(930,464)
Total Stockholders' Equity	**8,181,914**	8,035,673
Total Liabilities and Stockholders' Equity	**$11,654,821**	$10,667,779

CHAPTER 5

The Income Statement

The income statement, like the balance sheet and the statement of cash flows, presents information that is essentially historical in nature. It describes what has happened, rather than what will happen. Nonetheless, it is probably the single most important source of information for me when I try to evaluate whether our operating units are performing as planned.[1]

Key Chapter Issues

- What is the income statement, and what are its principal elements?
- What are the key accounting concepts and conventions underlying the income statement?
- What are the key principles used in measuring a company's revenues and expenses?
- What information does the income statement convey about a company's financial and operating performance?
- How precise is the net income figure?

[1]Glenn R. Simmons, CEO, Keystone Consolidated Industries, Inc.

As defined in Chapter 2, the income statement, or statement of earnings, summarizes transactions that produce revenue for a company as a result of selling a product or service and transactions that result in expenses for the company. By summarizing revenues and expenses, the income statement presents a picture of overall profitability of a company's operations.

Some argue that the income statement is the most important of the standard accounting statements because net income (or, colloquially, "the bottom line") is the basis for so many financial decisions. Management is rewarded or punished in large part depending on whether actual income is or is not equal to planned income. Stock prices rise or fall in large part because the company reports net income higher or lower than the market's expectations. And, because of the frequently immediate reaction to its announcement, net income for the year is often taken to be the essence of that year's business activity.

Because of the importance of net income, management is often under great pressure as it anticipates the preparation of the income statement for its company. Unfortunately, the normal, healthy pressure for results is sometimes translated into pressure for *reported* results, as the article in Exhibit 5.1 from *Business Week* demonstrates.

Perhaps because the evaluation of both companies and management depends largely on the basis of reported net income, the measurement of income under generally accepted accounting principles (GAAP) has been rigorously defined. Recorded net income does not attempt to measure changes in values of the assets owned by a company, nor does it measure the company's qualitative accomplishments during the year. An accounting system could be designed to capture and report some or all of that type of information. However, faced with a trade-off between the reliability and relevance of presented information, the financial community (including company management) has determined that a reliable measure of income is more important than a broader, perhaps more relevant measure of income.

Financial analysts, for example, have said that they would prefer to have companies quantify only those activities that can be reasonably measured and provide supplementary information about all other activities, such as the value inherent in new products or in the appreciation of a company's assets. Analysts believe that they can evaluate those qualitative developments more objectively on their own.

Most members of management have supported a narrow definition of "income" because they prefer to be measured by a more concrete, more predictable measure of performance. For example, asset appreciation is excluded from the income statement in part because it is so hard to measure, in part because it fluctuates and suggests that a company's results are unstable and in part because it is so completely out of management's control.

Fundamentally, management and analysts know that a living, functioning company is too complex to be represented simply by a single measure of performance. PepsiCo, for example, accomplished much more in 1994 than simply earning $2.18 per share. Thorough financial analysis requires considering all of the numbers in the income statement and asking about their relationships. What is the trend of net income? Does it appear that sales prices are keeping pace with cost increases or are they falling behind? To what degree was income depressed this year as a result of resolving a long-standing problem and therefore clearing the way for increased income in the future? The users of financial statements should also look beyond the income statement and ask about the company's cash flows and the strength of its balance sheet. Finally, to develop a complete picture of a company's results, financial statement users should go beyond the statements and investigate nonfinancial factors, including such things as a com-

EXHIBIT 5.1

Did a Shearson Unit Pad Its Profits?

Shearson Lehman Hutton's Boston Co. unit said it was investigating accounting transactions that may have overstated aftertax earnings by as much as $15 million in the first three quarters of 1988. President James von Germeten and two other senior executives have taken paid leaves of absence, apparently at least for the length of the inquiry.

Representatives wouldn't comment on the focus of the review, and von Germeten couldn't be reached. But outsiders and some Shearson executives speculated that von Germeten, under pressure to produce earnings, may have inflated revenues and improperly deferred expenses at a Boston Co. unit. The company, which has grown rapidly since Shearson acquired it in 1981, is expected to earn $150 million before taxes this year — accounting for a large chunk of Shearson's profits.

Source: Reprinted from the January 9, 1989, issue of *Business Week* by special permission. Copyright 1989 by the McGraw-Hill Companies.

pany's market share, customer loyalty, and new product development. A wise management provides footnotes and other textual commentaries describing the events of the year and encourages financial statement users to use the income statement only as a starting point for analysis.

Having said all of that, the financial community is occasionally too impatient to study a company in depth and, when pressured for immediate decisions, looks for shortcuts. Net income and earnings per share are the most commonly used shorthand measures of performance, and the income statement maintains its foremost position as *the* vehicle to report a company's financial results. The objective of this chapter is to help you understand the components of the income statement, how it is prepared, and how it can be used.

THE ELEMENTS OF THE INCOME STATEMENT

Terminology and Concepts

When first introduced to the income statement, people often think it strange that such an important topic should be encumbered by so many apparently overlapping and confusing terms. Perhaps the terminology problem can be traced to the attention given to the measurement of income — many people have looked at the subject from diverse viewpoints, and their different perspectives seem to have spawned many different words to express slightly different ideas. But it is simpler than that; perhaps the terminology problem is just a reflection of the inherent complexity of the subject. In any event, the words used are sometimes difficult. Because the topic is so important, it is useful to focus initially on the terminology used in connection with the income statement and to establish a common frame of reference for our subsequent discussions.

Revenues. The senior concept in the income statement, the term **revenues** refers to a company's actual, or promised, cash inflows resulting from a completed sale of the company's products or the satisfactory delivery of its services. (In some countries, the term *turnover* is used in lieu of *revenues.*) To help you distinguish between a company's revenues and its *cash receipts,* consider the following:

Revenue (a source of income)					Cash sales ↓	Gains and other income ↓	Credit sales ↓
Receipts (a source of cash flow)	↑ Proceeds from sales of stock	↑ Proceeds from bank loans	↑ Advances from customers for future work	↑ Collections on accounts receivable	↑ Proceeds from cash sales	↑ Proceeds from sale of other assets	

Cash inflows from the sale of stock or from borrowed money are not revenues but are financing transactions because the entity has continuing responsibilities to the providers of those funds. Cash deposits from a customer in advance of the delivery of a product or service are not revenues, nor will they be recognized as such until the "seller" completes its part of the bargain. In sum, revenues are those cash inflows (or expected cash inflows) that the company has earned and to which it is entitled to retain without qualification. Revenues are part of a company's income stream under accrual accounting. Some revenues also involve the receipt of cash, but others do not. Cash receipts, on the other hand, enter into the determination of a company's cash flows, which is the subject of Chapter 6.

Sales. A legal term, **sales** suggests that the title to property has passed from a seller to a buyer. Most legal sales transactions qualify as revenue, but the accounting world is more interested in the substance of a transaction than in its legal form. Not all legal sales qualify as revenues for accounting purposes, however, as we shall see.

Gains and losses. A **gain** is the net revenue a company earned as a result of a business transaction that is not a normal sale of products or delivery of services. For example, a company that sells an excess piece of land that it had purchased earlier for possible expansion will recognize a gain in its income statement to the extent that the sales price of the land is more than the original cost. Conversely, if the sales price is less than the land's cost, the company will recognize a **loss.**

Income. A generic term, **income** usually means revenue from sources other than product sales or from gain-producing transactions, such as interest income or rent income.

Expenses. This term encompasses all actual or expected cash outflows, or cost allocations from prior years' cash outflows, which cannot be justified as an addition to an asset account or a reduction in a liability. To help you distinguish between **expenses** and *cash expenditures*, consider the following chart:

Expenses (a reduction in income)				Expenses paid currently ↓	Expenses accrued now for later payment ↓	Expenses allocated from assets recorded in prior periods ↓
Expenditures (a reduction in cash flows)	↑ Payment for additions to assets	↑ Payment of prior accruals and debts owed to lenders and suppliers	↑ Payment of dividends to stockholders	↑ Payment of expenses currently		

As we said in Chapter 3, an accounting entry to record an expenditure must have two sides; the credit side is, of course, a reduction in cash, but whether the debit side is an increase in an expense or an increase in an asset (or a reduction in a liability) depends on a careful analysis of the reason for the expenditure. Principal payments on debt are not expenses because they are simply the repayment of funds provided earlier by a lender. Similarly, expenditures for the reacquisition of some of the company's stock, or dividends paid to the shareholders, are not expenses because they are transactions with the owners. (Remember from our work with Blue Ridge Hardware in Chapter 3 that interest is an expense and, therefore, a deduction from revenues in determining net income, but dividends are not an expense and instead are considered to be a distribution of net income to the shareholders.)[2] An expenditure that creates a future value for the company may be considered an asset. If no measurable future value results from an expenditure, it will be treated as an expense. Most often, an asset created in one year will become an expense in a future year — as with the annual allocation to expense that we call *depreciation*.

Cost. An awkward word, **cost** is best understood when used in conjunction with an explanatory adjective such as material cost, product cost, transportation cost, and so forth. You will hear businesspeople refer to the cost of a new machine, meaning the expenditure required for the asset. Or they will talk about the cost of a transaction, meaning the commission and delivery expenses incurred in connection with making a sale. The ambiguity of the term actually carries over to the traditional terminology used in preparing the income statement. For example, the biggest deduction from revenue in the measurement of net income is referred to as the *cost of goods sold,* which is the total cost of the products removed from inventory and delivered to customers as a result of sales. On the other hand, the other deductions from revenue on the income statement are *selling expenses* and *general and administrative expenses,* which are expenditures that were necessary for the operations of the business during the year.

Net income. The final financial result of all of an entity's operations for the year, **net income** is the difference between total revenues (including product and service revenues, net gains from other transactions, and interest and other income) and the total of the cost of goods sold and operating expenses. The phrases *net income* and *net earnings* are often used interchangeably, and the income statement itself is often referred to as the *earnings statement*. There are a number of intermediate designations on the income statement, such as *income from operations, income before extraordinary items,* and *income before taxes*. Consider again the basic accounting equation we studied in Chapter 2:

$$A = L + OE$$

Remember that we said that all changes in owners' equity between one year and the next are reported as either transactions with stockholders or as net income and that all net income items would be presented in the income statement. Conceptually, then,

Last year A = L + (CS + RE)
This year A = L + (CS + RE)

(difference in RE) = This year's income (excluding dividend considerations)

[2]Many financial economists consider the inconsistent accounting treatment of dividends and interest charges to be inappropriate. They argue that since interest is the cost of a company's debt financing, and dividends represent the cost of equity financing, the two items should be consistently accounted for. A counterargument, however, relates to tax considerations — in most countries, while interest charges are tax deductible, dividend payments are not.

Net income is the difference between revenues and expenses for the year, but it can also be seen as that part of the change in owners' equity from one year to the next that can be attributed to transactions with third parties — parties other than the owners.

Profit or loss. This is occasionally a synonym for income. Most often **profit** (or **loss**) is used to describe the income (or loss) effect of an *individual* transaction.

Unfortunately, some of these words are used casually in practice and are often used interchangeably. To understand what meaning is intended, it is important to consider the context in which a word is used and to focus on its meaning in that context.

Revenue and Revenue Recognition: Some Questions and Answers

Income statements always begin with revenue — sales, rent, services, or interest, depending on the nature of the business. Decisions about revenue recognition are among the most important accounting decisions a manager must make. For a simple transaction, for example, a retail sale of merchandise for cash, it is easy to determine which period's income statement should benefit: The revenue is recognized in the period when the merchandise and the cash are exchanged. For more complex transactions, such as the sale of a partially completed building in exchange for cash and a long-term note receivable, it is much more difficult to know whether a sale has really occurred and to decide when the revenue should be recognized. Should the sale be included in the income statement in (1) the period in which the parties agreed to the transaction, (2) the period in which the building is completed, or (3) the period in which the note is finally paid off in cash? Take a moment and think about when revenue should be recognized in the sale of a life insurance policy, the construction of a submarine for the navy, or the provision of legal services.

To make those **revenue recognition** decisions — that is, to decide whether a company is entitled to recognize revenue from a transaction in the current period — management must answer three important questions.

Has the buyer accepted substantially all of the risk associated with the product sold (or service provided)? A seller almost always retains some risk related to an item sold as the result of its customer service policies, which provide for product return or repair under warranty. To qualify for revenue recognition at the time of an exchange, however, the transaction must burden the seller with only ordinary business risks that can be estimated with a reasonable degree of certainty. Almost every consumer product company recognizes revenue when its products are delivered to the customer, and such companies simultaneously recognize an expense and a liability for the estimated warranty services that may be required. If those future expenses cannot be estimated with reasonable accuracy — because, for example, it is a very new product and there is not sufficient experience to suggest what the rate of warranty repair will be — the sale itself should not be recorded but should be treated as deferred revenue (a type of liability account). In such a case, the revenue would be deferred until the ultimate results from the transaction can be estimated more precisely.

Have we earned the right to the proceeds from this sale because we have completed our share of the transaction? The seller of a software package such as Lotus Notes™ can answer that question affirmatively when the disks and the manuals are delivered to the customer; in that case the delivery completes the earnings process because Lotus need do nothing more to the product to satisfy the customer. On the other hand, the producer of custom-designed software cannot answer that question affirmatively until the software has been programmed, debugged, and tested successfully on the customer's hardware. Only when all of that has been done can the seller say that the earnings process is complete for that transaction, and only then can the sale be recognized in the seller's income statement. In some very predictable long-term contract situations, the seller may be able to say that the earnings process is complete in phases and, as each phase is completed, recognize a pro rata share of the total expected revenue on the contract and the total expected cost of fulfilling that contract. This accounting convention is referred to as **percentage of completion** accounting (see Chapter 7 for further discussion). Aside from that unique exception, however, sale transactions can be recorded as revenue only when management can objectively affirm that the company's earnings process has been completed.

Can we estimate the collectibility of proceeds from this sale with a reasonable degree of certainty? Under accrual accounting, a seller makes no distinction between cash sales and credit sales on the assumption that collectibility of any resulting receivable is reasonably assured and that any credit loss can be estimated and recorded coincident with recognizing the revenue. However, when the terms of a transaction or the financial status of a buyer raise serious questions about the collectibility of the receivable resulting from the sale, recognition of the revenue should be deferred until that credit question is resolved. In some questionable collectibility situations, the seller may be entitled to recognize revenue on an installment basis; that is, the seller will recognize a pro rata portion of the total expected revenue and a pro rata portion of the total expected cost of the sale as the cash payments are received. The question of collectibility is similar to the first question regarding risk passage — management must be able to estimate reasonably the amount of loss the company will incur as the result of a possible bad debt. If that loss cannot be reasonably estimated based on experience, the recognition of the revenue must be deferred until that uncertainty is resolved.

Most companies' sales transactions are straightforward, and the financial statement user can assume that the preceding three questions were asked and answered in a routine fashion. However, when a company's business is complex, the footnotes to the financial statements will describe the revenue recognition policies being followed. For example, in General Motors' annual report, the company explains that it records a sale when it ships a car to an independent dealer rather than when the car is sold to the ultimate buyer. GM evidently follows that practice because it is confident that the dealer has assumed all substantive risk at the time of shipment to the dealer. General Motors' description of its revenue recognition policy is presented in a footnote, which is reproduced in Exhibit 5.2.

Occasionally a management group feels pressured to produce increasing net income numbers — the pressure may be from higher-level management or shareholders who want (expect) the company to perform well — and someone in the group will provide an inadequate or incorrect answer to one of the three revenue recognition questions. Unless one of the other members of the group protests, the company's income will be misstated. That misstatement may keep income high for a period and forestall a day of reckoning in the marketplace, but an incorrect answer to a revenue recognition question almost always becomes public, and the human and corporate cost to correct those misstatements is usually very great. Three cases involving misstatement are illustrated in Panel A of Exhibit 5.3. You will note that in several cases, more than one revenue recognition question was asked, and more than one wrong answer was given.

EXHIBIT 5.2

General Motors
Footnote Disclosure: Revenue Recognition Policy

Sales are generally recorded by the corporation when products are shipped to independent dealers. Provisions for normal dealer sales incentives and returns and allowances are made at the time of sale. Costs related to special sales incentive programs are recognized as sales deductions when these incentive programs are announced.

Certain sales under long-term contracts, primarily in the defense business, are recorded using the percentage of completion (cost-to-cost) method of accounting. Under this method, sales are recorded equivalent to costs incurred plus a portion of the profit expected to be realized on the contract, determined based on the ratio of costs incurred to estimated total costs at completion. Profits expected to be realized on contracts are based on the corporation's estimates of total sales value and cost at completion. These estimates are reviewed and revised periodically throughout the lives of the contracts, and adjustments to profits resulting from such revisions are recorded in the accounting period in which the revisions are made. Estimated losses on contracts are recorded in the period in which they are identified.

Source: Excerpted from the footnotes to General Motors' annual report.

EXHIBIT 5.3

Panel A — Revenue Recognition Questions and Answers

Case 1

A manufacturer of designer jeans maintained a policy to sell only to customers whose accounts receivable were current (i.e., only the most recent month's purchases were unpaid). However, at the end of a quarter when sales were below budget, an order came in from a major customer whose account was 90 days past due. At the direction of the CEO, the company recorded the sale in the period when the order was received but held the delivery, setting the jeans aside in the warehouse. The customer was told that the merchandise would be shipped when the account receivable was paid up to a current status. That transaction did *not* qualify for revenue recognition in the period when the order was received because by the manufacturer's own policies, there was a question as to the collectibility of the receivable. Because of its refusal to ship the merchandise, the manufacturer retained all risk on the goods "sold." (Who bore the risk, for example, of a fire in the warehouse or of a dramatic change in styles?) Revenue should have been recognized in the period when the customer's account status was acceptable and when the product was shipped to the customer.

Case 2

A manufacturer of computer equipment maintained a policy to recognize revenue when its products were shipped, pursuant to a valid customer order. So long as the products were on the leading edge of technology, the policy was appropriate because shipment by the manufacturer was the equivalent of customer acceptance. However, there came a time when the competition caught up with the company's products, and customers frequently accepted shipment *subject to* testing against a competing product in their own installations. (Had the customer accepted all risk for the equipment?) The company didn't always win those competitions, and many of its shipments were returned. When the business circumstances changed, the company's revenue recognition policies should have changed to recognize revenue only in the period when it had formal customer acceptance in hand. Only then could the company be sure that risk had passed on the "sales" and that collectibility could be estimated with any reasonable degree of certainty.

Case 3

An operator of a computer service bureau also ran a school in which students from disadvantaged neighborhoods were trained on word processors and other computer equipment. The teaching was provided by computer-driven programmed instruction, and the students worked on their programs in labs under the direction of proctors. The tuition was paid periodically by government grants as the students completed phases of the program. The company recognized all of the revenue from the course (less a provision for dropouts) as soon as a student signed up for the course. (Had the company essentially completed its portion of the transaction?) Revenue should *not*, however, have been recognized "up front" when the students signed up because to complete the earnings process and to ensure their estimates of dropouts, the company had to coach the students through the training and encourage their completion of the course work. Revenue should have been recognized only in the periods when the students completed phases of their course work, and the company completed that phase of its "earnings process."

EXHIBIT 5.3 concluded

Panel B — Expense Recognition Questions and Answers

Case 1

A manufacturer of high-tech products was faced with increasing competition and was forced to produce new models of its products before all of the engineering was complete. To meet production schedules, it was necessary to do significant handwork on each unit, which was very expensive. It was decided to send that handwork to a subcontractor because of its cheaper labor rate. Apparently arguing that a failure in tool design caused the production problem and required the handwork, management had the subcontractor bill the handwork as tooling. The manufacturer accounted for those tooling charges as long-term assets and depreciated them against income over five years. (Did the handwork have the potential to earn future cash flows?) The subcontractor agreed to the mislabeled billings because the job was important to its own income. Clearly, the handwork added no new value to the manufacturer and should have been accounted for as part of the current period's cost of sales. The fraud was uncovered when an employee of the subcontractor finally "blew the whistle" on the mislabeled billings.

Case 2

A cable TV company was experiencing much greater growth than it had anticipated. Management was concerned that the growth could not be sustained and so decided to "park" some of its current income for future years. To do so, it set up a reserve account (i.e. a contra asset) and charged current operations with expenses for possible inventory obsolescence. (Were all costs and expenses associated with the current year's revenues appropriately recognized?) In later years, the growth did begin to slow down and eventually slowed disastrously. Rather than recognizing the effect of that slowdown in the income statement, management drew down on that reserve, crediting current income with a reversal of the prior years' expenses. Those machinations only postponed the inevitable, however, and the company eventually entered bankruptcy. The shareholders sued management because they were misled on the up side and on the down side of the company's business cycle. The shareholders argued that they wanted to know the naked facts about the company's earnings, period by period, and that they had been misled by management's "smoothed" results.

Case 3

A bank had substantial loans outstanding to oil and gas producers at a time when oil prices collapsed. Looking at the collateral behind its loans, the bank realized that under current conditions, the collectibility of those loans was very questionable. Management delayed making any addition to the bank's loan-loss reserve (and taking a current period charge to bad debts expense) because it had some studies suggesting that oil prices would eventually recover. (Were the bank's judgments and estimates sufficiently conservative?) Oil prices did not recover sufficiently, however, and the bank's major borrowers eventually collapsed. When that occurred, the bank had to make a major addition to its loan-loss reserve. The shareholders sued, arguing that management knew about the probability of the loan-loss problem much earlier, and, had it accounted for the probable losses conservatively, the shareholders would have had a fairer picture of the bank's operations much sooner.

Expenses and Expense Recognition: Some Questions and Answers

In preparing the income statement, questions concerning the recognition of both revenue and expenses must be addressed. Although the challenges to revenue recognition may be the most dramatic questions posed to management in connection with the preparation of the income statement, measurement of net income is also affected by costs and expenses. And, in fact, management must address similar questions regarding the recognition of expenses.

Have we included in our income statement all of the costs and expenses associated with the benefits we realized during the year? In an accrual accounting system, management's first obligation is to match expenses with benefits in the accounting period in which the benefits are realized. Some benefits are transaction based — the obvious example being sales to customers. In the case of sales, the *matching principle* requires that all costs and expenses connected with the sale be recognized in the same accounting period as the related revenue. Those costs and expenses to be matched against sales include some prior period costs that have been deferred as inventory until the period in which the product is sold. Those costs include the actual current period costs to make the sale, including commissions and freight, as well as certain future costs, such as the estimated cost of warranty work and estimated losses due to uncollectible receivables. Some benefits also flow to the company with the passage of time. For example, interest expense is an expense of the current period because the company has had the use of the borrowed funds for the period. Or an insurance premium paid in advance to cover three years of insurance is recorded originally as an asset; that asset is then allocated to insurance expense, one-third in each of the covered years. The application of the matching principle requires some thought; management must look carefully at the benefits realized during the year and then think carefully about all the past, current, and future expenses that might be connected with those benefits.

As we prepared these financial statements, have our judgments and estimates been appropriately conservative? The decision as to whether an expenditure is an expense of the current year or whether it is an asset and is to be allocated to expense in future years is sometimes a difficult judgment. Some managers argue that an expenditure has a clear benefit and should therefore be allocated to future years. Others argue that the benefit is tenuous and the expense should therefore be recognized immediately. For example, some argue logically that an advertising campaign is sure to build product awareness and customer loyalty. Because those benefits will produce future sales, it might be argued that some portion of those advertising expenditures should be treated as an asset and deferred into future periods so that they can be matched against the future sales the campaign generates. However, because those future benefits are uncertain (and because they are difficult to measure), the *principle of conservatism* forces companies to recognize those expenditures as expenses in the period they are incurred.

In practice, management is often tempted to be optimistic. After all, an entrepreneur who has devoted three years to developing a new product must believe strongly in that product to have devoted so much time to it. It naturally follows that the entrepreneur is confident of success and therefore wants to match the costs of that product development with the expected future sales. Determining whether an entity has been appropriately conservative requires an extraordinary amount of objectivity from a responsible management group. It is also possible, however, to be too conservative. An overly conservative approach to the asset/expense decision results in an unduly pessimistic income statement for the current period and an unrealistically profitable picture in subsequent years. As in all key management decisions, the answer is balance: Management must balance its application of the matching principle, which requires the deferral of some expenditures until future periods, with its application of the conservatism principle, which stipulates that the only surprises that should arise in future years should be good surprises.

Do all of our assets still have the potential to earn future cash flows equal to their current costs? Have we recorded as liabilities all of the future expenditures we are likely to have to make? In addition to our challenge of the income statement, we ought to challenge the balance sheet as well. GAAP requires that an impairment of an asset and the recognition of a liability be recorded — and a charge to expense be recorded as well — when it is probable that an asset impairment or liability has occurred and when the amount of the expense can be estimated reasonably. In this context, "probable" is understood to mean that a future event is likely to confirm the impairment or liability incurrence.

Some expenses are probable because they are a natural consequence of a company's activities. For example, a company that sells a consumer product with a warranty will probably incur some warranty expense, and so an estimate of that expense is recorded in the period in which the sales are recorded. Other expenses are probable because of forces outside the company and so are recorded in the period that the outside events become probable. For example, a fashion goods manufacturer knows that its inventory is subject to obsolescence and so analyzes the inventory periodically and records an adjustment to the carrying value of its unsold products when they become unfashionable and difficult to sell.

Some expenses become probable over time as the asset impairment becomes more serious or the threat of a liability becomes more tangible. For example, when a company is sued, its attorneys are not likely to be able to estimate the probability of losing the suit or the possible cost of such a loss. As time goes on, however, they form a clearer picture of the litigation and have a better estimate of winning or losing. At an intermediate stage in the litigation, they may develop an opinion as to the probability of losing the suit, but they still may be a long way from being able to estimate the cost of such a loss. Thus, the company may be required to include a footnote to its financial statements warning of the possibility of such a loss, but the expected future liability is not recognized in the balance sheet, nor is the expense recognized in the income statement. Eventually, a time will come when a settlement is under discussion or when a judgment has been reached and the cost of that lawsuit can be reasonably estimated. At that time, the liability and the expense connected with that lawsuit are recorded in the financial statements.

As you have thought about the three revenue recognition questions and the three expense recognition questions, you have perhaps realized that the critical issues have to do with *timing*. Because the income statement presents the results of operations for a given period of time, all of the critical questions having to do with the preparation of the income statement are timing issues — when, in which period, should an event be recognized? For example, an expenditure for a new roof can be added to the cost of a building and depreciated over the building's remaining life, or it can be charged to maintenance expense all at once at the time of the expenditure. Intellectually, we might debate the nature of the expenditure — whether the new roof is an addition to the building or whether it is simple maintenance — but the practical effect of that debate would be a focus on the timing of the impact of that expenditure on net income. Because an income statement measures results over one period of time, and because income statements for a period of years measure trends of income, the timing of revenue recognition and expense recognition are critical. Management must make those decisions as objectively as possible to produce the fairest measure of results of operation for the period.

To help you review your understanding of expenses and expense recognition, return to Exhibit 5.3 and consider the three cases in panel B. Note the expense questions asked and how they were answered.

REPORTING THE RESULTS OF OPERATIONS: PEPSICO, INC.

Traditionally, income statements are prepared with revenues listed first, followed by various categories of expense deductions, to arrive at a "bottom line," or net income. Income statements may be condensed for brevity, as in the case of PepsiCo, Inc. (see Exhibit 5.4), or expanded for detail, providing many useful subtotals.[3] For example,

[3]Published income statements are almost always comparative, with the results for the current year and at least one, often two, prior years presented. The presentations are consistent, even if classifications in prior years have to be adjusted to conform to the current year's format.

EXHIBIT 5.4

PepsiCo, Inc.
Consolidated Statement of Income
(in millions except per share amounts)
Fifty-three weeks ended December 31, 1994, and 52 weeks ended December 25, 1993, and December 26, 1992

	1994	1993	1992
Net Sales	**$28,472.4**	$25,020.7	$21,970.0
Costs and Expenses, Net			
Cost of sales	**13,715.4**	11,946.1	10,611.7
Selling, general, and administrative expenses	**11,243.6**	9,864.4	8,721.2
Amortization of intangible assets	**312.2**	303.7	265.9
Operating Profit	**3,201.2**	2,906.5	2,371.2
Gain on joint venture stock offering	**17.8**	—	—
Interest expense	**(645.0)**	(572.7)	(586.1)
Interest income	**90.4**	88.7	113.7
Income before Income Taxes and Cumulative Effect of Accounting Changes	**2,664.4**	2,422.5	1,898.8
Provision for Income Taxes	**880.4**	834.6	597.1
Income before Cumulative Effect of Accounting Changes	**1,784.0**	1,587.9	1,301.7
Cumulative Effect of Accounting Changes			
Postemployment benefits (net of income tax benefit of $29.3)	**(55.3)**	—	—
Pension assets (net of income tax expense of $14.5)	**23.3**	—	—
Postretirement benefits other than pensions (net of income tax benefit of $218.6)	**—**	—	(356.7)
Income taxes	**—**	—	(570.7)
Net Income	**$ 1,752.0**	$ 1,587.9	$ 374.3
Income (Charge) per Share			
Before cumulative effect of accounting changes	**$ 2.22**	$ 1.96	$ 1.61
Cumulative effect of accounting changes			
Postemployment benefits	**(0.07)**	—	—
Pension assets	**0.03**	—	—
Postretirement benefits other than pensions	**—**	—	(0.44)
Income taxes	**—**	—	(0.71)
Net Income per Share	**$ 2.18**	$ 1.96	$ 0.46
Average shares outstanding used to calculate income (charge) per share	**803.6**	810.1	806.7

one important subtotal is the **gross margin** or **gross profit**, calculated as net sales minus the cost of sales or services. Another subtotal is **income from continuing operations**, which measures the profitability of a company's principal line of business activity.

Recurring and Nonrecurring Items

The results of a company's operations are frequently broken down into *recurring* and *nonrecurring* categories. Recurring (or continuing) results are those that can reasonably be expected to reoccur in future periods and are usually summarized as income from continuing operations. In the minds of many financial analysts, the income from recurring or continuing operations is the most important indicator of a company's performance because of its value in predicting future earnings performance. Nonrecurring income (or losses), on the other hand, refers to events or transactions that are *not* expected to recur in future periods. This category includes **unusual** and **extraordinary items** (such as loss due to fire or natural phenomena) as well as **discontinued operations.** Another example of nonrecurring income (or loss) consists of those additions to (or subtractions from) income resulting from a change in a company's accounting policies. PepsiCo's consolidated statement of income reveals, for example, that income was both increased (by $23.3 million) and decreased (by $55.3 million) as a consequence of various accounting policy changes undertaken by the company in 1994. GAAP defines (and provides explicit accounting treatment for) extraordinary items and discontinued operations. "Unusual" events are defined by financial statement users themselves, based on their reading of the footnotes, "Management's Discussion and Analysis," and other company news releases.

Discontinued Operations

When a company decides to divest itself of a division, a subsidiary, or other business segment (so long as it is a separate, major line of business), all of the final period's sales and expenses related to that segment should be netted together and reported in a single line on the next income statement with the designation **net income from discontinued operations.** That line item, for the period when the divestiture decision is made, also includes an estimate of the loss to be incurred on the sale of the division or segment (it would not include an estimated gain, of course). All prior periods' income statements presented for comparative purposes should be restated to place the results of that to-be-sold segment in the discontinued operations line.

For example, in 1990 (not reflected in Exhibit 5.4) PepsiCo sold a retail bakery operation, recognizing a $13.7 million aftertax loss. The results of the operations of the subsidiary, through the date of sale, were included in PepsiCo's consolidated income statement under the caption "Loss from discontinued operations."

Extraordinary Items

Because of the importance attached to the figure referred to as *net income,* only one figure in the income statement is so designated, and *all* items of revenue and expense are included in the determination of that amount. Certain events are so unusual and significant that they are called *extraordinary* and hence warrant separate identification on the income statement. When extraordinary items are reported on the income statement, an intermediate subtotal is designated **net income before extraordinary items**. To guard against the liberal use of the extraordinary item presentation, GAAP defines an extraordinary item as being both *unusual* (possessing a high degree of abnormality and clearly unrelated to the normal business of the entity) and *infrequent* (not reasonably expected to reoccur in the near future). As might be expected, extraordinary item presentation in published financial statements is rare.

As an example, Sears, Roebuck & Co. engaged in several debt retirement transactions in 1994 and 1993 that resulted in, respectively, a gain of $195 million and a loss of $211 million. These transactions were judged by the company to be sufficiently unrelated to normal operations (that is, unusual and infrequent) so as to qualify for disclosure as extraordinary items. Sears's 1994 and 1993 income statement and footnote disclosure of the extraordinary items are presented in Exhibit 5.5. It is worth noting that the criteria used in the U.S. to qualify an accounting event as extraordinary is not a global criteria. For example, historically in the U.K., restructuring costs and the disposal of a business segment were likely to qualify for such a designation.

EXHIBIT 5.5

Sears, Roebuck & Co.
Consolidated Statements of Income
(in millions, except per common share data)

	Year Ended December 31		
	1994	**1993**	**1992**
Revenues	**$54,559**	$51,486	$53,110
Expenses			
Costs and expenses	**51,390**	47,898	53,253
Restructuring	**154**	—	2,782
Interest	**1,339**	1,400	1,389
Total expenses	**52,883**	49,298	57,424
Operating income (loss)	**1,676**	2,188	(4,314)
Other income (loss)	**36**	149	(71)
Gain on sales of subsidiaries' stock	**—**	635	91
Income (loss) before income taxes (benefit) and minority interest	**1,712**	2,972	(4,294)
Income taxes (benefit)	**358**	404	(1,965)
Minority interest	**(110)**	(148)	18
Income (loss) from continuing operations	**1,244**	2,420	(2,311)
Discontinued operations	**15**	165	252
Income (loss) before extraordinary gain (loss) and cumulative effect of accounting changes	**1,259**	2,585	(2,059)
Extraordinary gain (loss) related to early extinguishment of debt	**195**	(211)	—
Cumulative effect of accounting changes	**—**	—	(1,873)
Net income (loss)	**$ 1,454**	$ 2,374	$ (3,932)
Earnings (loss) per common share, after allowing for dividends on preferred shares			
Income (loss) from continuing operations	**$ 3.12**	$ 6.25	$ (6.33)
Discontinued operations	**0.04**	0.43	0.68
Income (loss) before extraordinary gain (loss) and cumulative effect of accounting changes	**3.16**	6.68	(5.65)
Extraordinary gain (loss)	**0.50**	(0.55)	—
Cumulative effect of accounting changes	**—**	—	(5.07)
Net income (loss)	**$ 3.66**	$ 6.13	$ (10.72)
Average common and common equivalent shares outstanding	**388.9**	382.9	369.6

See accompanying notes and the summarized group financial statements.

Note 12. Extraordinary Items

On Nov. 7, 1994, the company transferred Sears Tower and all related assets and liabilities to a third party as trustee of a trust and was released from the related nonrecourse mortgages encumbering the building. The second mortgagee is the residual beneficiary of the trust. The company is the current income beneficiary but cannot receive distributions as beneficiary until all debt that encumbers Sears Tower is repaid. An affiliate of the second mortgagee is responsible for operating Sears Tower. As a result of this transfer, assets and long-term debt were reduced by $501 and $845 million, respectively, and other liabilities were increased by $25 million, resulting in an aftertax extraordinary gain of $195 million ($319 million pretax) related to the early extinguishment of debt.

During the second quarter of 1993, the company recorded an extraordinary loss of $145 million after taxes ($234 million pretax) related primarily to payments to terminate interest rate swaps associated with retired commercial paper that was allocated to the funding of discontinued operations.

In the third quarter of 1993, the company recorded an extraordinary loss of $66 million after taxes ($107 million pretax) related to the call of 7 percent deep-discount debentures due to mature Nov. 15, 2001.

Changes in Accounting Policies

The *consistency principle* discussed in Chapter 2 requires consistent application of the same accounting methods from one year's financial statements to the next to facilitate yearly comparisons of financial results. Consistency is a goal, however, not a categorical requirement. As the economic conditions that a company faces change, sometimes changing the accounting methods and policies it has used to depict its operations is also beneficial. In some instances, accounting policy changes may also be mandated by the Financial Accounting Standards Board (FASB) or the Securities and Exchange Commission (SEC).

When a company implements an accounting policy change, the current period's income statement is prepared using that new policy as if it had been adopted on the first day of the period. In addition, the effect of that change on the beginning balance sheet accounts is included in the current year's income statement as a separate line item designated as the **cumulative effect of a change in accounting principle.**

For example, during 1994, PepsiCo adopted a preferred method of calculating the market value of its pension plan assets, which in turn affected the determination of the company's annual pension expense. Exhibit 5.4 reveals that the cumulative effect of this policy change amounted to $23.3 million. Effective in the beginning of 1994, PepsiCo also adopted Statement of Financial Accounting Standard No. 112, "Employers Accounting for Postretirement Benefits," which negatively impacted the company's net income by $55.3 million.

Earnings per Share

Because the *absolute level* of net income is often difficult to compare between periods and among different companies (largely because the level of revenue-producing assets differs over time and between companies), it is accepted practice for companies to report a standardized measure of their performance. Under GAAP, net income is divided by the number of shares of a company's capital stock, and the resulting standardized measure of performance is called **earnings per share.**

Unfortunately, the rules followed in calculating earnings per share (EPS) are quite complex, and an in-depth discussion of those rules will be deferred until Chapter 7. For the moment, however, it is sufficient to understand only that *basic* earnings per share result from dividing the weighted average number of common shares outstanding during the year into the net income for the year which is available to the common shareholders (that is, the net income for the year reduced by any dividend payable to preferred shareholders). Companies that have preferred stock or debt that is convertible into common stock, and outstanding options and warrants that are exchangeable for common stock, may also have to provide a second earnings per share measure — *fully diluted* earnings per share — to show how the possible conversion of those securities might adversely affect the EPS calculation.

At the end of each quarter and the end of each year, publicly held companies release earnings information for the period, in total, and on a per share basis. Those quarterly reports are summarized in the financial press and then are used on an ongoing basis in calculating various stock market indicators, such as the price/earnings multiple (or P/E ratio) reported in the daily stock price tables. **Price/earnings multiples** are frequently used as a shorthand test of a company's stock price. An analyst might say, for example, "With a P/E multiple of 12, in an industry where the average multiple is 15, Company X's common stock appears to be a good buy." In addition, some analysts forecast a

EXHIBIT 5.6

Glaxo Plc
Consolidated Profit and Loss Account

	Audited 12 months to 30.6.94
	£m
Turnover	5,656
Operating costs less other income	3,837
Trading profit	1,819
Investment income less interest payable	21
Profit on ordinary activities before taxation	1,840
Taxation	525
Profit on ordinary activities after taxation	1,315
Minority interests	12
Profit attributable to shareholders	1,303
Dividends	823
Retained profit	480
Earnings per ordinary share	42.9p
Dividends per ordinary share	27.0p

company's earnings for the forthcoming year and, using the current P/E multiple, then forecast next year's expected stock price.

During 1994, for example, PepsiCo's common stock traded on the New York Stock Exchange at an average P/E multiple of 20. If earnings per share had been $2.05, what price might PepsiCo's stock have traded at? (Answer: $41)

The Income Statement: International Considerations

As we saw in Chapter 4, the basic concepts, conventions, and presentation format of financial statements may vary from one country to the next, and this is certainly true for the income statement. Exhibit 5.6 presents the consolidated profit and loss account (or income statement) of Glaxo Plc, a worldwide pharmaceutical company headquartered in Great Britain. (The letters "Plc" stand for "public limited company," the equivalent of an incorporated company in the United States.) Comparing Glaxo's income statement presentation with that of PepsiCo (see Exhibit 5.4) reveals a number of contrasts:

- Instead of "sales," Glaxo refers to its revenues as "turnover"; similarly, the term "profit" is used in lieu of "income."
- Glaxo provides little information about its various operating expenses (perhaps to avoid giving confidential information to its competitors), and thus a review of its footnotes (not provided in Exhibit 5.6) for this information would be essential.

Despite these terminology and presentation differences, the revenue and expense recognition practices followed by most British companies in the preparation of the income statement are essentially equivalent to those followed by U.S. companies. This is not to imply that the differences between U.S. and U.K. GAAP are minimal, because

EXHIBIT 5.7

Blue Ridge Hardware Co.
Income Statement
For the Year Ended March 31, 1995

		Income Statement	Common-Size Statement
Net revenues		$ 74,500	100%
Less: Cost of merchandise sold		(44,700)	60.0
Gross margin		29,800	
Less: Operating expenses			
Rent expense	$ 3,600		4.8
Wage expense	15,300		20.5
Utilities expense	650		0.9
Depreciation expense	1,000		1.3
		(20,550)	
Income from operations		9,250	
Less: Interest expense		(900)	1.2
Income before taxes		8,350	
Less: Federal and state income taxes		(2,900)	3.9
Net income		$ 5,450	7.3

in some areas of accounting the accepted practices of the two nations differ dramatically (such as the accounting for goodwill, to be discussed in Chapter 10). However, the basic revenue and expense recognition questions that must be addressed by a British company are essentially the same questions addressed by a U.S. company; and the answers are quite often the same.

As a final observation, while Glaxo does provide a presentation of its earnings per ordinary (or common) share, a presentation of EPS is not required in all countries. The IASC, however, recommends the presentation of both basic and fully diluted EPS; consequently, it is expected that the presentation of EPS data will soon become generally accepted throughout the world.

ANALYZING THE INCOME STATEMENT

The principal focus of the income statement is the current operations of a company and thus the overall *profitability* of those operations. An analysis of profitability may occur in two ways. First, the absolute level of revenues, gross margin, or net income, for example, can be investigated over time (a trend analysis). Second, a series of profitability ratios can be calculated.

As noted in Chapter 4, trend analysis is frequently aided by the use of common-size financial statements. A common-size income statement expresses all statement items as a percentage of gross revenues (see Exhibit 5.7).

Two widely used profitability ratios are the rate of return on total assets and the rate of return on owners' equity. The **return on total assets** (ROA) measures a company's overall performance or effectiveness in using its available resources to generate income. The ROA is also sometimes called the *return on investment* (ROI) and is calculated as

$$\text{Return on assets} = \frac{\text{Net income after tax}}{\text{Average total assets}}$$

Because net income is generated throughout an accounting period, it would be inappropriate to measure the ROA using the total assets at either the beginning or the end of the period. Both total asset figures represent only a single point in time and may be skewed (either high or low). Hence, in an effort to obtain an assessment of the level of assets available throughout the entire accounting period, an average of the total assets is used in the ROA denominator.

Technically, ROA should be computed using average "operating assets" and "operating" income. In most but not all situations, the operating numbers are the same as the totals reported in the financial statements. For example, in the PepsiCo case for 1994, we should base our calculation of ROA using income before the cumulative effect of accounting changes, and we should remove from the average assets any asset measures attributable to those accounting policy changes that might be included in the beginning and ending asset balances. We do not have the data to adjust PepsiCo's asset balances, so we leave the effect of the accounting policy changes in the income measure *and* in the asset measure. When making an ROA calculation and comparing one company's results against another, or one year's results against an array of prior years, it is important to be sure that the income and asset measures are determined consistently.

In general, the higher the ROA, the more profitable a company is thought to be. Since there is no ideal measure of ROA, it is important to compare the ROA to that of prior periods, to other competitor companies, and to industry averages.

The **return on owners' equity** (ROE) also measures a company's performance in using its assets to generate income; however, unlike the ROA, this measure relates a company's profitability only to the resources provided by its owners. The ROE is calculated as follows:[4]

$$\text{Return on equity} = \frac{\text{Net income after tax}}{\text{Average owners' equity}}$$

In general, the higher the ROE, the more profitable a company is thought to be.

Other useful profitability indicators are called the *profit margin ratios*. These ratios measure the relative profitability of a company's revenues. For example, the **gross profit margin ratio** is computed as follows:

$$\text{Gross profit margin} = \frac{(\text{Net Sales} - \text{Cost of goods sold})}{\text{Net sales}}$$

The gross profit margin ratio indicates the percentage of each dollar of revenue that is realized as gross profit after deducting the cost of goods or services sold. It represents the profit available to cover a company's other operating expenses, such as selling and administrative expenses, interest, and taxes. It provides an indicator of a company's pricing policies.

The most popular margin ratio is the *net profit margin ratio* or, as it is frequently referred to, the **return on sales** (ROS):

$$\text{Return on sales} = \frac{\text{Net income after tax}}{\text{Net sales}}$$

[4] If a company has both common and preferred stock outstanding, the ROE is usually calculated only for the common stock, as follows:

$$\text{Return on common equity} = \frac{(\text{Net income after tax} - \text{Preferred stock dividends})}{\text{Average common shareholders' equity}}$$

The common shareholders' equity includes the following accounts: Common Stock at Par (or Stated) Value, Paid-in Capital in Excess of Par (or Stated) Value, Retained Earnings, and Treasury Stock.

The ROS indicates the percentage of each dollar of sales revenue that is earned as net income and that may be retained in the company to support future operations or that may be paid to shareholders in the form of a dividend. Again, it is an indicator of a company's pricing policies and practices as well as its ability to control its ongoing expenses.

It is instructive to note that ROS is one of the component ratios that form the ROA ratio:

$$\text{Return on assets} = \text{ROS} \times \text{Asset turnover ratio}$$

$$= \frac{\text{Net income after tax}}{\text{Net sales}} \times \frac{\text{Net sales}}{\text{Average total assets}}$$

$$= \frac{\text{Net income after tax}}{\text{Average total assets}}$$

The asset turnover ratio is a measure of the effectiveness of a company's utilization of available resources to generate sales; it was discussed in Chapter 4.

It is noteworthy that the three profitability indicators, ROA, ROE, and ROS, are closely linked to the financial characteristic of *leverage,* as discussed in Chapter 4. So long as the cost of additional debt does not exceed the return generated from the borrowed assets, each of the profitability indicators should be enhanced. However, as increasing amounts of debt are assumed by a company, these profitability ratios, particularly the ROE, are threatened. We will have more to say about this in Chapter 12.

Using PepsiCo's consolidated statement of income (see Exhibit 5.4), we can calculate these profitability ratios, and they are as follows:

	1994	**1993**
Return on assets	7.2%	6.7%
Return on equity	26.0%	25.1%
Gross profit margin	51.8%	52.3%
Return on sales	6.3%	6.3%

As compared to 1993, PepsiCo's profitability in 1994 remained relatively stable. Although the return on assets and return on equity were up slightly (probably reflecting PepsiCo's significant growth by acquisition), the gross profit margin was down marginally, and the return on sales was flat. As compared to Coca-Cola in 1994, which achieved a gross profit margin of 61.9 percent and a return on sales of 15.8 percent, PepsiCo's results in that year were competitive, although not nearly so strong.

Management Issues

The income statement is a powerful analytical tool for managers as well as for investors and financial analysts. Just as investors and analysts focus on such profitability indicators as ROA, ROE, ROS, and EPS to help assess the desirability of investing in a particular company, managers likewise use these indicators to help them reach a variety of key decisions. On the one hand, management can use such measures to help identify which operating division or subsidiary would most benefit from further capital investment; and, on the other hand, these same measures can help show which subunits are performing well (that is, according to plan or budget), which are performing poorly, and hence which managers deserve a bonus and which don't. In essence, the profitability indicators can be used in three key management decision-making areas:

- Resource allocation decisions: Where should a company invest its limited economic resources to gain the most benefit?
- Control decisions: Which subunits are performing effectively, and for those subunits that aren't, why aren't they performing effectively?
- Compensation decisions: Which managers have performed most successfully and consequently merit additional compensation (such as a bonus)?

The importance of the income statement to the decision-making role of management also creates a particular accounting dilemma. As noted earlier in the chapter, the income statement (and the balance sheet as well) is significantly impacted by a variety of managerial decisions. For example, management must

- Select the appropriate revenue recognition method to be used in preparing the income statement.
- Estimate the expected useful life of any depreciable assets and their anticipated salvage value, as well as select the depreciation method to be used.
- Estimate the period's uncollectible accounts receivable expense and the expected sales returns.

These and many other accounting-related inputs to the preparation of the income statement are the responsibility of a company's management team. The dilemma is that those individuals with the greatest responsibility for the accounting decision inputs to the income statement are also those individuals most likely to be impacted by the income statement data in their performance evaluation and compensation. Needless to say, this dilemma should be (and usually is) carefully monitored by the board of directors and the company's independent auditors, both of which retain oversight responsibility for the income statement, in order to ensure that the income data fairly reflects the operations of the company.

Risk and Pro Forma Financial Statements

The analysis of profitability is not an end in itself but is often undertaken as part of a broader assessment of the relative riskiness of a company. In the case of a lending institution evaluating the desirability of lending funds to a company, the principal focus is on default risk, whereas in the case of an investment or brokerage house evaluating the desirability of investing funds in a company, the principal focus is on operational risk.

Default risk refers to the probability that a company will be unable to meet its short-term or long-term obligations. The liquidity and solvency ratios discussed in Chapter 4 provide a good assessment of the probability of default risk.[5] **Operational risk,** on the other hand, refers to the probability that a company will experience unforeseen or unexpected events or factors that consequently will reduce or impair its revenue and earnings streams (and implicitly its cash flow stream). These factors or events may be economywide (general inflation, recession, or high interest rates), industrywide (increased competition, changes in technology, or raw material/labor constraints), or firm specific (labor disputes, equipment failure, or product safety considerations).

[5]It is important to note that the liquidity and solvency ratios are not independent of the profitability ratios. Indeed, high volatility in current profitability, combined with low liquidity and solvency, may suggest a high degree of default risk.

Assessing the operational riskiness of a company involves, in part, developing an understanding of a company's marketplace, its competition, its sensitivity to inflation and interest rate changes, and its ability to respond to new opportunities. By analyzing the resiliency of past operations to prior economic changes, one can formulate assessments of how well (or poorly) current and future operations might respond to future economic changes and opportunities.

The ability to assess operational (and default) risk is tied in part to the ability to generate insightful pro forma financial statements. As discussed in Chapter 4, pro forma financial statements are projected or forecasted financial statements. These forecasts are crucial to lending and investment decisions, for example, because the repayment of debt and the payment of future dividends depend substantially on a company's future profitability.

To illustrate the development of a pro forma income statement, we return to our example of the Blue Ridge Hardware Co. In Chapter 3 we used the transactions of the Blue Ridge Hardware Co. as a basis to prepare financial statements after one year of operations (see Exhibits 3.4, 3.6, and 3.8). The income statement of Blue Ridge Hardware for the year ended March 31, 1995, was presented earlier in Exhibit 5.7.

As a starting point for preparing a pro forma income statement, it is useful to understand the relationship between the various income statement accounts. One way to do this is to prepare a common-size income statement. Earlier, Exhibit 5.7 presented such a statement for Blue Ridge Hardware for the first year of operations. If multiple periods of data are available, it is best to prepare common-size statements for several periods to determine whether the percentage relationships vary significantly between periods or at various levels of activity.

Since a common-size income statement relates all other account balances to the revenue figure, the most important projection is that of revenues. For illustrative purposes, let us assume that Blue Ridge Hardware is considering an advertising campaign as a means to generate additional future sales. On the basis of discussions with a local advertising agency, Blue Ridge anticipates an expenditure of $2,000 for print advertising to produce a 15 percent growth in sales.

To service the expected increase in customer demand, an additional investment in inventories will be required. However, the cost of merchandise is not expected to increase linearly with sales because volume purchase discounts will be available to lower the overall cost. Thus, the cost of merchandise sold is projected to decline to 57 percent of revenues from the 1995 level of 60 percent. All other outlays for operating expenses are expected to remain fixed in amount because no new employees or store operating hours will be required to handle the expected growth in sales. Further, income taxes are anticipated to remain at 35 percent of pretax income (that is, $2,900/$8,350).

Using these assumptions, it is possible to prepare a pro forma income statement for 1996 to assess the relative impact of the advertising campaign on Blue Ridge Hardware's profitability. Exhibit 5.8 presents a pro forma income statement for the year ended March 31, 1996, which reveals that net after tax income is projected to grow to $8,820, for an increase of $3,370. Thus, if our assumptions are reasonable, it is clear that the profitability of the company is substantially enhanced by the advertising campaign investment. Because advertising may help develop long-term customers, the effects may also have a carryover effect beyond 1996.

Pro formas may also be used to evaluate the desirability of lending money to or investing in a company. In Chapter 6 we will see how the pro forma income statement of Blue Ridge Hardware can be used to construct a pro forma statement of cash flows and a pro forma balance sheet.

EXHIBIT 5.8

Blue Ridge Hardware Co.
Pro Forma Income Statement*
For the Year Ended March 31, 1996

Net revenues		$85,675
Less: Cost of merchandise sold		(48,835)
Gross margin		$36,840
Less: Operating expenses		
Rent expense	$ 3,600	
Wage expense	15,300	
Utilities expense	650	
Depreciation expense	1,000	
Advertising expense	2,000	
		(22,550)
Income from operations		14,290
Less: Interest expense		(720)
Income before taxes		13,570
Less: Federal and state income taxes		(4,750)
Net income		$ 8,820

*Assumptions

1. Revenues will increase by 15 percent in response to an advertising campaign costing $2,000.
2. Because of volume purchase discounts, the cost of merchandise sold as a percentage of revenues will decline by 3 percent.
3. All other operating expenses will remain fixed.
4. Income taxes will average 35 percent of pretax income.

SUMMARY

The income statement summarizes transactions that produce revenue for a company as a result of selling a product or service and transactions that result in expenses. It measures the overall profitability of operations and reports the profitability in a number of ways: gross margin, income from continuing operations, net income, and earnings per share.

The measurement of profitability is guided by a number of revenue and expense recognition conventions, principally the accrual principle, the allocation principle, and the matching principle. Evaluating the profitability of operations may be accomplished through a trend analysis of net income or through the calculation of various profitability ratios such as the ROA, ROE, or ROS. It is important to consider pro forma income statements, which can be prepared using reasonable and realistic assumptions of future period activities.

NEW CONCEPTS AND TERMS

Cost (p. 209)
Cumulative effect of a change in accounting principle (p. 219)
Default risk (p. 224)
Discontinued operations (p. 217)
Earnings per share (p. 219)
Expenses (p. 208)
Extraordinary item (p. 216)
Gain (p. 208)
Gross margin (p. 216)
Gross profit (p. 216)
Gross profit margin ratio (p. 222)
Income (p. 208)

Income from continuing operations (p. 216)
Loss (p. 208)
Net income (p. 209)
Net income before extraordinary items (p. 217)
Net income from discontinued operations (p. 217)
Operational risk (p. 224)
Percentage of completion (p. 211)
Price/earnings multiples (p. 219)
Profit (p. 210)
Return on owners' equity (p. 222)
Return on sales (p. 222)
Return on total assets (p. 221)
Revenues (p. 207)
Revenue recognition (p. 210)
Sales (p. 208)
Unusual item (p. 216)

ISSUES FOR DISCUSSION

D5.1 Two accountants, arguing an income statement presentation issue, summarize the debate with these points:

Point: The income statement should report *only* the results of transactions directly related to the current period's operations of a company.

Counterpoint: The income statement should report *all* transactions affecting the owners' interest in a company, except those involving dividends and capital stock.

Evaluate these two perspectives — which one do you agree with, and why? Which of the following transactions do you feel should (or should not) be reported in a company's current income statement?

a. A gain on the sale of a subsidiary.

b. An unexpected loss due to a fire in the company warehouse.

c. The damages award received as settlement of a lawsuit.

d. A correction to the company's income statement from two years before.

e. Winning the grand prize of $40 million in the New York state lottery — the CEO purchased the ticket using company funds.

D5.2 It has frequently been noted that financial reporting can adopt either a balance sheet focus or an income statement focus, but that it is impossible to do both. The gist of such a statement is that if accounting focuses on the measurement of assets and liabilities, revenues and expenses become a function of how assets and liabilities are reported. Said another way, the basic equation must balance (A = L + OE), and if two of the three factors (A and L) are prescribed, the third (OE) is whatever it takes to balance the equation. On the other hand, if the measurement of OE's revenues and expenses is accounting's foremost concern, then the assets and liabilities reported on a balance sheet are determined by those revenue and expense measurements.

Comment on the juxtaposition of these two views.

D5.3 H.J. Heinz includes the following paragraph in its accounting policies footnote. Comment on each of the statements here (you may ignore the sentence that describes the tax policy) from the standpoint of a Heinz plant manager. What factors would the manager consider in the application of these policies, and how might those considerations affect the Heinz income statement?

> *Property, Plant, and Equipment:* Land, buildings, and equipment are recorded at cost. For financial reporting purposes, depreciation is provided on the straight-line method over the estimated useful lives of the assets. Accelerated depreciation methods are generally used for income tax purposes. Expenditures for new facilities and

improvements that substantially extend the capacity or useful life of an asset are capitalized. Ordinary repairs and maintenance are expensed as incurred. When property is retired or otherwise disposed, the cost and related depreciation are removed from the accounts and any related gains or losses are included in income.

D5.4 Flowers Industries bakes and distributes bread and other bakery products throughout the South. Recently, the company began a program of selling its distribution routes to its salespeople in an effort to give those people an increased stake in the business and provide them with an incentive to develop the territory more fully. Flowers includes the following footnote in its financial statements. Do you agree with Flowers's policy? Why or why not?

Long-Term Notes Receivable and Deferred Income

The company has sold a portion of its routes to independent distributors. The income from these sales is recognized as the cash payments are received.

The amounts due under the notes receivable from the distributors of $21,595,000 and $14,448,000 have also been included in deferred income at July 2, 19X2, and June 27, 19X1, respectively. At July 2, 19X2, and June 27, 19X1, $20,112,000 and $13,476,000, respectively, are included in other long-term assets.

D5.5 General Motors' income statement for 1990 included a special charge of $3.3 billion, which it described as a special provision for scheduled plant closings and other restructurings. The charge is described in Note 7 as follows:

Note 7 — Special Provision for Scheduled Plant Closings and Other Restructurings

In 1990 a special restructuring charge of $3,314.0 million was included in the results of operations to provide for the closing of four previously idled U.S. assembly plants, as well as provide for other North American manufacturing and warehouse operations that will be consolidated or cease operating over the next three years. As a result, consolidated net loss was increased by $2,087.8 million or $3.47 per share of $1-2/3 par value common stock.

A similar provision was made in 1986 in the amount of $1,287.6 million for costs associated with scheduled plant closings in the United States and other restructurings of foreign operations that were reasonably estimable at the time.

During 1990, 1989, and 1988, a net of $1,731.7 million, $148.1 million, and $218.6 million, respectively, was charged against these reserves.

Discuss the appropriateness of charging the 1990 income with this expense. Is it an appropriate charge against 1990, as opposed to 1991 or 1992? Why or why not? Why should it not be reallocated back to 1989 or prior years?

D5.6 The Boston Celtics Limited Partnership presents the following footnote in a recent annual report:

Revenue and Expense Recognition: Revenues and expenses are recognized when revenues and the related costs are earned or incurred. Ticket sales and television and radio broadcasting fees generally are recorded as revenues at the time the game to which such proceeds relate is played. Team expenses, principally player and coaches' salaries, related fringe benefits and insurance, and game and playoff expenses, principally National Basketball Association attendance assessments, arena rentals, and travel, are recorded as expense on the same basis. Accordingly, advance ticket sales and advance payments on television and radio broadcasting contracts and payments for team and game expenses not earned or incurred are recorded as deferred game revenues and deferred game expenses, respectively, and amortized ratably as regular season games are played. General and administrative and selling and promotional expenses are charged to operations as incurred.

Comment on the reasoning underlying such policies.

D5.7 Grumman Corp. produces jet fighters for the U.S. Navy and has other defense contracts for production and research projects. The company describes its revenue recognition policies in the following footnote:

> **Revenue Recognition**
> Sales under fixed-price production contracts are recorded at the time of delivery. Sales, including fees earned, under cost-reimbursement and research, development, test, and evaluation contracts are recorded as costs are incurred.
> Certain contracts contain cost and/or performance incentives. Such incentives are included in sales at the time actual performance can be related to the target and the earned amount can be reasonably determined. Accordingly, earnings recorded in one period may include adjustments related to sales recorded in a prior period. Losses on contracts are recorded when they become known.

Comment on the reasoning underlying such policies.

D5.8 Immediately following PepsiCo's income statement presented in the 1994 annual report is a report titled "Management Analysis — Results of Operations" (see Chapter 1). In that analysis a number of improvements in performance are cited as the company compares 1994, 1993, and 1992. Interpret these improvements from the standpoint of a prospective investor. Do you believe the improvements noted in net sales, expenses, operating profit, and provisions for taxes represent operating improvement and efficiencies as a result of outside circumstances, the impact of one-time events, or the result of creative accounting? Come to a conclusion on the individual factors cited by the company, and come to a conclusion regarding the improved operating results overall. Explain your conclusions.

D5.9 Goodyear Tire and Rubber Company has reported "unusual items" in its income statements in each of the last three years. The income statement from the 19X5 annual report to stockholders is as follows. Also presented is the company's footnote (see next page), which explains those unusual items.

	Year Ended December 31,		
(Dollars in millions, except per share)	**19X5**	**19X4**	**19X3**
Net Sales	$11,272.5	$10,869.3	$10,810.4
Other Income	180.6	216.1	217.6
	11,453.1	11,085.4	11,028.0
Cost and Expenses:			
Cost of goods sold	8,805.1	8,234.7	8,291.7
Selling, administrative and general expense	1,999.6	1,863.7	1,745.1
Interest expense	328.2	255.3	231.8
Unusual items	103.6	109.7	78.8
Other expenses	74.5	44.6	37.0
Foreign currency exchange	72.1	87.9	87.6
Minority interest in net income of subsidiaries	14.1	18.6	19.2
	11,397.2	10,614.5	10,490.5
Income before Income Taxes and Extraordinary Item	55.9	470.9	537.5
United States and Foreign Taxes on Income	94.2	281.5	187.4
Income (loss) before Extraordinary Item	(38.3)	189.4	350.1
Extraordinary Item — Tax Benefit of Loss Carryovers	—	17.4	—
Net Income (loss)	$ (38.3)	$ 206.8	$ 350.1

Comment on the designation of these items as "unusual" items, qualifying for separate identification in the income statement. Why are they not extraordinary items? Why are they not a normal part of the flow of transactions, which are included in costs and expenses?

Notes to Financial Statements
The Goodyear Tire & Rubber Company and Subsidiaries
(in millions)

	19X5	19X4	19X3
Unusual Items			
A summary of the pretax unusual charges follows:			
Restructuring	$ 66.4	$ 18.4	$27.9
Plant closure and sale of facilities	15.0	43.0	—
Discontinued segment—			
Environmental cleanup costs	22.2	—	—
Sale of assets	—	48.3	—
Pension settlement/asset reversion	—	—	50.9
	$103.6	$109.7	$78.8

19X5

The restructuring of United States tire operations during the second quarter resulted in a charge of $20.0 million ($12.2 million after tax) from the reduction of personnel in various sales, distribution, and other operations and other associated costs. The company also incurred restructuring charges of $46.4 million ($38.2 million after tax) during the third quarter. The costs resulted from a realignment of European tire marketing, distribution, and production operations, which will eliminate approximately 1,180 jobs; the phaseout of medium and heavy truck tire production at the Valleyfield, Quebec, Canada, plant, and the rationalization of certain tire and related production operations in Canada and Argentina.

The decision to close the New Bedford, Massachusetts, roofing systems plant resulted in a charge of $15.0 million ($9.2 million after tax) during the second quarter for personnel reduction and other plant closure costs.

The company recorded a charge of $22.2 million ($13.5 million after tax) during the third quarter for environmental cleanup costs associated with a business segment discontinued in 19X1.

19X4

The company accrued expenses of $18.4 million ($10.9 million after tax) for the reduction of bias-ply truck tire capacity at the Gadsden, Alabama, plant and from the realignment of the Canadian operations.

The company sold its South African tire and general products manufacturing subsidiary for $41.0 million. A loss of $43.0 million ($52.0 million after tax) was recorded in the second quarter, the majority of which was due to the recognition of the decreased value of the company's assets in South Africa arising form the devaluation of the South African Rand during the past several years.

The company's oil transportation subsidiary, All American Pipeline Company, sold about 435 miles of unused 30-inch pipe for $70.0 million in the second quarter. A loss of $48.3 million ($43.0 million after tax) was recorded on the sale.

19X3

The company, in an effort to reduce operating expenses, consolidated tasks and eliminated duplicate job responsibilities at a cost of $27.9 million ($17.1 million after tax) in the fourth quarter.

The company settled its pension liability for the principal domestic salary plan for all benefits accrued to June 30, 19X3, through the purchase of annuity contracts from major insurance companies during the fourth quarter. A loss of $10.9 million was recorded. In a related transaction excess assets of $400.0 million before taxes were reverted to the company. Excise tax of $40.0 million was incurred on the asset reversion making the total charge to Unusual Items $50.9 million. The combined effect of these transactions, together with the reversal of deferred tax recorded on the 19X1 pension settlement, resulted in an after tax charge of $9.7 million in 19X3. Proceeds to the company amounted to $210.0 million after deducting excise tax and federal and state income taxes. For further information regarding the tax effects on the transaction, see the note to the financial statements entitled Income Taxes.

D5.10 Pick up a current copy of the *Wall Street Journal* and refer to the page that gives you the statistics on the stocks that make up the Dow Jones Industrial Average. Pick two very different companies from that group of 30 and look up their stock trading data for that day from the table "New York Stock Exchange Composite Transactions." Explain why those two companies might have different price/earnings ratios. (You should review the annual reports to stockholders for your two companies, and you may have to review other business periodicals to get a fuller understanding of the factors affecting the companies.)

PROBLEMS

P5.1 Income statement preparation. On March 1, Click and Slick Snyder formed an auto repair business. The following data pertain to their first month's operations:

Cash received from customers	$33,000
Cash paid out:	
Purchased supplies	1,000
Purchased equipment	7,500
Paid employees	2,000
Paid March rent for garage space	2,500

The Snyders were blessed. Within days of opening the business, they signed two long-term contracts. One contract was with the local school board and it ran through the end of August. In exchange for monthly servicing of school buses, the school board would pay the Snyders $2,000/month. When the contract was signed, the Snyders asked for and received 3 months' payment in advance. The second contract was to take care of the local police department's patrol cars. This contract ran for 12 months. The financial terms agreed on by the police department were $1,500/month payable by the 5th of each month following the month in which services were rendered.

Required:

Assuming the equipment had a 3-year life and that supplies on hand at the end of March were $600, prepare an income statement for the Snyder's business for the month ended March 31.

P5.2 Transaction analysis: Cash versus accrual basis. Global Enterprises, Inc., began the year with $10,000 cash, some other assets, some vendor payables, and $8,000 in owners' equity. During this current year, Global Enterprises entered into a number of events, including the following:

Event	Income Statement		Cash Balance	
a. Paid utilities of $200.	______	______	______	______
b. Purchased a $10,000 truck, giving cash and a $9,000 note (interest rate of 8%).	______	______	______	______
c. Paid dividends of $1,000.	______	______	______	______
d. Paid consultant $1,500.	______	______	______	______
e. Sold additional common stock for $6,000 cash.	______	______	______	______
f. Used $500 of supplies previously purchased.	______	______	______	______
g. Used truck for 1/10 of useful life.	______	______	______	______
h. Collected a $75 account receivable.	______	______	______	______

Required:

Note the effect of each of the preceding events on the company's income statement and its cash balance. For the income statement effects, note the dollar amount and whether the event affected a revenue or an expense. For the cash balance effects, note the dollar amount and whether the cash balance increased or decreased. Where an event has no affect, please note it as such.

P5.3 Sales returns. In December, Barton Industries, Inc., disclosed that it would restate its results for the third quarter because a sale it had booked was returned during the fourth quarter. According to a news release by the maker of oil field equipment, the restatement would reduce its third quarter revenues from $8.1 million to $7.1 million and its net income from $1.0 million to $400,000.

Required:

Determine the accounting entries required for the third quarter restatement. Ignore any income taxes.

P5.4 Income measurement. At the beginning of 1995, M. Carlson, the owner and operator of a large agricultural concern, had no inventories on hand. During 1995, however, his company produced 80,000 bushels of corn, 100,000 bushels of soybeans, and 160,000 bushels of barley. Upon completion of the harvest, Carlson sold one-half of each of his crops at the following prices: corn, $4.50 per bushel; soybeans, $3.25 per bushel; and barley, $2 per bushel. At year-end, the remaining half of Carlson's crop was unsold.

To operate the company, Carlson incurred costs during 1995 of $370,000, including $100,000 in depreciation on his buildings and equipment. Moreover, Carlson estimates that his selling and delivery costs on the crops average $0.42 per bushel; these costs are included in his total operating costs given above. Finally, the commodities price quotations reported in the *Wall Street Journal* at year-end revealed that the current market price per bushel for each of the crops was as follows: corn, $5 per bushel; soybeans, $3.47 per bushel; and barley, $2.20 per bushel.

Presented below is the balance sheet for M. Carlson, Inc., as of January 1, 1995:

M. Carlson, Inc.
Balance Sheet
As of January 1, 1995

Assets			Liabilities and Equity	
Cash		$ 75,000	Liabilities	$ -0-
Land		300,000	Owners' equity:	
Buildings and equipment	$750,000		Capital stock	550,000
Less: Accumulated depreciation	(350,000)	400,000	Retained earnings	225,000
Total assets		$775,000	Total equities	$775,000

Required:

Prepare an income statement and balance sheet for the company as of December 31, 1995. Prepare a list of the accounting policy decisions that you made in arriving at these statements.

P5.5 Income statement concepts. Consider these juxtapositions, each of which suggest some important income statement ideas:

a. Gain versus income

b. Loss versus expense

c. Realized versus recognized

d. Deferred versus prepaid

Required:

Prepare a commentary on each of the above juxtapositions, explaining how the contrasted items are alike and how they are different, and how each of them might be considered in the presentation of the income statement.

P5.6 More income statement concepts. Consider the following juxtapositions, each of which suggest some important income statement decisions:

a. Asset versus expense

b. Earned versus unearned

c. Current period charge versus future period charge

d. Current period charge versus prior period charge

e. Operating items versus extraordinary items

Required:

Prepare a commentary on each of the above juxtapositions, explaining how the contrasted items are alike and how they are different, and the factors that might require them to be treated differently in the context of the income statement.

P5.7 Asset or expense. The King Corporation reported net income of $5,000,000 in 1994, and it appears that 1995 will be similar. During 1995 the company made the following expenditures:

1. $125,000 was spent to resurface the employee parking lot. The resurfacing has to be done about every five years.

2. $250,000 was spent to upgrade the air filtration system in the paint department. The system as it was had worked satisfactorily, but the U.S. Department of Labor had recently promulgated new rules (effective three years from today) that would have required the changes the company made voluntarily.

3. $450,000 was paid to an architect for the design of a new research center. The center was the dream of the prior CEO but has now been shelved because the new officers are more cautious about the future.

4. $300,000 has been spent this year on the development of a new computer-based order entry system. The idea behind the new system is that salespeople in the field will be able to enter orders into the system directly, electronically, so that they can be shipped the very next day. Everyone hopes that the new system will enhance customer service and help stop a sales slide. The system appears to be on track, but another $200,000 will have to be spent before it can be demonstrated that it will work as planned.

5. The company's Texas plant was shut down for about three months this year because of the slow economy. The company struggled to find a way to keep their employees busy so they could keep as many of them as possible. The employees agreed to accept half pay, and the company found maintenance work and training for them. At the end of the period, about 85 percent of the work force was still on the payroll, and when the company went back to work, production resumed without a hitch. The maintenance work done by the employees during this time cost about $500,000; the training time cost the company another $400,000.

Required:

Prepare a one-paragraph memo discussing each of these expenditures, including whether the other side of the entry should be an addition to an asset or an expense charge. Explain your position.

P5.8 Revenue recognition. Consider the following unique company situations:

1. The American Health Club sells lifetime memberships costing $1,200, which allow the member unlimited use of any of the company's 100 facilities around the country. The initiation fee may be paid in 24 monthly installments, with a 1 percent interest charge on the unpaid balance.
2. Universal Motors has always offered a limited, 24-month warranty program on its cars, but to counter the incredible competition in the industry, the company has come to the conclusion that they must do something more. With that in mind, they have developed a new program: For a $500 payment at the time of purchase, the customer can buy a five-year warranty that will cover replacement of almost all parts and labor. The purchased warranty expires at the end of five years or when the customer sells the car, whichever occurs first.
3. Community Promotions Corporation sells coupon books that give the holder a 10 percent discount (up to $10) from any of the 25 participating merchants. The buyer of the coupon book pays $50 for the book but obviously can realize up to $250 in benefits. Community Promotions convinces the merchants to participate in the program at no cost, arguing that they will build traffic and have the opportunity for repeat business from the coupon book holders.
4. Household Furnishings Emporium sells appliances and furniture with installment contracts. Those contracts usually carry interest rates of 16 percent or more. When the company has accumulated $200,000 of contracts with a year or more to go, they sell the contracts to a finance company on a nonrecourse basis. The company continues to service the contracts and is paid a service fee, which is based on the cash they collect and turn over to the finance company. If a contract goes bad, Household turns it over to a collection agency and has no further responsibility for it. In January the company sold contracts with a face value of $250,000 and received $275,000 in cash.
5. Neighborhood News, Inc., prints and distributes a weekly newspaper throughout the county. Local merchants order a certain number of the papers each week and pay for them on delivery. The company always takes back any unsold papers, however, and gives the merchant credit.

Required:

For each of these situations, prepare a short paper describing the revenue recognition policy the company ought to follow, explaining the basis for your recommendation.

P5.9 Income statement classification. Net income for The Multi Corporation, for the year just ended, is $10,000,000. There is some debate, however, about the presentation of the income statement and the classification of certain events that could be considered material to that net income. In thinking about these items, it is important to know that Multi manufactures and distributes a line of automobile aftermarket accessories, which are sold through Sears and other major retail outlets. The events that follow all occurred or were recognized during the year.

1. A fire destroyed a warehouse in New Jersey. The loss was $2,500,000, half of which was covered by insurance.
2. The company completed a defense contract that produced a $1,250,000 profit. The contract used excess capacity in the plant, and the gross margin went directly to the bottom line. The company hopes to bid on similar contracts but is not sure that there will be a repeat opportunity.
3. An order of seat covers for an East Coast auto parts chain was found to be defective and was returned and scrapped. The loss on the order was $250,000, and the company gave the customer an additional discount of $500,000 on future orders in hopes of protecting the relationship.

4. The company spent $1,000,000 on the development of a catalog, which is to be used to sell parts by direct mail. The catalog probably has a useful life of 24 months. In the first three months of the mail order operations, sales exceeded expectations substantially.

5. To ensure its source of merchandise, the company has made investments in several Pacific Rim supplier companies. An opportunity came to sell one of those investments at a substantial gain. The company agreed to the sale, received $4,000,000 in cash, realized a $2,000,000 gain, and invested the entire proceeds in a new supplier just beginning business in Mexico.

6. A loan to a manufacturer of car radios was written off this year. In fact, it had been clear for some time that the $1,500,000 note was worthless, but the radio maker was part of a complex of companies, some of whom were important to Multi. Multi's CEO had elected to keep a low profile with regard to the radio maker and had refused to press for payments of principal or interest for fear of alienating the other companies in the group. But now other sources had been found so that the complex was less significant as a supplier, and Multi forced the hand of the radio maker, pushing it into bankruptcy.

Required:

Prepare a paragraph discussing each event, describing how the item should be treated in Multi's income statement for the year just ended. Should the item be classified as unusual, extraordinary, or ordinary? Should the item be carried forward into next year (as an asset) or carried back to last year (as a prior period adjustment)? Be sure to explain the rationale for your decision.

P5.10 Quarterly income statements. Li'l Tyke sells toys in its own stores throughout the Midwest. It is a very seasonal business, with about 80 percent of sales coming in the period November 15 to December 31. Unfortunately, to have a presence in the market for those peak times, the store must remain open all year around. The company struggles to present a reasonable picture of its operations during the early part of the year, and it worries particularly about the requirement to present quarterly reports to its stockholders. The president has come up with several ideas to deal with this problem next year, and he asked you to consider these suggestions:

1. Everyone agrees that the company sells its toys at a higher markup during its peak season, but no one knows for sure how much the difference might be. The real margin for the year isn't known until the year-end inventory is counted and the real cost of sales is determined. The president proposes to use last year's actual gross margin percentage to determine the gross margin for each of the first three quarters of the next year. He will determine an actual gross margin for next year after the year-end inventory and will use that number to prepare the income statement for the year as a whole. That gross margin will also be used to develop the gross margins for the first three quarters of the succeeding year.

2. Most of the company's advertising is spread evenly over the period September 1 through December 15. The president has negotiated with the advertising agency to allow the company to pay for those advertisements during the month of December. He proposes to expense the advertising expense 20 percent in the third quarter and 80 percent in the fourth quarter — which is approximately proportional to the way sales are realized during that six-month period.

3. The president has also negotiated with the landlords of most of the store locations to allow the company to pay the rent in a lump sum total in the month of December. He proposes to expense the rent over the year on a pro rata basis, following the expected sales pattern.

Required:

Prepare a brief paragraph discussing each of the president's proposals for the Li'l Tyke's quarterly income statements. Do you agree with his plans? Why or why not?

P5.11 Balance sheet and income statement ratios. Business analysts often talk about the "DuPont Ratio" (so named because it was developed by financial analysts in the DuPont Corporation many years ago), and by that they mean this interconnection of balance sheet and income statement ratios ("leverage" is assets over equity):

Return on sales × Asset turnover	= Return on assets
Return on assets × Leverage	= Return on equity

Let us make some assumptions about two different companies, and state those assumptions in terms of their most important balance sheet and income statement ratios:

Suppose Co. X's financial results depict

2% (ROS) × 3.4 (Asset turnover)	= 7% (ROA)
7% (ROA) × 3 (Leverage)	= 21% (ROE)

whereas Co. Y's financials show

7% (ROS) × 1.5 (Asset turnover)	= 10.5% (ROA)
10.5% (ROA) × 2 (Leverage)	= 21% (ROE)

Required:

a. Which company would you rather manage? Why?

b. Which company would you rather invest in? Why?

P5.12 Working with income statement ratios. At lunch one day in the executive dining room of the Crest Investment Company, you notice a coworker lunching by herself and studying a set of financial statements. She seems frustrated and is talking to herself. You hear her say as she picks up her briefcase and leaves, "I do not understand what is going on with this company—none of this makes any sense to me." You start to follow her out when you notice that she has left a scratch sheet behind covered with figures; in fact, they appear to be a set of ratios, as follows:

	Last Year	This Year
AVG PRICE	$ 5.10	$ 4.80
ROS	8.23%	6.23%
SALES INCREASE	18.30%	−2.00%
GROSS MARGIN	37.50%	35.00%
R&D/SALES	8.17%	6.67%
G&A/SALES	10.62%	12.50%
EFF. TAX RATE	40.00%	42.50%
ASSET TURN.	0.95	1.08
ROA	8.68%	5.75%
ROE	20.98%	13.84%

Required:

Identify five important things that may have been going on with this company this year that may explain the ratios developed by your frustrated friend.

P5.13 Pro forma income statements. The Quandary Corporation is at a crossroads and must decide whether to expand a new product line or allow its mainline business to work toward liquidation. Income statements for the last three years are as follows:

The Quandary Corporation
Income Statements
(000s omitted)

	Two Years Ago	Last Year	This Year	Next Year	Two Years Out
Sales of old product	$10,000	$8,000	$7,000		
Cost of sales — old product	6,000	5,000	4,550		
Marketing costs — old product	1,500	1,280	1,225		
Depreciation — old product	500	450	400		
Interest — old product	200	180	150		
Contribution — old product	1,800	1,090	675		
Sales — new product	1,000	3,000	4,000		
Cost of sales — new product	750	2,175	2,800		
Marketing costs — new product	200	600	800		
Depreciation — new product	100	110	150		
Interest — new product	50	55	75		
Contribution — new product	(100)	60	175		
Corporate expenses	450	475	500		
Income before taxes	1,250	675	350		
Income taxes	500	270	140		
Net income	$ 750	$ 405	210		
Net assets employed — old prod.	5,000	4,800	4,600		
Net assets employed — new prod.	1,000	1,100	1,500		
Owners' equity	3,600	3,800	3,900		

Required:

Prepare two sets of pro forma income statements for next year and two years out, one set assuming that $10,000,000 is invested in an expansion of the new product line, and one set assuming that the new product line is abandoned. Prepare a memo for the president of Quandary, commenting on the pro forma statements. Your memo should explain the assumptions you made in preparing the pro forma statements and should interpret those statements to help the CEO decide what to do about the new product line.

P5.14 Revenue recognition. At the beginning of 1995 John Cornell decided to quit his current job as construction supervisor for Walsh, Inc., a construction company headquartered in Chicago, and formed his own company. When he resigned, he had a written contract to build a custom home in Evanston, Illinois, at a price of $400,000. The full price was payable in cash when the house was completed and available for occupancy.

By year-end 1995 Cornell's new company, Distinctive Homes, Inc., had spent $50,000 for labor, $107,740 for materials, and $3,800 in miscellaneous expenses in connection with construction of the home. Cornell estimated that the project was 70 percent complete at year-end. In addition, construction materials on hand at year-end cost $2,600.

During the year, Distinctive Homes, Inc., had also purchased a small run-down house for $95,000, spent $32,000 fixing it up, and then sold it on November 1, 1995, for $175,000. The buyer paid $25,000 down and signed a note for the remainder of the balance due. The note called for interest payments only, at a rate of 12 percent per year, with a balloon payment for the outstanding balance at the end of 1997.

John's wife, Karen, was employed to keep the accounting records for Distinctive Homes, Inc., and on December 31, she prepared the following statement:

Distinctive Homes, Inc.
Where We Stand at Year-End

Assets		Debts and Capital	
Cash	$ 21,000	Accounts payable	$ 44,600
Material on hand	2,600	Owner's investment	242,540
House renovation contract	150,000	Sale of renovated house	175,000
Construction in progress	161,540		
Cost of renovated house	127,000		
Total assets	$462,140	Total debts and capital	$462,140

After reviewing the statement, John and Karen got into a discussion concerning the level of income the company earned during the year. John argued that the entire profit on the sale of the renovated home, along with 70 percent of the expected profit from the construction contract, had been earned. Karen, on the other hand, maintained that the profit on the renovation should be recognized only to the extent of the cash actually collected and that no profit should be recognized on the new home construction until it was completed and available for occupancy.

After discussing the problem at length, John and Karen agreed that there were four possible alternative approaches to measuring the company's income:

1. Report the entire amount of renovation income and a proportionate amount of construction contract income.

2. Report the entire amount of renovation income but none of the construction contract income.

3. Report the renovation income in proportion to the amount of cash received and the construction contract income in proportion to the amount of work completed.

4. Report the renovation income in proportion to the amount of cash received but none of the construction contract income.

Required:

Prepare the balance sheets and income statements that would result under each of the four approaches. Which set of statements do you believe best reflects the results of Distinctive Homes, Inc., for 1995?

P5.15 Revenue recognition. Supercolider, Inc., is an independent research and development laboratory that undertakes contractual research for a variety of corporate and governmental clients. Occasionally, scientists at the laboratory undertake independent research, which, if successful (that is, if it results in new products, designs, or technology), is then marketed by the company.

In January 1992 scientists at Supercolider began work on a number of minor research projects involving high-speed atom smashing. During 1992 costs incurred in these efforts amounted to $363,000. In May 1993 promising results emerged and were reported to the U.S. Department of Energy. Development costs incurred in 1993 through the end of May totaled $204,000.

At this point Supercolider tried to secure a government contract to support the remainder of the research effort. The Department of Energy (DOE) was reluctant, however, to commit substantial sums until further tests had been completed. Nonetheless, to ensure that it retained the first right of refusal, the DOE gave Supercolider a seed grant of $50,000 to help support the continuation of the studies; this grant carried a stipulation that the DOE would retain the right to acquire the results, patents, and copyrights from the research any time on or before December 31, 1994, for $2,400,000.

Further testing proved favorable, although additional development costs incurred in 1993 amounted to $325,000 and to $210,000 in 1994. On December 28, 1994, the DOE exercised its right and agreed to purchase the results, patents, and copyrights from the research. As previously agreed, the DOE paid Supercolider $300,000 immediately, with the remainder of the contract price payable in seven equal annual installments beginning on December 31, 1995, through December 31, 2001. On March 1, 1995, Supercolider delivered all scientific and legal documents, test results, and samples to the DOE offices in Washington, D.C.

Required:

Evaluate the facts of this case and determine when Supercolider, Inc., should recognize the various revenue streams associated with its work on this project. Also determine when Supercolider should recognize the various developmental costs. Be prepared to substantiate your position.

P5.16 Profitability analysis. Digital Equipment Corporation presented its income statements in its annual report as follows (in thousands except per share data). (The companion balance sheet for Digital was presented in Case 4.4 as Company C.)

	19X5	19X4	19X3
Revenues			
Product sales	**$8,145,491**	$8,190,308	$7,541,241
Service and other revenues	**4,797,032**	4,551,648	3,934,205
Total operating revenues	**12,942,523**	12,741,956	11,475,446
Costs and Expenses			
Cost of product sales	**3,825,897**	3,468,307	3,042,172
Service expense and cost of other revenues	**2,968,529**	2,773,563	2,426,176
Research and engineering expenses	**1,614,423**	1,525,129	1,306,543
Selling, general, and administrative expenses	**3,971,059**	3,638,868	3,065,555
Restructuring charges	**550,000**	—	—
Operating income	**12,615**	1,336,089	1,635,000
Interest income	**142,015**	124,021	143,665
Interest expense	**30,641**	39,435	37,820
Income before income taxes	**123,989**	1,420,675	1,740,845
Provision for income taxes	**49,596**	348,065	435,212
Net income	**$ 74,393**	$1,072,610	$1,305,633
Net Income per Share	**$ 0.59**	$ 8.45	$ 9.90
Weighted average shares outstanding	**125,222**	127,008	131,923

Required:

Calculate all the profitability ratios for each of the three years presented. Perform other financial analysis you deem necessary in order to understand the financial health of Digital. Prepare a short commentary, summarizing the results of your work.

P5.17 Financial analysis in the United States and in Japan. Following are the income statements from the annual reports of Kansai Electric Power Co., Inc. (serving Osaka, Japan) and Commonwealth Edison Company (serving Chicago, Illinois, USA).

Required:

Perform a financial analysis regarding the profitability of both companies and determine which of the two appears to be more successful in generating profits. Also comment on the terminology used and the presentation employed in the two income statements.

The Kansai Electric Power Company, Incorporated
Statements of Income
Years ended March 31,

	Millions of Yen	
	19X5	**19X4**
Operating Revenues	¥2,245,007	¥2,075,296
Operating Expenses:		
Fuel	441,571	329,163
Purchased power	163,859	142,075
Maintenance	293,379	306,472
Depreciation	323,681	308,419
Taxes other than income taxes	140,383	132,957
Other	535,972	500,204
	1,898,845	1,719,290
Operating Income	346,162	356,006
Other (Income) Expenses:		
Interest expense	239,393	215,427
Exchange loss	—	14,369
Other, net	(2,953)	(1,722)
	236,440	228,074
Income before Provision for Reserve for Fluctuations in Water Level and Income Taxes	109,722	127,932
Provision for Reserve for Fluctuations in Water Level	1,668	6,525
Income before Income Taxes	108,054	121,407
Income Taxes	51,771	65,009
Net Income	**¥ 56,283**	**¥ 56,398**
Per Share of Common Stock:		
Net income —		
Primary	¥58	¥58
Assuming full dilution	¥57	¥56
Cash dividends applicable to period	¥50	¥49

Commonwealth Edison Company and Subsidiary Companies
Statements of Consolidated Income
(thousands except per share data)

		19X5	19X4	19X3
Electric Operating Revenues:	Operating revenues	$5,798,350	$5,782,850	$5,613,338
	Provisions for revenue refunds	(536,364)	(31,800)	—
		$5,261,986	**$5,751,050**	**$5,613,338**
Electric Operating Expenses and Taxes:	Fuel	$ 978,775	$ 951,350	$ 991,244
	Purchased and interchanged power — net	(27,209)	(44,836)	17,358
	Deferred (under)/overrecovered energy costs — net	8,415	(19,059)	(89,350)
	Operation	1,160,166	1,120,941	1,072,218
	Maintenance	489,463	435,664	434,402
	Depreciation	878,938	865,427	837,170
	Recovery of deferred plant costs	1,659	1,659	34,060
	Taxes (except income)	661,432	665,072	641,475
	Income taxes —			
	Current — federal	150,917	263,879	115,493
	— state	28,773	49,684	38,479
	Deferred — federal — net	19,456	162,088	220,873
	— state — net	17,299	38,445	47,144
	Investment tax credits deferred — net	(28,386)	(83,529)	9,582
		$4,339,698	$4,406,785	$4,370,148
Electric Operating Income		**$ 922,288**	**$1,344,265**	**$1,243,190**
Other Income and Deductions:	Interest on long-term debt	$ (648,603)	(620,589)	$ (648,871)
	Interest on notes payable	(577)	(7,685)	(8,607)
	Allowance for funds used during construction			
	Borrowed funds	13,840	17,898	39,726
	Equity funds	22,526	24,856	94,970
	Current income taxes applicable to nonoperating activities	(5,932)	2,445	17,669
	Disallowed Byron Unit 1 plant costs	(133,661)	(52,808)	—
	Income tax effect of disallowed Byron Unit 1 plant costs	(1,288)	5,570	(439)
	Miscellaneous — net	(40,302)	(20,269)	(117)
		$ (793,997)	$ (650,582)	$ (506,669)
Net income		**$ 128,291**	**$ 693,683**	**$ 737,521**
Provision for dividends on preferred and preference stocks		82,495	95,180	102,245
Net income on common stock		**$ 45,796**	**$ 598,503**	**$ 635,276**
Average number of common shares outstanding		212,032	211,647	211,233
Earnings per common share		**$ 0.22**	**$ 2.83**	**$ 3.01**
Cash dividends declared per common share		**$ 3.00**	**$ 3.00**	**$ 3.00**

P5.18 Financial analysis. Circuit City Stores, Inc., is a premier retail outlet for consumer electronics and major appliances in the United States. Presented below are five years of selected earnings and balance sheet data (years ended February 28 or 29).

	19X5	19X4	19X3	19X2	19X1
Consolidated Summary of Earnings					
(Amount in thousands except per share data)					
Net sales and operating revenues	$2,096,588	$1,721,497	$1,350,425	$1,010,692	$705,490
Cost of sales, buying, and warehousing	1,477,502	1,219,570	961,345	720,187	505,691
Gross profit	619,086	501,927	389,080	290,505	199,799
Selling, general, and administrative expenses	482,229	379,045	291,489	213,816	157,521
Interest expense	8,757	8,382	8,391	5,189	2,257
Total expense	490,986	387,427	299,880	219,005	159,778
Earnings before income taxes	128,100	114,500	89,200	71,500	40,021
Provision for income taxes	50,000	45,025	38,800	36,200	18,000
Net earnings	$ 78,100	$ 69,475	$ 50,400	$ 35,300	$ 22,021
Net earnings per common share:					
Primary and fully diluted	$ 1.70	$ 1.52	$ 1.12	$ 0.79	$ 0.50
Number of common shares outstanding at year end	45,860	45,234	44,802	44,380	43,780
Average common shares outstanding — primary	46,068	45,542	44,850	44,500	44,260
Consolidated Summary Balance Sheets					
(Amounts in thousands)					
Current assets	$ 442,208	$ 366,893	$ 265,364	$ 195,482	$135,939
Property and equipment, net	250,006	206,052	155,246	147,213	83,331
Deferred income taxes	6,460	3,023	354	—	1,637
Other assets	14,981	11,513	12,277	18,922	23,029
Total assets	$ 713,655	$ 587,481	$ 433,241	$ 361,617	$243,936
Current liabilities	$ 222,243	$ 192,150	$ 116,218	$ 98,162	$ 82,285
Long-term debt	93,882	94,674	96,676	101,149	40,005
Deferred income taxes	—	—	—	1,392	—
Deferred revenue, deferred credits, and other liabilities	38,244	27,040	18,934	11,643	9,874
Total liabilities	354,369	313,864	231,828	212,346	132,164
Stockholders' equity	359,286	273,617	201,413	149,271	111,772
Total liabilities and stockholders' equity	$ 713,655	$ 587,481	$ 433,241	$ 361,617	$243,936
Other Data					
Book value per share of common stock	$ 7.83	$ 6.05	$ 4.50	$ 3.37	$ 2.54
Cash dividends per share paid on common stock	$ 0.075	$ 0.055	$ 0.0375	$ 0.029	$ 0.024
Return on average stockholders' equity	24.6%	29.1%	28.7%	27.3%	22.0%
Funded debt to equity ratio	0.26 to 1	0.35 to 1	0.48 to 1	0.68 to 1	0.36 to 1
Number of employees at year-end	13,092	10,481	7,219	5,922	4,554
Number of retail units at year-end	149	122	105	87	69

Required:

Calculate all pertinent ratios. Prepare common-size financial statements. Explain the first four lines in the "other data" section. Overall, how has Circuit City Stores, Inc., been doing?

P5.19 Fortune 500 statistics. Presented below are selected return on sales (ROS), return on assets (ROA), return on equity (ROE), and sales per employee statistics for 19X5 and 19X4 Fortune 500 industry groupings.

Selected 19X5 (top line) and 19X4 Fortune 500 Industrials
Industry Medians

	ROS (%)	ROA (%)	ROE (%)	Sales/ Employees
Pharmaceuticals	14 13	13 14	26 25	$147,553 $142,807
Petroleum refining	4 3	5 4	14 10	613,084 537,026
Transportation equipment	3 3	4 3	9 11	120,859 109,539
Mining, crude-oil products	9 10	4 4	15 13	375,204 314,563
Apparel	3 4	4 7	13 20	64,869 58,232
Computers and office equipment	6 6	6 6	12 13	132,407 122,684
Chemicals	6 6	6 6	14 13	212,381 205,813
Food	3 3	6 5	17 15	223,584 211,323
Building materials	2 2	2 3	11 4	167,294 155,000
Aerospace	3 3	5 4	13 12	132,100 121,002
Electronics	3 4	4 5	13 14	111,478 101,190
Beverages	8 8	7 7	16 23	202,030 194,426
Industrial and farm equipment	3 4	4 4	11 12	125,570 112,091
Metals	4 5	4 6	11 18	185,079 195,750
Motor vehicles and parts	2 3	2 2	7 10	130,265 117,941
Scientific and photographic equipment	5 5	6 7	12 13	118,232 112,718
Textiles	0 2	0 3	3 10	89,391 80,901
Soaps and cosmetics	6 4	9 8	19 19	146,885 209,117
500 Industrials median	4 5	5 6	13 15	154,064 146,887

Required:

(This exercise assumes that you know something about the industries identified in the groupings. If you do not have a mental picture of the typical financial structure of the companies in the industry, some review of individual company financial statements may be in order.)

a. Identify the most significant differences in the ROS, ROA, and ROE performance of the industry groups, and explain why those extremes might occur.

b. Identify the most significant differences in results between 19X5 and 19X4, and explain what might have caused those differences.

c. How would you interpret the Fortune 500 industrial median statistics? Do you think they represent a historical low, high, or average period in industrial history? Explain your opinion.

P5.20 Presenting segment information. All public companies include in their annual reports a footnote presenting information about the results of operations of the segments of their companies. The following exhibits are the segment footnotes from Capital Cities/ABC, Brown-Foreman Corporation, and Teledyne. Also, note that PepsiCo presented its segment information as a part of its Management Discussion and Analysis (see Chapter 1). All four companies adhere to the GAAP pronouncement for the presentation of segment data, but each presentation is somewhat unique.

Brown-Foreman Corporation

6. Business Segment Information

The company's operations have been classified into two business segments: wine and spirits and consumer durables. The wine and spirits segment includes the production, importing, and marketing of wines and distilled spirits. The consumer durables segment primarily includes the manufacture and sale of china, crystal, and luggage. The "other" category principally involves the production and sale of jewelry and candles. The company has disposed of these businesses.

Summarized financial information by business segment is as follows *(in thousands)*:

	19X5	19X4	19X3
Net sales:			
Wine and spirits	**$ 974,846**	$1,002,112	$1,002,770
Consumer durables	**317,716**	284,967	248,134
Other	**—**	—	103,694
	$1,292,562	$1,287,079	$1,354,598
Operating income:			
Wine and spirits	**$ 204,484**	$ 178,710	$ 158,134
Consumer durables	**39,430**	47,519	39,788
Other	**—**	—	8,776
Corporate	**(18,970)**	(17,749)	(15,014)
	$ 224,944	$ 208,480	$ 191,684
Total assets:			
Wine and spirits	**$ 504,094**	$ 524,943	$ 520,492
Consumer durables	**395,639**	372,535	348,497
Corporate	**121,251**	105,794	63,295
	$1,020,984	$1,003,272	$ 932,284
Depreciation and amortization:			
Wine and spirits	**$ 19,250**	$ 17,614	$ 16,973

	19X5	19X4	19X3
Consumer durables	**14,406**	13,158	11,914
Other	**—**	—	2,990
Corporate	**175**	102	81
	$ 33,831	$ 30,874	$ 31,958
Capital expenditures:			
Wine and spirits	**$ 27,051**	$ 22,293	$ 15,907
Consumer durables	**22,365**	15,341	8,430
Other	**—**	—	907
Corporate	**651**	317	275
	$ 50,067	$ 37,951	$ 25,519

Classes of products that contributed 10% or more to consolidated net sales:

	19X5	19X4	19X3
American spirits	**$ 437,554**	$ 398,782	$ 372,373
Imported spirits	**224,084**	253,389	265,949
Wines and specialties	**313,208**	349,941	364,448
	$ 974,846	$1,002,112	$1,002,770

There were no significant intersegment sales or transfers. Operating income by business segment excludes interest income, interest expense, and net unallocated corporate expenses. Corporate assets consist principally of cash and cash equivalents, certain corporate receivables, and other assets.

Foreign assets and revenues and export sales each represents less than 10% of the company's total. No material amounts of the company's sales are dependent upon a single customer.

7. Stockholders' Equity

Changes in consolidated stockholders' equity during the three years ended April 30, 19X5, are shown in the accompanying consolidated statement of retained earnings and in the following table *(in thousands):*

	Capital in Excess of Par Value of Common Stock	Treasury Stock
Balance, April 30, 19X2	$89,747	$(118,780)
Acquisition of treasury stock (Class A, 625,849 shares; Class B, 3,487,800 shares)	—	(198,455)
Treasury stock issued in connection with employee benefit plans (Class B, 567 shares)	14	10
Balance, April 30, 19X3	$89,761	$(317,225)
Acquisition of treasury stock (Class A, 35 shares; Class B, 261 shares)	—	(16)
Balance, April 30, 19X4 and 19X5	$89,761	$(317,241)

The company acquired as treasury stock 625,849 shares of Class A and 3,487,800 shares of Class B common stock that were tendered to the company at $48 per share during 19X2.

Adjustments from foreign currency financial statement translations during the three years ended April 30, 19X5, were not material.

Capital Cities/ABC

8. Segment Data

The company's business operations are classified into two segments: Broadcasting and Publishing. Broadcasting operations include the ABC Television Network and eight television stations, the ABC Radio Networks and 21 radio stations, and cable television programming services. The publishing segment includes newspapers, shopping guides, various specialized business and consumer periodicals and books, research services, and database publishing. There are no material product transfers between segments of the company, and virtually all of the company's business is conducted within the United States. The segment data is as follows (000s omitted):

	19X5	19X4	19X3	19X2	19X1
Broadcasting					
Net revenues	$4,283,633	$3,899,989	$3,749,557	$3,433,749	$3,153,619
Direct operating costs	3,331,316	2,943,321	2,904,668	2,680,582	2,554,932
Depreciation	75,088	74,333	76,303	73,730	78,952
Amortization of intangible assets	46,772	46,186	46,415	46,527	45,200
Total operating costs	3,453,176	3,063,840	3,027,386	2,800,839	2,679,084
Income from operations	$ 830,457	$ 836,149	$ 722,171	$ 632,910	$ 474,535
Assets at year-end	$4,250,540	$4,177,132	$3,927,891	$4,018,775	$4,186,650
Capital expenditures	105,475	173,078	138,043	102,425	104,278
Publishing					
Net revenues	$1,101,969	$1,057,405	$1,023,896	$1,006,597	$ 970,755
Direct operating costs	934,022	891,542	858,102	822,123	778,201
Depreciation	18,363	17,971	18,361	18,878	15,353
Amortization of intangible assets	17,213	17,448	17,713	18,879	18,202
Total operating costs	969,598	926,961	894,176	859,880	811,756
Income from operations	$ 132,371	$ 130,444	$ 129,720	$ 146,717	$ 158,999
Assets at year-end	$ 916,346	$ 899,499	$ 898,608	$ 908,193	$ 920,896
Capital expenditures	14,450	13,015	15,085	13,114	48,589
Consolidated					
Net revenues	$5,385,602	$4,957,394	$4,773,453	$4,440,346	$4,124,374
Income from operations	$ 962,828	$ 966,593	$ 851,891	$ 779,627	$ 633,534
General corporate expense	(39,613)	(44,081)	(35,862)	(33,637)	(30,856)
Operating income	923,215	922,512	816,029	745,990	602,678
Interest expense	(168,859)	(174,417)	(182,362)	(190,806)	(185,511)
Interest and other income	83,424	103,032	53,609	8,794	5,576
Income before income taxes	$ 837,780	$ 851,127	$ 687,276	$ 563,978	$ 422,743
Assets employed by segments	$5,166,886	$5,076,631	$4,826,499	$4,926,968	$5,107,546
Cash investments and other corporate assets	1,529,301	1,282,876	1,262,372	451,404	83,870
Total assets at year-end	$6,696,187	$6,359,507	$6,088,871	$5,378,372	$5,191,416

Teledyne Corporation

Note 9. Business Segments

Teledyne is a diversified corporation comprised of companies that manufacture a wide variety of products. The company's major business segments include aviation and electronics, specialty metals, industrial and consumer.

Companies in the aviation and electronics segment produce aircraft and turbine engines, airframe structures, unmanned air vehicles, target drone systems, and equipment and subsystems for spacecraft and avionics. Other activities in this segment include the manufacture of military electronic equipment, aircraft monitoring and control systems, semiconductors, relays, and other related products and systems. Products in the specialty metals segment include zirconium, titanium, high-temperature nickel-based alloys, high-speed and tool steels, tungsten, and molybdenum. Other operations in this segment consist of processing, casting, rolling, and forging metals. The industrial segment is comprised of companies that manufacture a large range of air- and water-cooled, gasoline- and diesel-fueled engines, machine tools, dies, and consumable tooling. The consumer segment manufactures oral hygiene products, shower massages, water and air purification systems, and swimming pool and spa heaters, and provides other products and services.

Information on the company's business segments for the years ended December 31, 19X5, 19X4 and 19X3, was as follows (in millions):

	19X5	19X4	19X3
Sales:			
Aviation and electronics	**$1,339.2**	$1,471.4	$1,465.7
Specialty metals	**770.3**	853.7	922.7
Industrial	**763.6**	796.1	809.4
Consumer	**333.7**	324.6	333.4
	$3,206.8	$3,445.8	$3,531.2

Sales of operations that the company plans to sell or close were $514.8 million for the year ended December 31, 19X5, of which $368.8 million was in the industrial segment. Teledyne Monarch Rubber ceased operations in 19X5 and accounted for approximately $55 million in 19X5, $120 million in 19X4, and $135 million in 19X3 of industrial segment sales. Certain operations in the specialty metals segment were closed in 19X4 with sales of approximately $55 million in 19X4 and $90 million in 19X3.

The company's backlog of confirmed orders was approximately $1.9 billion at December 31, 19X5, and $2.2 billion at December 31, 19X4. Backlog of the aviation and electronics segment was $1.3 billion at December 31, 19X5, and $1.6 billion at December 31, 19X4.

The company's sales to the U.S. government were $1.1 billion in 19X5, and $1.2 billion in 19X4 and 19X3, including direct sales as prime contractor and indirect sales as subcontractor. Most of these sales were in the aviation and electronics segment. Sales by operations in the United States to customers in other countries were $535.6 million in 19X5, $447.4 million in 19X4, and $445.0 million in 19X3. Sales between business segments, which were not material, generally were priced at prevailing market prices.

	19X5	19X4	19X3
Income (Loss) of Operations before Income Taxes:			
Aviation and electronics	**$(18.3)**	$ 44.5	$ 92.1
Specialty metals	**45.8**	92.0	123.1
Industrial	**28.3**	48.4	78.0
Consumer	**19.4**	38.7	35.0
Operating profit	**75.2**	223.6	328.2
Corporate expenses	**56.1**	76.7	53.1
Interest expense	**61.9**	68.4	69.6
Other income	**(11.0)**	(17.9)	(26.2)
	$(31.8)	$ 96.4	$231.7

Operating profit in 19X5 included a restructuring charge of $107.6 million. The restructuring charge was $38.6 million in the aviation and electronics segment, $20.4 million in the specialty metals segment, $39.3 million in the industrial segment, and $9.3 million in the consumer segment.

Results of operations before tax for the aviation and electronics segment included provisions for losses from the performance of development and initial production fixed-price contracts of approximately $55 million in 19X5 and $90 million in 19X4. Operating profit in 19X4 for the industrial segment and the specialty metals segment was adversely affected by estimated losses on disposal of certain unprofitable operating companies. In addition, strikes at certain engine manufacturing locations in both the industrial segment and the aviation and electronics segment adversely affected 19X4 results. Corporate expenses for 19X4 included the effect of strengthening aircraft product liability reserves.

	19X5	19X4	19X3
Depreciation and Amortization:			
Aviation and electronics	**$ 23.2**	$ 29.5	$ 37.5
Specialty metals	**28.5**	27.1	24.1
Industrial	**18.2**	19.5	20.0
Consumer	**6.5**	6.8	7.3
Corporate	**7.7**	7.7	8.9
	$ 84.1	$ 90.6	$ 97.8
Identifiable Assets:			
Aviation and electronics	**$ 365.8**	$ 404.2	$ 405.5
Specialty metals	**316.0**	323.7	312.7
Industrial	**267.2**	294.3	272.2
Consumer	**108.9**	103.5	91.9
Corporate	**661.5**	550.6	505.1
	1,719.4	1,676.3	1,587.4
Net assets of discontinued insurance operations	**—**	—	1,880.8
	$1,719.4	$1,676.3	$3,468.2
Capital Expenditures:			
Aviation and electronics	**$ 16.8**	$ 19.7	$ 28.3
Specialty metals	**42.2**	49.4	52.3
Industrial	**19.9**	26.7	34.0
Consumer	**8.0**	10.9	21.2
Corporate	**10.7**	6.4	8.8
	$ 97.6	$ 113.1	$ 144.6

Required:

For all four companies, complete a ratio analysis on the segments reported, and prepare a separate commentary on the results of your analysis for each company. Prepare a fifth commentary, comparing and contrasting the four segment presentations and highlighting important differences between them. Which presentation did you prefer? Why?

CASES

C5.1 Revenue recognition under long-term contracts: Buildmore Construction Company. In June 1994 Buildmore Construction Company (BCC) was employed by the city of Houston, Texas, to assist in constructing its new World Trade Center complex. BCC was to construct the superstructure of a multistory office building as part of the city's downtown redevelopment. The construction agreement called for work to begin no later than August 1994 and required the company to construct the concrete frame for the complex.

Under the terms of the three-year contract, BCC was to receive a total of $10 million in cash payments from the city of Houston, to be paid as follows: 25 percent when the project was 30 percent complete, 25 percent when the project was 60 percent complete, and the remaining 50 percent when the project was fully completed (including all necessary building approvals). The contract, which was of a fixed price variety and hence did not provide for cost overrun recoupment, required that completion estimates be certified by an independent engineering consultant *before* any cash progress payments would be made.

In preparing its bid, BCC had estimated that the total cost to complete the project would be $8.3 million, assuming no cost overruns. Hence, under optimal conditions, the company anticipated a profit of approximately $1.7 million.

During the first year of the contract, BCC incurred actual costs of $2.49 million, and on June 30, 1995, the engineering consulting firm of C. Likert & Associates determined that the project had attained a 30 percent completion level. In the following year, BCC incurred actual costs of $3.1 million. As of June 30, 1996, the firm of C. Likert & Associates determined that the project had attained at least a 60 percent completion level. In their report to the City Authority, however, the consulting engineers noted that BCC might be facing a potential cost overrun situation. In response to this observation, the directors of BCC noted that they had anticipated that a number of economies of scale would arise during the final phases of construction and thereby offset any prior cost overruns.

By May 1997, BCC had completed the remainder of the project. Actual costs incurred during the year to June 30, 1997, amounted to $3.11 million. The firm received a certification for the fully completed work.

Accounting Decision

Prior to issuing the 1995 annual report, the controller's office of BCC determined that the proceeds from the World Trade Center contract would be accounted for using the *completed contract* method. Under this approach, the recognition of income is postponed until essentially all work on the contract has been completed. This method previously had been utilized by the company to account for construction contract income, and it appeared to be a prudent alternative, given the possibility of some cost overrun during the life of the current contract.

Under the completed contract approach, revenues (and thus expenses) are recognized on completion or substantial completion of a contract. In general, a contract is regarded as substantially complete if the remaining costs to complete the project are insignificant in amount. Funds expended under the contract are accounted for in an asset account, Construction in Progress, while progress payments received during the construction phase are accounted for in a Deferred or Unearned Revenue account. Although income is not recognized until completion of the contract, any expected losses should be recognized immediately when identified.

In the process of reaching the decision to use the completed contract method, the controller's office of the Buildmore Construction Company had reviewed *Accounting Research Bulletin No. 45*, "Long-Term Construction Type Contracts." This pronouncement identifies the *percentage of completion* method as the preferred method to account for long-term construction contract income, at least when the estimated costs to complete a contract and the extent of construction progress can be reasonably estimated. Under this method, revenues are recognized in proportion to the amount of construction actually completed in a given period.

Required:

a. Assuming that BCC had no other sources of revenues or expenses, determine the level of profits to be reported for the years ended June 30, 1995, 1996, and 1997, utilizing the following revenue recognition methods:

(1) Percentage of completion.
(2) Completed contract.
(3) Cash basis. (Note: Assume that the City Authority remits cash payments on the same day as work completion certification.)

b. Which set of results (from part *a*) best reflects the economic performance of the company over the period 1995–1997? What criteria did you apply in the foregoing assessment?

c. What are the advantages and disadvantages of each of the methods from part *a?*

C5.2 Revenue and expense recognition: Emergetel. Emergetel manufactures and sells two-way radio equipment used by police and fire departments and similar agencies. Unit sales have held steady over the last several years, but sales prices have been declining because of international competition. Earnings have been depressed, and so has the company's stock price.

California has become the company's most difficult sales territory. Because of the reduction in state and local tax rates in California, agencies responsible for purchasing radio equipment have sought to reduce costs and have turned to less expensive equipment from offshore suppliers. But even more frustrating, Emergetel's remaining California customers have become very demanding, insisting on top performance in very difficult circumstances — in intense urban environments and in rugged, hilly terrain. The Emergetel maintenance staff serving the California area is always the busiest of any in the company.

Harry Smith was assigned sales responsibility for the California territory in late 1989, just after the company lost a bid for a comprehensive new radio system in San Diego. That was a traumatic loss for the company because San Diego had used Emergetel equipment since 1952. The loss of an established customer hurt in three ways: The company lost the sales of the new equipment to be installed; it lost the service revenue on the ongoing maintenance; but perhaps most important, the company lost the opportunity to provide replacement and expansion equipment. Once a customer accepted a major new radio system, it was likely to stay with that supplier for ongoing enhancements. Over the life of a customer relationship, Emergetel estimated that the maintenance and add-on business was worth 10 times the original order.

Smith had worked the state tirelessly, although he had few sales to show for his effort. In late 1994 he came home with a *big* winner. He convinced the State Highway Patrol, the police departments from Los Angeles and the Bay Area, and the State Game and Wildlife Agency to go together and purchase a single radio system from Emergetel that would tie all four agencies' communication systems together. To satisfy the demands of each of those powerful agencies, Smith had promised spectacular performance. To meet the exacting specifications, Emergetel would be forced to redesign its basic equipment and create a "California Special Radio." The engineers estimated that the redesign and tooling involved would take three months and cost $8,000,000. The basic contract totaled $30,000,000. At that price, Emergetel would lose $2,000,000 after covering its direct costs, the design and tooling costs, and an appropriate share of fixed costs. Even so, the long-term potential of the contract was enormous, and Smith was awarded a bonus of $1,000,000, payable in three annual installments, beginning December 31, 1995.

The agencies also signed a combined five-year maintenance contract with Emergetel, providing for a fixed payment of $1,000,000 a quarter beginning March 31, 1996. Based on experience with similar systems, and factoring in the California environment, Emergetel estimated that there would be a 40 percent margin on that business.

The contracts were signed December 30, 1994. Prototype radios were to be delivered for testing by the agencies on March 31, 1995. The operational equipment was to be delivered in three equal stages: July 1995, September 1995, and November 1995. Everything was to be operational by December 30, 1995. The California agencies agreed to pay $6,000,000 on December 30, 1994, and four additional installments of $6,000,000 at the end of each quarter during 1995.

Required:

(Assume that Emergetel uses a calendar year-end for financial reporting purposes and prepares public financial statements every quarter.)

a. How much of the expected $2,000,000 loss on the basic contract should be recognized in Emergetel's quarterly income statements for these periods?

(1) When the contract is signed.	$________
(2) When the radios are delivered.	$________
(3) During the term of the maintenance contract.	$________
(4) When replacement or expansion radios are sold to the agencies.	$________
(5) Other.	$________

Explain the rationale for your answers.

b. How much of the $8,000,000 spent for redesign and tooling on the "California Special Radio" should be recognized in Emergetel's quarterly income statements for these periods?

(1) When the contract is signed.	$________
(2) When the radios are delivered.	$________
(3) During the term of the maintenance contract.	$________
(4) When replacement or expansion radios are sold to the agencies.	$________
(5) Other.	$________

Explain the rationale for your answers.

c. How much of Smith's $1,000,000 bonus should be recognized in Emergetel's quarterly income statements for these periods?

(1) When the contract is signed.	$________
(2) When the radios are delivered.	$________
(3) During the term of the maintenance contract.	$________
(4) When replacement or expansion radios are sold to the agencies.	$________
(5) Other.	$________

Explain the rationale for your answers.

C5.3 Revenue and expense recognition: Entertainment Arts, Inc. Entertainment Arts, Inc., (EAI) develops videotapes using animation (much like standard cartoons) and moving clay models (like the dancing raisins). The videos were prominent parts of cable TV fare during after-school hours. They had proven to be very popular with the 8–12-year-old market, and many of the featured characters were well known to the members of that age group. Each video cost about $150,000 to make, but because the target audience group was constantly being replenished, it could be shown an infinite number of times. As each video was made, its cost was added to an asset account; the cost was amortized over 10 years to reflect the possibility that changed styles would ultimately make the video obsolete. At the time of this case, EAI had 92 films in its asset pool, with an average age of 3.5 years and an aggregate unamortized cost of $11,000,000.

The company received a proposal for a license on EAI characters from an agent who represented a number of manufacturers of children's products. Three companies asked for an exclusive right to use EAI characters in their markets for a three-year period, and each proposed to pay EAI a 1 percent royalty on any of its products' sales where the product used an EAI character in its design. The agent asked EAI for a commission of $75,000 as compensation for bringing all of the parties together. EAI asked for details, and the agent explained the three companies' plans as follows:

	Planned Annual Sales of EAI Related Products
Lunch box manufacturer	$1,500,000
Clothing manufacturer	3,500,000
Toy manufacturer	5,000,000

EAI argued that it would be giving something up by signing this agreement and that it wanted more for its sacrifice than the 1 percent royalty proposed. So EAI countered with this proposal:

	Minimum Annual Royalty Payable	1% Royalty on Annual Sales Over
Lunch box manufacturer	$10,000	$1,000,000
Clothing manufacturer	25,000	2,500,000
Toy manufacturer	40,000	4,000,000

After some further negotiating, a three-year contract was signed. The manufacturers agreed on the guaranteed minimum royalty but insisted that the annual minimum payments would be paid at the end of each year, at the same time the obligation for any additional royalty was due. And, as a concession to complete the deal, the agent agreed to reduce her commission to $60,000.

1. What should EAI's revenue recognition policies be for this license agreement? Please explain all the considerations that entered into your policy proposal.
2. What should EAI's accounting policy be with regard to the aggregate unamortized cost of the videos ($11,000,000) as a result of this transaction? Please explain.
3. What should EAI's accounting policy be with regard to the $60,000 commission paid? Please explain.

C5.4 Revenue recognition and realization: Candela Laser Corporation.*

On November 2, 1988, the *Boston Globe* carried the following report:

> **Audit Problem Stops Candela's Public Offering**
> Candela Laser Corp., the Wayland (Mass.) company that is attempting to score big in the medical market with its laser technology, yesterday put off indefinitely a planned public stock offering after its auditors withdrew their opinion on the company's financial statements.
>
> The deferral puts pressure on Candela to reach agreement with its auditors, restate its offering, or find an alternative source of funding if the company is to proceed on schedule with its ambitious marketing plans.
>
> Candela said it deferred the planned secondary offering of 1,115,000 shares after its outside auditors, Deloitte, Haskins, & Sells, advised the company that it has withdrawn its opinion on Candela's June 30 year-end financial statements.
>
> "We have a difference of opinion on a technical accounting interpretation that relates to revenue recognition," said Richard J. Olsen, vice president and chief financial officer at Candela.
>
> Olsen said the disagreement relates to the timing of recognition of revenues of some sales of Candela's medical laser systems to independent distributors in the United States.

*This case was prepared by J. R. Anderson and D. Imbriani.

EXHIBIT 1

Candela Laser Corporation
Income Statement
For the Year Ended June 30, 1988
(before restatement)

Sales	$15,796,659
Cost of goods sold	6,268,348
Gross profit on sales	$ 9,528,311
Operating expenses	8,800,481
Income before taxes	$ 727,830
Income tax expense*	-0-
Net income	$ 727,830

*Because of tax loss carry-forwards, the company had no federal income tax obligation.

The disagreement between Candela and its auditors came just weeks after the company had announced record sales and profits for the fiscal year ended June 30, 1988 (see Exhibit 1). Reported sales had almost tripled from the preceding year, and the $727,830 profit represented a major turnaround from the $1.9 million in losses incurred over the two previous years. Candela's stock price reached an all-time high of $15 per share in September 1988 as the firm appeared to have emerged as a significant, profitable player in the medical laser market.

The auditors' decision to withdraw their unqualified opinion on the firm's financial statements forced Candela to delay raising over $10 million of much-needed equity capital and raised serious questions about the firm's ability to continue in business. The company's stock price dropped from $11.75 to $6 per share within a week following the announcement.

Company Background

Candela Laser Corporation designs, manufactures, and markets tunable dye lasers for medical, scientific, and defense applications. It was organized in 1970 by two physicists, Horace Furumoto and Harry Ceccon, who spent the next 10 years developing scientific lasers for sale to universities and federal agencies. The company remained quite small, with sales of less than $1 million per year.

In 1981 Furumoto began to collaborate with Dr. John Parrish of the Harvard Medical School on a prototype dermatology laser. Over the next three to four years, in conjunction with the Massachusetts General Hospital, Candela experimented with the use of tunable dye lasers in the treatment of birthmarks and kidney stones.

By 1985 Furumoto was convinced of the potential for his systems but needed to gain Food and Drug Administration approval and more capital to market the product. Investors were receptive, and the company raised $4.2 million in a June 1986 public stock offering at $3 per share (adjusted for a subsequent 2-for-1 stock split).

In late 1986 Candela received FDA approval to market both the dermatology and urology laser systems, and it began to ship the urology laser in April 1987, with the dermatology laser following in March 1988. Money from the initial public offering was soon exhausted, so the company raised another $5 million in a private offering to institutional investors. By fiscal year-end on June 30, 1988, medical laser systems accounted for 68 percent of Candela's sales, with units priced at $100,000 to $250,000 each.

After two years of extensive testing, Candela received FDA approval in June 1989 to sell a third laser, the MDL-1, for the photo-acoustic fragmentation of gallstones.

EXHIBIT 2

Candela Laser Corporation
Condensed Quarterly Income Statements

Quarter Ended →	9/30/86	12/31/86	3/31/87	6/30/87
Sales	$ 843,000	$ 799,000	$1,010,000	$2,900,000
Expenses	1,051,000	1,403,000	1,644,000	2,792,000
Profit/(Loss)	$ (208,000)	$ (604,000)	$ (634,000)	$ 108,000
Quarter Ended →	**9/30/87***	**12/31/87***	**3/31/88***	**6/30/88***
Sales	$2,800,000	$3,100,000	$3,910,000	$5,970,000
Expenses	2,642,000	3,264,000	3,758,000	5,389,000
Profit/(Loss)	$ 158,000	$ (164,000)	$ 152,000	$ 581,000

*As originally announced, before later restatement.

As the company's experience with the medical laser market grew, it recognized that competitive advantages in the industry did not necessarily flow from exclusive patents and superior technology. Instead, factors such as ease of use, customer training, product warranties, and well-trained sales personnel appeared to be decisive for most customers. Candela responded to this by dramatically increasing their investment in these areas. The company also greatly increased its research spending in an attempt to develop lasers that effectively treated common eye diseases and atherosclerosis (blocked arteries).

Financial Results

With FDA approval of the urology and dermatology lasers, Candela experienced rapid growth in sales volume. However, the company's research, marketing, and administrative costs also increased dramatically as it simultaneously tried to develop new products, sell existing products in a highly competitive market, and create an organization to service its growing customer base. Quarterly financial data is presented in Exhibit 2.

The strong results in the second half of fiscal 1987–88, as compared to the first half of the year, apparently convinced investors that Candela had matured from a developmental-stage enterprise into a fast-growing, profitable operation. The average stock price jumped 30 percent, and the company prepared to take advantage of this positive market position by selling over a million new common shares to the public. Prior to this planned sale, senior management and members of the board of directors owned approximately 40 percent of the common shares outstanding and additionally benefited from stock option plans allowing for the future purchase of 329,000 additional shares at an average price of $6.50 per share.

Auditor Disagreement

In early November 1988, however, just prior to the planned public stock offering, Deloitte, Haskins, and Sells announced that it was withdrawing its audit opinion on the June 30, 1988, Candela financial statements because of a disagreement over the firm's revenue and expense recognition policies. As shown in Exhibit 3, Candela's policy was to count revenue "when completed machines are shipped to customers." The "difference of opinion" between the auditors and Candela's management stemmed from the fact that a significant portion of Candela's shipments were to independent distributors who retained the right to return the product if they were unable to sell it to hospitals, clinics, or doctors. Deloitte argued that these shipments should not be counted as sales according to the provisions of *Statement of Financial Accounting Standards No. 48* (SFAS 48), which is summarized in Exhibit 4. While *SFAS 48* is quite clear in its basic requirements, it has been subject to liberal interpretation by many organizations and has not always been followed in practice. (See, for instance, Exhibit 5.)

EXHIBIT 3

Candela Laser Corporation
Excerpts from Notes to Financial Statements
Year Ended June 30, 1987

Summary of Significant Accounting Policies

Revenue Recognition:

Generally, the company recognizes revenue as completed machines are shipped to customers. On long-term contracts, the company recognizes revenues using the percentage-of-completion method of accounting based on the proportion of costs incurred on individual contracts to the total estimated contract costs . . .

. . . Warranty service contract revenue is recognized ratably over the contract period.

EXHIBIT 4

Summary of the Provisions of SFAS 48

When a buyer has the right to return merchandise purchased, the seller may not recognize income from the sale unless all of the following conditions are met:

1. The price charged the buyer is substantially fixed or determinable.
2. The seller has received full payment, or the buyer is indebted to the seller and the indebtedness is not contingent on the resale of the merchandise.
3. Physical destruction, damage, or theft of the merchandise would not change the buyer's obligation to the seller.
4. The buyer has an economic substance of its own and does not exist solely for the benefit of the seller.
5. No significant obligations exist for the seller to help the buyer resell the merchandise.
6. A reasonable estimate can be made of the future returns that will be allowed.

EXHIBIT 5

Revenue Recognition — Sales to Distributors

National Semiconductor Corporation

In 1981 the company adopted an accounting method that deferred the recognition of revenue on sales to distributors until final sale by the distributors. Since that time a clearly predictable pattern of returns from distributors and allowances to distributors has emerged. Consequently, the company has changed its accounting method from deferring such revenue to recognizing revenue when products are shipped to distributors. The company believes that the recognition of revenue at the time of shipment results in a more meaningful measurement of operations. Appropriate accruals for returns from distributors and for allowance granted to them are established at the time of shipment.

Although it was not mentioned in press coverage of the case, Deloitte also had concerns regarding Candela's accounting for

- Future warranty costs associated with current sales.
- Warranty revenue on extended service contracts.
- Obsolete or overstocked inventory.

Epilogue

In March 1989, almost nine months after its fiscal year-end, Candela issued restated 1988 financial statements (see Exhibit 6). These statements, reflecting major adjustments to sales, warranty revenue, warranty costs, and inventory, resulted in the firm's reported $727,000 profit being revised to a $3,690,000 loss. (See Exhibit 7 for a reconciliation of these adjustments.) The auditors also qualified their opinion because of questions about Candela's ability to continue as a going concern.

Accompanying the financial statements was a letter from the CEO, Dr. Horace Furumoto, indicating that Candela had "substantially modified its sales strategy to adapt to the new revenue recognition policy." He also discussed the effect that the auditor's withdrawal of opinion had on the company as a whole and indicated that a new independent auditor had been appointed for 1989.

In early 1989 Candela sold common stock to private investors for $8 million that was estimated to be worth nearly $13 million before the disagreement.

Required:

a. Using the financial statements and the profit reconciliation provided in Exhibits 6 and 7, reconstruct the adjusting journal entries required by the firm's auditors.

b. How could Candela's financial problems have been identified *before* the withdrawal of the auditor's opinion?

EXHIBIT 6

Candela Laser Corporation
Selected Excerpts: 1988 Annual Report

One Financial Center
Boston, Massachusetts 02111-2620
(617) 348-4000
Telex: 940161

Independent Auditors' Report

Board of Directors and Stockholders
CANDELA LASER CORPORATION AND SUBSIDIARY:

We have audited the accompanying consolidated financial statements of Candela Laser Corporation and its subsidiary, listed in the accompanying table of contents. These consolidated financial statements are the responsibility of the Company's management. Our responsibility is to express an opinion on the financial statements based on our audits.

We conducted our audits in accordance with generally accepted auditing standards. Those standards require that we plan and perform the audit to obtain reasonable assurance about whether the financial statements are free of material misstatement. An audit includes examining, on a test basis, evidence supporting the amounts and disclosures in the financial statements. An audit also includes assessing the accounting principles used and significant estimates made by management, as well as evaluating the overall financial statement presentation. We believe that our audits provide a reasonable basis for our opinion.

In our opinion, such consolidated financial statements present fairly, in all material respects, the financial position of the companies at June 30, 1988 and 1987, and the results of their operations and the changes in their financial position for each of the three years in the period ended June 30, 1988, in conformity with generally accepted accounting principles.

As discussed in Note 2 to the consolidated financial statements, the Company has restated its previously issued 1988 consolidated financial statements.

As discussed in Note 8 to the consolidated financial statements, the Company and certain of its directors and officers are defendants in litigation relating, in part, to the Company's previously issued 1988 consolidated financial statements. The ultimate outcome of the litigation cannot presently be determined. Accordingly, no provision for any loss that may result upon the resolution of this matter has been made in the accompanying consolidated financial statements.

The accompanying consolidated financial statements have been prepared assuming that the companies will continue as going concerns. As discussed in Note 1 to the consolidated financial statements, the companies' recurring losses from operations and increasing funds used for operations, the net stockholders' deficiency, and the termination of its primary lender relationship raise substantial doubt about their ability to continue as going concerns. Management plans concerning these matters are also described in Note 1. The consolidated financial statements do not include any adjustments that might result from the outcome of this uncertainty.

DELOITTE HASKINS & SELLS
March 8, 1989
Boston, Massachusetts

EXHIBIT 6 continued

Candela Laser Corporation and Subsidiary
Consolidated Statements of Operations
For the Years Ended June 30, 1988 (Restated), 1987 and 1986

	1988	1987	1986
Revenues:			
Sales	$11,086,691	$5,207,515	$1,502,899
Grants	443,972	433,303	363,713
Total	11,530,663	5,640,818	1,866,612
Costs of sales	6,078,415	3,042,852	1,132,284
Gross profit	5,452,248	2,597,966	734,328
Expenses:			
Marketing and selling	3,574,425	1,261,896	213,726
General and administrative	3,555,590	1,845,235	672,278
Research and development	1,740,906	852,765	274,676
Total	8,870,921	3,959,896	1,160,680
Loss from operations	3,418,673	1,361,930	426,352
Other (income) expense:			
Interest expense	492,707	121,290	42,409
Interest income	(101,291)	(116,635)	
Other	15,000	(28,953)	(2,083)
Total	406,416	(24,298)	40,326
Loss before minority interest and income taxes	3,825,089	1,337,632	466,678
Minority interest in net loss of subsidiary	134,950	—	—
Loss before income taxes	3,690,139	1,337,632	466,678
Provision (credit) for income taxes			(11,400)
Net loss	$ 3,690,139	$1,337,632	$ 455,278
Net loss per common and common equivalent share	$ 1.14	$ 0.45	$ 0.31
Weighted average number of common and common equivalent shares outstanding	3,238,113	2,995,817	1,482,272

EXHIBIT 6 continued

Candela Laser Corporation and Subsidiary
Consolidated Balance Sheets, June 30, 1988 (Restated) and 1987

	1988	1987
Assets		
Current Assets:		
Cash and equivalents — unrestricted	$ 241,542	$ 723,852
Cash and equivalents — restricted	2,001,071	—
Accounts receivable (less allowance for doubtful accounts of $75,661 in 1988)	3,025,242	2,518,359
Deferred distributor receivables	3,764,493	—
Inventory	3,183,042	2,069,598
Prepaid expenses and other	230,590	185,257
Total current assets	12,445,980	5,497,066
Property, Plant, and Equipment:		
Laser systems	811,268	447,230
Equipment	835,845	458,076
Office furniture and equipment	402,408	198,095
Leasehold improvements	43,433	21,566
Total	2,092,954	1,124,967
Less accumulated amortization	800,810	228,087
Property and equipment — net	1,292,144	896,880
Other Assets:		
Deferred financing costs — net	258,609	95,340
Patents — net	113,327	76,793
Deposits and other	47,784	33,441
Total other assets	419,720	205,574
Total	$14,157,844	$ 6,599,520
Liabilities and Stockholders' Equity (Deficiency)		
Current Liabilities:		
Note payable to bank	$ 2,750,000	$ 1,832,833
Deferred income	2,948,761	—
Current portion of long-term debt	179,668	24,338
Accounts payable	1,350,956	1,304,355
Accrued payroll and related expenses	607,856	316,191
Accrued warranty costs	229,350	20,000
Other accrued liabilities	640,562	139,832
Total current liabilities	8,707,153	3,637,549
Deferred Extended Warranty Revenue — Long-Term	709,500	222,000
Long-Term Debt — Net of Current Portion	5,054,601	92,746
Minority Interest	665,050	—
Stockholders' Equity (Deficiency):		
Redeemable convertible preferred stock, $0.01 par value: authorized, issued, and outstanding, 7,000 shares	70	70
Common stock, $0.01 par value: authorized, 15,000,000 shares; issued and outstanding, 3,051,172 and 3,037,882 shares in 1988 and 1987, respectively	30,512	30,379
Additional paid-in capital	4,220,128	4,155,807
Accumulated deficit	(5,229,170)	(1,539,031)
Stockholders' equity (deficiency)	(978,460)	2,647,225
Total	$14,157,844	$ 6,599,520

See notes to consolidated financial statements.

EXHIBIT 6 continued

Candela Laser Corporation and Subsidiary

Consolidated Statements of Changes in Financial Position for the Years Ended June 30, 1988 (Restated), 1987 and 1986

	1988	1987	1986
Operations:			
Net loss	$(3,690,139)	$(1,337,632)	$ (455,278)
Add (deduct) amounts not affecting funds:			
Depreciation and amortization	622,746	108,807	40,300
Minority interest in net loss of subsidiary	(134,950)	—	—
Deferred income taxes	—	—	(12,700)
Loss on sale of property	—	16,568	—
Deferred extended warranty revenue — long-term	487,500	222,000	—
Total	(2,714,843)	(990,257)	(427,678)
Changes in Working Capital Affecting Operations:			
Accounts receivable	(506,883)	(2,106,720)	(144,534)
Deferred distributor receivables	(3,764,493)		
Inventory	(1,113,444)	(1,258,319)	(410,276)
Prepaid expenses and other	(45,333)	(153,017)	(15,971)
Accounts payable	46,601	1,043,159	54,055
Accrued payroll and related expenses	291,665	170,816	84,353
Deferred income	2,948,761	—	—
Accrued warranty costs	209,350	20,000	—
Other accrued liabilities	500,730	56,769	53,718
Total	(1,433,046)	(2,227,312)	(378,655)
Total funds (used for) operations	(4,147,889)	(3,217,569)	(806,333)
External Financing Activities:			
Issuance of convertible subordinated notes	5,000,000	—	—
Increase in notes payable and long-term debt	5,349,806	3,047,885	984,102
Repayment of notes payable and long-term debt	(4,315,454)	(1,756,427)	(537,571)
Proceeds from minority interest	800,000	—	—
Issuance of common stock	64,454	588,675	3,382,511
Issuance of preferred stock	—	—	190,070
Total funds from external financing activities	6,898,806	1,880,133	4,019,112
Investing Activities:			
Additions to property and equipment	(967,987)	(841,325)	(126,190)
Other assets	(264,169)	(172,423)	(30,183)
Total funds (used for) investing activities	(1,232,156)	(1,013,748)	(156,373)
Transactions Not Affecting Funds:			
Cancellation of no-par common stock and treasury stock	—	—	(25,000)
Issuance of $0.01 par common stock	—	—	25,000
Issuance of $0.01 par value common stock for convertible preferred stock	—	—	200,000
Conversion of convertible preferred stock	—	—	(200,000)
Total transactions not affecting funds			—
Increase (Decrease) in Cash and Equivalents	1,518,761	(2,351,184)	3,056,406
Cash and Equivalents, Beginning of Year	723,852	3,075,036	18,630
Cash and Equivalents, End of Year	$ 2,242,613	$ 723,852	$ 3,075,036

See notes to consolidated financial statements.

EXHIBIT 6 continued

Candela Laser Corporation and Subsidiary
Notes to Consolidated Financial Statements

1. Basis of Presentation

The consolidated financial statements of Candela Laser Corporation and subsidiary (the "Company") have been presented on the basis that the companies are going concerns, which contemplates the realization of assets and the satisfaction of liabilities in the normal course of business.

In 1984, Candela Laser Corporation ("Candela") began the research and development of laser systems for medical applications, and in June 1987 Candela commercially introduced its first medical laser system. During the three-year period ended June 30,1988, Candela has changed its business focus from the sale of scientific lasers to the development and marketing of medical laser systems. This shift in focus resulted in substantial growth in sales in 1987 and 1988 and substantial increases in marketing, administrative, and research personnel costs since 1986. As a result, the Company experienced losses in 1986, 1987, and 1988. In addition, the Company has used funds for operations of $806,333, $3,217,569, and $4,147,889 for the years ended June 30, 1986, 1987, and 1988, respectively. The aggregate funds used for operations since 1986 of $8,171,791 have been provided principally from stock issuances of approximately $4,225,000 (including the proceeds from the Company's initial public offering) and approximately $7,770,000 proceeds from borrowings (including convertible subordinated notes) net of debt repayments.

At June 30, 1988, the Company had a stockholders' deficiency of $978,460 as a result of its recurring losses.

Subsequent to June 30, 1988, through the date of this report, the Company has continued to use substantial cash in its operations. The Company's operations during this period have been financed with bank borrowings and the proceeds of a private placement of 1,000,000 shares of the Company's stock (see Note 13). Candela is currently a defendant in litigation relating, in part, to its previously issued 1988 consolidated financial statements (see Notes 2 and 8).

All borrowings from Candela's former primary lender (note payable to bank in the accompanying consolidated financial statements) became due and payable on March 1, 1989, and were paid in full by March 8, 1989. The Company's management is currently seeking a new primary lender to finance its ongoing working capital needs. On March 8, 1989, Candela entered into an agreement in principle with one of its stockholders with respect to a private placement of 200,000 shares of the Candela's common stock for an aggregate purchase price of $1,000,000.

Even if the Company does obtain a replacement lender, its continued existence will remain dependent upon its ability to eliminate or substantially reduce the cash required by operations and, ultimately, to attain a positive cash flow. The Company is currently taking steps toward this goal, including a recent reduction in its current workforce of approximately 20 percent.

Management believes that it will be successful in obtaining the financing it currently needs and, ultimately, in attaining successful operations. Management also believes that the Company has the potential to continue its growth in a manner that will not put excessive pressure on cash flow. However, there can be no assurance that the Company will achieve these goals. The consolidated financial statements do not include any adjustments that might result if the companies are unable to continue as going concerns.

2. Restatement

The Company has restated the 1988 consolidated financial statements to reflect the changes in its revenue recognition methods from those utilized in its previously issued 1988 consolidated financial statements: namely its revenue recognition methods for recording sales to certain distributors, for recording revenues from extended warranties, and for the recording of commitments associated with certain sales. In addition, the Company restated the carrying value and classification of certain of its assets.

The following is a summary of the significant consolidated financial statement amounts that were affected by this restatement:

	Previously Reported	As Restated
For the year ended June 30, 1988:		
Total revenues	$15,796,659	$ 11,530,663
Gross profit	9,528,311	5,452,248
Net income (loss)	727,830	(3,690,139)
Net earnings (loss) per common and common equivalent share	0.22	(1.14)
June 30, 1988:		
Current assets	13,270,249	12,445,980
Current liabilities	5,525,220	8,707,153
Accumulated deficit	(811,201)	(5,229,170)
Stockholders' equity (deficiency)	3,439,509	(978,460)

3. Summary of Significant Accounting Policies

Organization

The Company designs, develops, manufactures, and markets flashlamp-excited tunable dye laser systems and related instruments and devices for medical and scientific applications. On December 19, 1987, Candela entered into a joint venture agreement to form Candela International Corporation to market the Company's products outside the United States. The Company contributed $1,200,000 to the joint venture in exchange for a 60 percent equity interest.

Basis of Consolidation

The consolidated financial statements include the accounts of Candela and its 60 percent owned subsidiary. Material intercompany balances and transactions have been eliminated.

EXHIBIT 6 concluded

Revenue Recognition

Product sales. Revenue from product sales, except sales to certain distributors and revenue from long-term contracts, is recognized at the time of shipment.

Shipments made to distributors, where payment is dependent on resale of the system, are not recognized until the system is sold by the distributor and reported to the Company. Upon shipment by the Company, amounts billed to such distributors are included in Deferred Distributor Receivables; inventory is relieved and the sale and estimated gross profit are deferred and recorded in Deferred Income until all conditions of sale are met.

On long-term contracts, the Company recognizes revenue using the percentage of completion method of accounting based on the proportion of costs incurred on individual contracts to the total estimated contract costs. Revisions in contract revenue and cost estimates during the course of a contract are reflected in the accounting period in which the facts requiring the revisions become known. Provision for estimated losses on contracts not yet completed is made in the period in which such losses become evident.

Grant Revenue. Grants represent revenues earned through government contracts granted under the Small Business Innovation Research program. Government contracts limit reimbursement to allowable direct and indirect costs reduced by a negotiated cost-sharing percentage to be absorbed by the Company (5 percent during the years ended June 30, 1988, 1987, and 1986). Revenues are recognized as costs are incurred.

Revenues from Extended Warranties. Revenue from the sale of extended warranties is deferred and recognized, on a straight-line basis, over the extended warranty period. The deferred extended warranty revenue scheduled to be earned over the succeeding fiscal year is included in Deferred Income, while the amount classified as long-term is scheduled to be earned in the second succeeding year.

Product Warranty Costs

Estimated future costs for initial product warranties are provided at the time of sale. The Company's warranty policy on direct sales of medical laser systems is one year on parts and labor. The Company warranties parts for one year on distributor sales to end users.

Income Taxes

In December 1987, the Financial Accounting Standards Board issued Statement No. 96 (SFAS 96), "Accounting for Income Taxes." SFAS 96 requires an asset and liability approach for financial reporting for income taxes and is effective for years beginning after December 15, 1989. Management has not determined if such statement will be adopted prospectively or retroactively but believes that the effect of its implementation on the Company's financial position and results of operations will not be material.

Cash and Cash Equivalents

Cash and equivalents include short-term investments stated at cost, which approximates market. The restricted cash and equivalents can only, by agreement of its 60 percent owned subsidiary's shareholders, be used in the operations of the subsidiary.

Accounts Receivable

Accounts receivable at June 30, 1988, includes a $100,000 promissory note dated September 3, 1987. The note bears interest at 8 percent and is payable on demand.

Inventory

Inventory is stated at the lower of cost (first-in, first-out method) or market.

Prepaid Expenses and Other

Prepaid expenses and other includes $67,391 of costs and estimated profit on contracts not yet completed at June 30, 1987. There were no such costs at June 30, 1988.

Property and Equipment

Purchased property and equipment are recorded at cost. Equipment leased under capital leases is recorded at the lesser of cost or the present value of the minimum lease payments required during the lease period. Laser systems are recorded at cost. Depreciation and amortization are provided using the straight-line method over the estimated useful lives of the related assets [three years for laser systems, five years for other assets, and over the lease term (two to five years) for capital leases].

Deferred Financing Costs

Costs incurred in the issuance of the convertible subordinated notes are amortized over the term of the related debt using the interest method (see Note 7). Accumulated amortization approximated $39,000 at June 30, 1988.

Patents

Legal costs incurred in obtaining patents are amortized using the straight-line method over their estimated useful lives. Accumulated amortization approximated $11,000 and $4,000 at June 30, 1988 and 1987, respectively.

Research and Development

Research and development costs are expensed as incurred.

Reclassifications

Certain amounts for 1987 and 1986 have been reclassified to conform to the 1988 presentation.

4. Inventory

Inventory consists of the following at June 30:

	1988	1987
Raw materials	$1,412,849	$ 895,300
Work in process	986,997	797,372
Finished goods	783,196	376,926
Total	$3,183,042	$2,069,598

5. Deferred Income

Deferred income consists of the following at June 30:

	1988
Shipments to distributors	$2,702,061
Extended warranty revenue	154,500
Other	92,200
Total	$2,948,761

EXHIBIT 7

Candela Laser Corporation: Reconciliation of 1988 Net Income from Original Announcement to Final Audited Net Loss

Net income, as originally reported	$ 727,830
Adjustments:	
To eliminate gross profit on sales to distributors	(2,702,061)
To defer the recognition of revenue from extended warranty contracts	(566,267)
To defer unspecified "other revenue"	(92,200)
To write off obsolete inventory	(824,269)
To provide for additional warranty expense on 1988 sales	(233,172)
Net loss, as restated	(3,690,139)

CHAPTER 6

The Statement of Cash Flows

Cash consciousness is figuring in virtually all aspects of corporate life, from major corporate strategic decisions to increased emphasis on such relatively humble functions as inventory control and contracts with suppliers.[1]

Key Chapter Issues

- What is the statement of cash flows, and what are its principal elements?
- How are statements of cash flows prepared?
- What information does a statement of cash flows convey about a company's health?
- How might future levels of cash flows be projected?

[1] I. Picker, "Going with the Flow," *Institutional Investor,* November 1990, p. 121.

For many years, the principle focus of all financial statement users — creditors, investors, and managers alike — was the accrual-based financial statements, namely the balance sheet and the income statement. These two statements were thought to be not only *necessary* but also *sufficient* to present a complete picture of the financial condition and operations of a company. In recent decades, however, financial statement user preference has shifted from a purely accrual-based information orientation to one that includes *both* accrual and cash flow information. In recognition of these changing preferences, the FASB in 1987 adopted SFAS No. 95, "Statement of Cash Flows," which specifies the format for a statement of cash flows that is now required in all U.S. published financial statements. The purpose of this chapter is to help students to gain an understanding of the information conveyed by the statement of cash flows and to learn how the statement is prepared and how it can be used and analyzed.

THE STATEMENT OF CASH FLOWS

A Historical Perspective

A noted authority on financial reporting once observed:

> For more than 500 years, until the 1930s, the central focus of financial reporting throughout the world was cash flow and solvency. So I find it somewhat amazing that for the past 50 years, which includes the entire lifespan of the Securities and Exchange Commission and the period of greatest development of external reporting in the United States, the financial community has been obsessed with the income statement and its all-important bottom-line figures — net income and earnings per share.[2]

To help explain the irony suggested by this observation, the following presents a brief historical perspective of the U.S. financial community. Until the 1920s, the investing public in the United States made relatively few stock investments, and when such stock investments were made, they were typically based on personal contacts and conversations between the investee and the officers of the investor company. In fact, the most common type of financing involved debt between a lending institution and a borrower. Consequently, the principal use of financial statements was to enable creditors to evaluate lending opportunities and to justify the loans that were made; stock investors made relatively little use of such information. Hence, it stands to reason that the financial reporting characteristic of that era focused on liquidity and credit-related information rather than on earnings and investment-related information.

With the advent of a broader public market for stock investments in the late 1920s, the focus of financial statement interest shifted to income and earnings per share. As the level of stock investing increased, the financial community became increasingly interested in earnings and other accrual-based measures. This shift in focus was logical, even if excessive, in that the net income reported by a company *is* a better predictor of future earnings than is cash flow.[3]

Only after a number of spectacular bankruptcies by companies that had reported positive earnings streams did this earnings fixation begin to subside, with the pendulum swinging back toward a more balanced view. Although some may argue that cash

[2] B.S. Thomas, "The Perils of Ignoring Cash Flow," *Directors and Boards,* Fall 1983, pp. 9–10.

[3] The interested reader is referred to Chapter 3 of *The Modern Theory of Financial Reporting* by L. Brown (Homewood, Ill.: BPI/Irwin, 1987).

is king in financial markets today, it is safe to say that an intelligent reader of financial statements looks at *both* the earnings picture and the cash flow picture.

The need for information to supplement the accrual-based income statement was first addressed in the United States in 1971 when the predecessor to the FASB, the Accounting Principles Board, required the inclusion of a statement of changes in financial position (SCFP) in published financial statements. (A similar phenomenon occurred in the United Kingdom in 1975 with the advent of the source and application of funds statement.) At that time, businesses were generally given the option of denominating the SCFP in terms of cash or working capital. Virtually all publicly held companies chose the seemingly more sophisticated working capital format for this statement.

The purpose of the SCFP was to explain how a company had funded its activities during the year, with *funds* defined as working capital. However, it did not take long for financial statement users to become disenchanted with the working capital approach to the SCFP because although working capital had a conceptual meaning (current assets minus current liabilities), it did not fully indicate the level of resources available for such normal operating functions as paying for purchases or investments.

This trend of increasing dissatisfaction with the SCFP was, in part, the result of a progressively more widespread call from the investing community for information pertaining to a business enterprise's cash flows. At about this same time, the FASB was also looking into the issue of cash flows. The board's study, begun in 1981, culminated with the issuance of SFAS No. 95, "Statement of Cash Flows," in November 1987. It was several years later that the British Accounting Standards Board issued its Financial Reporting Standard (FRS) No. 1, requiring publicly held companies to publish a cash flow statement as part of their 1992, and subsequent, annual reports. Likewise, in 1992 the International Accounting Standards Committee (IASC) revised International Accounting Standard (IAS) No. 7 to endorse the presentation of a statement of cash flows in lieu of a statement of changes in financial position (SCFP), operative for 1994 annual reports and thereafter. The formats adopted by both the British and the IASC parallel that detailed for U.S. companies in SFAS No. 95. It is interesting to note, however, that in some countries, like Japan, companies are currently not required to issue a cash flow statement or even a statement tantamount to a SCFP.

SFAS No. 95 requires businesses to include a statement of cash flows when issuing published financial statements. The FASB believes that this requirement will help readers and users of financial statements assess the following:

1. A business's ability to generate future cash flows.
2. Its ability to meet obligations and pay dividends.
3. The effectiveness with which its management has fulfilled its cash stewardship function.

In short, the required cash flow information is intended to aid in determining the amount, timing, and uncertainty of *future* cash flows.

Management Issues

Cash flows represent the most fundamental and prevalent economic events engaged in by businesses. In fact, talk to just about any small business owner, entrepreneur, banker, or chief financial officer and he or she will tell you that the "bottom line" of the income statement has little to do with staying solvent. It is cash planning—

specifically, understanding the sources and uses of current and future cash flows — that often makes the difference between corporate success and failure.

Businesses that manage cash effectively benefit in numerous ways. For example, they benefit by having lower financing costs. By accurately forecasting the amount and timing of cash flows, managers minimize their need to borrow, thus lessening their company's interest expense. In addition, improving the amount of cash generated from operations decreases the need to solicit external financing, thus preserving proportionate shareholder value and unused debt capacity.

Cash is also important to external users of management's financial statements. Shareholder and creditor interests are seldom settled by means other than cash. Therefore, cash flow information is very useful in enabling these users to assess a company's ability to (1) generate future positive cash flows from operations, (2) meet its maturing obligations, and (3) pay dividends.

Managers must be cognizant of the fact that accrual accounting often masks a company's underlying cash flows. Under the accrual basis of accounting, revenues are recognized at the time of sale, not when cash is received. Thus, credit sales increase net income but not current cash inflows. The accrual basis of preparing an income statement also reports such noncash expenses as depreciation, amortization, and accrued warranty estimates, which reduce net income and further widen the gulf between it and cash flows. For example, when a business enters into a loan agreement, the loan is reflected as an increase in loans payable on the balance sheet. As the loan is repaid, cash outflows increase and the loan's payable balance decreases. At no time, however, does any record of the cash outflow for the loan repayment appear in the income statement; only the interest expense appears there. For reasons such as this, the management of a business can easily find itself with an income statement that portrays an attractive net income number but without sufficient cash for tomorrow's tax bill, payroll, dividend, or loan payment. To ensure that such payments can be made, and that operations continue in an orderly manner, managers must manage both the timing and amount of cash flows.

THE ELEMENTS OF THE STATEMENT OF CASH FLOWS

The primary objective of the statement of cash flows (SCF) is to explain the change in cash and cash equivalents occurring during a given reporting period. Recall from Chapter 2 that this relationship can be portrayed as in Exhibit 6.1.

For purposes of the SCF, *cash* includes currency on hand and demand deposits and **cash equivalents,** which are short-term, liquid investments (such as U.S. Treasury bills) that are both readily convertible to cash and so close to maturity as to be essentially risk free. Companies must disclose which items are considered to be cash equivalents in their financial statements. Government securities of terms longer than three months, debt securities of terms longer than three months, and equity securities are not considered to be cash equivalents.

Statement Format

The SCF should clearly classify cash flows into one of three principal activities: operating, investing, and financing. **Investing activities** primarily affect the noncurrent asset accounts and include such transactions as making and collecting loans,

EXHIBIT 6.1

The Relationship between the Statement of Cash Flows and Consecutive Balance Sheets

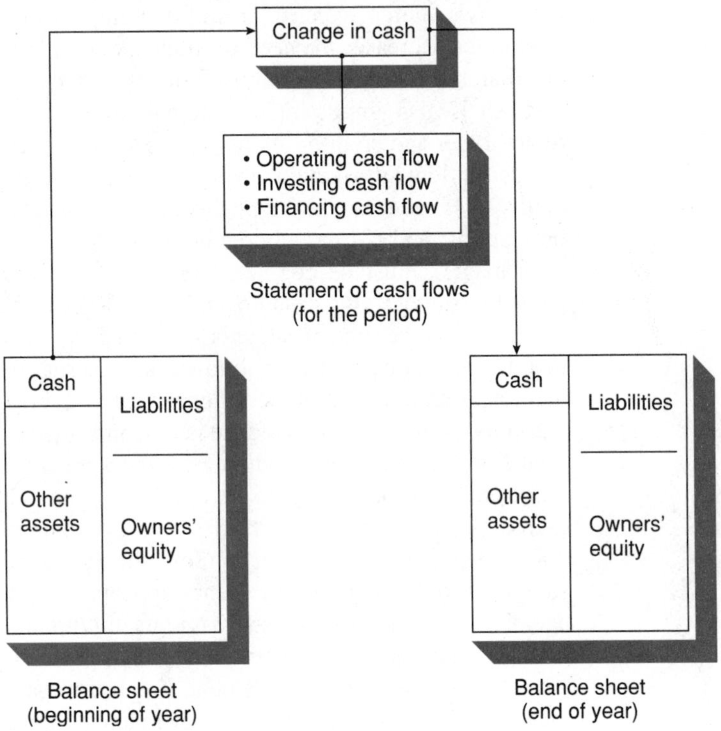

acquiring and disposing of other entities' debt instruments or equity investments, and buying and selling property, plant, equipment, and other long-lived productive assets. Cash flows from **financing activities** are the results of transactions generally affecting the noncurrent liability and shareholders' equity accounts and include such transactions as obtaining resources from owners and providing them a return *on* and a return *of* their investment and borrowing and repaying amounts borrowed. Finally, **operating activities** primarily affect the income statement and working capital accounts — in essence, the cash flows from sales of goods or services and cash payments for acquisition of the inputs used to provide the goods or services sold (for example, raw materials and labor). One helpful way to ascertain the appropriate categorization of a given business transaction is to think about the person who might be making the decision to engage in the transaction: Operations people generally make the *operating* decisions, the financial department is likely to be making the *investment* decisions, and the treasurer's office typically makes the *financing* decisions.

Operating activities. In regard to the operating activities section of the SCF, two presentation methods are permissible: the direct method and the indirect method (see Exhibit 6.2). The **direct method** presents major classes of cash receipts and payments. The direct method involves reporting, at a minimum, the **cash flows from operating**

EXHIBIT 6.2

The Statement of Cash Flows:
Direct versus Indirect Methods

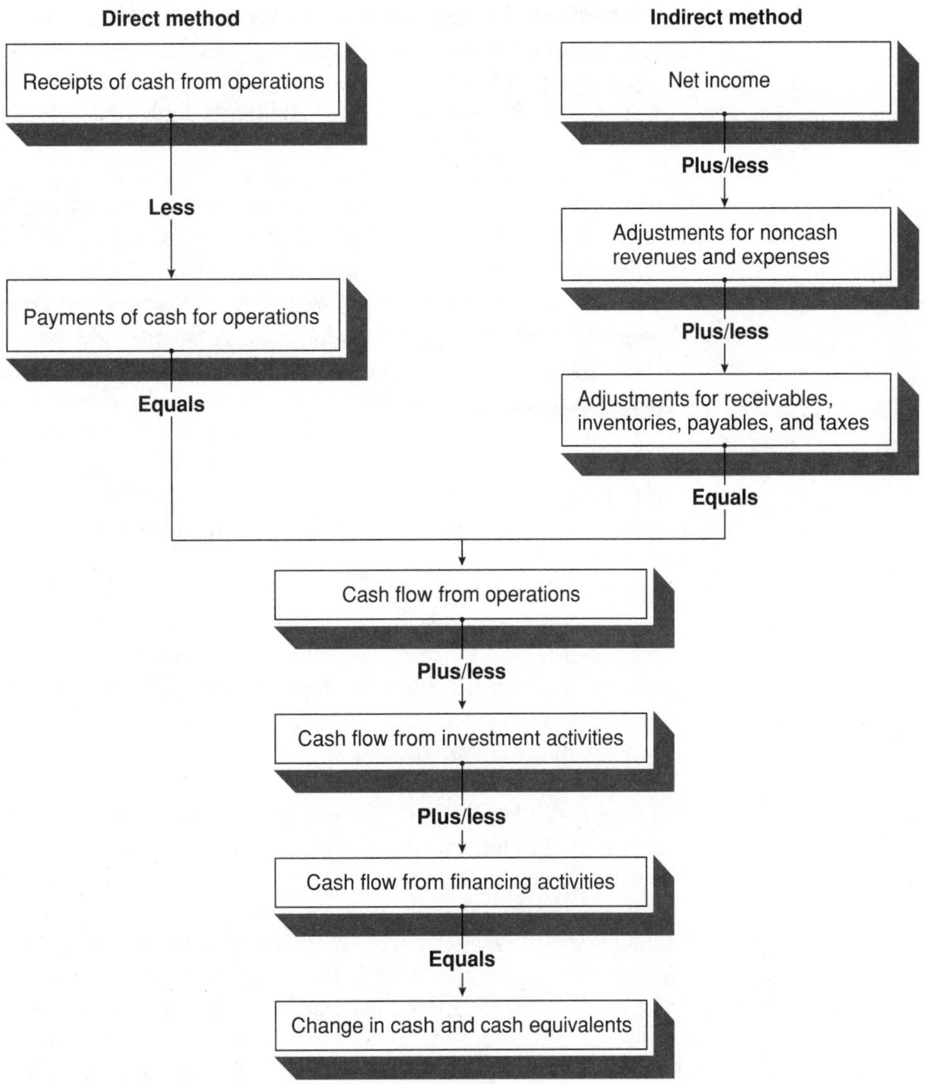

activities as the difference between the receipts and payments pertaining to the following separately reported items:

- Cash collected from clients and customers.
- Dividends and interest received.
- Other receipts of operating cash, if any, such as insurance and lawsuit settlements and refunds from suppliers.
- Cash payments for wages and other goods and services received.

- Interest paid.
- Taxes paid.
- Other operating cash payments, if any, such as charitable contributions.
- Refunds to customers and lawsuit settlements.

The distinctive feature of the **indirect method** of presenting the SCF is that it reconciles a company's accrual net income with its cash flows from operations. Beginning with net income (see Exhibit 6.3), the reconciliation process converts net income to its cash-basis equivalent by (1) adding back the noncash expenses (such as deferred income taxes, depreciation, and amortization expense) deducted that period in deriving net income, (2) subtracting the noncash revenues (such as undistributed earnings of affiliates) included in the period's net income, and (3) subtracting any gains and adding back any losses incurred on various transactions (such as the sale of a noncurrent asset or the early retirement of long-term debt) that will be reported in the investing and financing sections of the SCF. The first two types of adjustments are designed to eliminate any noncash items that are included in net income under the accrual basis of accounting, whereas the third type of adjustment is designed to avoid the double counting of certain cash flows. For example, if a long-term investment recorded on the books at $100,000 is sold for $120,000, the entire cash inflow of $120,000 should be reported on the SCF as an investing activity. To avoid double counting the $20,000 cash inflow representing the gain on the sale, the $20,000 gain included in accrual net income is subtracted from net income in deriving cash flow from operations in the SCF.

To complete the conversion of the accrual net income figure to the cash flows from operations figure under the indirect method, a final set of adjustments involving the operations-related current asset and current liability accounts is needed. Consider, for example, the fact that the sales figure in PepsiCo's income statement (most of which represents credit sales) is equal to this period's cash inflows from sales activities *only if* the year-end accounts receivable balance remains unchanged as compared to the receivable balance at the beginning of the period. This situation is reflected in Scenario 1 of Panel A in Exhibit 6.4. If, during the year, PepsiCo collected less than it billed its customers for credit sales, thereby creating an increase in the ending accounts receivable balance, the net income figure in the SCF would need to be reduced by the increase in receivables in order to approximate the period's true cash inflows from sales. Scenario 2 in Panel A of Exhibit 6.4 depicts this situation, as does PepsiCo's SCF for 1994, 1993, and 1992. Finally, a reduction in the ending receivable balance as compared to the beginning balance indicates that more cash had been collected than is reflected in the current period's sales figure. Thus, the amount of the reduction in the receivable balance should be added to the net income figure on the SCF in order to reflect this higher cash inflow. See, for example, Scenario 3 in Panel A of Exhibit 6.4.

This final set of adjustments needed to derive the cash flow from operations may involve more accounts than the Accounts Receivable account. Consider, for example, the case of inventory. Every period, service businesses accumulate billable time, merchandisers make new purchases, and manufacturers produce additional items. If reported inventory amounts have increased beyond the beginning of period balance (that is, purchases have exceeded sales of inventory), an increased outflow of cash has occurred. Thus, the net increase in inventory must be subtracted from the accrual-based net income to reflect accurately the total cash spent or invested in inventory. On the other hand, if the reported ending inventory amounts have declined relative to their beginning balances, the net decline represents a part of the cost of goods sold that is deducted in the income statement but for which no cash was expended this period. This

EXHIBIT 6.3

PepsiCo, Inc.
Consolidated Statement of Cash Flows
(in millions)
Fifty-three weeks ended December 31, 1994 and
fifty-two weeks ended December 25, 1993, and December 26, 1992

	1994	1993	1992
Cash Flows — Operating Activities			
Income before cumulative effect of accounting changes	**$1,784.0**	$1,587.9	$1,301.7
Adjustments to reconcile income before cumulative effect of accounting changes to net cash provided by operating activities			
Depreciation and amortization	**1,576.5**	1,444.2	1,214.9
Deferred income taxes	**(66.9)**	83.3	(52.0)
Other noncash charges and credits, net	**391.1**	344.8	315.6
Changes in operating working capital, excluding effects of acquisitions:			
Accounts and notes receivable	**(111.8)**	(161.0)	(45.7)
Inventories	**(101.6)**	(89.5)	(11.8)
Prepaid expenses, taxes, and other current assets	**1.2**	3.3	(27.4)
Accounts payable	**30.4**	143.2	(102.0)
Income taxes payable	**54.4**	(125.1)	(16.9)
Other current liabilities	**158.7**	(96.7)	135.2
Net change in operating working capital	**31.3**	(325.8)	(68.6)
Net Cash Provided by Operating Activities	**3,716.0**	3,134.4	2,711.6
Cash Flows — Investing Activities			
Acquisitions and investments in affiliates	**(315.8)**	(1,011.2)	(1,209.7)
Capital spending	**(2,253.2)**	(1,981.6)	(1,549.6)
Proceeds from sales of property, plant and equipment	**55.3**	72.5	89.0
Short-term investments, by original maturity:			
More than three months — purchases	**(218.6)**	(578.7)	(1,174.8)
More than three months — maturities	**649.5**	846.0	1,371.8
Three months or less, net	**(9.9)**	(8.3)	(249.4)
Other, net	**(268.3)**	(109.4)	(30.8)
Net Cash Used for Investing Activities	**(2,361.0)**	(2,770.7)	(2,753.5)
Cash Flows — Financing Activities			
Proceeds from issuances of long-term debt	**1,285.2**	710.8	1,092.7
Payments of long-term debt	**(1,179.5)**	(1,201.9)	(616.3)
Short-term borrowings, by original maturity:			
More than three months — proceeds	**1,303.8**	3,033.6	911.2
More than three months — payments	**(1,727.7)**	(2,791.6)	(2,062.6)
Three months or less, net	**113.8**	839.0	1,075.3
Cash dividends paid	**(540.2)**	(461.6)	(395.5)
Purchases of treasury stock	**(549.1)**	(463.5)	(32.0)
Proceeds from exercises of stock options	**97.4**	68.6	82.8
Other, net	**(43.5)**	(36.7)	(30.9)
Net Cash (Used for) Provided by Financing Activities	**(1,239.8)**	(303.3)	24.7
Effect of Exchange Rate Changes on Cash and Cash Equivalents	**(11.4)**	(3.4)	0.4
Net Increase (Decrease) in Cash and Cash Equivalents	**103.8**	57.0	(16.8)
Cash and Cash Equivalents — Beginning of Year	**226.9**	169.9	186.7
Cash and Cash Equivalents — End of Year	**$ 330.7**	$ 226.9	$ 169.9
Supplemental Cash Flow Information			
Cash Flow Data			
Interest paid	**$ 591.1**	549.5	574.7
Income taxes paid	**$ 663.1**	675.6	519.7
Schedule of Noncash Investing and Financing Activities			
Liabilities assumed in connection with acquisitions	**$ 223.5**	897.0	383.8
Issuance of treasury stock and debt for acquisitions	**$ 38.8**	364.5	189.5
Book value of net assets exchanged for investment in affiliates	**$ —**	60.8	86.7

EXHIBIT 6.4

Three Scenarios for Changes in Accounts Receivable and Accrued Wages Payable and Their SCF Reporting

Panel A: Accounts Receivable

Scenario	Accounts Receivable 12/31/96	Credit Sales included in 1997 Net Income	1997 Cash Collections	Accounts Receivable 12/31/97	1997 SCF Net Income Adjustment Related to a Change in Accounts Receivable
1	$10,000	$100,000	$100,000	$10,000	–0–
2	10,000	100,000	95,000	15,000	($5,000)
3	10,000	100,000	102,000	8,000	2,000

Panel B: Accrued Wages Payable

Scenario	Accrued Wages Payable 12/31/96	Wage Expense Deducted in 1997 Net Income	1997 Cash Outflow for Wages	Accrued Wages Payable 12/31/97	1997 SCF Net Income Adjustment related to a Change in Accrued Wages Payable
1	$ 4,000	$ 40,000	$ 40,000	$ 4,000	–0–
2	4,000	40,000	37,000	7,000	$3,000
3	4,000	40,000	43,500	500	(3,500)

means that the amount of the net decline must be added back to the accrual-based net income number to accurately reflect the actual cash outflows for inventory. Exhibit 6.3 depicts PepsiCo's adjustment to reduce accrual net income in 1994, 1993, and 1992 for an *increase* in inventories in deriving cash flow from operations.

Similar analyses apply to the accounts payable and to the accrued expenses payable that are a function of purchasing materials, supplies, and labor used in conducting a firm's operations. For example, an increase in accrued expenses payable (such as accrued wages payable) in effect represents a form of cash inflow because the business has not yet expended cash for some of the expenses currently deducted in the income statement (see Panel B in Exhibit 6.4). Alternatively, a decrease in accrued expenses payable in effect signifies an additional cash outflow for expenses booked on the current and/or prior income statement, thus necessitating a reduction in the cash-based net income estimate on the SCF in order to bring it into line with this period's actual cash outflows for expensed items.

It is important to understand fully these current asset and current liability adjustments. A way to facilitate one's understanding of the SCF working capital adjustments is to focus on the more intuitively obvious accounts as was done for accounts receivable and accrued wages payable in Exhibit 6.4. Once you become familiar with how the adjustments for these accounts relate to the SCF, the remaining working capital accounts can be viewed as extensions of the same logic but applied to different balance sheet accounts. Another means to achieve a greater level of understanding of these adjustments is to actually prepare an SCF — an opportunity for which is presented in a subsequent section of this chapter.

It is worth noting that accounts pertaining to the current portion of long-term debt and notes payable are more appropriately considered financing activities than operating activities and are therefore excluded from the conversion of net income to cash flows. Thus, the sum of net income plus all of the adjustments just described (as necessitated by the indirect method of preparing an SCF) results in the amount of cash generated internally by a company, or its *cash flows from operations*. Most companies (like PepsiCo) prefer the indirect method of presenting the SCF over the direct method because it provides a link to the income statement and balance sheet, and it is generally less costly to prepare. The FASB, on the other hand, prefers the direct method because it presents a company's major types of cash receipts and payments. As shown in Exhibit 6.2, the cash flows from operations are the same regardless of which method is used. Moreover, if the direct method is used, a reconciliation of net income to cash flow from operations must be presented in a separate schedule.

Cash flows from operations is arguably the most important cash flow indicator for users of financial statements because it demonstrates the ability of a company's operations to generate cash for its shareholders, creditors, or future investment. It informs the financial statement reader whether the business's core operations are a net provider or a net user of cash. If the operations of a business use more cash than they provide, cash must then be provided by liquidating investments, seeking further external financing, or decreasing the company's reserves of cash and cash equivalents. If, on the other hand, the operating activities provide cash, as is the case for PepsiCo, this additional cash will be available to invest in the business, to repay prior financing, to pay dividends, or merely to increase the cash reserves of the company. In 1994, PepsiCo's continuing operations generated a whopping $3.7 billion in cash flows, which was available to finance a variety of firm-related activities.

Investing activities. The next section of the SCF, as shown in PepsiCo's SCF (Exhibit 6.3), reports cash flows from investing activities. This section presents the uses and provisions of cash from investments, with the term *investment* used quite broadly. This section details the amounts a company has invested in its own business, equity investments in other firms, and dispositions and purchases of other assets. From Exhibit 6.3, we can see that in 1994 PepsiCo invested more than $315 million in new acquisitions and investments; invested more than $2.25 billion in purchases of property, plant, and equipment; and liquidated $421 million in various short-term investments. PepsiCo's 1994 SCF also reveals that the company received $55.3 million from the sale of property, plant, and equipment. Overall in 1994, PepsiCo's investing activities involved net cash outflows of $2,361.0 million.

Financing activities. The final section of an SCF is the cash flow from financing activities. This section details the changes in the capital structure of a company and payments made to provide a return to investors on (and of) their investments in the firm. If cash flows from operations are positive, the company may wish to reduce its debt load, pay dividends, or buy back some of its outstanding shares. These choices must be considered in light of the firm's capital expenditure needs. If, on the other hand, the cash flows from operations are negative, or if they are positive but investing activities used more cash than operations provided (for example, as for PepsiCo in 1992 as revealed in Exhibit 6.3), a firm might want to reconsider paying cash dividends; it could be argued that paying dividends under these circumstances involves a partial liquidation of the firm. Given PepsiCo's strong history of generating positive cash flows and the modest amount by which its 1992 net cash outflows for investing

EXHIBIT 6.5

Oakencroft Cabinet Company
Income Statement
(in thousands of dollars)

	For the Year Ended	
	December 31, 1996	December 31, 1995
Net sales	$ 419,991	$ 341,656
Costs and expenses:		
Cost of sales	(280,746)	(228,681)
Depreciation	(9,033)	(6,843)
Selling, general, and administrative	(85,469)	(65,610)
	(375,248)	(301,134)
Income from operations	44,743	40,522
Interest expense	(1,877)	(1,570)
Other income	2,081	2,807
Earnings before taxes	44,947	41,759
Federal income taxes*	(18,383)	(17,606)
State income taxes	(1,900)	(1,143)
Net income	24,664	23,010
Retained earnings, beginning of year	138,273	121,476
Less: Cash dividends	(6,920)	(6,213)
Retained earnings, end of year	$ 156,017	$ 138,273

*Federal income tax expense included the following:

	1996	1995
Current amount	$18,603	$17,456
Deferred amount	(220)	150
Total	$18,383	$17,606

activities exceeded the cash generated by operations, however, such a consideration was not warranted.

Noncash investing and financing activities. Businesses sometimes engage in **noncash investing and financing activities.** For example, the conversion of debt into owners' equity does not involve any cash inflows or outflows, nor does the acquisition of a piece of equipment financed entirely by the seller. Such noncash activities are either reported in a supplement to the SCF, as in Exhibit 6.3 for PepsiCo, or are disclosed elsewhere in the financial statements. Exhibit 6.3 reveals, for example, that PepsiCo issued $38.8 million in treasury stock and debt as part of the consideration given for various acquisitions of companies it made during 1994.

PREPARING A STATEMENT OF CASH FLOWS

With the preceding discussion in mind, the best way to gain a full understanding of the SCF is to prepare one. The following simplified example is designed to illustrate the preparation of an indirect method SCF, produced from the comparative income statements (Exhibit 6.5) and balance sheets (Exhibit 6.6) of the Oakencroft Cabinet Company.

EXHIBIT 6.6

Oakencroft Cabinet Company
Balance Sheet
(in thousands of dollars)

	As of		
	December 31, 1996	**December 31, 1995**	**Increase/ Decrease in Account Balance**
Assets			
Cash	$ 1,393	$ 2,419	$ (1,026)
Short-term treasury bills	21,172	13,305	7,867
Receivables, less allowances of $3,118 in 1996 and $2,814 in 1995	113,834	103,824	10,010
Inventories:			
Raw materials	19,541	15,305	
Work in process	17,143	14,771	
Finished goods	8,791	5,157	
	45,475	35,233	10,242
Other current assets	5,037	3,229	1,808
Total current assets	$186,911	$158,010	
Property, plant, and equipment:			
Land	3,586	2,842	
Buildings and fixtures	53,082	44,082	
Machinery and equipment	66,978	51,041	
	123,646	97,971	25,675
Less: Accumulated depreciation	50,115	41,082	(9,033)
	73,531	56,889	16,642
Other assets	9,445	18,095	(8,650)
Total assets	$269,887	$232,994	$36,893

In preparing Oakencroft's SCF, it is useful to recall the basic accounting equation regarding assets, liabilities, and owners' equity:

$$A = L + OE \tag{1a}$$

Moreover, it is useful to note that the change in total assets from one period to the next must equal the sum of the changes in the liability and owners' equity accounts over that same period. Thus, Equation (1a) can be restated as

$$\Delta A = \Delta L + \Delta OE \tag{1b}$$

where Δ is interpreted as "the change in." Remember also that assets and liabilities are both composed of current (C) and noncurrent (NC) portions, so Equation (1b) can be restated as

$$\Delta CA + \Delta NCA = \Delta CL + \Delta NCL + \Delta OE \tag{2a}$$

EXHIBIT 6.6 (continued)

	As of		
	December 31, 1996	December 31, 1995	Increase/ Decrease in Account Balance
Liabilities			
Notes payable	$ 6,099	$ 3,682	$ 2,417
Current portion of long-term debt	979	1,717	(738)
Accounts payable	20,134	11,033	9,101
Wages payable	15,941	13,144	2,797
Accrued liabilities	10,014	7,478	2,536
Accrued taxes	18,409	14,588	3,821
Total current liabilities	71,576	51,642	
Long-term debt	23,270	24,463	(1,193)
Deferred taxes	9,697	9,917	(220)
Total liabilities	$104,543	$ 86,022	
Stockholders' Equity			
Common stock	$ 10,714	$ 10,443	271
Retained earnings	156,017	138,273	17,744
	166,731	148,716	
Less: Treasury shares	(1,387)	(1,744)	357
Total stockholders' equity	$165,344	$146,972	
Total liabilities and stockholders' equity	$269,887	$232,994	$36,893

A further breakdown of current assets into their components of cash, accounts receivable, inventories, and prepaid expenses permits a restatement of Equation (2a) as

$$\Delta\ \text{Cash} + \Delta\ \text{AR} + \Delta\ \text{Inv} + \Delta\ \text{Ppd Exp} + \Delta\ \text{NCA} = \Delta\ \text{CL} + \Delta\ \text{NCL} + \Delta\ \text{OE} \quad (2b)$$

Rearranging this equation to isolate the change in cash, we see that

$$\Delta\ \text{Cash} = \underbrace{\Delta\ \text{CL} - \Delta\ \text{AR} - \Delta\ \text{Inv} - \Delta\ \text{Ppd Exp}}_{\text{Operating activities}} - \underbrace{\Delta\ \text{NCA}}_{\text{Investing activities}} + \underbrace{\Delta\ \text{NCL} + \Delta\ \text{OE}}_{\text{Financing activities}} \quad (3)$$

The dynamics of the statement of cash flows can easily be discerned from this alternative presentation of the accounting equation. For example, if a current liability such as accrued wages payable is increased, the effect is an increase in cash (or a positive cash flow) — in essence, a form of spontaneous financing. If, on the other hand, there is an increase in a current asset account such as Inventory or Prepaid Expenses, cash decreases.

As noted earlier, the starting point for preparing an SCF using the indirect method is the accrual net income for the period. From such a starting point, the net income number must be adjusted for the noncash revenues and expenses that are present in the income statement — primarily depreciation, amortization, deferred taxes,[4] and

[4]In the United States, a company may prepare its income tax return using different accounting principles than it uses to prepare its financial statements. To the extent that the amount of tax that would be due if the financial statement basis had been used is

the undistributed earnings of affiliate companies.[5] The 1996 Oakencroft income statement (see Exhibit 6.5) reveals, for example, that $9,033 was deducted as depreciation expense. Because depreciation of property, plant, and equipment requires no cash outlay, the $9,033 must be added back to net income in deriving an estimate of the cash flows from operations. Oakencroft's income statement reveals no other noncash revenues or expenses with the exception of deferred income taxes. From the balance sheet (see Exhibit 6.6), and the income statement footnote, in 1996 there was a decrease in the Deferred Taxes Liability account with a commensurate reduction in the total tax expense amount. The overall effect of this change represents an additional cash outlay this period for income taxes owed from an earlier accounting period; that is, the tax expense for this additional amount was recorded in an earlier accounting period but was not paid until this period. Thus, the decrease in deferred tax liabilities in 1996 represents a decrease in operating cash flows this period that was not revealed in the 1996 income statement where only $18,383 was deducted as tax expense. Remembering the relationships from Equation (3), we recognize that this decrease in a liability should, therefore, be subtracted from net income in the operating activities section.

As pointed out earlier, the objective of the SCF is to explain the change in cash and cash equivalents by reporting all of the changes in the noncash accounts. In a sense, this is like trying to define a word without using the word in the definition. In effect, the SCF provides a definition of the change in cash by examining all of the other balance sheet account changes. Thus, the next step in our efforts to develop Oakencroft's SCF (see Exhibit 6.7) is to focus on the adjustments to net income associated with changes in the current asset and current liability operations-related accounts.

From the balance sheet data in Exhibit 6.6, note that accounts receivable increased $10,010 from 1995 to 1996. This means that the company billed its customers for more than it collected from them, which represents sales for which collections have not yet been received. The amount is thus shown as a reduction to net income in the pursuit of converting an accrual-based net income amount to an operating cash flow estimate. With similar logic, the balance sheet data also reveal that accounts payable (along with wages payable and accrued liabilities) increased, indicating that the company was billed for more expenses than it paid; hence, this amount is like a provision of cash and is therefore shown as a positive cash flow. The sum of these items (that is, net income *plus/minus* the noncash revenues and expenses *plus/minus* the changes in working capital accounts) equals the cash flow from operating activities of $29,672.

The investment section of the SCF shows changes in the balance sheet for investments in property, plant, equipment (PP&E), in equity securities from other companies, and in other assets. Note that the balance sheet data indicate that PP&E increased by $25,675. The change in the accumulated depreciation account of $9,033 equals this

different from the taxes shown on the tax return, that difference is recorded as *deferred taxes*. Therefore, deferred taxes are different from taxes payable because the deferred taxes become a liability only at some future and uncertain time. Deferred taxes represent a form of interest-free borrowing by the company and are a reconciling item between earnings and cash flow. Taxes currently payable represent the amount of taxes shown on the current tax return, less any prepayments. This topic is discussed in Chapter 13.

[5]In certain circumstances, a company may include in its own income statement the income of another company that it controls. Those earnings are recognized as they are reported by the other company on the theory that the controlling company could cause those earnings to be remitted to it at any time. Obviously, to the extent that the earnings are not remitted to the parent company in cash, those earnings are an adjustment to accrual earnings to arrive at the operating cash flow. This topic is discussed in Chapter 10.

EXHIBIT 6.7

Oakencroft Cabinet Company
Statement of Cash Flows
(in thousands of dollars)

	For the year ended December 31, 1996
Operating activities	
Net income	$24,664
Add: Depreciation and amortization	9,033
Less: Noncash revenues	–0–
Adjustment for deferred taxes, decrease (increase)	(220)
Receivables, decrease (increase)	(10,010)
Inventories, decrease (increase)	(10,242)
Payables, increase (decrease)	14,434
Taxes, increase (decrease)	3,821
Other	(1,808)
	5,008
Cash flow from operating activities	$29,672
Investing activities	
Purchases of property, plant and equipment	(25,675)
Other	8,650
Cash flow from investing activities	($17,025)
Financing activities	
Proceeds from short-term notes payable	2,417
Payments on long-term loans	(1,931)
Sale of stock	271
Reissue of treasury stock	357
Cash dividends paid to stockholders	(6,920)
Cash flow from financing activities	($ 5,806)
Increase (decrease) in cash and cash equivalents	$ 6,841
Cash and cash equivalents, beginning of year	$15,724
Cash and cash equivalents, end of year	$22,565

period's depreciation expense, which has already been placed as an adjusting item in the operating section of Oakencroft's SCF. In the absence of any sales of PP&E during the year, the $25,675 figure equals the cost of *purchases* of PP&E made this year.

It is often helpful to construct a T-account for the PP&E accounts to facilitate these calculations. In this example, the T-accounts are very straightforward:

Property, Plant, and Equipment

1/1/96	97,971	
Purchases	25,675	
12/31/96	$123,646	

Accumulated Depreciation

	1/1/96	41,082
	This year's expense	9,033
	12/31/96	50,115

If, however, the financial statements had informed readers that PP&E originally costing $10,000 had been sold for $8,000 and the 1996 depreciation expense was $12,033, the reconstruction of the T-accounts would reveal the following:

Property, Plant, and Equipment

1/1/96	97,971	Cost of PP&E sold	10,000
PP&E purchases	35,675		
12/31/96	123,646		

Accumulated Depreciation

Accumulated depreciation on PP&E sold	3,000	1/1/96	41,082
		This year's expense	12,033
		12/31/96	50,115

Thus, in this hypothetical scenario where we were given the beginning and ending balances in the PP&E account and the cost of PP&E sold, it is possible to deduce purchases of PP&E totaling $35,675. In addition, it is also possible to determine that $3,000 of depreciation expense had been accumulated over the years for the particular PP&E item sold. In sum, then, the transaction to record the sale would have been as follows:

Dr. Cash (A)	(inc.) 8,000	
Dr. Accumulated Depreciation (CA)	(dec.) 3,000	
Cr. Property, Plant, and Equipment (A)		(dec.) 10,000
Cr. Gain on the sale of Property, Plant, and Equipment (G)		(inc.) 1,000

Under this scenario, the SCF would report a $1,000 subtracting adjustment to net income in the operations section and a line item of $8,000 for "proceeds of PP&E sale" in the investing section, as well as another line item of $35,675 for purchases of PP&E. Since in the base case we were not informed of any PP&E sales, we must assume the purchases of PP&E cost $25,675 and depreciation expense was $9,033.

The final section of the SCF, financing activities, shows the net changes in cash flows as a result of payments and proceeds from loans, stock sales and stock repurchases, dividends paid to shareholders, and other financing transactions. Note the increase in short-term notes payable of $2,417. This amount is a provision of cash for the company and is shown as a positive cash flow. In determining the payments on long-term debt ($1,931), both the amounts currently due and those that are noncurrent should be considered. Cash dividends paid to shareholders always represent a use of cash and thus are shown as a negative cash flow.

As a vehicle to verify that the entire change in the retained earnings balance has been accounted for in the SCF, it is useful to reconstruct the changes in this account balance using a T-account. In the Retained Earnings T-account following, note that the net income and dividend figures, both of which now appear in the SCF, fully explain the change in Oakencroft's Retained Earnings account for the period:

Retained Earnings

	1/1/96	138,273
1996 dividends 6,920	1996 net income	24,664
	12/31/96	156,017

The SCF format for reporting these results is shown in Exhibit 6.7. The sum of the three separate sections represents the increase (or decrease) in cash and cash equivalents for the period. When added to the beginning balance of cash and cash equivalents, the resulting sum should equal the ending cash and cash-equivalent balance on the latest balance sheet.

If all of the balance sheet changes reflected in Exhibit 6.6 have been included in the SCF, it should balance to the actual change in the cash and cash–equivalent balance ($6,841 for Oakencroft), and the SCF is then complete.

THE STATEMENT OF CASH FLOWS: INTERNATIONAL CONSIDERATIONS

As alluded to earlier, there is a growing global momentum toward accounting standards setters requiring an SCF as part of a company's published annual report. In some countries (such as Germany and Japan) such a financial reporting requirement does not exist. It is interesting to observe, however, that companies in those countries may actually exhibit a preference for publishing such a statement in an attempt to address the perceived information needs of an international investing community. For example, even though German accounting standards do not require an SCF, Hoechst AG (a German chemicals company) chose to present in its 1994 annual report an SCF "reflect[ing] the format recommended by the IAS [No. 7]." Exhibit 6.8 presents Hoechst's SCF, a review of which reveals the similarity in the SCF formats dictated by IAS No. 7 and SFAS No. 95.

It is important to acknowledge the fact that although a non-U.S. company may choose (or may even be required) to publish an SCF, it may be in a form quite different from that required in the United States or that suggested by the IASC. Again consider the German context where an SCF is not required. In Volkswagen's (a German auto maker) 1994 annual report, it presents cash flow-related information (see Exhibit 6.9). Volkswagen and Hoechst may be viewed as competing for the attention, confidence, and resources of the same international audience when they publish their annual reports, yet they do so quite differently in terms of an SCF. As we turn our attention next to analyzing cash flows, users of Volkswagen's cash flow disclosures, for example, must exercise care and caution in making direct comparisons to the cash flow disclosures of a U.S. company or, for that matter, Hoechst.

ANALYZING CASH FLOWS

By using the relationships depicted in Equation (3), the statement of cash flows itself, and some basic cash flow ratio analysis, financial statement users can increase their understanding of an enterprise and answer questions such as these:

- What is the relationship between cash flows and earnings?
- How are dividends being financed?
- How is debt repayment to be achieved?
- Does the company require outside financing?
- How are the cash flows from operations being used?
- Is management's financial policy reflected in the cash flows?

In Chapters 4 and 5, we saw that financial ratio analysis could be applied to income statement and balance sheet accounts to reveal various insights about a company. Traditional ratio analysis, and even the income statement itself, however, will not provide insights regarding issues such as the timing of cash flows or the effects of operations on liquidity. To obtain this kind of information it is necessary to analyze the information presented in the statement of cash flows.

EXHIBIT 6.8

Hoechst AG
Cash Flow Statement
For Years Ended December 31

	1994 DM m	1993 DM m
Net income for the year	1363	756
Depreciation of fixed assets and investments	3483	3322
Gain on disposals of fixed assets and investments	– 321	– 178
Undistributed earnings of associated companies	– 51	18
Foreign exchange gains (–)/losses	130	– 21
Changes in inventories	– 353	381
Changes in receivables and deferred items	–1753	–1015
Changes in provisions	1160	1257
Changes in liabilities (excluding corporate debt)	1006	313
Other	17	37
Cash flows from operating activities	4681	4870
Capital expenditure on tangible fixed assets	–3143	–3597
Investments in participating interests	– 459	–1664
Investments in intangible fixed assets	– 186	– 130
Proceeds from the sale of tangible and intangible fixed assets	388	129
Proceeds from the sale of investments	230	463
Additions (–)/disposal of marketable securities	– 192	630
Cash flows from investing activities	–3362	–4169
Capital increases		70
Increase in long-term corporate debt	1099	1509
Change in short-term corporate debt	–1616	–1342
Dividends paid	– 569	– 677
Other		– 28
Cash flows from financing activities	–1086	– 468
Effect of exchange rate changes on cash	– 53	11
Effect of consolidation changes on cash	57	67
Liquid assets excluding marketable securities, change in cash and cash equivalents	237	311
Status at beginning of year	1024	713
Status at end of year	1261	1024

Cash Flow Ratios

Some useful cash flow ratios are presented in this section.[6] The list is not comprehensive, but it does reveal the relative merit of analyzing the SCF by developing applicable ratios. Each ratio is discussed in light of the PepsiCo information presented in Exhibit 6.3. Individually, each ratio gives limited information as of a single point in time, but taken over a period of years and examined in conjunction with other ratios,

[6]See D. Giacomino and D.E. Mielke, "Preparation and Use of Cash Flow Statements," *The CPA Journal* (March 1987), pp. 30–35, for a more extensive presentation and discussion of cash flow ratios.

EXHIBIT 6.9

Volkswagen Group
1994 Cash Flow Presentation

Development of Short-Term Liquidity of the Volkswagen Group (DM million)

Net earnings	+ 150	
Depreciation and write-up of fixed assets	+ 9,838	
Increase in provisions	+ 2,485	
Other expenses and income not affecting payments	− 627	
Profit and loss on disposal of fixed assets	+ 32	
Increases and decreases in inventories, trade receivables, and other assets	+ 148	
Increase in trade payables and other liabilities	+ 1,601	
Change in other items	− 181	
Inflow of funds from current operations		**+13,446**
Inpayments from disposal of fixed assets	+ 2,614	
Outpayments for additions to fixed assets	−10,497	
Outflow of funds in respect of capital investments		**− 7,883**
Inpayments in respect of capital increase	+ 22	
Outpayments to stockholders (dividends)	− 120	
Inpayments and outpayments in respect of bonds and (financial) loans	− 45	
Outflow of funds in respect of financing operations		**− 143**
Change in funds		**+ 5,420**
Funds at start of period		**− 2,751**
Funds at end of period		**+ 2,669**

	Volkswagen Group Dec. 31, 94	Volkswagen Group Dec. 31, 93	Change
Liquid funds	13,317	11,157	+2,160
Securities	2,595	1,119	+1,476
Bonds (includes financial assets items)	959	191	+ 768
	16,871	**12,467**	**+4,404**
Short-term liabilities due to banks	−14,202	−15,218	+1,016
Total Funds	+ 2,669	− 2,751	+5,420

Determination of Cash Flow

Net earnings	+ 150	
Depreciation and disposal of fixed assets, minus write-ups	+ 7,785	
Depreciation and disposal of bonds	− 24	
Depreciation and disposal of leasing and rental assets	+ 4,914	
Increase in provisions for pensions and similar obligations	+ 607	
Decrease in special items with an equity portion and special item for investment subsidies	− 872	
Other charges not affecting liquidity	+ 22	
Cash flow		**+12,582**

the cash flow ratios can reveal trends that provide insights about the company and its industry.

Operating funds ratio. Calculated as net income divided by cash flows from operations, the **operating funds ratio** can be used to indicate the portion of operating cash flows provided by net income. Depreciation methods and the management of current asset and current liability accounts are the principal factors highlighted by this ratio because they are the principal adjustments to net income used in calculating the cash flows from operations. This ratio for PepsiCo in 1994 was 0.47, indicating that the cash flows from operations were greater than net income and that, on average, there were sizeable positive adjustments to accrual net income in deriving cash flow from operations. Given the capital-intensive nature of PepsiCo's business, there was indeed a large depreciation and amortization expense component ($1,576 million) to the income adjustments made to arrive at the cash flows from operations. Moreover, given the consistent, positive track record of PepsiCo's management, one would expect only minor fluctuations in the operations-related current asset or current liability accounts, with only a modest (and most probably positive) impact on cash flows.

Normal operating conditions are likely to yield ratios in the 0.25 to 1.0 range, but not all healthy companies have such ratios, and not all ratios in that range are necessarily good. Different management objectives and different industries tend to be characterized by different "normal" ratio ranges. For example, very high growth periods can result in ratios consistently greater than 1.0 because of the normal increases in receivables and inventories that characterize rapid growth. For example, Eli Lilly and Co., achieved a 10 percent growth in sales during 1991, and its operating funds ratio for that year was 1.05.

As with all ratios, one must be careful to examine the underlying events reflected by such ratios. A troubled company also may have especially high levels of receivables and inventory, giving rise to a high operating funds ratio. For example, the Grumman Corporation reported a decline in 1989 sales but an operating funds ratio of 1.4, reflecting a decline in its cash flow from operations due to a sizeable investment in unsold inventory.

Investment ratio. Calculated as capital expenditures divided by depreciation plus sales of assets, the **investment ratio** reveals the relative level of investment in capital assets and whether a company's productive asset base is expanding or shrinking. The ratio provides some insight regarding management's plans for the future and its analysis of the future economy. In 1994, this ratio for PepsiCo was 1.38. The fact that this ratio exceeds 1.0 indicates that PepsiCo's management increased the company's relative investment in property, plant, and equipment during the period. Ratio amounts less than 1.0 usually indicate a situation in which the management is, in effect, "harvesting" past investments in capital assets or is not investing in property, plant, and equipment at the same (or faster) rate than these productive assets are being consumed. For example, in the late 1980s, the Grumman Corporation was forced into a period of retrenchment, as revealed by its 1989 investment ratio of 0.58.

Cash flow adequacy ratio. The **cash flow adequacy ratio** is calculated as the cash flows from operations divided by long-term capital expenditures plus dividends and long-term debt repayment. This ratio helps reveal whether a business is providing sufficient funds through operations to match expenditures for its current capital structure and future asset base. In 1994, PepsiCo's cash flow adequacy ratio was 0.93, which indicates that slightly insufficient cash was being generated from operations to provide for the firm's expanded level of long-term investments, dividends, and debt repayment. In general, the closer this ratio is to zero, the greater is a company's dependency on creditors and owners for additional financing to execute plant and equipment expansion programs; the reverse is also true. Because expenditures for these types of items tend to vary from year to year, ratios less than 1.0 are not cause for alarm unless they are consistently below 1.0 for a number of accounting periods. In this regard, Grumman Corporation had a negative cash flow adequacy ratio in 1987, a 0.05 ratio in 1988, and 0.20 in 1989. Clearly, Grumman's ratio trend is in the appropriate direction, but the ratios have been so low that it must be concluded that Grumman's management faced a significant challenge to financially service its creditors and shareholders as well as its equipment replacement needs.

Cash sources percentages. This ratio (that is, individual cash flow sources divided by the total sources of cash) for each specific source of cash indicates the degree to which a company provides cash from operations, by external borrowing, or by other means. The 1994 PepsiCo cash flow statement shown in Exhibit 6.3 reveals that the total sources of cash (all of the positive cash flow entries) equaled $7,501.3 million. Individual ratios for each source can be calculated to show the relative importance of a particular activity to the cash flows of the company. For example, 17.1 percent of PepsiCo's cash inflows were provided by long-term borrowings ($1,285.2 ÷ $7,501.3), while 0.7 percent was generated by sales of property, plant, and equipment ($55.3 ÷ $7,501.3). Such percentages indicate PepsiCo's high need for short-term funds, suggesting that cash flow management is primarily a timing issue for PepsiCo rather than an inability to generate internally adequate levels of cash flows. Moreover, the 0.7 percent indicates a very low dependence on fixed asset liquidations for cash infusions. It is interesting to note that for 1989, the Grumman Corporation had a long-term borrowing-to-total cash inflows ratio that closely approximated PepsiCo's short-term borrowing-to-total cash inflows ratio. These ratios reflect Grumman's relative inability to generate cash flows internally and, consequently, the company's dependency on external sources of cash flows to operate.

Dividend payout ratio. Dividends are among the main concerns of a company's shareholders, and, consequently, the amount of cash dividends paid divided by available cash flows from operations is an important indicator for this group. The percentage of cash flow paid to shareholders is an indication of management's commitment to a company's dividend policy as well as high-return projects available to the company for investment. PepsiCo's dividend payout ratio in 1994 was 14.5 percent, a healthy level indicating that 85.5 percent of its cash flow from operations was available for investing and/or debt repayment purposes. A ratio greater than 100 percent is definitely cause for further investigation because it indicates that the company is paying dividends with funds not provided by the normal operations of the business. Moreover, as this ratio approaches 100 percent, concern should increase as to the ability of a company to maintain such dividend levels and it indicates that less internally generated cash will be available to cover other demands. For example, in 1989 Grumman Corporation's dividend payout ratio was 78 percent, indicating a relatively small amount of internally generated cash available to support the continuing operations of the company's businesses.

Many companies and industries use meaningful cash flow ratios that differ from those noted here. Thus, students are encouraged to consider ratios that are applicable to each industry or situation that they encounter.

Pro Forma Cash Flows

Just as it is instructive to examine various ratios based on the actual reported cash flow components, it is also useful to investigate a company's *expected* cash flows. In Chapter 5 we demonstrated that through the use of reasonable and realistic assumptions, it is possible to prepare forecast or pro forma financial statements. And, just as it is instructive to consider a pro forma income statement, it is useful to examine a pro forma statement of cash flows to anticipate the amount, sources, and uses of subsequent periods' available cash resources.

Using the pro forma income statement for Blue Ridge Hardware Co. (Exhibit 5.8 from Chapter 5) as a starting point, we can develop a pro forma statement of cash flows. To do so, however, requires several additional assumptions that might include the following:

1. The ending balance in accounts receivable increases by 10 percent of the growth in revenues (that is, 0.10 × $11,175).
2. The ending inventory increases by 5 percent of the existing value of goods currently on hand (that is, 0.05 × $12,700).
3. The ending balance of accounts payable increases by $200.
4. Because no new employees need to be hired and operating hours are not extended, the ending balances in wages and utilities payable remain unchanged.
5. Income taxes are paid quarterly; hence, at year-end, only the last quarter's taxes remain unpaid (that is, 0.25 × $2,900).
6. Because all of the equipment and fixtures are new, no asset purchases or replacements are required until 1997.
7. As required by the loan agreement, one-fifth of the outstanding bank loan is repaid (that is, 0.20 × $7,500).
8. Cash dividends remain at $2,000.

Using these assumptions, along with the Blue Ridge Hardware pro forma income statement from Chapter 5, we can prepare a pro forma statement of cash flows for Blue Ridge Hardware. As revealed in Exhibit 6.10, the cash flows from operating activities are projected to be $6,692 for the year ended March 31, 1996. After paying the cash dividends and the partial loan repayment, the cash balance is projected to increase by $3,192. Such a favorable increase may be viewed by interested parties as a healthy cushion of cash inflows over cash outflows, thus providing a relative amount of comfort regarding the company's ability to generate adequate cash resources in the coming year. (Those students interested in reviewing a slightly different approach to cash flow forecasting are referred to the appendix at the end of this chapter.)

By incorporating the assumptions used in the preparation of the pro forma income statement and the statement of cash flows, it is also possible to prepare a pro forma balance sheet for Blue Ridge Hardware Co. Exhibit 6.11 reveals that if our assumptions hold true, the level of total assets and equities will reach $31,895 by March 31, 1996.

EXHIBIT 6.10

Blue Ridge Hardware Co.
Pro Forma Statement of Cash Flows
For the Year Ended March 31, 1996

Operating Activities	
Net income	$ 8,820
Add: Depreciation on store equipment	1,000
Adjustments for working capital needs:	
Increase in accounts receivable	(1,118)
Increase in merchandise inventory	(635)
Increase in accounts payable	200
Increase in wages payable	–0–
Increase in utilities payable	–0–
Decrease in income tax payable	(1,575)
Cash flow from operating activities	$ 6,692
Investing Activities	$ –0–
Financing Activities	
Cash dividends paid	(2,000)
Partial repayment of bank loan	(1,500)
	$(3,500)
Increase in cash	$ 3,192
Cash, beginning of year	2,050
Cash, end of year	$ 5,242

EXHIBIT 6.11

Blue Ridge Hardware Co.
Pro Forma Balance Sheet
As of March 31, 1996

Assets		**Equities**	
Current assets:		Current liabilities:	
Cash	$ 5,242	Accounts payable	$ 4,000
Accounts receivable	5,318	Wages payable	700
Merchandise inventory	13,335	Utilities payable	200
Total current assets	$23,895	Income tax payable	725
		Total current liabilities	$ 5,625
Noncurrent assets:			
Store equipment	10,000	Noncurrent liabilities	
Less: Accumulated depreciation	(2,000)	Bank loan payable	6,000
Total noncurrent assets	$ 8,000	Total liabilities	$11,625
		Owners' equity:	
		Capital stock	10,000
		Retained earnings	10,276
			20,276
Total assets	$31,895	Total liabilities and owners' equity	$31,895

SUMMARY

Informed observers and businesspeople realize that the "bottom line" (that is, net income) has little to do with staying solvent and hence staying in business. Cash planning — specifically, the ability to understand the sources and uses of current and future cash flows — often makes the difference between business success and failure. Firms with excellent products, new equipment, and creative marketing efforts have gone out of business because they mistook earnings profitability for cash solvency.

A balance sheet, an income statement, and a statement of cash flows together provide managers, creditors, and investors alike with important information that is useful in developing a complete understanding of a company's financial status and health. Moreover, as we observed with regard to the balance sheet and income statement, it is possible to construct various ratios from the statement of cash flows that provide insights beyond the absolute level of cash provided or used. It would be quite misleading to suggest that information regarding cash flows is superior to that of earnings in providing a clear and true picture of a company's financial health. *Both* are important; but it is also worth noting the thoughts of one financial writer:

> Though my bottom line is black, I am flat upon my back,
> My cash flows out and customers pay slow.
> The growth of my receivables is almost unbelievable;
> The result is certain — unremitting woe!
> And I hear the banker utter an ominous low mutter,
> "Watch cash flow."[7]
>
> Herbert S. Bailey, Jr., with
> apologies to Edgar Allan Poe's
> *"The Raven"*

NEW CONCEPTS AND TERMS

Cash equivalents (p. 265)
Cash flow adequacy ratio (p. 281)
Cash flows from operating activities (p. 266)
Direct method (p. 266)
Dividend payout ratio (p. 282)
Financing activities (p. 266)
Indirect method (p. 268)
Investing activities (p. 265)
Investment ratio (p. 281)
Noncash investing and financing activities (p. 272)
Operating activities (p. 266)
Operating funds ratio (p. 281)

[7]R. Green, "Are More Chryslers in the Offing?" *Forbes,* February 2, 1981, p. 69.

APPENDIX 6

A Generalized Method of Forecasting Cash Flows from Operations

Managers and other users of financial statements are often interested in (1) ascertaining the sensitivity of a company's cash flows to varying economic factors and (2) estimating future cash flows from operations. Assume that you are such a user and you are again focusing on the Oakencroft Cabinet Company whose 1995 and 1996 balance sheets and 1996 income statement are presented in Exhibits 6.5 and 6.6. Assume that the company's projected 1997 sales figure is $540,000,000 and that the 1996 financial relationships will be the same in 1997. The task you are faced with is to forecast cash flows from operations and determine the effect on cash flow from operations due to (1) a possible sales decline of 10 percent from 1996, (2) a negative 2 percent net profit margin, and (3) a 50 percent increase in the relationship between the accounts payables and accruals amount versus the sales figure.

To forecast the cash flow from operations and to assess its sensitivity to various account balance changes, it is first necessary to develop a model of the underlying relationships. It is important to recall that the cash flows from operations figure is a function of net income, noncash expenses and noncash revenues, and the changes in the current asset and current liability accounts related to the company's operating activities. These latter items generally pertain to such items as accounts receivable and accounts payable. One model of these relationships is given by the following:[8]

Forecast cash flow from operations =

$$\left(\frac{NI}{S_c} + \frac{Depn}{S_c}\right) S_p + \frac{L}{S_c}(S_p - S_c) - \frac{A}{S_c}(S_p - S_c)$$

where

$\frac{NI}{S_c}$ = Current net income as a percentage of current net sales

[8]For a more extensive discussion of this approach, see J.R. Carter, "The Recession-Sensitive Borrower: Evaluating Cash Flow and Financial Structure," *Journal of Commercial Bank Lending*, July 1983, pp. 36–49.

$\frac{\text{Depn}}{S_c}$ = Current depreciation expense as a percentage of current net sales

$\frac{L}{S_c}$ = Liabilities that increase or decrease in proportion to increases or decreases in sales, expressed as a percentage of current net sales

$\frac{A}{S_c}$ = Assets that increase or decrease in proportion to increases or decreases in sales, expressed as a percentage of current net sales

S_c = Current year's net sales

S_p = Forecast annual net sales

Using the above equation, the following summarization of Oakencroft's 1996 financial statement relationships, and the fact that 1996 depreciation expense was $9,033,000, yield the following estimate of the cash flows from operations:

1996 Relationships

		Percentage of Sales
Assets:		
Receivables	$133,834,000	27.1
Inventories	45,475,000	10.8
		37.9
Liabilities:		
Payables	$ 36,075,000	8.6
Accruals	28,423,000	6.8
		15.4

1997 Forecast Cash Flows from Operations:

(0.059 + 0.022) 540,000,000 + 0.154 (540,000,000 – 419,991,000) – 0.379 (540,000,000 – 419,991,000) = 43,740,000 + 18,481,386 – 45,483,411 = $16,737,975

Thus, 1997 forecast net cash flows from operations equals $16,737,975, based on the assumed relationships. Clearly, this is a sizable amount, yet it is also considerably lower than the actual 1996 cash flows from operations of $29,672,000 (see Exhibit 6.7).

To see how sensitive this projection is to changes in the various assumptions, a sensitivity analysis can be undertaken. Remember that the 1996 relationships between the various financial statements remain constant *except for* the one change in assumption being focused on in the sensitivity analysis:

Sales Decline of 10 Percent:

Forecast sales = $378,000,000 (10% less than 1996 sales).

Hence,

$$0.081(378) + 0.154(378 - 419.9) - 0.379(378 - 419.9) = 30.62 - 6.45 + 15.88$$
$$= \text{Revised forecast cash flow from operations} = \$40{,}050{,}000.$$

This revised cash flow projection is a function of declining inventories and receivables (at 37.9 percent rate), which with profits and depreciation become a "source" of cash while declining payables and accruals (at a 15.4 percent rate) become a "use" of cash.

Negative 2 Percent Net Profit Margin:

$$(-0.02 + 0.022)540 + 0.154(540 - 419.9) - 0.379(540 - 419.9) = 1.08 + 18.5 - 45.52 = \text{Revised forecast cash flow from operations} = (\$25{,}940{,}000).$$

In this scenario, the net loss and the increase in receivables and inventories become a "use" of cash.

A 50 Percent Increase in the Accounts Payable Plus Accruals-to-Sales Ratio:

1996 Liabilities-to-sales ratio = 0.154; the 50 percent increase = 0.231.

Hence,

$$0.081(540) + 0.231(540 - 419.9) - 0.379(540 - 419.9) = 43.74 + 27.74 - 45.52 = \text{Revised forecast cash flow from operations} = \$25{,}960{,}000.$$

When assets are supported to a greater extent by payables and accruals than before, this means less is needed in the way of other sources of cash because cash flow from operations increases.

These simple examples and the basic approach to forecasting the cash flow from operations provide a simple but useful means for analysts, creditors, investors, and managers to assess more fully the amount and timing of a company's future cash flows.

ISSUES FOR DISCUSSION

D6.1 The statement of cash flows is a required financial statement for publicly held companies.

a. What are the objectives of the statement of cash flows?

b. Identify two types of transactions that would be disclosed in a separate schedule accompanying the statement of cash flows because they do not affect cash during the reporting period.

c. What effect, if any, would each of the following items have on the statement of cash flows assuming the *direct* method presentation is used to present cash flows from operations?
(1) Accounts receivable increase.
(2) Inventory decline.
(3) Depreciation expense.
(4) Deferred tax liability decrease.
(5) Signing of a mortgage for a building.
(6) Payment of this year's mortgage principal.
(7) Sale of a building resulting in a loss.

D6.2 A company acquired a building, making a cash downpayment and signing a mortgage note payable to the seller for the balance.

a. In a statement of cash flows, what amount is included in the investing activities section for the above transaction?

b. In a statement of cash flows, what amount is included in the financing activities section for the above transaction?

D6.3 Prior to SFAS No. 95 requiring a statement of cash flows, companies had the option to report their changes in financial condition on a cash flow or working capital basis. In 1972 fewer than 5 percent of publicly filed reports were on a cash flow basis, whereas just prior to the issuance of SFAS No. 95, approximately 70 percent had been. Discuss why this shift to a cash flow focus may have occurred and whether you see merit in such a shift.

D6.4 Which subgroup(s) of financial statement readers is (are) likely to be most interested in the statement of cash flows and why?

D6.5 Discuss in general the distinctions between accrual-based accounting and cash-based accounting.

D6.6 Why do you think the FASB chose to segregate the statement of cash flows into operating, financing, and investing activity sections? What other categorizations might have merit?

D6.7 One of the most frequent reasons for the failure of new businesses is poor cash flow management. Explain.

D6.8 Discuss the pros and cons of evaluating division managers on a "net cash provided by operations" basis.

D6.9 If you could receive only one cash flow figure from a company, what figure would you request? Why?

D6.10 Discuss the direct and indirect methods of presenting net cash flows from operating activities. Which do you find most useful? Why?

PROBLEMS

P6.1 Statement of cash flows (indirect method). Presented here are some items involving cash flows taken from the financial records of Tucson Equipment Company for the period ended December 31, 19X5:

Net income	$420,000
Payment of dividends	30,000
Ten-year bonds, issued at face value	250,000
Depreciation expense	50,000
Amortization expense	10,000
Beginning cash balance	28,000
Equipment purchased	96,000
Building purchased	114,000
Accounts receivable decrease	4,000
Accounts payable decrease	5,000
Inventories increase	5,000

Required:

Using the facts provided, prepare a statement of cash flows using the indirect method.

P6.2 Classification of cash flow items. Identify whether each of the following is properly classified as an operating, investing, or financing activity in a statement of cash flows. Explain your rationale.

a. Proceeds from sales of property, plant, and equipment.

b. Interest payments to creditors.

c. Proceeds from issuing shares of stock.

d. Payments to acquire GMAC long-term bonds.

e. Payments of dividends to shareholders.

P6.3 Cash flows from operations. The following information is available from Gravel Corporation's accounting records for the year ended December 31, 19X5:

Cash received from customers	$810,000
Rent received	19,000
Cash paid to suppliers	520,000
Taxes paid	140,000
Cash dividends paid	25,000

Required:

Determine the cash flow provided by operations for 19X5.

P6.4 and P6.5 Calculating cash flows. Problems P6.4 and P6.5 are based on the following information:

Dillon Corporation has estimated its business activity for December 19X5. Selected data from these estimated amounts are as follows:

Sales	$310,000
Gross profit (based on sales)	25%
Increase in accounts receivable during month	$13,000
Change in accounts payable during month	–0–
Decrease in inventory during month	$8,000

Total selling, general, and administrative expense (S, G, & A) is $29,000 per month plus 10 percent of sales. Depreciation expense of $15,000 per month is included in fixed S,G, & A. Accounts receivable written off were $2,000.

P6.4. On the basis of the data provided, what is the cash *inflow* from operating activities for December?

P6.5. On the basis of the data provided, what is the cash *outflow* from operating activities for December?

P6.6 Account analysis (multiple choice).

a. Over the course of the year, a company's accounts receivable declined. In the company's statement of cash flows (operating activities shown using the direct method), the cash collected from customers would be which of the following?

(1) Sales plus accounts receivable at the beginning of the year.

(2) Sales plus the year's net decrease in accounts receivable.

(3) Sales less the year's net decrease in accounts receivable.

(4) The same as sales.

(5) Sales plus accounts receivable at the end of the year.

b. In a statement of cash flows in which the operating activities section is prepared under the indirect method, a gain on the sale of a building should be presented as a (an)

(1) Addition to net income.

(2) Deduction from net income.

(3) Inflow of cash.

(4) Outflow of cash.

c. A company's taxes payable increased during the year. In the company's statement of cash flows in which the operating activities section is prepared under the direct method, the cash paid for taxes would be which of the following?

(1) Tax expense plus taxes payable at the beginning of the year.

(2) Tax expense plus the year's net increase in taxes payable.

(3) The same as tax expense.

(4) Tax expense less the year's net increase in taxes payable.

(5) Tax expense plus taxes payable at the end of the year.

d. A loss on the sale of a warehouse should be presented in a statement of cash flows (using the indirect method for cash flows from operations) as a (an)

(1) Deduction from net income.

(2) Inflow of cash.

(3) Addition to net income.

(4) Outflow of cash.

e. In a statement of cash flows using the indirect method for operating activities, an increase in inventories should be presented as a (an)

(1) Deduction from net income.

(2) Inflow of cash.

(3) Addition to net income.

(4) Outflow of cash.

f. The amortization of an acquired trademark should be presented in a statement of cash flows, using the indirect method for cash flow from operating activities, as a (an)

(1) Financing activity.

(2) Deduction from net income.

(3) Addition to net income.

(4) Investing activity.

P6.7, P6.8, and P6.9 Statement of cash flows. Problems P6.7, P6.8, and P6.9 are based on the following:

Dalton Corporation's balance sheet as of December 31, 19X6 and 19X5, and information relating to 19X6 activities are presented here.

	December 31, 19X6	December 31, 19X5
Assets		
Cash	$ 15,000	$ 90,000
Short-term investments	200,000	—
Accounts receivable (net)	590,000	440,000
Inventory	600,000	615,000
Long-term investments	310,000	390,000
Property, plant, and equipment	1,800,000	1,100,000
Accumulated depreciation	(500,000)	(500,000)
Goodwill (net)	95,000	105,000
Total assets	$3,110,000	$2,240,000
Liabilities and Stockholders' Equity		
Accounts payable and accrued liabilities	$ 900,000	$ 850,000
Short-term debt	190,000	—
Common stock, $10 par value	775,000	675,000
Additional paid-in-capital	380,000	300,000
Retained earnings	865,000	415,000
Total liabilities and stockholders' equity	$3,110,000	$2,240,000

Information Relating to 19X6 Activities

- Net income was $800,000.
- Cash dividends of $350,000 were declared and paid.
- Equipment costing $450,000 and having a book value of $200,000 was sold for $200,000.
- A long-term investment was sold for $150,000. There were no other transactions affecting long-term investments in 19X6.
- 10,000 shares of common stock were issued for $18 a share.
- Short-term investments consist of Treasury bills maturing on June 30, 19X7.

P6.7. Calculate Dalton's 19X6 net cash provided by operating activities.

P6.8. Calculate Dalton's 19X6 net cash used in investing activities.

P6.9. Calculate Dalton's 19X6 net cash provided by financing activities.

P6.10 and P6.11 Cash flow from investing and financing. Problems P6.10 and P6.11 are based on the following:

Nevada Corporation's transactions for the year ended December 31, 19X6, included the following:

- Acquired 40 percent of the common stock of Utah Corp. for $525,000 cash, which was borrowed from a bank.
- Issued 6,000 shares of its stock for mineral deposits having a fair value of $600,000.
- Issued 100 of its 10 percent bonds, due in five years, for $190,000 cash.
- Purchased a customer list for $300,000 cash.
- Paid $175,000 on a bank loan.
- Sold investments for $900,000.
- Had a net increase in advance payments to suppliers of $100,000.

P6.10. Determine Nevada's net cash flow from investing activities in 19X6.

P6.11. Determine Nevada's net cash flow from financing activities for 19X6.

P6.12, P6.13, P6.14, and P6.15 Account analysis. Problems P6.12, P6.13, P6.14, and P6.15 relate to data to be reported in the statement of cash flows of Wolfe Hardware Shops, Inc. based on the following information:

Wolfe Hardware Shops, Inc.
Balance sheets

	December 31	
	19X6	**19X5**
Assets		
Current assets:		
Cash	$ 400,000	$ 250,000
Accounts receivable	990,000	760,000
Merchandise inventory	710,000	400,000
Prepaid expenses	100,000	100,000
Total current assets	2,200,000	1,510,000
Long-term investments	100,000	—
Property, plant, and equipment	1,310,000	800,000
Less: Accumulated depreciation	110,000	80,000
	1,200,000	720,000
Total assets	$3,500,000	$2,230,000
Equities		
Current liabilities:		
Accounts payable	$ 550,000	$ 500,000
Accrued expenses	220,000	200,000
Dividends payable	70,000	—
Total current liabilities	840,000	700,000
Note payable — due in five years	500,000	—
Stockholders' equity:		
Common stock	1,500,000	1,380,000
Retained earnings	660,000	150,000
	2,160,000	1,530,000
Total liabilities and stockholders' equity	$3,500,000	$2,230,000

Wolfe Hardware Shops, Inc.
Income Statements

	Year ended December 31,	
	19X6	**19X5**
Net credit sales	$8,400,000	$6,000,000
Cost of goods sold	7,000,000	5,200,000
Gross profit	1,400,000	800,000
Expenses (including income taxes)	800,000	420,000
Net income	$ 600,000	$ 380,000

Additional information available included the following:

- All accounts receivable and accounts payable related to trade merchandise. No receivables were written off during 19X6.
- The proceeds from the note payable were used to finance a new building.

P6.12. Determine Wolfe's cash collected during 19X6 from accounts receivable.

P6.13. Determine Wolfe's cash payments during 19X6 on accounts payable.

P6.14. Determine Wolfe's net cash flow from financing activities for 19X6.

P6.15. Determine Wolfe's net cash flow from investing activities during 19X6.

P6.16. Cash flow analysis: Monsanto Company.* The Monsanto Company makes and markets high-value chemical and agricultural products, pharmaceuticals, low-calorie sweeteners, industrial process equipment, man-made fibers, plastics, and electronic materials. Monsanto's cash flow statements for a recent three-year period are presented here. Net sales for 19X2, 19X1, and 19X0 were $7,639, $6,879, and $6,747 million, respectively.

Monsanto Company
Statement of Consolidated Cash Flow
(in millions)

	19X2	19X1	19X0
Operating activities:			
Net income (loss)	$ 436	$ 433	$ (98)
Add: Income tax expense (benefit)	237	203	(170)
Deduct: Extraordinary gain			(30)
Income (loss) before income taxes and extraordinary gain	673 ~~687~~	636	(298)
Income tax payments	(229)	(221)	(273)
Items that did not use (provide) cash:			
Depreciation and amortization	679	780	599
Restructuring expense (income)	(32)	(158)	949
Other	37	(9)	(39)
Working-capital changes that provided (used) cash:			
Accounts receivable	(172)	117	2
Inventories	(22)	(2)	(54)
Accounts payable and accrued liabilities	13	(173)	—
Other	(19)	80	41
Nonoperating gains from asset disposals (before tax)	(26)	(90)	(392)
Cash provided by operations	902	960	535
Investing activities:			
Property, plant, and equipment purchases	(505)	(520)	(645)
Acquisition payments for Searle, net of cash acquired of $216			(2,538)
Acquisition and investment payments (other than Searle)	(59)	(29)	(78)
Investment and property disposal proceeds	75	503	1,469
Cash used in investing activities	(489)	(46)	(1,792)
Financing activities:			
Net change in short-term financing	150	33	(108)
Long-term debt proceeds	26	675	415
Long-term debt repayments	(122)	(1,139)	(555)
Searle acquisition financing proceeds			2,754
Short-term debt repayments (Searle acquisition)		(348)	(1,154)
Treasury stock purchases	(339)		(91)
Dividend payments	(212)	(199)	(188)
Other financing activities	33	45	18
Cash (used in) provided by financing activities	(464)	(933)	1,091
Decrease in cash and cash equivalents*	$ (51)	$ (19)	$ (166)

*Includes cash, time deposits, certificates of deposit, and short-term securities.

Required:

a. Historically, one of Monsanto's strong points has been its ability to provide significant cash flow from operations. Although operating income improved in 19X2, cash provided by operations declined. Briefly explain how this happened.

b. Cumulatively, over this three-year period, has Monsanto
(1) Experienced a net increase or decrease in inventories? How do you know?
(2) Been able to increase the level of cash provided by operations as a percentage of *total gross cash inflows?* If so, is this increase a sign of good management? Why? If not, is this a sign of bad management? Why?

c. Explain how depreciation and amortization can be the single largest source of cash in 19X2 and 19X1.

d. What might account for the fact that in 19X1 accounts receivable "provided" cash, whereas in 19X2 they "used" cash?

e. As of December 31, 19X2, Monsanto's ending retained earnings balance was $3,282 million. What was Monsanto's December 31, 19X1, retained earnings balance?

P6.17 Statement of cash flows (indirect method). Presented below are the balance sheet accounts of Carbide Cutters, Inc., as of December 31, 19X6 and 19X5.

	19X6	19X5
Assets		
Cash	$371,000	$207,000
Marketable equity securities, at market which approximates cost	240,000	325,000
Accounts receivable, net	650,000	615,000
Inventories	810,000	890,000
Investments in subsidiaries	320,000	290,000
Property, plant, and equipment	1,145,000	1,070,000
Accumulated depreciation	(345,000)	(280,000)
Patent, net	109,000	118,000
Total assets	$3,300,000	$3,235,000
Liabilities and Stockholders' Equity		
Accounts payable and accrued liabilities	$745,000	$860,000
Note payable, long-term	700,000	1,000,000
Deferred income taxes	190,000	190,000
Common stock, $10 par value	850,000	650,000
Additional paid-in capital	230,000	170,000
Retained earnings	585,000	365,000
Total liabilities and stockholders' equity	$3,300,000	$3,235,000

Additional Information

- On January 2, 19X6, Carbide Cutters sold equipment costing $55,000, with a carrying amount of $38,000, for $28,000 cash.
- On March 31, 19X6, Carbide Cutters sold one of its marketable equity securities for $119,000 cash. There were no other transactions involving marketable equity securities.
- On April 5, 19X6, Carbide Cutters issued 20,000 shares of its common stock for cash at $13 per share.

- On July 1, 19X6, Carbide Cutters purchased equipment for $130,000 cash.
  Carbide Cutters' net income for 19X6 is $315,000. Carbide Cutters paid a cash dividend of $95,000 on October 26, 19X6.

Required:

Prepare a statement of cash flows for Carbide Cutters, Inc., for the year ended December 31, 19X6, using the indirect method.

P6.18 Account reconstruction.

a. Presented below is the consolidated statement of cash flows from Guman Corporation's 19X2 annual report. Also presented is the company's consolidated balance sheet as of December 31, 19X2. In the empty column provided in Guman's consolidated balance sheet, please reconstruct the company's December 31, 19X1, balance sheet.

b. Explain the following:

(1) In 19X0 Guman paid $37,691 of cash dividends to its shareholders when earnings were only $35,650, a difference of $2,041; yet the cash balance went down only $1,612. Why? How can a company pay dividends in excess of earnings?

(2) How can a company have more depreciation and amortization than net income?

(3) (i) Over the three-year period, 19X0–X2, was Guman in a strong or weak cash flow condition? Please explain.

(ii) Please explain the most significant items that affected Guman's cash flow during this period.

Guman Corporation and Subsidiaries
Consolidated Statement of Cash Flow
($ in thousands)

	Year Ended December 31		
	19X2	**19X1**	**19X0**
Cash flows from operating activities			
Net income	$ 67,264	$ 86,465	$ 35,650
Items affecting cash from operations:			
Depreciation and amortization	112,402	113,854	103,593
Decrease/(increase) in:			
Accounts receivable and marketable securities (Note 1)	80,929	(207,912)	15,076
Inventories	(166,290)	(97,195)	(189,024)
Prepaid expenses	(13,110)	8,739	(21,274)
Increase/(decrease) in:			
Accounts payable, wages and employee benefits (Note 2)	6,158	73,978	9,912
Income taxes payable	12,470	31,800	(43,141)
Deferred income taxes	(17,900)	(13,200)	(41,560)
Other — Current liabilities	(33,814)	12,346	40,196
	(19,155)	(77,590)	(126,222)
Net cash provided/(required) by operating activities	48,109	8,875	(90,572)
Cash flows from investing activities:			
Capital expenditures	(65,725)	(118,119)	(177,700)
Proceeds from sale of capital assets	1,457	10,097	4,928
Net cash used in investing activities	(64,268)	(108,022)	(172,722)
Cash flows from financing activities:			
Increase/(decrease) in short-term debt	(18,000)	(30,549)	35,528
Proceeds from long-term debt	200,000	184,889	281,105
Repayment of long-term debt	(131,054)	(31,081)	(22,408)
Redemption of preferred stock	(2,525)	(2,502)	(2,375)
Common stock issued	5,526	5,726	7,573
Dividends paid	(37,288)	(37,436)	(37,691)
Net cash provided by financing activities	16,659	89,047	261,732
Net increase/(decrease) in cash for the period	500	(10,100)	(1,612)
Cash — January 1,	19,264	29,364	30,976
Cash — December 31,	$ 19,764	$ 19,264	$ 29,364

Note 1:	Marketable securities	($ 11,464)
	Accounts receivable	92,393
		$ 80,929
Note 2:	Accounts payable, wages, and employee benefits	
	Accounts payable	($ 12,681)
	Wages and employee benefits	18,839
		$ 6,158

Sales	**$3,506,348**	**$3,591,308**	**$3,325,062**

Guman Corporation and Subsidiaries
Consolidated Balance Sheet
($ in thousands)

	December 31	
	19X2	**19X1**
Assets		
Current assets		
Cash	$ 19,764	
Marketable securities (at cost, approximating market)	42,095	
Accounts receivable	709,560	
Inventories, less progress payments	1,028,924	
Prepaid expenses	48,187	
Total current assets	$1,848,530	
Property, plant, and equipment, less accumulated depreciation	539,207	
Noncurrent assets		
Long-term receivables	44,016	
Investments	87,194	
Other	72,115	
	203,325	
Total	$2,591,062	
Liabilities and Shareholders' Equity		
Current liabilities		
Short-term debt	$ 102,789	
Accounts payable	263,857	
Wages and employee benefits payable	96,491	
Income taxes	154,700	
Advances and deposits	21,943	
Other current liabilities	119,796	
Total current liabilities	759,576	
Long-term debt	846,423	
Deferred income taxes	46,069	
Other liabilities	83,762	
Preferred stock	37,561	
Common stock—$1.00 par value, authorized 80,000,000 shares; outstanding 32,966,991 and 32,720,816 shares (net of treasury stock)	296,056	
Retained earnings	521,615	
Total	$2,591,062	

CASES

C6.1 Cash flow statement preparation: FHAC Corporation. It was early 1996, and Ed Garrett was sitting at his desk staring at a set of financial statements. The financial statements (see following pages) were those of FHAC Corporation. They represented the raw materials for Garrett's first assignment as a credit analyst for Metroplex National Bank.

Garrett's immediate supervisor, Katherine Miller, had received the FHAC statements as part of a loan application package. Because FHAC was a privately held company, the statements did not have to conform to existing SEC disclosure requirements, and since the statements were unaudited, they did not fully conform to existing FASB requirements. The only significant omission from SEC/FASB standards that Miller had noticed was the absence of a cash flow statement. Rather than ask the new customer to provide one, she decided to ask Garrett to derive one from the existing financial data.

Required:

Prepare a statement of cash flows for FHAC for fiscal year 1995. On the basis of this statement and the other available statements, prepare an evaluation of the creditworthiness of FHAC assuming that the company is interested in (1) a short-term loan of $15 million for working capital purposes and (2) a $75 million five-year loan for capital asset purchases.

FHAC Corporation
Balance Sheet
(in thousands)

	As of December 31	
	1995	**1994**
Assets		
Current assets		
Cash	$ 14,696	$ 16,390
Receivables:		
Trade	20,378	10,808
Other	324	866
Inventories	15,967	3,843
Prepaid expenses	197	2,414
Total current assets	51,562	34,321
Noncurrent assets:		
Property, plant, and equipment (at cost)	258,908	152,145
Less: Accumulated depreciation	(34,224)	(11,516)
Total noncurrent assets	224,684	140,629
Deferred charges and other assets	2,041	1,666
Total assets	$278,287	$176,616
Liabilities and Shareholders' Equity		
Current liabilities		
Accounts payable	$ 20,160	$ 16,710
Accrued expenses payable	2,901	1,077
Income taxes payable	203	–0–
Current maturities on long-term debt	6,826	5,301
Total current liabilities	30,090	23,088
Long-term liabilities		
Convertible subordinated debentures	10,056	10,061
Notes payable	123,949	79,900
Deferred income taxes	44,730	20,464
Total long-term liabilities	178,735	110,425
Shareholders' equity		
Capital stock	1,380	912
Additional paid-in capital	19,949	16,552
Retained earnings	48,133	25,639
Total shareholders' equity	69,462	43,103
Total liabilities and shareholders' equity	$278,287	$176,616

FHAC Corporation
Statement of Income
(in thousands)

	As of December 31	
	1995	**1994**
Net revenue	$122,733	$60,095
Less: Costs and expenses		
Cost of operations	28,250	13,818
General and administrative	5,777	2,541
Interest	9,901	5,389
Depreciation and amortization	22,708	7,118
	66,636	28,866
Net income before income taxes	56,097	31,229
Provision for income taxes:		
Current	203	—
Deferred	24,266	12,804
Total	24,469	12,804
Net income after income taxes	$ 31,628	$18,425
Dividends paid	9,134	4,268
Transferred to retained earnings	$ 22,494	$14,157

C6.2 Cash flow statement preparation and interpretation: Compton Computing Systems (A)* Phillip Brantly, chief financial officer of Compton Computing Systems, sat in his office and considered the company's financial performance for 1995. He had reason to be pleased because just about every measure of financial performance had shown strong improvement for the first three quarters of 1995 and he had no reason to suspect that the last quarter would be any different. However, as he prepared for the final presentation of the 1996 budget to the board of directors, scheduled for December 11, he was uneasy about the economy and how it might affect Compton's financing and capital investment plans for next year. He knew that the board would have detailed discussions of alternative levels of expenditures and contingency financing plans for 1996. Thus, in the two weeks remaining before the meeting, he would need to complete his 1995 projected end-of-year financial statements. Using these statements as a base, he would then be able to determine whether sufficient funds from operations were being generated to portend a favorable cash flow in general through early 1996 and whether the company should proceed with the capital expenditures scheduled for early 1996.

The Company

Compton Computing Systems, headquartered in San Francisco, California, designed, manufactured, and serviced electronic products and systems for measurement and computation applications for general industry use. In addition to a full line of computers and computer-related hardware, Compton also produced and sold an impressive array of electronic test equipment, component parts, and medical test products. Compton's basic business purpose was to provide the capabilities and support needed to help customers worldwide improve their personal and business effectiveness.

The company was founded in 1958 to manufacture electronic measurement devices. It had started research into computers almost at founding and had marketed computers and computer systems since the early 1960s. Emphasis on quality and reliability allowed the company to grow

*This case was prepared by Mark E. Haskins and John B. Bristow.

rapidly. An increased need for capital forced the company to go public in 1962, and earnings had been sufficient to pay dividends to stockholders consecutively since 1965.

Through three quarters of 1995, financial performance had been strong. Orders were up 16 percent with net revenue up 25 percent. The fourth quarter, not yet complete, was one of great interest to Brantly. The United States and world economies were having a modest growth year, but predictions of economic slowdown were starting to surface. Many companies began to rethink their outlook for 1996.

Compton's budget for capital expenditures for 1996 had recently been revised and was now predicated on an immediate slowdown in demand for computers and computer systems domestically and worldwide. In addition, several contingency cost-reduction plans had been readied for implementation if and when revenues started declining. All in all, Brantly believed the company was positioned to withstand a recessionary year.

Preparation for the December Meeting

The 1996 budgetary process at Compton Computing Systems, begun in May 1995, was now complete except for the final approval of the board of directors. What concerned Brantly most was that, through November, indications pointed to a near-record quarter for orders. In fact, Compton's backlog of orders was increasing. National and international economic indicators also showed a strong business environment. The predicted downturn was not yet occurring. A retrenchment at the wrong time in the business cycle would be very costly to the company. Therefore, Brantly intended to go before the board prepared to discuss several alternative capital spending levels. This presentation would require 1996 pro forma financial statements for each of the economic scenarios and comparison with 1995's financial performance. Because actual 1995 financial statements would be unavailable prior to the end of the year, he would have to project those as well.

Brantly had spent most of the day gathering the information he needed to complete the 1995 financial statement projections and had now completed the balance sheets and income statements (presented below). All that remained was to complete the statement of cash flows (SCF) for 1995 by applying the indirect method to his recently completed income statement and comparative balance sheet. He knew from the data he had collected that, in 1995 and 1994, principal payments on the long-term debt had been $49 and $42 million, respectively. He also knew that the company had not disposed of any property or equipment in 1994 but in 1995 had disposed of a building originally costing $18 million, whose book value at the time of the sale was $10 million, for $10 million cash. After reviewing the 1994 SCF, he decided to complete this part of his task before leaving for home that evening.

Required:

Prepare a statement of cash flows for Compton Computing Systems for 1995.

Compton Computing Systems (A)
Consolidated Income Statements
(millions of dollars)

	For the Year Ended December 31		
	Projected 1995	Actual 1994	Actual 1993
Net revenue:			
Equipment	$6,315	$5,622	$5,267
Services	1,775	1,480	1,238
	8,090	7,102	6,505
Cost and expenses:			
Cost of equipment sold	2,723	2,479	2,423
Cost of services	1,062	874	743
Research and development	901	824	685
Marketing and selling	1,612	1,397	1,181
Administration and general	830	748	715
	7,128	6,322	5,747
Earnings before taxes	962	780	758
Provisions for taxes	318	264	269
Net earnings	$ 644	$ 516	$ 489
Notes to financial statements:			
Depreciation	$ 342	$ 321	$ 299

Compton Computing Systems (A)
Consolidated Balance Sheets
(millions of dollars)

	As of December 31		
	Projected 1995	Actual 1994	Actual 1993
Assets			
Cash and cash equivalents	$2,645	$1,372	$1,020
Accounts receivable	1,561	1,344	1,249
Inventories:			
Finished goods	480	427	401
Parts and assemblies	637	554	592
Other current assets	167	117	80
Total current assets	5,490	3,814	3,342
Property, plant, and equipment:			
Land	275	243	230
Buildings and improvements	2,081	1,891	1,653
Equipment	1,761	1,557	1,400
	4,117	3,691	3,283
Less: Accumulated depreciation	1,789	1,455	1,134
	2,328	2,236	2,149
Other assets	315	237	189
Total assets	$8,133	$6,287	$5,680
Liabilities			
Notes payable	$ 240	$ 229	$ 235
Accounts payable	364	285	268
Accrued wages and benefits	488	395	397
Accrued taxes	229	164	111
Deferred revenues	150	117	100
Other current liabilities	331	230	179
Total current liabilities	1,802	1,420	1,290
Long-term debt	827	110	102
Other liabilities	134	134	92
Deferred taxes	348	249	214
Total liabilities	3,111	1,913	1,698
Stockholders' Equity			
Preferred stock, $1 par	–0–	–0–	–0–
Common stock and paid-in capital in excess of $1 par (less Treasury stock of $68 in 1995, 1994, and 1993)	776	712	780
Retained earnings	4,246	3,662	3,202
Total stockholders' equity	5,022	4,374	3,982
Total liabilities and stockholders' equity	$8,133	$6,287	$5,680

Compton Computing Systems (A)
Statement of Cash Flows
For the Year Ended December 31, 1994
(numbers in parentheses indicate reductions in cash; millions of dollars)

Operations:	
Net income	$ 516
Depreciation and amortization	321
Adjustment for deferred revenue	17
Adjustment for deferred taxes	35
	889
Adjustments for:	
Increase in receivables	(95)
Decrease in inventories	12
Increase in accounts payable and other accruals	15
Increase in accrued taxes	53
Increase in other current assets	(37)
Increase in other current liabilities	51
	(1)
Cash flow — operations	888
Investing:	
Payments for additions to property, plant, and equipment	(408)
Increase in other assets	(48)
Cash flow — investing	(456)
Financing:	
Payments on notes payable	(6)
Proceeds from long-term debt	50
Payments on long-term debt	(42)
Increases in other liabilities	42
Repurchase of stock	(68)
Cash dividends paid	(56)
Cash flow — financing	(80)
Increase (decrease) in cash	352
Cash and equivalents — January 1	1,020
Cash and equivalents — December 31	$1,372

C6.3 Cash flow statement preparation and industry comparison: Compton Computing Systems (B)* Elizabeth Oakes, an outside director of Compton Computing Systems, sat watching the fog roll in over the Golden Gate Bridge from her office near the Embarcadero. A very familiar sight to her, the fog signaled evening and the close of another day. She had less than a week until the special board meeting at Compton's headquarters.

During the last meeting of the board of directors on December 11, Oakes had listened with great interest to CFO Phillip Brantly present information on the cash flow and cash position of Compton Computing Systems. There had been much debate regarding different economic scenarios and the appropriate management response to the uncertain economy. The meeting had ended with a number of questions unanswered, so the board had agreed to meet three weeks later — January 4 — to approve the final 1996 budget for the company. Prior to that meeting, Oakes wanted to review information on other companies, both inside and outside the computing

*This case was prepared by Mark E. Haskins and John B. Bristow.

industry to form an opinion on how Compton Computing Systems could respond to the changing economic environment. Her position as senior partner of Oakes, Glass, & Abernathy, a nationally known investment management firm, gave her ready access to financial information on a number of businesses with which to compare Compton. Her intention was to determine what other manufacturing companies had been doing recently regarding capital expenditures and the ways in which those expenditures were being financed. Her staff had provided the names of several suitable companies, and from that list she had chosen two to review that evening.

Background on Compton Computing Systems is found in Case 6.2.

Preparation for the January 4 Meeting

A trusted member of Oakes' staff had strongly recommended that she study the financial data on Reliant Information Technologies Corporation, a sizeable computer manufacturer competing directly in many of the same markets as Compton. Reliant Information Technologies designed, manufactured, and sold general-purpose computer systems and provided peripheral equipment, software, communications systems, and related products and services, including training and maintenance. Reliant Information Technologies marketed its systems to end users by its own sales force and a variety of third-party sales channels. Since its inception in 1968, it had installed more than 226,000 computer systems worldwide.

Oakes saw that Reliant Information Technologies had not been profitable in 1994. She was interested to determine how the loss would affect Reliant Information Technologies' cash flow from operations and whether the loss might have affected its 1995 capital expenditures relative to those for 1994. Reliant Information Technologies also had just embarked on a cost-reduction and restructuring program similar to the plan for Compton presented by Brantly at the last board meeting. As a part of this restructuring, Reliant Information Technologies had disposed of equipment with a net book value of \$3.669 million. The cash purchase price in that amount had been collected in the third quarter of fiscal 1995. Oakes also learned that new long-term loans in the amount of \$17.812 million had been subscribed during fiscal 1995.

The other company Oakes chose to study was Red Rock. Red Rock Company was a leading American brewer. In its 115-year history, it had become an increasingly diversified corporation, however, with operations in brewing, ceramics, aluminum, transportation, energy, food products, packaging, and biotechnology. Its ongoing success was based on an uncompromising commitment to quality, dedicated management, technological superiority, and talented employees.

Oakes chose Red Rock for review because it was a diversified, well-managed company that, like Compton, had limited stock distribution. While not nearly as closely held as Red Rock, Compton did have several substantial blocks of stock controlled by a few stockholders. Oakes wondered how this situation might affect dividend distributions, capital expenditures, and cash flows. Red Rock was also conservative regarding its use of debt financing. Compton had a low but increasing, long-term debt-to-equity ratio, and she wondered whether a company could effectively provide cash for expansion without use of significant debt. During 1995 Red Rock had not assumed any new long-term debt and, according to company sources, did not expect to in 1996. Red Rock did receive \$25.692 million in cash for selling plant assets with a net book value of that amount.

Oakes, Glass, & Abernathy's files had contained information on both Reliant Information Technologies and Red Rock, but because the 1995 annual statements for both companies had not yet been released, her staff had projected fourth-quarter financials in order to give Oakes annual 1995 financial statements. Before her were the 1994 and 1995 income statements and balance sheets for Reliant Information Technologies and the company's statement of cash flows for 1995, which she had completed. The Red Rock 1994 and 1995 income statements and balance sheets were also on her desk. She knew that, after completing a statement of cash flows for Red Rock, she would need to analyze thoroughly the information she had gathered.

Required:

a. Review the financial statements provided on Compton (from Case 6.2), Reliant Information Technologies, and Red Rock. Construct a 1995 statement of cash flows for Red Rock. While concentrating on the cash flow statements for the three companies, compare and contrast the companies and discuss the differences and similarities apparent from the financial statements concerning management's cash policies and debt policies, and make generalizations regarding the respective industries.

b. With Reliant Information Technologies having a loss for 1995, why was its cash flow from operations positive? What were the largest *uses* of cash from its statement of cash flows?

c. Why did Red Rock have a decrease in cash in 1995 when the income statement showed a positive net income?

d. How was Red Rock financing increases in investments?

e. What are the similarities and differences in the statements of cash flow of the three companies?

f. Were indications of management's policies and abilities discernible from the financial statements? Explain.

g. Which company was the best prepared to meet a recessionary market? A growing market? Why? What financial information led you to these conclusions?

h. What assumptions and associated limitations arise when you compare and contrast the Reliant Information Technologies and Red Rock statements of cash flow with Compton's?

i. What insights into the operations of a company might be gained by using the direct method that are not readily apparent using the indirect method for the statement of cash flows?

Reliant Information Technologies Corporation
Consolidated Income Statement
(in thousands)

	For the Year Ended December 31	
	Projected 1995	**Actual 1994**
Revenue:		
Equipment	$ 859,455	$ 868,269
Services	414,893	399,690
	1,274,348	1,267,959
Cost and expenses:		
Cost of revenues	608,810	639,574
Depreciation	107,727	92,657
Research and development	159,410	143,076
Marketing expenses	405,005	360,962
Other administrative expenses	53,800	11,000
	1,334,752	1,247,269
Income (loss) from operations	(60,404)	20,690
Other income	2,491	13,175
Interest expense	46,194	30,467
Income before income taxes and equity in net loss of unconsolidated affiliate	(104,107)	3,398
Income tax benefit (provision)	6,987	(945)
Net income before equity in net loss of unconsolidated affiliate	(97,120)	2,453
Equity in net loss of unconsolidated affiliate	(15,189)	(23,433)
Writedown of investment in unconsolidated affiliate	(14,769)	–0–
Net income (loss)	($ 127,078)	($ 20,980)

Reliant Information Technologies Corporation
Consolidated Balance Sheet
(in thousands)

	As of December 31	
	Projected 1995	Actual 1994
Assets		
Cash and cash equivalents	$ 136,676	$ 271,537
Marketable equity securities	–0–	30,126
Receivables, less allowance of $25,904 in 1995 and $21,744 in 1994	274,925	260,498
Inventories	189,538	237,585
Other current assets	34,858	23,350
Total current assets	635,997	823,096
Notes receivable	19,481	23,236
Property, plant, and equipment, net	398,944	367,422
Other assets including investment in affiliates	21,062	51,020
Total assets	$1,075,484	$1,264,774
Liabilities and Stockholders' Equity		
Notes payable	$ 38,740	$ 33,451
Accounts payable	103,441	75,536
Other current liabilities	245,369	210,935
Total current liabilities	387,550	319,922
Long-term debt	79,990	240,734
Deferred service revenue	13,378	14,144
Total liabilities	480,918	574,800
Stockholders' equity:		
Common stock	302,639	268,182
Retained earnings	279,749	406,827
Cumulative foreign currency translation adjustment	12,178	14,965
Total stockholders' equity	594,566	689,974
Total liabilities and stockholders' equity	$1,075,484	$1,264,774

Reliant Information Technologies Corporation
Projected Statement of Cash Flows
For the Year Ended December 31, 1995
(numbers in parentheses indicate reductions in cash; thousands of dollars)

Operations:		
Net income		($127,078)
Depreciation		107,727
Other noncash expenses		29,958
Adjustment for deferred taxes		(766)
		9,841
Adjustments for:		
Increase in receivables		(14,427)
Decrease in inventories		48,047
Increase in accounts payable		27,905
Increase in other current assets		(11,508)
Increase in other current liabilities		34,434
		$ 84,451
Cash flow — operations		$ 94,292
Investing:		
Payments for additions to property, plant, and equipment		($142,918)
Proceeds from sale of property, plant, and equipment		3,669
Net sales of marketable equity securities		30,126
Decrease in notes receivable		3,755
Cash flow — investing		($105,368)
Financing:		
Proceeds from notes payable		$ 5,289
Payments on long-term debt		(178,556)
Proceeds from long-term debt		17,812
Proceeds from sale of stock		34,457
Dividends		–0–
Cash flow — financing		($120,998)
Effect of exchange rate changes in cash		(2,787)
Increase (decrease) in cash		(134,861)
Cash and equivalents — January 1		271,537
Cash and equivalents — December 31		$136,676

Red Rock Company
Consolidated Income Statement
(in thousands)

	For the Year Ended	
	Projected December 27, 1995	**Actual December 28, 1994**
Sales	$1,503,805	$1,464,881
Less: Beer excise taxes	153,066	149,951
	1,350,739	1,314,930
Cost and expenses:		
Cost of goods sold	778,943	754,217
Marketing, general and administrative	362,293	336,528
Research and development	21,682	23,443
	1,162,918	1,114,188
Operating income	187,821	200,742
Other (income) expense:		
Interest income	(10,582)	(13,214)
Interest expense	2,604	3,219
Depreciation expense	99,240	91,968
Miscellaneous, net	10,511	8,376
Income before taxes	86,048	110,393
Taxes	37,900	51,000
Net income	$ 48,148	$ 59,393

Red Rock Company
Consolidated Balance Sheet
(thousands of dollars)

	Projected as of December 27, 1995	Actual as of December 28, 1994
Assets		
Cash and cash equivalents	$ 113,454	$ 150,464
Accounts and notes receivable	109,208	99,560
Inventories:		
Finished goods	17,254	18,464
In process	32,881	31,037
Raw materials	64,357	68,409
Packaging materials	40,208	38,632
	154,700	156,542
Prepaid expenses and other current assets	66,591	61,255
Tax prepayments	7,703	5,216
Total current assets	451,656	473,037
Properties, at cost, less accumulated depreciation	975,781	901,172
Excess of cost over net assets of businesses acquired, less accumulated amortization	3,356	3,538
Other assets	25,700	18,175
Total assets	$1,456,493	$1,395,922
Liabilities and Stockholders' Equity		
Accounts payable	$ 85,627	$ 75,203
Accrued salaries and benefits	39,132	43,772
Taxes, other than income	26,542	27,840
Income tax liability	9,418	10,759
Other accrued expenses	48,531	43,168
Total current liabilities	209,250	200,742
Accumulated deferred taxes	189,056	181,137
Other liabilities	26,376	17,903
Total liabilities	424,682	399,782
Stockholders' equity:		
Class A common, voting, $1 par	1,260	1,260
Class B common, nonvoting, no par	39,773	34,578
Retaining earnings	1,013,865	983,943
	1,054,898	1,019,781
Less: Class B treasury shares, 10,863,376 in 1995 and 11,123,876 in 1994	23,087	23,641
Total stockholders' equity	1,031,811	996,140
Total liabilities and stockholders' equity	$1,456,493	$1,395,922

CHAPTER 7

Analyzing and Understanding Corporate Financial Reports

Investors, whether novices or veterans, know that decisions about what and when to buy and sell are based upon a mix of fear, hopes, hunches, snatches of overheard conversations, and solid information. . . . [T]here is no substitute for information and knowledge . . . [but] while financial analysis can provide investors with a clear picture of a company's operations, it cannot tell them what individual stock prices will do tomorrow.[1]

Key Chapter Issues

- How can accounting data be used to develop an understanding of the financial health and performance of a company?
- What is ratio analysis?
- How does accounting information influence the behavior of investors and hence the movement of security prices?
- What special insights are revealed about a company from its statement of cash flows?

[1]T. L. O'Glove, *Quality of Earnings* (NY: The Free Press, 1987), pp. 1, xii.

In the previous six chapters we focused on developing an understanding of the basic financial statements, the fundamentals of the accounting system that produces those statements, and the institutional environment that surrounds the production of accounting information in general.

In this chapter we attempt to broaden your understanding of accounting information and its uses by considering a number of advanced topics in the analysis of financial statements. To begin, we return to some of the basics of ratio analysis and consider several alternative viewpoints using PepsiCo's financial statements. Attention then will be turned to the alternative GAAP methods available for use in financial statements and how alternative GAAP impacts ratio analysis and security prices. Finally, we return to the topic of evaluating a company's cash flows and developing pro forma statements from them.

To begin, when a potential investor considers acquiring the shares of a company like PepsiCo, a variety of information sources should be consulted. For example, an investor should access the following sources:

- The company's annual and quarterly financial reports.
- Recent articles or news releases appearing in the financial press (such as *Barrons, Business Week, Forbes, Fortune,* and *The Wall Street Journal*).
- Brokerage firm analyses and reports dealing with the company in particular and the industry in general.
- Investment service firms' reports and analyses (for example, Dun and Bradstreet, Moody's, Standard and Poors, and Value Line).

In this chapter we will consider how these information sources can be used to help an investor reach the very important resource allocation decision: to buy or not to buy.

ASSESSING THE QUALITY OF REPORTED EARNINGS AND FINANCIAL POSITION

Corporate financial reports are the primary means by which companies report their financial condition and performance to interested external parties. In the view of the FASB,

> Financial reporting should provide information that is useful to present and potential investors and creditors and other users in making rational investment, credit, and similar decisions.[2]

Implicit in these uses of financial reports are the concerns of users pertaining to a company's past performance, present condition, and future prospects. The first two of these are the primary focus of the financial statements, related footnotes, management discussion and analysis, and auditor's report. The latter is often the focus of management's letter to shareholders. Quite frankly, though, the assessment of future prospects is best served by users performing their own analysis of company performance and using supplementary third-party commentaries.

Many third-party sources of information about a company are readily available. To illustrate just one of these sources, Exhibit 7.1 presents the Value Line Investment Survey financial evaluation of PepsiCo, Inc., as of May 19, 1995. Not only does this report present abbreviated financial statements and many basic ratios calculated for those statements, but also it presents a brief assessment of the strengths and

[2]Financial Accounting Standards Board, *Statement of Financial Accounting Concepts No. 1*, "Objectives of Financial Reporting by Business Enterprises" (Stamford, Conn.: FASB, 1978).

EXHIBIT 7.1

Value Line Investment Survey Report for PepsiCo, Inc.

PEPSICO, INC. NYSE-PEP | RECENT PRICE 46 | P/E RATIO 19.4 (Trailing: 20.3 Median: 16.0) | RELATIVE P/E RATIO 1.35 | DIV'D YLD 1.7% | VALUE LINE 1546

TIMELINESS 1 Highest (Relative Price Performance Next 12 Mos.)
SAFETY 2 Above Average (Scale: 1 Highest to 5 Lowest)
BETA 1.10 (1.00 = Market)

	1985	1986	1987	1988	1989	1990	1991	1992	1993	1994	1995
High:	5.1	8.4	11.9	14.1	14.5	22.0	27.9	35.6	43.4	43.6	41.1	45.8
Low:	3.8	4.5	7.3	8.5	10.0	12.6	18.0	23.5	30.5	34.5	29.3	33.9

1998-00 PROJECTIONS

	Price	Gain	Ann'l Total Return
High	85	(+85%)	18%
Low	65	(+40%)	11%

Insider Decisions

	J	J	A	S	O	N	D	J	F
to Buy	0	0	0	0	0	0	0	1	0
Options	0	0	0	0	0	0	0	0	0
to Sell	0	0	0	0	0	0	0	0	0

Institutional Decisions

	2Q'94	3Q'94	4Q'94
to Buy	244	216	205
to Sell	292	281	293
Hld's(000)	435231	437962	434698

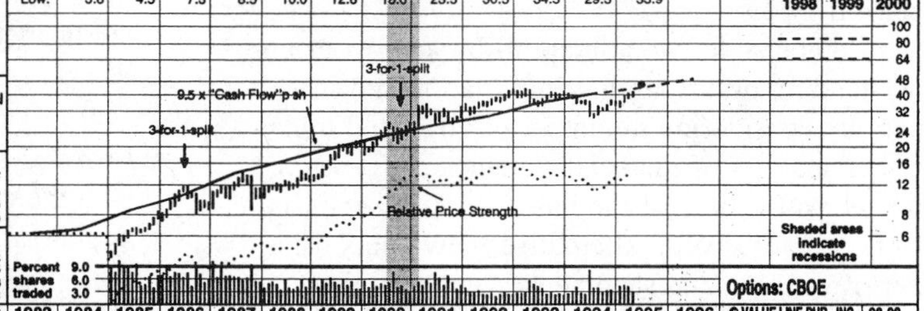

1979	1980	1981	1982	1983	1984	1985	1986	1987	1988	1989	1990	1991	1992	1993	1994	1995	1996	© VALUE LINE PUB., INC.	98-00
6.22	7.27	8.52	8.92	9.38	9.11	10.21	11.90	14.70	16.50	19.27	22.58	24.85	27.50	31.32	36.05	*39.50*	*42.95*	Sales per sh	*59.20*
.50	.56	.65	.64	.65	.69	.90	1.10	1.47	1.76	2.10	2.45	2.83	3.15	3.80	4.25	*4.65*	*5.20*	"Cash Flow" per sh	*7.50*
.32	.36	.40	.36	.33	.38	.50	.58	.74	.97	1.12	1.31	1.50	1.61	1.96	2.22	*2.40*	*2.70*	Earnings per sh B	*4.15*
.12	.14	.16	.18	.18	.19	.20	.21	.22	.27	.32	.38	.46	.51	.61	.70	*.78*	*.88*	Div'ds Decl'd per sh C■	*1.30*
.47	.54	.50	.57	.62	.68	1.00	1.13	.99	.92	1.19	1.50	1.85	1.94	2.48	2.85	*2.40*	*2.55*	Cap'l Spending per sh	*3.40*
1.54	1.74	1.99	1.96	2.13	2.19	2.33	2.64	3.21	4.01	4.92	6.22	7.03	6.70	7.94	8.68	*9.65*	*10.85*	Book Value per sh E	*16.60*
818.59	821.49	824.45	840.37	842.05	845.17	789.36	780.96	781.24	788.43	791.06	788.39	789.10	798.80	798.80	789.90	*785.00*	*780.00*	Common Shs Outst'g F	*760.00*
8.8	7.7	9.4	12.1	11.9	11.8	12.6	16.3	15.5	12.6	15.7	17.8	20.4	22.8	20.0	15.9	Bold figures are Value Line estimates		Avg Ann'l P/E Ratio	*18.0*
1.27	1.02	1.14	1.33	1.01	1.10	1.02	1.11	1.04	1.05	1.19	1.32	1.30	1.38	1.18	1.04			Relative P/E Ratio	*1.40*
4.4%	5.1%	4.2%	4.1%	4.5%	4.1%	3.1%	2.2%	1.9%	2.2%	1.8%	1.6%	1.5%	1.4%	1.6%	2.0%			Avg Ann'l Div'd Yield	*1.7%*
						8056.7	9290.8	11485	13007	15242	17803	19608	21970	25021	28472	*31000*	*33500*	Sales ($mill)	*45000*
						12.8%	13.1%	14.9%	15.3%	16.8%	16.6%	17.0%	16.3%	17.4%	16.8%	*17.0%*	*17.5%*	Operating Margin	*17.5%*
						290.8	400.7	563.0	629.3	772.0	884.0	1034.5	1214.9	1444.2	1576.5	*1750*	*1950*	Depreciation ($mill)	*2500*
						420.1	457.8	586.6	762.2	886.4	1050.0	1200.2	1301.7	1587.9	1784.0	*1900*	*2120*	Net Profit ($mill)	*3195*
						36.7%	32.7%	37.1%	33.0%	33.3%	33.0%	34.8%	31.4%	34.5%	33.0%	*35.0%*	*36.0%*	Income Tax Rate	*36.0%*
						5.2%	4.9%	5.1%	5.9%	5.8%	5.9%	6.1%	5.9%	6.3%	6.3%	*6.1%*	*6.3%*	Net Profit Margin	*7.1%*
						958.8	280.7	216.8	d608.9	d141.0	d689.1	844.0	517.9	d1411	d198.2	*d600*	*d580*	Working Cap'l ($mill)	*100*
						1162.7	2632.6	2279.9	2356.6	5777.1	5600.1	7806.2	7964.8	7442.6	8840.5	*8840*	*8840*	Long-Term Debt ($mill)	*8000*
						1837.7	2059.1	2508.6	3161.0	3891.1	4904.2	5545.4	5355.7	6338.7	6856.1	*7600*	*8475*	Net Worth ($mill)	*12600*
						16.9%	12.4%	14.5%	16.6%	11.8%	12.7%	11.3%	11.8%	12.9%	13.0%	*13.0%*	*13.5%*	% Earned Total Cap'l	*16.5%*
						22.9%	22.2%	23.4%	24.1%	22.8%	21.4%	21.6%	24.3%	25.1%	26.0%	*25.0%*	*25.0%*	% Earned Net Worth	*25.5%*
						14.1%	14.3%	16.4%	17.8%	16.6%	15.4%	15.5%	16.9%	17.8%	18.1%	*17.0%*	*17.0%*	% Retained to Comm Eq	*17.5%*
						38%	36%	30%	26%	27%	28%	29%	30%	29%	30%	*32%*	*32%*	% All Div'ds to Net Prof	*31%*

CAPITAL STRUCTURE as of 12/31/94
Tot.Debt $10506.5 mill. **Due in 5 Yrs** $5246.2 mill.
LT Debt $8840.5 mill. **LT Interest** $500.0 mill.
Incl. $298.2 mill. capitalized leases.
(Total interest coverage: 5.1x) (56% of Cap'l)

Leases, Uncapitalized Annual rentals $303.4 mill.

Pension Liability None

Pfd Stock None

Common Stock 789,900,024 shs. (44% of Cap'l)

CURRENT POSITION ($MILL.)	1992	1993	12/31/94
Cash Assets	2058.4	1856.2	1488.1
Receivables	1588.5	1883.4	2050.9
Inventory (FIFO)	768.8	924.7	970.0
Other	426.6	499.8	563.2
Current Assets	4842.3	5164.1	5072.2
Accts Payable	1164.8	1390.0	1451.6
Debt Due	706.8	2191.2	1666.0
Other	2452.8	2993.7	2152.8
Current Liab.	4324.4	6574.9	5270.4

ANNUAL RATES of change (per sh)	Past 10 Yrs.	Past 5 Yrs.	Est'd '92-'94 to '98-'00
Sales	13.0%	13.5%	*11.0%*
"Cash Flow"	19.0%	16.0%	*12.5%*
Earnings	18.5%	15.5%	*13.5%*
Dividends	13.0%	17.5%	*13.5%*
Book Value	14.0%	14.0%	*13.5%*

Cal-endar	QUARTERLY SALES ($ mill.) A Mar.Per	Jun.Per	Sep.Per	Dec.Per	Full Year
1992	4497	5126	5548	6799	21970
1993	5091	5890	6316	7724	25021
1994	5728	6557	7064	9122	28472
1995	6191	*7250*	*7800*	*9759*	*31000*
1996	*6800*	*7800*	*8400*	*10500*	*33500*

Cal-endar	EARNINGS PER SHARE A B Mar.Per	Jun.Per	Sep.Per	Dec.Per	Full Year
1992	.29	.47	.53	.32	1.61
1993	.32	.53	.56	.55	1.96
1994	.35	.55	.68	.64	2.22
1995	.40	*.60*	*.73*	*.67*	*2.40*
1996	*.43*	*.67*	*.85*	*.75*	*2.70*

Cal-endar	QUARTERLY DIVIDENDS PAID C■ Mar.31	Jun.30	Sep.30	Dec.31	Full Year
1991	.20D	.12	.12	--	.44
1992	.24D	.13	.13	--	.50
1993	.26D	.16	.16	--	.58
1994	.32D	.18	.18	--	.68
1995	.36D	.20			

BUSINESS: PepsiCo, Inc. operates three major businesses: Restaurants, accounting for 37% of 1994 sales, 22% of profits; Beverages, 34% and 37%; and Snack Foods, 29% and 41%. Int'l accounted for 29% of sales, 19% profits. Restaurants include Pizza Hut, KFC (formerly Kentucky Fried Chicken) and Taco Bell. Major soft drink products: *Pepsi-Cola*, *Diet Pepsi*, and *Mountain Dew*. Specialty snack foods: Frito-Lay (major product offerings include *Doritos*, *Ruffles*, and *Lay's*), Walker Crisps, Smiths Crisps. Has about 471,000 employees, 168,000 stockholders. Officers and directors own less than 1% of common. Chairman & Chief Executive Officer: D.W. Calloway. Inc.: NC Address: PepsiCo World Headquarters, Purchase, NY 10577. Tel.: 914-253-2000.

PepsiCo had a strong March quarter, and 1995 should generally be good, as well. The driving forces behind this year's gains will be beverages and snack foods, both of which are doing very well. And what's particularly impressive is that they are doing well even with the poor economic situation and currency devaluation in Mexico, PepsiCo's second largest market. Soft drink demand in the emerging markets of China and India looks particularly promising, and sales should also be strong in Brazil. In the U.S., the *Mountain Dew* and *Pepsi* brands should do well, and non-soft drink beverages, particularly *Lipton* iced tea, should see solid gains. The company's snack food market share should be up again, with more health-conscious items, such as *Rold Gold Fat Free Pretzels*, leading the way. Restaurant sales and profits should also improve, although same-store sales are likely to continue to be soft at Pizza Hut and Taco Bell, and **Moves to restructure the restaurant units could come fairly soon.** Our best guess is that the company will try to sell some portion of its owned units to franchisees. The cash generated by such a move could be then be used for various corporate purposes, most likely including the repurchase of stock.

Continued growth is likely for 1996 and the years out to 1998-2000. Soft drinks, snack food, and restaurants are all growth businesses, and we expect PepsiCo to fully partake in that growth. The largest potential over time is clearly in international markets, where PepsiCo is already a major factor in snack foods and a formidable (although much smaller than Coke) competitor in soft drinks. A joint venture in snack foods with General Mills in Continental Europe looks promising, and we also expect the company to expand through acquisitions. This year alone, before any restaurant restructuring, PepsiCo is likely to generate more than $500 million of free cash that can be used for acquisitions, debt repayment, or buying stock in the open market.

These shares, which are up about 20% since our February report, are still attractive on a six- to 12-month basis. Looking out 3 to 5 years, the appreciation potential is about average.

Stephen Sanborn, CFA *May 19, 1995*

(A) Quarters are 12, 12, 12 and 16 weeks. (B) Prim. earns. Ex. non-recur. chgs.: '79, 5¢; '80, 18¢; '81, 13¢; '82, 28¢; '84, 47¢; '91, 15¢; '92, $1.31. Ex. disc'd op. gains (losses): '84, 7¢; '85, 44¢; '87, (4¢); '90, (2¢). Ex. nonrecur. gains; '87, 7¢; '89, 4¢; '90, 6¢. Next earn. rep. due late July. (C) Next div. meeting late July. Goes ex early June. Pay. dates: Jan 1, March 31, June 30, Sept. 30. ■ Reinvest. plan avail. (D) Two payments in qtr. (E) Incl. intang. In '94: $7.84 bil., $9.92/sh. (F) In mil., adj. for stock splits.

Company's Financial Strength	A
Stock's Price Stability	85
Price Growth Persistence	90
Earnings Predictability	95

weaknesses of PepsiCo's operations, as well as a prognosis for the future. For example, the Value Line report highlights the following key points:

- PepsiCo had a strong first quarter, and the results for 1995 should generally be good.
- The beverage and snack foods segments were particularly strong, although restaurant sales were somewhat "soft."
- Lagging sales in the restaurant segment may result in some type of restructuring, possibly involving the sale of some company-owned units to franchisees.
- Continued growth in all segments is expected in 1996 and 1998–2000.
- This good-quality stock should be a standout performer in the foreseeable future, and even after a 20 percent share price run-up in the first five months of 1995, Value Line recommends its purchase with an "attractive buy" rating.

Note also that in terms of the Value Line investment rating system, PepsiCo earned a 2 (above average) on a scale of 1 to 5 in their Safety Ranking System, a 1 (highest) in their Timeliness Ranking System, and a Financial Strength Rating of A.

Because no one knows for certain what a company's future financial results will be, a great deal of emphasis is placed on past and present performance as indicators of the future. In projecting a link between the past and the future, issues falling under the general rubric of the **quality of earnings and financial position** become significant considerations. For example, although the amount of reported earnings is important, so too are the rate of earnings generated on available resources, the stability of earnings, the specific sources of earnings, and the accounting methods used to measure the earnings. Similarly, although it is useful to know the size and variety of asset categories, it is also important to determine their liquidity, operating capacity, and flexibility.

In previous chapters numerous financial ratios were suggested as sources of insight regarding a company's management of the various facets of its operations. For example, in Chapter 4 the accounts receivable turnover ratio was discussed as a means to estimate the rate at which a company's receivables were converted into cash. Chapter 5 presented the return on owners' equity ratio as an indication of the return earned by a company on noncreditor funds. Exhibit 7.2 summarizes the various ratios discussed throughout this text and also introduces a new category of indicators, the *return to investors.*

Return to Investors

For publicly held companies, the **return to investors** is one of the most frequently evaluated areas of company performance. Because investors are often the largest group of stakeholders (both in number and in dollars invested) in a company, how well they are rewarded for their investment is of considerable interest and importance. Most indicators of the return to investors are based on current income statement data and, in some cases, on actual stock market price data.

Earnings per share. Perhaps the most often cited measure of shareholder return is a company's **earnings per share,** or EPS. As noted in Chapter 5, EPS represents only those earnings of a company accruing to its voting, or common, shareholders, Thus, in the calculation of EPS, a company's earnings are first reduced for any dividends paid to the preferred shareholders.

EXHIBIT 7.2

Summary of Financial Statement Ratios

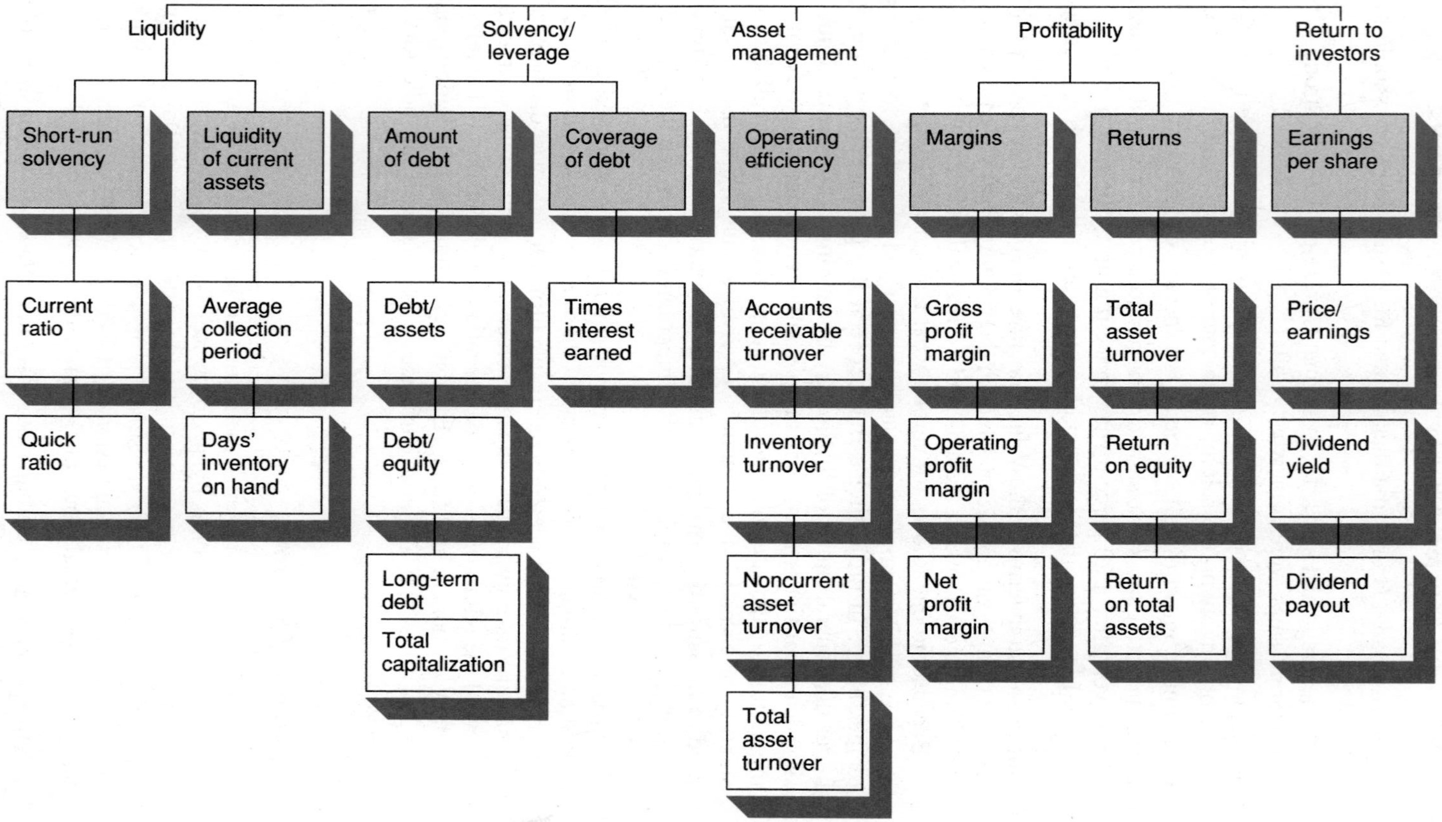

EXHIBIT 7.2 concluded

Summary of Financial Statement Ratios

Liquidity:

Current ratio = Current assets ÷ Current liabilities

Quick ratio = (Cash + Marketable securities + Receivables) ÷ Current liabilities

Average receivable collection period = (Average accounts receivable balance ÷ Net sales) × 365 days

Average number of days' inventory on hand = (Average inventory balance ÷ Cost of goods sold) × 365 days

Solvency/Leverage:

Total debt-to-total assets ratio = Total debt ÷ Total assets

Long-term debt to equity = Long-term debt ÷ Total owners' equity

Long-term debt to total capitalization ratio = Long-term debt ÷ (Long-term debt + Total owners' equity)

Times-interest-earned ratio = Net income before interest and income taxes ÷ Interest expense

Asset management:

Accounts receivable turnover = Net credit sales ÷ Average accounts receivable balance

Inventory turnover = Cost of goods sold ÷ Average inventory balance

Noncurrent asset turnover = Net sales ÷ Average noncurrent assets

Total asset turnover = Net sales ÷ Average total assets

Profitability:

Gross profit margin = (Net sales − Cost of goods sold) ÷ Net sales

Operating profit margin = Operating income ÷ Net sales

Net profit margin = Net income ÷ Net sales

Return on equity = Net income ÷ Average owners' equity

Return on total assets = Net income ÷ Average total assets

Return to investors:

Earnings per share (Net income − preferred stock dividends) ÷ Weighted-average common shares outstanding

Price-earnings ratio = Market price per common share ÷ Earnings per share

Dividend yield = Cash dividend per common share ÷ Market price per common share

Dividend payout ratio = Cash dividends paid to common stockholders ÷ (Net income − Preferred stock dividends)

The calculation of EPS can be quite complex, depending on whether a company has other securities outstanding that are convertible into, or exchangeable for, additional shares of common stock. In the simplest case in which a company has only common and preferred stock outstanding, the computation of basic EPS is straightforward:

$$\text{EPS} = \frac{\text{Net income} - \text{Preferred dividends}}{\text{Weighted-average number of common shares outstanding}}$$

Note that in the calculation of EPS, the divisor is not merely the number of shares outstanding at year-end but rather is an average of the shares outstanding, weighted by the proportion of a given year (or quarter) that the shares were actually in the hands of shareholders.

For a company with securities outstanding that are convertible (for example, convertible bonds or convertible preferred stock) or exchangeable (for example, stock options or warrants) for common stock, the calculation of EPS can be surprisingly difficult. Under these conditions, two calculations may be required — one for primary EPS and one for fully diluted EPS.

Primary EPS is calculated by dividing earnings applicable to common stock by the weighted-average number of common shares outstanding *plus* any common stock equivalents:

$$\text{Primary EPS} = \frac{\text{Earnings applicable to common stock}}{\text{Weighted-average common shares} + \text{Common stock equivalents}}$$

A **common stock equivalent** is "a security which is not, in form, a common stock but which usually contains provisions to enable its holder to become a common stockholder."[3] Stock options and stock warrants are considered to be common stock equivalents at all times; thus, *even if* an option or warrant is not exercised (exchanged for common stock) by the end of an accounting period, it is treated for primary EPS calculation purposes *as if* it had been exercised.

Determining whether a particular convertible security, such as convertible preferred stock or a convertible bond, is a common stock equivalent is more problematic. Current practice, however, relies on several well-reasoned, albeit arbitrary, rules in making such determinations. If a convertible security's effective yield at the time of issuance is less than 66⅔ percent of the then current average Aa corporate bond yield, it is considered to be a common stock equivalent. The rationale for this rule is the belief that the only reason an investor would purchase a convertible bond or convertible preferred stock yielding a rate of return substantially below the current market rate is the buyer's intent to convert the security into common stock at some future date. Notice, however, that this rule ignores any difference in investment risk between the convertible security and a corporate Aa bond.

Fully diluted EPS is calculated by including in the divisor *all* potentially dilutive securities in addition to any common stock equivalents:

$$\text{Fully diluted EPS} = \frac{\text{Earnings applicable to common stock}}{\begin{array}{c}\text{Weighted-average common shares +}\\ \text{Common stock equivalents +}\\ \text{Other potentially dilutive securities}\end{array}}$$

Thus, not only are all the common stock equivalents considered, as is done for primary EPS, but also all convertible securities not qualifying as common stock equivalents are assumed to have been converted, subject to one caveat: In determining either primary or fully diluted EPS, no security should be included in the calculation of EPS if its inclusion causes the EPS amount to increase (referred to as an **antidilutive effect**). Only common stock equivalents and convertible securities causing a *dilution* of the EPS are incorporated in the calculations. For example, assume the following EPS:

$$\text{EPS} = \frac{\$12{,}000{,}000 \text{ (net income)} - \$5{,}000{,}000 \text{ (preferred dividends)}}{\begin{array}{c}3{,}500{,}000 \text{ shares (average shares of}\\ \text{common stock outstanding)}\end{array}}$$

$$= \$2$$

If the outstanding convertible preferred stock is assumed to be converted at the beginning of the year into 1 million common shares, the following would be the new EPS:

$$\text{EPS} = \frac{\$12{,}000{,}000}{4{,}500{,}000} = \$2.67$$

Because the convertible preferred stock had an antidilutive effect, it would not be considered in the final EPS calculation.

As this example demonstrates, the earnings applicable to common stockholders for each convertible security included in the EPS denominator require an adjustment. For

[3]American Institute of Certified Public Accountants, *APB Opinion No. 15,* "Earnings per Share" (New York: AICPA, 1969).

example, if the number of common shares attributable to a convertible preferred stock is used to increase the EPS denominator, the numerator should be increased by the amount of preferred dividends that would no longer be required if the conversion took place. The one exception to this involves the exercise of stock options or warrants, which affect only the number of shares outstanding.

The International Accounting Standards Commission (IASC) recommends that only basic and fully diluted EPS be reported by companies. While the FASB has not, as yet, endorsed this position, it is anticipated that it will do so in the future.

Price-earnings (P/E) ratio. One of the most widely used indicators of a company's investment potential is the **price-earnings ratio,** or P/E multiple:

$$\text{P/E ratio} = \frac{\text{Market price per common share}}{\text{EPS}}$$

Because the market price of a share of stock is a function of investors' perceptions regarding a company's potential, the same factors that affect those perceptions affect the P/E ratio — factors such as a company's relative investment risk, past earnings record, and growth potential. Many investment houses use the P/E ratio as a criterion to advise their clients about when to buy or sell stocks. A typical rule of thumb followed by some investment advisers is that a company with a low P/E ratio, assuming it is a sound business enterprise, represents a bargain for potential investors *relative to* a company with a higher P/E ratio. Investing solely, or even principally, on the basis of P/E ratios can be a risky investment strategy. P/E ratios are significantly influenced by the level of reported earnings, and, as we will see shortly, it is possible for a company to artificially manage its reported results. Moreover, investing on the basis of P/E ratios ignores the fact that *current* stock prices frequently reflect all publicly available information about a company; thus, it is unlikely that an investor following such a strategy will be able to earn unusual or *abnormal* returns.

At year-end 1994, the P/E ratio for PepsiCo was 17; for Coca-Cola it was 25. If we assume that the two companies represent equivalent investment opportunities and that the P/E ratio is an effective means of identifying underpriced stocks, the year-end P/E ratios suggest that PepsiCo may have been a better investment opportunity at year-end 1994 than Coca-Cola.

Dividend yield. Some investors are principally interested in the actual level of cash distributed by a company to its shareholders. To these investors, the cash **dividend yield** is an important indicator:

$$\text{Dividend yield} = \frac{\text{Cash dividend per common share}}{\text{Market price per common share}}$$

This measure informs investors of the current cash rate of return on a given common stock, based on its current selling price. During 1994 PepsiCo's cash dividend yield was 1.9 percent based on the year-end market price; for Coca-Cola it was 1.5 percent. For an investor interested in current cash income, this measure readily facilitates investment choices.

Dividend payout ratio. A measure of the return actually paid to shareholders is captured in the cash **dividend payout ratio:**

$$\text{Dividend payout ratio} = \frac{\text{Cash dividends to common shareholders}}{\text{Net income} - \text{Preferred dividends}}$$

This ratio measures the percentage of a company's earnings that are actually distributed to its shareholders in the form of cash dividends. From an investor's point of view, a higher dividend payout ratio results in immediate increased cash inflows. On the other hand, from management's perspective, a growth-oriented company would want to maintain minimal payout ratios for the purpose of retaining funds to fuel continued growth, whereas a mature company (such as a utility company) would desire relatively high payout ratios to compensate for the fact that its potential stock appreciation is probably less than that of a growth-oriented company. In both 1993 and 1994 PepsiCo's cash dividend payout ratio was approximately 32 percent. These percentages are somewhat low when compared, for example, with the 41 and 39 percent amounts for Coca-Cola for the same periods.

FINANCIAL STATEMENT ANALYSIS: AN ILLUSTRATION

The topic of financial statement analysis has been a common thread linking the previous three chapters. As Exhibit 7.2 shows, the analysis of financial statements using ratios can be organized into five categories:

1. *Liquidity:* the assessment of a company's ability to meet current short-term obligations as they fall due.
2. *Solvency:* the assessment of a company's long-term debt payment ability.
3. *Asset management:* the assessment of how effectively a company utilizes its available resources.
4. *Profitability:* the assessment of a company's ability to generate revenues in excess of expenses.
5. *Return to investors:* the assessment of the earnings or cash flows accruing to the owners of a company.

Although each of these categories has been covered in detail elsewhere, it is instructive to review the ratios involved using PepsiCo's 1994 financial statements.

As Exhibit 7.3 reveals, PepsiCo's results for 1994 indicate both positive and negative trends. With respect to liquidity, the financial ratios indicate that the company was somewhat more liquid in 1993; however, with respect to solvency, on almost all measures PepsiCo's long-term debt position declined. Although profit margins were slightly down as compared to 1993, the return on equity and the return on total assets improved. Moreover, the asset management indicators reveal modest improvement between the two years with the exception of total asset turnover, which improved by almost 10 percent. Finally, with respect to the return-to-investors indicators, not only were the earnings per share up over 11 percent, but PepsiCo increased both its dividend yield and dividend payout. Despite these rather positive investor-related trends, PepsiCo's share price closed at $36.25 per share at year-end 1994, well below its 1993 year-end close of $41.88 per share.

Limitations of Ratio Analysis

Ratio analysis is undoubtedly the most widely used analytical technique for interpreting financial statement data. In spite of its widespread use, however, ratio analysis suffers from certain limitations and is subject to certain constraining assumptions.

EXHIBIT 7.3

PepsiCo, Inc.
Financial Statement Ratios

	1994	1993
Liquidity		
Current ratio	0.96:1	0.78:1
Quick ratio	0.67:1	0.56:1
Average receivable collection period	26.3	27.7
Average number of day's inventory on hand	25.9	28.3
Solvency/leverage		
Total debt-to-total assets ratio	72.3%	73.3%
Long-term debt-to-equity ratio	1.29:1	1.17:1
Long-term debt-to-total capitalization	45.3%	43.4%
Times-interest-earned ratio	5.1 times	5.2 times
Asset management		
Accounts receivable turnover	13.9 times	13.3 times
Inventory turnover	14.1 times	12.9 times
Noncurrent asset turnover	1.61 times	1.49 times
Total asset turnover	1.15 times	1.06 times
Profitability		
Gross profit margin	51.8%	52.3%
Operating profit margin	11.3%	11.6%
Net profit margin	6.3%	6.3%
Return on equity	26.0%	25.1%
Return on total assets	7.2%	6.7%
Return to investors		
Earnings per share	$2.18	$1.96
Price/earnings ratio*	17:1	21:1
Dividend yield*	1.9%	1.5%
Dividend payout	32.1%	31.1%

*Price = Fourth-quarter closing price.

For example, because a ratio involves *two* financial statement numbers (such as net sales divided by total assets), the analyst must be cautious in interpreting a cause when a change in a ratio is observed. Ratio changes may result from a change in either the numerator, the denominator, or both. Thus, when using ratios, the analyst must be prepared to look beyond the ratio itself in an effort to understand the economic event(s) causing the change.

Another concern is that, quite often, changes in financial statement data may be more cosmetic than real. For example, the trend analysis of PepsiCo's financial statement data reported in Exhibit 7.3 presupposes consistency in the basic relationships underlying the financial statement numbers. Consequently, any event — be it a real economic event or a cosmetic one — that disturbs an underlying relation will impact the reported ratios.

Although not an exhaustive listing, the following are examples of cosmetic events that will disturb the underlying financial statement relationships and thus must be taken into consideration by the astute reader:

1. A structural change in the accounting entity (such as a merger or an acquisition of another company).
2. A change in an accounting method or principle (such as a switch from a LIFO inventory cost flow assumption to FIFO).

3. A change in an accounting estimate (such as an increase in the estimated useful life of a depreciable asset).
4. A change in accounting classification (such as segregating the income (or loss) on a division recently sold from the income from operations).

These concerns are particularly relevant when accounting data are investigated for trends over a number of accounting periods. The analysis of financial statement data over multiple periods is frequently called **time-series analysis.**

As noted before, ratio analysis is most effective when the resulting ratios can be compared against some standard. Frequently, that standard is a similar ratio from a prior period, as in a trend analysis of time-series data. Another useful standard, however, is a ratio from a leading competitor or perhaps the industry in general. Unfortunately, the use of **cross-sectional analysis** — that is, the comparison of a given company's ratios with other companies' data or with industry averages — also involves certain restrictive assumptions, including these:

1. The individual company is assumed to be structurally similar to the competitor or the average of the industry, which is rarely the case.
2. The industry and the company under review are assumed to use a common set of accounting principles and accounting estimates. As we will see shortly, when a company under review uses one set of GAAP and the industry or comparative company uses another set, large cosmetic ratio differences tend to occur.
3. The company under review and the industry are assumed to experience a common set of external influences. A given company, however, may have undergone an unusual economic event (such as a labor strike) having multiple-period implications for its financial data that are not reflected in the industry standard.

Despite these concerns, ratio analysis can be a very powerful analytical tool so long as the analyst recognizes the following important maxim: *Ratios help the financial statement user identify important questions but seldom offer direct answers.* Only by a comprehensive review of the financial statements can answers be obtained.

Horizontal and Vertical Analysis

In addition to ratio analysis, two other types of financial statement analysis are frequently performed — horizontal analysis and vertical analysis. When comparative balance sheets or income statements are presented side by side, the statements can be made more meaningful if the dollar amount of increase or decrease and the percentage change is shown. This type of analysis is known as **horizontal analysis** because the data comparisons are made on a horizontal plane from left to right.

Exhibit 7.4 illustrates a horizontal analysis of PepsiCo's income statement. In this two-year comparison, the earlier year (1993) is the base year. The percentage changes are rounded to the nearest tenth of a percent. For PepsiCo, it is noteworthy that although 1994 net sales increased by 13.8 percent over 1993 sales, costs and expenses also increased but at a faster rate (14.3 percent). This increase, combined with certain tax benefits that lowered PepsiCo's effective income tax rate, produced a 11.2 percent growth in net income.

In **vertical analysis** three financial statement numbers — total assets, total equities, and net sales — are converted to a base of 100 percent. Each item within the assets and equities on the balance sheet, or each item on the income statement, is then expressed

EXHIBIT 7.4

PepsiCo, Inc.
Comparative Income Statements with Horizontal Analysis
For Years Ended December 31, 1994 and 1993
(in millions)

	1994	1993	Amount of Increase (Decrease) during 1994	Percentage Increase (Decrease) during 1994
Net sales	$28,472.4	$25,020.7	$3,451.7	13.8%
Costs and expenses				
Cost of sales	13,715.4	11,946.1	1,769.3	14.8
Selling, general, and administrative expenses*	11,555.8	10,168.1	1,387.7	13.6
Interest expense	645.0	572.7	72.3	12.6
Interest income	(90.4)	(88.7)	1.7	1.9
	25,825.8	22,598.2	3,227.6	14.3
Income from continuing operations before income taxes	2,646.6	2,422.5	224.1	9.3
Provision for income taxes	(880.4)	(834.6)	45.8	5.5
Net income	$ 1,766.2†	$ 1,587.9	$ 178.3	11.2%

*Includes amortization of intangible assets.

†Excludes gain on joint venture stock offering of $17.8 million and cumulative effect of accounting changes of $(32) million (that is, $55.3 – $23.3).

as a percentage of the base number. Since for any given set of financial statements the base numbers represent 100 percent, the restated financial statements are called **common-size statements.**

To illustrate vertical analysis, Exhibit 7.5 presents PepsiCo's common-size income statements for 1993 and 1994. An interpretation of vertical statements often parallels the interpretation of horizontal statements. Note that the common-size statements permit both within-period analysis (for example, in 1994 costs and expenses were approximately 90.8 percent of net sales) and across-period trend analysis (for example, costs and expenses as a percentage of net sales increased from 90.3 percent in 1993 to 90.8 percent in 1994).

ACCOUNTING INFORMATION AND STOCK PRICES

As will repeatedly be noted throughout this text, the reporting of earnings and financial position of a company involves both considerable latitude in selecting from the array of generally accepted accounting principles and the inevitable need for management to make numerous valuation estimates and judgments. Given the flexibility available to corporate management in the presentation of financial results, the very human desire to portray their companies in the best light possible, and their awareness of users' concerns about the quality of reported earnings and financial position, it is important to consider the subtle and not-so-subtle items that external users should look for in financial reports as they perform their evaluations of a company.

Consider, for example, the revenue recognition method decision that managers of construction companies must make. Under GAAP, the revenues of such companies may be presented using either the completed contract method or the percentage of

EXHIBIT 7.5

PepsiCo, Inc.
Comparative Common-Size Income Statements
For Years Ended December 31, 1994 and 1993
(in millions)

	1994	Common-Size Percentage	1993	Common-Size Percentage
Net sales	$28,472.4	100%	$25,020.7	100%
Costs and expenses				
Cost of sales	13,715.4	48.2	11,946.1	47.8
Selling, general, and administrative expenses*	11,555.8	40.6	10,168.1	40.6
Interest expense	645.0	2.3	572.7	2.3
Interest income	(90.4)	(0.3)	(88.7)	(0.4)
	25,825.8	90.8	22,598.2	90.3
Income from continuing operations before income taxes	2,646.6	9.3	2,422.5	9.7
Provision for income taxes	(880.4)	(3.1)	(834.6)	(3.3)
Net income	$ 1,766.2†	6.2	$ 1,587.9	6.4

*Includes the amortization of intangible assets.

†Excludes the gain on joint venture stock offering of $17.8 million and the net cumulative effect of accounting changes of $(32) million (that is, $55.3 – $23.3).

completion method. Under the **completed contract method,** management records no revenues until the work to be provided under a multi-period contract is fully completed. Under the **percentage of completion method,** management takes the position that revenue recognition is a function of the portion of work actually completed. Exhibit 7.6 provides a simple illustration contrasting the completed contract and percentage of completion methods for a hypothetical firm. The exhibit reveals that under the completed contract approach, FHAS Corporation would report no earnings in 1994 or 1995 and $1.7 million in earnings in 1996. Under the percentage of completion approach, however, a positive income stream ($0.4 million, $0.5 million, and $0.8 million, in 1994, 1995, and 1996, respectively) is reported in each year. The first method defers all income until 1996, whereas the second spreads the income across the three years as a function of the portion of work actually completed.

It is clear that although the aggregate results, viewed in their entirety over the three-year period, are equivalent, substantially different impressions are created in any individual year as to the relative success of FHAS Corporation in performing under the contract. It is important to recognize that either the completed contract or the percentage of completion method may be adopted for financial reporting purposes. Moreover, the decision to use one method or the other is exclusively a managerial decision, although the percentage of completion method is preferred by most accountants because it more closely reflects the accrual basis of accounting.

As we see from the data in Exhibit 7.6, the method that a company adopts to report its revenues or expenses may have a significant impact on its actual reported results. Not only will the level of revenues and expenses on the income statement be affected, but so too will be the level of reported assets and equities on the balance sheet, along with all the financial ratios calculated using those income statement and balance sheet values. Thus, when analyzing a company's reported performance and financial condi-

EXHIBIT 7.6

Alternative GAAP: Completed Contract versus Percentage of Completion Methods

In June 1994 FHAS Corporation signed a long-term construction contract to build a shopping center in Houston, Texas. Under the terms of the three-year contract, FHAS would receive a total of $12 million. During 1994, 30 percent of the project was completed at a cost of $3.2 million. In 1995, 40 percent of the project was completed at a cost of $4.3 million; in 1996, the project was completed at a cost of $2.8 million.

Under the completed contract method, FHAS would report earnings as follows:

	1994	1995	1996
Revenues	$–0–	$–0–	$12.0 million
Expenses	–0–	–0–	10.3
Net income	$–0–	$–0–	$ 1.7 million
Return on sales	–0–%	–0–%	14.2%

Under the percentage of completion method, FHAS would report earnings as follows:

	1994	1995	1996
Revenues	$3.6 million	$ 4.8 million	$ 3.6 million
Expenses	3.2	4.3	2.8
Net income	$0.4 million	$ 0.5 million	$ 0.8 million
Return on sales	11%	10.4%	22.2%

tion using either absolute figures or ratios, it is important to know just which accounting methods are being used and how those methods are likely to impact the reported values and calculated ratios. For example, in Exhibit 7.6, note how the trend in the return on sales dramatically differs for the two methods of reporting revenues.

Exhibit 7.7 provides further evidence of this analytical concern. This exhibit presents the income statement and selected financial indicators for two *economically identical* companies that differ *only* in regard to the accounting method used to value the cost of goods sold and ending inventory. A review of these financial data reveals that because inventory costs are rising, FIFO Company appears to be financially better off than LIFO Company: Earnings and working capital are higher by $7.8 million and $5.15 million, respectively, and the current ratio (liquidity), the debt-to-equity ratio (solvency), and the return on assets and on sales (profitability) are superior. Only the inventory turnover ratio (asset management) appears to be better for LIFO Company.

But are these financial indicators depicting the true economic reality? Holding the question of taxes aside, the answer is a resounding "No!" The two companies are economically identical in spite of the information revealed by the accounting data and the ratio analysis. If we now add the issue of income taxes and assume that each company uses the same inventory costing method for both IRS purposes and for financial statement purposes, our conclusion is even more startling — the LIFO company is actually superior in economic performance because larger cash flows (due to tax savings) are preserved within the company. (LIFO and FIFO are discussed at length in Chapter 9.)

EXHIBIT 7.7

Alternative GAAP and Financial Statement Analysis: LIFO versus FIFO

Presented below are the income statements and selected financial ratios for two companies that are identical in every respect except with regard to the method of inventory costing and the cost of goods sold:

	FIFO Company	LIFO Company
Net sales	$ 75,000,000	$ 75,000,000
Cost of goods sold	(34,500,000)	(42,300,000)
Gross margin	$ 40,500,000	$ 32,700,000
Other operating expenses	(15,000,000)	(17,000,000)
Net income	$ 25,500,000	$ 17,700,000
Ending inventory	$ 17,250,000	$ 9,450,000
Selected financial ratios:		
Earnings per share	$2.55	$1.77
Current ratio	1.67:1	1.42:1
Working capital	$10.8 m	$5.65 m
Inventory turnover	2:1	4.5:1
Debt-to-equity ratio	1:5.17	1:4.91
Return on assets	10.8%	7.8%
Return on sales	34.0%	23.6%

One thing is clear from these illustrations. The use of different financial accounting methods may produce very different impressions about the financial performance of a company and its management. Of importance, then, is whether these different accounting impressions are also reflected, or even should be reflected, in a company's stock price.

The Efficient Market Hypothesis

Although there is some disagreement over exactly what causes stock prices to move upward and downward, there is little disagreement over the notion that *accounting information* is at least partially responsible for stock price movements. Consider, for example, the news story reported in Exhibit 7.8. This *Wall Street Journal* article reports that PepsiCo's 1994 fourth-quarter earnings were up by 16 percent as compared to the 1993 fourth-quarter results. Record results in the beverage and snack food segments, however, were somewhat offset by a drop of 3 percent in the operating profits of PepsiCo's restaurant division. This apparently "mixed bag" of accounting results caused PepsiCo's stock price to fall by $0.75 per share, or 2 percent. Analysts and investors were apparently disappointed by the company's lower-than-expected results and responded by selling their shares.

This article and the resulting share price movement depict the role of accounting information for investors and the stock and bond markets in general. Using the latest accounting results, investors form expectations about the future of companies such as PepsiCo and accordingly determine how much they are willing to pay for a share of stock (or a bond) in the company. The negative share price reaction to the PepsiCo news indicates that investors' expectations about the future of PepsiCo were lowered by the announcement (and hence their unwillingness to pay a higher price for the stock). Notice also how quickly investors responded to the news release — the price of

EXHIBIT 7.8

PepsiCo's Net Jumped 16 Percent in Fourth Quarter

By ANITA SHARPE, *Staff Reporter of* THE WALL STREET JOURNAL

PepsiCo Inc., buoyed by record results in its beverage and Frito-Lay units, posted a 16 percent jump in fourth-quarter earnings.

But the company continued to battle problems in its restaurant division, where operating profit fell 3 percent in the quarter.

PepsiCo, based in Purchase, N.Y., said net income rose to $513.3 million, or 64 cents a share, in the fourth quarter from $442.5 million, or 55 cents a share, a year earlier. Revenue increased 18 percent to $9.12 billion from $7.72 billion.

Though the results were at the high end of most analysts' expectations, earnings per share received about a four-cent boost from a lower-than-expected tax rate, said Joseph Doyle, an analyst with Smith Barney. What's more, he said, while beverages and snack foods showed strong gains in the quarter, "They're tarnished by continuing disappointment in the restaurant division."

Indeed, worldwide operating profit at PepsiCo's restaurants fell to $238 million in the fourth quarter from $244.6 million a year earlier. Sales, however, rose 15 percent to $3.45 billion.

The mixed bag did little for PepsiCo's stock price, which fell 75 cents yesterday to $37.875 in late New York Stock Exchange trading.

Wayne Calloway, PepsiCo's chairman and chief executive, acknowledged in a prepared statement that "1994 was a tough year for our restaurants." Although KFC and Taco Bell posted profit gains, the results for the restaurant segment as a whole "declined for the first time in 15 years primarily because of weak results at Pizza Hut," he said.

That chain's fourth-quarter operating profit plunged 25 percent to $92.5 million as competitors rolled out their own value-priced items in response to Pizza Hut's efforts in that area. In addition, Mr. Doyle said, the lower-end dine-in concept "is tired." Restaurants like Pizza Hut are increasingly under siege from more diverse and upscale chains like Olive Garden and Chili's, he said.

PepsiCo's management "is aware of the problem, but it's tough to turn it around," Mr. Doyle added.

Mr. Calloway said that, in addition to reorganizing management in the restaurant division, the company "filled the pipeline with new product ideas for Pizza Hut and Taco Bell." The latter is expected to roll out a line of reduced-fat menu items at a news conference today.

On the positive side, worldwide operating profit in PepsiCo's beverage division increased 21 percent to $283 million in the fourth quarter, with sales advancing 18 percent to $2.94 billion. In the U.S., PepsiCo's Mountain Dew and Lipton tea brands led strong growth in bottler case sales.

Source: *The Wall Street Journal,* February 8, 1995. Reprinted by permission of *The Wall Street Journal*

PepsiCo's common stock declined by $0.75 very shortly after the story appeared on the Associated Press newswire. The story appeared in the *Wall Street Journal* on the day following the press release by PepsiCo, Inc.

The relationship between accounting information and stock prices is largely captured by a theory of the functioning of capital markets called the **efficient market hypothesis,** or EMH.[4] EMH is a widely accepted theory describing how stock and bond prices react to information. In fact, the theory is so well documented that it has been used by the U.S. Supreme Court to describe the behavior of U.S. capital markets.

Under EMH, stock prices are assumed to reflect fully (in terms of price) all publicly available information. When new information (such as the PepsiCo earnings announcement) is made public, share prices adjust very quickly to the new information. For example, on July 6, 1995, the *Wall Street Journal* reported that PepsiCo would report higher earnings for the second quarter of 1995. Specifically, a *Journal* staff reporter projected that PepsiCo's second-quarter earnings would increase by 9 percent over the same period in 1994 (i.e. $0.60 per share, versus $0.55 per share, respectively). Despite this seemingly positive news report, PepsiCo's share price declined by $1.25, or 2.8 percent, on the day the news was released to the market. PepsiCo

[4]See T. R. Dyckman and D. Morse, *Efficient Capital Markets and Accounting* (Englewood Cliffs, N.J.: Prentice Hall, 1986).

investors were apparently concerned about the company's rate of growth in earnings, consequently concluding that its then-current share price was unjustified.

Evidence also exists to suggest that the capital markets are not "fooled" by the differences in reported accounting numbers caused by the use of alternative GAAP; that is, sophisticated analysts and investors are apparently able to "see through" the differential accounting effects created by alternative GAAP (completed contract versus percentage of completion, LIFO versus FIFO, and so on) and are able to properly adjust share prices (by buying or selling) to reflect the true underlying economic value of a company.

An important implication of this theory is that managers of publicly held companies should be unable to manipulate the value of their companies' stock merely by selecting accounting methods that result in the highest level of reported earnings. Because stock prices reflect only *real* economic changes, they will be relatively unaffected by the cosmetic wealth changes associated with alternative GAAP. We will have more to say about the EMH in Chapter 16.

Unfortunately, it is sometimes possible to "fool" the stock market and its many investors by disclosing fraudulent financial data. Because share prices are based on all publicly available information, misleading or fraudulent financial information will often cause share prices to adjust inappropriately. The independent public auditor, however, does investigate a company's records to identify any material misstatements, and although not all fraudulent acts will be identified, most major errors (be they intentional or not) are identified as part of the annual audit investigation.

One approach used by many professional analysts and investors to evaluate a company's performance *independently* of the particular GAAP used to portray that performance is the analysis of cash flows, to which we now turn.

CASH FLOW ANALYSIS REVISITED

Cash flow is probably one of the most important elements of financial statement analysis. Not only are the reported cash flows invariant to the GAAP methods used to portray accrual net income, but cash is also the only asset without which a company cannot operate. As noted in Chapter 6, U.S. companies presenting audited financial reports are required to present a statement of cash flows.[5] The focus here is the analysis of those reported cash inflows and outflows.

Exhibit 7.9 presents a partial statement of cash flows for PepsiCo for 1993 and 1994. As the exhibit reveals, PepsiCo's cash and cash equivalents increased by $103.8 million during 1994. Continuing operations provided $3,716.0 million in cash inflows, financing activities consumed $1,239.8 million, and investing activities consumed $2,361.0 million in cash.

As discussed more thoroughly in prior chapters, an important aspect of financial analysis in general, and cash flow analysis in particular, is the development of pro forma financial statements. An initial step in developing a pro forma statement of cash flows is to identify those cash inflows and outflows that can reasonably be expected to recur in the future. With this in mind, we labeled the various items in Exhibit 7.9 *R*, for recurring, or left them unlabeled if the items are not expected to be recurring. Admittedly, this decision process is speculative, involving somewhat arbitrary classifications

[5]Although the IASC recommends that a statement of cash flows be presented, it is not a required financial statement disclosure in all countries (e.g., Japan).

EXHIBIT 7.9

PepsiCo, Inc.
Partial Consolidated Statement of Cash Flow
For Years Ended December 31, 1993 and 1994
(in millions)

	1993	1994	Classification*
Net cash provided by operating activities	$ 3,134.4	$ 3,716.0	R
Cash flows — investing activities			
Acquisitions and investments in affiliates	(1,011.2)	(315.8)	
Capital spending	(1,981.6)	(2,253.2)	R
Proceeds from sales of property and equipment	72.5	55.3	R
Short-term investments, net	259.0	421.0	
Other, net	(109.4)	(268.3)	
Net cash used for investing activities	(2,770.7)	(2,361.0)	
Cash flows — financing activities			
Proceeds from issuances of long-term debt	710.8	1,285.2	R
Payments of long-term debt	(1,201.9)	(1,179.5)	R
Short-term borrowings, net	1,081.0	(310.1)	
Cash dividends paid	(461.6)	(540.2)	R
Purchases of treasury stock	(463.5)	(549.1)	
Proceeds from exercises of stock options	68.6	97.4	
Other, net	(36.7)	(43.5)	
Net cash used for financing activities	(303.3)	(1,239.8)	
Effect of exchange rate changes on cash	(3.4)	(11.4)	
Net increase in cash and cash equivalents	$ 57.0	$ 103.8	

*R = Recurring.

by the financial statement user. But reasonable assertions are possible. For example, the current cash flows from continuing operations *are* likely to be a good estimate of the next period's cash flows from continuing operations, assuming that no material changes in operations occur. Dividends, although discretionary, are considered to be sacrosanct in most firms and thus are quite likely to be paid in the future. Finally, purchases of property, plant, and equipment are usually considered to be recurring because this type of investment is considered necessary for the continued survival and growth of a company such as PepsiCo.

Using this classification approach and a few assumptions regarding next period's operations, we can generate a rudimentary assessment of PepsiCo's cash flows for 1995. For example, if we assume that similar economic conditions will be experienced in 1995 and therefore that the level of operations will remain relatively constant, one estimate of the 1995 cash flows might be as follows:

Pepsico, Inc.
1995 Pro Forma Cash Flows

Net cash flows from continuing operations	$ 3,716.0
Net cash used for investing activities*	$(2,197.9)
Net cash used by financing activities	$ (434.5)
Net increase (decrease) in cash and cash equivalents	$ 1,083.6

*Assumes no new acquisitions or equity investments.

Obviously, this type of analysis depends heavily on the stability of PepsiCo's operations and on the classification decisions made by the analyst. As a company releases new information to the public, it is useful to incorporate this new data in any pro forma analysis. In so doing, the projected cash flows are likely to be as accurate as possible given the limited access to available corporate data.

SUMMARY

Almost all kinds of information — about a company specifically or about the economy in general — are likely to have some impact on a company's stock price. This is especially true for accounting information, which is frequently used by investors as a basis to predict future company performance, and, hence, stock value. Some of the specific indicators that investors use to evaluate current performance and to predict future company performance include earnings per share, the price-earnings ratio, dividend yield, and the payout ratio.

When evaluating a company's performance, investors need to consider the effects of alternative accounting methods (for example, LIFO versus FIFO or completed contract versus percentage of completion) on the ratios that they use. Failure to consider these accounting method effects may result in a misallocation of investor resources by overpaying when purchasing a company's shares. One way to examine a company's performance independent of the GAAP used to portray its results is to analyze its cash flows. By examining the financial statements in total and by considering the various trends revealed by ratio analysis, horizontal and vertical analysis, and cash flow analysis, the financial statement user should be able to develop a well-informed assessment of a company and its potential.

NEW CONCEPTS AND TERMS

Antidilutive effect (p. 318)
Common-size statements (p. 323)
Common stock equivalent (p. 318)
Completed contract method (p. 324)
Cross-sectional analysis (p. 322)
Dividend payout ratio (p. 319)
Dividend yield (p. 319)
Earnings per share (p. 315)
Efficient market hypothesis (p. 327)
Fully diluted EPS (p. 318)
Horizontal analysis (p. 322)
Percentage of completion method (p. 324)
Price-earnings ratio (p. 319)
Primary EPS (p. 317)
Quality of earnings and financial position (p. 315)
Return to investors (p. 315)
Time-series analysis (p. 322)
Vertical analysis (p. 322)

ISSUES FOR DISCUSSION

D7.1 Point: There are too many alternative methods under GAAP — accounting should be more standardized.

Counterpoint: Multiple alternative reporting approaches are necessary under GAAP to enable companies to portray the diverse circumstances that they face.

Evaluate the two viewpoints. Which one do you agree with, and why?

D7.2 PepsiCo's financial review indicates that the company's growth strategy involves two aspects: (1) internal growth (expansion of PepsiCo's current domestic and international markets) and (2) growth by acquisition of new companies and products. For example, Footnote 5 to PepsiCo's financial statements reveals that during 1994 PepsiCo completed acquisitions valued at approximately \$396 million (\$355 million in cash plus \$41 million in assumed debt).

A historical review of the company reveals that PepsiCo has long employed a strategy of growth by acquisition. In 1989, for example, the company completed acquisitions valued at more than \$3.4 billion, involving goodwill of approximately \$3.0 billion; hence, the fair market value of the identifiable tangible net assets was only \$0.4 billion.

Why would PepsiCo pay so much for the other companies in 1989 if the fair market value of the acquired net assets was only \$0.4 billion? Did PepsiCo overpay for those acquisitions?

D7.3 In early 1990 Lockheed Corporation's common stock was trading on the New York Stock Exchange at approximately \$25 per share. NL Industries, a company that already owned about 18 percent of Lockheed's shares, made a tender offer to buy Lockheed's remaining shares at \$40 per share, or a premium of \$15 per share above Lockheed's current market price per share.

Why would NL Industries offer a premium of 60 percent for the Lockheed shares? If the stock market is efficient, does this indicate that NL overpaid for the Lockheed shares?

D7.4 Identify at least three limitations of annual reports as a source of information about a company's profitability.

D7.5 Obtain a copy of any corporation's annual report to stockholders and consider the following questions:

a. What are the three most significant pieces of information you observe about the company's income statement?

b. What are the three most significant pieces of information you observe about the company's balance sheet?

c. How well did the company do in the most recent year?

d. Was the company better off at the end of the most recent year as compared with the preceding year?

e. How much was the company worth at the end of the most recent year?

f. Compare the company's book value and its market value per share. Why are these values different?

g. How do you explain the difference in the company's profit or loss for the year and its change in cash?

h. How do these five basic concepts affect the financial statements presented in the company's annual report?
(1) Business entity.
(2) Historical cost accounting.
(3) Use of estimates and exercise of judgment.
(4) Conservatism.
(5) Materiality.

D7.6 For what audience are a company's annual reports prepared? Do you think this audience has a good understanding of the information presented in a typical annual report? Explain.

D7.7 The text suggests that an analyst should learn as much as possible about a company and its environment.

a. Why?

b. To what sources should the analyst go?

c. Can you cite any specific instances in which knowledge of PepsiCo and its environment contributed to your understanding of PepsiCo's 1994 figures?

D7.8 It is often asserted that the return-on-investment ratio is open to many operationalizations.

a. For purposes of calculating return on investment, what are the pros and cons for measuring investment as the following? Which one do you prefer? Why?
(1) Total assets.
(2) Total assets plus accumulated depreciation on fixed assets.
(3) Total noncurrent assets.
(4) Total assets less current liabilities.
(5) The fair market value of total assets.

b. For purposes of calculating return on investment, what are the pros and cons for measuring return as the following? Which one do you prefer? Why?
(1) Net income plus interest and taxes.
(2) Net income exclusive of extraordinary items.
(3) Operating net income.
(4) Net income adjusted to show depreciation and cost of goods sold on a fair market value basis.
(5) Net income.

D7.9 In computing inventory turnover, which of the following do you prefer and why?

a. Cost of goods sold stated at LIFO should be divided by average inventory stated at LIFO.

b. Cost of goods sold stated at LIFO should be divided by average inventory stated at FIFO.

c. Cost of goods sold stated at FIFO should be divided by average inventory stated at FIFO.

d. Cost of goods sold stated at FIFO should be divided by average inventory stated at LIFO.

D7.10

a. If the numerator in computing earnings per share is subject to all the limitations of the income statement, how does one account for the concept being so widely quoted?

b. When earnings per share is coupled with market value per share to get the price-earnings ratio, also widely quoted, is the admonition to handle with care appropriate? If so, how so? If not, why not?

D7.11 In a comparison of reported earnings and shareholders' equity using U.S. and home-country GAAP, the following results were obtained:

	U.S. GAAP		Home-Country GAAP	
	Net Income	Shareholders' Equity	Net Income	Shareholders' Equity
SmithKline Beecham (U.K.) (pounds, millions)	474	4,113	638	743
Volvo (Sweden) (kronor, millions)	816	29,494	682	33,864

Required:

What generalizations would you draw from this data with respect to (1) U.S. versus U.K. GAAP and (2) U.S. versus Swedish GAAP?

D7.12 A survey of the reported performance of eight Japanese electronics companies revealed an average profit margin (that is, net income/net sales) of 6.31 percent using Japanese GAAP and an average price-earnings ratio of 41.4. Using U.S. GAAP, these same eight companies reported an average profit margin of 9.03 percent and an average price-earnings multiple of 26.33.

Required:

a. Based on the above data, what generalizations would you draw about the reported earnings and price-earnings ratios of U.S. companies (using U.S. GAAP) versus comparable Japanese companies (using Japanese GAAP)?

b. How should an efficient worldwide equity market respond to differences in accepted accounting practice between countries?

PROBLEMS: PART A

P7.1 Financial analysis: the income statement. Presented here are the consolidated statements of income for Coca-Cola Enterprises, Inc. Evaluate Coca-Cola's operations using whatever analyses (such as ratio analysis, trend analysis, vertical and horizontal analysis) you believe are appropriate.

Coca-Cola Enterprises, Inc.
Consolidated Statements of Income
(in thousands except per share data)

	Fiscal Year		
	19X5	**19X4**	**19X3**
Net operating revenues	**$4,034,043**	$3,881,947	$3,874,445
Cost of sales	**2,359,267**	2,313,032	2,268,038
Gross profit	**1,674,776**	1,568,915	1,606,407
Selling, general, and administrative expenses	**1,339,928**	1,258,848	1,225,238
Provision for restructuring	**9,300**	—	27,000
Operating income	**325,548**	310,067	354,169
Nonoperating income (deductions):			
Interest income	**6,566**	6,564	8,505
Interest expense	**(206,648)**	(200,163)	(210,936)
Other income (deductions) — net	**(519)**	10,463	12,183
Gain on sale of operations	**59,300**	11,000	103,800
Income before income taxes	**184,247**	137,931	267,721
Provision for income taxes	**90,834**	66,207	115,120
Net income	**93,413**	71,724	152,601
Preferred stock dividend requirements	**16,265**	18,217	9,882
Net income available to common shareholders	**$ 77,148**	$ 53,507	$ 142,719
Average common shares outstanding	**119,217**	129,768	138,755
Net income per common share	**$ 0.65**	$ 0.41	$ 1.03

P7.2 Financial analysis: the balance sheet. Presented next are the consolidated balance sheets for Coca-Cola Enterprises, Inc. Evaluate Coca-Cola's financial condition using whatever analyses (such as ratio analysis, trend analysis, vertical and horizontal analysis) you believe are appropriate. (Use the consolidated statement of income from P7.1 if necessary.)

Coca-Cola Enterprises, Inc.
Consolidated Balance Sheets
(In thousands except share data)

	December 28, 19X5	December 29, 19X4
Assets		
Current		
Cash and cash equivalents, at cost (approximates market)	$ 507	$ 9,674
Trade accounts receivable, less allowances of $18,754 and $13,472, respectively	296,822	297,098
Inventories	128,450	127,880
Prepaid expenses and other assets	69,562	58,735
Total current assets	495,341	493,387
Investments and other long-term assets	105,637	73,286
Property, plant, and equipment		
Land	157,008	129,591
Buildings and improvements	453,100	427,206
Machinery and equipment	1,302,938	1,243,969
Containers	37,238	34,830
	1,950,284	1,835,596
Less allowances for depreciation	723,856	665,999
	1,226,428	1,169,597
Construction in progress	146,319	116,748
	1,372,747	1,286,345
Goodwill and other intangible assets	3,046,871	2,878,928
	$5,020,596	$4,731,946
Liabilities and Shareholders' Equity		
Current		
Accounts payable and accrued expenses	$ 456,765	$ 395,069
Accounts payable to The Coca-Cola Company	21,396	51,657
Loans and notes payable and current maturities of long-term debt	576,630	549,396
Total current liabilities	1,054,791	996,122
Long-term debt	1,960,164	1,755,626
Deferred income taxes	335,008	266,086
Other long-term obligations	44,154	33,975
Shareholders' equity		
Preferred stock, $1 par value Authorized — 100,000,000 shares; Issued and outstanding — 2,500 shares, at aggregate liquidation preference	250,000	250,000
Common stock, $1 par value Authorized — 500,000,000 shares; Issued — 140,471,081 shares and 140,363,166 shares, respectively	140,471	140,363
Paid-in capital	1,262,755	1,262,288
Reinvested earnings	382,243	311,198
Common stock in treasury, at cost 25,636,358 shares and 17,317,010 shares, respectively	(408,990)	(283,712)
	1,626,479	1,680,137
	$5,020,596	$4,731,946

P7.3 Financial analysis: the statement of cash flows. Using the financial statements presented in P7.1 and P7.2, prepare a consolidated statement of cash flows for Coca-Cola Enterprises, Inc., as of fiscal year-end 19X5. Using this statement, identify the major sources and uses of cash by the company. How would you evaluate the company's overall cash position?

P7.4 Financial analysis by line of business. Review the business segments data for PepsiCo presented in Chapter 1. Using the financial analysis techniques discussed in Chapter 7, compare PepsiCo's three business segments (soft drinks, snack foods, and restaurants).

Required:

a. Which segment would you advise PepsiCo to emphasize, and why?

b. Is your recommendation the same for both domestic and international operations?

P7.5 Calculating earnings per share. Edna Lake, Inc., reported the following income data for 1995:

Income before extraordinary items	$174,000
Extraordinary loss (net of income taxes*)	(15,000)
Net income	$159,000

*Effective tax rate = 30 percent.

Throughout 1995 the company had 60,000 shares of common stock outstanding. The stock had traded at an average price of $25 and closed on December 31 at $30 per share. The company also had the following securities outstanding during all of 1995:

Common stock options for the purchase of 8,000 shares at a price of $20 per share.

10 percent convertible bonds, with a face value of $190,000. The bonds had been sold for $200,000 and yielded 9.4 percent when the average Aa corporate bond yield was 15 percent. The bonds were convertible into 7,600 shares.

9.2 percent convertible bonds, with a face value of $250,000. The bonds had been sold for $237,500 and yielded 9.7 percent when the average Aa corporate bond yield was 14 percent. The bonds were convertible into 10,000 shares.

Required:

a. Using the above data, calculate the basic EPS, the primary EPS, and the fully diluted EPS for Edna Lake, Inc., for 1995.

b. Which of the three EPS numbers most accurately reflects the company's actual performance during 1995?

P7.6 Calculating earnings per share. Assume that during 1995 FHAS Enterprises has the following securities outstanding:

1. 250,000 shares of common stock with an average market price of $25 per share.

2. Options granted to executives to purchase 4,000 shares of common stock during the next three years at a price of $20 per share.

3. Zero coupon convertible debentures with a maturity value of $10 million, which had been sold at a yield of 12 percent when the Aa corporate bond rate was 14.5 percent. Each $1,000 face value bond is convertible into 15 shares of common stock.

4. Convertible preferred stock, which had been sold at its par value of $100 to yield 9.5 percent. The preferred stock is convertible into 3 shares of common and 3,000 shares are outstanding.

During 1995, FHAS Enterprises earned $3.2 million after taxes. (Assume that taxes are calculated at 33 percent.)

Required:

Calculate the basic, primary, and fully diluted earnings per share for the company.

P7.7 Alternative GAAP: completed contract versus percentage of completion. Thunderbird Construction Company (TCC) was employed to construct a new office facility in downtown Phoenix, Arizona. The three-year project is projected to cost $100 million to complete and is expected to produce gross revenues of $150 million during the three-year period.

In anticipation of the preparation of financial reports covering the project, TCC's controller collected the following financial data (in millions) relating to the project:

	(in millions)		
	1993	1994	1995
Construction costs incurred	$400	$300	$325
Estimated costs to complete	600	350	—
Progress billings	500	500	500
Collections on billings	—	450	900
Administrative expense	25	25	25

Required:

a. Using the above data, prepare income statements for the company under (1) the completed contract method and (2) the percentage of completion method for each of the three years.

b. Which set of results do you believe most accurately depicts the performance of the company?

PROBLEMS: PART B*

P7.8 Restating financial statements: inventories.† Presented below are the condensed financial statements for Scott Furniture as of December 31, 1994, and 1995. In the company's 1995 annual report, the following statement appeared:

> If first-in, first-out had been in use, inventories would have been $1,960 million, $1,654 million, and $1,388 million higher than reported at December 31, 1995, 1994, and 1993, respectively.

Scott had used the LIFO method since 1960 for both tax and financial reporting purposes.

Required:

a. Assume a tax rate of 35 percent and that Scott had adopted the FIFO method (rather than LIFO) in 1960 and used FIFO through 1995. Restate Scott's balance sheets as of year-end 1994 and 1995 to reflect the use of FIFO.

b. By how much would Scott's net income change in 1994 and 1995 if FIFO were used instead of LIFO?

c. Calculate the following ratios for Scott for 1994 and 1995 under both LIFO and FIFO:
(1) Current ratio.
(2) Inventory turnover.
(3) Average number of days' inventory on hand.
(4) Total debt-to-equity ratio.

d. Under which method do the ratios look best?

*Some instructors may wish to return to Chapter 7 after completing coverage of Chapters 8-16. The problems in Part B are designed for use in those situations.

†P7.8, P7.9, and P7.10 are based on "A What If Exercise,"

Scott Furniture
Condensed Balance Sheets
As of December 31, 1995 and 1994
(in millions)

	December 31, 1995	December 31, 1994
Assets		
Cash and cash equivalents	$ 104	$ 147
Receivables	912	693
Inventories	1,750	1,670
Land	81	66
Building and equipment (net)	2,928	2,572
Long-term investments	103	85
Other assets and goodwill	220	146
Liabilities and Owners' Equity		
Payables and accruals	$1,067	$ 790
Income tax payable	198	133
Notes payable	430	404
Deferred income tax	23	(24)
Long-term debt (total)	948	1,011
Total	$2,666	$2,314
Owners' Equity		
Common Stock	$ 180	$ 177
Retained earnings	3,252	2,888
Total	$6,098	$5,379

Scott Furniture
Condensed Statement of Income
For the Years Ending December 31, 1995 and 1994
(in millions)

	1995	1994
Sales	$8,598	$7,613
Cost of goods sold	6,957*	6,172
Other expenses (net)	844	715
Income taxes	232	234
Total expenses	8,033	7,121
Income	$ 565	$ 492
Note:		
Depreciation for year	$ 370	$ 312
Dividends	$ 201	$ 182

*This figure includes depreciation allocable to cost of goods sold.

P7.9 Restating financial statements: depreciation. Scott Furniture's 1995 annual report included the following statement:

> Depreciation is computed principally using accelerated methods . . . for both income tax and financial reporting purposes. . . . If the straight-line method had always been in use, "Buildings, machinery, and equipment — net" would have been $504 million, $430 million, and $370 million higher than reported at December 31, 1995, 1994, and 1993, respectively, and depreciation expense for 1995, 1994, and 1993 would have been, respectively, $74 million, $60 million, and $48 million less.

Required:

a. Using the condensed financial statements presented in P7.8 and assuming a 35 percent tax rate, restate Scott's balance sheets for 1994 and 1995 to reflect the use of straight-line (rather than accelerated) depreciation. Assume that the straight-line method is used for financial reporting purposes and that accelerated depreciation is used for tax purposes.

b. By how much would Scott's net income change in 1994 and 1995 as a consequence of using the straight-line method?

c. Calculate the following ratios for Scott in 1994 and 1995 under both depreciation approaches:
(1) Return on sales.
(2) Return on total assets.
(3) Noncurrent asset turnover.
(4) Total asset turnover.

d. Under which method do the ratios look best?

P7.10 Restating financial statements: pooling versus purchase accounting. In 1975 Scott Furniture acquired the net assets of Erin Corporation by issuing 1,891,678 shares of Scott Furniture stock to the shareholders of Erin. Scott accounted for this transaction as a pooling-of-interests and, accordingly, included in its balance sheet only $32 million (the book value of Erin's net assets in 1975). The transaction was recorded on Scott's books as follows:

Dr. Net Assets (A)	(inc.) $32.0 million	
Cr. Capital Stock (OE)		(inc.) $ 3.0 million
Cr. Retained Earnings (OE)		(inc.) 29.0 million

At the time of the acquisition, Scott's capital stock was trading on the over-the-counter market at about $50 per share.

Assume that instead of a stock exchange, Scott had sold its shares for $95 million and had used the proceeds to buy Erin's net assets. Assume that the transaction was accounted for as a purchase and that the fair market value of Erin's identifiable net assets equals $32 million.

Required:

a. Restate Scott's 1994 and 1995 financial statements to reflect the use of purchase accounting rather than pooling-of-interests accounting.

b. By how much would Scott's net income in 1994 and 1995 change?

c. Calculate the following ratios for Scott in 1994 and 1995 under both purchase accounting and pooling-of-interests accounting:
(1) Total debt-to-total assets.
(2) Book value per share. (Assume that 86.5 million shares are outstanding.)
(3) Earnings per share.
(4) Return on equity.

d. Under which method do the ratios look best?

P7.11 Alternative GAAP: LIFO versus FIFO. The following information was taken from the 19X5 financial statements of General Electric Company, a major conglomerate with significant product lines in both industrial and consumer markets:

Inventories are valued on a last-in, first-out basis and carry the following balances (in millions) at December 31:

	19X5	19X4
Ending inventory	$3,158	$3,029

If FIFO had been used to value the inventories, they would have been $2,152 million higher than reported at December 31, 19X5 ($2,266 million higher at year-end 19X4). During 19X5, net reductions in inventory levels resulted in liquidations of LIFO bases of $114 million, and in 19X4, $163 million.

Required:

Presented following are the condensed financial statements of General Electric Company. Using this information, answer the following questions:

a. If GE had used FIFO instead of LIFO in all prior years, how would the company's 19X4 and 19X5 financial statements differ? (Ignore any effects on income taxes.)

b. Compare the income tax consequences of GE's use of LIFO rather than FIFO in 19X5.

c. Estimate the total tax savings that GE has received in all prior years as a consequence of using LIFO rather than FIFO. Assume a tax rate of 33 percent.

d. Calculate the following ratios for 19X5 for GE under both FIFO and LIFO:
(1) Current ratio.
(2) Quick ratio.
(3) Inventory turnover.
(4) Average number of days' inventory on hand.

General Electric Company
Statement of Financial Position
For the Year Ending December 31
(in millions)

	19X5	19X4
Assets:		
Quick assets	$ 7,754	$ 7,327
Inventories	3,158	3,029
Total current assets	$10,912	$10,356
Noncurrent assets	12,376	11,259
Total assets	$23,288	$21,615
Equities:		
Current liabilities	$ 8,688	$ 8,153
Long-term liabilities	3,162	3,099
Total liabilities	$11,850	$11,252
Owners' equity	11,438	10,363
Total equities	$23,288	$21,615

General Electric Company
Statement of Earnings
For the Years Ended December 31, 19X5, 19X4, and 19X3
(in millions)

	19X5	19X4	19X3
Sales of products and services rendered	$ 26,797	$ 26,500	$ 27,240
Cost of goods sold	(24,248)	(24,095)	(24,793)
Other income and expenses	450	312	167
Provision for income taxes	(975)	(900)	(962)
Net earnings	$ 2,024	$ 1,817	$ 1,652

P7.12 Alternative GAAP: leases. MCI is a telecommunications company that leases a substantial quantity of its noncurrent assets. For example, as of March 31, 19X3, MCI had leased more than one-third of its total noncurrent assets, and the obligations associated with those leases represented nearly 50 percent of the company's total long-term debt.

Presented below are condensed balance sheets for MCI as of March 31, 19X3. The company's footnotes revealed the following additional data:

Depreciation of noncurrent assets is calculated using straight-line depreciation, assuming an average useful life of 10 years, unless the lease life is shorter. (No salvage value is assumed.) The value of capitalized leases included in noncurrent assets was as follows (in thousands):

	March 31	
	19X3	19X2
Total capitalized leases	$227,582	$250,451

At March 31, 19X3, the aggregate minimum rental commitments under noncancelable leases were as follows:

Years Ending March 31,	Capital Leases	Other Leases	Total
19X4	$ 57,876,000	$ 16,610,000	$ 74,486,000
19X5	50,753,000	15,443,000	66,196,000
19X6	42,721,000	14,441,000	57,162,000
19X7	35,620,000	12,669,000	48,289,000
19X8	24,410,000	10,580,000	34,990,000
19X9 and thereafter	17,213,000	49,220,000	66,433,000
Minimum lease payments	228,593,000	$118,963,000	$347,556,000
Less — Amount representing interest	47,388,000		
Present value of future lease payments	$181,205,000		

Interest rates on capital lease obligations on a weighted-average basis approximate 12%.

Required:

Assuming that all "other leases" should be capitalized on the balance sheet, restate MCI's balance sheet as of March 31, 19X3. Calculate the following ratios both before and after restatement:

a. Long-term debt-to-owners' equity.

b. Total debt-to-total assets.

Comment on how the company's bond ratings might be affected following the capitalization of all "other leases."

MCI Communications Corporation
Balance Sheet
As of March 31, 19X3 and 19X2
(in thousands)

	19X3	19X2
Assets:		
Current assets	$228,428	$ 48,946
Noncurrent assets	631,970	417,946
Total assets	$860,398	$466,892
Equities:		
Current liabilities	$185,540	$ 73,729
Deferred income taxes	34,058	2,409
Long-term debt	400,018	242,707
Owners' equity	240,782	148,047
Total liabilities and owners' equity	$860,398	$466,892

P7.13 Alternative GAAP: LIFO versus FIFO. Presented below are the balance sheets and income statement of Phoenix Imports, Inc., as of December 31, 1995. In the company's annual report, the following statement appeared: "Inventories are valued on a FIFO basis. If LIFO had been used, inventories would have been valued at $889,000 at January 1, 1995, and at $1,270,000 at December 31, 1995."

Required:

Assume a tax rate of 50 percent and that Phoenix Imports had also been using FIFO for tax purposes. Restate the company's balance sheet and income statement for 1995 to reflect the use of LIFO instead of FIFO. (Would you recommend such a method change for income tax purposes also?) Calculate the following ratios for 1995 under both LIFO and FIFO:

a. Current ratio.

b. Inventory turnover.

c. Average number of days' inventory on hand.

d. Total debt-to-equity ratio.

Which method do you think Phoenix Imports should use, and why?

Phoenix Imports
Balance Sheet
As of December 31, 1995

Assets			Equities	
Current assets:			Current liabilities:	
Cash		$ 436,000	Accounts payable	$ 820,000
Trade receivables (net of allowance for uncollectible accounts)		828,000	Accrued expenses payable	80,000
Inventories		1,720,000	Total current liabilities	900,000
Prepaid expenses		30,000		
Total current assets		3,014,000		
Noncurrent assets:			Noncurrent liabilities:	
Property, plant, and equipment	$3,940,000		Notes payable	2,320,000
Less: Accumulated depreciation	(1,360,000)		Deferred federal income taxes	800,000
		2,580,000	Total Liabilities	4,020,000
Land		560,000	Owners' equity:	
Deferred research and development cost		1,150,000	Common stock, $1 par	2,000,000
			Retained earnings	1,284,000
Total assets		$7,304,000	Total equities	$7,304,000

Phoenix Imports
Income Statement
For the Year Ended December 31, 1995

Sales revenue		$4,950,000
Less: Cost of sales		
Beginning inventory	$1,205,000	
Cost of production	3,665,000	
Goods available for sale	4,870,000	
Less: Ending inventory	1,720,000	
		(3,150,000)
Gross margin		1,800,000
Less: Research and development expenses	350,000	
Licensing fees	100,000	
Selling and administrative expenses	400,000	
		(850,000)
Net income before taxes		950,000
Less: Income taxes	475,000	
Investment and research tax credits	(60,000)	
		(415,000)
Net income after taxes		$ 535,000

P7.14 Alternative GAAP: depreciation. Phoenix Imports' 1995 annual report included the following statement: "Property, plant, and equipment are depreciated on a straight-line method. If an accelerated method had been used, the depreciation expense for 1995 would have been $230,000 higher, and the year-end balance in the accumulated depreciation account $450,000 greater."

Required:

a. Using the financial statements presented in P7.13 and assuming a 50 percent tax rate, restate Phoenix Imports' financial statements for 1995 to reflect the use of accelerated depreciation rather than the straight-line method. Phoenix Imports reports all depreciation as a component of cost of goods sold. (What recommendation would you make for income tax purposes?)

b. Calculate the following ratios for 1995 under both accelerated and straight-line depreciation:
(1) Return on sales.
(2) Return on total assets.
(3) Noncurrent asset turnover.
(4) Total asset turnover.

c. Which method do you think Phoenix Imports should use, and why?

P7.15 Alternative GAAP: capitalizing versus expensing R&D. Phoenix Imports' 1995 annual report included the following statement:

> The research and development expense for 1995 represented one-half of the actual R&D expenditure for 1995; the remaining balance had been capitalized. The company's policy is to begin amortization of these capitalized costs once a commercially productive asset has been developed. To date, no productive assets have resulted from the research program represented by the currently capitalized R&D costs.

Required:

a. Using the financial statements presented in P7.13 and assuming a 50 percent tax rate, restate Phoenix Imports' financial statements for 1995 to reflect the full current expensing of all R&D costs. (What recommendation would you make for income tax purposes?)

b. Calculate the following ratios for 1995 under the old and new policies regarding expensing R&D expenditures:
(1) Return on sales.
(2) Return on total assets.
(3) Noncurrent asset turnover.
(4) Total asset turnover.

c. Which method do you think Phoenix Imports should adopt, and why?

P7.16 International accounting. To facilitate the orderly flow of capital among and between international capital markets, the International Accounting Standards Committee (IASC) is attempting to harmonize the reporting practices followed in different countries. To understand why harmonization is important, it is first necessary to understand the financial effects produced by differing disclosure and reporting practices.

Throughout the world, the accounting for inventories is usually limited to such well-known methods as LIFO (last-in, first-out), FIFO (first-in, first-out), and weighted average. Occasionally methods such as NIFO (next-in, first-out) or HIFO (highest-price-in, first-out) may be encountered. In the United States, LIFO accounting is the inventory method preferred by most publicly held companies.

Because FIFO is the most prevalent inventory method permitted internationally (probably because FIFO depicts the actual flow of inventory in the vast majority of settings), the IASC recently proposed to eliminate the use of LIFO accounting. (Note: in the end, the IASC retained LIFO as an acceptable method.)

Scenario: The 1990 financial statements of the Goodyear Tire & Rubber Company report that the company's inventories are valued using the LIFO method. The footnotes also reveal:

> The total costs of inventories on hand at year-end 1990, 1989, and 1988, were $1,346.0 million, $1,642.0 million, and $1,702.0 million, respectively. The costs of

> inventories using the LIFO method were less than the approximate current costs of inventories by $335.4 million at December 31, 1990, $330.6 million at December 31, 1989, and $306.6 million at December 31, 1988.

Goodyear's financial statements also disclosed that income before taxes was $55.9 million, $470.9 million, and $490.0 million in 1990, 1989, and 1988, respectively.

Required:

Assume that the IASC's proposal to eliminate the use of LIFO had been implemented. How much net income after tax (assume a 50 percent tax rate) would Goodyear have disclosed in 1989 and 1990? If this proposal were also implemented by the Internal Revenue Service, how would this affect the income taxes paid by Goodyear in 1989 and 1990? By how much?

CASES

C7.1 Ratio analysis: ratios tell a story.* Financial results vary among companies for a number of reasons. One reason for the variation can be traced to the characteristics of the industries in which the companies work. Some industries require large investments in property, plant, and equipment; others require very little. In some industries, the product-pricing structure allows companies to earn significant profits per sales dollar; in other industries, the product-pricing structure forces a much lower profit margin. In most low-margin industries, however, companies often experience a relatively high volume of product throughput in their businesses. A number of industries are also characterized by lenient credit terms; others sell for cash only.

A second reason for some of the variation in financial results among companies is the result of management policy. Some companies reduce their manufacturing capacity to more closely match their immediate sales prospects; others carry excess capacity to prepare for future expansion. Another policy-related difference is that some companies finance their assets with borrowed funds, but others avoid that leverage and finance their assets with equity.

Of course, one other reason for some of the variation in reported results among companies is the differing competencies of management. Given the same industry characteristics and the same management policies, different companies report different financial results simply because their management staff perform differently.

These differences in industry characteristics, in company policies, and in management performance are reflected in the financial statements and can be highlighted through the use of financial ratios.

Following are balance sheets, in percentage form, and selected ratios computed from fiscal 1993 balance sheets and income statements for 14 companies from the following industries:

1. Vehicle leasing/rental company.
2. Automobile manufacturer.
3. Chemical company.
4. Commercial bank.
5. Computer manufacturer.
6. Discount general merchandise store chain.
7. Electric utility.
8. Fast-food chain.

9. Wholesale food distributor.
10. Railroad company.
11. Supermarket chain.
12. Textile manufacturer.
13. Advertising agency.
14. Software development company.

These ratios were developed based on the following formulae:

1. Return on sales (ROS) = $\frac{\text{Net income before extraordinary items}}{\text{Net sales}}$

2. Asset turnover = $\frac{\text{Net sales}}{\text{Average total assets}}$

3. Return on assets (ROA) = $\frac{\text{Net income}}{\text{Average total assets}}$

   or = ROS × Asset turnover

4. Financial leverage = $\frac{\text{Liabilities + Owners' equity}}{\text{Owners' equity}}$

   or = $\frac{\text{Total assets}}{\text{Owners' equity}}$

5. Return on equity (ROE) = $\frac{\text{Net income}}{\text{Average total owners' equity}}$

   or = ROA × Financial leverage

6. Long-term debt to capital = $\frac{\text{LT debt}}{\text{LT debt + Owners' equity}}$

7. Current ratio = $\frac{\text{Total current assets}}{\text{Total current liabilities}}$

8. Inventory turnover = $\frac{\text{Cost of goods sold}}{\text{Average inventory}}$

9. Receivables collection = $\frac{\text{Average accounts receivable}}{\text{Net sales/365 days}}$

10. Depreciation as a percentage of average gross PP&E = $\frac{\text{Depreciation}}{\text{Average gross PP\&E}}$

Required:

a. Study the common size balance sheet profiles and the financial ratios listed for each of the 14 companies as presented on the next two pages. Your first assignment is to match each column in the exhibit with one of the industries listed previously. Be prepared to give the reasons for your pairings and identify those pieces of data that seem to contradict the pairings you have made.

b. Your second assignment is to identify those companies that are in similar industries (there are a number of comparables, although none are exact duplicates) but that report different results because they may have adopted different management policies. Be prepared to identify the different policies and the effect they have had. Also comment on the reason(s) the company may have had for adopting those policies.

Ratios Tell a Story

Fiscal Year End	1 6/93	2 12/93	3 12/93	4 12/93	5 6/93	6 12/93	7 12/93
% of total assets:							
Cash and equivalents	60.2	0.1	28.9	0.5	5.2	2.5	11.3
Receivables	8.9	9.7	67.0	22.2	7.9	6.9	2.7
Inventory	3.3	29.8	N/A	28.4	50.5	0.7	2.2
Other current assets	2.5	4.3	0.0	4.7	4.9	4.8	1.8
Total current assets	74.9	43.9	95.9	55.8	68.5	14.9	17.9
Net plant and equipment	22.8	20.5	1.7	39.7	28.4	83.0	71.0
Financial service assets	N/A	N/A	N/A	N/A	N/A	N/A	N/A
Goodwill and other intangibles	0.0	22.8	0.3	0.0	0.0	0.0	0.0
Other assets	2.3	12.9	2.0	4.5	3.0	2.1	11.1
Total assets	100.0%	100.0%	100.0%	100.0%	100.0%	100.0%	100.0%
Notes payable	0.0	0.0	11.0	0.0	3.9	1.4	0.0
Accounts payable	6.3	22.0	76.3	8.3	23.9	6.2	6.9
Accrued expenses	2.3	0.0	0.3	8.9	10.1	0.0	6.4
Income taxes	3.3	0.0	0.0	0.0	0.9	1.3	0.3
Other current liabilities	2.9	7.6	0.0	3.1	3.3	2.5	0.8
Total current liabilities	14.8	29.6	87.5	20.4	42.1	11.4	14.4
Long-term debt	0.0	21.5	2.1	39.8	0.0	14.1	20.1
Financial services liabilities	N/A	N/A	N/A	N/A	N/A	N/A	N/A
Deferred tax liability	0.0	0.9	0.0	0.0	0.0	20.2	4.1
Other liabilities	0.0	13.8	1.6	13.7	10.1	10.4	1.1
Total liabilities	14.8	65.8	91.2	73.9	52.2	56.1	39.7
Minority interest	N/A	N/A	N/A	N/A	N/A	N/A	N/A
Translation adjustment and other	N/A	(0.4)	N/A	(16.8)	N/A	N/A	(0.1)
Preferred stock	N/A	N/A	0.3	0.0	N/A	N/A	N/A
Capital stock and paid-in-excess	28.5	18.7	7.2	30.4	3.6	5.3	17.2
Retained earnings	56.7	15.9	1.3	12.6	44.1	38.8	43.2
Treasury stock	N/A	N/A	N/A	N/A	N/A	(0.2)	(0.0)
Total owners' equity	85.2	34.2	8.8	26.1	47.8	43.9	60.3
Total liabilities and equity	100.0%	100.0%	100.0%	100.0%	100.0%	100.0%	100.0%
Return on sales revenue	25.39%	0.29%	15.51%	1.50%	2.18%	12.30%	6.08%
Asset turnover	0.99	4.22	0.09	1.35	5.25	0.42	1.31
Return on assets	25.05%	1.21%	1.40%	2.03%	11.46%	5.22%	7.95%
Leverage	1.17	2.93	11.36	3.83	2.09	2.28	1.66
Return on owners' equity	29.40%	3.54%	15.93%	7.76%	24.00%	11.87%	13.19%
Long-term debt/total capital	0.00	38.61%	19.48%	60.38%	0.00	24.28%	25.03%
Current ratio	5.06	1.48	1.10	2.74	1.63	1.31	1.25
Inventory turnover	4.98	13.35	N/A	3.98	8.05	10.94	47.73
Days receivable O/S	33	8	2,705	60	5	60	8
Depreciation % PPE	14.00%	9.70%	13.80%	5.00%	8.00%	3.20%	6.30%

*Excluding financial services activity.

Ratios Tell a Story

8 (Auto) 12/93	9 12/93	10 (Film Serv) 12/93	11 1/93	12 (Bank) 12/93	13 (Electric) 9/93	14 12/93
2.0	3.3	6.2	0.1	4.9	1.9	11.2
4.1	10.1	22.3	2.6	1.6	6.3	53.2
1.1	9.9	9.2	45.1	2.8	1.1	N/A
1.5	6.7	1.1	1.9	2.0	2.2	5.4
8.6	30.0	38.8	49.6	11.3	11.5	69.8
63.5	33.6	22.9	47.6	11.6	85.5	7.6
N/A	N/A	37.5	N/A	69.0	N/A	N/A
0.0	17.4	0.0	0.0	1.3	0.0	17.1
27.8	19.0	0.8	2.8	6.8	3.0	5.5
100.0%	100.0%	100.0%	100.0%	100.0%	100.0%	100.0%
3.1	3.4	0.0	7.7	0.0	0.0	5.1
1.7	5.8	4.2	18.8	4.4	0.7	49.8
0.5	6.7	14.2	5.1	5.4	4.9	6.4
1.9	1.0	0.0	0.9	0.1	0.0	2.7
6.1	5.2	4.4	0.3	1.5	0.0	0.0
13.3	22.2	22.8	32.8	11.4	5.6	64.0
30.2	23.1	7.7	23.6	3.6	54.8	4.1
N/A	N/A	34.0	N/A	62.9	N/A	N/A
19.5	1.5	2.2	1.0	0.5	10.7	0.0
6.1	12.1	9.1	0.0	13.0	1.2	11.8
69.2	58.9	75.7	57.4	91.4	72.3	79.9
N/A	9.6	N/A	N/A	N/A	N/A	0.5
N/A	(1.2)	2.0	N/A	(0.5)	N/A	(4.9)
3.0	0.5	1.3	N/A	0.7	N/A	N/A
12.6	4.6	8.6	3.7	2.8	8.4	12.0
15.3	33.9	12.3	38.9	5.6	19.4	19.9
N/A	(6.3)	N/A	N/A	N/A	N/A	(7.3)
30.8	31.6	24.3	42.6	8.6	27.8	20.1
100.0%	100.0%	100.0%	100.0%	100.0%	100.0%	100.0%
8.17%	3.57%	–12.74%	3.60%	2.76%	7.44%	6.98%
0.37	0.71	0.77	2.70	0.46	0.44	0.63
2.99%	2.52%	–9.85%	9.70%	1.27%	3.89%	4.30%
3.24	3.17	4.11	2.35	12.77	3.60	5.09
9.69%	8.00%	–40.47%	22.77%	16.24%	14.03%	22.20%
49.49%	42.30%	23.94%	35.61%	31.26%	66.39%	17.31%
0.65	1.35	1.23	1.51	0.99	2.06	1.09
16.43	4.83	5.17	4.77	15.38	N/A	N/A
41	52	48	3	13	52	310
5.10%	7.20%	10.00%	8.00%	8.30%	11.80%	11.60%

C7.2 Accrual versus cash-basis financial statements: Lone Star Real Estate Corporation. Lone Star Real Estate Corporation is a land development and sales company located in Dallas, Texas. The company's audited financial statements for the year ended December 31, 1994, and unaudited financial statements for the first six months of 1995 are presented following. A review of the statements reveals that, among other things, the company is profitable, has a substantial net worth, and more than $14 million in liquid assets on hand.

In July 1995, however, the company approached its primary lender and requested a renegotiation of the terms of its outstanding notes payable. The president of Lone Star threatened that if the terms of the debt contracts were not suitably restructured, the company would be forced to file for voluntary bankruptcy.

Required:

Analyze the financial statements of Lone Star Real Estate Corporation to determine whether the company has a valid basis for requesting the debt restructuring. Be able to substantiate your position.

Lone Star Real Estate Corporation
Consolidated Balance Sheet
(in thousands)

	June 30, 1995 (Unaudited)	December 31, 1994
Assets		
Cash and investments	$ 14,313	$ 29,877
Accounts receivable (net):		
Other	890	519
Affiliates	1,949	1,693
Notes receivable (net):		
Other	2,545	855
Affiliates (including interest and fees)	44,038	18,592
Inventories of land	519,197	500,115
Rental real estate	13,244	13,438
Other assets	7,233	6,938
Total	$603,411	$572,027
Liabilities and Stockholders' Equity		
Notes payable:		
Other	$418,634	$408,008
Affiliates	1,413	2,447
Accounts payable and accrued liabilities:		
Other	20,902	23,808
Affiliates	6	9
Total liabilities	440,955	434,272
Stockholders' equity:		
Common stock	100	100
Additional paid-in capital	30,475	30,475
Retained earnings	131,881	107,180
Total stockholders' equity	162,456	137,755
Total	$603,411	$572,027

Lone Star Real Estate Corporation
Consolidated Statement of Income (Unaudited)
(in thousands)

	For the Six Months Ended June 30,	
	1995	**1994**
Revenues		
Sales of land	$ 13,819	$ 7,194
Management services income	356	215
Development services income	4,080	8,785
Interest and fee income	10,635	8,743
Total	28,890	24,937
Costs and expenses		
Bad debts expense (reversal)	(9,219)	6,640
Cost of land sold	5,592	3,325
Development services expense	3,712	9,145
Interest expense	22,707	19,569
Interest capitalized	(22,707)	(19,569)
Selling, general, and administrative expenses	4,104	3,216
Total	4,189	22,326
Income (loss) before income taxes	24,701	2,611
Charge equivalent to income taxes	11,362	1,201
Benefit from parent company	(11,362)	(1,201)
Net income (loss)	$ 24,701	$ 2,611

C7.3 Pro forma financial statements: Hofstedt Oil & Gas Company. The venture capital division of a major U.S. financial institution has elected to fund an investment in an oil and gas exploration and production company that will operate both onshore and offshore in Texas and Louisiana. The initial financing commitment from the bank is for $40 million.

The company's strategic plan calls for an aggressive drilling program to be carried out during 1996. Hofstedt Oil & Gas estimates that it will drill 50 wells at an average cost of $800,000 per well and that 30 of those wells will yield aggregate crude oil reserves of approximately 10 million barrels. The remaining 20 wells are expected to be dry or commercially unproductive. These forecasts were based on the expert opinion of geologists familiar with the properties and were confirmed by petroleum engineers employed directly by the bank.

The company's production plan calls for a maximum exploitation effort to earn the highest financial return. Tom Hofstedt, president of the company, developed the following production scenario:

Year	Number of Barrels to Be Produced	Estimated Selling Price per Barrel	Estimated Lifting Cost Per Barrel
1996	1,000,000	$30	$5
1997	1,500,000	30	5
1998	1,500,000	35	6
1999	2,500,000	40	7
2000	3,500,000	45	8

Hofstedt Oil & Gas is very concerned about the impact of this operation on its financial statements and on the company's stock price. Consequently, any available accounting policy choices loom as very important in the overall evaluation of the investment. As a result, Hofstedt sent a terse memo to the company's controller, the closing line of which stated, "Prepare pro forma statements showing the alternative accounting effects on cash flow, income before tax, and financial position if we elect to use the successful efforts method or the full-cost method."

Required:

For purposes of pro forma statement preparation, assume that the $40 million loan agreement will be repaid as follows: (1) $10 million principal repayment per year to be paid on December 31 beginning on December 31, 1997, and (2) interest payments of 10 percent per year on the balance of the loan outstanding as of the beginning of the year. Ignore income taxes and all other operations. Based on your pro forma cash flows, income statements, and balance sheets for the period 1996 through 2000, what accounting method (successful efforts or full cost) recommendation would you make to Hofstedt, and why?

C7.4 Pro forma financial statements: Brown's Fishing Reel Company.* Mike Brown, a machinist employed at General Gyro, Inc., liked to spend his free time fishing at local lakes. Over the years, he had developed several innovations in fishing equipment. Brown added the new fishing gear to his own equipment and occasionally made copies for friends to use.

As a consequence of the slowdown in defense-related products during the recession of 1991, Brown was among 1,500 employees laid off by General Gyro. He was troubled about the loss of income, as well as the fact that no one could predict when business might increase enough to put the laid-off employees back to work. Brown and his wife discussed the problems caused by the potential cash shortage faced by their family. Her current position as a dental technician would help, but they had become accustomed to spending their combined incomes. Living on just one income would result in many adjustments.

One of Brown's friends suggested the possibility of manufacturing fishing equipment as a full-time occupation. The Browns thought this could be the solution to their long-range income problem, although it would involve risk and sacrifices in the short run. The Browns had savings they had invested for several years. The total they believed they could use to start the new business was $70,000. When Brown's fishing friends heard about his plans, several of them said that they would like to provide part of the equity for the new venture. After talking it over with everyone who was interested in the investment, Brown knew he could count on total start-up equity capital of $170,000.

One of the investors, Tony Bartell, offered to help Brown develop plans for the first year of operations. The two decided to make conservative estimates of figures that would permit Bartell to construct pro forma financial statements. Meanwhile, Brown demonstrated his improved fishing reel to three national sporting goods retailers and two large catalog marketing organizations. With their initial orders and promises of repeat business, he felt confident that first-quarter sales would be $112,000 and that the quarterly growth rate in sales would be 5 percent.

Brown intended to watch operating costs carefully, doing much of the machining himself and hiring other laid-off General Gyro workers on a part-time contract basis. As sales became more predictable, permanent full-time employees would be hired. To reduce risk, Mike wanted costs to be as variable with sales as possible during the first year. He estimated that cost of goods sold could be held to 62 percent of sales.

To provide stable production of machined parts and finished reels, inventories would be maintained so that quarter-ending inventories would equal 95 percent of the next quarter's cost of goods sold. Twenty-five percent of inventory purchases would be paid in cash at the time of purchase; the remaining 75 percent would be paid in the following quarter.

Most sales would be credit sales, with 85 percent of sales dollars received at the end of the quarter following a sale. Small firms would pay cash for the reels shipped, accounting for the remaining 15 percent of collections.

*This case was prepared by Paul D. Cretien, Baylor University. Reprinted with permission.

Brown thought that the company should have a cash balance of $5,000 at all times to take care of regular transactions and possible emergency needs. If the projected cash balance fell below the $5,000 target balance at the end of any quarter, the company would use short-term bank credit to cover the deficit. On the other hand, if the pro forma statement indicated a cash surplus, the excess cash would be invested in short-term marketable securities. The company's bank assured Brown and Bartell that excess cash above $5,000 would be placed in money market deposits paying an annual interest rate of 5 percent. The interest on the securities would be received in the quarter following their investment.

Because of lower real estate prices and the numerous properties held by the Resolution Trust Corporation in the local business area, Brown found a building that could be purchased for the bargain price of $120,000. He estimated that $25,000 would be needed for equipment and building improvements to begin production. He decided to estimate total depreciation expense equal to 1.5 percent per month on the combined cost of the building and equipment.

Brown and Bartell approached the banker with a request for a term loan to assist in purchasing the building and equipment. After hearing their plans and viewing the projected figures, the bank officer agreed to provide a $60,000 term loan; principal and interest would be paid in equal quarterly installments over a five-year period. The annual interest rate on the term loan would be 8 percent. The banker suggested that the remaining credit should be in the form of a credit line, with interest paid in the quarter following the borrowing. The amount borrowed on the short-term working capital loan would depend on the financing needed to balance the company's statements at the end of each quarter. The annual rate of interest on short-term borrowing was 6.5 percent. Interest would be paid in the quarter following the one in which the credit was used.

In addition to the cost of goods sold, Brown estimated that the company's administrative and selling costs would be $15,000 per quarter. Start-up expenses, including travel and marketing costs already incurred, would total $6,900 by the time the company started business on January 1, 1992. Other operating expenses were expected to be 5 percent of sales; the company's average tax rate would be 30 percent.

After summarizing their estimated figures, Brown started to work on the statements he wanted to analyze. These included a beginning balance sheet (that is, the company's financial condition before starting production on December 31, 1991), pro forma quarterly balance sheets and income statements for the first four quarters and for the year ending December 31, 1992, and a pro forma cash flow statement (showing cash from operating activities, investing activities, and financing activities) for each quarter and for the year.

Brown and Bartell realized that the financial projections could determine whether or not Brown's Fishing Reel Company would be a successful venture. The company's investors had agreed that unless the business was expected to return at least 25 percent on stockholders' equity, the risk would be higher than justified by the potential returns.

Brown made several additional assumptions before constructing the pro forma statements: (1) beginning inventory at the end of Quarter 0 will be financed entirely by equity and bank loans; (2) financing with trade credit begins in Quarter 1; (3) income taxes will be calculated and paid at the end of each quarter; (4) any operating losses will be carried forward to offset future taxable income; (5) marketable securities and short-term bank loans are used as "plug" figures to balance the balance sheet, thus one of these accounts should be zero each quarter while the other contains a positive total; and (6) Brown's salary as a manager is included in administrative and selling expense. Otherwise, all stockholder profits are left to accumulate in retained earnings.

Required:

a. Complete the pro forma statements suggested by Brown and Bartell. A summary of the assumptions that will form the basis of the projected results is presented below. Also presented is a loan amortization table showing the payment schedule for the $60,000 term loan.

b. Comment on the expected profitability of the proposed venture. In view of the potential risks, explain why the investors should decide to (1) go ahead with the project or (2) cancel it.

Brown's Fishing Reel Company

Assumptions:	
Cost of goods sold (COGS) as percentage of sales	62.00%
Inventory as percentage of next month's COGS	95.00%
Percentage of merchandise orders paid in cash	25.00%
Percentage of orders paid in following quarter	75.00%
Percentage of sales that are for cash	15.00%
Credit sales as percentage of sales, paid next quarter	85.00%
Selling and administrative expenses per quarter	15,000
Other operating expense as percentage of sales	5.00%
Interest rate on long-term debt	8.00%
Interest rate on short-term debt*	6.50%
Depreciation expense as percentage of building cost	1.50%
Start-up expenses	6,900
Income tax rate	30.00%
Quarterly growth rate in sales	5.00%
Sales expected for first quarter	112,000
Building cost	120,000
Building improvements	25,000
Beginning inventory	87,250
Minimum cash balance	5,000
Owners' equity	170,000
Beginning term loan	60,000
Interest rate on marketable securities*	5.00%

*Interest on balancing accounts is received or paid in the following quarter.

Amortization Schedule: Term Loan

Term loan, initial balance	60,000
Annual interest rate	8.00%
Number of quarters to repay term loan	20
Quarterly payment	3,669

Quarter	Payment	Interest	Principal	Balance
0	—	—	—	60,000
1	3,669	1,200	2,469	57,531
2	3,669	1,151	2,519	55,012
3	3,669	1,100	2,569	52,443
4	3,669	1,049	2,621	49,822
5	3,669	996	2,673	47,149
6	3,669	943	2,726	44,423
7	3,669	888	2,781	41,642
8	3,669	833	2,837	38,805
9	3,669	776	2,893	35,912
10	3,669	718	2,951	32,961
11	3,669	659	3,010	29,951
12	3,669	599	3,070	26,880
13	3,669	538	3,132	23,748
14	3,669	475	3,194	20,554
15	3,669	411	3,258	17,296
16	3,669	346	3,323	13,972
17	3,669	279	3,390	10,582
18	3,669	212	3,458	7,124
19	3,669	142	3,527	3,597
20	3,669	72	3,597	(0)

C7.5 Common-size statements: The case of the unidentified industries.* Analyzing a company's financial statements requires an understanding of the environment in which a firm operates. Many characteristics of this environment are common to all firms in an industry and to some extent influence the financial statements.

Exhibit 1 presents condensed financial statement information for 11 U.S. firms in different industries. Balance sheet and income statement items are expressed as a percentage of total net revenues. To improve the representativeness and "resolution" of these items, they have been calculated as four-year averages instead of annual figures.

The companies represented in the exercise are in the following industries:

- Advertising agency services
- Aircraft manufacturing
- Airline
- Automobile manufacturing
- Brewing
- Computer manufacturing
- Discount retailing
- Grocery store
- Insurance underwriting
- Oil extraction
- Pharmaceutical manufacturing

Required:

Use the data in Exhibit 1 to match the companies with the industries listed above. Variations in SG&A expenses are principally due to differences in the level of advertising. Note also that CFFO stands for cash flow from operations.

*This case was prepared by Thomas I Selling.

EXHIBIT 1

Common-Size Four-Year Average Financial Statements

	1	2	3	4	5	6	7	8	9	10	11
Cash and cash equivalents	0.12	0.01	0.10	0.02	0.12	0.18	2.26	0.05	0.09	0.06	0.01
Net accounts receivable	0.07	0.06	0.20	0.20	0.27	0.73	0.14	0.09	0.12	0.16	0.00
Inventories	0.11	0.06	0.16	0.39	0.13	0.03	0.00	0.01	0.25	0.12	0.10
Total current assets	0.30	0.13	0.46	0.61	0.52	0.94	2.40	0.15	0.46	0.34	0.11
Property, plant, equipment at cost	0.41	0.98	0.28	0.37	0.58	0.24	0.47	1.01	0.59	1.60	0.22
Less: accumulated depreciation	0.19	0.32	0.10	0.14	0.16	0.12	0.19	0.40	0.20	0.79	0.08
Net property, plant, equipment	0.22	0.66	0.18	0.23	0.42	0.12	0.28	0.61	0.39	0.81	0.14
Other assets	0.09	0.14	0.05	0.05	0.01	0.17	0.12	0.15	0.10	0.07	0.49
Total Assets	0.61	0.91	0.69	0.89	0.95	1.23	2.80	0.91	0.95	1.22	0.74
Total current liabilities	0.23	0.14	0.19	0.33	0.35	0.91	1.79	0.26	0.44	0.26	0.11
Long-term debt	0.05	0.25	0.01	0.13	0.03	0.04	0.19	0.24	0.09	0.12	0.06
Other noncurrent liabilities	0.03	0.15	0.04	0.00	0.08	0.04	–0.04	0.19	0.07	0.03	0.03
Total liabilities	0.31	0.54	0.24	0.46	0.46	0.99	1.94	0.69	0.60	0.41	0.20
Owners' equity	0.30	0.38	0.47	0.43	0.49	0.23	0.86	0.22	0.35	0.81	0.54
Total Liabilities and Equity	0.61	0.92	0.71	0.89	0.95	1.22	2.80	0.91	0.95	1.22	0.74
Net Sales or Revenue	1.00	1.00	1.00	1.00	1.00	1.00	1.00	1.00	1.00	1.00	1.00
Cost of goods sold	0.81	0.60	0.61	0.78	0.36	0.58	0.74	0.78	0.75	0.83	0.79
Depreciation expense	0.01	0.05	0.05	0.01	0.05	0.04	0.01	0.07	0.05	0.02	0.01
SG&A expense	0.03	0.20	0.20	0.12	0.07	0.31	0.06	0.10	0.06	0.05	0.16
R&D expense	0.05	0.00	0.04	0.00	0.13	0.00	0.00	0.00	0.04	0.00	0.00
Interest expense	0.00	0.02	0.01	0.01	0.01	0.01	0.04	0.02	0.05	0.01	0.01
Income taxes	0.02	0.05	0.03	0.02	0.13	0.03	0.05	–0.01	0.00	0.06	0.02
Other expenses (net)	0.01	0.01	–0.02	0.02	0.19	0.01	0.04	0.08	0.00	0.01	0.00
Net Income	0.05	0.07	0.08	0.04	0.06	0.02	0.06	–0.04	0.05	0.02	0.01
CFFO/Capital Expenditures	2.11X	2.01X	2.11X	0.93X	1.94X	3.01X	52.33X	0.08X	0.86X	1.44X	3.30X

PART III

Measuring and Reporting Assets and Equities Using Generally Accepted Accounting Principles

CHAPTER 8

Trade Receivables and Marketable Securities

Your accounts receivable collection effort will be no better than the accuracy and timeliness of your accounting information.[1]

Market value accounting has been called a panacea by some and a placebo by others.[2]

Key Chapter Issues

- What are accounts receivable and marketable securities?
- At what value should these financial assets be reported on the balance sheet?
- How does the accounting for these assets affect the income statement?
- What management judgments and assumptions are necessary in order to account for these assets?
- What is "mark to market"?

[1]S. D. Popell, "Effectively Manage Receivables to Cut Costs," *Harvard Business Review,* January–February 1981, p. 49.

[2]J. T. Parks, "FASB 115: It's Back to the Future for Market Value Accounting," *Journal of Accountancy,* September 1993, p. 49.

In the previous chapters, we introduced some of the fundamental concepts involved in preparing and analyzing the three basic financial statements. In a sense, the preceding chapters attempted to demystify the process of constructing a set of financial statements. It is important, however, not to lose sight of the fact that many challenges are inherent in reporting on the financial condition and results of operations for a variety of companies that are engaged in diverse and different activities, have varied histories, and are run by managers with different ideas of how best to achieve certain results — all to the satisfaction of absentee owners who have their own agendas. In light of such circumstances, if the formulation of generally accepted accounting principles seems an imposing task, it is. We must remember that the overall objective of financial reporting is to provide useful information to decision makers. Such an objective necessitates a closer look at the various components making up those three basic financial statements so that you, the user of financial statement information, will be able to comprehend the financial story those statements tell.

Consider the fact that the assets reported on a company's balance sheet may be used in a variety of capacities to benefit the company. For example, one asset, cash, may be used to buy inventories or pay employee salaries. Inventories, another asset, may be sold to produce revenues and, hence, generate new cash inflows. Machinery and equipment may be used to produce new inventory units to sell to customers. Thus, each asset category on the balance sheet effectively serves one or more specialized functions within a company; and each has, as we will see, its own set of accounting challenges.

In this chapter we focus on the accounting for and valuing of trade receivables and marketable securities. Although these two assets differ as to their origin, they have some similar attributes. Both, for example, are **liquid assets**; i.e., they can be readily converted into cash. Both are subject to valuation adjustments for financial reporting purposes — accounts receivable are reported at their net realizable value (that is, the amount of cash flows expected to be realized when they are liquidated), and marketable securities are generally reported at fair value (that is, the amount of cash obtainable if they were sold today).

Our objective in this chapter is to learn how these assets arise, how they are accounted for, how they can be managed and utilized effectively, and how they may be analyzed. We begin with a consideration of trade receivables.

TRADE RECEIVABLES

In Chapter 6 we noted that managing accounts or trade receivables is an important component of the larger concern of managing a company's cash and cash flows. For most businesses, the extension of credit to customers is a normal part of generating sales. Credit sales, however, do not provide immediate cash inflows; indeed, they actually create some uncertainty regarding the timing and amount of expected future cash inflows. Consequently, prior to making a credit sale, management must weigh the cost of the anticipated benefit of increased sales by extending credit to customers who would normally not be willing to purchase goods on a strictly cash basis against the cost associated with the possible uncollectibility of a customer's promised payments of cash.

The accounting entry to record the receipt of a promise to be paid that is generated by a $1,000 credit sale of merchandise is:

Dr. Accounts Receivable (A)	(inc.) 1,000	
Cr. Sales (R)		(inc.) 1,000

Notice that in this transaction, even though cash is not received, the revenue is still considered to have been earned because the earnings process is assumed to be complete and is therefore recognized in the accounting period in which the sale is made.

When cash is subsequently collected on the account receivable generated by this credit sale, the following transaction is recorded:

Dr. Cash (A)	(inc.) 1,000	
Cr. Accounts Receivable (A)		(dec.) 1,000

Notice that this cash collection event does not affect the company's profitability nor does it change the level of total assets as of the recording date. The cash collection event is merely an exchange of one asset for another, and the accounting entry reflects that fact.

Management Issues

Conventional accounting practice is to use the account title Accounts Receivable or Trade Receivable only for those receivables arising from normal, recurring credit sales. From a manager's perspective, this practice permits the identification of amounts still to be collected from customers who have already received the goods purchased. Receivables generated by other events, for example by a cash advance to an employee, should not be commingled with the unremitted credit sales still reflected in the Accounts Receivable account. Separate accounts should be created for these other types of receivables to preserve the ease with which this monitoring of credit customer remittances, or lack thereof, may be done.

The primary reason that a company extends credit to customers is to increase sales. From a customer's point of view, credit purchases are preferable to cash purchases, in part because they are convenient and in part because they allow the customer to retain the use of cash for an additional period of time. From the seller's point of view, there is clearly a delay in obtaining the cash associated with having made a credit sale versus having made a cash sale. The managerial issue for the seller is whether the increase in sales as a result of offering the credit terms more than offsets the cost of granting credit. Moreover, if the Accounts Receivable balance increases during a period when credit sales are relatively stable, a manager should determine whether the increase is due to the collection department's ineffective job or due to more lenient credit terms having been offered to customers.

Besides the administrative costs associated with establishing the credit-granting and cash collection processes, two other costs are associated with extending credit to customers. There is the "time value of money"; that is, a dollar received tomorrow is not worth as much as a dollar received today. Because of this implicit cost of extending credit to customers, managers often offer discounts to credit customers to accelerate cash payments (that is, to induce credit customers to pay prior to the end of the normal credit period).

For example, consider the typical **credit sales terms** of 2/10, net/30. Translated, these terms mean that if a customer pays for a credit purchase within 10 days of being invoiced, a reduction of 2 percent in the amount due may be taken. If, on the other hand, payment is not remitted within the 10-day discount period, full payment is expected within 30 days. Thus, the key issue is whether the 2 percent discount will be seen as a sufficient inducement for a customer to pay 20 days early. In this case, the answer should be an emphatic "yes" in that the 2 percent savings, when annualized, is equivalent to an opportunity cost of 36 percent annually ($365/20 \times 0.02$). Thus, a credit customer would be well advised to borrow money from a bank, even at the usurious rate of 30 percent annually, to take advantage of a 2 percent discount offered by a seller.

Upon the taking of the discount by the credit customer, the seller would record a sales discount as follows:

Dr. Cash (A)	(inc.) 98	
Dr. Sales Discount (CR)	(inc.) 2	
Cr. Accounts Receivable (A)		(dec.) 100

The sales discount is a contra-revenue account and would be used in presenting the net sales figure in that period's income statement.

The second cost associated with extending credit to customers pertains to uncollectible receivables. Regardless of the care that managers take to investigate the creditworthiness of customers, some accounts receivable inevitably prove to be uncollectible. Knowing that such circumstances are probable in general (if management knew which specific customers would be the culprits there would be no credit sales made to them), sale prices must be set accordingly. Moreover, as will soon be discussed, sound financial reporting practices dictate that management record an expense for the estimated uncollectible amount.

Net Realizable Value and Uncollectible Accounts

From a financial reporting perspective, accounts receivable are to be reported in the balance sheet at their **net realizable value** (net collectible amount). The use of net realizable value as a valuation basis for accounts receivable stems, in part, from the fact that receivables are a current asset and financial statement users often compare the level of current assets with the level of current liabilities to assess a company's *liquidity,* or short-term default risk. Hence, to ensure that statement users obtain an accurate assessment of liquidity, receivables are valued at their net realizable or cash collectible amount.

One additional accounts receivable financial reporting concern evolves from the *matching principle*. As mentioned earlier, one of the costs of selling goods on credit is the cost involved in the likely event that not all customers will pay what they owe. Indeed, the experience of virtually all companies indicates that some customers will not pay the amounts owed. In view of this reality, the matching principle dictates that an expense for the cost of extending credit be recorded in the period in which the benefit (that is, the sales revenue) from doing credit business is recorded. Of course, if at the time of a credit sale management knew which specific customer would not pay, the credit sale would not be made. In the face of not knowing in advance which credit customer will default, and in order to achieve the matching principle and report the receivables at their net collectible amount, an *estimate* of their net realizable value that is consistent with prior experience involving customer defaults must be made. In reporting this estimated net realizable amount, the gross amount of the receivables account is reduced by establishing a contra-asset account called the **Allowance for Uncollectible Accounts.** To establish an appropriate allowance amount, managers may use one of two estimation approaches, both involving a historically based percentage: (1) a percentage of each period's credit sales or (2) a percentage of the year-end balance in accounts receivable. It is worth repeating that neither of these approaches identifies *specific* uncollectible accounts, but rather they *estimate* the dollar amount of possible uncollectible accounts.

The first approach to estimating the dollar value of uncollectible accounts is called the **percentage of credit sales** approach and it assumes that a certain proportion of a period's credit sales will never be collected. For example, if credit sales for the year are \$1 million and if 3 percent — the historical average of uncollected credit sales — is estimated to be the amount that will prove to be uncollectible, the following transaction is recorded at period-end:

Dr. Bad Debt Expense (E)	(inc.) 30,000	
Cr. Allowance for Uncollectible Accounts (CA)		(inc.) 30,000

Notice the income statement emphasis implicit in this method of estimating the net realizable value of accounts receivables: The $30,000 bad debt expense is derived from a calculation based on the period's credit sales and is thus a direct matching of expenses to related revenues. It is also important to note that a contra-asset account is used for the allowance account. The reason for this is that specific customer accounts have not yet been identified as uncollectible and therefore the Accounts Receivable account, which is an aggregation of *specific* customer receivables, cannot be reduced directly. In essence, the desired goal of reporting receivables in the balance sheet at their net realizable value is achieved by creating a contra-asset account that is netted against gross accounts receivable. For example, PepsiCo's consolidated balance sheet reveals the following presentation for accounts (and notes) receivable:

	(in millions)	
	1994	**1993**
Accounts and notes receivable, less allowance: $150.6 in 1994 and $128.3 in 1993	$2,050.9	$1,883.4

The contra-asset account serves to reduce the gross receivables amount to an estimated net collectible amount. This contra-asset account balance represents, as of a specific point in time, an amount believed to indicate the amount of outstanding customer accounts that will never be collected. Subsequently, if evidence is obtained that a specific customer account will not be collected (for example, a customer goes bankrupt), the receivables account can be directly reduced along with a similar reduction in the contra-asset account (in essence, a portion of the contra-asset account's balance is no longer needed). In summary, under the percentage-of-credit-sales method to estimate uncollectible accounts, the balance in the Allowance for Uncollectible Accounts is increased each period by an amount based on a percentage of credit sales (this amount is also the period's bad debt expense to be recorded under this method), and it is decreased by the dollar amount of specific accounts deemed uncollectible and therefore written off.

A second and perhaps more intuitively appealing implementation of the allowance method requires an **aging of the outstanding end-of-period accounts receivable.** In recognition of the fact that a large part of a given period's credit sales will already have been collected by period-end, this approach focuses only on those accounts yet to be collected. Under the aging method, outstanding accounts receivable are grouped according to the number of days they are past due. Typical "age" categories for the accounts receivable are current, 1–30 days overdue, 31–60 days overdue, 61–90 days overdue, and more than 90 days overdue. It is normally the case that as receivables become increasingly overdue, a larger percentage will prove to be uncollectible. Thus, for each of the increasingly overdue categories, a larger percentage estimate is applied to the respective receivables balance in determining an aggregate estimate of period-end uncollectible receivables.

The aging approach focuses on determining a targeted figure for the period-end balance in the allowance for uncollectible accounts, thus establishing a specific relationship between that balance and the accounts receivable balance. The difference between the targeted ending allowance for the Uncollectible Accounts balance and its existing balance is the *adjustment to be made* to the contra-asset account and is the amount recorded as that period's bad debt expense. The transaction recorded under this method is essentially the same as that shown in the percentage-of-credit-sales example, but the amounts are likely to differ.

Note that under either allowance method, specific uncollectible accounts receivable were not identified at the time of recording the bad debt expense and the increase to the contra-asset account. When a specific account receivable is finally identified as uncollectible, it is removed from the books. Under either of the allowance methods, adjusting the books to reflect this writing off of a specific account merely involves reducing the balance in the contra asset Allowance for Uncollectible Accounts and the balance in the asset Accounts Receivable. Such an entry has no income statement effect, nor does it affect the total assets, the total current assets, or the net realizable value of accounts receivable reported in the balance sheet. Indeed, the income statement and the balance sheet effects were anticipated and recognized at the time management recorded the estimate of the uncollectible accounts using either the percentage-of-credit-sales approach or the aging of outstanding receivables approach.

Under either of the allowance methods, if a specific account that has previously been removed from the books (that is, written off) subsequently turns out to be collectible, the prior entry made to reduce the receivable account and the contra-asset account is simply reversed. This transaction increases the balance in both the Accounts Receivable account and the Allowance for Uncollectible Accounts account by the amount now deemed to be collectible. As a final point, it is worth emphasizing that not only is the selection of the estimation method a managerial decision, but so are the percentage estimates that are used. For most firms, the percentage estimates of noncollectibility are based on the firm's actual historical experience and thus tend to be good indicators of future uncollectibility. It is also interesting to note that in some countries, the percentage estimates are prescribed by statute.

Comprehensive Illustration: Accounting for Receivables

As a comprehensive example of the financial reporting issues for accounts receivables posed thus far, consider the following information pertaining to United Department Stores, Inc. (UDS), for the fiscal year ending January 31, 1997. All amounts are in millions of dollars.

1. For the year, UDS had net sales of $10,512, of which $3,951 were credit sales.
2. The beginning Accounts Receivable balance as of February 1, 1996, was $1,623.5. The beginning balance in the Allowance for Uncollectible Accounts was $36.5.
3. Collections during the year were $3,953.
4. During the year, specific accounts receivable totaling $34.2 were deemed to be uncollectible and were written off (removed from the Accounts Receivable account).
5. Receivables totaling $2.0 that had been previously written off were subsequently deemed to be collectible.
6. As of January 31, 1997, the following aging schedule was prepared for UDS's accounts receivable:

	Amount
Uncollected billings on account:	
Current	$ 62.8
1 to 30 days past due	1,025.2
31 to 60 days past due	356.9
61 to 90 days past due	129.7
Longer than 90 days past due	14.7
Total accounts receivable outstanding	$1,589.3

7. In the judgment of UDS's management and based on past experiences of account collections, the following amounts were anticipated to be uncollectible:

1/4 of 1% of all current accounts:	0.0025 × 62.8	=	$ 0.16
1/2 of 1% of all accounts 1–30 days past due:	0.005 × 1,025.2	=	5.13
2.5% of all accounts 31–60 days past due:	0.025 × 356.9	=	8.92
10% of all accounts 61–90 days past due:	0.10 × 129.7	=	12.97
50% of all accounts more than 90 days old:	0.50 × 14.7	=	7.35
			$34.53

During the year, UDS would have recorded the following sales activity:

Dr. Cash (A)	(inc.) 6,561	
Dr. Accounts Receivable (A)	(inc.) 3,951	
Cr. Sales (R)		(inc.) 10,512

(In addition to the above sales entry, an entry would need to be made to adjust the Inventory and Cost of Goods Sold accounts — see Chapter 3.)

During the year, collections of the accounts receivable would be recorded as:

Dr. Cash (A)	(inc.) 3,953	
Cr. Accounts Receivable (A)		(dec.) 3,953

Next, the transactions recorded during the year to report accounts that were written off, as well as to reestablish the accounts previously written off that were later deemed to be collectible, should be recorded:

Dr. Allowance for Uncollectible Accounts (CA)	(dec.) 34.2	
Cr. Accounts Receivable (A)		(dec.) 34.2

Dr. Accounts Receivable (A)	(inc.) 2.0	
Cr. Allowance for Uncollectible Accounts (CA)		(inc.) 2.0

At year-end management must report the net realizable value of the outstanding accounts receivable. In this case UDS uses the aging method; thus, the *ending balance* in the Allowance for Uncollectible Accounts represents what management believes to be the offset to gross accounts receivables in arriving at their net realizable value. Using the balances in the aging schedule and the percentage estimates given by management, we determine that the ending balance in the contra-asset allowance account should be $34.53. Because the balance in the contra asset account after the previous two transactions were recorded is $4.3, the expense amount for uncollectible accounts for this period must be $30.23. In essence, the $30.23 (a plug figure) is the amount required to balance the contra asset allowance account to the targeted ending balance of $34.53. It is also the amount of the bad debt expense to appear on the current period's income statement. The transaction to record this would be as follows:

Dr. Bad Debt Expense (E) . . . . (inc.) 30.23
  Cr. Allowance for Uncollectible accounts (CA) . . . . (inc.) 30.23

A reconstruction of the contra asset allowance T-account is helpful in following the flow of these transactions:

Allowance for Uncollectible Accounts

Accounts written-off	34.2	Beginning balance (2/1/96)	36.5
		Restoration of previously written-off accounts	2.0
		Subtotal	4.3
		1997 bad debt expense	30.23
		Targeted ending balance (1/31/97)	34.53

If UDS had used the percentage-of-credit-sales method instead of the aging method, the recorded transactions would remain the same except for the last one involving the Bad Debt Expense account. Assuming that the percentage-of-credit-sales rate used by management was 1 percent, the estimate for uncollectible accounts would be $39.5 ($3,951 credit sales × 0.01). Recall that under the percentage-of-credit-sales approach, this amount is *not* the targeted ending balance for the allowance account but is the amount by which the allowance account is increased. Thus, in this case the year-end balance in the allowance account would become $43.8 ($39.5 + $4.3), and the period's bad debt expense would be $39.5. Take a moment to verify this.

It must be noted that a company that uses the percentage-of-credit-sales method must also carefully evaluate the resulting year-end balance in the allowance account. If that balance continues to increase from period to period, it suggests that the percentage of sales rate applied in prior periods is too high and does not reflect the company's real uncollectible accounts experience. If, on the other hand, that balance becomes negative (a debit balance), the percentage of sales rate used to estimate uncollectibles has been too low. In either event, management may decide to adjust the percentage factor to a rate more likely to result in increases to the allowance account that, over time, are similar to the amounts subsequently removed from the contra-asset account as specific receivables are found to be uncollectible.

This latter statement is true for both methods. This is so because, consistent with the matching principle, the methods attempt to match the cost of granting credit (the bad debt expense) to the period in which the benefit (the credit sale) was recorded. Thus, the increases and decreases to the contra asset allowance account indicate differences between the timing of recording an estimate for anticipated uncollectibles and the actual default of a specific account. Consequently, if the percentage factors used to estimate the future uncollectibles reflect the actual level of uncollectible accounts over a number of periods, the balance in the allowance account should achieve a steady state.

It may be helpful to visualize the operations of the two methods as presented in Exhibit 8.1. Notice that with the percentage-of-credit-sales method, the allowance account is adjusted *by* the calculated amount, whereas with the aging method, the allowance account is adjusted *to* a targeted, calculated amount.

There is one additional means to account for bad debts. The **direct write-off method** is not acceptable in the U.S. for publicly issued financial statements but is in fact the only acceptable method for tax purposes.[3] Only when evidence is available by

[3]In some countries, the direct write-off method is GAAP.

EXHIBIT 8.1

Illustration of Two Methods for Estimating Uncollectible Accounts

Panel A: Percentage-of-Credit-Sales Method

Panel B: Aging of Receivables Method

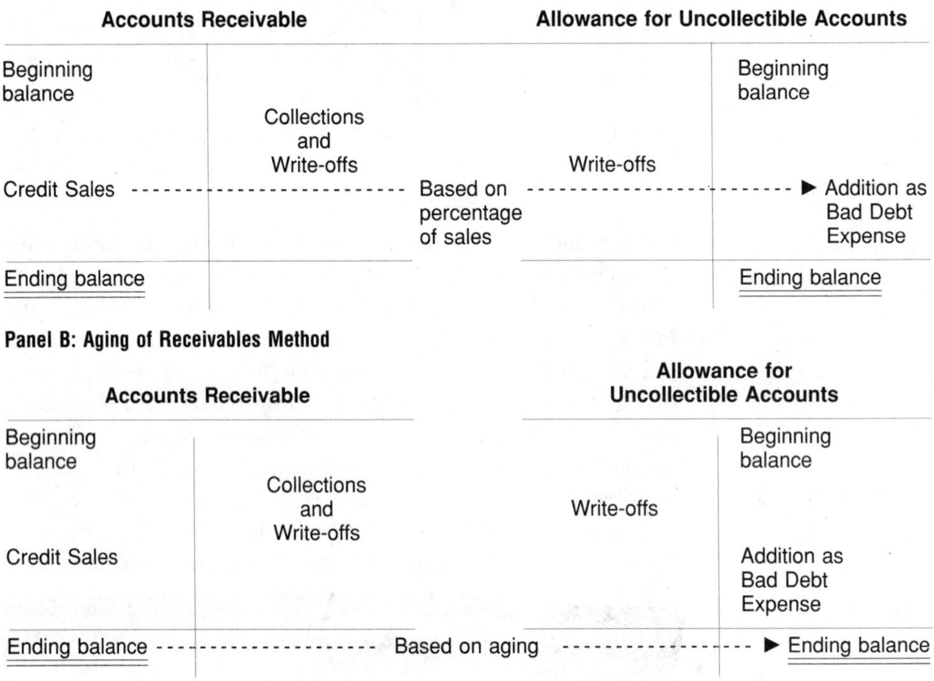

which management determines that a *specific* customer's account is uncollectible is a bad debt expense recorded and the Accounts Receivable account balance reduced to the net amount expected to be collected. Under this method, no allowance account is ever created, nor is there any attempt to record the bad debt expense amount in the period when the credit sale is made. The entry would be as follows:

Dr. Bad Debt Expense (E)	(inc.) 500	
Cr. Accounts Receivable (A)		(dec.) 500

From a managerial perspective, deciding to write off an account receivable, whether under one of the allowance methods or under the direct write-off method, can be problematic. Managers typically require convincing evidence that a specific account is indeed uncollectible before they delete it from their records. Indirect evidence such as a customer's declaration of bankruptcy or more direct evidence such as correspondence from the customer disputing the amount owed is generally considered to be sufficient evidence to warrant reducing the Accounts Receivable account. In spite of such evidence and despite recording the account write-off, management should continue to attempt to collect any outstanding amount.

more common.

EXHIBIT 8.2

Amoco Corporation
Current Assets
(in millions)

	December 31, 1994	December 31, 1993
Current assets:		
Cash	$ 166	$ 103
Marketable securities	1,623	1,114
Accounts and notes receivable (less allowances of $23 in 1994 and $65 in 1993)	3,180	3,196
Inventories	1,042	1,110
Prepaid expenses and income taxes	631	571
Total current assets	$6,642	$6,094

Trade Receivable Disclosures

As mentioned earlier, trade receivables appear in the balance sheet in the current assets section and are reported at their net realizable value. Most annual reports present the Trade Receivables account balance *net* of the Allowance for Uncollectible Accounts, with the balance in the allowance account either disclosed beside it or subtracted in the column of reported amounts. Exhibit 8.2, which presents the current asset section of Amoco Corporation's 1994 balance sheet, illustrates this typical method of receivable presentation.

Note that the reader learns from the balance sheet of the amount that Amoco management expects ultimately to collect ($3,180 million), as well as the amount of gross accounts receivable not expected to be collected ($23 million). The sum of these two figures is the amount of gross accounts receivable not yet collected as of year-end 1994.

Exhibit 8.3 illustrates another acceptable format for reporting accounts receivable. The balance sheet of Springs Industries presents only the net realizable value of receivables; the footnotes disclose the balance in the Allowance for Doubtful Accounts account. Such an approach is acceptable, although less common than the approach chosen by Amoco.

Factoring and Pledging

Most companies consider the management of accounts receivable (that is, the efforts undertaken to make sure that payments are promptly received) a normal part of their day-to-day operations. However, if a company decides that it does not want to expend the resources necessary to manage the accounts or finds itself short of cash, the company may *factor* its accounts receivable. **Factoring** is a process by which a company can convert its receivables into cash by selling them at face value less a service charge for processing the transaction and for the time value of money. Typically, the service charge for factoring receivables is very expensive, from 10 percent to as much as 50 percent or more. How much will be paid to a factor (usually a financial institution) is largely a function of whether the receivables are sold with or without recourse. **With recourse** means that the factor can return a receivable to the company and collect from

EXHIBIT 8.3

Springs Industries, Inc.
Current Assets Disclosure
(in thousands)

	December 31, 1994	January 1, 1994
Current assets:		
Cash and cash equivalents	$ 769	$ 2,790
Accounts receivable	312,739	315,834
Inventories	264,161	267,842
Other	39,335	40,073
Total current assets	$617,004	$626,539

Note 1. Summary of Significant Accounting Policies:

Accounts Receivable: Springs has a diverse customer base across a variety of industries. The company performs ongoing credit evaluations of its customers' financial condition and, generally, requires no collateral from its customers.

The reserve for doubtful accounts was approximately $7,067,000 and $6,235,000 in 1994 and 1993, respectively, which management believes is adequate to provide for expected credit losses.

the company if the receivable turns out to be unpaid as of a certain date. **Without recourse** means that the factor assumes the risk of any losses on collection. In either case, the customer owing the money may or may not be notified that a factor is the ultimate recipient of its payment. Panel A in Exhibit 8.4 typifies corporate disclosures pertaining to the factoring of accounts receivable.

Another way a firm can use accounts receivables to expedite its cash inflows is to pledge them as collateral for a short-term bank loan that may not have been obtainable without the pledge. In **pledging,** a company normally retains title to the accounts receivable but pledges that it will use the proceeds from collection of the receivables to repay the loan. Panel B in Exhibit 8.4 presents Bethlehem Steel's disclosures pertaining to the pledging of receivables and inventory against a revolving credit line.

Notes Receivable

Businesses sometimes accept promissory notes from customers in exchange for services or merchandise sold on credit or in place of an outstanding account receivable that a customer is unable to pay according to the original credit terms. A **promissory note** is a legal document that is signed by the customer (*the maker*) promising to pay to the company (*the payee*) a dollar amount (*the principal*) plus interest. The note may become due in total on a stated maturity date or in segments on several dates, at which time(s) the payee receives from the maker the stipulated amount(s) plus any accrued interest.

A promissory note, or note receivable, might be arranged by a seller if a customer is a high credit risk or needs a longer time than usual to pay. Companies often convert overdue accounts receivable to notes receivable so that the amount in question, the new payment date, and an interest charge for the extended payment time may all be formally and specifically stated and agreed to by the customer. Notes receivable classified as current assets are carried in the financial statements at net realizable value, that is, face value, less any allowance for uncollectible accounts. The evaluation process for possible uncollectible notes is exactly the same as for accounts receivable. If the

EXHIBIT 8.4

Accounts Receivables Disclosures

Panel A — Factoring

Cone Mills Corporation

On August 11, 1992, the company entered into an agreement with the subsidiary of a major financial institution, which allows the sale without recourse of up to $40 million of an undivided interest in eligible trade receivables. This agreement was amended on June 30, 1994, which made the agreement extendible to August 1997 and allowed the sale of up to $50 million in eligible trade receivables. The company acts as an agent of the purchaser by performing record keeping and collections functions of receivables sold. The cost of receivables sold by the company is the commercial paper rate plus 55 basis points calculated for the period of time from the sale of a receivable until its payment date. The resulting cost on the sale of receivables is included in cost of sales. Accounts receivable are shown net of $50 million sold at January 1, 1995, and net of $35 million sold at January 2, 1994, under this agreement. Cash flows provided by operating activities for the years 1994, 1993, and 1992 include the sale of accounts receivable of $15 million, $11 million, and $24 million, respectively.

Panel B — Pledging

Bethlehem Steel Corporation

Under the 1987 revolving credit agreement, the company may borrow a total of $500 million subject to collateral coverage requirements. On March 15, 1992, the maximum loan amount under this credit agreement will be reduced to $469 million and will continue to be reduced by $31 million on a quarterly basis over a four-year period. Accounts receivable and inventories are pledged as collateral for any borrowings and letters of credit under this credit agreement and for certain other debt obligations to participating banks. Borrowings outstanding at December 31, 1991, were $50 million and incur interest based on the prime rate, certificate of deposit rates, or LIBOR. The company pays a quarter of 1 percent per annum facility fee on the available credit and an eighth of 1 percent per annum commitment fee on the unused available credit.

notes receivables are more properly classified as noncurrent, they should be reported at the present value of the expected future cash flows. Later chapters will have more to say about such noncurrent accounts, their valuation, and the concept of present value.

Because promissory notes receivable are negotiable instruments, businesses sometimes sell or pledge notes receivable to a bank (or any other type of factor) to obtain cash prior to the due date of the note. Such transactions are similar to factoring and pledging accounts receivable in that the payee receives the face value of the note less some fee or discount.

Analyzing Trade Receivables

The level of investment a company might have in receivables at any particular time is affected by many conditions: seasonal, cyclical, or growth changes in sales; the market the company serves; the company's credit and collection policies; and inflation.

The investment in receivables is closely related to the volume of sales for the period immediately preceding a given balance sheet date. If sales during that period were low because of either seasonal or cyclical changes or declining markets, the accounts receivable balance should, all else being equal, be lower than in periods when credit sales were high.

The market a company serves also has a bearing on its receivables balance. In some markets, business cannot be conducted without using credit. Other markets, by custom, require longer or shorter credit terms than usual to facilitate commerce. For example, Wendy's Corporation requires prompt payment of a percentage of weekly sales from its franchisees, which primarily conduct business with customers on a cash basis. In the recent past, the average receivable collection period for Wendy's, Inc., was about six days. In contrast, many of the credit sales of Northrop Grumman Corporation are to the U.S. government, which relies on numerous administrative reviews before authorizing payment to its suppliers. Thus, it is not surprising that Northrop Grumman's financial statements reveal collection periods from the various segments of its government contracts (representing about 90 percent of sales) ranging from 60 days to more than two years.

A company's credit policy is an important competitive weapon. By allowing more and more potential credit customers to qualify for credit sales, a company's revenues and accounts receivable balances are likely to increase. At the same time, however, the carrying costs and potential losses from uncollectible accounts may also increase. Periods of high interest rates and periods of uncertain business conditions obviously raise the cost of carrying receivables. Thus, a company must weigh the costs of additional sales (increased interest expense and bad debts) against the benefits (increased revenues and increased cash inflows).

Inflation is another factor to be considered in managing a company's investment in receivables. During periods of inflation, the purchasing power of the dollar diminishes. Consequently, future collections of receivables represent collections of cheaper dollars. The lost purchasing power of those cheaper dollars is a cost of making credit sales. Indeed, the management of a company domiciled in a hyperinflationary economy, such as has historically been the case in Brazil, seeks to maintain minimal accounts receivable balances.

Many procedures can be used to evaluate the quality of a company's accounts receivable management. Most methods deal with ratio analysis, and the most common index is the average receivable collection period. As discussed in Chapter 4, the average collection period is computed as

$$\text{Average receivable collection period} = \frac{\text{Average accounts receivable balance}}{\text{Total net credit sales/365 days}}$$

The receivable collection period gives an approximate measure of the length of time that a company's accounts receivable have been outstanding.[4] A comparison of this measure with a company's credit terms, with the measure for other firms in the same industry, and with the figures for prior periods indicates a company's efficiency in collecting receivables and its trends in credit management.

Other receivable-related ratios may also be of interest to managers, creditors, and investors; these may include (1) the ratio of accounts receivable that are written off divided by credit sales or by total receivables and (2) the ratio of credit sales to total sales, which reveals how dependent a company is on credit sales. Ratios involving the written-off accounts receivable reveal how correct management has been in determining those customers to which to grant credit, as well as management's effectiveness in collecting those credit sales. In a similar vein, the aging schedule is a good indicator of the quality of the accounts receivables at a particular point in time. (Such information is usually not available to the public but is useful to management.) Frequent preparation of an aging schedule may be crucial to the timely management of credit.

Managers must use such analytical tools to manage their investment in accounts receivable throughout the credit cycle. This cycle, starting with the approval of a credit

[4]There are different ways to make this calculation. For example, rather than using the average accounts receivable balance, the year-end balance could be used. Another way would be to use credit sales for the fourth quarter divided by 91 days, divided into the year-end balance in accounts receivable.

sale and ending with the receipt of cash, is important to a company's continuing operations. Inattention to the details involved throughout the cycle often results in an opportunity cost because cash is needlessly tied up in accounts receivable and, in the worst case, may cause a firm to be critically short of cash.

MARKETABLE SECURITIES

As we have just seen, the management of accounts receivable involves managerial attention to collection of the promises to pay that a company has received from its customers. In contrast, the management of marketable securities principally involves the managerial concern of how best to invest a company's surplus cash until such funds are needed to support its regular operations.

Fair Value and Its Disclosure

As noted in Chapter 2, one of the long-standing cornerstones of U.S. financial reporting is the historical cost convention. In an attempt to achieve objectivity and reliability in the amounts reported for virtually all assets and liabilities, historical cost (such as purchase price paid) has traditionally been the designated reported amount. Unfortunately, historical cost values can quickly become outdated and hence of limited utility. There is, however, another attribute that could be reported — the asset's or liability's **fair value**.[5]

In a recent move toward providing more relevant information, the FASB now requires companies to disclose in their footnotes actual (or estimated if necessary) year-end market value data pertaining to financial instruments, which includes investments in marketable securities.[6] It should be obvious that as stock prices rise or fall, the historical cost of an investment in stocks becomes less relevant as an indicator of the financial wealth represented by those securities. Moreover, as interest rates climb (fall), the market value of bonds declines (rises), thus rendering the price paid for them less relevant as an indicator of their current market value. From an international perspective, it is important to note that *International Accounting Standard (IAS) No. 32* is compatible with U.S. GAAP. A typical U.S. corporate disclosure is presented in Exhibit 8.5, drawn from a recent J.C. Penney annual report. Considerable management judgment is involved in determining fair value, and companies must highlight the investments for which a fair value is not practicable to determine. Companies are also required to describe their means of determining fair value so that readers will have a sense of the reliability and subjectivity of the reported amount.

Mark-to-Market for Certain Investments in Debt and Equity Securities

In ascertaining where to invest corporate cash, managers frequently consider debt and/or equity security investments. Debt securities include such instruments as corporate bonds, government securities, and commercial paper. Equity securities include

---

[5]For our purposes, we may consider market value as synonymous with fair value. The FASB focuses on fair value because some assets and liabilities do not have active markets in which they are traded, so they do not have a "market value." The term *fair value* is used by the FASB to embrace the notion of an estimated market price for those assets and liabilities that do not have established markets for their buying and selling. An example is a share of stock in a closely held corporation.

[6]See SFAS No. 107.

EXHIBIT 8.5

J.C. Penney Company, Inc.
Fair Value Disclosures

Estimates of fair value are made at a specific point in time, based on relevant market prices and information about the financial instrument. The estimated fair values of financial instruments presented below are not necessarily indicative of the amounts the company might realize in actual market transactions. The carrying amount and fair value for the financial assets and liabilities on the consolidated balance sheet at each year-end were:

	1994		1993		1992	
(In millions)	Carrying Amount	Fair Value	Carrying Amount	Fair Value	Carrying Amount	Fair Value
Financial assets						
JCPenney Insurance fixed income securities	$ 661	$ 661	$ 670	$ 710	$ 541	$ 569
Asset-backed certificates	453	453	431	510	419	465
Other cash investments	148	148	1	1	2	1
Equity securities	97	97	80	80	29	29
Receivables, net	5,159	5,159	4,679	4,679	3,750	3,750
Cash and short-term investments	261	261	173	173	426	426
Financial liabilities						
Long-term debt (excluding capital leases)*	$3,231	$3,124	$2,802	$3,021	$3,030	$3,295
Bank deposits	702	698	581	581	538	541
Short-term debt	2,092	2,092	1,284	1,284	907	907
Current maturities of long-term debt	—	—	348	348	—	—

*The fair value of the off-balance-sheet interest rate swaps at the end of 1994, 1993, and 1992 was $(8) million, $13 million, and $4 million, respectively.

Fair values for fixed income securities, asset-backed certificates, and equity securities are based on quoted market prices. Fixed income securities and asset-backed certificates were carried at fair value on the consolidated balance sheet at year-end 1994 and were carried at amortized cost in 1993 and 1992. The company believes that the carrying value of existing customer and bank receivables is the best estimate of fair value because of their short average maturity, and bad debt losses can be reasonably estimated and have been reserved. The carrying amount for the company's cash and short-term investments, short-term debt, and current maturities of long-term debt approximate fair value due to their short maturities. The fair value for long-term debt, excluding capital leases, was determined based on the interest rate environment and the company's credit rating. The fair value of bank deposits was based on the discounted value of contractual cash flows. The fair value of interest rate swaps is estimated based on quotes from brokers and reflects the estimated amount that the company would receive or pay to terminate the contracts at the reporting date.

preferred stock, common stock, and stock options. Generally speaking, such investments are made in securities that have established, broad-based markets that render the investments quite liquid (that is, easily converted to cash) and easily valued at any point in time. For example, any issue of *The Wall Street Journal* provides market price quotes for an extensive variety of such securities.

Prior to 1975, publicly held U.S. companies reported their investments in these types of securities on a cost basis. From 1975 through 1993, publicly held U.S. companies reported their equity security investments in their balance sheets on a lower-of-cost-or-market basis (a practice still embraced by the International Accounting Standards Committee and followed in many countries including Brazil, France, Spain, and Korea), while investments in debt securities continued to be reported on a cost basis.[7] However, on December 15, 1993, U.S. GAAP again signif-

[7]For purposes of this discussion, equity investments are assumed to be passive, that is to say, at a noncontrolling and nonsignificant influence level, representing less than 20 percent ownership of the investee. Between 1975 and 1993, SFAS No. 12 governed

icantly changed the financial reporting requirements for debt and equity security investments.[8]

Consider for a moment two questions. First, what financial attribute of a debt or equity investment is most relevant to you as an interested observer of companies — a historical cost amount, an amount indicative of the lower of an investment's cost or market value, or the securities' market value? You probably selected the market value attribute as the most desirable because it can be reliably, objectively determined. Indeed, U.S. GAAP now focuses on fair values (that is, market values).

The second question to consider is, What are the possible intentions of management regarding investments in these securities? As depicted in Exhibit 8.6, the FASB assumes that limited investments in these securities manifest one of three management intents:

1. **Hold to maturity** — this intent is applicable to debt securities only, and the financial reporting practices germane to such securities are discussed in Chapter 12;
2. Actively trade the security in the near term for purposes of generating profits on short-term price differentials; and
3. Make the security available for sale when and if deemed appropriate — an intention that is less passive and less long-term than (1) but not as active or short-term as (2).

These three management investment intentions now drive the financial reporting practices for debt and equity security investments under U.S. GAAP. It is also important to observe that at its acquisition, a security must be placed in one of these three categories. Note also from Exhibit 8.6 that, except for trading securities, securities may be reported as either current or noncurrent assets, depending on the likely fruition of their intended purpose. Trading securities, by definition, are assumed to be current assets. Last, it is the hold-to-maturity, trading, and available-for-sale classifications that dictate the financial reporting of the security, not the security's designation as a current or noncurrent asset.

Trading securities. The fundamental objective of U.S. GAAP regarding investments classified as **trading securities** is that balance sheets report such investments at market value. As an example, consider the portfolio of securities portrayed in Exhibit 8.7. If a strict cost basis of reporting were followed, the investment account would be reported on the balance sheet at $75,000 as of the end of both Years 1 and 2. If, however, we assume all three securities are appropriately classified as trading securities, the investment account should be shown in the company balance sheet at $80,000 at the end of Year 1 and at $79,500 as of the end of Year 2.

More specifically, the entry to record these securities at their date of acquisition would appear as:

Dr. Trading security: ABC Corp. Bond (A)	(inc.) 20,000	
Dr. Trading security: 100 shares XT Co. Common stock (A)	(inc.) 30,000	
Dr. Trading security: 50 shares MN Inc. Preferred stock (A)	(inc.) 25,000	
Cr. Cash (A)		(dec.) 75,000

the U.S. accounting for marketable equity securities, and Accounting Research Bulletin No. 43 governed the U.S. accounting for marketable debt securities.

[8]See SFAS No. 115. It is important to note that SFAS No. 115 does not void the disclosure requirements of SFAS No. 107 that were discussed earlier.

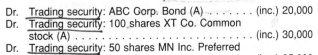

EXHIBIT 8.6

Financial Reporting of Equity and Debt Security Investments

Security	Management Intent at Date of Purchase	Balance Sheet Classification	Balance Sheet Valuation	Income Statement Effects*
Debt	Hold-to-maturity	Current asset if maturity date within one year Noncurrent asset if maturity date greater than one year	Amortized cost	• Interest income, including amortization of premium or discount • Realized gains/losses = net sales proceeds – unamortized cost
Debt or equity	Trading (actively trade in near term)	Current asset	Fair value	• Dividend income or interest income, including amortization of premium or discount • Realized gains/losses (which equal the net sales proceeds – latest balance sheet fair value) • Unrealized holding gains/losses
	Available-for-sale (securities not fitting into either of above categories)	Current asset if intent is to sell within one year Noncurrent asset if intent is to not sell within one year	Fair value; owners' equity adjusted for unrealized holding gains/losses	• Dividend income or interest income, including amortization of premium or discount • Realized gain/loss (which equal the net sales proceeds – latest balance sheet fair value ± security's owners' equity accumulated unrealized holding gain/loss balance)

*Realized gains/losses are those transaction-based gains/losses recorded at time of disposition of a security. Unrealized holding gains/losses are those gains/losses periodically recorded prior to disposition of a security.

The entry at the end of Year 1 to adjust their balance sheet amount would be as follows:

Dr. Valuation adjustment: ABC Corp. bonds (A)	(inc.) 1,000	
Dr. Valuation adjustment: XT Co. stock (A)	(inc.) 6,000	
Cr. Valuation adjustment: MN Inc. stock (A)		(dec.) 2,000
Cr. Unrealized holding gain (G)		(inc.) 5,000

And the entry at the end of Year 2 would be:

Dr. Valuation adjustment: XT Co. stock (A)	(inc.) 2,000	
Dr. Unrealized holding loss (Loss)	(inc.) 500	
Cr. Valuation adjustment: ABC Corp. bonds (A)		(dec.) 1,500
Cr. Valuation adjustment: MN Inc. stock (A)		(dec.) 1,000

From this simple example, it is important to note several things. First, the **mark-to-market** process (that is, the recording of market values) is done on an individual security

EXHIBIT 8.7

Hypothetical Portfolio of Debt and Equity Security Investment

	Year 1			Year 2		
	Recorded Cost	Market at Year-End	Gain (Loss)	Market at Beginning of Year	Market at Year-End	Gain (Loss)
ABC Corp. bond	$20,000	$21,000	$ 1,000	$21,000	$19,500	$(1,500)
XT Co. (100 shares of common stock)	30,000	36,000	6,000	36,000	38,000	2,000
MN Inc. (50 shares of preferred stock)	25,000	23,000	(2,000)	23,000	22,000	(1,000)
	$75,000	$80,000	$ 5,000	$80,000	$79,500	$ (500)

basis. This fact provides for a parallelism of market reality and the financial reporting picture painted for a specific security — reported amounts may rise (XT Co. stock), fall (MN Inc.), or rise and fall (ABC Corp.). Second, information pertaining to a security's original acquisition cost is retained by using the valuation adjustment account to capture its changes in market value. Third, for a security classified as a trading security, its yearly change in carrying value (that is, the change in reported market value) is recorded as an unrealized holding gain or loss that is then reported in that period's income statement. The rationale for this is that because such securities are regularly traded, their year-end measurement should reflect an "if sold" income statement impact.

In order to understand how to record the sale of a trading security, consider that during Year 2 the ABC Corp. bond was sold for $20,250 and the XT Co. shares were sold for $37,200. The entry to record the sale would look like this:

Dr. Cash (A)	(inc.) 57,450	
Cr. Realized gain on sale (G)		(inc.) 450
Cr. Valuation adjustment: ABC Corp. bonds (A)		(dec.) 1,000
Cr. Valuation adjustment: XT Co. shares (A)		(dec.) 6,000
Cr. Trading security: ABC Corp. bond (A)		(dec.) 20,000
Cr. Trading security: XT Co. shares (A)		(dec.) 30,000

Note that the gain on sale is reported as a "realized" gain, meaning that it was created by an actual disposition of the securities, not a year-end revaluation. Note also that the $450 realized gain is equivalent to the change in market value for the two sold securities since last revalued and not since the date of purchase. The total market gain/loss for the investment in the ABC Corp. bond and the XT Co. shares since their acquisition was $7,450 (original cost of $50,000 versus sales proceeds of $57,450). Why wasn't a realized gain of $7,450 recorded at the date of sale? The reason is that $7,000 of the gain had already been reported in Year 1's income statement, albeit as an unrealized holding gain netted against a $2,000 unrealized holding loss on MN Inc. shares.

Available-for-sale securities. Because **available-for-sale securities** are generally purchased with a more long-term intent than trading securities, the holding gains or losses highlighted by the securities' year-end balance sheet revaluation are reported not in the income statement but rather in the owners' equity (OE) section of the balance sheet as a separate line item.

Consider again the data in Exhibit 8.7 and the sales information presented in the prior section. If the securities shown in Exhibit 8.7 are classified as available for sale, the entry to record their acquisition is the same as shown earlier except for a change in designation from "trading security" to "available-for-sale security." The entry at the end of Year 1 would appear as:

Dr. Valuation adjustment: ABC Corp. bonds (A)	(inc.) 1,000	
Dr. Valuation adjustment: XT Co. stock (A)	(inc.) 6,000	
Cr. Valuation adjustment: MN Inc. stock (A)		(dec.) 2,000
Cr. Accumulated unrealized holding gain/loss (OE)		(inc.) 5,000

This entry is slightly different from the parallel entry when the securities were classified as trading securities. It is different in that the unrealized gain/loss is reflected (and will be accumulated year-to-year) in an owners' equity account; it is not reported as a yearly income statement amount. At the end of Year 2, the entry would be:

Dr. Valuation adjustment: XT Co. stock (A)	(inc.) 2,000	
Dr. Accumulated unrealized holding gain/loss (OE)	(dec.) 500	
Cr. Valuation adjustment: ABC Corp. bonds (A)		(dec.) 1,500
Cr. Valuation adjustment: MN Inc. stock (A)		(dec.) 1,000

As you may have anticipated, when a security classified as available for sale is sold, the reported *realized* gain/loss will be larger than if it had been classified as a trading security. This has to be the case because the year-to-year market revaluations of an available-for-sale security have not had any prior income statement effect, as is the case for trading securities. Consider again that during Year 2 the ABC bonds were sold for $20,250 and the XT Co. shares were sold for $37,200. Here is the entry to record their sale:

Dr. Cash (A)	(inc.) 57,450	
Dr. Accumulated unrealized holding gain/loss (OE)	(dec.) 7,000	
Cr. Valuation adjustment: ABC Corp. bonds (A)		(dec.) 1,000
Cr. Valuation adjustment: XT Co. shares (A)		(dec.) 6,000
Cr. Available-for-sale security: ABC Corp. bonds (A)		(dec.) 20,000
Cr. Available-for-sale security: XT Co. share (A)		(dec.) 30,000
Cr. Realized gain on sale of securities (G)		(inc.) 7,450

The $7,000 decrease to the OE account is to eliminate that part of the current balance in the Accumulated Unrealized Holding Gain/Loss account attributable to the sold securities. Moreover, as can be seen, the realized gain of $7,450 will be reported in the Year 2 income statement, and the gain equals the total income statement income reported when the securities were classified as trading securities; only the timing and labeling differ (all realized in Year 1 and some realized in Year 2 assuming a trading classification). Indeed, it is for these two differences that the classification of securities as trading or available for sale is important. These designations dictate the timing of an income statement effect and the amounts reported on any one income statement. It is therefore incumbent on managers to honestly acknowledge their intentions for a security and to classify it accordingly.

Reclassification of securities. We have just seen the importance of the classification of securities at the time of acquisition. Clearly, a security's classification need not be viewed as epitomizing management's intent forever. If that intent changes, the security should be reclassified at its market value. Consider the reclassification possibilities depicted in Exhibit 8.8, and in particular the four possibilities to and from the trading securities classification.

If a security is to be reclassified from the trading category it should be reported in its new classification at its market value as of the date of reclassification. There is no reversal of any previously recorded income statement unrealized holding gains/losses. Reclassifi-

EXHIBIT 8.8

Reclassifications of Investments in Debt and Equity Securities

	Reclassified from:		
Reclassified to:	Hold-to-maturity	Trading	Available-for-sale
Hold-to-maturity		A	D
Trading	B		B
Available-for-sale	C	A	

Accounting for gain/loss at reclassification date:

A = Record in income statement only the unrealized holding gain/loss arising since last valuation date.

B = Record in income statement any net unrealized holding gains/losses to date not reflected in prior income statements.

C = Record in owners' equity any net unrealized holding gains/losses to date not reflected in prior income statements.

D = The unrealized holding gain/loss already accumulated in an owners' equity account is amortized over the remaining life of the security as a yield adjustment.

cation does, however, necessitate recording in the income statement any unrealized holding gains/losses since the security's last revaluation. Consider the Exhibit 8.7 data and assume that during Year 3, the MN Inc. shares are to be reclassified from the trading to available-for-sale category. At the date of reclassification their market value is $22,750, and through the end of Year 2 $3,000 of unrealized losses have been reported in the income statement. The entry to record the reclassification looks like this:

Dr. Available-for-sale security: MN Inc. shares (A) . .	(inc.) 22,750	
Dr. Valuation adjustment: MN Inc. shares (A)	(inc.) 3,000	
Cr. Trading security: MN Inc. shares (A)		(dec.) 25,000
Cr. Unrealized holding gain on reclassification (G)		(inc.) 750

Assume the same facts except that the MN Inc. shares were classified as available-for-sale at acquisition and are now to be reclassified as trading securities. The entry to accomplish this reclassification would look like this:

Dr. Unrealized holding loss on reclassification (Loss)	(inc.) 2,250	
Dr. Trading security: MN Inc. shares (A)	(inc.) 22,750	
Dr. Valuation adjustment: MN Inc. shares (A)	(inc.) 3,000	
Cr. Available-for-sale security: MN Inc. shares (A)		(dec.) 25,000
Cr. Accumulated unrealized holding gain/losses (OE)		(inc.) 3,000

In this latter example the reclassification to a trading security prompts the recording to income of the reclassified security's net cumulative unrealized holding gains/losses since acquisition.

Permanent impairments of value. Declines in market value for held-to-maturity or available-for-sale securities that are deemed indicative of permanent value reductions should be reflected in that period's income statement.[9] Up to this point, we have only

[9]For trading securities, the normal year-end accounting valuation process is sufficient to reflect permanent impairments.

considered normal market appreciation/depreciation in a security's value. Drawing again on the Exhibit 8.7 data, assume that the XT Co. shares' market value dropped to $19,000 during Year 2 because their most profitable overseas division was appropriated by a new, hostile government in that country. The entry to reflect the decline in value as permanent would look like this:

Dr. Permanent impairment loss on XT Co. shares (Loss)	(inc.) 11,000	
Dr. Accumulated unrealized holding gains/loss (OE)	(dec.) 6,000	
Cr. Valuation adjustment: XT Co. shares (A)		(dec.) 6,000
Cr. Available-for-sale security: XT Co. Inc. shares (A)		(dec.) 11,000

In this case it is necessary to eliminate any valuation adjustment balance and accumulated owners' equity unrealized holding gains/losses pertaining to XT Co. because the asset must now be carried at a new cost figure, $19,000, not its original $30,000. The $11,000 loss is then recorded and reported in this period's income statement.

Providing informative disclosures. Earlier it was noted that U.S. GAAP has in the case of marketable securities, moved away from historical cost accounting by requiring certain financial statement adjustments for fair value. Exhibit 8.9 presents the fair value disclosures made by Chemical Banking Corporation in its 1994 annual report.

There are a variety of things of interest in Chemical's disclosure. In particular, the $546 million ($1,333 – $587) of 1994 net gross unrealized losses pertaining to Chemical's available-for-sale securities was used to decrease the asset's balance sheet carrying amount, and it also appears as a line item, net of taxes, in the owners' equity section of Chemical's 1994 balance sheet. On the other hand, the $460 million ($464 – $4) in net gross unrealized holding losses on held-to-maturity securities does not result in any balance sheet adjustments. Second, the bank discloses that the unrealized holding gains or losses stemming from fair value adjustments to its trading securities portfolio are reported in the income statement. Third, the bank reports the sales of securities in 1994 and 1993 as generating realized gains and losses reported in the income statement. Last, the aggregation of the available-for-sale and held-to-maturity securities into groupings of less than 1 year, 1 to 5 years, 6 to 10 years, and after 10 years provides an insight into the likely timing of the portfolios' liquidation. As can be seen, most of the portfolio will not mature for more than 10 years, and if Chemical were to classify its assets as current and noncurrent, the largest share of these two portfolios would be classified as noncurrent.

As you might have guessed by now, fair value disclosures tend to be most extensive for financial institutions such as banks and insurance companies. This is due to the simple fact that their stock in trade is financial instruments. For industrial and nonfinancial service companies, investments in financial instruments for noncontrolling purposes tend to be a relatively small portion of their total asset base. As such, their fair value disclosures are generally a bit less involved but are geared toward providing similar insights. Exhibit 8.10 presents such disclosures for ICN Pharmaceuticals, a company whose entire investment portfolio was classified as available for sale. Like Chemical Bank, ICN reflects its year-end tax adjusted net unrealized holding loss on that investment portfolio in stockholders' equity while carrying the investments in the asset section of the balance sheet at fair value.

It remains to be seen what change in investment behaviors, if any, will transpire as a result of the new fair value requirements. In a recent study of 74 financial institutions, Ernst & Young received the following responses to this question: Have your

EXHIBIT 8.9

Chemical Banking Corp.
Annual Report Fair Value Information

Panel A: Balance Sheet Excerpts

December 31, (in millions, except share data)	1994	1993
Assets		
Cash and due from banks	**$ 8,832**	$ 6,852
Deposits with banks	**5,649**	6,030
Federal funds sold and securities purchased under resale agreements	**12,797**	10,556
Trading assets:		
Debt and equity instruments	**11,093**	11,679
Risk management instruments	**17,709**	—
Securities:		
Held-to-maturity (market value: $8,106 and $10,288)	**8,566**	10,108
Available-for-Sale	**18,431**	15,840
Loans (net of unearned income: $460 and $477)	**78,767**	75,381
Allowance for credit losses	**(2,480)**	(3,020)
Premises and equipment	**2,134**	1,910
Due from customers on acceptances	**1,088**	1,077
Accrued interest receivable	**1,190**	1,106
Assets acquired as loan satisfactions	**210**	934
Assets held for accelerated disposition	**526**	—
Other assets	**6,911**	11,435
Total Assets	**$171,423**	$149,888
Stockholders' Equity		
Preferred stock	**1,450**	1,654
Common stock (authorized 400,000,000 shares, issued 254,009,187 shares in 1994 and 253,397,864 shares in 1993)	**254**	253
Capital surplus	**6,544**	6,553
Retained earnings	**3,263**	2,501
Net unrealized gain (loss) on securities available-for-sale, net of taxes	**(438)**	215
Treasury stock, at cost (9,497,533 shares in 1994 and 515,782 shares in 1993)	**(361)**	(12)
Total Stockholders' Equity	**10,712**	11,164
Total Liabilities and Stockholders' Equity	**$171,423**	$149,888

Panel B: Footnote excerpts

Trading Activities

Debt and equity instruments include securities, refinancing country loans, and money market and credit instruments held for trading purposes. These instruments are carried at fair value with gains and losses, including market value adjustments, reported on the income statement as trading revenue.

Held-to Maturity and Available-for-Sale Securities

Effective December 31, 1993, the corporation adopted Statement of Financial Accounting Standards No. 115, "Accounting for Certain Investments in Debt and Equity Securities" ("SFAS 115"). Securities that may be sold in response to or in anticipation of changes in interest rates and resulting prepayment risk, or other factors, are classified as available-for-sale and carried at fair value. The unrealized gains and losses on these securities are reported net of applicable taxes in a separate component of stockholders' equity. Securities that the corporation has the positive intent and ability to hold to maturity are classified as held-to-maturity and are carried at amortized cost.

The specific identification method is used to determine realized gains and losses on sales of securities, which are reported in securities gains. Individual securities are reduced through writedowns against securities gains to reflect other-than-temporary impairments in value.

EXHIBIT 8.9 continued

Held-to-Maturity Securities
The amortized cost and estimated fair value of held-to-maturity securities were as follows for the dates indicated:

December 31, 1994 (in millions)	Amortized Cost	Gross Unrealized Gains	Gross Unrealized Losses	Fair Value*
U.S. government and federal agency/corporation obligations:				
Mortgage-backed securities	$ 3,615	$ —	$209	$ 3,406
Collateralized mortgage obligations	3,871	—	237	3,634
Other, primarily U.S. Treasuries	130	—	2	128
Obligations of state and political subdivisions	118	1	—	119
Collateralized mortgage obligations†	140	1	4	137
Other, primarily asset-backed securities	692	2	12	682
Total Held-to-Maturity Securities	$ 8,566	$ 4	$464	$ 8,106

*The corporation's portfolio of securities generally consists of investment-grade securities. The fair value of actively traded securities is determined by the secondary market, while the fair value for non–actively traded securities is based on independent broker quotations.

†Collateralized mortgage obligations of private issuers generally have underlying collateral consisting of obligations of U.S. government and federal agencies and corporations.

Available-for-Sale Securities
The amortized cost and estimated fair value of available-for-sale securities at December 31 of 1994 and 1993 were as follows:

December 31, 1994 (in millions)	Amortized Cost	Gross Unrealized Gains	Gross Unrealized Losses	Fair Value*
U.S. government and federal agency/corporation obligations:				
Mortgage-backed securities	$ 8,151	$554	$ 593	$ 8,112
Collateralized mortgage obligations	354	1	28	327
Other, primarily U.S. Treasuries	6,414	8	359	6,063
Debt securities issued by foreign governments	2,736	16	134	2,618
Corporate debt securities	358	6	5	359
Collateralized mortgage obligations†	262	1	3	260
Other‡	702	1	11	692
Total Available-for-Sale Securities Carried at Fair Value §	$18,977	$587	$1,133	$18,431

*The corporation's portfolio of securities generally consists of investment-grade securities. The fair value of actively traded securities is determined by the secondary market, while the fair value for non–actively traded securities is based on independent broker quotations.

†Collateralized mortgage obligations of private issuers generally have underlying collateral consisting of obligations of U.S. government and federal agencies and corporations.

‡Comprised of all other debt, asset-backed and equity securities.

§See Note Five for loans accounted for pursuant to SFAS 115.

EXHIBIT 8.9 concluded

There were no sales of held-to-maturity securities in 1994. Cash proceeds from the sales of held-to-maturity securities during 1993 and 1992 were $152 million and $3,736 million, respectively. Cash proceeds from the sale of available-for-sale securities during 1994, 1993, and 1992 were $18,556 million, $5,352 million, and $684 million, respectively. Net gains from available-for-sale securities sold in 1994 and 1993 amounted to $66 million (gross gains of $141 million and gross losses of $75 million) and $139 million (gross gains of $178 million and gross losses of $39 million), respectively. Gross gains from held-to-maturity securities sold amounted to $3 million in 1993 (there were no losses from sales of such securities in 1993). Net gains from securities sold in 1992 were $53 million (gross gains of $140 million and gross losses of $87 million).

The amortized cost, estimated fair value, and average yield of securities at December 31, 1994, by contractual maturity are presented in the table that follows:

	Available-for-Sale Securities			Held-to-Maturity Securities		
Maturity Schedule of Securities December 31, 1994 (in millions)	**Amortized Cost**	**Fair Value**	**Average Yield***	**Amortized Cost**	**Fair Value**	**Average Yield***
Due in 1 year or less	$ 2,661	$ 2,658	6.85%	$ 194	$ 194	5.74%
Due after 1 year through 5 years	4,613	4,445	7.17	1,073	1,045	6.22
Due after 5 years through 10 years	2,371	2,665	6.67	1,450	1,386	6.68
Due after 10 years†	9,332	8,663	7.28	5,849	5,481	6.96
Total Securities	$18,977	$18,431	7.12%	$8,566	$8,106	6.80%

*The average yield is based on amortized cost balances at the end of the year. Yields are derived by dividing interest income, adjusted for amortization of premiums and accretion of discounts, by total amortized cost.

†Securities with no stated maturity are included with securities with a remaining maturity of 10 years or more. Substantially all of the corporation's mortgage-backed securities are due in 10 years or more based on contractual maturity. The weighted-average maturity of mortgage-backed securities, which reflects anticipated future prepayments based on a consensus of dealers in the market, is approximately 5 years.

investment strategies changed (or will they change) as a result of adopting the FASB's new fair value requirements?[10]

- "Our portfolio will become shorter in maturity and duration; yield will be lower, impacting profits."
- "Due to low interest rates, the impact of SFAS No. 115 on equity is positive. If interest rates rise, there will be greater reluctance to hold longer-term fixed rate [instruments]."
- "We will be reviewing the use of hedging to offset interest rate shock and its effect on our capital — currently, there is no intent to hedge in the near future."

Management Issues

As noted throughout the prior discussion, management's intent regarding its investments in financial instruments is the primary factor determining the mark-to-market accounting for those investments. In particular it should be apparent from the prior discussion that the trading versus available-for-sale classification has certain income statement implications: Holding gains/losses on trading securities are reflected in the income statement whereas those for available-for-sale securities are not. Likewise, management's reclassification and permanent impairment decisions, also have certain income statement implications. Therefore, the flexibility-inherent in each of these

[10]Ernst & Young, *A Follow-Up Survey on the Impact of SFAS 115* (New York: undated).

EXHIBIT 8.10

ICN Pharmaceuticals
Annual Report Fair Value Information

Panel A: Balance Sheet Excerpts

December 31 (in thousands except per share data)	1994	1993
Current Assets:		
Cash and cash equivalents	$ 42,376	$ 14,777
Restricted cash	1,425	—
Marketable securities (used to collateralize $10,000 note payable)	—	32,587
Receivables, net	81,951	43,277
Inventories, net	89,448	107,196
Prepaid expenses and other current assets	25,146	10,925
Total current assets	240,346	208,762
Marketable securities (used to collateralize $8,103 note payable)	33,179	—
Property, plant and equipment (at cost), net	128,623	78,718
Other assets	21,282	10,527
Goodwill and intangibles, net	18,043	4,010
	$441,473	$302,017
Stockholders' Equity:		
Common stock, $0.01 par value: 100,000 shares authorized: 28,028 and 20,101 shares issued and outstanding at December 31, 1994 and 1993, respectively	282	202
Additional capital	251,173	91,449
Retained earnings deficit	(142,946)	70,973
Foreign currency translation adjustment	(16,709)	(6,745)
Unrealized loss on marketable securities	(3,432)	—
Total stockholders' equity	$ 88,908	$155,879

Panel B: Footnote

Marketable Securities

In January 1994 the company adopted SFAS No. 115 ("Accounting for Certain Investments in Debt and Equity Securities"). This statement addresses the accounting and reporting for investments in equity securities that have readily determinable fair values and for all investments in debt securities. Those investments are to be classified as either held-to-maturity, trading securities, or available-for-sale. The company has classified its investment in corporate bond securities, with maturities ranging from 1999 to 2003, and its investment in equity securities as available-for-sale. The contractual maturity value of these corporate bond securities is approximately $33,700,000. The fair value of the company's investment in corporate bond securities is approximately $29,155,000. The fair value of these corporate bond securities is determined based on quoted market prices. Gross unrealized holding losses have been calculated on the specific identification method. Changes in market values of equity securities are reflected as unrealized gains or losses directly in stockholders' equity, as required, and accordingly have no effect on the consolidated statements of income. The adoption of SFAS No. 115 did not result in a cumulative effect adjustment in the consolidated statements of income.

management decisions presents an opportunity for the managing of net income — an unavoidable phenomenon but one that is hopefully not abused.

There is another issue imbedded in the management of an investment and/or debt portfolio of financial instruments: the level of **financial risk** assumed by having crafted a portfolio of certain instruments (such as stocks, bonds, derivatives) from certain issuers (corporate, governmental), of varying time horizons (short-term, long-term), and perhaps denominated in different currencies (such as dollars, yen, francs). What constitutes an acceptable level of financial risk for one company may be quite unacceptable to

EXHIBIT 8.11

Chemical Banking Corporation
Excerpted Risk Disclosures

Off-Balance Sheet Instruments Used in Asset/Liability Management Activities

As part of its asset/liability management activities, the Corporation may enter into interest rate futures, forwards, swaps and options contracts. Futures contracts are designated as hedges when they reduce risk and there is high correlation between the futures contract and the item being hedged, both at inception and throughout the hedge period. Interest rate forwards, swaps and options contracts are linked to specific assets or groups of similar assets, specific liabilities or groups of similar liabilities. Additionally, the Corporation uses interest rate swaps in place of cash market instruments. Asset/liability management instruments are accounted for on an accrual basis. Realized gains and losses on futures and forward contracts are deferred and amortized over the period for which the related assets or liabilities exposure is managed and are included as adjustments to interest income or interest expense. Settlements on interest rate swaps and options contracts are recognized as adjustments to income or interest expense over the lives of the agreements.

Interest rate contracts used in connection with the securities portfolio that is designated as available-for-sale are carried at fair value with gains and losses, net of applicable taxes, reported in a separate component of stockholders' equity, consistent with the reporting of unrealized gains and losses on such securities.

another and shareholders are not without their own risk preferences and perspectives that, in fact, may be congruent with or dissimilar to those of the management running the company whose stock they hold. With the intent of trying to provide a bit more insight into the type and level of risk imbedded in the financial instruments that a company has chosen to become a party to, U.S. companies are required to provide footnote disclosure pertaining to the extent, nature, and terms of the financial instruments' market risk (as well as insights into any concentrated levels of credit risk).[11] Such concerns are also addressed in the recommended disclosures put forth in IAS No. 32. Exhibit 8.11 provides the Chemical Banking Corporation's disclosures in this regard.

Analyzing Marketable Securities

The analysis of marketable securities, like that of accounts receivable, principally relates to the timing and uncertainties regarding the future cash flows represented by the investments. Because marketable securities are highly liquid, they constitute an important potential source of immediate cash inflows, thereby alleviating a company's need to borrow in the short term or to factor receivables. Thus, the larger a company's investment in marketable securities, the larger the available cash reserves at its disposal.

As noted above, investments in marketable securities are reported at their market value (unless they are classified as hold-to-maturity securities). The reporting of such a value provides a better indicator of the future cash flows likely to be realized from the securities' sale than if the securities were reported at cost or at the lower of cost or market. Moreover, the footnote disclosures depicting a company's year-to-year unrealized holding gains/losses on available-for-sale securities may be viewed as providing insights into management's astuteness of having chosen to continue to hold those securities and/or of having bought them in the first place. For example, a simple comparison of the portfolio's yearly appreciation or devaluation, in comparison to pertinent overall market indicators (such as the Dow Jones Industrials average), would indicate buy and hold decisions worse than or better than the market's average.

[11]See SFAS No. 105.

SUMMARY

Trade receivables and marketable securities are two key assets. Although not considered to be cash equivalents, they are nonetheless both readily convertible into cash. Trade receivables are evidence of a company's revenue production function. Although high receivable balances are not risky in and of themselves, the risk of noncollection of cash is inherent in all promised payments and thus should be closely monitored. Marketable securities represent the investment of cash into corporate securities. These investments are usually quite liquid to permit their easy conversion into cash when needed to support a company's operations.

NEW CONCEPTS AND TERMS

Aging of receivables (p. 360)
Allowance for uncollectible accounts (p. 359)
Available-for-sale securities (p. 373)
Credit sales terms (p. 358)
Direct write-off method (p. 363)
Factoring (p. 365)
Fair value (p. 369)
Financial risk (p. 380)
Hold-to-maturity security (p. 371)
Liquid assets (p. 357)
Mark-to market (p. 372)
Net realizable value (p. 359)
Percentage of credit sales (p. 359)
Pledging (p. 366)
Promissory note (p. 366)
Trading securities (p. 371)
With (without) recourse (p. 365)

ISSUES FOR DISCUSSION

D8.1 As a product manager, what concerns do you have regarding the company's bad debt expense and allowance for uncollectible accounts as they pertain to your accounts?

D8.2 What are the deficiencies of the direct write-off method for determining a company's periodic bad debt expense?

D8.3 What are the two basic allowance methods used to estimate a company's periodic bad debt expense, and what is the theoretical justification for each?

D8.4 Is the distinction between trade and nontrade receivables useful to the readers of financial statements? Explain.

D8.5 Should company management be concerned if revenues have remained steady but the company's accounts receivable balance has increased substantially? Why or why not? What action, if any, might they take?

D8.6 Discuss the significance of the net realizable value concept as it applies to receivables.

D8.7 Once a company writes off a specific account receivable, would you expect the company's collections effort to cease? Explain.

D8.8 Recreate the pro and con debate that most likely took place prior to the enactment of SFAS No. 115. Focus specifically on the question of retaining a strict historical cost perspective versus a lower-of-cost-or-market perspective versus a mark-to-market approach for marketable equity securities.

D8.9 Applying the mark-to-market rule to investments in available-for-sale marketable securities may result in the creation of a contra owners' equity account. One of the primary purposes served by such an account is to smooth reported net income. Discuss the pros and cons of such an objective and of such a technique for achieving that objective.

D8.10 Peruse the five latest issues of *The Wall Street Journal*, identifying two or three companies having a 52-week low in their stock prices, and report on whether such a decline in price is permanent. What issues did you focus on in making the judgment as to the permanent or temporary nature of the price?

D8.11 Might the desire for reporting a certain level of earnings have any bearing on whether certain investments in marketable securities are classified as trading, available-for-sale, or hold-to-maturity? Explain.

PROBLEMS

P8.1 Estimating bad debts expense. The trial balance of Sky Company at the end of 1996 included the following account balances:

Account	Debit	Credit
Accounts Receivable	$52,000	
Trade Notes Receivable	10,000	
Marketable Securities	20,000	
Allowance for Uncollectibles	4,000	
Sales		$600,000

The company has *not yet* recorded any bad debt expense for 1996.

Required:

Determine Sky Company's bad debt expense for 1996 assuming the following independent situations:

a. 85 percent of all sales are credit sales andhistorically, 2 percent of credit sales are never collected.

b. Use of a trade receivables aging schedule provides an estimate of uncollectible accounts of $2,000.

c. The Allowance for Uncollectible Accounts contra-asset account balance is targeted to equal 4 percent of outstanding trade receivables.

P8.2 Accounting for bad debts. Consider the following data pertaining to Noble Corp. during 1996:

1. The balance in the Allowance for Doubtful Accounts at January 1, 1996 was $550,000.
2. During 1996, Noble purged the Accounts Receivable accounts of $790,000 by a write off in that amount.
3. The company received a $60,000 check pertaining to a receivable they had written off in 1995.
4. The desired year-end balance in the Allowance for Doubtful Accounts account was $885,000.

Required:

a. Prepare the journal entries to reflect the data above assuming the following two independent situations:

(1) The allowance method for bad debts.

(2) The direct write-off method for bad debts.

b. What are the pros and cons of each method in light of the matching principle, conservatism principle, and historical cost principle?

P8.3 Valuing long-term receivables. Ken's Sub Shoppe, Inc., is a franchiser that offers for sale an exclusive franchise agreement for $30,000. Under the terms of the agreement, the franchisee will receive a variety of services associated with the construction of a Ken's Sub Shoppe, access to various product supply services, and continuing management advice and assistance once the retail unit is up and running. The contract calls for cash payments of $10,000 per year for three years.

Required:

How should Ken's Sub Shoppe, Inc., account for the sale of a franchise contract?

P8.4 Aging accounts receivables. The following data were taken from the accounts receivable records of Horner Products Company as of December 31, 1996:

Receivable Age Classification	Receivable Balances Outstanding	Probability of Noncollection
0–10 days	$200,000	1.0%
11–30 days	120,000	1.5
31–60 days	60,000	3.0
61–90 days	55,000	5.0
91–120 days	22,000	7.5
Over 120 days	4,000	10.0

A prior credit balance of $1,000 existed in the Allowance for Uncollectible Accounts account.

Required:

Determine the amount of bad debt expense to be recorded at year-end 1996 by Horner Products Company.

P8.5 Ratio analysis. Presented below are recent summary financial data for Coca-Cola Enterprises, Inc., and PepsiCo. Inc.

	Year 1	Year 2
Net sales (in millions):		
Coca-Cola Enterprises, Inc.	$ 3,882	$ 3,875
PepsiCo, Inc.	15,242	12,533
Net trade receivables (in millions):		
Coca-Cola Enterprises, Inc.	297	294
PepsiCo, Inc.	1,240	979

Required:

Using the data presented, calculate the accounts receivable turnover and average number of day's receivable collection period for each company. What is your evaluation of each company's credit management policy?

P8.6 Factoring and pledging receivables. Feed and Seed Stores, Inc., was experiencing a temporary shortage of cash. To make it through the next several weeks, the CFO was considering two options. The first was to sell some of the company's accounts receivables to a large, regional factor who agreed to buy as much as $2 million of the company's receivables without recourse at a fee of 15.5 percent of the receivables factored.

The second option was a 60-day loan of $2 million from a local bank, using the outstanding receivables as collateral for the loan. Under this agreement, Feed and Seed would receive

82 percent of the receivables assigned to the bank and would be charged 13 percent annual interest on the outstanding loan.

Required:

Which alternative is better from the company's perspective? Why? What are the entries for each transaction?

P8.7 Allowance account analysis. Selling Corporation had always estimated and booked an amount for estimated uncollectible accounts receivable on a *monthly*, 2 percent of credit sales basis. This approach continued through December 1996.

The balance in the Allowance for Doubtful Accounts account was $141,000 at January 1, 1996. During 1996, credit sales totaled $10,000,000; $90,000 of bad debts were written off; and recoveries of accounts previously written off amounted to $18,000. Selling's aging of accounts receivable was prepared for the first time as of December 31, 1996. A summary of the aging is as follows:

Month of Sale	Accounts Receivable as of December 31, 1996	Estimated Percentage Uncollectible
November–December 1996	$1,200,000	1%
July–October	700,000	12
January–June	500,000	30
Prior to January 1, 1996	220,000	80
Total receivable December 31, 1996	$2,620,000	

Based on a review of the accounts in the "Prior to January 1, 1996" aging category, receivables totaling $50,000 were written off on December 31, 1996 (these were included in the $220,000 and represent write-offs in addition to the $90,000 previously written off). In addition, for the year ended December 31, 1996, Selling wanted the Allowance for Doubtful Accounts account to be reported at the amount indicated by the year-end aging analysis of accounts receivable.

Required:

Recreate all the 1996 entries made to the allowance account. What is the December 31, 1996, allowance account balance?

P8.8 Accounting for marketable securities. Aspen Mining invests its excess idle cash in marketable equity securities. The following portfolio of stocks as of December 31, 1996, were all purchased in 1996.

	As of December 31, 1996	
	Cost	Market Value
Trading portfolio		
Nella Co.	$ 80,000	$ 72,000
Zen, Inc.	66,000	68,000
Aldon Co.	38,000	36,500
	$184,000	$176,500
Available-for-sale portfolio		
Leslie, Inc.	$ 36,000	$ 32,500
Diane Properties, Inc.	38,000	36,800
Stillfied Co.	24,000	26,000
	$ 98,000	$ 95,300

During 1997, all Zen, Inc., shares were sold. In addition, all Diane Properties, Inc., shares were transferred to the trading portfolio at a time when their market value equaled $34,000. As of December 31, 1997, the market value of the trading portfolio securities was: Nella, $82,000; Aldon, $39,000; and Diane Properties, $32,000. The remaining securities, composing the available-for-sale portfolio, had market values as of December 31, 1997 of: Leslie, $33,500 and Stillfield, $29,000.

Required:

a. Prepare all necessary *1996* entries pertaining to Aspen Mining's marketable equity security investments. You may ignore the purchase transaction.

b. Prepare all necessary *1997* entries pertaining to Aspen Mining's marketable equity security investments. You may ignore the sales transaction.

P8.9 Cost or market. Presented below is the marketable securities footnote taken from Exxon Corporation's 19X1 annual report:

	19X1	19X0
Trading investments:		
Marketable securities	$620,000,000	$908,000,000

Marketable securities are stated at market.

Marketable securities were purchased during 19X0 and at year-end were carried at market, which was $1 million less than their original cost. At year-end 19X1 marketable securities were carried at their market value, which was $5 million above original cost. There were no sales or purchases of securities during 19X1.

Required:

What aggregated entries did Exxon record at:

a. Year-end 19X0?

b. Year-end 19X1?

P8.10 Analyzing marketable securities. Presented below are some marketable securities investment footnote disclosures contained in Norwest Corporation's 1994 annual report.

In millions	1994 Amortized Cost	1994 Gross Unrealized Gains	1994 Gross Unrealized Losses	1994 Fair Value	1993 Amortized Cost	1993 Gross Unrealized Gains	1993 Gross Unrealized Losses	1993 Fair Value
Available for sale:								
Investment securities:								
U.S. Treasury and federal agencies	932.4	6.3	(15.4)	923.3	1,520.5	77.2	(2.8)	1,594.9
State, municipal, and housing-tax exempt	107.1	0.3	(3.9)	103.5	96.2	3.7	(0.1)	99.8
Other	321.2	97.0	(17.4)	400.8	384.5	188.8	(7.1)	566.2
Total investment securities available for sale	1,360.7	103.6	(36.7)	1,427.6	2,001.2	269.7	(10.0)	2,260.9
Mortgage-backed securities:								
Federal agencies	12,635.2	19.1	(642.4)	12,011.9	8,889.1	227.5	(7.5)	9,109.1
Collateralized mortgage obligations	165.8	0.5	(4.0)	162.3	132.5	2.7	(0.3)	134.9
Total mortgage-backed securities available for sale	12,801.0	19.6	(646.4)	12,174.2	9,021.6	230.2	(7.8)	9,244.0
Total investment and mortgage-backed securities available for sale	14,161.7	123.2	(683.1)	13,601.8	11,022.8	499.9	(17.8)	11,504.9

Total gross realized gains and gross realized losses from the sale of securities for each of the three years ended December 31 were as follows:

In millions	1994	1993	1992
Available for sale:			
Investment securities:			
Gross realized gains	$ 28.3	24.4	2.7
Gross realized losses	(75.9)	(3.4)	—
Net gains (losses)	(47.6)	21.0	2.7
Mortgage-backed securities:			
Gross realized gains	17.1	35.6	52.9
Gross realized losses	(48.5)	7.9	(0.1)
Net gains (losses)	(31.4)	27.7	52.8
Net realized gains (losses) on investment and mortgage-backed securities available for sale	$(79.0)	48.7	55.5

Required:

a. What is meant by the terms *realized* and *unrealized gains?*

b. What figure would appear in the asset section of Norwest's December 31, 1994, balance sheet for available-for-sale financial instruments?

c. Where in the financial statements would you find Norwest's 1994 gross unrealized loss of ($683.1) and its net realized loss of ($79.0)?

P8.11 Accounting for receivables.* Suppose that Tentex Company had the following balances in certain of its accounts on December 31, 1995 (in thousands of dollars):

Trade receivables	$350.0	(debit balance)
Allowance for estimated uncollectible accounts	10.2	(credit balance)

and that transactions during 1996 were as follows (in thousands of dollars):

1. Sales on account.	$1,585.0
2. Collections on account — $1,549.4 less cash discounts of $27.4.	1,522.0
3. Sales returns (from credit sales).	8.5
4. Accounts written off as uncollectible.	5.4
5. Accounts previously written off now determined to be collectible.	0.7
6. Provision for uncollectible accounts (based on percent of credit sales).	8.0

Required:

Prepare entries for the 1996 transactions. At what figure will Tentex show

a. Net sales in its 1996 income statement?

b. Net trade receivables in its balance sheet of December 31, 1996?

P8.12 Accounting for receivables.* Moss Products, Inc., was formed in 1982. Sales have increased on the average of 5 percent per year during its first 14 years of existence, with total sales for 1996 amounting to $350,000. Since incorporation, Moss Products has used the allowance method to account for bad debts. The company's fiscal year is the calendar year.

On January 1, 1996, the company's Allowance for Uncollectible Accounts had a *right-side* balance of $4,000. During 1996 accounts totaling $3,300 were written off as uncollectible.

Required:

a. What does the January 1, 1996, credit balance of $4,000 in the Allowance for Uncollectible Accounts represent?

b. Since Moss Products wrote off $3,300 in uncollectible accounts during 1996, was the prior year's bad debts estimate overstated?

c. Prepare the entries to record

(1) The $3,300 write-off during 1996.

(2) Moss Products' 1996 bad debts expense assuming these two independent situations: (i) Experience indicates that 1 percent of total annual sales prove uncollectible, and (ii) an aging of the December 31, 1996, accounts receivable indicates that potential uncollectible accounts at year-end total $4,500.

P8.13 Credit policy review.* The president, sales manager, and credit manager of Hacket Corporation were discussing the company's present credit policy and possible changes. The sales manager argued that potential sales were being lost to the competition because of Hacket Corporation's tight restrictions on granting credit to consumers. He stated that if credit were extended to a new class of customer, this year's credit sales of $2,500,000 could be increased by at last 20 percent next year with a corresponding increase in uncollectible accounts of only $10,000 over this year's figure of $37,500. With a gross margin on sales of 25 percent, the sales manager continued, the company would certainly come out ahead.

The credit manager, however, believed that a better alternative to easier credit terms would be to accept consumer credit cards like VISA or MasterCard for charge sales. The credit manager said that he had been reading on this topic and he believed this alternative offered the chance to increase sales by 40 percent. The credit card finance charges to Hacket Corporation would amount to 4 percent of the additional sales.

At this point, the president interrupted by saying that he wasn't at all sure that increasing credit sales of any kind was a good thing. In fact, he thought that the $37,500 figure was altogether too high. He wondered whether the company should discontinue offering sales on account.

Required:

a. Determine whether Hacket Corporation would be better off under the sales manager's proposal or the credit manager's proposal.

b. Address the president's suggestion that all credit sales be abolished.

P8.14 Accounting for marketable securities. Geisler Company reports its investments in marketable equity securities at market. At December 13, 1995, its account Trading Marketable Equity Securities Investments had a balance of $52,500, and the Valuation Adjustment for Trading Marketable Equity Securities account had a credit balance of $4,100. Analysis disclosed that on December 31, 1995, the facts relating to the securities were as follows:

	Cost	Market	Allowance Required
Brice Company	$21,000	$19,000	$(2,000)
Dunstan Company	12,000	9,000	(3,000)
Wilcox Company	19,500	20,400	900
	$52,500	$48,400	$(4,100)

During 1996, Dunstan Company stock was sold for $9,100. The market price of the remaining stocks on December 31, 1996, were Brice Company, $19,900; Wilcox Company, $20,800.

Required:

a. Prepare Geisler Company's journal entry to record the sale of Dunstan Company stock.

b. Prepare any additional entries necessary for Geisler Company at December 31, 1996, to reflect the facts on the balance sheet and income statement in accordance with generally accepted accounting principles. Explain.

P8.15 Accounting for marketable securities. Brownlee Bearings Company has the following securities in its trading portfolio of marketable equity securities on December 31, 1996:

	Cost	Market
2,000 shares of Miller Motors, common	$ 68,500	$ 60,250
10,000 shares of Erving, Inc., common	257,500	257,500
1,000 shares of Magic Ltd., preferred	52,500	56,000
	$378,500	$373,750

All of the securities were purchased in 1996.

In 1997 Brownlee Bearings trading completed the following securities transactions:

- March 1. Sold 2,000 shares of Miller Motors, common, at $30 per share less fees of $1,500.
- April 1. Bought 1,000 shares of American Steel, common, at $45 per share plus fees of $1,000.
- August 1. Transferred Magic Ltd., preferred, from the trading portfolio to the available-for-sale portfolio when the stock was selling at $50 per share.

Brownlee Bearings Company trading portfolio of marketable equity securities appeared as follows on December 31, 1997:

	Cost	Market
10,000 shares of Erving, Inc., common	$257,500	$291,000
1,000 shares of American Steel, common	46,000	41,000
	$303,500	$332,000

Required:

Prepare the accounting entries for the Brownlee Bearings Company for

a. The 1996 adjusting entry.

b. The sale of Miller Motors stock.

c. The purchase of American Steel stock.

d. The portfolio transfer of Magic Ltd.

e. The 1997 adjusting entry for the trading portfolio of securities.

P8.16 Accounting for reclassified securities. Hires, Inc., purchased marketable equity securities at a cost of $350,000 on March 1, 1996. When the securities were purchased, the company intended to have the investment available for sale. Therefore, the investment was reported in the company's balance sheet for the year ended December 31, 1996 at its then-market value of $300,000.

In October 1997, when the investment had a market value of $310,000, management reclassified the investment as a trading security because the company intended to sell it shortly. The market value of the investment was $325,000 on December 31, 1997.

Required:

a. At what amount should the investment be reported on October 30, 1997, after the decision to reclassify it?

b. How should the investment in the marketable equity securities be reported in the 1997 year end balance sheet and income statement of Hires Inc.?

P8.17 Bad debt policy review. Cooper Corporation accountant provides you, the sales manager, with the following list of accounts written off this year:

Date	Customer	Amount
March 31	Smith & Robertson, Inc.	$12,000
June 30	Lanahan Associates	7,000
September 30	Cheryl's Dress Shop	9,400
December 31	Haas Corporation	8,900

Cooper Corporation adheres to the direct write off method of recording bad debt expense. The accountant likes this approach because it is consistent with the Internal Revenue Service rules for recognizing bad debts.

Cooper Corporation follows the industry norm of extending sales credit on a 30-day basis. Sales for this year total $2,100,000. A recent summer intern's analysis indicated that bad debt losses historically were about 2 percent of sales.

Required:

a. Do you agree with Cooper Corporation's use of the direct write off method? Why?

b. If Cooper were to use the percentage of credit sales allowance method for recognizing bad debt expense, net income for this year would change by how much?

P8.18 Accounting for receivables. Prior to closing the books, the trial balance for Smith Consulting Company shows the following balances:

	Dr.	Cr.
Accounts Receivable	$99,000	
Allowance for Doubtful Accounts	4,600	
Sales		$410,000
Sales Returns and Allowances	5,200	

Required:

Using the data provided, prepare the accounting entries to record each of the following independent cases:

a. The company seeks to keep the Allowance for Doubtful Accounts account balance at 3 percent of gross accounts receivable.

b. To obtain a more timely influx of cash, Smith factors $16,000 of accounts receivable with Dallas Credit Corp. The factoring charge is 12 percent of the receivables factored.

c. To close the deal on a $55,000 loan, Smith assigns $64,000 of accounts receivable to Ace Banking. The finance charge is 6 percent of the loan.

P8.19 Financial statement disclosure: marketable securities.

a. Tub Factory Corporation invested its excess cash in some "hot" stocks during 1996. As of December 31, 1996, the portfolio of trading marketable equity securities consisted of the following common stocks:

		Per Share	
Security	**Quantity**	**Cost**	**Market**
Holden, Inc.	1,000 shares	$14	$19
Coates Corp.	3,000 shares	27	21
Carey Marine	2,000 shares	36	31

What information should be reported in Tub Factory's December 31, 1996, balance sheet relative to these investments?

b. On December 31, 1997, Tub Factory's portfolio of trading marketable equity securities consisted of the following common stocks:

Security	Quantity	Per Share Cost	Per Share Market
Holden, Inc.	1,000 shares	$14	$21
Holden, Inc.	2,000 shares	20	21
Lakeshore Company	1,000 shares	17	14
Carey Marine	2,000 shares	36	20

During 1997 Tub Factory sold 3,000 shares of Coates Corp. at a loss of $10,000 and purchased 2,000 more shares of Holden, Inc., and 1,000 shares of Lakeshore Company.

(1) What information should be reported in Tub Factory's December 31, 1997, balance sheet?

(2) What information should be reported to reflect the data in Tub Factory's 1997 income statement?

c. On December 31, 1998, Tub Factory's portfolio of trading marketable equity securities consisted of the following common stocks:

Security	Quantity	Per Share Cost	Per Share Market
Carey Marine	2,000 shares	$36	$47
Lakeshore Company	500 shares	17	15

During 1998 Tub Factory sold 3,000 shares of Holden, Inc., at a gain of $12,000 and 500 shares of Lakeshore Company at a loss of $2,300.

(1) What information should be reported in Tub Factory's December 31, 1998, balance sheet?

(2) What information should be reported to reflect the above in Tub Factory's 1998 income statement?

P8.20 Accounting for receivables. Due to the nature of its clientele, Holt Company has significant amounts of accounts receivable outstanding at any given time. Holt uses a commonly accepted allowance method to estimate bad debt expense. During the year, some specific overseas accounts were written off as uncollectible, and some that were previously written off were collected.

Besides its regular accounts receivable, Holt also has some interest-bearing notes receivable outstanding with a few of its more troublesome clients. The face amount of these notes plus interest, is due at maturity. The notes were signed on August 1, 1994, and are due on July 31, 1996.

Required:

a. How should Holt Company account for the collection of the accounts previously written off?

b. How should Holt Company report the effects of the notes receivable in its 1995 balance sheet and income statement? Explain.

P8.21 Estimating bad debts. Bolt Company's allowance for doubtful accounts had a credit balance of $10,000 at December 31, 1995. On a monthly basis during the year, for quick and ready reference purposes, Bolt accrues bad debt expense at 4 percent of credit sales. During 1996 Bolt's credit sales amounted to $1,500,000, and uncollectible accounts totaling $44,000 were judged worthless and thus were written off. The year-end aging of accounts receivable indicated that a $40,000 allowance for doubtful accounts balance was desirable at December 31, 1996.

Required:

What should Bolt's 1996 bad debt expense be? Explain.

P8.22 Accounting for receivables. Delta Company had the following information relating to its accounts receivable at December 31, 1995, and for the year ended December 31, 1996:

Accounts receivable at 12/31/95	$2,000,000
Allowance for uncollectible receivables at 12/31/95	120,000
Credit sales for 1996	10,600,000
Collections from customers during 1996	9,300,000
Accounts written off during 1996	140,000
Estimated uncollectible receivables per aging of receivables at 12/31/96	220,000

Required:

a. What is Delta's December 31, 1996, allowance for doubtful accounts balance?

b. What is Delta's December 31, 1996, gross accounts receivable balance?

CASES

C8.1 Accounting for bad debts: Omni Products Division. The following two scenarios should be analyzed independently.

Scenario A: The period-end analysis model. The manager of Omni Products Division, Harry Smith, was quite satisfied with all of his section leaders and had developed a high level of trust in their day-to-day decisions. Still, he insisted that he be involved in the critical, long-range judgments. For example, his accounting and control section was efficient and largely trouble-free. However, he carefully monitored the sensitive areas, including the status of collections on accounts receivable, the follow-up on slow-paying customers, and the reasonableness of the ongoing provision for estimated bad debt losses.

Smith's monitoring effort was complicated by the fact that Omni's average sale was less than $1,000 and that the division carried more than 10,000 open customer accounts. He found it difficult to put his hands around the situation because of the amount of detail in the file. To help him monitor the receivables–collections–bad debt situation, he had engaged a consultant some years ago to establish a statistical sampling system. Under the system, the Omni computer section produced a special report each quarter that analyzed the accounts receivable balances based on the dates of the unpaid invoices. This aging report was useful to Smith, helping him identify trends in the status of the receivables.

One of Smith's accounting people tracked a sample of accounts from each aging category and determined which of those sampled accounts were ultimately uncollectible. Based on a simple formula developed by the consultant, the clerk used those findings to calculate a factor for each aging category that would predict what proportion of those accounts would ultimately be uncollectible. The accounting clerk tested the results of the current studies against the numbers developed by the original study and always found that the original numbers were quite valid:

For Every Dollar in the Aging Category	Amount That Will Prove to Be Uncollectible
Current (0–30 days)	$0.00
1 month past due (30–60 days)	0.005
2 months past due (60–90 days)	0.05
3–4 months past due (90–150 days)	0.20
5–6 months past due (150–210 days)	0.50

Smith trusted the system and always had the accounting people adjust the period-end allowance for possible bad debts to the amount indicated by the quarterly aging report — the category totals multiplied by the table factors. In the interim months, he had his people record an estimated provision for possible bad debts, but the quarterly financial statements that were sent to the home office always included a revised provision for possible bad debt losses that was simply a plug number from the updated allowance account.

At March 31, 1992, the allowance account was adjusted to $2,658,000, the amount indicated by the aging-analysis process at that date. During the months of April, May, and June, accounts totaling $1,942,000 were turned over to the attorneys and written off. During April and May, Smith had his accounting people book $500,000 a month for possible bad debt losses. The aging of the accounts at June 30, 1992, showed the following:

	(000)
Current	$ 158,000
1 month past due	43,200
2 months past due	8,240
3–4 months past due	3,650
5–6 months past due	1,840
Total Accounts Receivable balance at June 30, 1992	$ 214,930

Required:

Determine the amount of the bad debt expense for the month of June 1992.

Scenario B: The percentage-of-credit-sales model. The manager of Omni Products Division, Harry Smith, was quite satisfied with all of his section leaders and had developed a high level of trust in their day-to-day decisions. Still, he insisted that he be involved in the critical, long-range judgments. For example, his accounting and control section was efficient and largely trouble-free. However, he carefully monitored the sensitive areas, including the status of collections on accounts receivable, the follow-up on slow-paying customers, and the reasonableness of the ongoing provision for estimated bad debt losses.

Smith's monitoring effort was complicated by the fact that Omni's average sale was less than $1,000 and that the division carried more than 10,000 open customer accounts. He found it difficult to put his hands around the situation because of the amount of detail in the file. To help him monitor the receivables–collections–bad debt situation, he had engaged a consultant some years ago to establish a statistical sampling system. Following the system, a clerk randomly selected a small number of credit sales each week and followed them through to their conclusion — either collection in cash after varying periods or a write-off because of the buyer's inability to pay. The system was easy to operate, and Smith had been assured that the results of the sample would give a very accurate reflection of the results to be expected from total credit sales. However, because the system required the clerk to follow each sampled credit sale to its conclusion, the results were not always available as quickly as Smith would have liked.

Over the past several years, the results of the system had tracked Smith's expectations, given the state of the economy in each period. The results of the study showed:

Report Dated	For the Year Ended	Average Period until Collection	Percentage of Sales Ultimately Written Off
July 5, 1988	December 31, 1987	14.2 weeks	5.5
July 8, 1989	December 31, 1988	12.4 weeks	4.8
July 7, 1990	December 31, 1989	10.5 weeks	4.6
June 28, 1991	December 31, 1990	9.3 weeks	4.5

Based on the trend through the July 1990 report, Smith had instructed his accounting people to record estimated losses from bad debts for the year ending December 31, 1990, at 4.6 percent of sales, and during the first half of 1991, the division had recorded possible bad debt losses using that 4.6 percent factor. When the June 1991 report came out, Smith was delighted. He had his accounting people reduce the expense for estimated bad debt losses to 4.5 percent of sales, effective with the July 1991 monthly financial statement. They continued with that estimate through the rest of 1991 and through the first six months of 1992. However, as the 1991 spring season wore on, Smith became anxious about the continued use of that low estimate because his customers were experiencing tighter times and the number of day's sales in the receivables balances was growing, suggesting that the trend of the late 1980s was reversing.

The allowance for possible bad debts had a balance of $2,152,000 at December 31, 1991, and through the first six months of 1992, an expense of $3,803,040 had been added to the allowance based on six-month sales of $84,512,000. During that same period of time, accounts totaling $4,203,000 had been turned over to the attorneys for collection and written off. When the results of the statistical study for the year ended December 31, 1991, was completed on July 15, 1992, it confirmed Smith's fears. It showed that credit sales made during the year ended December 31, 1991, took 11.2 weeks to turn to cash and that 4.7 percent of those sales were never collected but were written off. He called a meeting to review this situation with his sales and credit people. He got the sense that the ship had not been run as tightly as he would have liked, and he resolved to understand how that had happened. His immediate concern was the package of financial statements he was to send to the home office the next day for the month of June and the six months ended June 30, 1992. After consulting with his staff, he resolved to add to the allowance for possible bad debts. He instructed his accounting people to increase the six-month expense for possible losses from bad debts to 4.75 percent of sales, taking the effect of the new rate for the expense as a special charge against operations for June.

Required:

Calculate the revised allowance balance as of June 30, 1992.

C8.2 Accounting for trade receivables: A. H. Robins Company, Inc.* In mid-January 1985, Dave Bosher, director of corporate accounting for A. H. Robins in Richmond, Virginia, was faced with the task of estimating his company's provision for uncollectible trade receivables for 1984. Mr. Bosher was particularly concerned about the mounting trade receivable balance of one of the company's three major product lines, Caron Fragrances, because he believed that the collectibility of a large portion of this balance was questionable. Customers (several major U.S. retailers) had grown accustomed to taking large unauthorized deductions (referred to by A. H. Robins as "billbacks") on bills from their suppliers in order to widen their otherwise narrow profit margins. In December Mr. Bosher had given the Caron general manager three weeks to "do something about the receivables problem; at least get promises to pay from the major retailers or face a large write-off," but nothing had been done. Therefore, Mr. Bosher was faced with analyzing not only the total outstanding balance in the Caron receivables account, but also with the collectibility of the balance of unauthorized customer deductions. As a consequence of the problem, Mr. Bosher was also prepared to reconsider the company's policies for setting up trade receivables' allowances and writing off bad debts.

General Company Background

A. H. Robins Company was founded in 1866 as a small apothecary and manufacturing chemist's shop. The company had grown into a multinational corporation engaged primarily in the manufacture and marketing of ethical pharmaceutical products (such as Dimetapp and Reglan), consumer products (Robitussin, Chap Stick lip balm, and Sergeant's pet care products), and

*Certain case data have been disguised.

Caron Fragrance products (such as Nocturnes). Although sales in 1984 reached a historic high of \$632,000,000, the company showed a major loss for the first time. The loss resulted from establishing a \$615,000,000 reserve representing an estimate of the minimum costs for compensatory damages and legal expenses arising from the Dalkon Shield litigation. Also during 1984, the Caron trade account receivables grew to \$1,600,000, an amount equal to 146 days' sales, and the outstanding billback balance had expanded to \$411,902. Consistent with the company's desire to achieve a proper matching of revenues and expenses, recognize losses as early as possible, and reflect economic reality, Dave Bosher believed the time had come to review the company's accounts receivable reserves on all trade receivables.

Accounting for Trade Receivables

Mr. Bosher realized that the company's three major product lines were so diverse with respect to composition and distribution channels that each warranted an individual review of the policy for providing for uncollectible trade receivables. The ethical pharmaceutical product line consisted of pharmaceuticals promoted primarily to physicians, hospitals, and pharmacists; ethical pharmaceuticals were the original products carried by A. H. Robins and accounted for 57 percent of sales and 76 percent of profits. This product line was distributed by A. H. Robins through large wholesalers in the United States and abroad; approximately 88 percent of the sales in this category were to only 410 wholesalers.

Mr. Bosher pointed out that news spread quickly when a particular pharmaceutical wholesaler was in financial trouble, in which case A. H. Robins usually began quickly to monitor the activity in the customer's account closely or, if necessary, terminate Robins's extension of credit. To arrive at a yearly uncollectible receivables provision for the ethical pharmaceutical line, Mr. Bosher set up an allowance based on a review of the individual accounts. Then he prepared an aging schedule of those accounts that he believed posed collection problems. He typically set up an allowance for uncollectibles of 10 percent of the balances that were 1–30 days past due, 25 percent of the balances 31–60 days past due, and 50 percent of the balances over 60 days past due. In some instances, when he had particularly insightful financial information on a customer, he made his own subjective judgment as to the collectibility of the account. Historically, accounts actually going bad and thus necessitating a write-off had been less than 0.2 percent of net sales. The stability of these accounts allowed Mr. Bosher to make his estimates with reasonable confidence.

The distribution system for the consumer products category, which included cough preparations and pharmaceuticals marketed over the counter to the public, was far more complex than for the ethical pharmaceuticals. During 1984 the consumer products line accounted for 39 percent of sales and 23 percent of profits. It was sold not only to major wholesalers but also to thousands of small pharmacies and brokers. Therefore, the individual uncollectible accounts pertaining to consumer products customers were generally either very large or very small, depending on whether the account in trouble was a major wholesaler or one of the numerous "mom and pop" pharmacies. Because the number of accounts was far too many to review individually, Dave Bosher used an allowance method based on a percentage of sales. To date, for the fiscal year ended December 31, 1984, \$174,490 in consumer products accounts receivable had been determined to be totally uncollectible.

The Caron Fragrance line, with headquarters and production facilities in France, had become a wholly owned subsidiary of A. H. Robins in 1967. The product line was composed of five fragrances, which were marketed to both male and female upper-income groups. Caron accounted for less than 2 percent of A.H. Robin's sales and in 1984 was just breaking even in profitability. It was distributed in the United States only to major retailers in New York, Atlanta, Miami, Dallas, Chicago, Los Angeles, and San Francisco; over 80 percent of U.S. Caron sales went to only 35 retail distributors. Mr. Bosher was able to examine the financial standing of each of these customers individually and establish an allowance for bad debts using the same method he used for the ethical pharmaceutical line. For 1984, however, he decided also to use the direct write-off method for billbacks that he deemed uncollectible. Mr. Bosher had already determined that $40,000 in accounts receivable for Caron (not including the billbacks) had actually "gone bad" and were to be written off in 1984 and that the balance in the allowance account should total $59,383.

History of Collections for Trade Receivables

Prior to 1980, responsibility for the collection and accounting for trade receivables at A. H. Robins had been decentralized on a regional basis with separate credit and collections departments for pharmaceuticals, consumer products, and Caron. During those years, customer accounts were reviewed individually in order to derive an allowance for bad debts. In 1980, however, with the number of product lines and accounts growing, the company decided to centralize its receivables function and change its policy to combine an individual review of customer accounts with the percentage-of-sales method of establishing an allowance for bad debts. The company also developed a computerized aging schedule to aid in these computations. Mr. Bosher pointed out that the receivables department currently employed nine people, who spent approximately 40 percent of their time on the Caron accounts.

Since the receivables function had been centralized, Mr. Bosher noticed that the days' sales in trade receivables had shown a gradual improvement for both ethical pharmaceuticals and the consumer products. The receivables for ethical pharmaceuticals had been reduced from 65 days' sales in 1981 to its current balance of 47 days. The consumer products outstanding trade receivables had improved from the equivalent of 91 days' sales in 1982 to 77 day's sales in 1984.

Although centralization had helped the company control collectibility for these two product lines, the same was not true for Caron Fragrances. Here the receivables balance had grown from 73 days' sales in 1981 to 146 days in 1984. More importantly to Mr. Bosher, the disputed-claims portion of the receivables (the billbacks) was 25 percent of the total Caron receivables balance; it ranged from only 1 to 5 percent of the other two product lines. Summary financial data pertinent to the three product lines are shown in Exhibits 1 through 4.

The Billback Dilemma

At the end of 1984, the Caron Fragrance line in the United States had $411,902 in billbacks included in its $1,599,568 of trade receivables (see Exhibit 4). The billback was generated when a retailer made a payment for less than the invoiced amount. In response, A. H. Robins made a new invoice for the unpaid amount and sent it back to the retailer for payment. For example, a $20,000 invoice might be sent to Bloomingdale's, which might remit payment for only $15,000. A. H. Robins would record the original invoice as paid, originate a new invoice (a billback) for the unpaid amount of $5,000, and send it to Bloomingdale's for payment. Almost every Caron invoice had a subsequent billback, and the historical collectibility of these billbacks was considered poor. The history of one typical billback is detailed in Exhibit 5.

A common practice in the United States was for large retailers to take unauthorized deductions on the bills received from their suppliers and attribute the deduction to a promotion allowance, a product demonstration salary, or just an "unidentified deduction." Of the $411,900 in billbacks on Caron, Mr. Bosher decided that $205,000 was attributable to unidentified deductions. The rest Mr. Bosher explained as being more or less the result of a paperwork merry-go-round. Although A. H. Robins had agreements with many of the large retailers to pay for a portion of their promotions or demonstration salaries, the retailers refused to wait for the paperwork to go through to be reimbursed. Instead, they would just deduct the amount they believed they were owed from the goods' invoice amount, which made bookkeeping an extremely difficult task for A. H. Robins. While these practices were rampant in the perfume industry in the United States, they did not occur either with the Caron line in France or with A. H. Robins' other product lines.

EXHIBIT 1

A. H. Robins Company, Inc.
Sales and Receivables Data

	1981	1982	1983	1984
Sales				
Pharmaceuticals	$173,712,923	$128,519,975	$160,077,407	$194,951,564
Consumer products	118,653,484	123,229,687	132,557,961	128,532,000
Caron fragrances	5,132,689	3,860,305	4,899,240	3,993,933
Year-End Trade Receivables				
Pharmaceuticals	$ 30,691,204	$ 17,206,984	$ 20,364,088	$ 25,014,708
Consumer products	7,641,931	30,763,238	28,959,778	27,257,219
Caron fragrances	1,014,773	885,190	1,781,617	1,599,568
Billbacks (included in receivables figures above)				
Pharmaceuticals	$ 552,280	$ 159,908	$ 63,413	$ 218,000
Consumer products	58,932	294,517	1,476,500	1,305,000
Caron fragrances	24,456	319,000	563,097	411,902

Source: Company records.

EXHIBIT 2

A. H. Robins Company, Inc.
Accounts-Receivable Allowance and Write-off Data

	1981	1982	1983
Year-End Balance in Allowance Account			
Pharmaceuticals	$300,000	$203,669	$300,000
Consumer products	100,000	241,881	219,000
Caron fragrances	49,516	28,310	60,900
Account-receivable write-offs			
Pharmaceuticals	$249,494	$278,030	$152,283
Consumer products	250,600	474,267	685,671
Caron fragrances	19,991	21,206	100,038

Source: Company records.

Ideally, these large retail customers should have paid their suppliers for the goods received and then billed the suppliers for any agreed-upon shared expenses. Yet, despite the persistence of A. H. Robins' management, the retailers refused to cooperate. In fact, the situation had grown so serious with one retailer that A. H. Robins had stopped shipments for three weeks. In general, however, the Caron product line did not carry enough leverage with the major department stores to use such threats and actions to influence their behavior.

Mr. Bosher's Concern

As Dave Bosher was reviewing the receivables balances for the three product lines for the fiscal year ended December 31, 1984, he wondered what he should do about the mounting billback problem. He also needed a realistic estimate for the corporation's bad debt expense and the receivables allowance balance for 1984.

Required:

a. Recreate the accounting transactions that were made to recognize bad debt expense and accounts receivable write-offs during 1983 for each of the three product lines.

b. What is a reasonable estimate of the bad debt expense for 1984 for ethical pharmaceuticals? Consumer products? Caron fragrances?

Make the appropriate year-end accounting transactions for 1984 and set up t-accounts that show the year-end balance in the allowance accounts.

c. How should Dave Bosher resolve the billback problem with retail customers in the future? How could the accounting information system assist in successfully implementing your suggestions?

EXHIBIT 3a

A. H. Robins Company, Inc.
Example of Accounts Receivable for
Ethical Pharmaceutical Products
as of December 31, 1984
(credit terms 2/10, net 30)

Customer Name	Total Balance Due	Current Items	1–30 Days Past Due	31–60 Days Past Due	Over 60 Days Past Due
1.* Amfak Drug Co.	$ 51,193	—	—	—	$ 51,193
2.* Leigh Laboratories	20,996	$ 4,338	$ 16,658	—	—
3. Edwards Commissary	109,722	—	—	$ 35,802	73,920
4. Central Drug Supply	87,703	—	—	4,618	83,085
5.* Drug Service, Inc.	47,602	—	—	—	47,602
6. Ames Plaza Drugs	59,606	—	—	—	59,606
7. Johnson Drug Co.	56,884	—	—	56,884	—
8.* Armco Pharmac.	31,909	—	—	—	31,909
9.* Northern Medical Supplies	34,634	4,914	5,910	—	22,814
10. Medco Drugs	48,108	4,100	4,008	40,000	—
11. Reeds Drug Supplies	63,498	—	—	—	63,498
12. Remco, Inc.	54,022	—	—	—	54,022
13. Hampton Drug	60,929	—	—	—	60,929
14.* South Bay Drug Co.	36,401	36,401	—	—	—
15. Davis Laboratory Supplies	72,465	—	—	26,082	46,383
16. Ridgefield Drugs, Inc.	18,526	—	18,526	—	—
17. Geer Drug Corp.	49,101	24,312	24,789	—	—
18. Humdico Medical	77,670	18,070	59,600	—	—
19. Albertsons Drugs, Inc.	36,317	8,697	9,402	18,218	—
20. Pharmaceutical Supplies	26,965	—	—	—	26,965
21.* Virginia Drug, Inc.	28,324	—	—	—	28,324
22. Total other accounts (not considered doubtful)	23,942,138	23,942,138			
	$25,014,708	$24,042,970	$138,893	$181,604	$650,245

*See Exhibit 3b for additional financial information.

EXHIBIT 3b

A. H. Robins Company, Inc.
Excerpts from the 1984 Financial Press

Drug Service, Inc., to Post $900,000 Loss, Defaults on Bank Loan

San Jose, Calif. — Drug Service, Inc., said it expects to post a fiscal first-quarter loss of more than $900,000. The company also said it is in default on a $7 million bank loan.

The pharmaceutical wholesaler and distributor said it expects revenue for the quarter ended Sunday of about $3.5 million, down from $11.8 million a year earlier. In the earlier quarter, the company lost $600,000, and stock prices declined dramatically.

Drug Service, Inc. said it had planned to refinance the loan, which came due Sunday, by mortgaging some real estate, but that plan fell through.

******

Two Former Officers of South Bay Drug Plead Guilty to One Charge

New York — Two former officers of South Bay Drug Co., a small wholesaler for medical supplies and pharmaceuticals that entered bankruptcy law proceedings in December 1984, pleaded guilty in state court here to grand larceny, according to Robert Brams, New York state attorney general.

Rollin H. Need, former president of South Bay Drug Co. and Isaac Comerch, former operations officer, were indicted on charges of conspiracy, fraud, and grand larceny. The conspiracy and fraud charges were dropped when the two pleaded guilty to grand larceny, a spokesman for Mr. Brams said. Charges are still pending against another former officer, Terrence Whitney, who was chief financial officer, the spokesman said.

Mr. Need couldn't be reached for comment on the guilty plea. An attorney for Mr. Comerch said he declined to comment on the case. Mr. Whitney couldn't be reached for comment.

The attorney general said that Messrs. Need and Comerch were ordered to appear in court for sentencing Feb. 2.

******

Amfak Drug Co. Asks Lenders to Approve Debt Restructuring

Houston — Amfak Drug Co. said it submitted to its lenders a proposal to restructure $1 billion of debt to avert a cash shortage in the first quarter of 1985.

Under the proposal, Amfak Drug Co.'s secured lenders would receive interest and principal payments based on the company's available cash flow until about 1988. Principal payments of about $334 million for Amfak's secured debt are currently due through 1987. Amfak said payments under the debt restructuring would be less than the contracted amounts until 1988. After that, the original payment schedule would resume.

An Amfak spokesman said the company is "optimistic" that the lenders will accept the proposal. If approved, the debt restructuring will become effective Jan. 1. The spokesman said that if lenders don't agree to the proposal, a filing under Chapter 11 of the federal Bankruptcy Code would be considered only as a "last alternative."

******

Leigh Laboratories Says It May Dismiss up to 100 Employees

Lowell, Mass. — Leigh Laboratories Inc., hurt by slumping demand for its medical equipment, said it may dismiss as many as 100 employees in about 30 days.

The employees, who work at staff positions at the company's headquarters, represent a fraction of Leigh's 8,000 workers. But the layoffs would be the first in about 12 years for Leigh. For the third quarter ended Sept. 31, Leigh's earnings slumped 66 percent, the company's first downturn in quarterly earnings since 1975. For the quarter, Leigh earned 3.2 million, or 12 cents a share, on revenue of $152.7 million.

Leigh said if it isn't able to find alternative work for the 100 employees within 30 days, either at Leigh or at another employer, it would dismiss them with severance pay. Leigh didn't rule out additional layoffs.

******

Armco Pharmaceuticals Net from Operations Fell 23% in Its 3rd Quarter

Dayton, Ohio — Armco Pharmaceuticals reported a 23 percent drop in earnings from operations for its fiscal third quarter ended May 31.

The company also said its loss for the year ending Aug. 21 will total about $1.9 million, wider than the $1.4 million deficit projected in March.

For fiscal 1983, the wholesaler and distributor of drug products earned $3.1 million, or $1.29 a share. The company blamed its financial condition on the "generally weak industrial economy" and on foreign competition in the pharmaceuticals business.

For the third quarter, Armco Pharmaceuticals posted net income of $432,000, or 18 cents a share, compared with year-earlier profit from continuing operations of $530,000, or 22 cents a share.

******

Northern Medical Supplies Sets Plan to Close Two Distribution Sites, Cites Rise in Competition

Greenville, S.C. — Northern Medical Supplies said it will close two of its distribution warehouses in the Atlantic seaboard region that have been "most directly affected by the surge of imports over the last two years."

Northern Medical Supplies said its warehouse at Rockingham, N.C., which employs 180 people, will be phased out over a period of months.

Operations at its Anderson, S.C., facility, which has 475 employees, are to be reduced in size and eventually will be closed. The final closing date, however, isn't known yet, the company said.

Meanwhile, it said its East Coast distribution facilities will be consolidated at the Pickett facility in Rockingham.

******

Virginia Drug Company Seeks Buyer

Richmond, Va. — Va. Drug Company, which has filed a request to reorganize under the eye of the U.S. Bankruptcy Court here, is seeking a buyer, its president said yesterday.

James B. Farin, the Va. Drug Company president, said they hope to be bought by Seifer Inc. of Alexandria, Va. However, no written agreement has been made. Farin said Seifer is practically identical to the Richmond-based wholesaler of pharmaceutical drugs.

Va. Drug Co. had operated as many as six distribution outlets about two years ago. When it filed papers in bankruptcy court saying it planned to seek reorganization under Chapter 11, it listed assets of about $6.2 million and debts of about $9.9 million, including notes totaling about $8.5 million from Union Virginia Bank.

EXHIBIT 4

A. H. Robins Company, Inc.
Caron Outstanding Billbacks, December 1984

Codes	Outstanding No. of Billbacks	Current	Past Due: 1–30 Days	31–60 Days	61–90 Days	Over 90	Total
51 *	54	$ 6,571.63–	$ 2,154.43–	$ 3,838.88–	$ 1,650.00–	$ 6,268.40–	$ 20,483.34–
52 *	14	4,141.33–	2,965.48–	0.00	64.89–	880.90–	8,052.60–
53 *	60	2,412.67–	9,991.25–	1,210.71–	795.04–	10,953.36–	25,363.03–
54	488	50,283.27	35,072.97	25,031.08	5,947.62	88,635.20	204,970.14
55 *	43	1,791.29–	3,547.82–	2,358.47–	3,280.52–	3,725.40–	14,703.50–
56	18	54.00	278.66	113.10	217.90	643.84	1,307.50
58	92	5,917.00	333.78	843.41	1,212.36	14,184.41	22,490.90
60	1	.00	.00	.00	.00	252.00	252.00
62	119	8,414.87	274.21	3,368.49	14,785.02	19,303.54	46,146.13
64	7	.00	361.45	.00	154.26	469.44	985.15
66	31	1,749.20	744.14	399.08	233.95	582.38	3,708.75
67	6	48.63	.00	203.12	152.27	50.00	454.02
68	140	4,300.00	1,260.35	1,235.00	8,920.63	111,046.19	126,762.17
69	63	487.30	1,145.69	593.57	4,201.89	14,574.00	21,002.45
70	1	0.00	0.00	0.00	2,025.00	0.00	2,025.00
71	1	0.00	0.00	0.00	0.00	157.86	157.86
72	1	0.00	0.00	0.00	0.00	144.50	144.50
73	45	142.03	452.98–	510.75	121.08–	5,386.51	5,465.23
79	26	842.30	80.00	19.20	249.30	14,035.29	15,226.09
Totals	1,210	$60,904.26	$27,534.93	$29,625.68	$38,749.71	$255,087.90	$411,902.48

*A negative billback was generated when a customer made a payment for more than the invoice amount.

Source: Company records.

EXHIBIT 5

A. H. Robins Company, Inc.
History of a Typical Caron Fragrance Billback

Date	Description of Correspondence
2/20/83	Goods shipped to retailer.
3/1/83	Original invoice for $56,702 mailed to retailer (for example, Bloomingdale's).
5/1/83	Past-due notice sent.
7/1/83	Check for $30,000 received by A. H. Robins.
7/15/83	Billback invoice for $26,702 mailed to retailer.
9/1/83	Caron manager called customer regarding billback. Customer will look into outstanding balance.
10/1/83	Received letter from customer saying $26,702 discount taken was attributed to a product promotion booth.
10/15/83	Wrote letter to customer saying only $5,000 was authorized for promotion booth.
11/15/83	Caron manager called customer; customer said they'll take care of the discrepancy.
11/28/83	Received check for $6,000.
12/5/83	Billback #2 generated for $15,702.
1/30/84	Call to customer, who said they were trying to clear up outstanding invoices.
2/15/84	A. H. Robins's credit manager informed customer he was planning a visit to their NY office to clear up all outstanding bills.
3/1/84	Credit manager made NY trip. Customer happened to have billback #2 in their file. They'll check into it.
4/1/84	Received check for $7,000.
4/10/84	Call to customer, who said the balance not paid was for special product advertising.
5/1/84	Billback #3 generated for $6,702. (A. H. Robins allowed $2,000 special promotions discount.)
12/31/84	Billback #3 outstanding. No apparent resolution. Write off?

C8.3 Accounting for marketable securities: San Antonio Enterprises.* It was two weeks after the fiscal year ended August 31, 19X4, and Joan Compton, the controller of San Antonio Enterprises, was preparing the company's financial statements for the year. Over the past several years, San Antonio Enterprises had been successfully marketing leisure-time products in Texas. Last year, for the first time, the business had produced excess cash, which Joan invested in financial securities. Exhibit 1 details the investment portfolio as of the end of last year.

For the most part, San Antonio's stock investments had not advanced with last year's bull market. Their performance was fairly lackluster, but the decision had been made to hold onto them in the belief that at some point they would climb with the rest of the market. The stock market had slowed near the beginning of this year, and the growth of some of the stocks in San Antonio's portfolio also slowed — in some cases, even reversed.

Looking at the securities' market values as of the end of this year, shown in Exhibit 2, Joan was particularly concerned about the Borden stock. Borden's price had declined sharply during the year, and the current market value was below San Antonio's original purchase price. Joan called her broker, Jeff Fields, to find out what was happening.

"Well, the company is not expected to meet its projected earnings for the year, their credit rating has fallen from an A+ to a BBB, and they replaced their Chief Financial Officer (CFO) with a

EXHIBIT 1

San Antonio Enterprises
Investment Portfolio on August 31, 19X3

	Shares	Original Cost	Market Value
Equities			
Trading:			
ICN Pharmaceuticals	2,000	$ 14,000	$ 20,000
Sara Lee	2,000	52,000	40,000
Jefferson Bank	1,000	19,000	21,000
		$ 85,000	$ 81,000
Available for sale:			
Merck	1,000	$ 38,000	$ 32,000
Biocraft	2,000	50,000	58,000
Motorola	1,000	44,000	46,000
Mead	1,000	34,000	39,000
Blockbuster Video	2,000	64,000	54,000
American Cyanamid	1,000	48,000	44,000
Borden	3,000	48,000	36,000
		$326,000	$309,000
Bonds			
Available for sale:			
Ford Motor Company		$120,000	$121,500
Union Carbide		130,000	130,500
Hold to maturity:			
Xerox		100,000	100,750
		$350,000*	$352,750

*The bonds were purchased for an amount equal to their maturity value.

CFO from, of all things, the timber industry. I even hear Borden is contemplating selling Elsie the Cow."

"Okay, Jeff, thanks for the information. By the way, did you check the maturity dates on those bonds for me?"

"I sure did, None of your bonds are scheduled to mature this coming year. While I've got you on the line, Joan, I'd like to double-check those trigger prices at which you wanted me to sell some of your stocks: ICN Pharmaceuticals at 14, Sara Lee at 32, and Jefferson Bank Shares at 25. Do you still want these in effect?"

"Yes. By the way, you did sell American Cyanamid before the month ended, didn't you?"

"Sure did. It executed at 100. What a great run it had once American Home Products bid on it. By the way, let me know when you want to sell any of the others."

"Well, my attitude toward the Merck investment has changed. This health care debate in Congress seems like it could go on forever. If Merck inches up another couple of points, sell it. As always, if you have any hot tips, let me know."

"O.K. Anything else?"

"Nope. It's been good talking to you. Thanks for your time, Jeff."

Joan hung up the phone and contemplated the information Jeff had given her. She also decided it was time to study the reports she had seen in the business press (shown in Exhibits 3 and 4). Joan knew that 19X3 had been the first year San Antonio Enterprises had adopted a financial reporting rule for investments requiring something called mark-to-market accounting. She knew that she would have to set aside some time to recreate what was done last year in this regard. Joan also knew that her auditor wanted to see the financial statements at the end of the week, so she was determined to finish the books today.

EXHIBIT 2

San Antonio Enterprises
Investment Portfolio Market Values on August 31, 19X4

	# Shares	Market Value
Equities		
ICN Pharmaceuticals	2,000	$ 25,500
Sara Lee	2,000	39,000
Jefferson Bank	1,000	23,000
Merck	1,000	34,000
Biocraft	2,000	32,000
Motorola	1,000	51,000
Mead	1,000	50,750
Blockbuster Video	2,000	52,000
Borden	3,000	34,500
		$341,750
Bonds*		
Ford Motor Company		$120,500
Union Carbide		130,100
Xerox		100,200
		$350,800

*No bonds were purchased or sold during 19X4.

EXHIBIT 3

San Antonio Enterprises
Information Pertinent to the Borden Investment

Borden Considers Sale or Shutdown Of Dairy Business

BY SUEIN L. HWANG
Staff Reporter of THE WALL STREET JOURNAL

Borden, Inc., under growing pressure from creditors, is considering selling or shutting down its problem-plagued $1.3 billion dairy unit, people close to the company say.

Officials at Borden declined to comment, but people familiar with the situation say the fate of the beleaguered dairy business led the agenda of a board meeting on Tuesday. "Dairy isn't making any progress, and it's a real challenge to management," one executive says. "The [restructuring] plan isn't working."

One of the original cornerstones of the company, the dairy unit remains one of Borden's largest businesses, contributing 25 percent of total sales in 1993. With its familiar mascot Elsie the Cow, the dairy unit is perhaps most closely associated with the Borden name. Until recently, it had also been reasonably profitable, generating about $90 million in 1991.

But at a time when Borden is struggling to revamp its far-flung operations, the dairy unit has become a major headache. The business, which includes milk, cheese, and ice cream, had a loss of $35 million in 1993. Last month, Borden posted weaker-than-expected second-quarter results and said it might not reach its year-end projections. Analysts estimate the dairy unit had a loss of $30 million in the first half of this year.

Yesterday, Moody's Investors Service placed the ratings of $1.9 billion of Borden's long-term debt and commercial paper under review for a possible downgrade. The agency cited weaker-than-expected performance, particularly in the dairy and pasta businesses.

Getting rid of the dairy unit wouldn't be easy. Commodity costs are sky-high, leaving even healthy dairies struggling to eke out a profit. Chief Executive Officer Ervin Shames "is between a rock and a hard place," says John McMillin, an analyst at Prudential Securities Inc. "He can't write off the business without getting shareholders' equity into negative territory."

The problems in the dairy business reflect the turbulence that has plagued Borden in the last few years. After acquiring a number of regional dairies such as Meadow Gold, executives and analysts say the company did little to consolidate them. Last year, Borden finally did attempt a sweeping consolidation of its dairy operations, only to be badly hurt by an attempt to raise prices across the board. "They've changed courses a couple of times and it hasn't quite worked," says Nomi Ghez, an analyst at Goldman, Sachs & Co.

Since the end of 1993, the company has ousted Anthony S. D'Amato as chief executive, put its ailing snack-food unit on the block, and taken a $632 million restructuring charge. Executives say the many changes, which include the recruitment of six new executives into top posts at Borden, have stirred resentment among the old guard — particularly among the insular ranks of the dairy business. "There's been a lot of turnover, and this is a relationship business," says Mr. McMillin.

Source: *The Wall Street Journal,* August 18, 1994, p. A4. Reprinted by permission of *The Wall Street Journal*

EXHIBIT 4

San Antonio Enterprises
Information Pertinent to the Biocraft Investment

Biocraft Has Come to Terms with the FDA But Analysts Debate Whether to Buy Its Stock

BY JOHN R. DORFMAN AND ELYSE TANOUYE
Staff Reporters of THE WALL STREET JOURNAL

Can Biocraft Laboratories walk away unharmed from a car wreck?

The Fair Lawn, N.J., generic drug maker signed a tough consent agreement in July to settle a dispute with the Food and Drug Administration over manufacturing practices. Now, outside inspectors supervise Biocraft's operations. Proponents say most of Biocraft's troubles are behind it and the stock should rebound from Friday's close of 16⅛, which was down 57 percent from its 52-week high. But skeptics say a recovery won't be easy, and in this case, the pessimists make some compelling arguments.

A consent decree requiring outside supervision "is not the beginning of recovery," says Hemant Shah, an independent drug analyst with HKS & Co. in Warren, N.J. "What it tells you is that the FDA basically does not trust the company."

Biocraft didn't admit or deny wrongdoing. But tangles of this type can distract managers from running the business, slow down production, harm a company's stature among customers, and make regulators stingy with permission to manufacture more drugs, Mr. Shah says. He predicts Biocraft will only break even in the fiscal year ending next March and will need two years to get back on its feet.

David Saks of Gruntal & Co. disagrees. "The problems are obvious," he says. "They seemingly are being resolved. The company is a low-cost and important supplier of antibiotics." At today's price, Mr. Saks thinks the stock is worth buying even if full recovery is a way off.

Besides, Mr. Saks considers Biocraft takeover bait. "I usually like to see, right smack in my face, strong earnings," he says. "But I feel that the merger mania [in the drug industry] is a new factor. This firm has said that it would seek a strategic alliance or buyout. The CEO is 73 years old and not getting younger. He wants to have his family fortune become liquid."

Each of the dueling analysts boasts a good stock-picking record. In the most recent Wall Street Journal All-Star Analysts Survey, Mr. Saks ranked first for stock picking, Mr. Shah a close second.

Other analysts' opinions are mixed. Jack Lamberton of NatWest Securities calls the stock a buy, projecting fiscal 1997 earnings of $1.18 a share. "Usually consent decrees represent a trough in the fundamentals at any company," he says.

Stephen Buermann of Merrill Lynch considers Biocraft a buy in the long run but not the short run. He guesses the company will be unable to get new drugs approved for a while. Without new drugs, he says, profit margins will be susceptible to erosion. So he pegs this fiscal year's earnings at zero to 10 cents a share.

Bonnie Perkins of Fortaleza Asset Management in Chicago thinks highly of Biocraft's new "state-of-the-art" production facility in Mexico, Mo. But she isn't recommending either a purchase or sale of the stock.

The bears seem to have history on their side, citing slow recoveries by other companies that signed stringent consent orders. Operating under such an agreement "under all circumstances is harmful and expensive," says Neil Sweig of Ladenburg, Thalmann. Sales lost during the supervision period may not be easy to regain, he says.

According to Mr. Shah, Biocraft's revenue is running about 50 percent below normal. Jay T. Snyder, Biocraft's vice president of research and development, won't confirm or deny this figure. (Mr. Snyder is a member of the family that owns about two-thirds of Biocraft stock, and he is the son of the chief executive, Harold Snyder.)

Biocraft's earnings history has been "very spotty," says Mr. Shah. "The most it ever earned was $1.05 [a share] in 1988. It earned 59 cents a share in 1989, 23 cents in 1990, and 27 cents in 1991. It lost 48 cents a share in 1992. It made 42 cents in 1993."

People betting on a merger may care little about the earnings, but a merger isn't a sure thing. According to Mr. Shah, Biocraft has been dangled in front of prospective buyers for about two years, first by Wertheim Schroder and more recently by Goldman Sachs. No takers.

Biocraft Laboratories

Daily stock prices (NYSE symbol: BCL)

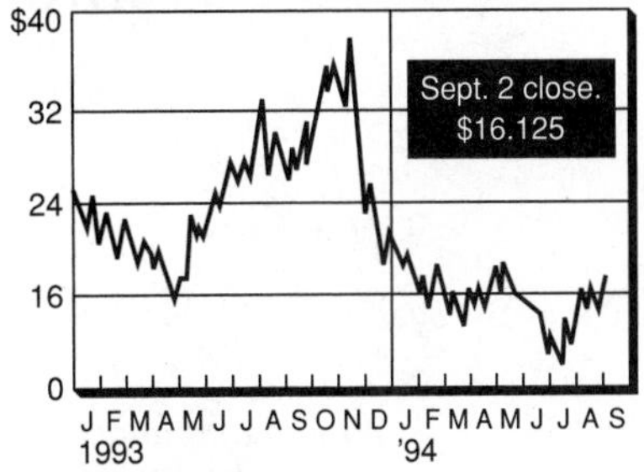

Source: *Baseline*

Business: Generic drug maker

Year ended March 31, 1994:

Sales: $143.1 million

Net Income: $6.1 million; or 43 cents a share

Fourth quarter, March 31, 1994:

Per-share earnings: 5 cents vs. 27 cents

Average daily trading volume:

67.071 shares

Common shares outstanding:

14.2 million

Biocraft's Mr. Snyder won't comment on takeover speculation except to say, "We'll be very successful in the future independently or in partnership with another firm."

Even though Biocraft's stock is down, it isn't cheap. The shares sell for 38 times the past four quarters' earnings and 78 times the average annual earnings for the past five years.

Source: *The Wall Street Journal,* September 6, 1994, p. C2. Reprinted by permission of *The Wall Street Journal*

Required:

Make all the judgments and financial statement adjustments necessary for preparing San Antonio's August 31, 19X4, year-end balance sheet. Prepare the investments part of that year-end balance sheet.

CHAPTER 9

Inventories and the Cost of Goods Sold

When companies are desperate to stay afloat, inventory fraud is the easiest way to produce instant profits and dress up the balance sheet.[1]

Key Chapter Issues

- What is inventory and what constitutes its cost?
- What are the physical flows versus cost flows for inventory?
- What do the acronyms LIFO, FIFO, LISH, and FISH mean?
- What financial reporting concerns and practices pertain to obsolete inventory?

[1]F. Pomerantz, quoted in L. Berton, "Inventory Chicanery Tempts More Firms, Fools More Auditors," *The Wall Street Journal,* December 14, 1992, pp. 1 and A4.

Visualize the items that are on the shelves of the Kroger grocery store. Visualize the millions of gallons of oil in various stages of refinement at Exxon sites around the world. Visualize a General Motors factory with various types of cars in various stages of assembly. Such images are the images of these companies' inventories — their stock in trade, composed of the goods purchased and/or manufactured to sell to their customers. On the balance sheet, inventories are regarded as current assets because they are expected to be sold and to benefit a business during the next operating cycle. The inventory items sold during a period, and therefore no longer on hand at period-end, are matched against that period's sales revenue and recorded in the income statement as the cost of goods sold. It must be quickly pointed out that in determining the amount to report for the cost of goods sold, however, management is accorded considerable leeway, and the alternative inventory accounting methods available to management can significantly affect both the balance sheet (the reported cost of ending inventory) and the income statement (the reported cost of goods sold attributable to that period).

How does PepsiCo, Exxon, General Motors, or Kroger account for its vast and varied inventories? As we will see, the inventory accounting method chosen by management depends on the nature of the industry, certain tax considerations, and a variety of other factors discussed in this chapter. The informed reader is advised to consider both the balance sheet and the income statement effects during the following discussion.

SOME BASIC RELATIONSHIPS: THE COST OF INVENTORY

For all companies, the principal accounting concept involved in valuing inventories is that all goods available for sale during a period must, at year-end, either have been sold or remain in ending inventory. For a *merchandising* business like Kmart, which simply buys goods and sells them as is, this relationship is depicted in Panel A of Exhibit 9.1 and in the following equations:

$$\text{Beginning inventory} + \text{Net purchases} = \text{Cost of goods available for sale} \quad (1)$$

$$\text{Cost of goods available for sale} - \text{Cost of goods sold} = \text{Ending inventory} \quad (2)$$

In accounting for a *manufacturing* company's inventory, such as that of General Motors, which transforms raw materials into a final product, the same basic principle applies, although the process is a bit more complicated and involves a larger number of costs. Manufactured inventories are usually composed of three categories: **raw materials** (RM), which include materials and purchased parts awaiting assembly or manufacture; **work in process** (WIP), which includes partially completed products still in the factory; and **finished goods** (FG), which include fully assembled or manufactured goods available for sale. Each of these three physical categories of inventory must be included in the accounting process.

Raw Materials

The accounting for a manufacturer's raw materials inventory is very similar to accounting for the inventory transactions of a merchandising company. The beginning inventory *plus* purchases *equals* the raw materials available for use. These raw materials available for use either remain unused at year-end (and thus in the inventory of unused raw materials at the end of the accounting period) or have been placed in production. This relationship is shown in the following equations:

EXHIBIT 9.1

Status of Inventory Items at Year-End

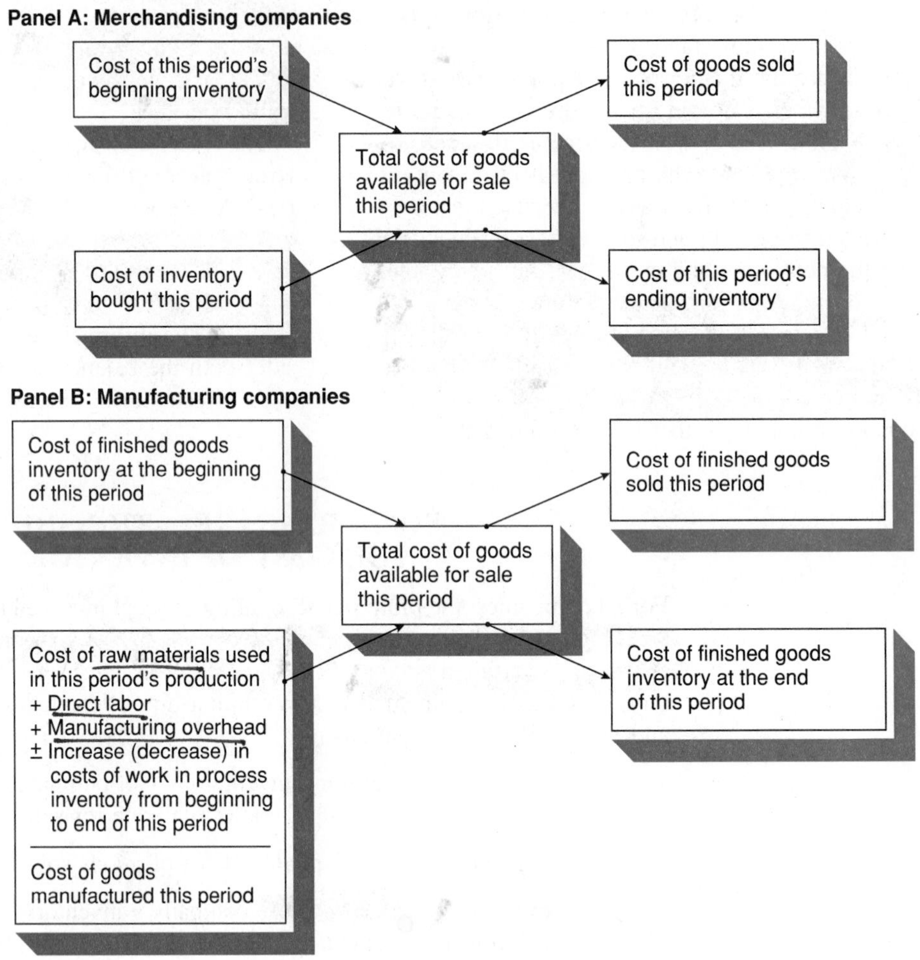

$$\text{Beginning RM inventory} + \text{Net purchases of RM} = \text{Cost of RM available for use} \quad (3)$$

$$\text{Cost of RM available for use} - \text{Ending RM inventory} = \text{Cost of RM used} \quad (4)$$

Work in Process

During the work in process phase of production, the cost of raw materials used, along with the cost of **direct labor** (the labor expended to convert raw materials to finished goods), and all *manufacturing overhead* costs must be assigned to the products being produced. Thus, beginning work in process inventory *plus* the cost of raw materials used during the period *plus* direct labor costs incurred during the period *plus* manufacturing overhead for the period *less* ending work in process inventory *equals* the cost of goods manufactured during the period. These relationships are shown in the following equations:

$$\text{Beginning WIP inventory} + \text{Cost of RM used} + \text{Direct labor cost} + \text{Manufacturing overhead costs} = \text{Total manufacturing costs} \quad (5)$$

$$\text{Total manufacturing costs} - \text{Ending WIP inventory} = \text{Cost of goods manufactured} \quad (6)$$

A word about the need and method to assign manufacturing overhead costs to work in process inventories is warranted. **Manufacturing overhead** is a phrase commonly used to describe all factory-related costs, other than raw materials and direct labor, involved in the production of a completed product: electricity, maintenance, supervision, depreciation of machines, and so on. Factory costs are considered to be **product costs** and thus need to be assigned to the cost of inventory rather than expensed on the income statement as incurred. The nonfactory-related costs of a manufacturer, such as selling expenses, are called **period costs** and are treated as expenses in the income statement in the period when they are incurred.

As an example, visualize a mattress manufacturing company that uses four raw materials in its production process: fabric, padding, lumber, and springs. To make one mattress, the production supervisor requisitions from the warehouse the appropriate quantity of each raw material (see Panel A, Exhibit 9.2). Once in the factory, the fabric and padding are used by workers to make the outer surface of the mattress. Other workers use the lumber to make the mattress frame. Additional labor is required to mount the springs on the frame and then to cover it with the padded surface. The cost of labor incurred in performing these tasks is as much a part of the final cost of a completed mattress as the actual materials in it and thus must be added to the inventory account. Manufacturing overhead costs related to these production operations are also incurred. These costs are for items such as equipment maintenance, cleaning supplies, and power, as well as the cost of insurance, taxes, and depreciation pertaining to the factory. A share of these overhead costs must be added to the primary product costs (raw materials and direct labor) to have a complete cost for a particular manufactured mattress (see Panel B, Exhibit 9.2) because they are a necessary part of the production process and, consequently, represent part of the total cost of the final product.

Notice in Exhibit 9.2 that the accounting process for manufactured inventories parallels the actual production process. When raw materials sit in a warehouse, their cost sits in the Raw Materials Inventory account. As raw materials and labor start being introduced into the manufacturing process, a Work in Process Inventory account accumulates such costs for the goods in various stages of partial production. Finally, when production is completed on an item, it is physically transferred to a finished goods warehouse or storeroom, and the costs accumulated for that finished item are likewise transferred from the Work in Process Inventory account to the Finished Goods Inventory account.

It is worth noting that a challenge arises when a company no longer manufactures only a single product. When it manufactures multiple products, it becomes necessary to determine just how much of the manufacturing overhead costs (such as factory depreciation, equipment maintenance, and supervisors' wages) should be included in the cost of Product A versus Product B. We can readily agree that each of two manufactured products contains a certain quantity of raw material and labor (for example, 40 springs for the deluxe queen mattress versus 15 for a crib-size mattress) and that it took five hours of labor to assemble one queen-size mattress but only two hours of

EXHIBIT 9.2

An Illustration of a Manufacturing Process and Associated Manufacturing Costs

Panel A: Manufacturing Process for One Queen-Sized Mattress

Beginning Warehouse Supply of Raw Materials	Supervisor's Requisition	Production/ Assembly Process	Finished Goods Produced
1,000 yds. fabric	10 yds. →	Covering	One mattress
1,000 yds. padding	10 yds. → (Covering)		
1,000 board ft. lumber	60 bd. ft. →	Frame	
1,000 springs	40 →	Springs	

Panel B: Inventory Accounts for Queen-Sized Mattress Paralleling Panel A's Manufacturing Process

Beginning Inventory Account of Raw Materials	Additions to Work in Process Inventory Account		Additions to Finished Goods Inventory Account
$3,000 fabric →	10 yds. @ $3/yd. →	$ 30	
$2,000 padding →	10 yds. @ $2/yd. →	$ 20	
$ 500 lumber →	60 bd. ft. @ $0.50/bd. ft. →	$ 30	
$ 800 springs →	40 springs @ $0.80/spring →	$ 32	
	Direct labor:		
	Covering (1 hr. @ $25/hr.)	$ 25	
	Frame (1 hr. @ $20/hr.)	$ 20	
	Assembly (1 hr @ $10/hr.)	$ 10	$195
	Manufacturing overhead*		
	Indirect labor	$ 5	
	Supplies	$ 4	
	Utilities	$ 1	
	Depreciation	$ 15	
	Other	$ 3	
		$195	

*The manufacturing overhead amounts are allocations from accumulated indirect cost pools based on some predetermined, estimated relationship (e.g., for every direct labor hour, $5 of depreciation is assigned to the cost of a single mattress). The raw materials and direct labor costs are determined by the actual quantity of materials and labor used in making the one mattress.

labor to assemble the crib-size mattress. However, no comparable objective assessments are possible for costs such as the factory building's depreciation, equipment maintenance, or supervisors' wages. Similarly, other manufacturing overhead costs such as inspection, warehousing, power, and so on are not easily quantifiable ingredients of each separate finished model.

The fact that there is no objectively measurable means to determine the manufacturing overhead costs incurred by each of two products does not, however, preclude the need to allocate such costs to the final cost of Products A and B for balance sheet reporting purposes. Ideally, the costs not *directly* attributable to inventory units but necessary for their production should be assigned to the finished products by astute managers on a basis reflecting the demands by the various products on those manufacturing resources. For example, manufacturing overhead costs are often allocated to products on the basis of direct labor hours required to produce the product, the machine hours required to produce it, production floor space devoted to the product, the number of production order changes required, or some other measurable allocation basis.

As a simple example of the allocation of factory overhead costs, assume that such costs are expected to total $1 million for the year. Assume further that the number of direct labor hours devoted to each of the two final products has been chosen as the allocation base and that the estimated total number of direct labor hours to produce the volume of products needed to fulfill projected sales is 40,000. These estimates result in an allocation scheme whereby, for every one hour of direct labor incurred in making a particular product, $25 of these manufacturing overhead costs are to be assigned to each finished product ($1 million ÷ 40,000 hours = $25/hour).

The issue of allocating manufacturing overhead costs to various product lines has received increasing attention from corporate managers as the direct material and direct labor cost components of manufactured products have been reduced through various overt cost-cutting measures. At the same time, the use of robotics and other technological innovations in production processes have helped to increase the relative share of overhead costs associated with manufactured products. In spite of the many systematic overhead allocation schemes devised over the years, in the final analysis, they are *all* arbitrary to some degree. Consequently, no single best, theoretically defensible method to allocate manufacturing overhead costs exists. Therefore, even though manufacturing overhead cost allocations are necessary to value a company's ending inventories in the balance sheet, managers must use caution when making strategic operating decisions based, at least in part, on allocated cost information. Given such a situation, it is not surprising that managers are continually searching for more accurate and informative allocation schemes to achieve a better matching of expenses to revenues and thus better measures of performance over time.

Finished Goods

At the end of the manufacturing phase, all costs associated with a completed product are transferred from work in process inventory to the finished goods inventory. Accounting for finished goods in a manufacturing firm is again very much like that for a merchandising company. The cost of beginning finished goods (FG) inventory *plus* the cost of goods manufactured (those costs transferred from work in process) *equals* the period's cost of goods available for sale. As of the end of a period, these costs must be attributed to either ending finished goods inventory (unsold goods) or to cost of goods sold. Hence, as depicted in Panel B of Exhibit 9.1, the following relationships exist:

$$\text{Beginning FG inventory} + \text{Cost of goods manufactured} \\ = \text{Cost of goods available for sale} \tag{7}$$

$$\text{Cost of goods available for sale} - \text{Cost of goods sold} \\ = \text{Ending FG inventory} \tag{8}$$

ACCOUNTING FOR INVENTORY COSTS

So far we have not mentioned the *physical* movement of inventory through a business. Clearly, purchased goods come into a company's facilities, and sold goods leave the premises. The following are pertinent questions that arise when a product is sold: Was that a sale of an item purchased or manufactured yesterday or last month? Does the answer to this question matter?

For a moment, visualize a business that makes and sells a large volume of a single model of chair. All during the year, the company incurs various costs to produce the chairs and to sell the finished product. Assume that you and another customer both arrive at the company's showroom simultaneously. You happen to walk in the west entrance, and the other customer walks in the east entrance. The showroom is full of identical chairs, and both of you select the first chair that you see. Unknown to either of you, the chair you selected was manufactured six months ago, and the one that the other customer chose was manufactured yesterday. Are the actual costs of manufacturing incurred by the company for your chair different than those of the other customer's chair? They *probably* are because of material cost increases or a few more minutes of labor devoted to one or the other of them. Does that fact result in the other customer paying a different price for a chair than you pay? *Probably not*. If the different costs do not result in different sales prices, there is no real need for the company even to bother keeping track of the fact that the other customer bought a chair from yesterday's production and you bought one from a prior month's production. But the company does have to record a reduction in the product costs accumulated in the Finished Goods Inventory account and assign them to the Cost of Goods Sold account as a result of its sales to both of you.

Several acceptable methods are used to determine what inventory costs to identify with a particular sale. These cost-flow methods are discussed shortly, and examples of each are presented later. It first must be noted, however, that the *accounting* cost-flow method chosen by management to assign inventory costs to the Cost of Goods Sold account need *not* match the actual *physical* flow of inventory items into and out of a company's warehouse or showroom. As satisfying as it may be to know that inventory item no. 59, produced on June 11, 1995, was the item actually sold on August 20, 1995, and its particular cost is the cost deducted from the Finished Goods Inventory account and added to the Cost of Goods Sold account, there are other considerations, providing more valued benefits, that diminish the importance of such a strict tracking of actual inventory items sold. These other considerations are discussed in the following sections.

Specific Identification Method

This cost-flow method is usually reserved for high-value, easily distinguishable items such as cars and jewelry and *does* require individual accounting for each inventory item. Under this approach, the costs associated with an inventory item are "attached" to it and remain in the inventory account as long as the specific item is on hand. The **specific identification method** is the only cost-flow approach that results in the costs flowing from the balance sheet (that is, ending inventory) to the income statement (that is, cost of goods sold) in a sequence exactly matching the product's physical flow from storeroom to customer.

Exhibit 9.3 is the inventory method footnote from the financial statements of Ryan Homes, Inc., a regional builder of residential dwellings in the mid-Atlantic and southeastern United States. It describes the company's use of the specific identification method and how a company's inventory cost-flow method might be presented in the financial statements. The decision by Ryan Homes to adopt this method appears quite reasonable — the company builds distinctive and expensive homes, which are generally sold one at a time.

The main disadvantage to the specific identification method is that its use is impractical for some types of businesses (such as mass merchandisers and mass manufacturers of homogeneous products) because of the very detailed inventory system required to track each item or each lot of goods purchased or manufactured. On the other hand,

EXHIBIT 9.3

Ryan Homes, Inc.
Inventory Method Disclosure: Specific Identification

Inventories

Inventories are stated at the lower of cost or market value. Cost of lots, completed and uncompleted housing units, and land in process of development represent the accumulated actual cost thereof. Field construction supervision salaries and related direct overhead expenses are included in inventory costs. Selling, general, and administrative costs are expensed as incurred. Upon settlement, the cost of the units is expensed on a specific identification basis.

the matching of cost of goods sold to the sales revenue of the period perfectly matches the physical flow of specific inventory items, consequently achieving a perfect income statement matching of revenue generated from the item sold with its actual cost.

Average Cost Method

The **average cost method** accounts for inventory costs in a manner that is especially useful when it is impossible (or at least impractical) to attempt to specifically identify the particular units of inventory sold, typically because large volumes of many types of similar products are sold. This is the case for such companies as food wholesalers, supermarkets, and retailers in general. For example, the Quaker Oats Company (see Exhibit 9.8, presented later in this chapter) uses the average cost method for about 35 percent of its ending inventory. With the advent of cost-effective electronic product label scanners, retailers' ability to track the physical flow of products, and thus their costs, has greatly improved. Whether managers of companies using such tracking devices will consequently abandon the simple average cost method has yet to be determined.

The average cost method is based on the assumption that the costs of the items sold and therefore charged against revenue should be the average unit cost of all the items of a like kind available for sale during the period. The average cost of a particular inventory item (such as Quaker Oats' raw oats) is determined simply by dividing the sum of the different unit costs incurred for the oats available for sale during the year by the number of different unit costs represented in that quantity of oats. The resulting unit cost is used to compute both the balance sheet ending inventory cost and the income statement cost of goods sold. The advantages of this approach are that it is very easy to compute and it is very objective in its determination of profits for the period. The disadvantage is that the cost attributed to a single item is not, in reality, a cost that has ever been paid for the item (that is, it is an average).

A variation of the average cost method is the **weighted-average cost method.** Under this method, the calculation of the cost of ending inventory (and cost of goods sold) is accomplished as under the average cost method except that each cost is weighted by the number of inventory units available at that cost. The weighted-average cost method is generally believed to be preferable to the average cost method because it takes into consideration the relative quantity of goods purchased at a given unit cost. Thus, if 100 units of inventory were purchased at \$10 each and 1,000 at \$14 each, the average cost method produces an average unit cost of only \$12 (that is, (\$10 + \$14) ÷ 2), which does not reflect the substantial difference in quantities purchased at the two costs. The weighted-average cost per unit, however, would be \$13.64 (that is, [(100 × \$10) + (1,000 × \$14)] ÷ 1,100 units), emphasizing the large volume of purchases at the higher cost of $14. The advantages and disadvantages of this method are the same as those for the average cost method.

First-in, First-out (FIFO)

The **first-in, first-out** cost-flow method accounts for inventory under the assumption that the first product physically purchased or manufactured is the first product physically sold. Remember that the actual physical flow of inventory does not need to be on a FIFO basis in order for a company to elect to account for its cost flow on a FIFO basis. Thus, under the FIFO method the costs assigned to the Cost of Goods Sold account for the products sold during the period are not the most recent costs paid, but they do represent an actual cost incurred for the item at some point in the past. In times of rapid inflation, the cost of goods sold under FIFO is likely to be low relative to a product's current replacement cost and current selling price, and will result in higher net income and thus higher income taxes payable vis-à-vis other inventory cost-flow methods. Because FIFO asserts a cost of goods sold focus, its equivalent for an ending inventory focus is **LISH — last in, still-here**. Thus, ending inventory account balances will approximate the product's current replacement cost, especially if inventory turnover is frequent (that is, if the inventory items are on hand for only a short period of time). Exhibit 9.4, Panel A, presents the inventory footnote disclosure of Tyson Foods, Inc., that indicates the company's use of the FIFO method, a choice that is intuitively appealing given the perishable nature of the product that this company sells. Panel B in Exhibit 9.4 presents the Swedish company Electrolux's FIFO disclosure. Electrolux is one of the world's largest white goods, floor care products, and industrial laundry companies. In contrast to the perishable goods rationale for Tyson's choice of FIFO, Electrolux's products do not provoke a similar conclusion. Nonetheless, all of the company's inventories are accounted for on the FIFO basis.

Last-in, First-out (LIFO)

The **last-in, first-out** cost-flow method accounts for inventory under the assumption that the last product physically purchased or manufactured is the first one physically sold, and therefore the **first in is still here (FISH)**. Following the reasoning of the FIFO method, this approach means that under LIFO, the cost of the products sold closely approximates the current replacement cost of the product (i.e., the most recent costs incurred in acquiring the item).

For company management, LIFO has advantages and disadvantages just the opposite of those of FIFO. Whereas FIFO presents ending inventory in the balance sheet at an approximation of current **replacement cost** (that is, the most recent cost incurred in acquiring the item), the LIFO method states the inventory balance at a mixture of costs incurred in the distant past. In times of high inflation (deflation), the reported ending balance of the inventory account under LIFO can be significantly lower (higher) than under FIFO. On the other hand, FIFO does not report cost of goods sold at the most recent costs; the LIFO method approximates current replacement cost in arriving at the cost reported in the income statement for each product sold (except, as will be discussed later, when the quantity of inventory sold during the period exceeds the quantity acquired during the period). Exhibit 9.5 presents the inventory footnote disclosure from the annual report of the General Motors Corporation, which describes that company's predominant use of the LIFO method.

The General Motors disclosures in Panel A of Exhibit 9.5 reveal a rich and useful set of inventory-related insights. For example, not all of the company's inventories are accounted for using the LIFO method. Indeed, the inventories of GM Hughes Electron-

EXHIBIT 9.4

Inventory Method Disclosure: FIFO

Panel A: Tyson Foods, Inc. (U.S. company)

Inventories, valued at the lower of cost (first-in, first-out) or market, consist of the following:

	(In Thousands)	
	1994	**1993**
Dressed and further-processed products	**$346,846**	$299,388
Live poultry and hogs	**255,904**	207,848
Seafood related products	**36,494**	53,064
Hatchery eggs and feed	**44,048**	40,110
Supplies	**70,898**	74,795
	$754,190	$675,205

Panel B: AB Electrolux (Swedish company)

Inventories are valued at the lower of acquisition cost and market value. Acquisition cost is computed according to the first-in, first-out method (FIFO). Appropriate provisions have been made for obsolescence.

Inventories comprise the following:

	Group		Parent Company	
	1994 SEKm	**1993 SEKm**	**1994 SEKm**	**1993 SEKm**
Raw materials	3,203	3,209	124	122
Work in progress	2,451	2,306	32	18
Finished products	12,860	11,183	355	280
Total	18,514	16,698	511	420

ics, Saturn Corporation, and overseas subsidiaries are accounted for not on a LIFO basis but on either FIFO or average cost. Moreover, the FIFO cost basis of the inventories that are accounted for on a LIFO basis is presented; the cost that would have been reported for ending inventory if the FIFO method had been used would have been $2,535.9 million higher than the reported 1994 LIFO cost. This difference in ending inventory value, often termed the **LIFO reserve,** also represents the *cumulative* decrease in pretax earnings (a part of OE) through 1994 that General Motors has experienced as a consequence of being on the LIFO method instead of the FIFO method. In other words, if GM's inventories would have been higher by this amount, the company's cost of goods sold would have been lower, resulting in $2,535.9 million higher pretax profits under the FIFO method. The portion of this decrease in pretax earnings for just 1994 is the difference between the 1994 cumulative inventory valuation differential and the 1993 cumulative inventory valuation differential, $2,535.9 million less $2,519.0 million, or $16.9 million. Given a 34 percent income tax rate for the company in 1994, taxes were $5.7 million less in 1994 than they would have been using a FIFO valuation for those inventory items accounted for under the LIFO method. Thus, in 1994 alone, more than $5.7 million in cash was saved on income taxes by using the LIFO method. Indeed, such tax consequences are a major motivation for U.S. companies to adopt the LIFO method.

EXHIBIT 9.5

General Motors Corporation
Inventory Method Disclosure: LIFO

Panel A

Inventories

Inventories are stated generally at cost, which is not in excess of market. The cost of substantially all U.S. inventories other than the inventories of Saturn Corporation (Saturn) and GMHE is determined by the last-in, first-out (LIFO) method. The cost of non-U.S., Saturn, and GMHE inventories is determined generally by FIFO or average cost methods.

(Dollars in millions)	1994	1993
Productive material, work in process, and supplies	**$ 5,478.3**	$4,671.9
Finished product, service parts, etc.	**4,649.5**	3,943.2
Total	**$10,127.8**	$8,615.1
Memo: Increase in LIFO inventories if valued at first-in, first-out (FIFO)	**$ 2,535.9**	$2,519.0

Panel B

As a result of decreases in U.S. inventories, certain inventory quantities carried at lower LIFO costs prevailing in prior years, as compared with the costs of current purchases, were liquidated in 1993 and 1992. These inventory adjustments improved pretax operating results by approximately $134.4 million in 1993, primarily from the sale of Allison Gas Turbine Division, and $294.7 million in 1992.

The PepsiCo annual report (see Chapter 1) presents the same type of information in its inventory footnote as shown for GM in Panel A of Exhibit 9.5, albeit arrayed somewhat differently. Only 38 percent of PepsiCo's 1994 inventory is accounted for using LIFO. PepsiCo's footnotes indicate that total inventory cost is $970.0 million for 1994 and that it would have been $964.5 million if LIFO had not been used for any of the items. This figure of $964.5 million approximates current costs (that is, the amount that would be the result of using a FIFO or average cost method). The $5.5 million decrement of current cost over LIFO cost is in the opposite direction of the $2,535.9 million noted in the GM disclosures. In the absence of further information, the direction of this difference suggests that PepsiCo's product costs have declined.

It is interesting to consider that from a balance sheet perspective, there is no sound conceptual basis for using LIFO. For example, if a company adopted LIFO in 1975, there simply is no merit to the possibility that its reported 1995 ending inventory figure would contain 1975 costs. Indeed, it is just this possibility that recently prompted the International Accounting Standards Committee to issue a draft proposal seeking to prohibit the use of LIFO for external financial statements. The proposal did gain a modicum of support, but in the end, the proposal was not approved. The committee's revised IAS No. 2 does, however, identify FIFO and weighted average as the preferred inventory cost-flow methods while merely acknowledging LIFO as an allowed alternative.[2] Worldwide, the most prevalent inventory methods are weighted-average and FIFO; LIFO is not available for use in all countries because of its conceptual deficiencies.

[2] In some countries, other inventory valuation methods similar to LIFO are also permitted. For example, in Japan, the HIFO method, or highest-in, first-out, is acceptable. NIFO, or next-in, first-out, is generally not available because most countries base the valuation of inventories on actual, as opposed to replacement, costs.

A Numerical Illustration

To assist you in understanding the calculations necessary to derive the cost of ending inventory to be presented in the balance sheet and the cost of goods sold for the income statement, we now consider a numerical illustration.

Assume that FHAS Company begins the year with 100 units of an item in inventory and makes the following additions to inventory:

	Quantity	Unit Cost	Total Cost
Beginning inventory:	100 units	@ $1.00	$100.00
Purchase no. 1	110 units	@ $1.10	121.00
Purchase no. 2	120 units	@ $1.25	150.00
Purchase no. 3	115 units	@ $1.50	172.50
Goods available for sale	445		$543.50

Assume further that the company sells 300 units for $2 cash per unit and has 145 units left in inventory at year-end. Reported ending inventory and cost of goods sold under the FIFO, LIFO, and weighted-average cost methods would be as follows:

FIFO

Sales (300 units at $2 per unit)			$600.00
Cost of goods available for sale		$543.50	
Less: Cost of goods sold			
100 units at $1.00	$100.00		
110 units at $1.10	121.00		
90 units at $1.25	112.50		
Cost of goods sold		(333.50)	(333.50)
Ending inventory (145 units) (115 units at $1.50 + 30 units at $1.25)		$210.00	
Gross profit			$266.50

Weighted-Average

Sales (300 units at $2 per unit)		$600.00
Cost of goods available for sale	$543.50	
Less: Cost of goods sold 300 units at $1.2213*	(366.39)	(366.39)
Ending inventory (145 units at $1.2213)	$177.11	
Gross profit		$233.61

*$543.50/445 units = $1.2213.

LIFO

Sales (300 units at $2 per unit)			$600.00
Cost of goods available for sale		$543.50	
Less: Cost of goods sold			
115 units at $1.50	$172.50		
120 units at $1.25	150.00		
65 units at $1.10	71.50		
Cost of goods sold		(394.00)	(394.00)
Ending inventory (145 units) (100 units at $1.00 + 45 units at $1.10)		$149.50	
Gross profit			$206.00

As these examples indicate, in times of rising costs and stable (or growing) ending inventory quantities, the cost of goods sold is highest using LIFO and lowest using

FIFO, with the weighted-average cost method falling between them. The valuation of the units remaining in inventory is highest using FIFO and lowest using LIFO, again with weighted-average cost falling between the two. These characteristics are important when managers are contemplating what picture of their company to portray in the year-end financial statements.

An important part of inventory accounting under the LIFO method is the notion of **inventory layers** and **inventory-layer liquidation**. During a given period, if the inventory purchased or manufactured exceeds the quantities sold, the result is the addition of a "layer" (increment) to the ending inventory balance. Such was the case in the simple numerical example just presented — 45 units were added during the period to the beginning inventory level of 100 units. This type of phenomenon is depicted in the 19X2 column in Exhibit 9.6. This 19X2 layer is distinct from the 19X1 layer preceding it in that it reflects an addition of units to ending inventory that will be reported at 19X2 costs. The 19X1 layer, on the other hand, will be costed at 19X1 costs. Together, the sum of the two layers' costs will be reported as the cost of inventory in the 19X2 balance sheet.

In Exhibit 9.6, the 19X2 ending inventory consists of 450 units, composed of a layer of 200 units from 19X1 and a layer of 250 units from 19X2. Both of these LIFO layers will be maintained in inventory through subsequent periods until a net *decrease* in inventory takes place when period sales exceed the period's production. When this occurs, the prior period's inventory layers are sequentially liquidated. For example, 19X3 witnessed a reduction of the 19X2 layer in the amount of 100 units. The liquida-

EXHIBIT 9.6

LIFO Layering
(all amounts are units of inventory)

	19X1	19X2	19X3	19X4
Beginning inventory	0	200	450	350
Purchases	1,000	1,550	900	1,100
Sales	(800)	(1,300)	(1,000)	(1,050)
Ending inventory	200	450	350	400

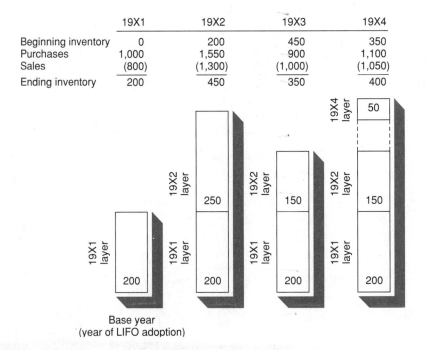

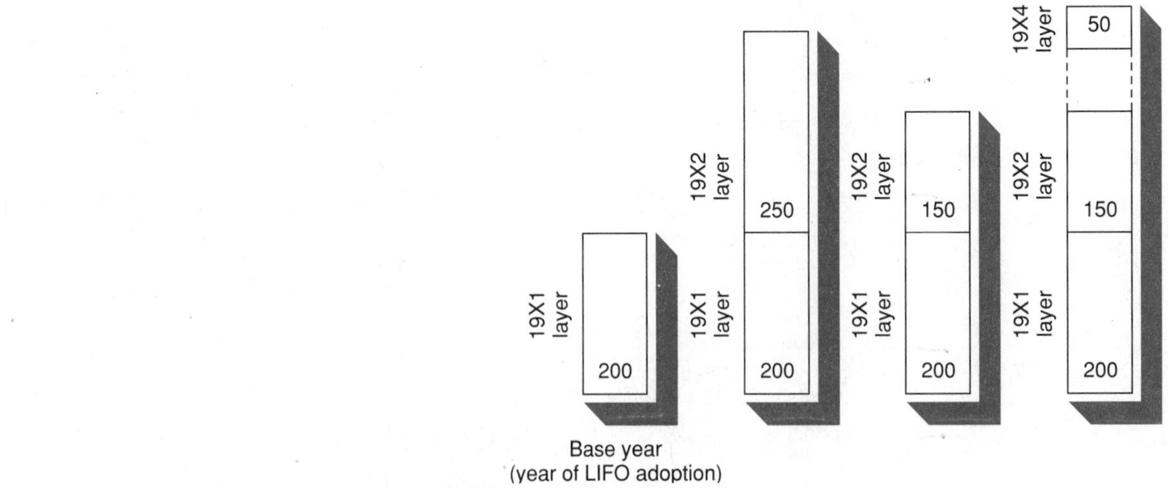

tion of a LIFO layer results in the inventory costs of a prior period being used to determine, in part, the current period's cost of goods sold deducted from the current period's revenue. Assuming annual cost increases, the matching of these old (perhaps as much as three or four years) costs with current revenues will result in higher profits than if only current period costs had been used in figuring the current period's cost of goods sold. Note that in Panel B of Exhibit 9.5, General Motors' LIFO-valued inventories for certain products were reduced in 1993, and net income before taxes was increased by $134.4 million. Such a boost to 1993 earnings was certainly anticipated and orchestrated by GM management as opposed to its being merely "a pleasant surprise." Indeed, many companies are reducing inventory quantities on hand through outsourcing of production and/or just-in-time production techniques. Lowering inventory levels is often motivated by a desire to reduce the annual carrying costs associated with storing, handling, and insuring large quantities of goods, as well as a desire to garner the capital tied up in goods on hand and to minimize potentially large losses associated with obsolescence.

A prior year's layer, once liquidated, will never be reestablished in subsequent periods. This is true in Exhibit 9.6 for 19X4 — a gap exists in the 19X2 layer for that part of the layer liquidated in 19X3, which will never be reestablished.

Inventory Systems: Periodic versus Perpetual

Determining how much of the goods available for sale during a period are still on hand and how much should be charged against income for the period is obviously critical to measuring a company's performance during a period. In addition to the cost-flow method decision, management must also adopt either a perpetual inventory system or a periodic inventory system to record ending inventory costs and cost of goods sold. Under a **periodic system**, the quantity of inventory on hand at any given time must be determined by physically counting the inventory items (usually once a year). The physical count, costed at an appropriate cost (LIFO, FIFO, or average), determines the balance sheet's ending inventory cost. The cost of goods sold for the period can then be determined from the basic relationship of beginning inventory *plus* purchases *minus* the costs attributable to ending inventory quantities. (A periodic system was assumed in the numerical examples above.)

When using a **perpetual system**, management maintains and regularly updates (often daily or, with computer assistance, continuously) an extensive inventory record-keeping system that is able to provide current inventory and cost of goods sold information on a moment's notice (rather than only after a physical count of items on hand). The perpetual system provides a continuous updating of both the Cost of Goods Sold and Ending Inventory account balances. Sound business practice suggests doing an occasional physical count of the inventory on hand to verify the accuracy of a perpetual system.

A final issue involving inventory systems, which will not be discussed at length here, involves the use of **standard product costs** rather than actual costs. Standard product costs are the estimated or projected costs of producing a product. Standard costs are widely used by managers for internal reporting and control purposes, and some companies carry this use over to external financial reporting. Inventory may be costed using standard cost estimates as long as the standard cost of the inventory is not materially different from actual costs. Regardless of whether management decides to use standard costs, decisions are still necessary regarding whether to use a periodic system or a perpetual system and what cost-flow method to adopt.

LOWER OF COST OR MARKET

As has been discussed to this point, the basis of accounting for inventories is historical cost (whether actual or standard), including all costs incurred to bring the goods to a salable condition. Such costs include, but are not limited to, transportation (inbound and/or outbound, depending on the circumstances), handling fees, labor costs, and overhead costs. Costs resulting from the marketing and selling activities of a company, even those directly related to a particular product, are normally not included as part of inventory costs.

A departure from the historical cost basis in reporting inventories is necessary when the "market value" of the ending inventory falls below its "cost" (as determined under one of the cost-flow methods). This can occur because of spoilage, obsolescence, or falling market prices for the goods. For example, consider a computer leasing company. Large quantities of computers may be technologically superseded by a newer generation of computers. Inventories of the older generation of computers are not likely to maintain their previous marketability — thus, they decline in market value. This decline in market value should be recognized as an expense of the period in which the reduction in value takes place, and the Inventory account balance should be adjusted to the lower value. Such a reduction represents the application of the **lower-of-cost-or-market principle.** Most companies maintain inventory control systems to help them monitor changing market values and inventory obsolescence.

Certain guidelines pertain to the determination of an inventory's current market value. Because there is no New York Stock Exchange equivalent for all the various items composing different businesses' investments in inventories, specifying a market value can be quite subjective, and thus the need for guidelines exists. To avoid gross manipulations of the lower-of-cost-or-market principle, the accounting profession has defined *market value* as the *replacement cost* of an item. Replacement cost is the cost that a company would incur today to reproduce or reacquire a similar item. Information pertaining to replacement cost is usually compiled from vendor catalogs, engineering estimates, and/or appraisals. Replacement cost is assumed to be the market value, subject to lower and upper boundaries, that should be compared to the recorded historical cost in determining whether a lower-of-cost-or-market adjustment is needed.

The upper boundary (or *ceiling*) has been defined by accounting standard setters as the net realizable value (NRV) of the inventory, that is, the company's selling price of the item less the costs of completing its production and of selling it. The lower boundary (or *floor*) for setting the market value is net realizable value less a normal profit margin. Both boundaries are generalized attempts to keep market value within a reasonable range given the nature of a particular company's inventory and its selling market. As long as replacement cost lies between these two values, it is considered to be a fair approximation of market value. If replacement cost is below the lower boundary, the lower boundary amount is used as the best approximation of market value. Similar considerations apply to the upper boundary. Once a market value is ascertained, inventories should be reported at the lower of their historical cost or market value.

If, for example, a write-down of $1,000 of the inventory's cost is required because its market value has fallen below cost, the following journal entry is made:

Dr. Cost of Goods Sold (E)	(inc.) 1,000	
Cr. Allowance for Decline in the Value of Inventory (CA)		(inc.) 1,000

Note that the decline in the inventory value is added to the cost of goods sold on the income statement, and an allowance account (a contra-asset account) is reported on the

EXHIBIT 9.7

Lower of Cost or Market for Inventory

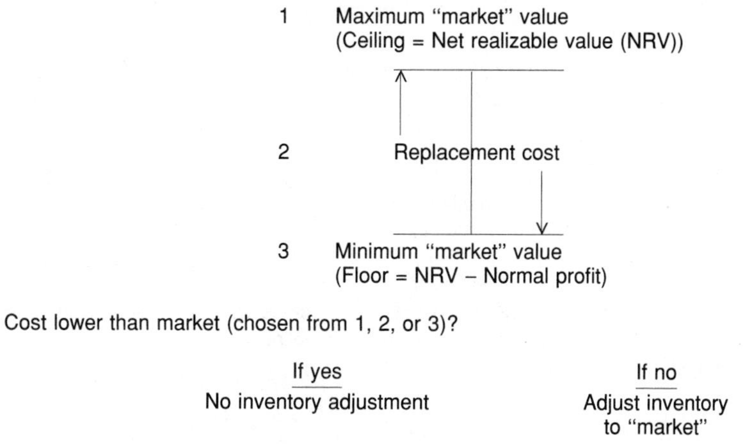

balance sheet as a deduction from the inventory account. In fact, the allowance account is rarely seen on the balance sheet; most often it is netted out against the balance in the inventory account. Some companies avoid the use of an allowance account by crediting the amount of the inventory reduction directly against the Inventory account. In either case, once inventory values have been written down, they cannot be written back up even if the value of the inventory recovers its previously lost value.[3] Exhibit 9.7 summarizes these lower-of-cost-or-market considerations.

FINANCIAL STATEMENT DISCLOSURE

In general, the requirements for financial statement disclosure for inventories include the following:

1. A description of the accounting principles a company used in determining reported inventory costs.
2. Reference to any accounting principles or methods of accounting peculiar to the industry in which a company operates.
3. Major categories of inventories.

Exhibit 9.8 presents the inventory disclosure from the annual report of the Quaker Oats Company. Notice that the disclosure reveals the costs attributable to three categories of inventory: finished goods, grains and raw materials, and supplies. Quaker Oats would not be expected to have a large work in process inventory category given the relatively short production time for its products. What amounts the company does have are probably included in the grains and raw materials category. Also note that the disclosures make explicit mention of the lower-of-cost-or-market valuation issue and that the LIFO method is utilized for the largest percentage of inventory items. With

[3]While under U.S. GAAP the value of inventory may not be written back up even if the inventory recovers in value, in some countries, an upward revaluation is permitted.

EXHIBIT 9.8

Quaker Oats Company
Inventory Disclosure
(in millions)

	June 30		
	1993	**1992**	**1991**
Inventories:			
Finished goods	$241.5	$302.8	$309.1
Grains and raw materials	73.1	93.7	86.7
Packaging materials and supplies	39.4	38.8	26.5
Total inventories	$354.0	$435.3	$422.3

Inventories. Inventories are valued at the lower of cost or market, using various cost methods, and include the cost of raw materials, labor, and overhead. The percentage of year-end inventories valued using each of the methods is as follows:

	June 30		
	1993	**1992**	**1991**
Last-in, first-out (LIFO)	53%	57%	61%
Average quarterly cost	35%	31%	27%
First-in, first-out (FIFO)	12%	12%	12%

If the LIFO method of valuing these inventories was not used, total inventories would have been $17.2 million, $13.9 million, and $18.9 million higher than reported at June 30, 1993, 1992, and 1991, respectively.

regard to LIFO, the disclosures reveal what the value of the LIFO-accounted inventories would have been if LIFO had not been used.

To maintain interperiod comparability, financial statement readers may assume the consistent application of cost-flow methods from period to period. If, however, a change in inventory accounting method is adopted (such as from FIFO to LIFO), company management is required to disclose the nature of the change and its effect on net income, including, whenever possible, a restatement of prior years' financial statements as if the new method had been in effect during those prior years. The disclosures by Kaiser Aluminum and Richfood Holding, Inc. (a grocery chain holding company), regarding their changes in inventory accounting methods are presented in Exhibit 9.9.

Note that in April 1990 Richfood Holding changed from FIFO to LIFO for virtually all of its inventory. For the year subsequent to that change, net income was $640,000 less than it would have been had the company remained with FIFO. Such an impact highlights the rising cost nature of this business and points to the fact that ending inventory at April 1991, under the newly adopted LIFO method, is lower than if it had continued to be reported at more recent costs, as the FIFO method would have done. Indeed, the note points to a $1,024,000 difference in ending inventory figures. The note also highlights the fact that prior years' financial statements cannot be restated as if they too had been prepared using the LIFO method. Such a restatement is simply not possible because ending inventory would have to be converted to the "oldest" costs, and it would be purely arbitrary to assume any base prior year start point other than this year — the year of making the change.

On the other hand, Kaiser discloses its change in 1985 from LIFO to FIFO and notes that a retroactive restatement is possible. Such a restatement actually results in the

EXHIBIT 9.9

Financial Statement Disclosures:
Inventory Method Changes

Panel A: Richfood Holding, Inc., Change to LIFO

1. Inventories
The company values its inventory at the lower of cost or market. Effective April 29, 1990, the company changed its method of determining cost from the first-in, first-out (FIFO) method to the last-in, first-out (LIFO) method for approximately 91 percent of its inventories. Remaining inventories are stated at the lower of cost or market using the FIFO method (see Note 3).

3. Inventories (in thousands)
As a result of the change to the LIFO inventory valuation method for the fiscal year ended April 27, 1991 (see note 1), net earnings decreased by $640, or $0.06 per share. There is no cumulative effect for this change on prior years since the ending inventory as previously reported at April 28, 1990, is the beginning inventory for LIFO purposes. Accordingly, pro forma results of operations for the prior years had LIFO been followed are not determinable. The current replacement cost of LIFO inventories exceeded reported cost by $1,024 at April 27, 1991. The company believes that the use the LIFO method better matches current costs of goods sold with current revenues from inventory sales.

Panel B: Kaiser Aluminum & Chemical Corp., Change to FIFO

Millions of dollars, except share amounts

4. Inventories
In 1985 the corporation changed its method of valuing its domestic aluminum raw materials, including primary aluminum, and certain industrial and specialty chemicals to the first-in, first-out (FIFO) method from the last-in, first-out (LIFO) method. The corporation is in the process of completing a refinancing of its bank debt, and the financial position of the corporation is of increasing interest to investors and others who extend credit to the corporation. The FIFO method of inventory valuation is a better measure to reflect the current value of such inventories and the financial position of the corporation. In addition, under the current economic environment of low inflation and the corporation's decreasing inventories and production costs, the FIFO method results in a better matching of costs and revenues as compared to the LIFO method.

The FIFO method of accounting has been applied retroactively, and prior-year financial statements have been restated. This change increased inventory value by $190.7 and retained earnings by $104.1 at December 31, 1985, and increased the net loss by $9.1 ($0.21 per share) because the effect of a FIFO cost write-down in 1985 exceeded the effect of liquidating a LIFO layer with higher unit costs than the current FIFO costs. The change increased the 1984 net loss by $43.5 ($0.99 per share) because a FIFO cost write-down was required by a market price decline in 1984. The 1983 net loss was reduced by $24.7 ($0.57 per share) because the FIFO inventory value increase of $82.6 exceeded the $57.9 benefit from the 1983 LIFO liquidation.

Operating supplies inventories were $72.4 and $76.5 at December 31, 1985 and 1984. Finished goods, work in process, and raw materials have been combined because they are sold at various stages of processing.

previously reported 1984 loss being increased by $43.5 million and the 1983 loss being reduced by $24.7 million. If additional prior years were reported in Kaiser's 1985 annual report, they too would be restated because for any previous year-end date, it is possible to determine what ending inventory costs would have been under FIFO. They would simply be those closest to that point in time. Notice that Kaiser and Richfood both claim that the change in method is prompted by a belief that a better matching of expenses and revenues is achieved by the new method.

Management Issues

A variety of inventory issues are of concern to merchandisers and manufacturers alike. One such issue pertains to the physical safeguarding of inventory items. Measures undertaken to prevent employee and/or customer theft often range from patrolling security personnel, to surveillance cameras, to limited access policies, to magnetic alarm strips, and unannounced physical inventory counting. In a related vein are the management concerns for precluding losses due to inventory obsolescence. Thus, we see that the dating of perishables (such as food and pharmaceuticals) and the minimization of inventory quantities or the production to order of fashionable items (such as clothes, computer games, and music CDs).

From a customer service vantage point, managers are concerned with avoiding stock outs. There is nothing quite so frustrating for a customer and a manager than to have a customer respond to a product ad, only to find it out of stock. Managers are fully aware of the customer ill will created by such experiences, and they try to maintain inventory levels to avoid such events. Carrying inventory, however, is costly. So while managers are trying to avoid stock outs they are also trying to minimize the company's funds tied up in inventory, their investment in warehouse space, and their inventory handling costs. Companies have studied the issue of inventory optimization and have, in many cases, implemented very sophisticated just-in-time (JIT) inventory management systems. Perhaps foremost among the innovators in addressing such concerns are Wal-Mart, American Hospital Supply, and Caterpillar.

Several management concerns are explicitly related to a choice to adopt the LIFO cost-flow method. First, if a U.S. company adopts LIFO for tax purposes, they generally are required by the U.S. Treasury to also use LIFO for externally published income statements. Thus, managers must weigh the cash tax savings that are achievable during periods of rising inventory quantities and costs against the lower earnings reported to shareholders. (The efficient-market hypothesis would assert that financial markets can see through this reporting convention and are not misled or misinformed about the firm's profitability.) Second, once on LIFO for tax purposes, U.S. companies wishing to subsequently switch to some other method must obtain permission to do so from the Internal Revenue Service. One other management LIFO issue pertains to the maintenance of the LIFO layers during periods of increasing costs. If near year-end it appears that a company's LIFO accounting for cost of goods sold will "dip into" a prior year's lower-cost LIFO layer due to this year's unit sales exceeding units purchased or manufactured, management may want to make a year-end purchase of inventory in order to preempt such a "dipping." Clearly, the efficacy of such a purchase, in the absence of any other business reason for it, needs to be considered by managers, if for no other reason than to avoid the additional taxes that are likely to result from a LIFO layer liquidation.

ANALYZING INVENTORIES

Analyzing a company's investment in inventories typically focuses on two questions: Is the investment in inventory likely to produce an adequate return to the company? Is the level of investment in inventory appropriate for anticipated future sales?

With respect to the first question, a widely used financial indicator is the **gross profit margin ratio**:

$$\text{Gross profit margin ratio} = \frac{\text{Gross profit margin}}{\text{Net sales}}$$

This ratio indicates the percentage of each sales dollar that is available to cover a company's period expenses and to provide a return to its owners *after* the cost of goods sold has been deducted. Clearly, the higher this ratio, the more profitable a company's sales of inventory will be. For 1994, PepsiCo's gross profit margin ratio is 0.52 [($28,472.4 − $13,715.4) ÷ $28,472.4], which is moderately high when compared to 0.24 for General Motors in 1994. An unacceptably low ratio may indicate several concerns: (1) the company is underpricing its products, or (2) when a product is competitively priced, the cost to manufacture it is too high, perhaps due to inefficiencies in the manufacturing process or in the purchase or raw materials or to the payment of excessively high wages to production employees. The gross profit margin ratio is important to managers because it allows them to determine whether the root of low earnings is attributable to the company's period costs or to its product costs. Likewise, this ratio is important to investors and creditors by enabling them to identify well-managed companies.

With respect to the second question above, two financial ratios are often reviewed: (1) the inventory turnover ratio, and (2) the average days inventory on hand. As discussed in Chapter 7, the **inventory turnover ratio** measures the number of times that the average level (or dollar investment) in inventory was sold, or "turned," during a given accounting period:

$$\text{Inventory turnover ratio} = \frac{\text{Cost of goods sold for the period}}{\text{Average inventory held during the period}}$$

In general, the higher the inventory turnover ratio, the better. A high turnover ratio such as PepsiCo's 14.5 ($13,715.4 ÷ 947.3) signals a reduced potential for losses attributable to product obsolescence, which in the case of PepsiCo indicates that it is probably incurring minimal costs to maintain an investment in inventory, and, simply given the nature of PepsiCo business, a high ratio is to be expected. GM's 1994 inventory turnover ratio is 12.5, indicating a fairly rapid transfer of inventory from GM's books to their dealers. Excessively high turnover ratios may be problematic if the cause is an insufficient investment in inventory. For example, when a company fails to maintain an adequate supply of inventory to meet its customers' needs, it may create order backlogs and customer dissatisfaction, not to mention the possibility of lost sales. On the other hand, a low ratio not warranted by the nature of the company's business may indicate excessive inventory that may not be salable.

The **average number of days' inventory on hand** ratio indicates the average number of days of inventory supplies on hand to meet customer needs, based on recent sales data:

$$\text{Average number of days' inventory on hand} = \frac{\text{365 days}}{\text{Inventory turnover ratio}}$$

The 1994 average number of days' inventory on hand for PepsiCo was 25 days (365 ÷ 14.5), and 20 days for GM. This ratio is important because it reveals whether there is an adequate quantity of inventory on hand or whether there is an excessive quantity; the latter indicates the need to slow or halt production. For both GM and PepsiCo, these figures appear about right — neither too high to cause worries of slow-moving products nor too low to cause worries of not being able to meet customer orders. Unfortunately, there is no ideal target for the average number of days' inventory on hand or for the inventory turnover ratio. In fact, these indicators vary substantially among industries and often within the same industry. As a general rule, potential investors, lenders, and managers are well advised to compare these indicators for a given company against the leading firm in that industry.

In conclusion, it is important to note that all of the financial indicators discussed are closely tied to the specific inventory cost-flow assumption utilized by a company. Thus, during a period of rising costs, it would be quite reasonable to expect that a FIFO-accounted company would have a higher gross profit margin ratio but lower inventory turnover ratio than would a LIFO-accounted company. In addition, for cross-company comparisons in which the companies use different cost-flow assumptions, the ending inventory and current period earnings amounts should be adjusted for the LIFO company so that it may be compared more appropriately to the FIFO company. Such adjustments would parallel those described earlier for General Motors (Exhibit 9.5). A comparison of these three ratios, with and without LIFO, is presented

EXHIBIT 9.10

1994 Inventory Ratio Analysis with and without LIFO Effects

	PepsiCo		General Motors	
	With LIFO	Without LIFO	With LIFO	Without LIFO
Gross profit margin ratio	0.52	0.52	0.24	0.26
Inventory turnover ratio	14.5	14.6	12.5	9.6
Average number of days' inventory on hand	25	25	29	38

for GM and PepsiCo in Exhibit 9.10. Note that a significant difference in GM's inventory turnover ratio occurs when the effects of LIFO are deleted from ending inventory and cost of sales. As higher costs are left in inventory and lower costs are assigned to cost of sales (as is the case for adjusting GM to FIFO), inventory turnover does not appear as good. Thus, as seen here, inventory-related financial indicators should be investigated with an eye toward determining the likely impact of the inventory accounting method on the ratios themselves.

SUMMARY

For most nonservice companies, inventories represent a significant current asset. For merchandising companies, inventories may represent the largest single asset category.

Inventories (and cost of goods sold) are usually valued using one of several common cost-flow methods: FIFO, LIFO, or average cost. In addition, the ending inventory must always be evaluated relative to its market (or replacement) value to ensure that the value reported on the balance sheet is not overstated and approximates its net realizable value.

The effective management and utilization of inventory is a hallmark of a well-run company. Thus, analyzing the nature of and investment in inventories is important to investors, creditors, and managers. In addition to reviewing the financial statement disclosure relating to inventories, the financial statement user would be wise to calculate such asset management ratios as the inventory turnover ratio and the average number of days' inventory on hand ratio. These ratios are useful indicators of the quality of a given company's inventory management.

NEW CONCEPTS AND TERMS

Average cost method (p. 413)
Average number of days' inventory on hand ratio (p. 425)
Direct labor costs (p. 408)
Finished goods inventory (p. 407)
First-in, first-out (FIFO) (p. 414)
First-in, still-here (FISH) (p. 414)
Gross profit margin ratio (p. 424)
Inventory layer (p. 418)
Inventory-layer liquidation (p. 418)
Inventory turnover ratio (p. 425)
Last-in, first-out (LIFO) (p. 414)
Last-in, still-here (LISH) (p. 414)
LIFO reserve (p. 415)
Lower-of-cost-or-market principle (p. 420)
Manufacturing overhead (p. 409)
Period costs (p. 409)
Periodic inventory system (p. 419)
Perpetual inventory system (p. 419)
Product costs (p. 409)
Raw materials inventory (p. 407)
Replacement cost (p. 414)
Specific identification method (p. 412)
Standard product costs (p. 419)
Weighted-average cost method (p. 413)
Work in process inventory (p. 407)

ISSUES FOR DISCUSSION

D9.1 For each of the companies below, are they likely to have, at any moment in time, more costs accumulated in raw materials, work in process, or finished goods ending inventory? Explain your rationale.

a. The Washington Post

b. Georgia Pacific Corp.

c. Harry's Custom-Made Furniture Reproduction Shop

d. PepsiCo, Inc.

e. Boeing Co.

D9.2 Consider a supermarket, a department store, an auto manufacturer, and a jewelry store. Which type of business is likely to have the highest inventory turnover ratio? The lowest inventory turnover ratio? Explain your rationale.

D9.3 In general, what criteria should be used to determine which costs to include in a published balance sheet's inventory account?

D9.4 Explain why the lower-of-cost-or-market convention is used to value inventory on published balance sheets.

D9.5 During periods of rising prices, a perpetual inventory system would result in the same dollar amount of ending inventory as a periodic inventory system under which inventory cost flow method(s)? Explain your answer.

D9.6 Identify and discuss three or four factors contributing to the particular investment in inventory that a company might chose to make.

D9.7 When performing a comparative ratio analysis on two companies of interest to you, and one uses LIFO and one uses FIFO to account for their inventory, what ratios will be affected by this accounting choice? Does this difference negate the possibility of a valid ratio comparison? Explain.

D9.8 Explain the rationale for the lower-of-cost-or-market principle. As a shareholder, are you in favor of this principle? Why or why not?

PROBLEMS

P9.1 Calculating inventory values. The following selected data were obtained from the accounting records of View for Pleasure, Inc., a distributor of videos.

	Jungle Warriors	The Blob
Inventory, January 1	16,000 copies at $1.00	8,000 copies at $3.00
Purchases: May 12	6,000 copies at 1.50	10,000 copies at 2.00
Aug. 20	6,000 copies at 2.00	6,000 copies at 1.50
Sales: March 3	12,000 copies at 2.50	7,000 copies at 3.50
July 8	3,000 copies at 3.00	4,000 copies at 3.50
September 21	10,000 copies at 2.50	3,000 copies at 3.50
Replacement cost: December 31	1.50	2.50

Required:

Using the information given, calculate the following:

a. The cost of goods sold for each of the two videos for the year assuming that the FIFO method is used in a *perpetual* inventory system.

b. The value of the ending inventory for each of the two videos assuming that the LIFO method is used in a *periodic* inventory system.

c. The value of ending inventory for each of the two videos assuming that the FIFO method is used in a *periodic* inventory system.

P9.2 Cost-flow identification. Fill in the blank beside each numbered statement below with one of the inventory cost flow methods discussed in the chapter.

_______ 1. Cost of goods sold is highest for a period wherein inventory purchase costs continuously rose.

_______ 2. The ending inventory is reported at the latest purchase cost.

_______ 3. Achieves best matching of current costs with current revenues in the income statement.

_______ 4. Provides the greatest cash tax savings in a period of rising purchase costs.

_______ 5. Results in the highest ending inventory valuation after a period of steadily declining purchase costs.

P9.3 Calculating inventory values. The following cost data were taken from the records of The Fertilizer Store:

Beginning inventory:	1,100 lbs. at $ 8	$ 8,800
Purchases:	2,100 lbs. at $10	21,000
	600 lbs. at $ 9	5,400
	1,200 lbs. at $12	14,400
	800 lbs. at $11	8,800
	200 lbs. at $10	2,000
		$51,600

Sales were $72,000 (4,500 lbs. at $16.00 per lb.).

Compute each of the following under LIFO and FIFO. In addition, apply the lower-of-cost-or-market principle under the assumption that the year-end market price is $10 per pound.

a. Cost of goods sold.

b. Ending inventory.

c. Gross profit.

P9.4 Evaluating inventory errors. Summit Corporation hired a new accountant during 19X5 who, it was discovered, had made at least four major mistakes (noted below). Note the 19X5 and 19X6 financial statement effect of each by completing the table below. Note the effect as: O = overstated, U = understated, and N = no effect. You may ignore taxes and assume that the company uses the periodic inventory system.

Mistake 1. The accountant did not record a $4,000 19X5 credit sale until 19X6. The merchandise was shipped in 19X5 and was not included in the 19X5 ending inventory. The customer paid for the goods in 19X6.

Mistake 2. The accountant did not record a $6,000 19X5 purchase on account until 19X6 when a check was cut to the supplier. The goods were also missed in the 19X5 year-end physical count.

Mistake 3. The accountant included $3,000 of obsolete inventory in the 19X5 year end inventory count. The obsolete inventory was finally written off in 19X6.

Mistake 4. The accountant treated $10,000 of 19X5 manufacturing overhead as a 19X5 period cost. In 19X6, all manufacturing costs were properly treated as product costs.

		Total Revenue	Total Expense	Net Income	Total Assets	Total Liabilities	Total Owners' Equity
19X5	Mistake 1						
	Mistake 2						
	Mistake 3						
	Mistake 4						
19X6	Mistake 1						
	Mistake 2						
	Mistake 3						
	Mistake 4						

P9.5 Inventory value calculation. Consider the following data for the We Made It Co.:

Raw materials inventory — April 1	$ 83
Raw materials purchased during April	715
Raw materials inventory — April 30	44
Other manufacturing costs	407
Direct labor	440
Work in process — April 1	66
Work in process — April 30	28
Finished goods inventory — April 1	99
Finished goods inventory — April 30	165
Gross margin	138
Selling and administrative expenses	39

Required:

Calculate the following:

a. The cost of raw materials used in April.

b. What was the cost of finished goods manufactured in April?

c. What was the cost of goods sold for April?

d. What was the sales revenue for April?

e. What was net income for April?

P9.6 Calculating cost of goods sold. The following information pertains to Skeen Manufacturing Corporation, a manufacturer of hotel bedroom furniture:

Beginning inventories:	
Raw materials	$ 11,000
Work in process	5,000
Ending inventories:	
Raw materials	16,500
Work in process	6,600
Raw materials used	77,000
Direct labor	55,000
Total manufacturing costs	167,000
Cost of goods available for sale	170,000
Cost of goods sold	159,000
Gross profit	135,000

Required:

Compute the following:

a. Raw materials purchased.

b. Raw materials available for use.

c. Manufacturing overhead.

d. Cost of goods manufactured.

e. Sales.

f. Beginning finished goods inventory.

g. Ending finished goods inventory.

P9.7 LIFO vs. FIFO. DFW, Inc., began business on January 1, 19X1, after taking over the business of Dallas–Ft. Worth Partnership. Partnership had been a manufacturer of custom souvenir products. At the time of the takeover, Partnership had on hand 7,500 Dallas Cowboy souvenir pennants valued at $1.35 each.

DFW, Inc., operated as a wholesale manufacturer from 19X1 through 19X6, selling its custom-designed pennants to various retail stores and distributors throughout the Texas area. During that period, the cost to produce and handle the pennants rose steadily, and by the end of 19X5, the cost had increased to $3 per pennant.

During 19X6, however, the price spiral finally broke. A general recession throughout the United States had caused a drop in the cost of labor (unemployment in Texas had exceeded 7 percent) and in the cost of many raw materials. By mid-19X6, the cost to produce a pennant had fallen to approximately $1.35.

Required:

Assume that DFW, Inc., ended 19X6 with 5,000 pennants on hand and that the manufacturer regularly maintained a base stock of at least 5,000 pennants at all times. Based on these facts, indicate whether each of the following statements is true or false, and explain your reasoning.

a. Both LIFO and FIFO would produce exactly the same total reported profit for the period 19X1–19X6.

b. LIFO would show a higher profit for 19X6.

c. FIFO would show a higher profit for 19X1.

d. The inventory of pennants on the balance sheet at year-end 19X3 would be valued higher if LIFO were used.

e. The inventory of pennants on the balance sheet at year-end 19X6 would be $6,750 under both LIFO and FIFO.

f. LIFO would show a lower profit than FIFO for each of the years 19X1 through 19X5.

P9.8 LIFO company versus FIFO company. Presented below are the financial statements of two companies that are identical in every respect except the method of valuing their inventories. The method of valuing inventory is LIFO for LIFO Company and FIFO for FIFO Company.

Comparative Income Statements

	FIFO Company	LIFO Company
Sales	$20,000,000	$20,000,000
Less: Cost of sales	9,200,000	11,280,000
Gross profit	$10,800,000	$ 8,720,000
Less: Operating expenses	5,000,000	5,000,000
Net income before tax	$ 5,800,000	$ 3,720,000

Comparative Balance Sheets

Assets		
Cash	$ 3,000,000	$ 3,000,000
Receivables	6,000,000	6,000,000
Inventory	3,800,000	1,720,000
Total current assets	$12,800,000	$10,720,000
Total noncurrent (net)	20,000,000	20,000,000
Total	$32,800,000	$30,720,000
Equities		
Current liabilities	$ 4,200,000	$ 4,200,000
Noncurrent liabilities	9,000,000	9,000,000
Total liabilities	$13,200,000	$13,200,000
Total owners' equity	19,600,000	17,520,000
Total	$32,800,000	$30,720,000

Required:

Using the two sets of financial statements, calculate the following ratios or financial indicators for each firm:

a. Current ratio.

b. Inventory turnover ratio.

c. Average days' inventory on hand.

d. Return on total assets.

e. Total debt to total assets.

f. Long-term debt to owners' equity.

g. Gross margin ratio.

h. Return on sales.

i. Return on owners' equity.

j. Earnings per share (assume 2 million shares outstanding).

Based on the above ratios in part (a)–(j), which company represents

k. The best investment opportunity?

l. The best acquisition opportunity?

m. The best lending opportunity?

P9.9 Ratio analysis. Presented below are some recent summary financial data for Coca-Cola Enterprises, Inc., and PepsiCo, Inc.

	Year 1	Year 2
Cost of goods sold (in millions):		
Coca-Cola Enterprises, Inc.	$2,313	$2,268
PepsiCo, Inc.	7,468	5,957
Year-end inventory (in millions):		
Coca-Cola Enterprises, Inc.	128	125
PepsiCo, Inc.	546	442

Required:

Using the above data, calculate the inventory turnover and the average number of days' inventory on hand for Year 1 for each company. What is your evaluation of each company's inventory management policy?

P9.10 Lower of cost or market. Sue Smith was the proprietor of a computer games store. She had recently decided to expand her inventory. To finance the increased inventory, she decided to approach the Wachovia Bank for a working capital loan.

In preparation for a meeting with her accountant to prepare the financial statements that she knew the bank would want, she collected the following information about some of her inventory.

	Computer Game				
	1	2	3	4	5
Cost	$15.00	$15.00	$15.00	$15.00	$15.00
Net realizable value	16.00	17.00	14.00	14.50	14.50
Net realizable value less her normal store profit	14.00	16.00	13.50	14.00	14.00
Replacement cost	16.50	15.50	13.00	14.30	14.75
Quantity in the store	10	8	15	20	15

Required:

For a balance sheet presentation, ascertain the carrying value of this part of Sue's computer games inventory.

P9.11 Estimating inventory values. Ball Sporting Goods Shops' accounting records indicated the following:

Inventory, 1/1/96	$ 500,000
Purchases during 1996	3,500,000
Sales during 1996	5,000,000

A physical inventory taken on December 31, 1996, revealed an ending inventory of $700,000. Ball's gross profit on sales averaged 35 percent in recent years. Ball suspects that a new employee has been stealing athletic equipment.

Required:

At December 31, 1996, what is the estimated cost of the missing inventory?

P9.12 Calculating cost of goods sold. The following data were obtained from Iowa Company's accounting records for the year ended December 31, 1996:

Decrease in raw materials inventory	$ 15,000
Increase in finished goods inventory	50,000
Increase in work-in-process inventory	10,000
Raw materials purchased	415,000
Direct labor	196,000
Factory overhead	298,000
Freight out	42,000

Because the company was a meat processor, there was no work in process inventory at day's end.

Required:

Calculate Iowa's 1996 cost of goods sold.

P9.13 Inventory valuation. Last year, Powell, Inc., was able to arrange what was thought to be a special purchase of a "rare" raw material for a new product that it manufactured. Powell had even hired a security guard to protect the raw material while it was in transit from the supplier. This year, unfortuantely, Powell management came to realize that the replacement cost of the raw material was above its net realizable value and both were below the original cost.

Powell has always used the average cost inventory method for raw materials. During the past two years, purchase costs had steadily declined for this particular raw material while its quantity in ending inventory had risen slightly.

Required:

a. How should Powell account for the security guard cost? Why?

b. Describe the amount that Powell's raw material inventory should be reported at on the balance sheet. Explain.

c. Describe the amount that Powell's raw material inventory should be reported at on the balance sheet if the company had always used LIFO, not the average cost inventory method. Explain.

P9.14 Inventory decisions. Noel Company sells food additives and uses LIFO inventory. One of the company's raw material inventory on January 1, 19X1, consisted of 3,000 lbs. costed at $20 per pound. Purchases and ending inventories in the subsequent years were as follows:

Year	Average Purchase Price per Pound during Year	Costs of Purchases	December 31 Inventory
19X1	25	$384,000	3,600 lbs.
19X2	28	352,000	2,600 lbs.
19X3	30	448,000	4,000 lbs.

Because of temporary scarcities, the raw material is expected to cost $40 per pound in 19X4. Sales for 19X4 are expected to require 7,000 pounds of the raw material. The purchasing agent suggests that the inventory be allowed to decrease to 600 pounds by the end of 19X4 and be replenished to 4,000 pounds in early 19X5. The controller argues that such a policy is foolish. She argues that if inventories are allowed to decrease, the company will pay a very large amount in income taxes (at its current income tax rate of 34 percent). She suggests that the company maintain a 19X4 year-end inventory of 4,000 pounds.

Required:

a. Calculate the cost of goods sold and the dollar value of ending inventory for 19X4 for both scenarios.

	Purchasing Agent	Controller
Cost of goods sold	$________	$________
Ending inventory	$________	$________

b. Calculate the tax savings for 19X4 if the advice of the controller is followed rather than that of the purchasing agent.

c. If you were making the decision, what other information might you consider in choosing whose advice to follow?

P9.15 Inventory disclosures. Presented below is the inventory footnote taken from a recent Merck & Co., Inc., annual report. When necessary, assume a 40 percent corporate income tax rate.

Merck & Co., Inc. and Subsidiaries
Notes to Financial Statements

Substantially all domestic inventories are valued using the last-in, first-out method (LIFO). Remaining inventories are valued at the lower of first-in, first-out (FIFO) cost or market.

	(in millions)	
Inventories at December 31 consisted of:	**19X1**	**19X0**
Finished goods	$359.6	$299.5
Raw materials and work in process	343.0	335.1
Supplies	46.4	41.5
Total (approximate current cost)	749.0	676.1
Reduction to LIFO cost	89.4	96.3
	$659.6	$579.8

Inventories valued at LIFO composed approximately 46 percent and 42 percent of inventories at December 31, 19X1 and 19X0, respectively.

Required:

a. What dollar amount for inventories appears in Merck's December 31, 19X1, balance sheet?

b. If Merck had used current costs for ending inventory valuation rather than those generated by LIFO:

(1) What dollar amount would have appeared for inventories in its December 31, 19X1, balance sheet?

(2) To what extent would its December 31, 19X1, retained earnings balance be different? Higher or lower?

(3) To what extent would its 19X1 net income be different? Higher or lower?

P9.16 Inventory disclosures. The 19X2 Reynolds Metals annual report contained the following footnote description of its accounting policies with respect to inventories:

Note A — Significant Accounting Policies

Inventories
Inventories are stated at the lower of cost or market. Cost of inventories of approximately $283 million in 19X2 and $321 million in 19X1 is determined by the last-in, first-out method (LIFO). Remaining inventories of approximately $422 million in 19X2 and $385 million in 19X1 are determined by the average or first-in, first-out (FIFO) methods. If the FIFO method was applied to LIFO inventories, the amount for inventories would increase by approximately $576 million at December 31, 19X2, and $498 million at December 31, 19X1. As a result of LIFO, costs and expenses increased by $78 million in 19X2 and $29 million in 19X1 and decreased by $60 million in 19X0. Included in the total LIFO effect are liquidations of prior year inventories of $26 million in 19X0.

Since certain inventories of the company may be sold at various stages of processing, no practical distinction can be made between finished products, in-process products, and other materials, and therefore inventories are presented as a single classification.

Required:

a. What would the balance sheet inventory amounts have been in 19X2 and 19X1 if *all* inventories had been reported on a FIFO basis?

b. Please explain the significance of using LIFO for some inventories and FIFO for others. Why do you think Reynolds Metals does this?

c. Explain what happened to Reynolds's inventories in 19X0.

d. Suppose Reynolds had always used FIFO for all inventories and assume the company's 19X2 income tax rate was 34 percent. What difference would it have made in its 19X2 income statement? The balance sheet as of December 31, 19X2? The 19X2 cash flow statement?

P9.17 Lower of cost or market. Doral Distribution Company has determined its December 31, 19X1, inventory on a FIFO basis at $206,000. Data pertaining to the inventory follow:

Estimated selling price	$219,000
Estimated cost of disposal	19,000
Normal profit margin	41,000
Current replacement cost	195,000

Required:

At December 31, 19X1, record the lower-of-cost-or-market inventory adjustment, if any, that Doral should book.

P9.18 Inventory method comparisons. During Fawcett Company's first two years of business, it sold a single product. During that time, Fawcett's inventory costs increased. Due to a model change, inventory quantities of the original product declined during 19X2 to zero. Assuming the periodic inventory system, which inventory cost method pairing below would report the highest amount for the two item headings?

	Inventory December 31, 19X1	Cost of Sales 19X2
a.	LIFO	LIFO
b.	LIFO	FIFO
c.	FIFO	FIFO
d.	FIFO	LIFO

Explain your answer.

CASES

C9.1 Inventory cost flows: Paragon Electronics, Inc.* One of the first tasks Greg Lemond was assigned on his recent appointment as assistant controller of Paragon Electronics, Inc., involved a review of Paragon's accounting for inventories. One of the specific requests made by Maria Sells, the controller, had been for Lemond to investigate the financial results of two different cost-flow methods: LIFO and weighted average. Paragon uses the periodic FIFO cost-flow method. Lemond contemplated what might be the most informative means to make the appropriate comparisons.

Paragon Electronics, Inc., was a small electronics firm that specialized in the design and production of state-of-the-art electronic systems for advanced Department of Defense projects. Under one particular new project, Paragon had a contract to supply a "package" of subassemblies that were used by a much larger prime contractor (Aero, Inc.) in the production of a new guidance system. Aero, Inc., made all but a select few of the subassemblies used to build the completed guidance system. For those that it did not make, it had chosen a single-source supplier, Paragon, in order to minimize contracting and administrative costs. Paragon manufactured all of the subassemblies contracted to it by Aero, Inc., except the pulsed integrated gyro accelerometer (PIGA). Paragon had found that it would be possible to purchase the PIGA subassemblies from an outside source at a price roughly equivalent to what Paragon's production costs would be. The option of purchasing the PIGAs allowed Paragon to (1) meet its component "package" contract with Aero, Inc., and (2) pursue other contract opportunities using the facilities that would otherwise have been used for PIGA production.

Lemond decided to use the PIGA inventory for his LIFO, FIFO, and weighted-average inventory method comparisons because, for a distinct component not produced internally, he would not have to be concerned with such issues as cost allocations, transfer prices, and so on. He recalled that under the Aero, Inc., contract, Paragon was to supply 500 PIGAs over a six-year period at a price of $950 per unit. Due to production constraints and demands from other programs, Paragon's sole-source supplier would commit to provide only 100 PIGAs a year over a five-year period. The PIGAs would be purchased at the beginning of the year. The unit costs for the PIGAs would increase the first two years due to the market's limited supply but then would decline as competitive sources came on line. Applicable freight and handling costs were included in the purchase price. Relevant selling and general and administrative expenses were expected to be $6,000 a year through 1990 and $2,000 in 1991. For analytical purposes, all purchases and sales between Paragon and its suppliers and customer could be assumed to be on a cash basis.

Lemond noted all of this information and developed a form (shown following) to analyze the PIGA pro forma inventories under the three different cost-flow assumptions. After completing the three relevant versions of this form, Lemond planned to analyze the impact of each of the three methods on each year's balance sheet (see the December 31, 1985, balance sheet), income statement, and cash flow (assuming a 46 percent income tax rate, the same inventory method was used for book and tax purposes, and all taxes are paid currently).

Required:

Perform the analysis Lemond intends to do.

LIFO

	PIGA Purchases by Paragon			Ending Inventory			Cost of Goods Sold		
Year Total	Units	Unit Cost	Units Sold to Aero, Inc.	Units	Unit Cost	Total	Units	Unit Cost	Total
1986	100	$700	80						
1987	100	800	110						
1988	100	850	92						
1989	100	750	104						
1990	100	650	94						
1991	–0–	N/A	20						

FIFO

1986	100	$700	80						
1987	100	800	110						
1988	100	850	92						
1989	100	750	104						
1990	100	650	94						
1991	–0–	N/A	20						

Weighted Average

1986	100	$700	80						
1987	100	800	110						
1988	100	850	92						
1989	100	750	104						
1990	100	650	94						
1991	–0–	N/A	20						

Paragon Electronics, Inc.
Balance Sheet
For the Year Ending December 31, 1985

Assets		**Liabilities & Owners' Equity**	
		Liabilities	
Cash	$ 500,000	Account payable	$ 300,000
Accounts receivable	140,000	Accrued expenses	100,000
Inventory	700,000	Current liabilities	400,000
Current assets	$1,340,000	Bond payable	200,000
		Total liabilities	$ 600,000
		Owners' Equity	
Property, plant, and equipment	2,000,000	Retained earnings	$1,140,000
		Common stock	1,600,000
Total assets	$3,340,000	Total equity	$2,740,000
		Total liabilities and owners' equity	$3,340,000

C9.2 LIFO valuation — Champion Spark Plug Company.* Champion Spark Plug Company was principally involved in manufacturing, distributing, and marketing spark plugs, windshield wipers, and other automotive components. Through various subsidiaries, however, Champion was also engaged in manufacturing coating application equipment, health care equipment, and cold-drawn steel. Champion made more than 850 types of spark plugs, diesel-starting glow plugs, and related items for a wide array of power-driven devices. Consider the following excerpts from Champion's 1980 annual report:

	(in millions)		
	1980	**1979**	**1978**
Net earnings	$ 36.9	$ 56.9	$ 55.3
Inventory	$261.4	$240.8	$227.1

In 1979 the company adopted the last-in, first-out (LIFO) method of determining costs for substantially all of its U.S. inventories. In prior years, inventory values had been principally computed under the lower-of-cost-or-market, first-in, first-out (FIFO) method. The effect of the change on the operating results for 1979 was to reduce net earnings by $5.8 million, or $0.15 per share.

Inventory balances at December 31, 1980 and 1979, would have been $26.8 million and $10.7 million higher, respectively, if U.S. inventory costs had continued to be determined principally under FIFO rather than LIFO. Net earnings on a primarily FIFO method basis would have been $45.6 million, or $1.19 per share [in 1980] compared to $62.7 million, or $1.64 per share, in 1979.

During 1980, certain inventory balances declined below the levels at the beginning of the year, resulting in a smaller increase in the LIFO reserve than would have occurred if these inventory levels had not declined. Net earnings in 1980 would have been $1.3 million ($0.03 per share) lower had the LIFO reserve addition not been affected by reduced inventories.

It was not practical to determine prior year effects of retroactive LIFO application.

Required:

Using the financial information provided, identify the unknowns in the table below. Assume that the effective tax rate for Champion during 1979 and 1980 was 46 percent. (Because the rate was actually a fraction less than 46 percent, any minor "unexplained" differences can be attributed to rounding errors.)

		1980	1979	1978
a.	Inventories on LIFO basis	$____	$____	NA
b.	Inventories on FIFO basis	$____	$____	$____
c.	Cumulative decrease in pretax earnings resulting from switch to LIFO	$____	$____	NA
d.	Single-year decrease in pretax earnings resulting from switch to LIFO	$____	$____	NA
e.	Single-year decrease in after-tax earnings resulting from switch to LIFO	$____	$____	NA

NA = Not available.

For 1987, Champion's inventory disclosures in the annual report provided the following information:

	(in millions)	
	1987	1986
Net earnings	$ 19.1	$ (17.2)
Inventory	$189.9	$ 174.6

Total inventory costs determined by the LIFO method were $94.3 million at December 31, 1987, and $94.9 million at December 31, 1986. LIFO inventories were $30.9 million and $29.0 million less than estimated current costs at December 31, 1987 and 1986, respectively.

During 1987, 1986, and 1985, certain inventory reductions resulted in liquidations of LIFO inventory quantities. The effect of the reductions was to increase 1987 net earnings by $0.5 million, decrease the 1986 net loss by $0.2 million, and decrease 1985 net earnings by $0.3 million.

In 1986, the company refined its classification of certain costs used in the valuation of domestic inventories. Such reclassifications resulted in a more uniform approach to the valuation of inventories by all domestic operations. The effect of these classification changes was to increase 1986 cost of goods sold by approximately $4.9 million.

Required:

f. What is Champion describing when it talks about "liquidations of LIFO inventory quantities?"

g. Were the reported LIFO inventory dollar balances affected by these liquidations at the end of each of these three years? If so, by what amount? If not, why not? (Note that in 1987 Champion's income tax rate changed from 46 percent to 40 percent.)

C9.3 LIFO valuation — Boyd Enterprises.* Boyd Enterprises is a manufacturer of parts used mainly in facsimile equipment and other small office machines. For many years, the company manufactured these parts in several states across the United States. Early in 1989, however, one of the company's principal customers announced its intention to buy machines completely ready for assembly from Japan. The news forced Boyd to close its Texas plant and dispose of its inventories at that location.

The company's 1989 annual report, which appeared early in 1990, disclosed that the closure of the Texas facility had precipitated a dramatic deterioration in its business accompanied by a significant liquidation of its inventories. The notes to the financial statements made the following facts about its inventories available to shareholders.

Note 1 — Summary of Significant Accounting Policies
Inventories are stated at the lower-of-cost-or market value. Cost of inventories is determined by the last-in, first-out method (LIFO), which is less than current cost by $87,609 and $55,952 at December 28, 1988, and December 30, 1989, respectively.

During 1989, inventory quantities were reduced, resulting in a liquidation of LIFO inventory quantities carried at lower costs prevailing in prior years as compared with the 1989 cost of production. As a result, income before taxes was increased by $62,310, equivalent to $2.10 per share after applicable income taxes, of which $26,190 before tax, equivalent to $0.88 per share after applicable income taxes, was reflected in cost of product sold; the balance was included as a reduction of the shutdown/disposal provision (see Note 6).

Note 6 — Shutdown Disposal Provision
In the third quarter of 1989, a provision was recorded for the closing of the Texas facilities, which are to be sold or otherwise disposed of. The after-tax provision of $55,595 is equivalent to $2.93 per common share and covers estimated losses on the disposition of property, plant, equipment, inventories, employee severance, and other costs. Net sales of products from these facilities included in consolidated sales totaled $92,465 in 1987, $121,012 in 1988, and $147,554 in 1989.

The note regarding quarterly results told a similar story.

Note 12 — Quarterly Results (Unaudited)
During the third and fourth quarters of 1989, inventory quantities were reduced, resulting in a liquidation of LIFO inventory quantities carried at lower costs prevailing in prior years as compared with the cost of 1989 production. As a result, income before taxes was increased by $62,310, equivalent to $2.10 per share after applicable income taxes, of which $36,120 before taxes, equivalent to $1.22 per share after applicable income taxes, was included as a reduction of the shutdown/disposal provision, with the balance reflected in cost of goods sold.

Examination of its situation revealed that in 1986 Boyd had moved from keeping its inventory on a first-in, first-out (FIFO) basis to a LIFO basis. A note to the financial statements at the time described the change.

Note 2 — Change in Inventory Valuation Method
In 1986 the company adopted the last-in, first-out (LIFO) method of determining costs for substantially all of its U.S. inventories. In prior years, inventory values were principally computed under the lower-of-cost-or-market, first-in, first-out (FIFO) method.

---

*This case was prepared by Kenneth R. Ferris and Michael F. van Breda.

The effect of the change on the operating results for 1986 was to reduce net earnings after tax by $4,714, or 25 cents per share. The inventory balance at December 31, 1986, would have been $7,365 higher if inventory costs had continued to be determined principally under FIFO rather than LIFO.

It was not practical to determine prior year effects of retroactive LIFO application.

The income statements for the years 1986 through 1989, along with the inventory shown in the balance sheet for each year, appear here. Details of the units purchased each year are also presented.

Boyd Enterprises
Selected Financial Data

	1986	1987	1988	1989
Revenue	$1,058,422	$1,236,091	$1,421,526	$1,277,107
Cost of sales	797,232	958,210	1,085,134	971,550
Gross margin	261,190	277,881	336,392	305,557
Selling and administration	192,775	207,332	209,884	212,567
Loss on write-off (net)	–0–	–0–	–0–	55,595
Income tax	24,629	25,398	45,543	33,476
Net income	43,785	45,151	80,965	3,919
Inventory (per ending balance sheet)	$ 147,304	$ 208,948	$ 232,006	$ 111,904

Required:

Using the 1986 footnote, explain the change in the inventory valuation from FIFO to LIFO. What are the costs and benefits of such an accounting change? Compute the LIFO reserve for each year and show how the company arrived at the effect of $62,310 for the liquidation of LIFO inventory in 1989. Assume an effective tax rate of 36 percent.

Boyd Enterprises
Inventory Summary

	Units	Unit Cost
Opening inventory	60,000	$ 2.00
Purchases in 1986	103,652	2.00
	293,920	2.10
Sales in 1986	383,920	
Purchases in 1987	282,220	2.20
	153,450	2.60
Sales in 1987	407,650	
Purchases in 1988	193,210	2.70
	202,250	2.90
Sales in 1988	386,920	
Purchases in 1989	196,320	2.90
	82,000	3.00
Sales in 1989	332,580	

CHAPTER 10

Active Investments and Business Combinations

Marriage is not just spiritual communion and passionate embraces; marriage is also three-meals-a day and remembering to carry out the trash.[1]

Key Chapter Issues

- Why is the accounting required for an active investment different than the accounting required for a passive investment?
- An investor can obviously own any proportion of the outstanding stock of an investee company; how does the accounting vary as that percentage of ownership increases?
- What difference does it make whether a parent company creates a new subsidiary starting with its own capital contribution, or whether the parent acquires the subsidiary from a prior investor?
- If the parent acquires an interest in another company by paying cash, isn't that the same as if it had bought those assets and liabilities individually? What happens if the parent makes that acquisition using common stock as consideration?
- The parent might buy a subsidiary in part to purchase its assets and liabilities but also in part to acquire its reputation. How is the value of that reputation recorded in the acquisition?

[1]J. Brothers, "When Your Husband's Affection Cools," *Good Housekeeping*, May 1972.

In Chapter 8 we discussed the accounting a company follows when it has a **passive investment** in another company. We said that mark-to-market accounting applies to any situation where the nature of the investment, or the size of the investment, was such that the investor company was just that — an investor. Mark-to-market accounting applies to situations where the investor *is not* in a position to exercise any significant amount of influence over the activities of the investee company (typically because the investor's ownership is in bonds or preferred stock or because the investor owns less than 20 percent of the investee's common stock). This chapter discusses the accounting for **active investments** — those investments where the investor company owns more than 20 percent of the common stock of another company and, as a result, *is* able to exercise a significant degree of influence over the policies and operations of that investee company. Active investments are those intercompany relationships where — as the quote from Dr. Joyce Brothers suggests — the two companies work together day-to-day for their common good.

First, however, this chapter looks at the nature of intercorporate investments and explores why the accounting for an active investment in another company might be different than the accounting required for a passive investment. Building on that understanding of intercorporate investing, the chapter then discusses the accounting to be followed when one company has an active investment in another company, focusing primarily on situations where the investee company was started by the investor company. Finally, the chapter looks at the accounting to be followed when the investor gains a significant ownership interest in an investee, acquiring that interest from a prior owner.

THE NATURE OF INTERCORPORATE INVESTMENTS

There are many reasons why one commercial company might make an investment in another. The simplest reason for such an investment is to earn a return on the funds invested. But an investor company might also invest in another so that the investee can grow (expand its distribution network, for example) and become a larger user of the investor's products. Or the reverse could be true: The investor could make an investment in an investee company to help it develop its capabilities (a natural resource, for example) and thereby become a more reliable supplier to the investor. Where the objective of the investment is exclusively to earn a financial return, or where the objective is a combination of earning a return and supporting the investee, the investor company can pick from a range of investment vehicles. The investment can be in the form of an informal advance, a formal loan, or a purchase of the investee's bonds, preferred stock, or common stock. Most often those investments will be passive investments because the investor usually must accept the decisions of investee management; if the investor is not happy with those decisions, the only recourse it usually has is to sell the investment.

Under normal circumstances, neither the making of a loan to a company nor the ownership of a company's bonds or preferred stock gives the investor any power or influence over the investee's operations. The only investment vehicle that gives the investor any voice in the activities of the investee is an investment in common stock. The distinguishing characteristic of an investment in common stock is the right it conveys to elect members of the investee's board of directors and, through the board, to influence decisions of the investee's management. It is that characteristic, the ability to vote for the board of directors and the ability to influence investee management, that is the focus of this chapter. Here we are interested only in investments in common stock and, further, only in situations where the size of that investment is large enough that the investor's wishes must, at the very least, be given serious consideration by investee management. The discussion in this chapter assumes that both the *investor* and the *investee* are corporations and not individuals; further, the discussion assumes that the companies are commercial corporations and not mutual funds or other financial institutions. Mutual fund accounting and the accounting for banks and insurance companies are both unique and beyond our inquiry here.

An investor company can own any amount of the common stock of the investee, and the degree of influence the investor will exercise will vary directly with the percentage of the investee's stock it owns. The most common investor–investee common stock relationship is a parent–subsidiary relationship. In those situations, the investor owns such a large percentage of stock that it is able to completely control the activities of the investee. When two companies are in such a close-knit relationship, the investor company is usually referred to as the **parent** and the investee as the **subsidiary.**

It is theoretically possible for a company to conduct all of its business through a single legal corporate entity. Only the smallest companies operate in that form, however. Most business entities of any size are composed of a parent corporation that owns the stock of various subsidiary corporations, which in turn might own the stock of still other sub-subsidiary corporations. For tax or legal reasons it may be important for the entity to conduct its business in one particular state, or in another country, or in the form of a separate corporation. For risk protection purposes, it may also be advisable to legally isolate certain aspects of the overall business in a separate subsidiary corporation.

From an accounting standpoint, the legal corporate structure is usually invisible; that is, as readers of the PepsiCo annual report, or even as investors, we will never know how many separate companies make up the PepsiCo network. In accounting, a substance-over-form perspective is adopted wherein if the parent company owns a controlling interest in the common stock of a subsidiary, the two legal entities are viewed as one business entity. That position is based on the understanding that a controlling shareholder can cause its subsidiary to do whatever the parent wishes. Because of its controlling stock ownership, a parent company can cause the subsidiary to pay dividends on command, transfer products at arbitrary prices, or even dissolve itself — subject only to certain legal protections for any minority shareholders. In other countries, the legal status of a corporation is more sacred than in the United States and there are many more restrictions on the actions a parent can cause a subsidiary to undertake. Nonetheless, even in the most legally oriented societies, it has become clear that the relationships between parent and subsidiary companies are so close (and non–arm's length in nature) that it is necessary to see them as parts of one larger, single entity; thus, we focus on the entity as a whole rather than on its parts.

In addition to the intercompany investments between a legal parent and its wholly owned or predominantly owned subsidiaries, the investor company might have investments in other entities where the size of the investment is significant but not controlling. As noted earlier, where the investor owns a controlling interest in the common stock of another company, there is a parent–subsidiary relationship. Where the investor owns enough common stock to be able to *influence* but not *control* the policies and activities of the investee company, the two companies are said to be **affiliates.**

The Significance of the Size of the Investment

It may be helpful to think of the different levels of investment one company might make in another as points along a spectrum:

← Investor Ownership →
of Investee Shares Outstanding

1% ———————————————————————— 100%

It should be apparent that the management of an investee company is likely to be more sensitive to the wishes of an investor with an investment at the right side of the continuum than at the left. In fact, an investor that owns 100 percent of the common stock of an investee will be in a position to completely direct the activities of the investee company just as though it was a branch of the investor. On the other hand, an investor that owns an investment at the far left of the continuum should not be accorded any more deference than any other investor. In between those two extremes are situations where the investor can exercise varying degrees of influence over the investee, based on the various degrees of ownership of common stock.

Looking across the spectrum, there are obviously many different stock ownership positions an investor company could have, and, conceptually, it would be nice to account for each specific intercompany investment according to the substance of the relationship that exists between the investor and investee. In reality, however, three different forms of accounting have evolved, and every intercorporate investment will be accounted for using one of these three forms. The three forms of accounting for intercorporate investments in common stock are as follows:

- Where the nature of the investment or the size of the investment is such that the investor is only a passive investor, the investment is accounted for using mark-to-market accounting as described in Chapter 8. Typically, that accounting is followed where the investment is in the form of bonds, preferred stock, or where the investor owns less than 20 percent of the investee's common stock.
- Where the investor owns enough common stock of the investee company to be able to exercise *significant influence* over the activities of the investee but is not in a position to control the investee, the investment is accounted for using **equity accounting** (described in the next section of this chapter). In practice, equity accounting is used where the investor owns more than 20 percent but less than 50 percent of the common stock of the investee.
- Where the investor owns enough of the investee's common stock to be able to *control* the activities of the investee company, consolidation accounting is used (described in the final section of this chapter). Typically, **consolidation accounting** is used when the investor owns more than 50 percent of the common stock of the investee company.[2]

[2]In general practice, a parent *may not use* consolidation accounting unless it owns 50 percent or more of the voting stock of the subsidiary; that rule has also been applied in the reverse, in that consolidation *has been required* whenever the parent owns 50 percent or more of the subsidiary's voting stock. However, in recent years it has been apparent that there are many ways for one company to control another beyond the ownership of a certain amount of voting stock. The Financial Accounting Standards Board has been studying the rules for consolidation accounting to see if there might be other ways to identify control siutations.

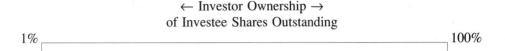

Referring back to the continuum presented earlier, the ownership positions and the accounting required can be visualized this way:

← Investor Ownership →
of Investee Shares Outstanding

1%	Mark-to-market accounting	20%	Equity accounting	50%	Consolidation accounting	100%

EQUITY ACCOUNTING

When the investor owns from 20 percent to less than 50 percent of the common stock of the investee, the investor must follow the provisions of equity accounting for that investment. The logic behind equity accounting goes something like this: Because the investor's ownership of a significant block of the investee's stock gives it the power to exercise significant influence over the operations of the investee company, the investor should be held accountable for the exercise of that power. Under equity accounting, the investor records its initial investment at the amount it paid to acquire the stock. That accounting is the same as for any other asset. But as time passes, equity accounting differs from ordinary asset accounting in that each year, as the investee reports its income or loss, the investor is obligated to recognize, in its own income statement, its proportionate share of the investee's net income or loss. Recognizing that the investor's recording of a share of the investee's net income will increase its own income and in turn its own retained earnings, the investor must also increase its Investment in Affiliate account by the same amount to keep the basic accounting equation in balance.

Let's create an example to illustrate these ideas. Assume that Johnson Paper Company joins with two other paper companies to build a wood pulp plant in Georgia. Each company agrees to purchase one-third of the output of the pulp plant for their further use in the manufacture of fine papers. The pulp plant will be owned and operated by a new company (let's call it Woodland, Inc.), which in turn will be owned by the three investor companies. Each of the investors puts in $1 million and is given 100,000 shares of stock in Woodland, Inc. Under the terms of their agreement, each investor company will be entitled to elect two directors to Woodland's board of directors. Each investor can be said to have significant influence over the operations of the investee company, Woodland, but none will be able to control it.

Johnson would record its initial investment with the following entry:

Dr. Investment in Woodland (A)	(inc.) 1,000,000	
Cr. Cash (A)		(inc.) 1,000,000

Notice that Johnson's investment account, on this first day in the life of Woodland, Inc., would be exactly equal to its proportionate share of Woodland's owners' equity account. But let's take the example forward. In its first year of operations, Woodland borrows additional funds from a bank and constructs the pulp plant. Because it is not yet in production, Woodland reports a loss of $600,000 in that first year. Using equity accounting, Johnson would record its share of that loss with the following entry:

Dr. Loss on equity investment (Loss)	(inc.) 200,000	
Cr. Investment in Woodland (A)		(dec.) 200,000

Notice that this entry reduces Johnson's investment account to $800,000 so that it is exactly equal to its one-third share of Woodland's net equity — the sum of Woodland's common stock ($3,000,000) and retained earnings (a negative 600,000). That investment–equity relationship is the objective of the equity accounting method.

Johnson's management might try to argue that the company should not have to record that $200,000 loss; after all, the loss was recorded by a separate legal entity, and there is no reason to believe that Johnson's investment in that entity is impaired in any way. They might argue that the value of the investment has grown now that the plant is almost complete and will soon be producing low-cost, high-quality raw material for Johnson's future benefit. However, the proponents of equity accounting would reply, the legal separation between Johnson Paper and Woodland is superficial. Johnson has at least an implicit obligation to Woodland (and its banker) because of its significant involvement in the new company and specifically because of its ability to influence the operations of the new company. Therefore, the accounting for the investment should ignore the legal separation between Johnson and Woodland and focus on the substance of the relationship. Equity accounting proponents would also argue that Johnson could have built this plant on its own but chose to share its cost and its potential with two other investors. If Johnson had built the plant on its own it would have incurred the start-up costs on its own. In this scenario, Johnson shares Woodland's losses with two other parties, and the one-third sharing of the initial loss is exactly the result produced for Johnson with equity accounting. Globally, equity accounting is firmly established as GAAP as a result of pronouncements from the Financial Accounting Standards Board, by statements of the International Accounting Standards Committee, and by practice in many other countries.

When Woodland begins operations, it will begin to earn profits. Assume that in its second year of operations Woodland's net income is $300,000. Under equity accounting, Johnson would record the following entry:

Dr. Investment in Woodland (A)	(inc.) 100,000	
Cr. Income on equity investment (Gain)		(inc.) 100,000

The theory behind this entry is that Johnson was in a position to exercise significant influence over Woodland, including its cost controls and its pricing policies. As a result of that ability to influence Woodland's operations, Johnson should recognize the results of those operations — or more correctly, its share of those operations. Further, the logic of equity accounting is based on the understanding that Johnson could have influenced its two other partners to cause Woodland to pay its earnings out as dividends. Johnson chose not to exert that pressure and so, in effect, agreed to invest its share of Woodland's earnings back into the company.

Suppose Woodland reports these results:

Year 1:	Net Loss of $600,000
Year 2:	Net Income of $300,000
Year 3:	Net Income of $450,000

In Year 3, Johnson would make an entry similar to the one it made for Year 2, increasing its investment account and recognizing its share of Woodland's income for the year. But suppose that the board of directors agrees to a dividend payout in Year 3 of $0.30 per share. Johnson would make the following entry to record that dividend:

Dr. Cash (A)	(inc.) 30,000	
Cr. Investment in Woodland (A)		(dec.) 30,000

As you think about the flow of these entries, you will see that equity accounting requires Johnson to account for its investment in Woodland on the accrual basis: Earnings from the investment are recorded when they are earned, not when the cash is paid out. That accounting is consistent with the notion that Johnson's 33 percent ownership of Woodland gives it the ability to influence the operations of Woodland. Because Johnson can influence Woodland's success or failure, it should recognize its share of that success or failure. Further, Johnson can influence the timing of Woodland's dividend payout, and so equity accounting treats the payout of the investee's earnings as being subject to Johnson's choice. Under equity accounting, Johnson treats the receipt of Woodland dividends as a partial liquidation of its investment in Woodland. The dividend is, in effect, a return *of* its investment as opposed to a return *on* its investment. Finally, notice that after three years' operations, Johnson's investment account is exactly equal to its one-third share of Woodland's net equity.

	Woodland's Equity Accounts	Johnson's Investment Account
Initial investment	$3,000,000	$1,000,000
First year's loss	–600,000	–200,000
Second year's income	300,000	100,000
Third year's income	450,000	150,000
Dividends paid	–90,000	–30,000
Balance at the end of the third year	$3,060,000	$1,020,000

Equity accounting requires the investor to maintain an investment account that reflects increases and decreases in its share of the equity of the investee, and it requires the investor to report that share of equity as an asset in its balance sheet. Similarly, equity accounting requires the investor to report its share of the investee's earnings or loss in its income statement. GAAP in the United States requires the equity investor to report that investment and that income (loss) as single-line entries in the investor's financial statements. GAAP in the United States does not permit an investor to report its share of the investee's individual assets and liabilities, nor its share of the investee's sales and expenses. That restriction is odd because the underlying theory of equity accounting would seem to support a proportionate consolidation, by the investor, of its share of the investee's assets and liabilities and its revenues and expenses. After all, if an investor can exercise significant influence over the investee's net assets, it ought to be able to exercise significant influence over the investee's individual assets and liabilities as well.[3] Similarly, if the investor has a large enough investment to influence the investee's net income, it would seem logical to assume that the investor has significant influence over its sales and expenses. But that so-called **proportional consolidation** approach — where the investor records and reports its share of all of the investee's assets and liabilities and its share of the investee's sales and expenses — is not GAAP in the United States but is in a few other countries (such as Australia).

The application of equity accounting (as practiced in the United States) is illustrated in the extracts from the 1994 annual report of Occidental Petroleum, Inc., presented in Exhibit 10.1. Note that in its income statement Occidental reports only its proportion-

[3]It may be helpful to go back to our earliest chapters and remember that the basic accounting formula is A = L + OE or, alternatively, A – L = OE = Net Assets. Because of this second presentation of the basic formula, where net assets are equal to owners' equity, we can say that the investor acquired an interest in the equity of the investee, and we can also say that the investor acquired an interest in the investee's net assets — its assets less its liabilities.

EXHIBIT 10.1

Occidental Petroleum Company
Equity Method Disclosures

From the Balance Sheet:

In millions, except share amounts	Assets at December 31 1994	1993
Current Assets		
Cash and cash equivalents	$ 129	$ 157
Receivables		
Trade, net of reserves of $17 in 1994 and $13 in 1993	831	539
Joint ventures, partnerships and other	134	128
Inventories	748	791
Prepaid expenses and other	416	319
Total current assets	2,258	1,934
Long-term Receivables, Net	131	93
Equity Investments (Note 13)	692	482
Property, Plant and Equipment, at cost		
Oil and gas operations	8,180	7,335
Natural gas transmission operations	8,383	8,364
Chemical operations	6,621	6,530
Corporate and other	202	199
	23,386	22,428
Accumulated depreciation, depletion, and amortization	(8,884)	(8,144)
	14,502	14,284
Other Assets	406	330
	$17,989	$17,123

ate share of the net income of its equity-accounting affiliates, not its share of their sales and expenses. Similarly, Occidental's balance sheet reports only the company's share of the net assets of its 20 to 50 percent owned equity-accounting affiliates.

The sentence in the middle of the Occidental footnote illustrates another interesting aspect of equity accounting: The company says that its investment in its affiliates exceeded its share of the underlying stockholders' equity reported by those companies by $150 million. (That difference explains why Occidental's share of the net equity in its affiliates as explained in the footnotes is not the same as the investment asset reported in the balance sheet.) That difference arises because Occidental purchased an interest in one or more of those companies on the open market and paid more than the book value of the stock for that acquisition. In the example we used earlier, based on Johnson Paper, the investors were all in on the project at the start, and their original investments were exactly equal to their original share of the investee's equity; equity accounting kept that relationship in place year by year. In Occidental's case, some of those investments were made after the investee company was under way, and Occidental was forced to pay a premium over the investee's historical book value to purchase that investment. GAAP requires any such excess contained in the acquiror's investment account to be amortized over a period not in excess of 40 years. Occidental will reduce its share of the earnings reported by those equity companies to reflect that amortization. We will have more to say about that excess purchase price amortization later.

EXHIBIT 10.1 continued

From the Income Statement:

	Net Income For the years ended December 31		
	1994	**1993**	**1992**
Revenues			
Net sales and operating revenues			
Oil and gas operations	**$2,451**	$1,702	$1,822
Natural gas transmission operations	**2,110**	2,378	2,491
Chemical operations	**4,677**	4,042	4,198
Interdivisional sales elimination and other	**(2)**	(6)	(17)
	9,236	8,116	8,494
Interest, dividends, and other income	**92**	347	446
Gains on disposition of assets, net	**15**	54	215
Income from equity investments	**73**	27	22
	9,416	8,544	9,177
Costs and Other Deductions			
Cost of sales	**6,726**	5,971	6,349
Selling, general, administrative, and other operating expenses	**984**	763	837
Depreciation, depletion, and amortization of assets	**882**	892	872
Environmental remediation charges	**4**	18	42
Exploration expense	**127**	102	112
Interest and debt expense, net	**584**	580	640
Minority interests in net income of subsidiaries and partnerships	**2**	1	4
	9,309	8,327	8,856
Income (Loss) from Continuing Operations before Taxes	**107**	217	321
Provision for domestic and foreign income and other taxes (Note 10)	**143**	143	195
Income (Loss) from Continuing Operations	**(36)**	74	126
Discontinued operations, net	**—**	221	(622)
Extraordinary gain (loss), net	**—**	(12)	(2)
Cumulative effect of changes in accounting principles, net	**—**	—	(93)
Net Income (Loss)	**$ (36)**	$ 283	$ (591)

EXHIBIT 10.1 concluded

Note 13: Investments

Investments in companies in which Occidental has a voting stock interest of at least 20 percent, but not more than 50 percent, and certain partnerships are accounted for on the equity method. At December 31, 1994, Occidental's equity investments consisted primarily of joint-interest pipelines, including a pipeline in the Dutch sector of the North Sea, an investment of approximately 30 percent in the common shares of CanadianOxy, and a chemical partnership. In the second quarter of 1993, Occidental sold its 45 percent nonvoting interest in Trident. The investment in Trident was in its preferred stock, and accordingly, no equity earnings had been recorded. In 1992 Occidental sold 12 million shares of its holdings in CanadianOxy. Equity investments paid dividends of $45 million, $33 million, and $60 million to Occidental in 1994, 1993, and 1992, respectively. Cumulative undistributed earnings since acquisition, in the amount of $102 million, of 50-percent-or-less-owned companies have been accounted for by Occidental under the equity method. At December 31, 1994, Occidental's investment in equity of investees exceeded the historical underlying equity in net assets by approximately $150 million, which is being amortized into income over periods not exceeding 40 years. The aggregate market value of the investment in CanadianOxy, based on the quoted market price for CanadianOxy common shares, was $453 million at December 31, 1994, compared with an aggregate book value of $185 million. Occidental and its subsidiaries' purchases from, and sales to, certain equity method pipeline ventures and the chemical partnership were $202 million and $225 million, respectively, during the year ended December 31, 1994.

The following table presents Occidental's proportional interest in the summarized financial information of its equity method investments (in millions):

For the years ended December 31	1994	1993	1992
Revenues	**$ 684**	$ 562	$ 518
Costs and expenses	**611**	535	496
Net income	**$ 73**	$ 27	$ 22
Balance at December 31,			
Current assets	**$ 273**	$ 170	
Noncurrent assets	**$ 917**	$ 950	
Current liabilities	**$ 168**	$ 146	
Noncurrent liabilities	**$ 543**	$ 544	
Stockholders' equity	**$ 479**	$ 430	

CONSOLIDATION ACCOUNTING

When the investor company owns 50 percent or more of the common stock of the investee, the investor must use consolidation accounting for that investment. Consolidation accounting assumes that the investor (the parent) can do more than just influence the activities of the investee and can in fact control the investee. An investor company will need to be sensitive to the legal rights of the investee's other shareholders — if any — but it is typically true that ownership of 50 percent or more of the stock of a company gives the investor the right to elect all of the members of the board of directors and to determine the policies and operations of the investee. Following on that understanding, GAAP requires any company that owns 50 percent or more of the stock of another to present only consolidated financial statements, combining the investee's assets, liabilities, sales, and expenses with its own.

When the Subsidiary Is Created by the Parent Company

Referring to the previous Johnson Paper example, assume that Johnson put up all of the $3,000,000 equity that was required to fund the beginning of Woodland, Inc., and thus was the sole shareholder. Also assume that Woodland is in the third year of operations of the plant and that it has reported these results during that three-year period:

Year 1:	Net loss of $600,000
Year 2:	Net income of $300,000
Year 3:	Net income of $450,000
Year 3:	Dividends of $90,000

With a 100 percent ownership, Johnson's investment in Woodland at the end of the third year would be $3,060,000; Woodland would have common stock equal to $3,000,000 and retained earnings of $60,000, for a total equity of $3,060,000. Because Johnson controls Woodland, consolidation accounting argues that we ought to look through the legal separation of the two companies and see them as one entity. The proponents of consolidation accounting are impatient with the idea that Johnson would only reflect an Investment in Woodland account on its balance sheet and instead insist on knowing what that investment represents in the way of specific assets, liabilities, revenues, and expenses. For example, assume the detailed balance sheets of Woodland and Johnson as of the end of Year 3 are as presented in the first two columns of this table:

Balance Sheets at the End of Year Three (000 omitted)

	Johnson Paper	Woodland, Inc.	Consolidated Johnson
Cash	$ 1,000	$ 500	$ 1,500
Accounts receivable	2,500	800	3,300
Inventory	2,800	900	3,700
Net property	5,200	3,400	8,600
Investment in Woodland	3,060	—	—
Total assets	14,560	5,600	17,100
Accounts payable	1,200	290	1,490
Long-term debt	300	2,250	2,550
Total liabilities	1,500	2,540	4,040
Net assets	$13,060	$3,060	$13,060
The equivalent net equity is represented by:			
Common stock	$ 8,000	$3,000	$ 8,000
Retained earnings	5,060	60	5,060
Total Equity	$13,060	$3,060	$13,060

Because Johnson has control over Woodland, when Johnson issues financial statements to its shareholders or its creditors, it must issue consolidated financial statements; no shareholder or creditor would be interested in the statements of the parent alone because everyone understands that the parent's operations are only part of the overall story. *In this situation where the parent company founded the wholly-owned subsidiary,* consolidation accounting simply combines the assets and liabilities of the two entities, eliminating the parent's investment account and the subsidiary's owners' equity accounts (see the third column in the above table). The parent's investment and the subsidiary's owners' equity accounts are eliminated to avoid double-counting: if they were not eliminated, the consolidated balance sheet would show an investment in the subsidiary and the outstanding stock of the subsidiary. Consolidation accounting assumes that the subsidiary is a branch of the parent, and that the parent acquired all of the subsidiary's assets directly and assumed all of the subsidiary's liabilities as its own. Consolidation accounting ignores the parent's investment and the subsidiary's equity which resulted from that investment. Some people explain consolidation accounting saying that it replaces the parent's single-line investment in the subsidiary with the details of the subsidiary's net assets (its assets less its liabilities).

In this same scenario, developing the consolidated income statement for Johnson is a little more complex than developing the balance sheet because there are significant intercompany transactions between the two companies. Assume that all of Woodland's sales are made to Johnson. The income statements of the two companies separately and the consolidated income statement for the third year of operations might look like this:

Income Statements for Year Three
(000 omitted)

	Johnson Paper	Woodland, Inc.	Consolidated Johnson
Sales	$28,750	$6,000	$28,750
Cost of sales	14,500	3,800	12,300
Gross profit	14,250	2,200	16,450
Expenses and taxes	9,400	1,700	11,100
Earnings of Woodland	500	—	—
Net income	$ 5,350	$ 500	$ 5,350

Consolidated cost of sales is calculated this way: Johnson's costs of $14,500 less the $6,000 of material it purchased from Woodland, plus Woodland's $3,800 cost of manufacturing those materials, all of which equals the consolidated cost of sales of $12,300.

The consolidated income statement would include all of the transactions the two companies had with outsiders but would eliminate all transactions that took place between the two companies. So consolidated sales include only the sales with Johnson's customers and do not include the sales Woodland made to its parent. The consolidated costs of sales include the costs Johnson paid to outsiders and the net cost of manufacturing the raw material it purchased from Woodland. The consolidated statements look through the legal division between the two companies and ignore any transactions between them; the consolidated statements look only for those transactions that took place with entities outside the corporate group.

When the Subsidiary Is Acquired Rather Than Created

Most parent-subsidiary relationships exist because the parent created the subsidiary for an explicit purpose, as in the Johnson Paper/Woodland example we have been discussing and as in the case of General Motors creating its wholly-owned subsidiary GMAC.

In those situations, the parent's investment in the subsidiary will always be equal to the subsidiary's net assets at their book value. Such subsidiary relationships are the most common intercompany relationship, but they are not the ones that get the most attention. Most arguments about the accounting for intercompany relationships occur because the parent did not create the subsidiary but instead acquired it from someone else. The distinctive feature of those acquired-subsidiary situations is that the seller usually demands a price in excess of the book value of the net assets of the company to be sold, and so the purchasing company's original investment will be in excess of the acquired company's recorded net assets.[4] It is very, very rare that an investor is able to acquire a company by paying a price exactly equal to the book value of the acquiree's net assets. Usually the seller demands a premium, arguing that the potential of the target company is greater than that indicated by the net book values reported on its balance sheet.

Accounting for that excess purchase price almost always raises questions and inspires spirited discussion within the purchasing parent's management team. As a result of the heated debates on this subject over the years, two methods of accounting for an acquired subsidiary have developed. The most prevalent method is the purchase method, which is discussed next. The alternative method, the pooling-of-interests method, is discussed in the following section of this chapter.

The Purchase Method of Accounting for Subsidiary Acquisitions

Under the **purchase method** of accounting for the acquisition of a subsidiary, the acquiring company records its investment at the price it pays to acquire the stock of the new subsidiary, just as it would record the cost of any asset. But what happens at year-end when consolidated financial statements need to be issued? At that time the parent cannot substitute its investment account for the net assets and liabilities of the subsidiary because its purchase price is more than its share of the net book value of the net assets of the subsidiary. Under the purchase method, the parent is required to allocate that *excess purchase price* following these three steps:

1. First the parent determines fair market values for all of the identifiable assets and liabilities owned and owed by its new subsidiary. Where there is a difference between the subsidiary's recorded cost for an asset and the fair market value of that asset, a portion of the parent's excess purchase price is allocated to that asset for the purpose of preparing a consolidated balance sheet. That process is applied to all of the subsidiary's assets and liabilities until (it is to be hoped) all of the excess purchase price is allocated away. The theory behind that allocation is that the parent purchased the subsidiary (by virtue of

[4]Think about the conversations an investor-company team might have as they evaluate a proposed acquisition of an existing company. As you visualize their conversations, it may be helpful to reread footnote 3. There we said that a reference to net assets is the same as a reference to owners' equity. A negotiating team in an acquisition may talk about buying the shareholders' equity in the investee, or they may talk about buying the investee's net assets. They are, of course, talking about the same acquisition but looking at it from a different perspective. Incidentally, an investor may occasionally decide that it is not interested in the investee's legal corporate entity (perhaps the investee is saddled with substantial litigation) and conclude that they are only interested in the actual assets owned by the investee company. It is possible to buy all of the assets of another company, just as it is possible to purchase an individual asset owned by another company. The accounting for any such basket purchase of assets is the same as the accounting accorded the purchase of an individual asset. It may be necessary to allocate the total purchase price over all the individual assets acquired, and if so, the allocation process described in the next section would apply. If such a basket purchase is made, the company from whom the assets were acquired continues to exist, with its previous shareholders.

the purchase of its stock), and so the accounting for that investment should reflect the current cost of the subsidiary's assets and liabilities. The purchase method determines the current cost of the individual assets and liabilities acquired by reference to their market values at the time of the purchase by the parent.

2. If the parent finds that not all of the excess purchase price can be explained away by differences between the subsidiary's recorded book values and the fair values of its assets and liabilities, the remaining excess purchase price will be put into a new account, for the purpose of preparing a consolidated balance sheet, referred to as **goodwill.** The theory behind that allocation of the residual excess purchase price is that the parent must have paid a fair price for its acquisition, and so the subsidiary must have had some additional assets that are not readily apparent. The excess purchase price that cannot be specifically allocated to the subsidiary's other assets must be a reflection of the value of those unseen assets. We call that unallocated excess purchase price "goodwill" to suggest that the unseen asset acquired in the transaction is reflected in the relationships the subsidiary has with its customers, its suppliers, and its employees.
3. In the rare situation where the purchase price was less than the net fair value of the assets acquired, the shortfall is often referred to as **negative goodwill.** That implied negative goodwill is allocated as a pro rata reduction in the fair market value of the new subsidiary's property, plant, and equipment.

Let's create a new example to illustrate the accounting required for an investee, where we purchase the investee rather than create it. Assume that a major computer company decides that it has been late in recognizing the value of the Internet and decides to catch up by acquiring a company that has developed state-of-the-art software for use on the Internet. The software company (let's call it NetWorld) has relatively little in the way of assets, but it does have great promise. The computer company (let's call it Power Computer) offers to exchange a new issue of preferred stock for each of the 100,000 common shares held by NetWorld's stockholders. An investor may use any form of consideration that is acceptable to the investee shareholders who are selling: cash, notes, bonds, preferred stock, or common stock. In any event, the cost of the acquisition is measured by the market value of the consideration given. Let us assume that the investment bankers tell us that the new issue of Power preferred stock will have a market value of $10 per share. If the NetWorld stockholders accept the exchange offer, Power would have paid $1 million for the acquisition.

The entry Power would make to record that acquisition would look like this:

Dr. Investment in NetWorld (A)	(inc.) 1,000,000	
Cr. Preferred stock (OE)		(inc.) 1,000,000

Let us assume that the balance sheets of the two companies just prior to the deal are as depicted in the first two columns of the following table. If we were to prepare a consolidated balance sheet immediately after the acquisition, it would appear as in the last column of the same table.

Balance Sheets at Date of NetWorld Acquisition
(000 omitted)

	Power Computer	NetWorld (Historical Cost)	NetWorld (Fair Value)	Consolidated Power
Cash	$1,550	$ 500	$ 500	$2,050
Accounts receivable	1,500	800	800	2,300
Inventory	1,800	600	600	2,400
Computer equipment, net of accumulated depreciation	2,200	750	800	3,000
Software, net	1,200	150	400	1,600
Other property, net	4,300	300	300	4,600
Other assets	500	50	50	550
Investment in NetWorld	1,000	—	—	—
Goodwill	—	—	—	250
Total assets	14,050	3,150	3,450	16,750
Accounts payable	1,900	450	450	2,350
Long-term debt	3,500	2,250	2,250	5,750
Total liabilities	5,400	2,700	2,700	8,100
Net assets	8,650	450	750	8,650
The equivalent net equity is represented by:				
Preferred stock	1,000	—		1,000
Common stock	2,850	100		2,850
Retained earnings	4,800	350		4,800
Total equity	$8,650	$ 450		$8,650

The goodwill in that consolidated balance sheet is calculated as follows:

Total Power purchase price	$1,000,000
NetWorld's net assets acquired (at historic costs)	450,000
Additional fair market values acquired, which were not recognized in NetWorld's recorded historic costs:	
Computer equipment	50,000
Software	250,000
Goodwill that must have been present at NetWorld	250,000

If we assume that the transaction took place on June 30, 1994, the consolidated income statement for the two companies at year-end December 31, 1994, might look like this:

Income Statements for 1994
(000 omitted)

	Power Computer		NetWorld		Consolidated Power
	Jan to June	July to Dec	Jan to June	July to Dec	1994
Sales	$7,900	$8,300	$1,500	$2,000	$18,200.0
Cost of sales	4,000	4,500	1,100	1,300	9,800.0
Gross margin	3,900	3,800	400	700	8,400.0
Selling expenses	750	850	300	400	2,000.0
Administrative expenses	400	480	100	125	1,005.0
Depreciation	200	225	50	75	500.0
Extra depreciation and amortization	—	—	—	—	27.5
Interest	100	120	100	125	345.0
Taxes	950	900	—	—	1,850.0
Total expenses	2,400	2,575	550	725	5,727.5
Net income	$1,500	$1,225	$(150)	$ (25)	$ 2,672.5

Note that the consolidated income statement includes the earnings of NetWorld for only the last six months of the year — since the date of the acquisition. Note also that there will be additional depreciation and amortization in the consolidated financial statements as compared with that reflected in the two separate set of books. That additional depreciation and amortization will be required to expense a portion of the new values that were recognized in the acquisition. The extra charge in this example assumes that NetWorld's computer and software assets had an average remaining life of 10 years; as a result, \$15,000 (\$30,000 annually, but half that for this six-month period) of the extra value allocated to NetWorld's property was charged as additional depreciation in the consolidated financial statements. The extra expense also assumes that Power management decided that the goodwill they acquired with their purchase of the NetWorld stock had a life of 10 years; as a consequence, the consolidated income statement reflects an amortization expense of \$12,500 (\$25,000 for the full year, but half that for this six-month period).[5]

The consolidated financial statements covering the period when the acquisition occurred will include a footnote describing the acquisition and explaining how the acquisition impacted the statements for the year. The footnote will usually include a pro forma table that shows what consolidated income would have looked like had the acquisition taken place at the first of the year. The example from Federal-Mogul Corporation's 1994 annual report, detailed in Exhibit 10.2, illustrates the disclosures required when the acquisition of new subsidiaries has been accounted for using the purchase method.

The income statement in Federal-Mogul's 1994 annual report provides this data (in millions):

	1994	1993	1992
Net earnings	\$63.3	\$40.1	\$4.4

Looking at the reported earnings (which include the results of operations of the acquired companies only since the date of their acquisition) and the pro forma information in the footnote, we can see that the acquired companies have had a dramatic effect on the growth in consolidated earnings. The income statement suggests that earnings grew 58 percent between 1993 and 1994. The data in the footnote do not tell us how much of that growth came from the original Federal-Mogul business, but the data do help us see that a substantial part of that growth came from the acquisitions. Had these companies all been together as of January 1, 1993, earnings would have grown from \$50.2 million to \$63.3 million, an increase of 26 percent. The remaining growth, to take the company up to the 58 percent reflected in the income statement, can be traced to the companies that were added to the combined entity as a result of the acquisitions.

The Pooling-of-Interests Method of Accounting for Subsidiary Acquisitions

The purchase method of accounting is quite logical because it records the net assets acquired (that is, the investee's assets and liabilities) at their fair value. Some managers, however, object to purchase accounting because it combines the assets of the

[5]GAAP in the United States sets a maximum life of 40 years for goodwill, and many companies use that maximum. In Japan, the maximum is 5 years. The International Accounting Standards Committee, which is working to establish one set of standards for use throughout the world, has said that the maximum life for goodwill should be 20 years. Most everyone in the financial world argues that we ought to have harmonized financial standards; it will be interesting to see how the conflicting views about the expected life of goodwill will be reconciled by those working on harmonization.

EXHIBIT 10.2

Federal-Mogul Corporation
Acquisition Accounting Disclosures:
Purchase Method

Acquisitions

On October 31, 1994, the company completed the transaction to purchase all the outstanding shares of Varex Corporation, Ltd, the largest independent auto parts distributor in South Africa. The acquisition has been accounted for as a purchase and, accordingly, the total cost of $58.3 million was allocated to acquired assets and assumed liabilities based on their estimated fair values as of the acquisition date. The excess of the consideration paid over the estimated fair value of net assets acquired of $49 million has been recorded as goodwill. The consolidated statement of earnings includes the operating results of the acquired business from July 1, 1994.

On October 26, 1993, the company completed its acquisition of SPX Corporation's United States and Canadian automotive aftermarket operations, Sealed Power Replacement (SPR). The acquisition has been accounted for as a purchase and, accordingly, the total cost of $167 million was allocated to the acquired assets and assumed liabilities based on their estimated fair values as of the acquisition date. The company and SPX Corporation also executed a noncompete agreement and a long-term trademark agreement making Federal-Mogul the sole distributor of engine and chassis parts sold under the Sealed Power and Speed-Pro brand names in North America. Federal-Mogul also acquired the right to use these trademarks throughout the rest of the world. The excess of the consideration paid over the estimated fair value of net assets acquired of $70 million has been recorded as goodwill. The earnings statement includes the operating results of the acquired business from October 26, 1993.

On October 20, 1992, the company acquired substantially all of TRW Inc.'s automotive aftermarket business (AAB). The acquisition had been accounted for as a purchase, and, accordingly, the total cost of $232 million was allocated to the acquired assets and assumed liabilities based on their estimated fair values as of the acquisition date. The company and TRW Inc. also executed a noncompete agreement and completed a long-term supply contract and a trademark agreement (valued at $48.2 million in the aggregate) making the company the exclusive supplier of TRW-brand engine and chassis parts to the independent automotive aftermarket. The excess of the consideration paid over the estimated fair value of net assets acquired of $34 million has been recorded as goodwill. The consolidated statement of earnings includes the operating results of the acquired business from October 20, 1992.

The following unaudited pro forma results of operations for the years ended December 31, 1993 and 1992, assume the acquisition of SPR and TRW occurred as of the beginning of the respective periods, after giving effect to certain adjustments, including amortization of intangible assets, increased interest expense on acquisition debt and related income tax effects, with the SPR acquisition impacting 1993 and the SPR and AAB acquisitions impacting 1992. The pro forma results do not include the acquisition of Varex as it would have had little impact on the results of operations in 1994, 1993, and 1992. The pro forma results have been prepared for comparative purposes only and do not purport to indicate the results of operations that would actually have occurred had the combination been in effect on the dates indicated, or that may occur in the future.

(millions of dollars, except per share amounts)

	1993	1992
Net sales	$1,705.3	$1,672.0
Earnings from continuing operations	74.3	42.0
Net earnings (loss)	50.2	(62.1)
Net earnings (loss) per common share:		
Primary	$ 1.50	$ (3.17)
Fully diluted	1.41	(3.17)

Operating results for 1993 include a $1 million ($0.02 per share) charge and for 1992 a $14 million ($0.34 per share) charge to provide for certain aspects of the rationalization of the company's present aftermarket business. This charge includes costs incurred for severance, eliminating redundant company facilities and equipment, and integrating the operations of the acquired businesses.

investee company at their fair market value with the assets of the investor company, which are still stated at their historic cost. Some managers also object to the inclusion of an intangible asset labeled *goodwill* on their balance sheet. They apparently believe that readers of the statements discount the value of such an intangible asset. Finally, on a more pragmatic note, some managers object to the purchase method because the higher asset values, including the newly recognized goodwill, result in increased amortization and depreciation expenses, which depress future consolidated earnings.

Because of such objections to the purchase method of accounting for acquired subsidiaries, an alternative has been established as GAAP. The **pooling-of-interests method** (or *merger accounting* as it is called in most European countries) takes an entirely different approach to the accounting for an acquired subsidiary. It may be used only in those very special situations where the parent acquires control of the target subsidiary by exchanging its own common stock for the common stock of the target company. A few other complex rules determine whether an acquisition qualifies for use of the pooling method, but primarily, the parent must use its common stock as consideration for the transaction, and it must contract with the shareholders of the target company to exchange parent company common stock for all of the target company common stock owned by those shareholders. Where such conditions have been met, along with a few other detailed provisions that we will ignore for this discussion, the acquisition qualifies for pooling-of-interests accounting.

The theory behind the pooling method is that the shareholders have simply pooled their interests in the two companies, and there has been no purchase of any assets. Because the owners have pooled their interests, there was no arm's-length transaction between them, and so it has not been possible to determine any new asset values. Because there was no purchase transaction, and because it has not been possible to determine any new asset values, the two companies bring only their historical costs to the consolidation. The parent company values its new investment at the historical cost of the new subsidiary's net assets — the historical cost of the subsidiary's assets less the historical costs of its liabilities.[6] Therefore, using pooling accounting, the consolidation of the two companies' balance sheets is simply a matter of adding the two individual companies' assets and liabilities together, eliminating the parent's Investment in Subsidiary account and the subsidiary's owners' equity. No current values are recognized. The end result is just as though the parent created the subsidiary at its very beginning.

Let's go back to the example of Power Computer and NetWorld that was used in the earlier discussion of the purchase method. Instead of issuing preferred stock in the acquisition of NetWorld, assume Power issues common stock because it wants to use the pooling method. Power would make the following entry to record the exchange of its common stock for the common stock of NetWorld:

Dr. Investment in NetWorld (A)	(inc.) 450,000	
Cr. Common stock (OE)		(inc.) 450,000

Note that the stock Power issued is valued at the historical cost of the net assets of NetWorld. It is important to understand that the real exchange of value involved in the transaction must be the same — the NetWorld shareholders will not be content to accept common stock from Power worth anything less than $1,000,000. To make the deal acceptable, Power must issue enough shares of its common stock so as to give the NetWorld shareholders the same value as they would have received with the preferred stock. If we assume that Power's stock trades at $20 per share, the company will issue 50,000 shares of its common stock in this transaction. Pooling accounting, however, ignores all current values involved in the transaction and records the Power stock issued at the historical-cost value of the net assets received from NetWorld — in this case at $9.00 a share ($450,000/50,000 shares). Pooling accounting assumes that the

[6] In light of what we have said about A − L = OE in the prior footnotes, it should be apparent that the historic cost of the subsidiary's net assets is the same as the subsidiary's historical cost net equity.

Power and the NetWorld shareholders have always been together, and there has been no purchase and no new valuation.

Because this is a common stock transaction, Power would not have issued the preferred stock as it did in our earlier purchase accounting transaction but rather would have issued common stock. We can assume, however, that all of the other asset and liability balances are the same as they were in that earlier example. If Power issued common stock as consideration for the transaction, and if Power used the pooling method to account for the transaction, the consolidated balance sheet just after the deal would look like this:

Balance Sheets at Date of NetWorld Acquisition
(000 omitted)

	Power Computer	NetWorld (Historical Cost)	NetWorld (Fair Value)	Consolidated Power
Cash	$1,550	$ 500	$ 500	$2,050
Accounts receivable	1,500	800	800	2,300
Inventory	1,800	600	600	2,400
Computer equipment, net of accumulated depreciation	2,200	750	800	2,950
Software, net	1,200	150	400	1,350
Other property, net	4,300	300	300	4,600
Other assets	500	50	50	550
Investment in NetWorld	450	—	—	—
Goodwill	—	—	—	—
Total assets	13,500	3,150	3,450	16,200
Accounts payable	1,900	450	450	2,350
Long-term debt	3,500	2,250	2,250	5,750
Total liabilities	5,400	2,700	2,700	8,100
Net assets	8,100	450	750	8,100
The equivalent net equity is represented by common stock:				
Prior issuances	2,850	100		2,850
New issuance	450	—		450
Retained earnings	4,800	350		4,800
Total equity	$8,100	$ 450		$8,100

Notice that under pooling accounting, the parent's investment exactly equals the net assets of the subsidiary, and so the consolidation is quite simple. Power's investment account is eliminated, as is the equivalent NetWorld owners' equity, and the remaining assets, liabilities, and owners' equity accounts are added across.[7] Notice also that the pooling method ignores any difference between the fair market values of NetWorld's assets and their historical costs; the consolidated balance sheet is prepared by combin-

[7]Most likely, the parent will make one further adjustment to the historical values as recorded in the two companies' balance sheets as the consolidation is prepared. Because this is a pooling of interests, it is assumed that the two companies have been together since the beginning. Given that assumption, the consolidated retained earnings should be the sum of the retained earnings originally reported by the two companies and the consolidated common stock amount is a plug figure to balance the consolidated balance sheet. The only restriction is that the parent's common stock account must not go below the par value of the shares outstanding. Assuming that limitation is not a factor in this case, the final consolidated equity presentation would look like this:

Common stock	$2,950
Retained earnings	5,150
Total equity	$8,100

ing the historical costs from both companies. Finally, notice that pooling ignores any goodwill that might have been implied in the transaction.

The other significant difference between the purchase method and the pooling-of-interests method arises in the preparation of the income statement. Remember that the theory supporting the pooling method argues that the two shareholder groups have simply merged their ownership interests and that no purchase has taken place. Building on that theoretical foundation, the pooling method ignores the transaction date and assumes that the companies have been together forever. Therefore, when the consolidated income statement is prepared, the sales, costs, and expenses reported by the two companies for the entire year are added together just as though the acquisition had taken place at the beginning of the year. In fact, when the consolidated annual report is prepared, *all* of the income statements presented, for a three-year period, a five-year period, or a 10-year period, will be combined in exactly the same way. Pooling accounting assumes that the two companies have been together from the beginning of their corporate lives. Assuming that the acquisition took place on June 30, 1994, the consolidated income statement for Power Computer for 1994 would look like this:

Income Statements for the 1994 Year
(000 omitted)

	Power Computer		Networld		Consolidated Power
	Jan to June	July to Dec	Jan to June	July to Dec	1994
Sales	$7,900	$8,300	$1,500	$2,000	$19,700
Cost of sales	4,000	4,500	1,100	1,300	10,900
Gross margin	3,900	3,800	400	700	8,800
Selling expenses	750	850	300	400	2,300
Administrative expenses	400	480	100	125	1,105
Depreciation	200	225	50	75	550
Extra depreciation and amortization	—	—	—	—	—
Interest	100	120	100	125	445
Taxes	950	900	—	—	1,850
Total expenses	2,400	2,575	550	725	6,250
Net income	$1,500	$1,225	$ (150)	$ (25)	$ 2,550

Notice that the results of the two companies for the entire year have been combined in the consolidated income statement for the year. Note also that there is no additional depreciation or amortization because there was no recognition of the current values inherent in NetWorld's assets and liabilities.

In the year of the acquisition, the footnotes to the financial statements will provide the details of the transaction and will describe the impact the acquisition had on the consolidated income statement. That disclosure is illustrated in Exhibit 10.3, which shows a footnote from AT&T describing its acquisition of McCaw Cellular Communications using the pooling method. At the time of this exchange, AT&T's shares traded at about $55, indicating that AT&T management thought that McCaw was worth $10.8 billion. Because of the start-up losses it had incurred setting up its cellular network, McCaw had reported losses in all of its prior years. The company reported a negative net equity $37.0 million in its balance sheet just prior to the acquisition. If purchase accounting had been used for this transaction, we can assume that *all* of AT&T's purchase price would have been allocated to additional asset values at

EXHIBIT 10.3

AT&T and Subsidiaries
Acquisition Accounting Disclosures:
Pooling Method

Merger with McCaw Cellular Communications, Inc. (McCaw)

On September 19, 1994, AT&T merged with McCaw. As a result, 197.5 million shares of McCaw common stock were converted into shares of AT&T common stock at an exchange ratio of one share of AT&T common stock for each McCaw share. In addition, AT&T assumed 11.3 million McCaw stock options, which were converted into AT&T stock options at the same exchange ratio, resulting in 11.3 million additional AT&T stock options at an average exercise price of $27.43. The merger was accounted for as a pooling of interests, and the consolidated financial statements were restated for all periods prior to the merger to include the accounts and operations of McCaw. Intercompany transactions prior to 1994 were not eliminated due to immateriality. Merger-related expenses of $246 million incurred in 1994 ($187 million net of taxes) were reported as selling, general, and administrative expenses. Certain reclassifications were made to McCaw's accounts to conform to AT&T's presentation. Premerger operating results of the companies in the current presentation were:

Dollars in millions	Nine Months Ended September 30, 1994	Year Ended December 31, 1993	Year Ended December 31, 1992
Sales and revenues			
AT&T	**$52,178**	$67,156	$64,904
McCaw	**2,062**	2,195	1,743
Eliminations	**(256)**	—	—
Total	**$53,984**	$69,351	$66,647
Net income (loss)			
AT&T	**$ 3,431**	$ (3,794)	$ 3,807
McCaw	**34**	(2,112)*	(365)
Eliminations	**(93)**	—	—
Total	**$ 3,372**	$ (5,906)	$ 3,442

*Includes a charge of $45 million previously reported as an extraordinary item for the early redemption of debt.

McCaw — and that a substantial amount of goodwill would have been recorded. It is easy to understand why AT&T might have wanted this transaction to be accounted for as a pooling: Not only did the company avoid the recognition of a very large amount of goodwill on the consolidated balance sheet, it avoided the future income charges from the depreciation of the extra asset values that would have had to been recorded and the amortization of that goodwill.

Although the pooling method is firmly entrenched in U.S. GAAP, its conceptual underpinnings are obviously weak. No one really believes that the shareholders of McCaw Cellular and AT&T pooled their equity interests and marched forward together into the wireless future. The pooling method really has appeal only because of the burdens that accompany the use of the purchase method. Because of the conceptual weaknesses behind the pooling method, the accounting rules governing its use are quite strict: GAAP sets forth 12 conditions that must be met if the transaction is to be accounted for as a pooling. If any one of those conditions is not met, the transaction must be accounted for using the purchase method.[8]

[8]Outside the United States, the accounting rules are even more prescriptive. The International Accounting Standards Committee has agreed somewhat reluctantly that pooling accounting may be appropriate in some rare circumstances. The IASC has established three overarching criteria that must be met if an acquisition is to be accorded pooling accounting. The criteria are as follows. (1) There must be no obvious acquiror in the transaction — the two parties must be of approximately the same size; management of the combining enterprises must continue in the management of the combined entity; and the shareholders must continue to share mutually in the risks and benefits of the combined entity. (2) There cannot be a substantial reduction in the rights attaching to the shares of one of the companies. (3) The shareholders must maintain substantially the same voting rights and interests in the combined entity after the combination as before.

Because the rules are restrictive, a management team that wants an acquisition to qualify for the pooling method must be very careful as they structure the deal. Conversely, where a management team wants an acquisition to qualify for purchase accounting, it is a relatively simple matter to break one of the pooling conditions and consequently be required to use purchase accounting.

Minority Interests

As discussed previously, consolidation accounting is relatively straightforward when the parent owns 100 percent of the stock of the subsidiary. Consolidation accounting can be a bit more complicated when the parent owns less than 100 percent of the common stock of the subsidiary. The basic process is as presented earlier, but now the parent cannot say that it owns all of the net assets of the subsidiary or that it earned all of the subsidiary's net income. The portion of the subsidiary's net assets that is owned by the other stockholders — in effect their share of the subsidiary's equity — is reflected in the consolidated balance sheet as a separate line item just after the liabilities, labeled **minority interest.** In the consolidated income statement, the minority owners' share of the earnings of the subsidiary is included as a single line expense item, positioned just before income taxes and referred to as *minority interest in earnings of subsidiaries*. Thus, in both the consolidated balance sheet and the consolidated income statement, all of the assets, liabilities, and the sales and expenses of the subsidiary are combined with those of the parent, with these additional minority interest lines subtracting out the net assets and net income ascribable to the minority owners.

The Essence of Consolidation Accounting

A large publicly held company can have thousands of subsidiaries, and the system required to gather the data from all of those entities and to keep track of their intercompany transactions can be extraordinarily complex. In reality, however, the process is quite simple: The preparation of consolidated financial statements for a multinational company is, by and large, a scaled-up version of the Johnson Paper and the Power Computer examples we have been discussing here. The essence of consolidation accounting, whether practiced by PepsiCo or the fictitious Johnson Paper or Power Computer, is this:

- The legal structure of the entities is ignored, and the accounting follows the substance of the relationship. Where the parent controls the subsidiary as a result of the parent's ownership of 50 percent or more of the subsidiary's common stock, the consolidated financial statements include all of the parent's assets and liabilities, combined with all of the subsidiary's assets and liabilities. Similarly, the two companies' sales and expenses are combined.
- Consolidation requires that all intercompany transactions be eliminated. Because they are intercompany transactions, they should not be included in the consolidated financial statements. Because they are intercompany transactions, each transaction in one company has a mirror image in the other. The effect of the transaction must be eliminated from each company's accounts to avoid double counting in the consolidation.
- Where the parent owns less than 100 percent of the subsidiary, any minority interest in the subsidiary's net assets is shown in the consolidated balance sheet as a credit balance; technically, the minority interest is neither debt nor owners'

equity — it is simply a balancing account needed to preserve the fundamental accounting equation A = L + OE. Any minority interest in the profit of the subsidiary is included in the consolidated income statement as a cost to the consolidated entity.

- Where the parent acquires its interest in the subsidiary from an earlier owner, the accounting will be determined by the form of the consideration given. Where the transaction fails to meet the tests for pooling accounting, purchase accounting must be used. Under purchase accounting, the purchase price paid by the parent will be allocated to the subsidiary's assets and liabilities in proportion to their individual fair values. Where there is excess purchase price that cannot be allocated to specific assets or liabilities, the remaining purchase price must be allocated to goodwill. The consolidated balance sheet reports the accounts of the newly acquired subsidiary at the current cost of the individual assets and liabilities acquired as a result of the purchase of the subsidiary's stock. The consolidated income statements will include the results of the two companies only from the date of acquisition; those consolidated income statements must include additional expense charges to cover the depreciation of the new asset values recognized and the amortization of any goodwill recorded.
- Where the parent acquires its interest in the subsidiary from an earlier owner, using common stock as the medium of exchange, it may be possible to use pooling accounting. Under pooling accounting, the common stock given up in the exchange will be valued at the historical cost values of the net assets acquired. It is not necessary to allocate the "purchase price" because there has been no purchase. Because the parent recognizes no new asset values, it is not necessary to recognize any goodwill. The consolidated balance sheet reports the assets and liabilities of the subsidiary at their original historical costs. Because there are no new asset values, there are no additional charges for depreciation or amortization. The income statements for the combined companies will include the operations of each company as of the beginning of each year presented, just as though the two companies had been together from the beginning of their respective lives.

TAXATION ISSUES

Under current U.S. tax laws, two companies may file a consolidated tax return only when both are U.S. companies, and only when the parent owns more than 80 percent of the subsidiary. Unfortunately, there is no such thing as equity accounting under tax law, and so in every other intercompany investment situation, each company involved in the relationship will be obligated to file a separate tax return and pay tax on its own earnings. For example, where Company A owns 75 percent of the stock of Company B, both of those companies will file tax returns and both will pay tax on their net income, as determined by their own stand-alone books. This is true even though Company A controls Company B and has a great deal to say about how much income Company B earns. To reduce the potential for double taxation in those kinds of intercompany relationships, however, the tax laws allow for a *dividend-received deduction.* A company that owns less than 20 percent of another may deduct up to 70 percent of the dividends it receives from that other company. When an investor owns between 20 percent and 80 percent of an investee company, it is entitled to deduct up to 80 percent of all dividends received from that other company. Notice that a company that

EXHIBIT 10.4

Rohm and Haas Company
Disclosure of Tax Status of International Subsidiaries

From the deferred tax footnote:
Provision for U.S. income taxes, after applying statutory tax credits, was made on the unremitted earnings of foreign subsidiaries and affiliates that have not been reinvested abroad indefinitely. Unremitted earnings, after provision for applicable foreign income taxes, were approximately $374 million at December 31, 1994. If the foreign subsidiary and affiliate earnings were remitted as dividends, the amount of additional U.S. income taxes, after applying statutory tax adjustments, would not be material.

is an investor but owns less than 80 percent of the investee will not be taxed on the investee's reported earnings, only on the dividends the investee pays — when and if they are paid. Even then, the dividend-received deduction substantially reduces the tax that would otherwise be due on that dividend distribution.

In situations where the investor owns more than 20 percent but less than 80 percent of the investee's stock, there will likely be a significant difference in the income the investor recognizes for its financial reports and the income it recognizes in its tax returns, assuming that the investee does not pay out all of its earnings as dividends. The investor should accrue a liability for the taxes it will have to pay when the earnings it recognized under the equity method, or under consolidation accounting, are eventually distributed in the form of dividends. Every year that accrued liability should be adjusted to recognize the tax that will be due as a result of any additional income reported but not distributed by the subsidiary. The tax expense that should be accrued against that currently recognized income will be reduced by (1) the expected dividend-received credit and (2) the possibility that because the investor can control or influence the investee, the earnings that have been retained by the investee will be permanently invested or distributed to the investor in a tax-free manner. Rohm and Hass explain their accrual for taxes on their subsidiary's earnings in Exhibit 10.4.

When an investor company acquires an investee, management has to decide whether the transaction is a pooling or a purchase for accounting purposes, and that decision will sometimes drive the structure of the transaction. If it is desirable that the transaction be accorded pooling accounting, it will have to be a stock for stock transaction, and the other detailed criteria will also have to be met. Management will also have to decide how to structure the transaction for tax purposes, depending on the needs of the parties to the negotiations. The tax rules for mergers and acquisitions are very complex, but they can be summarized this way:

- If the investor company acquires the stock of the investee company from the investee's shareholders and gives some form of equity such as common stock or preferred stock, the transaction is tax free to all parties.[9] The investee

[9]Technically, these transactions are not tax free but are tax deferred. The selling shareholders will not be obligated for any tax in a sale so long as they exchange one security for another; their cost for the new security is the same as their cost basis in the security they gave up. They will pay a tax when they sell any of the new securities, and the taxable gain will be the difference between the original cost basis and the current proceeds. In the same way, the investee company may avoid taxes on the gain suggested by the price paid by the investor; but when the investor causes the investee to sell any assets, that taxable gain on that sale will be calculated as the difference between the investee's original historical costs and the current proceeds — and that will be so whether the transaction is a purchase or a pooling for accounting purposes.

shareholders pay no tax until they sell the securities they received from the investor. The investee company continues to calculate its tax depreciation (and its gains and losses on asset sales) using its historical costs, and that depreciation is used in its own tax return or the consolidated return of the investee and investor. That is true whether the investor uses equity accounting for financial reporting purposes or consolidates the investee using purchase accounting or pooling accounting. Because this is a tax-free transaction to the investee company, neither the investor nor the investee gets any tax benefit from any new asset values that might otherwise have been implied in the purchase price. Obviously, this form of transaction is attractive to the investee-sellers but less so to the investor.

- If the investor acquires the stock of the investee company from the investee's shareholders and gives cash or notes, the investee shareholders pay tax on the capital gain they have realized — the difference between the value per share they received and the cost basis of the shares they held. Nonetheless, because this was a transaction between the investee shareholders and the investor company, the transaction is tax free to the investee company. The investee company continues to calculate its tax depreciation (and its gains and losses on asset sales) using its historical costs, and that depreciation will be used in the investee's tax return if the company files its own tax return, or it will be passed to the investor's consolidated tax return if the investor owns 80 percent or more of the investee. This is true whether the investor uses equity accounting for financial reporting purposes or consolidates the investee using purchase accounting or pooling accounting. As before, so long as the investee company is not subject to any tax on a gain in the transaction, neither the investor nor the investee gets any tax benefit from any new asset values that might otherwise have been implied in the purchase price.
- If the investor buys assets and liabilities directly from the original investee company and puts them into a newly created investee company, the new investee company (and, indirectly, the investor) may claim tax-deductible depreciation on all of the new asset values implied in the acquisition purchase price, including any goodwill. But of course the original investee company, which is now a shell, has an obligation to pay a tax on the gain implied in those new asset values.
- In our example where the investor buys the investee stock directly from the investee stockholders, it may be possible to obtain the tax benefit of the new values implied in the acquisition purchase price, but only as a result of a special tax election: The investor may elect to have the transaction treated as though it had purchased assets and liabilities directly from the company, thereby claiming depreciation on the new, purchase price–based asset values and similarly claiming a deduction for the amortization of the goodwill. However, to make that election, the investor would also have to agree to have its investee subsidiary pay the tax today on the gain implied in those new values. Only in a very unusual situation would the future benefit of those extra deductions be worth paying out the tax on the gain today.

In most situations, where purchase accounting is used for a consolidated subsidiary there will be significant differences between the tax bases of the assets and the new cost bases that are used for financial reporting in the consolidation. Those differences require deferred tax accounting, as described in Chapter 13.

OTHER MANAGEMENT CONSIDERATIONS

Segment Data and Deconsolidations

During the 1960s and 1970s, conglomerates were popular with Wall Street on the theory that a diverse company could protect a shareholder in the same way as a diverse portfolio might (that is, via risk diversification). Companies in cyclical industries sought investees in countercyclical businesses to balance their aggregate income stream. However, some conglomerates became so complex that it became difficult to evaluate how their assets were employed or what the sources of their revenues were. Accounting standard setters have attempted to deal with that problem by insisting that consolidated companies report supplemental, summarized line-of-business information. (See, for example, Chapter 1, which presents line-of-business information for PepsiCo, Inc.)

Even with the availability of line-of-business information, conglomerate companies have fallen out of favor with the investment community, in part because market analysts have become specialized by industry and no single analyst can follow a company as complex as, say, General Electric. Moreover, the more attractive components of a conglomerate were often ignored by the market, causing the stock price of such companies to languish. Given those problems, there has been a move to deconglomerate. Coca-Cola Company, for example, put most of its bottling business into one investee company and then sold 51 percent of the voting stock in that company (called Coca-Cola Enterprises, or CCE) to the public. The financial statements of Coca-Cola Co. report its share of the bottling business as a single line on its balance sheet and on its income statement. The bottling company has a higher leverage and a higher level of fixed assets than does the primary Coca-Cola business. The deconsolidation of the bottling business removed that debt and those fixed assets from the consolidated Coca-Cola Co. financial statements.

Exhibit 10.5 shows a footnote from Coca-Cola's 1994 annual report describing that relationship. In its balance sheet at December 31, 1994, Coca-Cola Co. reported that it had assets of $13.8 billion. That balance sheet included an entry for the Investment in CCE in the amount of $524 million. The company reported liabilities of $8.6 billion, which of course included none of the liabilities owed by CCE. Coca-Cola Co. reported net income of $2.5 billion; that income presumably included the company's share of the earnings of CCE, although the amount was too small to be reported on a separate line in the Coca-Cola Co. income statement.

Push-Down Accounting

In the examples we used to demonstrate the effects of purchase accounting, we have worried only about the increased asset values and the goodwill that resulted from the purchase when we prepared the consolidated financial statements. Occasionally, a subsidiary will be obligated to prepare financial statements covering only its own operations, either for a regulatory filing or to demonstrate compliance with a contract. When those separate financial statements of the subsidiary are required, they must include disclosures indicating the degree of control exercised by the parent. But that caution aside, the accounting world has debated what asset values ought to be used for those separate statements: Should the subsidiary's historical costs be used, or should the new costs paid by the parent and attributable to the subsidiary be used? A theory called **push-down accounting** has come to the fore; its proponents argue that the

EXHIBIT 10.5

Coca-Cola Company and Subsidiaries
1994 Annual Report Footnote Disclosures

Coca-Cola Enterprises, Inc.

Coca-Cola Enterprises is the largest soft drink bottler in the world. The company owns approximately 44 percent of the outstanding common stock of Coca-Cola Enterprises, and accordingly, accounts for its investment by the equity method of accounting. A summary of financial information for Coca-Cola Enterprises is as follows (in millions):

	December 31,	
	1994	**1993**
Current assets	**$ 809**	$ 746
Noncurrent assets	**7,928**	7,936
Total assets	**$8,737**	$8,682
Current liabilities	**$1,088**	$1,007
Noncurrent liabilities	**6,310**	6,415
Total liabilities	**$7,398**	$7,422
Share-owners' equity	**$1,339**	$1,260
Company equity investment	**$ 524**	$ 498

		Year Ended December 31,	
	1994	**1993**	**1992**
Net operating revenues	**$6,011**	$5,465	$5,127
Cost of goods sold	**3,703**	3,372	3,219
Gross profit	**$2,308**	$2,093	$1,908
Operating income	**$ 440**	$ 385	$ 306
Operating cash flow[1]	**$ 901**	$ 804	$ 695
Income (loss) before changes in accounting principles	**$ 69**	$ (15)	$ (15)
Net income (loss) available to common share owners	**$ 67**	$ (15)	$ (186)
Company equity income (loss)	**$ 30**	$ (6)	$ (6)

[1]Excludes nonrecurring charges.

The 1992 net loss of Coca-Cola Enterprises includes $171 million of noncash, aftertax charges resulting from the adoption of Statement of Financial Accounting Standards No. 106, "Employers' Accounting for Postretirement Benefits Other Than Pensions" (SFAS 106), and Statement of Financial Accounting Standards No. 109, "Accounting for Income Taxes" (SFAS 109), as of January 1, 1992. The company's financial statements reflect the adoption of SFAS 109 by Coca-Cola Enterprises as if it occurred on January 1, 1989.

The company's net concentrate/syrup sales to Coca-Cola Enterprises were $1.2 billion in 1994, $961 million in 1993, and $889 million in 1992. Coca-Cola Enterprises purchases sweeteners through the company under a pass-through arrangement, and accordingly, related collections from Coca-Cola Enterprises and payments to suppliers are not included in the company's consolidated statements of income. These transactions amounted to $254 million in 1994, $211 million in 1993, and $225 million in 1992. The company also provides certain administrative and other services to Coca-Cola Enterprises under negotiated fee arrangements.

The company engages in a wide range of marketing programs, media advertising, and other similar arrangements to promote the sale of company products in territories in which Coca-Cola Enterprises operates. The company's direct support for certain marketing activities of Coca-Cola Enterprises and participation with Coca-Cola Enterprises in cooperative advertising and other marketing programs amounted to approximately $319 million in 1994, $256 million in 1993, and $253 million in 1992. In addition, in 1994 the company committed to provide approximately $34 million to Coca-Cola Enterprises under a company program that encourages bottlers to invest in building and supporting soft drink infrastructure.

In January 1994 the company sold common stock representing a 9 percent voting interest in The Coca-Cola Bottling Company of New York, Inc. (CCNY) to Coca-Cola Enterprises, thereby reducing the company's ownership in CCNY below 50 percent.

If valued at the December 31, 1994, quoted closing price of publicly traded Coca-Cola Enterprises shares, the calculated value of the company's investment in Coca-Cola Enterprises would have exceeded its carrying value by approximately $490 million.

parent's costs for the subsidiary ought to be pushed down to take the place of the subsidiary's historical costs. They argue that the old costs are irrelevant because the subsidiary is now being run by new, different owners, and those new owners have different expectations for the subsidiary. The new owners measure success or failure of the new subsidiary against the investment they made, and that investment ought to be seen as the new cost basis for the subsidiary. The proponents of push-down accounting argue that the subsidiary's success or failure is being measured against those new values, and therefore those new values ought to be the basis for the subsidiary's financial reports. In those situations where there has been a substantial change in ownership in a transaction that qualifies for purchase accounting, push-down accounting is GAAP for any separate financial statements subsequently required for the subsidiary.

That discussion raises an interesting management accounting issue, also. If the subsidiary is to be measured by how well it does against the new costs implied in the acquisition price, should not the managers of the subsidiary be measured against those new costs as well? Even if it is not necessary to publish separate financial statements for the subsidiary, it makes sense to push the values from the purchase down into the subsidiary's accounts so that measures such as return on assets, return on equity, and other ratios are prepared using the costs that the parent understands to be embedded in the subsidiary. In fact, it makes sense to do that whether the acquisition of the subsidiary was accounted for as a pooling or as a purchase. Even if the transaction is accounted for as a pooling for financial reporting purposes, the values implied by the consideration given up by the parent ought to be used in measuring the performance of the subsidiary management.

SUMMARY

In today's complex business community, it is quite common to find that companies invest in each other. These long-term intercorporate investments are undertaken for a variety of reasons, such as to gain control over a major competitor or supplier, to diversify business risk, and to produce additional income and cash flows.

The financial reporting of these investments is largely dictated by the extent of the investor's stockholdings in the investee. When a relatively small (less than 20 percent of the outstanding shares) amount of stock is owned, the investor most commonly reports its investment using mark-to-market accounting. When the size of the investment is sufficient to influence the operating activities of the investee (usually 20 to 50 percent stockholding), equity accounting is most likely to be used. Finally, when an investor gains control of an investee (that is, its stockholding exceeds 50 percent of the outstanding voting shares), the financial results of the two companies must be reported on a consolidated basis. Such investments may be accounted for using the purchase method or, under certain circumstance, the pooling-of-interests method.

NEW CONCEPTS AND TERMS

Active investment (p. 443)
Affiliates (p. 444)
Consolidation accounting (p. 445)
Cumulative Translation Adjustment account (p. 471)
Current rate method (p. 471)
Economic exposure (p. 471)
Equity accounting (p. 445)
Foreign exchange risk (p. 470)
Functional currency (p. 471)
Goodwill (p. 455)
Minority interest (p. 463)
Negative goodwill (p. 455)
Parent company (p. 444)
Passive investment (p. 443)
Pooling-of-interests method (p. 459)
Proportional consolidation (p. 448)
Purchase method (p. 475)
Push-down accounting (p. 467)
Subsidiary company (p. 444)
Transaction exposure (p. 471)
Translation exposure (p. 470)

APPENDIX 10

Accounting for Foreign Operations

There appears to be a fairly well-established pattern of evolution for most business enterprises: After successfully establishing a local market, the enterprise then seeks out other new markets. Thus, it is not at all surprising to find that most mature, successful U.S. companies have expanded their area of operations beyond the borders of the United States. When a company does establish operations outside the United States, a question arises: How best to financially portray those foreign operations.

Essentially, there are two choices. First, the company may prepare financial statements for its foreign operations (that is, subsidiary, affiliate, or division) using the generally accepted accounting principles of the host foreign country, expressing those statements in the currency (such as the dollar in Canada, the yen in Japan, or the peso in Mexico) of the host country. Second, the company may prepare financial statements for its foreign operations using U.S. GAAP and translating the value of those foreign operations into U.S. dollars.

Because of the diversity in GAAP among countries, the FASB has determined that the second option is the most informative one for U.S. analysts, creditors, and investors, and it is required for companies issuing publicly traded securities on U.S. exchanges. Consequently, in this appendix we focus on how such companies translate their foreign operations into U.S. equivalents and how that information can be used to understand the foreign activities of a company. In Chapter 15 we consider the topic of GAAP in foreign countries, focusing specifically on the accounting practices followed by companies in Japan and the United Kingdom to illustrate the diversity of accounting practices between countries.

Foreign Exchange Risk

In prior chapters we discussed the various types of *risk* that companies face as part of their normal business operations. The two principal types of risk are operating risk and default risk. When a company maintains foreign operations, however, it is also subject to a third type of risk — **foreign exchange risk.** This type of risk occurs because the exchange rates between the U.S. dollar and foreign currencies are rarely stable, creating value changes in international operations.

Foreign exchange risk is usually thought to result from three elements: translation exposure, transaction exposure, and economic exposure. **Translation exposure** occurs as a result of the need to translate (or convert) the financial statements of a foreign division or subsidiary into U.S. dollars in order to prepare consolidated financial statements for the entire company. This type of exposure is solely the result of the *consolidation process* and, consequently, is sometimes referred to as *accounting exposure*. **Transaction exposure** occurs during the normal course of international business transactions when a lag occurs between the date on which a contract is signed or goods delivered and the date of payment. This type of exposure has real cash flow consequences if the exchange rate changes between the date the transaction occurs and the date the currency exchange occurs. **Economic exposure** is a prospective concept focusing on the impact of exchange rate fluctuations on the future operations of a foreign division or subsidiary. As exchange rates change, the competitive position of companies operating in that country change: As the local currency strengthens, exports are easier, and vice versa.

Translation of Foreign Operations

Current U.S. GAAP stipulates that the translation of foreign operations should be undertaken using a "functional currency" approach. A company's (or subsidiary's) **functional currency** is defined to be the currency of the primary economic environment in which it operates. Thus, a subsidiary that does business exclusively or principally in Japan has a functional currency of the yen. Moreover, the foreign subsidiary's accounts should be determined (or redetermined, as the case may be) using U.S. GAAP and initially reported in terms of its functional currency. The foreign subsidiary's financial statements thus prepared are then *translated* into U.S. dollars using the **current rate method.** Under this approach, the subsidiary's income statement is converted into U.S. dollars using the average exchange rate for the period, and its balance sheet is converted at the exchange rate existing on the date of the translation (for example, December 31).

Gains and losses due to translation (or accounting) exposure are accumulated into an owners' equity account, the **Cumulative Translation Adjustment account,** and have no effect on current income. Gains and losses due to transaction exposure are reported as a separate line item on the company's income statement.

Exhibit 10A.1 illustrates the translation process for FHAS, Inc., a company which operates in another country where the currency is the fictitious zlot. Note that since the exchange rate of the U.S. dollar declined relative to the zlot (or, alternatively, the zlot increased in value relative to the U.S. dollar), the value of FHAS's subsidiary's net assets and operations increased over the 1994 fiscal year. As a consequence, the prior accumulation in the Translation Adjustment account, representing an exchange loss, was eliminated, ultimately ending the period in a gain position. This gain remains unreported until the subsidiary is sold or its operations discontinued.

The translation process illustrated in Exhibit 10A.1 was accomplished using a few basic conventions:

1. Assets and liabilities on the balance sheet are translated at the end-of-period exchange rate.
2. Owners' equity (in this case, common stock and retained earnings) is translated at the exchange rate in effect when the account balance was created.
3. The income statement is translated at the average exchange rate for the period.
4. Dividends are translated at the actual exchange rate at the time of payment.

EXHIBIT 10A.1

FHAS, Inc.
Translation of Foreign Financial Statements

FHAS, Inc., is a U.S. corporation with a foreign subsidiary operating principally in one other country. The foreign subsidiary, hereafter called Pty. Limited, was founded in 1980 and had a cumulative translation adjustment of $(10,780) as of January 1, 1994. The exchange rates between the zlot and the U.S. dollar in 1994 were as follows:

January 1:	.75	(1Ƶ = $0.75 U.S.)
December 31:	.78	(1Ƶ = $0.78 U.S.)
Average:	.76	

Pty. Limited
Statement of Income
December 31, 1994

	Local Country Zlots (Functional Currency)	Exchange Rate	U.S. Dollars
Sales	Ƶ1,148,000	.76	$872,480
Costs and expenses:			
Cost of sales	Ƶ 588,000	.76	$446,880
Depreciation	56,700	.76	43,092
General and administrative	101,500	.76	77,140
Interest	35,000	.76	26,600
	Ƶ 781,200		$593,712
Net income before taxes	366,800		278,768
Income taxes	186,200	.76	141,512
Net income	Ƶ 180,600		$137,256

Take a moment to review the income statement and balance sheet in Exhibit 10A.1 and consider the reconciliation of the ending balance in the Retained Earnings and Cumulative Translation Adjustment accounts.

As a consequence of the translation process, financial statement users are able to view, in a single set of financial statements, all of a company's operations — both foreign and domestic — using a consistent set of accounting methods (U.S. GAAP). Thus, the process of determining whether a company's overall performance has increased (or declined) is made easier. Note that the process of translating the various accounts of a foreign subsidiary into their U.S. dollar equivalents is a necessary step *preceding* the consolidation of those accounts with the U.S. parent. Once the translation process is complete, the consolidation process as described in Chapter 10 can be undertaken.

ISSUES FOR DISCUSSION

D10.1 What accounting should be used for an investment in marketable common stock of other companies that represent a 5 percent ownership in that company? What rationale supports that accounting? How should fluctuations in the current market value of that investment affect the income statement of the investing company? Why? Is that decision influenced by the size of the investee's holdings? Why?

EXHIBIT 10A.1 concluded

Pty. Limited
Balance Sheet

	Beginning-of-Year			End-of-Year		
	Local Country Ƶ	Exchange Rate	United States $	Local Country Ƶ	Exchange Rate	United States $
Assets						
Cash	Ƶ 28,000	.75	$ 21,000	Ƶ 63,000	.78	$ 49,140
Accounts receivable	84,000	.75	63,000	103,600	.78	80,808
Inventory	98,000	.75	73,500	140,000	.78	109,200
Property, plant, and equipment (net)	476,700	.75	357,525	462,000	.78	360,360
Total assets	Ƶ686,700		$515,025	Ƶ768,600		$599,508
Liabilities						
Accounts payable	Ƶ 84,700	.75	63,525	56,000	.78	43,680
Long-term debt	350,000	.75	262,500	280,000	.78	218,400
Total liabilities	Ƶ434,700		$326,025	Ƶ336,000		$262,080
Stockholders' equity:						
Common stock	Ƶ 42,000	H*	$ 25,830	Ƶ 42,000	H*	$ 25,830
Retained earnings	210,000	H*	173,950	390,600		311,206
Cumulative translation adjustment	—		(10,780)	—		392
Total equity	Ƶ252,000		$189,000	Ƶ432,600		$337,428
Total liabilities and equity	Ƶ686,700		$515,025	Ƶ768,600		$599,508

Reconciliation of ending balance in retained earnings:

	U.S. dollars
Retained earnings, 1/1/1994	$ 173,950
Net income (restated)	137,256
Retained earnings, 12/31/1994	$ 311,206

Reconciliation of Cumulative Translation Adjustment account:

Balance, 1/1/1994	$ (10,780)
Adjustment for beginning net assets, with increase in exchange rate from \$0.75 to \$0.78: \$252,000 × \$0.03	7,560
Adjustment for net income, with increase in exchange rate from average of \$0.76 to \$0.78: \$180,600 × \$0.02	3,612
Balance, 12/31/1994	$ 392

*Refers to the historic exchange rate in effect when the account balance was created.

D10.2 Fully describe the purpose, use, and rationale of the equity method of accounting for investments in voting common stock.

D10.3 What factors must managers consider as they deliberate between the use of the mark-to-market method and the equity method?

D10.4 The equity method has been termed a "one-line" consolidation. What does that expression mean to you? Is it a fair description of equity accounting?

D10.5 You were president of QR Inc., all the company's outstanding common stock was just purchased by Conglomerate Inc. who paid twice QR's recorded net book value. The good news is, you get to stay on as vice president of the QR Division — the bad news is, Conglomerate's

CFO is intrigued with the idea of push down accounting. Explain why the CFO might be in favor of this and why you might not be.

D10.6 World Wide, Inc., had just completed its acquisition of Local Manufacturing, and the acquisition team was now assessing their prize. The purchase price had been $25,000,000. Local had paid off all of its liabilities prior to the acquisition. The fair value of Local's receivables and inventory seemed to be about the same as the book value, at $8,000,000. The $5,000,000 net book value in equipment and trucks was also approximately equal to fair value. The appraisers were having a hard time coming up with a fair value for Local's plant and land, however. One appraiser came in with a value of $5,000,000 for the building and $2,000,000 for the land. Another appraiser came in with values of $6,000,000 for the building and $4,000,000 for the land. Assume that World Wide management pushed the appraisers to reconcile their differences but without success: The variation in the appraisal numbers remained.

As the chief executive officer of World Wide, outline the factors you would consider in making your decision about the appropriate values for Local's plant and land.

D10.7 The pooling-of-interests method is based on the understanding that two companies of roughly equal size come together to form a new entity; it makes less sense to think of a pooling as a large firm acquiring a smaller one. At what point should pooling be unacceptable due to a relative difference in size between the two firms? Be specific! For example, should it be three times assets, or four times revenues?

D10.8 Some analysts refuse to acknowledge purchased goodwill as an asset. If purchased goodwill is not an asset, what should be done with the difference that exists when the purchase price of an acquisition exceeds any fair values that could be assigned to the net assets acquired? Of all the alternative treatments of purchased goodwill that you can identify, what is the best solution?

D10.9 A few years back, Coca-Cola Co. popularized the "49 percent solution" when it spun off the Coca-Cola Enterprises bottling business, a previously wholly owned subsidiary, retaining only a 49 percent ownership. Why might Coca-Cola Co. have done this?

PROBLEMS

P10.1 Accounting for intercorporate investments: the equity method. In January 1994 Contran Corp. acquired a 40 percent ownership interest in the National Lock Company, paying $3.5 million. During the year, National Lock declared (and paid) its usual dividends totaling $240,000. Following a year-end audit by its independent auditors, National Lock released its 1994 earnings report, which showed earnings of $850,000 for the year.

Bill Montgomery, controller for Contran, considered this information and how it should be reflected in Contran's 1994 financial statements. With some concern, he also noted that as of December 31, 1994, Contran's original investment was now worth only $3.25 million according to National Lock's quoted share prices in the over-the-counter market. He was confident, however, that the market price decline was only temporary, and he expected a full recovery in 1995.

Required:

How should Contran value its investment in National Lock at year-end 1994? Assume that National reported a *loss* of $300,000 for 1994. How would Contran's valuation of National Lock change?

P10.2 Applying the equity method — a further example. On October 1, 1994, Westover Corporation purchased 35 percent of the outstanding common stock of Graydon Corporation for $500,000. For the quarter ending December 31, 1994 Graydon Corporation declared and paid a dividend totaling $80,000. For the same quarter, Graydon Corporation reported net income of $160,000, even though net income for the year was only $10,000.

Required:

a. Prepare Westover's 1994 entries for its investment in Graydon Corporation.

b. What line item(s) and amount(s) will appear on Westover's 1994 balance sheet, income statement, and statement of cash flows related to its investment in Graydon?

P10.3 Accounts affected by purchase accounting. On January 1, 1995, Acquiror issued stock to Acquiree's stockholders for all of Acquiree's outstanding shares. The market value of Acquiror's stock involved in that exchange was $40,000. At that time, the appraised value of Acquiree's net assets was equal to its recorded book value except for the PP&E which was appraised at $54,000.

	12-31-94 Preacquisition Balance Sheets	
	Acquiror	**Acquiree**
Cash	$ 6,000	$ 1,000
Accts. Receivable	14,000	8,000
Inventory	22,000	12,000
PP&E (net)	80,000	50,000
Other Assets	4,000	2,000
	$126,000	$73,000
Accts. Payable	$ 10,000	$ 2,500
Other Current Liab.	10,000	1,500
Bonds Payable	24,000	35,000
Common Stock	50,000	25,000
Retained Earnings	32,000	9,000
	$126,000	$73,000

Required:

Prepare two consolidated balance sheets as of January 1, 1995 using:

a. The purchase method.

b. The pooling-of-interests method.

P10.4 Long-term investment exercise (A): Purchase accounting.* The statements of financial position of Company P and Company Q and the fair value of Company Q's assets at December 31, 1994, were as follows (in thousands of dollars):

	Historical Costs: Company P	Historical Costs: Company Q	Company Q Fair Value
Assets:			
Cash	$1,100	$ 50	$ 50
Trade receivables	500	225	225
Inventories	1,000	125	175
Property, plant, and equipment (net)	2,500	250	450
	5,100	650	900
Deduct liabilities	750	100	100
Net assets	$4,350	$550	800
Stockholders' equity:			
Capital stock (no par)	3,000	200	
Retained earnings	1,350	350	
	$4,350	$550	

Market value per share at 12/31/94 was $200 for Company P's stock and $400 for Company Q's.

Required:

The management of Company P was considering several approaches to the acquisition of Company Q.

Approach 1. If, as of December 31, 1994, Company P negotiated to purchase the assets and assumed the liabilities of Company Q for $800,000 cash:

a. What entry(ies) would Company P make? Company Q?

b. How would the statements of financial position look for Company P and Company Q after these entries had been made?

c. What entry(ies) would Company P and Company Q make, and how would the financial statements look afterward, if the purchase price was $900,000 in cash?

Approach 2. If, as of December 31, 1994, Company P negotiated to purchase all of Company Q's assets and assumed all of Company Q's liabilities, as in Approach 1, but instead of cash payment, the purchase price was 4,000 shares of Company P stock:

d. What entry(ies) would Company P make? Company Q?

e. How would the statements of financial position look for Company P and Company Q after these entries were made?

f. What entry(ies) should Company P and Company Q make, and how would the financial statements look afterward, if the purchase price were paid to Company Q by issuance of 4,500 shares of Company P's stock?

Approach 3. If, as of December 31, 1994, Company P negotiated to purchase from the stockholders of Company Q their 2,000 shares for $400 cash per share (Company Q was to become a subsidiary of Company P):

g. What entry(ies) would Company P make? Company Q?

h. How would the consolidated statement of financial position for Companies P and Q look at December 31, 1994?

i. What entry(ies) would Company P and Company Q make, and how would the consolidated statement of financial position look afterward, if the price paid for each Company Q share was $450?

Approach 4. If, as of December 31, 1994, Company P negotiated with the stockholders of Company Q to issue 4,000 shares of its voting common stock in exchange for the 2,000 shares of outstanding Company Q's stock (Company Q was to become a subsidiary of Company P):

j. What entry(ies) would Company P make? Company Q?

k. How would the consolidated statement of financial position of Company P and Company Q look at December 31, 1994? (Assume the pooling method is not permissable here.)

l. What entry(ies) would Company P and Company Q make, and how would the consolidated statement of financial position look afterward, if Company P were to exchange 4,500 shares of its stock for all of the 2,000 shares of Company Q?

P10.5 Contrasting the equity method and the mark-to-market method. The balance sheet of DAE Corporation at December 31, 1994, shows a long-term investment in the common stock of Wallace Corporation of $350,000. The investment was purchased by DAE in January 1991, and the following information pertaining to Wallace Corporation is available:

Year	Income or (Loss)	Dividends Paid
1991	($30,000)	-0-
1992	120,000	$50,000
1993	150,000	60,000
1994	200,000	80,000

Market value of the investment in Wallace Corporation at December 31, 1994, was $350,000.

Required:

a. Assuming that DAE Corporation's investment is classified as available for sale and that it represents a 10 percent interest in Wallace, determine how much DAE paid for Wallace's stock in January 1991.

b. Assuming that DAE Corporation's investment represents a 25 percent interest in Wallace Corporation, determine how much DAE paid for Wallace's stock in January 1991.

P10.6 Long-term investment exercise (B): Contrasting pooling-of-interests and purchase accounting.* Preacquisition balance sheets of Al and Syd corporations are shown below:

	Preacquisition Balance Sheets (in thousands)	
	Al Corporation	**Syd Corporation**
Assets		
Cash	$ 8,000	$ 2,500
Marketable securities	5,000	3,500
Accounts receivable (net)	7,500	5,000
Inventories (LIFO)	19,000	9,500
Fixed assets (net)	38,000	23,000
Other assets	4,500	1,500
Total assets	$82,000	$45,000
Liabilities and Stockholders' Equity		
Accounts payable	$ 9,500	$ 7,500
Other current liabilities	4,000	3,000
Bonds payable	11,000	—
Other long-term debt	7,500	12,500
Common stock ($10 par)	12,000	—
Common stock ($5 par)	—	6,000
Capital in excess of par	7,000	2,000
Retained earnings	31,000	14,000
Total liabilities and stockholders' equity	$82,000	$45,000

Subsequent to a six-month period of intense negotiating, Al Corporation agreed to purchase all of the outstanding common stock of Syd Corporation at a price of $29.4 million. In arriving at this price, Al Corporation placed the following fair market values on Syd Corporation's assets:

Asset	Fair Market Value (thousands)
Cash	$ 2,500
Marketable securities	4,500
Accounts receivable (net)	3,500
Inventories	13,000
Fixed assets (net)	28,000
Other assets	0
Total	$51,500

According to the terms of the agreement, Al Corporation was to issue one share of its common stock in exchange for each share of Syd Corporation's outstanding common stock. Subsequent to the exchange of common stock, Syd Corporation was to become a wholly owned subsidiary of Al Corporation. The current market price of Al Corporation's common stock was $24.50 per share.

Required:

Al Corporation expects to be able to account for its acquisition of Syd Corporation using the pooling-of-interests method. There is, however, some question about a possible violation of one of the numerous pooling criteria. You have been asked by Al Corporation's management to prepare a consolidated balance sheet to reflect the acquisition of Syd Corporation under both the pooling-of-interests and the purchase methods of accounting.

P10.7 Application of the pooling-of-interests method of accounting. On November 9, 1994, Shea & Shea Corporation merged with Garbo Associates by an exchange of one share of Shea & Shea for one share of Garbo. Shea & Shea issued 1,891,678 of its shares and accounted for the transaction using the pooling-of-interests rather than the purchase method. In accounting for the issue of 1,891,678 shares, Shea & Shea increased its no-par common stock account by $3,300,000.

Garbo's net assets on November 9, 1994, can be approximated as follows:

Capital stock (1,891,678 shares)			$3.3 million
Retained earnings at 12/31/93		$25.5	
Net income 1/1/94 to 11/9/94 (313 days) 313/365 of $6.2	$5.3		
Less dividends from 1/1/94 to 11/9/94	(2.1)	3.2	
			$28.7 million
Garbo's estimated owners' equity (net assets)			$32.0 million

For purposes of the questions to follow, assume that the market value of Shea & Shea stock at November 9, 1994, was $50 a share, or a total of $94.6 million for the 1,891,678 shares issued in the exchange.

Required:

a. What entry did Shea & Shea make to record the acquisition of Garbo? Why?

b. What difference(s) would it have made if Shea & Shea had treated the transaction under the purchase method rather than the pooling-of-interests method?

c. If you had been a Garbo stockholder, are there any reasons that you would have preferred one share of Shea & Shea stock for each Garbo share you owned rather than $50 in cash?

d. If you were a part of Shea & Shea's management, are there any reasons you would have preferred treating the share-for-share exchange under the pooling-of-interests method rather than under the purchase method?

P10.8 Application of consolidation accounting. Joann Jones was the plant manager of World Wide Incorporated's (WWI) California assembly plant. She was pulling together the material for the company's year-end reporting package to send to World Wide's home office. Her systems people gave her the following data pertaining to the suppliers her plant had used during the year:

	Actual Invoice Cost		
Suppliers	Beginning Inventory	Purchases	Ending Inventory
WWI subsidiaries:			
Arizona	$25,000	$175,000	$20,000
Northeast	15,000	125,000	18,000
Southwest	12,000	250,000	10,000
Outside contractors:			
National	14,000	85,000	12,000
Amalgamated	8,000	62,000	6,500

World Wide's home office told Jones that the Arizona plant had experienced a 25 percent profit rate during the last several years, Northwest had experienced a 20 percent rate, and Southwest had experienced a 15 percent rate.

Required:

Calculate for Jones the value of her plant's ending inventory and the materials cost component of the cost of goods sold for the year.

CASES

C10.1 Consolidated vs. unconsolidated reporting: UFS Corporation. "Why me?" thought Connie Likert. "My first day on the job at the bank and instead of getting a company with a nice single set of financial statements, I get five separate sets of statements that supposedly fit together."

Likert had just started as a new credit analyst for the First National Bank of Bruceton Mills, having just completed an MBA degree with a major in finance at the local university. From the loan officer responsible for this client, Likert learned the following information about each of the four companies associated with UFS Corporation and about UFS Corporation itself.

UFS Corporation. UFS Corporation is a manufacturing company whose principal products are microwave ovens, refrigerators, and conventional ovens. The company has had a long history (more than 50 years) of selling high-quality, high-priced home appliances; however, recent reductions in the price of competitor products forced UFS to consider ways to provide assistance to its customers to help them buy its products. As a consequence, UFS started its own finance subsidiary, the UFS Acceptance Corporation, to assist customers in financing their purchases.

UFS Corporation is also associated with three other companies. It holds an 80 percent interest in Scrub-All, a company that makes automatic dishwashers. UFS purchased this interest in Scrub-All because the company's product line complemented its own items, and the products were of a quality that UFS would have had difficulty duplicating. Further, to ensure a steady supply of chrome parts for its appliances, UFS obtained a 10 percent interest in the common stock of Acme Chrome Company. Well over 50 percent of Acme's sales were attributed to purchases by UFS and Scrub-All. Further, to compete in the low-end market for various appliances, UFS Corporation formed a joint venture with Whirlwind Products Co. to produce such appliances.

UFS Acceptance Corporation. Created nearly five years ago, UFS Acceptance Corporation is a wholly owned subsidiary that purchases consumer notes from its parent, UFS Corporation. UFS Acceptance borrows funds from several banking institutions on a medium- and long-term basis and uses the margins between the short-term interest rates on the consumer notes and the rates on its medium- and long-term liabilities to cover its overhead costs. The parent company guarantees all of the borrowings of UFS Acceptance Corporation.

Scrub-All Company. With an ownership interest of 80 percent of the common stock of Scrub-All, UFS Corporation controls the tactical and strategic policies of Scrub-All Company through an interlocking board of directors. Scrub-All, like UFS, sold its consumer notes to UFS Acceptance Corporation. The family that originally started Scrub-All still holds a 20 percent ownership interest in the common stock of the company.

Acme Chrome Company. To guarantee a steady supply of chrome parts and a quality cadre of people who could work with the engineers of UFS in the design of new parts, UFS purchased a 10 percent interest in Acme Chrome Company. Over the years, a strong relationship had developed between UFS and Acme. For example, Acme schedules the production runs of its other customers around the production needs of UFS and Scrub-All.

Spotless Appliance Company. Both UFS Corporation and Whirlwind Products Company (an otherwise unrelated company) contributed half of the funds necessary to start Spotless Appliance Company. Spotless Appliance Company makes low-end appliance models that are sold under the Spotless trade name or are labeled with various department store names. The board of directors of Spotless Appliance Company consists of an equal number of members voted in by each of UFS Corporation and Whirlwind Products Company and three members from outside either of the respective companies. Any debt of Spotless is guaranteed by both UFS Corporation and Whirlwind Products Company.

Kirk Tennant, the loan officer responsible for UFS, provided Likert with the financial statements of the five companies (presented on the following pages) and asked her to answer some basic credit review questions concerning an expansion loan application that had been received from UFS management. Before Likert could complete the credit review, she identified the following questions that needed to be answered so that she could understand the relationship between the various companies.

Required:

a. Why are the investments in Acme Chrome and Spotless Appliance Companies shown on the UFS Corporation balance sheet while the investments in Scrub-All and UFS Acceptance Corporation are omitted?

b. What is meant by the carrying value "at equity" for the investment in Spotless Appliance Company?

c. Why is the investment in Acme Chrome Company shown "at cost"?

d. Explain the Goodwill account. What other name is sometimes used instead of *goodwill,* and to what company is this account related?

e. What is meant by "minority interest," and to what company is this account related? Is this a liability or an equity account?

f. What are UFS Corporation's current ratio, debt-to-equity ratio, and debt-to-asset ratio? Are these ratios at an acceptable level?

g. How would the balance sheet of UFS Corporation appear if Spotless Appliance Company were consolidated? Would you recommend consolidation for Spotless?

h. How would the ratios calculated in part (f) differ after the consolidation of Spotless Appliance? Can an argument be made for consolidating Acme Chrome Company?

i. How would the balance sheet of the parent company appear without including any of the consolidated subsidiaries? Which balance sheet would you use to make this credit decision?

UFS Corporation
Consolidated Statement of Financial Position
December 31, 1994

Assets	
Current assets	$ 37,500,000
Notes receivable	58,000,000
Investment in stock of Spotless Appliance at equity (50%)	1,750,000
Investment in stock of Acme Chrome Company (10%) at cost*	5,600,000
Other assets	101,500,000
Goodwill	3,200,000
Total assets	$207,550,000
Liabilities and Stockholders' Equity	
Current liabilities	$ 31,500,000
Long-term liabilities	102,100,000
Minority interest	7,500,000
Common stock	15,000,000
Retained earnings	51,450,000
Total liabilities and stockholders' equity	$207,550,000

*Cost approximates market value.

UFS Acceptance Corporation
Statement of Financial Position
December 31, 1994

Assets	
Current assets	$ 8,000,000
Notes receivable	58,000,000
Other assets	6,500,000
Total assets	$72,500,000
Liabilities and Stockholders' Equity	
Current liabilities*	$ 5,000,000
Long-term debt	47,100,000
Common stock ($1 par)	10,000,000
Retained earnings	10,400,000
Total liabilities and equities	$72,500,000

*$3,000,000 of the current liabilities is a promissory note to UFS Corporation. UFS Corporation accounts for this as a long-term receivable in other assets.

Scrub-All Company
Statement of Financial Position
December 31, 1994

Assets	
Current assets	$16,400,000
Other assets	52,600,000
Total assets	$69,000,000
Liabilities and Stockholders' Equity	
Current liabilities	$13,350,000
Long-term liabilities	18,150,000
Common stock	12,000,000
Retained earnings	25,500,000
Total liabilities and stockholders' equity	$69,000,000

Acme Chrome Company
Statement of Financial Position
December 31, 1994

Assets	
Current assets	$14,750,000
Other assets	36,250,000
Total assets	$51,000,000
Liabilities and Stockholders' Equity	
Current liabilities	$5,000,000
Long-term liabilities	15,000,000
Capital stock	18,750,000
Retained earnings	12,250,000
Total liabilities and stockholders' equity	$51,000,000

Spotless Appliance Company
Statement of Financial Position
December 31, 1994

Assets	
Current assets	$ 8,500,000
Other assets	16,000,000
Total assets	$24,500,000
Liabilities and Stockholders' Equity	
Current liabilities	$ 3,000,000
Long-term debt	18,000,000
Common stock ($1 par)	6,000,000
Retained earnings	(2,500,000)
Total liabilities and equities	$24,500,000

C10.2 Purchase vs. pooling: The Steady Growth saga. Steady Growth, Inc. (SGI), began business in 1974 as part of an effort to popularize natural foods, a subject that was of passionate interest to its founders. The founding group was part counterculture and part agricultural engineer. It successfully developed a line of alternative, organic fertilizers and pesticides. Sales grew modestly but steadily and by 1981 had reached $25 million a year. SGI produced 30 different items, all sold under the Steady Growth trade name. Organic farmers marketed their products explaining that they used only Steady Growth products; natural food stores specifically advertised products as "grown the Steady Growth way." To provide funds for its own growth and to share the benefits of the business, SGI sold stock in 1982 to the natural food wholesale and retail community. The founding group retained about 60 percent of the stock, but the publicly held shares traded occasionally on the Pacific Coast Exchange at prices that approximated SGI's book value per share, about $20.

In early 1992 the press was full of stories about chemical contamination of apples and other fruit crops. Overnight, the general public became interested in organically grown produce, and SGI found itself swamped with orders. As the spring planting season began, SGI's inventory was completely sold out, and production capacity for the year was committed by orders taken in March. SGI management looked at its order books and decided that the company might be ready finally to move into the really "big time." They worked with a team of financial advisers and developed a plan for a management-led leveraged buyout. They arranged to borrow the requisite funds and proposed a cash repurchase of all the stock in the hands of the public at $30 a share.

But SGI was not the only company to notice the public interest in natural foods. Enormous, Inc., a large food chain, notified SGI's board of directors that it would be interested in acquiring the company. Later SGI's board received a similar proposal from an international chemical concern. A spirited bidding war ensued. After several weeks of intense negotiations, SGI's board agreed to recommend to the shareholders that they tender their stock to Enormous in a share-for-share exchange. Enormous's shares were actively traded, and on the day of the announcement, the market price of its stock was $40 a share.

The exchange was completed on September 30, 1992, and SGI became a wholly owned subsidiary of Enormous. Some of the founders of SGI took their newfound wealth and left to pursue other interests. Some stayed on, in part because of the salary promised by Enormous and in part because they still believed in the need to promote the cause of natural foods. Enormous sent in a team of transitional managers to help get SGI into the mainstream. As part of their initial review, the Enormous team members determined that the book value of SGI's assets and liabilities equaled their market values, with a few exceptions: SGI's land had appreciated to a current market value of $4,500,000, and the equipment (which had all been handmade) had a current value of $6,000,000. On the other hand, SGI had been rather lenient with its credit policies, and the Enormous staff determined that an additional doubtful account allowance of $500,000 was required. The transitional team also noted that SGI had paid $1,250,000 for a 15 percent interest in a fruit drink business, which was now worth only $1,000,000. SGI had been committed to the fruit drink company, but as part of the planning for the leveraged buyout, management had decided to sell the investment and had transferred the asset to the current category. Finally, SGI's original funding had been in the form of a government-subsidized loan, which had carried a 5 percent interest rate. Because of the low interest rate, the present value of the loan was now only $17,500,000.

The trade name Steady Growth was registered to SGI and was now an Enormous asset. Unfortunately, none of the industry experts on the transitional team was able to put a market value on that asset.

Required:

a. Using the preacquisition historical data presented next, prepare consolidated balance sheets for Enormous as of September 30, 1992, giving effect to the acquisition of SGI. Prepare one balance sheet assuming that the purchase method was used in the acquisition and one assuming the pooling-of-interests method was used.

b. What consolidated earnings will Enormous report in its interim report for the nine months ended September 30, 1992?
(1) Under the purchase method?
(2) Under the pooling-of-interests method?

c. When will the extra $500,000 allowance for doubtful accounts appear as a provision in an income statement under the pooling-of-interests method? Under the purchase method?

d. At what amount did you record SGI's appreciated land? At what amount did you record Enormous' appreciated long-term investments? Did you treat them the same? If not, why not?

e. At what amount did you record the stock issued to the SGI shareholders? Did you record the stock issued at the same amount for both the purchase and pooling-of-interests methods? If so, why? If not, what happened to the difference?

f. Outline the pros and cons that might be presented in arguments for or against the pooling-of-interests and purchase methods of accounting in this situation.

Enormous, Inc.
Preconsolidated Balance sheet
September 30, 1992
(millions)

	Preacquisition Historical Data	
	Enormous	**SGI**
Current assets		
Cash	$ 31.0	$ 2.0
Accounts receivable	15.0	4.5
Inventories	27.0	0.5
Investments		1.0
Total current assets	73.0	8.0
Fixed assets (net of accumulated depreciation)		
Machinery and equipment	25.0	5.0
Buildings	112.0	18.0
Trucks	54.0	0.5
Land	19.0	2.5
Net fixed assets	210.0	26.0
Investments (market value $12)	12.0	
Goodwill	2.0	
Total assets	$ 297.0	$ 34.0
Current liabilities		
Accounts payable	$ 25.0	$ 6.0
Accrued expenses	12.0	3.5
Total current liabilities	37.0	9.5
Mortgages and loans payable	165.0	18.0
Owners' equity		
Common stock		
Retained earnings		
Total owners' equity	95.0	6.5
Total liabilities and equity	$ 297.0	$ 34.0
Earnings, 1/1/92 to 9/30/92	$ 3.02	$ 2.78
Shares outstanding	3,250,000	325,000
Market price per share of common stock	$40	$20

C10.3 Analyzing consolidated statements: Sony Corporation. On the following pages are the consolidated balance sheets of the Sony Corporation's 1990 annual report. Footnote 1 of the annual report included the following:

Basis of consolidation and accounting for investments in affiliated companies

The consolidated financial statements include the accounts of the parent company and, with minor exceptions, those of its majority-owned subsidiary companies. All significant intercompany transactions and accounts are eliminated. Investments in 20 percent to 50 percent owned companies are stated, with minor exceptions, at cost plus equity in undistributed earnings; consolidated net income includes the company's equity in current earnings of such companies, after elimination of unrealized intercompany profits.

The excess of the cost over the underlying net equity of investments in consolidated subsidiaries and affiliated companies accounted for on an equity basis is allocated to identifiable assets based on fair market value at the date of acquisition. The unassigned residual value, which is recognized as goodwill, is amortized on a straight-line basis principally over a 40-year period, with the exception of minor amounts that are charged to income in the year of acquisition.

Footnote 2 was as follows:

U.S. dollar amounts

U.S. dollar amounts are included solely for convenience. These translations should not be construed as representations that the yen amounts actually represent, or have been or could be converted into, U.S. dollars. As the amounts shown in U.S. dollars are for convenience only, the rate of ¥157 = U.S. $1, the approximate current rate at March 30, 1990, has been used for the purpose of presentation of the U.S. dollar amounts in the accompanying financial statements.

Footnote 3 included the following paragraphs pertaining to acquisitions:

Acquisitions

On January 5, 1988, the company acquired from CBS Inc. all of the outstanding common stock of CBS Records Inc. and its affiliates, which are operating primarily in the record business, for approximately U.S. $2 billion in cash. The purchase agreement provides for an additional payment in the form of a dividend to CBS Inc. from the acquired company based on its net worth at the acquisition date. The amount of the additional payment is still subject to the determination of net worth.

In November 1989 the company acquired all of the outstanding shares of common stock of Columbia Pictures Entertainment, Inc. (CPE) and The Guber-Peters Entertainment Company (GPEC), which are operating primarily in the film business, for approximately U.S. $3.4 billion and U.S. $0.2 billion, respectively.

All of the acquisitions were accounted for as purchases, and the company's consolidated financial statements include operating results of the acquired companies for the periods from the dates of acquisition. The excess of the purchase price over the net assets acquired has been allocated to identifiable assets such as inventories, land, property, plant, equipment, and intangible assets (primarily artist contracts and music catalogs), based upon the estimated fair value of such assets. The excess of the acquisition costs over the amounts preliminarily assigned to identifiable assets less liabilities assumed is recognized as goodwill.

Property, plant, and equipment and various intangible assets, after the above allocations, are depreciated or amortized based on estimated useful lives. In the case of artist contracts and music catalogs, the amounts are amortized on a straight-line basis principally over 16 years and 21 years, respectively. Goodwill is being amortized on a straight-line basis principally over a 40-year period.

Required:

Part 1

a. Sony acquired CBS Records in 1988 and Columbia Pictures in 1989. Where, if at all, do these investments appear on the balance sheets of Sony Corporation presented on the following pages?

b. Footnote 1 refers to investments carried "at cost plus equity in undistributed earnings." What does this mean? What are some reasons why an investment such as this might *decline* in its carrying value?

c. Footnote 1 also says that "consolidated net income includes the company's equity in current earnings of such companies, after elimination of unrealized intercompany profits."
(1) What is meant by "unrealized intercompany profits"?
(2) Why are unrealized intercompany profits eliminated?

Part 2 We now concern ourselves with Sony's acquisition of Columbia Pictures. In November 1989 Sony acquired all of the common stock of Columbia Pictures for ¥534 billion (U.S. $3.4 billion) cash. You may assume that Sony did *not* revalue any of Columbia's assets or liabilities when it brought Columbia onto its (Sony's) books.

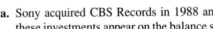

The condensed March 31, 1990, balance sheet for Sony is given in Column 1; Column 2 presents Columbia Pictures' balance sheet just prior to acquisition (converted into yen). Of course, there could be differences in Sony's balance sheet between the date of acquisition of Columbia in November 1989, and the published March 31, 1990, financial statements, but we will ignore them. We assume that Column 1 depicts Sony's consolidated balance sheet immediately *after* the acquisition of Columbia.

(All figures are given in billions of yen.)

	(1) Sony and Columbia Consolidated	(2) Columbia Pictures
Current assets	2,197	126
Film inventories (total)	173	173
Property and investments (net)	1,037	125
Goodwill and other assets	963	125
Total assets	4,370	549
Total liabilities	2,923	392
Minority interests	17	—
Net assets	1,430	157
Common stock	698	173
Retained earnings	695	(16)
Other	37	—
Total equity	1,430	157

d. Using the summary information just presented, prepare a balance sheet for the Sony Corporation as it would have appeared *before* the acquisition of Columbia.

e. Prepare a consolidated balance sheet for the Sony Corporation and its Columbia Pictures subsidiary subsequent to the acquisition assuming Sony had acquired Columbia by issuing 66.75 million common shares (market value ¥534 billion) and had accounted for the acquisition under the pooling-of-interests method.

Sony Corporation and Consolidated Subsidiaries
Consolidated Balance Sheets

	Millions of yen		Thousands of U.S. dollars (Note 2)
	March 31		March 31, 1990
	1989	1990	
Assets			
Current assets:			
Cash and cash equivalents	¥297,889	¥451,668	$2,876,866
Time deposits	33,665	182,533	1,162,631
Marketable securities	91,115	54,784	348,943
Notes and accounts receivable, trade	432,692	696,950	4,439,172
Allowance for doubtful accounts and sales returns	(32,957)	(46,560)	(296,561)
Inventories	483,648	692,966	4,413,796
Income tax prepayments	51,408	57,637	367,115
Prepaid expenses and other current assets	76,338	111,555	710,541
Total current assets	1,433,798	2,201,533	14,022,503
Noncurrent inventories — film	—	168,788	1,075,083
Investments and advances			
Affiliated companies	16,015	14,834	94,484
Officers and employees	2,445	2,315	14,745
Security investments and other	94,975	151,213	963,140
	113,435	168,362	1,072,369
Property, plant, and equipment			
Land	86,964	114,002	726,127
Buildings	267,351	415,835	2,648,631
Machinery and equipment	726,564	908,646	5,787,554
Construction in progress	24,611	90,693	577,663
	1,105,490	1,529,176	9,739,975
Less — Accumulated depreciation	560,714	661,048	4,210,497
	544,776	868,128	5,529,476
Other assets			
Intangibles	141,779	168,748	1,074,828
Goodwill	59,168	629,401	4,008,923
Other	71,819	165,125	1,051,752
	272,766	963,274	6,135,503
	¥2,364,775	¥4,370,085	$27,834,936

	Millions of yen		Thousands of U.S. dollars (Note 2)
	March 31		March 31, 1990
	1989	1990	
Liabilities and Stockholders' Equity			
Current liabilities:			
Short-term borrowings	¥224,637	¥757,017	$4,821,764
Current portion of long-term debt	12,797	76,715	488,631
Notes and accounts payable, trade	468,784	580,932	3,700,204
Notes payable, construction	21,323	27,375	174,363
Dividends payable	6,461	8,770	55,860
Accrued income and other taxes	84,752	112,664	717,605
Other accounts payable and accrued liabilities	266,568	432,418	2,754,254
Total current liabilities	1,085,322	1,995,891	12,712,681
Long-term liabilities:			
Long-term debt	220,790	645,969	4,114,452
Accrued pension and severance costs	61,319	70,949	451,904
Deferred income taxes	36,928	46,493	296,134
Other long-term liabilities	33,699	163,846	1,043,605
	352,736	927,257	5,906,095
Minority interest in consolidated subsidiary companies	14,901	16,879	107,510
Stockholders' equity			
Common stock, ¥50 par value —			
Authorized — 920,000,000 shares			
Issued: 1989 — 282,602,923 shares	114,641		
1990 — 331,928,730 shares		278,038	1,770,943
Additional paid-in capital	232,050	419,417	2,671,446
Legal reserve	10,535	13,566	86,408
Retained earnings appropriated for special allowances	16,313	20,547	130,872
Retained earnings	600,184	674,962	4,299,121
Cumulative translation adjustment	(61,907)	23,528	149,860
	911,816	1,430,058	9,108,650
Commitments and contingent liabilities			
	¥2,364,775	¥4,370,085	$27,834,936

The accompanying notes are an integral part of these statements.

C10.4 Purchase vs. pooling: Alliance Corporation. Subsequent to an unsuccessful hostile takeover attempt, Alliance Corporation entered into friendly negotiations for the acquisition of Felker Corporation. Following two months of discussions, Alliance Corporation agreed to purchase all of the outstanding common stock of Felker Corporation at a price of $36 million. In arriving at this price, Alliance Corporation placed the following fair market values on Felker Corporation's assets at the time of acquisition:

Felker's Assets	Fair Market Values ($ thousands)
Cash	$ 1,300
Marketable securities	1,800
Accounts receivable (net)	1,900
Inventories	10,700
Fixed assets (net)	21,400
Patents	5,500
Other assets	-0-
Goodwill	-0-
Total	$42,600

According to the terms of the agreement, Alliance Corporation was to issue *two* shares of its common stock in exchange for each share of Felker Corporation's outstanding common stock. Subsequent to the acquisition, Felker was to become a wholly owned subsidiary of Alliance. The market price of Alliance Corporation's common stock at the time of the acquisition was $45 per share.

Required:

Alliance Corporation expects to be able to account for its acquisition of Felker Corporation using the pooling-of-interests method. The resulting consolidated balance sheet under this method follows. Also shown is Felker Corporation's preacquisition balance sheet. Using these two balance sheets and the information provided above, prepare the preacquisition balance sheet for Alliance Corporation and the consolidated balance sheet, assuming the acquisition is accounted for using the purchase method.

	Preacquisition Balance Sheets ($ thousands)		Consolidated Balance Sheets ($ thousands)	
	Alliance Corp.	Felker Corp.	Purchase Method	Pooling-of-Interests Method
Assets				
Cash	______	$ 1,300	______	$ 4,800
Marketable securities	______	1,500	______	3,900
Accounts receivable (net)	______	2,100	______	7,300
Inventories	______	11,800	______	35,500
Fixed assets (net)	______	18,600	______	60,000
Patents	______	1,700	______	5,700
Other assets	______	500	______	2,800
Goodwill	______	1,500	______	1,500
Total	$ ______	$39,000	$ ______	$121,500
Liabilities and Stockholders' Equity				
Accounts payable	______	$ 2,700	______	$ 11,200
Other current liabilities	______	1,400	______	4,400
Long-term debt	______	8,000	______	28,000
Common stock (no par)	______	1,400	______	20,100
Retained earnings	______	25,500	______	57,800
Total	$ ______	$39,000	$ ______	$121,500

CHAPTER 11

Noncurrent Assets: Fixed Assets, Intangible Assets, and Natural Resources

As CEO of a capital-intensive company, I can assure you that the management of our noncurrent asset base is critical to our long-term success. The accelerating pace of technology, coupled with rapidly evolving markets, requires that we "get it right" on the front end, maintain peak performance of equipment throughout its useful life, and look beyond our customers' current requirements to invest in capital assets meeting tomorrow's customer needs.[1]

Key Chapter Issues

- What are fixed assets, and how are they valued on the balance sheet?
- Why, and how, is the cost of fixed assets allocated to the various periods benefiting from those assets?
- What are intangible assets and natural resources, and how are they accounted for on the balance sheet and the income statement?
- What special management issues arise regarding the accounting for noncurrent assets?

[1]Michael A. Snetzer, CEO, Medite Corporation.

Noncurrent assets represent the principal long-term revenue-producing assets of most companies. In the case of a manufacturing company, the fixed assets (or property, plant, and equipment) are used to manufacture the products that are ultimately sold to customers. In the case of a computer software development company, a copyright on a computer software package provides the company with the monopolistic right to the earnings stream associated with the sale of the package. In the case of an oil and gas company, the oil and gas properties or leaseholds the company owns provide it with access to new salable reserves.

The focus of this chapter is on the analysis and financial reporting issues pertaining to these three types of noncurrent assets. Two important financial reporting questions characterize the financial management of these assets: What cost should be assigned to the asset (that is, capitalized to the balance sheet)? How should the asset's cost systematically be expensed (matched) against the revenues produced by the asset?

FIXED ASSETS AND DEPRECIATION

Fixed assets are long-lived tangible assets owned by a company for the purpose of deriving a benefit from their *use* rather than from their resale. Fixed assets include such *property, plant, and equipment* (PP&E) as buildings; land used or held as factory and office locations (not depreciable); land improvements such as landscaping and parking lots; machinery and equipment; office furniture and fixtures; and vehicles.

The primary financial reporting issues associated with fixed assets that must be addressed by managers are the following:

1. Determining the cost to be recorded in the balance sheet at the time of acquisition (the **capitalization** issue).
2. Determining the annual income statement depreciation expense to be reported (the **allocation** issue). In this regard, decisions must be made regarding the preferred depreciation method, the estimated useful life of the asset, and its estimated salvage value.
3. Distinguishing between those fixed asset–related expenditures made subsequent to the initial acquisition (such as repairs and improvements) that should be expensed when incurred and those that should be capitalized (added to the asset's reported balance sheet value) and subsequently depreciated over future periods.
4. Determining if, and when, the revenue-generating capacity of such long-lived assets has diminished as a consequence of factors other than normal day-to-day use, and thus whether a write-down of the balance sheet value of the assets should be recorded in the company's financial statements.
5. Accounting for the sale or other disposition of an asset.

Determining Original Cost: The Capitalization Issue

Fixed assets are initially reported in the balance sheet at their original cost (that is, the outlay of cash or cash equivalents at the date of purchase). The original acquisition cost of a fixed asset includes *all* costs incurred in getting the asset ready for its intended use. For example, surveying costs, title searches, the costs of clearing unwanted trees and buildings, and the costs of soil and water tests are all a part of the land's original

EXHIBIT 11.1

Determining the Cost of an Asset

Omar Corporation paid $200,000 for a tract of land that had an old gas station on it. The gas station was razed at a cost of $10,000, and a new warehouse was constructed at a cost of $250,000. In addition, several other costs were incurred:

Legal fees (for the purchase of the land)	$ 5,000
Architect's fees	22,000
Interest on construction loan	18,000

Omar Corporation should record two assets as follows:

Dr. Land (A)	(inc.) $215,000	
Cr. Cash (A)		(dec.) $215,000

(The value of the land is determined as follows: $200,000 + $10,000 + $5,000 = $215,000.)

Dr. Building (A)	(inc.) $290,000	
Cr. Cash (A)		(dec.) $290,000

(The value of the building is determined as follows: $250,000 + $22,000 + $18,000 = $290,000.)

It is important to distinguish between the land and the building because only the building will be depreciated. The land will not be depreciated but will continue to be reported at its original cost until it is sold.

cost. In addition, when a company contracts with another party to construct a new building, all construction-related costs incurred are part of its original cost. In this regard, architect's fees, inspection costs, payments to the contractor, and interest on the construction loan would all be properly included in the building's original cost. In the case of machinery and equipment, original cost includes purchase price, freight in, and the cost of initial setup and installation. An example regarding these items is presented in Exhibit 11.1.

As an incentive to purchase and promptly pay for a particular piece of equipment, sellers often offer discounts to potential purchasers. When a cash discount is received on the purchase of equipment (or any other asset, for that matter), the equipment's cost should be reported net of the discount. Another means to attract potential buyers involves various seller-sponsored financing plans. For example, a buyer's recorded cost when fixed assets are bought on an installment payment plan is not the sum of the total payments to be made but rather the *present value* of the installment obligation (that is, today's cash-equivalent purchase price) as of the date of purchase. (Present value will be discussed in Chapter 12.) Fixed assets also may be acquired by issuing capital stock. In this case, the cash-equivalent value of the issued stock, as of the date of the transaction, is used to cost the assets. Sometimes an old asset is traded in on a new one (for example, a used truck for a new one). In such an arrangement the market value of the old asset plus the cash paid for the new one is the original cost of the new asset to be reported on the balance sheet.

It is important to note that a popular means by which corporate managers may obtain property is to lease it under a long-term, noncancelable lease. If the lease meets certain criteria, generally accepted accounting principles stipulate the recording of a leasehold right as an asset and a lease obligation as a liability. Under these circumstances, the leased asset would be depreciated in the same way as any other fixed asset owned by the company, except that the depreciation period may be limited by the lease term. A more detailed description of lease accounting is provided in Chapter 13.

Depreciation: The Allocation Issue

The purpose of recording depreciation is to reflect the "using up" of the productive capacity of a company's PP&E and to match this cost of doing business with the revenues that the PP&E helped generate. The process of recording depreciation is nothing more than allocating the depreciable cost (that is, original cost less estimated salvage value) of a company's PP&E to the accounting periods during which the PP&E is used. Depreciating PP&E is, however, not intended to establish a market valuation process for the PP&E. (A word of caution: Sometimes the business use of the term *property, plant, and equipment* is meant to include the land owned by a company on which its plant, offices, loading terminals, and so forth are built. In such circumstances, even though the gross dollar amount reported for PP&E on the balance sheet may include the cost of land, such costs are *not* depreciable. In such circumstances, land is not viewed as being "used up" and therefore is not depreciated.)

The periodic amount of PP&E cost allocated to the income statement is called *depreciation expense* and serves to reduce the net income of the period. In determining a given period's depreciation expense, corporate financial managers must assess the useful lives and salvage values of the PP&E items, as well as select a systematic method to allocate the costs of the PP&E items over their respective estimated useful lives. These three management decisions (useful life, salvage value, and depreciation method) involve considerable discretion and judgment and may frequently have a significant financial effect on a company's reported earnings. Each of these decisions is discussed at length in the following sections. It is important to remember that it is possible that a PP&E item that has been fully depreciated in the accounting records may still be an integral part of a company's operations and/or may be sold to another company at a significant price. It is also important to note that **net book value** (that is, original cost less accumulated depreciation) does not approximate an asset's fair market value, nor is it intended to.

Useful life. In estimating the useful lives of various PP&E components, managers must consider the manner in which the assets are expected to be used and maintained. Generally, useful lives are established based on the assumption that normal repairs and maintenance will be made to keep the assets in good operating condition. In situations in which maintenance programs deviate from what is considered normal, estimated useful lives should be adjusted accordingly.

The two primary factors that managers should consider when estimating the useful lives of their PP&E are physical life and technological life. **Physical life** refers to the length of time an asset can reasonably be expected to last before it physically wears out. When physical life is influenced more by the passage of time than by use (as for a building) or when it is difficult to assess the level of usage, useful life is usually expressed in terms of years. When physical life is influenced more by use (as for a machine or a vehicle) than by the passage of time, useful life is often expressed in terms of expected output (such as units produced or miles driven).

For a great many PP&E items, the concept of technological life has a greater relevance to managers in estimating useful life than does physical life. **Technological life** refers to the length of time an asset can reasonably be expected to generate economic benefits before it becomes obsolete. Two types of obsolescence must be considered: product obsolescence and process obsolescence. **Product obsolescence** pertains to the market lives of the products that are produced by the PP&E. For example, auto manufacturers normally depreciate tooling costs over two or three years because of the product obsolescence brought about by frequent model changes even though the physical life of the tooling equipment may be many more years. **Process obsolescence** pertains to the PP&E item itself becoming obsolete because of subsequent technological improvements. For example, the useful lives of computer equipment have generally been set with the expectation that process obsolescence would occur prior to the time the equipment was physically worn out.

It is important to note that this discussion of estimating useful lives of PP&E pertains solely to financial reporting. As discussed in a later section of this chapter, a country's tax code often specifies useful-life rules for income tax purposes.

Depreciation methods. For financial reporting purposes in the U.S., corporate management has a choice of several generally accepted methods for allocating the depreciable cost of PP&E over an asset's estimated useful life. The common element among these alternatives is that they each result in a systematic process of cost allocation.

1. **Straight-line method** — The annual depreciation expense is determined by dividing the *depreciable cost* of an asset by its estimated life. The *depreciable cost* is the original cost less the estimated salvage value; hence,

   Annual depreciation expense = (1/n) (Cost – Salvage value)
   where n = estimated life in years

   For example, consider an asset with an original cost of $8,000, an estimated salvage value of $500 (and thus a depreciable cost of $7,500) and an estimated useful life of five years. Under straight-line depreciation, the depreciable cost of $7,500 is divided by 5 to give an annual depreciation figure of $1,500 for each of the five years of the asset's estimated useful life.

2. **Double-declining-balance method** — This method requires the calculation of the straight-line percentage rate (1/n), which is then doubled and applied each year to the PP&E's decreasing *net book value* (that is, the recorded cost less depreciation taken to date). The amount of depreciation taken to date for a particular asset is often referred to as the asset's **accumulated depreciation.** Salvage value is ignored in determining net book value, but the recording of depreciation expense should stop when the asset's net book value equals its salvage value. Hence,

   Annual depreciation expense = (2/n) (Net book value)

   Consider again an asset with an original cost of $8,000, salvage value of $500, and an estimated life of five years. The straight-line percentage rate is 20 percent (1/5 years) and the double-declining-balance rate is 40 percent (2/5). Thus, under the declining-balance method, depreciation is 40 percent of $8,000, or $3,200 for the first year; 40 percent of $4,800 ($8,000 less $3,200), or $1,920, for the second year; 40 percent of $2,880 ($8,000 less $5,120), or $1,152, for the third year. In the final two years, the depreciation calculation will often be converted to a straight-line basis. When the accumulated depreciation recorded for this asset reaches $7,500, its depreciation expensing stops.

3. **Sum-of-the-years' digits method** — Just as the double-declining-balance method results in the recording of larger depreciation expense amounts in the early years of an asset's life (referred to as an *acceleration of depreciation*), so also does the sum-of-the-years' digits (SYD) method.

Under this method, declining fractions are applied to the asset's *depreciable cost*. The denominator of the fraction is the sum of the digits of the years of useful life (SYD = n(n + 1)/2). The numerator is the number of years of useful life remaining, including the present year. The only rationale behind the mechanics of the SYD method is that it is systematic and results in higher depreciation expense amounts earlier in an asset's life than under the straight-line method.

Consider again an asset costing $8,000 with an estimated salvage value of $500, a depreciable cost of $7,500, and an estimated life of five years. The sum of the years' digits (1, 2, 3, 4, and 5) is 15. Hence, depreciation expense for the first year is 5/15ths of $7,500, or $2,500; for the second year, it is 4/15ths of $7,500, or $2,000; for the third year it is 3/15ths of $7,500, or $1,500, and so on.

4. Physical-unit methods.
   a. **Machine-hour method** — The number of hours a machine is to be used during its useful life is often a better basis for determining depreciation expense than the mere passage of time. Under the machine-hour method, depreciation expense is determined according to the number of hours the asset is actually used during an accounting period relative to the total number of hours it can ultimately be used (that is, the usage or productivity rate):

$$\text{Annual depreciation expense} = \frac{\text{Actual machine hours used in this period}}{\text{Total estimated machine hours}} \times (\text{Cost} - \text{Salvage value})$$

   Referring again to the asset with a cost of $8,000, an estimated salvage of $500, and a depreciable cost of $7,500, its estimated lifetime hours are 15,000 and the hours actually used during the first year are 1,800. The depreciable cost of $7,500 divided by the total hours of 15,000 yields $0.50 to be allocated to each hour of use. Depreciation expense for the first year on this machine is therefore $900 (1,800 times $0.50 per hour of use).

   b. **Units-of-production method** — This method is conceptually similar to the machine-hour method except that an estimate is made of the number of units to be produced by a machine during its useful life. Depreciation expense for a period is then determined according to the number of units actually produced during the period relative to the estimated lifetime potential of the machine.

   Again using the example of an asset with a cost of $8,000 and an estimated salvage value of $500, assume that its projected units of production are 25,000. The asset's depreciable cost of $7,500 divided by 25,000 units yields $0.30 depreciation expense per unit produced. Thus, if in its first year of use, 5,000 units are produced, the depreciation expense for that year is $1,500.

The double-declining-balance and sum-of-the-years' digits methods are often referred to as **accelerated methods of depreciation.** The phenomenon captured by accelerated depreciation methods is that more depreciation expense is recorded in the early years of an asset's life as compared to the amount that would be recorded under the straight-line method. Rationales frequently given for using accelerated methods include (1) an asset is more useful to management when newer because it is more efficient; and (2) repairs and maintenance costs complement an asset's yearly accelerated depreciation in deriving a year-by-year cost of owning and using the asset; i.e., repair and maintenance expenses are normally greater in later years when the accelerated depreciation expense amount has lessened. This latter notion may be more clearly understood through the following graphic representation:

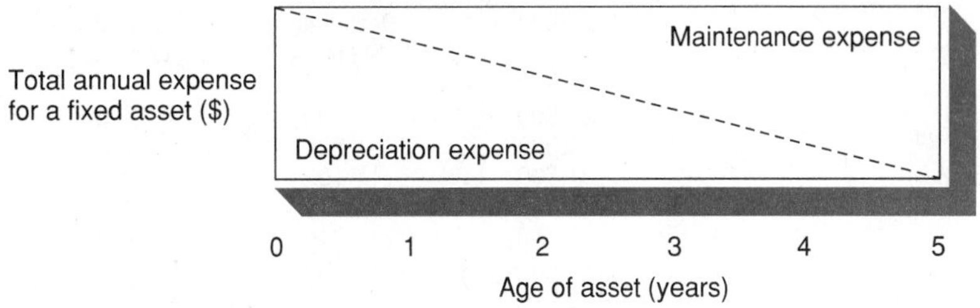

Exhibit 11.2 summarizes the results of the five depreciation method examples. Note the variability across the different methods for any given year. In spite of this variability, however, the *total* depreciation expense reported over the life of an asset must be the same under each of the methods. Thus, it can be seen that the financial reporting of depreciation is fundamentally a decision concerning the *timing* as to when an asset's cost is systematically allocated to the income statement in the form of depreciation expense to reflect the cost of using the asset.

The accounting entry to record the annual depreciation expense on an asset appears as follows:

Dr. Depreciation Expense (E)	(inc.) 4,000	
Cr. Accumulated Depreciation (CA)		(inc.) 4,000

Note that the cost basis of the asset is preserved in the PP&E account because the credit entry is to a contra-asset account. Using this approach, the balance sheet will reveal not only the original cost of the asset but also its total depreciation taken to date and its remaining undepreciated cost. From this information, it is possible to make rough estimates of the age of a company's assets — the larger the net book value (that is, cost minus accumulated depreciation) relative to the original cost of the PP&E, the newer (on average) are the company's assets.

Presented in Exhibit 11.3 are the financial statement disclosures of three companies pertaining to their choices of asset lives and depreciation methods. In reviewing those examples, consider the impact of the different lives and methods on the companies' reported depreciation expense and depreciable fixed assets. In particular, note that for machinery and equipment, Snap-On-Tools Corporation generally uses shorter estimated lives than Kmart Corporation and uses mostly accelerated depreciation methods rather than the straight-line method. Clearly, Snap-On-Tools Corporation records a larger depreciation expense deduction sooner than Kmart, all other things being equal. Also note that Ace Hardware Corp., which has somewhat different asset lives than the other two companies, uses a variety of depreciation methods and has five categories of PP&E versus four and three for Snap-On-Tools and Kmart, respectively. Such variations between companies highlight some of the latitude left to management as they decide how best to depreciate their assets.

Capitalizing depreciation. The depreciation allocated to each accounting period may be charged, in part, against net income as a period expense (as has already been discussed) and, in part, to work-in-process inventory as manufacturing overhead (see

EXHIBIT 11.2

Comparison of Depreciation Methods*

	Depreciation Method				
Year	Straight-Line	Double-Declining-Balance	Sum-of-the-Years' Digits	Machine-Hour	Units-of-Production
1	$1,500	$3,200	$2,500	$ 900	$1,500
2	1,500	1,920	2,000	1,500	1,650
3	1,500	1,152	1,500	1,600	1,950
4	1,500	614	1,000	3,000	1,950
5	1,500	614	500	500	450
	$7,500	$7,500	$7,500	$7,500	$7,500

*Assumptions: A machine with an original cost of $8,000 is estimated to have a useful life of five years and an estimated salvage value of $500; the machine is assumed to be operated for the following number of hours, producing the following number of units:

Year	Hours Operated	Units Produced
1	1,800	5,000
2	3,000	5,500
3	3,200	6,500
4	6,000	6,500
5	1,000	1,500
	15,000	25,000

Chapter 9). To the extent that the depreciation costs are incurred "under the factory roof" (that is, are a part of the costs of manufacturing a product), management should capitalize them as a product cost by increasing the Work-in-Process Inventory account instead of recording depreciation expense on the income statement. If added to Work-in-Process Inventory, the depreciation will become a deduction in the income statement only when the finished goods with which it is associated are sold and an accounting entry for the cost of goods sold is made.

Changes in Depreciation Accounting Policy

During the course of depreciating either a particular asset or an entire array of fixed assets, corporate financial managers may decide to modify or adjust their initial estimates and decisions underlying the calculation of depreciation. For example, a change in the depreciation method from the double-declining-balance method to the straight-line method might be undertaken because other similar companies are predominantly using the straight-line method. In this case, the decision to change depreciation methods is probably motivated by management's desire to appear to be using the industry-preferred method, as well as a desire to improve the firm's within-industry comparative financial standing. When such a change in accounting method is made, its cumulative effect is recorded on a net-of-taxes basis in the current financial statements, and all subsequent financial statements reflect the use of the new method.

To illustrate such a change, consider again the data presented in Exhibit 11.2. Assume, for example, that in Year 3 a change from the double-declining-balance method (DDB) to the straight-line method is to be made. Through the end of Year 2, depreciation totaling $5,120 has been taken under the DDB method, whereas if the

EXHIBIT 11.3

Selected Depreciation-Method and Asset-Life Disclosures

Panel A — Snap-On-Tools Corporation

Property and equipment

Land, buildings, machinery, and equipment are carried at original cost. Depreciation and amortization are provided for primarily by using accelerated depreciation methods on all property acquired prior to December 31, 1989. For financial statement purposes, the company adopted the straight-line depreciation method for all property acquired after December 30, 1989. The company believes the new method will more accurately reflect its financial results by better matching costs of new property over the useful lives of these assets. In addition, the new method more closely conforms with that prevalent in the industry. The effect of the change was not material to the current year financial results.

The estimated service lives of property and equipment are as follows:

Buildings and improvements	5 to 45 years
Machinery and equipment	3 to 15 years
Furniture and fixtures	3 to 15 years
Transportation vehicles	2 to 5 years

Panel B — Ace Hardware Corp.

Depreciation expense is computed on both straight-line and accelerated methods based on estimated useful lives as follows:

	Useful Life (Years)	Principal Depreciation method
Buildings and improvements	10–40	Straight line
Warehouse equipment	5–10	Sum of years
Office equipment	3–10	Various
Manufacturing equipment	3–20	Straight line
Transportation equipment	3–7	Straight line

Panel C — Kmart Corporation

Depreciation

The company computes depreciation on owned property principally on the straight-line method for financial statement purposes and on accelerated methods for income tax purposes. Most store properties are leased and improvements are amortized over the term of the lease but not more than 25 years. Other annual rates used in computing depreciation for financial statement purposes are 2% to 4% for buildings, 10% to 14% for store fixtures, and 5% to 33% for other fixtures and equipment.

---

straight-line method had been used, only $3,000 in depreciation deductions would have been recorded. Thus, at the beginning of Year 3, an entry to restate the depreciation account balances would be needed as follows:

Dr. Accumulated Depreciation (CA)	(dec.) 2,120*	
Cr. Cumulative Effect of Change in Accounting Method (Income)		(inc.) 2,120

*($5,120 – $3,000 = $2,120)

The account Cumulative Effect of Change in Accounting Method is reported on the company's Year 3 income statement and thus will increase the period's net income. Because of the unusual nature of this account, it is separately and prominently disclosed on the income statement if material in amount. In addition to the above entry to reflect the change in depreciation method, the regular Year 3 depreciation expense under the new method also needs to be recorded:

Dr. Depreciation Expense (E)	(inc.) 1,500	
Cr. Accumulated Depreciation (CA)		(inc.) 1,500

Another depreciation-related change often made by corporate financial managers involves the estimated useful life of an asset or a group of assets. This type of change involves a change in an *estimate* rather than in a *method* and is usually dealt with on a prospective, or future, basis. For example, if in Year 3 management decided that the expected useful life of an asset being depreciated was really eight

EXHIBIT 11.4

Changes in Depreciation Methods and Estimates

Panel A — AT&T

Accounting Change

Effective January 1, 1989, for certain network equipment, AT&T changed its method of depreciation from straight-line to sum-of-the-years' digits, shortened the estimated depreciable lives, and decreased the estimated net salvage. These changes were implemented to better match revenues and expenses because of rapid technological changes occurring in response to customer requirements and competition. The new depreciation method was applied retroactively to all digital circuit, digital operator services, and radio equipment and was applied to digital electronic switching equipment placed into service after December 31, 1988. Other network equipment, principally lightguide cable and central office buildings, continues to be depreciated on a straight-line basis. The changes in estimates of depreciable lives and net salvage were made prospectively. The effect of these changes on 1989 results was to decrease net income by approximately \$393 million or \$0.36 per share. The cumulative prior years' effect of the change in depreciation method was not material.

Panel B — Owens-Corning Fiberglas Corporation

Depreciation of Plant and Equipment

During 1993 the company completed a review of its fixed asset lives. The company determined that as a result of actions taken to increase its preventative maintenance and programs initiated with its equipment suppliers to increase the quality of their products, actual lives for certain asset categories were generally longer than the useful lives for depreciation purposes. Therefore, the company extended the estimated useful lives of certain categories of plant and equipment, effective April 1, 1993. The effect of this change in estimate reduced depreciation expense for the year ended December 31, 1993, by \$14 million and increased income before cumulative effect of accounting change by \$8 million (\$0.19 per share).

years instead of five, no accounting entry would be required to restate the previous years' depreciation deductions. Instead, all future depreciation calculations would be based on a remaining estimated life of six rather than three years. Thus, an estimate change such as this does not affect prior published financial statements but only future reported results.

When accounting method or estimate changes are undertaken by management, the effect of the change on the current financial statements must be described in the company's footnotes. Exhibit 11.4 presents such footnote disclosures made by two very prominent corporations — AT&T and Owens-Corning Fiberglas Corporation. Note in Panel A that AT&T changed three things — depreciation method, estimated useful lives, and estimated salvage value. All three changes were effective beginning in 1989 and had the combined effect of decreasing 1989 net income by almost \$400 million. AT&T mentions that the portion of this decrease attributable to the cumulative effect of just the change in depreciation method is not material and thus not reported separately in the note or in the income statement. On the other hand, the financial effect of Owens-Corning's change is to increase pretax earnings by \$8 million. The change made by Owens-Corning, however, did not involve a change in depreciation method but only in estimated useful lives, and even though material, it is thus not required to be shown separately in the income statement. It is important to note that although Owens-Corning's pretax earnings increased due to this accounting change, there was *no* increase in the company's operating cash flows, nor was there any increase in the operating efficiency of the company (the same can be said for AT&T). Finally, PepsiCo's "Management Analysis — Overview" (see section titled "Certain Factors Affecting Comparability" in Chapter 1) reveals that in 1994 the company extended the depreciable lives on certain domestic Pizza Hut delivery assets. The effect of this estimate change was to increase 1994 operating income by approximately \$11.3 million.

Depreciation Myths

A number of myths exist concerning depreciation. One myth states that for financial reporting purposes, depreciation expense reflects the decline in the market value of the depreciable asset and that the asset's net book value approximates the asset's current fair market value. On the contrary, the recording of depreciation is a process of cost allocation, not of valuation. Accordingly, depreciation expense is not intended to equal the change in an asset's market value, nor is its net book value intended to reflect the market value of the asset at the end of any period.

A second depreciation myth is that the depreciation accounting process provides the means for replacement of the asset at the end of its useful life. On the contrary, the costs allocated to depreciation expense are costs *already incurred,* not some budgeted amount for a future period's purchase of a replacement asset. In fact, the recording of depreciation is not even premised on a belief that the asset will be replaced when it wears out.

Another myth is that depreciation provides cash. As discussed in Chapter 6, the statement of cash flows usually lists net income first among the sources of operating cash flows. To adjust this figure to a cash-based net income approximation, depreciation is added back. The sum of net income plus depreciation and other pertinent items is then labeled *cash flow from operations.* As a consequence of this separate listing of depreciation in the statement of cash flows, some financial statement readers have been led to the false conclusion that depreciation provides cash. This is *not* so! Depreciation is a noncash expense that is recognized under the accrual basis of accounting but in no way constitutes a cash inflow. Depreciation does, however, reduce the taxable net income amount reported on a company's tax return and thus lowers the amount of taxes to be paid. So to the extent that depreciation reduces the cash outflow for taxes otherwise due, it can be thought of as having an indirect cash flow benefit.

Tax Depreciation

In 1986 Congress passed the Tax Reform Act of 1986 — the second time in 5 years and the fourth time in 25 years that the tax rules concerning depreciable assets had undergone revision.[2] Each successive piece of legislation sought to restrict the diversity of depreciation practices employed by different corporate managers for similar assets (for example, to standardize the estimated useful life of similar assets) and reflected a particular fiscal policy of the U.S. government at the time of passage (such as the use of shorter estimated asset lives as an attempt to stimulate increased corporate investment in capital assets). Under rules put in place by the 1986 Tax Reform Act, the **Modified Accelerated Cost Recovery System** (MACRS) is the only accelerated depreciation method acceptable for tax purposes; straight-line, machine-hours, and units-of-production methods are also still acceptable methods.

MACRS defines nine classifications of fixed asset lives and uses the term *cost recovery* in place of the term *depreciation:*

[2]For assets put in service before 1962, IRS *Bulletin F* rules apply. For assets placed in service after 1962 and before 1971, managers may choose general depreciation rules or the Class Life System (CLS). After 1971 but before 1981, the taxpayer may choose from the Asset Depreciation Range (ADR) System or the general depreciation rules. In 1981 the Economic Recovery Tax Act of 1981 inaugurated the use of the Accelerated Cost Recovery System (ACRS), which applies to all assets placed in service between 1981 and 1986. Assets placed in service after 1986 are subject to MACRS.

MACRS Classification	Asset Description
3-year property	Race horses and some special-use tools
5-year property	Autos, trucks, R&D equipment, certain technological equipment, computers, office machinery
7-year property	Office furniture, railroad track and rolling stock, some agricultural structures, and other unclassified property
10-year property	Vessels, barges, and tugs
15-year property	Communications equipment and water treatment facilities
20-year property	Some real property, sewage treatment facilities, and general-use agricultural buildings
27.5-year property	Residential real property
39-year property	Most building and plant facilities
50-year property	Railroad gradings and tunnel bores

Under MACRS, the cost of 3-year, 5-year, 7-year, and 10-year property may be recovered using the double-declining-balance method over 3, 5, 7, and 10 years, respectively. The cost of 15-year and 20-year property may be recovered using the 150 percent-declining-balance method over 15 and 20 years; the costs of 27.5-year, 39-year, and 50-year property are to be recovered using only the straight-line method. When using MACRS, estimated salvage value is *not* considered.

For tax purposes, all asset classes except the 27.5-year, 39-year, and 50-year classes must also conform to the **half-year convention.** An asset is said to have been put in service or disposed of at the mid-point of the year regardless of the date actually placed in service or disposed of, thereby allowing one-half of a year's depreciation in the year in which the asset was placed in service and one-half year's depreciation in the year in which the asset is disposed of. Moreover, for those classes of assets using one of the declining-balance methods, a switch to the straight-line method is permitted at the time during an asset's life when the prospective annual straight-line depreciation amount, recalculated using the net book value and remaining life as of that instant, exceeds that year's declining-balance method amount.

For new and used assets placed into service after December 31, 1986, the current tax law requires the use of MACRS as the only accelerated method. Companies must continue to use previously adopted tax depreciation methods on all fixed assets put into service prior to 1987. Those methods might include ACRS, sum-of-the-years' digits, various declining-balance methods, or other methods previously acceptable to the IRS.

Financial reporting and tax depreciation. The depreciation expense that a company records for external financial reporting is usually not the same amount as is reported on its income tax return. This may occur for a variety of legitimate reasons. For example, a company may choose to use the straight-line method of depreciation for its external financial statements but the MACRS method (as required by the IRS) for its income tax return.

For external financial statements, corporate financial managers typically adopt depreciation methods that result in a total depreciation expense for the year that indicates the cost of utilizing their fixed assets for the period while also striving to maximize reported net income. For tax return purposes, management should use the method permitted by the IRS that gives them the greatest tax savings. As a result, many corporate managers choose accelerated methods of depreciation and IRS lives for income tax return purposes but the straight-line method and longer estimated useful lives for financial reporting purposes.[3] In such cases, the income tax actually owed (per the tax return) is not the same amount as the income tax due based on the income reported in the published annual report. In general, the tax liability (per the tax return), tax expense (per the accounting records), and related difference are recorded in an accounting entry such as the following:

Dr. Income Tax Expense (E)	(inc.) 120	
Cr. Income Taxes Payable (L)		(inc.) 100
Cr. Deferred Income Taxes (L)		(inc.) 20

A detailed discussion of the Deferred Income Taxes account noted in this entry is left until Chapter 13. For now, it is important only to recognize the need for such an account in order to reconcile the difference between the tax expense and the tax liability accounts. In this illustration, the deferred income tax account is classified as a liability because the account presumably will be reduced in later years when the depreciation deducted on the income tax return becomes less than the depreciation expense reported in the published income statement.

Exhibit 11.5 presents the depreciation disclosures of the Pacific Gas & Electric Company (PG&E) that highlight the differences in financial reporting and tax return depreciation. To illustrate the effect of such differences, we assume that PG&E purchased a piece of production equipment costing $100,000 that is classified under MACRS as five-year property. Assume further that PG&E's chief financial officer has decided to use straight-line depreciation for financial reporting purposes and estimates that the equipment will be used for eight years and will have a salvage value of $20,000 at the end of the eighth year. If the corporation uses a half-year convention for both tax and financial reporting purposes, the depreciation schedules for both tax and financial reporting purposes will be as follows:

Year	MACRS Tax-Return Depreciation Expense	Financial Reporting Depreciation Expense
1	$ 20,000	$ 5,000
2	32,000	10,000
3	19,200	10,000
4	11,520	10,000
5	11,520*	10,000
6	5,760	10,000
7	0	10,000
8	0	10,000
9	0	5,000
Total	$100,000	$80,000

*Beginning in Year 5, the straight-line method over the asset's remaining years (1.5) provides a depreciation amount greater than that from the continued use of the double-declining-balance method; thus, Year 5's allowable depreciation switches to a straight-line amount.

In Year 1, PG&E will show depreciation expense of $5,000 in its income statement but will deduct $20,000 in its tax return for cost recovery under MACRS. This procedure will cause income on the company's tax return to be $15,000 less than its

[3]In some countries (such as Germany, Japan, and Sweden), the amount of depreciation expense deducted for tax purposes is limited to the depreciation charge taken for financial reporting (or book) purposes. As a consequence, no deferred income taxes result because the depreciation deductions for book and tax purposes are equivalent.

EXHIBIT 11.5

Pacific Gas & Electric Co.
Financial Reporting versus Tax-Return Depreciation

Depreciation
For financial reporting purposes, depreciation of plant in service is computed using a straight-line remaining life method. For federal income tax purposes, the most liberal depreciation methods allowed by the Internal Revenue Code generally are used.

accounting income and, at a 34 percent tax rate, will defer $5,100 in taxes to subsequent years. In its income statement, PG&E will show its tax expense based on its income statement profit and, as a result, will recognize a deferred tax liability of $5,100 in its balance sheet.

Two additional aspects of this example are important to note. First, capital investment decisions involving net present value and internal rate of return techniques employing the cash flows resulting from depreciation-generated tax savings should be based on tax return depreciation deductions, not those reported for financial reporting purposes (these topics are usually part of a managerial finance course). Second, as noted earlier, MACRS ignores the salvage value of an asset, and this permits greater tax return depreciation deductions over the life of an asset than would otherwise be taken in the published income statement. On the other hand, the IRS has reduced the amount of flexibility available to a company preparing its tax return by eliminating those decisions relating to the length of an asset's life, the expected salvage value, and effectively, the method of depreciation.

Repairs, Maintenance, and Betterments

Costs incurred for the purpose of maintaining the existing service level of PP&E are classified as *repairs and maintenance* and should be treated by managers as expenses of the period in which they are incurred. Costs incurred to improve an asset beyond its original service potential are viewed as betterments and should be capitalized rather than expensed in the period incurred. Capitalizing betterments increases an asset's book value because their costs are added to the asset's original recorded cost. The capitalized cost is subsequently expensed over future periods as an additional component of depreciation. The first part of Phelps Dodge Corporation's PP&E footnote (see Panel B, Exhibit 11.8) makes this same distinction.

Distinguishing between an ordinary repair or maintenance expenditure and an asset betterment expenditure is difficult in many instances. For both financial accounting and income tax purposes (in this area, financial reporting and tax guidelines are the same), management's rationale for a particular expenditure and the nature of the asset alteration itself are important factors in determining whether the expenditure is properly recorded as a repair/maintenance expense item or as a betterment item. For example, replacing a roof on a production plant after 2 years is probably a repair item to be expensed, whereas replacing a roof after 20 years is probably best treated as a betterment item to be capitalized on the balance sheet. Similarly, servicing the engines of a fleet of trucks every 5,000 miles represents a normal maintenance expense, but rebuilding the engines after 100,000 miles of use represents a betterment expenditure because the life of the asset has been extended.

The reporting of these asset-related expenditures should attempt to reflect the intended purpose of the expenditure. For financial reporting purposes, managers generally argue for capitalizing such expenditures in order to keep current reported profits as high as possible (by reducing the current level of deductions against net income). For tax purposes, however, the greatest benefit is achieved by expensing as many of these PP&E-related expenditures in the current period as is permitted. Once again, this situation presents another instance about which there may be disagreements between corporate management and the IRS as to what constitutes a repair/maintenance and what constitutes a betterment. It does stand to reason, however, that the logic applied to a particular expenditure would lead to a single classification that should be used for both tax and financial reporting purposes.

Impairment

A long-standing concern regarding the reporting and valuation of long-lived assets has been the recognition and timing of asset impairments. Because assets are valuable to an entity by virtue of their revenue-producing capacity, an **impairment** occurs whenever that revenue-generating ability is diminished or reduced. Consider, for example, a real estate development company holding land whose market value has fallen below its original cost. If this decline in value is not expected to recover in the foreseeable future, it is reasonable to conclude that the land's future revenue-producing capacity for the company has been impaired; and consequently, a write-down (that is, a loss) on the carrying value of the land should be recorded on the company's financial statements.

Regrettably, it is often quite difficult to unequivocally conclude that an asset's revenue-generating ability has declined or, alternatively, in the context of our real estate example above, that the drop in real estate prices is anything but temporary. To help resolve this issue, the FASB has developed criteria for financial statement preparers to help identify when an asset impairment has definitively occurred, and consequently, when a loss should be recorded. The accounting entry might appear as follows:

Dr. Loss on Asset Impairment (Loss)	(inc.) 2,000,000	
Cr. Property, Plant, and Equipment (A)		(dec.) 2,000,000

The FASB concluded that all long-lived assets (including identifiable intangibles and goodwill) should be reviewed for possible revaluation whenever events or changes in circumstances indicate that the carrying amount of the assets may not be fully recoverable. Examples of such events or changes in circumstances may include the following:

- A significant decline in the market value of an asset.
- A significant change in the extent or manner in which an asset is used.
- A significant adverse change in the business climate that affects the value of an asset.
- An accumulation of capitalized costs significantly in excess of the amount originally expected to acquire or construct the asset.
- A forecast suggesting that the use of the asset will be associated with continuing losses.

If any of these events or circumstances are present, the company should estimate the future cash flows expected to result from the use of the asset and its eventual disposition. If the sum of the *undiscounted* future net cash flows is less than its carrying value,

EXHIBIT 11.6

Asset Impairment Disclosures

Panel A — Coca-Cola Enterprises, Inc.

Impairment of Long-Lived Assets

In the event that facts and circumstances indicate that the cost of franchise assets or other assets may be impaired, an evaluation of recoverability would be performed. If an evaluation is required, the estimated future undiscounted cash flows associated with the asset would be compared to the asset's carrying amount to determine if a write-down to market value or discounted cash flow value is required.

Panel B — Stone Container Corporation

Goodwill

Goodwill is amortized on a straight-line basis over 40 years and is recorded net of accumulated amortization of approximately $129 million and $107 million at December 31, 1993 and 1992, respectively. The company assesses at each balance sheet date whether there has been a permanent impairment in the value of goodwill. This is accomplished by determining whether projected undiscounted future cash flows from operations exceed the net book value of goodwill as of the assessment date. Such projections reflect price, volume, and cost assumptions. Additional factors considered by management in the preparation of the projections and in assessing the value of goodwill include the effects of obsolescence, demand, competition, and other pertinent economic factors and trends and prospects that may have an impact on the value or remaining useful life of goodwill.

an impairment loss should be immediately recorded. Panel A of Exhibit 11.6 illustrates a general statement regarding impairment as disclosed by Coca-Cola Enterprises, Inc. Panel B presents the goodwill impairment policy of the Stone Container Corporation.[4]

Accounting for the Sale or Disposition of an Asset

When a PP&E item is sold or otherwise disposed of, both the original cost and the associated accumulated depreciation must be removed from the books. If the proceeds from the disposal exceed the asset's net book value, a gain is recognized. If the proceeds are less than the net book value, a loss is recognized. For example, if a machine with an original cost of $90,000 and accumulated depreciation of $70,000 is sold for $30,000 cash, the entry to record the sale is as follows:

Dr. Cash (A)	(inc.) 30,000	
Dr. Accumulated Depreciation (CA)	(dec.) 70,000	
Cr. Machine (A)		(dec.) 90,000
Cr. Gain on Sale (Gain)		(inc.) 10,000

The $10,000 gain on sale appears in the income statement covering the period in which the sale was made. Consistent with the reporting of gains from the sale of inventory, the gain on the sale of PP&E is reported in the period in which the sales event takes place rather than in the period in which the asset's market value appreciated above its net book value. This latter possibility, as discussed in Chapter 8, is the approach followed for marketable equity securities classified as trading securities. The principal difference between these two approaches relates to the degree of objectivity present in attempts to assess when the appreciation in asset value occurred. In the absence of a market mechanism, like the stock market, to establish appreciated value

[4]Similar issues also pertain to the loan receivable assets that a creditor (e.g., a bank or savings and loan) reports on its balance sheet. The issue of impairment is addressed by SFAS No. 114. A loan receivable is impaired if it is probable that the creditor will be unable to collect all amounts due. In such a situation, the impairment would be measured as the difference between the contractual cash flows and the present value of the currently expected future cash flows, discounted at the loan's effective interest rate.

EXHIBIT 11.7

Northrop Corporation
Income Statement
(in millions)

Year Ended December 31	1990	1989
Net sales	$5,489.8	$5,248.4
Cost of sales:		
Operating costs	4,747.7	4,691.9
Administrative and general expenses	450.5	533.2
Operating margin	291.6	23.3
Other income (deductions):		
Gain (loss) on disposals of property, plant, and equipment	103.0	(8.6)
Interest income	2.8	2.0
Other, net	10.0	(4.5)
Interest expense	(94.9)	(123.7)
Income (loss) before income taxes and cumulative effect of accounting change	312.5	(111.5)
Federal and foreign income taxes (benefit)	102.1	(31.0)
Income (loss) before cumulative effect of accounting change	210.4	(80.5)
Net income (loss)	$ 210.4	(80.5)
Weighted average common shares outstanding	47.0	47.0
Earnings (loss) per share before cumulative effect of accounting change	$ 4.48	$ (1.71)
Earnings (Loss) per share	$ 4.48	$ (1.71)

continued

objectively, GAAP relies on the occurrence of an actual sale transaction as a signal to record value appreciation (that is, a gain on sale).

In contrast to a gain on the sale of inventory, which is considered to be operations related, the gain (or loss) on the sale of PP&E is considered to be a nonoperating event because it is assumed that the company is not in the business of selling its PP&E. Thus, in the statement of cash flows (Chapter 6) and in the income statement (Chapter 5), PP&E sales are reported, but not as part of continuing operations. Exhibit 11.7 depicts the fact that Northrop Corporation reported gains and losses from sales of PP&E as a separate line item in its income statement and statement of cash flows. Moreover, in order to report the total proceeds from such sales, which would include amounts recognized as gains, the operating cash flows section in Northrop's statement of cash flows shows an adjustment for the gains and losses, and the total proceeds are then shown in the investing activities section.

Financial Statement Presentation and Disclosure

In the balance sheet, PP&E are shown in the noncurrent asset section. Land is reported at its original cost, whereas buildings, machinery, vehicles, and equipment are shown at original cost less the portion of that cost previously allocated as depreciation.

The annual expense for depreciation may or may not be shown in the body of the income statement. If it is not reported separately in the income statement, the amount expensed may be found in the notes to financial statements or as a line item in the

EXHIBIT 11.7 (concluded)

Partial Consolidated Statement of Cash Flows
(in millions)

Year Ended December 31	1990	1989
Reconciliation of Net Income (Loss) to Net Cash Provided by (Used in) Operating Activities		
Net income (loss)	$ 210.4	$ (80.5)
Adjustments to reconcile net income (loss) to net cash provided (used):		
Depreciation and amortization	186.6	220.6
Common stock issued to employees	3.7	5.1
Amortization of restricted award shares	1.3	4.9
Loss (gain) on disposals of property, plant, and equipment	(103.0)	8.6
Noncash pension cost (income)	(53.3)	7.3
Amortization of deferred gain on sale/leaseback	(2.3)	
Loss (gain) on sale of subsidiaries and affiliates		6.8
Gain on sale of direct financing leases		(12.9)
Decrease (increase) in		
Accounts receivable	(1,085.4)	(1,209.0)
Inventoried costs	49.7	(85.9)
Prepaid expenses	0.4	(4.3)
Refundable income taxes	8.1	1.2
Increase (decrease) in		
Progress payments	1,204.2	1,137.5
Accounts payable and accruals	(211.2)	54.2
Provisions for contract losses	(41.0)	59.9
Deferred income taxes	93.3	(34.0)
Income taxes payable	6.2	0.8
Other noncash transactions	(1.6)	(1.7)
Net cash provided by (used in) operating activities	$ 266.1	$ 78.6
Investing Activities		
Additions to property, plant, and equipment	(121.2)	(186.8)
Proceeds from sale of property, plant, and equipment	252.1	14.3
Proceeds from sale of subsidiaries and affiliates		1.1
Proceeds from sale of direct financing leases		21.9
Dividends from affiliate, net of investments	0.1	
Other investing activities	(2.3)	4.8
Net cash provided by (used in) investing activities	128.7	(144.7)

statement of cash flows. The notes to the financial statements include substantial information regarding a company's fixed assets, depreciation policies, and related expenditures. Complete examples of the required financial statement disclosures for PP&E are presented in Exhibit 11.8.

Managerial Issues

The property, plant, and equipment purchase decision is one of the most important decisions a manager makes because of the size of the investment and the long-term nature of the asset and related financing. A number of financial considerations that parallel some of this chapter's earlier discussions are involved in such purchase decisions. If the decision to buy a piece of equipment is determined, in part, on the asset's estimated net present value or internal rate of return (two very common capital budget-

EXHIBIT 11.8

Fixed Asset Disclosure Excerpts

Panel A — Stone Container Corp.

Property, Plant, Equipment, and Depreciation

Property, plant, and equipment are stated at cost. Expenditures for maintenance and repairs are charged to income as incurred. Additions, improvements, and major replacements are capitalized. The cost and accumulated depreciation related to assets sold or retired are removed from the accounts, and any gain or loss is credited or charged to income.

For financial reporting purposes, depreciation is provided on the straight-line method over the estimated useful lives of depreciable assets, or over the duration of the leases for capitalized leases, based on the following annual rates:

Type of Asset	Rates
Machinery and equipment	5% to 33%
Buildings and leasehold improvements	2% to 7%
Land improvements	4% to 7%

Effective January 1, 1990, the company changed its estimates of the useful lives of certain machinery and equipment at its paper mills. Mill asset depreciation lives that previously averaged 16 years were increased to an average of 20 years, while mill asset depreciation lives that previously averaged 10–12 years were increased to an average of 14–16 years. These changes were made to better reflect the estimated periods during which such assets will remain in service. The change had the effect of reducing depreciation expense by $39.8 million and increasing net income by $20.2 million, or $0.34 per common share, in 1990.

Panel B — Phelps Dodge Corp.

Property, Plant, and Equipment

Property, plant, and equipment are carried at cost. Cost of significant assets includes capitalized interest incurred during the construction and development period. Expenditures for replacements and betterments are capitalized; maintenance and repair expenditures are charged to operations as incurred.

The principal depreciation methods used are the units of production method for mining, smelting, and refining operations and, for other operations, the straight-line method based upon the estimated lives of specific classes or groups of depreciable assets. Upon disposal of assets depreciated on a group basis, cost less salvage is charged to accumulated depreciation.

Values for mining properties represent mainly acquisition costs or pre-1932 engineering valuations. Depletion of mines is computed on the basis of an overall unit rate applied to the pounds of principal products sold from mine production.

Mine exploration costs and development costs to maintain production of operating mines are charged to operations as incurred. Mine development expenditures at new mines and major development expenditures at operating mines that are expected to benefit future production are capitalized and amortized on the units of production method over the estimated commercially recoverable minerals.

ing techniques), then the asset's estimated useful life, periodic tax depreciation amount, salvage value, initial cost, and gains or losses on disposal of the assets being replaced are important factors to be considered. These factors are important because they influence the amount and timing of the cash flows generated by the particular asset under consideration and, thus, are an integral part in calculating the asset's net present value.

Some observers of corporate financial reporting have sarcastically observed that corporate accounting departments have become the best-performing profit centers for many companies — a comment that reflects the bottom-line impact attributable to the various financial reporting alternatives available under GAAP. Recall from Chapter 9, for example, the discussion of how net income could be significantly influenced by management's choice of LIFO versus FIFO for purposes of valuing ending inventory and the cost of goods sold. A similar concern exists with regard to fixed assets: Management's choice of depreciation method, expected useful life, and anticipated salvage value can have a material, direct effect on the company's bottom line. Recall our earlier example involving Owens-Corning, which increased 1993 net income by more than $8 million through discretionary PP&E accounting policy decisions. Although managers do have this flexibility available to them under GAAP, changes in accounting methods and estimates must be documented in the published financial statements. Such changes should be infrequent to avoid the appearance of overt earnings management.

Other, less critical management concerns include reducing the clerical costs associated with the accounting for fixed assets. In this regard, most companies, as a matter of policy, set a lower limit (for example, $500) for capitalizing assets. The purchase of any item costing less than this amount is expensed. This policy reduces the number of items that must be depreciated on a periodic basis even though many of those assets expensed will be used for more than one year. Because of the immateriality of these small dollar items, they do not affect the overall accuracy of the financial statements.

Another clerical-saving policy involves depreciating assets for a half-year in the year of acquisition and in the final year of their planned life rather than using the actual fractional parts of the year. Many companies adopt a half-year depreciation convention for the year of acquisition. Under this convention, capitalized property is depreciated on a six-month basis for the first year regardless of when it was acquired. A similar convention is normally adopted for the year of disposition if the asset is not fully depreciated at the time of disposition. Fortunately, in the U.S. the IRS recognizes the validity of this convention.

Time and money also can be saved by using similar policies for both accounting and tax purposes when possible. Adopting the same depreciation method for general accounting as that used for tax purposes, for example, minimizes the amount of work required to maintain two sets of records. Managers still must ensure, however, that fixed asset costs are allocated for accounting purposes in a rational and systematic manner. Managers also should be concerned with preserving cash flows to the company through well-planned tax depreciation policies.

INTANGIBLE ASSETS

Accounting for assets such as inventories and property, plant, and equipment seems relatively straightforward because these items are tangible in nature and their revenue-producing potential as assets is readily apparent. In contrast, the accounting for an intangible asset may not be so readily apparent because such assets do not physically produce goods or services. The term **intangible asset** refers to "certain long-lived legal rights and competitive advantages developed or acquired by a business enterprise"[5] exemplified by such items as patents, trademarks, and franchises. In the following section we will focus on such questions as, What cost figure should be assigned to a trademark on the balance sheet? Should a trademark be depreciated? If so, what is its useful life?

The financial reporting for most intangible assets is similar to that for fixed tangible assets such as property, plant, and equipment. At the date of acquisition, an intangible asset's cost must be determined and recorded at the fair market value of the consideration given up or the item acquired, whichever is more clearly determinable. When payment is noncash, every effort should be made to determine the market value of the noncash payment. If that is not possible, then the corporate financial manager should attempt to determine the market value of the intangible asset received. The consideration given (or the value of the asset received) becomes the basis for recording the asset — in effect, its recorded cost.

---

[5] *1988 GAAP Guide* (New York: Harcourt Brace Jovanovich, 1987), p. 21.02.

Consider, for example, the purchase of a franchise agreement for a combination of cash and capital stock. At the time of the purchase, the capital stock has a market value of $250,000; hence, the accounting entry to record the acquisition of the franchise appears as follows:

Dr. Franchise (A)	(inc.) 300,000	
Cr. Cash (A)		(dec.) 50,000
Cr. Capital Stock (OE)		(inc.) 250,000

Over its useful economic life, the intangible asset's recorded cost must be allocated to the periods benefited. GAAP assumes that the economic utility (the useful potential) of an intangible asset declines (is used up) over its life, and therefore the total cost should be systematically allocated as a period expense against the income of the company. This process, which is similar to the depreciation of fixed assets, is referred to as **amortization**. The period of time over which the recording of amortization takes place depends on the estimated economic life of the asset and varies from case to case. Generally accepted accounting principles provide the following insights:

> The recorded costs of intangible assets should be amortized by systematic charges to income over the periods estimated to be benefited. . . . The cost of each type of intangible should be amortized on the basis of the estimated life of that specific asset. . . . The period of amortization should not, however, exceed 40 years.[6]

Amortization of an intangible asset normally relies on the straight-line method over the estimated economic life of the asset unless an alternative method can be shown to comply more closely with the "using up" of the asset. By convention, amortization expense usually results in a direct reduction to the intangible asset account rather than an increase to a contra-asset allowance account as is done for depreciation charges related to property, plant, and equipment. In the previous franchise example, if the contractual term of the franchise agreement was 10 years, the accounting entry to record each year's amortization expense is as follows:

Dr. Franchise Amortization Expense (E)	(inc.) 30,000	
Cr. Franchise (A)		(dec.) 30,000

As with any asset, when intangible assets are disposed of, sold, or exchanged, they must be removed from the accounts, and any gain or loss must be recorded at that time. Continuing with the previous example, assume that after eight years the franchise is sold for a cash payment of $80,000. The entry appears as follows:

Dr. Cash (A)	(inc.) 80,000	
Cr. Franchise (A)		(dec.) 60,000
Cr. Gain on Sale of Franchise (Gain)		(inc.) 20,000

A Taxonomy for Intangible Assets

Intangible assets may differ from one another in several ways. Depending on these key dimensions, the accounting for the intangible asset under consideration may differ from that just described for the franchise example.

From a financial reporting perspective, managers must consider three key characteristics of intangibles. The first characteristic is *identifiability and separability:* Can the

[6] Accounting Principles Board, *Opinion No. 17 "Intangible Assets"* (APB, 1970), par. 9.

intangible asset be considered separately and distinctly from the other assets of the company? The usual test for separate identity is to determine whether the asset can be sold individually (as can a patent) or is so intertwined with the company that it cannot be separated (as is customer goodwill). The second issue pertains to the *manner of acquisition:* Was the intangible asset developed internally (like a proprietary manufacturing process) or was it purchased externally (like a franchise or an exclusive license)? A final issue pertains to the expected *period of benefit:* What is the economic life of the intangible asset? For some intangible assets, such as patents and franchises, the maximum economic life is legally or contractually determined. For others, such as trademarks, the economic life is not easily determined because of the potential for continual legal renewals and extensions. Moreover, the useful life of an intangible asset, like a trademark or patent, may be affected by product or process obsolescence, competitors' actions, and changes in technology. The only guidelines available to managers of U.S. companies in choosing an appropriate useful life is that the period selected should not be longer than the intangible's legal life, if it has one, and it cannot exceed 40 years in any case.

Exhibit 11.9 presents a summary of these dimensions with a taxonomy for a variety of intangible assets that distinguishes between those that are specifically identifiable and separable and those that are not and between those assets developed internally and those acquired externally.

Accounting Guidelines

Internally developed intangibles. The costs associated with internally developed intangible assets that are not specifically identifiable and separable are expensed against income in the period incurred. Stated in the language of current financial reporting standards, costs " . . . inherent in a continuing business and related to the enterprise as a whole — such as [customer] goodwill — should be deducted from income when incurred."[7] On the other hand, internally incurred costs associated with identifiable and separable intangible assets are expensed unless they are incurred under contract to an outside party. A classic example are R&D expenses incurred under a contractual agreement for the benefit of another entity. These expenses should be capitalized as an inventory-type item (that is, one held for sale) as opposed to a depreciable asset (one held for internal production).

On the other hand, consider the issue of in-house research and development costs. Prior to 1975, accounting convention was to capitalize R&D expenses, based on the observation that such expenses were investments in the products and operations of the future and were thus a cost of bringing those future assets to a usable condition. However, because of practical realities (less than 1 in 10 new product ideas ever go to market, and the ability to predict which one will be successful is highly uncertain), capitalizing R&D expenditures seldom achieved the ultimate matching of revenues and expenses it sought to achieve.

A recent case highlights the nontrivial issue of accounting for R&D expenditures. During the 1980s, Burroughs Wellcome spent and expensed more than $80 million on R&D that ultimately led to the AIDS drug AZT. As the R&D was being incurred, management did not know whether the outcome would result in an effective, marketable AIDS drug. All expenditures therefore were expensed, as were another $700 mil-

[7]Accounting Principles Board, *Opinion No. 17.*

EXHIBIT 11.9

Classification Taxonomy for Intangible Assets

Method of acquisition	Asset specifically identifiable and separable	Asset not specifically identifiable and separable
Internally developed	I • R&D costs • Costs specifically attached to development of proprietary products or processes **Expense**	II • Customer relations • Quality reputation **Expense**
Externally developed	III • Costs of obtaining a - patent - copyright - trademark or tradename - franchise • Organization costs • Beneficial contracts • Government concessions **Capitalize**	IV • Excess purchase price paid on acquisition (goodwill) **Capitalize**

lion of R&D on other diseases that produced nothing of significance. On the day that the Food and Drug Administration approved AZT, it became a valuable asset that was not and could not be reported on the balance sheet. In setting the retail price for AZT, however, Wellcome managers asked this question: What is the cost of the product? Various stakeholders in the pricing decision argued for quite different points of view. Some argued that only the $80 million specifically associated with the AZT product development should be considered; others argued that AZT pricing had to be sufficient to recover the entire R&D budget of $780 million. Still others argued that the price should be merely the cost involved in manufacturing the drug. This debate illustrates the divergent views that exist as to whether R&D should be considered part of a product's cost, and, if so, whether only direct R&D costs or both direct and indirect costs be considered. Financial reporting practice does not help management in this case because it requires the conservative "solution" of treating R&D expenditures as a period cost rather than a product cost. In so doing, GAAP emphasizes objectivity over subjectivity and conservatism over optimism, resulting in a decoupling of accounting policy from strategic management decisions.

Externally developed intangibles. The consideration paid to external parties for control of specifically identifiable and separable intangible assets (Exhibit 11.9, Quadrant III) should be capitalized and systematically amortized over the economic life of the asset (but not to exceed 40 years). Examples include government concessions (such as licenses to develop a country's resources), beneficial contracts for goods or services below market rates, and trademarks.

Patents, for example, are exclusive legal rights to products registered with the United States Patent Office; they recognize the holder's right to use, manufacture, dispose of, and control in every way the patented product or process without hindrance from others. Patents have a legal life of 17 years, but their economic life may be much shorter because of technological obsolescence. Similarly, *copyrights* are legal rights of protection given to the creators of published materials. Copyright law has recently been changed so that copyrights now extend protection for the life of the creator plus 50 years, or if the copyright is held by a corporation (deemed to have an indeterminate life), 75 years from the date of first publication. *Franchises* are the rights granted by one company to another to use a specific designation in their business; use can be limited in term by contract or be renewable indefinitely to create essentially an indeterminate life. If a franchise is renewable indefinitely, it should be amortized over a period not to exceed 40 years. PepsiCo's largest intangible asset noted in its footnote is for its franchises. *Trademarks* are federally registered claims of ownership to names, symbols, slogans, or other devices providing distinctive identity of a product. Although they have no legally limited life, trademarks often have limited economic life. If an estimate of the economic life can be made, it should be used as the term for amortization of the asset. If no estimate of economic life can be made, the asset should be amortized over a period not to exceed 40 years. As noted in Exhibit 11.9 (Quadrant III), the costs of obtaining a patent, copyright, franchise, or trademark should be capitalized as intangible assets. It is important to note that the costs of producing an asset (for example, a feature motion picture) should be reported as an asset separate from the costs incurred in obtaining the copyright on the film.

Exhibit 11.10 presents several corporate disclosures for intangible assets representing different approaches to amortization. Note in particular McDonnell Douglas's statement as to the variety of intangible assets reported in its balance sheet and to the fact that they are being amortized over 3 to 10 years. Rockwell International, on the other hand, chooses to amortize somewhat similar items over 5 to 20 years. Air Products' disclosure points out that internally incurred costs leading to a patent are expensed whereas externally incurred costs associated with acquisition of a patent are capitalized. Last, note how Polaroid Corp. reports the patents on all of its very valuable, highly lucrative proprietary products and processes — at $1. Because the bulk of such costs were internally incurred, and because the patent filing costs were probably immaterial relative to the asset's value, all such costs were expensed. In order to draw the reader's attention to their patented propriety processes and products, however, Polaroid chooses to report them, albeit at the unique cost figure of $1.

Goodwill: Special considerations. As has already been mentioned, costs associated with internally created goodwill (such as public service expenditures, employee development, charitable contributions, customer service expenses, and so on) are not capitalized. They are expensed in the period in which they are incurred. As discussed in Chapter 10, the acquisition of another business, however, often creates the need to identify and record a goodwill intangible asset pertaining to the acquired company (Exhibit 11.9, Quadrant IV). Consider for a moment the fact that the only reason Dresser Industries management was willing to pay in excess of $122 million more for Bredero Price Holding B.V. than the fair market value of Bredero's net assets was the customer loyalty, managerial talent, sound reputation, and so on already built up by Bredero Price (see Exhibit 11.11). Although Bredero Price was never permitted to

EXHIBIT 11.10

Intangible Asset Disclosures

Panel A — Rockwell International Corp.

Intangible assets are summarized as follows (in millions):

September 30	1994	1993
Goodwill, less accumulated amortization (1994, $174.0; 1993, $149.2)	$589.3	$581.5
Patents, product technology, and other intangibles, less accumulated amortization (1994, $348.7; 1993, $321.2)	187.7	195.6
Intangible assets	$777.0	$777.1

Goodwill represents the excess of the cost of purchased businesses over the fair value of their net assets at date of acquisition and generally is being amortized by the straight-line method over periods ranging from 10 to 40 years.

Patents, product technology, and other intangibles relate principally to Allen-Bradley and are being amortized on a straight-line basis over their estimated useful lives, generally ranging from 5 to 20 years.

Panel B — McDonnell Douglas Corp.

Intangible Assets

Intangible assets consist of capitalized computer software and the unamortized balances of the excess of the cost of acquired companies (or significant interests therein) over the values assigned to net tangible assets. The latter amounts have been assigned to government programs, computer software, leaseholds, and goodwill. These intangibles are being amortized over 3 to 10 years, except goodwill, which has various periods up to 40 years.

Panel C — Polaroid Corp.

Patents and Trademarks

Patents and trademarks are valued at $1.

Panel D — Air Products, Inc.

Patents

Expenses related to the development of patents are deducted from income as they occur. Patents acquired from other companies are recorded at their purchase price and charged to income over the remaining life of the patent.

record an intangible asset for such goodwill-related factors, the external acquisition of Bredero Price by Dresser Industries was an event that justified Dresser's recording of Bredero's goodwill. In essence, a marketplace valuation of that goodwill had been made and confirmed via the payment of a price for Bredero Price in excess of Bredero's net assets' appraised fair market value. This premium paid was recorded as goodwill on Dresser's books. In the U.S., such goodwill is assumed to be of indeterminate life but, by convention, is amortized over a life not to exceed 40 years.

Beginning in 1994, goodwill became tax-deductible in the United States over an amortizable life of 15 years. When a company's estimated amortizable life of goodwill for accounting purposes (usually 40 years) differs from that assumed for tax purposes, the effect of this difference is captured in the deferred income tax account. (There will be more on this topic in Chapter 13.)

NATURAL RESOURCES

Natural resources include such assets as timber, oil, gas, iron ore, coal, and uranium. Like intangible assets, natural resources may be either internally or externally developed. When these assets are externally developed, they are reported on the balance sheet at their acquisition cost less any depletion taken subsequent to acquisition. Alternatively, when they are internally developed, several valuation approaches may be adopted.

The two principal valuation alternatives that exist for companies in the extractive industries are the full cost method and the successful efforts method. Under the **full cost method,** *all* costs associated with the exploration for and development of natural resources are capitalized to the natural resource accounts on the balance sheet. There is

EXHIBIT 11.11

Dresser Industries' Disclosure for Bredero Price Holding Acquisition

Effective February 1, 1993, the company acquired all the outstanding stock of Bredero Price Holding B.V., a Netherlands corporation, from Koninklijke Begemann Groep N.V. for approximately $161.5 million in cash. Bredero Price is a multinational company that provides pipe coating for both onshore and offshore markets.

Effective April 1, 1993, the company acquired TK Valve & Manufacturing, Inc., from Sooner Pipe & Supply Corporation, Tulsa, Oklahoma, for approximately $143.5 million in cash. TK Valve supplies ball valves for the oil and gas production and transmission industry.

The purchase price exceeded the fair value of the net assets acquired by approximately $122 million for Bredero Price and approximately $92 million for TK Valve. Both acquisitions were accounted for as purchases. The resulting goodwill is being amortized on a straight-line basis over 40 years. The consolidated statement of earnings includes the results of operations of Bredero Price from February 1, 1993, and TK Valve from April 1, 1993.

little disagreement over this method *except* when unsuccessful exploration activities are involved. Under the full cost method, the costs of unsuccessful exploration activities are also capitalized to the balance sheet under the philosophy that the development of new resource reserves is a speculative activity involving some inherent failure. In contrast, under the **successful efforts method,** only the costs associated with successful exploration and development activity are capitalized to the balance sheet accounts. The costs of any unsuccessful activity are expensed against net income.

Both the full cost and the successful efforts methods are generally accepted, and thus both are available for use by managers of natural resource companies in the extractive industries. In practice, however, only small resource companies tend to use the full cost method, whereas larger companies tend to prefer the successful efforts method (see panels A, B, and C, Exhibit 11.12), which is also the method of choice among most preparers of financial statements. Under both methods, however, the costs capitalized to the balance sheet are subject to certain constraints in a manner similar to the effect that the lower-of-cost-or-market method has on inventory. In the event that the current market value of a company's reserves of natural resources declines substantially, it may become necessary to write down the value of the capitalized balance sheet values. Thus, just as the lower-of-cost-or-market method prevents the overstatement of inventories, this "ceiling test" similarly constrains the value of natural resources on the balance sheet.

Natural resource companies not involved in the extractive industries, such as a timber company, usually capitalize all of their initial expenditures while expensing their ongoing maintenance and development costs. Except in those cases involving forest fires, which destroy substantial portions of a company's timber reserves, the initial capitalized cost is carried on the balance sheet until the reserves are harvested (see Panel D, Exhibit 11.12).

Depletion

Depletion refers to the periodic expensing of the capitalized natural resource cost. Unlike depreciation, there is only one generally accepted depletion approach, the units-of-production method, which is conceptually and procedurally similar to the units-of-production method of depreciation sometimes used by companies for machinery and equipment. The first step is to estimate the number of units — barrels of crude oil, tons of ore, or board feet of timber — in a well, mine, or tract of forest. Next, a

EXHIBIT 11.12

Natural Resource Disclosures

Panel A — Homestake Mining Co.

Exploration costs, including those incurred through partnerships and joint ventures, are charged to operations in the year incurred.

Preoperating and development costs relating to new mines and major programs at existing mines are capitalized. Ordinary mine development costs to maintain production and underground equipment acquisitions are charged to operations as incurred.

Depreciation, depletion, and amortization of mining properties, mine development costs, and major plant facilities are computed principally by the units-of-production method (based on estimated proven and probable ore reserves). Proven and probable ore reserves reflect estimated quantities of commercially recoverable reserves that the company believes can be recovered in the future from known mineral deposits. Such estimates are based on current and projected costs and product prices.

Panel B — Amoco Corporation

Costs Incurred in Oil and Gas Producing Activities
The corporation follows the successful efforts method of accounting. Costs of property acquisitions, successful exploratory wells, all development costs (including CO_2 and certain other injected materials in enhanced recovery projects), and support equipment and facilities are capitalized. Unsuccessful exploratory wells are expensed when determined to be nonproductive. Production costs, overhead, and all exploration costs other than exploratory drilling are charged against income as incurred.

Depreciation, Depletion, and Amortization
Depletion of the cost of producing oil and gas properties, amortization of related intangible drilling and development costs, and depreciation of tangible lease and well equipment are computed on the units-of-production method.

The portion of costs of unproved oil and gas properties estimated to be nonproductive is amortized over projected holding periods.

Panel C — Mobil Corp.

Oil and Gas Accounting Method
Mobil follows the "successful efforts" method of accounting prescribed by Financial Accounting Standard (FAS) 19, Financial Accounting and Reporting by Oil and Gas Producing Companies.

Exploration and Mineral Rights (Leases)
Direct acquisition costs of unproved mineral rights (leases) are capitalized and then amortized in the manner stated below. Payments made in lieu of drilling on nonproducing leaseholds are charged to expense currently.

Geological, Geophysical and Intangible Drilling Costs
Geological and geophysical costs are charged to expense as incurred. Intangible drilling costs of all development wells and of exploratory wells that result in additions to proved reserves are capitalized.

Depreciation, Depletion, and Amortization
Annual charges to income for depreciation and the estimated cost for restoration and removal of major producing facilities are computed on a straight-line basis over the useful lives of the various classes of properties or, where appropriate for producing properties, on a unit-of-production basis by individual fields.

Costs of producing properties are generally accumulated by field. Depletion of these costs and amortization of capitalized intangible drilling costs are calculated on a unit-of-production basis.

Capitalized acquisition costs of significant unproved mineral rights and unamortized costs of significant developed properties are assessed periodically on a property-by-property basis to determine whether their values have been impaired; where impairment is indicated, a loss is recognized.

Capitalized acquisition costs of other unproved mineral rights are amortized over the expected holding period. When a mineral right is surrendered, any unamortized cost is charged to expense. When a property is determined to contain proved reserves, the mineral right then becomes subject to depletion on a unit-of-production basis.

Panel D — Stone Container Corp.

Timberlands
Timberlands are stated at cost less accumulated cost of timber harvested. The company amortized its private fee timber costs over the total fiber that will be available during the estimated growth cycle. Cost of nonfee timber harvested is determined on the basis of timber removal rates and the estimated volume of recoverable timber. The company capitalizes interest costs related to premerchantable timber.

depletion rate per unit must be determined. For example, if the estimated number of tons of ore in a mine was 200,000 and the mine's original cost (less estimated residual value) was $820,000, the depletion rate per ton would be $4.10. Last, the depletion expense for the year is figured. So if during the first year 22,000 tons were taken out, the depletion expense for the year would be 22,000 times $4.10, or $90,200. The accounting entry follows:

Dr. Depletion Expense (E)	(inc.) 90,200	
Cr. Allowance for Depletion (CA)		(inc.) 90,200

The Allowance for Depletion account is conceptually similar to the Accumulated Depreciation account. The depletion example above is referred to as *cost depletion,* and it is generally used only for financial reporting purposes. U.S. tax law allows another method, referred to as *percentage depletion.* This method is not permissible for financial reporting purposes because it is not an allocation approach based on the asset's cost basis. Under percentage depletion, depletion expense for a period is figured by multiplying the gross income generated by the natural resource asset that period by a percentage rate legislated in the tax law (for example, 22 percent). Over the asset's life, for tax purposes, the accumulated depletion amount can exceed the cost of the resource, whereas for accounting purposes, the accumulated depletion cannot exceed the original cost of the resource less its estimated residual value. The difference between the two depletion methods results in a permanent difference between tax accounting and financial accounting. As will be explained in Chapter 13, no deferred taxes are recognized for such permanent differences.

INTERNATIONAL CONSIDERATIONS

Fixed assets. The accounting for noncurrent assets can vary dramatically from one country to the next. While U.S. GAAP rigidly adheres to the historical cost concept as the basis for valuing these assets, many countries permit, and some even require, a departure from the historical cost principle. Italy, for example, periodically passes legislation that requires publicly held companies to revalue their noncurrent assets using governmentally approved price indexes. This process insures that all Italian companies consistently restate their balance sheet values to reflect the effects of inflation in that country. In yet other countries, such as Australia and the United Kingdom, revaluation of noncurrent assets is not required but is widely practiced.

Consider for example, Exhibit 11.13, which presents the asset revaluation disclosures of Coca-Cola Amatil Ltd., an Australian-based bottler of Coca-Cola products (such as Coke, Fanta, and Sprite soft drinks). This exhibit reveals that Amatil revalues some of its buildings and freehold land every three years. The revaluations are provided in some cases by licensed independent appraisers and in others by the company's directors. The exhibit also reveals that the depreciation expense taken on the revalued property is based on the adjusted amounts, not historical cost. Proponents of revaluation argue that the process results in a more fairly stated balance sheet presentation of a company's net worth,[8] and that since depreciation is based upon revalued amounts, the reported net income more accurately reflects a company's true (inflation-adjusted) earnings. The accounting entry for the revaluation of PP&E might appear as follows:

Dr. PP&E (A)	(inc.) £10,000	
Cr. Asset Revaluation Reserve (OE)		(inc.) £10,000

Intangible assets. Considerable diversity also exists around the world in the accounting for intangible assets. While under U.S. GAAP all intangible assets must be amortized against net income, in some countries (such as France), amortization is not required where the value of an intangible asset can be shown to be increasing or where the end of the useful economic life of the asset cannot be foreseen. With respect to

[8]Revaluation proponents suggest that the balance values of companies using U.S. GAAP are inherently conservatively biased, possibly to the extent of being misleading.

EXHIBIT 11.13

Asset Revaluation Disclosures: Coca-Cola Amatil Ltd.

Panel A — Statement of Accounting Policies

Valuation of Noncurrent Assets
Freehold land and buildings are revalued at three-year intervals. The value of the land and buildings is assessed on their worth to the group on an existing use basis and does not exceed the net amount expected to be recovered from their continued use and subsequent disposal. Other noncurrent assets are carried at the lower of cost and recoverable amount. The expected net cash flows included in determining the recoverable amounts of noncurrent assets have been discounted to their present value.

Depreciation and Amortization of Noncurrent Assets
Noncurrent assets are depreciated or amortized over the useful life of each asset where the amount charged would be material. Where assets have been revalued, depreciation or amortization is charged on the adjusted amount.

Panel B — Notes to Financial Statements

	CCA Group		CCA Entity	
	1994 $M	**1993 $M**	**1994 $M**	**1993 $M**
12. Property, Plant, and Equipment				
Freehold and leasehold land and buildings at cost	**92.3**	171.7	—	—
Provision for depreciation and amortization	**(3.3)**	(4.0)	—	—
	89.0	167.7	—	—
Freehold and leasehold land and buildings				
at independent valuations —				
1994*	**147.8**	—	—	—
1991	—	102.5	—	—
at directors' valuations —				
1994	**129.2**	—	—	—
1991	—	35.4	—	—
	277.0	137.9	—	—
Provision for depreciation and amortization	**(1.7)**	(6.1)	—	—
	275.3	131.8	—	—
Total property	**364.3**	299.5	—	—
Plant and equipment at cost	**1,077.2**	884.7	**46.1**	32.0
Provision for depreciation	**(405.2)**	(330.7)	**(13.4)**	(10.6)
	672.0	554.0	**32.7**	21.4
Plant and equipment at directors' valuation 1984	—	7.0	—	—
Provision for depreciation	—	(6.4)	—	—
	—	0.6	—	—
Total plant and equipment	**672.0**	554.6	**32.7**	21.4
Total property, plant, and equipment	**1,036.3**	854.1	**32.7**	21.4

*Independent valuations of freehold land and buildings at 31 August 1994 were made by licensed valuers of the firm Edward Rushton.

research and development expenditures, U.S. GAAP requires that most of these expenditures be expensed in the period in which they are incurred. In other countries (such as Brazil), capitalization of R&D outlays is permitted, in large measure as an incentive to companies to invest in the development of new products. Finally, as noted in Chapter 10, while goodwill is capitalized to the balance sheet under U.S. GAAP, in other countries (such as Sweden and the United Kingdom) it is more commonly expensed in total in the year of acquisition by reducing shareholders' equity; that accounting entry might appear as follows:

Dr. Retained Earnings (OE)	(dec.) £50,000	
Cr. Goodwill (A)		(dec.) £50,000

The charge-to-equity treatment of goodwill avoids the "drag" on future corporate income that results from the amortization of goodwill under U.S. GAAP. Even in countries that require the capitalization of goodwill, there is considerable diversity in the allowable amortizable life, as the following data reveal:

Country	Maximum Amortizable Life (in Years)
Australia	20
Canada	40
Germany	5
Italy	10
Japan	5
United States	40

SUMMARY

Noncurrent assets are the principal long-term revenue-producing assets of most companies. Because of the significant dollar investment in these assets, the accounting methods adopted for them may have a material impact on both the balance sheet and the income statement of a company. Although the initial cash outflow to acquire these assets affects the statement of cash flows, the periodic amortization of intangibles, the depreciation of fixed assets, and the depletion of natural resources do not affect it; amortization, depreciation, and depletion expenses are added back to net income to adjust the accrual operating results for these noncash expenses to arrive at the cash flows from operations.

When evaluating the performance of a company or its management, it is important to consider how effectively the noncurrent assets were utilized. Such ratios as the asset turnover ratio and the return on noncurrent assets, as discussed in Chapter 4, are instructive indicators in this regard.

NEW CONCEPTS AND TERMS

Accelerated methods of depreciation (p. 496)
Accumulated depreciation (p. 495)
Allocation (p. 492)
Amortization (p. 511)
Capitalization (p. 492)
Depletion (p. 516)
Double-declining-balance method (p. 495)
Fixed assets (p. 492)
Full cost method (p. 515)
Half-year convention (p. 502)
Impairment (p. 505)
Intangible asset (p. 510)
Machine-hour method (p. 496)
Modified Accelerated Cost Recovery System (p. 501)
Net book value (p. 494)
Physical life (p. 494)
Process obsolescence (p. 495)
Product obsolescence (p. 494)
Straight-line method (p. 495)
Successful efforts method (p. 516)
Sum-of-the-years' digits method (p. 495)
Technological life (p. 494)
Units-of-production method (p. 496)

ISSUES FOR DISCUSSION

D11.1 Point: Research and development expenditures should be expensed when incurred.

Counterpoint: Research and development expenditures should be capitalized until it is known whether a commercially viable product will result. If none results, then R&D should be expensed.

Required:
Evaluate the two viewpoints. Which one do you agree with, and why?

D11.2 Does the booking of depreciation provide for the replacement of a fixed asset? Explain.

D11.3 Is depreciation a source or use of cash? Is amortization a source or use of cash? How are these two items handled in the statement of cash flows? Explain.

D11.4 Can depreciation be treated as a period cost? product cost? Explain.

D11.5 What guidelines should be used when determining the original cost to book for a machine? Explain.

D11.6 During a period of slack production, Amos Company decided to remodel part of its plant using some of its own workers. Should the company capitalize the cost of its workers who did the remodeling? Explain. Should the company capitalize some of its plant general overhead costs incurred during the remodeling period? Explain.

D11.7 If an intangible asset such as a patent is fully amortized, can a company continue to benefit from it? If so, can the company continue to record amortization expense based on the matching principle? Explain.

D11.8 What change in management estimates might occur related to a building? a trademark? Does the change have accounting implications? Explain.

D11.9 If toxic waste is discovered beneath a company's warehouse and the government orders the warehouse permanently closed or the waste cleaned up, explain the accounting issues that arise.

D11.10 How should a company account for normal repairs and maintenance on its office building? For a replacement of the carpet? For a technological renovation of the building comprised mostly of running fibre optic cable, increasing the number of computer work stations, and the installation of a keyless security system? Explain.

PROBLEMS

P11.1 Estimating depreciation and book value. Equipment costing $29,000, with a scrap value of $3,000, was purchased on January 1, 1995, by Global Communications, Inc. The estimated useful life of the equipment was four years and it was expected to generate 80,000 finished units of production. Units actually produced were 14,000 in 1995 and 20,000 in 1996. Complete the following table.

	Depreciation Expense		Net Book Value	
Depreciation Method	1995	1996	12/31/95	12/31/96
Straight line	6,500	6,500	22,500	16,000
Sum-of-the-years' digits	10,400	7,800	18,600	21,200
Double-declining balance	14,500	750	14,500	7250
Units of production	4,550	6,500	24,450	22,500

P11.2 Income statement preparation. Ottawa Oil Corporation paid $4,000,000 for land with proven oil reserves. The company spent another $300,000 building roads and water run off ponds. The petroleum engineers were certain of at least 1 million barrels of oil and perhaps as many as 1.5 million. In 10 to 12 years, when the wells dry up, the derricks will be dismantled at a cost estimated to be equivalent to the land's then market value.

A record of other capital expenditures made during the year, exclusive of the $300,000 costs previously mentioned, is as follows:

Asset	Estimated Service Life	Cost
Field office building	20 years	$400,000
Derricks	12 years	700,000
Miscellaneous equipment	7 years	200,000

The miscellaneous equipment (comprised of trailers, trucks, and crude oil assaying equipment) is movable to other sites.

During the oil field's first full year of operation, Ottawa experienced the following:

Barrels of oil extracted and sold at $15 per barrel	200,000
Field labor and other operating costs (exclusive of depreciation and depletion)	$800,000
Selling and administrative expenses	$100,000

Required:

Prepare an income statement for the first full year of the oil field's operations. (Assume every well dug, struck oil.)

P11.3 Accounting for the sale of an asset. On January 1, 1991, Home Computing Consulting Corporation purchased a number of pieces of new equipment, including a new, state-of-the-art printer. The printer cost $8,000 and was expected to last 8 years. Home used the double-declining-balance method of depreciation for both financial reporting and tax purposes. By December 1995, the home computing consulting business had begun to slow down. The company found itself with underutilized employees and equipment. Near the end of 1995, the company sold the printer in exchange for a $1,000 note receivable that required three annual payments of $333. The original estimated salvage value was zero.

Required:

a. What entry(ies) should Home make regarding the printer for the year ended December 31, 1995?

b. What entry(ies) should Home make regarding the printer for the year ended December 31, 1995, if the note is agreed on in principle in 1995 but not signed until early January 1996?

P11.4 Fixed asset accounting policy. At the beginning of the year, Constance Dado acquired a sophisticated document scanner to be used in her business. The scanner was delivered by the office products company, installed by Dado Corporation personnel, and placed into operation. The estimated useful life of the scanner is five years, and its estimated salvage value is about 20 percent of its original cost.

During the year, Dado also sold for cash one of her fully depreciated delivery trucks.

Required:

a. What costs should be capitalized for the scanner?

b. Can the purchaser of the delivery truck depreciate it even though Dado had already fully depreciated it?

c. How should Dado account for the disposal of the delivery truck?

P11.5 Depreciation policy. USX Corporation provided the following footnote in a recent set of financial statements detailing its depreciation policies.

> *Property, plant, and equipment* — Except for oil and gas producing properties, depreciation is generally computed on the straight-line method based upon the estimated lives of the assets. The corporation's method of computing depreciation of steel assets modifies straight-line depreciation based on the level of production. The modification ranges from a minimum of 80 percent at a production level of 50 percent of capacity and below, to a maximum of 130 percent for a 100 percent production level. No modification is made at the 85 percent production level, considered the normal long-range level.
>
> Depletion of the cost of mineral properties, other than oil and gas, is based on rates that are expected to amortize the cost over the estimated tonnage of minerals to be removed.
>
> Depreciation and depletion of oil and gas producing properties are computed at rates applied to the units of production on the basis of proved oil and gas reserves as determined by the corporation's geologists and engineers.
>
> When a plant or major facility within a plant is sold or otherwise disposed of by the corporation, any gain or loss is reflected in income. Proceeds from the sale of other facilities depreciated on a group basis are credited to the depreciation reserve. When facilities depreciated on an individual basis are sold, the difference between the selling price and the remaining undepreciated value is reflected in income.

Required:

a. In your own words, explain USX's depreciation policy for steel assets.

b. What rationale would support USX's depreciation policy?

P11.6 Repair and maintenance expense. During 1995, Cemex S.A. made the following expenditures relating to plant, machinery and equipment:

- Overhaul of several machines at a cost of $50,000 to improve efficiency in production over their remaining five-year useful lives. The overhaul was completed on December 31, 1995.
- Regularly scheduled repairs at a cost of $25,000.
- A broken cooling pump on a machine was replaced at a cost of $4,000.

Required:

What amount should be expensed as repairs and maintenance in 1995?

P11.7 Cost capitalization. Belpre, Inc., had just completed the reconfiguration of its production line to increase its efficiency. Belpre estimated that benefits from the changes would be realized over the remaining five-year useful lives of the machines. The following costs were incurred:

Moving	$50,000
Set up and testing	40,000
Maintenance	10,000

Required:

Which of these costs should be capitalized? Explain.

P11.8 Estimating depletion expense. In January 1995, Craig Mining Corporation purchased a mine for $5 million with ore reserves estimated at 2,600,000 tons. The property has an estimated value of $500,000 as a landfill after the ore has been extracted. Craig incurred $1.2 million of development costs preparing the property for its mining operation. During 1995, 300,000 tons were removed and 250,000 tons were sold.

Required:

For the year ended December 31, 1995, Craig should include what amount of depletion in its cost of goods sold? Explain.

P11.9 Estimating amortization expense. Curtis Company bought a trademarked learning system for use in its consulting practice from Kent Corporation on January 1, 1995, for $200,000. Curtis expected to be able to market the system for at least another 10 years. Kent's accounting records reported no figure for the system. Curtis wanted to amortize the trademark over 40 years.

Required:

How much should be amortized for the year ended December 31, 1995? Explain.

P11.10 Accounting for intangible assets. Global Enterprises, Inc., had a balance sheet loaded with intangible assets. During 1995 four additional decisions were required regarding various intangible asset-related expenditures.

Required:

a. Should the legal fees incurred in successfully defending a copyrighted song be capitalized? Explain.

b. Should the costs of creating customer goodwill be capitalized? Explain.

c. Should the purchase of a customer list be capitalized and expensed? Explain.

d. Should the legal fees incurred by a company in a successful defense of its CEO against a discrimination suit be capitalized? Explain.

P11.11 Accounting for intangible assets. Mitsui Corporation incurred $3,000,000 of research and development costs to develop a product for which a patent was granted. Legal fees associated with registration of the patent totaled $40,000 and the legal fees paid by Mitsui in a successful defense of the patent totaled $100,000.

Required:

How much should be capitalized for this patent? Explain.

P11.12 Accounting for asset exchanges. On June 30, 1995, Clay, Inc., exchanged 5,000 shares of North Corp. $1 par value common stock it owned for a patent owned by South Co. The North stock had been purchased some years earlier at a cost of $25,000. At the exchange date, the North common stock was selling at $35 per share, and the patent had a net book value of $90,000 on South's books.

Required:

Clay should book the patent at what amount? Explain.

P11.13 Accounting for asset exchanges. On September 1, 1995, Ruane, Inc., exchanged several excess lap top computers it owned for a used tractor suitable for its landscaping needs. Ruane bought the lap tops in 1993 for $18,000. As of September 1, 1995, the lap tops had a book value of $7,000 and a fair market value of $5,000. Ruane gave $3,000 in cash in addition to the lap tops as part of this transaction. The previous owner of the tractor had been advertising it for sale at $10,000.

Required:

At what amount should the tractor be recorded in Ruane's books?

P11.14 Accounting for fixed assets. Kraft, Inc., included the following footnote in one of its recent annual reports:

> Properties are stated at cost. Depreciation is determined on a straight-line basis over estimated useful lives. For certain machinery and equipment, depreciation is determined on a composite basis over estimated group lives. The estimated useful lives are principally 10 to 40 years for buildings and improvements and 2 to 25 years for machinery and equipment.
>
> On routine disposals of depreciable assets accounted for on a composite basis, the gross book value less the proceeds or salvage value is charged to accumulated depreciation. On all other sales or retirements of property, plant, and equipment, gain or loss is recognized. Expenditures for maintenance and repairs are charged to expense.

Required:

a. What does Kraft mean when it refers to depreciation "being determined on a composite basis"? Why might management have chosen this approach?

b. Do gains/losses on routine disposals of depreciable assets accounted for on a composite basis affect current period income? Explain.

c. Do gains/losses on all other sales or retirements of property, plant, and equipment affect current period net income? Explain.

P11.15 Estimating book values. Kaiser Aluminum and Chemical Corporation provided the following footnote in one of its recent financial statements regarding its property, plant, and equipment:

Property, Plant, and Equipment and Long-Term Leases

December 31	19X1	19X0
Land and improvements	$ 171.5	$ 157.8
Buildings	386.8	359.0
Machinery and equipment	2,342.3	2,206.1
Construction in progress	52.9	62.7
Total property — at cost (includes idle facilities: $215.8 in 19X1 and $215.9 in 19X0	2,953.5	2,785.6
Accumulated depreciation (includes idle facilities: $130.8 in 19X1 and $126.1 in 19X0)	1,467.7	1,253.9
Property, plant, and equipment — net	$1,485.8	$1,531.7

The idle facilities shown consist of the corporation's Chalmette, Louisiana, aluminum smelter, which is temporarily closed because of high energy and other costs and the market conditions for primary aluminum. In addition, production of alumina at Alumina Partners of Jamaica (ALPART) was temporarily suspended in August 19X0 due to the continuing adverse economic conditions impacting the aluminum industry. ALPART, a 50%-owned partnership, has an alumina plant in Nain, Jamaica. At December 31, 19X1 and 19X0, investments and advances include $32.5 and $32.0 for ALPART, which is accounted for by the equity method. The corporation is obligated to pay $72.4 and $79.0 of ALPART's debt at December 31, 19X1 and 19X0.

Management believes that market conditions will improve and that operating costs of the idle facilities can be reduced sufficiently to permit economic operation of these facilities in the future. The corporation's policy is to continue normal depreciation for temporarily closed facilities.

Required:

a. What is the net book value (NBV) of Kaiser's idle facilities at 12/31/X1?

b. If, as of 12/31/X1, an independent appraiser determined that the fair market value of the idle facilities was $50 million less than Kaiser's NBV, should the NBV be adjusted? Why or why not?

c. If the appraisal were $50 million more than NBV, should it be adjusted? Why or why not?

d. Why is Kaiser depreciating its idle facilities?

e. What rationale would support a decision not to continue depreciating facilities?

P11.16 Capitalization policy. On January 2, 1995, Keystone Plc. replaced its truck and dolley system of moving product around its factory with a computerized conveyor system. The following information was available on that date:

Purchase price of new conveyor	$100,000
Book value of trucks and dolleys	4,000
Fair value of trucks and dolleys	10,000
Installation cost of new conveyor (primarily Keystone labor)	6,000

The small fleet of trucks and dolleys was sold for $10,000.

Required:

The new conveyor should be recorded at what amount?

P11.17 Accounting for fixed assets. Presented below are selected PP&E disclosures from a recent Manville Corporation annual report:

Manville Corporation
Consolidated Balance Sheets
December 31, 19X2 and 19X1
(thousands of dollars)

Assets	19X2	19X1
Current assets		
Cash (including time deposits of $5,742 in 19X2, $14,621 in 19X1)	$ 9,309	$ 19,180
Marketable securities, at cost (approximates market)	276,061	240,094
Receivables (net of allowances of $8,026 in 19X2, $8,998 in 19X1)		
Trade	254,302	233,303
Other	30,939	44,343
Inventories	164,398	140,886
Prepaid expenses	17,288	21,902
Total current assets	752,297	699,708
Property, plant, and equipment, at cost (Note 2c)		
Land and land improvements	93,395	97,202
Buildings	308,421	302,909
Machinery and equipment	1,120,733	1,056,009
	1,525,549	1,456,120
Less accumulated depreciation and depletion	512,590	471,868
	1,012,959	984,252
Timber and timberlands, less cost of timber harvested	391,886	395,004
Property, plant, and equipment, net	1,404,845	1,379,256
Other assets (principally long-term receivables)	181,002	174,298
	$2,338,144	$2,253,262

Note 2 — Summary of Significant Accounting Policies
Property, Plant, and Equipment, and Depreciation

Gains and losses from the normal retirement or replacement of property, plant, and equipment are reflected in accumulated depreciation with no effect on current period earnings. Gains and losses arising from abnormal dispositions are included in operations currently.

Depreciation and amortization are computed using the straight-line method based on estimated useful lives of the related assets. Depletion of mineral properties is calculated using the unit-of-production method. Expenditures for replacements and betterments are capitalized, while maintenance and repairs are charged against operations as incurred. The company is engaged in a reforestation program that was initiated in 1972. Currently, the company uses a 30-year rotation cycle, which will convert its natural forest to timber plantations over approximately the next 18 years. Cost of timber harvested is based on the unit cost rates calculated using the total estimated yield of timber to be harvested during the conversion period and the unamortized timber costs.

Manville Corporation
Schedule V — Property, Plant, and Equipment
for the Years Ended December 31
(thousands of dollars)

Classification	Balance at Beginning of Period	Additions at Cost	Retirements	Other Deductions*	Balance at End of Period
19X2					
Land, including mineral properties, and land improvements	$ 97,202	$ 3,342	$ 3,723	$ (426)	$ 96,395
Buildings	302,911	11,052	2,829	(2,713)	308,421
Machinery and equipment	1,056,007	100,674	26,101	(9,847)	1,120,733
	1,456,120	115,068	32,653	(12,986)	1,525,549
Timber and timberlands	395,004	6,701	22	(9,797)	391,886
	$1,851,124	$121,769	$ 32,675	$(22,783)	$1,917,435
19X1					
Land, including mineral properties, and land improvements	$ 108,002	$ 2,210	$ 12,590	$ (420)	$ 97,202
Buildings	331,802	6,718	32,462	(3,147)	302,911
Machinery and equipment	1,090,337	99,409	124,993	(8,746)	1,056,007
	1,530,141	108,337	170,045	(12,313)	1,456,120
Timber and timberlands	402,034	2,359	4	(9,385)	395,004
	$1,932,175	$110,696	$170,049	$(21,698)	$1,851,124
19X0					
Land, including mineral properties, and land improvements	$ 119,174	$ 1,237	$ 10,724	$ (1,685)	$ 108,002
Buildings	363,308	2,861	26,905	(7,462)	331,802
Machinery and equipment	1,202,490	53,348	139,488	(26,013)	1,090,337
	1,684,972	57,446	177,117	(35,160)	1,530,141
Timber and timberlands	406,205	3,837	581	(7,427)	402,034
	$2,091,177	$ 61,283	$177,698	$(42,587)	$1,932,175

*Includes the current year translation of the company's foreign operations and amounts for the cost of timber harvested.

3.

Building

BB 302,911	
Purchase 11,052	2829 Sales
	2713 MIS
308,421	

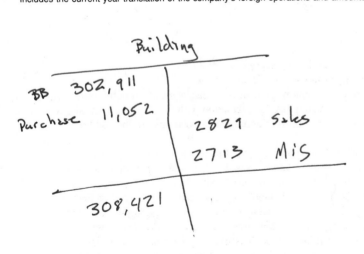

Manville Corporation
Schedule VI — Accumulated Depreciation, Depletion and Amortization of Property, Plant, and Equipment for the Years Ended December 31 (thousands of dollars)

Classification	Balance at Beginning of Period	Additions Charged to Costs and Expenses	Retirements	Other Charges Add (Deduct)*	Balance at End of Period
19X2					
Mineral properties and land improvements	$ 36,134	$ 2,624	$ 2,450	$ (115)	$ 36,193
Buildings	102,350	10,099	2,494	(859)	109,096
Machinery and equipment	333,384	56,852	20,370	(2,565)	367,301
	$471,868	$69,575	$ 25,314	$ (3,539)	$512,590
19X1					
Mineral properties and land improvements	$ 43,494	$ 2,761	$ 10,090	$ (31)	$ 36,134
Buildings	120,315	10,503	27,774	(694)	102,350
Machinery and equipment	382,903	55,395	102,920	(1,994)	333,384
	$546,712	$68,659	$140,784	$ (2,719)	$471,868
19X0					
Mineral properties and land improvements	$ 43,669	$ 3,435	$ 5,109	$ 1,499	$ 43,494
Buildings	113,225	11,535	14,067	9,622	120,315
Machinery and equipment	367,853	61,931	72,535	25,654	382,903
	$524,747	$76,901	$ 91,711	$ 36,775	$546,712

*Includes the current year translation of the company's foreign operations and in 19X0 includes $48,120 permanent impairment provision in the carrying amount of assets related to the company's open-pit mining operation at Asbestos, Quebec, Canada.

Required:

a. Explain the first two sentences in Manville's Note 2, Property, Plant, and Equipment, and Depreciation.

b. Prepare the entry to reflect Manville's 19X2 building retirements.

c. Between 19X1 and 19X2, the balance in Manville's buildings account increased by $5,512, yet 19X2 depreciation expense on the buildings was less than 19X1 building depreciation expense by $404. Explain how this could happen.

d. Why did Manville use the units-of-production method for mineral properties rather than the straight-line method?

e. If Manville spent $1,000 on betterments and $800 for maintenance, how would these transactions be recorded?

f. Explain why "timber and timberlands" are classified under property, plant, and equipment, not as inventory in the balance sheet.

g. According to Manville's Note 2, cost of timber harvested "is based on the unit cost rates calculated using the total estimated yield of timber to be harvested during the conversion period and the unamortized timber costs." Explain how this is accomplished.

P11.18 Analyzing income statement data. The top part of a recent Pioneer income statement is as follows:

	(In thousands)		
	19X2	19X1	19X0
Net sales	$874,871	$839,878	$884,726
Operating costs and expenses:			
Cost of goods sold	$399,464	$416,640	$426,768
Research and development	54,484	49,866	45,618
Selling	195,046	185,206	189,598
General and administrative	79,507	70,786	55,781
Restructuring and early retirement	—	—	12,913
Provision for plant closings	4,176	1,912	5,643
Loss on discontinued business	27,269	—	—
	$759,946	$724,410	$736,321
Operating income	$114,925	$115,468	$148,405

The top part of Pioneer's most recent cash flow statement is as follows:

	(in thousands)		
	19X2	19X1	19X0
Cash flows from operating activities			
Net income	$ 65,128	$ 53,939	$ 73,753
Noncash expenses included in net income:			
Depreciation	46,890	44,709	36,648
Amortization	3,023	2,924	3,055
Loss on disposal of property and equipment	7,044	4,962	6,919
Other	1,698	2,625	6,028
Foreign currency exchange losses	3,737	4,362	4,196
Change in assets and liabilities net of effects from purchase of subsidiaries:			
(Increase) in receivables	(17,343)	(16,995)	(36,272)
(Increase) decrease in inventories	41,427	22,655	(21,915)
Increase (decrease) in accounts payable and accrued expenses	26,614	(718)	22,281
Increase (decrease) in income taxes payable	11,102	(31,639)	4,137
Other prepaids, deferrals and accruals, net	(4,151)	10,153	(6,881)
Net cash provided by operating activities	$185,169	$ 96,977	$ 91,949
Cash flows from investing activities			
Purchase of property and equipment	$ (67,841)	$ (72,768)	$ (93,576)
Proceeds from sale of property and equipment	7,362	4,434	5,477
Purchase of subsidiaries, net of cash and cash equivalents acquired	(6,159)	—	(7,271)
Other	(4,390)	132	(1,059)
Net cash (used in) investing activities	$ (71,028)	$ (68,202)	$ (96,429)

On the 19X2 and 19X1 balance sheets, Pioneer included the following:

	(in thousands)	
Assets	19X2	19X1
Property and equipment	$ 46,457	$ 43,638
Buildings	237,298	214,368
Machinery and equipment	290,558	262,930
Construction in progress	12,451	27,008
	$586,764	$547,944
Less accumulated depreciation	201,285	170,781
	$385,479	$377,163

Required:

a. The cash flow statement shows $46.89 million for depreciation for 19X2, yet this figure does not seem to appear on the consolidated statements of income. Please explain.

b. This $46.89 million of depreciation does not seem to explain the change in the accumulated depreciation figures that exists between the 19X1 and 19X2 balance sheets. Please explain; use figures as necessary.

c. The purchase of property and equipment shown on the cash flow statement of $67.84 million in 19X2 does not agree with the change in the property, plant, and equipment figures between the 19X1 and 19X2 balance sheets. Please explain; use figures as necessary.

P11.19 Accounting for goodwill. In May 1994, the Swiss pharmaceutical company Roche Holdings Ltd. acquired Syntex Corporation (a U.S. company) for $5.3 billion. And one month later, Sandoz Ltd., another Swiss pharmaceutical company, offered $3.7 billion for Gerber Products Co.

According to analysts familiar with the two transactions, the purchases were motivated by two factors. First, a strong Swiss franc relative to the U.S. dollar made the acquisition of Syntex and Gerber appear relatively inexpensive despite the high U.S. dollar price tag. Second, a dramatic change in International Accounting Standards Committee (IASC) guidelines with respect to the accounting for goodwill would become effective at year-end 1994. (Goodwill refers to the amount paid for a company in excess of its fair market value. For example, Roche's offer price exceeded Syntex's fair market value by approximately $3.0 billion, and Sandoz's offer for Gerber exceeded that company's fair market value by about $2.0 billion.)

Prior to 1995, most European companies had a choice as to how they accounted for goodwill: They could either capitalize goodwill to the balance sheet and then amortize it against earnings, or they could write the goodwill off in total against existing shareholders' equity. Most European firms, including Roche and Sandoz, chose the latter method. Beginning in 1995, the charge-to-equity method would no longer be available for many European companies as part of the IASC's harmonization efforts.

Required:

a. What is the advantage of the charge-off method of accounting for goodwill to companies like Roche and Sandoz? Why would they prefer it to the alternative of capitalizing and amortizing goodwill?

b. How do U.S. companies account for goodwill?

c. Which method do you prefer, and why?

P11.20 International accounting. To facilitate the orderly flow of capital between international capital markets, the International Accounting Standards Committee (IASC) is attempting to harmonize the reporting practices followed in different countries. To understand why harmonization is important, it is first necessary to understand the financial effects produced by differing disclosure and reporting practices. This problem focuses on two controversial areas: the accounting for goodwill and for research and development costs.

Presented below are two different case scenarios. Analyze each scenario independently, and identify the financial statement effect of each alternative accounting or reporting practice.

Goodwill

Throughout the world, it is commonly accepted that "goodwill" is said to result when an acquiring company (the acquiror) purchases another company (the acquiree) and pays more than the fair market value for the acquiree's net assets. How this excess purchase price — or goodwill — is accounted for varies considerably from country to country. In the United States, for example, goodwill is capitalized to the acquiror's balance sheet and then is amortized off against earnings over the goodwill's expected useful life (but not in excess of 40 years). In the United Kingdom, however, goodwill is frequently charged off in total against an equity reserve account (usually the Profit and Loss Account) at the time of an acquisition. Contrary to both of these treatments, the IASC has proposed that when goodwill arises as a consequence of a merger or acquisition, it should be capitalized to the acquiror's balance sheet and then amortized against earnings over a period not to exceed 20 years, and preferably over only 5 years.

> **Scenario:** During 1991 the American Telephone and Telegraph Company (AT&T) made a successful acquisition bid for the NCR Corporation. The initial bid of $6.12 billion (U.S.) came at a time when NCR's net assets were reportedly worth $1.77 billion (U.S.).

Required:
Calculate the effect on AT&T's annual earnings of accounting for the NCR goodwill under each of the the above three approaches (the United States, the United Kingdom, and the IASC). Does the accounting treatment for goodwill affect the price that an acquiror would be willing to pay for an acquiree in a merger or acquisition?

Research and Development Costs

The accounting for research and development costs around the world is quite diverse. In some countries, such as the United States, all R&D costs must be expensed against earnings in the year in which they are incurred. In other countries, however, R&D costs may be capitalized to the balance sheet and then amortized against earnings over the expected period of benefit. Currently, the IASC has proposed to permit the capitalization of R&D costs if a company can prove that a market does (or will) exist for its proposed product.

> **Scenario:** The 1990 financial statements of Goodyear Tire and Rubber Company reveal that R&D costs deducted against earnings totaled $331.3 million, $303.3 million, and $304.8 million in 1990, 1989, and 1988, respectively.

Required:
Assume that the IASC proposal for R&D is implemented and that Goodyear is able to demonstrate that a market will exist for its proposed products. Calculate the aftertax dollar effect on Goodyear's 1989 and 1990 earnings assuming the capitalization of R&D costs. (Assume a tax rate of 50 percent).

CASES

C11.1 Fixed assets and natural resources: Salem Coal Company. Near the end of 1993, Andrew and Michael Miller formed the Salem Coal Company. According to the charter of incorporation, the purpose of the new business was to "locate, develop, extract, and transport" coal reserves in the state of West Virginia. The company remained closely held until January 1995, at which time a small public offering of common shares was held. According to the prospectus, the funds raised through the public offering would be used to acquire coal reserves and removal and transportation equipment and to construct miscellaneous facilities for the administration of the company's coal operations.

Approximately $4 million was raised through the offering and was dispersed during 1995 as follows:

1. In February, the Salem Coal Company paid $2.35 million for a tract of land in Grant District (Preston County) containing estimated coal reserves of 3.5 million tons. Following extraction and reclamation, it was anticipated that the land would have a resale value of $280,000 for agricultural purposes. In addition, the purchase price included a $50,000 reclamation bond that would be refunded if the reclamation work met certain standards established by the West Virginia Department of Natural Resources.
2. The following equipment was purchased:

Quantity	Item	Estimated Useful Life	Per Unit Price
1	Bulldozer	15 years	$195,000
1	Earthmover with dragline and stripping bucket	10 years	425,000
3	Dump trucks	5 years	75,000

The scrap value of the equipment at retirement was anticipated to be nominal. Signed checks for the equipment were delivered to the vendors on March 1.

3. A storage facility was constructed on the site at a cost of $150,000. It was anticipated that it would not be economically feasible to remove the building from the land after coal operations had terminated. In addition, it was uncertain whether the facilities might have alternative uses to subsequent landowners. Construction was completed by mid-May.

During May and June 1995, the company spent an additional $200,000 to prepare the site for operations. Finally, by mid-June, extraction operations began. By the end of 1995, 700,000 tons of coal had been mined and sold to the Monongahela Power Company at an average price of $15 per delivered ton.

Operating expenses (exclusive of depreciation and depletion) and selling and administrative expenses incurred in connection with the mining operations totaled $550,000.

Required:

a. Before financial statements can be prepared for the year ended December 31, 1995, a number of accounting policy decisions must be made. Prepare a list of those policy decisions and describe what accounting methods you would adopt and why. Assume that these decisions are to be made for financial reporting purposes only.

b. On the basis of your policy selections in part (a), prepare an income statement and a partial balance sheet as of December 31, 1995. Assume an average tax rate of 34 percent.

c. Assume that (1) coal producers are eligible for a 10 percent "statutory percentage depletion allowance" and (2) a firm may choose to deplete its natural resources for *tax purposes* using either a unit of production approach *or* the statutory percentage depletion approach. Which method should the Salem Coal Company use, and why?

C11.2 Amortization policy: Blockbuster Entertainment Corp. In May of 1989, Lee J. Seidler, a senior managing director and accounting analyst for Bear, Stearns & Co., issued a report critical of the accounting policies followed by Blockbuster Entertainment Corporation, the largest video store chain in the United States. In essence, Seidler suggested that Blockbuster's stock price was overvalued because of various questionable accounting policies used by the company. A portion of Seidler's comments are produced (with permission) below:

Have You Ever Seen a 40-Year-Old Video Store?

Some of Blockbuster's mergers have been accounted for as purchases, others as poolings of interests. Pooling is usually more attractive, but Blockbuster Video (BV) takes most of the sting out of purchase accounting.

In a merger treated as a purchase, the price paid is first allocated to the fair values of assets that can be kicked, picked up, or painted. Any excess becomes goodwill, which Blockbuster labels "intangible assets relating to acquired businesses." APB Opinion No. 17 requires that goodwill be amortized to income over 40 years or less.

In the past, many companies automatically adopted 40-year amortization. Current practice, which is usually required by the SEC, is to relate the amortization period to the nature of the business acquired. Thus, in a typical hi-tech acquisition the SEC requires goodwill to be amortized over five to seven years; in bank purchases, over 15 to 20 years.

Have you ever seen a 40-year-old videotape store? Will you ever see one? It is difficult to support the notion that goodwill associated with a videotape store has a life of more than a few years. The 10-K notes:

Both the company and a franchise owner have relocated a number of Blockbuster Video Superstores during the three-year period ended December 31, 1988.

Reiterating this point, eight (of 80) company-owned stores that appeared in the 1987 10-K are not in the 1988 list. The maximum term of the company's franchise agreement is 25 years.

There is no "correct" amortization period for this goodwill. Our guess is that five years would be reasonable for videotape stores. More important, we suspect that if the SEC considers this item it will require BV to bring its amortization period into this range. Applying five-year amortization to BV's goodwill, rather than 40, would reduce 1988 EPS by $0.14.

Stretching Videotape Amortization Way Out

BV drastically slowed its amortization of "hit" videotapes at the start of 1988. The change raised 1988 EPS $0.11, of a total of $0.57. In 1989 we estimate the change will add another $0.13 to EPS.

Analysis of the impacts of the change is complicated by BV's confusing disclosure. The 1988 Form 10-K describes 1987 amortization differently than 1987 amortization was described in the original 1987 10-K. Discussions with the company clarified matters.

In 1987 BV amortized its rental videotapes of hits, which are 20 percent to 25 percent of total inventory, over nine months straight-line. At the start of 1988, it switched to 36 months accelerated. The financial statements do not disclose how accelerated the curve is, but the company says it uses 150 percent of straight-line, computed on a monthly basis.

The resulting amortization is not very accelerated. The cost of hit tapes is amortized as follows:

First 12 months	40%
Second 12 months	30%
Third 12 months	30%

This is pretty close to straight-line. In effect, BV quadrupled the life of hit tapes.

BV seemed to imply that the longer amortization was demanded by the SEC, a comment that we doubt and that did not appear in the 10-K describing the change. Note that nine months is not necessarily right nor 36 months wrong. The right period (and curve) is the one that approximates revenue flows. By that standard, this curve seems slow for hit tapes.

Even with the slower curve, BV's 1989 earnings will face much higher amortization expense. In 1988 amortization was $15.7 million, mainly caused by purchases of $15.6 million of tapes in 1987. In 1988 the company purchased $53.6 million of tapes. We estimate that the 1989 amortization will total $38 million (excluding charges from merged companies). That increase in amortization will require a substantial increase in tape rental revenue to maintain earnings.

Bear Stearn's analyst Steve Eisenberg suggests the necessary growth may not be forthcoming. Videotape "rental tape" shipments for the total industry grew at an average 57 percent annual rate in the 1984–1988 period. Eisenberg predicts only 8.2 percent annual growth in 1989–1993.

Blockbuster EPS Recalculated

Following the adjustments proposed by Seidler, Blockbuster's 1988 earnings per share would be restated as follows:

EPS, as originally reported	$ 0.57
Less: Adjustment for faster goodwill amortization	(0.14)
Adjustment for change in tape amortization	(0.11)
Restated EPS	$ 0.32

In response to Seidler's report, Blockbuster's shares plunged $3.375 a share to $30⅛. On the following day, the share price fell another $3.875 a share to close at $26¼.

Required:

Evaluate Seidler's arguments with respect to the Blockbuster accounting policies. Do you agree with him? If so, why? If not, why not? Assuming that the market received no other information, do you agree that the price of the Blockbuster stock should have fallen by $7.25 per share following Seidler's report?

C11.3 Depreciation policy: Freshman Products. Freshman Products International specializes in injection-molded, plastic trim parts for the auto industry (dash board knobs, etc.), supplying the Big Three U.S. companies and the domestic plants of the Japanese companies. Because of Freshman's reputation for service, one of the Big Three automakers asked if the company would bid on a new part — the pinch welt, which finishes off the inside edge of the door frame. Each car has at least 15 feet of that trim (it's about an inch in diameter), and all manufacturers use the same basic product. Even in a modest year, the industry requires about 40,000 miles of the welt. There are several welt manufacturers who already service the market, but all are subsidiaries of much larger companies. Freshman management believes that they can be successful with this new product by applying their brand of customer attention, thereby setting themselves apart from their competition.

The welt, however, is an extruded part, and Freshman has no experience with extruded plastics and has no extruding equipment. Two extruding machines would be required to handle the volumes required by the bid, and they are estimated to cost $250,000 each. Used machines are available at less cost, but the new equipment is more energy efficient. There is excess space in the plant for this project, but the floor would have to be strengthened if the heavy extrusion equipment were to be moved in. Cost of the floor reinforcement would be $50,000. Shipping the new machines to the Freshman plant would likely cost $25,000; installation would probably cost $50,000; lighting in the new machine area would have to be improved at a cost of $30,000.

Extruded parts, like injected parts, are produced by the basic machine working on a die. The tool and die makers estimated that the two welt dies required for the extrusion machines would cost about $50,000 each.

The company uses straight-line depreciation in its financial reports prepared for the banks. Management has estimated a 30-year life on the plant (now 15 years old) and has set a six-year life for all equipment because the injection machines (which are the biggest component of that asset class) tend to wear out over that period due to completing 100 stamping cycles an hour. Dies are depreciated over three years, not because they wear out, but because the customer product cycle runs about that long. All equipment and dies are assumed to have a 10 percent salvage value.

For tax purposes, the building is depreciated on the same basis and uses the same life as in the financial statements. The equipment and the dies are depreciated on the double-declining-balance (DDB) method for taxes, using the same lives as for the financial statements.

The manufacturer of the extrusion equipment claims that it will last at least 10 years with normal maintenance — the extrusion process is evidently not as self-destructive as is the injection process. The pinch welt is a generic product, which has been unchanged for at least the last 12 years: the auto companies have redesigned interiors a number of times recently, but they have continued to use the same welt design as they did when the product was first introduced. Freshman has never used a die for its complete physical life and so does not know how long these new welt extrusion dies might last. The tool and die makers have said that their best guess would be about five years.

Required:

Part 1

a. What depreciable life would you use for:

(1) The extrusion machines? Why?

(2) The other costs to be incurred in connection with the acquisition of those machines? Why?

(3) The dies to be used in the extrusion process? Why?

b. Would you recommend using the same depreciation lives and methods for the tax returns and for the financial statements? Please explain your answer.

Part 2

Without regard to the answers you gave in *Part 1*, assume that the dies are depreciated on a straight-line method over *five* years for financial statement purposes and on a DDB method over *three* years for tax purposes. Calculate the depreciation expense for each of those five years, for book and for tax.

	Year 1	Year 2	Year 3	Year 4	Year 5
Depreciation expense per books	______	______	______	______	______
Depreciation expense per tax return	______	______	______	______	______

Part 3

c. Assuming that income before depreciation on the dies and before tax expense was $100,000 in each year, prepare the book entries to record the dies' depreciation expense *and* the tax expense for Year 1. (Assume a 34 percent tax rate.)

C11.4 Accounting for noncurrent assets: three examples.*

I. General Motors' Depreciation Policy Revisions

On October 28, 1987, both the *New York Times* and *The Wall Street Journal* published articles that discussed General Motors corporation (GM) at considerable length. The majority of the discussion in each article was devoted to GM's third-quarter earnings announcement. The announcement included details of a change in financial reporting policies.

Specifically, GM announced that it was lengthening estimates of the remaining service lives of its plant, equipment, and special tools for financial reporting purposes. GM indicated that the new assumptions were better estimates of the useful lives of its capital investments and were more similar to those used by Ford and Chrysler.

GM's change in accounting estimates was made retroactive to the beginning of 1987, and the year's cumulative effect to date would be included in the company's third-quarter income. Net income for the third quarter would be a reported $812 million; however, excluding the effects of the accounting change, GM would have reported an operating loss of $537 million. As a result of overproduction of cars and the use of expensive incentives to clear out backlogged inventories, GM would have recorded its third consecutive third-quarter operating loss had the accounting change not been made. And the current third-quarter loss would have been the company's largest ever reported.

Analysts gave GM's accounting change mixed reviews. Harvey E. Heinbach, an analyst with Merrill Lynch & Company, was quoted as saying "there is no doubt they were more conservative than the industry, and this brings them into line with other companies. It troubles me, though, that they are doing it to mask disappointing operating performance."

Other items covered in the articles included a discussion of GM's recent contract with the United Auto Workers union, a change in the company's sales mix toward less profitable models, declining market share, and cost reduction efforts. It was also pointed out that recent earnings announcements by Ford and Chrysler revealed a growth in profitability for both companies.

Exhibit 1 contains stock data for dates surrounding the announcement of the accounting change.

Required:

a. What might GM have been trying to accomplish with the accounting change?

b. What are the possible economic effects of such a change?

---

*This case was prepared by Thomas I. Selling.

EXHIBIT 1

Opening GM Share Prices and DJIA Indices (10/26/87–10/30/87)

Date	GM Common	Percentage Change	DJIA	Percentage Change
10/26/87	$57.50	—	1793.93	—
10/27/87	55.50	−3.478%	1846.49	2.930
10/28/87	59.375	6.982	1846.82	0.018
10/29/87	57.875	−2.526	1938.33	4.955
10/30/87	59.125	2.160	1993.53	2.848
11/2/87	58.875	−0.423	2014.09	1.031

II. GM Takes a Big Write-Off Related to Plant Closing

The October 29, 1990, "Heard on the Street" column of *The Wall Street Journal* reported rumors that GM would reclassify four plants from "indefinitely idled" status to "permanently closed." If this were to be the case, accounting recognition of $1 billion or more in write-offs would reduce the company's third-quarter net income. Analysts estimated that GM would earn approximately $109 million in the quarter before any such special charges.

The article indicated that the write-offs "would be welcome by most analysts" because they would signal that GM was "tackling some overdue housecleaning." In addition, there was some concern that if the write-offs weren't sufficient, more write-offs would be needed in the future. There was also some speculation that three additional plant closings might be announced.

Two days later, GM announced it would charge off $2.1 billion to cover the closing of seven plants in the United States and Canada. Three plants would not begin closing until the end of 1991. GM chairman Robert Stempel said that the closings were a "major element in GM's long-term strategic plan to improve the competitiveness and profitability of its North American operations." The company's chief financial officer, Robert T. O'Connell, indicated that the huge write-offs cover all foreseeable circumstances and include plant closings that won't actually occur for two or three years.

Exhibit 2 contains stock price data for dates surrounding the events just described.

Required:

a. Compare these 1990 developments to those that occurred in 1987.

b. Why do you think these decisions were made? What do you think GM is trying to accomplish?

III. Software Development Costs

Anyone who owns or uses a computer can have some appreciation of the recent rapid growth of the computer software industry. As a result of this growth, a wide variety of accounting practices emerged among software developers that give rise to large differences in the content of financial reports. *Statement of Financial Accounting Standards No. 86 (SFAS No. 86),* "Accounting for the Costs of Computer Software to Be Sold, Leased, or Otherwise Marketed" was released in August 1985 in response to the growing need for guidelines in this area.

SFAS No. 86 provides that costs incurred prior to the time that technological feasibility of software is achieved are to be expensed as R&D. Additional costs incurred toward achieving a "product master" are to be capitalized as a noncurrent asset and amortized over future periods.

EXHIBIT 2

Opening GM Share Prices and DJIA Indices (10/25/90–10/30/90)

Date	GM Common	Percent Change	DJIA	Percent Change
10/25/90	$38.625	—	2484.16	—
10/26/90	38.25	–0.971	2436.14	–1.933%
10/27/90	37.25	–2.614	2430.2	–0.244
10/28/90	37.00	–0.671	2448.02	0.733
10/29/90	36.625	–1.014	2442.33	–0.232
10/30/90	36.75	0.341	2454.95	0.517
10/31/90	36.875	0.340	2490.84	1.462

Costs incurred beyond this point of development are to be treated as production costs (that is, charged to inventory and flowed through to cost of sales as the software is sold). A review of the state of affairs in accounting for software costs prior to the issuance of *SFAS No. 86* was provided on April 4, 1984, by the following *Wall Street Journal* article:

Software Firms Debate Method of Accounting by Lee Berton

A battle is raging in the computer industry that could spell success or failure for many of the nation's fledgling computer software companies.

The battle isn't over complex technological fare, such as "windowing" or "user friendliness," but over complex accounting fare like "capitalization" and "expensing." The question is whether the computer programs that the companies lease or license are assets or expenses.

Most software companies treat the programs as expenses, so they deduct all development costs from profits in the year those costs are incurred. But a growing number of software companies treat the software as assets. That allows them to capitalize the costs, deducting them from profits slowly over several years.

The Financial Accounting Standards Board, the chief rule-making body for accountants, will begin considering which approach to endorse when it meets today. Gregory Ray, a project manager for the FASB, concedes that the software accounting question will not be easy to resolve. "It's got so many ramifications involving the bottom line, taxes, and borrowing power that we want to make sure we make a decision that makes accounting sense and leads to more comparable financial reporting," he says.

For software companies that capitalize the costs, a change that would force them to expense more — or expense completely — could cut deeply into earnings. International Business Machines Corporation, for example, capitalizes only a small portion of its software costs. But if it couldn't capitalize any of the costs, the company's 1983 per-share earnings would drop to $8.60 from the $9.04 it reported.

For a company such as Compserve Corporation, an Eagan, Minnesota, software company that capitalizes a major portion of its software development costs, the effect would be much more dramatic. Compserve reported a profit of $1.6 million, or 49 cents a share, in 1982, but would have had a loss of more than $3 million had it deducted all such costs from income immediately.

"Expensing or capitalizing software costs is probably one of the most important bottom-line issues for the rapidly growing software industry today," says Alfred R. Berkeley, managing director of Alex, Brown & Sons, an investment banking firm active in public financing of software companies.

Last August, the Securities and Exchange Commission banned the use of capitalizing software costs, unless the company had previously done it, until the FASB resolves the question. The SEC felt that capitalizing gave too many companies an opportunity to create instant earnings — by reducing reported expenses — and that it was leading to too much diversity in financial reporting in the software industry.

Some fledgling software companies have been capitalizing software development costs because such a move enables them to list the development costs as an asset on their balance sheets. They can then borrow against that asset. A survey by the National Association of Accountants, an organization of management accountants, shows that bank lending officers are much more likely to lend money to software companies that capitalize.

Still, many companies prefer to use the expense method, and they are worried that the FASB will force a change. Policy Management Systems Corporation, a Columbia, South Carolina, software producer, deducts all software planning, design, and construction costs in the year they're incurred. "We think it's very difficult to prove that software is a tangible asset like a building, and capitalization gives companies so many choices that earnings comparisons would be impossible," says G. Larry Wilson, the company's president.

Other companies prefer expensing because it reduces profits — and, therefore, taxes. Abraham Paznanski, treasurer of Computer Associates International, Inc., a small Jerico, New York, software company, expenses its development costs. "We are now getting the tax benefits of reporting lower earnings," he says. For the year ended March 31, 1983, Computer Associates reported earnings of 64 cents a share. If it had capitalized 50 percent of its software development costs, its per-share net would have jumped to 89 cents a share.

Some companies have been able to get that tax benefit while at the same time capitalizing the development costs. That's because the Internal Revenue Service allows software companies that capitalize some development costs to deduct all those costs for tax purposes in the year they're incurred. In other words, these companies keep two sets of books — one for tax purposes, the other for reporting to shareholders.

Specialists in the field worry that, if the FASB opts for mandatory capitalization of part of these costs, the IRS might tell companies that they can't treat the development costs differently for tax purposes, forcing the companies to report higher earnings and pay more taxes.

"It could be a very logical position for the IRS to take that, if software is judged to be physical property and is amortized or depreciated, earnings are therefore higher and taxes should be, too," says Mr. Berkeley.

The IRS is remaining mum on the subject. But an IRS public hearing on the tax treatment of software is scheduled for May 21, 22, and 23, and such questions could come up.

Source: *The Wall Street Journal*, April 4, 1984. Reprinted by permission of *The Wall Street Journal* ©1984, Dow Jones & Co., Inc. All Rights Reserved Worldwide.

Required:

a. What issues are raised by *The Wall Street Journal* article?

b. Do you think that *SFAS No. 86* resulted in improved accounting for software companies?

C11.5 American Toy Company — The Zapper.* Karen McNeely, general manager of the Modern Toy Division of American Toy Company, had just met with her design engineering staff regarding their proposed new laser toy, the Zapper. They had presented an exciting and persuasive argument that the toy was a surefire hit from both production and market standpoints. Ms. McNeely had been convinced of the merits of the project and was now preparing new budget pro formas for the division that included the Zapper line prior to sending a formal request for funds to the chief financial officer of American Toy. She was specifically interested in what effect putting the toy into production would have on the asset book value base and net income of her division. If successful, the new laser toy could significantly help Ms. McNeely meet her division's return-on-assets goal for the current fiscal year, now a little over a week old.

American Toy

American Toy Company, a midsized toy manufacturer based in Denver, Colorado, produced toys for a wide range of age groups. The company developed ideas for toys and often adapted general-purpose machines to produce complementary toys for its established lines in successful or promising markets.

American Toy had been very successful in the past five years. Sales had increased from $11.6 million to just over $40 million; the sales-to-assets ratio was currently 0.96; and net income on last year's $40.132 million in sales was $2.849 million, for a 7.1 percent return on sales.

The company was conservatively capitalized with a bank debt–to–total equity ratio of 0.15. Existing company policy for depreciation of fixed assets was to use the straight-line method over an asset's economic life. The company's tax rate on profits was 34 percent.

Zapper

Zapper would be another product in a line of light-activated personal combat toys known to most consumers as laser tag toys. A fairly simple toy to produce, it consisted of a light-generating device (LGD) powered by replaceable batteries housed inside a pressure-formed plastic housing shaped to resemble a futuristic gun. The LGD was activated by applying pressure to the "trigger," which sent a thin beam of light toward wherever the gun was aimed. A "kill" was scored when the beam of light hit a sensor, usually worn by an opponent on his or her chest. Most of the existing products on the market had an effective range of approximately 25 yards. The range of the Zapper would be 60 yards under ideal conditions.

To make Zapper, American Toy would need to purchase a rather sophisticated piece of machinery to produce the LGDs. With the attachments and modifications necessary to produce at the high volume required by the operating plan, the machine would cost $520,000 delivered. Wiring and lighting modifications to the factory to accommodate the machine would total $19,000. Installation of a vent and hood for part of the line (to vent unpleasant fumes from part of the process, which included an acid treatment) would cost $11,000. Conversion of a previously unused portion of the factory to a warehouse for storing the finished products before shipping would cost $25,000.

While the new warehouse section would be usable for any subsequent products introduced by American Toy, the LGD machine would not be adaptable for any other use and would have virtually no salvage value. The warehouse alterations were not expected to increase the salvage value of the factory. Salvage values on other, more general-use machinery were estimated to be 10 percent of their respective costs, while salvage values on special-purpose machines historically equaled their removal costs.

The manufacturing process would also require the use of a six-year-old plastic-molding machine (originally purchased to produce a toy that had since been discontinued), which had been idle for six months. The machine (#12 molder) had cost $455,000 when new and was thought to have had a 10-year economic life. It was also considered to have a scrap value of $45,000. To adapt the machine to produce the Zapper, it would be modified to handle larger pieces. The cost of those modifications was estimated to be $30,000, and the modifications would probably not change the machine's salvage value.

In addition, a packaging machine would be required. Although American Toy's packaging lines were currently operating almost at full capacity, Ms. McNeely knew there was a packaging machine (#164 packager) being used intermittently for overflow work in a different part of the warehouse. The machine had been moved to its present location when the new packaging line was designed and installed three years previously. As far as the production staff could ascertain, it still functioned well, albeit more slowly than the new line. The machine was now 12 years old and was fully depreciated. Expenditures to move the machine into position for use on the Zapper line and to perform initial setup tests would cost $8,000.

Ms. McNeely had investigated purchasing a new packager, but the price was over $420,000. Thus she decided that as long as the old machine could be placed into service, she would recommend that alternative.

Financial Considerations

The effect of Zapper on her division's return on assets was important to Karen McNeely. The Modern Toy Division's ROA for the previous year was 5.68 percent, and Ms. McNeely hoped that new projects would help her improve that return.* Her forecasts for divisional sales for the next two years were $10,002,700 and $11,703,200, respectively. Of these amounts, she estimated Zapper would contribute $840,000 and $1,741,500. The division's fixed assets for the previous year are given in Exhibit 1; divisional financial statements are in Exhibit 2.

Ms. McNeely knew that net income and the asset base could be significantly affected by decisions regarding which costs to include in the basis of an asset, the depreciation method chosen, the economic life of the asset in question, and the salvage value assigned to the asset. Last year at a local university's executive management program, she had learned the potential advantages and disadvantages of the most commonly accepted depreciation methods — such as straight-line, declining-balance, and sum-of-the-years' digits. She was considering which one of these to adopt for the Zapper-related fixed asset additions when she heard that another American Toy general manager had recently proposed the adoption of the unit-of-production method for his division; so Ms. McNeely made a mental note to talk with him that afternoon about the advantages of that method over the other commonly used methods.

She was uncertain what life the machines should be assigned. She had been told by the company producing the LGD machine that she could expect a 10-year physical life, at least, for the machine, and she had been told by the controller that the asset recovery period for tax purposes should be five years. She also knew, however, that the average product life cycle for toys was only three years; some lasted only six months, while a few (such as Etch A Sketch™ and Hoola Hoops™) lasted 25 years or more. The Product Design Group of American Toy estimated that a purchaser could expect the Zapper, with normal use, to operate for approximately 18 months. She wondered which of these lives would be appropriate for the assets under consideration.

Ms. McNeely also needed to consider the possibility of not producing the toy. In this case, the division would not need the idle plastic molder. The molder, which had a current market value of $188,000, had been purchased six years ago through an unsecured line of credit from First National Bank. That line had been converted to an unsecured term loan and currently had an outstanding balance of $154,796. If Zapper were not produced, she planned to sell the idle molder.

All these decisions could potentially affect the reported profitability of both Ms. McNeely's division and the company. Each decision involved several considerations, and she needed to have her recommendations ready for the weekly managers' meeting in the morning.

*Managers at American Toy were evaluated on the basis of the achieved ROA for their business unit compared with a projected ROA negotiated and agreed upon by the unit manager and his or her supervisor. Below the corporate level, American Toy computed ROA by dividing business unit profit before taxes (PBT) by average total assets employed, and any adjustments for the cumulative effect of a change in accounting principle did not need to be considered.

EXHIBIT 1

American Toy Company — The Zapper
Modern Toy Division Fixed Asset Ledger
(End of Latest Fiscal Year)

Asset	Age (years)	Original Cost	Book Value	Economic Life (Years)	Year's Depr.
#12 molder	6	$ 455,000	$ 209,000	10	$ 41,000
High-speed packager	3	1,140,000	986,100	20	51,300
Wood lathes	4	210,000	102,000	7	27,000
Metal presses	6	1,185,000	545,100	10	106,650
#6 molders	2	1,896,000	1,213,440	5	341,280
Electro-former	1	100,000	75,000	4	25,000
#164 packager	12	348,000	34,800	10	-0-
Misc. tools	7	135,000	72,000	15	9,000
Fork lifts	2	138,000	88,320	5	24,840
Building	7	1,970,000	1,473,560	25	70,920
		$7,577,000	$4,799,320		$696,990

EXHIBIT 2

American Toy Company — The Zapper
Modern Toy Division Financial Statements
(for Most Recent Fiscal Year)

Sales	$8,427.7
Cost of goods sold	5,225.2
Gross margin	3,202.5
Selling, general, and administrative	1,953.5
Depreciation	697.0
Profit before tax	$ 552.0
Current assets	$5,012.3*
Plant assets	4,799.3
Total assets	$9,811.6
Current liabilities	$2,179.3
Equity from parent	7,632.3
Total liabilities and equity	$9,811.6

*Because of corporate policy, cash is not included in this total.

Required:

Help Ms. McNeely decide the best course of action.

CHAPTER 12

Accounting for Liabilities: Basic Concepts, Payables, Accruals, and Interest-Bearing Debt

Many companies are beginning to examine the notion that they ultimately will be responsible for the costs of recycling and final disposition of their products, a responsibility variously labeled life-cycle assessment, take-back principle, or cradle-to-grave responsibility. The related notion of full cost accounting requires companies to gather all of the costs related to a product, including the environmental costs, and apply them to both products and divisions.[1]

Key Chapter Issues

- When does an obligation become a liability and how are liabilities valued?
- What obligations are not recognized in financial statements and why?
- Why are some liabilities recorded at present value when others are not?
- Which liabilities are only estimated as opposed to being measured and why?
- What are contingent liabilities and how are they described in the financial statements?
- What are the special problems of valuing interest-bearing debt?
- What are derivatives and how are they recorded or described?

[1]Marc Epstein, "Environmentally Responsible Corporations," *Management Accounting,* April 1994, p. 74.

As discussed in previous chapters, assets are the tangible and intangible resources owned or controlled by an entity. They represent the *uses* of cash and other funds of the firm. The *sources* of these funds are the entity's liabilities and owners' equity. Thus, when one looks at the assets on the balance sheet and wonders, "Where did the money for these assets come from?" the answer is that part came from the owners — the owners' equity — and the rest came from creditors — the liabilities. Creditors are any parties to which an entity owes money or other consideration and may include lenders, suppliers, employees, or governmental agencies (such as the IRS). For many corporations, creditors are the largest source of funding. For example, as of December 31, 1994, more than 72 percent of PepsiCo's assets were funded by creditors.

Corporate liabilities present a number of accounting and valuation problems. Some liabilities are current and must be paid within a few days; others may extend 50 years or more. Some are for definite amounts that can be established from invoices, employment agreements, tax filings, and other documents; others, such as the provisions for anticipated warranty expenses, pensions, lawsuits, and deferred taxes, can only be estimated.

The purpose of this chapter is to consider the questions "What liabilities does a company have?" and "How should those liabilities be valued?" The three types of liabilities that present the most difficult valuation issues are saved for Chapter 13; these include leases, pensions, and deferred income taxes. As we shall see in this chapter, in theory, *all* liabilities are to be reported at the present value of their related cash outflows. In reality, however, only some obligations are actually valued in this way. Students unfamiliar with the concept of present value, or the calculation of discounted cash flows, are urged to review Appendix A of this chapter before proceeding.

CONCEPTUAL OVERVIEW

Every entity has a variety of obligations; only some of these are recognized in the financial statements as liabilities. Obligations are recognized as liabilities when they can be determined with reasonable precision, cannot be avoided, and are created by an event that has already occurred. Obligations that do *not* meet these three tests include, for example, a signed, binding contract to purchase certain products when the goods have not been received and a lawsuit for which damages have not yet been assessed.

As a general rule, short-term liabilities are recorded at their **face amount** (such as the amount printed on a bank note or an invoice), and long-term liabilities are recorded at their **present value** (that is, the value *today* of receiving — or paying — a given sum of money). Although the conventional practice is to ignore present values on relatively short-term items such as accounts payable and accrued expenses payable (because the difference between the present value and face value of such a claim is usually insignificant), some current liabilities (such as the current portion of a mortgage payable) are nevertheless reported at their present values. Conversely, most long-term liabilities are carried at their present values, but a few are not, as shown in Exhibit 12.1.

CURRENT LIABILITIES: PAYABLES AND ACCRUALS

Current liabilities are those obligations to be repaid during the next year or during the next operating cycle (if longer than a year in length). All other liabilities are noncurrent.

EXHIBIT 12.1

A Taxonomy of Liabilities

	Current liabilities	Noncurrent liabilities
Valued at face amounts	Accounts payable Accrued expenses Income taxes payable Dividends payable Unearned revenue Warranty obligations	Unearned revenue Warranty obligations
Valued at present value	Loans payable Current portion: Notes payable Bonds payable Leases payable	Loans payable Notes payable Bonds payable Leases payable Pension obligations
Shown at some other value	Deferred taxes	Deferred taxes Other liablilties

Accounts payable are the normally recurring obligations of a business for the purchase of materials, parts, fuel, and other items used in manufacturing or for purchases of merchandise to be resold, as in retailing. These liabilities are the easiest to value because an invoice or electronic transmission from the supplier provides the exchange price, and a receiving report from within the company indicates proper receipt of the item(s). The primary accounting policy issue a business entity faces here is whether to record the payable at its *gross* or *net* value.

If the merchandise is purchased for $10,000 and the payment terms are 2/10, net 30, the firm may pay the net amount ($9,800) within 10 days (that is, net of the 2 percent discount), or it must pay the gross amount of $10,000 within 30 days. The transaction to record the cash disbursement is relatively straightforward, but how should the company record the liability originally? Companies typically choose one accounting policy and follow it for all such purchases, even if they sometimes take the discount but do not at other times. If a company chooses to use the **gross method** (that is, all purchases are initially recorded at the gross amount), when a discount is taken, the amount is recorded in the Purchase Discount account and appears on the income statement as miscellaneous revenue or as a reduction to the cost of sales. If, on the other hand, the **net method** is used (that is, all purchases are initially recorded at the net amount), when a discount is missed because the entity did not pay on time, an expense entry to an account such as Purchase Discounts Lost or Interest Expense is generated. The latter is the most common policy in large firms. It is typically called the "sore thumb" choice because any discounts lost are highlighted.

Using the example just discussed, the transactions would be recorded as follows:

Gross method

At the time of purchase:

Dr. Inventory (A)	(inc.) 10,000	
Cr. Accounts Payable (L)		(inc.) 10,000

If the discount is taken:

miscellaneous revenue

Dr. Accounts Payable (L)	(dec.) 10,000	
Cr. Cash (A)		(dec.) 9,800
Cr. Purchase Discounts (R)		(inc.) 200

If the discount is not taken, the liability is satisfied by a cash payment of $10,000.

Net method

At the time of purchase:

Dr. Inventory (A)	(inc.) 9,800	
Cr. Accounts Payable (L)		(inc.) 9.800

If the discount is taken, as is assumed by this method, the liability is satisfied by a payment of $9,800. If the discount is not taken, the entry looks like this:

Interest Expense

Dr. Accounts Payable (L)	(dec.) 9,800	
Dr. Purchase Discounts Lost (E)	(inc.) 200	
Cr. Cash (A)		(dec.) 10,000

Accrued expenses payable includes the obligations to employees for wages earned but not paid, the employer's portion of any salary or wage taxes due the government, and any amounts accrued for interest or rent expense. For example, if a company owes $15,000 for computer rental charges but payment is not due for another 10 days, the amount would be accrued by the following entry:

Dr. Computer Rental Expense (E)	(inc.) 15,000	
Cr. Accrued Expenses Payable (L)		(inc.) 15,000

Payables and accruals, including current income taxes payable and dividends payable, are valued at their face amounts, not at their present value. The time and trouble to determine their present value is generally not worth the effort for such a slight difference in value (and it would be needlessly confusing to many readers of financial statements). For example, the present value of the $15,000 of accrued computer rentals due in 10 days is $14,959.02, assuming a discount rate of 10 percent. The purist might argue that this amount should be recorded as the liability, with the difference of $40.98 recorded as interest expense. Fortunately for both the readers of financial statements and the preparers, this practice is not followed unless the amounts are material.

Unearned revenue (or deferred income) is another current liability not usually reported at its present value; rather, it is shown at the amount received less whatever has been taken into income (earned) to date. For example, when an airline sells a ticket for $1,000 cash 30 days in advance of a scheduled flight, the transaction is recorded as follows:

Dr. Cash (A)	(inc.) 1,000	
Cr. Unearned Revenue (L)		(inc.) 1,000

Because the service has not yet been rendered, the revenue has not been earned and thus cannot be recognized. When the passenger actually takes the flight and the airline receives the flight coupon, the transaction is recorded as follows:

Dr. Unearned Revenue (L)	(dec.) 1,000	
Cr. Revenue (R)		(inc.) 1,000

Warranty obligations arise when a company sells a product and agrees to repair it and/or provide certain other services if the product fails. An automobile manufacturer, for example, may guarantee free repairs for four years or 60,000 miles, whichever comes first (it also may provide a loaner car while the repairs are being made). The accounting challenge for such obligations is one of *matching*. The sale is recorded when the buyer takes delivery of the car, but the repairs may not occur until some time far into the future. To match expenses with related revenues and avoid overstating income at the time of sale, the warranty costs associated with each car sale are estimated. These estimates are based on historical analysis, engineering assessments, and management judgment. At the time of sale or at the end of the sale's accounting period, an entry to record the expected warranty obligation is made:

Dr. Warranty Expense (E)	(inc.) 500	
Cr. Estimated Warranty Obligation (L)		(inc.) 500

When a cash payment is made by a dealer for warranty services provided to a customer, the following entry is made:

Dr. Estimated Warranty Obligation (L)	(dec.) 100	
Cr. Cash (A)		(dec.) 100

Note that this accrual-oriented method to account for warranties has the effect of reflecting the *total* estimated warranty obligation and the *total* estimated warranty costs at the time of the sale. Hence, there will be no income statement impact in future periods for this particular car when warranty repairs are actually made. From time to time, adjustments are necessary to the estimating procedures to ensure that the total outstanding warranty obligation is a reasonable approximation of the total warranty costs yet to be incurred.

Exhibit 12.2, taken from PepsiCo's 1994 annual report, illustrates a typical format for reporting current liabilities. With the exception of short-term borrowings, each of the current liabilities is shown at its actual or face amount without considering its present value. PepsiCo's footnotes provide further information about these current obligations — for example, the composition of the short-term borrowings and the income taxes due to federal, state, or foreign taxation authorities.

EXHIBIT 12.2

PepsiCo, Inc., and Subsidiaries
Current Liabilities Section
As of December 31, 1994 and December 25, 1993
(in millions)

	1994	1993
Current Liabilities		
Accounts payable	**$1,451.6**	$1,390.0
Accrued compensation and benefits	**753.5**	726.0
Short-term borrowings	**678.5**	2,191.2
Income taxes payable	**671.7**	823.7
Accrued marketing	**546.2**	400.9
Other current liabilities	**1,168.9**	1,043.1
Total Current Liabilities	**5,270.4**	6,574.9

LOANS, BILLS, NOTES, AND BONDS

Loans and securities are two basic types of interest-bearing debt. *Loans* are monetary agreements between two parties. The parties negotiate and sign an agreement that sets forth the terms and conditions of the loan. Loans may be of a short duration or may extend for many years. Although almost anyone can borrow or lend money, commercial banks are typically the primary source of business loans for short and intermediate-term borrowing (that is, up to five years). Life insurance companies, on the other hand, have been the traditional source of business loans with maturities of 10 or more years.

Debt in the form of *securities* includes bills, certificates, notes, and bonds. For these obligations, the borrower formalizes the terms and conditions of the loan in a document, which is then sold. The most common type of bill is a T-bill, or U.S. Treasury bill — a short-term U.S. government debt obligation. The most common type of certificate is the **certificate of deposit,** or CD — an obligation of a commercial bank. Notes and bonds are the most common form of intermediate and long-term debt securities issued by *corporations*. Bills, certificates, and, in some cases, notes, are short-term obligations with maturities of less than a year. The maturity period for notes is usually 1 to 10 years, and for bonds, usually more than 10 years.

Current Loans Payable

Loans, notes, certificates, bills, and other current interest-bearing debt (which will henceforth be called *current loans payable*) are recorded at their present value. For example, suppose a company borrows $100,000 for six months at 10 percent with interest payable monthly. Essentially, the company receives $100,000 upon signing the loan agreement and agrees to pay a total of $5,000 ($833.33 per month) in interest over six months and a lump sum representing the repayment of the principal of $100,000 in six months. Thus, the cash flows for this loan appear as follows:

	Cash Flow at End of Month							Total
	Now	**1**	**2**	**3**	**4**	**5**	**6**	
Loan proceeds	100,000							
Interest payments		(833)	(833)	(833)	(833)	(833)	(833)	(5,000)
Principal payment							(100,000)	(100,000)

This agreement calls for the company to repay $105,000 in total, but accounting practice for short-term loans (and long-term ones, for that matter) is to record them at their discounted or *present value*.[2] Thus, the entry to record the loan at its inception looks like this:

Dr. Cash (A) . . . . (inc.) 100,000
  Cr. Loan Payable (L) . . . . (inc.) 100,000

Each month an entry for the accrued interest is also necessary:

Dr. Interest Expense (E) . . . . (inc.) 833
  Cr. Loan Interest Payable (L) . . . . (inc.) 833

[2]A financial calculator can be used to verify that the present value of the six monthly interest payments of $833, plus the principal payment of $100,000 in the sixth month, is indeed $100,000 when the interest rate is 10 percent (that is, FV = −100,000, PMT = −833, N = 6, I = 0.833, 10%/12).

A complication with some short-term loans is that they are often issued on a discounted basis, as if the interest were prepaid. For example, a company may agree to pay $100,000 in six months and receive only $95,000 now. Convention is to record this note at $100,000, with the difference going to a contra-liability (CL) account. Thus, the transaction would be recorded as follows:

Dr. Cash (A)	(inc.) 95,000	
Dr. Discount on Notes Payable (CL)	(inc.) 5,000	
Cr. Notes Payable (L)		(inc.) 100,000

Of course, this note is stated at its present value ($95,000), but the rate is not quite 10 percent (the effective rate is 10.53 percent). Each month an entry is made of the accrual of the prepaid interest:

Dr. Interest Expense (E)	(inc.) 833	
Cr. Discount on Notes Payable (CL)		(dec.) 833

After six months the contra-liability account will be zero, and the liability will reflect its maturity value of $100,000.

Sometimes a company may sign a note when it does not know the implicit interest rate; perhaps it knows only the actual payments to be made over time. (For example, the notes could be in exchange for a special, one-of-a-kind machine for which the buyer does not know the market value.) Conventional practice is to discount the payments at a rate that matches the risk characteristics of the note. For example, if the note is noncancelable, a low-risk debt rate such as the prime rate or the company's incremental borrowing rate may be used.

Bonds, Notes, and Loans: Long-Term Debt

The term **bond** refers to a variety of long-term obligations evidenced by a document that may be sold or traded. The entity issuing a bond is the borrower, and the buyer of those bonds is the lender. **Debentures,** for example, are general obligation bonds issued by a company. **Mortgage bonds** and **revenue bonds** are examples of bonds in which particular corporate assets are pledged as security for the debt.

Bond liabilities are recorded at their present value in a manner similar to that used for current loans payable. The present value of the combined interest and principal payments on a bond is the same as the principal outstanding on the bond when discounting is done at the effective interest rate on the bond. (If this concept is not clear, refer to Appendix 12A for examples and an explanation.)

If bonds are issued or sold at their face amount, the accounting is straightforward. For example, assume that a company issues $50 million of 11 percent, 20-year debentures with annual interest payments. The entry to record the initial borrowing looks like this:

Dr. Cash (A)	(inc.) 50,000,000	
Cr. Bonds Payable (L)		(inc.) 50,000,000

This entry assumes that the company sold the bonds itself and thus incurred no transaction costs. In reality, most companies hire a bond underwriter to place or sell debt securities and thus incur certain transaction fees when debt securities are sold.

When the annual interest payment is made, the following entry is recorded:

Dr. Interest Expense (E)	(inc.) 5,500,000	
Cr. Cash (A)		(dec.) 5,500,000

Assuming that the bonds are retired on the maturity date, we make the following entry:

Dr. Bonds Payable (L)	(dec.) 50,000,000	
Cr. Cash (A)		(dec.) 50,000,000

Like discounted notes, bonds present accounting problems because the amount printed on the face of a bond certificate may not be what the issuing company (the borrower) ultimately receives in cash, and from the buyers' perspective, it may not be what the purchaser (the lender) ultimately has to pay. Bonds often sell at a **premium** or **discount** when first issued because of interest rate changes in the bond market between the time the bonds are priced (and the certificates printed) and the time customers actually buy them. Most corporate bonds issued in the United States come to market at a slight discount because it is psychologically easier to sell a security at a discount than at a premium.

From the bond buyer's perspective, money is lent when the bonds are purchased. In exchange for cash the buyer receives a promise of a stream of cash flows (the annuity interest payments) over the life of the bond plus a terminal cash flow payment (the lump-sum principal repayment) at the **maturity date.** The value of these cash flows depends upon the interest rate, or **yield rate,** used to discount them. Interest (yield) rates change continually due to market forces such as world political conditions, the general health of the economy, inflation, and investor expectations, to name just a few.

For example, a $1,000, 20-year, 11 percent, annual interest payment bond may come to market when the yield rate for the class and risk of bond has just increased to 11⅛ percent. Because of the rise in interest rates, the bond will actually sell for only $990.13, or a discount of $9.87.[3] Suppose an entire issue of these bonds with a face value of $50 million were sold in the market and brought the issuing firm $49,506,333. Note that 11 percent bonds pay $5.5 million per year in interest (the coupon amount), and $50 million (the **maturity value**) is to be repaid at the end of the 20th year. The present value of these payments at 11 percent is, of course, $50 million, whereas at 11⅛ percent, the **effective rate,** the present value is only $49,506,333, which is the amount of cash that the bond-issuing company can expect to receive if the bonds are sold to yield 11⅛ percent. The difference between the face amount of $50 million and the selling price of $49,506,333 is the *bond discount,* which must be amortized over the 20-year life of the debt. The following is the accounting challenge in a situation like this:

1. To show the bond liability at its present value,'not its face amount.
2. To show the annual interest expense at the effective rate (11⅛ percent), not the stated or **coupon rate** (11 percent).

The transaction to record the sale of bonds for this example is as follows:

Dr. Cash (A)	(inc.) 49,506,333	
Dr. Bond Discount (CL)	(inc.) 493,667	
Cr. Bonds Payable (L)		(inc.) 50,000,000

Thus, the bonds would be recorded initially on the balance sheet at $49,506,333, the present value at the time of issuance. At the end of each year, two transactions are required: one to record the interest paid on the bonds and the second is to amortize the

[3]To verify this number using a financial calculator, the keying if FV = 1,000, PMT = 110 (that is, 11% × $1,000), N = 20, I = 11.125 (11⅛%).

bond discount. Bond discounts (or premiums) are typically amortized over the life of a bond using the **effective interest method** rather than straight-line amortization. To facilitate the preparation of the two transactions, the borrower usually prepares a bond amortization schedule similar to that in Exhibit 12.3. This schedule adjusts the actual interest expense, based on 11⅛ percent on $49,506,333 in the first year, by amortizing the bond discount of $493,667. The key to Exhibit 12.3 is that the total yearly interest expense (column 2) is always 11⅛ percent (the effective rate) of the outstanding net liability (column 5). Of course, the net liability is also equivalent to the present value of the future payments (cash interest to be paid plus the principal) at 11⅛ percent.

Another way to think about this is that in terms of face amounts, $50 million is being borrowed for 20 years on which $5.5 million per year (or $110 million in total) of interest will be paid in cash. In fact, however, only $49,506,333 is borrowed, although a full $50 million will be repaid in 20 years. The difference of $493,667 represents additional interest, and, thus, the total interest expense paid over the life of the debt is $110,493,667. By spreading the $493,667 over 20 years (as revealed in column 3 of Exhibit 12.3), the borrower's income statement shows an interest expense equal to 11⅛ percent of the bond value as reported on the company's balance sheet (*not* 11 percent of $50 million).

The entries for Year 1 for this bond would be recorded as follows:

Dr. Interest Expense (E)	(inc.) 5,500,000	
Cr. Cash (A)		(dec.) 5,500,000

and

Dr. Interest Expense (E)	(inc.) 7,580	
Cr. Bond Discount (CL)		(dec.) 7,580

The two separate entries can also be combined into one as follows:

Dr. Interest Expense (E)	(inc.) 5,507,580	
Cr. Cash (A)		(dec.) 5,500,000
Cr. Bond Discount (CL)		(dec.) 7,580

The income statement reflects total interest expense of $5,507,580 for Year 1. Note that this expense is exactly 11⅛ percent of the outstanding bond liability (11⅛ percent × 49,506,333 = $5,507,580).

For financial statement purposes, the details of each bond issue should be disclosed in the footnotes and should reveal the aggregate present value of all bond liabilities and the aggregate principal payments to be made for each over the next five years. Bond liabilities are shown in the balance sheet net of any premium or discount. On the balance sheet, the current principal obligation is classified as a current liability; the remainder is included under noncurrent liabilities. Thus, for the bonds under discussion here, at the end of Year 1, the balance sheet shows nothing related to these bonds under current liabilities (because no *principal* repayments are to be made in Year 2 and the accrued interest was paid in cash). The balance sheet reports $49,513,913 under noncurrent liabilities reflecting the *net* bond liability:

Bonds payable	$50,000,000
Less: Unamortized bond discount	486,087
Bonds payable (net)	$49,513,913

EXHIBIT 12.3

Amortization of a Bond Discount

Year	(1) Coupon Interest (11.0%)	(2) Effective Interest (11.125%)	(3) Discount Amortization (2-1)	(4) Unamortized Discount (4-3)	(5)j Present Value of Bond ($50,000,000-4)
				$493,667	$49,506,333
1	$ 5,500,000	$ 5,507,580	$ 7,580	$486,087	$49,513,913
2	5,500,000	5,508,423	8,423	477,664	49,522,336
3	5,500,000	5,509,360	9,360	468,304	49,531,695
4	5,500,000	5,510,401	10,401	457,904	49,542,096
5	5,500,000	5,511,558	11,558	446,345	49,553,655
6	5,500,000	5,512,844	12,844	433,501	49,566,499
7	5,500,000	5,514,273	14,273	419,228	49,580,722
8	5,500,000	5,515,861	15,861	403,367	49,596,663
9	5,500,000	5,517,625	17,625	385,742	49,614,258
10	5,500,000	5,519,586	19,586	366,156	49,633,844
11	5,500,000	5,521,765	21,765	344,391	49,655,604
12	5,500,000	5,524,187	24,187	320,204	49,679,796
13	5,500,000	5,526,877	26,877	293,327	49,706,673
14	5,500,000	5,529,867	29,867	263,459	47,736,541
15	5,500,000	5,533,190	33,190	230,269	49,769,731
16	5,500,000	5,536,883	36,883	193,387	49,806,631
17	5,500,000	5,540,986	40,986	152,401	49,847,599
18	5,500,000	5,545,545	45,545	106,855	49,893,145
19	5,500,000	5,550,612	50,612	56,243	49,943,757
20	5,500,000	5,556,243	56,243	–0–	50,000,000
Total	$110,000,000	$110,493,667	$493,667		

Exhibit 12.4 is from the 1994 annual report of International Game Technology, the only gaming machine manufacturer licensed to do business in every regulated gaming jurisdiction in the world. The presentation format describing notes payable and capital lease obligations is typical of the footnote disclosure required by U.S. GAAP, but the information contained within this particular footnote is quite interesting. The company's 1991 $115 million, 5½%, convertible subordinated notes were issued at a discount of almost 20%.[4] It's not clear why the company chose to do this, but a good guess would be that the actual cash interest payments, $6.3 million, were less using a steeply discounted note than if they'd simply borrowed $89.4 million at 8.5%, the going rate at that time, which would have resulted in a $7.6 million annual cash interest payment. This suspicion is reinforced by their action in 1994: They called the old notes, triggering a conversion of these notes to common stock, and issued $100 million more debt in the form of 7.84% senior notes with a deferred repayment schedule beginning in 1998. The 1995 through 1999 principal repayment schedule reflects this new senior note and also the Australian cash advance. The company was expanding rapidly to meet the growth in the midwestern riverboat and Native American gambling markets; they were conserving cash wherever they could.

Although rare, bonds are also sometimes sold at a premium. It is more difficult to sell securities at a premium for psychological reasons. Consequently, bond issuers

[4]Convertible means that the notes are exchangeable into a certain number of common shares. Subordinated means that in the event of bankruptcy some other liability is "senior," probably the bank line of credit, and would be repaid before any payment could be made to these note holders.

EXHIBIT 12.4

International Game Technology
Notes Payable and Capital Lease Liabilities

Notes payable and capital lease obligations consist of the following as of:

(Dollars in thousands)	September 30, 1994	1993
Senior notes (see Note 11)	$100,000	$ —
Australian cash advance facility (see Note 11)	13,212	—
Capital lease obligations (see Note 8)	632	1,079
Other notes payable	237	—
Total	114,081	1,079
Less current maturities	(2,613)	(462)
Long-term notes payable and capital lease obligations, net of current maturities	$111,468	$ 617

Future fiscal year principal payments of these notes and capital lease obligations at September 30, 1994, are as follows:

(Dollars in thousands)

1995	1996	1997	1998	1999	2000 and later
$2,613	$4,709	$4,556	$16,503	$14,300	$71,400

11. Debt Offerings

Convertible Subordinated Notes

In May 1991, the Company completed a $115,000,000 public offering of 5-½% Convertible Subordinated Notes (the "Notes") maturing June 1, 2001.

The Notes were issued at a price of 80.055% of the principal amount due at maturity, representing an original issue discount of 19.945% from the principal amount payable at maturity. Semiannual interest payments at 5-½% along with the original issue discount represented a yield of 8.5% per annum. Net proceeds from the issue and sale of the Notes were $89,426,800.

The Company, as permitted under the terms of the Notes, called all the outstanding Notes for redemption on June 1, 1994. The redemption price was 84.414% of the principal amount due at maturity together with accrued and unpaid interest to the date of redemption. At the option of the holder, the Notes were convertible into common stock of the Company at a conversion rate of 129.384 shares per each $1,000 principal amount until May 31, 1994. All the outstanding notes were converted prior to the redemption date. During fiscal 1994 and 1993, notes with a face amount of $72,180,000 and $42,719,000 were converted into 9,339,000 and 5,527,000 shares, respectively, of the Company's common stock.

Senior Notes

In September 1994, the Company completed a $100,000,000 private placement of 7.84% Senior Notes (the "Senior Notes"). The Senior Notes require annual principal payments of $14.3 million commencing in September 1998 through 2003 and a final principal payment of $14.2 million in September 2004. Interest is paid quarterly. The Senior Notes contain covenants that limit the financial commitments the Company may make and require the maintenance of a minimum level of consolidated net worth. The net proceeds from the Senior Notes of $99.6 million will be used to finance the construction of a new manufacturing and headquarters facility and for general corporate purposes.

Australian Cash Advance Facility

In August 1994, the Company was advanced $18,000,000 (Australian), from an Australian bank under a cash advance facility. Annual principal payments (Australian) are $3,000,000, $6,000,000, $6,000,000 and $3,000,000 at September 30, 1995, 1996, 1997, and June 30, 1998, respectively. Interest is paid quarterly in arrears at a blended rate comprised of fixed and floating rates. The proceeds of the loan were used to acquire manufacturing and administrative facilities in Sydney, Australia.

usually err on the discount side when setting the interest rate to be printed on their bonds. When market interest rates are lower than a bond's coupon (stated) rate, however, a bond premium results. Conceptually, accounting for bond premiums is the reverse of accounting for bond discounts. Suppose, for example, that the $50 million in bonds actually sell for $50,501,800, resulting in an effective yield of only 10⅞ percent.[5] The transaction for the issuer at the time of sale looks like this:

Dr. Cash (A)	(inc.) 50,501,800	
Cr. Bonds Payable (L)		(inc.) 50,000,000
Cr. Bond Premium (L)		(inc.) 501,800

When the first interest payment is made at the end of Year 1, the two transactions necessary to record the interest payment and the amortization of the premium are as follows:

Dr. Interest Expense (E)	(inc.) 5,500,000	
Cr. Cash (A)		(dec.) 5,500,000

and

Dr. Bond Premium (L)	(dec.) 7,928	
Cr. Interest Expense (E)		(dec.) 7,928

These two separate entries can be combined into a single one as follows:

Dr. Interest Expense (E)	(inc.) 5,492,072	
Dr. Bond Premium (L)	(dec.) 7,928	
Cr. Cash (A)		(dec.) 5,500,000

Note that the premium is amortized in a manner similar to that illustrated in Exhibit 12.3, except that the effect is to reduce the effective interest expense, not to raise it.

If a company chooses to retire its debt early (that is, prior to its scheduled maturity date as printed on the bond certificate) by exercising call provisions or purchasing its debt securities in the open market, accounting practice requires that any gain or loss from the extinguishment of debt retirement be recognized in the current income statement as an extraordinary item.[6] For example, suppose that the $50 million in 11 percent bonds, sold at a premium, were retired after one year by repurchase of the bonds for an aggregate of $52 million. Because the book value of the bonds after one year is $50,493,872 ($50,501,800 – 7,928), the *seller* records a loss of $1,506,128:

Dr. Loss on Early Retirement (Loss)	(inc.) 1,506,128	
Dr. Bonds Payable (L)	(dec.) 50,000,000	
Dr. Bond Premium (L)	(dec.) 493,872	
Cr. Cash (A)		(dec.) 52,000,000

The costs incurred to actually issue the bonds such as for underwriting, engraving, printing, and registration should be capitalized and amortized over the life of the bonds; amortization should be based on the effective interest method. Often these costs are expensed on a straight line basis because of materiality.

[5]To determine the present value of these bonds using a financial calculator, the keying is FV = –50,000,000, PMT = –5,500,000, N = 20, I = 10.875.

[6]Early retirement of debt is a common occurrence. At first glance, it may seem inappropriate to treat the associated gains or losses as *extraordinary;* however, generally accepted accounting practice is to do just that to prevent corporations from attempting to "manage earnings" by retiring selected bonds as needed to raise or lower reported accounting income.

Purchasers of bonds sold at a premium or discount simply record the securities at their cost. They are carried at cost, and the premium or discount is amortized over the lifetime of the bonds.[7] For example, suppose that a company purchased the entire issue of $50 million in the above example at a cost of $49,506,333. (This could happen only if the underwriter received no commission and there were no other transaction fees or expenses.) At the end of the first year, the entry on the purchaser's books to record the receipt of interest income appears as follows:

Dr. Cash (A)	(inc.) 5,500,000	
Dr. Investment in Corporate Bonds (A)	(inc.) 7,580	
Cr. Interest Income (R)		(inc.) 5,507,580

The result of this entry is that total interest income for the year is 11⅛ percent of the bond asset. The cash received is only $5.5 million, or 11.11 percent of the bond asset ($49,506,333), but the effective interest income becomes 11⅛ percent once the bond discount is amortized.

As the business activities of American corporations become more global and as borrowing arrangements become more complex, the valuation of short- and long-term debt becomes ever more important. Accordingly, the footnote disclosures of these debts have become more extensive.[8] PepsiCo, Inc., again provides an illuminating example. In Exhibit 12.5 the footnote disclosures for short-term borrowings and long-term debt from the 1994 annual report describe PepsiCo's commercial paper, notes, bonds, and other long-term liabilities. Note that PepsiCo has debt denominated in Swiss francs, Japanese yen, and, of course, U.S. dollars.

The zero coupon notes are interesting because the disclosed yield to maturity, 14.6 % as of December 31, 1994, is so much higher than the market rate of interest for that type of risk and maturity. The explanation is that these zeros were issued in the early 1980s when prevailing rates were much higher, and the notes are being amortized over their life following schedules established at the time of original issue. Of course, against a "fair value" basis, those zeros today would have a much lower yield to maturity.

The Swiss franc 400 million perpetual Foreign Interest Payment bonds are also interesting. Interest on these bonds is paid in U.S. dollars, whereas the principal is to be paid in Swiss francs. Apparently, PepsiCo has protected itself against foreign exchange losses through some type of hedging arrangement because the value of the bonds at the initial issue price in U.S. dollars was $214 million, almost the same as the current carrying value.

Exhibit 12.6 was taken from the 1994 annual report of SBC Communications Inc., formerly Southwestern Bell Corporation. It illustrates not just the required disclosure for long-term debt, Note 4, but also the fair value of these financial instruments. Beginning in 1992, SFAS 107 required the disclosure of fair values not just for debt and equity securities owned but also for long-term debt outstanding. It is interesting that in 1993 the fair values of the debt exceeded the book values by a small amount while the reverse was true in 1994. Although there was a small change in the actual debt outstanding from one year to the next, the swing in fair values is no doubt due to a rise in prevailing interest rates.

---

[7] Bonds classified as hold-to-maturity are not subject to the mark-to-market considerations of SFAS No. 115 (see Chapter 8). If, however, there is a permanent impairment of a bond's market value, it should be written down accordingly.

[8] Liability footnote disclosures found in other countries tend to be less detailed than those found in U.S. corporate annual reports. Moreover, debt valuation practices also differ around the world. For example, the International Accounting Standards Committee permits liabilities to be valued at either present value or face/settlement value. Despite the many merits of using the present value approach, many countries (e.g., Japan) do use the settlement value as the basis to value all liabilities.

EXHIBIT 12.5

PepsiCo, Inc.
Footnote Disclosure for Short-Term Borrowings and Long-Term Debt

Note 9: Short-Term Borrowings and Long-Term Debt

	1994	1993
Short-Term Borrowings		
Commercial paper (5.4% and 3.3%) **(A)**	**$ 2,254.4**	$ 3,535.0
Current maturities of long-term debt issuances **(A)**	**987.5**	1.183.1
Notes (5.4% and 3.5%) **(A)**	**1,492.4**	394.0
Other borrowings (6.5% and 6.3%)	**444.2**	529.1
Amount reclassified to long-term debt **(B)**	**(4,500.0)**	(3,450.0)
	$ 678.5	$ 2,191.2
Long-Term Debt		
Short-term borrowings, reclassified **(B)**	**$ 4,500.0**	$ 3,450.0
Notes due 1995 through 2008 (6.6% and 6.5%) **(A)**	**3,724.7**	3.873.8
Euro notes, 8% due 1997	**250.0**	—
Zero coupon notes, $795 million due 1995–2012 (14.6% and 14.4% annual yield to maturity)	**219.2**	327.2
Japanese yen 3.3% bonds due 1997 **(D)**	**200.8**	—
Swiss franc perpetual Foreign Interest Payment bonds **(C)**	**213.0**	212.2
Swiss franc 5¼% bearer bonds due 1995 **(D)**	**99.7**	90.1
Swiss franc 7⅛% notes due 1994 **(D)**	—	69.8
Capital lease obligations (See Note 11)	**298.2**	291.4
Other, due 1995–2015 (8.1% and 6.6%)	**322.4**	311.2
	9,828.0	8,625.7
Less current maturities of long-term debt issuances	**(987.5)**	(1,183.1)
	$ 8,840.5	$ 7,442.6

The interest rates in the above table indicate, where applicable, the weighted average rates at year-end 1994 and 1993, respectively.

The carrying amount of long-term debt includes any related discount or premium and unamortized debt issuance costs. The debt agreements include various restrictions, none of which are presently significant to PepsiCo. Subsequent to year-end 1994, PepsiCo issued $150 million of Notes through February 7, 1995.

The annual maturities of long-term debt through 1999, excluding capital lease obligations and the reclassified short-term borrowings, are: 1995–$1.0 billion; 1996–$1.1 billion; 1997–$1.0 billion; 1998–$1.2 billion; and 1999–$280 million.

See Management's Analysis — Overview on page 24 for a discussion of PepsiCo's use of interest rate swaps and currency exchange agreements and its management of the inherent credit risk.

(A) The following table indicates the notional amount and weighted average interest rates, by category, of interest rate swaps outstanding at year-end 1994 and 1993, respectively. The weighted average variable interest rates that PepsiCo pays, which are indexed primarily to either commercial paper or LIBOR rates, are based on rates as of the respective balance sheet date and are subject to change. Terms of interest rate swap agreements match the debt they modify and terminate in 1995 through 2008. The differential to be paid or received on interest rate swaps is accrued as interest rates change and is charged or credited to interest expense over the life of the agreements. The carrying amount of each interest rate swap is reflected in the Consolidated Balance Sheet as a receivable or payable under the appropriate current asset or liability caption.

	1994	1993
Receive fixed-pay variable:		
Notional amount	**$1,557.0**	$570.0
Weighted average receive rate	**5.89%**	5.96%
Weighted average pay rate	**6.12%**	3.28%
Receive variable-pay variable:		
Notional amount	**$1,008.5**	$465.0
Weighted average receive rate	**4.90%**	3.81%
Weighted average pay rate	**5.99%**	3.17%
Receive variable-pay fixed:		
Notional amount	**$ 215.0**	$265.0
Weighted average receive rate	**6.56%**	3.84%
Weighted average pay rate	**8.22%**	7.46%

The following table identifies the composition of total debt (excluding capital lease obligations and the effect of the reclassified amounts from short-term borrowings) after giving effect to the impact of interest rate swaps. All short-term borrowings are considered variable interest rate debt for purposes of this table.

	1994		1993	
	Carrying Amount	Weighted Average Interest Rate	Carrying Amount	Weighted Average Interest Rate
Variable interest rate debt:				
Short-term borrowings	**$5,178.5**	**6.19%**	$5,641.2	4.11%
Long-term debt	**1,102.5**	**6.25%**	567.6	4.75%
	6,281.0	**6.20%**	6,208.8	4.17%
Fixed interest rate debt	**2,939.8**	**6.96%**	3,133.6	6.95%
	$9,220.8	**6.44%**	$9,342.4	5.10%

EXHIBIT 12.5 concluded

(B) At year-end 1994 and 1993, PepsiCo had unused revolving credit facilities covering potential borrowings aggregating $3.5 billion. Effective January 3, 1995, PepsiCo replaced its existing credit facilities with new revolving credit facilities aggregating $4.5 billion, of which $1.0 billion expire in 1996 and $3.5 billion expire in 2000. At year-end 1994 and 1993, $4.5 billion and $3.5 billion, respectively, of short-term borrowings were classified as long-term debt, reflecting PepsiCo's intent and ability, through the existence of the unused credit facilities, to refinance these borrowings. These credit facilities exist largely to support the issuances of short-term borrowings and are available for acquisitions and other general corporate purposes.

(C) The coupon rate of the Swiss franc 400 million perpetual Foreign Interest Payment bonds issued in 1986 is 7½% through 1996. The bonds have no stated maturity date. At the end of each 10-year period after the issuance of the bonds, PepsiCo and the bondholders each have the right to cause redemption of the bonds. If not redeemed, the coupon rate will be adjusted based on the prevailing yield of 10-year U.S. Treasury Securities. The principal of the bonds is denominated in Swiss francs. PepsiCo can, and intends to, limit the ultimate redemption amount to the U.S. dollar proceeds at issuance, which is the basis of the carrying amount. Interest payments are made in U.S. dollars and are calculated by applying the coupon rate to the original U.S. dollar principal proceeds of $214 million.

(D) PepsiCo has entered into currency exchange agreements to hedge its foreign currency exposure on these issues of non-U.S. dollar-denominated debt. At year-end 1994, the carrying amount of this debt aggregated $301 million and the receivables and payables under related currency exchange agreements aggregated $50 million and $2 million, respectively, resulting in a net effective U.S. dollar liability of $253 million with a weighted average interest rate of 6.6%. At year-end 1993, the aggregate carrying amount of the debt and the receivables under related currency exchange agreements were $160 million and $41 million, respectively, resulting in a net effective U.S. dollar liability of $119 million with a weighted average fixed interest rate of 6.5%. The carrying amount of each currency exchange agreement is reflected in the Consolidated Balance Sheet as a receivable or payable under the appropriate current and noncurrent asset and liability captions. Changes in the carrying amount of a currency exchange agreement resulting from exchange rate movements are offset by changes in the carrying amount of the related non-U.S. dollar-denominated debt, as both amounts are based on current exchange rates.

CONTINGENT LIABILITIES

What happens when there is only the possibility of a liability, such as in the case of a lawsuit or, in more recent times, for environmental liabilities? Lawsuits against corporations and partnerships can be huge with much contingent on a judgment, settlement, petition, or judicial finding. For example, the Price Waterhouse accounting firm was sued for $11 billion by the liquidators of the failed BCCI bank. Costs to clean up the known hazardous waste sites in the United States are estimated to run into the hundreds of billions of dollars. The accounting challenge is to determine when and how these potential obligations are to be recognized.

GAAP defines a **contingent liability** as

> an existing condition, situation, or set of circumstances involving uncertainty as to possible . . . loss . . . to an enterprise that will ultimately be resolved when one or more future events occur or fail to occur. Resolution of the uncertainty may confirm the . . . impairment of an asset or incurrence of a liability.

An expense entry and offsetting liability must be recorded when both of the following conditions are met:

1. [I]t is probable that an asset has been impaired or a liability has been incurred at the date of the financial statements.
2. The amount of the loss can be reasonably estimated.[9]

[9]Source: SFAS No. 5, "Accounting for Contingencies," (Financial Accounting Standards Board: Norwalk, CT, 1975), para. 8.

EXHIBIT 12.6

SBC Communications Inc.
Footnote Disclosure for Debt and the Fair Value of Financial Instruments

4. Debt

Long-term debt, including interest rates and maturities, is summarized as follows at December 31:

	1994	1993
Telephone Company debentures		
4.50%–5.88% 1995–2006	**$ 700.0**	$ 700.0
6.12%–6.88% 2000–2024	**1,050.0**	1,050.0
7.00%–7.75% 1994–2025	**1,200.0**	1,400.0
8.25%–8.30% 1996–2017	**650.0**	650.0
	3,600.0	3,800.0
Unamortized discount — net of premium	**(31.2)**	(34.2)
Total Telephone Company debentures	**3,568.8**	3,765.8
Telephone Company notes		
5.04%–7.35% 1994–2010	**815.9**	900.0
Unamortized discount	**(5.2)**	(4.8)
Total Telephone Company notes	**810.7**	895.2
Other notes		
4.28–6.95% 1994–2000	**607.8**	191.5
7.00%–9.00% 1994–2004	**888.0**	736.1
	1,495.8	927.6
Unamortized discount	**(24.6)**	—
Total other notes	**1.471.2**	927.6
Guaranteed obligations of employee stock ownership plans*		
8.41%–9.40% 1994–2000	**308.4**	354.3
Capitalized leases	**9.3**	11.7
Total long-term debt, including current maturities	**6,168.4**	5,954.6
Current maturities	**(320.1)**	(495.2)
Total long-term debt	**$5,848.3**	$5,459.4

*See Note 7.

SBC recorded an extraordinary loss on the refinancing of long-term debentures by the telephone company of $153.2 in 1993, net of related income tax benefits of $92.2.

At December 31, 1994, the aggregate principal amounts of long-term debt scheduled for repayment for the years 1995 through 1999 were $320.1, $423.2, $705.7, $299.5 and $442.9, respectively. As of December 31, 1994, SBC was in compliance with all covenants and conditions of instruments governing its debt.

Debt maturing within one years consists of the following at December 31:

	1994	1993
Commercial paper	**$1,348.5**	$ 890.5
Current maturities of long-term debt	**320.1**	495.2
Total	**$1,668.6**	$1,385.7

The weighted average interest rate on commercial paper debt at December 31, 1994 and 1993 was 5.9% and 3.3%, respectively. SBC has entered into agreements with several banks for lines of credit totaling $1,020.0. All of these agreements may be used to support commercial paper borrowings. The majority of these lines are on a negotiated fee basis with interest rates negotiable at time of borrowing. There were no borrowings outstanding under these lines of credit at December 31, 1994.

5. Financial Instruments

SBC does not have any financial instruments held or issued for trading purposes. The carrying amounts reported in the Consolidated Balance Sheets for cash and cash equivalents, other short-term investments and commercial paper debt approximate fair values. The carrying amounts and fair values of SBC's long-term debt, including current maturities, are summarized as follows at December 31:

	1994		1993	
	Carrying Amount	**Fair Value**	**Carrying Amount**	**Fair Value**
Telephone company debentures	**$3,568.8**	**$3,169.3**	$3,765.8	$3,830.8
Telephone company notes	**810.7**	**730.2**	895.2	915.1
Other notes	**1,471.2**	**1,450.9**	927.6	983.6
Guaranteed obligations of employee stock ownership plans	**308.4**	**321.0**	354.3	398.5

The fair value of SBC's long-term debt was based on quoted market prices, where available, or on discounted future cash flows using current interest rates.

EXHIBIT 12.7

The Dow Chemical Company
Footnote Disclosure for Commitments and Contingent Liabilities

In millions, except for share amounts

Q Commitments and Contingent Liabilities

In January 1994, Dow Corning Corporation (Dow Corning), in which Dow is a 50 percent shareholder, announced a pretax charge of $640 ($415 after tax) for the fourth quarter of 1993. In January 1995, Dow Corning announced a pretax charge of $241 ($152 after tax) for the fourth quarter of 1994. These charges included Dow Corning's best estimate of its potential liability for breast implant litigation based on the settlement approved by Judge Sam C. Pointer, Jr. of the U.S. District Court for the Northern District of Alabama (the Court); litigation and claims outside of this breast implant settlement; and provisions for legal, administrative and research costs related to breast implants. The charges for 1993 and 1994 included pretax amounts of $1,240 and $441, respectively, less expected insurance recoveries of $600 and $200, respectively. The 1993 amounts reported by Dow Corning were determined on a present value basis. On an undiscounted basis, the estimated liability above for 1993 was $2,300 less expected insurance recoveries of $1,200.

As a result of the Dow Corning actions, the Company recorded its 50 percent share of the charges, net of tax benefits available to Dow. The impact on the Company's net income was a charge of $192 for 1993 and a charge of $70 for 1994.

The Company is separately named as a defendant in many of the breast implant claims and lawsuits. It is the opinion of the Company's management that the possibility is remote that the litigation of these claims will have a material adverse impact on the Company's consolidated financial statements.

Numerous lawsuits have been brought against the Company and other chemical companies alleging that the manufacture, distribution or use of pesticides containing dibromochloropropane (DBCP) has caused, among other things, property damage, including contamination of groundwater. To date, there have been no verdicts or judgments against the Company in connection with these allegations. It is the opinion of the Company's management that the possibility is remote that the resolution of such lawsuits will have a material adverse impact on the Company's consolidated financial statements.

The Company has accrued $234 at December 31, 1994, for probable environmental remediation and restoration liabilities, including $29 for the remediation of Superfund sites. This is management's best estimate of these liabilities, although possible costs for environmental remediation and restoration could range up to 50 percent higher. It is the opinion of the Company's management that the possibility is remote that costs in excess of those accrued or disclosed will have a material adverse impact on the Company's consolidated financial statements.

Whether or not the contingent liability is recognized, the circumstances must be disclosed, the possible losses described, and any amounts accrued identified. Exhibit 12.7 contains a selected set of paragraphs from footnote Q, "Commitments and Contingent Liabilities," in the 1994 annual report of Dow Chemical. It provides a number of interesting illustrations of these requirements. The first paragraph discloses the charges taken by Dow Corning, a 50 percent owned, unconsolidated subsidiary of Dow Chemical, related to breast implant litigation. Note that Dow Corning's total pretax charge over the two years was $1,681 million and that this was net of expected insurance recoveries, on a present value basis (at least the 1993 portion was). Disclosing contingent liabilities net of estimated recoveries and at present value have been controversial issues for some time.

Paragraphs two and three of Exhibit 12.7 discuss significant lawsuits but conclude that the likelihood of a material loss is remote.

During the 1970s a series of environmental catastrophes (such as the Love Canal crisis in Niagara, New York) brought the problem of hazardous wastes to public attention. The U.S. Congress reacted to the problem by passing the Resource Conservation and Recovery Act (RCRA) in 1976 and the Comprehensive Environmental Response, Compensation, and Liability Act (CERCLA) in 1980. With this legislation began the Superfund National Priorities List — a list of designated locations having hazardous waste problems. Currently there are over 1,200 waste sites on the list, with another 30,000 potential locations under review as Superfund candidates.

Under CERCLA, entities suspected of having contaminated a given site are identified as *potentially responsible parties,* or PRPs. Whenever possible, the Environmental Protection Agency (EPA) compels PRPs to clean up sites they created or contributed to creating. If the EPA is unable to identify PRPs for a given site, the agency will itself pay for site cleanup using Superfund Trust funds authorized by Congress. In many instances businesses are identified as the PRPs for a site, and thus issues arise as to the appropriate accounting and reporting that should be adopted.

From a contingent liability perspective, if an environmental contingency loss is "probable" and can be reasonably estimated, a loss reflecting the expected cost to restore the environment and settle any related litigation (such as health claims) must be accrued on the company's financial statements. Alternatively, if the loss is only "reasonably probable" or "remote," no disclosure is required.

The last paragraph of Exhibit 12.7 describes what Dow Chemical's management concluded about its own Superfund liability; obviously, they decided the loss both was probable and could be estimated (at $234 million) although they said the possible costs could be 50 percent more. Dow does not identify whether this amount is net of expected recoveries or at present value; however, in 1993 the Emerging Issues Task Force (EITF) of the FASB and later the SEC ruled that environmental liabilities should be reduced by expected recoveries only when the claim for recovery is probable of realization; discounting is permitted only if the amounts and timing of the cash payments for cleanup are reliably determinable, and only on a site-by-site basis. It seems likely that Dow's accrued liability is not a net figure and is not discounted.

The EITF has also concluded that not all costs associated with environmental contingencies need be deducted from current earnings. Consider, for example, the situation of a property owner who acquires a building in which asbestos fibers have been used as insulation. Various federal, state, and local laws now require the removal or containment of "dangerous asbestos." The EITF has determined that the costs incurred to treat or remove asbestos (within a reasonable period of time after a property with a known asbestos problem is acquired) *should* be capitalized as part of the cost of the acquired property as a betterment. The EITF has determined that while, in general, environmental contamination treatment costs should be charged to expense, some costs may be capitalized if they are recoverable, as indicated by the following criteria:

1. The costs extend the life, increase the capacity, or improve the safety or efficiency of property owned by the company.
2. The costs mitigate or prevent environmental contamination that has yet to occur and that otherwise may result from future operations or activities.
3. The costs are incurred in preparing the property for sale.

The costs of complying with today's and tomorrow's environmental regulations and society's expectations pose interesting questions for accountants. These issues will take on greater importance in the years to come. For example, in the summer of 1995, Shell Oil agreed to abort their planned dumping of the Brent Spar oil-storage rig in the North Atlantic after protests instigated by Greenpeace. Whatever the merits of the case, whether dumping or salvage on land was environmentally better, the cost differential was £36 million. Over 200 rigs in the North Sea must be salvaged eventually. How should the owners of those rigs provide for this teardown cost, and when? And what about the costs for recycling old automobiles, railroad cars, chemical plants, office towers, and shipyards? Aren't they obligations of someone? When should they be recorded as liabilities? Where should the costs of those liabilities be charged? Are we miscosting products and services by not including these costs? It doesn't take long to appreciate the seriousness of this issue.

DERIVATIVES AND OTHER OFF-BALANCE-SHEET RISKS

Another set of corporate obligations not considered liabilities under U.S. GAAP are repurchase agreements, letters of credit written, interest swaps, forward purchase agreements for securities or commodities, options, and variations of these types of transactions. These agreements are termed **financial instruments** if they impose an obligation or right to exchange cash or some other financial instrument under potentially unfavorable terms. A simple example of a financial instrument might be a repurchase agreement or "repo." In this situation, Company X might sell a package of securities to Company Y, subject to an agreement whereby Y sells them back at the same price one year later. This is rather common. A corporation with temporarily surplus funds might buy some bonds from a brokerage firm. During the period of the agreement the corporation earns interest on the bonds but risks no loss of principal because under the terms of the repo it will resell the bonds to the brokerage firm for what it paid for them. Brokerage firms like these agreements because they usually include a provision that permits substitution of one bond for another of comparable risk, maturity, yield, and so on. This is how brokerage firms keep a large inventory of bonds available for sale to their customers: The bonds out on repo can be sold and replaced with a similar bond. It's a win-win proposition: The company earns interest on the bonds with no principal risk, and the brokerage gets a large inventory of bonds without putting up any cash.

This simple repo raises serious accounting issues for both parties. Both face the possibility of a significant loss. The brokerage firm could suffer a major loss if the value of the bonds declined — this is the **market risk.** The corporation faces a **credit risk** because the brokerage firm may not be around to honor the agreement, and, consequently, the corporation faces the same market risk as the brokerage firm because it may be left holding worthless bonds.

Financial instruments have **off-balance-sheet risk** "if the risk of loss, even if remote, exceeds the amount recognized, if any, in the financial statements."[10] The repo is a good example of just such a situation. During the period when the repo is outstanding, the balance sheet does not reflect the possibility that the brokerage firm could suffer a big principal loss, a loss far greater than any fee income recognized on the sale of the bonds. In the same vein, the corporation could suffer a big principal loss — far greater than any interest income earned on those bonds during the period of the repo agreement. The matter is important because the amount of off-balance-sheet risk assumed by U.S. corporations, under this definition, is huge. For example, in 1994 many people first heard of *derivatives* when Orange County, California, discovered it had lost $1.7 billion on a $7.5 billion investment pool and a number of corporations reported big losses from derivatives, losses that surprised both shareholders and corporation directors. In fact, derivatives and derivative contracts have been routinely used by corporations to help manage risk for decades.

[10]J. R. Williams, *Miller's Comprehensive GAAP Guide* (New York: Harcourt Brace Jovanovich, 1995).

Derivative financial instruments are off-balance-sheet options, forwards, futures, swaps, and similar agreements that provide the owner with a benefit or loss based on the underlying value of an asset or index. The instrument or contract "derives" its value from some other asset or index. A simple example of a derivative financial instrument might be the following. Imagine two people debating who has the best terms on a home mortgage. Each thinks the other has the better deal: "I think you will be better off next year because you've got a fixed rate and I think rates are rising." The other person may disagree: "Actually, I think you're better off with a variable rate because my big concern is that rates will drop." (Assume that both parties pay the same interest rate now and have the same principal outstanding.) All that's missing is for someone to say, "Well, if that's the way you feel, then let's agree to pay each other's interest payments for a year. Here, let's write a letter of understanding." They may not know what to call is, but they have just created a derivative financial instrument.

The corporate version of this neighborhood vignette is an interest rate swap wherein Company X, with outstanding debt at a fixed rate, is able to enter into a contract with some other party, say Company Y, whereby Y pays a fixed rate of interest to X over the period of the agreement and, in return, X agrees to pay Y a variable rate of interest linked to some index like a bank lending rate. The effect of the agreement is to transform X's fixed-rate debt into a variable rate. In fact, Company X will receive a series of fixed payments from Y and will give Y a series of payments linked to some index. The derivative is like an off-balance-sheet receivable to X from Y — and an off-balance-sheet payable from X to Y.

Appendix 12B describes off-balance-sheet risks and derivatives in more detail and illustrates the required accounting and footnote disclosures under GAAP with examples drawn from several current annual reports. But for our purposes here, a summary explanation is sufficient. Information on all financial instruments with off-balance-sheet risk (as just defined) must be disclosed in the footnotes and must include

- The contractual amounts.
- The nature of the agreement.
- The terms and conditions.
- The market and credit risk.
- The cash requirements and the related accounting policies.

Additional disclosure requirements for derivatives used for trading purposes require fair value reporting as well as disclosure of trading gains and losses by class of activity. Ordinarily, accounting for trading and speculative activities using financial instruments requires that they be marked to market and that unrealized gains and losses be included in income. Derivatives not used for trading, such as hedging, require a different accounting and another set of disclosures that focus on the reasons for using hedges, descriptions of the types of derivatives used, and the risks being hedged.

Many of the most common derivatives, such as interest rate swaps, when used to hedge as opposed to trading, qualify for **hedge accounting** (explained in Appendix 12B); accordingly, these instruments are recorded at cost and are amortized over the life of the instrument. Changing interest rates or price levels are recognized each period as actual receipts and payments are made under the swap. As a consequence of hedge accounting, the gains or losses on the swap or hedging instrument are recognized at the same time as the losses or gains on the asset or liability being hedged. For example, if an interest rate swap is used to hedge interest rate risk on the company's outstanding debt, say by transforming variable-rate debt to fixed, then if interest rates rise, the gain from the swap should offset the rising interest expense on the debt. If interest rates fall, a loss on the swap will offset the declining interest expense on the original debt.

It can become quite complex, but not all companies use every different type of derivative. Understanding what is happening with derivatives does require careful study of footnotes. Exhibit 12.8 is an example of the disclosure made by Dresser Industries in its 1994 annual report. In January 1994, Dresser acquired Baroid Corporation and its $150 million, 8 percent senior notes, which Dresser subsequently guaranteed. To hedge their risk as they saw it, they entered into a three-year reverse swap arrangement as described in the footnote. It works like this:

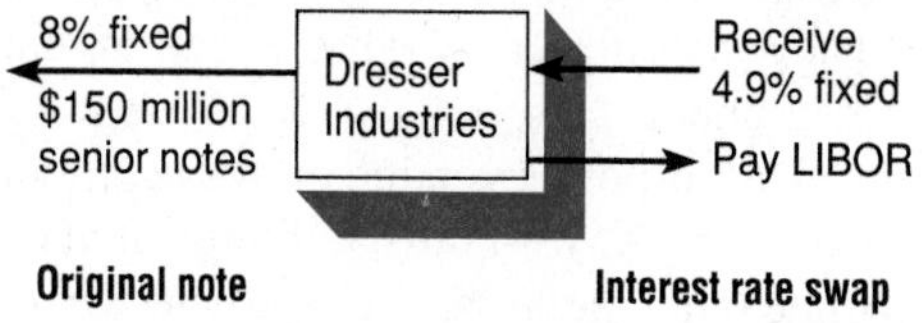

Look carefully at the wording — it's not a misprint. The effect of the swap together with the outstanding notes is such that Dresser has converted its 8 percent fixed-rate notes into a 3.1 percent fixed-rate note plus a trailing six-month variable London Interbank Offered Rate (LIBOR) as follows, all based on the $150 million face amount:

Original note	Pay 8% fixed
Swap	Receive 4.9% fixed Pay LIBOR (6-month trailing)
Net of the above	Pay 3.1% fixed Pay LIBOR (6-month trailing)

In Exhibit 12.5 PepsiCo disclosed three classes of interest rate swaps:

1. "Receive fixed-pay variable" means they transformed fixed-rate debt into variable-rate debt on $1,557 million face amount of debt. The weighted average interest rate on the amounts *received* from the swap (that is, the fixed amounts received) was 5.89%. The average rate paid as of December 31, 1994, was 6.12 percent. In common parlance, this is a "fixed to variable" swap.
2. In a similar fashion, the "Receive variable-pay variable" means that PepsiCo must have swapped some $1,008 million of variable-rate debt based on one set of indexes to variable-rate debt based on another set of indexes such as LIBOR or a bank CD rate. This is a "variable for variable" swap.
3. Finally, "Receive variable-pay fixed" means they have transformed some set of variable-rate debt to a fixed rate. Fortunately, as we will see in some other annual reports, not all companies use such obscure wording in describing what they have done with derivatives.

In each of the situations it is important to remember that the swap is a contract or agreement all by itself that is technically, and legally, independent of the loan agreement it seeks to modify. The swaps themselves, netting the future payments and receipts, appear in the balance sheet as current assets or current liabilities even though the terms of the swap might extend several years. Presumably this is because the swaps

EXHIBIT 12.8

Dresser Industries
Footnote Disclosure of Derivatives

Baroid entered into a three year reverse interest rate swap beginning May 7, 1993 and ending May 7, 1996. Under terms of the swap agreement, the Company receives a fixed interest payment of 4.9% and pays six-month LIBOR for the prior six months on $150 million. The effect of the reverse interest rate swap is to convert the first three years of the 8% Senior Notes from a fixed rate obligation to a floating rate obligation (composed of a fixed payment of 3.1% plus a floating payment based on six-month LIBOR for the prior six months). If on the date to set the interest rate, six-month LIBOR is less than 4.9%, the Company pays an effective floating rate of less than 8.0% and conversely if six-month LIBOR is greater than 4.9% the Company pays an effective floating rate greater than 8.0%. The effect of the swap is accrued monthly based upon current LIBOR estimates. The swap agreement increased interest expense $1.0 million in 1994 and decreased interest expense $1.2 million in 1993.

can be and are resold as market conditions change. The swaps can be netted on the balance sheet because both the pay and receive sides are from and to the same party. After being netted and discounted, the amount is usually pretty small and probably appears in the balance sheet buried in Other Current Receivables or a similar title. It still represents an off-balance-sheet risk because of the potential for a sharp market rate loss.

For example, in 1994 Procter and Gamble (P&G) announced the loss of $157 million on just two derivative contracts. Using interest rate swaps in an effort to save 75 basis points (0.75 percent) on $200 million of debt, or $1.5 million saved each year for five years (0.3 percent of P&G's total yearly interest expense) the company found itself on the wrong end of rising interest rates in 1993 and 1994, and eventually was locked into paying 14.12 percent *above* commercial paper rates for almost five years! P&G's 1994 annual report remarked soberly, "Leveraged options can magnify the impact of interest rate changes." Indeed they can!

Note that PepsiCo also provided a summary table showing how much debt is at a fixed or variable rate as a consequence of the swaps. For PepsiCo, the swaps transformed about $1.3 billion of fixed-rate debt to a variable rate.

MANAGEMENT CONSIDERATIONS

In earlier chapters we discussed the need to manage the components of working capital so as to minimize the amount of idle cash. We also observed that an important aspect of management's job was to balance:

- The need to maintain an adequate working capital position (to be able to pay bills when they come due) against the cost of maintaining that liquid position.
- The need for inventory (to be able to fill orders promptly) against the cost of carrying that inventory.
- The need to extend credit (to be able to expand sales) against the cost of carrying those receivables.

This chapter's discussion of the liability side of the balance sheet has noted that the source of some of the costs involved in maintaining too liquid a position, namely tying up funds in cash, in inventory, or in receivables, could alternatively be used to reduce interest-carrying debt. To the extent that management can reduce the cost of that debt, it also reduces the cost of carrying working capital and thereby makes the balancing job easier and less critical.

Management can reduce some of the cost of carrying inventory by slowing down payments to suppliers. But suppliers are important stakeholders in the company, and an extended payment program is likely to cost the company in the long run. For example, suppliers may decide to cover their own costs of carrying a receivable due from a company by raising their prices. Or they may simply decide not to do business with the company at any price. Worse, an extended payout program may force the supplier into an illiquid position or even cause bankruptcy, resulting in the loss of a critical resource for the company. Clearly, the management of payables requires delicate balancing.

The other liability accounts can be managed in a similar fashion to provide a certain amount of no-cost financing. Employees are occasionally content to defer their compensation because they can also defer their own personal taxes. Those deferred compensation plans can also fund the company's operations. The IRS allows the deferral of some income taxes, sometimes only from one year to the next, in other situations for the life of the company (such as when the company continues to add to its fixed asset base so that the tax effects of accelerated depreciation never roll over — a topic discussed in the next chapter).

Liabilities need to be managed in much the same way as a company's assets to produce the greatest return on the shareholders' funds as is practical and consistent with the company's long-term goals and ethical values. Even the interest-bearing liabilities need to be managed for the benefit of shareholders. If a company earns 10 percent after tax on its assets, and shareholders expect a 20 percent return on their investment, it would appear to be foolish to borrow money for an expansion if borrowing costs are 12 percent. It would appear better to ask the shareholders for an additional infusion of capital. But interest on debt is tax deductible, whereas the dividends paid to stockholders are not. Therefore, the cost of a loan in this situation is really only 8 percent if we assume a 35 percent tax rate. With that perspective, borrowing makes sense because shareholders earn the extra 2 percent on the newly acquired assets *without* investing any more capital.

In theory, a company could borrow all of its funds and provide an infinite rate of return to its shareholders. It stands to reason, however, that no creditor would lend on that basis. Lenders require some equity protection for their risk, and as that protection decreases, their risk rises; and accordingly, they will charge more for their borrowings. Most managements today carefully manage their company's leverage ratio to operate with the least amount of shareholder capital, consistent with the most cost advantageous credit rating from their borrowers. Managing that relationship requires careful attention to the credit markets and to the attitudes of the company's credit suppliers.

Payables and accruals require only minor amounts of management's attention; typically they are driven by the purchase of assets or the incurring of wage or operating costs. The key decision is almost always, "Should we recognize this event as an asset (or a cost), and at what value?" The liability side of the transaction is usually quite simple. However, many liabilities require serious management attention as to whether, in fact, a liability exists, and if so, at what value. One of the toughest accounting tasks managers face is to define all of a company's liabilities. Stock options, promised pension benefits, lawsuits brought against the firm, forward contracts for the purchase or delivery of a product or service, and environmental cleanup obligations are all common examples of the nature of the task.

Debt placements or sales raise another set of issues. Thoughtful managers must consider a host of factors before obligating the organization to a particular form of debt. Should it be short- or long-term? Denominated in what currency? Collateralized by what assets or contracts? Hedged by what kinds of financial instruments? Good borrowing decisions require a keen understanding of risk management. Obviously one does not want to borrow long-term and invest short-term, thereby running the sort of risk that the U.S. savings and loan companies faced in the 1980s. U.S. companies with substantial overseas sales often borrow from the same markets into which they sell so as to match their risks of changes in exchange rates. They may also hedge their borrowing to manage interest, exchange rates, or both.

Derivatives themselves are another thorny issue for managers. They are essential elements for any company facing market price risks or risks of currency exchange or interest rate fluctuations; but how can management ensure that derivatives are not being abused or that the business has not taken on another, undetected risk without management knowledge? Finally, there is the issue of what can be explained to the shareholders and the other readers of financial statements.

SUMMARY

Liabilities are the short- and long-term obligations of a company, usually involving the repayment of cash. In this chapter we learned that most current liabilities are valued at their face value, whereas most long-term liabilities are valued at their present value. The present value of a liability represents the amount of cash (or other assets) necessary to satisfy a liability *today,* as opposed to its maturity date in the future.

Understanding the extent of obligations that are present in a company is important. If a company has borrowed too much, it may face a high degree of *default risk* for nonpayment of its obligations. On the other hand, for most companies, borrowing some level of funds is usually advantageous so long as the company is able to produce a return on the borrowed funds that exceeds the cost of borrowing.

NEW CONCEPTS AND TERMS

Accounts payable (p. 546)
Accrued expenses payable (p. 547)
Annuity (p. 570)
Bond (p. 550)
Call option (p. 574)
Certificate of deposit (p. 549)
Compound interest (p. 568)
Contingent liability (p. 558)
Coupon rate (p. 551)
Credit risk (p. 562)
Current liabilities (p. 545)
Debenture (p. 550)
Derivative financial instruments (p. 563)
Discount (p. 551)
Discounted value (p. 569)
Effective interest method (p. 552)
Effective rate (p. 551)
Face amount (p. 545)
Financial instrument (p. 562)
Forward (p. 575)
Futures (p. 574)
Gross method (p. 546)
Hedge accounting (p. 563)
Market risk (p. 562)
Maturity date (p. 551)
Maturity value (p. 551)
Mortgage bond (p. 550)
Net method (p. 546)
Off-balance-sheet risk (p. 562)
Options (p. 574)
Premium (p. 551)
Put option (p. 575)
Present value (p. 545)
Revenue bond (p. 550)
Time value of money (p. 568)
Unearned revenue (p. 547)
Value at risk (p. 578)
Warranty obligation (p. 548)
Yield rate (p. 551)

APPENDIX 12A

The Time Value of Money

One of the most important and pervasive concepts in business is the **time value of money.** We take it for granted, for example, that when we deposit a sum of money in a bank or savings institution, we will receive *interest* on those deposited funds. In effect, the deposited funds have an income-producing feature — the time value of money. By allowing a bank or savings institution to use the funds, perhaps to loan them to someone else, we receive a fee (interest income).

Even when funds are not deposited in a financial institution, they are assumed to have a time value of money. For example, some automobile manufacturers advertise that a customer may buy their product, pay for the purchase over 48 months, but incur no interest charges. Realistically, it is improbable that any manufacturer is able to finance its customers' purchases over extended periods without charging some interest costs; in any case, such practice makes very little business sense. In most cases in which zero interest is advertised, the manufacturer has added an *implicit* cost of financing the purchase over time into the consumer's purchase price. When this occurs, the consumer is faced with an accounting dilemma, namely to determine the true cost of the item versus the implicit cost of paying for the purchase over 36, 48, or 60 months.

To illustrate, suppose that on December 31, 1995, Cavalier Company purchased a new delivery van from a local truck dealer, Keller Auto & Truck Company. According to the agreement between the two companies, Cavalier will pay Keller $20,000 on December 31, 1997 — two years hence — and issues a non-interest-bearing note in that amount. On the basis of recent conversations with a loan officer at a bank, executives at Cavalier are aware that they could have borrowed the $20,000 for the two-year period at 10 percent interest. Thus, the accounting dilemma is to answer the following questions: What amount did Cavalier pay for the van? At what value should Cavalier's note payable be shown on the company's December 31, 1995, balance sheet?

Both questions can be answered by determining the cash equivalent value of the Cavalier note on December 31, 1995. Obviously, this figure is less than the $20,000 to be paid on December 31, 1997, because of the time value of money. If Cavalier had borrowed $1 from its banker at 10 percent, it would become $1.10 at the end of one year, and this $1.10 would become $1.21 at the end of a second year (if interest is compounded annually).[1] Thus, the problem is to determine the value of the Cavalier

[1]The concept of **compound interest** is based on the assumption that interest earned on a savings deposit in the current period will be left on deposit so that in subsequent periods, interest will be earned not only on the original deposit but also on the interest on deposit from prior periods.

note *exclusive* of the time value of money. To accomplish this, we must look to present value concepts for help.

Present value or **discounted value** refers to *today's* value of receiving (or paying) a given sum of money. For example, if we are able to deposit \$1 in a bank today and interest is compounded annually at 10 percent, the value of our deposit will be \$1.10 at the end of one year. The value to be received at the end of one year is known as the *future value* and, computationally, is given by the following equation:

$$F_{n,i} = (1 + i)^n$$

where $F_{n,i}$ is the future (compounded) value of \$1 at interest rate i for n periods. Thus,

$$F_{1,0.10} = (1 + 0.10)^1 = 1.10$$

To understand the concept of present value, it is a simple matter to consider merely the reverse (or inverse) of the concept of *future value*. For example, if we are to receive \$1.10 in one year, and if interest is calculated at 10 percent annually, what is the value of that payment today? Using the equation for present value computations,

$$P_{n,i} = \frac{1}{(1 + i)^n}$$

we can readily determine that the present value of receiving \$1 in one year at 10 percent interest is 0.90909. To determine the present value (PV) of receiving \$1.10 in one year, it is a simple matter to multiply the two figures together:

$$PV = \$1.10\ (0.09090) = \$1$$

Thus, the present value today of receiving \$1.10 in one year at 10 percent interest is \$1.

With these concepts in mind, we can now approach the problem of determining the cash equivalent value of the Cavalier note. The present value of Cavalier's \$20,000 so-called non-interest-bearing, two-year note should bear the same relationship to \$20,000 as \$1 does to \$1.21. Hence,

$$\begin{aligned} \$PV/\$20{,}000 &= \$1.00/\$1.21 \\ \$PV &= \$20{,}000 \times (\$1.00/\$1.21) \\ \$PV &= \$20{,}000 \times 0.82645 \end{aligned}$$

Thus, the present value factor for 10 percent compounded annually for two years is 0.82645. Therefore, \$20,000 times 0.82645 is \$16,529, the figure at which the note payable (and the van) should be shown on Cavalier's December 31, 1995, balance sheet.

To verify this figure, consider the perspective of Cavalier's banker. If the bank lent Cavalier the \$16,529.00 on December 31, 1995, at 10 percent interest, the compounded amount owed one year later, at December 31, 1996, would become \$18,181.90 (\$16,529 × 1.10) and two years later, at December 31, 1997, would become \$20,000 (\$18,181.90 × 1.10). Thus, \$16,529.00 at December 31, 1995, is equivalent, at 10 percent interest compounded annually, to \$20,000 two years later. Stated alternatively, \$16,529.00 is the present value of \$20,000 in two years at 10 percent interest compounded annually. Generalized factors for determining the present value of a single, lump sum amount are given in Exhibit 12A.1.

EXHIBIT 12A.1

Present Value of $1 Received at End of Period Indicated
$PV = 1/(1 + i)^n$

End of Period	2%	4%	6%	8%	10%	12%	14%	16%	18%	20%	25%	30%
1	0.98	0.96	0.94	0.93	0.91	0.89	0.88	0.86	0.85	0.83	0.80	0.77
2	0.96	0.92	0.89	0.86	0.83	0.80	0.77	0.75	0.71	0.70	0.64	0.59
3	0.94	0.89	0.84	0.79	0.75	0.71	0.67	0.64	0.61	0.58	0.51	0.46
4	0.93	0.86	0.79	0.73	0.68	0.63	0.59	0.55	0.52	0.48	0.41	0.35
5	0.90	0.82	0.75	0.68	0.62	0.57	0.52	0.47	0.44	0.40	0.33	0.27
6	0.89	0.79	0.71	0.63	0.56	0.51	0.46	0.41	0.37	0.34	0.26	0.20
7	0.87	0.76	0.66	0.59	0.51	0.45	0.40	0.36	0.31	0.28	0.21	0.16
8	0.85	0.73	0.63	0.54	0.47	0.41	0.35	0.30	0.27	0.23	0.17	0.12
9	0.84	0.70	0.59	0.50	0.42	0.36	0.31	0.26	0.22	0.19	0.13	0.10
10	0.82	0.68	0.56	0.46	0.39	0.32	0.27	0.23	0.19	0.16	0.11	0.07
11	0.81	0.65	0.52	0.43	0.35	0.29	0.23	0.20	0.16	0.14	0.09	0.06
12	0.79	0.63	0.50	0.40	0.32	0.26	0.21	0.17	0.14	0.11	0.07	0.04
13	0.77	0.60	0.47	0.37	0.29	0.23	0.18	0.14	0.12	0.09	0.05	0.03
14	0.76	0.58	0.44	0.34	0.26	0.20	0.16	0.13	0.10	0.08	0.04	0.03
15	0.74	0.55	0.42	0.31	0.24	0.18	0.14	0.11	0.08	0.07	0.04	0.02
20	0.67	0.45	0.31	0.22	0.15	0.10	0.07	0.05	0.04	0.03	0.01	0.01
25	0.61	0.37	0.23	0.15	0.09	0.06	0.04	0.03	0.02	0.01	*	*
30	0.55	0.31	0.17	0.10	0.06	0.03	0.02	0.01	0.01	*	*	*
35	0.50	0.25	0.13	0.07	0.04	0.02	0.01	0.01	*	*	*	*
40	0.45	0.21	0.10	0.05	0.02	0.01	*	*	*	*	*	*

Present Value of an Annuity

The Cavalier Company illustration is an example of determining the present value of a future lump sum to be paid (or received). Let us assume that it is necessary to know the present value, at 6 percent annually, of three year-end payments of $8,000 each. Such a uniform amount payable (or receivable) each period for a stated number of periods is called an **annuity**. One way to find the present value of an annuity of $8,000 for three years, is to compute the present value of each payment and then sum the three present value amounts:

End of Period	Present Value Factor (Exhibit 12A.1)	Present Value of $8,000 Payable
1	0.94	$ 7,520
2	0.89	7,120
3	0.84	6,720
	2.67	$21,360

A more expeditious way of determining the present value of this annuity is to use a table of present value annuity factors, factors that are merely successive sums of present value, single payment factors. Exhibit 12A.2 shows a factor of 2.67 for three years at 6 percent; this factor multiplied by the $8,000 annuity amount results in the present value figure of $21,360.

EXHIBIT 12A.2

Present Value of $1 Received at End of Period for N Periods

$PV = 1/i[1 - 1/(1 + i)n]$

End of Period	2%	4%	6%	8%	10%	12%	14%	16%	18%	20%	25%	30%
1	0.98	0.96	0.94	0.93	0.91	0.89	0.88	0.86	0.85	0.83	0.80	0.77
2	1.94	1.88	1.83	1.79	1.74	1.69	1.65	1.61	1.56	1.53	1.44	1.36
3	2.88	2.77	2.67	2.58	2.49	2.40	2.32	2.25	2.17	2.11	1.95	1.82
4	3.81	3.63	3.46	3.31	3.17	3.03	2.91	2.80	2.69	2.59	2.36	2.17
5	4.71	4.45	4.21	3.99	3.79	3.60	3.43	3.27	3.13	2.99	2.69	2.44
6	5.60	5.24	4.92	4.62	4.35	4.11	3.89	3.68	3.50	3.33	2.95	2.64
7	6.47	6.00	5.58	5.21	4.86	4.56	4.29	4.04	3.81	3.61	3.16	2.80
8	7.32	6.76	6.21	5.75	5.33	4.97	4.64	4.34	4.08	3.84	3.33	2.92
9	8.16	7.43	6.80	6.25	5.75	5.33	4.96	4.60	4.30	4.03	3.46	3.02
10	8.98	8.11	7.36	6.71	6.14	5.65	5.22	4.83	4.49	4.19	3.57	3.09
11	9.79	8.76	7.88	7.14	6.49	5.94	5.45	5.03	4.65	4.33	3.66	3.15
12	10.58	9.39	8.38	7.54	6.81	6.20	5.66	5.20	4.79	4.44	3.73	3.19
13	11.35	9.99	8.85	7.91	7.10	6.43	5.84	5.34	4.91	4.53	3.78	3.22
14	12.11	10.57	9.29	8.25	7.36	6.63	6.00	5.47	5.01	4.61	3.82	3.25
15	12.85	11.12	9.71	8.56	7.60	6.81	6.14	5.58	5.09	4.68	3.86	3.27
20	16.35	13.59	11.47	9.82	8.51	7.47	6.62	5.93	5.35	4.87	3.95	3.32
25	19.52	15.62	12.78	10.68	9.08	7.85	6.88	6.09	5.47	4.95	3.99	3.33
30	22.40	17.30	13.76	11.26	9.43	8.06	7.01	6.18	5.52	4.98	4.00	3.33
35	25.00	18.67	14.49	11.65	9.64	8.18	7.07	6.21	5.54	4.99	4.00	3.33
40	27.36	19.80	15.04	11.92	9.78	8.25	7.11	6.23	5.55	5.00	4.00	3.33

To verify this calculation, let us again assume the perspective of a lender. If a financial institution lent $21,360 repayable in three annual installments of $8,000 each, the debtor would record the receipt of $21,360 in cash and the associated liability for the same amount. At the end of each year, however, a $8,000 cash disbursement must be made to the bank, for a total outflow of $24,000 over the life of the loan. Clearly, each of the $8,000 payments contains amounts applicable to (1) the interest income required by the bank in exchange for forgoing the use of the $21,360 loaned to the debtor and (2) the repayment of the loan principal. The following table depicts the annual parts of each payment attributable to interest and principal:

		Portion of $8,000 Applied to	
Year	**Loan Principal at Beginning of Year**	**Interest at 6%**	**Principal Repayment**
1	$21,360.00	$1,281.60	$ 6,718.40
2	14,641.60	878.50	7,121.50
3	7,520.10	451.20	7,548.80
		$2,611.30	$21,388.70*

*Not precisely equal to $21,360 due to rounding.

Present value annuity factors are appropriate to use when the stream of cash flows are equal amounts and occur at the end of a constant sequence of periods. It is worth noting again that the Exhibit 12A.2 factors are merely the successive sums of the factors from Exhibit 12A.1.

An Illustration

Assume that Cavalier Company wanted to raise $10 million by issuing bonds payable due five years from the date of issue, with 8 percent interest payable annually. As a simplification, assume further that the net proceeds the company receives from the issuance of the bonds is the full $10 million. What liability should Cavalier report on its balance sheet?

The company will pay $14 million over the five-year period, but the present value, at 8 percent, is only $10 million:

Year	Interest (End of Year) (Millions)	Principal at End of year	Factor at 8% (Exhibit 12A.1)	Present Value Amount (Millions)*
1	$0.8	—	0.93	$0.744
2	0.8	—	0.86	0.688
3	0.8	—	0.79	0.632
4	0.8	—	0.73	0.548
5	0.8	—	0.68	0.544
		10.0	0.68	6.800
				$9.992

*A shorter way to do this problem would be to use an Exhibit 12A.2 factor: 3.99 (8 percent; 5 years) times $0.8 million annual interest cash outflows, which equals $3,192,000, and this plus $6,800,000, the present value of the single $10 million principal amount ($10 million times Exhibit 12A.1 factor of 0.68), gives $9,992,000.

Note that debt issued at a yield rate equal to its coupon rate will be sold at an amount equal to its face value.

Now assume that two years after these bonds were issued, an investor wanted to buy $100,000 of the bonds at a price that would yield a 10 percent return. How much should the investor pay?

Graphically, the cash flows of such an investment involve an annuity stream of $8,000 in annual interest inflows (or 8 percent of $100,000) and a one-time principal receipt of $100,000. Using an effective interest rate of 10 percent, the investor should pay $95,000 (or $94,920 rounded off):

Cash Flows at End of Year			Exhibit 12A.1 Factors at 10%	Present Value Amount
1	2	3		
$8,000			0.91	$ 7,280.00
	$8,000		0.83	6,640.00
		$ 8,000	0.75	6,000.00
		100,000	0.75	75,000.00
				$94,920.00

Note that the appropriate present value interest factors were selected using the real (or effective) rate of interest (10 percent) on the bonds, not the coupon or stated rate of interest (8 percent). Even though the bonds carry a stated rate of 8 percent, the price at which the bonds may be bought (or sold) will fluctuate to enable the investor to earn a fair (market) rate of return.

APPENDIX 12B

Derivatives and Other Off-Balance-Sheet Risks

Financial instruments, including derivatives, have become very important tools for many corporations and for the financial community in general. The number of derivative contracts has grown dramatically, involving trillions of dollars, and they are steadily growing in their complexity as well. Unfortunately, they are not well understood by either investors or creditors. The FASB began studying derivatives in 1986. Since then they have issued three standards that directly or indirectly affect the accounting for derivatives:

	Date	Subject
SFAS 105	March 1990	Financial Instruments and Off-Balance Sheet Risks
SFAS 107	December 1991	Fair Value of Financial Instruments
SFAS 119	October 1994	Derivatives and Fair Values

This appendix describes off-balance-sheet financial instruments and each of the four basic kinds of derivatives. We also describe the accounting and the disclosures that are required under U.S. GAAP together with examples from recent annual reports.

Off-Balance Sheet Risk

As defined in Chapter 12, certain financial agreements expose an entity to substantial risk and yet do not appear as such in the balance sheet. Examples of such off-balance-sheet risks include

- Obligations arising from financial instruments sold short.
- Receivables sold with recourse.
- Repurchase agreements.
- Options.
- Loan commitments.
- Interest rate caps and floors.
- Financial guarantees.
- Letters of credit.

- Interest rate swaps.
- Currency swaps.
- Financial futures contracts (hedges and nonhedges).
- Financial forward contracts (hedges and nonhedges).

Some of these agreements are conditional, like an option; others are unconditional, as with a forward or futures contract. Note that some off-balance-sheet financial instruments are associated with a balance sheet liability, such as an interest rate swap. Some are associated with an asset, such as a repo agreement tied to securities owned; and some are associated with neither an asset nor a liability, such as a forward interest agreement.

Derivatives

Derivatives are a subset of these off-balance-sheet risks. There are four important types of derivatives, each with many variations:

1. Financial futures contracts
2. Options
3. Interest rate swaps
4. Financial forward contracts

Futures

Futures contracts were the first derivatives, and they have been used for generations. In the classic agricultural future, a farmer enters into an agreement to sell a certain quantity (and prescribed quality) of a commodity at a certain price and at a certain time, usually at the end of the harvest. It might be to deliver 10,000 bushels of number 2 yellow corn for $2.74 per bushel on the Cargill elevator in Omaha. This agreement or futures contract can be resold to someone else. There is a market for corn and one for corn futures. Commodity exchanges in the United States routinely trade futures in corn, wheat, oats, cattle, hogs, and dozens of other products. The important thing to understand about a futures contract is that it is an unconditional agreement to sell; it is not like an option. In addition to commodities, futures can be used for securities as well. Security exchanges trade U.S. treasury futures, currency futures, and futures based on certain other financial instruments. The commodities and financial futures exchanges, and the futures contracts that they trade, permit companies to hedge against changes in the price of corn or oil, the prices of Japanese yen and German marks. And, of course, some entities buy and sell futures contracts on speculation rather than to hedge a business price risk.

Accounting for futures is prescribed by SFAS No. 80, "Accounting for Futures Contracts." It requires that all futures contracts be marked to market and, if the futures contract is a hedge (that is, an attempt to offset or eliminate some type of risk exposure), that gains or losses on the contract must be deferred until gains or losses on the hedged item are realized.

Options

Options are conditional contracts concerning the sale or purchase of a currency or commodity at some time in the future. A **call option** permits the holder to purchase a certain security or commodity at some given date. For example, an individual, called the holder, may have the right, but not an obligation, to purchase a thousand shares of Intel Corporation stock at $75 per share on, or prior to, a certain date, say, six months from today. Such an agreement requires two parties: the purchaser or holder of the call option and the issuer or writer of the option, who has the contractual obligation to sell those shares of stock in six months if the holder so demands.

A **put option** works much the same way, but in reverse: The owner or holder has the right to sell a particular security or commodity for a set price at some time in the future — and the issuer or writer of the put option is then obligated to buy at that price if so instructed by the holder. The Wall Street expression "He can really *put* it to you" captures the essence of a put option. You can force someone to buy a security at a price way above market.

Accounting for options purchased is somewhat more complex than for futures because a futures contract is a binding agreement while an option is a right, not an obligation. In general, options are marked to market unless they are designated hedges, in which case the marked-to-market adjustment is deferred. Because the premium paid for an option includes both intrinsic value and time value, the two elements are separated. The time value is amortized over the life of the option; the intrinsic value, if any, is recorded as an asset and marked to market at the end of each accounting period.[1]

Interest Rate Swaps

Interest rate swaps have already been described in the text. The 1994 PepsiCo annual report illustrated the disclosure required by U.S. GAAP for such transactions. Interest rate swaps are typically used to provide a degree of protection against a feared change in interest rates, but they actually exchange one risk for another. Interest rate floors and caps can be thought of as variations of the basic interest rate swap from a fixed rate to a variable one. When the variable rate is capped, floored, or both, there is less risk; accordingly, there is an additional cost either in a fee paid or in some other fashion. Caps and floors can also be added to an existing variable rate instrument. The important point here is that these contracts are like side agreements. Their effect is to modify the company's risk position in some fashion. The exact effect depends upon future events. Finally, there are almost an infinite number of variations.

Forwards

Forwards are a type of financial futures contract. The financial futures market trades standardized amount contracts with standard time periods, such as a million dollars for 12 months. Forwards are customized or tailored financial futures contracts that can be used by the buyer to hedge a specific risk over a specific time period, such as the purchase of DM 6.3 million (deutsche marks) on September 20.

Hedge Accounting

Organizations such as brokerage firms, swap dealers, investment companies, hedge funds, and pension funds are, by definition, traders and must account for financial instruments on a mark-to-market basis. However, firms that are using derivatives as hedges to reduce their exposure to changing interest rates or commodity price changes,

[1]Accounting for options sold is beyond the scope of this appendix.

for example, may qualify for **hedge accounting.** The general idea behind hedge accounting is one of matching: Gains or losses on the hedge should be recognized in the same time period as the loss or gain on the hedged item — that is, the debt instrument or commodity. For example, if a hedge transaction is undertaken so as to reduce the exposure of the firm to a steep drop in the value of a commodity, then unrealized gains on the hedge may be recognized only to the extent of a corresponding write-down in the carrying value of the inventory item — that is, the commodity itself. Beyond that, all unrealized gains or losses are deferred until the hedge is terminated or the hedged item is expensed. Interest rate swaps are treated in a similar fashion: Since the underlying debt item, a note or bond outstanding, is not marked to market, it is not appropriate to realize gains or losses on the swap contract used to hedge that interest rate exposure. Accordingly, the interest expense for a given period on an interest rate swap is the net of the interest received and the interest paid on the swap. This offsets the interest expense on the underlying debt. The resulting net expense is at the revised or transformed interest rate. In other words, if the original debt item was at a variable rate and the swap transformed the debt into a fixed rate of 7 percent, then hedge accounting will result in a combined or net interest expense for the period of 7 percent, if it's a perfect swap. If the swap was to transform fixed-rate debt to a variable rate, then the resulting interest expense will be at that variable rate.

The swap itself is carried as either a receivable or payable, usually as a current item, at historical cost. This means that the two sides — the future receipts and the future payments — are netted and discounted at the fixed rate specified in the swap. For many interest rate swaps today, this difference is small or is zero; it is amortized to income over the life of the swap.

It is inappropriate to recognize gains or losses on the value of the swap except if the underlying asset or liability being hedged is adjusted. Unrealized gains or losses do appear in the footnote disclosures, however.

There are three conditions for the use of hedge accounting; each instrument must be examined on a case-by-case basis. The requirements are these:

1. *Risk.* The item being hedged must expose the company to a real risk. Debt at a fixed rate is not such a risk because the cash flow implications are certain.
2. *Reduced exposure.* The hedge must reduce the exposure to that risk. Hedges are often created using a basis other than the exact asset or index of the item being hedged; this is called *cross-hedging.* The firm must be able to establish that the hedge actually reduces exposure to risk associated with the underlying asset or liability.
3. *Purpose of hedging.* The hedge must be so identified from the start. The firm cannot designate an instrument as a hedge after the fact.

Required Disclosures

The requirements for financial disclosure of financial instruments with off-balance-sheet risk is defined by SFAS No. 105. Disclosure must include the following:[2]

- The face or contract amount (or the notional amount if there is no face or contract amount).

[2] J. R. Williams, *Miller's Comprehensive GAAP Guide* (New York: Harcourt Brace Jovanovich, 1995).

- The nature and terms, including, at a minimum, a discussion of credit and market risk, cash requirements of the instrument, and the related accounting policies.

With certain exceptions, the following must also be disclosed for each class of off-balance-sheet risk:[3]

- The maximum amount of accounting loss that would be incurred if any party failed to perform completely according to the terms of the financial instrument with off-balance-sheet risk, even if this is a remote possibility, and the collateral or other security for the amount due, if any, was absolutely worthless (in other words, a worst-case scenario).
- The entity's policy for determining the amount of collateral or other security required to support financial instruments subject to credit risk, information about the entity's access to that collateral or other security, and the nature and a brief description of the collateral or other security (in other words, an entity's policy for requiring security and a brief description of the security supporting financial instruments with off-balance-sheet risk of accounting loss).

Specifically excluded from this requirement are most insurance contracts, unconditional purchase obligations, pensions, stock options, leases, and certain other items.

In addition to these disclosure requirements, SFAS No. 107 requires disclosure of the fair values of financial instruments using quoted market prices or estimates based on market prices. If fair values are not practicable to estimate, that must be explained; then the details of the instrument must be disclosed as well.

Derivatives have an additional set of disclosure requirements found in SFAS No. 119. If they are used for trading, the following disclosure must be made:

1. The average and end-of-period amounts of fair value, distinguishing between assets and liabilities.
2. The net gains or losses (often referred to as net trading revenues) arising from derivative financial instruments trading activities during the period, disaggregated by class, business activity, risk, or another category consistent with management of those activities and when those net trading gains and losses are reported in the income statement.[4]

If derivatives are used for purposes other than trading, the disclosure requirements are as follows:

1. A description of the entity's objectives for holding or issuing the derivative financial instrument, the context needed to understand those objectives, and the entity's strategies for achieving those objectives.
2. A description of how the derivative financial instruments are reported in the financial statements, including
   a. Policies for recognizing and measuring the derivative financial instruments held or issued.
   b. When recognized, and where those instruments are reported in the statement of financial position and income statement.

[3]Williams, *Miller's Comprehensive GAAP Guide.*

[4]Williams, *Miller's Comprehensive GAAP Guide.*

3. For derivative financial instruments that are held or issued for the purpose of hedging anticipated transactions:
   a. A description of the anticipated transactions for which risks are hedged with derivative financial instruments, including the period of time until the anticipated transactions are expected to occur.
   b. A description of the classes of derivative financial instruments used to hedge the anticipated transactions.
   c. The amount of hedging gains and losses explicitly deferred.
   d. A description of the transactions or other events that result in the recognition of earnings of gains or losses deferred by hedge accounting.[5]

The FASB also urged, but did not require, that firms disclose even more information about their derivatives and other financial instruments, including information about interest rates, commodity prices, foreign exchange, or whatever risks were germane to the firm. In particular, the FASB urged disclosing the hypothetical impact of large (±100 or 200 basis points) shifts in interest rates or comparable movements in commodities prices or value at risk from derivatives and other financial instruments. **Value at risk** is the expected loss from adverse market movements at a specified probability and specific time frame. For example, value at risk simulation models might be used to state that the net value of a pool of financial instruments could be expected to change by no more than a certain percent on 95 out of a 100 trading days in response to either interest rate or currency exchange rates.

Examples

Probably the best way to understand what these requirements mean in practice is to examine some representative corporate disclosures. Exhibit 12B.1 shows Note 16, "Financial Instruments," from Chrysler's 1994 annual report. Note that the company disclosed fair values for securities owned, and debt, currency exchange agreements, and long-term receivables of its credit corporation. Except for the debt, where fair values are somewhat higher than book values, there's no surprise in these figures. The off-balance-sheet financial instruments disclosure is quite interesting because Chrysler has interest rate swaps (and caps), interest rate forwards, currency forwards, and options.

The next to the last paragraph of this footnote is important because it illustrates the worst case disclosure requirement of SFAS No. 105, discussed previously. In this case, Chrysler Finance Corporation (CF), a wholly owned subsidiary, has a possible worst-case loss of up to $27 million attributable to one unidentified party. On the surface, the magnitude of Chrysler's derivatives seems moderate when judged against the size of the company, its international operations, and the extent of its credit company financing and its outstanding debt. However, with derivatives, it's what's below the surface that can really do harm.

Exhibit 12B.2 presents a similar disclosure in a much different format. It is taken from the 1994 annual report of CPC International, a $7 billion branded food products company with less than 40 percent of its revenues in North America. One would expect a company like this to be active in hedging currency risks, interest rate risks, and exposure to commodity price changes; indeed, this firm is active in all three categories. Note that CPC explains the purposes for its hedging activities on foreign exchange and also what the company does not do — act as a trader.

[5] Williams, *Miller's Comprehensive GAAP Guide.*

EXHIBIT 12B.1

Chrysler Corporation
Disclosure of Financial Instruments

NOTE 16. FINANCIAL INSTRUMENTS

The estimated fair values of financial instruments have been determined by Chrysler using available market information and the valuation methodologies described below. However, considerable judgment is required in interpreting market data to develop the estimates of fair value. Accordingly, the estimates presented herein may not be indicative of the amounts that Chrysler could realize in a current market exchange. The use of different assumptions or valuation methodologies may have a material effect on the estimated fair value amounts.

Amounts related to Chrysler's financial instruments were as follows:

	DECEMBER 31, 1994		DECEMBER 31, 1993	
In millions of dollars	Carrying Amount	Fair Value	Carrying Amount	Fair Value
Balance Sheet Financial Instruments				
Marketable securities	$ 3,226	$ 3,218	$ 1,055	$ 1,061
Finance receivables and retained interests[1]	10,524	10,494	8,252	8,345
Debt[2]	13,309	13,735	11,550	12,588
Currency exchange agreements[3]	220	241	121	145

(1) The carrying value of finance receivables excludes $2.0 billion of direct finance and leveraged leases classified as finance receivables in the consolidated balance sheet at December 31, 1994 and 1993. The carrying value of retained interests excludes $41 million and $57 million of retail lease securities at December 31, 1994 and 1993, respectively.

(2) The carrying value of debt excludes $17 million and $22 million of obligations under capital leases classified as debt in the consolidated balance sheet at December 31, 1994 and 1993, respectively.

(3) Currency exchange agreements are recorded on the consolidated balance sheet as a reduction to the carrying value of debt.

	DECEMBER 31, 1994		DECEMBER 31, 1993	
In millions of dollars	Contract/ Notional Amount	Unrealized Gains/ (Losses)	Contract/ Notional Amount	Unrealized Gains/ (Losses)
Off-Balance-Sheet Financial Instruments				
Interest rate swaps				
With unrealized gains	$101	$ 4	$ 314	$ 15
With unrealized losses	676	(16)	1,107	(95)
Interest rate caps	134	—	403	—
Forward interest rate contract	500	1	—	—
Currency forward contracts				
With unrealized gains	—	—	1,285	61
With unrealized losses	326	(17)	437	(8)
Purchased currency options	901	(21)	116	2

The carrying values of cash and cash equivalents, accounts receivable and accounts payable approximated fair values due to the short-term maturities of these instruments.

The methods and assumptions used to estimate the fair values of other financial instruments are summarized as follows:

Marketable securities

The fair values of marketable securities were estimated using quoted market prices.

Finance receivables, retained interests in sold receivables and other related amounts–net

The carrying value of variable-rate finance receivables was assumed to approximate fair value since they are priced at current market rates. The fair value of fixed-rate finance receivables was estimated by discounting expected cash flows using rates at which loans of similar maturity would be made as of the date of the consolidated balance sheet. The fair values of excess servicing cash flows and other amounts due CFC arising from receivable sale transactions were estimated by discounting expected cash flows.

Debt

The fair value of public debt was estimated using quoted market prices. The fair value of other long-term debt was estimated by discounting future cash flows using rates currently available for debt with similar terms and remaining maturities.

Currency exchange agreements

The fair values of currency exchange agreements were estimated by discounting the expected cash flows using market exchange rates and relative market interest rates over the remaining terms of the agreements. Currency exchange agreements are more fully described in **Note 1. Summary of Significant Accounting Policies** and **Note 6. Debt.**

EXHIBIT 12B.2

CPC International
Disclosure of Financial Instruments

Financial instruments

Fair value of financial instruments— The carrying values of cash equivalents, accounts receivable, accounts payable, and short-term debt approximate fair values. The fair value of long-term debt at December 31, 1994, and 1993 was $870 million and $899 million, respectively. The fair value of long-term debt was based on quotes obtained from brokers.

Foreign exchange contracts— The Company's policy is to hedge its exposure to foreign currency cash flows resulting from planned dividends, fees and royalties, intercompany loans, and other similar transactions. The Company also hedges certain net investments in foreign operations with foreign exchange contracts or with borrowings denominated in the particular foreign currency. As a matter of policy, the Company does not speculate on foreign currencies. Gains and losses, both realized and unrealized, on financial instruments that hedge operating activities and related cash flows, flow through income in the same period as the items being hedged. Gains and losses, both realized and unrealized, on financial instruments that hedge the Company's investments in foreign operations are recognized as part of the cumulative translation adjustment in stockholders' equity.

At December 31, 1994, the Company had forward exchange contracts to deliver $414 million of foreign currencies comprising $137 million in German marks, $87 million in British pounds, $14 million in Swiss francs, $71 million in Italian lira, $26 million in Dutch guilders, $52 million in French francs, and $27 million in various other currencies. The Company also had, at December 31, 1994, contracts to purchase $56 million worth of foreign currencies consisting of $15 million in Italian lira, $13 million in Austrian schillings, and $28 million in other currencies. At December 31, 1993, the Company had forward exchange contracts to deliver $376 million of foreign currencies comprising $192 million in German marks, $90 million in British pounds, $35 million in French francs, $33 million in Dutch guilders, and $26 million in various other currencies. The Company also had, at December 31, 1993, contracts to purchase $31 million in foreign currencies, primarily German marks. Most of the forward currency contracts outstanding mature within 90 days of the respective balance sheet dates.

Interest rate swaps— The Company utilizes interest rate swap agreements to minimize its financing costs and to balance its current and noncurrent asset levels with floating and fixed-rate debt positions. The Company's risk related to swap agreements is limited to the cost of replacing such agreements at current market rates. The Company continually monitors its positions and credit ratings of its counterparties and limits the number of agreements it enters into with any one party. Management believes the risk of incurring a material loss is remote. Any interest rate differential on interest rate swaps is recognized as an adjustment to interest expense over the term of the agreement.

At December 31, 1994, the Company had $280 million notional amount of interest rate swap agreements outstanding. A portion of the Company's variable interest rate debt position was hedged with $100 million notional amount of swap agreements with a weighted average receive rate of 6.50% and a weighted average pay rate of 5.09%. The remaining agreements with maturity dates through 2000 effectively convert fixed interest rate debt into variable interest rate debt with a weighted average receive rate of 5.89% and a weighted average pay rate of 6.50%. At December 31, 1993, the Company had $300 million notional amount of interest rate swap agreements outstanding. A portion of these agreements with maturity dates through 1995 effectively converted an aggregate principal amount of $100 million variable interest rate debt into fixed interest rate debt with a weighted average receive rate of 7.21% and a weighted average pay rate of 3.44%. The remaining agreements with maturity dates through 2000 also effectively converted $200 million of fixed interest rate debt into a variable interest rate debt with a weighted average interest receive rate of 5.88% and a weighted average pay rate of 5.09%. Net unrealized gains and losses at December 31, 1994 and 1993 were not significant.

Commodities— The Company follows a policy of fixing the cost, with commodities futures contracts, of certain of its key North American raw material purchases in line with production requirements to minimize cost risk due to market fluctuations. Such raw materials may or may not be hedged at any given time based on management's decisions as to the need to fix the cost of such raw materials. In addition, commodity futures contracts are employed to fix the raw material cost of certain fixed price sales contracts of the corn refining business. Gains and losses arising from such hedging transactions are included with the cost of raw material purchases.

The Company's products are manufactured from a number of raw materials, including soybean and other edible oils, peanuts, corn, and wheat, all of which are, and are expected to continue to be, in adequate supply. However, as market prices of these materials depend on a number of unpredictable factors, such as farm plantings and weather, resulting fluctuations may have an effect on the Company's earnings to the extent such fluctuations cannot, for competitive reasons, be passed on immediately through pricing adjustments of the Company's products. It is the possible exposure to such relatively short-term cost/pricing imbalances that the Company attempts to cover through fixing, when appropriate, the costs of certain commodities in the short term by using commodities futures contracts.

At December 31, 1994, and 1993, the Company had commodity futures contracts to purchase primarily corn totaling $138 million and $111 million, respectively. The commodity futures contracts at December 31, 1994, principally call for delivery in the period January to July 31, 1995. Contracts for delivery beyond March 31, 1995, aggregate about $89 million, of which $46 million is due in May, $38 million in July, and the balance later in the year. At December 31, 1994, the Company had unrealized gains of $2 million on these contracts.

CPC disclosed the details of its interest rate swaps in the same fashion as PepsiCo: Fixed-rate debt is being transformed into variable-rate debt. And, as with Chrysler, the magnitudes of these contracts are also disclosed:

- $414 million forward currency exchange delivery contracts.
- $56 million forward currency exchange purchase contracts.
- $280 million face amount interest rate swaps.
- $111 million commodities futures contracts to purchase.

These contracts do not seem large relative to the size of the corporation. Of course, without value at risk one can not assess what might happen if interest rates or corn prices or currencies were to change dramatically. The directors of Procter & Gamble did not think they had much of a problem with their two derivatives tied to a $200 million piece of debt, but they ended up losing almost the entire $200 million in less than a year! The FASB still has more work to do in helping investors and creditors understand the potential exposure that derivative financial instruments can present.

ISSUES FOR DISCUSSION

D12.1 Compare and contrast the following transactions:

a. Tom Barry borrows $3,000 from his local bank, agreeing to repay a total of $3,600 in principal and interest over the coming year.

b. Dana Howard signs a noncancelable, nontransferable lease on an apartment for one year, agreeing to pay $3,600 in rent payments over the coming 12 months.

How would you account for each of these transactions?

D12.2 In 1981, American Airlines introduced its frequent flyer program, the Advantage Program, as a means to attract new and retain old customers. By 1995, the program had been copied by many carriers; an estimated 34 million individuals belonged to these programs. British Airways alone acknowledged it had 5 billion unused air miles outstanding. How should an airline account for the unused miles earned by its frequent flyer club members?

D12.3 What is the effect of purchase discounts on the manufactured costs of a product? What circumstances are possible in this situation? What is the impact of each on a product's cost?

D12.4 The following appeared in Philip Morris Companies Inc. 1994 annual report in the footnote titled Contingencies:

> In May 1994, an action was filed in Mississippi state court against the leading United States cigarette manufacturers and others, including the Company, by the Attorney General of Mississippi seeking reimbursement of Medicaid and other expenditures by the State of Mississippi claimed to have been made to treat smoking-related diseases. Plaintiff also seeks an injunction barring defendants from selling or encouraging the sale of cigarettes to minors. In June 1994, defendants removed the case to the United States District Court for the Southern District of Mississippi. In that same month, plaintiff moved to remand the case back to state court. Plaintiff's motion was granted on August 17, 1994 and the case remanded to state Chancery Court. In September 1994, the plaintiff moved to strike defendants' challenges to the sufficiency of the complaint and the subject matter jurisdiction of the Chancery Court. Also in September 1994, defendants moved to transfer the case from the Chancery Court to the Circuit Court. In October 1994, defendants moved for judgment on the pleadings. All three motions are presently pending. In December 1994, the Governor of the State of Mississippi filed an amicus brief in support of defendants' motions.

> In August 1994, an action was filed in Minnesota state court against the leading United States cigarette manufacturers and others, including the Company, by the Attorney General of Minnesota and Blue Cross and Blue Shield of Minnesota seeking reimbursement of Medicaid and other expenditures by the plaintiffs claimed to have been made to treat smoking-related diseases. Plaintiffs assert causes of action of negligent performance of a voluntary undertaking, violation of Minnesota antitrust laws, violation of consumer protection statutes, restitution, and conspiracy.

These are 2 of 13 cases in which significant developments occurred in 1994. Are these liabilities? How should they be reported? Why?

D12.5 The following footnote appeared in the 1990 annual report of Bausch & Lomb, Inc.:

> The terms of a revolving credit and term loan agreement provide for a 364-day revolving credit line with a six-month term loan provision thereafter, under which the company may borrow up to $100,000,000. A commitment fee at a rate of .05 percent is charged on the unused portion. For any six-month period during the year the agreement includes a provision that allows the company to increase its borrowings up to an additional $150,000,000. A commitment fee of $62,500 per year is paid under this provision. The interest rate for total borrowings under the agreement is the prime rate or, at the company's option, a mutually acceptable market rate. At December 19, 1990, this revolving credit and term loan agreement supported $100,000,000 of unsecured promisory notes that have been classified as long-term debt. While the company intends to refinance these obligations, the level of the outstanding debt may fluctuate from time to time.

What business event has occurred? Bausch & Lomb's fiscal year ended December 29, 1990. What would you expect on its 1990 balance sheet and on the 1990 income statement related to this footnote?

D12.6 In April 1995, the Federal National Mortgage Association (Fannie Mae) issued new debentures as follows:

> $400,000,000
> 8% debentures
> Dated April 10, 1995
> Due April 13, 2005
> Interest payable on October 13, 1995 and semiannually thereafter
> Callable on or after April 13, 1998
> Price 99.921875%

The debentures were not obligations of the United States government and were not guaranteed by it.

Explain what happened. What are the accounting issues?

D12.7 In accounting, a distinction is made between the concept of an *obligation* and a *liability*. Prepare a list of the different types of nonliability obligations that a company might have. What prevents each type from being a liability?

D12.8 What is the difference between *accounts payable* and *accrued expenses?* If an accrued item is not yet due, how can it be considered a liability?

D12.9 Consider the accounting for a deposit or prepayment. Why is this receipt of cash a liability? Does such an event leave the business better off or worse off than it was before?

PROBLEMS

P12.1 Purchase discounts. Olympic Distributors of Seattle, Washington, distributes general hardware items to more than a thousand retail customers in the Northwest. Olympic's management manages its cash flow carefully and almost always takes the purchase discounts offered by its suppliers. Recently, many manufacturers have reduced their discounts or have changed the terms and conditions. Occasionally, Olympic has lost discounts by choosing to pay later. Naomi Herring, Olympic's accounts payable supervisor, set out to bring some order to the process. The company has a long-standing revolving loan agreement with a local bank whereby the effective interest rate is one point over prime; thus, Olympic is currently paying 9.5 percent on its short-term borrowing. In the past three years, that cost has been as high as 14 percent and as low as 8.5 percent.

Herring rummaged through the pile of invoices on her desk, noting the different purchase discounts, terms, and conditions given by various vendors. Most fell into one of three categories:

1. 1/10 days, net 30.
2. 2/10 days, net 30.
3. Net 30 days, 2 percent monthly finance charge on balances over 30 days.

Required:

a. Prepare a table with interest rates from 10 to 20 percent, indicating for each of the three types of conditions whether Olympic should take the discounts for prompt payment or not.

b. How would you explain to a new employee why the typical 2/10, net 30 terms and conditions are really a good deal for a company paying (or earning) 12 percent on its money?

P12.2 Bond valuation. MTF, Inc., was a manufacturer of electronic components for facsimile equipment. The company financed the expansion of its production facilities by issuing $10 million, 10-year bonds carrying a coupon rate of 8 percent, with interest payable annually on December 31.

The bonds had been issued on January 1, and at the time of the issuance, the market rate of interest on similar risk-rated instruments was 6 percent. Hence, the bonds were sold into the market at a price reflecting an effective yield of 6 percent.

Two years later, the market rate of interest on comparable debt instruments had climbed to a record high level of 12 percent. The CEO of MTF, Inc., realized that this might be an opportune time to repurchase the bonds, particularly because an unexpected surplus of cash made the outstanding debt no longer necessary.

	Present Value of $1 to Be Received at the End of Year n			Present Value of $1 to Be Received at the End of Each Year for n Years		
n	6%	8%	12%	6%	8%	12%
1	0.9434	0.9259	0.8930	0.9434	0.9259	0.8930
2	0.8900	0.8573	0.7970	1.8334	1.7833	1.6900
3	0.8396	0.7938	0.7120	2.6730	2.5771	2.4020
8	0.6274	0.5403	0.4040	6.2098	5.7466	4.9680
9	0.5919	0.5002	0.3610	6.8017	6.2469	5.3280
10	0.5584	0.4632	0.3220	7.3601	6.7101	5.6500

Required:
Using the present value data in the table, calculate the following:

a. The proceeds received by the company at initial issuance.

b. The interest expense to be reported in each of the two years that the bonds were outstanding.

c. The amount of cash needed to retire the debt after two years, assuming a yield rate of 12 percent.

d. Evaluate the merits of retiring the bonds early. Do you agree with the CEO?

P12.3 Accounting for zero-coupon debentures. In December 1990, Alza Corp. of Palo Alto, California, offered for sale $750 million of zero-coupon debentures. The bonds were offered for sale at $221.87 for each $1,000 face amount. Alza, a pharmaceutical products maker, expected to receive $166.4 million from the debt sale.

Required:

How would Alza Corp. account for the proceeds from the sale of bonds? Why would Alza want to sell zero-coupon bonds? Why would anyone buy them?

P12.4 Debt retirement. In March 1987, Continental Airlines sold $350 million of aircraft bonds. The bonds took their name from the fact that Continental had secured the debt with a pool of 53 airplanes and 55 engines, initially valued at $467 million.

By 1990, however, Continental was experiencing serious financial difficulties and lacked sufficient cash flows to continue operations. Consequently, with bondholder approval, Continental removed some of the planes from the pool and sold them to raise cash to support operations. After taking the airplanes from the asset pool, Continental was required (within a reasonable period of time) either to replenish the pool or to retire some of the bonds. Continental chose the latter option, and in late 1990 went into the market and repurchased $167 million (face value) of its aircraft bonds at a price of $0.58 on the dollar.

Required:

a. Assuming that Continental initially issued the aircraft bonds at par value, how would the company account for the debt repurchase?

b. Was the decision to retire the debt a good one?

P12.5 Accounting for long-term bonds. On March 1, 1996, Proctor Company sold $10,000,000 principal amount of its 8 percent bonds. The maturity date of the bonds was March 1, 2016 and interest was due semiannually each September first and March first. The sale of the bonds netted $10,400,000.

a. Did the buyers of the bonds make a mistake in paying more than the face amount for the bonds? Explain.

b. What specific accounts and amounts pertaining to the bonds would appear on Proctor's balance sheet at December 31, 2005, and on its 2005 income statement?

c. Assuming the bonds are allowed to mature in 20 years, the total interest expense for Proctor, related to those bonds, would total what amount?

P12.6 Issuing bonds at a discount. Hopewell, Inc., issued $5,000,000 face value of its 10 percent bonds on January 1, 1996. The bonds matured in 10 years, and interest was payable semiannually. Hopewell, Inc. netted $4,800,000 from the issue.

Required:

a. What is the entry for the January 1, 1996 bond issue?

b. What are the 1996 semiannual journal entries?

c. What is the December 31, 2005 journal entry, assuming the bonds have matured then?

P12.7 Issuing bonds at a discount. This past December 1, 1995, James Cable Corporation issued $2,500,000 of 14 percent bonds, due December 1, 2005. Interest is payable quarterly and the company netted $2,440,000 from the issue.

Required:

a. Prepare the December 1, 1995 journal entry to record James Cable's bond issue.

b. In regards to this bond issue, will James Cable's 1995 interest cash payments be less than or greater than its 1995 interest expense? Provide amounts and explain.

c. Prepare any necessary December 31, 1995 journal entries related to this bond issue.

d. Prepare any necessary March 1, 1996 entries related to this bond issue.

e. What is the total amount of bond interest expense that James Cable will book over the life of the bond?

P12.8 Accounting for purchase discounts. Suppose two companies were similar except that the first, NetCo, usually takes all purchase discounts available from its vendors and thus records all purchases at net. The second company, GrossCo, does not usually take such discounts and, accordingly, records all purchases at invoice cost.

Required:

a. What entries would the two companies make if they purchase $10,000 of materials under the conditions of 2/10, net 30 (if you pay within 10 days, you may subtract 2 percent from the bill; otherwise, the bill is due in 30 days).

b. What entries would the two companies make on Day 9 if they both decided to take the discount?

c. What entries would the two companies make if they wait to pay the bill on Day 29?

d. What is the income statement impact of parts (b) and (c) on NetCo and GrossCo? What should these income statement items be called?

12.9 Amortization of debt discount. In October 1989, Sun Microsystems, Inc., sold $135 million of 6⅜ percent convertible subordinated debentures due October 15, 1999. They were sold at 84.9 percent of face value, with an effective annual yield to maturity of 8.67 percent. Interest is to be paid semiannually beginning April 1990. As of June 30, 1991, the debentures were valued at $117,013 on Sun's balance sheet.

Required:

Assuming no early retirements or conversions, what will these debentures be valued at on June 30, 1992?

P12.10 Accounting for zero-coupon debentures. Woody Corporation issued $40 million face value of 10 year, zero coupon debentures on January 1, 1983 to one purchaser. The company netted $18 million. Assume that on December 31, 1991, interest rates for bond instruments posing similar risks was 8 percent.

Required:

a. Prepare the January 1, 1983 and December 31, 1983 journal entries for both the seller and the buyer of the debentures.

b. At what amounts would these debentures be reported on the two companies' balance sheets at December 31, 1991?

c. Estimate the market price of these debentures as of December 31, 1991.

d. Assume the purchaser of the Woody zeros sold them on January 2, 1992 to a third party. Prepare the journal entries that Woody and the original buyer need to make at that date.

P12.11 Accounting for warranties. Signal Communications provides certain warranties for its products. As of January 1, 1996, the Provision for Estimated Warranty Costs account stood at $72,500. Warranty costs were estimated to be 0.5 percent of sales. Prepare entries related to warranties for the years 1996, 1997, and 1998 using the following:

	Sales (Millions)	Actual Warranty Costs
1996	$6.5	$53,200
1997	7.9	49,800
1998	5.8	61,100

Required:

a. What will appear on the income statements for each of these three years relating to warranties?

b. What will be the amount in the Provision for Estimated Warranty costs account at December 31, 1998?

P12.12 Mortgages. A mortgage is a type of loan that is secured by property. Suppose a company acquired a building financed with a 20-year, 9½ percent mortgage with level payments to be made monthly. An amount of $20 million was to be borrowed under this mortgage.

Required:

a. What would the payments be?

b. How would the mortgage appear in the company's balance sheet after the third year?

Suppose that after three years the building is refinanced with a new 20-year mortgage; this time the rate is 8 percent. The amount of the new loan is to be the exact principal amount of the loan it replaces.

c. What difference would it make in the monthly payments?

d. What transactions would be made to repay the old loan and consummate the new one? Explain.

P12.13 Accounting for mortgages in the United Kingdom. Most home mortgages in the United Kingdom are of a variable-rate type. At the time the mortgage is issued, a monthly payment is determined by the bank or building society holding the mortgage. As interest rates change, the monthly payment typically remains constant (at least during the early years) while the principal is adjusted to account for the change in interest rates. The following is an example to see how this might work.

Suppose one had a £100,000, 20-year mortgage established when interest rates were 10 percent. Monthly payments would be £965. Now suppose the following:

Month	Interest Rate Percentage
1	10
2	11
3	12
4	11
5	10
6	9

Required:

At the end of six months, what is the outstanding principal on this mortgage? How much interest has been paid?

P12.14 Analyzing debt securities. On January 16, 1992, Dayton-Hudson announced its intent to sell $200 million of debentures due January 15, 2012, with a coupon of 8.6 percent, priced at 99⅞ percent.

Required:

What does this mean? (Explain the business event.) What will such an investment yield? (Assume the debentures paid interest semiannually.)

P12.15 Accounting for debt securities. In the Dayton-Hudson debentures described in P12.14 (the $200 million at 8.6 percent due January 15, 2012), what would the yield be if the debentures sold for only $199 million? What entry would be made at the time of sale? What entry would be made at December 31, 1992?

P12.16 Accounting for debt securities. Again with respect to the Dayton-Hudson debentures in P12.14, interest rates began falling rapidly in January 1992. Suppose that the 8.6 percent debentures due January 15, 2012, actually sold at a price yielding 8.495 percent.

Required:

How much would Dayton-Hudson receive? What accounting entry would be made when the bonds were sold? What entry would be made on December 31, 1992? On January 15, 1993?

P12.17 The making of a derivative. Global United, Inc., was concerned about declining interest rates and its exposure on a $100 million, 7½ percent fixed rate note. The note had three years to run and could not be called. The LIBOR was then 6 percent. Global wished to hedge against any further decline in interest rates and so approached Gotham Bank in hopes of securing an interest rate swap on their $100 million note.

Gotham responded by informing Global that three-year, fixed-to-variable swaps on LIBOR were then paying 7 percent. In other words, Global would receive 7 percent over the three-year period and would pay LIBOR, then at 6 percent, based on a three-month trailing rate. It would look like this to Global:

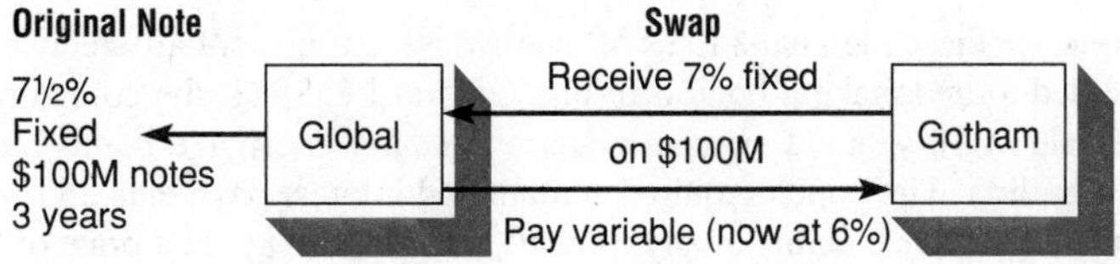

Global responded by asking, "But how do we make that swap fit our situation, we're not paying 7½ percent!" Gotham's answer was to scale up the notional amount to

$$(7.5/7) \times 100 = 107 \text{ million.}$$

Eventually they agreed to do the swap at 110 million:

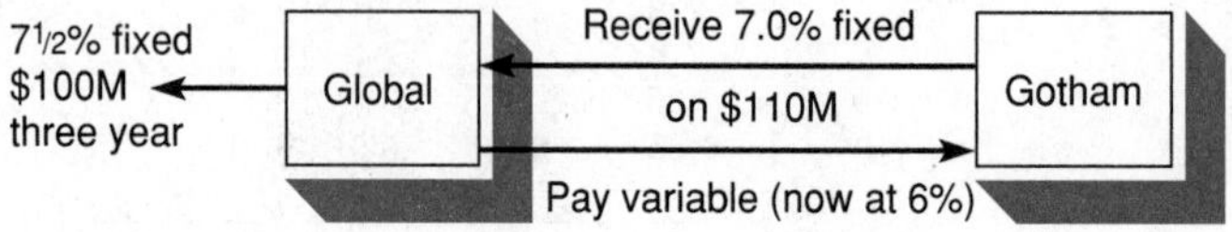

Required:

Let's look at three scenarios:

1. Status quo — no change in interest rates.
2. Rising LIBOR. At the end of the first quarter, LIBOR has moved to 6.25 percent and Global must pay 6.25% × 110/4 million or $1,718,750. Rates keep rising 25 basis points per quarter.
3. Rates fall. LIBOR at the end of quarter 1 is 5.57 percent and then the first quarter's payment to Gotham is $1,581,250. Rates will continue to drop 25 basis points a quarter.

For each scenario:

a. What are the cash flows?

b. What accounting should Global make at the time the derivative is executed? At the end of each quarter?

c. What is the fair value at the end of each quarter?

d. What alternative accounting should be considered for such swaps?

e. Assume Gotham owns the other side of this swap. What entries should they make?

CASES

C12.1 Bond valuation: R.J. Miller, Inc. R.J. Miller, Inc., is a real estate development company headquartered in Charleston, West Virginia. Since its inception in 1970, the company had been involved in the development of numerous shopping centers and apartment complexes in Virginia, West Virginia, and Maryland. In 1976, the company went public with an initial offering of 2.5 million shares of common stock. The public offering was quickly sold out at $10 per share. Over the next six years, the price of the common shares more than doubled.

Other than the initial public offering of stock, the company generated capital for its development projects primarily through the sale of limited partnership interests and bank borrowing. By 1979, however, interest rates had begun to climb sharply, and by 1980, the prime rate of interest (the rate charged by banks to their most preferred customers) had reached 20 percent. R.J. Miller, Inc., was not considered a preferred customer and consequently found itself facing the prospect of borrowing funds at nearly 22 percent.

To escape these high bank rates of interest, which substantially reduced profit margins, the firm decided to undertake a bond offering. On April 1, 1981, the company successfully completed the sale of 10-year, 15 percent coupon rate, first mortgage bonds having a maturity value of $40 million. The bonds required semiannual interest payments and were sold to yield 16 percent. They were callable at any time after April 1, 1986, at a price of $105 per bond, and were also convertible into R.J. Miller common stock ($1 par value) at any time after April 1, 1983, at a rate of 58.82 shares of common per $1,000 bond.

Over the next two years, interest rates fell by more than 50 percent. By April 1983, the prime rate of interest had fallen to 10½ percent. The stock market, in turn, had moved into a bullish trend with the Dow Jones Industrial Average breaking the 1,200 point barrier. In response to these market trends, the price of R.J. Miller common rose to $25 per share.

Required:

Use the charts that follow in solving these problems:

a. Determine the amount of the proceeds from the April 1, 1981, sale of bonds (ignore transaction costs). Illustrate the December 31, 1981, balance sheet disclosures related to the debt. (Use the effective interest method and use specific dollar amounts.)

b. Determine the amount of interest expense to be deducted during the year ended December 31, 1982 (*Note:* Use the effective interest method.)

c. Assume that bonds having a maturity value of $5 million are converted into common stock on April 1, 1983. Describe the balance sheet and income statement effects of the conversion. (Use specific dollar amounts.)

d. Assume that the market yield on the outstanding bonds is 12 percent per annum and that the price per share of common is $18.75. Assume also that on April 1, 1986, the firm decides to repurchase in the open market bonds having a maturity value of $20 million. Describe the balance sheet and income statement effects of this transaction. (Use specific dollar amounts.) Do you agree with this decision?

e. Assume that the company decides to force the conversion of the remaining outstanding bonds by calling the bonds as of December 31, 1988. Assume that on that date the company's common stock was trading at $28 per share. Show the journal entries needed to record (1) the calling of the bonds and (2) the conversion of the bonds. If you were a bondholder, what option would you take?

Present Value of $1

Period	6%	8%	12%	15%	16%
1	0.943	0.926	0.893	0.870	0.862
2	0.890	0.857	0.797	0.756	0.743
3	0.840	0.794	0.712	0.658	0.641
4	0.792	0.735	0.636	0.572	0.552
5	0.747	0.681	0.567	0.497	0.476
6	0.705	0.630	0.507	0.432	0.410
7	0.665	0.583	0.452	0.376	0.354
8	0.627	0.540	0.404	0.327	0.305
9	0.592	0.500	0.361	0.284	0.263
10	0.558	0.463	0.322	0.247	0.227
11	0.527	0.429	0.287	0.215	0.195
12	0.497	0.397	0.257	0.187	0.168
13	0.469	0.368	0.229	0.163	0.145
14	0.442	0.340	0.205	0.141	0.125
15	0.417	0.315	0.183	0.123	0.108
16	0.394	0.292	0.163	0.107	0.093
17	0.371	0.270	0.146	0.093	0.080
18	0.350	0.250	0.130	0.081	0.069
19	0.331	0.232	0.116	0.070	0.060
20	0.312	0.215	0.104	0.061	0.051

Present Value of $1 Per Period

Period	6%	8%	12%	15%	16%
1	0.943	0.926	0.893	0.870	0.862
2	1.833	1.783	1.690	1.626	1.605
3	2.673	2.577	2.402	2.283	2.246
4	3.465	3.312	3.037	2.855	2.798
5	4.212	3.993	3.605	3.352	3.274
6	4.917	4.623	4.111	3.784	3.685
7	5.582	5.206	4.564	4.160	4.039
8	6.210	5.747	4.968	4.487	4.344
9	6.802	6.247	5.328	4.772	4.607
10	7.360	6.710	5.650	5.019	4.833
11	7.887	7.139	5.938	5.234	5.029
12	8.384	7.536	6.194	5.421	5.197
13	8.853	7.904	6.424	5.583	5.342
14	9.295	8.244	6.628	5.724	5.468
15	9.712	8.559	6.811	5.847	5.575
16	10.106	8.851	6.974	5.954	5.668
17	10.477	9.122	7.120	6.047	5.749
18	10.828	9.372	7.250	6.128	5.818
19	11.158	9.604	7.366	6.198	5.877
20	11.470	9.818	7.469	6.259	5.929

C12.2 Accounting for warranty costs: NoHo Manufacturing Co. NoHo Manufacturing Company has been selling equipment for many years. It is well known to consumers because of its excellent customer service reputation. NoHo sells three types of machines: A, B, and C. When you purchase equipment from NoHo, you receive a six-year warranty. Estimating the warranty costs that would be incurred in the future is a complex issue for NoHo. Accuracy is important.

At the beginning of 1987, NoHo set up a new expense pool for warranty costs. The following exhibit presents the estimated number of sales units in each of the company's product lines and the estimated warranty expense for each year beginning in 1987. This number was calculated by multiplying the average estimated warranty cost per unit of $809 (see below for this calculation) by the total number of units sold. The actual warranty costs incurred are also reported. For example, the estimated warranty expense for 1987 was $1,781 million, or $809 × 2,201,000 sales units. Actual warranty costs incurred during 1987 for equipment sold during 1987 were $426 million. (Warranty costs actually incurred for sales in model years before 1987 were charged to the old warranty expense pool.)

The column titled End-of-Year Accumulated Warranty Liability was calculated by subtracting the actual warranty costs from the pool. The EOY Accumulated Warranty Liability account increased each year. By 1995 it was $2.305 billion, although the actual warranty cost incurred that year was only $1,762 million. Thus, there was a great discrepancy between the actual and the predicted.

	Units Sold (000s)				(000s)		
	A	B	C	Total	Actual Warranty	Estimated Warranty	End-of-Year Accumulated Warranty
1987	237	1,147	817	2,201	$ 426,098	$ 1,780,609	$1,354,511
1988	243	1,125	849	2,217	1,241,539	1,793,553	1,906,525
1989	255	1,077	882	2,214	1,591,220	1,791,126	2,106,431
1990	267	1,010	921	2,198	1,773,030	1,778,182	2,111,583
1991	276	991	961	2,228	1,797,337	1,802,452	2,116,698
1992	287	953	985	2,225	1,805,745	1,800,025	2,110,978
1993	318	943	1,037	2,298	1,794,114	1,859,082	2,175,946
1994	317	901	1,043	2,261	1,786,900	1,829,149	2,218,195
1995	334	874	1,077	2,285	1,761,788	1,848,565	2,304,972
				20,127	$13,977,771	$16,282,743	

Estimated Warranty Expense
($ Per Unit)

Warranty Year	A	B	C	AVG $
1	126	281	97	168
2	437	558	80	358
3	210	238	60	169
4	86	108	48	81
5	10	25	27	21
6	11	9	15	12
				809

Based on a study done during 1986, reflecting proposed changes in future model year products.

The following tables present the actual number of units sold in each category as well as the actual warranty costs associated with them.

Actual Number of Units Sold

	1987	1988	1989	1990	1991	1992	1993	1994	1995
Unit A	237	244	258	268	281	292	310	322	336
Unit B	1,147	1,105	1,088	1,042	1,008	987	964	924	885
Unit C	817	851	870	903	943	975	1,001	1,021	1,088

Actual Warranty Costs per Unit A ($)

Warranty Year	1987	1988	1989	1990	1991	1992	1993	1994	1995	AVG $
AVG $										
1	127	130	134	135	136	134	134	138	141	134
2	436	440	433	444	442	443	442	440		441
3	218	221	230	221	224	219	217			221
4	78	79	83	76	69	67				75
5	12	6	4	−1	−8					3
6	9	4	7	8						7

Negative figures are adjustments to previous costs.

Unit A Actual Warranty Costs per Year

										Total Costs
1987	30,999									30,099
1988	103,332	31,600								134,932
1989	51,666	107,252	34,699							193,617
1990	18,486	53,780	113,015	36,258						221,539
1991	2,844	19,348	59,329	119,106	38,288					238,910
1992	2,133	1,352	21,319	59,422	124,227	39,096				247,548
1993		994	1,143	20,289	62,954	129,383	41,649			256,414
1994			1,880	(328)	19,316	64,073	136,895	44,300		266,136
1995				2,051	(960)	19,604	67,117	141,579	47,268	276,660

Actual Warranty Costs per Unit B ($)

Warranty Year	1987	1988	1989	1990	1991	1992	1993	1994	1995	AVG $
1	279	286	287	291	291	289	289	294	291	289
2	560	556	559	559	559	556	555	553		553
3	235	237	240	243	247	253	246			243
4	111	110	110	110	109	108				110
5	22	21	14	12	11					16
6	12	12	19	17						15

Unit B Actual Warranty Costs per Year

										Total Costs
1987	320,013									320,013
1988	642,320	315,527								957,847
1989	269,545	613,966	312,449							1,195,960
1990	127,317	262,082	607,678	303,361						1,300,438
1991	25,234	121,129	260,883	581,954	293,248					1,282,548
1992	13,764	22,882	119,887	252,642	563,762	285,355				1,258,298
1993		13,342	15,291	114,486	249,453	549,084	278,714			1,220,360
1994			20,334	12,898	109,735	249,565	534,954	271,357		1,198,841
1995				17,297	10,885	106,961	237,236	511,136	257,642	1,141,158

Actual Warranty Costs per Unit C ($)

Warranty Year	1987	1988	1989	1990	1991	1992	1993	1994	1995	AVG $
1	93	94	95	102	101	93	101	103	110	99
2	84	77	80	81	85	84	81	79		81
3	65	63	62	70	72	78	78			70
4	43	39	37	44	40	39				40
5	25	23	22	17	22					22
6	17	9	7	13						12

Unit C Actual Warranty Costs per Year

										Total Costs
1987	75,981									75,981
1988	68,628	80,132								148,760
1989	53,105	65,965	82,572							201,643
1990	35,131	54,058	69,386	92,478						251,053
1991	20,425	33,104	53,732	73,232	95,386					275,879
1992	13,889	19,566	32,067	63,533	80,502	90,348				299,905
1993		7,872	18,723	39,802	67,733	81,922	101,284			317,341
1994			5,888	15,732	37,793	76,145	80,987	105,378		321,923
1995				12,046	20,702	37,915	78,586	80,269	114,207	343,727

Required:

Is the pool too high or too low? Explain with figures to prove your case. If the pool were to be adjusted, what accounting entry would be required? Explain.

C12.3 Estimating warranty liabilities: General Motors.* Roger Smith, the chairman of General Motors, kept his promise to drive the first automobile produced at the Saturn Automobile Subsidiary. In the new, integrated manufacturing and assembly facility at Spring Hill, Tennessee, the ceremony was a brief and quiet one because GM did not wish to associate its name with the new cars; Saturn was to be a new American automobile. After eight years of planning and a total cost of more than $3 billion, the new high-tech automobiles went on sale in November 1990. The new company was steering clear of its GM ownership as much as it could. There were no corporate GM officials at the introduction of the cars, nor was there any mention of GM in any Saturn advertising. By December 1 only 2,162 cars had been built, but the 1991 plan targeted a volume of 120,000 units. Saturn's goal in its first year was to attract 55 percent of its buyers from non-GM owners.

With a base price of $7,995, the Saturn was predicted to get 27 miles a gallon in the city and 37 on the highway. To overcome the reluctance of car buyers to try a brand-new model that had not been tested in the real world, Saturns were offered with a guarantee. Initial buyers of the 1991 cars, if not completely satisfied, could return them for a full refund within 30 days or 1,500 miles. The guarantee presented a real challenge to those who had to estimate the costs of its warranty.

The 2,400-acre site of the Saturn complex is one of the most vertically integrated parts production and vehicle assembly plants ever built at a single location by the U.S. automotive industry.

*Prepared from publicly available sources of information.

The equipment for the casting plant, including the metal melting systems, casting production equipment, and robots, has been designed for simplicity of operation, reliability, and durability. The plant has a modified "skillet" system, or moving sidewalk, that substantially increases manufacturing quality while reducing worker fatigue. Unlike typical U.S. auto assembly operations, major components are on site at the six-building Saturn plant.

The automobiles produced in this complex are quite different from those of other complexes. Some 35 percent of the exterior and interior components are produced in plant at Spring Hill. They have stylish aerodynamic design facilitated by the freedom of plastics. GM management considers the operation in Spring Hill to be the last word in auto production with plastic. Fender and rear quarter panels are injection molded of polyphenylene ethernylon alloy; door outers are of a special grade of Dow Chemicals' Pulse polycarbonate ABS ally, and front and rear facias are of thermoplastic olefin elastomers. The vertical side panels are made of plastic to eliminate annoying parking lot dents and dings. The plastic molds can be switched quickly, making for fast styling changes. Steel is used for the horizontal panels — the hood, roof, and trunk lid.

All Saturns have aluminum engines. The sedan comes with a single overhead-cam engine, and the sport coupe has a twin-cam, multivalve engine. The sedan was expected to accelerate from 0 to 60 miles per hour in less than eight seconds — good for its class. The power train plant is Saturn's most high-tech operation. The engine block and heads, the crankshaft, and the differential housing are formed by a newly perfected method called *lost-foam casting*. Molten metal is poured into molds containing plastic foam patterns of the desired parts. The plastic vaporizes, producing more intricate parts with greater precision, which then need less costly machining to meet exacting dimensions, which translates into 30 percent less spending on tools and machinery. Lost-foam casting has been around for years, but Saturn is the first to apply it to high-volume production of large components such as engine blocks.

In addition, Saturn machines and assembles both manual and automatic transmissions on the same line in any sequence, a first for an American manufacturer. Doing both on the same line allows an exact match to car production, with no inventory buildup and at a lower investment. GM had never tried it before. In the past, the engineers designing automatics and those designing manuals worked for different divisions. The power train also was designed for ease of manufacturing, which reduced the number of operations required. One supplier estimated that production costs on the power train lines should be 20 to 40 percent lower than those of conventional engine plants.

The steps to world-class manufacturing in the engineering context began with an understanding of the benefits of designing the product and the process together and the need for quickly getting product concepts to market. The emphasis was not on technological solutions but on how people integrated solutions. The conventional practice of dividing product development into separate tasks to be done sequentially was not followed. Instead, the organization used simultaneous engineering so that projects were shaped by teams. Represented on these teams were finance, marketing, product design, manufacturing, engineering, and material engineering departments.

As part of its assault on rivals Toyota and Honda, Saturn's materials management operation developed a strict approach to finding the right transportation partners for the just-in-time manufacturing plant. Saturn sought carriers that were willing to enter into a long-term relationship and that had a proven performance record, a quality program in place, and a commitment to continuous improvement. GM also developed a strategy to train its 3,000-person workforce at the Saturn plant. The strategy combined the theories of GM, Japanese carmakers, United Auto Workers (UAW) members, and other leading U.S. firms such as Hewlett-Packard and IBM. The individualized training plan recognized each worker's knowledge base and learning speed. Saturn cars were to be built using the teamwork concept with teams of 7 to 15 employees. Saturn trainers adopted a needs-driven, competency-based approach: Team members learned at their own pace and advanced only after they mastered a required task. The average employee received 300–600 hours of training, including team concepts and leadership skills. Thirteen days of training per employee per year were written into the UAW contract.

Required:

How should GM go about estimating the warranty liabilities for its new and very different Saturn car?

C12.4 Procter & Gamble Long-term debt disclosures Enclosed are the financial instruments footnote from Procter & Gamble's (P&G) 1994 annual report; the long-term debt footnote in that statement; and the balance sheet.

Based upon these documents, respond to the following questions:

a. What business events led P&G to lose $157 million on "two out-of-policy leveraged interest rate swaps"?

b. What is an interest rate swap? What is an out-of-policy interest rate swap?

c. What event caused this loss?

d. What is the $3,542 million "notional amount" as of June 30, 1994? What is the net fair value and carrying value for those same items? How can the values be so different?

e. What's the difference between hedging and speculation? Does P&G speculate in derivatives?

f. How do the derivatives relate to P&G's long-term debt? Or do they? Explain.

g. What is a forward exchange contract as used by P&G? Why do they use them? How does that differ from the use of options to hedge currency exchange risks?

h. The footnote explains that the notional amount of forward currency contracts is $1.873 billion, but the carrying value is only $10 million, and it is negative. Why does P&G carry such a big contract at such a small value?

Following the balance sheet is the sort of statement one rarely finds in an annual report. It too was taken from P&G's 1994 annual report.

i. From the evidence you have, what is your assessment of the statement "our policy on derivatives is to not engage in speculative leveraged transactions"?

6. FINANCIAL INSTRUMENTS

The Company is subject to market rate risk from exposure to changes in interest rates and currency rates and enters into various financial instrument transactions to manage these exposures. Financial instruments used for these purposes are evaluated against the Company's policies in areas such as counterparty exposure and hedging practices, and are monitored using techniques such as market value and sensitivity analyses.

Interest Rate Instruments

The Company's financing and cash management activities entail market rate risk from exposure to changes in interest rates. The Company assesses the exposure of its overall financing position on a net basis, after considering the extent to which variable rate liabilities can be offset with variable rate assets, typically cash equivalents and marketable securities. The Company's objective is to optimize interest expense consistent with maintaining an acceptable level of exposure to the risk of interest rate fluctuation. In order to achieve this objective, the Company targets a mix of fixed and variable rate debt based on an assessment of interest rate trends. To obtain this mix in a cost efficient manner, the Company primarily utilizes interest rate swaps, including foreign currency interest rate swaps, that have the effect of converting specific debt obligations of the Company from fixed to variable rate, or vice versa, as required. Amounts due to or from the counterparties to interest rate swaps are reflected in interest expense in the periods in which they accrue.

A portion of interest rate exposure is managed through the use of options to manage the Company's overall risk profile and reduce interest expense. When using written option contracts, the Company receives a premium in exchange for providing a counterparty the right to enter into a swap. Gains and losses on such options are recognized currently. The notional amounts of such instruments were $1,094 and $845 at June 30, 1994 and 1993, respectively. The fair values were $40 at June 30, 1994 and $14 at June 30, 1993, reflecting the approximate cost to terminate the options.

The net effect of interest rate instruments on interest expense for 1994 and 1993 was insignificant, but this measurement does not capture the value to the Company of managing to a targeted mix of fixed and variable rate debt.

The option portions of the two out-of-policy leveraged interest rate swaps entered into during 1994 were closed in the January–March quarter. The related $157 charge in the quarter to close these options is reflected in other income/expense, net. Leveraged options can magnify the impact of interest rate changes. At June 30, 1994 no such instruments were in our portfolio and it is the Company's intent not to enter such leveraged contracts in the future.

Based on the Company's overall variable rate exposure at June 30, 1994, including interest rate swaps and options, a 300 basis point interest rate change would not have a material effect on earnings.

The following information includes all interest rate instruments. The notional amount is the reference point for determining amounts due or receivable under the contracts. The fair value approximates the cost to settle the outstanding contracts. The carrying value includes the net amount due to counterparties under swap contracts, the marked-to-market value of written options, and currency translation associated with currency interest rate swaps.

June 30	1994	1993
Notional amount	$3,543	$3,773
Fair value: gains	13	77
losses	252	199
Net fair value	239	122
Less: carrying value	193	74
Estimated unrealized loss	46	48

The estimated unrealized losses shown above represent the incremental charge to earnings to immediately settle all interest rate swaps. However, it is the Company's current intention to leave these instruments outstanding until maturity over various periods extending to the year 2004, in which case no incremental charge to earnings will be realized.

Currency Instruments

The Company is subject to market rate risk from exposure to changes in currency exchange rates primarily in three areas: commercial transactions, intercompany financings and net investments in foreign subsidiaries.

The primary purpose of the Company's foreign currency hedging activities is to protect against the risk that local currency cash flows associated with purchase transactions will be adversely affected by changes in exchange rates. Although this foreign currency exposure is managed locally, corporate policy prescribes the range of hedging activity into which the subsidiary operations may enter. To execute this policy, the Company utilizes forward exchange contracts and options with durations of generally less than twelve months. The impact of changes in the value of these instruments typically offsets changes in the value of the underlying transactions. For accounting purposes, gains and losses on option contracts that hedge identifiable anticipated transactions and on forward contracts that hedge firm commitments are included in the measurement of the related transaction. Gains and losses on instruments used for other purposes are recognized currently.

The Company manages its foreign exchange exposure associated with intercompany financing transactions primarily using foreign currency swaps. Gains and losses on such instruments mitigate the impact on earnings of currency exchange rates changes on the underlying transactions.

The impact of net asset exposures related to investments in foreign subsidiaries are managed primarily through local currency financing, and by foreign currency denominated debt issued by the parent company. As discussed in the interest rate instruments section, the Company has also entered into currency interest rate swaps, which effectively convert the principal and interest cash flows of certain existing debt to foreign currency obligations. The currency translation associated with these obligations is designated as a hedge of the net investment in the foreign subsidiaries and reflected in the currency translation adjustment in shareholders' equity.

Currency instruments outstanding at June 30, 1994 were as follows:

( ) = Liability	Notional Amount	Carrying Value
Forward contracts	$1,873	$(10)
Currency options	1,138	10
Currency swaps	646	(62)
	3,657	(62)

The aggregate notional amount of currency instruments with off-balance sheet risk at June 30, 1993 was $2,409. The aggregate notional amount of currency instruments outstanding at June 30, 1994 increased over the prior year primarily due to an increased level of transaction hedging activity by our international subsidiaries, a timing change related to certain purchased option contracts, and the impact of a weaker dollar at year end which increased the notional value in dollars. The major currency exposures hedged by the Company include the German mark, Japanese yen and British pound sterling.

The aggregate fair value of currency instruments at June 30, 1994 and 1993 included the following unrealized amounts: $11 in net gains ($16 in gains, offset by $5 in losses), and $17 in net gains ($36 in gains, offset by $19 in losses), respectively.

Other Financial Instruments

The carrying value of other financial instruments approximated fair value at June 30, 1994 and 1993.

Credit Risk

Credit risk arising from the inability of a counterparty to meet the terms of the contracts is generally limited to the amounts, if any, by which the counterparties' obligations exceed the obligations of the Company. It is the Company's policy to only enter into financial instruments with a diversity of creditworthy counterparties. Therefore, the Company does not expect to incur credit losses on financial instruments.

Market Valuation Methods

The estimated fair value amounts of financial instruments presented have been determined using available market information and valuation methodologies, primarily discounted cash flow analysis. Such estimates require considerable judgments in interpreting market data, and changes in assumptions or estimation methods may significantly affect the fair value estimates.

5. LONG-TERM DEBT

The following presents the carrying value of outstanding long-term debt:

June 30	1994	1993
9½% notes due 1998	**$ 200**	$ 200
6¼% notes due 1995	**200**	200
8% notes due 2003	**200**	200
7.1% notes due 1994	**200**	200
6.85% notes due 1997	**200**	200
7⅜% debentures due 2023	**175**	175
8.7% notes due 2001	**175**	175
5.2% notes due 1995	**150**	150
9⅝% notes due 2001	**150**	150
8½% notes due 2009	**149**	149
10⅞% Canadian dollar bonds due 2001	**145**	157
Commercial paper	**765**	423
9.36% ESOP debentures, Series A, due 2021, guaranteed by the Company	**1,000**	1,000
8.08%–8.33% serial ESOP notes, due 1994–2004, guaranteed by the Company	**787**	836
Other, due in varying amounts through 2036	**978**	1,609
	5,474	5,824
Less amounts included in debt due within one year	**494**	650
Total long-term debt	**4,980**	5,174

The following payments are required during the next five fiscal years: 1995 — $494; 1996 — $468; 1997 — $416; 1998 — $322; and 1999 — $293.

The fair value of the underlying long-term debt, excluding amounts due within one year, was $5,205 and $5,656 at June 30, 1994 and 1993, respectively.

Certain commercial paper balances have been classified as long-term debt. The Company has the intent and ability to renew the commercial paper obligations on a long-term basis and has entered into swap arrangements that convert them to fixed rate obligations.

Consolidated Balance Sheet

June 30 (Millions of Dollars)	1994	1993
ASSETS		
Current Assets		
Cash and cash equivalents	$ 2,373	$ 2,322
Marketable securities	283	306
Accounts receivable	3,115	3,111
Inventories	2,877	2,903
Deferred income taxes	716	740
Prepaid expenses and other current assets	624	593
	9,988	9,975
Property, Plant, and Equipment	10,024	9,485
Goodwill and Other Intangible Assets	3,754	3,762
Other Assets	1,769	1,713
Total	$25,535	$24,935
LIABILITIES AND SHAREHOLDERS' EQUITY		
Current Liabilities		
Accounts payable–trade	$ 2,604	$ 2,269
Accounts payable–other	660	642
Accrued liabilities	2,961	2,838
Taxes payable	440	726
Debt due within one year	1,375	1,812
	8,040	8,287
Long-Term Debt	4,980	5,174
Other Liabilities	3,336	3,850
Deferred Income Taxes	347	183
	16,703	17,494
Shareholders' Equity		
Convertible Class A preferred stock	1,942	1,969
Common stock–shares outstanding: 1994–684,348,359; 1993–681,754,226	684	682
Additional paid-in capital	560	477
Currency translation adjustments	(63)	(99)
Reserve for employee stock ownership plan debt retirement	(1,787)	(1,836)
Retained earnings	7,496	6,248
	8,832	7,441
Total	$25,535	$24,935

Statement of Financing Philosophy

The derivatives write-off, which resulted in a $102 million charge to third-quarter earnings, warrants special comment to our shareholders.

Procter & Gamble is in the business of developing and marketing consumer products of superior value in a broad range of categories. The financing objective is in support of this business. Our philosophy about the use of financial instruments is to manage risk and cost. Our policy on derivatives is to not engage in speculative leveraged transactions.

The company has taken steps to substantially increase the oversight of the company's financial activities, including the formation of a Risk Management Council.

The council's role is to insure that the policies and procedures approved by the board of directors are being followed within approved limits, that transactions are properly analyzed prior to implementation, and that they are regularly monitored once implemented.

The Risk Management Council goes well beyond normal corporate operating controls. With these new procedures in place, the shareholders of the corporation can be assured that the company's management has taken the appropriate steps so that the situation that led to the third-quarter write-off will not happen again.

CHAPTER 13

Leases, Retirement Benefits, and Deferred Income Taxes

It was a matter of equity that current taxpayers not have to foot the bill for future retirement costs.[1]

Key Chapter Issues

- When does a lease become, in substance, a purchase of assets with a built-in financing program?
- How should leased assets be valued on the balance sheet? What about the lease liability?
- How should the pension obligations of an organization appear in the financial statements? Are they liabilities?
- Are the investments set aside to pay the pensions and other retirement benefits corporate assets, or do they belong to the pensioners?
- Should organizations recognize an expense today for employees that might not retire for 30 years or might not even live to retire?
- On the matter of income taxes, why is it that the income tax expense in the income statement is almost never what the company actually must pay? Are there two sets of books?
- Why can some organizations defer paying taxes indefinitely while others cannot?
- How can an organization have both deferred tax assets and deferred tax liabilities at the same time? What are they?

[1]"The Whitman Effect," *The New York Times*, July 9, 1995, p. 14 (section 4).

In the previous chapter we considered the valuation processes for current and noncurrent liabilities in general. In this chapter we consider three unique liabilities that frequently arise in the financial statements of publicly held companies: leases, retirement benefits, and deferred income taxes. Deferred taxes do not depend on present-value concepts for their measurement, while the other two items do. Our focus in this chapter is similar to that of Chapter 12; namely, we consider two questions: "Do these obligations exist?" "If so, how should they be valued on the financial statements?"

LEASES

Leasing of assets is a common activity for many corporations, governmental agencies, and not-for-profit entities. It is used by large organizations and small ones, by the financially strong as well as the weak. Some types of leases result in the reporting of both assets and liabilities on the balance sheet, but others do not. Just about any kind of asset can be leased — computers, copy machines, vehicles, aircraft, naval vessels, buildings, and manufacturing equipment, to name just a few.

Companies lease assets for many reasons. They use leases, for example, as a form of financing that permits a company to acquire an asset without the immediate cash consequences of purchasing it. Moreover, companies with weak credit ratings sometimes find borrowing money difficult. Thus, for these companies, leasing may be the only way to obtain the assets they need to carry on their business. Financially healthy companies, on the other hand, often lease simply because they have better alternatives for investing their cash. Sometimes the decision to lease an asset is driven by tax considerations. Finally, many companies lease assets because they find the ancillary services provided by leasing companies to be attractive. Leasing specialists often become experts at purchasing, installing, and maintaining the assets that they lease. They frequently make it easy to upgrade an asset and thereby obtain access to the latest available technology. Moreover, these leasing specialists often tailor the lease payments to the particular cash flow circumstances of the lessee.

As one might expect, there are some drawbacks to leasing. The interest rate implicit in the lease payments is frequently somewhat higher than long-term borrowing rates. In addition, lessees often face restrictions as to how an asset can be used. For example, if a purchased computer becomes redundant or is no longer needed, it can be sold, whereas with a leased computer, the lessee may be unable to cancel the lease without incurring a costly penalty.

From an accounting perspective, there are only two types of leases. **Operating leases** are nothing more than short-term rental agreements. For example, a grocery store (the *lessee*) may lease a new delivery vehicle from an auto dealership (the *lessor*) for one year. Accounting for such a lease is simple: Each month, an entry is made for the lease expense, which is deducted from revenues in the income statement. No lease asset or lease liability appears on the balance sheet. Since the company has use of the asset without having to purchase it, this type of arrangement is often referred to as **off-balance-sheet financing**.

Other leases are simply long-term purchase agreements structured as leases; essentially, they are installment purchases. The grocery store, for example, might sign a noncancelable agreement to lease a delivery vehicle for four years at amounts sufficient to cover the cost of the vehicle, interest, and administrative costs and with an option to purchase the vehicle for a nominal sum at the end of the lease period. The substance of this type of lease agreement is clear: The company has acquired an asset and has incurred a liability. Except for legal distinctions, it is equivalent to borrowing the money and buying the asset outright. Leases of this type are called **capital leases** and appear as both assets and liabilities on the lessee's balance sheet. The periodic lease payments are discounted (see Appendix 12A) at either the interest rate implicit in the lease or the lessee's borrowing rate, whichever is lower, and this present value amount is used to value both the leased asset and the lease liability on the balance sheet.

For many years executives, accountants, leasing companies, and the Internal Revenue Service have considered which lease arrangements constitute a capital lease and thus necessitate disclosure on the balance sheet. In general, capital leases are leases whose terms meet *any one* of the following four tests:

1. Ownership is transferred to the lessee by the end of the lease (the *ownership test*).
2. The lease contains an option to purchase the asset at a bargain price (the *alternative ownership test*).
3. The lease term is equal to 75 percent or more of the remaining estimated economic life of the asset (the *economic life test*).
4. The present value of the minimum lease payments (excluding any "executory" costs for insurance, maintenance, taxes, and the like) equals or exceeds 90 percent of the fair market value of the asset (the *value test*).

If none of these conditions is met, the lease agreement is considered to be an *operating lease*.[2]

Accounting for Capital Leases

Terminology is critical to any discussion of leases. There are capital-lease *assets* and capital-lease *liabilities* and, of course, lease interest *expense* for lessees and lease *revenues* for lessors. The agreement itself is called the **lease.** From a **lessee's** perspective, the accounting issues related to capital leases involve measuring the lease liability and asset, the cost of financing (interest expense), and the cost of the use of the asset (amortization expense). The related accounting issues for a **lessor,** the owner of the asset, pertain to the valuation of the lease asset and the amount of lease revenue.

The following example will be used to illustrate lease accounting for a lessee.[3]

Suppose American Airlines decides to acquire the use of a new Boeing 747 valued at $125 million. Because of its current cash position, the airline does not want to purchase the aircraft outright at this time. Instead, it decides to approach several insurance companies that might be interested in purchasing the aircraft and then leasing it to them. Assume that the best terms are available from Prudential Insurance Co. for a 10-year, quarterly installment, level payment, full-payout lease, with a quarterly payment of $5,250,000. Assume further that the airline's bank borrowing rate is 9½ percent, that the lease transfers ownership of the 747 to the airline after the last payment, and that the airline is to perform all maintenance and repairs and is responsible for insuring the aircraft.

---

[2]Some leases clearly fall in the middle, but no one has created any "middle ground" accounting rules. Many computer leases fit this description in that they run for most of the technological life of an asset and are noncancelable, but the leasing company (the lessor) keeps the asset, and the deal is structured so that the lessor will actually lose money unless it can release or sell the asset at a good price at the end of the initial lease term.

[3]The accounting for lessors is discussed in Appendix 13A, "Leases in Detail."

From the lessee's point of view, the agreement should be considered a capital lease. It meets both the ownership and the valuation tests of the capital-lease decision rules. The interest rate implicit in the lease is 8 percent (2 percent per quarter), which can be derived by simple present value techniques.[4] Because the implicit rate is lower than the company's incremental borrowing rate (that is, 9½ percent per year), the lease payments are discounted at the 2 percent quarterly rate. The present value of the capital-lease liability and the capital-lease asset is $125 million; hence, American Airlines would record the lease at signing as follows:

Dr. Leased Aircraft (A)	(inc.) 125,000,000	
Cr. Capital Lease (L)		(inc.) 125,000,000

The lease liability will be amortized using an interest amortization schedule similar to a mortgage payment table that separates the lease payments into two parts, principal repayment and interest expense. The interest amortization schedule for the American Airlines/Prudential lease is shown in Exhibit 13A.1 in Appendix 13A to this chapter. The following entry illustrates how the quarterly lease payment at the beginning of the second quarter would be recorded:

Dr. Capital Lease (L)	(dec.) 2,069,468	
Dr. Interest Expense (E)	(inc.) 2,410,403	
Cr. Cash (A)		(dec.) 4,479,871

The lease asset also must be depreciated following the asset-depreciation policies that American Airlines uses for similar assets.

Assuming that American Airlines depreciates the leased asset over 12 years (or 48 quarters), the quarterly depreciation expense would be $2,604,167 ($125,000,000/48), and the accounting entry would look like this:

Dr. Depreciation Expense (E)	(inc.) 2,604,167	
Cr. Accumulated Depreciation (CA)		(inc.) 2,604,167

Capitalized leases for buildings and equipment are ordinarily included with other property, plant, and equipment, net of the accumulated depreciation, in the balance sheet. In classified balance sheets, the next year's principal reduction is shown as a current liability, and the noncurrent liabilities section includes the capital-lease liabilities less any current portion.

As can be seen in Exhibit 13.1 (Panel A), AMR Corporation, the parent company of American Airlines, listed its flight equipment acquired with capital leases separately from its other fixed assets. The capital-lease liability appeared, in part, as a current liability and the remainder as noncurrent. Thus, as of December 31, 1994, AMR Corporation valued its equipment and property under capital leases at $1,878 million; the principal outstanding on these leases was $2,403 million ($128 million current and $2,275 long term). Note that the capital-lease liability exceeds the capital lease asset, no doubt because the asset was amortized on a straight-line basis while the effective interest method is used to amortize the capital-lease liability. Footnote 4 (Panel B of Exhibit 13.1) includes additional details of these leases and also describes other flight equipment under operating leases. It shows that most of the lease payments for both capital and operating leases are deferred into the next century. It is interesting that so

[4]Using a financial calculator, this can be easily derived. Because lease payments are made at the beginning of a period, set the calculator to *begin*. (The default option on many popular financial calculators assumes that cash flows occur at the end of a period.) Then, enter PV = 125,000,000, I = 2, N = 40 to obtain PMT = –4,479,871.05 — or a quarterly payment of $4.48 million.

EXHIBIT 13.1

AMR Corporation
Lease Disclosures

(in millions)	December 31, 1994	1993
Panel A: Partial balance sheet		
Equipment and Property		
Flight equipment, at cost	13,323	12,841
Less accumulated depreciation	3,435	3,058
	9,888	9,783
Purchase deposits for flight equipment	116	350
	10,004	10,133
Other equipment and property, at cost	4,046	3,984
Less accumulated depreciation	2,030	1,856
	2,016	2,128
	12,020	12,261
Equipment and Property under Capital Leases		
Flight equipment	2,508	2,229
Other equipment and property	268	247
	2,776	2,476
Less accumulated amortization	898	760
	1,878	1,716
Liabilities and Stockholders' Equity		
Current Liabilities		
Accounts payable	$ 920	$ 921
Accrued salaries and wages	619	507
Accrued liabilities	1,184	1,219
Air traffic liability	1,473	1,460
Current maturities of long-term debt	590	200
Current obligations under capital leases	128	110
Total current liabilities	4,914	4,417
Long-Term Debt, Less Current Maturities	5,603	5,431
Obligations under Capital Leases, Less Current Obligations	2,275	2,123
Other Liabilities and Credits		
Deferred income taxes	279	310
Deferred gains	733	786
Postretirement benefits	1,254	1,090
Other liabilities and deferred credits	1,048	893
	3,314	3,079

continued

much of AMR's leases are operating as opposed to capital leases. The 15 Boeing 767-300ER's are on a 10-year lease with renewal provisions for another 10 to 12 years; yet they are cancelable upon 30 days notice! This cancellation clause certainly keeps the leases from meeting the test for capitalization of a lease; but one has to wonder what penalties or fees are associated with the cancellation. It raises the basic question about leases: Is the substance of this transaction a purchase with long-term financing or is it a short-term rental? With the airliner market as soft as it was in the mid-1990s, would Boeing build and rent 15 big planes under leases with such short cancellation periods unless they were protected in some fashion? And if Boeing is protected, then isn't AMR bearing the risk of ownership?

EXHIBIT 13.1 concluded

Panel B: Footnote

4. Leases

AMR's subsidiaries lease various types of equipment and property, including aircraft, passenger terminals, equipment, and various other facilities.

The future minimum lease payments required under capital leases, together with the present value of net minimum lease payments, and future minimum lease payments required under operating leases that have initial or remaining noncancelable lease terms in excess of one year as of December 31, 1994, were (in millions):

Year Ending December 31,	Capital Leases	Operating Leases
1995	$ 273	$ 946
1996	300	924
1997	280	920
1998	276	931
1999	270	912
2000 and subsequent	2,440	15,378
	3,839*	$20,011†
Less amount representing interest	1,436	
Present value of net minimum lease payments	$2,403	

*Future minimum payments required under capital leases include $390 million and $216 million guaranteed by AMR and American, respectively, relating to special facility revenue bonds issued by municipalities.

†Future minimum payments required under operating leases include $6.3 billion guaranteed by AMR relating to special facility revenue bonds issued by municipalities.

At December 31, 1994, the company had 216 jet aircraft and 123 turboprop aircraft under operating leases, and 82 jet aircraft and 63 turboprop aircraft under capital leases.

The aircraft leases can generally be renewed at rates based on fair market value at the end of the lease term for one to five years. Most aircraft leases have purchase options at or near the end of the lease term at fair market value, but generally not to exceed a stated percentage of the defined lessor's cost of the aircraft. Of the aircraft American has under operating leases, 15 Boeing 767-300ERs are cancelable upon 30 days' notice during the initial 10-year lease term. At the end of that term in 1998, the leases can be renewed for periods ranging from 10 to 12 years.

Rent expense, excluding landing fees, was $1.3 billion for 1994, 1993, and 1992.

In many countries (Switzerland and India, for example), leases are not capitalized; instead, they are all treated like operating leases. This could represent a significant off-balance-sheet asset and liability for many companies reporting in other countries. The International Accounting Standards Committee's *IAS No. 17* does deal, however, with classifying a lease as a finance lease (equivalent to the U.S. notion of a capital lease) or operating lease. Indeed, the IASC and U.S. criteria are even similar except that the IASC is not as specific as U.S. GAAP is. For example, where U.S. GAAP stipulates the existence of a capital lease if the lease term is greater than or equal to 75 percent of the asset's useful life, the IASC's guidelines are if "the lease term is for the major part of the useful life of the asset." Clearly, such a criterion is more susceptible to different interpretations in a given situation than the more precise, albeit arbitrary, U.S. notion of 75 percent. The IASC plans to revisit leases during its 1995–1999 work plan.

In summary, at the inception of a capital lease, the present value of the future lease payments is the value assigned to the capital-lease liability (net of any executory costs). Lease payments are discounted at the lessee's incremental borrowing rate unless the rate implicit in a lease is at a lower rate; then the implicit rate is used. The capital-lease asset is also valued at the present value of the lease payments. From that moment on, the two figures are rarely the same. Assets acquired under capital leases are depreciated using the straight-line (or some accelerated) method as if the assets were owned. Capital-lease liabilities are amortized using the effective interest method as if they were bonds.

Financial Disclosures for Capital Leases

At a minimum, the footnotes to a lessee's financial statements must show the following information for all capital leases:

1. The gross (undiscounted) lease payments.
2. The gross lease payments for each of the next five years and the total lease commitment (reduced by imputed interest).
3. The minimum rentals to be received under noncancelable subleases.
4. The total contingent rentals this year (leases based on something other than the simple passage of time).

For example, Exhibit 13.2 contains the PepsiCo, Inc., 1994 annual report footnote pertaining to its leases. The gross amount of these capital leases, most of which are for restaurants, was $538.1 million. The present value of these lease obligations, $298 million, is included on the balance sheet as debt; the rest is interest and executory costs. Most of PepsiCo's leases are of the operating type and do not appear as liabilities.

Lessors follow rules similar to those for lease capitalization so long as there are no uncertainties as to the amounts to be received or any question as to their collectibility. Lease assets and liabilities for lessors must be shown separately on the balance sheet, and there are substantial footnote disclosure requirements as well. The accounting followed by lessors is discussed in Appendix 13A, "Leases in Detail."

Management Issues

Most large leases are carefully structured to meet the needs and constraints of both parties. Often there is considerable negotiation or even competitive bidding. One of the first considerations is often one of accounting: "Will this be a capital lease?" No doubt many leases have been designed so as to skirt the accounting requirements for capitalization. Just as important are the terms and conditions. Some leases tailor the payment amounts and dates to the expected cash availability of the lessee (or cash requirements of the lessor). Issues related to terminating or extending the lease may receive more attention than anything else. Lessees want to protect themselves against surprises; lessors want the same protection. For example, one of the biggest concerns in equipment leasing is the threat of technological obsolescence. Some companies lease computers to protect themselves against the risk, although they, in fact, pay a premium for this protection one way or the other. Sometimes the lessor permits an upgrade or expansion by rolling or pushing the unrecovered costs into the new lease. Sometimes this is done through a negotiated set of penalties for early termination or a schedule of residual values.

EXHIBIT 13.2

Pepsico, Inc.
Lease Disclosures

Note 11: Leases
PepsiCo has noncancelable commitments under both capital and long-term operating leases, primarily for restaurant units. Certain of these units have been subleased to restaurant franchisees. In addition, PepsiCo is lessee under noncancelable leases covering vehicles, equipment, and nonrestaurant real estate. Capital and operating lease commitments expire at various dates through 2088 and, in many cases, provide for rent escalations and renewal options. Most leases require payment of related executory costs, which include property taxes, maintenance, and insurance.

Future minimum commitments and sublease receivables under noncancelable leases are as follows:

	Commitments		Sublease Receivables	
	Capital	Operating	Direct Financing	Operating
1995	$ 58.9	$ 313.0	$ 3.2	$ 9.6
1996	53.9	276.4	3.0	8.8
1997	46.7	247.3	2.7	7.7
1998	65.2	228.7	2.3	6.7
1999	34.4	203.3	2.0	6.0
Later years	279.0	1,072.1	7.1	24.2
	$538.1	$2,340.8	$20.3	$63.0

At year-end 1994, the present value of minimum payments under capital leases was $298 million, after deducting $1 million for estimated executory costs and $239 million representing imputed interest. The present value of minimum receivables under direct financing subleases was $13 million after deducting $7 million of unearned interest income.

Rental expense and income were as follows:

	1994	1993	1992
Rental expense			
Minimum	**$433.5**	$392.3	$351.5
Contingent	**31.7**	27.5	27.5
	$465.2	$419.8	$379.0
Rental income			
Minimum	**$ 11.7**	$ 12.2	$ 10.2
Contingent	**3.5**	4.4	4.5
	$ 15.2	$ 16.6	$ 14.7

Contingent rentals are based on sales by restaurants in excess of levels stipulated in the lease agreements.

RETIREMENT BENEFITS

Of all the obligations of a corporation (or a government), pensions and other retirement benefits probably present some of the most complex accounting issues. The size of the private U.S. pension system is enormous. Perhaps one-half of the full-time U.S. workforce is covered by private pension plans, with thousands of billions of dollars being managed by pension-fund administrators. One private pension fund, TIAA-CREF, had more than $100 billion of invested pension assets. Some major corporations today have more pensioners than employees! Almost everyone has a stake in the pension system: current employees and retirees, corporate executives, investment managers and advisers, unions, government officials, the IRS, accountants and actuaries, shareholders, lenders, and even the Financial Accounting Standards Board.

As one might expect, one must learn a unique vocabulary before understanding the subject of pensions. In simple terms, a **pension** is a promise to pay certain benefits to employees as specified in an agreement (the plan). The terms *contribution* and its derivatives appear frequently in any discussion of pensions. Unfortunately, *contribution* can refer either to the amounts paid into the plan or to the amounts paid out of the plan to the pensioner. In regard to payments to a plan, *contributory* pension plans are those to which employees may be required to contribute. *Noncontributory* plans are the most common; the employer makes all the payments to such plans. On the payout side, regardless of who makes the actual contributions, defined-contribution and defined-benefit plans are the two broad types of pension plans.

Defined-Contribution Pension Plans

Under a **defined-contribution plan** an employer promises to pay a specific amount per month (or quarter or year) to an employee's union or to an independent pension-fund administrator on behalf of an employee. The retirement plans for college professors are a good example.

Many U.S. colleges and universities pay a set percentage of a professor's salary each month to TIAA-CREF, a pension organization founded just for this purpose. If the professor moves from one university to another, the new employer begins paying to TIAA-CREF (assuming the new employer also uses TIAA-CREF for this purpose, and most universities do). TIAA-CREF invests the money and keeps track of the contributions made on behalf of each professor and the related earnings on those contributions. Upon retirement, the faculty member then begins receiving a monthly pension check based on his or her accumulated pension account balance. The college or university really has no pension liability to the professors beyond making those monthly payments. A professor's retirement benefits are purely a function of the total contributions he or she earns over the years from various employers, plus the earnings on those funds (and his or her retirement age and certain choices made as to payout options). Thus, the more contributions made and the better the earnings record of the invested contributions, the larger the professor's retirement income.

Accounting for defined-contribution pension funds is a simple task. Each month, the employer makes an entry to record the pension expense and the accrued pension liability. Within a few days or weeks, the liability is satisfied by a check written to the pension fund.

Defined-Benefit Pension Plans

These types of plans are more common than defined-contribution plans and much more complex. As the name suggests, **defined-benefit plans** specify the *future* amount an employee will receive on retirement. The amount is usually a function of age, years of service, and salary level; other factors may also affect the amount. Companies must estimate the *current* cost of these future pension benefits and record this cost as the pension expense for the current year. The offsetting entry is a current pension liability. Ordinarily, the company then eliminates this pension liability by paying cash (called *funding*) to an independent, third-party trustee. The trustee invests these funds and pays the retirees when they become eligible. This process is illustrated in Exhibit 13.3.

EXHIBIT 13.3

Money Flow for Defined-Benefit Pension Plans

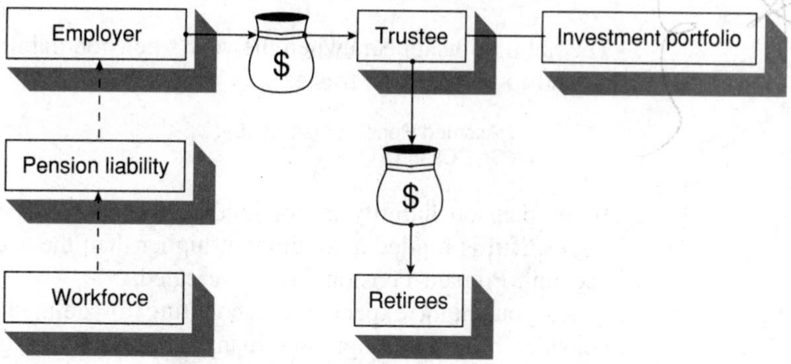

The assets of a pension fund appear on the books of the pension trustee, not on the books of the employer. It is important to understand that the trustee is only the agent of the employer. *The employer's obligation remains even after it has made the payments to the trustee.* If the trustee makes poor investments and runs out of money, the employer is still obligated to pay the pensions for the committed retirement benefits.

Ideally, the trustee should have just enough funds to satisfy the terms of the pension agreement. Occasionally, however, a fund becomes overfunded and an employer may either stop contributing to the fund for a while or may request that the trustee return the excess funds.

It is important to note that in the United States, corporations are *not* required to provide pensions to their employees. However, if they choose to do so, there are laws that prescribe how pensions are to be administered. The Employee Retirement Income and Security Act of 1974 (**ERISA**) is such a law. Moreover, tax regulations prescribe how much pension cost can be deducted for income tax purposes (usually it is the amount actually paid in cash by the company to the trustee). And, of course, generally accepted accounting practices specify how such costs are to be expensed, how liabilities are to be valued, and what supplemental information is to be disclosed in the footnotes.

Pension Expense

GAAP for defined-benefit pension plans requires that the cost of pension benefits be recognized during the period in which those benefits are earned. For example, suppose that a particular pension plan promised an employee a monthly pension of 1.5 percent of her salary at retirement for each year of service to a company. Consequently, if the employee worked 30 years prior to retirement, she would receive a monthly pension equal to 45 percent of her monthly salary at retirement. Assuming that she worked from 1990 to 2020, she would begin receiving her pension payments in 2021. Clearly, however, some portion of the payments received in 2021 were earned in 1990. Consequently, the cost of that portion of her expected pension benefit, adjusted for various estimates, including the present value, must be recognized as **pension expense** in 1990.

A typical pension expense entry recorded by an employer while its future retirees are currently working would appear as follows:

Dr. Pension Expense (E)	(inc.) 10,000	
Cr. Accrued Pension Liability (L)		(inc.) 10,000

The liability disappears when the year's pension liability is funded (that is, when cash is paid to the pension trustee):

Dr. Accrued Pension Liability (L)	(dec.) 10,000	
Cr. Cash (A)		(dec.) 10,000

If the pension liability is not funded, the accrued pension liability remains on the books. If it is funded at an amount higher than the accrued pension liability, an asset account, Prepaid Pension Cost, is created.

As you might expect, the accounting for defined-benefit pension plans requires considerable estimating: How many employees will qualify for pensions? How long will they work? How many will live to retirement age? What salaries will they be receiving? How long will they live while retired? How much will the trustee earn on the funds? What must the company pay now to satisfy all of its future obligations? If the pension fund is underfunded, how should the company "catch up"?

For many years, defined-benefit pension plans were considered to be economic obligations but not accounting liabilities. This is still the case in many countries today. It was argued that an employer did not legally have a liability to an employee *until* that employee actually reached retirement age — and then the only liability was to make one month's benefit payment! If the retiree lived another month, another month's benefit payment was due, and so on. How could pension promises made to employees with many years still to work be considered accounting liabilities when no one could know what future salary levels would be?

For example, Cable & Wireless, a company with some $10 billion of assets, prepares its accounts under U.K. GAAP. The company and its subsidiaries operate pension and retirement programs for the majority of their employees. In a footnote in their 1994 annual report, they reported the following:

The pension costs as shown in Note 6 comprise:	**1994 £m**	**1993 £m**
Regular costs	**41.6**	49.9
Amortization of surplus	**7.0**	(31.2)
	48.6	18.7
Special contribution	—	17.2
	48.6	35.9

Pension schemes other than the principal schemes are accounted for on the basis of local custom and practice. Pension prepayments of £42.3m (1993 — £35.4m) are included in other debtors (Note 18). Provisions for obligations to pay terminal gratuities on retirement to staff who are not members of the pension and retirement schemes are included in provisions for pensions (Note 23).

That is it! No assessments of ultimate liability are attempted. Nowhere is there a mention of plan assets or what they might be.

In view of the history of this issue, U.S. pension accounting represents a compromise. Employers must record as expense the current cost of pension benefits earned by employees, but estimates of the total pension obligation are relegated to the footnotes,

EXHIBIT 13.4

Exxon Corporation
Pension Disclosures

15. Annuity Benefits
Exxon and most of its affiliates have defined benefit retirement plans which cover substantially all of their employees. Plan benefits are generally based on years of service and employees' compensation during their last years of employment.

Assets are contributed to trustees and insurance companies to provide benefits for many of Exxon's retirement plans. All U.S. plans that are subject to funding requirements meet federal government funding standards. Certain smaller U.S. plans, and a number of non-U.S. plans, are not funded because of local tax conventions and regulatory practices which do not encourage funding. Book reserves have been established for these plans to provide for future benefit payments.

The discount rate used in calculating the year-end pension liability for financial reporting purposes is based on the year-end rate of interest on high quality bonds, as required by current accounting standards. This discount rate reflects the rate at which pension benefits could be effectively settled, either by matching the liability with a bond portfolio or buying annuities from an insurance company. Interest rates rose in many countries in 1994, and the resultant higher discount rates have decreased the actuarial present value of the benefit obligation from the previous year. When measured on this basis, the assets and book reserves of the U.S. plans are greater than the projected benefit obligation at the end of 1994. While assets and book reserves for non-U.S. plans are less than the projected benefit obligation, they are greater than the accumulated benefit obligation through the end of 1994.

In contrast to the discount rate, which is limited to current bond interest rates, the assumed rate of return on funded assets is based on anticipated long-term investment performance. The majority of pension assets, for both U.S. and non-U.S. plans, are invested in equities that have historically had returns which exceeded bond interest rates. In the U.S., the expected long-term rate of return for funded assets is 10 percent, and the average actual return over the past 10 years was 12 percent. This expected long-term rate of return is utilized in reporting to appropriate federal government authorities. On this basis, all of Exxon's funded plans in the U.S. are fully funded.

continued

and the emphasis is on the projected benefits at current salary levels. Only under a special circumstance, when the total pension obligation significantly exceeds total pension plan assets, is the pension obligation recorded as a balance sheet liability. Such a liability would be in addition to any yearly accrued pension liability amount arising from a particular year's underfunding of pension expense.

Financial Disclosures for Pensions

Because of the importance of pensions and the complexity presented by their accounting, GAAP requires extensive footnote disclosure. Three items — pension expense, projected benefit obligation, and the plan assets at fair value — deserve special attention in these disclosures. We have already discussed the concept of pension expense. The **projected benefit obligation,** or PBO, is the present value of all future pension benefits earned by employees as of a particular date. Of course, it must reflect expected mortality, future wage levels, and some of the other assumptions we have already mentioned. The term **plan assets at fair value** refers to the market value of the investment portfolio held by the pension trustee as of the employer company's balance sheet date.

Exhibit 13.4 illustrates typical employer company pension disclosures. It is taken from the 1994 annual report of Exxon Corporation. The total pension expense (net pension cost) for 1994 was \$189 million, consisting of \$146 million current service cost, \$354 million interest cost on pension liabilities, and a \$44 million gain for the year on investing the pension plan assets and certain adjustments. These calculations are explained more fully in Appendix 13B. The gain on plan assets was small

EXHIBIT 13.4 concluded

Annuity plans net pension cost/(credit)	U.S. Plans 1994	U.S. Plans 1993	U.S. Plans 1992	Non-U.S. Plans 1994	Non-U.S. Plans 1993	Non-U.S. Plans 1992
			(millions of dollars)			
Cost of benefits earned by employees during the year	**$ 146**	$ 111	$ 108	**$ 163**	$ 144	$ 152
Interest accrual on benefits earned in prior years	**354**	350	352	**483**	482	515
Actual (gain)/loss on plan assets	**(44)**	(463)	(150)	**76**	(742)	(258)
Deferral of actual versus assumed return on assets	**(286)**	146	(203)	**(423)**	437	(73)
Amortization of actuarial (gain)/loss and prior service cost	**10**	(35)	(51)	**67**	52	16
Net pension enhancement and curtailment/settlement expense	**9**	(13)	(8)	**35**	6	11
Net pension cost for the year	**$ 189**	$ 96	$ 48	**$ 401**	$ 379	$ 363

Annuity Plans Status	U.S. Plans Dec. 31 1994	U.S. Plans Dec. 31 1993	Non-U.S. Plans Dec. 31 1994	Non-U.S. Plans Dec. 31 1993
		(millions of dollars)		
Actuarial present value of benefit obligations				
Benefits based on service to date and present pay levels				
Vested	**$3,357**	$3,749	**$ 5,080**	$ 5,418
Non-vested	**378**	438	**243**	220
Total accumulated benefit obligation	**3,735**	4,187	**5,323**	5,638
Additional benefits related to projected pay increases	**647**	901	**738**	921
Total projected benefit obligation	**4,382**	5,088	**6,061**	6,559
Funded assets (market values)	**3,298**	3,512	**3,980**	3,997
Book reserves	**1,098**	1,215	**2,015**	1,941
Total funded assets and book reserves	**4,396**	4,727	**5,995**	5,938
Assets and reserves in excess of/(less than) projected benefit obligation	**$ 14**	$ (361)	**$ (66)**	$ (621)
Consisting of:				
Unrecognized net gain at transition	**$ 312**	$ 374	**$ 26**	$ 37
Unrecognized net actuarial gain/(loss) since transition	**(186)**	(635)	**194**	(457)
Unrecognized prior service costs incurred since transition	**(112)**	(100)	**(286)**	(201)
Assets and reserves in excess of accumulated benefit obligation	**$ 661**	$ 540	**$ 672**	$ 300
Assumptions in projected benefit obligation and expense (percent)				
Discount rate	**8.75**	7.25	**5.0–10.0**	5.0–9.0
Long-term rate of compensation increase	**5.00**	5.00	**3.0–7.0**	4.0–9.0
Long-term annual rate of return on funded assets	**10.00**	10.00	**5.0–10.0**	6.0–10.0

compared to 1993, probably because the U.S. stock market was flat or even slightly down during 1994.

The footnote also shows the funded status of the plan. The PBO for Exxon Corporation's U.S. workforce as of December 31, 1994 was $4,382 million, a drop of $700 million from the previous year. Part of the drop reflects the decline in the number of employees as the company's restructuring efforts continue; but as the text in the footnote explains, the other explanation is that a higher interest rate was assumed, thus reducing the present value of the annuity. Exxon's trustees have assets valued at $3,298 million plus another $1,098 million of unfunded liability for these pensions still on Exxon's balance sheet. For the U.S. and non-U.S. plans combined, Exxon's unfunded liability is over $3 billion ($1.098 + $2.015)! Put another way, at year-end 1994, total PBO was $10.443 billion, an approximation of the current cost of settling all of the pension liabilities, and the assets held by the trustees were only $7.278 billion, leaving a $3.165 billion unfunded pension liability. And $3.113 billion is the amount the company has accrued, although it's only a coincidence that the two numbers are almost the same. One wonders why Exxon is not fully funding its pension promises. Exxon recognized them through the income statement, but the company has not written the check to the trustees.

It is important to note that neither the PBO nor the plan assets appear on an employer company's balance sheet. GAAP for pensions is specified in SFAS No. 87, which requires the recording of a portion of the PBO as a pension liability on the balance sheet, but *only* when the PBO is "significantly underfunded." The test used to decide how much of the pension obligation should be recorded as a liability is based on a fourth figure, the **accumulated benefits obligation,** or ABO. The ABO is the present value of all pension benefits earned based on *current* salary levels. Thus, it is the same as the PBO but without the projection of future salary increases. A pension liability is recognized on the balance sheet only to the extent to which the ABO exceeds the plan assets:

Accumulated benefits obligation
Less: Plan assets
Minimum pension liability

If this minimum pension liability must be recognized, the entry reduces owners' equity unless the minimum liability arises because of changes in the plan that increase benefit levels and for certain other technical reasons. When this is the cause of the minimum liability, an asset account called the **Unfunded Pension Cost** is created. In summary, if a minimum pension liability arises as a consequence of an increase in pension benefits, the following entry is made:

Dr. Unfunded Pension Cost (A)	(inc.) XX	
Cr. Pension Liability (L)		(inc.) XX

But if a minimum pension liability results as a consequence of underfunding, the entry is as follows:

Dr. Unfunded Pension Cost (COE)	(inc.) XX	
Cr. Pension Liability (L)		(inc.) XX

The test for the minimum pension liability is made each time financial statements are prepared. If a new minimum pension liability is applicable, the old entry is reversed and a new entry is made as just explained. Exxon did not face the Unfunded Pension Cost requirement because their plan assets together with their "book reserves" exceeded the ABO. Book reserves, as used by Exxon, result when pension expense of the form

Dr. Pension Expense (E)	(inc.) XX	
Cr. Pension Liability (L)		(inc.) $XX

results in a liability that is not fully funded. Exxon's position is really one of "expensed but not funded." This means a particular pension plan can be in one of three states at any moment:

- Overfunded — plan assets exceed ABO.
- Underfunded — it has been necessary to record an entry for Unfunded Pension Cost.
- The Exxon situation — plan assets plus yearly accrued pension expenses not funded exceed ABO.

EXHIBIT 13.5

PepsiCo, Inc.
Pension Disclosures

Note 13 — Pension Plans
PepsiCo sponsors noncontributory defined benefit pension plans covering substantially all full-time domestic employees as well as contributory and noncontributory defined benefit pension plans covering certain international employees. Benefits generally are based on years of service and compensation or stated amounts for each year of service. PepsiCo funds the domestic plans in amounts not less than minimum statutory funding requirements nor more than the maximum amount that can be deducted for federal income tax purposes. International plans are funded in amounts sufficient to comply with local statutory requirements. The plans' assets consist principally of equity securities, government and corporate debt securities and other fixed income obligations. For 1994 and 1993, the domestic plan assets included 6.9 million shares of PepsiCo Capital Stock, with a market value of $227.2 million and $265.7 million, respectively. Dividends on PepsiCo Capital Stock of $4.7 million and $4.0 million were received by the domestic plans in 1994 and 1993, respectively.

The international plans presented below are primarily comprised of those in the U.K. and Canada for all three years as well as those in Mexico and Japan for 1994 and 1993. Information for 1992 has not been restated, since complete information for plans in Mexico and Japan was not available. Inclusion of the plans in Mexico and Japan increased the 1994 and 1993 pension expense by $7.9 million and $5.5 million, respectively.

The net pension expense (income) for company-sponsored plans included the following components:

	Domestic Plans			International Plans		
	1994	**1993**	**1992**	**1994**	**1993**	**1992**
Service cost of benefits earned	**$ 69.8**	$ 57.1	$ 52.3	**$ 15.0**	$ 12.4	$ 8.6
Interest cost on projected benefit obligation	**84.0**	75.6	72.0	**15.4**	15.0	10.9
Return on plan assets:						
Actual loss (gain)	**19.7**	(161.5)	(61.3)	**8.1**	(40.8)	(36.0)
Deferred (loss) gain	**(130.5)**	70.9	(26.2)	**(32.5)**	20.4	18.6
	(110.8)	(90.6)	(87.5)	**(24.4)**	(20.4)	(17.4)
Amortization of net transition (gain) loss	**(19.0)**	(19.0)	(19.0)	**(0.2)**	0.3	—
Net other amortization	**9.1**	8.8	8.2	**1.7**	1.7	(6.5)
	$ 33.1	$ 31.9	$ 26.0	**$ 7.5**	$ 9.0	$ (4.4)

continued

PepsiCo's footnote disclosure from its 1994 annual report is shown in Exhibit 13.5. It illustrates all of these points concerning the accounting for pensions. The company funds a number of defined-benefit plans. Total pension expense for 1994 was $40.6 million ($33.1 million plus $7.5 million), although the current service cost for benefits earned in the year was over twice that amount, $84.8 million ($69.8 plus $15.0 million). While PepsiCo has some plans where plan assets exceed the PBO and some where the reverse is true, its total plan assets exceed PBO by only a small amount. PepsiCo has not left large excess pension assets in the hands of the trustees. It should also be noted that PepsiCo significantly increased the assumption used to discount the PBO from 7.0 percent to 9.0 percent; otherwise the PBO would have been much higher.

OTHER RETIREMENT BENEFITS

In addition to the accounting for pensions, corporations must also accrue the expected cost of providing any promised retiree health care, life insurance, and other postretirement benefits. In general, the accounting is similar to that for pensions. Moreover, the employer's obligation for these benefits must be fully recognized by the date the employee became eligible for the benefits, and the accrual period must begin at the employee's hire date.

EXHIBIT 13.5 concluded

Reconciliations of the funded status of the plans to the pension liability are as follows:

	Domestic Plans				International Plans			
	Assets Exceed Accumulated Benefits		Accumulated Benefits Exceed Assets		Assets Exceed Accumulated Benefits		Accumulated Benefits Exceed Assets	
	1994	1993	1994	1993	1994	1993	1994	1993
Actuarial present value of benefit obligation:								
Vested benefits	**$(774.0)**	$ (726.0)	**$(21.6)**	$(192.8)	**$(124.4)**	$(138.8)	**$(22.8)**	$(28.0)
Nonvested benefits	**(97.4)**	(99.0)	**(1.6)**	(28.3)	**(2.3)**	(3.4)	**(7.4)**	(5.4)
Accumulated benefit obligation	**(871.4)**	(825.0)	**(23.2)**	(221.1)	**(126.7)**	(142.2)	**(30.2)**	(33.4)
Effect of projected compensation increases	**(111.1)**	(131.6)	**(47.6)**	(41.7)	**(24.1)**	(22.9)	**(10.1)**	(18.4)
Projected benefit obligation	**(982.5)**	(956.6)	**(70.8)**	(262.8)	**(150.8)**	(165.1)	**(40.3)**	(51.8)
Plan assets at fair value	**1,133.0**	1,018.7	**2.8**	185.2	**213.4**	221.7	**15.5**	17.3
Plan assets in excess of (less than) projected benefit obligation	**150.5**	62.1	**(68.0)**	(77.6)	**62.6**	56.6	**(24.8)**	(34.5)
Unrecognized prior service cost	**30.6**	11.7	**30.0**	49.9	**3.5**	3.2	**0.3**	0.5
Unrecognized net (gain) loss	**(71.3)**	16.0	**3.7**	26.1	**14.0**	11.9	**(3.1)**	7.7
Unrecognized net transition (gain) loss	**(73.1)**	(89.0)	**0.3**	(2.8)	**(1.8)**	(2.6)	**4.9**	8.1
Adjustment required to recognize minimum liability	**—**	—	**—**	(33.0)	**—**	—	**—**	(4.3)
Prepaid (accrued) pension liability	**$ 36.7**	$ 0.8	**$(34.0)**	$ (37.4)	**$ 78.3**	$ 69.1	**$(22.7)**	$(22.5)

The assumptions used to compute the information above were as follows:

	Domestic Plans			International Plans		
	1994	1993	1992	1994	1993	1992
Discount rate–pension expense	**7.0%**	8.2	8.4	**7.3%**	9.0	9.5
Expected long-term rate of return on plan assets	**10.0%**	10.0	10.0	**11.3%**	10.8	10.8
Discount rate–projected benefit obligation	**9.0%**	7.0	8.2	**9.3%**	7.4	9.0
Future compensation growth rate	**3.3%–7.0%**	3.3–7.0	3.3–7.0	**3.0%–8.5%**	3.5–8.5	5.0–7.0

The discount rates and rates of return for the international plans represent weighted averages.

The year-to-year fluctuations in the discount rate assumptions primarily reflect changes in interest rates. The discount rates represent the expected yield on a portfolio of high-grade (AA rated or equivalent) fixed-income investments with cash flow streams sufficient to satisfy benefit obligations under the plans when due. The higher assumed discount rates used to measure the 1994 projected benefit obligation compared to the assumed discount rate used to measure the 1993 projected benefit obligation changed the funded status of certain plans from underfunded to overfunded.

In 1994, PepsiCo changed the method for calculating the market-related value of plan assets used in determining the return-on-asset component of annual pension expense and the cumulative net unrecognized gain or loss subject to amortization. Under the previous accounting method, the calculation of the market-related value of assets reflected amortization of the actual capital return on assets on a straight-line basis over a five-year period. Under the new method, the calculation of the market-related value of assets reflects the long-term rate of return expected by PepsiCo and amortization of the difference between the actual return (including capital, dividends and interest) and the expected return over a five-year period. PepsiCo believes the new method is widely used in practice and preferable because it results in calculated plan asset values that more closely approximate fair value, while still mitigating the effect of annual market-value fluctuations. Under both methods, only the cumulative net unrecognized gain or loss which exceeds 10% of the greater of the projected benefit obligation or the market-related value of plan assets is subject to amortization. This change resulted in a noncash benefit in 1994 of $37.8 million ($23.3 million after-tax or $0.03 per share) representing the cumulative effect of the change related to years prior to 1994 and $35.1 million in lower pension expense ($21.6 million after-tax or $0.03 per share) related to 1994 as compared to the previous accounting method. Had this change been applied retroactively, pension expense would have been reduced by $16.4 million ($10.7 million after-tax or $0.01 per share) and $9.5 million ($6.5 million after-tax or $0.01 per share) in 1993 and 1992, respectively.

As with pensions, there is a delayed recognition of changes in benefit levels, and gains or losses in plan assets in excess of long-term earnings assumptions are recognized systematically over future periods. In the case of health care benefits, corporations must estimate *participation rates* for their workforce, retirement ages, per capita claims costs by age, health care cost trends, and Medicare reimbursement rates, as well as the sorts of assumptions required in pension accounting: Employee turnover, dependency status, mortality, and the rates of return on plan assets. What makes health care estimating different than that for pension costing is the sensitivity of some of the assumptions. For example, vested pension benefits become corporate obligations even if the employee changes jobs, but most corporate postemployment health benefit programs are restricted to employees who work right up to normal retirement. So estimates of employee turnover are particularly important, as are estimates of dependency, because most plans extend benefits to a spouse and other dependents. Even the age of expected retirement is key because of the copayments or coverage available through other health plans or Medicare. Finally, health care costs are especially sensitive to estimates of longevity. Because of such sensitivity, SFAS No. 106 also requires that the employer disclose the impact on current health care costs and the accumulated postretirement benefit (APB) for health care benefits of a 1-percentage-point increase in the cost of health care cost trends. This is the first time that the FASB has required this type of "what if" information on a prospective basis.

The required disclosure for postretirement benefits other than for pensions is illustrated in Exhibit 13.6, taken from the 1994 annual report of General Electric (GE) Company. The current cost for GE's retiree health and life insurance plans in 1994 was $545 million ($280 million plus $265 million) which is about the cost of pensions (pension expense was $574 million). The PBO for pensions, however, is eight times that for retiree health care obligations. The reader must wonder if this is reasonable. GE's footnote explains the assumptions they used to project future health care costs and what might happen if their assumptions are wrong. In particular, note that a 1 percent increase in the estimated trend of health care costs would increase the APB obligation by $54 million and add $5 million to the 1994 benefit cost and interest cost.

Accounting for postretirement health care and related benefits is prescribed by SFAS No. 106, which became effective in 1991. In that year GE recorded a $1.8 billion charge reflecting this accounting change, which lowered reported earnings per share by $2.07, about the size of the annual dividend. Obviously it made a big difference in reported results, although GE did not fund this provision. As of December 31, 1994, it remained on GE's balance sheet as a liability. Clearly, SFAS No. 106 is a change that was long overdue. Corporations have been promising health care benefits to retirees for decades. With rising health care costs and no government takeover of health care plans, the magnitudes of these corporate obligations have become huge. This is a good example to show where better accounting, as mandated by SFAS No. 106, should have been adopted long ago.

Before we move on to the next obligation, income taxes, there should be one final word about pensions. The three companies highlighted in this chapter (PepsiCo, Exxon, and GE) reflect different management decisions regarding provisions for pensions. From the vantage point of 1995, GE had not made a pension contribution since 1987 because the company considers its plan "overfunded" under the assumptions adopted. Exxon had funded only 70 percent of its obligation, as the company estimated, but had expensed off the rest and carried it as a balance sheet liability. PepsiCo was at a point where plan assets equaled the obligation, but one could argue that their assumptions were robust. The management trade-offs are clearly apparent in these

EXHIBIT 13.6

General Electric Corporation
Costs for Retiree Health and Life Plans

Note 6: Pension and Other Retiree Benefits
GE and its affiliates sponsor a number of pension, retiree health and life insurance, and other retiree benefit plans. Principal plans are discussed below; other plans are not significant individually or in the aggregate.

Principal pension plans are the GE Pension Plan and the GE Supplementary Pension Plan.

The GE Pension Plan covers substantially all GE employees and 55 percent of GECS employees in the United States. Generally, benefits are based on the greater of a formula recognizing career earnings or a formula recognizing length of service and final average earnings. Benefit provisions are subject to collective bargaining. At the end of 1994, the GE Pension Plan covered approximately 459,000 participants, including 139,000 employees, 143,000 former employees with vested rights to future benefits, and 177,000 retirees and beneficiaries receiving benefits.

The GE Supplementary Pension Plan is an unfunded plan providing supplementary retirement benefits primarily to higher-level, longer-service U.S. employees.

Principal retiree benefit plans generally provide health and life insurance benefits to employees who retire under the GE Pension Plan with 10 or more years of service. Benefit provisions are subject to collective bargaining. At the end of 1994, these plans covered approximately 248,000 retirees and dependents.

Transfer of aerospace businesses in 1993 resulted in associated transfers of GE Pension Plan assets of $1,169 million and projected benefit obligations of $979 million to new pension plans. The 1993 gain on transfer of discontinued operations included pension plan curtailment/settlement losses of $125 million before income taxes and retiree health and life plan curtailment/settlement gains of $245 million before income taxes.

Pension, retiree health and life insurance benefits of the discontinued securities broker-dealer were not significant.

Actuarial assumptions used to determine benefit obligations for principal plans at December 31, 1994, included a discount rate of 8.5% (7.25% at December 31, 1993) and an average rate of future increases in benefit compensation of 5.5% (4.25% at December 31, 1993).

The assumed rate of future increases in per capita cost of health care benefits (the health care cost trend rate) was 9.5% for 1994, decreasing to 9.0% for 1995 and gradually decreasing to 5.0% after the year 2022. Increasing the health care cost trend rates by one percentage point would increase the December 31, 1994, accumulated postretirement benefit obligation by $54 million and would increase annual aggregate service and interest costs by $5 million.

Recognized return on plan assets was determined by applying the expected long-term rate of return of 9.5% to the market-related value of assets.

Gains and losses that occur because actual experience differs from actuarial assumptions are amortized over the average future service period of employees. Amounts allocable to prior service for plan amendments are amortized in a similar manner.

Employer costs for principal pension and retiree health and life insurance benefit plans follow.

continued

examples: There is a long-term obligation to employees for the promised retirement benefits, and at the same time there are year-to-year pressures on reported results and cash flows. As we saw in this chapter's opening quotation, Governor Whitman sees the issue in an even different way, and perhaps for a state that has general taxing powers, her view is correct; but for corporations, GAAP requires that the costs of these promises be recognized today.

Management Issues

Pensions present a wealth of management issues, not the least of which is the decision of whether to have a pension plan at all. ERISA does not require a business to offer a pension plan to its employees, but if one is offered, ERISA does prescribe rules as to eligibility, vesting, funding, termination insurance, fiduciary standards, disclosure, and reporting. Faced with large numbers of pensioners or pensioners-to-be and smaller

EXHIBIT 13.6 continued

Cost (income) for pension plans

(In millions)	1994	1993	1992
Benefit cost for service during the year — net of employee contributions	$ 496	$ 452	$ 494
Interest cost on benefit obligation	1,491	1,486	1,502
Actual return on plan assets	(316)	(3,221)	(1,562)
Unrecognized portion of return	(1,951)	1,066	(584)
Amortization	(294)	(352)	(436)
Pension plan cost (income)	$ (574)	$ (569)*	$ (586)*

* Amounts excluding discontinued Aerospace operations were $(555) million for 1993 and $(494) million for 1992.

Cost (income) for retiree health and life plans

(In millions)	1994	1993	1992
Retiree health plans			
Benefit cost for service during the year	$ 78	$ 49	$ 62
Interest cost on benefit obligation	191	192	203
Actual return on plan assets	—	(3)	(4)
Unrecognized portion of return	(1)	1	—
Amortization	(3)	(26)	(40)
Retiree health plan cost	265	213	221
Retiree life plans			
Benefit cost for service during the year	24	21	24
Interest cost on benefit obligation	105	111	110
Actual return on plan assets	(2)	(152)	(78)
Unrecognized portion of return	(120)	.42	(20)
Amortization	8	7	2
Retiree life plan cost	15	29	38
Total	$280	$242*	$259*

* Amounts excluding discontinued Aerospace operations were $224 million for 1993 and $213 million for 1992.

Funding policy for the GE Pension Plan is to contribute amounts sufficient to meet minimum funding requirements set forth in employee benefit and tax laws plus such additional amounts as GE may determine to be appropriate from time to time. GE has not made contributions since 1987 because the fully funded status of the GE Pension Plan precludes current tax deduction and because any Company contribution would require the Company to pay annual excise taxes. Subject to limits imposed by tax laws, GE funds the present value of future life insurance benefits for retirees. In general, retiree health benefits are paid as covered expenses are incurred.

The following table compares the market-related value of assets with the present value of benefit obligations, recognizing the effects of future compensation and service. The market-related value of assets is based on cost plus recognition of market appreciation and depreciation in the portfolio over five years, a method that reduces the short-term impact of market fluctuations.

Funded status of principal plans

December 31 (In millions)	1994	1993	1992
Pension plans			
Market-related value of assets	$25,441	$24,532	$24,204
Projected benefit obligation	19,334	20,796	17,999
Retiree health and life plans			
Market-related value of assets	1,346	1,252	1,220
Accumulated postretirement benefit obligation	3,701	4,120	3,743

Trust assets consist mainly of common stock and fixed-income investments. GE common stock represents less than 3% of trust assets and is held in part in an indexed portfolio.

Schedules reconciling the benefit obligations for principal plans with GE's recorded liabilities in the Statement of Financial Position are shown on the following page.

continued

workforces, companies have been struggling to curtail their expensive retirement benefits, such as health care programs and pensions, without demoralizing the existing employees. In this regard, companies face the same issue as does the U.S. Congress with respect to health care.

EXHIBIT 13.6 concluded

Reconciliation of Benefit Obligation with Recorded Liability

December 31 (in millions)	Pension Plans 1994	Pension Plans 1993	Retiree Health Plans 1994	Retiree Health Plans 1993	Retiree Life Plans 1994	Retiree Life Plans 1993
Benefit obligation	$ 19,334	$ 20,796	$2,386	$2,586	$ 1,315	$ 1,534
Fair value of trust assets	(26,166)	(27,193)	—	(13)	(1,323)	(1,317)
Unamortized balances						
SFAS No. 87 transition gain	923	1,077	—	—	—	—
Experience gains (losses)	2,548	2,371	(112)	(654)	(198)	(206)
Plan amendments	(602)	(395)	188	580	130	—
Recorded prepaid asset	4,489	3,840	—	—	76	—
Recorded liability	$ 526	$ 496	$2,462	$2,499	$ —	$ 11

The portion of the projected benefit obligation representing the accumulated benefit obligation for pension plans was $18,430 million and $19,890 million at the end of 1994 and 1993, respectively. The vested benefit obligation for pension plans was $18,305 million and $19,732 million at the end of 1994 and 1993, respectively.

Details of the accumulated postretirement benefit obligation are shown below:

Accumulated Postretirement Benefit Obligation

December 31 (in millions)	1994	1993
Retiree health plans		
Retirees and dependents	$1,858	$2,017
Employees eligible to retire	101	119
Other employees	427	450
	$2,386	$2,586
Retiree life plans		
Retirees	$1,099	$1,147
Employees eligible to retire	55	79
Other employees	161	308
	$1,315	$1,534

Other than the issues of benefits and changes to benefits, the biggest pension and retirement benefits decision for many companies is the one of funding or fund recoveries. Firms with "overfunded" plans have been recovering assets from their plan trustees or have simply stopped further funding of pension costs. Firms driven by the concepts of "shareholder value" and "economic value-added" often look at every asset, every cost, and every employee questioning, "What's the value proposition for the item?" As a consequence, pension plans have become targets for cash recoveries.

DEFERRED INCOME TAXES

Income taxes represent one of the largest obligations arising from operations that a company must satisfy. Some of these taxes must be paid currently; others may be postponed for many years. This section focuses on those income taxes that, because of the particular provisions of the U.S. Internal Revenue Code, may be postponed until some future date.

Because of differences between GAAP and tax accounting, the amounts due to the taxation authorities for a given period are not necessarily the accounting income tax expense of that period. The accounting issue behind deferred taxes is one of matching: Income tax expense is the periodic cost associated with particular revenue and expense items recognized in that accounting period's financial statements. This cost, however, is independent of when those particular revenue and expense items are recognized for income tax return purposes. If revenues and expenses are recorded in this year's income statement, the related income tax expense should also appear in this year's income statement *even* if the recognition of those revenues and expenses (and their associated income tax liability) can be deferred until some later date for tax purposes. This process is called **interperiod tax allocation;** it is really just another form of accrual accounting. It recognizes business events (in this case, the income tax expense) at some moment more appropriate than simply when the tax bill appears or must be paid in cash. Without interperiod tax accounting, a company's operating results can fluctuate wildly because of tax accounting conventions, even if the basic operations of the business are stable.

Almost all business events have the potential to be recognized at different times for tax purposes than for accounting purposes, but the most common accounting-tax differences leading to deferred income taxes are those listed in Exhibit 13.7. In the following illustration, we will use depreciation accounting to demonstrate the role of interperiod tax allocation.

An Illustration: Sample Company

Ideally, in published financial statements, the cost of an asset is assigned to various years in whatever manner best reflects the use of the asset over its lifetime. Tax accounting also expenses that same cost over the asset's life but often with different amounts being charged to different years. One often hears the expression that "U.S. companies keep two sets of books"; what this means is simply that tax rules are often different from GAAP. Moreover, companies have much different objectives when reporting income to the IRS than when reporting income to owners and potential shareholders. Thus, in the case of depreciation, although both tax and accounting statements reflect the same *total* depreciation expense over the life of an asset, the tax depreciation is typically accelerated or "front loaded" while the accounting depreciation is usually flat or straight-line.

Imagine that a company purchases an asset costing $1,000 that, because of special tax incentives, can be depreciated for tax purposes over only two years (50 percent each year) and that, for accounting purposes, can be depreciated over four years (25 percent per year). For simplicity, assume that the company is subject to a 40 percent tax rate. The differences between the accounting depreciation and tax depreciation deductions are as follows:

	Year 1	Year 2	Year 3	Year 4
Accounting depreciation	$250	$250	$250	$250
Tax depreciation	500	500	–0–	–0–
Difference	(250)	(250)	250	250
Tax impact of difference at 40 percent	($100)	($100)	$100	$100

EXHIBIT 13.7

Common Business Events Associated with Deferred Income Taxes

Event	Prevalent Accounting Treatment	Prevalent Tax Treatment
Depreciation of long-term assets	Straight-line method	Accelerated methods
Installment sales	Immediate recognition	Recognized when cash is received
Bad debt expense	Estimated and recognized in the period corresponding with the actual credit sale	Recognized when written off
Warranty expense	Estimated and recognized in the period of product sale	Recognized when paid
Environmental cost	Estimated and accrued	Recognized when paid
Retiree health cost	Estimated and accrued	Recognized when paid

In essence, $250 *more* tax depreciation will be taken in Years 1 and 2 and $250 *less* tax depreciation will be taken in Years 3 and 4. Take a moment and consider the implications of these differences. The taxes actually due in Years 1 and 2 will be $100 *lower*; in Years 3 and 4, the actual taxes due will be $100 *higher* than will be reflected in the accounting income statements. In total, however, over the four-year period, the amount of taxes will be the same under either system. If this were the only accounting-tax difference that the company had, the accounting income tax *expense* in Years 1 and 2 would simply be the taxes actually due plus $100. In Years 3 and 4, this process would be reversed — the accounting income tax *expense* would be the taxes actually due minus $100.

Exhibit 13.8 illustrates the effect of these accounting-tax differences, as well as the use of interperiod tax allocation to account for these differences. In this example, we assume that revenues for each period are $1,000 and that all other expenses other than depreciation total $400 per year. Note that the income tax *liability* (per the tax return) for each of the first two years would be only $40 and then would increase to $240 per year for the next two years. On the accounting income statement, the total income tax *expense* is adjusted to eliminate what would otherwise be a distortion caused by the special tax depreciation allowances. The additional $100 of income tax *expense* in Years 1 and 2 increases the Deferred Tax Liability account. Note that this account builds up in Years 1 and 2 and then reverses in Years 3 and 4 when the total income tax *liability* is higher than the total income tax *expense*. Also note that the events that gave rise to this situation were the purchase of an asset and the decision to use different accounting and tax depreciation schedules.

The use of a Deferred Tax Liability account on the balance sheet eliminates the distortion that would otherwise occur if the current tax liability (per the tax return) were considered to be the income tax expense for the year. Deferred tax accounting makes the total income tax expense in the income statement conform to the accounting treatment used for depreciation in that statement.

The Deferred Tax Liability account at the end of Years 1, 2, and 3 is a liability in the sense that someday income taxes will be payable *in excess of what the accounting statements would otherwise suggest*. In simple terms, Sample Company temporarily

EXHIBIT 13.8

Sample Company
Deferred Income Taxes

Income tax returns of Sample Corporation

	1	2	3	4	Total
Sales	$1,000	$1,000	$1,000	$1,000	
Depreciation	500	500			
All other expenses	400	400	400	400	
Taxable income	100	100	600	600	
Income tax @ 40%	40	40	240	240	560

On the balance sheets of Sample Corporation

	1	2	3	4
Deferred tax liability	$100	$200	$100	$0

Income statement of Sample Corporation

	1	2	3	4	Total
Sales	$1,000	$1,000	$1,000	$1,000	
Depreciation	250	250	250	250	
All other expenses	400	400	400	400	
Taxable income	350	350	350	350	
Current income tax expense	40	40	240	240	
Deferred income tax expense	100	100	–100	–100	
Total income tax expense	140	140	140	140	560
Net income	210	210	210	210	

Deferred tax liability

	0 Balance
	100 Year 1
	100 Balance
	100 Year 2
	200 Balance
Year 3 100	
	100 Balance
Year 4 100	
	0 Balance

avoided $100 of income tax payments in Year 1 because it used a more rapid method of depreciation for tax reporting than was used for accounting purposes. Someday that advantage will reverse; the fast depreciation write-offs will run out with straight-line depreciation continuing on the accounting records. At that time, the tax return will reflect higher taxable income than the accounting statements, and the tax bills coming into the company will be far higher than what would be predicted from the figure for income before tax on the accounting income statement. Like a buffer, the Deferred Tax Liability account is used to prevent such distortions. Expenses are credited to this account when temporary tax advantages lower taxable income, and when the differences reverse, the buffer is drawn down.

Temporary and Permanent Differences

Temporary differences. Interperiod tax allocation is used when tax returns and the accounting reports reflect **temporary differences,** as with depreciation. By definition, temporary differences always reverse themselves at some point: Tax depreciation may exceed accounting depreciation for a while for any particular asset, but eventually the reverse will occur, and by the end of the life of the asset, the sum of the differences (positives and negatives) will always be zero. Accordingly, the deferred tax liability associated with this asset may increase for a few years on the balance sheet, but then it will decline and eventually become zero.

Even though the temporary difference that triggered the deferred tax liability (or asset if the account has a debit balance) will always reverse itself for any particular item having a temporary difference, it is possible for an account such as the Deferred Tax Liability to keep increasing *in total*, for example, if a business is growing and more assets are being acquired.

Permanent differences. Depreciation differences between tax and accounting statements illustrate a temporary difference because for any given asset, the total difference over time is zero. **Permanent differences,** on the other hand, arise when an item is included for accounting purposes but will never appear in the determination of taxable income (or vice versa). For example, interest on municipal bonds is a revenue item for accounting purposes but is not taxable in the U.S. — it represents a permanent difference in the income reported to the IRS versus the income reported to shareholders. Historically, amortization of purchased goodwill is another example — it is an accounting expense that did not become tax deductible until passage of the Omnibus Budget Reconciliation Act in 1993. Deferred taxes are never calculated for permanent differences; they are simply ignored in the interperiod tax allocation process.

Events that lead to temporary differences. Temporary accounting differences may arise as a result of two types of events:

1. An accounting asset balance is greater than its tax return asset balance. This often arises when: (a) Expenses (or losses) become tax deductible *before* before being expensed for accounting purposes. (The most frequent example of this is depreciation and the related PP&E accounts in the early years of the PP&E's life where straight-line depreciation is used for accounting purposes and MACRS for tax return purposes); and (b) Revenues (or gains) become taxable *after* they are recognized in the accounting income statement. (For example, certain types of installment sales are recognized as accounting sales immediately but generate a deferred gross profit liability account on the tax books because they are treated as taxable income only as payments are received.)
2. An accounting liability balance is greater than its tax return liability balance. This often arises when: (a) Expenses (or losses) become tax deductible *after* the recognition of the expense. (This happens when a company provides warranties or guarantees on a product or service. Generally accepted accounting principles require such a company to estimate the expense and liability for warranties when the revenue is recognized; tax rules permit no deductions for anticipated warranty work, only for repairs actually made); and (b) Revenue (or gains) become taxable *before* being recognized as accounting income. (Rent collected in advance is such an item and is recorded as unearned revenue (a liability) for GAAP purposes but is treated as revenue when the cash is collected for tax purposes.)

It should be noted that in the first instance, accounting income exceeds taxable income, thus giving rise to a deferred tax liability; in the latter example, the reverse is true: There is a deferred tax asset that, in simple terms, is like a prepaid income tax. (To be precise, it is the income tax benefit of future deductions.) Many companies have both, perhaps a deferred tax liability because of different depreciation policies and a deferred tax asset because of the alternative treatment of warranty expenses.

Accounting for Deferred Taxes

The FASB's current accounting standard for deferred taxes, SFAS No. 109, embraces the **liability method.** Under this opinion, which was discussed and debated at the Financial Accounting Standards Board for 10 years, companies must recognize the current and future tax consequences of events that have been recognized in either the financial statements or the tax returns. A deferred tax liability (or asset) must be recognized for all tax effects due to temporary differences as alluded to in the prior section, the key to SFAS No. 109 is that any temporary book-tax difference in the value of an asset or liability will result in taxable or tax-deductible amounts in future periods. Such items must be valued using the marginal tax rates expected to apply to taxable income in future periods. Deferred tax assets, which may result from such book-tax difference, may need to be adjusted by a *valuation allowance* if it is "more likely than not" that some portion of the deferred tax asset will not be realized.

Applying the liability method of SFAS No. 109 to our example of Sample Company (Exhibit 13.8), recall that tax depreciation was figured on a two-year basis and accounting depreciation was taken over four years and that the asset's original cost was $1,000. The asset's account balance per the tax books and the accounting books would be as follows:

	Tax Calculations		Accounting Calculations	
Year	Yearly Depreciation	End-of-Year Undepreciated Asset Cost	Yearly Depreciation	End-of-Year Undepreciated Asset Cost
1	$500	$500	$250	$750
2	500	–0–	250	500
3		–0–	250	250
4		–0–	250	–0–

At the end of Year 1, the balance sheet of Sample Company reflects an asset valued at $750:

Asset (at cost)	$1,000
Less: Accumulated depreciation	(250)
Asset (net)	$ 750

However, this asset has an undepreciated cost basis of $500 on the tax books, and the difference between the two cost bases is $250. When the accounting basis temporarily differs from the tax basis for an asset (or a liability) like this, it means that a deferred tax liability (or asset) must be recognized.

In this case, at the end of Year 1, an additional tax liability will occur in the future because of the temporary accounting-tax difference. If tax rates are expected to remain at 40 percent, there will be a $100 additional tax liability (0.40 × $250) in the future.

Thus, the Deferred Tax Liability account at the end of Year 1 should be $100, and the Deferred Tax Expense amount to be recorded in Year 1 is also $100 (the beginning Deferred Tax Liability account was zero). The deferred taxes would be calculated as follows for the four years for the Sample Company:

	End of Year			
	1	2	3	4
Accounting asset NBV*	$750	$500	$ 250	$ –0–
Tax asset NBV	500	–0–	–0–	–0–
Difference	$250	$500	$ 250	$ –0–
Tax rate (during the year)	0.4	0.4	0.4	0.4
Deferred tax liability	$100	$200	$ 100	$ –0–
Deferred tax expense	$100	$100	$(100)	$(100)

*(NBV = net book value.)

In reviewing these figures, it is important to recall the purpose of deferred tax accounting: Deferred tax liabilities (and assets) measure the future tax expenditures (or benefits) that a company faces due only to the differences between tax accounting and financial statement accounting.

Using the above data for Sample Company, the asset's tax basis at the end of Year 1 is $250 below its accounting basis, so there should be a $100 deferred tax liability *associated with this asset* (that is, 0.40 × $250). In the following year the difference in the two cost bases is $500, so the deferred tax liability must be $200. To increase the liability requires an expense in Year 2 of $100; hence,

Years 1 and 2
Dr. Income Tax Expense (E) . . . . (inc.) 100
  Cr. Deferred Tax Liability (L) . . . . (inc.) 100
Years 3 and 4
Dr. Deferred Tax Liability (L) . . . . (dec.) 100
  Cr. Income Tax Expense (E) . . . . (dec.) 100

Note that at the end of Year 1, it was determined that the ending balance for the Deferred Tax Liability account should be $100. Since there was no beginning balance in this account, so the deferred tax expense is also $100. At the end of Year 2, it was determined that the ending balance for the Deferred Tax Liability account should be $200. Since there was a beginning balance of $100, the account requires another $100 increase which is also Year 2's deferred tax expense.

Deferred Tax Liability

	Beginning of Year 1	$ 0
	(Plug) Deferred tax expense	100
	End of Year 1	$100
	(Plug) Deferred tax expense	100
	End of Year 2	$200

In simple terms, each asset or liability that may reflect a temporary accounting-tax difference in carrying value is analyzed separately. The taxable or tax-deductible amounts in future years are projected, and the deferred tax assets or liabilities are calculated each year at the incremental tax rate *expected to apply* to taxable income in *future periods* when the deferred tax assets and liabilities are realized. The deferred tax expense for each year is then the difference in the deferred tax liability or asset from the beginning of the year to the end of the year (that is, a "plug"). In other words, the liability is calculated first and then the expense figure is derived to obtain the new balance for the deferred tax liability.

The accounting for some items, such as warranties, is the reverse of that for depreciation. For example, the balance sheet may show a reserve for future warranty claim or some such liability. This represents a liability with an accounting-tax difference the other way: Expensing on the accounting statements has preceded its tax deduction. A deferred tax asset must be created to reflect this difference. Consider the following warranty example:

	At the End of Year		
	1	2	3
Accounting basis of warranty liability	$(500)	$(400)	$(200)
Tax basis of warranty liability	–0–	–0–	–0–
Difference	$(500)	$(400)	$(200)
Tax rate (during the year)	0.40	0.40	0.40
Deferred tax asset	$ 200	$ 160	$ 80
Deferred tax expense (benefit) for the year	$(200)	$ 40	$ 80

Suppose that during Year 1 a liability for future warranty expense was established for the first time at $500. Because *estimated* warranty expenses cannot be deducted for tax purposes, at the end of Year 1 there is a liability with an accounting-tax difference, in this case $500. The deferred tax asset related to this liability is $200 (0.40 × $500). The difference between the beginning and ending deferred tax assets is thus $200. As a consequence, a $200 deferred tax adjustment (or negative expense) exists. At the end of Year 2, the warranty liability is $400, indicating no further accounting warranty estimates were made on the incurrence of $100 of actual warranty costs or, more likely, it means that the actual warranty cost recognized on the tax return exceeded the warranty expense reflected in the accounting statements by $100. Because the end of Year 2 accounting-tax warranty liability difference is $400, the deferred tax asset's end of Year 2 balance should be $160 (0.40 × $400). To reduce the deferred tax asset account from its opening balance of $200, a deferred tax expense of $40 will be recorded in Year 2. A similar situation occurs in Year 3.

Financial Disclosures for Deferred Taxes

GAAP requires disclosure of the primary categories of deferred tax asset and liability such as the following from the 1994 annual report of Hasbro, Inc., an international manufacturer of children's toys:

(thousands)	1994	1993
Deferred tax assets:		
Accounts receivable	$ 27,782	30,049
Inventories	12,600	12,090
Net operating loss and other loss carryovers	16,923	11,073
Operating expenses	33,948	32,393
Postretirement benefits	11,487	8,675
Other	41,223	39,554
Total gross deferred tax assets	143,963	133,834
Valuation allowance	(11,829)	(10,376)
Net deferred tax assets	132,134	123,458
Deferred tax liabilities:		
Property rights and property, plant, and equipment	64,743	68,614
Other	7,786	6,468
Total gross deferred tax liabilities	72,529	75,082
Net deferred income taxes	$ 59,605	48,376

Think about why each of the items is associated with a deferred tax asset or liability. Take accounts receivable for example: On Hasbro's balance sheet, receivables are valued at $717,890 thousand as of December 31, 1994. The $27,782 thousand is certainly due to the company's provision for uncollectible accounts, which gives rise to a book-tax difference in the carrying value of receivables. A good estimate of the December 31, 1994 tax basis for accounts receivable would be $797,267 ($717,890 + $27,782/0.35) assuming a 35 percent tax rate.

The classification of deferred tax assets and liabilities in the balance sheet must reflect the classification of the liabilities and assets with which they are associated. Thus, deferred tax liabilities resulting from accounting-tax depreciation differences are always classified as noncurrent because the assets associated with them, fixed assets, are always classified as noncurrent. Although it is possible to have four deferred tax items in a balance sheet — current and noncurrent liabilities, and current and noncurrent assets — current deferred tax assets must be netted against current deferred tax liabilities; the same is true for noncurrent deferred tax assets and liabilities unless the assets and liabilities are attributable to different tax-paying components of the corporation.

The footnotes must also reconcile the U.S. **federal statutory tax rate** to the **effective tax rate** — that is, to a rate defined to be:

$$\text{Effective tax rate} = \frac{\text{Income tax expense}}{\text{Income before income tax}}$$

Exhibit 13.9 shows the income tax rate reconciliation from Hasbro's 1994 annual report. They determined the effective tax rate to be 38.5 percent. The table at the top of the exhibit describes all the components of income tax expense; the total for 1994 was $112,254 thousand. The table at the very bottom of the exhibit reports that the total income before tax that year was $291,569. The ratio of the two figures is, of course, 38.5 percent.

Here is another way to understand the effective tax rate disclosures. Exhibit 13.10 contains an illustration of where the components of this calculation can be found. Total income tax expense has two parts: the current tax expense from the U.S. tax return and all the other income tax returns the company must file, and the deferred income tax expense, which is determined by an examination of all temporary book-tax differences as we have discussed previously.

EXHIBIT 13.9

Hasbro, Inc.
Income Tax Disclosures

Income Taxes

Income taxes attributable to earnings before income taxes are as follows:

	1994	1993	1992
Current			
Federal	**$ 60,539**	81,770	64,825
Foreign	**42,543**	28,614	33,147
State and local	**10,417**	12,541	13,012
	113,499	122,925	110,984
Deferred			
Federal	**1,924**	315	2,612
Foreign	**(3,349)**	1,817	(663)
State and local	**180**	149	279
	(1,245)	2,281	2,228
	$112,254	125,206	113,212

The cumulative effect of the change in accounting principles resulting from the adoption of Statement of Financial Accounting Standards No. 109, "Accounting for Income Taxes," increased 1992 net earnings by $12,349.

Certain tax benefits are not reflected in income taxes on the consolidated statements of earnings. Such benefits of $9,800 in 1994, $6,299 in 1993, and $12,583 in 1992 relate primarily to stock options and cumulative effect of changes in accounting principles.

A reconciliation of the statutory U.S. federal income tax rate to the company's effective income tax rate is as follows:

	1994	1993	1992
Statutory income tax rate	**35.0%**	35.0%	34.0%
State and local income taxes, net of federal income tax effect	**2.4**	2.6	3.0
Amortization of goodwill	**1.6**	1.4	1.4
Foreign earnings taxed at rates other than the U.S. statutory rate	**(0.7)**	—	(0.6)
Other, net	**0.2**	(0.5)	0.9
	38.5%	38.5%	38.7%

The components of earnings before income taxes are as follows:

	1994	1993	1992
Domestic	**$177,672**	243,820	190,268
Foreign	**113,897**	81,390	102,108
	$291,569	325,210	292,376

Although the International Accounting Standards Committee has proposed the adoption of the liability method to account for temporary differences, in line with U.S. GAAP, it has yet to be adopted. In the meantime, practice varies widely from country to country because some countries do not have accounting-tax differences by statute (e.g., Japan) and thus do not need deferred income-tax accounting while others have accounting-tax differences (e.g. U.K.) but are not required to adopt deferred income tax accounting.

EXHIBIT 13.10

Calculation of Effective Income Tax Rate

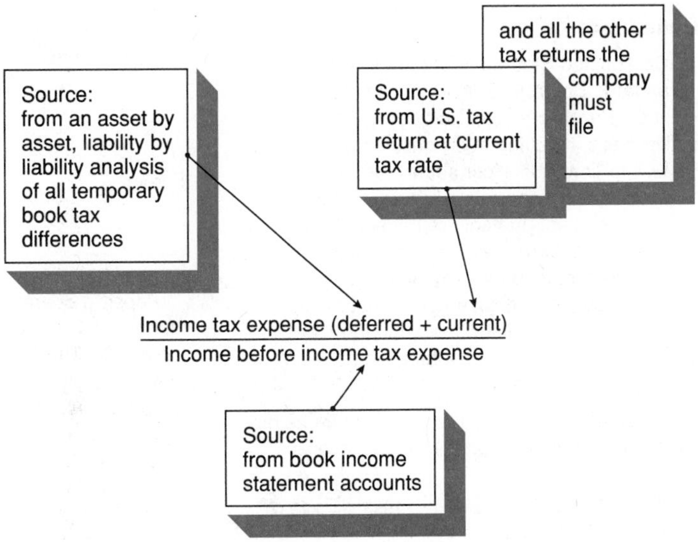

Exhibit 13.11 is the income tax footnote from PepsiCo's 1994 annual report. It illustrates each of the points we have discussed plus one we have not yet mentioned. When PepsiCo adopted the current income tax reporting standards in 1992 it was obligated to record a one-time charge of $570.7 million to put the company's accounting for deferred taxes on a liability-method basis as opposed to the earlier standard. The current income tax expense for the year 1994 was $947.3 million, and there was a deferred tax *benefit* of $66.9 million in 1994.

In 1993 the U.S. federal government increased corporate income tax rates by 1 percent. This required PepsiCo to refigure the deferred tax liabilities and assets stemming from all temporary book-tax differences at the new tax rate, effective in 1993. Indeed, deferred tax assets and liabilities must be based upon tax rates expected to be in force in the future. If the tax rates change, as they did in 1993, all deferred tax assets and liabilities must be revalued. Tax rate changes are explained more fully in Appendix 13C. The point we have not yet mentioned pertains to PepsiCo's 1994 deferred tax asset valuation allowance of $319.3 million. Just as with any asset whose value lies in future economic benefits, deferred tax assets may need to be adjusted to reflect their approximated net realizable future value. As PepsiCo notes, its valuation allowance springs from the belief that some potentially deductible operating losses will expire, for tax purposes, before the pertinent subsidiary is able to use them to offset positive levels of profit. More on valuation allowances is presented in Appendix 13C.

PepsiCo's effective tax rate was 33.0 percent in 1994 ($880.4 million/$2,664.4 million). The differences between that and the U.S. statutory tax rate are due to state income tax rates, lower tax rates in other countries, and the other adjustments described in the footnote. The biggest items leading to deferred taxes for PepsiCo are

EXHIBIT 13.11

PepsiCo, Inc.
Income Taxes

Note 17: Income Taxes

In 1992 PepsiCo adopted Statement of Financial Accounting Standards No. 109 (SFAS 109), "Accounting for Income Taxes." PepsiCo elected to adopt SFAS 109 on a prospective basis, resulting in a noncash tax charge in 1992 of $570.7 million ($0.71 per share) for the cumulative effect of the change related to years prior to 1992. The cumulative effect primarily represented the recording of additional deferred tax liabilities related to identifiable intangible assets, principally acquired trademarks and reacquired franchise rights, that have no tax bases. These deferred tax liabilities would be paid only in the unlikely event the related intangible assets were sold in taxable transactions.

Detail of the provision for income taxes on income before cumulative effect of accounting changes was as follows:

		1994	1993	1992
Current	Federal	**$642.0**	$466.8	$413.0
	Foreign	**174.1**	195.5	170.4
	State	**131.2**	89.0	65.7
		947.3	751.3	649.1
Deferred	Federal	**(63.9)**	78.2	(18.8)
	Foreign	**(1.8)**	(12.5)	(33.5)
	State	**(1.2)**	17.6	0.3
		(66.9)	83.3	(52.0)
		$880.4	$834.6	$597.1

In 1993 a charge of $29.9 million ($0.04 per share) was recorded to increase net deferred tax liabilities as of the beginning of 1993 for a 1 percent statutory income tax rate increase under 1993 U.S. tax legislation. The effect of the higher rate on the 1993 increase in net deferred tax liabilities through the enactment date of the legislation was immaterial.

U.S. and foreign income before income taxes and cumulative effect of accounting changes were as follows:

	1994	1993	1992
U.S.	**$1,762.4**	$1,633.0	$1,196.8
Foreign	**902.0**	789.5	702.0
	$2,664.4	$2,422.5	$1,898.8

PepsiCo operates centralized concentrate manufacturing facilities in Puerto Rico and Ireland under long-term tax incentives. The foreign amount in the above table includes approximately 50 percent (consistent with the allocation for tax purposes) of the income from U.S. sales of concentrate manufactured in Puerto Rico. See "Management's Analysis — Overview" on page 26 for a discussion of the reduction of the U.S. tax credit associated with beverage concentrate operations in Puerto Rico.

Reconciliation of the U.S. federal statutory tax rate to PepsiCo's effective tax rate on pretax income, based on the dollar impact of these major components on the provision for income taxes, was as follows:

	1994	1993	1992
U.S. federal statutory tax rate	**35.0%**	35.0%	34.0%
State income tax, net of federal tax benefit	**3.2**	2.9	2.3
Effect of lower taxes on foreign income (including Puerto Rico and Ireland)	**(5.4)**	(3.3)	(5.0)
Adjustment to the beginning-of-the-year deferred tax assets valuation allowance	**(1.3)**	—	—
Reduction of prior year foreign accruals	**—**	(2.0)	—
Effect of 1993 tax legislation on deferred income taxes	**—**	1.1	—
Nondeductible amortization of domestic goodwill	**0.8**	0.8	0.9
Other, net	**0.7**	—	(0.8)
Effective tax rate	**33.0%**	34.5%	31.4%

continued

intangible assets such as marketing costs not yet expensed. Deduction of these items for tax purposes has preceded book accounting because the cash has already been spent. The overall impact of the temporary accounting-tax differences for PepsiCo is to defer almost $1.8 billion of income taxes.

EXHIBIT 13.11 concluded

Detail of the 1994 and 1993 deferred tax liabilities (assets) was as follows:

	1994	1993
Intangible assets other than nondeductible goodwill	**$ 1,627.8**	$ 1,551.0
Property, plant, and equipment	**506.4**	552.3
Safe harbor leases	**171.2**	177.5
Zero coupon notes	**110.6**	103.5
Other	**336.7**	549.0
Gross deferred tax liabilities	**2,752.7**	2,933.3
Net operating loss carryforwards	**(306.0)**	(241.5)
Postretirement benefits	**(248.3)**	(268.0)
Self-insurance reserves	**(71.2)**	(10.8)
Deferred state income taxes	**(69.1)**	(39.9)
Restructuring accruals	**(15.8)**	(42.0)
Various accrued liabilities and other	**(551.2)**	(686.8)
Gross deferred tax assets	**(1,261.6)**	(1,289.0)
Deferred tax assets valuation allowance	**319.3**	249.0
Net deferred tax liability	**$ 1,810.4**	$ 1,893.3
Included in:		
Prepaid expenses, taxes, and other current assets	**$ (166.9)**	$ (138.2)
Other current liabilities	**4.4**	23.9
Deferred income taxes	**1,972.9**	2,007.6
	$ 1,810.4	$ 1,893.3

The valuation allowance related to deferred tax assets increased by $70.3 million in 1994 primarily resulting from additions related to current year net operating losses, partially offset by reversals related to prior year net operating losses. The net operating loss carryforwards largely related to a number of state and foreign jurisdictions and generally expire over a range of dates.

Deferred tax liabilities have not been recognized for basis differences related to investments in foreign subsidiaries and joint ventures. These differences, which consist primarily of unremitted earnings intended to be indefinitely reinvested, aggregated approximately $3.8 billion at year-end 1994 and $3.2 billion at year-end 1993, exclusive of amounts that if remitted in the future would result in little or no tax under current tax laws and the Puerto Rico tax incentive grant. Determination of the amount of unrecognized deferred tax liabilities is not practicable.

Tax benefits associated with exercises of stock options of $27.1 million in 1994, $23.4 million in 1993, and $57.5 million in 1992 were credited to shareholders' equity. A change in the functional currency of operations in Mexico from the U.S. dollar to local currency in 1993 resulted in a $19.3 million decrease in the net deferred foreign tax liability that was credited to shareholders' equity.

SUMMARY

Leases, pensions, and deferred income taxes are significant obligations that present unique valuation issues. Capital leases are reported in the balance sheet at their present value; pension obligations are disclosed in the footnotes at their present value, and, under some circumstances, a portion of this obligation may appear on the balance sheet as a liability. Deferred income taxes, on the other hand, are not reported at their present value but are reported in the balance sheet.

Many types of leases exist, but only those that meet one or more of the four tests (that is, ownership, alternative ownership, economic life, or value) are considered to be capital leases. Capital leases are recorded on the books of the lessee as both an asset and a liability at their present value at the time the lease is signed. Lease assets are amortized in a manner similar to other depreciable assets as if the asset were owned. Lease liabilities, on the other hand, are amortized using the effective interest method as one would amortize a bond.

Pensions and other retirement benefits are important because of the sheer magnitude of the dollars involved. They are complex because of the variety of estimates one must make to value an entity's retirement obligations. No matter how a pension is to be funded, whether by contributions from the employer, the employee, or both, the two basic types are defined-contribution and defined-benefit plans. The latter is more complex because accountants, actuaries, and management must estimate future benefits, employee mortality, retirement ages, and the future earnings rate of pension assets. In situations in which the accumulated benefit obligation (or ABO) is less than the plan assets, a pension liability may be created reflecting this difference.

Differences between the accounting procedures adopted for tax purposes and for financial reporting purposes may result in deferred tax liabilities and/or assets and deferred tax expenses and/or benefits. Some items result in permanent accounting-tax differences and are not subject to deferred tax accounting. Only temporary differences, such as those created by differences in depreciation, result in interperiod income tax allocations.

Three special appendixes are included with this chapter. They are designed to further explain the accounting for leases, pensions, and deferred income taxes, and they contain additional examples of each.

NEW CONCEPTS AND TERMS

Accumulated benefits obligation (p. 613)
Capital lease (p. 602)
Defined-benefit plan (p. 608)
Defined-contribution plan (p. 608)
Effective tax rate (p. 627)
ERISA (p. 609)
Federal statutory tax rate (p. 627)
Interperiod tax allocation (p. 620)
Lease (p. 602)
Lessee (p. 602)
Lessor (p. 602)
Liability method (p. 624)
Off-balance-sheet financing (p. 601)
Operating leases (p. 601)
Pension (p. 608)
Pension expense (p. 609)
Permanent differences (p. 623)
Plan assets at fair value (p. 611)
Projected benefit obligation (p. 611)
Temporary differences (p. 623)
Unfunded pension cost (p. 613)

APPENDIX 13A

Leases in Detail

Chapter 13 introduced the concepts of operating and capital leases and discussed the accounting for both types of leases from the lessee's perspective. Here we will explain more fully the calculations underlying the accounting for capitalized leases for both the lessee and the lessor. The accounting and required disclosures for capitalized leases for lessors, including the *direct-financing type* and *sales-type leases*, are also described.

We will continue to use the example of the Boeing airplane leased by American Airlines from Prudential Insurance Co. Recall that the present value of the lease was $125 million and that the lease asset will be depreciated and the lease liability will be amortized.

Amortization of the Lease Liability

Exhibit 13A.1 presents the lease amortization schedule for the American Airlines lease liability. Column 2 is the quarterly payment due at the beginning of each quarter, and columns 3 and 4 identify the interest expense portion and the principal reduction portion of this payment. Thus, the first quarter's payment is all principal reduction. After this payment, the principal is then $120,520,129.

The key to Exhibit 13A.1 is the way that the interest expense and principal reduction portions of the payment are separated. We know that the interest rate per quarter is 2 percent. Thus, for the second payment, the interest expense portion must be 0.02 × $120,520,129, or $2,410,403. Because the payment is always $4,479,871 per quarter for this lease, the remainder is the principal reduction, or $2,069,468 (that is, $4,479,871 – $2,410,403). Because the principal balance is reduced by this amount, the ending principal balance for Quarter 2 is $118,450,660, or $120,520,129 – $2,069,468. Each quarter's payment is separated in this manner. Note that the last payment's principal reduction, $4,392,030, is almost the same as the outstanding principal of $4,392,031. The difference is due to rounding at the penny level.[1]

[1]One might ask why there is any interest portion at all in the last payment since the payment is made at the *beginning of the period*. The explanation is that annuities such as this lease with 40 payments, with payments made at the beginning of the period, are really liabilities that extend over only 39 periods. It is as if one borrowed $120,520,129 and repaid it at $4,479,871 per quarter for 39 quarters, with payments made at the end of the period — when the interest expense for that period had been accrued.

EXHIBIT 13A.1

Lease Amortization Schedule: Aircraft Financing Example (in millions)

Quarter	Payment	Interest Portion	Principal Reduction	Ending Principal
0				$125,000,000
1	$ 4,479,871	$ —	$ 4,479,871	120,520,129
2	4,479,871	2,410,403	2,069,468	118,450,660
3	4,479,871	2,369,013	2,110,858	116,339,803
4	4,479,871	2,326,796	2,153,075	114,186,728
5	4,479,871	2,283,735	2,196,136	111,990,591
6	4,479,871	2,239,812	2,240,059	109,750,532
7	4,479,871	2,195,011	2,284,860	107,465,672
8	4,479,871	2,149,313	2,330,558	105,135,114
9	4,479,871	2,102,702	2,377,169	102,757,945
10	4,479,871	2,055,159	2,424,712	100,333,233
11	4,479,871	2,006,665	2,473,206	97,860,027
12	4,479,871	1,957,201	2,522,671	95,337,356
13	4,479,871	1,906,747	2,573,124	92,764,232
14	4,479,871	1,855,285	2,624,586	90,139,646
15	4,479,871	1,802,793	2,677,078	87,462,568
16	4,479,871	1,749,251	2,730,620	84,731,948
17	4,479,871	1,694,639	2,785,232	81,946,716
18	4,479,871	1,638,934	2,840,937	79,105,779
19	4,479,871	1,582,116	2,897,755	76,208,024
20	4,479,871	1,524,160	2,955,711	73,252,313
21	4,479,871	1,465,046	3,014,825	70,237,488
22	4,479,871	1,404,750	3,075,121	67,162,367
23	4,479,871	1,343,247	3,136,624	64,025,743
24	4,479,871	1,280,515	3,199,356	60,826,387
25	4,479,871	1,216,528	3,263,343	57,563,044
26	4,479,871	1,151,261	3,328,610	54,234,434
27	4,479,871	1,084,689	3,395,182	50,839,251
28	4,479,871	1,016,785	3,463,086	47,376,165
29	4,479,871	947,523	3,532,348	43,843,817
30	4,479,871	876,876	3,602,995	40,240,823
31	4,479,871	804,816	3,675,055	36,565,768
32	4,479,871	731,315	3,748,556	32,817,212
33	4,479,871	656,344	3,823,527	28,993,686
34	4,479,871	579,874	3,899,997	25,093,688
35	4,479,871	501,874	3,977,997	21,115,691
36	4,479,871	422,314	4,057,557	17,058,134
37	4,479,871	341,163	4,138,708	12,919,425
38	4,479,871	258,389	4,221,483	8,697,943
39	4,479,871	173,959	4,305,912	4,392,031
40	4,479,871	87,841	4,392,030	0
Totals	$179,194,842	$54,194,842	$125,000,000	

minimum lease payment receivable
unearned revenue
Present value of the future lease payments

Note one more thing about Exhibit 13A.1: The total payments are $179,194,842, of which $54,194,842 is interest and the rest principal. Thus, in American Airlines' footnotes, this capital lease would be disclosed as follows:

Future minimum lease payments	$179,194,842
Less: Amount representing interest	54,194,842
Present value of minimum lease payments	$125,000,000

Depreciation of the Lease Asset

In Chapter 13 we learned that the depreciation policies for capital-lease assets are the same as those that a lessee adopts for similar owned assets. If, however, American Airlines depreciates its other aircraft over 12 years on a straight-line approach, it has an interesting problem: What time frame should it use to depreciate the leased asset when the lease runs for 10 years and the asset's normal depreciable life is 12 years?

Convention is to use the economic life of a leased asset if ownership is expected to transfer to the lessee and to use the lease lifetime only if the lease qualifies for capitalization because it meets the economic-life or valuation tests (but not one of the ownership tests). In the airline case, the asset-depreciation period should be 12 years or 48 quarters; hence, the leased asset will be depreciated at the rate of $10,416,667 per year (or $125 million divided by 12 years).

Accounting for the Lessor

If a lease meets *any* of the four capital lease tests discussed in Chapter 13, the lessor treats the agreement as a capitalized lease if it meets two *additional* tests: (1) There is reasonable assurance that the lease payments will be received and (2) there are no other major uncertainties as to costs or revenues. The need for these two additional tests is obvious: A lease asset (lease receivable) must not be recorded if collectibility is in doubt, and the amount of the receivable must be known at the inception of the lease for an accounting entry to be recorded. Assuming that a lease meets these criteria, it is then necessary for the lessor to determine whether the lease is a *direct-financing-type* or a *sales-type* capital lease. This decision rests on whether or not the asset's market value is the same as the lessor's cost of the asset.

In the case of the airplane lease, the insurance company enters into a typical *direct-financing lease* arrangement when, at the lease date, the airplane's cost to the lessor (Prudential Insurance Co.) is the same as its current market value. The insurance company first buys the airplane and carries it on its books as an asset. Later, when the lease is signed, the airplane asset will be replaced by a capital-lease asset (that is, a receivable). As lease payments are received, the reported amount of the lease receivable will decline according to the amortization schedule. The insurance company's profit on the transaction will come from the interest income associated with the lease payments (that is, from financing the airline's purchase of the aircraft).

When Prudential purchases the airplane from Boeing, the transaction is recorded as follows:

Dr. Aircraft (A)	(inc.) 125,000,000	
Cr. Cash (A)		(dec.) 125,000,000

When the lease agreement is signed, the asset is removed from the insurance company's books and is replaced by two accounts: Minimum Lease Payment Receivable (the total undiscounted lease receivable) and Unearned Revenues (the future interest payments to be received). Referring to Exhibit 13A.1, note that the total payments are to be $179,194,842. In the leasing industry, this figure is called the *minimum lease payment receivable*. The $54,194,842 is the unearned revenue, and the $125 million is the present value of the future lease payments (it is also the market value of the asset). Clearly,

Minimum lease payment receivable =
Unearned revenue + Present value of lease payments.

Thus, the insurance company makes the following entry when the lease is signed:

Dr. Minimum Lease Payment Receivable (A)	(inc.) 179,194,842	
Cr. Unearned Revenue (L)		(inc.) 54,194,842
Cr. Aircraft (A)		(dec.) 125,000,000

Each quarter, Prudential will make entries to record the receipt of the lease payment and to recognize its portion of the revenue earned. For example, the second-quarter entries would look like this:

Dr. Cash (A)	(inc.) 4,479,871	
Cr. Minimum Lease Payment Receivable (A)		(dec.) 4,479,871
Dr. Unearned Revenue (L)	(dec.) 2,410,403	
Cr. Interest Revenue (R)		(inc.) 2,410,403

At 2 percent per quarter, the quarterly interest income is 2,410,403 ($0.02 \times 120{,}520{,}129 = 2{,}410{,}403$).

In contrast to the direct-financing lease example just described, when a manufacturing company makes a product and then leases it, it generates a *sales-type lease* (that is, the asset's market value is not the same as the lessor's cost of the asset). The accounting issues become (1) how much profit the company should show on the sale of the product itself, as opposed to the interest revenue on the lease, and (2) when it should be shown.

Let us return to the American Airlines example and suppose that the Boeing Company, instead of a third-party insurance company, was to be the lessor at the same terms as those offered by Prudential. Suppose also that Boeing's cost of manufacturing the airplane was $100 million. When the lease is signed, Boeing makes an entry for this sales-type lease that recognizes a profit (or loss) on executing the lease (thus the origin of the "sales-type" label). The following is the "sale" entry:

Dr. Cost of Goods Sold (E)	(inc.) 100,000,000	
Dr. Minimum Lease Payment Receivable (A)	(inc.) 179,194,842	
Cr. Sales (R)		(inc.) 125,000,000
Cr. Unearned Revenue (L)		(inc.) 54,194,842
Cr. Inventory (A)		(dec.) 100,000,000

Under this type of lease, Boeing will make entries each quarter to record the receipt of the lease payment and to recognize the portion of the interest revenue earned as if it were a direct-financing lease. For example, these would be the second-quarter entries:

Dr. Cash (A)	(inc.) 4,479,871	
Cr. Minimum Lease Payment Receivable (A)		(dec.) 4,479,871
Dr. Unearned Revenue (L)	(dec.) 2,410,403	
Cr. Interest Revenue (R)		(inc.) 2,410,403

Disclosure for Lessors

Lessors with significant leasing activities have extensive disclosure requirements for both operating and capitalized leases. Exhibit 13A.2 contains the leasing footnotes from Comdisco, Inc.'s 1994 annual report. This company is a major lessor of computing equipment with three kinds of leases: direct financing, sales-type, and operating leases. The company has done a careful job of explaining its accounting for each. From Note 3, the two items that will appear in the September 30, 1994, balance sheet are Net

EXHIBIT 13A.2

Comdisco, Inc.
Lessor's Lease Accounting Disclosures

Leasing
Note 2: Lease Accounting Policies
FASB Statement of Financial Accounting Standards No. 13 requires that a lessor account for each lease by either the direct financing, sales-type or operating method.
Leased Assets:

- Direct financing and sales-type leased assets consist of the present value of the future minimum lease payments plus the present value of the residual (collectively referred to as the net investment). Residual is the estimated fair market value at lease termination.
- Operating leased assets consist of the equipment cost, less the amount depreciated to date.

Revenue, Costs and Expenses:

- Direct financing leases — Revenue consists of interest earned on the present value of the lease payments and residual. Revenue is recognized periodically over the lease term as a constant percentage return on the net investment. There are no costs and expenses related to direct financing leases since leasing revenue is recorded on a net basis.
- Sales-type leases — Revenue consists of the present value of the total contractual lease payments which is recognized at lease inception. Costs and expenses consist of the equipment's net book value at lease inception, less the present value of the residual. Interest earned on the present value of the lease payments and residual, which is recognized periodically over the lease term as a constant percentage return on the net investment, is included in direct financing lease revenue in the statement of earnings.
- Operating leases — Revenue consists of the contractual lease payments and is recognized on a straight-line basis over the lease term. Costs and expenses are principally depreciation of the equipment. Depreciation is recognized on a straight-line basis over the lease term to the company's estimate of the equipment's fair market value at lease termination, also commonly referred to as "residual" value.
- Equity transactions — The company enters into equity transactions with third-party investors who obtain ownership rights, which include tax depreciation deductions and residual interests. The company retains control and the use of the equipment generally throughout its economic life by leasing back the equipment from the third-party investor. Accordingly, the leased asset cost related to the period of control remains on the balance sheet. Revenue consists of the profit recognized on equity transactions and is included in operating lease revenue. Profit is recognized on a straight-line basis over the leaseback term (life of the transaction).
- Initial direct costs related to operating and direct financing leases, including salespersons' commissions, are capitalized and amortized over the lease term.

Note 3: Leased Assets
The components of the net investment in direct financing and sales-type leases as of September 30 are as follows:

(in millions)	94	93
Minimum lease payments receivable	$ 2,177	$ 2,080
Estimated residual values	260	305
Less: unearned revenue	(293)	(312)
Net investment in direct financing and sales-type leases	$ 2,144	$ 2,073

Unearned revenue is recorded as leasing revenue over the lease terms. Operating leased assets include the following as of September 30:

(in millions)	94	93
Operating leased assets	$ 3,132	$ 3,308
Less: accumulated depreciation and amortization	(1,436)	(1,474)
Net	$ 1,696	$ 1,834

continued

Investment in Direct Financing and Sales-Type Leases, $2,144 million, and Operating Leased Assets — Net, $1,696 million. Notes 4 and 5 contain a lot of interesting information not always shown by lessors. Perhaps the reason for disclosing this information is to convince the reader that the volume of leases is increasing (Note 4) even if the computer marketplace seems to be moving away from mainframes to small machines, and also that the company's projected cash flows from existing contracts (Note 5) were substantial. Comdisco had been suffering from declining revenues and low profitability, and it had cut its dividends on common stock. The last sentence in Note 6 suggests that the company has also sold its interest in some of the leases.

EXHIBIT 13A.2 concluded

Note 4: Lease Portfolio Information

The size of the company's lease portfolio can be measured by the cost of leased assets at the date of lease inception. Cost at lease inception represents either the equipment's original cost or its net book value at termination of a prior lease. The following table summarizes, by year of lease commencement and by year of projected lease termination, the cost at lease inception for all leased assets recorded at September 30, 1994 (in millions):

		Projected year of lease termination				
Year lease commenced	Cost at lease inception	95	96	97	98	99 and after
1990 and prior	$ 936	$ 659	$ 166	$ 69	$ 18	$ 24
1991	1,017	441	399	93	78	6
1992	1,514	612	387	409	53	53
1993	1,473	234	557	323	278	81
1994	1,582	83	334	662	270	233
	$6,522	$2,029	$1,843	$1,556	$697	$397

The following table summarizes the estimated net book value at lease termination for all leased assets recorded at September 30, 1994. The table is presented by year of lease commencement and by year of projected lease termination (in millions):

		Projected year of lease termination				
Year lease commenced	Net book value at lease termination	95	96	97	98	99 and after
1990 and prior	$ 73	$ 64	$ 7	$ 1	$ 1	$—
1991	97	47	47	3	—	—
1992	179	89	41	44	—	5
1993	193	36	68	40	36	13
1994	241	20	56	101	40	24
	$783	$256	$219	$189	$77	$42

Note 5: Owned Equipment — Future Noncancelable Lease Rentals and Disaster Recovery Subscription Fees

Presented below is a summary of future noncancelable lease rentals on owned equipment and future subscription fees on noncancelable disaster recovery contracts (collectively, "cash in-flows"). The summary presents expected cash in-flows, except for cash to be received on non-owned equipment of $35 million, due in accordance with the contractual terms in existence as of September 30, 1994. The table also presents the amounts to be received by financial institutions for leases discounted on a nonrecourse basis (see Note 6 of Notes to Consolidated Financial Statements).

	Years ending September 30,					
(in millions)	95	96	97	98	99 and after	Total
Expected future cash in-flows:						
Operating leases	$ 737	$ 441	$190	$ 58	$ 22	$1,448
Direct financing and sales-type leases	912	645	361	160	99	2,177
Disaster recovery contracts	190	149	101	58	27	525
Total	1,839	1,235	652	276	148	4,150
Less: To be received by financial institutions						
Operating leases	391	234	94	19	3	741
Direct financing and sales-type leases	405	286	159	77	30	957
Total	796	520	253	96	33	1,698
To be received by the company	$1,043	$ 715	$399	$180	$115	$2,452

EXHIBIT 13A.3

The Boeing Company
Disclosure of Sales-Type Leases

Note 4: Customer Financing
Long-term customer financing, less current portion, at December 31 consisted of the following:

	1994	1993
Notes receivable	$1,189	$1,396
Investment in sales-type leases	1,235	768
Operating lease aircraft, at cost, less accumulated depreciation of $269 and $220	747	895
	3,171	3,059
Less valuation allowance	(100)	(100)
	$3,071	$2,959

Financing for aircraft is collateralized by security in the related asset, and historically, the Company has not experienced a problem in accessing such collateral. The operating lease aircraft category includes new and used jet and commuter aircraft, spare engines and spare parts.

Principal payments from notes receivable and sales-type leases for the next five years are as follows:

1995	1996	1997	1998	1999
$250	$266	$56	$51	$46

The Company has entered into interest rate swaps with third-party investors whereby the interest rate terms differ from the terms in the original receivable. These interest rate swaps related to $358 of customer financing receivables as of December 31, 1994.

Interest rates on fixed-rate notes ranged from 6.5% to 11%, and effective interest rates on variable-rate notes ranged from the London Interbank Offered Rate (LIBOR) to 4.125% above LIBOR.

Sales and other operating revenues included interest income associated with notes receivable and sales-type leases of $183, $153 and $57 for 1994, 1993 and 1992, respectively.

Exhibit 13A.3 is the Boeing Company's footnote disclosure for its customer financing, which includes leases. It appears that Boeing disclosed its sales-type leases ($1,235 million as of December 31, 1994) on a net basis without bothering to break out the gross amount less the amount attributable to unearned income or future interest, perhaps for reasons of materiality. It is interesting that Boeing chose to disclose its derivative activities in this footnote, or at least that part associated with customer financing programs. A word of caution: Do not expect to find those 15 leased 767-ER's that AMR reported in this list of leased aircraft from Boeing. AMR did not necessarily lease them from the Boeing Company.

APPENDIX 13B

Pensions in Detail

This appendix presents some basic pension terminology and illustrates the calculations necessary to determine a company's pension expense. It explains the significance of the required footnote disclosures for defined-benefit plans and interprets an actual pension footnote. Finally, an example of pension accounting is presented.

Terminology

To understand the valuation of defined-benefit pension obligations and the disclosure of pension expense, and liability and asset information reflected in corporate annual reports, one must first learn the language of pension accounting. The following concepts and definitions are essential for a complete understanding of pension accounting.

Plan assets — the market value of the assets in a pension fund under the control of a trustee. These assets are owned by the pension fund or trust, a separate legal entity, and appear on the balance sheet of the trust, not of the employer-company.

Accumulated benefit obligation (ABO) — the present value of the projected payments a company must make in the future to satisfy the retirement benefits that have already been earned by employees and retirees. Discounting of the future cash outflow is done using an interest rate termed the *settlement rate*, an external market rate reflecting the return on high-quality, fixed-income investments. Projections are made using only *current* salary levels but with assumptions for mortality and so on. Conceptually, if a company were to terminate a pension agreement now and seek to settle whatever obligations it had to employees and retirees by making a single payment now to an external pension administrator, the ABO would be the amount it owed. Note that an employer can cancel a pension agreement, but it is obligated to pay benefits for the accumulated years of service each employee has earned until the agreement is canceled. Also note that, as each year passes, qualified employees "earn" another year of benefits.

Projected benefit obligation (PBO) — an obligation similar to the ABO except that it is based on projected or future salary levels. Consequently, the PBO is usually higher than the ABO. The PBO is the present value (using the settlement rate) of the pension benefits that have been earned to date by employees and retirees. It reflects expected mortality, expected salary increases, and expectations about employee turnover.

Expected rate — the expected long-term rate of return on a pension fund's assets. This rate is used to estimate what the trustee will earn on a fund's invested assets.

Vested benefits — *vested* means that an employee has met the minimum plan tenure requirements and is qualified to receive pension benefits. In most corporate pension plans, employees must work full-time for a defined period of time, say two years, before they become eligible for a pension. For example, suppose that two people joined a company at the same time and that one quit after two years and the other left after four years. If the company had a three-year vesting requirement, the first person would receive no pension. The second person would be eligible for a pension based on the four years of service. A company's PBO for all employees and retirees might be $130 million, but perhaps only $110 million for vested employees and retirees — those with more than the required years of service (that is, the vesting period).

Funded status of the plan — the difference between the projected benefit obligation (PBO) and a plan's assets at market value.

Net gain or loss — the difference between the actual earnings of a plan for a year and the expected earnings (expected rate times beginning of the year value of the plan's assets). If the difference is included in pension expense, it is considered "recognized." If it is accumulated and amortized at some later date, it is termed *the accumulated, unrecognized net gain or loss*. Generally accepted accounting practice is to recognize the net gains or losses only when they exceed a threshold (10 percent of the higher of the PBO or the plan assets).

Financial Accounting Standard 87 (SFAS No. 87) — the current U.S. GAAP for pensions.

Financial Accounting Standard (SFAS No. 106) — the current U.S. GAAP for retirement benefits other than pensions.

Net obligation — the difference between the PBO and the plan assets at the time SFAS No. 87 was adopted. It is also called the *transition asset (or liability)*. It is amortized or recognized in the income statement on a straight-line basis over the expected working lives of the workforce at the time SFAS No. 87 was adopted.

Accrued or prepaid pension cost — the cumulative total of the unfunded pension expense or, if funding has exceeded the cumulative expenses, the cumulative prepaid pension cost.

Service cost (or **current service cost** or **normal cost**) — the present value of the benefits earned in the current year by the existing employees in a plan. Perhaps the best way to conceptualize service cost is the following. As each year goes by, the employees should say to themselves, "I've just put in another year of service toward retirement. I'll get another X percent of my ending salary in each retirement check." The employer must predict just how many of those employees will survive to begin collecting their retirement and how long that retirement will last. The present value cost of this obligation, for just this year, is the *service cost*. Calculating the service cost requires projections of mortality and future salary levels. Discounting the future payments is done at the settlement rate.

Prior service cost — when a pension plan is first adopted, an employer often gives credit to existing employees for their years of service prior to the adoption of the plan. For example, 63-year-old employees will suddenly be treated as if they had been in the plan since they were hired. They may get 35 or 40 years of service "with the stroke of a pen." The present value of this prior (or past) service is estimated by using projected salary levels, mortality, and the settlement rate. The same thing happens when a plan's benefit levels are increased and made retroactive.

Interest cost — for the year, the beginning of the year PBO times the settlement rate. Conceptually, interest cost is like saying "At the beginning of this year, our total pension obligation (as measured by the PBO) on a discounted basis was $320 million.

We are now at the end of the year, one year closer to the payouts. Hence, the value of the obligation has increased by a year's interest."

Actual return on plan assets — the total actual earnings of the pension-fund assets for a year.

Actuarial gains and losses — a catchall category for the favorable and unfavorable adjustments arising from changes in expected mortality (and other actuarial) assumptions.

Additional minimum liability — an amount in addition to any current accrued or prepaid pension cost that may be required to be shown as a pension liability when a plan's assets are less than the ABO.

Accounting for Defined-Benefit Plans

Each year, actuaries and accountants project the number of an employer's present workforce who will survive to retirement and the life expectancies for those projected retirees. Salary levels are projected, benefits calculated, and an expected pension payout schedule is prepared as of the end of each accounting period. This payout schedule is then discounted using a *settlement rate* to derive a *projected benefit obligation* (PBO). A similar calculation, the *accumulated benefit obligation* (ABO), is prepared using only current salary levels. Thus, there are two liability figures — one assuming current salary levels and one assuming salary progression. It is important to note that these "liabilities" do not necessarily appear in the employer's balance sheet; at this stage, they are simply calculations.

Under SFAS No. 87, the *pension expense* for a given year to be reported by an employer is the net of the following four items:

1. The *service cost* for the year (that is, the present value cost of future benefits earned by employees for this year only).
2. *Plus* the *interest cost* on the PBO as of the beginning of the year, which is like the debt service cost on the total pension liability as of the beginning of the year.
3. *Less* the *actual return on plan assets* for the year (what the pension fund actually earned). In an ideal world, the pension fund's assets at the beginning of the year would equal only the PBO at the beginning of the year. During the year, the fund would earn only the year's interest cost on the PBO, so items 2 and 3 would offset one another.
4. *Plus/minus* four miscellaneous adjustments:
   a. The difference between the actual return on plan assets and the expected return on plan assets for the year. The effect is to replace the actual return on plan assets with the *expected return on plan assets*. The differences between actual and expected returns are accumulated and, if they exceed a threshold, are amortized over the expected working lifetime of the employees. This adjustment smooths the recognition of differences between the actual and expected earnings rate.
   b. Actuarial gains and losses are treated the same way.
   c. The difference between the PBO and the total fund assets at the time SFAS No. 87 was adopted is called the *net obligation* or *transition amount*. It too is amortized over the expected workforce service life.
   d. If the plan is modified in later years and these modifications lead to prior service costs, this cost is also amortized.

The concept underlying this complex calculation of the yearly expense is based on the following logic: In a perfect world, a company's pension expense should be only its current pension service cost. This amount would be paid to the pension trust, which would add it to the fund's assets. Each year, the fund's invested assets would earn just what was expected. In such situation, the PBO (the present value of the total pension obligation) would always equal the fund's assets. The following exemplifies this "perfect world" situation:

Beginning balance of PBO	**$100**
Plus: Current service	10
Plus: Interest cost	8
Ending balance	$118

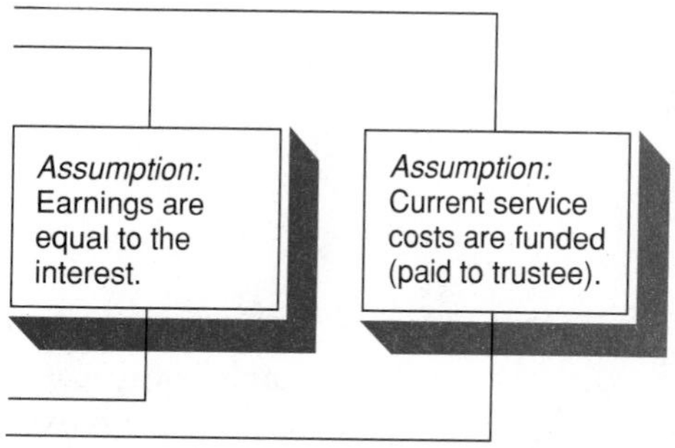

Pension asset

Beginning balance	$100
Plus: Earnings	8
Plus: Funding	10
	$118

In such a world, the pension assets would always be equal to the pension obligation. In the real world, however, many things are different:

- Actual earnings are rarely equal to expected earnings. The effect of SFAS No. 87 is to substitute the expected return for the actual return and then amortize the accumulated differences between the two over time if the cumulative amount gets "too big" (that is, it smooths out the effects of stock and bond market swings).
- Sometimes management increases the benefits level. This has an immediate impact on the PBO (it increases it). The new obligation created by these plan modifications (prior service costs) is amortized over time — another smoothing activity.
- Sometimes the actuaries change their mortality tables or make similar changes to their assumptions. This can immediately either raise or lower the PBO. SFAS No. 87 smooths this by amortizing the actuarial gain or loss over time.
- Finally, when SFAS No. 87 was first adopted, most companies had a PBO different from their fund assets. This difference, or transition amount, is amortized over time.

The consequence of all of these smoothings and adjustments is to ensure that for a company that funds its pension costs on a timely basis, the plan assets approximate the PBO over time without causing the annual pension expense to fluctuate widely.

Disclosure Requirements for Defined-Benefit Plans

Companies with defined-benefit pension programs must disclose the nature of their programs, types of benefits, funding policies, and actuarial methods. They must also disclose both the settlement rate and the expected earnings rate, the major elements of the actual pension expense, the ABO, and the PBO. The cumulative overfunded and underfunded status of different pension plans for a single employer cannot be netted together.

The 1994 footnote disclosure of PepsiCo, Inc., presented earlier in Exhibit 13.5 is typical of footnotes under the disclosure requirements of SFAS No. 87.

PepsiCo's 1994 pension expense for its domestic plans, for example, was \$33.1 million, and this is the amount that is included in the income statement for that year. It consists of \$69.8 million of service cost (the present value of benefits earned by employees during the year), \$84.0 million of interest cost on the PBO (simply because of the passage of time), and an actual loss during 1994 on the plan's assets of \$19.7 million. Apparently the expected earnings on the plan assets were \$110.8 million as follows:

Expected earnings	\$110.8 million
Actual loss	19.7
Expected − Actual	\$130.5 million

The \$130.5 million difference is added to the "smoother." In 1993 the reverse was true: Earnings exceeded expectations and the smoother was reduced by \$70.9. Over time the smoother is expected to net to zero; otherwise, the assumptions about earnings on the plan's assets must be revised. We can also see that for most plans the PepsiCo pension assets exceeded the PBO at the time it adopted SFAS No. 87 because the amortization of the transition amount, \$19 million a year for the domestic plans, reduced the overall pension expense.

Defined-Benefit Pension Liability on the Balance Sheet

Under certain circumstances, a pension liability other than a particular year's accrued or prepaid pension cost amount discussed earlier could appear on a company's balance sheet. SFAS No. 87 requires that, whenever total pension fund assets are less than the ABO (that is, the present value of the projected benefits *without* salary progression), a minimum liability is to be recognized in the employer's balance sheet even though the pension assets are under the control of and on the books of the pension plan.

Three situations are possible. When there is no current accrued or prepaid pension cost, the additional minimum liability is just the ABO minus the plan assets — *the unfunded ABO*. When there is a current *prepaid* pension cost, the additional liability is the unfunded ABO plus the prepaid pension cost. When there is a current accrued pension liability, the additional liability is the unfunded ABO less the accrued pension cost (except that when the unfunded liability is less than the accrued pension liability, there is no additional minimum liability).

For example, consider the following situation:

Accumulated benefit obligation (ABO)	\$(3,500)
Provision for salary progression	(2,100)
Projected benefit obligation (PBO)	\$(5,600)
Fair value of plan assets	3,000
Funded status of plan (underfunded)	\$(2,600)
Unrecognized net gain or loss	400
Unrecognized net obligation	1,800
(Accrued) prepaid pension cost	\$ (400)

The unfunded ABO is thus $500:

ABO	$(3,500)
Plan assets	3,000
	$ 500

The additional minimum liability is $100:

Unfunded ABO	$ 500
(Accrued) prepaid pension cost	(400)
	$ 100

The requirement to reflect this minimum liability on the employer's balance sheet was the result of a compromise by the FASB between the dictates of accounting theory and the realities of business practice. One might easily argue that when the pension assets are less than the *PBO*, the difference is an obligation of the employer that should be recognized just like any other liability. The compromise resulted in the FASB's decision that a liability must be recognized in the balance sheet only when the plan assets are less than the *ABO*.

In the previous example, the difference between the ABO and the plan assets is $500, but the firm already has a $400 accrued pension liability. This portion of the liability has already been recognized and expensed but has not yet been funded. Hence, the additional, minimum liability to be shown on the balance sheet is $100. This is what Exxon did, as explained in Chapter 13.

Conditions leading to the recognition of a minimum liability usually arise when a new plan is adopted and benefits are granted for prior service. The "goodwill" created in the workforce by the new plan is considered to be an intangible asset, and an entry would be made as follows:

Dr. Unamortized Pension Cost (A)	(inc.) 100	
Cr. Pension Liability (L)		(inc.) 100

Each year the previous year's minimum liability and related asset are removed from the books, and a new liability and asset are added if conditions indicate that an unfunded ABO exists. Some critics refer to this as a "post-it" entry that appears each year as a different figure as long as the fund's assets do not exceed the value of the ABO.

If the ABO exceeds the fund's assets *by an amount in excess of the unrecognized prior period costs and the unrecognized net obligation*, the excess amount is deducted from the recorded pension asset and is a contra equity. In other words, if the ABO exceeds the fund assets for reasons other than the cost of prior service, the plan is essentially underfunded, and it should appear as a liability without any offsetting asset. In the example just discussed, this would not be the case because the unrecognized net obligation or transition amount is $1,800.

Pension accounting is complex because pensions are complex. SFAS No. 87 introduced many new and potentially confusing concepts such as the PBO and ABO, the additional minimum liability, and the unrecognized net obligation. It may be some time before readers of financial statements become thoroughly familiar with this information, but its impact on reported net income and the statement of financial position is not likely to be significant for most large publicly traded corporations because most have funded some or all of their pensions. The same cannot be said about a related issue — postretirement medical costs. These costs are predicted to rise rapidly in the next decade. Most corporations have provided no funding or reserves for such costs. SFAS No. 106, effective for 1993 fiscal year, added significant liabilities to U.S. corporate balance sheets for these future obligations.

Effective with SFAS No. 106 a company must report its annual expense for medical, life insurance, and other postretirement benefits segmented into

- Current service cost
- Interest on the PBO
- Actual return on plan assets
- Amortization of the unrecognized transition obligation

and other adjustments. It must also disclose

- Fair value of plan assets
- ABO

and details of remaining unamortized prior service cost, transition obligation, and net gain/loss on plan assets. These disclosures closely parallel the pension disclosures.

Many companies expensed their entire PBO when they adopted SFAS No. 106, although for most it was a noncash expense because the liability was not funded. Otherwise companies would have had to amortize the transition obligation over the working lifetimes of their employees (for that portion of the PBO obligated to current employees), which would have reduced net income each year going forward. For many, the onetime, noncash catch-up charge was preferable.

A Complete Example

Exhibit 13B.1 reports the pension expense for a hypothetical company that adopted SFAS No. 87 in 1987; Exhibit 13B.2 illustrates the derivation of accrued or prepaid pension cost following the format used in most U.S. annual reports today. In this particular illustration, the company experiences five years when the expected returns exceed the actual returns on the invested plan assets. Then the reverse is true. In addition, the actuarial assumptions change in 1990 and 1993. In 1989 the plan is amended to grant retroactive (prior service) benefits to employees. The effects of these events will be reflected in the pension assets and liability.

To begin, consider the first three lines of Exhibit 13B.2. The company's pension liability (PBO) at the beginning of 1987 was $400 larger than the pension assets of $3,000. Note that in this illustration the pension liability rises steadily (in years such as 1989, it seems to jump considerably), and the plan assets lag behind for several years, resulting in a sharp increase in the unfunded PBO. Beginning in 1993, however, the fund's assets increase dramatically. In spite of these large changes in assets, the PBO, and the funded status of the plan, the pension expense (Exhibit 13B.1) reflects only gradual changes, which is exactly what SFAS No. 87 attempts to achieve.

In following the calculations, perhaps the first thing that one should note is that at the time of adoption of SFAS No. 87, the difference between the PBO and the plan assets is the unrecognized net obligation ($400). This amount is amortized over 10 years (the projected average working lifetime of the present employees) and becomes a part of the pension expense for those years. If the company funds the expense each year by giving money to the pension trust, this will add to the assets and in

EXHIBIT 13B.1

Calculation of Pension Expense

	1987	1988	1989	1990	1991	1992	1993	1994
Service cost	300	310	320	330	340	350	360	370
Interest cost	340	404	475	605	708	813	930	1,039
Actual return on plan assets	(240)	(267)	(201)	(214)	(567)	(847)	(1,103)	(1,114)
Net amortization (see below)	(20)	(17)	(141)	(193)	88	252	366	212
Pension expense	380	430	454	528	569	568	553	506
Explanation of net amortization:								
Amortization — unrecognized net (gain)/loss	–0–	–0–	–0–	–0–	2	–0–	–0–	–0–
Actual — expected earnings	(60)	(57)	(231)	(283)	(4)	162	276	122
Amortization — unrecognized net obligation	40	40	40	40	40	40	40	40
Amortization — unrecognized prior service cost	–0–	–0–	50	50	50	50	50	50
Net amortization	(20)	(17)	(141)	(193)	88	252	366	212

EXHIBIT 13B.2

Reconciliation of (Accrued) Prepaid Pension Cost

	Begin	End of Year							
	1987	1987	1988	1989	1990	1991	1992	1993	1994
Projected benefit obligation	(3,400)	(4,040)	(4,754)	(6,049)	(7,084)	(8,133)	(9,296)	(10,386)	(11,794)
Fair value of assets	3,000	3,240	4,317	4,972	5,713	6,850	8,265	9,921	11,542
Funded status of plan	(400)	(800)	(437)	(1,078)	(1,371)	(1,283)	(1,031)	(464)	(253)
Unrecognized prior service cost		–0–	–0–	450	400	350	300	250	200
Unrecognized net (gain) loss		60	117	348	731	733	571	94	(27)
Unrecognized net obligation	400	360	320	280	240	200	160	120	80
(Accrued) prepaid pension cost	–0–	(380)	–0–	–0–	–0–	–0–	–0–	–0–	–0–

10 years will close the gap between the assets and PBO if there are no other variances between what is expected and what actually happens.

One should next note Exhibit 13B.3, the calculation of the PBO. Each year, the PBO is increased by the current year's service cost and interest on the beginning of the year's PBO. The PBO is also increased when the terms of the pension plan are changed, giving additional benefits to employees based on their past years of service. This benefit increase is called *prior service cost.* Note that this is assumed to occur in 1989. Actuarial adjustments also change the PBO as depicted in 1990 and 1993. The reader should note also what does not change the PBO: actual funding by the employer and earnings on the plan assets. The PBO is reduced as retirees begin receiving their benefits (that is, when the projected payouts are actually made). To simplify matters, this example assumes that there are as yet no retirees and their expected working life continues to be 10 years.

Exhibit 13B.4 illustrates the calculation of the plan assets. They are increased by company funding and the earnings on the fund. They decline when payouts are made to retirees.

Referring back to Exhibit 13B.1, the periodic pension expense is composed of service cost, interest on the PBO, actual return on the plan assets, and net amortization.

EXHIBIT 13B.3

Calculation of Projected Benefit Obligation

	1987	1988	1989	1990	1991	1992	1993	1994
Projected benefit obligation — Beginning	(3,400)	(4,040)	(4,754)	(6,049)	(7,084)	(8,133)	(9,296)	(10,386)
Add: Service cost	(300)	(310)	(320)	(330)	(340)	(350)	(360)	(370)
Interest	(340)	(404)	(475)	(605)	(708)	(813)	(930)	(1,039)
New prior service cost	–0–	–0–	(500)	–0–	–0–	–0–	–0–	–0–
Actuarial adjustment	–0–	–0–	–0–	(100)	–0–	–0–	200	–0–
Deduct: Pension benefits paid	–0–	–0–	–0–	–0–	–0–	–0–	–0–	–0–
Projected benefit obligation — end	(4,040)	(4,754)	(6,049)	(7,084)	(8,133)	(9,296)	(10,386)	(11,794)

EXHIBIT 13B.4

Calculation of Fair Value of Assets

	1987	1988	1989	1990	1991	1992	1993	1994
Fair value of assets — beginning	3,000	3,240	4,317	4,972	5,713	6,850	8,265	9,921
Add: Actual return on plan assets	240	267	201	214	567	847	1,103	1,114
Amount funded	–0–	810	454	528	569	568	553	506
Deduct: Pension benefits paid	–0–	–0–	–0–	–0–	–0–	–0–	–0–	–0–
Fair value of assets — end	3,240	4,317	4,972	5,713	6,850	8,265	9,921	11,542

(The actual derivation of service cost is not explained in this example.) Note that the interest cost is based on the beginning of the period PBO and the settlement rate, here assumed to be 10 percent. Pension expense is reduced by the actual earnings on the plan assets, or $240 in 1987.

The net amortization consists of four elements. The first is the amortization of the unrecognized net gain or loss. The logic of this adjustment is that over time most gains and losses (actual minus expected returns) should cancel one another. Only if the cumulative difference gets too large should one increase (or decrease) the level of expensing and funding. SFAS No. 87 chose the threshold of 10 percent. Hence, as long as the cumulative gain/loss on plan assets is less than 10 percent of the greater of the PBO or the plan assets, no amortization is necessary. If the net gain or loss exceeds this threshold, the amount in excess of 10 percent is amortized over the remaining working lifetime of the employees.

As explained in Exhibit 13B.5, only in 1992 does the cumulative deficit in expected earnings exceed the 10 percent level. The calculation of the unrecognized gain/loss is explained in Exhibit 13B.6. Note that it is decreased by amortization and increased (or decreased) by the difference between the expected and actual investment performance of the plan. Note also that it is affected by actuarial gains and losses. In this illustration, the actuarial changes in 1990 increased the unrecognized loss; in 1993, the change was a gain.

Returning to Exhibit 13B.1, note that the adjustment for the actual – expected earnings, when combined with the actual return on plan assets, results in the pension expense reflecting the expected return. Only if the accumulated actual – expected earnings is outside the 10 percent corridor does it affect pension expense. The two remaining items to be amortized have already been mentioned: the $400 unrecognized

EXHIBIT 13B.5

Calculation of Amortization of Unrecognized Gain/Loss

	1987	1988	1989	1990	1991	1992	1993	1994
Unrecognized (gain)/loss — Beginning of year	–0–	60	117	348	731	733	571	94
10% of the greater of the PBO or fair value	340	404	475	605	708	813	930	1,039
Unrecognized (gain)/loss subject to amortization	–0–	–0–	–0–	–0–	22	–0–	–0–	–0–
Amortization of unrecognized (gain) loss	–0–	–0–	–0–	–0–	2	–0–	–0–	–0–

EXHIBIT 13B.6

Calculation of Unrecognized Gain (Loss)

	1987	1988	1989	1990	1991	1992	1993	1994
Unrecognized (gain)/loss — Beginning of year	–0–	60	117	348	731	733	571	94
Less: Amortization	–0–	–0–	–0–	–0–	2	–0–	–0–	–0–
Unrecognized (gain)/loss — before adjustment	–0–	60	117	348	729	733	571	94
Add: Actuarial net (gain) loss	–0–	–0–	–0–	100	–0–	–0–	(200)	–0–
Net asset (gain) loss (actual – expected)	60	57	231	283	4	(162)	(276)	(122)
Unrecognized (gain)/loss — end of year	60	117	348	731	733	571	94	(27)

EXHIBIT 13B.7

Calculation of Unrecognized Prior Service Cost

	1987	1988	1989	1990	1991	1992	1993	1994
Prior service cost — beginning of year		–0–	–0–	450	400	350	300	250
Add: New prior service cost	–0–	–0–	500	–0–	–0–	–0–	–0–	–0–
Less: Amortization of prior service cost	–0–	–0–	50	50	50	50	50	50
Prior service cost — end of year	–0–	–0–	450	400	350	300	250	200

net obligation (on adoption of SFAS No. 87) and the prior service cost (calculated in Exhibit 13B.7).

A final word about this example. SFAS No. 87 requires a reconciliation of PBO and plan assets back to prepaid or accrued pension cost. If the pension expense is actually funded each year (as illustrated in all years except 1987), there should be no accrued prepaid pension cost because the funded status of the plan should just be the sum of the following:

- Unamortized net obligation (transition amount to SFAS No. 87).
- Unamortized net gain or loss (cumulative actual – expected earnings).
- Unamortized prior service cost (since inception of SFAS No. 87).

APPENDIX 13C

Deferred Income Taxes in Detail

The concept of *interperiod tax allocation* and the recognition of deferred tax liabilities and deferred tax assets were explained in Chapter 13. This explanation did not discuss one of the most important complications arising from deferred tax accounting: What happens when tax rates change? Furthermore, it did not discuss the important limits on recognizing deferred tax assets required by SFAS No. 109. These two items are explained in this appendix.

When Tax Rates Change

Chapter 13 explained the fundamentals of deferred tax accounting by using an illustration of the calculation of deferred tax expense and the associated deferred tax liability from Sample Company:

	End of Year			
	1	2	3	4
Accounting asset NBV	$750	$500	$ 250	$ –0–
Tax asset NBV	500	–0–	–0–	–0–
Difference	$250	$500	$ 250	$ –0–
Tax rate (during the year)	0.4	0.4	0.4	0.4
Deferred tax liability	$100	$200	$ 100	$ –0–
Deferred tax expense	$100	$100	$(100)	$(100)

We will again refer to this example to explain what happens when income tax rates change.

SFAS No. 109 requires that when tax rates change, the changes are to be reflected in the accounting for deferred taxes when the legislation is enacted (signed by the president). This means that if, for example, the corporate income tax rates are increased in 1996, effective 1997, the effect of the change to the deferred tax liability and deferred tax assets is to be recorded in 1996. In the case of depreciation, perhaps the single largest cause of deferred taxes, this would mean higher deferred tax liabilities and, immediately, higher deferred tax expense.

Using this same example, if at the beginning of Year 3 the income tax rates were reduced to 30 percent, the changes (called *reversals*) in the accounting-tax differences at the new tax rate would yield a revised (and lower) deferred tax liability:

Year	Accounting-Tax Difference	Tax Rate	Deferred Tax Liability
3	$250	0.3	$ 75
4	250	0.3	75
	$500		$150

This change in the deferred tax liability and the related deferred tax benefit of $50 would be reflected in the first quarter of Year 3. At the end of Year 3, the deferred tax liability would be $75. The *net* deferred tax benefit for Year 3 is $125: $50 is the immediate benefit reflecting the effect of the lower income tax rate, and $75 reflects the Year 3 difference between accounting and tax depreciation — at the 30 percent rate.

The four-year summary table reflects exactly what will happen to Sample Company:

Accounting asset NBV	$750	$500	$250	$–0–
Tax asset NBV	500	–0–	–0–	–0–
Difference	$250	$500	$250	$–0–
Tax rate (during the year)	0.4	0.4	0.3	0.3
Deferred tax liability	$100	$200	$ 75	$–0–
Deferred tax expense (benefit)	100	100	(125)	(75)

In Years 3 and 4, the depreciation deductions on the tax return exceed the accounting depreciation expense. The deferred tax benefit adjusts for this difference, drawing down the balance in the deferred tax liability buffer. Year 3 also reflects the catch-up or adjustment to the deferred tax liability because of the changed tax rate. The impact of this catch-up is clearly seen in the revised income statements for Sample Company:

	Year 1	Year 2	Year 3	Year 4
Sales	$1,000	$1,000	$1,000	$1,000
Depreciation	250	250	250	250
All other expenses	400	400	400	400
Taxable income	350	350	350	350
Current income tax expense	40	40	180	180
Deferred income tax expense	100	100	–125	–75
Total income tax expense	140	140	55	105
Net income	210	210	295	245

The net income in Year 4 is higher than in years 1 and 2 because tax rates are lower. The Year 3 net income is even higher, by $50, because the tax rate was lowered before the deferred tax liability was reduced by the reversal of the accounting-tax depreciation charges. In effect, in Years 1 and 2, a total of $500 of taxable income was deferred by Sample Corporation into Years 3 and 4 when the tax rates were lower by 10 percent.

This immediately saved \$50 ($0.10 \times$ \$500), which is reflected in Year 3, the year the tax rate changes were announced.

Deferred Tax Assets

No doubt the most controversial aspect of SFAS No. 109 is the valuation of deferred tax assets; in certain circumstances, the full amount of the deferred tax assets may *not* be included in the financial statements even though a company must include all deferred tax liabilities. For example, consider an event for which the expense deduction for tax purposes lagged behind the deduction for accounting purposes, as in the provision for warranty expenses. Diagrammatically,

The provision for warranty expenses (not for taxes)

leads to

A temporary accounting-tax difference in warranty liability book values

that leads to

A deferred tax asset and deferred income tax benefit

that leads to

Lower tax expense and higher accounting net income

This is just the mirror image of the accelerated depreciation example but with the reverse effect: The income tax expense is shown at a lower amount than the current income taxes payable, and accounting net income is higher.

The logic may be consistent, but the FASB concluded that permitting deferred tax *benefits* due to accounting-tax differences on liabilities (such as warranty reserves) could violate the principal of conservatism in that a company would have to assume that it would make profits in the future and therefore have to pay taxes and consequently actually have tax liabilities against which to offset its tax benefits. SFAS No. 109 prescribes that a *valuation allowance* be established if it is "more likely than not" that all or a portion of the deferred tax assets will not be realized. Such a valuation allowance is to be based upon management's judgment as to the likelihood of future taxable income. A firm with continuing losses and a real issue of "going concern" might need to establish a valuation allowance up to or equal to the amount of the deferred tax asset. In practice, deferred tax assets typically relate to

- Bad debt allowances.
- Inventory reserves.
- Restructuring reserves.
- Litigation reserves.

EXHIBIT 13C.1

Amgen, Inc.
Income Taxes

The provision for income taxes includes the following (in thousands):

	Years ended December 31,		
	1994	1993	1992
Current provision:			
Federal	$231,306	$165,822	$178,609
State	34,855	25,856	34,937
Total current provision	266,161	191,678	213,546
Deferred provision (benefit):			
Federal	516	19,723	(8,012)
State	1,927	6,394	—
Total deferred provision (benefit)	2,443	26,117	(8,012)
	$268,604	$217,795	$205,534

Deferred income taxes reflect the net tax effects of net operating loss carryforwards and temporary differences between the carrying amounts of assets and liabilities for financial reporting purposes and the amounts used for income tax purposes. Significant components of the Company's deferred tax assets and liabilities as of December 31, 1994 and 1993 are as follows (in thousands):

	December 31,	
	1994	1993
Deferred tax assets:		
Net operating loss carryforwards	$ 89,478	$ 3,913
Expense accruals	78,481	42,834
Fixed assets	17,018	7,280
Royalty obligation buyouts	11,772	12,936
State income taxes	9,499	6,501
Research collaboration expenses	8,033	7,865
Other	7,215	6,969
Total deferred tax assets	221,496	88,298
Valuation allowance	(79,497)	(17,805)
Net deferred tax assets	141,999	70,493
Deferred tax liabilities:		
Purchase of technology rights	(25,708)	(9,608)
Other	(5,649)	(1,948)
Total deferred tax liabilities	(31,357)	(11,556)
	$110,642	$ 58,937

The net change in the valuation allowance for deferred tax assets during the year ended December 31, 1994 was $61,692,000. This change primarily relates to the net operating loss carryforwards acquired through the purchase of Synergen (Note 2).

- Operating loss carryforwards.
- Capital loss and tax credit carryforwards.
- Postretirement employee benefit accruals.

When companies with a history of profits record valuation allowances, they are usually associated with

- Unique sources, such as foreign tax credits that must be matched with taxable income in a particular country.
- Jurisdictional issues, such as operating loss carryforwards in a particular state.
- Unique timing issues, such as reversal patterns on pensions and other postretirement benefits that might run 30 years or more.[1]

For example, Exhibit 13C.1 is the income taxes footnote of Amgen, Inc.'s 1994 annual report. On a consolidated basis, Amgen has paid well over half a billion dollars in taxes during the 1992–1994 time period, and yet the company has a valuation allowance of $79.5 million. As the last sentence in its footnote explains, most of this valuation is associated with net operating loss carryforwards of an acquisition, Synergen. Apparently, the $61.7 million loss carryforward at Synergen is not applicable to the rest of Amgen.

ISSUES FOR DISCUSSION

D13.1 Point: All leases should be capitalized on the balance sheet as liabilities.

Counterpoint: Only capital leases should be treated as liabilities.

Evaluate the two viewpoints. Which one do you agree with, and why?

D13.2 The 1994 annual report of Warner Lambert contained three footnotes on retirement benefits that are reproduced here. Based on the information contained in the footnotes, answer the following pension-related questions:

a. Explain what is meant by a noncontributory plan. Are these plans defined benefit or defined contribution?

b. What is the total amount of Warner Lambert's pension expense shown in the company's 1994 income statement?

c. What is meant by
(1) Vested benefit obligation?
(2) Accumulated benefit obligation?
(3) Projected benefit obligation?

d. Why is one of the components of the pension cost the interest cost on the projected benefit obligation? How is the amount determined?

e. The actual return on plan assets has changed considerably from 1992 to 1994. Does this result in a very volatile annual pension expense figure for the defined-benefit plans? Explain.

f. Are Warner Lambert's defined-benefit pension plans overfunded as of 1994? How do you know?

[1]T. R. Petree; G. J. Gregory; and R. J. Vitray, "Evaluating Deferred Tax Assets," *Journal of Accountancy*, March 1995, pp. 71–77.

Warner-Lambert

NOTE 12 — PENSIONS:

The company has various noncontributory pension plans covering substantially all of its employees in the U.S. Benefits covering most employees are based on years of service and average compensation during the last years of employment. Current policy is to fund these plans in an amount that ranges from the minimum contribution required by ERISA to the maximum tax-deductible contribution. Certain foreign subsidiaries also have various plans, which are funded in accordance with the statutory requirements of the particular countries.

Pension costs for the plans included the following components:

	Years Ended December 31,		
	1994	1993	1992
Service cost — benefits earned during the year	**$ 50.9**	$ 44.9	$ 42.0
Interest cost on projected benefit obligation	**134.3**	130.1	122.6
Return on assets	**(24.2)**	(199.2)	(127.2)
Net amortization and deferral	**(124.5)**	59.4	(5.5)
Net pension expense	**$ 36.5**	$ 35.2	$ 31.9

Net pension expense attributable to foreign plans and included in the above was $21.4, $17.9 and $18.2 in 1994, 1993 and 1992, respectively.

The 1993 restructuring charge, discussed in Note 3, included a $4.6 curtailment loss representing a decrease in unrecognized prior service costs resulting from a reduction in domestic plan participants.

The plans' funded status at December 31 was as follows:

	Plans in Which Assets Exceed Accumulated Benefits		Plans in Which Accumulated Benefits Exceed Assets	
	1994	1993	1994	1993
Plan assets at fair value	**$1,583.9**	$1,605.9	**$ 70.5**	$ 80.6
Actuarial present value of accumulated benefit obligation:				
Vested	**1,421.5**	1,464.9	**140.3**	141.6
Nonvested	**45.4**	30.3	**9.4**	10.4
	1,466.9	1,495.2	**149.7**	152.0
Estimated future salary increases	**138.5**	171.5	**27.6**	35.7
Projected benefit obligation	**1,605.4**	1,666.7	**177.3**	187.7
Excess of projected benefit obligation over plan assets	**(21.5)**	(60.8)	**(106.8)**	(107.1)
Unrecognized net (asset) obligation	**(22.0)**	(38.1)	**7.2**	7.8
Unrecognized prior service cost	**36.2**	41.8	**2.7**	3.0
Unrecognized net actuarial loss	**150.8**	208.5	**21.5**	28.7
Minimum liability adjustment	**—**	—	**(18.6)**	(19.0)
Net pension asset (liability) included in consolidated balance sheets	**$ 143.5**	$ 151.4	**$ (94.0)**	$ (86.6)

continued

Plan assets are composed primarily of investments in equities and bonds.

Foreign plan assets at fair value included in the preceding table were $570.1 in 1994 and $524.1 in 1993. The foreign plan projected benefit obligation was $596.4 in 1994 and $536.2 in 1993.

The assumptions for the U.S. plans were:

	Years Ended December 31,		
	1994	**1993**	**1992**
Expected long-term rate of return on plan assets	**10.5%**	10.5%	10.5%
Expected increase in salary levels	**4.0**	4.0	5.0
Weighted average discount rate	**8.8**	7.5	8.8

Assumptions for foreign plans did not vary significantly from the U.S. plans.

NOTE 13 — POSTEMPLOYMENT BENEFITS:
The company adopted the provisions of SFAS No. 112, "Employers' Accounting for Postemployment Benefits," effective January 1, 1993. This accounting change resulted in a cumulative effect adjustment which decreased net income upon adoption by $17.0 ($27.0 pretax) or $0.13 per share. SFAS No. 112 requires employers to recognize an obligation for postemployment benefits to former or inactive employees after employment but before retirement. This one-time charge primarily represented the present value of medical and life insurance costs for employees receiving long-term disability benefits.

NOTE 14 — OTHER POSTRETIREMENT BENEFITS:
The company provides other postretirement benefits, primarily health insurance, for domestic employees who retired prior to January 1, 1992 and their dependents. Although the plans are currently noncontributory, the company has implemented a cap which limits future contributions for medical and dental coverage under these plans. The company is generally self-insured for these costs and the plans are funded on a pay-as-you-go basis. Domestic employees retiring after December 31, 1991 will receive additional pension benefits based on years of service in lieu of these benefits.

The annual cost of providing other postretirement benefits for domestic retirees amounted to $15.0, $14.0 and $13.4 in 1994, 1993 and 1992, respectively. These amounts primarily represent the accrual of interest on the present value obligation.

A reconciliation from the plans' benefit obligation to the liabilities recognized in the consolidated balance sheets as of the latest actuarial valuations was as follows:

	December 31,	
	1994	**1993**
Accumulated postretirement benefit obligation	**$179.3**	$ 180.2
Unrecognized prior service cost	**1.8**	2.0
Unrecognized net actuarial loss	**(49.4)**	(45.9)
Accrued postretirement benefit cost recognized in the consolidated balance sheets	**$131.7**	$ 136.3

The health care cost trend rate used to develop the accumulated postretirement benefit obligation for those retirees under age 65 was 12.3 percent in 1994 declining to 6 percent over 12 years. For those 65 and over, a rate of 8 percent was used in 1994 declining to 6 percent over 7 years. A one percentage point increase in the health care cost trend rate in each year would increase the accumulated postretirement benefit obligation as of December 31, 1994 by $5.8 and the interest cost component of the postretirement benefit cost for 1994 by $0.5. The weighted average discount rate used to develop the accumulated postretirement benefit obligation was 8.8 percent, 7.5 percent and 8.8 percent for 1994, 1993, and 1992, respectively.

Other postretirement benefit costs for foreign plans expensed under the cash method in 1994, 1993 and 1992 were not material.

D13.3 Point: Deferred income taxes represent a liability.

Counterpoint: Deferred income taxes represent owners' equity.

Evaluate the two viewpoints. Which one do you agree with, and why?

D13.4 Suppose you are the chief financial officer of a corporation and a director has some questions about your annual report. The director notes that accounts called *deferred tax* appear both on the asset and the liability sides of the balance sheet, and asks, "What are those things supposed to be?" How would you explain them to the director?

D13.5 Who benefits from a company-sponsored pension plan? When do those benefits happen? If there is a benefit, there is no doubt a cost somewhere. What are the costs of those benefits just identified? When are those costs paid?

D13.6 As an employee, would you prefer to receive a defined-benefit pension or a defined-contribution pension, assuming the pension benefits appeared to be about the same during that important first year of retirement?

D13.7 The 1994 annual report of Johnson & Johnson (J&J) contained the following footnote pertaining to income taxes. Explain what this footnote says. What was the income tax expense in those three years? What caused the taxes to be deferred? Are there deferred tax assets or liabilities shown on the J&J balance sheets? Why is J&J's tax rate so much lower than that of most corporations? What was J&J's 1994 net income after tax?

Johnson & Johnson

6 Income Taxes

The provision for taxes on income consists of:

(Dollars in millions)	1994	1993	1992
Currently payable:			
U.S. taxes on domestic income	**$318**	190	179
U.S. taxes on international income	**(30)**	(1)	(14)
International taxes	**404**	345	403
U.S. state and local taxes	**49**	30	22
	741	564	590
Deferred:			
U.S. taxes	**(36)**	(26)	(29)
International taxes	**(30)**	7	21
	(66)	(19)	(8)
	$675	545	582

Deferred taxes result from the effect of transactions which are recognized in different periods for financial and tax reporting purposes and relate primarily to employee benefits, depreciation and other valuation allowances.

Effective December 30, 1991, the Company adopted the provisions of Statement of Financial Accounting Standard (SFAS) No. 109, "Accounting for Income Taxes." The cumulative effect of $35 million, or $0.05 per share, is reported as a one-time charge in the 1992 Consolidated Statement of Earnings. Prior years' financial statements have not been restated to apply the provisions of SFAS No. 109. The standard required a change from the deferred to the liability method of computing deferred income taxes. Deferred income taxes are recognized for tax consequences of "temporary differences" by applying enacted statutory tax rates, applicable to future years, to differences between the financial reporting and the tax basis of existing assets and liabilities.

Temporary differences and carryforwards for 1994 are as follows:

	Deferred Tax	
(Dollars in millions)	Asset	Liability
Postretirement benefits	$ 255	—
Postemployment benefits	104	—
Employee benefit plans	93	—
Depreciation	—	214
Non-deductible intangibles	—	157
Alternative minimum tax credits	101	—
International R&D capitalized for tax	81	—
Reserves & liabilities	286	—
Income reported for tax purposes	112	—
Miscellaneous international	65	157
Miscellaneous U.S.	237	126
Total deferred income taxes	$1,334	654

A comparison of income tax expense at the federal statutory rate of 35% in 1994 and 1993, and 34% in 1992 to the Company's effective tax rate is as follows:

(Dollars in millions)	1994	1993	1992
Earnings before taxes on income:			
U.S.	**$1,317**	1,006	863
International	**1,364**	1,326	1,344
Worldwide	**$2,681**	2,332	2,207
Statutory taxes	**$ 938**	816	750
Tax rates:			
Statutory	**35.0%**	35.0%	34.0%
Puerto Rico & Ireland operations	**(9.2)**	(9.7)	(9.6)
Research tax credits	**(0.5)**	(0.7)	(0.3)
Domestic state and local	**1.2**	0.8	0.7
International subsidiaries excluding Ireland	**(1.8)**	(2.4)	0.7
All other	**0.5**	0.4	0.9
Effective tax rate	**25.2%**	23.4%	26.4%

The increase in the 1994 worldwide effective tax rate was primarily due to the increase in income subject to tax in the United States.

For 1994, the Company has subsidiaries operating in Puerto Rico under a grant for tax relief expiring December 31, 2007. The Omnibus Budget Reconciliation Act of 1993 includes a change in the tax code which will reduce the benefit the Company receives from its operations in Puerto Rico by 60% gradually over a five-year period. In addition, the Company has subsidiaries manufacturing in Ireland under an incentive tax rate expiring on December 31, 2010.

D13.8 Explain the significance of vested versus nonvested pension benefits. Is a nonvested benefit a real obligation of a company? Does it meet the test of a liability? Present the arguments on both sides of this issue.

D13.9 IBM included the following in its 1994 annual report:

The significant components of deferred tax assets and liabilities included on the balance sheet were as follows:

	At December 31	
(Dollars in millions)	**1994**	**1993***
Deferred Tax Assets		
Retiree medical benefits	$ 2,500	$ 1,961
Restructuring charges	2,446	5,253
Capitalized R&D	2,057	1,739
Foreign tax credits	1,380	885
Alternative minimum tax credits	738	729
Inventory	633	621
Foreign tax loss carryforwards	469	989
Doubtful accounts	453	480
General business credits	452	452
Equity alliances	445	309
State and local tax loss carryforwards	370	566
Employee benefits	363	480
Intracompany sales and services	357	440
Depreciation	249	234
U.S. federal tax loss carryforwards	230	1,093
Warranty	163	125
Retirement benefits	127	124
Software income deferred	78	186
Other	2,685	2,521
Gross deferred tax assets	16,195	19,187
Less: Valuation allowance	4,551	5,035
Total deferred tax assets	$11,644	$14,152
Deferred Tax Liabilities		
Sales-type leases	$ 2,862	$ 3,118
Depreciation	1,653	1,537
Software costs deferred	1,283	1,824
Retirement benefits	1,061	1,069
Other	823	1,379
Gross deferred tax liabilities	$ 7,682	$ 8,927

*Reclassified to conform with 1994 presentation.

The valuation allowance applies to U.S. federal tax credit and net operating loss carryforwards, state and local net deferred tax assets and net operating loss carryforwards, and net operating losses in certain foreign jurisdictions that may expire before the company can utilize them. The net change in the total valuation allowance for the year ended December 31, 1994, was a decrease of $484 million.

Explain each of the lines in this figure. What is the impact, if any, of these figures on the income, assets, owners' equity, and cash flow of the company?

D13.10 What entry would one use to establish a *valuation allowance* in conjunction with a deferred tax asset? What kind of account is this asset? How would a person calculate the allowance?

D13.11 IBM included the following in its 1994 annual report:

Plant, Rental Machines, and Other Property

(Dollars in millions)	At December 31: 1994	1993
Land and land improvements	$ 1,437	$ 1,422
Buildings	13,093	13,314
Plant, laboratory, and office equipment	27,084	29,829
	41,614	44,565
Less: Accumulated depreciation	26,299	28,576
	15,315	15,989
Rental machines and parts	3,206	2,939
Less: Accumulated depreciation	1,857	1,407
	1,349	1,532
Total	$16,664	$17,521

Investments and Sundry Assets

(Dollars in millions)	At December 31: 1994	1993
Net investment in sales-type leases*	$15,838	$17,518
Less: Current portion — net	6,351	6,428
	9,487	11,090
Deferred taxes	4,533	4,521
Prepaid pension cost	1,528	532
Noncurrent customer loan receivables	1,311	882
Installment payment receivables	817	703
Investments in business alliances	380	650
Goodwill, less accumulated amortization (1994, $648; 1993, $462)	427	646
Other investments and sundry assets	1,643	1,663
Total	$20,126	$20,687

*These leases relate principally to IBM equipment and are generally for terms ranging from three to five years. Net investment in sales-type leases includes unguaranteed residual values of approximately $535 million and $760 million at December 31, 1994 and 1993, and is reflected net of unearned income at these dates of approximately $2,600 million and $3,100 million, respectively. Scheduled maturities of minimum lease payments outstanding at December 31, 1994, expressed as a percentage of the total, are approximately as follows: 1995, 40 percent; 1996, 33 percent; 1997, 18 percent; 1998, 7 percent; 1999 and after, 2 percent.

a. What is meant by rental machines and parts? Are these items included in IBM's $9,487 million net investment in leases as of December 31, 1994? Explain.

b. In the text at the bottom of the exhibit, reference is made to $2,600 million and $3,100 million, respectively, of unearned income. Where, if at all, does this unearned income appear in the figures of the above footnotes? Why is it unearned? What does IBM have to do to earn it?

c. How does the Deferred Taxes item, $4,533 million and $4,521, respectively, for December 31, 1994 and 1993, relate to the schedule in D13.9?

PROBLEMS

P13.1 Accounting for leases: the lessee.* SC Company leases an asset with a market value of $200,000 under conditions by which the company agrees to pay $47,479.28 each year for five years (assume annual payments at year-end). The agreement is noncancelable; five years is the expected economic life of the asset; there is no expected residual value to the asset. (Thus, the lease is to be capitalized.) The lease is executed on January 1, 1996.

Required:

a. What entry does the lessee make on January 1, 1996?

b. What entry does the lessee make at the end of 1996 to record the cash payment of $47,479.28?

c. For 1996, what expenses will be reflected on the income statement with respect to the lease?

d. How will the lease asset and liability items appear on the books as of January 1, 1996? 1997? 1998? 1999? 2000? 2001?

e. How much of the lease liability will appear as a current item in the balance sheet as of December 31, 1996? How much of the leased asset will appear as a current item on that date?

P13.2 Accounting for leases: the lessor.* SC Company leased the asset referred to in P13.1 from AC Manufacturing Company. The cost of the asset that AC Manufacturing Company leases to SC Company is $150,000. (This is a sales-type lease.)

Required:

a. What entry does the lessor make on January 1, 1996?

b. What entry does it make at the end of 1996 to record the cash received of $47,479.28? What other entry is required?

c. For the year 1996, what will be reflected on the income statement with respect to the lease?

d. What items will appear on the lessor's balance sheet as of December 31, 1996? 1997? 1998? 1999? 2000?

P13.3 Accounting for leases.* Kenyon Auto Company owns land on which it can build a new showroom at a cost of $60,000. As an alternative, Kenyon can have Robbin Leasing Company build the showroom and Kenyon can lease it for $7,010 a year for 15 years, which is the estimated useful life of the building. Kenyon would pay all maintenance and insurance costs. The $7,010 a year will give Robbin an 8 percent return on its investment of $60,000. Lease payments would be made at the end of each year.

Required:

a. How should a lease of this type be classified, and why?
(1) By the lessee.
(2) By the lessor.

b. If Kenyon decides to lease the showroom from Robbin, what entry(ies) will Kenyon make in its books on January 2, 1996, the date the lease would begin?

c. If Kenyon decides to lease the showroom from Robbin, what entry(ies) will Kenyon make on its books on December 31, 1996, the end of the lease year and the company's fiscal year?

P13.4 Deferred income taxes. The consolidated balance sheet of Sprint Corporation contains an item listed in the liabilities and shareholders' equity section titled Deferred Income Taxes in the amount of $882.4 million. What does this number represent? If Sprint had the opportunity to either increase or decrease the amount of this item, which would it prefer to do? Why?

P13.5 Deferred income taxes. The income tax footnote contained in the 1994 annual report for Curtiss-Wright Corporation (C-W) is presented next. Based on the information contained in it, answer the following questions:

a. How much income tax expense will C-W report in its income statement for 1994?

b. How much income tax for 1994 does C-W actually owe?

c. It appears that C-W's deferred income taxes are caused by a variety of factors. Explain why environmental cleanup is one of the causes and whether it was a benefit or a detriment to C-W in 1994.

Curtiss-Wright Corp. and Subsidiaries

7. Income Taxes.

Effective January 1, 1993, the Corporation adopted SFAS No. 109, "Accounting for Income Taxes." It requires an asset and liability approach for financial accounting and reporting for deferred income taxes. Pursuant to SFAS No. 109, the Corporation recognized a net tax benefit of $5,861,000 in 1993 (of which $3,764,000 or $0.74 per share was recognized as a cumulative effect of changes in accounting principles), primarily from the utilization of its capital loss carryforward, and correspondingly recorded a valuation allowance to offset this deferred tax asset, based on management's assessment of the likely realization of future capital gain income. During 1994, the Corporation realized $1,697,000 of capital gain income resulting in a reduction to the valuation allowance of $594,000. An additional valuation of $193,000 was recorded for an unrealized loss on securities. The net valuation allowance decreased by $401,000. The Corporation had available, at December 31, 1994, net capital loss carryforwards of $11,110,000 and $3,940,000 that will expire on December 31, 1995 and December 31, 1997, respectively.

Earnings (loss) before income taxes and cumulative effect of changes in accounting principles for domestic and foreign operations are:

(In thousands)	1994	1993	1992
Domestic	$24,009	$ (1,639)	$28,246
Foreign	4,748	2,969	4,471
Total	$28,757	$ 1,330	$32,717

The provisions for taxes on earnings before cumulative effect of changes in accounting principles consist of:

(In thousands)	1994	1993	1992
Federal income taxes currently payable	$4,755	$3,100	$11,367
Foreign income taxes currently payable	1,991	1,035	1,531
State and local income taxes currently payable	668	1,411	1,925
Deferred income taxes	1,603	(5,303)	(3,130)
Adjustment for deferred tax liability rate change	—	453	(663)
Federal income tax on net capital gains	594	367	998
Utilization of capital loss carryforward	(594)	(367)	(998)
Valuation allowance	193	3,586	—
	$9,210	$4,282	$11,030

The rates used in computing the provision for federal income taxes vary from the U.S. Federal statutory tax rate principally due to the following:

	1994	1993	1992
U. S. Federal statutory tax rate	35.0%	35.0%	34.0%
Add (deduct):			
Utilization of capital loss carryforward	(2.1)	(78.8)	(3.6)
Dividends received deduction and tax-exempt dividends	(1.9)	(85.9)	(0.3)
Increase (decrease) in deferred tax liability for change in tax rate	—	34.0	(2.0)
State and local taxes	2.3	106.1	5.9
Valuation allowance	0.7	269.7	—
All other	(2.0)	41.9	(0.3)
	32.0%	322.0%	33.7%

The components of the Corporation's deferred tax assets and liabilities at December 31 are as follows:

(In thousands)	1994	1993
Deferred tax assets:		
Environmental clean-up	$ 7,323	$ 8,688
Postretirement/employment benefits	3,912	3,632
Inventories	2,032	1,665
Facility closing costs	1,081	1,290
Legal matters	1,147	1,190
Net capital losses and tax carryforward	5,460	5,861
Other	4,158	4,460
Total deferred tax assets	25,113	26,786
Deferred tax liabilities:		
Pension	9,830	8,414
Depreciation	6,600	7,733
Contracts in progress	—	1,030
Other	1,465	1,220
Total deferred tax liabilities	17,895	18,397
Deferred tax asset valuation allowance	(5,460)	(5,861)
Net deferred tax assets	$(1,758)	$(2,528)

Deferred tax assets and liabilities are reflected on the Corporation's consolidated balance sheets as follows:

(In thousands)	1994	1993
Current deferred tax assets	$(8,204)	$(8,882)
Non-current deferred tax liabilities	6,446	6,354
Net deferred tax assets	$(1,758)	$(2,528)

Income tax payments of $7,586,000 were made in 1994, $10,491,000 in 1993, $18,100,000 in 1992.

P13.6 Deferred income taxes. Target Corporation is to begin its operations on January 1, 1996. Pro forma income statements for the new corporation are shown below. No provision has been made for deferred taxes, but there is a temporary book-tax difference due to depreciation.

Required:

a. Use a 35 percent tax rate and complete (and correct if necessary) the preparation of these pro forma statements.

b. What will Target show on its balance sheet each year (1996–2000) for deferred taxes?

c. Can you explain the company's calculation of current income tax expense in 1998?

Target Corporation
(millions)

	1996	1997	1998	1999	2000
Sales	3,400	3,604	3,820	4,049	4,292
less: CGS	1,598	1,712	1,834	1,964	2,103
Gross margin	1,802	1,892	1,986	2,085	2,189
Operating costs	633	681	729	777	826
Depreciation expense*	325	330	337	343	356
Income before tax	844	881	920	965	1,007
Current income tax	195	239	296	346	391
Deferred income tax	?	?	?	?	?
Income tax expense	195	239	296	346	391
Net income	649	642	624	619	616
*Note					
Book depreciation	325	330	337	343	356
Tax depreciation	612	528	411	320	245
Book value — assets	980	978	1,012	1,114	1,099
Tax value — assets	693	493	453	578	674

P13.7 Deferred income taxes. Suppose that Target Corporation were to revise its pro forma statements to include an accrual for estimated warranty expense (in addition to the effects of P13.6), but the recognition of these expenses would be delayed for tax purposes as follows:

	1996	1997	1998	1999	2000
Book warranty expense	112	132	137	128	119
Tax warranty expense	13	39	78	143	141

Required:

a. How would this affect the balance sheets? The income statements?

b. Would the balance sheets still balance?

P13.8 Changing income tax rates. What would happen to the pro forma statements in P13.7 if, in 1998, Congress overrode the president's veto and raised the corporate income tax rate to 38 percent effective in 1999?

P13.9 Pension accounting. It was December 31, 1995 and Mr. Joe Wadkin, controller of Schroeder-Price Manufacturing (SP), was at his desk organizing a pile of papers. He had just talked to his son Earl, about the impact of SFAS No. 87 on pension accounting and reporting. SP had just gone public the first of the year and found it now necessary to prepare financial statements in total conformity with GAAP.

Mr. Wadkin had overall responsibility for managing the pension fund. He had read several articles on SFAS No. 87 and was specifically interested in what actions he should take to insure his company's accounting was in line with the new pension standard.

Earl and Mr. Wadkin had decided that the following information was important:

1. The pension plan was established on January 1, 1988 but Mr. Wadkin had declared it retroactive to the start of the company on January 1, 1986.
1. Since the company was located in a small town, all 80 of the original employees still worked at SP. The assumption was made that all 80 would stay with the company until retirement and none would leave or die prior to retirement.
3. The average age of the employees was 24 when the company opened its doors.
4. The settlement rate was 8%, the expected rate of return on plan assets was 9%, and the 1995 actual return on the beginning of the year pension balance of $149,200 was 11%.
5. Retirement was mandatory at age 65 with benefits of $35 per month for every year of service paid for a period of 16 years to the retiree or a designated beneficiary.
6. The amount funded for 1995 was to be the same as the amount expensed, and the decision was made to adopt the pension accounting and reporting standards from SFAS No. 87 as of January 1, 1995.

Mr. Wadkin spent a few hours writing down some questions for Earl to answer the following day after the family's New Year's meal. He certainly hoped that Earl would be able to answer them.

Required:

a. What does the timeline look like for the company's pension plan?

b. What was the actuarial present value of the past service cost as of January 1, 1988, the date the plan was adopted?

c. Calculate the actuarial present value of the projected benefit obligation as of January 1, 1995.

d. Calculate the amount of the 1995 pension expense as follows:

1. Service Cost
2. Interest Cost
3. Actual return on plan assets
4. Actuarial adjustment to convert actual return on plan assets to expected return on plan assets
5. Amortization of Transition amount

e. What is the total 1995 pension expense?

f. What is the amount of pension liability to be shown in the balance sheet assuming adoption of the "minimum liability" provision of SFAS No. 87?

g. What are six actuarial assumptions that are usually needed when determining the amount of annual pension expense? Were all of them needed for this plan? Why?

P13.10 Pension disclosures. The pension disclosures from Bethlehem Steel Corporation's 1994 annual report are reported in footnote H on a subsequent page.

Required:

a. What was the total pension expense appearing in Bethlehem's income statement for 1994?

b. What do you consider to be the pension liability for Bethlehem as of the end of its 1994 year? Explain.

c. What are the total pension assets as of the end of the 1994 year? Do these assets exceed the total liability?

d. How much of this, if any, appears on the corporation's balance sheet?

e. Reference is made to a "minimum liability." How was that determined? Does it appear on the balance sheet? If so, where?

Bethlehem Steel

H. Postretirement Pension Benefits
We have noncontributory defined benefit pension plans which provide benefits for substantially all employees. Defined benefits are based on years of service and the five highest consecutive years of pensionable earnings during the last ten years prior to retirement or a minimum amount based on years of service. We fund annually the amount required under ERISA minimum funding standards plus additional amounts as appropriate.

The following sets forth the plans' actuarial assumptions used and funded status at year end together with amounts recognized in our consolidated balance sheets:

	December 31	
(Dollars in millions)	**1994**	**1993**
Assumptions:		
Discount rate	9.0%	7.5%
Average rate of compensation increase	3.1%	2.9%
Actuarial present value of benefit obligations:		
Vested benefit obligation	$4,246.9	$4,816.4
Accumulated benefit obligation	4,392.9	4,979.4
Projected benefit obligation	4,578.8	5,208.6
Plan assets at fair value:		
Fixed income securities	1,758.6	1,955.0
Equity securities	1,371.4	1,232.2
Cash and marketable securities	145.8	178.6
Total plan assets	$3,275.8	$3,365.8
Projected benefit obligation in excess of plan assets	1,303.0	1,842.8
Unrecognized net loss	(82.1)	(289.7)
Remaining unrecognized net obligation resulting from adoption of Statement No. 87	(255.2)	(293.5)
Unrecognized prior service cost from plan amendments	(275.2)	(307.1)
Adjustment required to recognize minimum liability — Intangible asset	426.6	600.6
— Additional paid-in capital (pre-tax) (Note L)	—	60.5
Pension liability	$1,117.1	$1,613.6

The assumptions used in each year and the components of our annual pension cost are as follows:

(Dollars in millions)	**1994**	**1993**	**1992**
Assumptions:			
Return on plan assets	8.75%	9.50%	9.50%
Discount rate	7.50%	8.50%	8.50%
Pension cost:			
Service cost — benefits earned during the period	$ 51.9	$ 39.3	$ 45.0
Interest on projected benefit obligation	375.7	380.4	394.2
Return on plan assets — actual	60.3	(308.8)	(250.0)
— deferred	(365.3)	4.3	(62.2)
Amortization of initial net obligation	36.7	37.7	37.8
Amortization of unrecognized prior service cost from plan amendments	32.7	19.8	18.8
Total defined benefit plans	192.0	172.7	183.6
PBGC premiums, administration fees, etc.	11.1	10.9	5.1
Total cost	$203.1	$183.6	$188.7

P13.11 Health care and life insurance benefits. Footnote I of Bethlehem Steel Corporation's 1994 annual report is shown below.

Required:

a. What is the difference between the "pay-as-you-go" approach and the accrual basis required by SFAS No. 106? Will the new treatment be better for employees? For shareholders?

b. How much of these amounts appears in the company's balance sheet? Income statement?

c. How sensitive is the company's forecast for health care cost trends?

Bethlehem Steel

I. Postretirement Benefits Other Than Pensions
In addition to providing pension benefits, we currently provide health care and life insurance benefits for most retirees and their dependents.

Information regarding our plans' actuarial assumptions, funded status, and liability follows:

(Dollars in millions)	December 31 1994	1993
Assumptions:		
Discount rate	9.0%	7.5%
Trend rate — beginning	9.0%	9.0%
— ending (year 2000)	4.6%	4.6%
Accumulated postretirement benefit obligation:		
Retirees	$1,427.6	$1,506.7
Fully eligible active plan participants	99.7	126.8
Other active plan participants	160.4	236.1
Total	1,687.7	1,869.6
Plan assets at fair value:		
Fixed income securities	135.5	158.5
Accumulated postretirement benefit obligation in excess of plan assets	1,552.2	1,711.1
Unrecognized net gain (loss)	27.2	(130.5)
Total obligation	1,579.4	1,580.6
Current portion	(138.0)	(132.3)
Long-term obligation	$1,441.4	$1,448.3

The assumptions used in each year and the components of our postretirement benefit cost follow:

(Dollars in millions)	1994	1993	1992
Return on plan assets	8.75%	9.50%	9.50%
Discount rate	7.50%	8.50%	8.50%
Trend rate			
— beginning	9.00%	9.50%	9.50%
— ending (2000)	4.60%	5.50%	5.50%
Service cost	$ 11.1	$ 9.0	$ 9.0
Interest on accumulated postretirement benefit obligation	138.8	144.1	139.0
Return on plan assets — actual	4.7	(17.9)	(18.4)
— deferred	(17.6)	3.8	4.5
Total cost	$137.0	$139.0	$134.1

A 1 percent increase or decrease in the assumed health care trend rate would increase or decrease the accumulated postretirement benefit obligation by about $120 million and 1994 expense by about $20 million.

P13.12 Deferred income taxes. Early in 1996, Strafford Corporation acquired a $100,000 asset that was to be depreciated on a straight-line basis for accounting purposes and on an accelerated basis for taxes according to the following schedules:

	Straight-Line	Accelerated
1996	$ 8,333	$ 16,667
1997	16,666	27,778
1998	16,667	18,519
1999	16,667	12,347
2000	16,667	8,230
2001	16,667	8,230
2002	8,333	8,230
	$100,000	$100,000

Required:

Prepare a schedule illustrating the annual deferred tax entries for each year associated with this asset. Use a 35 percent tax rate. When will the deferred income tax liability begin to reverse?

P13.13 Lessee accounting. FHAC Corporation was considering the purchase of a mini-supercomputer. Under a proposal from Convex Computer Co., FHAC could acquire the computer under a 10-year lease agreement. The lease proposal called for quarterly lease payments of $3,655.57 and carried an implicit interest rate of 8 percent. At the end of the lease agreement, FHAC would be entitled to purchase the computer for its expected residual value, currently estimated to be $10,000. Alternatively, FHAC could purchase the computer outright at a price of $115,000, inclusive of installation costs.

Required:

Evaluate the above proposals. Should FHAC lease or buy? How would each option (lease or buy) affect FHAC's financial statements?

P13.14 Lessee accounting. Sybra, Inc., a newly incorporated research and development company, decided to lease additional laboratory space. The lease commenced on January 1, 1996, and was to extend through the 20-year period ending December 31, 2015. The annual rental rate on the new facility was $115,200 (exclusive of property taxes, maintenance, and insurance costs, which were also to be paid by Sybra). Because of the length of the lease and the generally poor rental market in Austin, Texas, Sybra had negotiated so that rent payments would be made only once a year on December 31.

The facility's original construction cost had been approximately $480,000, but its current market value was now in excess of $1 million. On the basis of conversations with the lessor, Sybra's chief financial officer determined that the lease payments included implicit interest at the rate of 10 percent per annum. Further, as of 1996, the facility was estimated to have a remaining useful life of 25 years. At the end of the initial 20-year lease period, Sybra would have the option of renewing for another 10 years at a rate equal to one-half of the annual lease rate during the initial lease period.

Required:

a. What accounting treatment should be adopted for the above lease? Why?

b. Illustrate the balance sheet and income statement effects in 1996 for the lease agreement, assuming that it is to be accounted for as (1) an operating lease and (2) a capital lease.

P13.15 Leases. On January 2, 1996, Lion Metal Forming, Inc., entered a lease for a new 50-ton hydraulic press costing $75,000 and having an estimated life of eight years. The management of Lion Metal believes the new press will be much more efficient than equipment presently in use and that it will allow Lion Metal to manufacture certain items that it previously had to subcontract out. The noncancelable term of the lease is seven years, at which time the press is returned to the lessor. The residual value is expected to be minimal. Rental payments of $16,433 are due at the *end* of each year. All executory costs are to be paid directly by Lion Metal, which depreciates its fixed assets on the straight-line basis. Its incremental borrowing rate is 15 percent.

Required:

a. Calculate the lessor's implicit interest rate in the lease.

b. Why does this lease qualify as a *capital lease* to Lion Metal for financial reporting purposes?

c. For questions (c) and (d), assume the implicit rate is 12 percent. Prepare the entry that Lion Metal should make to record the lease on January 2, 1996.

d. What amounts (properly labeled) related to the lease will appear in Lion Metal's
(1) Balance sheet as of December 31, 1996?
(2) Income statement for the year ending December 31, 1996?

P13.16 Deferred income taxes. Jerris Corporation was incorporated in late 1995 for the purpose of entering the quick-copy industry. At the beginning of 1996, it purchased copying equipment having a value of $60,000, an economic life of four years, and no anticipated salvage value. Lacking sufficient capital, Jerris's equipment purchase was financed by the manufacturer, who subsequently sold the note to Metroplex National Bank (MNB). Under the terms of the note, Jerris Corporation was required to submit periodic financial statements to MNB to ensure that the company was in compliance with the note's various covenants.

For purposes of the financial statements submitted to MNB, Jerris Corporation adopted the straight-line method of depreciation for the equipment; for Internal Revenue Service purposes, the company was required to use the Modified Accelerated Cost Recovery System (MACRS) with a three-year tax life.

At December 31, 1996, Jerris's accounting records revealed that the company had earned a pretax income of $14,000, *including* $1,000 of life insurance premiums on its CEO (not deductible on its tax return because the company was the policy beneficiary). Mr. Jerris, the owner, decided that the company was likely to achieve that level of income for the next three years. In anticipation of preparing the financial statements for MNB and the tax return for the IRS, Jerris determined the following:

1. The current income tax rate was 35 percent and was expected to be 30 percent in 1997 and 40 percent thereafter.

2. Under the MACRS, a three-year asset would be depreciated at the following rates:

Year	Percentage
1	33.34
2	44.45
3	14.81
4	7.40
	100.00

Required:

Assist Mr. Jerris in preparing the company's financial statements for MNB by determining the deferred income taxes for 1996 through 1999.

CASES

C13.1 Leases: Wendy's International, Inc. Presented next is the footnote pertaining to leases from the 1994 annual report of Wendy's International, Inc.

Wendy's International, Inc. — Leases

Note 3: Leases

The company occupies land and buildings and uses equipment under terms of numerous lease agreements expiring on various dates through 2027. Terms of land only and land and building leases are generally for 20 to 25 years. Many of these leases provide for future rent escalations and renewal options. Certain leases require contingent rent, determined as a percentage of sales, when annual sales exceed specified levels. Most leases also obligate the company to pay the costs of maintenance, insurance, and property taxes.

At each year-end capital leases consisted of the following:

(In thousands)	1994	1993
Buildings	**$ 63,531**	$ 64,148
Accumulated amortization	**(31,764)**	(29,972)
	$ 31,767	$ 34,176

At January 1, 1995, future minimum lease payments for all leases, and the present value of the net minimum lease payments for capital leases, were as follows:

(In thousands)	Capital Leases	Operating Leases
1995	$ 9,965	$ 24,670
1996	9,858	23,744
1997	9,442	22,510
1998	8,553	21,333
1999	6,809	18,437
Later years	25,280	88,801
Total minimum lease payments	69,907	$199,495
Amount representing interest	(24,457)	
Present value of net minimum lease payments	45,450	
Current portion	(5,432)	
	$40,018	

Total minimum lease payments have not been reduced by minimum sublease rentals of $1.1 million under capital leases, and $23.9 million under operating leases due in the future under noncancelable subleases.

Rent expense for each year is included in company restaurant operating costs and amounted to:

(In thousands)	1994	1993	1992
Minimum rents	**$28,510**	$28,425	$28,346
Contingent rents	**7,035**	7,238	6,544
Sublease rents	**(3,224)**	(3,256)	(3,283)
	$32,321	$32,407	$31,607

In connection with the franchising of certain restaurants, the company has leased land, buildings, and equipment to the related franchise owners.

Most leases provide for monthly rentals based on a percentage of sales, while others provide for fixed payments with contingent rent when sales exceed certain levels. Lease terms are approximately 10 to 20 years with one or more five-year renewal options. The franchise owners bear the cost of maintenance, insurance, and property taxes.

The company generally accounts for the building and equipment portions of the fixed payment leases as direct financing leases. The land portion of leases and leases with rents based on a percentage of sales are accounted for as operating leases.

At each year-end the net investment in financing leases receivable, included in other assets, consisted of the following:

(In thousands)	1994	1993
Total minimum lease receipts	**$ 36,315**	$ 45,548
Estimated residual value	**4,542**	4,662
Amount representing unearned interest	**(19,659)**	(25,806)
Current portion, included in accounts receivable	**(927)**	(911)
	$ 20,271	$ 23,493

At each year-end assets leased under operating leases consisted of the following:

(In thousands)	1994	1993
Land	**$ 54,230**	$ 52,063
Building	**83,130**	81,060
Equipment	**15,911**	16,288
	153,271	149,411
Accumulated amortization	**(43,685)**	(41,090)
	$109,586	$108,321

At January 1, 1995, future minimum lease receipts were as follows:

(In thousands)	Financing Leases	Operating Leases
1995	$ 3,008	$ 2,934
1996	2,984	2,948
1997	3,003	2,656
1998	2,990	2,602
1999	2,866	2,398
Later years	21,464	13,697
	$36,315	$27,235

Net rental income for each year is included in other revenues and amounted to:

(In thousands)	1994	1993	1992
Minimum rents	**$ 1,868**	$ 1,860	$ 1,182
Contingent rents	**9,685**	8,255	7,180
	$11,553	$10,115	$ 8,362

Required:

a. According to the footnote, Wendy's is both a lessee and a lessor. From a cash flow perspective, does it appear that leasing activities will result in a net cash use or cash source for Wendy's in 1995? Explain (include specific dollar amounts where possible).

b. The footnote states that Wendy's occupies land and buildings and uses equipment under terms of numerous lease agreements. It also discloses that the company's leases are classified as either capital leases or operating leases.
(1) Explain the difference between a capital lease and an operating lease from a risk and reward of ownership perspective.
(2) It appears that building leases are treated as capital leases and that land and equipment leases are treated as operating leases. Of the four accounting criteria for capital leases, which *two* criteria were most likely met in regard to the building leases? Briefly explain your reasons.

c. How much interest expense relating to capital leases does Wendy's expect to incur in 1995?

d. How much rent expense did Wendy's show in its 1994 income statement?

e. What lease-related assets and liabilities, including dollar amounts, appeared in Wendy's December 31, 1994, balance sheet?

Current assets:	Current liabilities:
Long-term assets:	Long-term liabilities:

f. In calculating the present value of net minimum lease payments for capital leases, as a lessee, Wendy's deducted an amount representing interest. How would Wendy's go about deciding on the appropriate interest rate to use?

g. The footnote states that certain leases that entitle Wendy's to occupy buildings require the company to pay contingent rent, determined as a percentage of sales, when annual sales exceed specified levels. Give *two* reasons why Wendy's might want a "contingent rent" provision included in its leases.

C13.2 Leases: Nelson Leasing Company. In November 1995, Nelson Leasing Company requested an increase in its loan from Boston Trust Company. The operations of such a leasing company involve buying capital equipment (anything from computers to automobiles) and renting it to a user. The leasing company first finds a customer for the equipment. Then it negotiates with its bank for a loan with which to buy the equipment. The bank always requires an assignment of the lease payment, and it usually secures the loan further with a chattel mortgage on the equipment being leased. The lease contract is characteristically written in such a binding fashion that the lessee must make his or her lease payments for the equipment whether or not it is used, unless the lessee goes into bankruptcy or resorts to similar legal proceedings.

The initial lease period might run for one to five years, occasionally longer, depending on the normal economic life of the equipment. The sum of the lease payments during the life of the lease normally exceeds by a small amount the total of (1) the price of the equipment, (2) its installation cost, and (3) the cost of interest on the leasing company's note. The leasing company makes its profit on renewals of the lease subsequent to its original term. Typically, the leasing company's note has a face amount equal to the total of the lease payments; this note is discounted at a rate that would give the leasing company sufficient cash to pay for and install the equipment.

When Nelson Leasing Company requested an increase in its loan, the company's most recent balance sheet was requested by the bank (see below). This balance sheet was taken to the loan committee meeting at which Nelson Leasing Company's request was discussed. The bank's senior vice president, Karla Walker, raised the following question: Should the bank lend money to a company that showed a deficit in working capital? Walker's experience had been primarily in the bank's trust department, but her present position required that she be aware of what was going on in the commercial loan department as well. To help clarify Nelson's working capital position, it was explained that a loan due within one year was classified as a current liability on the leasing company's balance sheet; on the other hand, accounting practice forbade showing as a current asset the future leasing income, although it was almost certain to be received because of the financial standing of the lessees, and although it would be sufficient in amount to cover payments to the bank on the company's note.

Further, it was noted that each time the leasing company completes a series of transactions of borrowing from the bank and buying and leasing equipment, its stated working capital decreases.

Nelson Leasing Company
Balance Sheet as of Year Ending June 30, 1995
($ millions)

Assets	
Cash and marketable securities	47
Notes receivable	
Accounts receivable (net)	
Inventory	
Total current assets	47
Deferred receivables	
Deferred charges and prepaid expenses	15
Equipment on lease (net)	175
Land and buildings	
Machinery and fixtures	
Total fixed assets	
Less: Depreciation	
Net fixed assets	
Other assets	4
Total	241
Equities	
Notes payable — bank	
Notes payable — trade	
Due officers	6
Accounts payable — trade	23
Miscellaneous accruals	3
Taxes accrued and reserved	
Due bank — current Portion (secured)	79
Total liabilities — current	111
Due bank — deferred portion (secured)	120
Total liabilities	231
Capital stock — preferred	
Capital stock — common	15
Earned surplus — deficit	(5)
Net worth (excluding intangibles)	10
Total	241
Working capital — deficit	(64)
Current ratio	0.42
Net sales	35
Net profit (loss)	(5)
Dividends or withdrawals	—

For example, when Nelson Leasing Company bought a $1,000 machine and borrowed $1,000 from the bank, it added $1,000 to fixed assets, $330 to current liabilities, and $670 to long-term liabilities (for the second and third years of a three-year lease). Thus, stated working capital was lowered by $330, although the company was actually no worse off due to this transaction. This explanation satisfied Walker and, after further discussion, the loan request was granted.

Boston Trust Company
Alternative Balance Sheets
($ millions)

	6/30/95 Alternative 1	6/30/95 Alternative 2
Assets		
Cash and marketable securities	47	47
Notes receivable		
Accounts receivable (net)		
Inventory		
Lease income — current	79	
Total current assets	126	47
Deferred receivables — lease income	120	
Deferred charges and prepaid expenses	15	15
Equipment on lease (net)	175	175
Land and buildings		
Machinery and fixtures		
Total fixed assets		
Less depreciation		
Net fixed assets		
Other assets	4	4
Total	440	241
Equities		
Notes payable — bank		
Notes payable — trade		
Due officers	6	6
Accounts payable — trade	23	23
Miscellaneous accruals	3	3
Taxes accrued and reserved		
Due bank — current (secured)	79	
Total current liabilities	111	32
Due bank — deferred (secured)	120	199
Contingent liability to bank		
Total liabilities	231	231
Deferred lease income	199	
Capital stock — preferred		
Capital stock — common	15	15
Earned surplus	(5)	(5)
Net worth (excluding intangibles)	10	10
Total	440	241
Total current assets	126	47
Total current liabilities	111	32
Working capital	15	15
Current ratio	1.13	1.47
Net sales	35	35
Net profit	(5)	(5)
Dividends and withdrawals	—	—

Nevertheless, Philip Cannon, the officer in charge of this loan, wondered if it might not be possible to make future explanations of this type unnecessary by altering the way in which the bank records the leasing companies' balance sheets. Cannon asked Jan DuBois, a member of the bank's credit department, to try to present a more accurate picture of the leasing company's real position via the balance sheet (generally the only statement used by the bank for credit analysis). DuBois developed the two alternative balance sheets shown above.

Required:

What recommendation would you make to the bank?

C13.3 Dunlap Corporation.* Dunlap Corporation was a small, privately held manufacturer of custom cabinets for the commercial and residential markets. It was incorporated in the Commonwealth of Pennsylvania in November 1979 and commenced operations on January 2, 1980. Corporate headquarters and the company's sole manufacturing plant were located near Philadelphia.

During the early years, the company initiated a profit-sharing plan but did not have a formal pension plan. Then, in 1982, management began investigating the establishment of either a defined-contribution or a defined-benefit plan. By year-end, the decision was made to adopt a noncontributory defined-benefit plan effective January 1, 1983, and to grant retroactive credit to all employees for the time of employment prior to the inception of the pension plan. Of the 110 employees originally hired in January 1980, six left the company in 1981 and four more left in 1982. No new employees had been hired to replace those that left. Of the 100 employees that remained, all were approximately 28 years old at the time the pension plan was adopted.

The terms of the plan called for full vesting after five years of service and stipulated mandatory retirement at age 65. Pension benefits of $50 per month for each year of service were to be paid to the employee or the employee's beneficiary for a period of 15 years subsequent to retirement. For fiscal years 1983–1985, Dunlap Corporation recognized annual pension expense equal to normal cost plus an amount for past service cost based upon a 30-year amortization schedule, which was in accordance with the requirements of APB Opinion No. 8. During this period, no employees left the company and no new employees were hired.

At the board of directors meeting in March 1986, the decision was made to adopt the pension accounting and reporting standards specified by SFAS No. 87 that had been issued by the Financial Accounting Standards Board in December 1985. At fiscal year-end, the following information was assembled for use in determining the pension-related items to be presented in the company's December 31, 1986, balance sheet and 1986 income statement:

1. The estimated rate at which the pension benefits could be effectively settled (such as by purchasing annuity contracts from an insurance company) was 10 percent.
2. The long-term expected rate of return on pension assets was 10 percent.
3. The fair value of pension assets as of January 2, 1986 (which included the amount funded for 1985) was $90,000. For 1986 the actual return on plan assets was 12 percent.
4. The amount funded for 1986 was to be the same as the amount expensed.

Required:

a. Assuming a 10 percent return, calculate the actuarial present value of the past service cost as of January 1, 1983, the date the pension plan was adopted. $__________

 Case prepared by E. Richard Brownlee, II.

b. Calculate the actuarial present value of the projected benefit obligation as of January 1, 1986. $________

c. Calculate the amount of the 1986 pension cost (that is, pension expense) as follows:

(1) Service cost	$________
(2) Interest cost	$________
(3) Actual return on plan assets	$________
(4) Amortization of unrecognized prior service cost	$ –0–
(5) Actuarial adjustment to convert actual return on plan assets to expected return on plan assets	$________
(6) Amortization of transition amount	$________
1986 pension cost	$________

d. Calculate the amount of the pension liability to be shown in the balance sheet. $________

e. Calculate the amount of the intangible asset to be shown in the balance sheet. $________

f. Are the pension liability and intangible pension asset calculated above amortized? If so, how? If not, will they continue to appear in subsequent balance sheets?

CHAPTER 14

Owners' Equity

It seems to me that the realities of stock options can be summarized quite simply. If options aren't a form of compensation, what are they? If compensation isn't an expense, what is it? And, if expenses shouldn't go into the calculation of earnings, where in the world should they go?[1]

Key Chapter Issues

- What is owners' equity and how does a company acquire it? Can it be lost?
- What difference does it make if an organization is legally a proprietorship or partnership rather than a corporation? What is a Subchapter S corporation, and what difference does this make in accounting?
- What happens when a company sells new shares of its common stock? What happens when it buys some of them back?
- What is par value common stock? What happens if new shares are issued at prices that exceed par value?
- What's the difference between common stock and treasury stock? What is preferred stock?
- How do cash dividends, stock dividends, and stock splits affect owners' equity? How do they affect the income statement?
- What are stock options and why are they so controversial? How does the accounting for stock options affect owners' equity?
- Some corporations include a foreign currency translation adjustment in owners' equity. What is this, and why is it in owners' equity? Are shareholders better or worse off because of it?

[1]Mr. Warren Buffett's chairman's letter from the 1992 Berkshire Hathaway Inc. annual report.

According to the basic accounting equation (A = L + OE), owners' equity is simply the difference between a company's assets and its liabilities. It is the amount that would be left over if the assets were liquidated at their book values and the liabilities were then paid off. Owners' equity is also sometimes referred to as the **net worth** or the *net book value* of a company. However, owners' equity can also be considered on its own terms — as one of the three elements of the accounting equation — rather than only the residual of assets minus liabilities.

Owners' equity usually takes two principal forms: **contributed capital,** as represented by the capital stock of a company, and **retained capital,** as represented by the cumulative retained earnings of a company. For many companies, transactions involving the owners' equity accounts are simple and straightforward. In fact, some publicly held companies bypass the presentation of a formal statement of owners' equity and provide what little detail might be of interest to financial statement users as a part of a footnote or as part of the income statement. To a very large degree, the owners' equity accounts are of more interest to attorneys than to management or accountants because the attorneys are responsible for a company's legal status and because many of the transactions in the owners' equity accounts have to do with a company's legal life. However, the owners' equity accounts are always of interest to a company's shareholders because these accounts measure the shareholders' residual interest in the net assets of the company. For this reason, owners' equity is also sometimes called *shareholder equity.*

In the first section of this chapter we consider the various ways in which a company can be legally organized and explore some of the activities common to the corporate form of organization. In the second section we examine some of the most common transactions affecting the owners' equity accounts, the accounting entries that are required, and the financial statement presentation that is conventionally followed. In the final section we illustrate the typical owners' equity disclosures using data from PepsiCo's annual report.

THE FORM OF A BUSINESS ENTITY

Business entities can be organized in different ways, and the differences can be important. A business entity can be a proprietorship, a partnership, or a corporation, depending on the legal structure of the entity's ownership.

Many small businesses are organized as proprietorships or partnerships because both types are relatively simple and inexpensive to form. To establish a proprietorship, one simply obtains the required permits to do business from a local or state governmental agency. The same is true for a partnership except that, in addition, the partners typically execute a written contract among themselves detailing the terms of their financial arrangements. The desirability of having a written agreement is as great for a two-person partnership as it is for partnerships composed of hundreds of partners. Some of the items usually detailed in a partnership agreement include the amount of each partner's investment, the rights of partners to withdraw funds, the manner in which profits and losses are to be divided, and the procedure to be followed in admitting a new partner.

The Partnership

We can make some general statements about **partnerships** (and proprietorships) that flow in part from the legal characteristics accorded to partnerships and in part from the way businesspeople have applied these legal forms in practice:

- *Limited ownership:* As a practical matter, most partnerships have relatively few partners.

- *Owners as managers:* The partners frequently manage the business.
- *Mutual agency:* Each partner, acting within the scope of reasonable partnership activities, acts as an agent for the business entity, and any single partner may act on behalf of all the other partners.
- *Unlimited liability:* Ordinarily, each partner is personally liable for all of the debts of the partnership.
- *Division of profit and loss:* Partnership profits and losses may be divided in whatever manner the individual partners agree.
- *Withdrawal of resources:* Unless the partners agree otherwise, they may withdraw resources from the business in an amount equal to their total investment in the partnership any time they wish to do so.
- *Limited life:* Unless the partners agree otherwise, the death or withdrawal of a partner automatically dissolves a partnership.
- *Taxes:* The partnership itself is not subject to income tax. Income earned (or a loss incurred) by the partnership is taxable income for the partners, whether or not it is distributed. This requirement is sometimes an advantage (as in the early years of a real estate partnership when depreciation throws off large tax losses) and sometimes a disadvantage (as in the early years of a growing company that generates earnings but must retain the operating cash flow for reinvestment).

The Corporation

The creation of a corporation is a more complex legal procedure than the creation of partnerships and proprietorships. The incorporators (the initial shareholders) must first apply to a state commission, requesting permission to form a corporation. When a state agency grants that permission, a new entity comes into being. The newly incorporated entity's **charter of incorporation** thereby creates a legal entity that can sell shares to stockholders, own property, borrow money and incur obligations, and sue and be sued, all in its own name independently of its owners.

Again, we can make some general statements about the operations of corporations, in part because of their legal characteristics and in part because of the way corporate life has evolved in practice:

- *Diverse ownership:* The owners of a corporation are called *stockholders,* and ownership in a corporation is evidenced by shares of capital stock. The number of stockholders a corporation may have is not limited. In most states, a corporation can be formed with just a few stockholders. On the other hand, a corporation may be owned by a very large number of stockholders (General Motors' shares were owned by more than a million investors in December, 1994), and the shares may be traded in a public market like the New York Stock Exchange. The stock of a corporation may be held by individuals, mutual funds, or other corporations.
- *Separation of ownership and management:* The management of public corporations often owns only a small percentage (or none) of the company.
- *Limited liability:* As a separate legal entity, a corporation is responsible for its own debts. Stockholders are not personally liable for a corporation's debts, and the maximum financial loss that stockholders can incur is the amount of their investment in the corporation.

- *Withdrawal of resources:* Stockholders are entitled to withdraw resources from a corporation only in the form of dividends and only after the board of directors has authorized a dividend payment. Dividends are paid to all stockholders in proportion to their ownership of the corporation, unless otherwise provided in the stock agreement.
- *Transferability of ownership:* Stockholders may buy and sell shares of capital stock in a corporation without interfering with the activities or the life of the corporation whose shares they are buying. Most of the millions of shares that are traded daily on the stock exchanges represent private transactions between independent buyers and sellers. The activities of the corporations themselves are unaffected by such transactions.
- *Government regulation:* Although a corporation exists as a result of a charter granted by a state agency, no significant legal implications flow from the chartering process. For instance, no state charter requires any corporation to prepare financial statements or file annual reports with the state. A publicly held corporation — that is, one with more than 500 stockholders and more than $5 million in assets — is subject to the federal securities laws by virtue of the public distribution of its stock. It must register its stock with the Securities and Exchange Commission; and the SEC's regulations *do* impose significant legal obligations on the corporation, including the periodic public distribution of financial statements.
- *Taxes:* As separate legal entities, corporations pay federal and state income taxes on their earnings. When any part of these earnings is subsequently distributed to stockholders in the form of dividends, the stockholders also pay income taxes on the amount of dividends received. This separation of entity and ownership results in double taxation.[2]

A Glimpse of Corporate Life

Typically, individual stockholders have very little say in the management of the company they own. Small stockholders "vote with their feet," selling their stock if they conclude that the company is not going forward. Major stockholders can be more assertive and use their voting rights to elect a board of directors to represent them (and all stockholders). In most companies, the board of directors is responsible for the corporation's overall direction. The board of directors elects and oversees the corporate officers who are directly responsible for the day-to-day management of the corporation. The officers usually include a president, vice president, secretary, and treasurer.

The officers report periodically to the board of directors and at least once a year to the shareholders. The officers usually present a business plan for the board's approval and request the board's advice and concurrence regarding major decisions. The board members, on the other hand, prepare employment agreements for the officers and generally monitor their progress in moving the company forward according to the

[2]Under certain conditions specified by the Internal Revenue Code, U.S. corporations with no more than 35 shareholders may elect to be treated as a partnership for tax purposes and thus pay no corporate income tax. Instead, the owners of these companies, called *S corporations,* pay personal income taxes on their respective share of the business's earnings regardless of whether the earnings are actually withdrawn from the business.

approved business plan. Board members and officers have significant legal obligations, as fiduciaries, to always work in the best interests of a company's stockholders.

Corporations typically hold an annual meeting of stockholders subsequent to the end of each fiscal year. A **fiscal year** is the 12-month period a corporation selects as its accounting year; it may or may not be the calendar year. The annual meeting is held for purposes such as reviewing the past year's performance; discussing business, economic, and political issues of importance to the corporation; selecting an independent auditor; electing directors; and voting on any other business that requires stockholders' ratification. The board of directors also decides — depending on the corporation's earnings' history, expectations for the future, cash position and needs, and (last but not least) expectations of the stock market — how much of the corporation's earnings should be paid out as dividends.

Even though corporate stock can be bought and sold without affecting the company, corporations must keep track of stockholder transactions to know who is entitled to receive dividends and who is entitled to vote at shareholder meetings. A small corporation can keep track of its stockholders relatively easily because it has few transactions involving the stock. For a large, publicly held company, however, keeping track of its stockholders is very difficult because its shares trade in large volumes every day on the public stock exchanges. In fact, many corporations engage the services of a transfer agent and registrar to record stockholder transactions, cancel old stock certificates, issue new ones, and maintain a current record of stockholders and the number of shares each owns. Transfer agents and registrars are usually banks or trust companies.

Publicly held companies whose stock is registered with the SEC must publish quarterly and annual reports for use by stockholders and other interested parties. These reports generally include status reports on a company's progress, from both the chairperson of the board and the president, and financial statements for the period. The financial statements in the annual report are accompanied by a report from an independent accounting firm, stating the accountants' opinion as to whether the financial statements are presented fairly, in all material respects, in conformity with generally accepted accounting principles. Similar, but not identical, requirements exist in other countries where, for example, Japanese public corporations must file financial statements with the Ministry of Finance and Brazilian corporations must file with the Comissao de Valores Mobiliários.

OWNERS' EQUITY TRANSACTIONS

The most common transactions affecting the owners' equity accounts include the recognition of revenue and expenses for the year (which result in net income), the payment of dividends, and the sale or repurchase of capital stock.

Sales of Stock

A corporation may sell stock to new stockholders or to its existing stockholders. Those stock sales are recorded in the owners' equity account at the net cash (or other consideration) that the company receives for the stock sold. The journal entry is:

Dr. Cash (A)	(inc.) 50,000	
Cr. Capital Stock, at Par Value (OE)		(inc.) 1,000
Cr. Paid-In-Capital in Excess of Par Value (OE)		(inc.) 49,000

Note that if the sale price of the stock exceeds the *par* (or *stated*) value of the purchased shares, the excess is recorded in the Paid-In-Capital in Excess of Par Value account. Thus, the sum of the Capital Stock account and the Paid-In-Capital in Excess of Par Value account represents the aggregate contributed capital of a company.

As noted earlier in this text, par value (and stated value) is a legal value required by some state incorporation commissions. Originally, it was meant to be the minimum capital required to be contributed to, and maintained in, a company by the stockholders. That concept has eroded in practice, however, and today the concept has very little practical significance. Nonetheless, most financial statements continue to distinguish between par value and paid-in capital in excess of par value.

Most often, stock is issued for cash and so the value of the capital received in the exchange is easy to determine. However, companies sometimes exchange their stock for other forms of assets, including the stock or bonds of another corporation. In these exchanges, the total capital received (and, in turn, the assets received) are valued at the market value of the stock issued or the asset received, whichever provides the most reliable measure of value. When shares of stock are actively traded, the per share market price from those trades is usually considered the most reliable measure of the value involved in a swap of stock for other forms of assets. When the stock is not actively traded, the transaction may have to be valued at the value of the asset exchanged. When the asset cannot be readily valued either, the transaction may have to be valued at the contributor's (the asset owner's) cost.

Every corporation issues **common stock** as its basic, senior equity security. But it is also possible to raise capital by selling other equity securities with special terms. **Preferred stock,** for example, is an equity security with some of the characteristics of a bond. Preferred stocks usually carry a specific dividend rate, stated as an amount per share or as a percentage of its par value. A preferred stock is "preferred" in that its dividend requirements have a first claim on a company's earnings before any claims of the common shareholders. Thus, in the event that earnings are limited, the preferred shareholders must receive their full dividend before common shareholders receive any. Should a company be liquidated, the preferred stockholders are entitled to secure the par value of their shares before any distribution is made to the common stockholders.

A preferred stock may also be **cumulative;** that is, its dividend preferences accumulate year to year even if the company has not earned enough to pay the dividend in any one year.[3] Preferred stock may be **participating** in that it may share in a company's earnings in excess of its stated dividend requirements, along with the common stock. It may also be **convertible** into a stated number of common shares. It also may be **callable** in that a company may have the right to call the security for redemption, usually at a premium above the stated or par value of the stock.

Class B common stock usually has the same provisions as a company's regular common stock regarding liquidation and dividend rights, but it may have disproportionate (usually lower) voting rights. For example, in some companies, the class B stock carries only one-tenth the voting power of a company's class A common stock. In many cases the class B stock is traded publicly, but the class A stock can be exchanged only between members of the company's founding family. Class B stocks are very popular with European companies who do not want to dilute home-country ownership power and thus the Class B stock is used in the foreign equity markets

[3]Unpaid accumulated dividends are called **dividends in arrears,** and although not representing a liability of a company until the dividends are declared, they must be disclosed in the footnotes to the financial statements.

where they seek to raise capital. Class B stocks have also become popular in the U.S. as a defense mechanism against hostile takeovers.

The terminology used to describe equity accounts in other countries is somewhat different. In the United Kingdom and other Commonwealth nations (such as Canada and Australia), the terms are as follows:

United States	Commonwealth Nations
Common Stock	Ordinary Share or Called-up Share Capital
Preferred Stock	Preference Share
Additional Paid-in Capital	Share Premium
Retained Earnings	Profit and Loss Account

It is also not uncommon to find accounts termed "reserves" in the equity sections in the United Kingdom, Japan, Sweden, Germany, and other countries. Typically these reserves pertain to foreign currency translation adjustments, provisions for goodwill, legal reserves required by law, accruals for future expected expenses, and/or asset write-up revaluations.

For example, the equity section of the balance sheet in Carlton Communications' 1993 annual report is as follows:

£M	1993	1992
Capital and reserves		
Called-up share capital	18,190	18,143
Share premium account	7,880	3,228
Revaluation reserve	2,346	11,977
Other reserves	30,659	40,214
Profit and loss account	365,658	309,730
Total	424,733	383,292

Carlton Communications is a U.K.-based telecommunications company. The "other reserves" item for this company is primarily related to requirements under the Companies Act of 1985 and the prevalent British practice of charging goodwill, in total, to owners' equity.

Retained Earnings Transactions: Net Income

As we saw in Chapter 3, revenue and expense-producing transactions affect many balance sheet accounts — cash, accounts receivable, inventory, fixed assets, liabilities — but ultimately, the effects of these transactions are recorded in the Retained Earnings account. It may be useful at this point to recall the relationship between the balance sheet and the income statement. As the following chart (from Chapter 2) depicts, these two statements are linked by the Retained Earnings account:

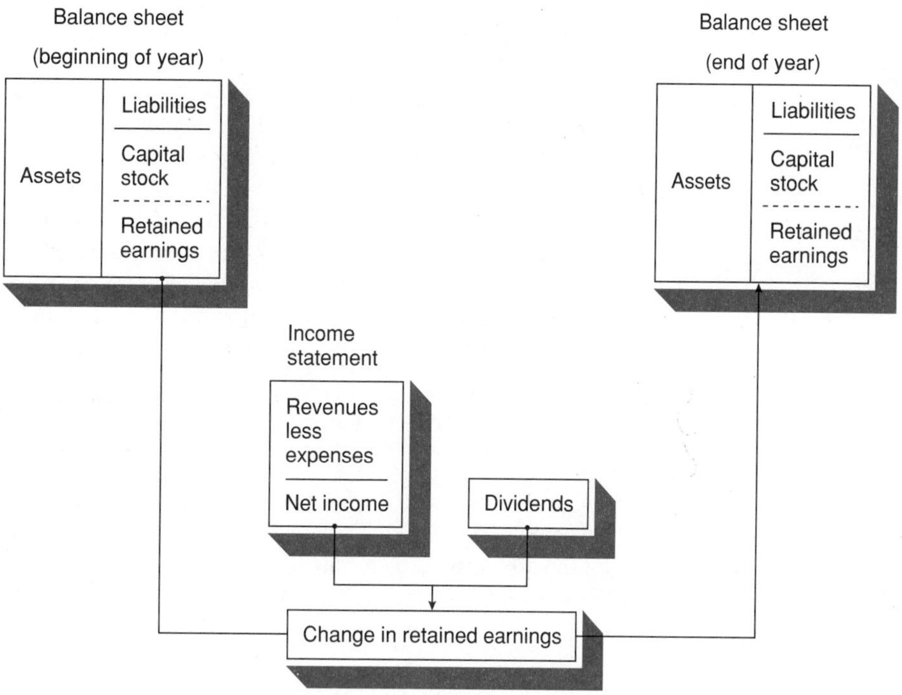

The net income for the period, less any dividends declared, is added to the Retained Earnings account on the balance sheet. This addition reflects the shareholders' increasing ownership interest in the net worth of the company.

Retained Earnings Transactions: Dividends

After net income, the second most common entry to the Retained Earnings account is the payment of dividends. We have said this several times, but it is worth repeating — dividends are a distribution of a company's income to its shareholders but are not an expense of the business. The accounting entry to record a $5,000 cash dividend on the **date of declaration** by the board of directors looks like this:

Dr. Retained Earnings (OE)	(dec.) 5,000	
Cr. Dividends Payable (L)		(inc.) 5,000

and on the **date of payment,**[4] it looks like this:

Dr. Dividends Payable (L)	(dec.) 5,000	
Cr. Cash (A)		(dec.) 5,000

To be entitled to receive a dividend, a shareholder must own the stock on the **date of record,** which is set by the board of directors. For example, on January 31, 1996

[4]Technically, the entry recording the *declaration* of a $5,000 cash dividend is

Dr. Dividends Declared (COE)	(inc.) 5,000	
Cr. Dividends Payable (L)		(inc.) 5,000

and at the end of the accounting period, before preparation of the financial statements, Dividends Declared is then netted against the Retained Earnings account.

Exxon Corp. declared a $0.75 quarterly dividend payable March 11, 1996 to shareholders *of record* as of February 12, 1996.

Typically, dividends are paid in cash. Growth-oriented companies that have profitable places to invest their cash internally, however, may pay a **stock dividend** instead. The shareholders — who now own a few more shares than they did before the stock dividend — can then ride along with a company's expected growth, or they can liquidate part of their shareholdings by selling the stock dividend and converting it to cash. The accounting entry for a stock dividend is conceptually the same as for a cash dividend, except that the credit portion of the entry is an increase in common stock rather than a decrease in cash. The dollar value of the entry is measured by the fair market price of the stock issued at the date the dividend was declared:

Dr. Stock Dividends Declared (OE)	(dec.) 5,000	
Cr. Capital Stock, at Par Value (OE)		(inc.) 500
Cr. Paid-in-Capital in Excess of Par Value (OE)		(inc.) 4,500

(This entry assumes that the fair market value of the shares issued was $5,000 and that the par value was $500.) As with a cash dividend, the Stock Dividend Declared account must be closed to Retained Earnings at the end of the accounting period and thus has the effect of transferring a portion of retained earnings to the capital stock accounts.

Stock Splits versus Stock Dividends

A company may "split" its stock for any number of reasons, but most often it is to reduce the market value of each share. The theory supporting a stock split is that investors will be more interested in a stock with a current market value of $25 than in one with a current market value of $100. Ordinarily, no journal entry is required for a stock split, although the number of shares outstanding increases and the par value (or stated value) of each share decreases proportionately. In a 2-for-1 stock split, for example, the number of shares outstanding doubles and the par value is halved, leaving the aggregate value of owners' equity unchanged. A **stock split** is, quite simply, a pro rata issuance of new shares to all existing shareholders.[5]

Sometimes a stock split is accounted for without changing a stock's par value. For example, on July 26, 1990, PepsiCo declared a 3-for-1 stock split. PepsiCo did not change the par value ($0.0167) of its capital stock but transferred an amount equal to the total par value of the new shares from the Capital in Excess of Par Value account to the Capital Stock account.

The economic substance of a stock split is not very different from that of a stock dividend; however, the accounting implications are quite different. Note that a stock dividend transfers some part of a company's retained earnings to the capital accounts whereas (usually) the accounting for a split simply reallocates the paid-in capital over a larger number of shares. That theoretical accounting difference is perhaps justifiable when a split is large — 2 for 1 or 4 for 1. That difference is less justifiable, however, with a smaller split. In fact, the American and New York Stock exchanges have adopted reporting rules that have become general practice. They have said that a stock split is any distribution of stock in *excess* of 25 percent of the previously outstanding shares, whereas a distribution of *less* than 25 percent is always considered a stock

[5]A stock split may be either a *forward* split or a *reverse* split. A forward split increases the number of shares outstanding; a reverse split reduces the number of shares outstanding.

dividend. Thus, for example, under stock exchange rules, a stock distribution equal to 10 percent of the previously outstanding shares must be accounted for as a stock dividend even if it is legally described as a stock split. In that situation, the fair market value of the newly distributed shares is transferred from retained earnings to the capital accounts.

Many countries make no distinction between stock splits and stock dividends. They simply appear under a heading such as "free share distribution" or a similar title. For example, ISCOR, the South African Steel Company, reported the following in its 1994 annual report:

> As was the case at the interim when a capitalisation share award was declared in the ratio of 1,2 new fully paid ordinary shares of R1 each in Iscor for every 100 ordinary shares, the directors again elected the allocation of a final capitalisation share award, in order to preserve cash resources.

Essentially, the company declared a 1.2 percent stock dividend on their one Rand par value common stock. (Note that in many countries the use of the comma and the decimal point to delineate thousands and fractional amounts is reversed. While we might write 132,843.12 in the United States, the same amount might appear as 132.843,12 in many other countries. That is one reason why Americans are often confused when they see a tag reading 73.035,50 hanging on a T-shirt in Florence.)

Treasury Stock Transactions

In the United States, companies may, at the discretion of management, buy back a proportion of their own outstanding stock. A company may, for example, repurchase its own stock because it has commitments for future issuances of stock to satisfy various stock options, stock warrants, or convertible securities (to be discussed shortly). Or a company may reacquire some of its own shares because it has excess cash and because the board of directors believes that the company's own stock represents the best investment opportunity for that cash. A company may also buy some of its outstanding shares because management believes that the current market price of the stock is too low, and it hopes to raise that price by reducing the supply of available shares.

If the reacquired shares are to be held and reissued sometime in the future, they are accounted for in a contra owners' equity account titled **Treasury Stock.** The reacquired shares are usually recorded in the Treasury Stock account at the cost paid to repurchase the shares:

Dr. Treasury Stock (COE)	(inc.) 15,000	
Cr. Cash (A)		(dec.) 15,000

Note that under U.S. GAAP a company's investment in its own stock is not considered to be an asset; instead, it is treated as a reduction in owners' equity. Also note that practice varies from country to country. Many countries forbid companies from buying and then reissuing their own stock. In other countries, such as Italy and France, treasury stock is carried as an asset, often in the Long-Term Investments account.

When treasury stock is reissued as a result of a sale, to satisfy stock options or for the conversion of convertible bonds, the cost of the reissued shares is removed from the Treasury Stock account. If the proceeds related to that reissuance differ from the cost of the treasury shares issued, that difference is added to (or subtracted from) the Paid-in Capital account. For example, suppose that Smith Company purchased 100 shares of its own stock at $12 a share in anticipation of the exercise of its $10 stock options by its employees. The entry to record that purchase is an increase in its Treasury Stock account (a contra owners' equity account) for $1,200 and a decrease in the Cash account of like amount. Assuming that options for 100 shares are exercised, the following accounting entry is made:

Dr. Cash (A)	(inc.) 1,000	
Dr. Paid-in Capital in Excess of Par Value (OE)	(dec.) 200	
Cr. Treasury Stock (COE)		(dec.) 1,200

If a company reacquires its own shares with no intention of reissuing them, it formally, legally retires them. Instead of a debit entry to the Treasury Stock account, the company debits the cost of the stock acquired to the Common Stock (at Par) account and the Paid-in Capital account for any difference. If the difference between the par value and the per-share cost of the reacquired shares is more than the average per-share paid-in capital from prior issuances of stock, that difference may have to be charged against retained earnings.

Other Stock Transactions

Stock options. Many companies maintain **stock option plans** for their employees, and issuances of stock in satisfaction of those commitments are frequent owners' equity transactions. A stock option plan might work this way: Assume that Smith Company is on the verge of a new business cycle and that its board of directors concludes that management motivation will be a major factor in the company's success. At the present time, the company's $1 par value stock is selling at $10 a share. The board might agree to grant 100 options to key management people entitling them to purchase shares of the company's stock at $10 a share (the market price of a share at date of grant) any time after five years from today (the vesting period), thereby creating a financial incentive for the executives to manage the company over the next several years so that its stock price appreciates.

Under most stock option plans, no accounting entry is necessary when such an option is granted. The entry to record the issuance of those shares when the employees exercise their options assumes that the transaction is simply a sale of stock at $10 a share — even if the stock price is $20 a share on the exercise date:

Dr. Cash (A)	(inc.) 1,000	
Cr. Common Stock, at Par Value (OE)		(inc.) 100
Cr. Paid-in Capital in Excess of Par Value (OE)		(inc.) 900

Some stock option plans produce no tax deductions for a corporation; similarly, the employee has no taxable income as a result of the award of the option or the exercise of the option. The most common situation, however, is that the corporation is able to deduct, for tax purposes, the difference between the fair value of the stock and the exercise price at the time the options are exercised and the employee also experiences a commensurate taxable gain at exercise date. The employee will experience another taxable gain when the stock is sold, with that gain based on the difference between the ultimate sale price of the stock and its option (purchase) price.

In recent years, a great variety of stock option plans have come into use, some of which do require the company to recognize an option expense, for financial statement purposes, over the option period and do require the employee to recognize taxable income. Companies establish one plan or another (sometimes a combinations of plans) depending on the impact of the plans on their earnings and their tax position, as well as the needs of their employees.

For many years there has been controversy about accounting for stock options because they are used so often by corporations and the values associated with them are clearly material in many instances. Warren Buffett's quote at the beginning of this chapter illustrates one position in the debate. On June 30, 1993, the FASB issued an exposure draft titled *Accounting for Stock-Based Compensation.* It would require the *fair-value based method* of valuation for all options at the time of their grant. The previous approach was termed the *intrinsic-value based method* because only the excess of the market value of the stock over the exercise price, the intrinsic value, is recognized as expense when the options are *granted.* Under the proposed standard, the *value of the options* granted would be amortized to earnings as a compensation expense over the vesting period and the credit would be to owners' equity. The value of options granted without any vesting period would immediately be recognized as an expense.

Let's look at the fair-value based method a bit more in depth. Companies could select one of several binomial option pricing models to value the options at the grant date. One of the most popular of these is the Black-Scholes model, which is widely used in the financial community and frequently studied in business schools. These models are sensitive to the current stock price, the exercise price, the expected dividend yield, stock price volatility, the option exercise term, and the prevailing interest rate.[6] They do not depend upon earnings growth or forecasts of future market prices.

For example, assume a company grants 900,000 options to employees as of January 1, 2000, when the company's stock price was \$50, and the exercise price is also \$50. The options vest after three years; the expected life of the options is six years; and the maximum term of the options is 10 years. Expected dividend yield is 2.5 percent; the risk-free rate of interest is 7.5 percent; and the volatility is 30 percent. *Volatility* is the standard derivation of the continuously compounded rates of return of the stock over a specified period. Finally, assume that each year during the vesting period, 3 percent of the options are canceled because of employee attrition. These are the assumptions necessary to value a stock option using one of the binomial models.

Using these assumptions and the Black-Scholes option pricing model modified for dividends, the value of each option at the grant date is \$17.15. (The Black-Scholes calculations are not shown here, but they are discussed in Appendix 14A.) Thus, the value of the options at the grant date is

$$\$17.15 \times 900{,}000 \times 0.97 \times 0.97 \times 0.97 = \$14{,}087{,}108$$

Under the fair value accounting rules proposed by the FASB, the value of the options granted would be amortized over the service period. Typically this means the vesting period; consequently, at the end of years 2000, 2001, and 2002, the following entry would be recorded:

Dr. Compensation Expense (E)	(inc.) 4,695,703	
Cr. Additional Paid-in Capital — Options (OE)		(inc.) 4,695,703

A deferred tax asset would also be established for the temporary difference related to compensation expense.

[6]F. Black and M. Scholes, "The Pricing of Options and Corporate Liabilities," *Journal of Political Economy* 81 (May–June 1973), pp. 637–54. See also R. C. Merton, "Theory of Rational Option Pricing," *Bell Journal of Economics and Management Science* 4 (Spring 1973), pp. 141–83.

If the options are all exercised in 2005, when the stock price is 70, the entry to record the sale of stock, assuming 821,406 shares are issued, looks like this:

Dr. Cash (A)	(inc.) 41,070,300	
Dr. Additional Paid-in Capital—Options (OE)	(dec.) 14,087,108	
Cr. Capital Stock (OE) . . . . (divided appropriately between common stock and other paid-in capital)		(inc.) 55,157,408

Entries would also erase any accumulated deferred tax asset and record the income tax benefit of the options when exercised if the options produce a tax deduction to the issuer. The effect of this approach to valuing options is to increase the capital stock accounts by the sum of the exercise price (what the grantees actually paid in cash for their stock) and the value of the options at the grant date (valued using Black-Scholes or one of the other option pricing models), which was earlier charged to compensation expense. The market value of the shares at the exercise date is ignored. The intrinsic-value based method, in contrast, values stock issued via options at the exercise price only.

In summary, fair value accounting for stock options would result in charges to net income for the cost of options granted based on a valuation model. These expenses are recognized over the vesting period. When the options are exercised, the value of the options exercised plus the proceeds from the issuance of the new shares are recorded as an increase in capital stock. If the options are tax-deductible compensation, the actual tax consequences of the stock option are based on the difference between the exercise price and the market value of the shares at the exercise date. This is explained more fully in Appendix 14A.

The impact of the FASB proposed stock option accounting could have been significant, particularly for start-up companies. In the end, the FASB backed down. Effective for fiscal years beginning after December 31, 1995, companies must describe the general characteristics of the plan and they must disclose the number and weighted-average exercise prices of options in each of the following categories, together with the weighted-average grant-date fair value of options granted during the year and the methods and assumptions employed to establish these valuations:

- Outstanding at the beginning of the year.
- Outstanding at the end of the year.
- Exercisable at the end of the year.
- Granted during the year.
- Exercised during the year.
- Forfeited during the year.
- Expired during the year.

However, under the new opinion, SFAS No. 123, companies may elect to recognize the value of options granted as a compensation expense or merely footnote the pro forma net income and earnings per share effect of the options vested using the fair value method. In the end, companies were left to choose whether to bring the cost of options granted to their balance sheets and income statements. The intention of many companies on this point was clear: They had no intention of booking the value of options granted as an expense.

A sample disclosure under SFAS No. 123 is contained in Appendix 14A. No published annual reports reflecting this new opinion were available as of the publication date of this book but the reader can anticipate the likely impact from an examination of current disclosures. The following was excerpted from the Stock Purchase and Award Plans footnote of Medtronic, Inc.'s 1995 annual report:

> Under the provisions of the 1994 stock award plan, nonqualified stock options and other stock awards are granted to officers and key employees at prices not less than fair market value at the date of grant. In addition, awards granted under the previous nonqualified stock option and stock award plans remain outstanding though no additional awards will be made under these plans.
>
> A summary of option transactions in 1995 follows:

Nonqualified Options	Option Price Range Per Share	Number of Shares	Expiration Date
Outstanding at beginning of year	$3.34–$49.00	3,185,830	1995–2004
Granted	37.88– 70.00	479,675	2000–2005
Exercised	3.34– 53.00	368,421	1995–2005
Canceled	15.06– 53.00	41,942	2000–2005
Outstanding at end of year	5.34– 70.00	3,255,142	1996–2005
Exercisable at end of year	5.34– 53.00	1,842,079	1996–2005

Beginning with their 1997 fiscal year (commencing May 1, 1996), Medtronic must either adopt the fair value method of reporting stock options, amortizing the value at grant date of stock options over a one-year period as compensation expense (because Medtronic's options vest in one year), or they must use the footnote disclosure approach, showing what the effect on net income and EPS would have been. Whichever election the company makes, it must continue to disclose in a footnote the details of its option transactions, but it must do so for each year for which it publishes an income statement (three years for Medtronic), and it must show the fair values of the options granted during each year.

In other countries, stock options outstanding are frequently disclosed in a footnote similar to that of Medtronic. In some countries they are not disclosed at all; in others, only the awards to officers and directors are disclosed. Exhibit 14.1, from the 1994 annual report of Reckitt & Colman, a U.K. consumer goods firm, illustrates the type of disclosure typical in Commonwealth countries.

Stock warrants. A cash-short firm that is going through a difficult period may find that it is unable to sell new shares of stock at a price it believes is reasonable. In lieu of a stock sale, a company may sell **stock warrants,** which enable the holder to purchase shares of stock at a fixed price at some time in the future. The proceeds from the sale of warrants are simply added to the Paid-in Capital in Excess of Par Value account:

Dr. Cash (A)	(inc.) 5,000	
Cr. Paid-in Capital in Excess of Par Value (OE)		(inc.) 5,000

When a warrant is exercised, the proceeds are added to the common stock account using the same theory followed for the exercise of stock options. Sometimes warrants for the purchase of common stock are issued in connection with the sale of a bond to make the bonds more attractive to potential purchasers. In those situations, some portion of the proceeds of the bond sale are allocated to the Paid-in Capital in Excess account, just as though the company had sold the bonds and the warrants separately.

EXHIBIT 14.1

Reckitt & Colman Plc
British Stock Option Disclosures

Called-up Share Capital
Options unexercised at 31 December 1994:

Executive Share Option Schemes			Savings-Related Share Option Scheme		
Number of shares	**Price to be paid**	**Exercisable by**	**Number of shares**	**Price to be paid**	**Exercisable by**
32,498	376.9p	April 1997	34,209	379.7p	June 1995
76,018	323.6p	April 1998	90,838	386.0p	July 1995
279,842	420.8p	April 1999	30,949	308.2p	June 1996
169,671	442.9p	April 2000	78,500	385.2p	June 1996
45,826	481.6p	Oct 2000	131,884	548.2p	June 1997
253,402	578.4p	April 2001	52,807	386.0p	July 1997
91,544	685.5p	Oct 2001	50,815	385.2p	June 1998
363,670	628.2p	April 2002	329,869	426.7p	June 1998
282,413	532.4p	Sept 2002	72,069	548.2p	June 1999
247,079	594.6p	April 2003	125,381	489.9p	June 1999
323,334	612.4p	Sept 2003	171,158	426.7p	June 2000
281,459	602.5p	April 2004	199,738	477.1p	July 2000
			42,175	489.9p	June 2001
			61,227	477.1p	July 2002

Shares to be Issued (Including Premium)	Number of Shares	£m
Share capital — ordinary shares of 10p each	46,983,898	4.70
Share premium account (after costs of issue)		224.60
		229.30

Convertible securities. Many companies sell **convertible bonds** that enable the holder to exchange a bond for shares of common stock at a predetermined ratio (the conversion ratio). Convertible bonds are usually less expensive for the issuing corporation because they can be sold with a lower interest rate than would otherwise be required (because the conversion feature itself has value). Convertible bonds are attractive to the holder because they ensure a steady stream of interest income for a certain number of years, as well as the possibility of sharing in any potential appreciation of the common stock. The proceeds from the sale of a convertible bond increase the cash account and increase the bond account. If some of the bonds are subsequently converted, a pro rata share of the bond's carrying value is transferred from the Bond Payable account (a decrease) to the Common Stock and Paid-in Capital accounts (increases). Similar accounting is followed for convertible preferred stock.

Hybrid Transactions

Earlier we indicated that all transactions involving the owners' equity accounts that relate to stock issuances are reported in the statement of owners' equity and that all owners' equity transactions that involve revenue and expenses are reported in the income statement. For many years, the dividing line between the two types of transactions was clearly defined and stoutly defended. The accounting profession argued that it was important to include *all* income and expense items (and *only* those items) in the determination of income for the period. Recently, the line between income and equity transactions has become blurred. Today, under GAAP, two nonstock events are reported in the statement of owners' equity, not in the income statement. The two nonstock events are (1) the residual that results from translating the foreign currency value of assets and liabilities held outside the United States into U.S. dollars and (2) the residual that results from adjusting the carrying value of available-for-sale investments to their current market value.

To describe the **currency translation adjustment,** it may be easiest if we use an example. Assume that a U.S.-based company has a subsidiary in Germany with receivables, inventory, equipment, and payables denominated in German marks. Obviously, adding together the company's dollar-stated accounts and its mark-stated accounts would not be appropriate. If the exchange rate stayed the same from one year to the next (for example, 1 mark = $0.50 or $1 = 2 marks), it would be easy to convert the mark-stated accounts into their U.S. dollar equivalents and then to add those dollar-equivalent accounts to the U.S. dollar-stated accounts.

Exchange rates do fluctuate, however, and sometimes they change dramatically. In previous years, the exchange rate between the U.S. dollar and the German mark has been 1 to 4, with a mark being equal to $0.25 U.S. Hence, a piece of equipment purchased for a company's German operations at that time might have cost 1 million marks and would therefore have had a U.S. dollar cost of only $250,000. With an exchange rate of $1 to 2 marks, the translated dollar cost for that piece of equipment would be $500,000. Accountants and businesspeople have been concerned about the appropriate accounting for that extra $250,000. No one wanted to include the apparent increase in asset value in the income statement because it did not seem to be a revenue item. In addition, the exchange rates might reverse in a subsequent period, and consequently companies would report fluctuations in earnings induced by the exchange markets rather than due to operations. Instead, it was agreed (in SFAS No. 52) that all such translation adjustments be included as a unique element of owners' equity until those assets or liabilities were liquidated, converted to U.S. dollars, and repatriated. Only after those non-U.S. assets (or liabilities) are realized in dollars is the resulting gain or loss recognized in the income statement.

The second unique element of owners' equity builds on the same logic as the translation adjustment. A company that owns less than 20 percent of the stock of another company, and whose intent is that such shares are available for sale if the right circumstances come along, must report that investment at its market value in the balance sheet. As elaborated on more fully in Chapter 8, if the market value of the available-for-sale shares held has changed since the last balance sheet report date, the Investment asset account must be adjusted, and the resultant unrealized holding gain or loss carried to an account in the owners' equity section of the balance sheet. In essence, this owners' equity account acts as a holding account for the shares' market appreciation or diminution until such time that the shares are actually sold and the realized gain or loss, based on original cost, is then recognized in that period's income statement. Once the shares have been sold, the owners' equity holding gain or loss account pertaining to the shares would no longer be needed and thus would be zeroed out.

OWNERS' EQUITY DISCLOSURES

To illustrate the typical annual report disclosures involving owners' equity, we again refer to the 1994 PepsiCo, Inc., annual report. Exhibit 14.2 presents the shareholders' equity section of the PepsiCo consolidated balance sheet. This exhibit presents summary information concerning PepsiCo's shareholder equity accounts, whereas detailed information is presented in Exhibit 14.3 in the consolidated statement of shareholders' equity.

From these two exhibits, the following facts can be determined:

- PepsiCo has one class of capital stock — a \$0.0167 par value, common stock. It is *authorized* to issue 1.8 billion shares, and as of December 31, 1994, 863.1 million shares had been *issued.* Only 789.9 million shares were *outstanding;* 73.2 million shares were held in treasury as of December 31, 1994.
- The aggregate contributed capital at year-end 1994 was \$948.8 million (14.4 + 934.4), whereas total shareholders' equity was \$6,856.1.
- The aggregate cost of the 73.2 million shares of capital stock held as treasury stock was \$1,361.2 million. An interesting sidenote: PepsiCo has bought back, in dollar terms, more capital stock than that contributed by shareholders when the new shares were originally issued. If the company were to cancel the shares held as treasury shares, the capital stock and capital in excess of par value would be negative. In lieu of creating such a circumstance, the company would attribute part of the cost of treasury shares to the capital stock at par value (\$14.4 million) and the rest would be apportioned between capital in excess of par value and retained earnings.
- In 1994, 15 million shares were purchased at a cost of \$549.1 million; 4.9 million shares were reissued for stock options being exercised; and 0.9 million shares were issued as part of the compensation for acquisitions.
- Retained earnings at year-end 1994 were \$7,739.1 million. Net income in 1994 was \$1,752.0 million, and cash dividends were \$554.8 million. These two items explained the net change in retained earnings from the beginning to the end of the 1994 fiscal year.

EXHIBIT 14.2

PepsiCo, Inc.
Shareholders' Equity Section
As of December 31, 1994, and December 25, 1993
(in millions)

	1994	**1993**
Shareholders' Equity		
Capital stock, par value 1⅔¢ per share: authorized 1,800.0 shares, issued 863.1 shares	**\$ 14.4**	\$ 14.4
Capital in excess of par value	**934.4**	879.5
Retained earnings	**7,739.1**	6,541.9
Currency translation adjustment and other	**(470.6)**	(183.9)
	8,217.3	7,251.9
Less: Treasury stock, at cost: 73.2 shares and 64.3 shares in 1994 and 1993, respectively	**(1,361.2)**	(913.2)
Total Shareholders' Equity	**\$ 6,856.1**	\$6,338.7

EXHIBIT 14.3

PepsiCo, Inc., and Subsidiaries
Consolidated Statement of Shareholders' Equity
(in millions except per share amounts)
Fifty-three weeks ended December 31, 1994 and 52 weeks ended December 25, 1993, and December 26, 1992

	Capital Stock							
	Issued		Treasury		Capital in Excess of Par Value	Retained Earnings	Currency Translation Adjustment and Other	Total
	Shares	Amount	Shares	Amount				
Shareholders' Equity, December 28, 1991	863.1	$14.4	(74.0)	$ (745.9)	$476.6	$ 5,470.0	$ 330.3	$5,545.4
1992 Net income	—	—	—	—	—	374.3	—	374.3
Cash dividends declared (per share — $0.51)	—	—	—	—	—	(404.6)	—	(404.6)
Currency translation adjustment	—	—	—	—	—	—	(429.3)	(429.3)
Shares issued in connection with acquisitions	—	—	4.3	44.2	115.3	—	—	159.5
Stock option exercises, including tax benefits of $57.5	—	—	6.3	65.3	74.9	—	—	140.2
Purchases of treasury stock	—	—	(1.0)	(32.0)	—	—	—	(32.0)
Other	—	—	0.1	1.4	0.8	—	—	2.2
Shareholders' Equity, December 26, 1992	863.1	$14.4	(64.3)	$ (667.0)	$667.6	$ 5,439.7	$ (99.0)	$5,355.7
1993 Net income	—	—	—	—	—	1,587.9	—	1,587.9
Cash dividends declared (per share — $0.61)	—	—	—	—	—	(485.7)	—	(485.7)
Currency translation adjustment	—	—	—	—	—	—	(77.0)	(77.0)
Purchases of treasury stock	—	—	(12.4)	(463.5)	—	—	—	(463.5)
Shares issued in connection with acquisitions	—	—	8.9	170.2	164.6	—	—	334.8
Stock option exercises, including tax benefits of $23.4	—	—	3.4	46.0	46.1	—	—	92.1
Pension liability adjustment, net of deferred taxes of $5.1	—	—	—	—	—	—	(7.9)	(7.9)
Other	—	—	0.1	1.1	1.2	—	—	2.3
Shareholders' Equity, December 25, 1993	863.1	$14.4	(64.3)	$ (913.2)	$879.5	$ 6,541.9	$(183.9)	$6,338.7
1994 Net income	—	—	—	—	—	**1,752.0**	—	**1,752.0**
Cash dividends declared (per share — $0.70)	—	—	—	—	—	**(554.8)**	—	**(554.8)**
Currency translation adjustment	—	—	—	—	—	—	**(294.6)**	**(294.6)**
Purchases of treasury stock	—	—	**(15.0)**	**(549.1)**	—	—	—	**(549.1)**
Stock option exercises, including tax benefits of $27.1	—	—	**4.9**	**80.8**	**44.5**	—	—	**125.3**
Shares issued in connection with acquisitions	—	—	**0.9**	**15.1**	**13.7**	—	—	**28.8**
Pension liability adjustment, net of deferred taxes of $5.1	—	—	—	—	—	—	**7.9**	**7.9**
Other	—	—	**0.3**	**5.2**	**(3.3)**	—	—	**1.9**
Shareholders' Equity, December 31, 1994	**863.1**	**$14.4**	**(73.2)**	**$(1,361.2)**	**$934.4**	**$ 7,739.1**	**$(470.6)**	**$6,856.1**

- The cumulative foreign currency translation account totaled ($470.6) million at year-end 1994 — a decrease of $294.6 million from the prior year, reflecting a substantial weakening of foreign currencies relative to the U.S. dollar in those areas where PepsiCo maintains operations.

Because of the importance of employee stock option and stock compensation plans, the principal features of these plans are detailed in the footnotes to the financial statements. Exhibit 14.4 presents the footnote disclosure for PepsiCo's employee incentive plan.

Management Issues

Most of the decisions that managers are called upon to make concerning the accounting for owners' equity issues are episodic — such as a new issue of common stock, a new preferred stock, stock splits, acquisitions paid for with common stock, and the decision to repurchase common stock. Managers give a good deal of attention to these decisions because they can have an immediate impact on a firm's stock price — usually the single most important measure of how well management is performing its job. Because they are infrequent and of a critical importance, companies often bring in experts to help with the decisions. Investment bankers, public accountants, and lawyers are almost always present when these big equity events are being considered. The overriding issue is typically "What's this going to do to our stock price? What signal will be given to the market? What will the analysts say about this?" Because of the direct and immediate link between these equity decisions and the share price, most executives have a detailed knowledge of the implications of each alternative being considered. As more public attention is brought to bear on stock options, this too will become a priority concern for senior executives. If the FASB returns to the issue of accounting for options when they are granted, then the stock option programs of most large companies will attract the same degree of management attention as is now devoted to other equity matters.

SUMMARY

The owners' or shareholders' equity represents the residual value of a company, or its assets minus its liabilities. The transactions affecting the shareholder equity accounts are summarized in the statement of owners' equity. The principal owners' equity transactions include the sale of capital stock, the results of operations (that is, the net income or net loss resulting from a company's principal business activity), the payment of dividends (either cash or stock), the exercise of stock options or warrants, the conversion of convertible preferred stock or debentures, and the purchase or reissuance of treasury stock. In addition to these transactions involving individuals or organizations outside the company, the statement of owners' equity also depicts two hybrid transactions: (1) the adjustment for foreign currency changes when consolidating the results of foreign operations and (2) the adjustment for valuation changes in the long-term investment portfolio.

The owners' equity of a company is also referred to as its *net worth* or *book value*. In many cases the market value of a company, as defined by the market price of its capital stock, far exceeds the company's net worth or book value. Why this may be the case was the focus of Chapter 7.

EXHIBIT 14.4

PepsiCo, Inc.
Selected Footnote Disclosures:
Employee Incentive Plans

Note 18: Employee Incentive Plans
PepsiCo has established certain employee incentive plans under which stock options are granted. A stock option allows an employee to purchase a share of PepsiCo Capital Stock (stock) in the future at a price equal to the fair market value on the date of the grant.

Under the PepsiCo SharePower Stock Option Plan, approved by the board of directors and effective in 1989, essentially all employees other than executive officers and part-time and short-service employees may be granted stock options annually. The number of options granted is based on each employee's annual earnings. The options generally become exercisable ratably over five years from the grant date and must be exercised within 10 years of the grant date. SharePower options were granted to approximately 128,000 employees in 1994, 118,000 employees in 1993, and 114,000 employees in 1992.

The shareholder-approved 1987 Long-Term Incentive Plan (the 1987 Plan), which has provisions similar to prior plans, provides incentives to eligible senior and middle management employees. In addition to grants of stock options, which are generally exercisable between 1 and 15 years from the grant date, the 1987 Plan allows for grants of performance share units (PSUs) to eligible senior management employees. A PSU is equivalent in value to a share of stock at the grant date and vests for payment four years from the grant date, contingent upon attainment of prescribed corporate performance goals. PSUs are not directly granted, as certain stock options granted may be surrendered by employees for a specified number of PSUs within 60 days of the option grant date. During 1994, 1,541,187 stock options were surrendered for 513,729 PSUs. At year-end 1994, 1993, and 1992, there were 629,202, 491,200, and 484,698 outstanding PSUs, respectively.

Grants under the 1987 Plan are approved by the compensation committee of the board of directors (the committee), which is composed of outside directors. Payment of awards other than stock options is made in cash and/or stock as approved by the committee, and amounts expensed for such awards were $7 million, $5 million, and $11 million in 1994, 1993 and 1992, respectively. Under the 1987 Plan, a maximum of 54 million shares of stock can be purchased or paid pursuant to grants. There were 7 million, 20 million, 22 million, and 32 million shares available for future grants at year-end 1994, 1993, 1992, and 1991, respectively. The committee does not intend to grant future awards under the 1987 Plan.

On May 4, 1994, PepsiCo's shareholders approved the 1994 Long-Term Incentive Plan (the 1994 Plan). The 1994 Plan continues the principal features of the 1987 Plan and authorizes a maximum of 75 million shares of stock, which may be purchased or paid pursuant to grants by the committee. The first awards under the 1994 Plan were made as of January 1, 1995.

1994, 1993, and 1992 activity for the stock option plans included:

(options in thousands)	SharePower	Long-Term Incentive
Outstanding at December 28, 1991	23,801	27,834
Granted	8,477	12,653
Exercised	(1,155)	(5,155)
Surrendered for PSUs	—	(503)
Canceled	(2,327)	(1,839)
Outstanding at December 26, 1992	28,796	32,990
Granted	9,121	2,834
Exercised	(1,958)	(1,412)
Surrendered for PSUs	—	(96)
Canceled	(2,524)	(966)
Outstanding at December 25, 1993	33,435	33,350
Granted	**11,633**	**16,237**
Exercised	**(1,820)**	**(3,052)**
Surrendered for PSUs	—	**(1,541)**
Canceled	**(3,443)**	**(2,218)**
Outstanding at December 31, 1994	**39,805**	**42,776**
Exercisable at December 31, 1994	**16,115**	**18,439**
Option prices per share:		
Exercised during 1994	$17.58 to $36.75	$4.11 to $38.75
Exercised during 1993	$17.58 to $36.75	$4.11 to $36.31
Exercised during 1992	$17.58 to $35.25	$4.11 to $29.88
Outstanding at year-end 1994	$17.58 to $36.75	$7.69 to $42.81

NEW CONCEPTS AND TERMS

Callable preferred stock (p. 681)
Charter of incorporation (p.678)
Common stock (p. 681)
Convertible bonds (p. 690)
Contributed capital (p.677)
Convertible preferred stock (p. 681)
Cumulative preferred stock (p. 681)
Currency translation adjustment (p. 691)
Date of declaration (p. 683)
Date of payment (p. 683)
Date of record (p. 683)
Dividends in arrears (p. 681)
Fiscal year (p. 680)
Net worth (p. 677)
Participating preferred stock (p. 681)
Partnership (p. 677)
Preferred stock (p. 681)
Retained capital (p. 677)
Stock dividend (p. 684)
Stock options plans (p. 686)
Stock split (p. 684)
Stock warrant (p. 689)
Treasury stock (p. 685)

Stock Options in Detail

In its simplest form, a stock option is a right to purchase a certain number of shares of company stock at a set price during some future period of time beyond the grant date. Typically, the shares are the common stock of the corporation and the exercise price is the market price of the stock on the grant day so as to avoid any income tax issues. Options typically have vesting restrictions; that is, one must be employed for so many months in order to exercise the first block of options, so many months for the next set, and so on. With what are called *American options,* owners may exercise their options at any time beyond the vesting date up to the expiration date. *European options* can be exercised only on the expiration date. Options are used as a type of incentive compensation, and it is common for directors, officers, and managers (and sometimes all employees) to receive stock options. Some companies have promised to sell millions of shares of stock under these option agreements. As of June 30, 1994, Microsoft Corporation, for example, estimated that the *net* value of its outstanding options was $3.2 billion!

The Debate over Accounting for Stock Options

Between 1993 and 1995, while the proposed accounting standard that would require companies to book a compensation expense for the value of stock options at their granting date was being discussed by the FASB, the debate about its merits raged throughout the financial community. For example, under a headline of "FASB's Folly," Malcolm S. Forbes Jr., Editor-in-Chief of *Forbes* magazine wrote the following in an editorial:

> The Financial Accounting Standards Board will soon hold pro forma hearings on one of its most asinine, destructive proposals ever. It wants to force companies to put a value on grants of stock options and expense them against profits.
>
> The idea is utterly illogical. How can a company know what its stock will be worth several years down the road? By definition the valuation is totally arbitrary, no matter how highfalutin the computer models used to come up with the numbers.
>
> The ruling will severely impact new companies. Many start-ups depend heavily on stock options to attract top-rate people. Coercing these outfits to penalize what are already anemic earnings with a capricious charge for options will make it even more difficult for them to attract good talent and fresh capital.[1]

[1]*Forbes,* Jan. 31, 1994, p. 25.

A *Harvard Business Review* editorial countered with the following:

> But that's precisely the point, the FASB says. Since stock options make up the difference between a market-level salary at an established company and a below-market salary at a start-up, options have a calculable value. If you can calculate them, and they have an effect on your financial condition and the condition of your stock, then you must count them as an expense.[2]

Actually the debate began much earlier; the issue had been on the FASB agenda for 10 years. One of the sharpest criticisms of the old accounting came from Warren Buffett in his chairman's letter in the 1992 Berkshire Hathaway Inc. annual report:

> Shareholders should understand that companies incur costs when they deliver something of value to another party and not just when cash changes hands. Moreover, it is both silly and cynical to say that an important item of cost should not be recognized simply because it can't be quantified with pinpoint precision. Right now, accounting abounds with imprecision. After all, no manager or auditor knows how long a 747 is going to last, which means he also does not know what the yearly depreciation charge for the plane should be. No one knows with any certainty what a bank's annual loan loss charge ought to be. And the estimates of losses that property-casualty companies make are notoriously inaccurate.
>
> Does this mean that these important items of cost should be ignored simply because they can't be quantified with absolute accuracy? Of course not. Rather, these costs should be estimated by honest and experienced people and then recorded. When you get right down to it, what other item of major but hard-to-precisely-calculate cost — other, that is, than stock options — does the accounting profession say should be ignored in the calculation of earnings?
>
> Moreover, options are just not that difficult to value. Admittedly, the difficulty is increased by the fact that the options given to executives are restricted in various ways. These restrictions affect value. They do not, however, eliminate it. In fact, since I'm in the mood for offers, I'll make one to any executive who is granted a restricted option, even though it may be out of the money: On the day of issue, Berkshire will pay him or her a substantial sum for the right to any future gain he or she realizes on the option. So if you find a CEO who says his newly issued options have little or no value, tell him to try us out. In truth, we have far more confidence in our ability to determine an appropriate price to pay for an option than we have in our ability to determine the proper depreciation rate for our corporate jet.

Mr. Buffett, one of America's best-known investors, prided himself on being able to "look through" GAAP accounting to see the reality of an economic situation.

Almost as if in answer to Mr. Buffett's charge, Microsoft Corporation published the following statement and table in their 1994 annual report:

> At Microsoft, every employee is eligible to become a stockholder in the company through the company's employee stock purchase and stock option plans. Management believes stock options have made a major contribution to the success of the company by aligning employee interests with those of other stockholders. Stock options are in widespread use today, and many of the company's competitors have similar programs. During the last several years there has been considerable debate about the appropriate accounting for stock options. Questions in this ongoing discussion include how stock options should be measured; whether they should be recorded in traditional financial statements, subject to already complex and increasingly difficult

[2] "Taking Account of Stock Options," *Harvard Business Review,* January–February 1994.

rules; whether they should be highlighted in a separate new financial statement or table; or whether further information concerning stock options should be disclosed in footnotes to financial statements. Pending resolution of these outstanding issues, on the accompanying page [see below] we have provided a table of outstanding common shares and net options and changes in their computed values based on quoted prices for the company's stock. It provides a clear understanding of the company's equity, its equity holders, and the value or possible value of their vested and unvested holdings.

In this table, common shares are those outstanding. Net vested and unvested options represent the number of common shares issuable upon exercise of such stock options less the number of common shares that could be repurchased with proceeds from their exercise. Computed values are calculated based on the closing price of the company's common stock on the Nasdaq National Market System on the dates indicated.

(In millions)	June 30				
	1992	Change	1993	Change	1994
Outstanding Common Shares and Options					
Directors' and officers' common shares	273	(13)	260	(21)	239
Employees' and directors' net vested and unvested stock options	78	(11)	67	(5)	62
Employees' and directors' shares and options	351	(24)	327	(26)	301
Other investors' common shares	271	34	305	37	342
Total	622	10	632	11	643
Nasdaq closing price per share	$ 35		$ 44		$ 51⅝
Computed Values					
Directors' and officers' common shares	$ 9,579	$1,886	$11,465	$ 845	$12,310
Employees' and directors' net vested and unvested stock options	2,714	245	2,959	269	3,228
Employees' and directors' shares and options	12,293	2,131	14,424	1,114	15,538
Other investors' common shares	9,486	3,930	13,416	4,259	17,675
Total	$21,779	$6,061	$27,840	$5,373	$33,213

To compute what Microsoft calls "net vested and unvested stock options" the company subtracted the amount to be paid on the option from the market value to get a net figure, then divided this by the market value of the shares to calculate the number of option shares outstanding.

SFAS No. 123

The FASB decision on the matter, announced in October of 1995, was presented in Chapter 14 of the text. Essentially, the FASB urged the adoption of the fair value method of accounting for options granted, but stopped short of making it mandatory. If a company did not adopt SFAS No. 123, it must report the pro forma impact on net income and EPS in the footnotes. Whatever election is made, the footnotes must also disclose the details of the company's options programs and must show fair values for all options granted.

Let's use the example from Chapter 14 to look more closely at fair value accounting for stock options.[3] Recall the details of the example:

Stock price at grant date	$50
Exercise price	$50
Vesting	January 1, 2003
Expected life of options	6 years
Maximum term of options	10 years
Expected dividend yield	2.5%
Risk-free rate of interest	7.5%
Expected volatility	30%
Expected cancellation rate	3%/year
Black-Scholes valuation	$17.15/share

For simplicity, the Black-Scholes valuation used in this example is actually based on the assumption that all options are exercised in six years, as if they were European options. Black-Scholes itself is particularly sensitive to the expected life of the option and the volatility. For example, the following table shows the Black-Scholes valuation for different combinations of volatility and expected life.

Black-Scholes Valuations of the $50, January 1, 2003, Options

		Expected life of options (in years)							
		1	2	3	4	5	6	7	8
Volatility	0.20	5.10	7.67	9.71	11.41	12.86	14.11	15.18	16.11
	0.23	5.56	8.27	10.38	12.12	13.59	14.85	15.92	16.84
	0.25	6.02	8.87	11.06	12.85	14.34	15.60	16.68	17.58
	0.28	6.48	9.47	11.75	13.58	15.10	16.38	17.45	18.35
	0.30	6.94	10.08	12.43	14.32	15.87	17.15	18.22	19.12
	0.33	7.40	10.69	13.12	15.06	16.63	17.93	19.00	19.89
	0.35	7.87	11.29	13.81	15.80	17.40	18.71	19.78	20.66
	0.38	8.33	11.90	14.50	16.53	18.16	19.48	20.56	21.43

Thus, if the volatility is only 0.25 (about the average for New York Stock Exchange stocks) and the life is just two years, the options are valued at only $8.87 over a $50 exercise price. The assumptions used in the example were for a volatility of 0.3 and a life of six years, thus the value of $17.15.

Returning to the example begun in Chapter 14, the yearly compensation expense over the vesting period would be net of applicable income taxes. U.S. income tax regulations permit deductions for stock options, generally the excess of the market price at the time of exercise over the exercise price. Following fair value accounting rules, the compensation expense will be based on the option pricing model's valuation of the option at the grant date. Thus, the tax deductions will be at different amounts and at different times than the financial statement compensation expense.

The process is illustrated below. Recall the transaction to record the compensation expense in year 2000, 2001 and 2002 was:

Dr. Compensation Expense (E)	(inc.) 4,695,703	
Cr. Additional Paid-in Capital-Options (OE)		(inc.) 4,695,703

[3]This example is taken from SFAS No. 123.

Assuming a 35 percent federal tax rate, the entry to establish the deferred tax asset each year over the vesting period would look like this:

Dr. Deferred tax asset (A)	(inc.) 1,643,496	
Cr. Deferred tax expense (E)		(dec.) 1,643,496

The net aftertax effect on net income is thus $3,652,207 per year ($4,695,703 – $1,643,496).

If the options are all exercised in 2005, when the stock price is 70, the entry based upon 821,406 shares will be as follows:

Dr. Cash (A)	(inc.) 41,070,300	
Dr. Additional Paid-in Capital — Options (OE)	(dec.) 14,087,108	
Cr. Capital Stock* (OE)		(inc.) 55,157,408

*(divided appropriately between common stock and other paid-in capital)

The difference between the market price of the stock on the exercise date and the exercise price is deductible for tax purposes. Thus ($70 – $50) × 821,406 or $16,428,120 is deductible; therefore, the tax benefit realized on the tax return is $16,428,120 × 0.35, or $5,749,842. The accounting entries are

Dr. Deferred tax expense (E)	(inc.) 4,930,488	
Cr. Deferred tax asset (A)		(dec.) 4,930,488

to reverse the cumulative effect of the three years of deferred tax entries in years 2000, 2001, and 2002 and:

Dr. Current taxes payable (L)	(dec.) 5,749,842	
Cr. Current tax expense (E)		(dec.) 4,930,488
Cr. Additional paid-in capital — Stock options (OE)		(inc.) 819,354

to recognize the tax benefit of the options that are deductible when the options are exercised.

Options that vest partially over time — for example, 25 percent the first year, 25 percent the second year, and 50 percent the third year — are simply treated as if they were three different options. Each would have its own vesting and exercise periods and its own option valuation.

Some stock option plans are based upon performance measures such as revenues, profits, or share of market. The maximum number of options is specified at the grant date and then a schedule is established specifying how many options vest by Year 1 if various performance targets are met, how many options vest by Year 2, and so on. For such performance-based stock options, the application of the fair-value based method of accounting requires an assumption of expected performance. Adjustments to these estimates would be made over the life of the performance period (which corresponds to the vesting period). Thus, the compensation costs of performance-based stock options are based on valuations using appropriate option pricing models and at performance levels estimated by management on a prospective basis. Employee stock purchase rights are also included in SFAS No. 123. An example of such a disclosure, taken from Appendix B of SFAS No. 123, is presented in Exhibit 14A.2, together with disclosures of simple stock option plans and a performance-based plan.

Let's step through the disclosure. The first paragraph is key. If the company adopts the fair-value based method of accounting for stock options, the compensation cost will include the amortized portion of stock options granted, including options granted in an earlier period. If the company had elected not to follow the fair value method,

EXHIBIT 14A.1

Stock Option Plan Disclosure

At December 31, 2006, the Company has four stock-based compensation plans, which are described below. The Company applies APB Opinion 25 and related Interpretations in accounting for its plans. Accordingly, no compensation cost has been recognized for its fixed stock option plans and its stock purchase plan. The compensation cost that has been charged against income for its performance-based plan was $6.7 million, $9.4 million, and $0.7 million for 2004, 2005, and 2006, respectively. Had compensation cost for the Company's four stock-based compensation plans been determined based on the fair value at the grant dates for awards under those plans consistent with the method of FASB Statement No. 123, the Company's net income and earnings per share would have been reduced to the pro forma amounts indicated below:

		2004	2005	2006
Net income	As reported	$347,790	$407,300	$479,300
	Pro forma	$336,828	$394,553	$460,398
Primary earnings per share	As reported	$1.97	$2.29	$2.66
	Pro forma	$1.91	$2.22	$2.56
Fully diluted earnings per share	As reported	$1.49	$1.73	$2.02
	Pro forma	$1.44	$1.68	$1.94

Source: *FASB Statement of Financial Accounting Standards No. 123, Accounting for Stock-Based Compensation* is copyrighted by the Financial Accounting Standards Board, 401 Merritt 7, P.O. Box 5116, Norwalk, CT 06856-5116, U.S.A. Portions are reprinted with permission. Copies of the complete document are available from the Financial Accounting Standards Board.

then the first paragraph would be replaced with one like that shown in Exhibit 14A.1 (the reference to APB Opinion No. 25 is to the earlier accounting standard employing the intrinsic-value based method). It is here that the company would disclose the pro forma impact of SFAS No. 123 on net income and EPS.

The disclosure in Exhibit 14A.2 describes each of the company's stock-based plans. Note that the level of detail is such that any reader equipped with their own Black-Scholes valuation model could test the sensitivity of the valuations, although they could not recreate the actual compensation expenses because some of the other assumptions made by management, such as projected forfeiture rates, have not been disclosed. Note that the fair value of the options granted under the Fixed Stock Option Plan was $15.90 in 2004 and $16.25 under the Performance-Based Stock Option Plan:

Fiscal Year 2004

	Shares	Value	Total
Fixed stock options	900,000	$15.90	$14,310,000
Performance-based options	850,000	16.25	13,812,500
			$28,122,500

This $28.1 million is not the same as the $23.3 million compensation expense in 2004 (see next page) for the stock-based plan for several reasons:

- The 2004 awards vest over time, not immediately on the award date.
- Awards from earlier years may have vesting periods that span 2004.
- Management has made certain assumptions about forfeitures that reduce the estimated cost.

EXHIBIT 14A.2

Stock Option Plan Disclosures: Fair-Value Method

Stock Compensation Plans

At December 31, 2006, the Company has four stock-based compensation plans, which are described below. The Company accounts for the fair value of its grants under those plans in accordance with FASB Statement 123. The compensation cost that has been charged against income for those plans was $23.3 million, $28.7 million, and $29.4 million for 2004, 2005, and 2006, respectively.

Fixed Stock Option Plans

The Company has two fixed option plans. Under the 1999 Employee Stock Option Plan, the Company may grant options to its employees for up to 8 million shares of common stock. Under the 2004 Managers' Incentive Stock Option Plan, the Company may grant options to its management personnel for up to 5 million shares of common stock. Under both plans, the exercise price of each option equals the market price of the Company's stock on the date of grant and an option's maximum term is 10 years. Options are granted on January 1 and vest at the end of the third year under the 1999 Plan and at the end of the second year under the 2004 Plan.

The fair value of each option grant is estimated on the date of grant using the Black-Scholes option-pricing model with the following weighted-average assumptions used for grants in 2004, 2005, and 2006, respectively: dividend yield of 1.5 percent for all years; expected volatility of 24, 26, and 29 percent, risk-free interest rates of 6.5, 7.5, and 7 percent for the 1999 Plan options and 6.4, 7.4, and 6.8 percent for the 2004 Plan options; and expected lives of 6, 5, and 5 years for the 1999 Plan options and 5, 4, and 4 years for the 2004 Plan options.

A summary of the status of the Company's two fixed stock option plans as of December 31, 2004, 2005, and 2006, and changes during the years ending on those dates is presented below:

	2004		2005		2006	
Fixed Options	**Shares (000)**	**Weighted-Average Exercise Price**	**Shares (000)**	**Weighted-Average Exercise Price**	**Shares (000)**	**Weighted-Average Exercise Price**
Outstanding at beginning of year	4,500	$34	4,600	$38	4,660	$42
Granted	900	50	1,000	55	950	60
Exercised	(700)	27	(850)	34	(800)	36
Forfeited	(100)	46	(90)	51	(80)	59
Outstanding at end of year	4,600	38	4,660	42	4,730	47
Options exercisable at year-end	2,924		2,873		3,159	
Weighted-average fair value of options granted during the year	$15.90		$17.46		$19.57	

The following table summarizes information about fixed stock options outstanding at December 31, 2006:

	Options Outstanding			Options Exercisable	
Range of Exercise Prices	**Number Outstanding at 12/31/06**	**Weighted-Average Remaining Contractual Life**	**Weighted-Average Exercise Price**	**Number Exercisable at 12/31/06**	**Weighted-Average Exercise Price**
$25 to 33	1,107,000	3.6 years	$29	1,107,000	$29
39 to 41	467,000	5.0	40	467,000	40
46 to 50	1,326,000	6.6	48	1,326,000	48
55 to 60	1,830,000	8.5	57	259,000	55
$25 to 60	4,730,000	6.5	47	3,159,000	41

continued

EXHIBIT 14A.2 concluded

Performance-Based Stock Option Plan

Under its Goals 2010 Stock Option Plan adopted in 2002, each January 1 the Company grants selected executives and other key employees stock option awards whose vesting is contingent upon increases in the Company's market share for its principal product. If at the end of 3 years market share has increased by at least 5 percentage points from the date of grant, one-third of the options under the award vest to active employees. However, if at that date market share has increased by at least 10 percentage points, two-thirds of the options under the award vest, and if market share has increased by 20 percentage points or more, all of the options under the award vest. The number of shares subject to options under this plan cannot exceed 5 million. The exercise price of each option, which has a 10-year life, is equal to the market price of the Company's stock on the date of grant.

The fair value of each option grant was estimated on the date of grant using the Black-Scholes option-pricing model with the following assumptions for 2004, 2005, and 2006, respectively: risk-free interest rates of 6.5, 7.6, and 7.4 percent; dividend yield of 1.5 percent for all years; expected lives of 6, 6, and 7 years; and volatility of 24, 26, and 29 percent.

A summary of the status of the Company's performance-based stock option plan as of December 31, 2004, 2005, and 2006, and changes during the years ending on those dates is presented below:

	2004		2005		2006	
Performance Options	**Shares (000)**	**Weighted-Average Exercise Price**	**Shares (000)**	**Weighted-Average Exercise Price**	**Shares (000)**	**Weighted-Average Exercise Price**
Outstanding at beginning of year	830	$46	1,635	$48	2,533	$51
Granted	850	50	980	55	995	60
Exercised	0		0		(100)	46
Forfeited	(45)	48	(82)	50	(604)	51
Outstanding at end of year	1,635	48	2,533	51	2,824	55
Options exercisable at year-end	0		780	46	936	47
Weighted-average fair value of options granted during the year	$16.25		$19.97		$24.32	

As of December 31, 2006, the 2.8 million performance options outstanding under the Plan have exercise prices between $46 and $60 and a weighted-average remaining contractual life of 7.7 years. The Company expects that approximately one-third of the nonvested awards at December 31, 2006, will eventually vest based on projected market share.

Employee Stock Purchase Plan

Under the 1987 Employee Stock Purchase Plan, the Company is authorized to issue up to 10 million shares of common stock to its full-time employees, nearly all of whom are eligible to participate. Under the terms of the Plan, employees can choose each year to have up to 6 percent of their annual base earnings withheld to purchase the Company's common stock. The purchase price of the stock is 85 percent of the lower of its beginning-of-year or end-of-year market price. Approximately 75 to 80 percent of eligible employees have participated in the Plan in the last 3 years. Under the Plan, the Company sold 456,000 shares, 481,000 shares, and 503,000 shares to employees in 2004, 2005, and 2006, respectively. Compensation cost is recognized for the fair value of the employees' purchase rights, which was estimated using the Black-Scholes model with the following assumptions for 2004, 2005, and 2006, respectively: dividend yield of 1.5 percent for all years; an expected life of 1 year for all years; expected volatility of 22, 24, and 26 percent; and risk-free interest rates of 5.9, 6.9, and 6.7 percent. The weighted-average fair value of those purchase rights granted in 2004, 2005, and 2006 was $11.95, $13.73, and $15.30, respectively.

Source: *FASB Statement of Financial Accounting Standards No. 123, Accounting for Stock-Based Compensation* is copyrighted by the Financial Accounting Standards Board, 401 Merritt 7, P.O. Box 5116, Norwalk, CT 06856-5116, U.S.A. Portions are reprinted with permission. Copies of the complete document are available from the Financial Accounting Standards Board.

ISSUES FOR DISCUSSION

D14.1 Assume that you and two of your friends are about to form a business. Anticipating a meeting with your attorney, what factors should you consider in deciding between establishing a partnership or forming a corporation? Why might these factors be important to your planning?

No personal liability, Corp → easier to raise capital. limited liability.

D14.2 Point: Treasury stock should be accounted for as an asset; after all, a company's resources must be expended to repurchase the shares.

Counterpoint: Treasury stock should be accounted for as a contra owners' equity account in that the shares held in the treasury represent a reduction in the total shares outstanding.

Comment on the two viewpoints. Which one makes most sense to you, and why?

D14.3 Point: Investors who have agreed to buy shares in a growing company and who have signed notes for their stock subscriptions represent real stockholders, and their notes should be counted as assets and equity, even though they have not yet been paid in cash. That, after all, is what accrual accounting is all about.

Counterpoint: Stock subscriptions should not be recorded as assets because the funds are not available for the company's use until the notes are paid. We should treat notes receivables from stockholders differently than we treat notes from customers or creditors because the notes do not arise in the ordinary course of business. More importantly, the users of the financial statements are entitled to assume that shareholders' equity is really in place and is fully ready to absorb the deepest layer of business risk facing the company.

Comment on the two viewpoints. Which one makes the most sense to you, and why?

D14.4 What does the expression "vote with their feet" mean to you? Why should it be necessary for shareholders to vote with their feet? What message might management look for from such a voting process?

D14.5 Brown-Foreman Corporation has class A and class B common shares outstanding. Both the A and the B shares carry a par value of $0.15, and both are paid the exact same dividend. The shares appear to be the same in every respect, except that the class A shares have a vote, whereas the class B shares do not. There are 12 million class A shares outstanding and 26.6 million class B shares outstanding. In the last quarter of 1990, the class A shares traded in a range between $75 and $$57\frac{1}{2}$ a share; the class B shares traded in a range between $$78\frac{7}{8}$ and $$58\frac{3}{8}$ per share. Why would the company have these two classes of common stock outstanding? Would you expect the two classes to trade in the market at the same or at different prices? How would you interpret the price data in this case? What are the implications of that data for other companies that might be contemplating a two-class stock program?

D14.6 In 1988 the directors of Schuchardt Software Systems, Inc., declared a 2,000-for-1 stock split. SSS, Inc., a California-based publisher of business software, was organized in 1983, and each founding stockholder paid $5,000 per share. At that time, 84 individuals purchased stock in the company. Since then, the founding shareholders have sold a few shares between themselves at prices varying between $5,800 and $6,800 a share. The company is preparing itself for its initial offering of stock to the public.

Required:

a. Why would the directors decide on a 2,000-for-1 split?

b. Assume that the presplit par value of the company's stock was $100 per share. How could the company account for the stock split? (Provide an entry.)

c. According to a company spokesperson, at the time of the stock split announcement, Schuchardt had not yet earned any income. Would this fact change your answer to part (b) above?

d. Assume that the company declared a 2,000 percent stock dividend instead of a stock split. How would you account for the stock dividend? (Provide an entry.)

D14.7 Georgia Pacific Corporation made the comment below in its 1990 annual report to shareholders:

> **Dividends and Share Repurchases** In the past five years, we have distributed approximately $1.7 billion to our shareholders through a combination of dividends and stock repurchases.
>
> Our policy is to pay dividends at a rate of approximately one-third of sustainable earnings, recognizing the cyclical nature of our business. Following four consecutive years with fourth-quarter dividend increases, we left our quarterly dividend unchanged in 1990.
>
> We view the dividend payout in conjunction with our share repurchase program. Our board of directors authorized a share repurchase program that began in 1987 as a means of distributing excess cash to our shareholders and maintaining our ratio of debt to capital within a target range, currently set at 40 to 45 percent. In 1989, for example, cash provided by operations exceeded our capital expenditures and dividend payments by $729 million. Of this free cash flow, $468 million was used to repurchase 9.7 million shares of common stock. This brought total share repurchases since 1987 to 26.2 million at a cost of $1.1 billion.
>
> In October 1989 we suspended our share repurchase program, anticipating the higher leverage that resulted from the Great Northern Nekoosa acquisition. Our board's authorization to repurchase shares remains in effect, however, and we expect to resume our share repurchase program after we reduce debt to an appropriate level.

Required:

a. Is the company justified in its position that dividends and share repurchases should be considered in the same way? Why or why not?

b. How are they the same and how are they different in their impact on the company?

c. How are they the same and how are they different in their impact on the shareholders?

D14.8 Quick Start, Inc., had a public offering of stock in 1991, and as a result, it had 250,000 common shares outstanding. Because of its need for cash, the company had never paid a dividend. Quick Start had been moderately successful, but it was subject to the seasonality that affected the automobile industry. Results for the last five years were as follows (in thousands):

Year	Net Income	Cash Flow from Operations
1991	$20,000	$32,000
1992	8,000	14,000
1993	12,000	15,000
1994	16,000	20,000
1995	19,000	22,000

The company has debt and lease commitments that require about $18,000,000 a year. Its capital expansion plans are now at a level at which they could be met by additional borrowing, and the company has open credit lines of $75,000,000 available. Retained earnings are $90,000,000.

Because of pressure from the public stockholders, Quick Start's board of directors is considering making a dividend payment in 1996.

Required:

a. Outline all of the factors you might want the board to address as it considers the possibility of making a dividend payment. How much should the 1996 dividend be?

b. Suggest and justify a range of per share amounts that the board might consider.

PROBLEMS

P14.1 Stock issuances and dividend payments. Mesa Corporation was incorporated on January 1, 1993, and issued the following stock, for cash:

1,000,000 shares of no-par common stock were authorized; 100,000 shares were issued on January 1 at $18 per share.

200,000 shares of $1 par value, 10 percent cumulative preferred stock were authorized, and 50,000 shares were issued on January 1, 1995, at $14 per share.

The year 1995 went relatively well. Net income was $700,000, and the board of directors declared dividends of $200,000 and paid them by year end.

Required:

Prepare the entries required to record the issuances of the shares of stock and the payment of the dividends.

P14.2 Issuing stock to the founders. Three entrepreneurs have come together to exploit an invention that one of them recently patented. The inventor has very little cash, but he is willing to put his patent into the venture. Similarly, the second entrepreneur has very little cash, but he has a manufacturing plant he can contribute to the venture. (The plant is presently vacant but can be used to manufacture the inventor's product. The plant was recently appraised as having a value of between $180,000 and $225,000.) The third entrepreneur has plenty of cash, and she is willing to put $200,000 into the new venture. They agree to form a corporation and that each will receive 2,000 shares of common stock for the contributions of cash, the building, and the patent.

Required:

Prepare the entries required to record the issuance of the stock. Explain your rationale for the entries you made and the numbers you used.

P14.3 Preferred stock characteristics. Netway Corporation has four issues of preferred stock outstanding in addition to its common stock. All of these issues are detailed in the following footnote. Describe in your own words the characteristics of each of these preferred stock issues.

Netway Corporation and Subsidiaries

10. Capital Stock
The number of shares of capital stock outstanding is as follows:

	December 31	
	1995	**1994**
5% Cumulative preferred — $50 par value. Authorized, 585,730.	**407,718(a)**	407,718(a)
$5.50 Dividend cumulative convertible preferred — no par value — $20 stated value (each share convertible into 4.5 shares of common; maximum liquidation value, $3,252,900 and $3,476,800). Authorized, 1,164,077.	**32,529**	34,768
$4.50 Dividend cumulative preferred — $100 par value. Authorized, 103,976.	**103,976**	103,976
$4.30 Dividend cumulative preferred — no par value — $100 stated value. Authorized, 1,069,204.	**836,585**	836,585
Common — $1 par value. Authorized, 60,000,000.	**22,414,564(b)**	22,404,494(b)
After deducting treasury shares		
(a) 5% cumulative preferred	**178,012**	178,012
(b) Common	**4,822,088**	4,822,066

P14.4 Stock splits. The following table was taken from Brown-Foreman's 1995 annual report and was titled Consolidated Selected Financial Data. Notice the 3-for-1 stock split in 1994. Why doesn't this show up in the earnings per share figures, or does it? Where else does it show up? Explain.

(Expressed in thousands, except per share amounts and ratios)

Operations	For Fiscal Year Ended April 30, 1995	1994	1993
Net sales	$1,679,630	1,628,482	1,658,426
Excise taxes	$ 259,418	263,693	277,152
Net sales less excise taxes	$1,420,212	1,364,789	1,381,274
Gross profit	$ 823,904	790,245	791,490
Operating income	$ 267,785	240,361	255,382
Interest income	$ 1,903	3,984	3,113
Interest expense	$ 22,630	17,195	15,918
Income before cumulative effect of accounting changes	$ 148,629	161,069	156,190
Cumulative effect of accounting changes	$ —	(32,542)	—
Net income	$ 148,629	128,527	156,190
Weighted-average common shares outstanding	68,996	78,657	82,664
Earnings per common share:			
Income before cumulative effect of accounting changes	$ 2.15	2.04	1.88
Cumulative effect of accounting changes	$ —	(0.41)	—
Net income	$ 2.15	1.63	1.88
Cash dividends per common share	$ 0.97	0.93	0.86
Common stock splits		3-for-1	

P14.5 Treasury stock transactions. Smith Company has sold stock to its employees and to outsiders at various times during its life, as follows:

1990	100,000 shares originally sold at par value for $100,000 in cash.
1990	10,000 shares issued to an employee as an inducement to sign an employment contract; no cash exchanged.
1991	25,000 shares sold to an independent investor for $50,000 in cash.
1992	100,000 shares sold to a group of 25 investors at $30 a share.
1993	A 2-for-1 stock split declared.
1994	500,000 shares sold in a public offering through Merrill Lynch at $25 a share.
1995	100,000 shares given to the top management as a bonus. The market price was then $20.

In 1996 the company purchased 50,000 shares on the open market at $12 a share.

Required:

a. Prepare the entry required to record the 50,000 share purchase, assuming the company plans to reissue the shares as a bonus to its employees at a future date.

b. Prepare the entry required to record the share purchase, assuming the company plans to retire the reacquired shares.

P14.6 Convertible preferred stock. In 1995 Clever Corp. raised $1,000,000 in capital by the sale of 10,000 shares of convertible preferred stock, par value $100. The preferred stock required an annual dividend of only $4 a share even though the prime rate at the time was

8 percent. Each share of preferred stock was convertible into five shares of Clever common stock, which had a market value of $10 at the time of the preferred stock issuance.

Required:

a. Prepare the entry to record the sale of the preferred stock. How would you propose to recognize the value of the conversion feature in the financial statements? Please provide the rationale for your answer.

b. Why would Clever want to issue convertible preferred instead of regular preferred or additional common stock? less dividends, conserve cash.

c. Why would an investor buy the Clever convertible preferred when it pays only a $4 dividend?

P14.7 Convertible preferred, revisited. In 1996 all of the holders of Clever Corp. convertible preferred stock (discussed in P14.6) turned in their shares for conversion and were given five shares of common stock for each share of preferred stock.

Required:

a. Why would the holders of the preferred stock turn their shares in for redemption at this time?

b. What entry would Clever Corp. make at the time of the conversion?

P14.8 Stock options. Aggressive Corporation was doing very well with its new product line, and it seemed as though the company could double in size over the next three years. It was a tense time for the management people, however, and the good fortune brought its own questions. Do we have enough inventory to meet demand? Should we expand the plant to accommodate one more assembly line? If we encourage sales by granting extended credit terms, how will we pay our own bills? Nonetheless, management had worked very hard for a long time with very little reward, and members were delighted to bask in the prospects of the future. The board of directors was pleased, too, and at the end of the year awarded the top five people stock options, which would enable each of them to buy 10,000 shares of the company's stock at $9, the current market price. It was indeed a happy new year.

Required:

a. Why might Aggressive's board of directors have believed it appropriate to issue the stock options to the top management people at this time at $9 a share?

b. How might you feel about the stock options if you were one of the top management people? Why? How might you feel if you were a nonmanagement shareholder in the company?

c. Assuming SFAS No. 123 is not yet applicable, prepare the entry required to recognize the issuance of the options at the issue date. Explain the reasons for your entry.

d. Now assume that SFAS No. 123 is applicable and that the value of the options is calculated to be $2.15. What accounting would be required?

P14.9 Stock options exercised. Three years after Aggressive's board of directors issued the stock options to its top five employees (see P14.8) the company's sales had grown nearly three times and profits were up 250 percent. The stock market had recognized the company's success, and the shares regularly traded at $32. Three of the top five employees exercised their options in full, but the other two had not as yet done so.

Required:

a. Prepare the entries required under both the intrinsic-value based method and the fair value method of accounting to recognize the exercise of the options for 30,000 shares. Explain the rationale for your entry and then explain the source of your numbers.

b. What factors might have motivated the three management people to have exercised their stock options? What factors might have motivated the other two to hold on to the options, at least for the time being?

P14.10 Describing stock options. Seagram Company, Ltd., began a stock option program for its employees in 1989. The status of the program, as of the end of each of the last three years, is described in footnote 3 to the company's 1990 report to stockholders as follows:

	Twelve Months Ended January 31,		
Stock Option Activity	**1991**	**1990**	**1989**
Options outstanding at the beginning of the period	1,357,025	830,975	—
Granted	1,025,125	870,660	855,035
Average grant price	$77.75	$69.75	$54.37
Exercised	(191,950)	(291,285)	—
Average exercise price	$63.62	$54.37	—
Canceled	(90,180)	(53,325)	(24,060)
Options outstanding at the end of the period	2,100,020	1,357,025	830,975
Average exercise price	$70.58	$64.00	$54.37
Exercisable	1,106,545	507,015	—
Shares reserved for options at the end of the period	2,416,745	3,351,690	4,169,025

Under the company's employee stock option plan, options may be granted to purchase the company's common shares at not less than the fair market value of the shares on the date of the grant. The options become exercisable commencing one year from the grant date and expire 10 years after the grant.

Required:

In your own words, describe the events depicted by each of the line items in the table from the footnote. What do the numbers in the table mean? What might the sources of those numbers be?

P14.11 Accounting for stock warrants. Poorboy had been through difficult years, but management was hopeful that the recent financial restructuring and product reorganization would turn things around. The company needed cash to carry out its new strategy, but the banks had refused any further credit extension. The stock was trading at an all-time low, around $2.50 per share. (Interestingly, the par value of the company's common stock was also $2.50.) An investment adviser suggested that the company consider selling warrants. After some negotiation, the adviser helped the company sell 1,000,000 warrants, each good for the purchase of a share of common stock at $5 in eight years. The warrant sale raised $500,000.

Required:

a. Why might the market pay $500,000 for warrants to purchase Poorboy's stock at $5 a share eight years from now when the company has been through such difficult times and when that same market has concluded that the company's common stock is worth only $2.50?

b. Prepare the entry required to record the sale of the warrants. Explain the rationale for your entry and your numbers.

P14.12 Stock warrant redemptions. Five years after Poorboy's reorganization and its sale of warrants, things were finally looking up. Sales were growing, earnings were up very nicely, and cash flow was finally looking strong. The common stock was trading at about $10 a share. Management looked for a place to put the excess cash flow and decided to buy some of the company's stock back. An investment adviser suggested buying the warrants back because the same impact on the outstanding common stock could be had with a little less cash outflow. (The warrants were then trading at about $6.25.) Poorboy published an offer to buy and subsequently did purchase all of the outstanding warrants at $7.50 each.

Required:

a. Prepare the entry to record the purchase of the warrants, assuming they will be retired after acquisition.

b. Prepare the entries that would have been required had the company purchased $7,500,000 of common stock instead of the warrants and had all warrant holders tendered their warrants for conversion.

c. What do you think of the company's warrant buyback?

P14.13 Stock compensation programs. Footnote 10 from the annual report to shareholders from the Snap-On Tools Corporation reads as follows:

Note 10 Corporation Stock Option and Purchase Plans

The corporation has a stock option plan for directors, officers, and key employees with expiration dates on the options ranging from 1996 to 2004. The plan provides that options be granted at exercise prices equal to market value on the date the option is granted.

	Number of Shares	Option Price Per Share
Options outstanding at December 28, 1991	1,890,032	$20.56–38.13
Granted	150,025	33.75–34.75
Exercised	(151,116)	20.56–35.50
Surrendered	(54,934)	20.56–38.13
Options outstanding at January 2, 1993	1,834,007	20.56–38.13
Granted	532,619	31.75–35.00
Exercised	(361,057)	20.56–35.50
Surrendered	(106,905)	20.56–35.50
Options outstanding at January 1, 1994	1,898,664	20.56–38.13
Granted	40,500	36.75–37.25
Exercised	(203,445)	20.56–35.00
Surrendered	(182,502)	20.56–31.75
Options outstanding at December 31, 1994	**1,553,217**	**$20.56–38.73**
Shares reserved for future grants	**1,738,093**	
Shares exercisable at December 31, 1994	**1,498,004**	

The corporation offers shareholders a convenient way to increase their investment in the corporation through a no-commission dividend reinvestment and stock purchase plan. Participating shareholders may invest the cash dividends from all or a portion of their common stock to buy additional shares. The program also permits shareholders to invest cash for additional shares that are purchased for them each month. For 1994, 1993, and 1992, shares issued under the dividend reinvestment and stock purchase plan totaled 17,991, 15,485, and 17,587. At December 31, 1994, 933,501 shares were reserved for issuance to shareholders under this plan.

Employees of the corporation are entitled to participate in an employee stock purchase plan and are entitled to purchase shares up to the maximum allowed by the Internal Revenue Code. The purchase price of the common stock is the lesser of the closing market price of the stock on the beginning date (May 15th) or ending date (May 14th) of each plan year. The board of directors may terminate this plan at any time. For 1994, 1993, and 1992, shares issued under the employee stock purchase plan totaled 43,205, 44,563, and 66,554. At December 31, 1994, shares totaling 94,282 were reserved for issuance to employees under this plan, and the corporation held contributions of approximately $1.3 million for the purchase of common stock.

Franchised dealers are entitled to participate in a dealer stock purchase plan. The purchase price of the common stock is the lesser of the closing market price of the stock on the beginning date (May 15th) or ending date (May 14th) of each plan year. For 1994, 1993, and 1992, shares issued under the dealer stock purchase plan totaled 50,126, 4,683, and 348. At December 31, 1994, 144,843 shares were reserved for issuance to franchised dealers under this plan, and the corporation held contributions of approximately $1.5 million for the purchase of common stock.

In 1993, shareholders approved the Directors' 1993 Fee Plan. Under this plan, nonemployee directors receive a mandatory minimum of 25 percent and an elective maximum of up to 100 percent of their fees and retainer in shares of corporation stock. Directors may elect to defer receipt of all or part of these shares. For 1994 and 1993, shares issued under the Directors' Fee Plan totaled 1,545 and 184. Additionally, receipt of 602 and 1,004 shares were deferred in 1994 and 1993. At December 31, 1994, 196,665 shares were reserved for issuance to directors under this plan.

Required:

Comment on each of the following:

a. From the company's perspective, what is the purpose of each of these five stock plans?

b. How do the programs differ in terms of impact on the participants and on the company?

c. What accounting is afforded each of the programs?

P14.14 Shareholders' equity on a per share basis. Hercules Incorporated presents selected financial data as the first page of its annual report to stockholders. You will note that it reports stockholders' equity per share as $41.35 as of December 31, 1990. In a later section of the report, the company presents the market prices of its stock for the past two years. That table reports that the stock closed at $31⅝ on December 31, 1990.

	1990	1989	1988	1987	1986
For the year					
Net sales	$3,199.9	$3,091.7	$2,802.1	$2,693.0	$2,615.1
Profit (loss) from operations	190.1	(121.3)	129.7	176.9	185.4
Income (loss) before cumulative effect of changes in accounting principles	96.0	(96.4)	120.4	820.7	226.7
Net income (loss)	96.0	(81.3)	120.4	820.7	226.7
Dividends	105.0	103.6	92.9	98.5	93.8
Per share of common stock					
Earnings (loss) before cumulative effect of changes in accounting principles	2.04	(2.09)	2.55	14.74	4.02
Earnings (loss)	2.04	(1.76)	2.55	14.74	4.02
Dividends	2.24	2.24	2.00	1.84	1.72
Research and development	92.2	78.5	74.4	73.8	71.1
Depreciation	191.1	179.3	144.9	134.4	125.3
Capital expenditures	272.6	292.6	251.0	205.0	256.9
At year-end					
Working capital	692.0	615.6	949.2	1,299.0	660.1
Current ratio	1.8	1.7	2.8	3.6	2.6
Property, plant, and equipment — at cost	3,063.6	2,924.5	2,349.3	2,153.2	2,240.2
Total assets	3,699.6	3,653.2	3,325.3	3,492.1	2,914.3
Long-term debt	601.0	575.7	428.6	488.5	546.1
Stockholders' equity	1,942.0	1,897.2	2,044.5	2,189.9	1,703.2
per share	41.35	40.77	44.58	44.88	31.11
Common shares outstanding	47.0	46.5	45.9	48.8	54.8
Number of common stockholders	25,342	26,015	27,080	25,995	26,733
Number of employees	19,867	23,290	22,718	23,152	25,120

Required:

Explain why the stockholders' equity per share as reported in the selected financial data is not the same as the closing market price. What might cause the difference between the two numbers?

P14.15 Shareholder transactions. Wal-Mart's 1995 annual report contained the following statement of consolidated changes in shareholders' investment:

(Amounts in millions except per share data)	Number of Shares	Common Stock	Capital in Excess of Par Value	Retained Earnings	Foreign Currency Translation Adjustment	Total
Balance — January 31, 1992	1,149	$115	$626	$ 6,249	$ —	$ 6,990
Net Income				1,995		1,995
Cash dividends ($0.11 per share)				(241)		(241)
Two-for-one stock split	1,150	115	(115)			—
Other	1		16			16
Balance — January 31, 1993	2,300	230	527	8,003	—	8,760
Net Income				2,333		2,333
Cash dividends ($0.13 per share)				(299)		(299)
Other	(1)		9	(50)		(41)
Balance — January 31, 1994	2,299	230	536	9,987	—	10,753
Net Income				2,681		2,681
Cash dividends ($0.17 per share)				(391)		(391)
Foreign currency translation adjustment					(256)	(256)
Other	(2)		3	(64)		(61)
Balance — January 31, 1995	2,297	$230	$539	$12,213	$(256)	$12,726

Required:

a. Is Wal-Mart's common stock no par or par? Explain.

b. Explain to a stockholder owning 100 shares of stock just what happened in the two-for-one stock split in 1992.

P14.16 Shareholders' transactions with treasury stock. Footnote 5 from the 1989 annual report of the H. J. Heinz Company follows:

	Cumulative Preferred Stock — Third, $1.70 First Series $10 par	Common Stock — Issued		Common Stock — In Treasury		Additional Capital
(In thousands)	Amount	Amount	Shares	Amount	Shares	Amount
Balance April 30, 1986	$1,141	$71,850	143,700	$227,374	10,283	$ 85,882
Reacquired	—	—	—	236,165	5,471	—
Conversion of preferred into common stock	(171)	—	—	(1,295)	(77)	(1,124)
Stock options exercised	—	—	—	(10,430)	(619)	4,763
Reduction in par value of common stock	—	(35,925)	—	—	—	35,925
Other, net	—	—	—	166	3	—
Balance April 29, 1987	$ 970	$35,925	143,700	$451,980	15,061	$125,446
Reacquired	—	—	—	123,519	2,703	—
Conversion of preferred into common stock	(128)	—	—	(972)	(58)	(843)
Stock options exercised	—	—	—	(27,598)	(1,638)	11,013
Other, net	—	—	—	809	14	269
Balance April 27, 1988	**$ 842**	**$35,925**	**143,700**	**$547,738**	**16,082**	**$135,885**
Reacquired	—	—	—	**97,508**	**2,056**	—
Conversion of preferred into common stock	**(85)**	—	—	**(693)**	**(38)**	**(608)**
Conversion of subordinated debentures	—	—	—	**(30,906)**	**(1,150)**	**3,784**
Stock options exercised	—	—	—	**(35,379)**	**(1,756)**	**6,293**
Other, net	—	—	—	**1,390**	**25**	**236**
Balance May 3, 1989	**$ 757**	**$35,925**	**143,700**	**$579,658**	**15,219**	**$145,590**
Authorized Shares — May 3, 1989	**76**	—	**600,000**	—	—	—

Capital Stock: The preferred stock outstanding is convertible at a rate of one share of preferred stock into 4.5 shares of common stock. The company can redeem the stock at $25.50 per share.

In September 1986 the shareholders approved an increase to the authorized common stock of the company from 300,000,000 shares to 600,000,000 shares and changed the par value of the common stock from 50 cents per share to 25 cents per share.

On May 3, 1989, there were authorized, but unissued, 2,200,000 shares of third cumulative preferred stock for which the series had not been designated.

Required:

For each of the five transactions highlighted above:

a. Describe in your own words the underlying event, explaining in particular (1) the factor(s) that triggered the event and (2) the probable source of the numbers used.

b. Prepare the probable entry(ies) that were required.

P14.17 Stock for debt exchange. In 1989 RJR Nabisco, Inc., was taken private by Kohlberg Kravis Roberts & Co. in a leveraged buyout. As part of the buyout, RJR Nabisco issued large amounts of high-yield "junk bonds." For example, one part of the leveraged buyout involved the issuance of $2.86 billion of 17 percent bonds due in 2007.

Beginning in late 1990, KKR & Co. began efforts to reduce the level of debt carried on the books of RJR Nabisco. One such proposal involved the issuance of 82.8 million shares of RJR stock and $350 million of cash in exchange for $753 million (face value) of the 17 percent bonds.

Assume that the RJR Nabisco stock has a par value of $1; the stock, being privately held, has no readily determined market value; and the bonds are trading at their face value.

Required:

a. Why would the company make that exchange at this time?

b. What entry would the company make at the time of the exchange?

c. What entry would be made if the bonds were trading at $830 rather than $1,000 face value?

P14.18 Paying stock dividends. The following disclosures, pertinent to a General Host Corporation declaration of a stock dividend, were made in the company's fiscal 1994 annual report.

Consolidated Statements of Changes in Shareholder's Equity

(Dollars in thousands)	Shares of Common Stock		Common Stock Issued	Capital in Excess of Par Value	Retained Earnings	Cost of Common Stock in Treasury	Notes Receivable from Exercise of Stock Options	Total Shareholders' Equity
	Issued	In Treasury						
Balance at January 31, 1993	31,752,450	(13,676,692)	31,752	88,937	165,405	(129,640)	(2,096)	154,358
Net loss					(56,060)			(56,060)
Cash dividends					(7,422)			(7,422)
Stock dividends		1,000,788		(3,106)	(6,380)	9,486		
Acquisition of equity interest In Sunbelt Nursery Group, Inc.		1,940,000		(686)		18,389		17,703
Note repayments							135	135
Balance at January 30, 1994	31,752,450	(10,735,904)	31,752	85,145	95,543	(101,765)	(1,961)	108,714
Net income					8,585			8,585
Stock dividend declared on March 1, 1995		1,054,307		(3,668)	(6,326)	9,994		
Restricted stock grants issued		68,300		(306)		648		342
Issuance of common stock		1,800		(8)		17		9
Balance at January 29, 1995	31,752,450	(9,611,497)	$31,752	$81,163	$ 97,802	$ (91,106)	$(1,961)	$117,650

Note 1 (In Part): Accounting Policies
Subsequent to fiscal 1994 a 5% stock dividend was declared by the Board of Directors for shareholders of record on March 17, 1995. The stock dividend is payable on April 7, 1995 and all stock related data in the consolidated financial statements reflect the stock dividend for all periods presented.

Required:

a. What entry did the company make as of the fiscal year ended January 29, 1995?

b. The company's footnote states that the stock dividend is payable April 7, 1995 to shareholders of record on March 17, 1995. Both of these dates are *after* the fiscal year end. What rationale prompted the company to book the stock dividend in fiscal 1994 anyway?

P14.19 Convertible preferred stock. On August 16 *The Wall Street Journal* carried an advertisement concerning Baker Hughes. The following is from that advertisement: "Baker Hughes Incorporated has called for redemption of all its $3.50 Convertible Preferred Stock."

According to the advertisement, Baker Hughes had decided to exercise the redemption feature on its outstanding preferred stock and to redeem the stock at a price of $52.45 per share plus accrued dividends of $0.16, for a total of $52.61, on August 31. The preferred stock also carried a conversion feature that would permit the owner to convert the preferred stock into 1.9608 shares of common stock (par value of $1). The market price of the common stock on August 13 was $32.625 per share. The advertisement emphasized that the conversion feature of the preferred stock expired on August 27.

Required:

a. Assume that Baker Hughes has 1 million shares of preferred stock outstanding and that its par value is $5. How would the company account for (1) the redemption of all shares and (2) the conversion of all shares?

b. If you held 100 shares of Baker Hughes preferred stock, which alternative (conversion or redemption) would you choose, and why?

c. If you were the CEO of Baker Hughes, which alternative would you prefer, and why?

P14.20 Translation of foreign financial statements. Graham International, Inc., is a subsidiary of a U.S.-based corporation, The Graham Group. Graham International is headquartered in Mexico City, Mexico, although it represents the parent company worldwide.

Presented below are Graham International's income statement for 19X5, expressed in pesos, and its balance sheets as of December 31, 19X4, and December 31, 19X5, also expressed in pesos. Assume the exchange rate between the Mexican peso and the U.S. dollar was as follows:

12/31/X4	$0.0004 (1 peso = $0.0004 U.S.)
12/31/X5	$0.00036 (1 peso = $0.00036 U.S.)
19X5 average	$0.00038

Graham International had been in existence since 19X2, when it was capitalized with an investment of 3,000,000 pesos. At that time, the exchange rate was 1,800 pesos to the U.S. dollar. Since then, the company has earned (after taxes and dividends) 15,000,000 pesos, with a translation value of $7,500 U.S.

Required:

a. Prepare the translated (in U.S. dollar equivalents) financial statements of Graham International, Inc., at December 31, 19X5.

b. Determine the balance (if any) required in the Translation Adjustment account for the equity section of The Graham Group's 19X5 balance sheet.

Graham International, Inc.
Statement of Income
For the Year Ended December 31, 19X5
(in thousands of pesos)

Sales	82,000
Less: Costs and expenses	
Costs of sales	42,000
Depreciation	4,050
Selling, general, and administrative expenses	7,250
Interest	2,500
	55,800
Net income before taxes	26,200
Less: Income taxes	13,300
Net income	12,900
Dividends paid to parent (12/31/X5)	1,500

Graham International, Inc.
Balance Sheet
As of December 31
(in thousands of pesos)

	19X4	19X5
Assets:		
Cash	2,000	3,000
Accounts receivable	6,000	7,400
Inventory	7,000	10,000
Total current assets	15,000	20,400
Plant and equipment	39,000	42,000
Less: Accumulated depreciation	(4,950)	(9,000)
Net plant and equipment	34,050	33,000
Total assets	49,050	53,400
Equities:		
Liabilities		
Accounts payable	6,050	4,000
Long-term debt	25,000	20,000
Total	31,050	24,000
Owners' equity:		
Capital stock	3,000	3,000
Retained earnings	15,000	26,400
Total	18,000	29,400
Total equities	49,050	53,400

P14.21 Stock options. On January 1, 1997, Biotrack, Inc., planned to announce a new employee stock option program under which certain officers, directors, and employees would be eligible to purchase the company's $1 par value common shares. The details were as follows:

1. A total of 900,000 options to be awarded
2. Market price of shares at grant date: $60.00
3. Option price: $60.00

4. Expiration date: January 1, 2005

5. Expected exercise date: 3 years after vesting

6. Vesting: 1/3 on January 1, 1998
   1/3 on January 1, 1999
   1/3 on January 1, 2000

7. Estimated forfeitures: 2%/year

8. Volatility on company shares: 20%

9. Risk free borrowing rate: 5%

10. Dividend rate: 3%

Assume that Biotrack has opted to adopt the fair-value based method of accounting for stock options. Ignore income taxes.

(The following table may be used in this problem. It is based on a Black-Scholes option pricing model adapted for dividends, and it assumes a 5 percent borrowing rate and a 3 percent dividend payout rate.)

Black-Scholes Options Pricing Model
Adapted for Dividends
Assumptions: 5% Borrowing Rate, 3% Dividend Payout

		Expected Lifetime in Years							
		1	2	3	4	5	6	7	8
Volatility	0.15	3.38	4.89	6.04	6.97	7.74	8.40	8.97	9.45
	0.18	3.85	5.53	6.78	7.78	8.61	9.30	9.89	10.39
	0.20	4.33	6.17	7.52	8.60	9.48	10.21	10.82	11.33
	0.23	4.80	6.80	8.26	9.41	10.35	11.11	11.75	12.28
	0.25	5.27	7.44	9.01	10.23	11.21	12.01	12.67	13.22
	0.28	5.75	8.08	9.75	11.04	12.07	12.91	13.59	14.15
	0.30	6.22	8.71	10.48	11.85	12.93	13.80	14.51	15.08
	0.33	6.69	9.35	11.22	12.65	13.78	14.68	15.41	15.99

Required:

a. What entry should the company make on January 1, 1997, when the options are granted? What entry is made at year-end 1997?

b. What entry is made to record the compensation expense associated with these options for the fiscal year 1998?

c. Suppose that the assumption as to forfeiture was reduced on January 1, 1999. It now appeared that there would be 290,000 options vesting as of December 31, 1999. What entry is made to record the compensation expense associated with these options for the fiscal year 1999?

d. Suppose that 400,000 options were exercised during December 2000, when the average market price was $80.00. What entry would the company make?

e. Suppose that 400,000 options were exercised during December 2001, when the average market price was $90.00. What entry should the company make?

f. Suppose that the last of the options to be exercised, 55,000, were exercised during December 2002, when the average market price was $100.00. What entry would the company make?

g. Over the whole program, how many options were exercised? How many were canceled or lapsed? What was the overall effect on owner's equity? What other entries would be necessary?

P14.22 Stock options subject to income tax deductions. Refer to problem P14.21. Assume that Biotrack's planned stock option program can be structured so that the corporation is eligible to deduct the excess of the market value of the stock, on the day of exercise, over the exercise price on their income tax return.

Required:

a. What entry should the company make on January 1, 1997, when the options are granted? What entry is made at year-end 1997?

b. What entry is made to record the compensation expense associated with these options for the fiscal year 1998?

c. Suppose that the assumption as to forfeiture was reduced on January 1, 1999. It now appeared that there would be 290,000 options vesting as of December 31, 1999. What entry is made to record the compensation expense associated with these options for the fiscal year 1999?

d. Suppose that 400,000 options were exercised during December 2000, when the average market price was $80.00. What entry would the company make?

e. Suppose that 400,000 options were exercised during December 2001, when the average market price was $90.00. What entry would the company make?

f. Suppose that the last of the options to be exercised, 55,000, were exercised during December 2002, when the average market price was $100.00. What entry would the company make?

g. Over the whole program, how many options were exercised? How many were canceled or lapsed? What was the overall effect on owner's equity? What other entries would be necessary?

CASES

C14.1 Two classes of stock: World Wide, Inc. World Wide, Inc., had almost completed its acquisition program. It had acquired companies in the raw material segment of its industry, in the fabrication segment, and most recently in the distribution segment. Management bristled at the suggestion that the company was becoming a conglomerate; they preferred to think of it as a fully integrated company. Still, the company's stock price had languished, and some critics on Wall Street had begun to question its strategy. There was talk that the company would be worth more in parts than it was in total.

Lindsey Toma, the chief financial officer, was very concerned about activity in the company's stock. It appeared that someone was accumulating a block of stock, perhaps with the intention of instituting a raid. Toma suggested at a meeting of the World Wide board that it adopt some defensive strategies. She said, "We have worked very hard to build this company, and we are close to realizing the potential of our plans. If we fail to act defensively now, some raider will be able to come in and reap the benefits of our work before the stock price rewards our long-time stockholders for their patience."

The company's attorney urged the board to look into the possibility of creating a two-class stock arrangement. He said he knew of a number of two-class situations, and he promised to find some good examples. Later that day, he sent all of the members of the board copies of pertinent portions of a recent annual report for Dow Jones & Company and a *Business Week* article (reproduced on the following pages) that reported on a challenge to two-class stock plans.

The attorney's letter transmitting these two documents made two other points for perspective:

- The SEC had adapted some rules regarding two-stock plans, but those rules address only the most seriously disenfranchising plans. He said he was confident that his law firm could come up with a plan much like the Dow Jones Plan that would clear the SEC rule.
- The Dow Jones class B stock was originally issued a few years earlier as a 50 percent stock dividend. He urged the board to authorize him to begin drafting such a plan for World Wide.

You have been a member of the board of World Wide for the last five years, and you have agreed with the acquisition program because you believe that the economies available to an integrated company will pay real benefits. However, you also have been concerned that the acquisitions have not come together as well as had been predicted, and you have become a little impatient with management's promises that the payoff is just around the corner.

Your academic training in economics has been a strong influence in your business life. You have been a passionate advocate for free market forces and have resisted the efforts of World Wide management to claim tariff protection from offshore competition.

Required:

Study the material in the exhibits and outline the advantages and disadvantages of adopting a two-class stock plan for World Wide. How will you vote if such a plan is eventually recommended to the board by the attorney?

Dow Jones & Co.
Recent Annual Report Excerpts

	19X2	19X1
Stockholders' equity:		
Common stock, par value $1 per share; authorized 135,000,000 shares; issued 78,626,190 shares in 19X2 and 77,961,638 shares in 19X1	**78,626**	77,962
Class B common stock, convertible, par value $1 per share; authorized 25,000,000 shares; issued 23,554,831 shares in 19X2 and 24,219,383 shares in 19X1	**23,555**	24,219
	102,181	102,181
Additional paid-in capital	**150,031**	149,557
Retained earnings	**1,185,426**	940,989
	1,437,638	1,192,727
Less: Treasury stock at cost, 1,355,892 shares in 19X2 and 1,345,560 shares in 19X1	**32,437**	32,152
Total stockholders' equity	**1,405,201**	1,160,575
Total liabilities and stockholders' equity	**$2,688,336**	$2,111,781

Note 8: Capital Stock

The common stock and class B common stock have the same dividend and liquidation rights. The class B common stock has 10 votes per share and free convertibility into common stock on a one-for-one basis and can be transferred in class B form only to members of a stockholder's family and certain others affiliated with a stockholder.

The SEC's Tough Call on One Share, One Vote

Call it "junk stock." That's the label Roland M. Machold, the State of New Jersey's portfolio manager, has pinned on the rash of common stock being issued with limited voting rights — or none at all. "In the absence of a vote, you have to look at what a security is. It's nothing," says Machold, who also is co-chairman of the Council of Institutional Investors, a group of more than 40 public and private pension funds. With no leverage on companies to maintain returns, "It's worse than junk bonds," he adds.

Such objections were the focus of Securities & Exchange Commission hearings on Dec. 16–17 that examined the New York Stock Exchange's proposal to drop its one-share, one-vote rule in favor of one permitting multiple classes of common stock. But the argument transcends the issue of stock value and attendant voting rights. It's the focus of a controversy about who should control Corporate America.

MEDIA BLITZ. The debate comes as both large and small shareholders — not just gadflies — are showing greater interest in how companies operate, forcing disinvestment in South Africa or demanding compliance with environmental laws. "The old Wall Street rule — vote with your feet — is being replaced with a more activist role. I think that shareholders are just starting to recognize their responsibility to vote," notes Lawrence S. Speidell, trustee and portfolio manager for Batterymarch Financial Management in Boston, which always votes against multiclass stock proposals.

The SEC faces a tough decision. It is under pressure from a wide range of interests to turn thumbs down on the Big Board proposal. The opposition ranges from the Council of Institutional Investors to Senator Howard Metzenbaum (D-Ohio) to ordinary shareholders.

Takeover artist T. Boone Pickens Jr. has mounted a media and mailing campaign against the proposal and formed a group called the United Shareholders' Association. "You are witnessing the ultimate in takeovers," he says. He argues that abandoning one share, one vote lets management take over companies internally by concentrating voting power in the hands of friendly stockholders.

Even NYSE Chairman John J. Phelan Jr. appears uneasy about the proposal. While he thinks the Big Board shouldn't dictate recapitalization decisions, he says, "I like my right to vote, whether I exercise it or not." But exchange officials feel they have little choice. Some of the best-known names on the Big Board, including General Motors Corp. and Dow Jones & Co., have adopted multiple classes of common stock and would have to be delisted if the rules aren't changed.

The NYSE has put a temporary hold on delisting for violations of the rule, and more companies may issue nonvoting stock for a variety of reasons. Moreover, without a rule change, NYSE companies could flee to the American Stock Exchange or the over-the-counter market, which allow dual classes.

American Stock Exchange chairman Arthur Levitt Jr. told commissioners he shares some of Phelan's concerns, even though he wants further easing of AMEX rules on dual-class listings. "Public shareholder voting is a key element of corporate accountability," he said as he pleaded for some shareholder safety standard. Commissioner Joseph A. Grundfest, remarking on the exchanges' dilemma, joked, "You're asking us to stop you before you kill again."

Despite the pervasive qualms, an unpublished SEC staff study of 65 cases of dual-class common stock could buttress agency approval of the rule change. "There is no evidence that the dual-class recapitalizations we have seen have been against shareholder interests," says Gregg A. Jarrell, the SEC's chief economist and co-author of the study.

The SEC study suggests that dual classes of stocks haven't been used often by widely held public companies. In 54 of the 65 companies, "insider holdings," usually with a family, accounted for an average of 50 percent of the outstanding stock before the recapitalization plan was announced. Share prices weren't hurt by the change, according to the study, though Jarrell wouldn't predict future price behavior. And proponents of the rule change argue that family-run companies should be able to use equity financing while retaining corporate control.

WHICH WAY? The commissioners' cautious questioning at the hearing makes it hard to tell which way they will go, though Chairman John S. R. Shad has in the past backed the idea of one share, one vote. An NYSE requirement that multiple listings be approved by a majority of current holders and independent directors may satisfy the commissioners. Or, worried that Congress may override an attempt to end the NYSE tradition, the SEC could revive efforts to encourage the exchanges to devise uniform voting standards. The commission may also O.K. the NYSE proposal on the ground that states have traditionally handled internal corporate-governance issues.

The commissioners' decision, which could come as early as March, will be a wrenching one — with broad consequences. "Dual-class stock is perhaps the most violent of developments to date regarding shareholders' rights," says Robert A. G. Monks, president of Institutional Shareholder Services Inc., a Washington-based consulting group. "Once the shareholders have been disenfranchised by a company, there's no way to reverse it."

By Vicky Cahan, with Patricia Kranz, in Washington and Anthony Bianco in New York

---

C14.2 Performance-oriented stock: General Motors. In 1984 and 1985 General Motors acquired Electronic Data Systems (EDS) and Hughes Aircraft Company (Hughes), giving cash and newly created shares of stock, GM-E and GM-H, respectively. The notes in the 1990 GM financial statements describe those transactions as follows:

Acquisitions and Intangible Assets

Effective December 31, 1985, the corporation acquired Hughes Aircraft Company (Hughes) and its subsidiaries for $2.7 billion in cash and cash equivalents and 100 million shares of General Motors Class H common stock having an estimated total value of $2,561.9 million and carrying certain guarantees.

The acquisition of Hughes was accounted for as a purchase. The purchase price exceeded the net book value of Hughes by $4,244.7 million, which was assigned as follows: $500.0 million to patents and related technology, $125.0 million to the future economic benefits to the Corporation of the Hughes Long-Term Incentive Plan (LTIP), and $3,619.7 million to other intangible assets, including goodwill. The amounts assigned to the various intangible asset categories are being amortized on a straight-line basis: patents and related technology over 15 years, the future economic benefits of the Hughes LTIP over five years, and other intangible assets over 40 years. Amortization is applied directly to the asset accounts.

For the purpose of determining earnings per share and amounts available for dividends on common stocks, the amortization of intangible assets arising from the acquisition of Hughes is charged against earnings attributable to $1⅔ par value common stock. The effect on the 1990, 1989, and 1988 earnings attributable to $1⅔ par value common stock was a net credit (charge) of $24.9 million, $17.8 million, and ($31.6) million, respectively, consisting of the amortization of the intangible assets arising from the acquisition, the profit on intercompany transactions, and the earnings of GMHE attributable to $1⅔ par value common stock.

On October 18, 1984, the corporation acquired Electronic Data Systems Corporation (EDS) and its subsidiaries for $2,501.9 million. The acquisition was consummated through an offer to exchange EDS common stock for either (a) $44 in cash or (b) $35.20 in cash plus two-tenths of a share of Class E common stock plus a nontransferable contingent promissory note issued by GM. This note is payable seven years after closing in an amount equal to .2 times the excess of $31.25 over the market price of the Class E common stock at the maturity date of the note. Contingent notes were issued in denominations termed "Note Factors," each of which represents five contingent notes. Holders were allowed to tender their notes for prepayment at discounted amounts beginning in October 1989. There are currently approximately 21.0 million contingent notes issued and outstanding. The maximum possible liability to the corporation for such notes is approximately $654.7 million.

If the market price of Class E common stock at the maturity date of the notes were to equal the market price at December 31, 1990, $38.625 a share, no additional consideration for contingent notes outstanding at December 31, 1990, would be required.

The acquisition of EDS was accounted for as a purchase. The purchase price in excess of the net book value of EDS, $2,179.5 million, was assigned principally to existing customer contracts, $1,069.9 million, computer software programs developed by EDS, $646.2 million, and other intangible assets, including goodwill, $290.2 million. The cost assigned to these assets is being amortized on a straight-line basis over five years for computer software programs (fully amortized in 1989), about seven years for customer contracts, 10 years for goodwill, and varying periods for the remainder. Amortization is applied directly to the asset accounts.

For the purpose of determining earnings per share and amounts available for dividends on common stocks, the amortization of these assets is charged against earnings attributable to $1⅔ par value common stock. The effect on the 1990, 1989, and 1988 earnings attributable to $1⅔ par value common stock was a net charge of $111.3 million, $225.1 million, and $286.1 million, respectively, consisting of the amortization of the intangible and other assets arising from the acquisition less related income tax effects, the profit on intercompany transactions, and the earnings of EDS attributable to $1⅔ par value common stock.

Both of those companies have been quite successful. GM management described the results of EDS and Hughes in the management discussion and analysis section of its 1990 annual report as follows:

Electronic Data Systems Corporation

Reflecting the continued strong growth of its non-GM business, Electronic Data Systems Corporation (EDS) achieved another record performance in 1990. Separate consolidated net income of EDS rose 14.2 percent to $496.9 million. Earnings per share attributable to Class E common stock were $2.08, up from $1.81 in 1989 and $1.57 in 1988, and are based on the Available Separate Consolidated Net Income of EDS (described in Note 10 to the Financial Statements).

EDS continues as the world leader in systems integration and communications services. Sales to sources outside GM and its affiliates rose 16.9 percent in 1990 to $2,787.5 million, reflecting EDS's continued success in obtaining new business as well as growth through acquisitions. Additionally, EDS continued to assist GM in a variety of automation projects being implemented in the corporation's factories and offices.

continued

EDS financial statements do not include the amortization of the $2,179.5 million initial cost to GM of EDS customer contracts, computer software programs, and other intangible assets, including goodwill, arising from the acquisition of EDS by GM in 1984. This cost, plus the $343.2 million cost of contingent notes purchased in 1986, less certain income tax benefits, was assigned principally to intangible assets, including goodwill, and is being amortized by GM over the estimated useful lives of the assets acquired. Such amortization was $205.7 million in 1990, $348.9 million in 1989, and $386.6 million in 1988.

For the purpose of determining earnings per share and amounts available for dividends on common stocks, such amortization is charged against earnings attributable to GM's $1⅔ par value common stock. The effect of EDS operations on the earnings attributable to $1⅔ par value common stock was a net charge of $111.3 million in 1990, $225.1 million in 1989, and $286.1 million in 1988, consisting of the previously described amortization less related income tax benefits, profit on intercompany transactions, and the earnings of EDS attributable to $1⅔ par value common stock. The net charge does not reflect any estimate of the savings realized by GM from the installation of new computer systems within GM operations.

Summary Financial Data — EDS

(Dollars in millions except per share amounts)	Years Ended December 31, 1990	1989	1988
Revenues			
Systems and other contracts			
GM and affiliates	$3,234.2	$2,988.9	$2,837.0
Outside customers	2,787.5	2,384.6	1,907.6
Interest and other income	87.1	93.3	99.5
Total revenues	6,108.8	5,466.8	4,844.1
Costs and expenses	5,320.1	4,786.5	4,254.7
Income taxes	291.8	245.0	205.3
Separate consolidated net income	$ 496.9	$ 435.3	$ 384.1
Available separate consolidated net income*	$ 194.4	$ 171.0	$ 160.3
Average number of shares of Class E common stock outstanding (in millions)	93.5	94.5	101.8
Earnings attributable to Class E common stock on a per share basis	$ 2.08	$ 1.81	$ 1.57
Cash dividends per share of Class E common stock	$ 0.56	$ 0.48	$ 0.34

*Separate consolidated net income of EDS multiplied by a fraction, the numerator of which is the weighted average number of shares of Class E common stock outstanding during the period and the denominator of which is currently 239.3 million shares. The denominators during 1989 and 1988 were 238.7 million and 243.8 million shares, respectively. Available Separate Consolidated Net Income is determined quarterly.

GM Hughes Electronic Corporation

Earnings of GM Hughes Electronics Corporation (GMHE) declined 7.1 percent to $726.0 million, while revenues increased 3.2 percent to a record $11,723.1 million. Earnings per share attributable to Class H common stock were $1.82 in 1990, compared with $1.94 in 1989 and $2.01 in 1988, and are based on the Available Separate Consolidated Net Income of GMHE (described in Note 10 to the Financial Statements).

Earnings were down slightly as the result of reduced defense spending, lower motor vehicle production volumes, and a higher effective tax rate, which were only partially offset by ongoing cost reduction efforts and increased electronic content in GM vehicles.

GMHE is the world leader in automotive and defense electronics and in commercial communications satellites. GMHE also provides direct support to GM through projects to automate the corporation's factories and by supplying components and technologies for GM vehicles.

Both of GMHE's principal subsidiaries — Hughes Aircraft Company and Delco Electronics Corporation — achieved revenue increases in 1990. This improvement reflected growth in the commercial market for business communications networks and increasing demand for electronic components and systems in cars and trucks. In addition, these GMHE subsidiaries continued to pursue new business opportunities by entering into joint ventures and teaming arrangements with other companies. Included was the formation of a subsidiary, H E Microwave Corporation, to manufacture high-technology electronics for both automotive and military applications.

For the purpose of determining earnings per share and amounts available for dividends on common stocks, the amortization of intangible assets arising from the acquisition of Hughes in 1985 is charged against earnings attributable to GM's $1⅔ par value common stock. The effect of GMHE operations on the 1990, 1989, and 1988 earnings attributable to $1⅔ par value common stock was a net credit (charge) of $24.9 million, $17.8 million, and ($31.6) million, respectively, consisting of amortization of the intangible assets, profit on intercompany transactions, and the earnings of GMHE attributable to $1⅔ par value common stock. The net credit (charge) does not reflect any estimate of the savings and improvements in product development or plant operation resulting from the application of GMHE technology to GMs operations.

Summary Financial Data — GMHE

(Dollars in millions except per share amounts)	Years Ended December 31, 1990	1989	1988
Revenues			
Net sales			
Outside customers	$ 8,091.3	$ 7,647.7	$ 7,518.2
GM and affiliates	3,534.5	3,521.8	3,482.8
Other income — net	97.3	189.5	242.6
Total revenues	11,723.1	11,359.0	11,243.6
Costs and expenses	10,684.7	10,371.3	10,259.7
Income taxes	461.2	355.3	349.3
Income before cumulative effect of accounting change	577.2	632.4	634.6
Cumulative effect of accounting change	—	—	18.7*
Separate consolidated net income	577.2	632.4	653.3
Available separate consolidated net income			
Adjustments to exclude the effect of purchase accounting†	148.8	148.8	148.8
Earnings of GMHE, excluding purchase accounting adjustments	$ 726.0	$ 781.2	$ 802.1
Available separate consolidated net income‡	$ 160.0	$ 188.1	$ 256.9
Average number of shares of Class H common stock outstanding (in millions)	88.1	95.7	127.9
Earnings attributable to Class H common stock on a per share basis			
Before cumulative effect of accounting change	$1.82	$1.94	$1.96
Cumulative effect of accounting change	—	—	0.05
Net earnings attributable to Class H common stock	$1.82	$1.94	$2.01
Cash dividends per share of Class H common stock	$0.72	$0.72	$0.44

*Effective January 1, 1988, accounting procedures at Delco Electronics were changed to include in inventory certain manufacturing overhead costs previously charged directly to expense.

†Amortization of intangible assets arising from the acquisition of Hughes Aircraft Company.

‡Earnings of GMHE, excluding purchase accounting adjustments, multiplied by a fraction, the numerator of which is the weighted average number of shares of Class H common stock outstanding during the period and the denominator of which is currently 399.7 million shares. The denominator during 1989 and 1988 was 400.0 million shares. Available Separate Consolidated Net Income is determined quarterly.

Footnote 10 from the GM 1990 annual report explains how the company computes earnings per share for its three classes of common stock:

Note 10: Earnings (Loss) per Share Attributable to and Dividends on Common Stocks

Earnings (Loss) per share attributable to common stocks have been determined based on the relative amounts available for the payment of dividends to holders of $1⅔ par value, Class E, and Class H common stocks. Prior to 1990, the effect on earnings per share of $1⅔ par value common stock resulting from the assumed exercise of outstanding options, the delivery of stock awards, the assumed conversion of the preference shares discussed in Note 17, and the assumed exercise of the put options discussed in Note 1 were not material. However, for 1990, the loss per share attributable to $1⅔ par value common stock has been computed by dividing such loss by the average number of common and equivalent shares outstanding. The operations of the EDS and GMHE Incentive Plans and the assumed exercise of stock options do not have a material dilutive effect on earnings per share of Class E or Class H common stocks, respectively, at this time.

Dividends on the $1⅔ par value common stock are declared out of the earnings of GM and its subsidiaries, excluding the Available Separate Consolidated Net Income of EDS and GMHE.

Dividends on the Class E and Class H common stocks are declared out of the Available Separate Consolidated Net Income of EDS and GMHE, respectively, earned since the acquisition by GM. The Available Separate Consolidated Net Income of EDS and GMHE is determined

continued

quarterly and is equal to the separate consolidated net income of EDS and GMHE, respectively, excluding the effects of purchase accounting adjustments arising at the time of acquisition, multiplied by a fraction, the numerator of which is the weighted average number of shares of Class E or Class H common stock outstanding during the period and the denominator of which is currently 239.3 million shares for Class E and 399.7 million shares for Class H. The denominators during 1989 and 1988 were 238.7 million and 243.8 million shares, respectively, for Class E and 400.0 million shares for Class H.

The denominators used in determining the Available Separate Consolidated Net Income of EDS and GMHE are adjusted as deemed appropriate by the board of directors to reflect subdivisions or combinations of the Class E and Class H common stocks and to reflect certain transfers of capital to or from EDS and GMHE. In this regard, the board has generally caused the denominators to decrease as shares are purchased by EDS or GMHE and to increase as such shares are used at EDS or GMHE expense for EDS or GMHE employee benefit plans or acquisitions.

Dividends may be paid on common stocks only when, as, and if declared by the board of directors in its sole discretion. The board's policy with respect to $1⅔ par value common stock is to distribute dividends based on the outlook and the indicated capital needs of the business. At the February 4, 1991 meeting of the board, the quarterly dividend on the $1⅔ par value common stock was reduced from $0.75 per share to $0.40 per share. This action was taken as a part of a comprehensive cost-cutting and cash conservation program to strengthen GM's competitive position. The current policy of the board with respect to the Class E and Class H common stocks is to pay cash dividends approximately equal to 30 percent and 35 percent of the Available Separate Consolidated Net Income of EDS and GMHE, respectively, for the prior year. At the February 4, 1991, board meeting, the dividend on the Class E common stock was increased by 14 percent to a quarterly rate of $0.16 per share from a rate of $0.14 per share in 1990. The quarterly dividend on Class H common stock was continued at $0.18 per share.

GM's balance sheet and income statement from its 1990 annual report to stockholders are presented below. Read the above information and study the two GM financial statements.

Required:

a. How do the GM shareholders benefit from the results of EDS and Hughes? How do the holders of GM-E and GM-H shares benefit from the results of those two companies?

b. Why might GM have used these special shares in its acquisition program? What advantages did GM gain from the use of those special shares?

c. What operations and accounting problems might those shares have created for General Motors management? Outline your ideas for management of those problems.

General Motors
Statement of Consolidated Income*

(Dollars in millions except per share amounts)	1990	1989	1988
	Years Ended December 31,		
Net sales and revenues			
Manufactured products	$107,477.0	$109,610.3	$107,815.2
Financial services	11,756.3	11,216.9	10,664.9
Computer systems services	2,787.5	2,384.6	1,907.6
Other income	2,684.3	3,720.1	3,253.9
Total net sales and revenues	124,705.1	126,931.9	123,641.6
Costs and expenses			
Cost of sales and other operating charges, exclusive of items listed below	96,155.7	93,817.9	92,506.0
Selling, general, and administrative expenses	10,030.9	9,447.9	8,735.8
Interest expense	8,771.7	8,757.2	7,232.9
Depreciation of real estate, plants, and equipment	5,104.1	5,157.8	5,047.0
Amortization of special tools	1,805.8	1,441.8	1,432.1
Amortization of intangible assets	451.7	568.6	601.9
Other deductions	1,288.3	1,342.4	1,351.0
Special provision for scheduled plant closings and other restructurings	3,314.0	—	—
Total costs and expenses	126,922.2	120,533.6	116,906.7
Income (loss) before income taxes	(2,217.1)	6,398.3	6,734.9
United States, foreign, and other income taxes (credit)	(231.4)	2,174.0	2,102.8
Income (loss) before cumulative effect of accounting change	(1,985.7)	4,224.3	4,632.1
Cumulative effect of accounting change	—	—	224.2
Net income (loss)	(1,985.7)	4,224.3	4,856.3
Dividends and accumulation of redemption value on preferred and preference stocks	38.2	34.2	26.0
Earnings (loss) on common stocks	($ 2,023.9)	$ 4,190.1	$ 4,830.3
Earnings (loss) attributable to common stocks			
$1⅔ par value before cumulative effect of accounting change	($ 2,378.3)	$ 3,831.0	$ 4,195.0
Cumulative effect of accounting change	—	—	218.1
Net earnings (loss) attributable to $1⅔ par value	($ 2,378.3)	$ 3,831.0	$ 4,413.1
Class E	$ 194.4	$ 171.0	$ 160.3
Class H before cumulative effect of accounting change	$ 160.0	$ 188.1	$ 250.8
Cumulative effect of accounting change	—	—	6.1
Net earnings attributable to Class H	$ 160.0	$ 188.1	$ 256.9
Average number of shares of common stocks outstanding (in millions)			
$1⅔ par value	601.5	604.3	615.7
Class E	93.5	94.5	101.8
Class H	88.1	95.7	127.9
Earnings (Loss) Per Share Attributable to Common Stocks			
$1⅔ par value before cumulative effect of accounting change	($4.09)	$6.33	$6.82
Cumulative effect of accounting change	—	—	0.35
Net earnings (loss) attributable to $1⅔ par value	($4.09)	$6.33	$7.17
Class E	$2.08	$1.81	$1.57
Class H before cumulative effect of accounting change	$1.82	$1.94	$1.96
Cumulative effect of accounting change	—	—	0.05
Net earnings attributable to Class H	$1.82	$1.94	$2.01

Certain amounts for 1989 and 1988 have been reclassified to conform with 1990 classifications.

*Notes to financial statements not reproduced here.

General Motors
Consolidated Balance Sheet*

(Dollars in millions except per share amounts) **Assets**	December 31, 1990	1989
Cash and cash equivalents	$ 3,688.5	$ 5,625.4
Other marketable securities	4,132.9	4,587.9
Total cash and marketable securities	7,821.4	10,213.3
Finance receivables — net	90,116.2	92,354.6
Accounts and notes receivables (less allowances)	5,731.3	5,447.4
Inventories (less allowances)	9,331.3	7,991.7
Contracts in process (less advances and progress payments of $2,353.1 and $2,630.7)	2,348.8	2,073.3
Net equipment on operating leases (less accumulated depreciation of $2,692.6 and $3,065.9)	5,882.0	5,131.1
Prepaid expenses and deferred charges	4,751.6	3,914.7
Other investments and miscellaneous assets (less allowances)	7,252.5	5,050.2
Property		
Real estate, plants, and equipment — at cost	67,219.4	63,390.7
Less accumulated depreciation	38,280.8	34,849.7
Net real estate, plants, and equipment	28,938.6	28,541.0
Special tools — at cost (less amortization)	7,206.4	5,453.5
Total property	36,145.0	33,994.5
Intangible assets — at cost (less amortization)	10,856.4	7,126.3
Total assets	$180,236.5	$173,297.1
Liabilities and Stockholders' Equity		
Liabilities		
Accounts payable (principally trade)	$ 8,824.4	$ 7,707.8
Notes and loans payable	95,633.5	93,424.8
United States, foreign, and other income taxes	3,959.6	5,671.4
Other liabilities	38,255.2	28,456.7
Deferred credits (including investment tax credits — $723.0 and $915.4)	1,410.1	1,403.9
Total liabilities	148,082.8	136,664.6
Stocks subject to repurchase	2,106.3	1,650.0
Stockholders' Equity		
Preferred stocks ($5.00 series, $153.0; $3.75 series, $81.4)	234.4	234.4
Preference stocks (E $0.10 series, $1.0; H $0.10 series, $1.0 in 1989)	1.0	2.0
Common stocks		
$1⅔ par value (issued, 605,592,356 and 605,683,572 shares)	1,009.3	1,009.5
Class E (issued, 100,220,967 and 48,830,764 shares)	10.0	4.9
Class H (issued, 34,450,398 and 35,162,664 shares)	3.5	3.5
Capital surplus (principally additional paid-in capital)	2,208.2	2,614.0
Net income retained for use in the business	27,148.6	31,230.7
Subtotal	30,615.0	35,099.0
Minimum pension liability adjustment	(1,004.7)	—
Accumulated foreign currency translation and other adjustments	437.1	(116.5)
Total stockholders' equity	30,047.4	34,982.5
Total liabilities and stockholders' equity	$180,236.5	$173,297.1

Reference should be made to the notes to financial statements.

*Notes to financial statements not reproduced here.

C14.3 Trading stock with another corporation: Colorado Mining Corporation. Colorado Mining Corporation owned the mineral rights to a silver claim in the northeast corner of the state. The mine itself had been inactive for some time, although the rights had been bought and sold several times in the last five years. CMC had purchased the rights most recently from a group of Denver attorneys, paying $50,000 in cash and giving two notes totaling $250,000. One note, for $100,000, bore interest at 10 percent and was due in 12 months; the other, for $150,000, carried a 5 percent interest rate and was due in five years.

Immediately on taking possession of the claim, CMC regraded the access roads and cleared the accumulated debris from the property. It hired a maintenance worker who began to pump water from the mine so that it could be worked. He brought out a few samples and had them processed and evaluated by an independent laboratory; the results showed that the samples contained good quality ore, although in small traces. The company also sent out a photographic team who took pictures of the activity, and the president managed to get a Denver newspaper to run a story on CMC's plans for reactivating the mine. The company spent about $15,000 on this start-up activity.

Latenight Entertainment, Inc., had once been a high-flying record and video producer, but its stars had fallen out of favor and the company was now inactive. In its glory days, the stock had an active following and had once traded as high as $12. There was no trading now, although there were still 150,000 shares outstanding, and there was a stockholder list with 350 names.

CMC purchased the stockholder list from a company called Corporate Brokers, Inc., and sent the Latenight shareholders a proposal whereby CMC would exchange its mining claim in exchange for 850,000 shares of Latenight stock. It also proposed that the name "Latenight Entertainment, Inc." be changed to Colorado Mining Corporation. In the offering document sent to the Latenight shareholders, CMC stated that the mine had the potential to produce $3,000,000 worth of silver in the next five years. On that basis, the offering document stated that the property was worth at least $1,000,000 and that the value of the Latenight shares would be worth $1 after the exchange was consummated. The exchange was approved by a majority of Latenight shareholders, and the transaction was completed as planned.

Required:

a. What accounting would be appropriate for *all* of the above acquisitions and exchanges in the affected companies' accounts? Please explain your proposed accounting.

b. Why would CMC want to enter into this exchange? What would you expect the next step in its plan to be? How might your accounting in part (a) help or frustrate that plan?

C14.4 Foreign operations: Moon Computers, Inc. Moon Computers manufactures IBM-compatible personal computers (PC) and computer-based workstations. The production takes place in various offshore and domestic locations. Final assembly takes place at the company's main plant in California, which is where all customer shipments originate.

The sales price for the basic computer model to the company's distributors is $500. Occasionally, a large distributor negotiates a 10 percent discount as a result of a very large (250 units) order. Moon's full-absorption cost is about $375, and so there is not a great deal of negotiation room in the wholesale pricing.

In mid-1994 Shana Royo, the vice president of sales, took a vacation in Italy, ostensibly to look at art but also to taste the wine. Royo met an Italian industrialist, however, and the conversation went from art to wine to computers. Royo came home with an order for 1,000 basic machines. The Italian customer wanted Moon's standard PC and opted to make the purchase using Moon's normal five-year lease. The customer pushed hard on prices, and Royo agreed to terms that would recover full-absorption manufacturing cost as well as cover the cost of money over the lease term.

An order of this size was exciting but awesome. The company was not in a position to finance such a large lease program with internal funds. After some investigation, the management team came up with this approach:

1. A new Swiss subsidiary was set up to handle the transaction. The new company would borrow 375,000 Swiss francs from a local Swiss bank with repayment terms that matched the expected cash flow from the Italian lease. The loan carried a 5 percent interest rate.

2. The Swiss subsidiary bought the computers from the U.S. parent for $375 each, using the proceeds of the bank loan. (For purposes of this discussion, we will assume that the conversion rate of the dollar and the franc was 1:1 at the time of the sale.)

3. The lease, payable in lira, carried an implicit interest rate of 10 percent. At that rate (and assuming a franc-to-lira exchange rate of 1:4), the present value of the lease was 500,000 francs.

All of this was accomplished just before the end of 1994. As a result of this transaction, the U.S. parent recorded an all-cash, break-even sale to its subsidiary. The Swiss subsidiary treated the lease as a sales-type lease and recorded a profit on the transaction of 125,000 francs. The following is the subsidiary's income statement for the period ended December 31, 1994 (in Swiss francs):

Sales	500,000
Cost of sales	375,000
Swiss income tax	25,000
Net income	100,000

The following is from the Swiss subsidiary's balance sheet at December 31, 1994 (in Swiss francs):

Lease receivable	500,000
Loan payable	375,000
Taxes payable	25,000
Equity	100,000
Total liability and equity	500,000

The parent created an investment account, picking up the subsidiary's income as its initial investment.

Dr. Investment in Swiss Subsidiary (A)	(inc.) 100,000	
Cr. Subsidiary's income (R)		(inc.) 100,000

When the consolidated income statement was prepared, the parent's one-line income from the subsidiary was replaced with the subsidiary's sale of $500,000, cost of $375,000, and tax expense of $25,000. (Technically, the subsidiary's cost of sales of $375,000 was eliminated against the parent's sale so that the consolidated income statement reflected the subsidiary's $500,000 sale and the parent's manufacturing cost of $375,000.) When the consolidated balance sheet was prepared, the $100,000 investment in the subsidiary was expanded to reflect the lease receivable, the bank debt, and the tax payable. (This plan assumes that payments are due on December 31 each year.)

The planned workout of this transaction looked like this:

	Swiss Bank Loan (sf)			Italian Lease (l)		
		Applied to			Applied to	
Year	Total Payment	Principal	Expense	Total Payment	Principal	Income
1995	87	68	19	528	328	200
1996	87	71	15	528	360	167
1997	87	75	12	528	396	131
1998	87	79	8	528	436	92
1999	87	82	5	528	480	48
		375			2,000	

We are now getting ready to prepare Moon's consolidated financial statements for the year ended December 31, 1996. Assume that the exchange rates stayed the same throughout 1995 but that during 1996 the lira weakened so that at the end of the year it was 5 lira to the franc, and the dollar weakened so that at the end of the year a franc was worth $1.20. Assume that the lease and loan payments were made on time each year at December 31. Assume that the Swiss taxes due each year were paid (or are due) in March of the following year.

Required:

a. Develop the balance sheet and income statement for the Swiss subsidiary for the year ended December 31, 1996, and prepare the entries required to record the activities of the Swiss subsidiary in the parent's books.

b. Explain how the Swiss subsidiary's assets, liabilities, and results of operations will be presented in the Moon consolidated financial statements for the year ended December 31, 1996. To do this, you may want to prepare the consolidation entry that distributes the parent's investment in the Swiss subsidiary, or you may want to prepare the Swiss subsidiary's translated balance sheet and income statement, which will be required for the preparation of the U.S. consolidated financial statements.

PART IV

Special Considerations in Preparing and Using Accounting Data

CHAPTER 15

Financial Reporting in Two Other Countries

The major roadblock to foreign companies listing their . . . stock on U.S. exchanges has long been the big difference between accounting standards in the U.S. and abroad.[1]

Key Chapter Issues

- Are the financial reporting practices in other countries different from those adhered to in the United States? If so, in what ways do they differ?
- What are some of the contextual factors that shape a country's financial reporting practices?
- Is it possible to develop global financial reporting standards? To what extent has such a circumstance evolved?
- If I pick up the annual report of a non-U.S. company, at a minimum, what should I know in order to begin to understand it?

[1] L. Berton, "All Accountants Soon May Speak the Same Language," *The Wall Street Journal,* August 29, 1995, p. A15

With the existence of a global economy, the production, dissemination, and use of financial information is no longer restricted by national borders. The knowledge needed to interpret and understand foreign financial statements goes beyond merely acquainting oneself with the accounting methods and practices used in preparing the documents (though of course this is important). Even if complete standardization of international accounting practices were achieved — which is unlikely to happen for some time to come — one would still need important contextual information to assess the significance of a given piece of financial data. For example, what should we conclude if we find that the equity of a Japanese steel-making firm is only 10 percent of its total capitalization and its current ratio is 0.75? Contextualizing the information from other nations imposes special demands on both managers and investors. The premises on which financial data are constituted in other parts of the world are now a matter of crucial importance.

The focus of this chapter, thus, is on providing an overview of the financial reporting practices unique to two other countries. We will consider the contextual factors that influence those accounting practices.

CONTEXTUAL FACTORS

Tax and Political Environment

A fundamental issue in trying to understand the financial reporting practices used in other countries is the relationship between a country's financial reporting system and its tax law. In the United States and the United Kingdom, for example, the influence of tax provisions on the calculation of accounting income is minimal. Companies may report one set of figures in their financial statements and a substantially different set in their tax returns. In many other countries, however, taxable income is more closely related to accounting income. For example, in Japan and Germany, expenses must be recorded in the financial statements to qualify as deductible on a company's tax return.

The requirement that accounting and tax income be substantially the same naturally prompts companies to measure income as conservatively as legally possible. Certain expenses, most notably depreciation, are calculated according to legislative requirements instead of business experience. Consequently, accountants and auditors are less concerned with fair presentation than with legal compliance. Because tax law is formulated by nationalistic legislative bodies in response to varying political and economic agendas, its influence on financial reporting is one of the most obvious hindrances to establishing a common set of international reporting standards.

Although corporate tax law and its relationship to financial reporting have a more direct effect on accounting standards, individual tax laws are also a factor. Tax incentives for individuals are among the tools that governments use to encourage (or discourage) share ownership among small investors. As share ownership among small investors increases, so too does the demand for understandable, pertinent, and timely financial disclosures. Nations eager to develop stronger stock exchanges — Italy is a good example — are not only adjusting governmental regulation to ensure fair and free markets, they are also implementing shareholder-oriented financial reporting practices. If this trend persists, it is likely to move foreign accounting standards in the direction of the more extensive disclosure Anglo-American model.

Other legal and political factors impinge on accounting systems as well. For example, the role of government in formulating financial reporting principles and standards versus the private sector, the volatility of the political system (which may affect the frequency of reform), and the existence of external pressures (such as membership in the European Economic Community) on governments to revamp systems all affect a country's financial reporting practices.

Business Environment

Because modern notions of financial accountability result from the development of the publicly held corporation, with its separation of ownership and management, the dominant form of business in an economy can have a material effect on a country's financial reporting standards. In Italy, for example, the continuing prominence of small, family-owned companies (and large ones as well) has undoubtedly contributed to the slow development of public-minded financial reporting standards in that country. Although every developed nation recognizes some version of the publicly owned corporation as a primary business entity, the reporting requirements imposed on such companies vary widely. Company law in most countries distinguishes between public and closely held corporations and between "large" and "small" companies (however they may be defined) and adjusts reporting requirements accordingly.

The role and prominence of a country's capital markets is also a factor. The nature of financial reporting standards and the fundamental purpose of the entire reporting system depend on customary sources of capital. In such countries as Germany and Japan, where banks have long played a very powerful role in fueling economic growth, public financial disclosure tends to be deemphasized because these lenders (who are usually major investors as well) generally have access to internal corporate information. In addition to the banking system, the development of stock exchanges, the distribution of share ownership, the effectiveness of regulation, and the stringency of listing requirements have a powerful effect on financial reporting standards and the extent of disclosure.

A sophisticated and modern system of financial disclosure also requires an accounting profession that is well educated and large enough to ensure its proper functioning. This is readily apparent in countries such as the U.K. and the United States, where the accounting profession has significant responsibility for creating financial reporting standards. But even in nations where financial reporting standards are largely a matter of government legislation, the sophistication and training of the accounting profession noticeably affects the quality of financial reporting (usually because it serves as an adviser to the legislature and is itself charged with developing auditing standards). Swedish multinationals, for example, under the guidance of a professional elite, consistently publish some of the best annual reports in the world even though Swedish accounting standards are largely dictated by commercial law.

Cultural Environment

It is possible to argue that the culture of a particular country is the root influence on the nature of its legal, political, tax, business, and financial reporting systems. For example, in a very egalitarian society committed to a broad array of government social programs supported by an extensive corporate tax system (such as Sweden), the financial reporting disclosures required of companies will, in part, be geared toward highlighting a company's role in supporting that social agenda. Thus, in Sweden we see extensive tax and labor-related disclosures in the corporate annual reports. In another vein, consider a people's propensity for risk-taking and/or tolerance of uncertainty. Americans, as an example, are often noted as being very entrepreneurial — willing to take a risk. On the other hand, the Japanese are generally viewed as opting for tradition and therefore less likely to embrace change. Thus, in the United States we see financial reporting standards geared to the highlighting of business risks (such as SFAS No. 105) so that investors can make their own risk/return judgments, whereas in Japan no such disclosures are required; Japanese investors generally assume that their country's large corporations have the public's best interest at heart and that the Japanese government would not allow the companies to risk the peoples' or the nations' welfare.

One other example of culture's influence can be seen in a people's faith in those in positions of authority and power. If a populace (such as the Japanese) tends to honor and trust those in high leadership positions (such as heads of business), they will demand less sharing of insights and information from those leaders than will people who tend not to trust and honor those in high position (as in the United States). Such different contexts may, in part, account for quite different levels of financial disclosures across countries.

INTERNATIONALIZING ACCOUNTING STANDARDS

The desire to standardize international accounting standards has become a major focal point for multinational companies attempting to communicate with investors and lenders in foreign domains. With no universally accepted set of international financial reporting and disclosure guidelines, multinationals have responded with a variety of strategies ranging from merely translating the text of annual reports into various languages ("convenience translations") to preparing several sets of statements that report results in different languages and currencies according to different countries' accounting principles ("multiple reporting").

Obviously, financial reporting strategies that ignore differences in local accounting principles present problems for analysts and investors; those that take them into account require considerably more time and expense on the part of the preparer. Either way, someone must absorb the costs of divergent principles and standards of financial reporting, and generally it has been the multinational company. No wonder, then, that many multinationals are supporting **harmonization** of accounting practices because it promises to reduce the differences in financial reporting requirements across countries and to make investing more transparent and rational.

International Accounting Standards Committee

Among professional organizations that have greatly contributed to the codification of international accounting practice to date is the **International Accounting Standards Committee** (IASC). The IASC was founded in 1973 by a group of professional accounting organizations from nine countries and has since grown to include groups from about 80 nations. An association of professional accountancy bodies, the IASC is headquartered in London and is the most widely recognized professional group in charge of developing and issuing international accounting standards. The purpose of the IASC, as stated in its constitution, is as follows:

a. To formulate and publish in the public interest, accounting standards to be observed in the presentation of financial statements and to promote their worldwide acceptance and observance;
b. To work generally for the improvement and harmonization of regulations, accounting standards, and procedures relating to the presentation of financial statements.

Given the myriad political and technical barriers that hinder the harmonization process, the IASC has made considerable headway, issuing over 30 **international accounting standards** (each known as an IAS) since its founding.

Lacking the authority to enforce observance of its standards, the IASC has had to exercise considerable diplomacy and discretion both in formulating standards and in pushing for their adoption by national standard-setting bodies. It must continually weigh the benefits of greater uniformity in financial reporting practices against the social and economic costs of retooling accounting systems, and it must bear in mind that many financial reporting practices arise from legitimate local needs. Consequently, a typical IAS sets broad principles and leaves details of application to national officials. Often it allows alternative treatments and permits some adaptation to national circumstances.

The IASC has focused principally on obvious targets — financial reporting practices that are clearly arbitrary or unsound — in the belief that filtering out such practices is an important first step toward harmonization. In countries that have not yet issued financial reporting standards or that allow more than one accounting treatment of a given transaction, the IASC has urged local officials to adopt uniform practices consistent with existing international accounting standards. In short, rather than pushing toward complete uniformity, it has instead sought to reduce needless diversity.

Predictably, the IASC has drawn considerable criticism from some quarters. It has been accused of allowing industrialized nations to dominate the standard-setting process, of legislating with little regard for the needs of practitioners and financial analysts, and of serving multinationals and ignoring smaller domestic enterprises. The IASC, however, owes no allegiance to any nation and makes a point of including developing nations on its governing board. It consults with analysts, executives, managerial accountants, and industry groups as standards are developed, and it recognizes that the acceptance of each IAS depends on its usefulness to users and preparers of statements. Small domestic companies as well as giant multinationals are included in its jurisdiction, a fact that the IASC implicitly recognizes by trying to make its standards concise, clear, and simple enough to be useful around the world.

Two other complaints, somewhat broader in scope, are sometimes leveled against the IASC. The first and most common is that the IASC is ineffectual. The lack of an enforcement mechanism has undoubtedly slowed progress toward harmonization, but one can hardly blame the IASC itself for the limitations imposed on it by the politics of national sovereignty. In the endeavor in which the IASC may properly be held accountable — winning acceptance of its standards by dint of negotiation and consultation — the general consensus is that it is making significant progress. Moreover, the IASC has begun forging a close relationship with the International Organization of Securities Commissions (IOSCO), a body that does have enforcement power over its members. Thus, as IOSCO endorses IASC accounting standards as a minimal set of requirements for its member agencies (e.g., IAS No. 7 on statements of cash flows), the standards then have an enforcement mechanism not available via the IASC itself.

The other charge, made less frequently but more serious, is that the IASC is too concerned with technical conformity and not sensitive enough to the cultural and economic issues underlying national accounting systems. This is a more problematic charge, one that ultimately calls into question the feasibility of harmonization. It implicitly asks us to consider what level of reform is necessary for the creation of meaningful international standards. Is it enough to change an accounting system alone, or must legislation, economic habits, and even basic cultural attitudes be altered as well? This is a difficult question to answer because we simply do not yet know enough about the interaction between cultural contexts and financial reporting norms.

FINANCIAL REPORTING IN TWO FOREIGN COUNTRIES

The remaining pages of this chapter provide an introduction to the reporting practices and contextual issues of two countries: Japan and the United Kingdom. Of necessity, the discussion of each will be brief but, we hope, enlightening.

Japan

Although scholars have devised several classifications of international financial reporting systems, Japan's system is difficult to fit into any particular global grouping. Largely because of the cultural differences between Japan and most other developed nations, its system bears no kinship to another system in the way that the American and British systems or the Swiss and German systems, for example, are related. Although Japanese financial reporting practices may share certain technical features in common with foreign systems, it is equally true that a variety of unique cultural factors condition the actual application of its methods in a way that sets Japanese financial reporting apart from its Western analogues.

Cultural environment. Japanese corporations, except for a handful of unusually progressive firms that cultivate an international image, tend to reveal much less in their financial statements than their American counterparts. Beyond providing translations of statements, most Japanese multinationals do little to accommodate foreign readers (or Japanese readers, for that matter). It is still rare to find Japanese corporate financial results restated in accordance with U.S. GAAP; nor do the Japanese provide much supplementary information in notes. For example, the recent financial statements of Nippon Kokan (NKK), a steel-making and shipbuilding concern, include just over three pages of notes, probably half of which provide only general explanations of accounting policies with little or no reference to actual numbers. (NKK's recent summary of accounting policies appears in Exhibit 15.1.) Needless to say, many foreign investors and financial analysts have complained about such a cautious approach to sharing financial information.

One of Japan's most pervasive and influential cultural features is *dantai ishiki,* or group consciousness, with its related social values of interdependence and harmony. This cultural value profoundly affects the nature of Japanese business relationships and conditions attitudes toward external reporting of financial results. It has become widely known in the West, for example, that Japanese group consciousness creates a level and quality of loyalty within business organizations rarely seen in other cultures, and that it can often cut across lines of loyalty that we would consider normal. For example, Japanese unions tend to be organized by company and corporate group rather than by trade, suggesting that the members' hierarchy of loyalties is not the same as, say, a U.S. teamster or coal miner. What may be less appreciated by a Westerner is that, as a result, the Japanese expect business relationships to proceed on the basis of implicit and mutual trust rather than on the basis of legally mandated disclosure. "Fairness" in financial reporting — that elusive yet indispensable concept undergirding the attest function in the United States — in Japan is more apt to be measured by the needs of the immediate corporate community than by appeal to the judgment of

EXHIBIT 15.1

Nippon Kokan K.K.
Notes to Financial Statements

1. SUMMARY OF SIGNIFICANT ACCOUNTING POLICIES

(a) Basis of preparation

The accompanying financial statements include only the accounts of NIPPON KOKAN K.K. (the "company"). The accounts of its subsidiaries are not consolidated.

The accompanying financial statements have been prepared from accounts and records maintained by the company in accordance with the provisions set forth in the Commercial Code of Japan and in conformity with generally accepted accounting principles and practices in Japan. Certain items presented in the original financial statements have been reclassified for the convenience of readers outside Japan.

As permitted by the Commercial Code of Japan, amounts less than one million yen have been omitted. As a result, the totals shown in the accompanying financial statements do not necessarily agree with the sum of the individual amounts.

(b) Foreign Currency

All assets and liabilities denominated in foreign currencies other than those that were covered by forward exchange contracts are translated into Japanese yen at the historical rates. All revenues and expenses associated with foreign currencies are translated at the rates of exchange prevailing when such transactions are made. Translation gains and losses are credited or charged to income currently. Translation gains and losses arising from long-term forward exchange contracts are deferred and amortized over the remaining lives of those contracts.

(c) Recognition Basis of Sales and Profit on Contracts

The company has principally adopted the completed contract method for the recognition of sales and gross profit on contracts. Under this method, sales and gross profit applicable to each contract are not recorded until construction is completed and delivery is made to customers.

In the case of installment contract sales, profit on such sales is recognized in the period in which installment payments become due. The amounts of such deferred profits are included in other current liabilities in the accompanying balance sheets. Related amounts are charged (or credited) to cost of sales.

(d) Securities

Marketable and investment securities are carried at cost or less. Appropriate write-downs are recorded for securities that incurred substantial losses and are not expected to recover such losses in the near future.

(e) Inventories

Inventories are valued at cost, being determined by the following methods:

Finished goods and raw materials	Moving average method
Work in process	Specific identification method
Supplies	Total average method

(f) Property, Plant, and Equipment

Depreciation of machinery at the Keihin Works, other than that of medium diameter seamless pipe mill, which is depreciated under the straight-line method, is computed under the declining balance method; other plant and equipment at the Keihin Works and plant and equipment at the Fukuyama Works under the straight-line method; plant and equipment at other locations under the declining balance method, based on the estimated useful lives of the assets as prescribed by the Japanese income tax regulations.

Maintenance and repairs, including minor renewals and betterments, are charged to income as incurred.

(g) Research and Development Expenses

Research and development expenses are charged to income as incurred.

(h) Income Taxes

Income taxes are calculated on taxable income and charged to income on an accrual basis. Deferred income taxes pertaining to timing differences between financial and tax reporting are not provided.

(i) Estimated Termination Allowances

Employees of the company are generally entitled to receive termination pay when they leave the company. The payment of termination allowance is determined on the basis of length of service and basic salary at the time of termination.

The company provides for these termination allowances at 50 percent of the amount required to be paid if all employees retired as of the balance sheet date.

The termination plans are not funded.

continued

EXHIBIT 15.1 concluded

(j) Amounts Per 100 Shares of Common Stock

The computation of primary net income per 100 shares is based on the average number of shares of common stock outstanding during each year.

Amounts per 100 shares of common stock assuming full dilution are not significantly different from the per 100 shares data shown in the accompanying statement of income.

Cash dividends per 100 shares of common stock are based on an accrual basis and include, in each year ended March 31, dividends approved by shareholders after such March 31.

outsiders. Hence, more traditional Japanese managers may not see the desirability of an outside evaluation of internal control systems or of an independent audit of financial statements.

One might argue further that the reluctance of Japanese management to share large amounts of information with investors is related to the strong cultural bias toward risk aversion. Disclosure, whether by an individual or an organization, by its very nature involves a measure of risk. Thus, it would be logical for a manager who wants to maximize his or her control of circumstances (and what manager does not?) to seek to restrict or at least to manage disclosure in order to lower potential risks. In a cultural setting that automatically understands and accepts risk avoidance as a value but does not automatically see the importance of legally mandated disclosure, one might expect a bias in the direction of less disclosure rather than more.

Given the different position of investors in Japanese corporate culture, readers of Japanese statements should be aware of several possible pitfalls. One will not find, for example, supplementary information disclosing assets, sales, and profits by activity or geographic region. Even Sony, a relatively "user-friendly" Japanese multinational that is listed on the New York Stock Exchange and that has adopted limited restatement according to U.S. GAAP, did not include segment information in its 1992 annual report — and, consequently, it received a qualified opinion from Price Waterhouse, its auditor.

Legal and political environment. Many first-time readers of Japanese financial statements are struck by the extremely low net income reported by most Japanese firms. For example, Mitsubishi Electric Corp. reported earnings of 36,074 million yen on sales of 3,343,271 million yen in fiscal 1992 — about 1 percent. General Electric's net income to sales for 1992 was about 8.5 percent. Such relatively small earnings, combined with the historically strong performance of Japanese stocks on the Tokyo stock market, have created dizzyingly high price-earnings ratios. P/E ratios have ranged up to 60 and beyond in Japan in recent years, compared to an average of 15 or so for most American stocks. Such numbers have led some Western analysts to claim that the Tokyo market is highly overpriced. But before we reach any kind of conclusion, we need to consider several legal and political factors surrounding Japanese reporting that conspire to depress earnings and thereby pump up the P/E ratio.

The most important and obvious reason that Japanese companies report low net income in their financial reports is that Japanese law requires that accounting income equal taxable income. With effective tax rates on undistributed corporate income exceeding 50 percent, companies have a strong incentive to keep reported earnings down, chiefly by taking advantage of favorable depreciation provisions allowed by the Ministry of Finance. Some analysts have accordingly observed that substituting a price-net cash flow ratio for the traditional P/E ratio can provide a sounder basis for comparison between Japanese companies and their American counterparts. Linking tax policy to accounting income inevitably distorts the financial statements by encouraging managers to maximize tax benefits rather than to report economic substance.

Japanese firms also report lower earnings than their U.S. counterparts because their managers are less interested in short-term profitability than in continuous long-term growth. One reflection of this emphasis on the long run is Japanese managers' freedom from the quarterly earnings reports that American companies issue. In this respect, Japanese managers reflect the macroeconomic strategy pursued by the nation's political and financial leaders. Market share, technological progress, and corporate harmony constitute the top priorities of Japanese managers and Japanese political culture. The sacrifice of immediate rewards and comforts for the sake of greater economic power in the future is a central tenet of the national consensus (supported by the cultural ideal of group consciousness) that has helped make possible the country's economic progress in recent decades. One could say, then, that the typically low net income reported by Japanese firms can be attributed in part to policies adopted by that nation's government and ratified by its managers, its workers, and its people.

Business environment. The dominant form of business organization in Japan is the **kabushiki kaisha** (KK), a type of limited liability company similar to an American corporation. The Japanese Commercial Code requires that a KK elect a statutory auditor to examine the performance of the company's directors and report to shareholders annually. However, there is no requirement that the statutory auditor be independent or qualified to perform the job, and in fact he or she is often a company employee. A large KK — one with stated capital of 500 million yen or liabilities of 20 billion yen — must appoint an independent, professional auditor.

Japanese managers can focus on long-term objectives without having to worry about takeovers because of the pattern of stable shareholding established by corporate families, or **keiretsu,** which dominate the Japanese economy. These giant alliances of companies grew out of the American attempt in the late 1940s to break up the great industrial conglomerations (known as *zaibatsu*) of prewar Japan. When U.S. occupation ended in 1948, companies quietly and informally began to form new ties — generally under the aegis of a major bank and a large trading company — by lending each other money, establishing interlocking directorates, buying each other's stock, and creating helpful patterns of trade within the group. *Keiretsu* tend to be highly diversified, each attempting to form within itself an economic microcosm so as to minimize risk and maximize benefit to individual members.

As Exhibit 15.2 illustrates, group members do not purchase large enough blocks of stock to trigger consolidation requirements. *Keiretsu* (literally, "headless combines") involve no holding company and no controlling board of directors. Although the group as a whole often owns a significant percentage of the voting stock of each of its core members, that ownership is dispersed among a number of companies.

Keiretsu influence the capital structure of Japanese corporations by altering the relationship between debt and risk and, hence, by changing the way in which we should interpret a Japanese balance sheet. Many Japanese firms carry a load of debt that would often prove fatal to an American business. NKK's 1994 balance sheet, for instance, shows that debt accounts for 87 percent of total assets. Commentators have offered a variety of explanations for this phenomenon: Equity costs more and is scarcer in smaller Asian markets; Japanese workers tend to save rather than invest in stocks; Japanese banks historically have played a central role in the economy because they were the primary sources of capital for reconstruction. Each of these explanations is valid, although some of the national characteristics they describe may be changing.

EXHIBIT 15.2

Toyota Motors' Interlocking Shareholdings (1995)

Major Shareholder	Percent Shareholding in Toyota	Toyota Shareholding in Affiliate
Sanwa Bank	4.9%	2.2%
Tokai Bank	4.9	5.0
Sakura Bank	4.9	2.5
Toyoda Automatic Loom Works	4.9	23.0
Nippon Life Insurance Co.	3.7	—
LTCB	3.1	—
Daiwa Bank	2.4	—
Mitsui Trust	2.4	1.7
	31.2%	

Source: *Japan Company Book: Summer 1995* (Tokyo, Japan: Toyo Keizai, Inc.).

The rise of investment trusts suggests that Japanese workers may be looking for equity investment vehicles, and the liquidity created by success in export markets has made some large trading companies less dependent on banks. But such factors address necessities and constraints rather than the reasons that debt financing has worked well in Japan for so many years. In fact, many debt-laden Japanese corporations have survived and prospered because of the uniquely cooperative patterns of behavior between members of *keiretsu.*

Much of the debt on a typical Japanese balance sheet has been provided by other members of the *keiretsu* — banks, insurance companies, trading companies — which means that less risk is attached to high levels of debt than would be the case elsewhere. Under normal circumstances, much of the firm's short-term bank debt is automatically rolled over, making it in fact a form of long-term debt. Trade credit, by virtue of extremely favorable terms of payment, also serves as a kind of semipermanent financing provided by major trading companies to their friends. When a group member runs into trouble, its creditors — if it has properly maintained its alliances — rather than abandoning it will in fact extend credit, buy stock, and, if necessary, lend managerial expertise.

Accounting principles. The following are several principles and practices of Japanese accounting of which you should be aware.

Asset valuation. Japanese companies closely adhere to the historical cost principle applied conservatively — a practice that no doubt reflects the relatively low rate of inflation experienced by Japan. Inventories are valued at cost or at market, if market is significantly lower and the value is not expected to recover. In the case of marketable equity securities, lower of cost or market is applied individually but not on a portfolio basis. Fixed assets are stated at cost less accumulated depreciation.

Intercorporate investments. Because Japan's Commercial Code requires neither consolidated statements (in fact, it forbids them) nor comparative data, securities laws have been the primary tool by which the Japanese government has propagated Anglo-American consolidation methods and the inclusion of prior year information. As a result of this approach, however, only those companies whose securities are registered with the Ministry of Finance are subject to consolidation rules, which require firms to publish both consolidated and parent-only financial statements. The ministry essentially accepts the American definition of control, and it requires companies to account for unconsolidated affiliates (20–50 percent owned) under the equity method, but only in their consolidated statements. On unconsolidated (parent-only) financial statements, companies must show investments in other companies at cost or less.

Doubtful accounts. A bad debt allowance is calculated using percentages of receivables predetermined by tax law. It is considered acceptable to charge the allowance up to the legal limit.

Goodwill. When goodwill is acquired through acquisition, it may be capitalized and amortized over a five-year period, usually using the straight-line method.

Leases. Most leases are accounted for as operating leases by both lessor and lessee. However, a 1978 regulation requires some leases to be capitalized, including those that contain a bargain purchase clause, those that involve machinery built specifically for the lessee that cannot be leased to others, and those for which the leased property is land or buildings.

Interest. Interest costs are usually not capitalized, except in the case of real estate development companies.

Appendix 15A presents the financial review section of the annual report of Kawasaki Steel Corporation and illustrates many of the above principles and practices.

The United Kingdom

As the first great industrial power of the modern era, the United Kingdom has had a broad and enduring influence on financial reporting practices around the world. Although the historical importance and geographical reach of British practices grow directly out of Britain's former role as a world power and pioneer of capitalism, its continuing influence on international accounting standards is more that of an elder partner than a ruler. This shift in the dynamics of power is reflected in the United Kingdom's changing trade patterns, which have moved away from its colonies and dependencies of the 19th century to its current membership in the European Union (EU) and close ties with the United States.

Cultural environment. British attitudes toward business and its social responsibilities are deeply divided and have been since the development of modern capitalism in that country. Even as the landmark Companies Acts of the 1840s through the 1860s were granting legal existence and limited liability to corporations, social legislation was attempting to provide controls over the new force that had been unleased. The advent of capitalism, with its unprecedented potential for working both good and ill, had by the end of the 19th century posed one of the central questions of the 20th century: How much and in what way must government involve itself in economic enterprise?

The belief that corporations must look beyond the maximization of profit has become a permanent if oft-debated element in British public opinion. A by-product of this belief is the search for progressive ways to report the results of business operations — new methods to depict the corporation as a locus of cooperation rather than as a unit of competition. One of the most widespread and best-known experiments in this direction is the **value added statement**, which a significant minority of European firms began to include in their corporate reports in the 1970s. (See Exhibit 15.3 for an example of a value added statement taken from the annual report of Imperial Chemicals Industries Plc.) Although the popularity of value added statements has declined in recent years as questions have been raised about their usefulness, they continue to be presented along with more traditional documents by a number of prominent British firms.

EXHIBIT 15.3

Imperial Chemicals Industries Plc
Sources and Disposal of Value Added
Years Ended 31 December

	1994			1993		
	Continuing operations £m	Discontinued operations £m	Total £m	Continuing operations £m	Discontinued operations £m	Total £m
SOURCES OF INCOME						
Sales turnover	**9,189**	—	**9,189**	8,430	2,202	10,632
Royalties and other trading income	**82**	—	**82**	113	32	145
Less materials and services	**(6,556)**	—	**(6,556)**	(6,111)	(1,351)	(7,462)
Value added by manufacturing and trading activities	**2,715**	—	**2,715**	2,432	883	3,315
Share of profit less losses of associated undertakings	**14**	—	**14**	45	2	47
Value added related to exceptional items taken below trading profit	**(37)**	—	**(37)**	(52)	(47)	(99)
Total value added	**2,692**	—	**2,692**	2,425	838	3,263
DISPOSAL OF TOTAL VALUE ADDED						
Employees						
Employee costs charged in arriving at profit before tax	**1,791**	—	**1,791**	1,742	514	2,256
Governments						
Corporate taxes	**164**	—	**164**	199	70	189
Less grants	**(8)**	—	**(8)**	(10)	(1)	(11)
	156	—	**156**	109	69	178
Providers of capital						
Interest cost of net borrowings	**88**	—	**88**	90	63	153
Dividends to shareholders						
Cash	**199**	—	**199**	199	—	199
Demerger				363	—	363
Minority shareholders in subsidiary undertakings	**56**	—	**56**	42	—	42
	343	—	**343**	694	63	757
Reinvestment in the business						
Depreciation	**413**	—	**413**	417	88	505
(Loss) profit retained	**(11)**	—	**(11)**	(537)	104	(433)
	402	—	**402**	(120)	192	72
Total disposal	**2,692**	—	**2,692**	**2,425**	**838**	**3,263**

Devised by a U.S. Treasury official in the 18th century, the concept of *value added* has since been used by governments as a measure of national income. In the 1970s it was adopted by corporations, on the recommendation of the British government and the accounting profession, to provide additional information to shareholders, to serve as the basis of employee incentive programs, and to improve public and employee relations by showing what a company does with the wealth it creates.

The basic numerical definition of *value added* is sales less purchases. A refinement on this definition distinguishes gross value added (as just defined) from net value added, which subtracts depreciation as well as purchases from sales. Depending on who is doing the calculating, depreciation may be figured on a historical cost basis or a current cost basis. Governments typically attempt to calculate depreciation using the latter. The interest in value added has also spawned a variety of ratios (such as value added/payroll costs and operating profit/value added) designed to provide company planners with a new perspective on operations and to express the efficiency of a company in terms that are more easily understandable to the general public.

Legal and political environment. With very few exceptions, such as formation by Royal Charter, British companies are incorporated under the companies act currently in force. (The most recent one at this writing is the Companies Act of 1985.) The act requires all corporations to maintain accounting records that include information sufficient to give a "true and fair view" of the company's financial position and its operations. The phrase "true and fair view" is an important one in British accounting and auditing. Even though its meaning is difficult to ascertain with precision (as is likely to be the case with any standard of "fairness"), it is the key phrase by which auditors express an opinion on a set of financial statements. Companies must present audited financial statements and a directors' report to shareholders at the annual meeting. In addition, they must file these documents with the Registrar of Companies.

The investor orientation that has traditionally dominated British financial reporting is reinforced by British tax law, which gives individuals several important incentives to invest in stocks. Capital gains are taxable, but they are eligible for tax breaks favoring small investors: Net gains less losses carried forward are indexed to eliminate the effects of inflation. An annual exemption, which in 1994 amounted to £5,000, further decreases the taxable portion of any gain.

The United Kingdom is one of the relatively few nations in the world in which corporate tax law does not serve as the basis for financial reporting. In many countries firms must keep their books in accordance with the dictates of tax regulations, a procedure that subjects financial reporting practices to the whims of legislators and greatly hinders comparability across national boundaries. In the United Kingdom, however, the process is reversed — income statements are prepared according to British GAAP and then, for tax return purposes, are adjusted to arrive at taxable income.

Business environment. The dominant British business entity is the **limited liability company,** also referred to as a *company limited by shares.* A limited liability company may be incorporated as a private or a public concern, the latter having the right to issue securities to the public. Both public and private companies must have at least two stockholders, and public companies must have at least two directors as well. For a limited liability company to be incorporated as a public entity, it must have a minimum share capital of 50,000 pounds and include **public limited company** (or Plc) in its name. A private company is subject to no minimum capital requirement and must include the word *Limited* (or Ltd.) at the end of its name.

Despite government efforts, organized labor still exerts a significant if somewhat diminished influence over British society. Whereas membership in U.S. labor unions has never reached 40 percent and currently stands at less than 20 percent, British trade unions represent around 45 to 50 percent of the workforce, or about 11 million people. Although labor relations have had little direct impact on accounting methods and conventions, they have undoubtedly affected the disclosure requirements imposed on British corporations. The Companies Act of 1985, for example, requires certain disclosures pertaining to directors' fees and management salaries exceeding £30,000. Specifically, the company must reveal the amount paid to the chairperson and (if not the same person) to the highest paid director, and it must indicate where remuneration paid to the other directors and to management falls on a pay scale broken into £5,000 increments. The company must also disclose wage and salary expenses, social security costs, and pension costs paid to or on behalf of employees. All of this information may be of interest to union negotiators as well as investors.

British law does not mandate employee representation on company boards (as is the case in Sweden); however, a firm employing 250 or more workers must disclose its policy concerning employee consultation programs. Many individual companies and the Confederation of British Industry (an association of employers) have responded to the legal requirement by publicly supporting voluntary programs for employee participation on the firm level. In addition, many firms encourage share ownership among employees. B.A.T. Industries, the tobacco and retailing conglomerate, touches on these themes in the following summary included in its directors' report, presented in a recent annual report:

> **Employee Involvement in the United Kingdom**
> B.A.T. Industries actively encourages the development of systems of employee involvement in operating companies. Progress is regularly monitored and reported to the board and statements on employee involvement are included in the annual reports of U.K. subsidiaries.
>
> The details of direct involvement processes are appropriately different in each operating company in ways that reflect both individual local needs and the working environment. Typically, however, they include staff committees, briefing groups, in-house newspapers, and videos.
>
> The company believes that financial participation is a fundamental constituent of employee involvement and is an innovator in this area within both the United Kingdom and other European community countries in which it operates. The U.K. Share Participation Scheme is in its fifth year and shares valued at £18.5 million have been appropriated for the benefit of 14,150 employees of the continuing group. A U.K. Save-As-You-Earn Share Option Scheme also attracts a great deal of support.
>
> **Employment of the Disabled in the United Kingdom**
> The group's policy on recruitment is based on the ability of a candidate to perform the job. Full and fair consideration is given to applications for employment from the disabled where they have the skills and abilities to perform the job.
>
> If a disabled applicant proves a suitable candidate for employment, modification of facilities and the provision of special equipment is considered favourably. If employees become disabled during the course of their employment and as a result are unable to perform their normal jobs, every effort is made to offer suitable alternative employment, to provide assistance with retraining, and to deal with their cases compassionately.
>
> It is group policy to encourage the training and development of all its employees where this is of benefit to the individual and to the company. This includes the provision of training to meet the special needs of disabled employees.

Although B.A.T. would undoubtedly like to be considered progressive, its policy statement is similar to those of other British multinational firms.

Accounting terminology and practices. Several terms used in British financial statements may confuse or mislead unwary foreign readers. *Fixed assets,* for example, refers to all assets retained for continuous use in the business, not only to property, plant, and equipment (which the British call *tangible fixed assets*). The term *stocks* generally means inventory. Receivables may be lumped under the laconic heading *debtors,* with payables simply listed as *creditors.* On the income statement, called the *profit and loss account,* sales are referred to as *turnover.* Alternatively, *profit and loss* *account* and *reserves* or *retained profits* may refer to retained earnings or some component thereof. As these examples suggest, one must cultivate a judicious suspicion of familiar terminology; it may be camouflaging a distinctively British usage.

Accounting principles. The following illustrate some of the unique British reporting and disclosure practices. (Appendix 15B presents the financial section of the Rolls-Royce Plc 1994 annual report.)

Format. Although the format of British financial statements varies in a number of ways from that used in American statements, the most noticeable difference is in the arrangement of the balance sheet. British balance sheets following the **horizontal format** resemble American balance sheets but run from *low* liquidity to *high* liquidity; hence, fixed assets appear above current assets, and shareholders' equity above liabilities. Companies that adopt the **vertical format** offset current assets against current liabilities, then offset total assets against current liabilities, balancing this figure against long-term liabilities and stockholders' equity. The balance sheet of B.A.T. Industries (see Exhibit 15.4) provides an example of the horizontal format. The Rolls-Royce Plc balance sheet (see Appendix 15B) illustrates the vertical format.

Consolidation. The Companies Act requires companies with subsidiaries to prepare "group accounts." Although theoretically the law would accept group accounts prepared on some basis other than consolidation, they almost always use the consolidation form. (Implementation of the EU's Seventh Directive, effective in 1990, removes the option of using bases other than consolidation.) Companies must present separate balance sheets for the group and the parent company, but only a group income statement is required. Control is defined as more than a 50 percent share in equity capital (not necessarily voting) or as a smaller shareholding with the power to control the membership of the board of directors.

Valuation of assets. A British company may choose to value its assets according to historical cost principles or alternative valuation rules. According to historical cost rules, current assets should be carried at the lower of cost or net realizable value, and fixed assets at cost less accumulated depreciation (if applicable) and any permanent decline in value. LIFO is not permitted as a basis for inventory valuation for either tax or financial reporting.

The alternative valuation rules allow assets to be written up above cost as follows:

- Inventories, current investments, tangible fixed assets, and intangible fixed assets (except goodwill) may be written up to current cost.
- Long-term investments and tangible fixed assets may be written up to market value as of the date of the last valuation (even if it differs from the balance sheet date).
- Investments in 20 percent or more of an affiliate's stock may be accounted for under the equity method.

It is not uncommon for a firm to revalue its land and buildings periodically, taking the surplus to a revaluation reserve account in the owners' equity section of the balance sheet. This reserve, however, is not available for distribution to shareholders. Companies are required to disclose the bases of valuation for inventories, investments, and fixed assets. In light of the valuation options open to British companies and their possible impact on the balance sheet, a careful reader will surely want to check this information.

Goodwill. Purchased goodwill is defined as the difference between the fair value of consideration given up and the aggregate fair values of the assets received. Normally, neither goodwill nor negative goodwill is carried on the balance sheet; both are written

EXHIBIT 15.4

B.A.T. Industries
Balance Sheets — Horizontal Format
31 December

£ millions	Group 1994	Group 1993	Company 1994	Company 1993
Assets				
Commercial and corporate activities				
Tangible fixed assets	1,684	1,487	4	5
Investments in group companies			2,596	1,930
Other investments and long-term loans	76	81		
Fixed assets	1,760	1,568	2,600	1,935
Stocks	2,146	1,991		
Debtors	1,269	953	3,357	2,990
Current investments	188	333	3	
Short-term deposits	971	503	59	
Cash and bank balances	99	135		1
	6,433	5,483	6,019	4,926
Financial services general business				
Interest in underwriting associations	1,497	1,583		
Investments	3,870	3,956		
Associates	34	34		
Tangible fixed assets	324	342		
Other assets	1,905	2,115		
Cash and bank balances	50	43		
	7,680	8,073		
Financial services life business				
Investments	22,679	23,227		
Securitised mortgages	245	290		
Nonrecourse financing	(245)	(290)		
Associates	33	19		
Interest in life businesses	1,009	1,020		
Tangible fixed assets	102	99		
Other assets	1,167	1,278		
Cash and bank balances	116	121		
	25,106	25,764		
Investments in associates	766	614		
Total assets	39,985	39,934	6,019	4,926
Funds Employed				
Capital and reserves				
Share capital	770	770	770	770
Share premium account	7	2	7	2
Capital reserves	109	260		
Deferred investment gains	117	321		
Profit and loss account	3,585	3,647	1,041	1,020
Interest of B.A.T. Industries' shareholders (equity)	4,588	5,000	1,818	1,792
Minority shareholders interest including nonequity	438	403		
	5,026	5,403	1,818	1,792
Commercial and corporate activities				
Provisions for liabilities and charges	870	682		
Borrowings	3,439	2,975	314	314
Creditors	2,810	2,160	3,887	2,820
	7,119	5,817	4,201	3,134
Financial services general business				
General business insurance funds	3,848	4,041		
Borrowings	461	232		
Other liabilities	701	752		
	5,010	5,025		
Financial services life business				
Long-term assurance funds	21,557	22,124		
Borrowings	33	48		
Other liabilities	1,240	1,517		
	22,830	23,689		
Total funds employed	39,985	39,934	6,019	4,926

off immediately against owners' equity. Companies may choose, however, to capitalize purchased goodwill (but not negative goodwill) and amortize it over its estimated economic life. (This latter approach, as of this writing, is being given serious consideration as the required approach.)

Research and development. Research expenditures are written off immediately, but development costs may be capitalized if they fulfill a number of requirements concerning the technical and commercial feasibility of the project to which they are related. Deferred development expenditures must be reviewed at the end of each period and written off immediately if they no longer meet these feasibility requirements.

Leases. Accepted accounting principles distinguish between operating leases and finance leases, requiring the latter to be capitalized by lessees in financial statements. Finance leases are deemed to be those that essentially transfer the risks and benefits of ownership to the lessee. Lessees should record an asset to be depreciated over the shorter of the lease term (including likely renewals) or the asset's useful life, a liability for future payments to the lessor, and apportion interest payments between interest expense and repayment of principal. The lessor should record a receivable for the total minimum lease payments plus any residual value, less any provision for bad debts.

Interest costs. The Companies Act allows interest on financing for the construction of assets — both fixed and current — to be capitalized. The generality of the law on this point permits capitalization in cases that would not be acceptable under U.S. GAAP.

Earnings per share. Contrary to current U.S. practice (which is likely to change soon), basic earnings per share (called *primary earnings per share* in the United States) are calculated without regard to common stock equivalents. The basis for calculating earnings per share must be disclosed in the notes.

Reconciliation of U.S. and British GAAP. Because British firms are frequently listed on U.S. stock exchanges, some publish a reconciliation of net income and stockholders' equity calculated according to the accounting principles of the two countries. The excerpted schedule and explanatory notes from the Hanson Plc annual report (see Exhibit 15.5) illustrate how the differences just listed may affect these figures. Notice that the differing treatment of goodwill is particularly important in Hanson's case.

Management Issues

One of the management issues related to differences in financial reporting practices around the world springs from the need (or interest) for raising capital in other countries. For example, if a U.S. company wants to list on a foreign stock exchange, one of the listing requirements may be the recasting of the U.S. GAAP-based financial statements into the GAAP of the host country. So far, global reciprocity of financial statements does not exist. Thus, managers must consider the costs of recasting their financial statements as well as understand how the recasting will alter the financial picture presented.

Another issue pertains to the management of a multinational company where the results from different business units around the world must be understood and codified into one set of consolidated financial statements. For example, local financial reporting practice in a particular country may not recognize such a thing as a capital lease. Thus, in negotiating leases, the local management would typically give no consideration to the possibility of having to record a large lease liability. For purposes of reporting to the parent company domiciled where capitalizing of certain leases is required, however, a new challenge arises for parent company management to educate local country

EXHIBIT 15.5

Hanson Plc and Subsidiaries
Reconciliation to U.S. Accounting Principles

The following is a summary of the estimated material adjustments to profit and ordinary shareholders' equity that would be required if U.S. Generally Accepted Accounting Principles (U.S. GAAP) had been applied.

	Years ended September 30,			
	1993 £ million	**1992 £ million**	**1993 $ million**	**1992 $ million**
Profit available for appropriation as reported in the consolidated profit and loss account	**734**	1,089	**1,098**	1,628
Estimated adjustments:				
Goodwill amortization	**(94)**	(95)	**(141)**	(142)
Foreign currency translation	**(7)**	(11)	**(10)**	(16)
Pensions	**34**	52	**51**	78
Timberlands depletion and reforestation	**(32)**	(36)	**(48)**	(54)
Taxation	**(22)**	(96)	**(33)**	(144)
	(121)	(186)	**(181)**	(278)
Estimated profit available for appropriation (net income) as adjusted to accord with U.S. GAAP	**613**	903	**917**	1,350
Arising from:				
Continuing operations	**561**	701	**839**	1,048
Discontinued operations — income (loss) from operations	**19**	44	**29**	66
— gain (loss) on disposals	**33**	158	**49**	236
	613	903	**917**	1,350
	Per share		Per ADR	
Earnings	**p**	p	**$**	$
Undiluted — continuing operations	**11.6**	14.5	**0.87**	1.09
— discontinued operations	**1.1**	4.2	**0.08**	0.31
— profit available for appropriation	**12.7**	18.7	**0.95**	1.40
Diluted — continuing operations	**11.6**	14.4	**0.87**	1.08
— discontinued operations	**1.1**	4.2	**0.08**	0.31
— profit available for appropriation	**12.7**	18.6	**0.95**	1.39
Ordinary shareholders' equity as reported in the consolidated balance sheet	**3,953**	4,224	**5,912**	6,317
Estimated adjustments:				
Goodwill and other intangibles	**4,379**	3,340	**6,549**	4,995
Revaluation of land and buildings	**(166)**	(166)	**(248)**	(248)
Pensions	**223**	189	**333**	283
Timberlands depletion and reforestation	**(105)**	(60)	**(157)**	(90)
Taxation	**(320)**	(102)	**(479)**	(153)
	4,011	3,201	**5,998**	4,787
Estimated ordinary shareholders' equity as adjusted to accord with U.S. GAAP	**7,964**	7,425	**11,910**	11,104

The exchange rate used to translate the above figures was that ruling at the 1993 balance sheet date ($1.4955 to £).

The following are the main U.S. accounting principles that differ from those generally accepted in the United Kingdom as applied by Hanson in its financial statements:

Goodwill and Other Intangibles

Goodwill and other intangible assets arising on the acquisition of a subsidiary are written off in the year in which that subsidiary is acquired. Under U.S. GAAP such

continued

EXHIBIT 15.5 concluded

goodwill is capitalized and is amortized through the profit and loss account over its estimated useful life, not exceeding 40 years.

Taxation

Deferred taxation is not provided where, in the opinion of the directors, no liability is likely to arise in the foreseeable future. However, under U.S. GAAP, deferred taxation would be provided on a full deferral basis.

U.K. GAAP permits the reduction of the tax charge by the use of tax losses available at the time of acquisition. However, U.S. GAAP requires that the benefit of such losses be adjusted through goodwill and tangible fixed assets.

Revaluation of Land and Buildings

Periodically land and buildings are revalued on an existing use basis by professionally qualified external valuers, and such assets are written up to the appraised value. Depreciation is, where applicable, calculated on these revalued amounts. When revalued properties are sold, the gain or loss on sale is calculated based on revalued carrying amounts and reflected in income, and any revaluation surplus thus realized is reclassified directly to retained earnings. Under U.S. GAAP such revaluations would not be reflected in financial statements, and the gain or loss on sale would be calculated based on original cost and reflected in income. The amount of additional depreciation charged in respect of the revalued properties is not material.

Timberlands

Reforestation costs are charged to the profit and loss account when incurred, and depletion of timberlands is provided only to the extent that the amount of timber harvested exceeds the estimated growth of standing timber. Under U.S. GAAP depletion on a unit of production basis is charged to the profit and loss account and reforestation costs are capitalized as part of the carrying cost of timberlands.

Foreign Currencies

Revenues, expenses, assets, and liabilities relating to overseas subsidiaries are translated at the year-end rate. Under U.S. GAAP assets and liabilities are translated as under U.K. GAAP; however, revenues and expenses are translated at average rates for the year.

Pensions

The accounting policy of the group has not been to account for exceptional past pension surpluses, when surpluses do not revert to the employer. Under U.S. GAAP, such surpluses are recognized and credited over an appropriate future period.

---

management about such a practice and consideration. In turn, local management would have to engage in a business leasing decision with a slightly different perspective than they would normally be accustomed to doing in order to be sure the lease would not have to be capitalized when reporting local financial results to parent company management. Such nuances in financial reporting practices would need to be understood by local and parent-company management.

One other scenario where it is incumbent on management to understand the financial reporting practices common to businesses in another country is when they are considering the acquisition of a company domiciled in another country. In any corporate acquisition, one of the things a potential buyer does is determine a value for the possible acquisition target. A common valuation process is to apply an industry P/E multiple to the company's reported earnings. Clearly, reported earnings are a function of the accounting practices used. Therefore, before using that earnings figure, one must have a thorough understanding of how it was determined and in particular how its determination differs from the results that would be determined according to the buyer country's GAAP.

SUMMARY

With the passage of time, there has been an increasing blurring of the economic boundaries between countries. Japanese cars, for example, are no longer made only in Japan but are also manufactured in Tennessee and Ohio, among other locations in the United States. Similarly, British consumer goods are so prevalent in the U.S. marketplace today that consumers rarely view them as foreign products.

Just as consumers have come to accept foreign-produced goods as an everyday occurrence, so have managers and investors come to recognize the opportunities for investing abroad. The ability to identify the best British partner for a European joint venture, for example, and the best Japanese company to invest in depends significantly on a manager's or investor's understanding of the accounting and reporting practices followed by companies of those countries.

In this chapter, we have examined the accounting principles, practices, and business environment of two countries, Japan and the United Kingdom. Exhibit 15.6 compares and contrasts the prevailing accounting practices in these two with those found in the United States (and discussed in the previous 14 chapters). It is apparent that although many similarities exist, differences can be quite significant. The manager or investor contemplating foreign investment would be wise to develop an understanding of the accounting and business practices prevalent in that country.

NEW CONCEPTS AND TERMS

Harmonization (p. 737)
Horizontal format (p. 748)
International accounting standards (p. 738)
International Accounting Standards Committee (p. 737)
Kabushiki kaisha (p. 742)
Keiretsu (p. 742)
Limited liability company (p. 746)
Public limited company (p. 746)
Value added statement (p. 744)
Vertical format (p. 748)

EXHIBIT 15.6

Financial Reporting Practices in Three Countries

UNITED STATES

Accounting Standards

- Basis of financial statement is principally historical cost.
- Consolidated information provided by most.
- Inventory costing method predominantly used is LIFO.
- Depreciation is principally on straight-line method.
- Excess depreciation not allowed.
- Valuation method for long-term investments between 20–50% of equity is equity method.
- Valuation method for long-term investments less than 20% of equity is mark-to-market method.
- Long-term financial leases are capitalized.
- Deferred taxes are recorded when accounting income is not equal to taxable income.
- Pension expenses are usually provided.
- Funding pension liabilities to outside trustees is common.
- Accounting method for acquisition is usually purchase method.
- Goodwill is capitalized and amortized.
- Foreign currency translation is determined by current rate method.
- Gains or losses from foreign currency translation are taken to income statement and/or shareholders' equity.
- Contingent liabilities disclosed by most.
- Discretionary/nonequity reserves are not used in general.

Reporting Practices

- Notes to the financial accounts are extensively utilized.
- Income statement format is sales less expenses with more than two years of comparative figures reported by most.
- Foreign exchange gains/losses are reported if material.
- Extraordinary gains/losses are reported by many.
- Balance sheet format is total assets = liabilities + shareholders' equity with two years of comparative figures reported.
- Arrangement is by decreasing liquidity.
- Other intangibles are disclosed by most.
- Preferred stock is separately reported by many.
- Changes in shareholders' equity reported by most.
- Appropriation of retained earnings is disclosed by most.
- Changes in cash flows required; statement format is net income, investing activities, and financing activities on cash basis.
- Product segmentation disclosed by most with sales, operating income, and identifiable assets by product line.
- Geographic segmentation disclosed by most with sales, operating income, and identifiable assets by area. Exports are reported by many.
- Earnings per share reported by most. Numerator of EPS is based on the net income after preferred dividend. Denominator is the average number of shares outstanding during period.
- Dividend per share reported by most.
- Shareholders:
  Major shareholding is reported by some and names of the shareholders are disclosed by some.
- Subsidiary information is reported with name, domicile, and percentage held by parent.
- Number of employees reported by most on a worldwide basis.
- Management information:
  Names and titles of principal officers are reported by most.
  List of board members is reported by most.
  Company shares owned by directors/officers are not reported at all.
  Remuneration to directors/officers is reported by some.
- Research and development expenses disclosed by most on worldwide basis.
- Capital expenditures disclosed by most on a worldwide basis.
- Subsequent events disclosed by most.

Interim Reports

- Frequency: Quarterly.
- Consolidation is done.
- Audit not required.

Other Observations

Accounting Standards

- Some consolidation of investments between 20% and 50%, depending on management control.
- Revaluation of accounts generally not allowed.

Reporting Practices

- Language of the financial statement is English.
- Accounts receivable are separated by short and long term and reported in net.
- Diluted earnings per share are disclosed by most.
- Changes in capital are most frequently achieved through new issues, stock dividends, splits, and right issues.
- Multiple classes of common shares are utilized by many.

continued

EXHIBIT 15.6 continued

UNITED KINGDOM

Accounting Standards

- Cost basis of financial statement is on historical cost with revaluation permitted.
- Consolidated information provided by most.
- Inventory costing method predominantly used is first-in-first-out method (FIFO).
- Depreciation principally on straight-line method.
- Excess depreciation is not allowed.
- Valuation method for long-term investments between 20–50% of equity is equity method.
- Valuation method for long-term investments less than 20% of equity is cost method, with revaluation permitted.
- Long-term financial leases are capitalized.
- Deferred taxes recorded when accounting income is not equal to taxable income.
- Pension expenses are usually provided.
- Funding pension liabilities to outside trustees is common.
- Accounting method for acquisition is purchase method; pooling (merger) accounting permitted in limited cases.
- Goodwill usually taken to owners' equity reserves.
- Foreign currency translation determined by current rate method.
- Gains or losses from foreign currency translation are taken to income statement and/or shareholders' equity.
- Contingent liabilities are disclosed by most.
- Discretionary/nonequity reserves are specific reserves.

Reporting Practices

- Notes to the financial accounts are extensively utilized.
- Income statement format is sales less expenses with two years of comparative figures.
- Foreign exchange gains/losses reported by many.
- Extraordinary gains/losses reported by many.
- Balance sheet format is fixed assets + net working capital – long-term debts = shareholders' equity with two years of comparative figures reported by majority.
- Arrangement is by increasing liquidity.
- Other intangibles are disclosed by most.
- Preferred stock is separately reported.
- Reserves are reported as statutory/legal reserves by most.
- Changes in shareholders' equity are reported by most.
- Appropriation of retained earnings disclosed by most.
- Changes in cash flows are reported; statement format uses headings of operating activities, returns on investments and servicing of finance, taxation, investing activities, and financing.
- Product segmentation disclosed by most with sales and operating income by product line.
- Geographic segmentation is disclosed by most with sales only by area. Exports are reported by many.
- Earnings per share is reported by most. Numerator of EPS is based on net income before extraordinary items. Denominator is the average number of shares outstanding during period.
- Dividend per share is reported by most.
- Shareholders:
  Major shareholding is reported by many and names of the shareholders frequently disclosed.
- Subsidiary information reported with name, domicile, and percentage held by parent.
- Number of employees reported by most on a worldwide basis.
- Management information:
  Names and titles of principal officers are reported by most.
  List of board members is reported by most.
  Company shares owned by directors/officers are reported by most.
  Remuneration to directors/officers is reported by most.
- Research and development expenses disclosed infrequently.
- Capital expenditures disclosed by most on a worldwide basis.
- Subsequent events are reported by some.

Interim Reports

- Frequency: Semiannually.
- Consolidation is done.
- Audit not required.

Other Observations

Accounting Standards

- Some consolidation of investments between 20% and 50%, depending on management control.

Reporting Practices

- Language of the financial statement is English.
- Accounts receivable are separated by short and long term and reported in net.
- Total assets can be computed indirectly from balance sheet.
- Diluted earnings per share are disclosed by many.
- Changes in capital are most frequently achieved through new issues, stock splits, and right issues.
- Multiple classes of common shares are utilized by many.
- Differences in multiple shares are usually in voting rights.

continued

EXHIBIT 15.6 concluded

JAPAN

Accounting Standards

- Cost basis of financial statement is entirely on historical cost basis.
- Consolidated information is provided by many.
- Inventory costing method predominantly used varies with different inventories.
- Depreciation is principally on accelerated method.
- Excess depreciation is not allowed.
- Valuation method for long-term investments between 20–50% of equity is cost and/or equity method.
- Valuation method for long-term investments less than 20% of equity is cost method.
- Long-term financial leases are capitalized and/or expensed.
- Deferred taxes are not recorded when accounting income is not equal to taxable income.
- Pension expenses are usually provided.
- Accounting method for acquisition is purchase method by many.
- Goodwill is capitalized and amortized over 5 to 10 years.
- Foreign currency translation is determined by temporal method and/or current rate method.
- Gains or losses from foreign currency translation are taken to income statement and/or deferred.
- Contingent liabilities disclosed by many.
- Discretionary/nonequity reserves are general-purpose reserves.

Reporting Practices

- Notes to the financial accounts are extensively utilized.
- Income statement format is sales less expenses with two years of comparative figures reported by most.
- Foreign exchange gains/losses are reported by many.
- Extraordinary gains/losses are reported by many.
- Balance sheet format is total assets = liabilities + shareholders' equity with two years of comparative figures reported by majority.
- Arrangement is by decreasing liquidity.
- Other intangibles are disclosed by most.
- Preferred stock is rarely used.
- Reserves are reported as statutory/legal reserves by most.
- Changes in shareholders' equity are reported by most.
- Appropriation of retained earnings is disclosed by most.
- Changes in working capital or cash flows are reported by many; statement format is net income, sources/uses, or investing/financing activities on cash basis.
- Product segmentation is disclosed by most with sales only by product line.
- Geographic segmentation disclosed by some. Exports are reported by many.
- Earnings per share is reported by most. Numerator of EPS is based on the net income after preferred dividend. Denominator is the fiscal year-end shares outstanding.
- Dividend per share is reported by most.
- Shareholders:
  Major shareholding is reported by most, and names of the shareholders are also disclosed by most.
- Subsidiary information is reported with name, domicile, and percentage held by parent.
- Number of employees is reported by most on parent company only.
- Management information:
  Names and titles of principal officers are reported by most.
  List of board members is reported by most.
  Company shares owned by directors/officers are reported by most.
  Remuneration to directors/officers is not reported at all.
- Research and development expenses usually disclosed by many on parent company basis.
- Capital expenditures disclosed by many on parent company basis.
- Subsequent events reported by many.

Interim Reports

- Frequency: Semiannually.
- Consolidation is infrequent.
- Audit not required.

Other Observations

Accounting Standards

- Only domestic majority-owned subsidiaries are consolidated; others carried at cost method.
- No consolidation of investments between 20% and 50%.
- Revaluation of accounts not allowed.

Reporting Practices

- Language of the financial statement is equally distributed between local language and English.
- Changes in capital are most frequently achieved through new issues, stock dividends, and conversions of securities.

Based on V. A. Bavishi, *International Accounting and Auditing Trends,* 2nd ed. (Princeton, N.J.: Center for International Financial Analysis and Research, Inc., 1991). Used with permission.

APPENDIX 15A

Kawasaki Steel Corporation 1994 Annual Report — Excerpts

KAWASAKI STEEL CORP. 1994 ANNUAL REPORT

MESSAGE FROM THE PRESIDENT

Performance

Fiscal 1993, ended March 31, 1994, was another tough year for Japan's steel industry. In fact, it was worse than we had anticipated. Annual raw steel production in Japan fell 1.8%, to 97 million metric tons, the third consecutive year of lower output and the second consecutive year that the industry total fell short of 100 million tons.

The steel industry bore the brunt of Japan's unrelenting recession, and Kawasaki Steel was not alone in posting losses. The Corporation fared better than many of its competitors, however, thanks to concerted efforts to boost profitability and cut costs. Non-consolidated net sales dropped 7.9%, to ¥1,005.3 billion, chiefly because of low demand and price reductions. We also posted extraordinary losses, including losses on investments in subsidiaries, and expenditures related to the past service portion of pension costs.

To counter these outlays, we sold marketable securities and fixed assets while limiting costs. These actions undoubtedly buoyed our bottom line, but we recorded an operating loss of ¥7.5 billion and a net loss of ¥39.1 billion, our worst performance ever. Regrettably, because of these results and the gloomy prognosis for the steel industry in fiscal 1994, Kawasaki Steel was unable to pay cash dividends in fiscal 1993.

Operating Environment

The operating environment was bleak in fiscal 1993. Despite indications of economic recovery in Japan, the nation remained mired in recession. Lackluster personal spending and a considerable decline in capital investment fed a cool demand impasse, while the high yen, an unusually inclement summer and delayed action on public works projects further compounded the difficult climate.

Our steel operations suffered the most. Raw steel production, at 9.9 million metric tons, was down 0.2% from fiscal 1992. Production of steel products dipped 1.9%, to 9.6 million metric tons.

These declines paralleled faltering business for two of our main customer groups—the domestic automotive and construction industries. Automakers faced pressure from sluggish domestic demand and the high yen's detrimental impact on exports, while construction companies found that a rebound in housing starts was not enough to compensate for diminished corporate investment. In addition, as demand dwindled in the electric appliance, industrial machinery and civil engineering sectors, orders for steel from these client groups tumbled.

In the export arena, weak market conditions offset volume increases in overseas steel shipments, especially to the People's Republic of China. Moreover, because of the high yen, dollar-based prices yielded lower transaction values in yen terms.

In our other operating segments, sales of chemical products languished, owing to the recession. On a brighter note, revenues from engineering activities grew, due to the completion of several large projects.

Topics Addressed

For as long as Kawasaki Steel's main steel customers face their own slump, domestic demand for steel will languish. Calls for lower prices are inevitable and we will likely have to comply, as we did in fiscal 1993.

In exports, the high yen is bound to hamper sales and heighten the already tough environment. Competition, both on domestic and international fronts, will intensify in the medium term as demand for steel reaches its saturation point.

With these conditions in mind, Kawasaki Steel established medium- and long-term goals geared toward a firmer profit base more responsive to changes in Japan's economic structure. In fiscal 1993, we began divisionwide implementation of "Common Sense Challenge," a program that encourages the questioning of preconceived notions and conventional wisdom to spur innovation and efficiency.

In the Steel Division, we initiated a program to achieve better profits through internationally competitive pricing and also strengthened our item-specific profit management system. In the Chemical Division, we reinforced each existing field of endeavor but emphasized the ongoing expansion of our engineering-plastics compound and soft ferrite operations.

KAWASAKI STEEL CORP. 1994 ANNUAL REPORT

Shinobu Tosaki, President

In the Engineering and Construction Division, we continued to promote existing operations while vigorously developing new fields, such as environmental engineering and social development engineering. In a strategic and technical move, we absorbed the bridge operations of Kawaden Co., Ltd., and set up the Bridge and Steel Structure Division. The integration of our large-scale steel structure construction activities and those of Kawaden Co. will enhance overall engineering expertise.

The LSI Division designed and manufactured high-performance products to meet the sophisticated requirements of semiconductor makers and their clients, while the Integrated Systems and Electronics Division continued to work with Kawasaki Steel Systems R&D Corporation (KSD), pooling operating resources to expand our systems integration business.

To nurture the activities outlined above, Kawasaki Steel streamlined its management structure. Our responses were better attuned to the times and to the difficulties of the current operating environment. In this tough business climate, it is more imperative than ever to realize a profit structure that generates stable earnings.

While the business environment is a critical focus these days, we cannot ignore the natural environment. We have numerous programs that utilize the most recent breakthroughs to conserve resources and limit pollution. With the understanding and cooperation of the public, we will persevere in both entrepreneurial and societal areas.

Fiscal 1994

To date, the first half of fiscal 1994 has been tough and will likely remain so into the second half. But we are hardier than the recession. With the determined efforts of employees throughout the Corporation and the Group, Kawasaki Steel will overcome the operating hurdles and return to net income growth.

On behalf of the Board, I would like to thank our customers, stockholders, employees and business partners for their support, especially during these lean times. With your continued encouragement, I am confident that Kawasaki Steel can ride out the recession and capitalize on long-term opportunities.

June 29, 1994

Shinobu Tosaki
President

KAWASAKI STEEL CORP. 1994 ANNUAL REPORT

MANAGEMENT'S DISCUSSION AND ANALYSIS

Net Income Analysis

Japan's recession persisted in fiscal 1993, ended March 31, 1994. The domestic steel industry was beset by sluggish domestic demand for steel, unfavorable exchange rates on exports and heightened competition from overseas steelmakers. For Kawasaki Steel, these conditions squeezed profit margins in most divisions, especially the Steel Division, and led to non-consolidated net sales of ¥1,005.3 billion, a drop of 7.9% from fiscal 1992. For the first time in its history, Kawasaki Steel recorded an operating loss.

Efforts to control expenditures undoubtedly buoyed the bottom line. Although reduced steel production, prompted by slow demand, led to higher production costs, the average cost of materials for steelmaking was down, thanks to lower variable costs and maximized use of employees. Yen appreciation, while hurting export profits, lowered the cost of raw materials procured from abroad.

Unfortunately, the negative effects of the operating environment overshadowed cost-cutting measures, and Kawasaki Steel recorded an operating loss of ¥7.5 billion. Net other expenses totaled ¥31.3 billion, as extraordinary losses on investments in subsidiaries and expenditures related to the past service portion of pension costs countered other income derived from the disposal of marketable securities and fixed assets. The net loss on Kawasaki Steel's fiscal 1993 statements of operations was ¥39.1 billion.

Net Income Analysis	**1994**	1993	1992	1991	1990
Net sales (Millions of yen)	**¥1,005,316**	¥1,092,099	¥1,208,067	¥1,185,435	¥1,112,274
Operating income (loss) (Millions of yen)	**(7,524)**	37,052	78,944	117,988	149,230
Net income (loss) (Millions of yen)	**(39,133)**	143	27,476	38,107	50,164
Total assets (Millions of yen)	**1,888,915**	1,943,828	1,921,529	1,888,297	1,765,351
Stockholders' equity (Millions of yen)	**525,948**	565,081	583,531	576,683	558,169
Net income (loss) per share (Yen)	**(12.03)**	0.04	8.45	11.71	16.45
Dividends per share (Yen)	**0.00**	6.00	6.00	6.00	6.00
Operating margin (%)	**(0.7%)**	3.4%	6.5%	10.0%	13.4%
Return on sales (%)	**(3.9)**	0.0	2.3	3.2	4.5
Return on assets (%)	**(2.1)**	0.0	1.4	2.0	2.9
Return on equity (%)	**(7.4)**	0.0	4.7	6.6	11.0

Sales Breakdown (Billions of yen; % of net sales)	**1994**	1993	1992	1991	1990
Steel	**¥ 715.1**	¥ 822.6	¥ 926.0	¥ 915.1	¥ 904.3
	(71.1%)	(75.3%)	(76.6%)	(77.2%)	(81.3%)
Chemical	**43.0**	46.7	50.3	52.9	40.2
	(4.3)	(4.3)	(4.2)	(4.5)	(3.6)
Engineering and Construction, and Diversified Businesses	**247.0**	222.6	231.7	217.3	167.6
	(24.6)	(20.4)	(19.2)	(18.3)	(15.1)
Total	**¥1,005.3**	¥1,092.0	¥1,208.0	¥1,185.4	¥1,112.2
	(100.0%)	(100.0%)	(100.0%)	(100.0%)	(100.0%)
Export ratio	**22.4%**	21.6%	20.9%	22.2%	25.6%

KAWASAKI STEEL CORP. 1994 ANNUAL REPORT

Steel Performance

Demand for steel in Japan fell as the unrelenting recession put pressure on major steel customers, specifically the construction, automotive and industrial and electric machinery industries. As a result, Kawasaki Steel posted a considerable decline in domestic sales volume, down 633 thousand metric tons. On a positive note, export volume expanded 649 thousand metric tons, thanks to increased shipments to China and Southeast Asia. Thus, overall sales volume edged up 0.2%, or 16,000 metric tons, to 9.8 million metric tons.

Weak market conditions triggered a drop of ¥11,094/metric ton in the average price of steel. Sales value thus declined 13.1%, or ¥107.5 billion, to ¥715.1 billion. Yen-based export performance succumbed to lower U.S. dollar-based prices, the result of greater competition from steelmakers in South Korea and Europe, and yen appreciation.

Steel Data	**1994**	1993	1992	1991	1990
Sales (Billions of yen)	**¥ 715.1**	¥ 822.6	¥ 926.0	¥ 915.1	¥ 904.3
Raw steel production (Millions of metric tons)	**9.9**	9.9	10.7	11.3	11.0
Shipments (Millions of metric tons)	**9.8**	9.8	10.4	10.5	10.3
Average price per ton (Yen)	**¥72,870**	¥83,964	¥88,809	¥87,344	¥88,076

Steel Orders by Market (%)	**1994**	1993	1992	1991	1990
Domestic					
Fabrication and construction	**12.0%**	12.5%	13.7%	14.9%	14.8%
Machinery	**6.7**	7.3	9.8	9.8	9.2
Shipbuilding	**4.6**	5.0	4.5	4.4	4.1
Automotive	**14.5**	15.9	16.3	15.8	14.7
Distributors	**10.5**	10.2	11.4	11.2	11.8
Miscellaneous	**16.5**	21.4	18.6	21.2	21.6
Export	**35.2**	27.7	25.7	22.7	23.8
Total	**100.0%**	100.0%	100.0%	100.0%	100.0%

Steel Product Mix (Domestic and import %)	**1994**	1993	1992	1991	1990
Sheets, strips, plates	**76.1%**	77.0%	76.7%	75.2%	74.8%
Bars	**8.2**	8.5	9.7	10.4	10.3
Pipes, tubes	**11.6**	12.4	12.3	10.6	11.1
Other	**4.1**	2.1	1.3	3.8	3.8
Total	**100.0%**	100.0%	100.0%	100.0%	100.0%

Steel Export Shipments by Area (%)	**1994**	1993	1992	1991	1990
Southeast Asia and Taiwan	**47.9%**	55.4%	56.5%	57.3%	45.1%
China	**28.5**	14.3	12.1	9.1	18.1
United States	**8.4**	9.2	10.6	15.5	16.1
Middle East	**4.3**	7.8	6.3	4.7	4.9
Commonwealth of Independent States (C.I.S.)*	**2.9**	1.2	1.6	1.4	3.4
Other	**8.0**	12.1	12.9	12.0	12.4
Total	**100.0%**	100.0%	100.0%	100.0%	100.0%

*C.I.S. figures are for 1994, 1993 and 1992 only. Previous years' figures are for the U.S.S.R.

KAWASAKI STEEL CORP. 1994 ANNUAL REPORT

Steel Market Analysis and Outlook

Several indicators point toward economic recovery in Japan. Housing starts are growing and commodity prices are stabilizing. However, the employment rate remains unfavorable and levels of capital investment are down because yen appreciation has encouraged manufacturers to shift production overseas. Thus, the Japanese economy currently lacks sufficient strength to sustain a full-fledged recovery, and the prevailing weak conditions will certainly influence the steel industry.

Exports will remain at a high level. In fiscal 1993, steel exports from Japan to China grew even more than anticipated and soared 5.1 million metric tons, to 24.5 million metric tons. Although demand began to wane in the second half of fiscal 1993, Kawasaki Steel expects shipments to China will surge again in fiscal 1994. Sustained improvement of the U.S. economy bodes well for increased exports of semifinished goods to that market in fiscal 1994.

While imports continued to fall in fiscal 1993, the decline seems to be slowing. The drop of 250 thousand metric tons, to 5.4 million metric tons, in the year to March 31, 1994, is due to the recession. In fiscal 1994, user procurement strategies are likely to change, because of the high yen, and will reverse the downward trend in steel imports.

Economic recovery in Japan hinges on an upswing in capital investment and the current delay will likely suppress demand for steel for the fourth consecutive year. Kawasaki Steel estimates fiscal 1994 raw steel production in Japan to fall between 96 million and 97 million metric tons.

Engineering and Construction

Revenues from steelmaking plant activities boosted engineering and construction revenues 10.2%, to ¥186.2 billion, an all-time high. The percentage of high-profit orders contributing to revenues in fiscal 1993 dropped, compared with the fiscal 1992 level, but was compensated for by a sizable increase in lower-profit orders.

Chemical

Sales of chemical products decreased 7.9%, to ¥43.0 billion. Lackluster market conditions caused the prices of benzene, phthlatic anhydride and carbon black oil to fall, and reduced sales volume exacerbated the situation.

The high yen and an overseas shift by users led to a drop in demand for hard ferrite, prompting Kawasaki Steel's decision to pull out of the faltering hard ferrite market in fiscal 1994. Soft ferrite shows promise, thanks to continuing application of the product in electric sources and for limiting electromagnetic noise. The Corporation reinforced its soft ferrite business with the November 1993 establishment of Kawatetsu Ferrite, which assumed the soft ferrite operations of Kawatetsu Magnex. Concerted efforts to rationalize chemical operations were offset by lower market prices.

Large-Scale Integrated Circuits

Sales of LSIs jumped 23.5%, to ¥8.7 billion, primarily the result of a rise in domestic and overseas foundry services. Kawasaki Steel expects the tough LSI operating environment to persist. Operations at the LSI Utsunomiya Works have been upgraded to handle higher demand, but unit prices for LSIs have fallen.

Integrated Systems and Electronics

Fiscal 1993 sales were down 6.0%, to ¥2.4 billion, primarily because of lower sales of computers. Increased product development costs contributed to the decline in sales.

Financial Condition and Liquidity

The lackluster business environment caused profitability to falter. Total funds from operations, buoyed by ¥120.3 billion in depreciation, fell ¥29.4 billion, to ¥99.9 billion. Consequently, despite higher proceeds from the sale of straight bonds, an increase in long-term loans and proceeds from sales of property, plant and equipment, total source of funds dropped ¥31.1 billion, to ¥215.5 billion. Total application of funds amounted to ¥287.8 billion, because a decrease in long-term debt offset a reduction in investments in securities. Working capital dropped ¥72.3 billion.

KAWASAKI STEEL CORP. 1994 ANNUAL REPORT

As a result, interest-bearing liabilities increased ¥67.1 billion, to ¥936.5 billion. The debt/equity ratio reached 1.8:1, from 1.5:1. The equity ratio slipped to 27.8%, from 29.1%.

At March 31, 1994, total assets stood at ¥1,888.9 billion, down ¥54.9 billion from fiscal 1992 year-end. This decrease is attributed to a reduction in inventories and valuation losses on stock and other equity in Group subsidiaries and affiliates.

Financial Condition	1994	1993	1992	1991	1990
Depreciation (Billions of yen)	**¥120.3**	¥121.3	¥117.1	¥102.4	¥104.7
Capital expenditures (Billions of yen)	**133.2**	139.8	167.1	184.8	125.0
Interest-bearing liabilities (Billions of yen)	**936.5**	869.4	813.4	742.8	690.3
Interest coverage ratio (Times)	**0.1**	1.2	2.1	2.9	3.5
Equity ratio (%)	**27.8%**	29.1%	30.4%	30.5%	31.6%

Capital Expenditures

In line with the revised goals of its Five-Year Plan, Kawasaki Steel gave priority to investments that have the greatest direct impact on efficiency and rationalization. Consequently, investment in plant and equipment remained at a high level, and on a construction-cost basis, capital expenditures reached ¥133.2 billion in fiscal 1993.

Kawasaki Steel has focused investment on the modernization of the Chiba Works. Management aims to turn the works into the world's most cost- and quality-competitive steelmaking facility of the 21st century and earmarked ¥260.0 billion for new plants and equipment. Construction of the No. 4 steelmaking shop was completed during fiscal 1993 and will start operations in July 1994. The No. 3 hot-strip mill is slated to go on-stream in May 1995, but the pickling line inside this mill began operations in January 1994.

Because of the importance of modernization at the Chiba Works, management will keep capital investment at a higher level than depreciation until fiscal 1995. From fiscal 1996 onward, management will refrain from major facilities investments and thereby substantially curb capital expenditures.

Consolidated Information

On a consolidated basis, net sales fell 9.6%, to ¥1,185.0 billion. This decrease is attributed to faltering parent-company performance and lower net sales from Group subsidiaries and affiliates, particularly those in steel-related fields, due to the recession.

The Corporation posted a consolidated operating loss of ¥5.6 billion, primarily because of its own operating loss.

The absence of extraordinary losses, such as those recorded in fiscal 1992 for major restructuring at ASC, buoyed the bottom earnings line but failed to overt a consolidated net loss of ¥22.0 billion for the Corporation in fiscal 1993.

Consolidated Results	1994	1993	1992	1991	1990
Net sales (Millions of yen)	**¥1,185,081**	¥1,310,210	¥1,378,554	¥1,314,393	¥1,214,296
Operating income (loss) (Millions of yen)	**(5,639)**	53,493	93,562	127,046	156,546
Net income (loss) (Millions of yen)	**(22,019)**	(30,041)	14,395	43,517	55,869
Operating margin (%)	**(0.5)**	4.1	6.8	9.7	12.9
Return on sales (%)	**(1.9)**	(2.3)	1.0	3.3	4.6
Net income (loss) per share (Yen)	**(6.77)**	(9.23)	4.42	13.38	18.32

Segment Information

Segment information for fiscal 1993 was as follows:

	Steel	Engineering and Construction	Other	Total	Elimination	Consolidated total
Net sales (Millions of yen)	¥822,980	¥306,341	¥259,222	¥1,388,544	¥(203,463)	¥1,185,081
Operating expenses (Millions of yen)	817,913	301,632	272,042	1,391,589	(200,868)	1,190,721
Operating income (loss) (Millions of yen)	5,066	4,708	(12,820)	(3,044)	(2,595)	(5,639)

Note: Segment sales are not included in net sales.

KAWASAKI STEEL CORP. 1994 ANNUAL REPORT

NON-CONSOLIDATED BALANCE SHEETS
March 31, 1994 and 1993

ASSETS	Millions of yen		Thousands of U.S. dollars (Note 1)
KAWASAKI STEEL CORPORATION	1994	1993	1994
Current assets:			
Cash and time deposits	¥ 43,749	¥ 121,993	$ 424,132
Marketable securities (Note 3)	185,098	95,269	1,794,463
Receivables:			
Trade notes	3,853	4,546	37,360
Trade accounts	55,674	62,465	539,747
Subsidiaries and affiliates	145,139	136,319	1,407,072
Other	8,818	8,225	85,488
Less allowance for doubtful receivables	(1,400)	(1,100)	(13,572)
	212,086	210,457	2,056,095
Inventories (Note 4)	249,440	300,508	2,418,233
Other current assets	3,912	5,994	37,930
Total current assets	694,287	734,223	6,730,853
Property, plant and equipment, at cost:			
Land	104,563	104,268	1,013,700
Buildings and structures	565,875	555,353	5,485,951
Machinery and equipment	2,114,487	2,099,804	20,499,148
Construction in progress	85,576	40,805	829,629
	2,870,502	2,800,232	27,828,428
Less accumulated depreciation	(1,991,782)	(1,927,219)	(19,309,573)
	878,719	873,012	8,518,855
Investments and other assets:			
Investments in securities	35,468	36,345	343,850
Investments in and advances to subsidiaries and affiliates (Note 5)	221,111	239,449	2,143,588
Other assets	59,328	60,797	575,169
	315,907	336,592	3,062,607
Total	¥ 1,888,915	¥ 1,943,828	$ 18,312,315

KAWASAKI STEEL CORP. 1994 ANNUAL REPORT

LIABILITIES AND STOCKHOLDERS' EQUITY

KAWASAKI STEEL CORPORATION

	Millions of yen		Thousands of U.S. dollars (Note 1)
	1994	1993	1994
Current liabilities:			
Short-term loans (Note 6)	¥ 194,280	¥ 201,960	$ 1,883,471
Current portion of long-term debt (Note 8)	158,409	39,235	1,535,724
Payables:			
Trade notes	481	582	4,669
Trade accounts	61,499	78,120	596,212
Subsidiaries and affiliates	65,491	70,598	634,913
Other	22,508	17,681	218,209
	149,980	166,981	1,454,003
Accrued taxes	2,233	2,223	21,650
Other current liabilities, including dividends payable (Note 7)	143,316	205,371	1,389,397
Total current liabilities	648,219	615,772	6,284,245
Long-term liabilities:			
Long-term debt (Note 8)	576,059	620,621	5,584,676
Allowance for employees' retirement benefits	91,879	93,273	890,740
Allowance for special repairs (Note 9)	41,524	41,806	402,566
Other long-term liabilities	5,283	7,272	51,221
Total long-term liabilities	714,747	762,974	6,929,203
Contingencies (Note 14)			
Stockholders' equity:			
Common stock			
Authorized 6,000,000,000 shares			
Issued (par value ¥50 per share):			
3,251,553,095 shares as of March 31, 1994	239,643	—	2,323,253
3,251,553,095 shares as of March 31, 1993	—	239,643	—
Capital surplus	119,610	119,610	1,159,579
Legal reserve (Note 10)	36,306	36,306	351,982
Retained earnings (Note 11)	130,387	169,520	1,264,053
Total stockholders' equity	525,948	565,081	5,098,867
Total	¥1,888,915	¥1,943,828	$18,312,315

KAWASAKI STEEL CORP. 1994 ANNUAL REPORT

NON-CONSOLIDATED STATEMENTS OF OPERATIONS

Years ended March 31, 1994 and 1993

	Millions of yen		Thousands of U.S. dollars (Note 1)
KAWASAKI STEEL CORPORATION	**1994**	1993	**1994**
Net sales (Note 12)	**¥1,005,316**	¥1,092,099	**$9,746,158**
Cost of sales (Note 12)	**903,579**	935,893	**8,759,859**
Gross profit	**101,736**	156,206	**986,299**
Selling, general and administrative expenses	**109,260**	119,154	**1,059,242**
Operating income (loss)	**(7,524)**	37,052	**(72,943)**
Non-Operating Profit (Loss):			
Interest income	**8,108**	10,244	**78,604**
Interest expense	**(40,538)**	(42,886)	**(393,005)**
Dividends received	**3,951**	5,460	**38,307**
Miscellaneous	**3,717**	(2,326)	**36,041**
	(24,761)	(29,508)	**(240,053)**
Ordinary Profit (Loss)	**(32,285)**	7,543	**(312,996)**
Extraordinary Profit:			
Profit on sale of tangible fixed assets	**8,569**	3,755	**83,074**
Profit on sale of marketable securities	**18,963**	—	**183,841**
	27,532	3,755	**266,915**
Extraordinary Loss:			
Loss on disposal of tangible fixed assets	**368**	1,243	**3,568**
Loss on devaluation of investments in subsidiaries and affiliates	**27,154**	—	**263,255**
Past service portion of pension cost	**6,627**	9,468	**64,253**
Expenses related to litigation	**—**	265	**—**
	34,150	10,976	**331,076**
Income (loss) before income taxes	**(38,903)**	323	**(377,157)**
Income taxes (Note 13)	**230**	180	**2,230**
Net income (loss)	**¥ (39,133)**	¥ 143	**$ (379,387)**
		Yen	U.S. dollars
Amounts per share of common stock:			
Net income (loss)	**¥ (12.03)**	¥ 0.04	**$ (0.12)**
Cash dividends	**—**	6.00	**—**

KAWASAKI STEEL CORP. 1994 ANNUAL REPORT

NON-CONSOLIDATED STATEMENTS OF STOCKHOLDERS' EQUITY
Years ended March 31, 1994 and 1993

KAWASAKI STEEL CORPORATION

	Number of shares of common stock (Thousands)	Millions of yen Common stock	Capital surplus	Legal reserve	Retained earnings
Balance at March 31, 1992	3,251,553	¥ 239,643	¥ 119,610	¥ 34,347	¥ 190,930
Net income		—	—	—	143
Cash dividends paid		—	—	—	(19,509)
Bonuses to directors and statutory auditors		—	—	—	(84)
Transfer to legal reserve		—	—	1,959	(1,959)
Balance at March 31, 1993	3,251,553	239,643	119,610	36,306	169,520
Net loss		—	—	—	(39,133)
Cash dividends paid		—	—	—	—
Bonuses to directors and statutory auditors		—	—	—	—
Transfer to legal reserve		—	—	—	—
Balance at March 31, 1994	**3,251,553**	**¥ 239,643**	**¥ 119,610**	**¥ 36,306**	**¥ 130,387**

	Number of shares of common stock (Thousands)	Thousands of U.S. dollars (Note 1) Common stock	Capital surplus	Legal reserve	Retained earnings
Balance at March 31, 1993	3,251,553	$ 2,323,253	$ 1,159,579	$ 351,982	$ 1,643,440
Net loss		—	—	—	(379,387)
Cash dividends paid		—	—	—	—
Bonuses to directors and statutory auditors		—	—	—	—
Transfer to legal reserve		—	—	—	—
Balance at March 31, 1994	**3,251,553**	**$2,323,253**	**$1,159,579**	**$351,982**	**$1,264,053**

KAWASAKI STEEL CORP. 1994 ANNUAL REPORT

NON-CONSOLIDATED STATEMENTS OF CHANGES IN FINANCIAL POSITION

Years ended March 31, 1994 and 1993

KAWASAKI STEEL CORPORATION	Millions of yen 1994	Millions of yen 1993	Thousands of U.S. dollars (Note 1) 1994
Source of funds:			
Operations—			
Net income (loss)	¥ (39,133)	¥ 143	$ (379,387)
Add income changes:			
Depreciation	120,363	121,306	1,166,874
Provision for employees' retirement benefits	10,023	4,370	97,175
Provision for special repairs	1,657	1,854	16,068
Loss from disposal of property, plant and equipment	7,002	1,642	67,888
Total from operations	99,912	129,316	968,618
Proceeds from sale of straight bonds	30,000	30,000	290,839
Increase in long-term loans	84,317	86,907	817,423
Proceeds from sales of property, plant and equipment	1,285	398	12,465
Total source of funds	215,515	246,622	2,089,345
Application of funds:			
Decrease in long-term debt	158,879	40,130	1,540,280
Cash dividends paid	—	19,509	—
Bonuses to directors and statutory auditors	—	84	—
Capital expenditures	133,220	139,888	1,291,517
Increase (decrease) in investments in securities, and investments in and advances to subsidiaries and affiliates	(19,215)	40,518	(186,291)
Other, net	15,015	14,049	145,566
Total application of funds	287,899	254,181	2,791,072
Decrease in working capital	¥ (72,383)	¥ (7,559)	$ (701,727)
Changes in components of working capital:			
Increase (decrease) in current assets:			
Cash and time deposits	¥ (78,244)	¥ (17,514)	$ (758,552)
Marketable securities	89,829	(7,039)	870,862
Receivables, less doubtful accounts	1,628	2,158	15,790
Inventories	(51,067)	(1,786)	(495,082)
Other current assets	(2,081)	(9,988)	(20,182)
Decrease in current assets	(39,936)	(34,170)	(387,164)
Increase (decrease) in current liabilities:			
Payables	(17,001)	(6,517)	(164,823)
Short-term loans	(7,680)	1,840	(74,455)
Current portion of long-term debt	119,174	(22,074)	1,155,351
Other current liabilities	(62,045)	139	(601,510)
Decrease in current liabilities	32,447	(26,611)	314,563
Decrease in working capital	¥ (72,383)	¥ (7,559)	$ (701,727)

KAWASAKI STEEL CORP. 1994 ANNUAL REPORT

NOTES TO NON-CONSOLIDATED FINANCIAL STATEMENTS
March 31, 1994 and 1993

KAWASAKI STEEL CORPORATION

1 Basis of preparation

(a) The accompanying non-consolidated financial statements were prepared from the accounts and records maintained by Kawasaki Steel Corporation (the "Company") in accordance with the relevant provisions of the Commercial Code of Japan and in conformity with generally accepted accounting principles and practices in Japan.

In preparing the non-consolidated financial statements for inclusion in this report, certain items presented in the originally published financial statements have been reclassified for readers outside Japan.

(b) Preparation of non-consolidated statements of changes in financial position is not required in Japan. They are, however, presented in this report to provide additional information. In addition, the accompanying notes include information that is not required under generally accepted accounting principles and practices in Japan but is presented herein as additional information.

(c) As permitted by the Securities and Exchange Law of Japan, all amounts in the financial statements and notes are stated in millions of yen by rounding off fractional amounts of less than one million. As a result, the totals in yen shown in the financial statements and notes do not necessarily agree with the sums of the individual amounts.

(d) The translation of yen amounts into U.S. dollar amounts is included solely for convenience and has been made as a matter of arithmetical computation only, at the rate of ¥103.15=US$1, the prevailing rate on the Tokyo foreign exchange market on March 31, 1994.

The translation should not be construed as a representation that the yen amounts have been or could be readily converted, realized or settled in U.S. dollars at that or any other rate.

2 Summary of significant accounting policies

(a) Foreign currency translation
Short-term receivables and payables in foreign currencies are translated at the exchange rates prevailing on the transaction dates. Those hedged by forward foreign exchange contracts are translated at the contracted rates.

Long-term receivables and payables in foreign currencies are translated at the exchange rates prevailing on the transaction dates. Those hedged by forward foreign exchange contracts are translated at the contracted rates. Deferred translation gain arising from differences between the historical exchange rates and the contracted exchange rates is deferred and amortized over the period from the date of the forward exchange contract to its maturity date.

The remaining unamortized balances of the deferred translation gain are included in "Other long-term liabilities" in the accompanying non-consolidated balance sheets.

(b) Sales recognition
Sales of finished goods are generally recognized when the goods are shipped to the customers.

Sales and the related costs of certain long-term construction contracts (for which the period of construction is more than one year and the acceptance amount of the contract exceeds ¥7 billion) are recognized by the percentage of completion method.

(c) Inventories
Inventories are carried at cost as determined by the last-in, first-out method, except for inventories of the Engineering and Construction Division, which are valued by the individual identification method; inventories of LSI Division by the first-in, first-out method; supplementary supplies by the moving-average method; and ingot cases and rolls by the average method.

Effective April 1, 1993, the Company changed its valuation method for raw materials and supplies, except for ingot cases and rolls, from the average method to the last-in, first-out method. Given the recent rapid fluctuations in foreign exchange rates, this change was made for a more appropriate matching of costs and revenues as well as for a more accurate reflection of the fluctuations in the prices of raw materials for cost accounting purposes.

The effect of this change was to increase income before taxes by ¥1,627 million ($15,778 thousand) for the year ended March 31, 1994.

KAWASAKI STEEL CORP. 1994 ANNUAL REPORT

(d) Marketable securities and investments in securities
All securities are valued at cost as determined by the moving-average method. However, in cases where there has been a substantial decline in value and the Company does not expect a significant recovery in the foreseeable future, such securities have been written down to a level that the Company considers to be fair and reasonable in the circumstances.

(e) Depreciation
Depreciation is provided by the declining-balance method based on the useful lives of the assets as prescribed by the Corporation Tax Law of Japan. The range of useful lives is principally from 15 to 65 years for buildings and structures and from 5 to 15 years for machinery and equipment.

Maintenance and repairs, including minor renewals and betterments, are charged to income as incurred.

(f) Research and development expenses
Research and development expenses are charged to income as incurred.

(g) Income taxes
Income taxes are calculated on taxable income and charged to income on an accrual basis. Deferred income taxes pertaining to timing differences between financial and tax reporting are not provided.

(h) Retirement allowances and pension plans
Employees of the Company are generally entitled to lump-sum retirement allowances when they leave the Company. The amount of the retirement allowance is determined on the basis of length of service and basic salary at the time of retirement.

In the case of involuntary retirement, the employee is entitled to a higher payment than in the case of voluntary retirement.

The Company provides for these retirement allowances by the present value method, based on the amounts which could be required to be paid if all employees retired voluntarily as of the balance sheet date.

Retirement allowance provisions are not funded by the Company.

Effective March 1, 1990, the Company introduced a qualified defined pension plan, replacing a part of the lump-sum retirement allowance, which provides a lump-sum payment, as defined, to employees who terminate employment with the Company at age 50 or older.

Normal costs of the plan are charged to expenses as incurred. Past service cost is being amortized by the declining-balance method (30% of the unamortized balance each year), as prescribed by Japanese tax law.

(i) Net income (loss) per share and cash dividends per share
The computation of net income per share is based on the weighted average number of shares of common stock issued during each year, but is not adjusted for the potentially dilutive effects of the conversion of outstanding convertible bonds or the exercise of outstanding warrants.

Cash dividends declared subsequent to the end of an accounting year and designated as applicable to the earnings of the year are accrued and charged to retained earnings as of the end of such accounting year.

3 Marketable securities

Marketable securities and the aggregate values of listed equity securities were as follows:

	Millions of yen		Thousands of U.S. dollars (Note 1)
As of March 31,	**1994**	1993	**1994**
Listed equity securities	**¥131,051**	¥ 85,195	**$1,270,496**
Bonds and other marketable securities	**54,047**	10,073	**523,967**
Total	**¥185,098**	¥ 95,269	**$1,794,463**
Market value of listed equity securities	**¥264,916**	¥234,592	**$2,568,264**

KAWASAKI STEEL CORP. 1994 ANNUAL REPORT

4 Inventories

Inventories as of March 31, 1994 and 1993 were as follows:

As of March 31,	Millions of yen 1994	Millions of yen 1993	Thousands of U.S. dollars (Note 1) 1994
Finished goods	¥ 38,850	¥ 49,071	$ 376,640
Semifinished goods	55,547	62,122	538,513
Work in process	57,531	78,764	557,749
Raw materials and supplies	97,510	110,549	945,331
Total	¥249,440	¥300,508	$2,418,233

5 Investments in and advances to subsidiaries and affiliates

Investments in and advances to subsidiaries and affiliates consisted of the following:

As of March 31,	Millions of yen 1994	Millions of yen 1993	Thousands of U.S. dollars (Note 1) 1994
Subsidiaries:			
Kawasaki Steel Holdings (USA), Inc.	¥ 71,952	¥ 93,792	$ 697,550
Philippine Sinter Corporation	20,197	20,225	195,803
Kawatetsu Magnex Corporation	12,130	9,801	117,596
Kawatetsu Steel Products Corporation	4,975	4,975	48,238
Kawaden Co., Ltd.	4,594	4,594	44,538
Kawatetsu Transportation Co., Ltd.	3,979	3,979	38,583
Daiwa Steel Corporation	3,800	3,800	36,845
Kawatetsu Galvanizing Co., Ltd.	3,391	3,391	32,877
Mizushima Ferroalloy Co., Ltd.	3,359	3,359	32,570
Kawatetsu Kizai Kogyo Kaisha, Ltd.	2,916	2,916	28,274
Kawasaki Steel Techno-Wire Corporation	2,856	2,856	27,692
Kawatetsu Metal Fabrica Corporation	2,359	2,359	22,872
Kawatetsu Ferrite Corporation	2,030	—	19,680
Other	11,990	12,908	116,245
	¥150,533	¥168,960	$1,459,363
Affiliates:			
Kawasaki Enterprises Inc.	29,378	27,360	284,818
Nihon Semiconductor, Inc.	17,500	17,500	169,657
Kawasho Corporation	6,016	6,016	58,323
Kawatetsu Rockfiber Corporation	2,575	2,805	24,964
Mizushima Joint Thermal Power Co., Ltd.	1,937	1,937	18,783
Other	13,170	14,870	127,680
	¥ 70,577	¥ 70,489	$ 684,225
Total	¥221,111	¥239,449	$2,143,588

KAWASAKI STEEL CORP. 1994 ANNUAL REPORT

6 Short-term loans

Short-term loans bore interest at 4.00% per annum as of March 31, 1993 and 4.40% per annum as of March 31, 1994, the prime rates in effect at those dates.

7 Other current liabilities

Other current liabilities as of March 31, 1994 and 1993 consisted of the following:

	Millions of yen		Thousands of U.S. dollars (Note 1)
As of March 31,	1994	1993	1994
Accrued expenses	¥ 76,679	¥ 85,156	$ 743,382
Advances received	49,473	80,025	479,629
Cash dividends payable and bonuses to directors and statutory auditors	—	9,838	—
Other	17,162	30,351	166,386
Total	¥143,316	¥205,371	$1,389,397

Cash dividends and bonuses to directors and statutory auditors are paid subsequent to approval by the stockholders at the relevant annual general meeting of stockholders.

8 Long-term debt

Long-term debt as of March 31, 1994 and 1993 consisted of the following:

	Millions of yen		Thousands of U.S. dollars (Note 1)
As of March 31,	1994	1993	1994
7.3% to 8.2% domestic mortgage bonds due in annual installments from 1988 to 1996	¥ 24,000	¥ 27,200	$ 232,671
7.5% dual currency U.S. dollar/yen notes issued April 1, 1986, due 1996[1]	10,000	10,000	96,946
Reverse floating rate/fixed rate yen notes issued September 9, 1986, due 1996	10,000	10,000	96,946
4.875% yen notes issued April 8, 1987, due 1994[1]	18,572	18,572	180,054
7.25% yen notes issued August 22, 1991, due 1999	30,000	30,000	290,839
7.25% yen notes issued August 22, 1991, due 2000	30,000	30,000	290,839
6.00% yen notes issued June 10, 1992, due 1997	30,000	30,000	290,839
3.0% domestic bonds issued December 20, 1993, due 1999	30,000	—	290,839
1.6% domestic convertible bonds issued May 18, 1989, due 2004[2]	69,614	69,614	674,881
1.5% domestic convertible bonds issued May 18, 1989, due 1998[2]	79,363	79,363	769,394
3.9% domestic bonds with warrants issued September 20, 1990, due 1994[3]	50,000	50,000	484,731
5.0% U.S. dollar bonds with warrants issued September 20, 1990, due 1994[1, 3]	47,423	47,423	459,750
Loans, at interest rates from 0.75% to 9.5%, principally from banks and insurance companies, due from 1994 to 2012	305,496	257,684	2,961,671
	734,469	659,857	7,120,400
Less current portion of long-term debt	(158,409)	(39,235)	(1,535,724)
	¥ 576,059	¥620,621	$ 5,584,676

[1] These bonds and notes are fully or partially covered by forward exchange or currency swap contracts.
[2] These bonds were convertible into shares of common stock at the rate of ¥1,082.20 per share as of the date of this report.
[3] The initial subscription price of the warrants attached to these bonds was ¥441 per share.

KAWASAKI STEEL CORP. 1994 ANNUAL REPORT

Assets pledged as of March 31, 1994 and 1993 to secure the Company's long-term debt were as follows:

As of March 31,	Millions of yen 1994	Millions of yen 1993	Thousands of U.S. dollars (Note 1) 1994
Accounts receivable	¥ 4,109	¥ 8,219	$ 39,843
Marketable securities and investments in securities	31,196	34,750	302,431
Land	11,877	11,908	115,147
	¥47,183	¥54,878	$457,421

Mortgage bonds of ¥24,000 million ($232,671 thousand) in the aggregate, were secured by a mortgage on all the Company's property and assets.

As is customary in Japan, substantially all of the bank borrowings, including short-term borrowings, are subject to general agreements with each bank which provide, among other things, that the bank may require the borrower to provide collateral (or additional collateral) or guarantees for these loans and may treat any collateral so furnished as collateral for all present and future indebtedness. In addition, the bank shall have the right to offset cash deposits against obligations that have become due or, in the event of default, against all obligations payable to the bank.

Under certain loan agreements relating to long-term debt, the lenders may require the Company to submit proposals for appropriations of earnings, including payment of dividends, for the creditors' review and approval prior to presentation to the stockholders. The Company has never received a request of the kind described.

In 1989, the Company entered into an agreement with overseas subsidiaries (the "agreement") to deposit amounts in U.S. dollars equivalent to the principal and accrued interest due on the Company's 10.5% U.S. dollar notes due 1995 guaranteed by a bank, in consideration for which the bank undertook to assume the Company's obligation for payment thereunder. Consequently, although the Company remains the primary obligor for such notes in the event of default by the bank, it regards the likelihood of such default as being sufficiently remote that neither the obligation of the Company for the notes nor the amounts paid to the bank under the agreement have been recognized in the accounts of the Company subsequent to the date of the agreement.

The aggregate annual maturities of long-term debt subsequent to March 31, 1994, are summarized as follows:

Year ending March 31,	Millions of yen 1994	Thousands of U.S. dollars (Note 1) 1994
1995	¥158,410	$1,535,725
1996	29,470	285,700
1997	87,405	847,358
1998 and thereafter	459,183	4,451,604
Total	¥734,468	$7,120,387

9 Allowance for special repairs

Blast furnaces and hot blast stoves, including related machinery and equipment, periodically require substantial repairs and replacement of components. Such work normally occurs approximately every 7 to 10 years for blast furnaces and every 14 to 20 years for hot blast stoves. The estimated future costs of such maintenance are provided and charged to income on a straight-line basis over the periods to the respective dates of such anticipated replacements and repairs. Differences between the estimated costs and the actual costs are charged or credited to income as incurred.

10 Legal reserve

The Commercial Code of Japan provides that a portion of retained earnings equal to at least 10% of cash dividends and bonuses to directors and statutory auditors paid with respect to each financial period be appropriated as a legal reserve until such reserve equals 25% of the common stock. This reserve is not available for dividends, but may be capitalized by resolution of the Board of Directors or used to eliminate a deficit by resolution of the stockholders.

KAWASAKI STEEL CORP. 1994 ANNUAL REPORT

11 Retained earnings

Retained earnings include the reserves under the Special Taxation Measures Law. The schedule of these reserves is summarized as follows:

As of March 31,	Millions of yen 1994	Millions of yen 1993	Thousands of U.S. dollars (Note 1) 1994
Reserve for accelerated depreciation	¥14,067	¥14,724	$136,375
Reserve for losses on overseas investments	149	214	1,450
Reserve for advanced depreciation of property	21,240	13,547	205,921
Total	¥35,457	¥28,486	$343,746

The Special Taxation Measures Law permits the Company to deduct for income tax purposes, transfers to certain reserves that are not required for financial accounting purposes, if recorded on the books as profit appropriations or charges to income, and to restore them to taxable income in future years.

12 Sales to and purchases from subsidiaries and affiliates

Sales to and purchases from subsidiaries and affiliates for the years ended March 31, 1994 and 1993 were as follows:

	Millions of yen 1994	Millions of yen 1993	Thousands of U.S. dollars (Note 1) 1994
Sales	¥624,768	¥653,198	$6,056,890
Purchases	293,165	296,731	2,842,128

13 Income taxes

Income taxes applicable to the Company consist of corporate, enterprise and inhabitants' taxes. Income taxes shown in the statements of operations include corporate and inhabitants' taxes. Enterprise tax is included in operating expenses. Accrued taxes reflected on the balance sheets consist of the above-mentioned taxes.

14 Contingencies

The Company had the following contingent liabilities as of March 31, 1994:

Year ending March 31,	Millions of yen 1994	Thousands of U.S. dollars (Note 1) 1994
Trade notes discounted	¥7,800	$75,618
Guarantees of loans	5,709	55,349
Notes under debt assumption agreements (Note 8)	5,207	50,484

As of March 31, 1994, the Company had cancelable long-term lease agreements, principally for computer equipment, office space and employees' housing, under which the Company was contingently liable for annual lease payments of approximately ¥7,026 million ($68,121 thousand) in the aggregate for the year ended March 31, 1994.

KAWASAKI STEEL CORP. 1994 ANNUAL REPORT

15 Subsequent event

The following appropriations of retained earnings, which have been reflected in the accompanying financial statements for the year ended March 31, 1994, were approved at the annual meeting of the stockholders held on June 29, 1994:

	Millions of yen	Thousands of U.S. dollars (Note 1)
Year ending March 31,	**1994**	**1994**
Cash dividends	¥ —	$ —
Transfer to legal reserve	—	—
Bonuses to directors and statutory auditors	—	—

REPORT OF THE INDEPENDENT CERTIFIED PUBLIC ACCOUNTANTS ON THE NON-CONSOLIDATED FINANCIAL STATEMENTS

The Board of Directors
Kawasaki Steel Corporation

We have examined the non-consolidated balance sheets of Kawasaki Steel Corporation as of March 31, 1994 and 1993, and the related non-consolidated statements of operations, stockholders' equity and changes in financial position for the years then ended, all expressed in yen. Our examinations were made in accordance with auditing standards generally accepted in Japan and, accordingly, included such tests of the accounting records and such other auditing procedures as we considered necessary in the circumstances.

In our opinion, the accompanying non-consolidated financial statements present fairly the financial position of Kawasaki Steel Corporation at March 31, 1994 and 1993, and the results of its operations and changes in its financial position for the years then ended, in conformity with accounting principles generally accepted in Japan consistently applied, except for the change, with which we concur, in the valuation method of raw materials and supplies as discussed in Note 2 (c) to the non-consolidated financial statements.

The U.S. dollar amounts in the accompanying non-consolidated financial statements with respect to the year ended March 31, 1994 are presented solely for convenience. Our examination also included the translation of yen amounts into U.S. dollar amounts and, in our opinion, such translation has been made on the basis described in Note 1 to the non-consolidated financial statements.

SHOWA OTA & CO.

Osaka, Japan
June 29, 1994

KAWASAKI STEEL CORP. 1994 ANNUAL REPORT

CONSOLIDATED BALANCE SHEETS
March 31, 1994 and 1993

ASSETS	Millions of yen		Thousands of U.S. dollars (Note 1)
KAWASAKI STEEL CORPORATION	1994	1993	1994
Current assets:			
Cash and time deposits	¥ 65,071	¥ 141,064	$ 630,843
Marketable securities	195,765	113,923	1,897,870
Notes and accounts receivable	208,180	216,370	2,018,234
Less allowance for doubtful receivables	(1,897)	(1,709)	(18,396)
Inventories	306,593	354,388	2,972,311
Other current assets	93,147	70,031	903,026
Total current assets	866,861	894,069	8,403,888
Property, plant and equipment, at cost:			
Land	128,299	124,909	1,243,814
Buildings and structures	636,291	620,930	6,168,606
Machinery and equipment	2,318,124	2,276,936	22,473,337
Construction in progress	92,488	44,824	896,636
	3,175,203	3,067,600	30,782,393
Less accumulated depreciation	(2,159,966)	(2,076,648)	(20,940,049)
	1,015,237	990,952	9,842,344
Investments and other assets:			
Investments in securities	46,153	76,478	447,443
Investments in and advances to unconsolidated subsidiaries and affiliates	110,906	128,422	1,075,200
Deferred income taxes	8,130	7,576	78,827
Other assets	80,200	82,931	777,510
	245,391	295,407	2,378,980
Deferred assets:			
Expenses for the issuance of new shares	—	1	—
Expenses for research and development	67	53	650
Total deferred assets	67	55	650
Excess of investment costs over equity in net assets of consolidated subsidiaries	3,435	3,036	33,310
Translation adjustments	33,391	47	323,719
Total	¥ 2,164,385	¥ 2,183,569	$ 20,982,891

KAWASAKI STEEL CORP. 1994 ANNUAL REPORT

LIABILITIES AND STOCKHOLDERS' EQUITY

KAWASAKI STEEL CORPORATION

	Millions of yen 1994	Millions of yen 1993	U.S. dollars (Note 1) 1994
Current liabilities:			
Notes and accounts payable	**¥ 182,034**	¥ 207,889	**$ 1,764,758**
Short-term loans	**290,014**	275,866	**2,811,581**
Current portion of long-term debt	**169,309**	48,925	**1,641,387**
Accrued taxes	**3,838**	5,812	**37,211**
Other current liabilities	**182,569**	247,595	**1,769,942**
Total current liabilities	**827,766**	786,088	**8,024,879**
Long-term liabilities:			
Long-term debt	**650,481**	667,424	**6,306,171**
Allowance for employees' retirement benefits	**108,163**	109,032	**1,048,607**
Allowance for special repairs	**42,242**	42,523	**409,522**
Other long-term liabilities	**9,943**	12,358	**96,401**
Total long-term liabilities	**810,831**	831,339	**7,860,701**
Minority interests in consolidated subsidiaries	**24,455**	26,862	**237,090**
Contingencies (Note 4)			
Stockholders' equity:			
Common stock			
Authorized 6,000,000,000 shares			
Issued (par value ¥50 per share):			
3,251,553,095 shares as of March 31, 1994	**239,643**	—	**2,323,253**
3,251,553,095 shares as of March 31, 1993	**—**	239,643	**—**
Capital surplus	**119,610**	119,610	**1,159,579**
Legal reserve	**36,306**	36,306	**351,982**
Retained earnings	**105,777**	143,722	**1,025,476**
Less treasury stock at cost			
19,482 shares at March 31, 1994			
13,506 shares at March 31, 1993	**(7)**	(4)	**(69)**
Total stockholders' equity	**501,331**	539,279	**4,860,221**
Total	**¥2,164,385**	¥2,183,569	**$20,982,891**

KAWASAKI STEEL CORP. 1994 ANNUAL REPORT

CONSOLIDATED STATEMENTS OF OPERATIONS
Years ended March 31, 1994 and 1993

	Millions of yen		Thousands of U.S. dollars (Note 1)
KAWASAKI STEEL CORPORATION	**1994**	1993	**1994**
Net sales	**¥1,185,081**	¥1,310,210	**$11,488,917**
Cost of sales	**1,034,129**	1,088,469	**10,025,488**
Gross profit	**150,952**	221,740	**1,463,429**
Selling, general and administrative expenses	**156,592**	168,246	**1,518,105**
Operating income (loss)	**(5,639)**	53,493	**(54,676)**
Non-operating profit (loss):			
Interest income	**10,183**	12,419	**98,727**
Interest expense	**(47,595)**	(50,508)	**(461,420)**
Dividends received	**3,071**	4,268	**29,780**
Miscellaneous	**2,979**	(3,529)	**28,885**
	(31,360)	(37,349)	**(304,028)**
Ordinary profit (loss):	**(37,000)**	16,144	**(358,704)**
Extraordinary profit:			
Profit on sale of tangible fixed assets	**8,536**	3,878	**82,756**
Profit on sale of marketable securities	**18,963**	—	**183,841**
	27,499	3,878	**266,597**
Extraordinary loss:			
Loss on disposal of tangible fixed assets	**(505)**	(1,281)	**(4,903)**
Loss on devaluation of investments in subsidiaries and affiliates	**(5,314)**	—	**(51,525)**
Past service portion of pension cost	**(7,022)**	(9,935)	**(68,083)**
Expenses related to litigation	**—**	(265)	**—**
	(12,843)	(11,482)	**(124,511)**
Income (loss) before income taxes	**(22,344)**	8,540	**(216,618)**
Income taxes:			
Current	**3,003**	6,583	**29,117**
Deferred	**(554)**	(567)	**(5,380)**
Minority interests in net loss (income) of consolidated subsidiaries	**2,495**	(2,537)	**24,196**
Amortization of investment cost over equity in net assets of consolidated subsidiaries	**(840)**	(432)	**(8,151)**
Equity in net income (loss) of affiliates	**1,147**	(29,372)	**11,129**
Translation adjustments	**(29)**	45	**(287)**
Net income (loss)	**¥ (22,019)**	¥ (30,041)	**$ (213,468)**
		Yen	U.S. dollars
Amounts per share of common stock:			
Net income (loss)	**¥ (6.77)**	¥ (9.23)	**$ (0.066)**
Cash dividends	**—**	6.00	**—**

KAWASAKI STEEL CORP. 1994 ANNUAL REPORT

CONSOLIDATED STATEMENTS OF STOCKHOLDERS' EQUITY
Years ended March 31, 1994 and 1993

KAWASAKI STEEL CORPORATION

	Number of shares of common stock (Thousands)	Millions of yen			
		Common stock	Capital surplus	Legal reserve	Retained earnings
Balance at March 31, 1992	3,251,553	¥239,643	¥119,610	¥34,347	¥195,885
Net loss		—	—	—	(30,041)
Cash dividends paid		—	—	—	(19,509)
Bonuses to directors and statutory auditors		—	—	—	(217)
Transfer to legal reserve		—	—	1,959	(1,959)
Decrease in retained earnings mainly due to addition of consolidated subsidiaries or to application of equity method to certain affiliates		—	—	—	(595)
Translation adjustments		—	—	—	159
Balance at March 31, 1993	3,251,553	239,643	119,610	36,306	143,722
Net loss		—	—	—	(22,019)
Cash dividends paid		—	—	—	—
Bonuses to directors and statutory auditors		—	—	—	(87)
Transfer to legal reserve		—	—	—	—
Decrease in retained earnings due to restatement of a consolidated subsidiary's financial statements [Note 2 (d)]		—	—	—	(20,250)
Translation adjustments		—	—	—	4,412
Balance at March 31, 1994	**3,251,553**	**¥239,643**	**¥119,610**	**¥36,306**	**¥105,777**

	Number of shares of common stock (Thousands)	Thousands of U.S. dollars (Note 1)			
		Common stock	Capital surplus	Legal reserve	Retained earnings
Balance at March 31, 1993	3,251,553	$ 2,323,253	$ 1,159,579	$ 351,982	$ 1,393,332
Net loss		—	—	—	(213,468)
Cash dividends paid		—	—	—	—
Bonuses to directors and statutory auditors		—	—	—	(849)
Transfer to legal reserve		—	—	—	—
Decrease in retained earnings due to restatement of a consolidated subsidiary's financial statements [Note 2 (d)]		—	—	—	(196,317)
Translation adjustments		—	—	—	42,777
Balance at March 31, 1994	**3,251,553**	**$2,323,253**	**$1,159,579**	**$351,982**	**$1,025,475**

KAWASAKI STEEL CORP. 1994 ANNUAL REPORT

NOTES TO CONSOLIDATED FINANCIAL STATEMENTS

March 31, 1994 and 1993

KAWASAKI STEEL CORPORATION

1 Basis of preparation

(a) The accompanying consolidated financial statements were prepared from the accounts and records maintained by Kawasaki Steel Corporation (the "Company") and its 35 major subsidiaries (together, the "Companies." See Note 2 (a) below.) The Companies maintain their accounts and records in accordance with the relevant provisions of the Securities and Exchange Law of Japan and in conformity with accounting principles and practices generally accepted in Japan.

In preparing the consolidated financial statements for inclusion in this report, certain items presented in the originally published financial statements have been reclassified for readers outside Japan.

(b) As permitted by the Securities and Exchange Law of Japan, all amounts in the financial statements and notes are stated in millions of yen by rounding off fractional amounts of less than one million. As a result, the totals in yen shown in the financial statements and notes do not necessarily agree with the sums of the individual amounts.

(c) The translation of yen amounts into U.S. dollar amounts is included solely for convenience and has been made as a matter of arithmetical computation only, at the rate of ¥103.15=US$1, the prevailing rate on the Tokyo foreign exchange market on March 31, 1994. The translation should not be construed as a representation that yen amounts have been or could be readily converted, realized or settled in U.S. dollars at that or any other rate.

2 Summary of significant accounting policies

(a) Principles of consolidation

The Company had 112 wholly-owned or majority-owned subsidiaries as of March 31, 1994. The consolidated financial statements include the accounts of the Company and 35 of its subsidiaries. The 35 subsidiaries consolidated with the Company are listed below:

Kawatetsu Galvanizing Co., Ltd.
Daiwa Steel Corporation
Kawatetsu Steel Products Corporation
Kawasaki Steel Container Co., Ltd.
Kawatetsu Transportation Co., Ltd.
Kawaden Co., Ltd.
Kawasaki Steel Systems R&D Corporation
Kawasaki Refractories Co., Ltd.
Mizushima Ferroalloy Co., Ltd.
Kawatetsu Kizai Kogyo Co., Ltd.
Kawatetsu Techno-Construction Co., Ltd.
Kawatetsu Electric Engineering Co., Ltd.
Kawatetsu Warehouse Co., Ltd.
Kawatetsu Metal Fabrica Corporation
Kawatetsu Advantech Co., Ltd.
River Building Materials Co., Ltd.
Kawasaki Steel Holdings (USA), Inc.
Philippine Sinter Corporation
Kawasaki Wafer Technology, Inc.*
Kawasaki Thermal Systems, Inc.*
Kawasaki Steel America, Inc.*
Kawasaki Steel Investments, Inc.*
KSCA, Incorporated*
Kawasaki Steel International (USA), Inc.*
KS San Diego, Inc.*
KS Development America, Inc.*
KSC Hawaii, Inc.*
KSEC America, Inc.*
Kawasaki Chemical Holding Co., Inc.*
Kawasaki LNP, Inc.*
LNP Plastics Nederland B.V.*
LNP Engineering Plastics, Inc.*
River-America, Inc.*
KSC Capital of America, Inc.*
Kawasaki Steel Trade Funding (USA), Inc.*

*These 17 companies are consolidated subsidiaries of Kawasaki Steel Holdings (USA), Inc.

Kawasaki Steel Holdings (USA), Inc., its consolidated subsidiaries and Philippine Sinter Corporation adopt a fiscal year ending on December 31. These subsidiaries do not prepare for consolidated purposes statements for the period corresponding with the fiscal period of the Company, because the effects of the intervening events are considered immaterial.

KAWASAKI STEEL CORP. 1994 ANNUAL REPORT

Intercompany transactions and account balances among the Companies have been eliminated in consolidation.

The remaining 77 unconsolidated subsidiaries whose combined assets, sales and net income are not significant in the aggregate (essentially less than 10% in relation to those of the Companies), have, therefore not been consolidated with the Companies.

Any difference between the acquisition cost of a consolidated subsidiary and the underlying equity in its net assets is treated as an asset or liability, and is amortized over a period of five years on a straight-line basis.

The legal reserves of the consolidated subsidiaries are transferred to retained earnings in the consolidated statements in accordance with the Securities and Exchange Law of Japan.

(b) Investments in unconsolidated subsidiaries and affiliates
Investments in certain unconsolidated subsidiaries (wholly-owned and majority-owned) and affiliates (owned 20% to 50% by the Company) are accounted for by the equity method.

Although the Company had 77 unconsolidated subsidiaries and 70 affiliates at March 31, 1994, the equity method was applied only to the investments in 14 affiliates since the investments in the remaining unconsolidated subsidiaries and affiliates were not material in relation to the net income (loss) of the Companies in the consolidated financial statements.

(c) Change in accounting principles
See Note 2 (c) of the Notes to Non-Consolidated Financial Statements.

(d) Restatement of a consolidated subsidiary's financial statements
In December 1993, Armco Steel Company, L.P. ("ASC"), an affiliate of Kawasaki Steel Holdings (USA), Inc. ("KSH", a consolidated subsidiary of the Company), the investment in whom is accounted for by the equity method in the consolidated financial statements of KSH, adopted Statement of Financial Accounting Standards No. 106, "Employer's Accounting for Postretirement Benefits Other than Pensions" (SFAS 106), retroactive to January 1, 1990.

SFAS 106 requires ASC to accrue the estimated cost of retiree benefit payments during the years the employee provides services. ASC previously expensed the cost of these benefits, which are principally health care, as claims were incurred. SFAS 106 allows recognition of the cumulative effect of this obligation in the year of the adoption or the amortization of the obligation over a period of up to 20 years. ASC elected to recognize this obligation immediately effective January 1, 1990 and recorded $491.6 million as the cumulative effect of this change in 1990. ASC restated its financial statements for the years 1990 through 1992, and accordingly, KSH restated the 1992 consolidated financial statements by adjusting the accumulated deficit at December 31, 1991 and its share of the 1992 loss of ASC.

3 Account balances with unconsolidated subsidiaries and affiliates

Account balances of the Companies with unconsolidated subsidiaries and affiliates as of March 31, 1994 and 1993 are summarized as follows:

	Millions of yen		Thousands of U.S. dollars (Note 1)
As of March 31,	**1994**	1993	**1994**
Due from unconsolidated subsidiaries and affiliates	**¥213,803**	¥191,495	**$2,072,743**
Due to unconsolidated subsidiaries and affiliates	**77,609**	96,423	**752,398**

4 Contingencies

As of March 31, 1994 and 1993, the Companies were contingently liable as follows:

	Millions of yen		Thousands of U.S. dollars (Note 1)
As of March 31,	**1994**	1993	**1994**
Trade notes discounted	**¥20,336**	¥24,290	**$197,156**
Trade notes endorsed	**66**	25	**641**

KAWASAKI STEEL CORP. 1994 ANNUAL REPORT

REPORT OF THE INDEPENDENT CERTIFIED PUBLIC ACCOUNTANTS ON THE CONSOLIDATED FINANCIAL STATEMENTS

The Board of Directors
Kawasaki Steel Corporation

We have examined the consolidated balance sheets of Kawasaki Steel Corporation and its consolidated subsidiaries as of March 31, 1994 and 1993, and the related consolidated statements of operations and stockholders' equity for the years then ended, all expressed in yen. Our examinations were made in accordance with auditing standards generally accepted in Japan and, accordingly, included such tests of the accounting records and such other auditing procedures as we considered necessary in the circumstances.

In our opinion, the accompanying consolidated financial statements present fairly the financial position of Kawasaki Steel Corporation and its consolidated subsidiaries at March 31, 1994 and 1993, and the results of their operations for the years then ended, in conformity with accounting principles generally accepted in Japan consistently applied, except for the change, with which we concur, in the valuation method of raw materials and supplies as discussed in Note 2 (c) to the consolidated financial statements.

The U.S. dollar amounts in the accompanying consolidated financial statements with respect to the year ended March 31, 1994 are presented solely for convenience. Our examination also included the translation of yen amounts into U.S. dollar amounts and, in our opinion, such translation has been made on the basis described in Note 1 to the consolidated financial statements.

Showa Ota & Co.

SHOWA OTA & CO.

Osaka, Japan
June 29, 1994

APPENDIX 15B

Rolls-Royce Plc 1994 Annual Report — Excerpts

ROLLS-ROYCE PLC 1994 ANNUAL REPORT

Corporate Profile

Rolls-Royce is a high integrity engineering group bringing advanced cost-effective technology to aerospace and industrial power systems markets worldwide.

With extensive international experience and outstanding technological skills Rolls-Royce is a world leader in its chosen product fields: aero, marine and industrial gas turbines, power generation, nuclear engineering and materials handling.

Rolls-Royce operates through two main units: the Aerospace Group, specialising in gas turbines for civil and military aircraft; and the Industrial Power Group which designs, constructs and installs complete power generation, transmission and distribution systems and major equipment for marine propulsion, oil and gas pumping, offshore and defence markets.

Today's Rolls-Royce is a significant supplier wherever cost-effective engineering solutions are required. In 1994 more than 70 per cent of its sales were achieved overseas.

ROLLS-ROYCE PLC 1994 ANNUAL REPORT

Chairman's Statement

Sir Ralph Robins, Chairman of Rolls-Royce plc

Rolls-Royce has continued to improve its competitive position in international markets. This has involved a significant investment programme in new products and an enormous drive to reduce costs. Market conditions have remained depressed but we have been able to improve our financial position. We enter the second half of the nineties with a sound balance sheet and a broad range of competitive products which will be further enhanced by the proposed acquisition of the Allison Engine Company. This will strengthen our position as a world-leading power systems company.

1994 was an important year for Rolls-Royce. Our financial performance continued to improve though market conditions remained challenging. Profit before tax, at £101 million, compared with £76 million in the previous year. Sales were £3,163 million, compared with £3,518 million in 1993.

This performance reflects the excellent progress with our development programmes and our drive to increase efficiency and reduce costs. The major restructuring programme, which we embarked upon early in 1993, is nearing completion and has resulted in significant consolidation of our manufacturing sites and a reduction in the work force by more than 20 per cent. It is a tribute to our employees that we have been able to complete such an extensive exercise whilst continuing to meet our commitments around the world.

In November we announced that we had reached agreement to buy the Allison Engine Company. We are making good progress with the necessary regulatory approvals and hope soon to be able to announce the successful conclusion of this deal.

The aerospace industry globally has been hit by the combined impact of cyclic depression in the civil market and reduced defence budgets in the military market. This has led to further consolidation of the industry and a continuing trend towards collaboration. I firmly believe that the acquisition of Allison, along with successful joint ventures such as BMW Rolls-Royce and Industria de Turbo Propulsores, places Rolls-Royce in a much better position to compete in this changing world.

Allison will add considerable strength to our Aerospace Group with its complementary range of engines. Rolls-Royce, with Allison, will have an installed engine base of more than 50,000 engines and one of the most comprehensive product families of all aero engine manufacturers. Most importantly, we will have established a manufacturing base in the USA, the leading market-place for aerospace products.

ROLLS-ROYCE PLC 1994 ANNUAL REPORT

We took further steps within the Industrial Power Group to strengthen our access to world power generation markets with the formation of Rolls-Royce Power Ventures Limited. This company will exploit new opportunities in independent power projects around the world, drawing on the resources of the Industrial Power Group.

The key to our future success lies in our ability to bring new and competitive products to the market-place. 1994 saw further progress in the development of our product range. In particular, our new aero engine, the Trent, launched as a development programme almost seven years ago, has now entered service with Cathay Pacific's Airbus A330s. The Trent 800 became the first aero engine ever to be certificated at 90,000lb thrust, three months ahead of schedule, at the beginning of 1995.

We have established an extensive family of engines which is well matched to current and future aircraft applications. Whilst the progress we have made with our development programmes has enabled a reduction in research and development expenditure, we remain committed to investing for the future.

In the Industrial Power Group we have increased our investment in new products and intensified our programme to exploit our core engine technology across the group. As a result new machines, such as the WR-21 advanced marine engine being developed in collaboration with Westinghouse for the US Navy and the 50MW Industrial Trent, have passed significant programme milestones and will soon be in our product portfolio.

At the end of 1994, Mr John Sandford returned to Rolls-Royce Inc., in Virginia, having completed his assignment in Rolls-Royce plc. He is succeeded as Managing Director, Aerospace Group by Mr John Rose. Both will continue as Directors of Rolls-Royce plc.

I was pleased to welcome Lord Moore of Lower Marsh to the Board as a non-executive director, last July. His distinguished career in both business and Government brings valuable experience to the Board.

Several employees received Birthday honours and New Year honours: Nigel Clothier, a generator engineer, Geoffrey Collis, Head of Programme Management – Materiel, Colin Johnson, an armature winder and Kenneth Dodsworth, former garage manager, all received MBEs. John Allen, a director of Clark Chapman received an OBE. We offer them all our congratulations.

Prospects

Rolls-Royce is well-placed to emerge from this period of very difficult market conditions in a good competitive position.

In Aerospace we have developed a comprehensive range of engines. Our new engines benefit from our technological strengths and incorporate the features of quality, reliability and value for money expected of Rolls-Royce products. Like our established engines we believe they will distinguish themselves in service and that they will win leading market positions.

We are confident that commercial aerospace represents a long-term growth market and expect to benefit as the market recovers from its current depressed state, although we do not anticipate that this will impact upon manufacturers until 1996 at the earliest.

Similarly, we see improving conditions for our military products in 1996, as volumes reflect improved exports.

1994 was a frustrating year for the Industrial Power Group with the move towards complex independent power projects leading to protracted contract negotiations. However, we believe the formation of Rolls-Royce Power Ventures Limited, the further development of the strategic alliance with Westinghouse, and the introduction of new and improved products will help us to strengthen our global position in one of the world's largest long-term growth markets.

The proposed acquisition of Allison will benefit both sides of our business, bringing us access to new market sectors for aero and industrial engines.

We can look forward with some confidence to the second half of the decade.

Dividend

Your Board has recommended a final dividend payment of 3.00p a share making a total of 5.00p for the year, unchanged on the 1993 level.

Ralph Robins

Sir Ralph Robins
Chairman
March 8, 1995

ROLLS-ROYCE PLC 1994 ANNUAL REPORT

Finance Director's Review

Michael Townsend, Finance Director

Our financial performance reflects the continuing difficult market conditions faced by the Group. However, we have improved our profitability as a result of the restructuring programme and reduced research and development expenditure through good progress on our development programmes. The Group has a sound balance sheet and a good order book.

Results for the year

Turnover fell by 10 per cent to £3,163 million reflecting falls in both the Aerospace and Industrial Power Groups.

In Aerospace, civil engine deliveries were marginally lower than in 1993 and no improvement was seen in our spares business. Military turnover was significantly lower, as we predicted last year.

Industrial Power turnover fell by 13 per cent as a result of a general reduced level of business and the significant time taken to conclude contract negotiations on independent power projects.

Sales achieved overseas were £2,321 million representing 73 per cent of total sales.

Profit before tax was £101 million (1993 £76 million), a small fall in trading profit being more than offset by reduced research and development expenditure and the elimination of interest payable. The dollar exchange rate had only a marginal impact on the results.

Net research and development expenditure, at £218 million was reduced substantially in comparison with the 1993 level of £253 million. This was achieved through progress made with the Trent engine. The reduction in the level of research and development expenditure is expected to continue in 1995, as we make further progress with the Trent 800.

Profit attributable to shareholders was £81 million (1993 £63 million), resulting in earnings per share of 6.62p (1993 5.95p).

As an associated undertaking BMW Rolls-Royce GmbH (BRR) contributes neither a profit nor a loss because its costs are offset by subvention payments. We provide against operating profit for a proportion of the Group's contribution (included in other debtors) towards the financing of BRR, having regard to the fact that certain other sources of finance are repayable in priority. The Group currently estimates that it will begin to share in a positive return from BRR around the year 2000.

ROLLS-ROYCE PLC 1994 ANNUAL REPORT

The restructuring provision, established in our 1992 accounts, fell by £95 million during 1994 as we completed the major part of the programme. The number of employees at the end of the year was 41,000, a reduction of 9 per cent during the year.

The order book at £5.9 billion was maintained at the level announced with our half-year results.

The dividend, which was maintained at 5.00p per share was covered 1.3 times.

Current liquidity

The Group Cash Flow statement is shown on page 26. Net cash balances stood at £285 million, compared to £397 million at the end of 1993, representing an outflow of £112 million. This was largely attributable to the expenditure on restructuring.

The 1993 figure has been restated from £473 million to reflect the requirements of Financial Reporting Standard 5, which was introduced in 1994, and to reflect the reclassification of obligations under finance leases as borrowings.

The year end cash balance is not representative of our average position throughout the year as seasonal factors lead to a large inflow towards the year end. The average cash balance in 1994 was £118 million (1993 £159 million overdrawn). The position in 1994 reflects the proceeds of the rights issue, made towards the end of 1993, which contributed approximately £230 million of the improvement.

The Group maintains a significant margin over convenants entered into with its lenders.

Proposed acquisition of Allison Engine Company, Inc.

In November 1994 we announced the proposed acquisition of the Allison Engine Company, Inc. We intend to fund this acquisition largely through the issue of new shares upon obtaining the necessary regulatory approvals.

Foreign exchange management

The Group's dominant currency exposure is to the US dollar/sterling exchange rate. Net US dollar income represents approximately 22 per cent of Group sales.

The Group hedges its foreign currency exposure by entering into a variety of financial instruments. It thereby has removed, on average, approximately 85 per cent of its exposure to the fluctuation of the US dollar exchange rate.

US dollar cover extends for periods of up to ten years, but is primarily in the 1-5 year time horizon. Total cover currently represents approximately three years net dollar income. The majority of cover is in the form of standard forward exchange contracts. Some cover, primarily in the 5-10 year time horizon, includes instruments on which exchange rates may be dependent on interest rates. Cover is only taken to hedge forecast net dollar income according to parameters set by the Board.

The Group's exposure and forward cover is closely monitored, regularly reviewed by the Board and considered in detail by a specialist committee on a quarterly basis. Factors taken into consideration include credit limits (by counterparty) and market risk exposures.

Sales financing

The provision of financing support to customers is a feature of our main business sectors.

This support can include guarantees as to the future value of aircraft, or the provision or guarantee of finance to the airline customer both prior to and following delivery of the aircraft. Such guarantees are, in general, secured on the aircraft.

During 1994 the Group was notified by a customer that it intended to exercise its rights under a guarantee provided by the Group. Subsequently the Group negotiated a refinancing of the related aircraft without crystallisation of the guarantee.

The Group's contingent liability in respect of sales financing activities is described in note 26 to the financial statements.

In order to support our marketing activities we are strengthening our sales financing capability. We are looking at acquiring the balance of 60 per cent held by other partners in Rolls-Royce & Partners Finance Limited in order to increase the focus on aerospace markets.

In the Industrial Power Group we formed Rolls-Royce Power Ventures Limited (RRPV). This company will focus its efforts in the primary power market and will enter into joint venture arrangements with project sponsors, development companies and other combinations as required. RRPV can provide long-term equity commitments to the projects in which it has an involvement.

ROLLS-ROYCE PLC 1994 ANNUAL REPORT

Taxation

As in 1993, there is no mainstream UK corporation tax payable on the 1994 profits. This is due largely to the set-off of brought forward losses in Rolls-Royce plc and to the effect of the expenditure on restructuring provided for in the 1992 accounts. The Group's UK tax losses carried forward have reduced to £275 million from £325 million in 1993 and are available for offset against future UK trading profits.

Because there is no UK corporation tax payable in respect of 1994, all the advance corporation tax (ACT) generated by the 1994 dividends has been written-off. At the end of 1994 £156 million (1993 £141 million) of ACT was available to offset future corporation tax liabilities.

The 1994 tax charge therefore represents, principally, ACT written off and tax on overseas earnings and associated undertakings. Because of the high ACT element and the Group's tax losses, the amount of tax charge remains relatively constant.

Internal controls

The directors are responsible for the Group's system of internal financial control. Such a system can provide only reasonable and not absolute assurance against material misstatement or loss. In discharging this responsibility, the Group has an Audit Committee which comprises solely non-executive directors and which meets with the executive directors and with the external and internal auditors several times a year. Separate audit committees operate in Canada and South Africa. The Group also has an internal audit department which works closely with the external auditors and operates to a work programme agreed with the Audit Committee.

There is a comprehensive budgeting system with an annual budget approved by the directors. Monthly actual results are reported against budget and revised forecasts for the year prepared regularly.

Key financial management issues such as foreign exchange management, sales financing and risk management are reported regularly to the Board.

Additionally, finance and general management of operating units are required to acknowledge by interview and in writing, that they are aware of their responsibility to operate internal financial control systems and that their results are properly stated in accordance with Group and statutory requirements and are appropriate for inclusion in the Group financial statements.

Share capital

The Company's share price varied between 161p and 203.5p in 1994. Over the year it out performed the FTSE 100 index by 20 per cent.

The Company's Articles of Association contain a restriction on the total foreign share ownership to 29.5 per cent of the issued share capital. The actual level of foreign ownership varied between 24 and 25 per cent during the year.

ROLLS-ROYCE PLC 1994 ANNUAL REPORT

Board of Directors

on March 8, 1995

Sir Ralph Robins BSc, F Eng[3]
Chairman
Elected to the Board in 1982. He joined Rolls-Royce in 1955, became Managing Director in 1984 and was appointed Chairman in 1992. Age 62.

Dr Terence Harrison DL, BSc, F Eng[3]
Chief Executive
Elected to the Board in 1989 and appointed Chief Executive in 1992. He joined Clark Chapman, part of NEI, in 1957. Age 61.

L. John Clark BS, MBA[1,3]
Non-Executive Director
Elected to the Board in 1993. He is Chief Executive and Managing Director of BET plc. Age 53.

Sir Gordon Higginson BSc, PhD, F Eng[2,3]
Non-Executive Director
Elected to the Board in 1988. Age 65.

Richard H. Maudslay BSc, F Eng
Managing Director – Industrial Power Group
Elected to the Board on January 1, 1994. He joined Bruce Peebles, part of NEI, in 1968. Age 48.

Stewart C. Miller CBE, BSc, HonDTech, F Eng
Director – Engineering and Technology
Elected to the Board in 1985. He joined Rolls-Royce in 1954. Age 60.

Lord Moore of Lower Marsh, PC[1]
Non-Executive Director
Elected to the Board on July 4, 1994. He is Chairman of Credit Suisse Asset Management Limited. Age 57.

Harold G. Mourgue FCA[1,2,3,4]
Non-Executive Director
Elected to the Board in 1985. He is Chairman of Kenwood Appliances plc. Age 67.

Sir Robin Nicholson FRS, F Eng[2,3]
Non-Executive Director
Elected to the Board in 1986. He is an Executive Director of Pilkington plc. Age 60.

John E.V. Rose MA
Managing Director – Aerospace Group
Elected to the Board in 1992. He joined Rolls-Royce in 1984. Age 42.

John W. Sandford MSc
President and Chief Executive Officer of Rolls-Royce Inc.
Elected to the Board in 1993. He joined Rolls-Royce in 1990. Age 60.

Michael Townsend MA, FCA
Finance Director
Elected to the Board in 1991. He joined Rolls-Royce in 1990. Age 53.

Richard T. Turner OBE, BA
Group Marketing Director
Elected to the Board in 1992. He rejoined Rolls-Royce in 1991 having previously been with the Company from 1965 to 1988. Age 52.

Company Secretary and General Counsel
Clyde R. Harris
Appointed 1993. Solicitor. He joined Rolls-Royce in 1960. Age 61.

[1]Member of the Audit Committee.
[2]Member of the Remuneration Committee.
[3]Member of the Nomination Committee.
[4]Chairman of the Trustees of The Rolls-Royce Pension Fund.

Note: Committees 1 and 2 are made up entirely of non-executive directors

The Board of Rolls-Royce plc.
Front row from left to right: Michael Townsend, Dr Terence Harrison. *Standing from left to right:* Richard Turner, Sir Gordon Higginson, Harold Mourgue, Sir Ralph Robins, Stewart Miller, John Clark, John Rose, Clyde Harris, Richard Maudslay, John Sandford, Lord Moore. *Absent from photograph:* Sir Robin Nicholson.

ROLLS-ROYCE PLC 1994 ANNUAL REPORT

Report of the Directors

The directors present their report and the financial statements of the Group for the year ended December 31, 1994.

Principal activities

The Corporate Profile (page 1) describes the Group's principal activities.

Results for the year

The Chairman's Statement, the Chief Executive's Review of Activities and the Finance Director's Review together give information relating to the year's operations, research and development activities and future prospects.

The directors recommend a final dividend of 3.00p a share. With the interim dividend of 2.00p a share, paid on January 9, 1995, this will make a total dividend of 5.00p a share for the year. Subject to approval of the recommended final dividend, the total cost of dividends for 1994 is £61m. If approved, the Company will pay the final dividend on July 3, 1995 to shareholders registered on April 6, 1995 and £20m will be added to Group reserves.

Employment

The number of Group employees at the end of the year was 41,000 (1993 45,800) of whom 22,700 (1993 25,900) were in Aerospace and 18,300 (1993 19,900) were in Industrial Power.

The Group's policy is to provide, wherever possible, employment opportunities and training for disabled people, to care for employees who become disabled and to make the best possible use of their skills and potential. It also operates an equal opportunities policy, details of which are available to all employees.

There are various forms of communication across the Group, each adapted to the particular needs of individual businesses. The Group consults with employees and their elected representatives on a comprehensive range of topics which relate to its overall business objectives. Management and employee representatives hold regular meetings at every location to discuss problems and opportunities.

Health, safety and the environment (HS&E)

In 1994 industrial accidents remained at a level substantially below the average for similar UK engineering companies. There were, however, two health and safety prosecutions by the Health and Safety Executive but no environmental prosecutions during 1994. The corporate HS&E committee, chaired by the Chief Executive, continues to oversee the Group's activities and review its performance.

The involvement of the workforce in HS&E is increasing beyond the traditional activities of safety representatives and safety committees. The level of training and briefing has increased at all levels within the Group.

The issue of a unified policy document on HS&E is seen as a substantial step forward in integrating these disciplines into business management. Issued to all managers and supervisors as a booklet, the document contains the new policy, a definition of responsibilities and the HS&E management system. This is backed by a new manual of standards and guidance notes on HS&E.

The first round of Group audits of health and safety and an environmental review of facilities has been completed.

The strength of commitment to the environment can be seen in actions which have led to a significant reduction in the use of solvents, including the virtual elimination of ozone-depleting substances in aerospace manufacturing. Considerable efforts have been made during site closures to ensure that they are left as safe and environmentally sound as is practical.

Copies of the Group's HS&E policy are available on written request to the Company Secretary.

ROLLS-ROYCE PLC 1994 ANNUAL REPORT

Training

1994 saw a change in employee development with greater emphasis on individual competence, and more customer and commercial awareness at all levels.

186 new trainees joined the Industrial Power Group, an increase over 1993. The Aerospace Group did not take on any new trainees.

All trainees will be able to complete their training and more than 90 per cent of those who completed their training in 1994 are now employed on a full-time basis.

Rolls-Royce has 790 trainees engaged in a wide range of training and personal development activities. National vocational qualifications have been addressed in youth training programmes and Rolls-Royce has participated in the development of modern apprenticeship schemes and the setting of standards for the whole engineering industry.

During 1994 Rolls-Royce continued to fulfil its social responsibilities, as well as contributing to regional regeneration, by operating youth training programmes for unemployed school leavers: 152 were recruited, making a total of 248 receiving training of this kind during the year. The majority have found employment with local employers.

Training needs are identified against job requirements and a variety of training programmes have been delivered to meet these needs. These programmes include engineering skills training to develop and maintain core competence and skills. A management development curriculum for all managers and potential managers was also launched.

The quality of Rolls-Royce training programmes has been recognised by the receipt of a national training regional award for the Advanced Design Engineering Planning Training (ADEPT) course in engineering.

In further recognition of the quality of training for young people, three engineering technician trainees from Derby, Simon Bennett, Ian Stevenson and Lee Webb, won the Business and Technology Education Council (BTEC) prize in the Young Engineer for Britain competition.

Directors

The directors listed on page 18 were in office throughout 1994 apart from Lord Moore of Lower Marsh who was appointed on July 4, 1994.

The directors retiring by rotation at the Annual General Meeting on May 24, 1995 are Sir Robin Nicholson, Mr J.W. Sandford, Mr M. Townsend and Mr R.T. Turner. Lord Moore, the new director, also retires at the Annual General Meeting. They all offer themselves for re-election.

Mr M. Townsend and Mr R.T. Turner have service agreements which are subject to two years notice of termination. Mr J.W. Sandford has a fixed term service agreement which expires within one year. Lord Moore and Sir Robin Nicholson do not have a service agreement. All are subject to re-election by rotation every three years.

The Company has renewed an insurance policy to indemnify its directors and officers against liability when acting for the Company.

The Board is not aware of any significant contract with the Company or its subsidiary undertakings in which a director has, or has had, a material interest.

Note 22 to the financial statements gives details of directors' share interests.

Going concern

After making enquiries, the directors have a reasonable expectation that the Group has adequate resources to continue in operational existence for the foreseeable future. For this reason they continue to adopt the going concern basis in preparing the financial statements.

The auditors, KPMG, have confirmed to the directors that they are satisfied that the directors' comments above:

i) comply with the guidance issued to directors on reporting on going concern, in accordance with the Code of Best Practice;
ii) are consistent with the information of which they are aware, based on their normal audit work.

KPMG has not carried out any additional work necessary to give an opinion that the Company has adequate resources to continue in operational existence.

Corporate governance

The Company has complied throughout the financial year with those elements of the Code of Best Practice, issued by the Committee on the Financial Aspects of Corporate Governance, that were in force for the year.

Guidance for directors on reporting on internal controls was issued in December 1994

ROLLS-ROYCE PLC 1994 ANNUAL REPORT

and is not regarded as effective for the period of the financial statements. A brief description of internal controls is set out in the Finance Director's Review.

The auditors have confirmed that they are satisfied that this statement appropriately reflects the Company's compliance with the Code of Best Practice, insofar as it relates to the other paragraphs of the Code which the London Stock Exchange has specified for their review.

Members of the Audit Committee, Remuneration Committee and Nomination Committee are identified on page 18.

Fixed assets

Group expenditure on tangible fixed assets related mainly to manufacturing and engineering facilities and supporting computer equipment. Movements in tangible fixed assets during the year are set out in note 10 to the financial statements.

At the end of 1994 a review of the Company's land and buildings was carried out by professional valuers, which suggests a value marginally greater than the figure shown in the financial statements.

Notes 11 and 12 to the financial statements give the movements on investments.

Donations

During 1994 the Group made charitable donations amounting to £248,000. The annual donations budget is administered by a committee of the Board and by local site committees to a policy predominantly directed towards assisting military services benevolent associations and charities associated with engineering, scientific and educational objectives as well as objectives connected with the Group's business and place in the community.

A political contribution of £35,000 was made to the Conservative and Unionist Party.

At the Annual General Meeting a resolution will be proposed to give the directors authority, for three years, to make political donations.

Close company status

The close company provisions of the Income and Corporation Taxes Act 1988 do not apply to the Company.

Share capital

Note 22 to the financial statements gives details of the share capital and employee share schemes.

At the Annual General Meeting a resolution will be proposed to give the directors authority, for a further year, to allot shares for cash both by way of rights issues and, for a limited number of ordinary shares, to people other than existing shareholders.

The following has a notifiable interest in the Company's ordinary shares:

	% of issued share capital
S.G. Warburg Group plc	12.20

of which 12.19 per cent is held by its subsidiary, Mercury Asset Management plc.

Auditors

On February 6, 1995 the auditors changed the name under which they practise from KPMG Peat Marwick to KPMG.

A resolution to reappoint the auditors and to authorise the directors to determine their remuneration will be proposed at the 1995 Annual General Meeting.

By order of the Board

C. R. Harris
Company Secretary
March 8, 1995

ROLLS-ROYCE PLC 1994 ANNUAL REPORT

Group Five Year Review

for the years ended December 31

Profit and loss account	1994 £m	1993 £m	1992 £m	1991 £m	1990 £m
Turnover	3,163	3,518	3,562	3,515	3,670
Trading profit[1]	309	329	325	335	468
Exceptional items	—	—	(268)	(58)	(50)
Research and development (net)*	(218)	(253)	(229)	(216)	(237)
Share of profits of associated undertakings	9	12	6	6	2
Net interest receivable (payable)	1	(12)	(18)	(16)	(7)
Profit/(loss) on ordinary activities before taxation	101	76	(184)	51	176
Taxation	(20)	(18)	(25)	(32)	(36)
Profit/(loss) on ordinary activities after taxation	81	58	(209)	19	140
Attributable to equity minority interests	—	5	7	5	(6)
Profit/(loss) attributable to the shareholders	81	63	(202)	24	134
Dividends	(61)	(56)	(48)	(70)	(69)
Transferred to/(from) reserves	20	7	(250)	(46)	65
Earnings/(loss) per ordinary share					
Net basis	6.62p	5.95p	(20.39)p	2.43p	13.60p
Nil distribution basis	7.84p	7.18p	(19.29)p	3.44p	14.93p
Net basis before exceptional items	6.62p	5.95p	6.46p	8.12p	18.68p
Dividends per ordinary share	5.00p	5.00p	5.00p	7.25p	7.25p
*Research and development (gross)	(452)	(451)	(482)	(498)	(480)

Balance sheet	1994 £m	Restated 1993 £m	Restated 1992 £m	Restated 1991 £m	1990 £m
Fixed assets	907	950	936	885	827
Current assets	2,195	2,392	2,177	2,181	2,020
	3,102	3,342	3,113	3,066	2,847
Liabilities and provisions	(1,847)	(2,107)	(2,199)	(1,917)	(1,645)
	1,255	1,235	914	1,149	1,202
Share capital	245	244	194	193	192
Reserves	997	981	705	929	972
Equity shareholders' funds	1,242	1,225	899	1,122	1,164
Minority interests in subsidiary undertakings	13	10	15	27	38
	1,255	1,235	914	1,149	1,202

The figures for 1991 to 1993 have been restated to reflect the requirements of Financial Reporting Standard 5.

No material discontinued operations have occurred.

[1]Trading profit represents gross profit less commercial, marketing, product support, general and administration costs but is stated before exceptional items.

ROLLS-ROYCE PLC 1994 ANNUAL REPORT

Directors' Responsibilities for the Financial Statements

Company law requires the directors to prepare financial statements for each financial year which give a true and fair view of the state of affairs of the Company and the Group and of the profit for that period.

In preparing those statements, the directors are required to:

i) select suitable accounting policies and then apply them consistently.
ii) make judgements and estimates that are reasonable and prudent.
iii) state whether applicable accounting standards have been followed, subject to any material departures disclosed and explained in the financial statements.
iv) prepare the financial statements on a going concern basis unless it is inappropriate to presume that the Group will continue in business.

The directors are responsible for keeping proper accounting records which disclose with reasonable accuracy at any time the financial position of the Company and to enable them to ensure that the financial statements comply with the requirements of the Companies Act 1985. They have general responsibility for taking such steps as are reasonably open to them to safeguard the assets of the Group and to prevent and detect fraud and other irregularities.

Report of the Auditors to the Members of Rolls-Royce plc

KPMG

We have audited the financial statements on pages 24 to 48.

Respective responsibilities of directors and auditors
As described above, the Company's directors are responsible for the preparation of financial statements. It is our responsibility to form an independent opinion, based on our audit, on those statements and to report our opinion to you.

Basis of opinion
We conducted our audit in accordance with Auditing Standards issued by the Auditing Practices Board. An audit includes examination, on a test basis, of evidence relevant to the amounts and disclosures in the financial statements. It also includes an assessment of the significant estimates and judgements made by the directors in the preparation of the financial statements, and of whether the accounting policies are appropriate to the Group's circumstances, consistently applied and adequately disclosed.

We planned and performed our audit so as to obtain all the information and explanations which we considered necessary in order to provide us with sufficient evidence to give reasonable assurance that the financial statements are free from material misstatement, whether caused by fraud or other irregularity or error. In forming our opinion we also evaluated the overall adequacy of the presentation of information in the financial statements.

Opinion
In our opinion the financial statements give a true and fair view of the state of affairs of the Company and the Group as at December 31, 1994 and of the profit of the Group for the year then ended and have been properly prepared in accordance with the Companies Act 1985.

KPMG
Chartered Accountants, Registered Auditors

London
March 8, 1995

ROLLS-ROYCE PLC 1994 ANNUAL REPORT

Group Profit and Loss Account
for the year ended December 31, 1994

	Notes	1994 £m	1993 £m
Turnover	2	3,163	3,518
Cost of sales	3	(2,646)	(2,995)
Gross profit		517	523
Commercial, marketing and product support costs		(117)	(105)
General and administrative costs		(91)	(89)
Research and development (net)		(218)	(253)
Operating profit		91	76
Share of profits of associated undertakings		9	12
Profit on ordinary activities before interest	2	100	88
Net interest receivable (payable) and other similar charges	4	1	(12)
Profit on ordinary activities before taxation	3	101	76
Taxation	5	(20)	(18)
Profit on ordinary activities after taxation		81	58
Attributable to equity minority interests in subsidiary undertakings		—	5
Profit attributable to the shareholders of Rolls-Royce plc		81	63
Dividends	6	(61)	(56)
Transferred to reserves	23	20	7
Earnings per ordinary share	7		
Net basis		6.62p	5.95p
Nil distribution basis		7.84p	7.18p

No material acquisitions or discontinued operations have occurred.

As permitted by the Companies Act 1985, a separate profit and loss account for the Company has not been included in these financial statements. Of the Group 'Profit attributable to the shareholders of Rolls-Royce plc', a profit of £138m (1993 £44m) has been dealt with in the profit and loss account of the Company.

ROLLS-ROYCE PLC 1994 ANNUAL REPORT

Balance Sheets

at December 31, 1994

	Notes	Group 1994 £m	Group Restated 1993 £m	Company 1994 £m	Company Restated 1993 £m
Fixed assets					
Tangible assets	10	836	882	605	639
Investments – subsidiary undertakings	11	–	–	347	339
– associated undertakings	12	71	68	50	53
		907	950	1,002	1,031
Current assets					
Stocks	13	595	611	468	466
Debtors – amounts falling due within one year	14	714	714	509	478
– amounts falling due after one year	15	205	176	236	500
Short-term deposits and cash		681	891	596	792
		2,195	2,392	1,809	2,236
Creditors – amounts falling due within one year					
Borrowings	16	(11)	(84)	(2)	(57)
Other creditors	17	(1,162)	(1,179)	(882)	(909)
Net current assets		1,022	1,129	925	1,270
Total assets less current liabilities		1,929	2,079	1,927	2,301
Creditors – amounts falling due after one year					
Borrowings	18	(385)	(410)	(156)	(493)
Other creditors	19	(129)	(133)	(321)	(324)
Provisions for liabilities and charges	21	(160)	(301)	(113)	(233)
		1,255	1,235	1,337	1,251
Capital and reserves					
Called up share capital	22	245	244	245	244
Share premium account	23	509	506	509	506
Revaluation reserve	23	109	120	105	115
Other reserves	23	20	20	261	261
Profit and loss account	23	359	335	217	125
Equity shareholders' funds		1,242	1,225	1,337	1,251
Minority interests in subsidiary undertakings					
Equity interests		10	7	–	–
Non-equity interests		3	3	–	–
		1,255	1,235	1,337	1,251

The figures for 1993 have been restated to reflect the requirements of Financial Reporting Standard 5 (see notes 14, 15, 16 and 18) and the reclassification of obligations under finance leases (see notes 16 and 18).

The financial statements on pages 24 to 48 were approved by the Board on March 8, 1995 and signed on its behalf by:

Sir Ralph Robins
Chairman
M Townsend
Director

ROLLS-ROYCE PLC 1994 ANNUAL REPORT

Group Cash Flow Statement

for the year ended December 31, 1994

		1994 £m	Restated 1993 £m
Net cash inflow from operating activities	A	11	275
Returns on investments and servicing of finance			
Interest received		38	21
Interest paid		(34)	(34)
Interest element of finance lease payments		(2)	(2)
Dividends paid to the shareholders of Rolls-Royce plc		(51)	(44)
Net cash outflow from returns on investments and servicing of finance		(49)	(59)
Taxation			
UK and overseas tax paid		(17)	(20)
Investing activities			
Purchases of tangible fixed assets		(105)	(130)
Disposals of tangible fixed assets		24	16
Disposals of subsidiary undertakings (see below)		16	22
Purchase of minority interest in subsidiary undertaking		—	(3)
Loan repayment from associated undertaking		2	—
Investment in associated undertaking		—	(1)
Net cash outflow from investing activities		(63)	(96)
Net cash (outflow)/inflow before financing		(118)	100
Financing			
Proceeds of ordinary share issues		(4)	(324)
Expenses paid in connection with the rights issue		—	9
Investment by minority interest in subsidiary undertaking		(3)	—
(Decrease)/increase in short-term deposits (more than 3 months to maturity when acquired)		(90)	111
New borrowings		—	(208)
Repayment of borrowings		68	178
Capital element of finance lease payments		8	4
Net cash inflow from financing	B	(21)	(230)
(Decrease)/increase in cash and cash equivalents	C	(97)	330
		(118)	100

	1994 £m	Restated 1993 £m
Disposals of subsidiary undertakings		
Tangible fixed assets	4	3
Non-cash equivalent working capital	9	13
	13	16
Purchased goodwill charged to profit and loss account	—	4
Profit on disposals	3	2
Cash consideration	16	22

The figures for 1993 have been restated to reflect the requirements of Financial Reporting Standard 5 (see notes 14, 15, 16 and 18) and the reclassification of obligations under finance leases (see notes 16 and 18).

ROLLS-ROYCE PLC 1994 ANNUAL REPORT

Reconciliation of operating profit to net cash inflow from operating activities	1994 £m	Restated 1993 £m
Operating profit	91	76
Depreciation of tangible fixed assets	109	105
(Profit) on disposals of tangible fixed assets	(3)	–
(Profit) on disposals of subsidiary undertakings	(3)	(2)
(Decrease) in provisions for liabilities and charges	(138)	(107)
Decrease in stocks	6	74
(Increase)/decrease in debtors	(36)	107
(Decrease)/increase in creditors	(15)	22
Net cash inflow from operating activities	11	275

Payments in 1994, relating to 1992's £230m exceptional items provision for restructuring and customer problems, have been £95m (1993 £92m).

Changes in financing			
At January 1		(1,114)	(882)
Net cash inflow from financing		(21)	(230)
Finance leased tangible fixed assets		(2)	(7)
Minority interests in subsidiary undertakings – share of loss for year		–	5
Exchange adjustments		1	–
At December 31		(1,136)	(1,114)
Consisting of:			
Called up share capital		(245)	(244)
Share premium account		(509)	(506)
Minority interests in subsidiary undertakings		(13)	(10)
Long-term borrowings	1	(385)	(410)
Items having more than 3 months to maturity when acquired:			
Short-term deposits and cash	2	22	112
Short-term borrowings	3	(6)	(56)
		(1,136)	(1,114)

Changes in cash and cash equivalents			
At January 1		751	421
(Decrease)/increase in cash and cash equivalents		(97)	330
At December 31		654	751
Consisting of:			
Items within 3 months of maturity when acquired:			
Short-term deposits and cash	2	659	779
Short-term borrowings	3	(5)	(28)
		654	751

Reconciliation with Group Balance Sheet (page 25):			
Short-term deposits and cash	2	681	891
Borrowings – amounts falling due within one year	3	(11)	(84)
– amounts falling due after one year	1	(385)	(410)
		285	397

ROLLS-ROYCE PLC 1994 ANNUAL REPORT

Group Statement of Total Recognised Gains and Losses

for the year ended December 31, 1994

	1994 £m	1993 £m
Profit attributable to the shareholders of Rolls-Royce plc	81	63
Exchange adjustments on foreign currency net investments	(12)	(4)
Total recognised gains and (losses) for the year	69	59

Group Historical Cost Profits and Losses

for the year ended December 31, 1994

	1994 £m	1993 £m
Profit on ordinary activities before taxation	101	76
Realisation of property revaluation gains of previous years	7	—
Difference between the historical cost depreciation charge and the actual depreciation charge for the year calculated on the revalued amount	3	4
Historical cost profit on ordinary activities before taxation	111	80
Historical cost transfer to reserves	30	11

Reconciliation of Movements in Shareholders' Funds

for the year ended December 31, 1994

	Group		Company	
	1994 £m	1993 £m	1994 £m	1993 £m
At January 1	1,225	899	1,251	944
Total recognised gains and (losses) for the year	69	59	138	44
Ordinary dividends (net of scrip dividend adjustments)	(56)	(52)	(56)	(52)
New share capital issued	4	324	4	324
Expenses paid in connection with the rights issue	—	(9)	—	(9)
Goodwill transferred to the profit and loss account in respect of disposals of businesses	—	4	—	—
At December 31	1,242	1,225	1,337	1,251

ROLLS-ROYCE PLC 1994 ANNUAL REPORT

Notes to the Financial Statements

1 Accounting policies

Basis of accounting
The financial statements have been prepared in accordance with applicable accounting standards on the historical cost basis, modified to include the revaluation of land and buildings.

The requirements of Financial Reporting Standard 5 became effective in 1994. Adjustments have been made to comparative figures to put them on a consistent basis with the current year.

Basis of consolidation
The Group financial statements include the financial statements of the Company and all of its subsidiary undertakings made up to December 31, together with the Group's share of the results of associated undertakings up to December 31. Any subsidiary and associated undertakings sold or acquired during the year are included up to, or from, the dates of change of control.

Goodwill, which represents the excess of the value of the purchase consideration for shares in subsidiary and associated undertakings over the fair value to the Group of the net assets acquired, is written off to reserves in the year of acquisition.

The profit or loss on the disposal of a previously acquired business takes into account the attributable amount of purchased goodwill relating to that business.

Turnover
Turnover excludes value added tax. Long-term contracts are included in turnover on the basis of the sales value of work performed during the year by reference to the total sales value and stage of completion of these contracts.

Research and development
The charge to the profit and loss account consists of total research and development expenditure incurred in the year less known recoverable costs on contracts, contributions to shared engineering programmes and matching government assistance.

Foreign currencies
Assets and liabilities denominated in foreign currencies are translated into sterling at the rate ruling at the year end or, where applicable, at the estimated sterling equivalent, taking account of future foreign exchange and similar contracts. The trading results of overseas undertakings are translated at the average exchange rates for the year or, where applicable, at the estimated sterling equivalent, taking account of future foreign exchange and similar contracts. Exchange adjustments arising from the retranslation of the opening net investment, and from the translation of the profits or losses at average rate, are taken to reserves. Other exchange differences, including those arising from currency conversions in the usual course of trading, are taken into account in determining profit on ordinary activities before taxation.

Pension costs
Contributions to Group pension schemes are charged to the profit and loss account so as to spread the cost of pensions at a substantially level percentage of payroll costs over employees' working lives with the Group.

Certification costs
Costs paid to airframe manufacturers in respect of meeting regulatory certification requirements for new civil engine/aircraft combinations are carried forward in prepayments to the extent that they can be recovered out of future sales and are charged to the profit and loss account over five years following certification.

ROLLS-ROYCE PLC 1994 ANNUAL REPORT

Notes to the Financial Statements continued

1 Accounting policies continued

Taxation
Provision for taxation is made at the current rate and for deferred taxation on all timing differences where a liability is expected to crystallise in the foreseeable future. Advance corporation tax which is not recoverable in the immediate future by offset against United Kingdom corporation tax liabilities is included in the taxation charge for the year.

Scrip dividends
The amounts of dividends taken as shares instead of in cash under the scrip dividend scheme have been added back to reserves. The nominal value of shares issued under the scheme has been funded out of the share premium account.

Stocks and long-term contracts
Stocks are valued at the lower of cost and net realisable value. Provided that the outcome of long-term contracts can be assessed with reasonable certainty, such contracts are valued at cost plus attributable profit earned to date. Full provision is made for estimated losses to completion.

Progress payments received, when greater than recorded turnover, are deducted from the value of work in progress except to the extent that payments on account exceed the value of work in progress on any contract where the excess is included in creditors. The amount by which recorded turnover of long-term contracts is in excess of payments on account is classified as 'amounts recoverable on contracts' and is separately disclosed within debtors.

Accounting for leases
Assets financed by leasing agreements which give rights approximating to ownership (finance leases) have been capitalised at amounts equal to the original cost of the assets to the lessors and depreciation provided on the basis of Group depreciation policy. The capital elements of future obligations under finance leases are included as liabilities in the balance sheet and the current year's interest element is charged to the profit and loss account. The annual payments under all other lease arrangements, known as operating leases, are charged to the profit and loss account on an accruals basis. Rentals receivable as lessor under operating leases are included in turnover for the year on an accruals basis.

Depreciation

i) Properties
Depreciation is provided on the valuation of properties adopted at December 31, 1985 and on the original cost of purchases since 1985 and is calculated on the straight line basis at rates sufficient to reduce them to their estimated residual value. Estimated lives, as advised by the Group's professional valuers, are:
   a) Freehold buildings – 10 to 45 years (average 20 years).
   b) Leasehold land and buildings – lower of valuers' estimates or period of lease.

   Depreciation is not provided on freehold land.

ii) Plant and equipment
Depreciation is provided on the original cost of plant and equipment and is calculated on the straight line basis at rates sufficient to reduce them to their estimated residual value. Estimated lives are in the range five to 25 years (average 15 years).

ROLLS-ROYCE PLC 1994 ANNUAL REPORT

2 Analysis of turnover, profit and net assets

	Turnover		Profit before interest		Net Assets[1]	
	1994 £m	1993 £m	1994 £m	1993 £m	1994 £m	Restated 1993 £m
Analysis by business:						
Aerospace	1,962	2,139	34	20	726	631
Industrial Power	1,201	1,379	66	68	244	207
	3,163	3,518	100	88	970	838
Geographical analysis by origin:						
United Kingdom	2,831	3,161	95	80	856	715
Other	332	357	5	8	114	123
	3,163	3,518	100	88	970	838
Geographical analysis by destination:						
United Kingdom	842	997				
Rest of Europe	334	379				
USA	1,182	1,151				
Canada	131	137				
Asia	428	558				
Africa	101	165				
Australasia	107	81				
Other	38	50				
	3,163	3,518				
Exports from United Kingdom	1,989	2,165				
Sales to overseas subsidiaries	(128)	(118)				
Sales by overseas subsidiaries	460	474				
Total overseas	2,321	2,521				

[1]Net assets exclude net cash balances of £285m (1993 £397m). The figures for 1993 have been restated to reflect the requirements of Financial Reporting Standard 5 and the reclassification of obligations under finance leases as borrowings.

3 Profit on ordinary activities before taxation

	1994 £m	1993 £m
After crediting		
Operating lease rentals receivable	3	5
After charging		
Depreciation of owned tangible fixed assets	104	100
Depreciation of tangible fixed assets held under finance leases	5	5
Operating lease rentals payable – hire of plant and equipment	23	21
– hire of other assets	19	16

Auditors' fees were as follows during the year:

Audit 1994 £1.5m (1993 £1.1m)

Other 1994 – United Kingdom £0.4m (1993 £0.7m)

– Rest of World £0.2m (1993 £0.3m)

ROLLS-ROYCE PLC 1994 ANNUAL REPORT

Notes to the Financial Statements continued

4 Net interest receivable (payable) and other similar charges

	1994 £m	1993 £m
Interest payable on:		
Borrowings repayable within five years	(17)	(26)
Borrowings repayable after five years	(17)	(8)
Finance leases	(2)	(2)
	(36)	(36)
Interest receivable	37	24
	1	(12)

5 Taxation

	1994 £m	1993 £m
United Kingdom – corporation tax at 33%	1	–
– advance corporation tax written off	15	13
– double tax relief	(1)	–
– in respect of prior years	–	(3)
	15	10
Overseas	3	5
Associated undertakings	2	3
	20	18

The UK mainstream corporation tax charge has been reduced by the impact of restructuring expenditure provided for in the 1992 accounts.

6 Dividends – ordinary shares

	1994 £m	1993 £m
Interim 2.00p (1993 2.00p) per share	24	19
Final proposed 3.00p (1993 3.00p) per share	37	37
	61	56

ROLLS-ROYCE PLC 1994 ANNUAL REPORT

7 Earnings per ordinary share

Earnings per ordinary share on the net basis are calculated by dividing the profit attributable to the shareholders of Rolls-Royce plc of **£81m** (1993 £63m) by **1,224 million** (1993 1,058 million) ordinary shares, being the average number of ordinary shares in issue during the year.

Earnings per ordinary share on the nil distribution basis are calculated as for the net basis but after adjusting for the irrecoverable advance corporation tax attributable to dividends paid and proposed of **£15m** (1993 £13m). This calculation is shown as recommended by Statement of Standard Accounting Practice No. 3 'Earnings per share'.

Dilution of the earnings per ordinary share figure based upon outstanding share options is not material.

8 Employee information

	1994 Number	1993 Number
Average weekly number of Group employees during the year		
United Kingdom	36,800	41,400
Overseas	6,700	7,800
	43,500	49,200
Aerospace	24,500	27,900
Industrial Power	19,000	21,300
	43,500	49,200

	£m	£m
Group employment costs		
Wages and salaries	866	914
Social security costs	80	82
Other pension costs (note 27)	52	50
	998	1,046

ROLLS-ROYCE PLC 1994 ANNUAL REPORT

Notes to the Financial Statements continued

9 Emoluments of directors

The total emoluments of the directors, including the Chairman who was also the highest paid director, were as follows:

	Total		Chairman	
	1994 £000	1993 £000	1994 £000	1993 £000
Salary and benefits	1,705	1,532	321	308
Performance related bonuses	324	58	60	–
Fees	107	84	–	–
	2,136	1,674	381	308
Pension contributions	207	171	25	36
	2,343	1,845	406	344

In 1993 the Chairman waived a performance related bonus of £7,000.

The emoluments, including performance related bonuses but excluding pension contributions, of directors working wholly or mainly in the United Kingdom were:

£	1994 Number	1993 Number	£	1994 Number	1993 Number
5,001 to 10,000	1	–	215,001 to 220,000	1	–
15,001 to 20,000	1	3	230,001 to 235,000	1	–
20,001 to 25,000	2	–	240,001 to 245,000	1	–
30,001 to 35,000	–	1	250,001 to 255,000	1	–
35,001 to 40,000	1	–	255,001 to 260,000	–	1
185,001 to 190,000	1	–	305,001 to 310,000	–	1
190,001 to 195,000	–	2	310,001 to 315,000	1	–
200,001 to 205,000	1	2	380,001 to 385,000	1	–

Executive directors' salaries, bonuses (which are performance related) and executive share options are determined by the Remuneration Committee of the Board (see page 18). The members of this committee are all non-executive directors, none of whom receives salaries or bonuses or holds options.

The salary levels take into account the skill and experience of the individual, the scope of the duties performed and personal contribution. Account is also taken of the level of remuneration for comparable jobs in the UK engineering and aerospace industries, based upon information provided by independent remuneration consultants.

A performance improvement bonus scheme is in operation and membership is restricted to executive directors and senior executives. The scheme is based on the achievement of profit and cash performance targets for the relevant business group or trading company during the year in question. Such bonuses have a ceiling of 20% of year end salary.

Executive share options are provided to executive directors and to certain other personnel, in accordance with the terms of the Executive Share Option Scheme. These options encourage executives to take a long-term view of the Group's performance and are granted at the market value at the date of issue. No options were granted in 1994 nor in 1993 (note 22).

Under the Sharesave Scheme, options over shares are offered to all employees including executive directors. The latest offer (1992) was at a discount of 15% to the market value at the date of offer.

Fees of non-executive directors are determined by reference to independent market surveys and comprise a basic fee, plus additional fees for Board Committee membership.

ROLLS-ROYCE PLC 1994 ANNUAL REPORT

10 Tangible fixed assets

	Group			Company		
	Land & buildings £m	Plant & equipment £m	Total £m	Land & buildings £m	Plant & equipment £m	Total £m
Cost or valuation:						
At January 1, 1994	371	1,331	1,702	244	910	1,154
Exchange adjustments	(10)	(6)	(16)	—	—	—
Additions at cost	19	78	97	13	53	66
Disposals/write-offs	(17)	(142)	(159)	(10)	(77)	(87)
At December 31, 1994	363	1,261	1,624	247	886	1,133
Depreciation:						
At January 1, 1994	85	735	820	60	455	515
Exchange adjustments	(4)	(4)	(8)	—	—	—
Provided during year	13	96	109	10	77	87
Disposals/write-offs	(4)	(129)	(133)	(3)	(71)	(74)
At December 31, 1994	90	698	788	67	461	528
Net book value 1994	273	563	836	180	425	605
Net book value 1993	286	596	882	184	455	639

Tangible fixed assets include:	Group 1994 £m	Group 1993 £m	Company 1994 £m	Company 1993 £m
Net book value of finance leased assets	38	44	18	339
Assets held for use in operating leases:				
Cost	74	79	—	—
Depreciation	(46)	(52)	—	—
Net book value	28	27	—	—
Land and buildings at cost or valuation comprise:				
Valuation at December 31, 1985[1]	174	186	163	173
Cost	189	185	84	71
	363	371	247	244
Land and buildings at net book value comprise:				
Freehold	251	263	170	174
Long leasehold	20	21	8	8
Short leasehold	2	2	2	2
	273	286	180	184
On an historical cost basis the net book value of land and buildings would have been as follows:				
Cost	294	295	172	165
Depreciation	(130)	(129)	(97)	(96)
Net book value	164	166	75	69

[1]At December 31, 1985 specialised properties were revalued on a depreciated replacement cost basis and the remainder by reference to their open market value for existing use.

ROLLS-ROYCE PLC 1994 ANNUAL REPORT

Notes to the Financial Statements continued

11 Investments – subsidiary undertakings

	£m
Company	
Shares at cost at January 1, 1994	339
Additions	7
Transfer from associated undertakings	1
Shares at cost at December 31, 1994	347

The principal subsidiary undertakings are listed on pages 45 and 46.

12 Investments – associated undertakings

	Shares at cost £m	Share of post acquisition reserves £m	Loans £m	Total £m
Group				
At January 1, 1994	53	12	3	68
Repayments	—	—	(2)	(2)
Retained profit	—	7	—	7
Transfer to subsidiary undertakings	(1)	(1)	—	(2)
At December 31, 1994	52	18	1	71
Company				
At January 1, 1994	50	—	3	53
Repayments	—	—	(2)	(2)
Transfer to subsidiary undertakings	(1)	—	—	(1)
At December 31, 1994	49	—	1	50

The principal associated undertakings are listed on pages 47 and 48.

13 Stocks

	Group		Company	
	1994 £m	1993 £m	**1994 £m**	1993 £m
Raw materials	65	75	37	47
Work in progress	277	291	182	183
Long-term contract work in progress	25	25	—	—
Finished goods	376	387	360	355
Payments on account	17	11	16	20
	760	789	595	605
Progress payments against:				
Long-term contract work in progress	(8)	(14)	—	—
Other stocks	(157)	(164)	(127)	(139)
	595	611	468	466

ROLLS-ROYCE PLC 1994 ANNUAL REPORT

14 Debtors – amounts falling due within one year

	Group 1994 £m	Group Restated 1993 £m	Company 1994 £m	Company Restated 1993 £m
Trade debtors[1]	437	445	279	262
Amounts recoverable on contracts	63	60	2	3
Amounts owed by – subsidiary undertakings	—	—	65	47
– associated undertakings	93	119	91	118
Corporate taxation	3	2	—	—
Other debtors	34	27	6	4
Prepayments and accrued income	84	61	66	44
	714	714	509	478

[1]The Group has amended its accounting policies to comply with Financial Reporting Standard 5. Discounted promissory notes, previously offset against debtors, are now included in borrowings. The figures for 1993 have been restated by £20m.

15 Debtors – amounts falling due after one year

	Group 1994 £m	Group Restated 1993 £m	Company 1994 £m	Company Restated 1993 £m
Trade debtors	75	75	43	28
Amounts owed by – subsidiary undertakings	—	—	92	385
– associated undertakings	3	21	3	21
Other debtors[1]	46	18	46	18
Prepayments and accrued income	43	33	43	33
Prepaid pension contributions	38	29	9	15
	205	176	236	500

[1]As described in note 14, the figures for 1993 have been restated by £18m.

16 Borrowings – amounts falling due within one year

	Group 1994 £m	Group Restated 1993 £m	Company 1994 £m	Company Restated 1993 £m
Bank loans and overdrafts	5	51	—	—
Acceptance credits and promissory notes[1]	—	27	—	20
Obligations under finance leases[2]	6	6	2	37
	11	84	2	57

[1]As described in note 14, the figures for 1993 have been restated by £20m.
[2]The comparative figures have been adjusted to reclassify obligations under finance leases (previously included in note 17) as borrowings as in the opinion of the directors this more fairly reflects their nature.
Company obligations under finance leases include **£nil** (1993 £36m) owed to a subsidiary undertaking.

ROLLS-ROYCE PLC 1994 ANNUAL REPORT

Notes to the Financial Statements continued

17 Other creditors – amounts falling due within one year

	Group 1994 £m	Group 1993 £m	Company 1994 £m	Company 1993 £m
Payments received on account	144	214	91	101
Trade creditors	488	451	355	299
Amounts owed to – subsidiary undertakings	—	—	38	100
– associated undertakings	46	57	46	57
Corporate taxation	29	26	23	21
Other taxation and social security	40	44	15	17
Other creditors	308	294	226	230
Accruals and deferred income	46	37	27	28
Interim dividend since paid	24	19	24	19
Final proposed dividend	37	37	37	37
	1,162	1,179	882	909

18 Borrowings – amounts falling due after one year

	Group 1994 £m	Group Restated 1993 £m	Company 1994 £m	Company Restated 1993 £m
Unsecured				
11⅝% Notes 1998[1]	150	150	150	150
7⅛% Notes 2003[1,2]	198	198	—	—
Other loans 1996-2006 (interest rates nil)	2	2	—	—
Preference shares issued by a subsidiary undertaking[3]	9	10	—	—
Promissory notes[4]	—	18	—	18
Obligations under finance leases payable[5]:				
Between one and two years	6	6	1	38
Between two and five years	17	18	4	111
After five years	3	8	1	176
	385	410	156	493
Repayable				
Between one and two years – by instalments	6	8	1	38
– otherwise	9	—	—	—
Between two and five years – by instalments	17	36	4	129
– otherwise	150	160	150	150
After five years – by instalments	5	8	1	176
– otherwise	198	198	—	—
	385	410	156	493

[1]Notes are the subject of interest swap agreements under which counterparties have undertaken to pay amounts at fixed rates of interest in consideration for amounts payable by the Company at variable rates of interest.
[2]The Group has borrowed US $300m through a subsidiary, Rolls-Royce Capital Inc., in order to provide a fixed rate loan for general Group purposes. This has been translated into sterling after taking account of future contracts. The loan is guaranteed by the Company.
[3]Cumulative preference shares, redeemable in 1996, have been issued by NEI Africa Operations Limited. The share issue is guaranteed by the Company.
[4]As described in note 14, the figures for 1993 have been restated by £18m.
[5]The comparative figures have been adjusted to reclassify obligations under finance leases (previously included in note 19) as borrowings as in the opinion of the directors this more fairly reflects their nature. Company obligations under finance leases include **£nil** (1993 £318m) owed to a subsidiary undertaking.

ROLLS-ROYCE PLC 1994 ANNUAL REPORT

19 Other creditors – amounts falling due after one year

	Group 1994 £m	Group 1993 £m	Company 1994 £m	Company 1993 £m
Payments received on account	63	41	63	41
Amount owed to subsidiary undertaking	—	—	198	198
Other creditors	47	77	46	73
Accruals and deferred income	15	12	14	12
Accrued pension costs	4	3	—	—
	129	133	321	324

20 Deferred taxation

	Group 1994 £m	Group 1993 £m	Company 1994 £m	Company 1993 £m
Full potential liability/(asset):				
Fixed asset timing differences	73	77	62	(6)
Other timing differences	(62)	(78)	(65)	(70)

No provision for deferred taxation has been made.

At December 31, 1994, the Company had tax losses of approximately **£275m** (1993 £325m), which are available for relief against future trading profits of the Company.

At December 31, 1994 advance corporation tax of **£156m** (1993 £141m) for the Group, including **£137m** (1993 £122m) for the Company, is available for carry forward against future corporation tax liabilities.

21 Provisions for liabilities and charges

	Restructuring and customer problems £m	Other £m	Total £m
Group			
At January 1, 1994	138	163	301
Net charge to profit and loss account	—	22	22
Utilised	(95)	(68)	(163)
At December 31, 1994	43	117	160
Company			
At January 1, 1994	126	107	233
Net charge to profit and loss account	—	—	—
Utilised	(85)	(35)	(120)
At December 31, 1994	41	72	113

Other provisions include, principally, warranty relating to sales up to the year end and estimated future losses on current contracts.

ROLLS-ROYCE PLC 1994 ANNUAL REPORT

Notes to the Financial Statements continued

22 Share capital

	Non-equity Special share of £1	Equity Ordinary shares of 20p each	Nominal value £m
Authorised			
At January 1 and December 31, 1994	1	1,750,000,000	350
Issued and fully paid			
At January 1, 1994	1	1,220,783,882	244
Exercise of share options	—	2,602,007	—
In lieu of paying dividends in cash	—	3,066,831	1
At December 31, 1994	1	1,226,452,720	245

Subject to the provisions of Companies Act 1985, the special rights redeemable preference share (special share) may be redeemed by the Treasury Solicitor at par at any time. The special share confers no right to dividends or to vote at general meetings and in the event of a winding-up shall be repaid in priority to any other shares.

At December 31, 1994 the following ordinary shares were subject to options:

	Date of grant	Number	Exercise price	Exercisable dates
Executive Share Option Scheme	1987	1,456,931	200p	1995-1997
	1988	137,612	110p	1995-1998
	1989	295,048	183p	1995-1999
	1990	2,799,755	174p	1995-2000
	1991	2,484,823	140p	1995-2001
	1992	110,700	149p	1995-2002
	1992	3,859,125	126p	1995-2002
Sharesave Scheme	1987	3,964,680	180p	1995
	1988	3,912,075	109p	1995-1996
	1990	11,659,553	146p	1996/1998
	1992	17,802,343	107p	1998/2000

Under the terms of the Executive Share Option Scheme, options granted to 82 directors and senior executives were outstanding at December 31, 1994. Under the terms of the Sharesave Scheme the Board may grant options to purchase ordinary shares in the Company each year to those employees who enter into an Inland Revenue approved Save As You Earn (SAYE) contract for a period of either five or seven years.

The directors at December 31, 1994 had the following beneficial interests, including options, in the ordinary share capital of the Company:

	Holdings		Options				
	Jan 1[1] 1994	Dec 31 1994	Jan 1 1994	Exercised in 1994	Dec 31 1994	Exercise price	Exercisable dates
Sir Ralph Robins	7,700	7,909	259,940		259,940	200p	1995-1997
			125,255		125,255	174p	1995-2000
			124,743		124,743	140p	1995-2001
			178,350		178,350	126p	1995-2002
			688,288		688,288	165p[2]	
Dr T. Harrison	27,263	27,263	57,862	57,862[3]	—		
			137,760		137,760	174p	1995-2000
			116,133		116,133	140p	1995-2001
			180,400		180,400	126p	1995-2002
			492,155		434,293	145p[2]	

ROLLS-ROYCE PLC 1994 ANNUAL REPORT

22 Share capital continued

	Holdings		Options				
	Jan 1[1] 1994	Dec 31 1994	Jan 1 1994	Exercised in 1994	Dec 31 1994	Exercise price	Exercisable dates
Mr R.H. Maudslay	4,000	4,066	53,300		53,300	174p	1995-2000
			26,855		26,855	140p	1995-2001
			74,825		74,825	126p	1995-2002
			5,535[4]		5,535	146p	1998
			5,674[4]		5,674	107p	1998
			166,189		166,189	144p[2]	
Mr S.C. Miller	5,022	5,022	97,478		97,478	200p	1995-1997
			19,065		19,065	110p	1995-1998
			161,643		161,643	174p	1995-2000
			56,888		56,888	140p	1995-2001
			128,125		128,125	126p	1995-2002
			463,199		463,199	159p[2]	
Mr J.E.V. Rose	1,250	1,250	33,005		33,005	200p	1995-1997
			34,133		34,133	174p	1995-2000
			66,830		66,830	140p	1995-2001
			102,500		102,500	126p	1995-2002
			236,468		236,468	147p[2]	
Mr J.W. Sandford	12,746	13,092	–		–		
Mr M. Townsend	1,250	1,250	85,383		85,383	174p	1995-2000
			54,633		54,633	140p	1995-2001
			117,875		117,875	126p	1995-2002
			7,093[4]		7,093	107p	1998
			264,984		264,984	144p[2]	
Mr R.T. Turner	2,409	2,409	110,700		110,700	149p	1995-2002
			129,150		129,150	126p	1995-2002
			239,850		239,850	137p[2]	
Mr L.J. Clark	5,937	5,937	–		–		
Sir Gordon Higginson	3,125	3,125	–		–		
Lord Moore	5,000	5,000	–		–		
Mr H.G. Mourgue	5,937	5,937	–		–		
Sir Robin Nicholson	5,937	5,937	–		–		

[1]Or date of appointment if later.
[2]Weighted average exercise price.
[3]The exercised price was 130p and the market price at date exercised was 192p.
[4]Sharesave scheme options.

Sir Ralph Robins, Mr R.H. Maudslay, Lord Moore and Mr J.W. Sandford took shares, 89, 46, 56 and 148 respectively, instead of cash dividends in January 1995. Otherwise there has been no change in the directors' interests set out above between December 31, 1994 and March 8, 1995.

The market price of the Company's ordinary shares ranged between 161p and 203.5p during 1994 and was 179.5p on December 31, 1994.

ROLLS-ROYCE PLC 1994 ANNUAL REPORT

Notes to the Financial Statements continued

23 Reserves

	Non-distributable			
	Share premium £m	Revaluation reserve £m	Other reserves £m	Profit and loss account £m
Group				
At January 1, 1994	506	120	20	335
Exchange adjustments	—	(1)	—	(11)
Scrip dividend adjustment	—	—	—	5
Ordinary shares issued relating to scrip dividend	(1)	—	—	—
Arising on share issues	4	—	—	—
Transfers between reserves	—	(10)	—	10
Profit for the year	—	—	—	20
At December 31, 1994	509	109	20	359
Company				
At January 1, 1994	506	115	261	125
Scrip dividend adjustment	—	—	—	5
Ordinary shares issued relating to scrip dividend	(1)	—	—	—
Arising on share issues	4	—	—	—
Transfers between reserves	—	(10)	—	10
Profit for the year	—	—	—	77
At December 31, 1994	509	105	261	217

Goodwill, written off against other reserves, cumulatively amounts to **£243m** (1993 £243m).

The undistributed profits of overseas subsidiary and associated undertakings may be liable to overseas taxes and/or United Kingdom tax (after allowing for double tax relief) if remitted as dividends to the UK.

24 Capital expenditure commitments

	Group		Company	
	1994 £m	1993 £m	**1994 £m**	1993 £m
Contracted but not provided	23	18	14	14
Authorised but not yet contracted	40	23	36	18

25 Operating lease annual commitments

	Group		Company	
	1994 £m	1993 £m	**1994 £m**	1993 £m
Leases of land and buildings which expire:				
Within one year	2	2	1	1
Between one and five years	3	4	1	1
After five years	4	4	2	2
Other leases which expire:				
Within one year	2	1	—	—
Between one and five years	11	8	3	4
After five years	7	12	—	—

ROLLS-ROYCE PLC 1994 ANNUAL REPORT

26 Contingent liabilities

In connection with the sale of its products, on some occasions the Company enters into individually and collectively significant long-term contingent obligations. These can involve, inter alia, guaranteeing financing for customers, guaranteeing a proportion of the values of both engine and airframe, entering into leasing transactions and in certain circumstances could involve the Company assuming certain of its customers' entitlements and related borrowing or cash flow obligations until the value of the security can be realised.

At December 31, 1994 having regard to the estimated net realisable value of the relevant security the net contingent liabilities on all delivered aircraft amounted to **£48m** (1993 £11m). Sensitivity calculations are complex, but, for example, if the value of the relevant security was reduced by 20%, a net contingent liability of approximately **£130m** would result. There are also net contingent liabilities in respect of undelivered aircraft but it is not considered practicable to estimate these as deliveries can be many years in the future and the related financing will only be put in place at the appropriate time.

At the date these accounts are approved the directors regard the possibility that there will be any significant loss arising from these contingencies, which cover a number of customers over a long period of time, as remote. In determining this, and the values above, the directors have taken account of advice, principally from Airclaims Limited, professional aircraft appraisers, who base their calculations on a current and future fair market value basis assuming an arms length transaction between a willing seller and a willing buyer.

Contingent liabilities exist in respect of guarantees provided by the Group in the ordinary course of business for engine delivery, performance and reliability. The Company and some of its subsidiary undertakings have, in the normal course of business, entered into arrangements in respect of export finance, performance bonds, countertrade obligations and minor miscellaneous items. There are claims outstanding which arise under contracts carried out by the Group. The directors do not expect any of these arrangements or claims, after allowing for provisions already made, to result in significant loss to the Group.

The Group and Company enter into forward exchange and swap transactions, including interest rate swaps, to improve the achieved rate and limiting exposure to exchange rate movements in the medium and long-term.

In addition to the guarantees referred to in note 18, there are other Company guarantees in respect of financial obligations of subsidiary undertakings **£55m** (1993 £68m) and associated undertakings **£63m** (1993 £30m).

27 Pensions

The Group's pension schemes are mainly of the defined benefit type and the assets of the schemes are held in separate trustee administered funds.

The pension cost relating to the UK schemes is assessed in accordance with the advice of independent qualified actuaries using the projected unit method. The latest actuarial valuations of the principal schemes were as at April 5, 1992 (for NEI) and March 31, 1994 (for Rolls-Royce). The principal assumptions used were that in the long-term the average return on investments would be respectively 1.5% and 2.5% per annum higher than the average increase in pay and between 4.5% and 5.5% per annum higher than the average increase in pensions. Assets have been valued using the discounted income method assuming that UK equity dividends increase at a rate of between 4.5% and 4.75% per annum less than the return on investments. The pension cost relating to overseas schemes is calculated in accordance with local best practice and regulations. The total pension cost for the Group was **£52m** (1993 £50m) of which **£5m** (1993 £4m) relates to the overseas schemes.

The aggregate of the market values of the UK schemes at the dates of the latest actuarial valuations was **£2,422m**. The actuarial value of the assets of the principal schemes represented respectively 119.0% (for NEI) and 94.2% (for Rolls-Royce) of the value of the projected accrued liabilities. The difference between the value of the assets and the value of the projected accrued liabilities (after allowing for expected future increases in earnings and discretionary pension increases) is being amortised as a percentage of scheme earnings over periods of between eight and 13 years, being the average remaining service lives of the pensionable employees.

Prepayments of **£38m** (1993 £29m) are included in debtors and accruals of **£4m** (1993 £3m) are included in creditors, being the differences between the accumulated amounts paid into the pension funds and the accumulated pension costs.

ROLLS-ROYCE PLC 1994 ANNUAL REPORT

Notes to the Financial Statements continued

28 Other commitments

Acquisition of Allison Engine Company, Inc. (Allison)

On November 21, 1994 Rolls-Royce announced that it had agreed to acquire Allison from Clayton, Dubilier and Rice, Inc. subject to the necessary regulatory approvals.

Allison had profit before tax of £4m and retained profit of £2m for the year ended December 31, 1994 which after estimated adjustments to reflect Rolls-Royce accounting policies amounted to £2m and £1m respectively. These figures have been derived from Allison's unaudited financial statements for the year ended December 31, 1994.

Acquisition of Rolls-Royce & Partners Finance Limited (RRPF)

Rolls-Royce is considering acquiring the remaining 60% of the shares of RRPF which it does not already own.

RRPF had profit before tax of £4m and retained profit of £3m for the year ended December 31, 1994. These figures have been derived from RRPF's unaudited financial statements for the year ended December 31, 1994.

Proforma statement of net assets of the enlarged group

The following illustrative proforma statement of the combined net assets of the enlarged group is based on the December 31, 1994 unaudited consolidated balance sheets of Allison and RRPF. The proforma balance sheet has been prepared as if the interests had been acquired by Rolls-Royce on December 31, 1994. No fair value adjustments have been made.

	Rolls-Royce Group £m	Allison £m	RRPF £m	Adjustments £m	Enlarged Rolls-Royce Group £m
Tangible fixed assets	907	184	104	12	1,207
Short-term deposits and cash	681	82	1	(21)	743
Borrowings	(396)	(122)	(60)	109	(469)
Other assets and liabilities	63	(84)	(11)	(5)	(37)
	1,255	60	34	95	1,444

The proforma consolidated balance sheet includes adjustments reflecting the following:

i) the issue of ordinary Rolls-Royce shares to fund the acquisition of Allison and repay Allison's borrowings,

ii) the payment of cash consideration with respect to the acquisition of RRPF and adjustments in respect of existing arrangements with Rolls-Royce,

iii) adjustments to reflect significant differences between the accounting policies of Allison and Rolls-Royce including: treatment of intangible assets, depreciation of tangible fixed assets, valuation of inventory, basis of calculation of provisions and deferred taxation.

ROLLS-ROYCE PLC 1994 ANNUAL REPORT

Principal Subsidiary Undertakings

at December 31, 1994

Registered in England	
Aerospace Group	
Rolls E.L. Turbofans Limited	– FJ44 engine support services/holding company
Rolls-Royce Aero Engine Services Limited[1]	– Overhaul and repair
Rolls-Royce Commercial Aero Engines Limited[1]	– Sale and support of aero gas turbine engines and parts
Rolls-Royce Engine Controls Limited	– Holding company
Rolls-Royce International Support Services Limited	– Product support services
Rolls-Royce Military Aero Engines Limited[1]	– Sale and support of aero gas turbine engines and parts
Sawley Packaging Company Limited	– Specialised packaging
Industrial Power Group	
Allen Power Engineering Limited[2]	– Diesel engines, small steam turbines, compressors and valves
Clarke Chapman Limited[2]	– Cranes and mechanical handling equipment
International Combustion Limited[2]	– Power station boilers and combustion systems
NEI Brantford International Limited (51%)[3]	– Freight forwarding
NEI Control Systems Limited[2]	– Control systems for power stations and industrial applications
NEI Overseas Holdings Limited[3]	– Holding company
Parsons Power Generation Systems Limited[2]	– Large steam turbine generators
Peebles Electric Limited[2]	– Transformers and electric motors
Reyrolle Limited[2]	– Electrical switchgear and protection equipment
Rolls-Royce and Associates Limited	– Nuclear submarine propulsion systems
Rolls-Royce Industrial & Marine Gas Turbines Limited[1]	– Aero-derived gas turbines
Rolls-Royce Industrial Power (India) Limited[3]	– Power station construction
Rolls-Royce Nuclear Engineering Limited[4]	– Management company
Rolls-Royce Nuclear Engineering Services Limited[2]	– Refurbishment and modification of nuclear power plant
Rolls-Royce Power Engineering plc	– Holding company
Thompson Defence Projects Limited[2]	– Military bridging systems
Thompson Kennicott Limited[2]	– Water treatment plant
Corporate	
Middle East Equity Partners Limited	– Holding company
Rolls-Royce International Limited	– Support and commercial information services in Australia, Brazil, China, Dubai, France, Hong Kong, India, Indonesia, Japan, Korea, Malaysia, Mexico, Singapore and Thailand
Rolls-Royce Leasing Limited	– Leasing of engines
Rolls-Royce Overseas Holdings Limited	– Holding company
Rolls-Royce Power Ventures Limited	– Provision of project development capabilities

[1]These subsidiaries act as agents of Rolls-Royce plc.
[2]The interests are held by Rolls-Royce Power Engineering plc and these companies act as agents of that company.
[3]The interests are held by Rolls-Royce Power Engineering plc.
[4]This subsidiary acts as agent of Rolls-Royce Power Engineering plc.

Except where otherwise stated, the above companies operate principally in Great Britain and the effective Group interest is 100%.

ROLLS-ROYCE PLC 1994 ANNUAL REPORT

Principal Subsidiary Undertakings continued

Incorporated overseas		
Aerospace Group		
Brazil	Motores Rolls-Royce Limitada	– Overhaul and repair
France	Rolls-Royce Technical Support SARL[1]	– Project support
Industrial Power Group		
Australia	Rolls-Royce Industrial Power (Pacific) Limited[3]	– Electrical, mechanical and construction engineering
Canada	Bristol Aerospace Limited[6]	– Servicing of aircraft engines and airframes
	Ferranti-Packard Transformers Limited[6]	– Power transformers
	Parsons Turbine Generators Canada Limited[6]	– Turbine generator overhaul
	Rolls-Royce Canada Limited[6]	– Industrial gas turbines and aero engine sales, service and overhaul
	Rolls-Royce Gas Turbine Engines (Canada) Inc.[6]	– Industrial gas turbines
	Rolls-Royce Holdings Canada Inc.	– Holding company
	Rolls-Royce Industries Canada Inc.[5]	– Holding company
Mexico	Ferranti-Packard de Mexico SA De CV[7]	– Power transformers
New Zealand	Rolls-Royce Industrial Power (New Zealand) Limited[8]	– Electrical switchgear and industrial engineering
South Africa	NEI Africa Holdings Limited (60.33%)[3]	– Holding company
	Northern Engineering Industries Africa Limited (56.36%)[4] (The effective interest in South African Companies is 35.20%.)	– Energy conversion and distribution equipment
Zambia	Cutler Hammer Zambia Limited[3]	– Low voltage motor control equipment
	NEI Zambia Limited[3]	– Diesel engines, distribution switchgear
Zimbabwe	NEI Holdings Zimbabwe (Private) Limited[3]	– Boilers, distribution switchgear
Corporate		
Australia	Rolls-Royce of Australia Pty. Limited	– Service facilities
Guernsey	Nightingale Insurance Limited[1]	– Insurers
Saudi Arabia	Rolls-Royce International Turbines (Saudi Arabia) Limited (51%)	– Operation and maintenance of electrical generating plant
USA	Rolls-Royce Holdings Inc.[1]	– Holding company for US operations
	Rolls-Royce Inc.[2]	– Engineering research; marketing and support
	Rolls-Royce Capital Inc.[2]	– Financial services

[1]These interests are held by Rolls-Royce Overseas Holdings Limited.
[2]The interest is held by Rolls-Royce Holdings Inc.
[3]The interests are held by NEI Overseas Holdings Limited.
[4]The interest is held as follows: 53.34% by NEI Africa Holdings Limited, 3.02% by NEI Overseas Holdings Limited.
[5]The interests are held by Rolls-Royce Holdings Canada Inc.
[6]The interests are held by Rolls-Royce Industries Canada Inc.
[7]The interest is held as follows: 37% by Rolls-Royce Industries Canada Inc., 63% by NEI Overseas Holdings Limited.
[8]The interest is held by Rolls-Royce Industrial Power (Pacific) Limited.

The above companies operate principally in the country of their incorporation and the effective Group interest is 100% unless otherwise stated.

A list of all subsidiary undertakings will be included in the Company's next annual return.

ROLLS-ROYCE PLC 1994 ANNUAL REPORT

Principal Associated Undertakings

at December 31, 1994

Registered in England or Scotland*	Class	% held by Rolls-Royce plc	% of total equity held by Rolls-Royce plc
Aerospace Group			
Rolls-Royce Turbomeca Limited (England & France)	A Shares	–	50
– Adour and RTM 322 engines collaboration	B Shares	100	
Rolls Smiths Engine Controls Limited[1]	A Ordinary	–	50
– Digital engine controls	B Ordinary	50	
RS Leasing Limited[2]	A Ordinary	50	50
– Aircraft leasing	B Ordinary	–	
Turbo-Union Limited (England, Germany & Italy)	Ordinary	40	40
– RB199 engine collaboration	A Shares	37.5	
Industrial Power Group			
Rolls Wood Group (Repair & Overhauls) Limited*	A Ordinary	100	50
– Overhaul and repair	B Ordinary	–	
Cooper Rolls Limited[3]	Ordinary	50	50
– Sale of mechanical drive units			
Rolls Laval Heat Exchangers Limited	A Ordinary	50	50
– Design, development and manufacture of heat exchangers	B Ordinary	–	
Corporate			
Rolls-Royce & Partners Finance Limited	Ordinary	40	40
– Financial services			

Incorporated overseas			
Aerospace Group			
Germany			
BMW Rolls-Royce GmbH (England & Germany)	Ordinary	49.5	49.5
– BR700 engine development			
EUROJET Turbo GmbH (England, Germany, Italy & Spain)	Ordinary	33	33
– EJ200 engine collaboration			
MTU, Turbomeca, Rolls-Royce GmbH (England, France & Germany)	Ordinary	33.3	33.3
– MTR 390 engine collaboration			
Spain			
Industria de Turbo Propulsores SA	Ordinary	45	45
– Component design and manufacture; engine overhaul			
Switzerland			
IAE International Aero Engines AG (England, Germany, Italy, Japan & USA)	A Shares	100	30
– V2500 engine collaboration	B Shares	–	
	C Shares	–	
	D Shares	–	
	E Shares	–	
USA			
Williams-Rolls, Inc.[4] (Europe & North America)	Common	15	15
– FJ44 engine collaboration			

ROLLS-ROYCE PLC 1994 ANNUAL REPORT

Principal Associated Undertakings continued

Incorporated overseas continued	Class	% held by Rolls-Royce plc	% of total equity held by Rolls-Royce plc
Industrial Power Group			
Canada			
Cooper, Rolls Corporation[5] – Sale and marketing of mechanical drive units	Common	50	50
India			
Belliss India Limited[6] – Steam turbines	Ordinary	40	40
Easun Reyrolle Relays and Devices Limited[7] – Protection, relays and systems and power supplies	Ordinary	24.4	24.4
USA			
Cooper Rolls Incorporated (Europe & North America) – Sale and marketing of mechanical drive units	Common	50	50
Corporate			
Saudi Arabia			
Middle East Propulsion Company Limited[8] – Overhaul and repair facility	Ordinary	16.6	16.6
USA			
R-H Component Technologies, L.C.[9] – Component refurbishment	Ordinary	50	50

[1]The interest is held by Rolls-Royce Engine Controls Limited.
[2]The interest is held by Rolls-Royce Leasing Limited.
[3]The interest is held by Cooper Rolls Incorporated.
[4]The interest is held by Rolls E.L. Turbofans Limited.
[5]The interest is held by Rolls-Royce Industries Canada Inc.
[6]The interest is held by Belliss & Morcom Holdings Limited.
[7]The interest is held by Rolls-Royce Power Engineering Limited.
[8]The interest is held by Middle East Equity Partners Limited.
[9]The interest is held by Rolls-Royce Inc.

The countries of principal operations, if other than the country of registration, are stated in brackets after the company's name.

ROLLS-ROYCE PLC 1994 ANNUAL REPORT

Shareholders' Information

Financial calendar	
Ex dividend date for final dividend	March 20, 1995
Calculation period for scrip dividend	March 20-24, 1995
Qualifying date for final dividend	April 6, 1995
Last date for new scrip dividend instructions	May 19, 1995
Annual General Meeting	May 24, 1995
Payment of final/scrip dividend	July 3, 1995
Press advertisement of 1995 Interim Results*	September 1, 1995
Ex dividend date for interim dividend	October 16, 1995
Calculation period for scrip dividend	October 16-20, 1995
Qualifying date for interim dividend	October 26, 1995
Last date for new scrip dividend instructions	November 16, 1995
Financial year end	December 31, 1995
Payment of interim/scrip dividend	January 8, 1996
Press advertisement of 1995 Preliminary Results*	March, 1996
1995 Annual Report published	April, 1996

*Note: Preliminary and Interim Results are notified by press advertisement only.

Analysis of ordinary shareholders at December 31, 1994

Size of holding	Number of holdings	% of total holdings	% of total shares
1 – 150	187,377	41.34	2.09
151 – 500	227,822	50.27	4.32
501 – 10,000	36,183	7.98	4.89
10,001 – 100,000	1,033	0.23	2.80
100,001 – 1,000,000	594	0.13	17.34
1,000,001 and over	206	0.05	68.56
	453,215	100.00	100.00

Details of special low cost dealing services in the Company's shares may be obtained from Hoare Govett Corporate Finance Limited (telephone 0171 601 0101) and from NatWest Stockbrokers Limited (telephone 0171 895 5454). Both are members of the Securities and Futures Authority and NatWest Stockbrokers Limited is a member of the London Stock Exchange.

If you have any queries about your shareholding please write to or telephone the Registrar at the following address:

The Royal Bank of Scotland plc
Registrar's Department
PO Box 82
Caxton House
Redcliffe Way
Bristol BS99 7NH
Telephone: 0117 930 6600

You can obtain the current market price of the Company's shares by telephoning 0839 500 232.

If you would prefer to receive new shares instead of cash dividends please ask the Registrar for a Scrip Dividend Mandate.

The Company operates a free of charge service for consolidating the individual shareholdings of immediate members of a family. Please ask the Registrar for details if you are interested.

ISSUES FOR DISCUSSION

D15.1 Assume the existence of four underlying financial reporting dimensions* as described here:

1. *Professionalism versus statutory control*—a preference for the exercise of individual professional judgment and the maintenance of professional self-regulation as opposed to compliance with prescriptive legal requirements and statutory control.
2. *Uniformity versus flexibility*—a preference for the enforcement of uniform accounting practices between companies and for the consistent use of such practices over time as opposed to flexibility in accordance with the perceived circumstances of individual companies.
3. *Conservatism versus optimism*—a preference for a cautious approach to measurement to cope with the uncertainty of future events as opposed to a more optimistic, laissez-faire, risk-taking approach.
4. *Secrecy versus transparency*—a preference for confidentiality and the restriction of disclosure of information about the business only to those who are closely involved with its management and financing as opposed to a more transparent, open, and publicly accountable approach.

Be prepared to discuss your personal preferences along these dimensions and where you perceive the financial reporting standards in the United States, Japan, and the United Kingdom to be along these dimensions.

D15.2 The average year-end 1994 price-earnings ratios for the publicly traded companies in the United Sates, Japan, and the United Kingdom, monitored in the *Emerging Stock Markets Factbook: 1995* (Washington, D.C.: International Finance Corporation, May 1995), were 16.9, 97.3, and 14.8, respectively. Discuss the possible causes for the disparity in Japan's P/E ratio when compared to that for the United States and the United Kingdom. What are the resulting implications of this disparity for investors, money managers, and financial analysts?

D15.3 It has been argued that a number of factors contribute to the harmonization of worldwide financial reporting practices, including the business press, textbooks, multinationals, the Big Six accounting firms, international capital markets, international lenders, the top business schools, the IASC, the United Nations, and the European Union. Among the factors thought to deter harmonization are national pride, different intended audiences, and different legal and tax systems.

a. Discuss the role of each of the factors contributing to harmonization. Are there others? Are some more important than others? If so, which ones?

b. Discuss the role of each of the deterring factors. Are there others?

c. Discuss the "battle" between the contributing and deterring factors. Can you predict the outcome?

D15.4 What are the costs and benefits associated with comparability in financial reporting practices for financial statement preparers in different countries? Should national standards continue in effect with domestic preparers required to reconcile income and owners' equity under two sets of standards (one domestic and one international)?

D15.5 Compile a list of as many differences as you can identify between the Rolls-Royce annual report presented in Appendix 15B and what you would expect to find in General Electric's annual report for the same period.

---

*The source for these four items is S. J. Gray, "Toward a Theory of Cultural Influence on the Development of Accounting Systems Internationally," *Abacus*, vol. 24, no. 1 (1988), pp. 1–15.

a. Discuss the significance of the differences in trying to come to an understanding of the financial profile of Rolls-Royce.

b. Discuss what the differences might tell you about the business environment and culture in the United Kingdom.

D15.6 Compile a list of as many differences as you can identify between the Kawasaki Steel annual report presented in Appendix 15A and what you would expect to find in U.S. Steel Group's annual report for the same period.

a. Discuss the significance of the differences in trying to come to an understanding of the financial profile of Kawasaki Steel.

b. Discuss what the differences might tell you about the business environment and culture in the Japan.

D15.7 As an external user of financial reports, assign a letter grade in each of the following categories for both the Kawasaki Steel and Rolls-Royce annual reports. In class, compare your grades to those given by your classmates and discuss the differences in terms of the following:

a. Informativeness

b. Understandability

c. Relevance

D15.8 In a *European Accounting Review* (Nov. 2, 1993 pp. 387–96) article, K. Van Hulle reported the views on financial reporting harmonization expressed by two CFOs from two major international companies:

> Mr. Hugh Collum of SmithKline Beecham — There are only two major stock exchanges in the world: London and New York. The accounting standard-setting bodies of the U.K. and the U.S. should therefore get together and develop the accounting standards. The rest of the world should merely follow their lead.
>
> Mr. Gegard Liener of Daimler-Benz — During the last few decades the English language has become the world language without a resolution of the U.N. or any other institution. It just happened. Well, something very similar is happening in international accounting. The Anglo-Saxon principles are gaining more ground and thus getting nearer and nearer to becoming the world's accounting language.
>
> The expression "Anglo Saxon" . . . as used by Mr. Leiner . . . does not include the U.K. . . . [it] is clearly an option for U.S. GAAP.

Prepare an essay discussing your agreement or disagreement with the above statements. Do not devote space in your essay to summarizing or paraphrasing the comments above. Your thoughts and rationale are important.

PROBLEMS

P15.1 International standard setting. Prepare a one- or two-page brief, to be handed in, spelling out what you believe the __________ role should be in the international standard-setting process. The blank is to be filled in according to the following:

First Letter in Your Last Name	Fill in Blank With
A to D	FASB's
E to K	SEC's
L to N	NYSE's
O to Z	multinationals'

P15.2 France. This chapter does not include information on France. France is clearly an important country in the world economy, especially in the EU. France is home to a number of major multinationals, including Michelin, Lafarge, Peugot, and Renault. Find a recent set of financial statements for one of these French companies. Select a partner in the class and prepare a 10-page (approximate) paper reviewing the annual report you have chosen and its national context.

The major thrust of the paper should be directed to the company's annual report; you might devote one-third of the paper to context and two-thirds to your analysis of the company. The paper should provide the following:

a. An overview of the French business climate, its legal structure, its capital tradition, and the resulting accounting and reporting situation.

b. The same analysis of the company's accounting and reporting as was developed in the chapter for Japan and the United Kingdom:
(1) How do these financial statements differ from what you might have expected from a U.S. company in the same industry?
(2) How do these statements illustrate the unique characteristics of the French capital and financial reporting environment?

P15.3 Analyzing the results of Kawasaki Steel Corporation. Presented in Appendix 15A are excerpts from the financial statements of Kawasaki Steel Corporation. Using the analytical techniques discussed in Chapter 7, prepare an analysis of Kawasaki Steel. Develop specific conclusions regarding the company's liquidity, solvency, asset management, and profitability. Identify those financial ratios that you believe are most likely to be influenced by the business and cultural environment of Japan.

P15.4 Analyzing the results of Rolls-Royce Plc. Presented in Appendix 15B are excerpts from the financial statements of Rolls-Royce. Using the analytical techniques discussed in Chapter 7, prepare an analysis of Rolls-Royce. Develop specific conclusions regarding the company's liquidity, solvency, asset management, and profitability. Identify those financial ratios that you believe are most likely to be influenced by the business and cultural environment of the United Kingdom.

P15.5 U.S. versus Japanese P/Es. A recent survey of the reported performance of eight Japanese electronics companies revealed an average profit margin (net income/net sales) of 6.31 percent using Japanese GAAP and an average price-earnings ratio of 41.4. Using U.S. GAAP, these same eight companies reported an average profit margin of 9.03 percent and an average price-earnings multiple of 26.33.

Required:

(a) Based on these data, what generalizations would you draw about the reported earnings and price-earnings ratios of U.S. companies (using U.S. GAAP) versus comparable Japanese companies (using Japanese GAAP)?

(b) How should an efficient worldwide equity market respond to differences in accepted accounting practice between countries?

P15.6 Valuation of the firm and goodwill accounting in the United Kingdom. In late 1994, Browning-Ferris Industries (BFI) launched a hostile takeover bid for Attwoods Plc, a British waste service company. The BFI offer of £364 million (or approximately $570 million) was flatly rejected by Attwoods' management on grounds that it was grossly underpriced. BFI executives, on the other hand, argued that the offer represented a premium of more than 115 percent above Attwoods's current value.

According to the BFI offer document, if Attwoods followed U.S. GAAP for goodwill, Attwoods' 1993 reported earnings of 5.3 pence per share would be halved to 2.5 pence per share. Based on average price-earnings multiples for waste companies in the United States, the value of one ordinary Attwoods share would be approximately 50 pence, or 19 times earnings. Hence, BFI's offer of 109 pence for each ordinary share could be seen to be quite generous. (Just prior to the BFI offer, Attwoods' ordinary shares had traded at 105 pence on the London Stock Exchange.)

BFI executives expressed concern that Attwoods' earnings were inflated when considered under U.S. accounting standards. In Great Britain, goodwill is written off directly against retained earnings, whereas in the United States it is capitalized to the balance sheet and typically amortized against earnings over a 40-year expected life. Through 1993, Attwoods had written off against owners' equity over £179 million in goodwill.

Required:
Evaluate the merits of BFI's offer for Attwoods. Is it generous, as BFI executives claim, or grossly underpriced as Attwoods's management argues? Justify your position.

CHAPTER 16

Communicating Corporate Value[1]

We all want, above all, to be heard—but not merely to be heard. We want to be understood—heard for what we think we are saying, for what we know we meant. With increased understanding of the ways [we] use language should come a decrease in frequency of the complaint "You just don't understand."[2]

Key Chapter Issues

- What is the role of financial reporting in communicating corporate value?
- What factors inhibit the communication of corporate value?
- How does the efficient market hypothesis help us understand the role of financial communications in establishing security market prices?
- How might a business report differ from a financial report?
- As the economy evolves to more service industries, what implications does that have for financial reporting and the communication of corporate value?

[1]Earlier versions of this chapter were presented during the Ira Shapiro/Beta Alpha Psi Distinguished Lecture Series in 1991 at The University of Maryland at College Park, and as part of the 1992 Price Waterhouse Speaker Series at Miami University, Oxford, Ohio. We want to thank both universities for their support and encouragement.

[2]D. Tannen, *You Just Don't Understand: Women and Men in Conversation* (New York: Ballantine, 1990), p. 48.

Professor Tannen's words seem particularly appropriate as the introduction to the capstone chapter for this text. Her thought-provoking book helped many understand the enormously complex process of interpersonal communication. Indeed, she illustrated how the effectiveness of communication depends on the background of the speaker and of the listener; on the way language is used; on what the parties expect from the conversation; and on the context of the discussion. We believe all of these factors apply in business communication as well as in interpersonal communication. Moreover, we believe business communication is inhibited by a set of additional factors that include the use of specialized language, the intensity of commercial competition, and the existence of legal restraints.

The focus of this chapter is on the communications between a company and its financial stakeholders. It is very different from the previous 15 chapters in that it seeks to highlight the critical thinking applicable to today's accounting debates. It should be read not with the idea that you will find resolutions for those debates here, but rather that you will join the search for more effective business and financial communications. Indeed, this search is one that engages most financial managers at some time in their career. For example, managers of growing but cash-hungry companies often complain that despite their hard work to create a flourishing business, no one outside the management team really understands how truly wonderful their company is.[3] Clearly part of their frustration is an outgrowth of their natural bias about their company, but very often their frustration is based in fact. With but a moment's reflection, it should be obvious that it is an impossible task to set forth the total essence of a complex company in a set of numbers or even in a verbal description. If management does find a way to tell the company's story somewhat effectively, telling that story in a way that then attracts the interest of potential stakeholders is still difficult. To the extent that the communication between the company and its financial stakeholders fails to fully inform, there is a real cost to the company. At best, the company's stock may be underpriced and its capital costs excessive. At worst, the company is vulnerable to a hostile takeover or a forced restructuring.

Communicating to outsiders the real value inherent in a company is subject to a number of natural impediments:

- Management will always have a better understanding of their company than will ever be possible for an outside financial stakeholder.
- In financial communications, the speaker and the listener will almost always have dramatically different contexts.
- Outside stakeholders will have many other companies clamoring for their attention (there are more than 12,000 companies registered with the Securities and Exchange Commission), and the attention those stakeholders can allocate to any particular company's story is, of necessity, limited.
- All financial communication is subject to the antifraud statutes, and all managers understand the risk of being subjected to that legal web. A manager with good news to report is faced with a difficult trade-off: There is a natural temptation to announce the news quickly so as to impound that information into the stock price; but caution suggests delaying that announcement until the facts are ironclad and there is little possibility of a subsequent disappointment likely to spawn a follow-on lawsuit.
- The language used in communications with financial stakeholders is primarily accounting-based, and for many reasons the language of accounting is an imperfect communication device. In particular, financial reporting is an imperfect communication vehicle (1) because of the estimates that are required in preparing a financial report, (2) because of the politics and personalities that shape accounting rules, and (3) because reporting conventions represent compromises aimed to meet the needs of those who want accounting to measure the past and those who want it to predict the future.

[3]A poll by Louis Harris and Associates found that 60 percent of executives surveyed believed that the shares of their companies were undervalued. See "Companies Feel Underrated by the Street," *Business Week*, February 20, 1984, p. 14.

AN ACCOUNTING PERSPECTIVE ON COMMUNICATING WITH FINANCIAL STAKEHOLDERS

The 1960s generated a good deal of concern about accounting in general and about the accounting standard-setting process in particular. The decade came to be characterized as the "Go-Go Years," and many of the excesses that plagued the financial marketplace during those years were attributed to accounting and the accountants. In response to such criticisms, the financial community in the early 1970s established two task forces. The first was to explore alternative ways of establishing timely accounting standards and to make sure that the resultant standards met the needs of the financial community as a whole. The second was to rethink the role of accounting and to set a conceptual course for the future of accounting standard setting. The deliberations of the first task force resulted in the dismantling of the Accounting Principles Board (APB) and the formation of the Financial Accounting Standards Board (FASB). The deliberations of the second task force resulted in the publication of an important report titled "The Objectives of Financial Statements." Here are perhaps the most important assertions of that report:

- The basic **objective of financial statements** is to provide information useful for making economic decisions.
- An objective of financial statements is to provide information useful to investors and creditors for predicting, comparing, and evaluating potential cash flows to them in terms of timing and related uncertainty.
- An objective of financial statements is to serve primarily those users who have limited authority, ability, or resources to obtain information and who rely on financial statements as their principal source of information about an enterprise's economic activities.[4]

These conclusions may seem elemental, but like all fundamental statements, they communicate important truths. In essence, the conclusions of the report challenged the accounting profession to work to meet the needs of users. The report also concluded that users needed to have information to help them make investment decisions. Finally, the report concluded that the users to be served were those who depended on the financial reporting process as their primary source for investment information. Thus, the report informed the accounting profession what their real mandate was, what their customers wanted, and who their customers were.

After many years of study — while dealing concurrently with many specific accounting issues — the FASB issued a series of releases referred to as its **conceptual framework** that attempted to codify and clearly state the primary underpinnings of the financial reporting process. The first of those releases built on the work of the earlier "Objectives" task force; here are two of the key points from *Concepts Statement No. 1*:

- Financial reporting should provide information that is useful to present and potential investors and creditors and other users in making rational investment, credit, and similar decisions.

[4]*Report of the Study Group on the Objectives of Financial Statements (The Trueblood Report)*, (New York: American Institute of Certified Public Accountants, 1973), pp. 13, 17, 20.

- Financial reporting should provide information to help present and potential investors and creditors and other users in assessing the amounts, timing, and uncertainty of prospective cash receipts from dividends, interest, and the proceeds from the sale, redemption, or maturity of securities or loans.[5]

Hindsight might suggest that the FASB has at times lost sight of those objectives and has failed to focus on the user. For example, in the late 1980s the FASB devoted substantial efforts to the accounting for income taxes and the accounting for pensions and health benefits. During those two major efforts, the FASB frequently found itself caught up in the same kinds of conceptual preoccupations and politicking that its predecessor the APB had found so unproductive. Indeed, the impetus for the new income tax accounting was a concern that the prior approach resulted in balance sheet numbers (deferred tax assets and liabilities) that did not meet the conceptual definition of either assets or liabilities. However, some critics have argued that the end result of the FASB's eight years of work on income taxes (SFAS No. 109) still failed to meet the objective of providing information to help assess the "amounts, timing, and uncertainty of prospective cash receipts."[6] Similarly, the accounting community became concerned about the growing obligation companies had as a result of their commitment to employees and retirees for health care benefits. As a result of that concern, the FASB published a complex standard (SFAS No. 106) that requires the accrual of very large liabilities to recognize those commitments. However, in a subsequent article on the editorial page of *The Wall Street Journal*, an actuary suggested that the actual benefits to be paid were subject to so many variables as to make the accounting pension accruals meaningless. He concluded, "Information about the future is useful only when it allows us to make better decisions today. Unless a 50-year commitment to retiree health benefits has been made, the best thing a manager can do with the FASB rule is to do what the financial analysts have done so far — ignore it . . . "[7]

While the FASB was devoting incredible time and effort toward these specific issues, several important environmental shifts were under way, suggesting that all was not well with the overall financial reporting process:

- The proportion of shares owned by individual investors in the U.S. shrank, and the proportion owned by institutional investors grew. According to a report by the Securities Industry Association (SIA), the percentage of stocks held by individuals fell to 49.7 percent in the second quarter of 1992, down from 71 percent in 1980 and 84 percent in 1965.[8] Further, institutional investors came to dominate the activity in the market, accounting for more than two-thirds of the trading volume of common stocks on United States' markets. There are many explanations for the rise of the institutions and the relative decline in the role of individual investors; unfortunately, it is very likely that one explanation is that individuals have decided that corporate communications are too complex. It may very well be that the average individual investor has been forced to conclude that only a full-time

[5]"Objectives of Financial Reporting by Business Enterprises" FASB Statement of Concepts No. 1, para. 34 and 37, The Financial Accounting Standards Board, November 1978.

[6]See, for example, several articles and an editorial in the June 1989 issue of *Accounting Horizons*, published by the American Accounting Association.

[7]Jeffery Peteril, "Ignore the Retiree Health Benefits Rule," *The Wall Street Journal*, February 21, 1992, p. 14.

[8]The SIA study was reported in an article by Michael Siconolfi in *The Wall Street Journal*, November 13, 1992, page C1.

professional can discern the value of a company's stock by interpreting the bewildering display of corporate financial information included in published annual reports.

- In the 1980s, a large number of savings and loan associations collapsed, shortly after issuing an apparently healthy balance sheet supported by an unqualified opinion from a CPA firm. Some argued that Congress was at fault because of the industry-specific accounting rules they had set for the S&Ls, and that the accountants were simply following those rules. That argument, however, was counterproductive: It only served to reinforce the notion that accounting and accountants had become so rule-oriented that the financial reporting system was unable to communicate financial reality.
- During the 1980s, while the accounting standard setters were debating how to measure assets and liabilities, the major CPA firms were facing unprecedented litigation.[9] The most notorious lawsuits charged CPAs with failure to find management fraud at such companies as Lincoln Savings, Phar Mor, MiniScribe, and Regina. There was also a related concern that financial reporting (and the audit of those financials) had become so mechanical that it did not communicate the real risks and opportunities in a business. In response, CPA firms expressed concern that the public had unrealistic expectations for the financial reporting process.

These trends and events suggested that there had been a basic change in the environment for accounting. In response, the American Institute of Certified Public Accountants (AICPA) commissioned another introspective endeavor, establishing a special committee to look into the future of financial reporting. The special committee's report, often referred to as the Jenkins Committee Report, reiterated the primary role of accounting as a vehicle to communicate information. The report concluded, however, that the information to be communicated for effective decision making was much broader than that encompassed by existing notions of corporate accounting systems. The report suggested that **business reporting** take the place of **financial reporting.** Here are some of the key suggestions contained in the report:

- Business reporting serves a critical role in supporting effective capital allocation. In many respects, it serves that role well, providing those who use it with essential information. However, profound, accelerating changes affecting business threaten the continued relevance of business reporting. To stay relevant, it must change in response to users' evolving needs for information.
- To meet users' changing needs, business reporting must
  - Provide more information about plans, opportunities, risks, and uncertainties.
  - Focus more on the factors that create longer-term value, including nonfinancial measures indicating how key business processes are performing.
  - Better align information reported externally with the information reported internally to senior management to manage the business.[10]

The committee's focus on "business reporting" rather than on "financial reporting" is particularly relevant to us in this chapter as we focus on communicating

[9]In 1992, *Business Week* reported that insurance premiums for the Big 6 CPA firms had increased tenfold since 1985, and that for some firms premiums and legal fees consume up to 25 percent of what would otherwise go to partners. See, "The Big 6 Are in Trouble," *Business Week*, April 6, 1992, pp. 78–79.

[10]*Improving Business Reporting—A Customer Focus (The Jenkins Committee Report)*, American Institute of Certified Public Accountants, New York, 1994, p. 3.

corporate value. For example, the call for increased emphasis on reporting those "factors that create long-term value" in the business might suggest that accounting step away from the traditional concern for the reliability of the numbers and focus more on the usefulness of the information presented. That might suggest, for instance, that a "business report" for General Mills should report the market share trend of its various cereals — certainly the value of General Mills is not in its plant and equipment but in its presence on the supermarket shelves. Further, a frank discussion of "plans, opportunities, risks, and uncertainties" that was set forth in a way to help the user see the company as management sees it might help users understand the potential value in a biotech firm that consistently reports losses under GAAP accounting but is on the verge of introducing a dramatic new cancer drug. Today's accounting for R&D prevents any attempt to measure the potential in that new product, yet that is clearly where the value of a biotech company lies. The direction suggested by the Jenkins Committee report is exciting because it urges a focus on the communication of value-creating factors. To do that, however — to move toward business reporting — the accounting profession and the FASB must find a way to avoid the conceptual debates and the details that have plagued it in the past. And corporate financial management must find a way to avoid knee-jerk rejections of calls for more disclosure. Toward that end, some have argued that the legal climate must be eased to encourage more open disclosure and to discourage punitive lawsuits.[11] In any event, it will take a communitywide effort if we are to realize the promise in the Jenkins Committee report.[12]

A FINANCE PERSPECTIVE ON COMMUNICATING WITH FINANCIAL STAKEHOLDERS

Researchers in accounting and finance have devoted considerable effort over the years to studying the relationship between a company's financial information and the market price for its stock. The result of that research has been the development (and at least partial support) of an idea called the **efficient market hypothesis** (EMH). The EMH argues that where there are enough players in an active auction-type market, the price paid for a security in that market will reflect its real value.

Some theorists argue a **strong form of the EMH,** claiming that the market price for a security at any time must reflect all information that pertains to that security whether the information has been publicly disseminated or not. The strong form of the EMH is based on the assumption that the market is composed of a great many curious and motivated players who will search for, find, and obtain *all relevant* information to a company whether or not that information is publicly available. Once they have the information they will act on it, and their actions will be reflected in the market price of the security. That understanding of the marketplace assumes the total interest and

---

[11]In December 1995 Congress did pass a litigation reform bill that contains a more effective safe harbor for disclosure of forward-looking information, restrictions on class action suits, and a change in the way damages are assessed from the prior joint-and-several approach to a contributory-share approach.

[12]It is interesting that the two study groups, 20 years apart, both argued for a focus on the needs of the user. But it is especially significant that the Jenkins Committee redefined the users not as those who depend on financial reporting for their information but as the financial analysts who presumably have the power and the tools to get the information they need in other ways. That definition of the user of financial reporting — as a professional analyst — recognizes the increased influence and power of institutional investors and their professional advisers. It has obvious implications for communication: On the positive side, it will be easier for corporate management to tell their story to and through a professional analyst because the analysts can be located more easily than a diverse group of individual shareholders, and because they will usually be better-informed listeners. But conversely, because of the concentration of ownership in the institutions, the analysts have a concentrated power. If they do not understand or do not believe the company's story, there is no one else to whom management can appeal.

completely dedicated ingenuity of the players in the market, and that degree of assumed interest and ingenuity is a bit too hypothetical for most of us to accept. Most theorists argue a **semistrong form of the EMH:** They argue that the players in an active market will be motivated to analyze information that is available to them and to act on opportunities that information illuminates. As a consequence, *all available* information will be incorporated in the trading price for a security, and no one can expect to profit from information once it is in the public domain. However, the semistrong form of the EMH also acknowledges that there will be information about a company that has not been discovered and cannot be deduced, and that the market price of that company's securities can reflect only the information that is publicly available. The semistrong form of the EMH has gained fairly wide acceptance, in part because research has demonstrated its validity and in part because it seems consistent with the day-to-day observations that the market price of a stock reacts to new information and that once that new information has been digested, a new equilibrium price is established.

The following quotation succinctly captures the essence of the semistrong form of the EMH and introduces some questions that are important to our study here:

> A securities market is defined as efficient if (1) the prices of the securities traded in that market act as though they fully reflect all available information and (2) these prices react instantaneously or nearly so, in an unbiased fashion, to new information. We note in passing that even if the view of a sophisticated market embedded in the EMH is valid, individual investors may still make wrong decisions. Hence the hypothesis requires "experts" (or arbitragers) of significant numbers or wealth to produce an efficient market. Furthermore, the hypothesis refers to the total market. It is quite possible that for a particular stock at a particular time the hypothesis may not be true. As with all hypotheses, the EMH is an approximation of the world, and those who hold this idea believe it to be substantially accurate and operationally useful.[13]

Most financial people would agree with the semistrong form of the EMH, but most would also agree with the penultimate sentence in the quotation: "It is quite possible that for a particular stock at a particular time, the hypothesis may not be true." Certainly the EMH has some applicability to the market as a whole and to a security over time. But those involved in the financial markets also know from experience that at various times there will be information about a company that has not yet been digested in the public marketplace. Moreover, where an equilibrium price seems to have been established, prices for a security may fluctuate around that equilibrium, occasionally quite widely. In this chapter's discussion of the role of corporate communication in setting stock prices, we believe that as long as there is an interested, inquiring, liquid market for a company's security, the prices established in an auction for that security will, over the long term, reflect the value of all of the information regarding that company that is publicly available and has been absorbed by the key stakeholders in the market.

Note the three important caveats imbedded in our notion of the EMH:

1. There must be a significant number of players in the market, and they must be interested in and curious about a particular company and objective and unbiased in their valuation judgments.

[13] T. Dyckman, D. Downes, and R. Magee, *Efficient Capital Markets and Accounting: A Critical Analysis*. (Englewood Cliffs, N.J.: Prentice Hall, 1975), p. 4. This booklet, one in a series titled Contemporary Topics in Accounting, provides both a useful introduction and a more exhaustive exploration of the EMH and its implication for accounting.

2. Over some period of time, the average market prices will reflect the reality of the information available for the market as a whole and — given enough time — for a particular company's security.
3. To have an impact on a security's price, information must be available to and understood by the participants in the public financial marketplace.

We now will explore each of these three EMH caveats and their implications for financial managers. A popular finance text states, "For the corporate treasurer who is concerned with issuing or purchasing securities, the efficient market theory has obvious implications. In one sense, however, it raises more questions than it answers. The existence of efficient markets does not mean that the financial manager can let financing take care of itself."[14] The EMH caveats that we have just outlined suggest some important challenges for financial managers — in particular, communication challenges.

Caveat Number One: The marketplace for a particular company's stock is composed of a sufficient number of interested and curious players who are unbiased and objective in their judgments. Although there is strong empirical evidence to support the semistrong form of the EMH as it applies to the securities markets in the United States, there is also anecdotal evidence that raises continuing doubts. For example, the financial market has invented a name for companies whose stock is publicly held but that are not followed by a research analyst. Such available but professionally ignored companies are referred to as **wallflowers.** There are 12,000 companies whose securities trade publicly in the United States, but the most popular investment advisory service, Value Line, reports on only 1,800 companies. How important is it for a company to have the attention of an investment advisory service? How much does it cost the company if its shares are relegated to wallflower status? In theory, the EMH would argue that arbitragers would see the value in a wallflower company and keep its price in a fair range. However, a *New York Times* article dealing with the wallflower phenomenon said, "for these neglected stocks, the question of efficient market prices is more problematic. Is all 'available information' about them reaching the buyers and sellers whose daily decisions are determining the stock's price? Of course not, say the experts. And the result is an inefficient market, one in which investors who do extensive homework can often find bargains — and those who do not are vulnerable to some very nasty surprises."[15]

The fact that an independent investment analyst follows a company helps that company's stock price move toward its real value in part because the analyst's report provides one more vehicle for the dissemination of the company's story, in part because the analyst's report provides some assurance that the company's message is understood, and in part because the attention provided by an analyst's coverage attracts the attention of busy market participants. And, of course, the converse is true — the lack of analyst coverage can cost the company in terms of reduced share prices.

While there are a great many potential buyers in an equity market as large as that of the United States, there are also a great many investment opportunities, and more arrive every day.[16] The size of the marketplace in the United States adds to its overall

[14]R. Brealey and S. Myers, *Principles of Corporate Finance*, 4th ed. (New York: McGraw Hill, 1991), p. 310.

[15]Diana B. Henriques, "The Wallflowers of Wall Street," *The New York Times*, April 14, 1991, section 3, page 12.

[16]According to A. Raghavan in "Underwriters Revel in a Robust Year as Interest Rates Drop," *The Wall Street Journal*, January 2, 1996, p. R38, 572 companies went through an initial public offering in the United States in 1995, raising more than $30 billion.

efficiency, but it can also bury a company that is unable to attract enough attention. Individual investors have little chance to identify prospective investments on their own and so depend upon the advice of brokers or investment advisory services in making their selection. If a company is not on the screen of an advisory firm, few individual investors will know about it or take the chance of investing in it. We might expect the larger, institutional investors to be more interested in searching out investment opportunities and to be less dependent on reports from advisory services for their initial introduction to a company. Still, why should the manager of an institution such as a state pension fund make the effort to look for values in an unknown stock when there are enough other well-analyzed investments to pick from? Why should the financial analyst take the risk of investing the pension fund's assets in such an unknown company when there are plenty of other companies where other analysts have already digested the most important data? In fact, to protect themselves from charges of recklessness, some fiduciarily-minded institutional investors have a policy to not invest in a company's securities unless it is covered by at least two independent advisory services. Corporate financial officers do have an obligation to tell their company story, but first they have to have someone to tell the story to. Therefore, one of the first obligations of a corporate financial officer, in addition to merely crafting the company's financial story, is to develop and cultivate a cadre of investment advisors who will follow the company's stock.

Another Wall Street saying that informs this inquiry is a movement called the "herd mentality." The EMH assumes a group of players each independent of the other, each free from any bias or influence. But there is no line of human endeavor where that is true. Most of us would agree that a national election in the United States is a reasonably efficient marketplace because it involves the votes of tens of millions of individuals. We recognize that human emotion and a herd mentality enter into those election results, but we take comfort in the fact that those human factors are lost in the grand total of the participants and that the end result is reasonably efficient in reflecting the true sentiment of the populace. That overall perspective may be true for an election of a president, but the analogy fails when it is compared to a stock market. In a stock market there is no voting as to whether a security is good or bad; rather, an attempt is being made to determine the fair value of a security at a particular time. As much as management may wish to have the market's approval of their company, they want even more to have the market price of the stock fairly valued.[17]

The emotions of the time, good or bad, will drive the values established for a company's stock, and those emotion-driven values may or may not reflect the real value in the company. What proportion of a stock's value (or its shortfall from its

[17]In 1988, an important case in this area was decided by the U.S. Supreme Court. The officers and directors of Basic Inc., together with the company itself, were sued in an action alleging that the officers had misled the market. It had been rumored that the company was about to be acquired by Combustion Engineering, but each time they were asked about those rumors the officers denied that any merger negotiations were under way; they were evidently trying to protect the negotiations and wanted to control the timing of the announcement according to their own schedule. Eventually the merger was completed and announced, and the shareholders who had bought on the strength of the rumor but sold on the strength of the denials sued. The Court, relying on the EMH, ruled in favor of the suing shareholders, saying that the officers' denials had misled the market and therefore had misled the suing shareholders; the Supreme Court sent the case back to a lower court for determination of damages. Two justices dissented to that decision, arguing against the strong forms of the EMH and providing backhanded confirmation of the semistrong form by saying, "We note that there may be a certain incongruity between the assumption that Basic shares are traded on a well-developed, efficient, and information-hungry market, and the allegation that such a market could remain misinformed, and its valuation of Basic shares depressed, for 14 months, on the basis of the three public statements." But even as they affirmed the semistrong form of the EMH, the dissenting justices raised the question of valuation, saying, "the fraud-on-the-market theory produces the "economically correct result" . . . but . . . the question of damages under the theory is quite problematic. Not surprisingly, the difficult damages question is one that the Court expressly declines to address today."

value) is due to the herd mentality on the street? No one knows the answer to that question, but the reality of this phenomenon was demonstrated in the incredible growth in prices that were accorded any company having to do with the Internet in 1995,[18] or the variations that were accorded the "technology stocks" as one or another of the companies in that group reported good news or bad news during 1995. There were plenty of players in those markets, but given the movements in the stock prices, it would be hard to argue that they all were objective and unbiased.

Finally, an efficient market says that a security's fair value is its equilibrium value — that is, the value at which there are an equal number of interested sellers and interested buyers. It may be true that such a balancing of supply and demand produces an equilibrium price, but the extension of that thesis, which then says that the equilibrium price is the fair price, is not necessarily true. Consider the phenomenon of discounts and premiums on closed-end mutual funds. A closed-end fund is a mutual fund that owns stocks, bonds, and cash just as traditional mutual funds do. However, the common stock of a closed-end fund is traded between individual shareholders just as the stock of a commercial company might be. At the end of each accounting period, management of the closed-end fund values the securities in the fund's portfolio and reports the fund's net assets on a market value basis. It is a simple matter to take that aggregate net asset value and divide it by the number of shares outstanding to determine a net asset value per share. Because the fund's assets consist solely of marketable securities — each of which have a value determined in an efficient market — we might expect that the fund's own shares would trade at a price exactly equal to the inherent value of the securities in the fund. But that is almost never true. Unlike the shares of traditional mutual funds, which can be redeemed at their net asset value at any time, the shares of closed-end funds almost always trade at a premium or discount to their net asset values — usually a discount of from 5 to 10 percent.[19]

Why should that be? Why should a seller be willing to sell a share in a fund at a price that is less than the fundamental values of the securities in that fund? The answer is that there are not enough buyers who will pay a higher price. And it follows that we ought to ask why open-end funds trade exactly at their net asset value. The answer is that the fund itself stands ready to buy its shares from anyone who wants to sell. In effect, a traditional open-end fund makes a market in its own shares, and because it is willing to redeem its shares at their net asset value, the market value of those shares is equal to the market value of the securities it holds. On the other hand, a closed-end fund depends on the players in the auction market to buy and sell its shares and to establish the equilibrium price, regardless of the underlying value of the assets. The phenomenon of the closed-end fund illustrates that the market price for securities is influenced in part by the underlying value of the entity and in part by factors of supply and demand. That understanding can be applied to the stock of a commercial company

---

[18]Netscape Communications Corp. came to the market in 1995 at the height of the market's enthusiasm for anything having to do with the Internet. At the time of the offering, Netscape reported a loss for the nine months ended September 30, 1995, and earnings of only $0.04 for the latest quarter. However, the company did have an intriguing product that promised to become the industry standard for surfing the net. The stock that was to be issued in the IPO was valued by the underwriters at $28 a share, but trading opened at $71. The shares closed the year at $139.

[19]In 1995, The Global Privatization Fund, Inc., a closed-end fund investing in large-scale privatization projects throughout the world, was merged into the Worldwide Privatization Fund, an open-end fund. Both were operated by Alliance Capital Management, and both had similar objectives — in fact, the two funds held many of the same securities. Because it was a closed-end fund, Global had traded at discounts of between 6 percent and 19 percent since its public offering, whereas the Worldwide fund had sold and redeemed its shares at their net asset value. The board of directors of Global concluded that it would be in the best interests of its shareholders to be merged with the Worldwide Fund so as to eliminate the discount and provide for greater liquidity for the shareholders. The shares of Global were exchanged share for share with Worldwide, and the shareholders of Global found themselves with an immediate increase in share value.

as well: There is more to the pricing of a company's shares than the underlying value in the company, and more even than the full and fair telling of the company's story. The pricing of a company's securities will depend on the *development* of an adequate demand.

Caveat Number Two: The market prices of well-followed stocks will average out to reflect aggregate fair values over a period of time, but those average, aggregate market prices will not necessarily be the fair price for a particular security at a particular time. Some have suggested that companies should consider a program to manage their stock prices on a day-to-day basis. For example, C. Callard observes: "Unlike the CEO, who attempts to achieve longer-term value, the security analyst makes judgments about the margin of short-term change, which may or may not become permanent."[20] Mr. Callard also suggests that management has a responsibility to manage the company's cost of capital by managing both the long-term growth of the company *and* by buying and selling the company's stock when the short-term trading price of the stock deviates significantly from its "warranted value." Warranted value is a calculated value for the stock, given the company's steady-state asset growth, its current earnings, and the prevailing cost of capital and management should look for opportunities to buy or sell the company's stock when the current price is outside a range based on the warranted value. The notion of managing a company's stock price in this way is oddly controversial. Consider the following:

- Few managers will publicly acknowledge that they have a **target** (or **warranted) price** for their company's stock because they understand that they might then be expected to take action to achieve that price. However, we know that managers *do* watch their company's stock price — they trade in their company's stock for their personal accounts, and they manage the timing and the amounts of shares to be purchased under the company's share repurchase programs.
- Some managers will argue that the stock market decides its own value for the stock and that the value of the stock can only be the current trading price. They argue that they cannot develop a value that is more accurate than the market does itself. And yet those managers develop capital expenditure budgets that are based on hurdle rates, which in turn are designed to earn a return to support or increase a targeted stock value.
- Some managers argue that their job is to manage the company and not the stock price. They argue that the market ought to be left to its own devices and to value their management efforts as the market players see fit. And yet, the fact is that shareholders are interested in the operations of the company only as those operations can be converted into an increased stock price. A shareholder might well argue that management's ultimate job is not the management of the company but is instead the management of the value of the stock.

It is impossible to know how many companies actively manage their day-to-day stock prices by buying into and selling out of price opportunities. It is well known, however, that many companies have authorized share repurchase plans that are implicitly designed to support a stock price floor.

[20]The ideas outlined here are more fully explained by C. G. Callard in "Managing Today's Stock Price," *Planning Review* (March/April 1988), pp. 34–39. The contents of Exhibits 16.1 and 16.2 are reprinted from *Strategy & Leadership* (formerly *Planning Review*), (March/April 1988) with permission from the Strategic Leadership Forum (formerly The Planning Forum), The International Society for Strategic Management.

EXHIBIT 16.1

Abbott Laboratories: Shareholder's Wealth Relative to S&P 500

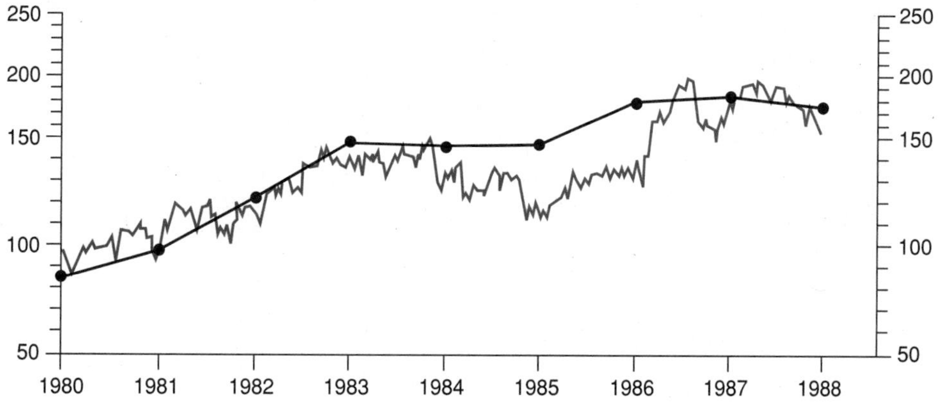

Note: The weekly values compare shareholder wealth (price appreciation plus dividends) relative to a corresponding calculation for the S&P 500. The annual values are the stock's warranted value for the beginning of each fiscal year, but plotted relative to the beginning year Abbott/S&P price ratio. Because cost of capital (COC) changes during the year, it is necessary to focus on the longer-term asset growth strategy and the earnings factor without being disturbed by short-term changes in COC. Hence, the objective is to fix a beginning year COC and let price reflect changing expectations for asset growth and earnings. The bullets (•) above reflect such a calculation. See footnote 20.

Mr. Callard illustrates his main thesis by determining a warranted price for the stock of Abbott Laboratories over a period of years and plotting those prices to the S&P 500 as shown in Exhibit 16.1.

The results do suggest that the short-term swings in the market price of a company's stock move in a random fashion around some norm. But what is particularly interesting for the discussion in this chapter is the set of explanations offered by the author for the short-term declines in the stock price, which are presented in Exhibit 16.2.

Note, for instance, the gap in 1979 and 1980, which is explained as "relative overvaluation," and the gap in 1984, which is described as "momentum error." Abbott Labs may have been fortunate that the momentum atrophied and that the stock price recovered to its norm without incident. Similarly, Abbott was probably fortunate that the relative overvaluation in the early 1980s was not followed by a shareholder suit as the correction worked its way out. This case example illustrates that the stock market may be efficient, but, if so, it achieves that efficiency only over a long period of time. That understanding has significant implications for the manager who has the obligation to assure a fair valuation of the company's stock and the power — through communications — to help the market correct over and under valuations. Although the market on its own might come to see the value in the company's stock over time, in the interval the company will be forced to pay higher capital costs and will be at risk for a stock market raid or forced restructuring. In less dynamic times than today, it may have been possible for a company to wait out the market and hope that the real value in the company would be discovered. Today, however, with the concentration of marketplace power in institutional hands, the enormous liquidity created by junk bonds, and the relatively relaxed attitude toward take-overs that prevails in Washington, a raid or a stockholder rebellion can come with lightning swiftness. Every financial executive has an obligation to monitor the company's stock price against a target and — based on the

EXHIBIT 16.2

Short-Term Relative Declines Exceeding 10 Percent

Peak Date	Price: Abbott	Price: S&P	Length of Decline (Weeks)	% Change: Abbott	% Change: S&P 500	% Change: Net	Classification
12/28/79	10.25	107.84	9	−8.9%	6.7%	−14.6%	Relative overvaluation
9/19/80	13.69	129.25	10	−7.3	7.6	−13.9	" "
6/26/81	15.81	132.56	11	−24.1	−9.4	−16.2	" "
9/24/82	18.44	123.32	21	2.4	19.7	−14.5	Relative earnings decline
10/28/83	25.32	163.37	6	−14.1	1.3	−15.2	" "
2/17/84	22.50	155.74	3	−10.3	2.2	−12.2	Momentum error
8/31/84	23.63	166.68	6	−18.0	−2.4	−16.0	" "
8/01/86	51.50	234.91	13	−16.5	3.9	−19.6	Relative overvaluation
6/05/87	62.38	293.45	17	−2.4	11.8	−12.7	Relative earnings decline
Average			11	−11.0%	4.6%	−15.0%	

Note: See footnote 20.

length of *time* the values are out of line or the *degree* to which the values are skewed — take action to protect the company and its shareholders.

Another provocative article on this subject outlines a number of important levers that managements can control to enhance the value of their company's shares.[21] Increasing the dividend payout is the first obvious answer, but it is important to note that one can increase shareholder value by reducing the perceived risk attributed to the company and by increasing the perceived value of future cash flows by better communication of future prospects. This particular article concludes that long-term market values are not driven by quarterly earnings or other short-term events but are more heavily influenced by "the market's perception of the present value of the stock in the future." To support that point, an interesting experiment is described wherein the author looked at the stock market's valuation for the companies that make up the Dow Jones Industrials. The dividend payout from each of those firms was aggregated over a 10-year period, 1975–1984, and added to the actual stock price at the end of 1984. Those actual numbers were then discounted back to the beginning of 1975 using discount rates that recognized each company's risk profile. Finally, that aggregate present value was compared with the market price for those stocks at the beginning of 1975. The results of that experiment demonstrated several things:

1. On average, only 42 percent of the value of a stock is in its dividend payout, with the rest coming from the expected terminal value.
2. The market is generally optimistic — that is, almost all of the beginning-of-period stock prices were higher than would have been justified by the results during the following period. On average, the market overvalued the Dow Jones Industrials by about 33 percent.
3. Within that average, several companies were considerably overvalued, and several were considerably undervalued. The standard deviation of the averages in that sample was 65 percent.

[21] A. H. Seed, "Winning Strategies for Shareholder Value Creation," *Journal of Business Strategy* (Fall 1985), pp. 44–51.

EXHIBIT 16.3

Comparison of Expected Stock Values
(as Reflected in Beginning-of-Period Quoted Prices)
with Actual Cash Returns from the
Dow Jones Industrials for 1981–1991

	Present Value of Actual Cash			Expected Cash	Expected Cash
Company*	Dividends	End-of-period Value	Total	(Beginning-of-period Value)	as a Percentage of Actual Value
Alcoa	5.83	9.65	15.49	25.625	165.43%
American Brands	4.58	8.63	13.21	9.470	71.69%
American Express	2.46	2.52	4.97	10.590	213.08%
Chevron	10.09	11.95	22.04	38.625	175.25%
DuPont	3.99	7.11	11.10	12.625	113.73%
Eastman Kodak	6.64	9.33	15.97	28.890	180.90%
Exxon	8.04	12.86	20.90	15.380	73.59%
General Electric	4.85	10.25	15.10	14.090	93.31%
General Motors	8.31	10.40	18.71	22.250	118.92%
Goodyear	6.08	8.57	14.65	17.625	120.31%
IBM	16.96	15.90	32.86	54.000	164.33%
International Paper	4.89	10.23	15.13	19.875	131.36%
Merck	3.53	32.24	35.77	14.130	39.50%
3M	7.77	16.20	23.97	27.250	113.68%
Procter & Gamble	6.58	19.38	25.96	18.530	71.38%
Sears	6.78	5.86	12.64	16.125	127.57%
Texaco	13.76	12.73	26.49	33.750	127.41%
Union Carbide	4.57	2.90	7.47	16.120	215.80%
US Steel	5.20	5.12	10.32	32.000	310.08%
United Tech	5.36	8.05	13.41	22.630	168.75%
Westinghouse	2.47	2.44	4.91	6.250	127.29%
Woolworth	2.42	4.25	6.67	4.750	71.21%
		Average excess expected			136.12%
		Standard deviation			59.63%

*The original experiment we describe in the chapter omitted those companies that were not included in the Dow Jones Industrials throughout the entire period. Our repeat of his experiment also left those companies out of the database, and it also omitted Bethlehem Steel, which went into and came out of bankruptcy in the 1981–1991 time period.

We replicated that experiment using the 10-year period 1981 through 1991. The results of that experiment are reflected in Exhibit 16.3.

As is apparent from Exhibit 16.3, the use of more current data produced results that were very close to the original study: the average excess was around 35 percent and the standard deviation of the average results was around 60 percent. Rerunning the experiment using shorter, different time periods produced the following results:

- Using the data for the first five years of the period produced an average excess of 9 percent and a standard deviation of 46 percent.
- Using the data for the last five years of the period produced an average excess of 42 percent and a standard deviation of 59 percent.
- Using the data for the last three years of the period produced an average excess of 28 percent and a standard deviation of 41 percent.

Interestingly, the average excess varied considerably as shorter, different time periods were used. Nonetheless, the standard deviation remained quite high. That continued variability in the ability of the market to predict the results that an investment will produce suggests an enormous opportunity for management. Because management understands the company and its prospects better than any outside member of the market ever will, and because that understanding of the future is so important to the valuation of the stock price, it is incumbent on the management team to explain that future as effectively as it can. Looking again at the results in Exhibit 16.3, we have to feel sympathy for the managers at Merck, at American Brands, at Procter & Gamble, and at Woolworth as they saw the market's consistent undervaluation of their efforts. It may be that it was difficult to value those companies because the key valuation information was not disseminated in any organized way: Merck's assets are in its product pipeline, the value of which has been expensed as R&D costs; the real assets that Procter & Gamble and American Brands bring to bear are their important product franchises, the value of which is expensed as advertising and promotion costs; Woolworth has a consumer franchise too, but its value has deteriorated as the retail market has changed. In the case of Woolworth, the market may have been correct in its long-term valuation of the company's prospects, but it misvalued the cash flow potential from the company in the interim.

There is no reason to think that the results of this experiment would be any different if we used a set of companies other than the Dow Jones Industrials; in fact, it would be reasonable to conclude that the results would be more extreme for companies that have less of a following on Wall Street. The results of this experiment provide a solid argument for a proactive movement on the part of financial managers to communicate the values that are inherent but latent in their companies.

Caveat Number Three: To have an impact on a security's price, information must be available to and understood by the players in the public financial marketplace. The accounting and finance literature provide a number of illustrations of the ability of the marketplace to react to information when it first becomes available. One of the most interesting looked at stock price values before and after 1970, when the SEC first required presentation of revenue and earnings data by business segment.[22] The research had the benefit of business segment data for the current year as well as retrospective disclosures of segment data for the two prior years. The research found that the stock prices in 1970 were closer to a target value than they had been in the earlier years when the segment data had not been publicly available.

But it is not just that the data must be available to the market; it must be interpreted by the players in the market, and that fact makes the job of the financial manager much more difficult. One other Wall Street phenomenon often heard discussed is the "conglomerate discount." At one time conglomerates were greatly in favor because it was felt that a company could assure its shareholders more stable returns if it developed a portfolio of businesses whose business cycles might smooth each other out. In recent years, however, the financial markets have penalized conglomerates, and managements of those companies have been under pressure to break them up. Often, in those disputes, it is reported that the breakup value of the conglomerate is 5 to 10 percent more than the quoted stock price.

Why should that be? So long as the company provides good business segment information, should not the market be able to value the company as a whole by simply valuing its individual components? A number of explanations are offered for the conglomerate discount including (1) the concern that management cannot manage a diverse group of companies and that its attention will therefore be diluted or (2) that

---

[22] D. Collins, "SEC Product Line Reporting and Market Efficiency," *Journal of Financial Economics*, 1975. Cited in *Efficient Capital Markets and Accounting* by T. Dyckman, D. Downes and R. Magee (Englewood Cliffs, N.J.: Prentice Hall, 1975).

the market focuses only on the most obvious of the components and values the income stream from the entire entity at the earnings multiple applicable to that business, so that the more valuable entities in the company are undervalued. All such explanations may be true, but other nagging concerns suggest that the problem is more complex. The process of investment analysis is multifaceted because the investment adviser must understand the company's industry. Very few analysts focus on individual companies, but most do focus on individual industries. If it makes sense to concentrate your analytical expertise on an industry-by-industry basis (and it seems intuitively logical to do so), how would you field a team to prepare an investment analysis of a company like USX, with its very different steel and oil operations? If you were developing an expertise in the oil industry, why would you devote your time to USX? Would you not prefer to concentrate your analysis effort on a relatively "pure play" like Shell or Exxon? It is entirely likely that some portion of the conglomerate discount is attributable to the structural weakness inherent in the conglomerate form. But it is also very likely that some part of the conglomerate discount can be traced to the market. If so, one of the key tasks of the financial executive is to ensure that the players in the market understand the company's various businesses and have reason to be interested in their results.

A CASE STUDY

J. Walter Thompson (JWT) was one of the premier advertising agencies in the world, with a consistent record of award-winning advertising campaigns and a loyal following from a blue-ribbon clientele. The company began operations in 1864, selling advertising space in religious magazines. By 1986, more than 120 years later, JWT had revenues in excess of $650 million and employed more than 10,000 people in 200 offices around the world.

An advertising agency is different from a merchandising or manufacturing company in that an advertising company's assets are almost exclusively its people. Those people will stay with an agency as long as they feel challenged and rewarded. In turn, clients are drawn to an agency because of its creative people, and they will stay with an agency only as long as the creative people stay. Advertising is unique in other, more prosaic ways, as well: Advertising is a surprisingly seasonal business, with peak revenues in the second and fourth quarter of the calendar year, and it is very vulnerable to the ups and downs of the business cycles. For example, in the mid 1980s a combination of declining advertising volume and pressure on fees depressed the financial results of almost every agency in the industry. However, there was a good bit of hope in the international sector as the European countries moved toward commercial television; it was expected that the need for advertising services in that market would grow enough to offset any decline in the U.S. market.

JWT had been through a particularly difficult period in the 1970s but had been rescued by the creative energies of Don Johnston, who had become chairman in 1975. In the years from 1975 to 1986, JWT made a number of important acquisitions and grew its volume substantially. Unfortunately, profits were erratic: The company earned $16 to $29 million in each of the years 1980, 1983, 1984, and 1985. However, in 1982 the company took a substantial earnings hit as a result of a fraud reported in its overseas operations and only broke even for the year. The company's strong earnings in 1985 were surprising, given the general problems of the industry. But then, in 1986, earnings dropped to approximately $6 million as a result of a number of factors —

including the costs of an expanded staff (anticipating the overseas expansion of TV advertising), the costs of absorbing a complex merger (it was a pooling and so the costs the two companies incurred in closing duplicate facilities all were charged to reported income for the year), and a very high effective tax rate (the company had losses overseas that it could not offset against its earnings at home).

The stock market had rewarded the company for its rather extraordinary results in 1985 (earnings in the fourth quarter of 1985 set a record), and the stock closed the year at $41 a share. But when the 1986 results began to be apparent, quarter by quarter, the stock sank to $30. The analysts who followed JWT concluded that the company's abilities and its people should enable it to grow revenues by 10 to 15 percent a year. It was also felt that with a cost containment program, the company could grow its earnings by 25 percent a year. When the 1986 financial statements showed the expected increase in revenues but also showed costs that had grown even faster, the analysts became discouraged. One analyst said, "He [Johnston] has not been willing to accept a partner in running the agency in those areas — financial controls and business organization — where he is weak." It was true — between 1979 and 1986 there had been four different CFOs at JWT.

All of that might have been simply one more episode in a history of boom and bust years. However, while all of this was going on at JWT, the world was changing: The British pound strengthened against the dollar, and the fiscal conservatism of Prime Minister Thatcher in the U.K. was in full swing. On June 10, 1987, when JWT's stock was trading at $30, WWP Ltd., a newly formed company in the United Kingdom, bid $45 a share for all of JWT's shares. After a brief struggle (which resulted in an increase in the bid to $55 a share) the board of directors of JWT was forced to agree to the tender. JWT and its component parts were absorbed into WWP, and the 120-year-old company disappeared.

PULLING IT ALL TOGETHER

The financial market's response to a particular company's stock will be in part a reaction to its industry and the overall economy. The market's response will also be in part a reaction to the company's actual results, its expected results, the strategy it has outlined, and its demonstrated ability to execute that strategy. Finally, the reaction of the market to a company's stock will be in part a reaction to the way the company tells its story and the trust earned by the management team. This chapter has been devoted to an exploration of these latter factors, which are most clearly the purview of the financial executive. The discussion in this chapter and the experiences of companies such as JWT suggest a few observations for your consideration and debate:

- We must move accounting standards toward presentations that will help users see the inherent values in the company. For example, the FASB has taken on a new project to define "comprehensive income," and we hope that such a project will result in a standard which will help measure and report income in such a way that readers can more effectively use the income statement to predict future results. Any such standard must force a distinction — in the income statement — between core and noncore operations. While we wait for the FASB to move in that direction, chief financial officers can use the SEC's required management discussion and analysis (MD&A) to help the reader isolate the effects of unusual or nonrecurring items that might be buried in the current year's income.

- Now that Congress has established a more effective safe harbor for forward-looking information,[23] companies might experiment with supplemental presentations in their financial reports, including such things as fair-value presentations and forecasts. The Rouse Company, for example, has for many years provided fair-value balance sheets, helping the reader understand the value inherent in its portfolio of properties. Other companies that have substantial property investments (such as the fast-food chains) might consider a similar presentation. In our financial society, forecasts of company operations are provided by the investment analysts who follow the company; those forecasts are based on data developed by the analysts and also on data provided by the company. Some companies have provided data willingly, while some have left the analysts to develop information on their own; some managers have ignored the analysts' forecasts, and some have commented on forecasts that seem out of line. Now that the new safe harbor is in place, we might expect that companies will be more open with the analysts working on a forecast and might be more outgoing in their comments on the forecasts, which have heretofore been prohibited. Still, given the new safe harbor, why should analysts be the purveyors of financial forecasts? Why shouldn't management provide forecasts of their companies' future results, directly? Again, the MD&A required by the SEC provides a vehicle for companies to provide that information, now in a more protected forum.
- Our traditional accounting system and conventions are designed for merchandising and manufacturing companies and do not lend themselves to communicating the value of service companies, whose assets are talented people. Managers of those companies must be permitted to report new ways of explaining their results (such as revenues per employee, growth in number of employees, average tenure of employees, and so on), and it will be especially important for them to find ways to describe the investment they make in employees and productivity each year. Given the time lag between an investment in people and the return that might be expected, disclosure of forecasts and plans will be important. It may even be that because of the financial communication difficulties inherent in these companies (consider JWT), they ought not depend on the stock market for their capital.
- Top managers must focus on the quality of the product or service that the company produces, but they cannot ignore the expectations and needs of the capital market. Today every public company is vulnerable to a takeover raid. It will be important for managers to have a target price in mind for their stock and to take action when the trading price falls too far below that target. One manager explained that his company talked about things as being "BT and AT," referring to a takeover raid on the company by a well-established financier, and events or decisions as being before or after that takeover raid. The manager explained that in the past, management had not worried much about the potential reaction of the financial market as they made various decisions on running the company. But as a result of the takeover raid they learned to anticipate the market's reaction as they considered every decision, from strategic actions to accounting choices. (As you mull the JWT case, you might reflect

[23]See footnote 10.

on these questions: Would the company have been vulnerable to a raid and a takeover at $55 a share if the stock had been at $40 rather than $30? How far away from a targeted price can the market be before the company is vulnerable? Would management have been so hopeful in their hiring of people for Europe if they had considered the impact of those hirings on the current financial results and on the stock price? Would the market have reacted so dramatically to the 1986 results if the CFO had been in place for a number of years and had been able to demonstrate that investments in people in one year had paid off in the future? Would the market have reacted so negatively to the 1986 results if the acquisition had been a purchase rather than a pooling, and if the merger expenses been allocated to goodwill rather than to the operations of the year?)

- The top officers of the company must be prepared to go before the financial analyst community and communicate personally. In a large company it may be possible to delegate some part of that contact to a stockholder relations person, but in most firms the analysts will insist on a personal contact with a senior executive. One senior financial manager explained that 40 percent of his time was devoted to making analyst presentations and answering analyst phone calls. A CEO explained to us that he devoted several days each quarter to visits with the top people in the institutions that owned the majority of his company's shares. He was careful to explain that he told each investor team the same story so as to avoid any suggestion of favoritism or charges of revealing inside information. But if that is the case, why is it necessary for him to visit each of those major investors personally? Why not invite them to a central location and tell his story to the group? He explained that it is important for him to be seen personally because only in a personal interview can those major investors make an assessment of his management abilities. They want to assess his candor, his grasp of the facts, and frankly, his health. They want to be assured that he is in charge of the company and managing their investment.
- A company that operates in a seasonal business must have a store of credibility built up with the financial community. Managers must be able to say (and demonstrate) that any slowdown is due to outside forces, the effects of which they can manage. It will be important for them to be able to say (and demonstrate) that they are in control of the company during good times and bad. One financial manager explained that his company had carefully studied the expectations for raw material prices and had decided that they would not need to hedge against cost increases. Results proved them wrong, and earnings for that next year were significantly depressed. The manager said that he met the analysts who followed the company and explained that the extra-high raw material costs were not due to a management error but were due to a conscious decision that in hindsight turned out to be wrong. The market accepted his explanation — because of the reputation for integrity that he had developed with the analyst group over many prior years — and the price of the stock stayed steady even after the dramatic drop in earnings. He had demonstrated that the company was under control, and the blip in the earnings stream created by the high material costs was an aberration not likely to be repeated.

One of the more practical ways to make such personal contact is to establish a conference call linkup the day after an important announcement is made, as, for instance, after quarterly results are released. In establishing such conference calls, any analyst who has expressed an interest in the company is usually invited to join in to hear the CFO (and often the CEO) discuss the results for the period and outline the directions of the company's future. Those presentations are important because they give the company a chance to explain the numbers and to humanize those numbers. One analyst explained that he often participates in such calls not to ask questions himself but to hear what questions others ask and to listen to the way management responds. One senior manager explained that he conducts those calls in a conference room lined with chalkboards: When questions are asked, staff people write the answers on the board or refer him to an answer in a preprepared briefing book. His goal is to provide honest answers to questions posed but also to demonstrate his command of the company's operations. If managers do their job well in these conference calls — answering questions forthrightly and with a minimum of hype — they will build trust in the company and reduce the market's level of uncertainty about the company's future prospects.

- Corporate management should seek regular criticism of its relationships with the financial community and its communications program and should be prepared to take action necessary to rectify identified problems. These steps might include, for instance, a stock buyback program to increase the cash flow to the shareholders and to demonstrate the company's confidence in its own future. If the company does not have an adequate following in the analyst community, it may be necessary to do some institutional advertising or to make some dramatic reporting moves to attract some attention. Or a company might engineer a stock sale to a major supplier or customer whose participation will attract one or more large institutions. Of course, any such challenge ought to include a careful scrutiny of the financial reporting practices followed by the company to assure that they tell the company's story as fully as possible and that they are perceived as honest and straightforward.
- All of the prior discussion has assumed a chief financial officer in the United States interfacing with the United States' financial market. But think about the role of business reporting in a different market setting, such as Germany, where equity investments are largely held by banks. In those countries, where the equity market is more of a closed system, the communication of value-creating factors ought to be easier. Very often the banks who hold a strong equity position in a company have representation on the company's board of directors, and so the communication can be immediate and in as much detail as is necessary. Even if there are no representatives on the board, the CFO will surely know the bank people personally, and the legal environment will make it possible to talk to those primary equity holders one-on-one. The reverse is also true, however; as those companies come to the United States and the United Kingdom, with their more egalitarian marketplaces, their managers will have to rethink their financial communications because the same norms, rules, and expectations cannot be presumed to apply.[24]

[24]See for example, "Planes, Trains and Automobiles," a *Financial Times* interview with Jurgen Schrempp, the newly appointed chairman of Daimler-Benz. The company recently listed its equity securities on the New York Stock Exchange; it was the first German company to do so. In the interview, the author reported, "he peppered his rapid-fire conversation with talk of shareholder value" and quoted Mr. Schrempp as saying, "I introduced the notion in this company; now everybody talks about it." *Financial Times*, November 7, 1995, p. 15.

SUMMARY

Accounting and financial reporting are complex and interesting subjects that warrant the attention of every manager and therefore every student of business. This text is an attempt to help you master the language of accounting. It is important, however, to keep things in perspective: The real goal of all of accounting is to help owners understand the real value in a company. Financial reporting plays a critically important part in the communication process between managers and owners. We believe that traditional accounting reports are only a tool in the communications process and only one of the many tools available. Managers understand that their communication program must be a comprehensive program, integrating such components as the financial statements, the MD&A, the annual report, quarterly reports, meetings with analysts, news releases, and conference calls. Such a communications program must be driven toward one goal — a full understanding of the company by the marketplace and a fair value for the stock.

NEW CONCEPTS AND TERMS

Business reporting (p. 830)
Conceptual framework (p. 828)
Efficient market hypothesis (EMH) (p. 831)
Financial reporting (p. 830)
Objectives of financial statements (p. 828)
Semistrong form of the EMH (p. 832)
Strong form of the EMH (p. 831)
Target price (p. 836)
Wallflowers (p. 833)
Warranted price (p. 836)

ISSUES FOR DISCUSSION

D16.1 Pick one publicly held company that interests you, and find several magazine and newspaper articles that discuss the company and its prospects. Make some notes from that reading, outlining things about the company that you like and things that might worry you as a stockholder. Then read the company's annual report (the president's letter, the MD&A, and the financial statements). Look for amplification of the positive things you highlighted, and look for reassurance about the things you were concerned about. Prepare a short essay on your findings, and come to class prepared to talk about them.

D16.2 Select one industry that interests you, and think about the factors that drive the value of the companies in that industry. Identify three companies in that industry and study their annual reports (the president's letter, the MD&A, and the financial statements) to see how each company reports on those value drivers. Prepare a short essay describing your findings and offering suggestions to the companies themselves, and to the standard setters, suggesting how the accounting policies and rules for that industry might be modified to focus on those value drivers.

D16.3 Select a company that interests you, and find an analyst's report on the company that includes an estimate of the company's earnings and its future stock price. What factors did the analyst consider in the development of the forecast earnings and forecast stock price? Read the company's annual report and quarterly reports, looking to see how the company reports on those factors that were evidently important to the analyst. To what degree is the information used by the analyst provided by the company in its formal reports? If it is not available in the annual report, why is it not? Where might the analyst find that information if it is not readily available in public reports?

D16.4 Study two Statements of Financial Accounting Standards issued by the FASB in the last five years (other than No. 106 and No. 109) and prepare an essay, critiquing the accounting that results from those standards against a goal that says that the accounting is to "provide information to help present and potential investors and creditors . . . in assessing the amounts, timing and uncertainties of prospective cash receipts . . ."

D16.5 Study the report from the AICPA, "Improving Business Reporting — A Customer Focus" (the Jenkins Committee Report), and make some notes about the kinds of information that might be provided in a "business report" that are not likely to be included in a traditional "financial report." Select a company that interests you and read the annual report provided by the company. To what degree would the annual report have to change if it was to be a "business report" as contemplated by the Jenkins Committee? Would those changes be made in the chairman's letter section of the annual report? In management's discussion and analysis? In the formal financial statements? How would you feel about making those changes if you were the CFO? How would you feel about making those changes if you were the CPA?

D16.6 Recently the FASB issued an invitation to comment on the recommendations in the Jenkins Committee Report. Study the Jenkins Report and prepare your own letter to the FASB suggesting specific projects that the Board ought to add to its agenda to implement the report's recommendations. Be sure that your letter provides a solid rationale for your recommendations.

D16.7 The professional association of Chartered Financial Analysts, the Association for Investment Management and Research (AIMR), evaluates the financial communications from major companies within industry groupings each year. The following chart shows the AIMR rankings for the food, beverage, and tobacco companies during the 1993–1994 period. Select one of the companies at the top of the list and one near the bottom, and critically read their annual reports. Why might the AIMR have ranked them as they did? Assume that you have been appointed chief financial officer of the company you selected near the bottom of the list; what changes would you make in the annual report to raise the company's ranking next year?

Food, Beverage, and Tobacco Evaluations, 1993–1994

Rank	Company	Number of Responses	Average Score	Annual Report		Interim Reports		Investor Relations		Meetings and Other	
				Score	Rank	Score	Rank	Score	Rank	Score	Rank
1	PepsiCo Inc.	14	88	90	1	90	1*	90	1*	80	2*
2	Sara Lee Corporation	13	83	80	5*	80	4*	90	1*	80	2*
3	Coca-Cola Company	16	82	85	2*	85	3	75	9*	83	1
4	McDonald's Corporation	10	80	85	2*	90	1*	80	4*	63	12*
5	Quaker Oats Company	12	79	80	5*	80	4*	80	4*	77	4*
6*	RJR Nabisco Inc.	13	76	75	9*	70	8*	80	4*	77	4*
6*	General Mills Inc.	17	76	80	5*	70	8*	75	9*	77	4*
8*	Hershey Foods Corporation	15	75	75	9*	70	8*	80	4*	73	8*
8*	Coca-Cola Enterprises	10	75	85	2*	75	7	75	9*	63	12*
10	Philip Morris	13	74	80	5*	80	4*	80	4*	57	17*
11	Sysco Corporation	6	73	75	9*	65	13*	75	9*	77	4*
12	CPC International	16	72	60	16*	70	8*	85	3	73	8*
13	Campbell Soup Company	12	68	70	13*	65	13*	70	14*	67	10*
14*	Tyson Foods	7	66	70	13*	65	13*	70	14*	60	14*
14*	UST Inc.	13	66	75	9*	60	16*	70	14*	57	17*
14*	ConAgra Inc.	13	66	60	16*	60	16*	75	9*	67	10*
17	Anheuser-Busch Cos. Inc.	14	65	70	13*	70	8*	60	17*	60	14*
18	Grand Metropolitan PLC	6	59	60	16*	55	18*	60	17*	60	14*
19	Universal Corporation	9	58	60	16*	55	18*	60	17*	57	17*
20	Seagram Company Ltd.	6	53	55	21*	55	18*	50	23*	50	20*
21	Brown-Forman Corporation	9	52	55	21*	55	18*	55	21*	43	22*
22	American Brands	10	51	55	21*	55	18*	55	21*	40	25*
23	H. J. Heinz Company	12	50	50	24*	40	25	60	17*	50	20*
24*	Kellogg Company	16	48	60	16*	45	24	45	25*	43	22*
24*	Adolph Coors	6	48	50	24*	50	23	50	23*	43	22*
26	Ralston Purina Group	13	35	40	26*	35	26*	40	27	23	28
27	Dole Food Company	4	34	40	26*	35	26*	20	29	40	25*
28	Archer Daniels Midland	9	34	35	28	25	28*	45	25*	30	27
29	Borden Inc.	8	25	30	29	25	28*	25	28	20	29

*Tie.

Source: Reprinted, with permission, from *An Annual Review of Corporate Reporting Practices, 1993–94.*

D16.8 Obtain a copy of the annual report of a major company whose securities are not registered for sale in the United States, and compare the discussions and communications contained in that report with the presentation in the annual report of a United States company in the same industry (for example, Bayer/Dow or Toyota/Ford).

D16.9 The SEC requires each company to include in its annual report a quarterly summary of its stock price movement. Prepare an essay arguing for and against this statement:

> The inclusion of stock price information in the annual report, along with the audited financial statements and the other required disclosures, directs the stockholders to short-term thinking about their company. There is no need to include that stock price information in the annual report, inasmuch as it is available from other sources. More importantly, its inclusion carries an implication suggesting that the shareholder has invested in a stock, when we should be encouraging the understanding that the shareholder has invested in a company.

D16.10 Select a company that interests you, and study its annual report from a year ago and an analyst's report from the same period. Think about the factors that might influence the company's stock price, including, for example, its earnings and its P/E ratio, its net assets, and its ratio of net assets to market value. Using those characteristics and others that seem appropriate to you, develop a target price for the stock. Then chart the actual movement of the stock, month by month, over the next year. Read the president's letter and the MD&A from the current year's annual report and a current analyst's report on the company. Prepare a short essay explaining how the stock price moved compared to your target, and outline some of the factors that might have caused that movement. Comment on what the company (and the analyst) had to say about the movement of the stock during the year and the factors that might have caused that movement.

CASES

C16.1 Goodyear Tire and Rubber Company (B). The annual reports issued by the Goodyear Tire and Rubber Company for the years 1984, 1985, and 1986 describe eloquently the trauma that washed over one of America's oldest and largest companies:

> In 1984 Goodyear reported record sales ($10 billion) and earnings ($411 million). Also, the 1984 report reflected a dramatic move in Goodyear's diversification program as a result of the acquisition of the Celeron Company, an energy firm, for $860 million in stock. The mood of the 1984 report was captured by a cartoon on the front cover that portrayed three threatening figures hovering over an eager young man: The in-charge young character says, "See what you can do when you don't listen to what 'they' say." The common stock closed the year at $31½, down $5 from its high in 1983.
>
> The 1985 report was more prosaic, featuring a picture of Celeron's California — Texas oil pipeline, which was under construction. Sales for 1985 were flat, but costs rose and income from continuing operations fell to $360 million. However, the spin-off of Celeron's gas activities (to focus on oil) resulted in a gain and pushed total net income to $412.4 million. The president's letter explains the decline in operating income "as a result of laying foundations for the future" in that the company incurred costs of $46 million related to workforce reduction. The president's letter concluded, "Our success in changing the composition and thrust of the company, in concert with markets and operating conditions, reflects the quality and dedication of our employees." The stock closed the year at $31¼.
>
> In 1986 the composition and thrust of the company was changed more dramatically than anyone could have anticipated. A hostile takeover bid forced the company to buy back $2 billion of its own stock, reducing shareholder's equity by 60 percent and increasing the level of debt to 77 percent of total capital. To manage that debt the company was forced to put all of its nontire activities up for sale. The president's letter in the 1986 annual report said, "The restructuring program is proceeding according to plan as we take steps necessary to reduce the additional debt involved in the repurchase of nearly half of our outstanding shares." Net income for 1986 dropped dramatically in part because of costs related to the restructuring. But 1986 earnings were also reduced because of a first-quarter write-down — to market — in the value of the Celeron oil properties. Ironically, the common stock closed the year at $50 a share.

The Company

Goodyear Tire and Rubber Company was formed in 1898 by Mr. Frank Seiberling, with $13,500 of borrowed funds. It was one of several U.S. tire and rubber companies that flourished as the automobile industry exploded in the years before and after World War II. During the late 1960s excess capacity in the industry intensified competition, and the commodity tire business moved offshore. The premium tire market was growing and profitable, but it included a number of large international competitors, including Michelin in Europe and Bridgestone in Japan. In this tumultuous environment, Goodyear more than held its own and, in the words of one investment analyst, was "pulling away from the pack." Many of the other companies in the industry merged, moved into chemical or other related industries, or simply closed their doors.[1] Goodyear was big, however, and its size helped it get bigger.

In 1985 Goodyear was a $10 billion sales company with $3.5 million in net worth. The company was owned by 72,000 shareholders, but 64 percent of its stock was held by institutions. Goodyear did business in 27 countries and employed 134,000 people. It ranked 31st in the Fortune 500 and was one of the 30 firms in the Dow Jones Industrial index.

All of the major tire companies had invested heavily in research and development in an effort to automate the production of tires; tire production had always required a great deal of labor content because it had been necessary to lay up each ply by hand. Goodyear's R&D budget was equal to the total of all of its domestic competitors, and it showed. The company developed a proprietary process for manufacturing tires, and invested $250 million each in new semiautomated plants in Texas and Oklahoma. That competitive advantage distanced the company from its domestic competitors and protected it from foreign firms that might otherwise have considered establishing a productive capacity in the United States.

In the 1970s Michelin developed the radial tire, and that very important new technology was another factor that drove the smaller tire companies out of the business. The cost of converting from the production of bias tires to radial tires was prohibitive for all but the strongest companies. Goodyear was able to convert to radial production and then took a market lead with the first all-season radial tire. Michelin failed to exploit its initial advantage, and by 1985 Goodyear led in seven of the eight tire market categories, ceding only heavy truck radials to Michelin.

Because a radial tire lasts three times as long as a bias tire, the replacement tire business began to flatten. Unit tire sales grew 22 percent in the four-year period of 1981–1984 but were expected to drop 6 percent in the 1984–1987 period. Things were not totally bleak: As the industry consolidated it was expected that prices would strengthen, and as the new production technology came on stream it was thought that costs would come down. As a result of these developments, it was expected that the companies remaining in the business would become more profitable. Nonetheless, it was hard to see the tire business as a growth industry.

Exhibit 1 presents the company's income statement, balance sheet, and cash flow statement from the 1985 report to stockholders. Exhibit 2 presents the segment data, and Exhibit 3 presents the president's letter from that 1985 annual report.

[1]For example, in 1985 Uniroyal put its tire business into a joint venture with Goodrich and in June 1986 announced plans to pay off its debts and liquidate its remaining business units. Goodrich had been developing its chemical business over the years, and in 1988 it sold off its interest in the tire joint venture with Uniroyal and so became a specialty chemical producer.

EXHIBIT 1

The Goodyear Tire & Rubber Company and Subsidiaries
Consolidated Statement of Income

(Dollars in millions, except per share)	Year Ended December 31, 1985	1984	1983
Net sales	**$9,585.1**	$9,628.5	$9,031.6
Other income	**118.2**	85.5	61.4
	9,703.3	9,714.0	9,093.0
Cost and expenses:			
Cost of goods sold	**7,635.1**	7,581.9	7,073.5
Selling, administrative, and general expense	**1,469.6**	1,357.7	1,316.1
Interest and amortization of debt discount and expense	**105.2**	117.3	108.6
Plant closures and sale of facilities	**(2.4)**	(9.8)	73.8
Foreign currency exchange	**32.7**	45.8	55.6
Minority interest in net income of foreign subsidiaries	**6.6**	6.4	6.4
	9,246.8	9,099.3	8,634.0
Income from continuing operations before income taxes and extraordinary item	**456.5**	614.7	459.0
United States and foreign taxes on income	**155.2**	253.8	226.5
Income from continuing operations before extraordinary item	**301.3**	360.9	232.5
Discontinued operations	**111.1**	50.1	37.9
Income before extraordinary item	**412.4**	411.0	270.4
Extraordinary item — gain on long-term debt retired	**—**	—	35.1
Net Income	**$ 412.4**	$ 411.0	$ 305.5
Per share of common stock:			
Income from continuing operations before extraordinary item	**$ 2.81**	$ 3.40	$ 2.33
Discontinued operations	**1.03**	0.47	0.38
Extraordinary item — gain on long-term debt retired	**—**	—	0.35
Net Income	**$ 3.84**	$ 3.87	$ 3.06

continued

EXHIBIT 1 (continued)

The Goodyear Tire & Rubber Company and Subsidiaries
Consolidated Balance Sheet

(Dollars in millions, except per share)	December 31, 1985	1984
Assets		
Current assets:		
Cash and short-term securities	$ 139.0	$ 143.4
Accounts and notes receivable	957.4	1,370.1
Inventories	1,378.5	1,333.4
Prepaid expenses	83.3	53.6
Total current assets	2,558.2	2,900.5
Other assets:		
Investments in nonconsolidated subsidiaries and affiliates, at equity	181.3	158.2
Long-term accounts and notes receivable	126.8	39.6
Investments and miscellaneous assets, at cost	30.6	25.5
Deferred charges	31.6	33.8
	370.3	257.1
Properties and plants	4,025.0	3,036.7
	$6,953.5	$6,194.3
Liabilities and Shareholders' Equity		
Current Liabilities:		
Accounts payable — trade	$ 657.4	$ 582.5
Accrued payrolls and other compensation	347.4	298.4
Other current liabilities	219.1	192.4
United States and foreign taxes:		
Current	173.2	204.6
Deferred	58.8	84.3
Notes payable to banks and overdrafts	116.3	157.4
Long-term debt due within one year	35.2	38.8
Total current liabilities	1,607.4	1,558.4
Long-term debt and capital leases	997.5	656.8
Other long-term liabilities	301.6	293.9
Deferred income taxes	475.3	448.9
Minority equity in foreign subsidiaries	64.3	65.0
Shareholders' Equity:		
Preferred stock, no par value:		
Authorized, 50,000,000 shares		
Outstanding shares, none	—	—
Common stock, no par value:		
Authorized, 150,000,000 shares		
Outstanding shares, 108,110,085 (106,492,709 in 1984)	94.1	92.5
Capital surplus	655.4	613.6
Retained earnings	3,172.2	2,931.1
	3,921.7	3,637.2
Foreign currency translation adjustment	(414.3)	(465.9)
Total shareholders' equity	3,507.4	3,171.3
	$6,953.5	$6,194.3

continued

EXHIBIT 1 (concluded)

The Goodyear Tire & Rubber Company and Subsidiaries
Consolidated Statement of Changes in Financial Position

(Dollars in millions, except per share)	Year Ended December 31, 1985	1984	1983
Funds provided from operations:			
Income from continuing operations before extraordinary item	**$ 301.3**	$ 360.9	$ 232.5
Noncash items:			
Depreciation and depletion	**300.5**	292.3	280.3
Other	**65.9**	39.3	154.4
Accounts and notes receivable reduction (increase)	**412.7**	157.3	(95.7)
Long-term accounts and notes receivable (increase) reduction	**(87.2)**	11.1	(16.2)
Inventories (increase) reduction	**(45.1)**	(114.5)	86.1
Other items	**23.7**	25.9	79.2
	971.8	772.3	720.6
Income from discontinued operations	**111.1**	50.1	37.9
	1,082.9	822.4	758.5
Funds provided from (used for) financing:			
Notes payable to banks and overdrafts (reduction) increase	**(41.1)**	2.8	149.8
Long-term debt and capital lease reduction	**(234.7)**	(112.4)	(383.2)
Long-term debt and capital lease increase	**571.8**	101.1	104.8
Long-term debt retired in exchange for common stock	**—**	—	(199.4)
Less extraordinary gain on long-term debt retired	**—**	—	35.1
Common stock issued and acquired	**43.4**	25.2	189.0
	339.4	16.7	(103.9)
Funds used for investment:			
Capital expenditures	**(1,667.6)**	(610.9)	(478.7)
Property and plant dispositions	**415.9**	37.0	27.3
Other transactions	**(55.3)**	48.2	49.8
	(1,307.0)	(525.7)	(401.6)
Dividends paid	**(171.3)**	(158.7)	(125.2)
Foreign currency translation adjustment reduction (increase)	**51.6**	(122.4)	(118.9)
Cash and short-term securities (reduction) increase	**$ (4.4)**	$ 32.3	$ 8.9

EXHIBIT 2

The Goodyear Tire & Rubber Company

Industry Segments (In millions)	1985	1984	1983
Sales to unaffiliated customers			
Tires	**$6,190.2**	$6,237.5	$5,959.4
Related transportation products	**1,485.4**	1,469.6	1,363.1
Tires and related transportation products	**7,675.6**	7,707.1	7,322.5
Industrial rubber, chemical, and plastic products	**1,102.0**	1,137.9	974.1
Aerospace	**707.5**	659.2	610.6
Oil and gas	**36.5**	49.1	57.6
Other products and services	**63.5**	75.2	66.8
Net sales	**$9,585.1**	$9,628.5	$9,031.6
Income			
Tires and related transportation products	**$ 461.2**	$ 609.7	$ 537.3
Industrial rubber, chemical, and plastic products	**82.7**	91.5	53.4
Aerospace	**73.0**	71.5	68.6
Oil and gas	**7.9**	13.9	7.8
Other products and services	**15.1**	21.0	20.2
Total operating income	**639.9**	807.6	687.3
Interest and amortization of debt discount and expense	**(105.2)**	(117.3)	(108.6)
Foreign currency exchange	**(32.7)**	(45.8)	(55.6)
Equity in income of affiliated companies	**2.6**	2.8	0.8
Minority interest in net income	**(6.6)**	(6.4)	(6.4)
Corporate expenses and revenues	**(41.5)**	(26.2)	(58.5)
Income from continuing operations before income taxes and extraordinary item	**$ 456.5**	$ 614.7	$ 459.0
Assets			
Tires and related transportation products	**$4,428.5**	$4,318.8	$4,249.6
Industrial rubber, chemical, and plastic products	**464.3**	479.2	451.4
Aerospace	**186.2**	188.4	168.3
Oil and gas	**1,296.1**	430.0	345.3
Other products and services	**101.0**	100.1	93.4
Total identifiable assets	**6,476.1**	5,516.5	5,308.0
Corporate assets	**296.1**	519.6	526.0
Investments in affiliated companies	**181.3**	158.2	151.5
Assets at December 31	**$6,953.5**	$6,194.3	$5,985.5
Capital expenditures			
Tires and related transportation products	**$ 586.8**	$ 438.6	$ 341.6
Industrial rubber, chemical, and plastic products	**48.5**	34.0	31.6
Aerospace	**28.2**	17.8	14.1
Oil and gas	**992.4**	113.5	86.4
Other products and services	**11.7**	7.0	5.0
For the year	**$1,667.6**	$ 610.9	$ 478.7
Depreciation and depletion			
Tires and related transportation products	**$ 247.7**	$ 237.2	$ 221.2
Industrial rubber, chemical, and plastic products	**26.8**	20.7	23.3
Aerospace	**14.0**	12.7	11.3
Oil and gas	**9.4**	19.4	22.1
Other products and services	**2.6**	2.3	2.4
For the year	**$ 300.5**	$ 292.3	$ 280.3

EXHIBIT 3

President's Letter from the 1985 Annual Report to Stockholders

To the Shareholders of The Goodyear Tire & Rubber Company

The global nature of today's competition pervades virtually every market in the world, and successful companies must accept this reality. This was high in the conduct of Goodyear's business in 1985.

We continued our dedication to being competitive in all markets in which we choose to operate, and our strategy was directed to that objective.

In line with that strategy, it was a year in which major investments were made to "clean up" a good part of our operations, both to strengthen our ability to be world competitive in every facility, and to market product lines with the widest possible consumer acceptance.

Strengthening our core business in tires continued to be a dominant factor in our current and future planning.

Our strategy to meet changing conditions in our various business environments has resulted in decisions that have produced nonrecurring gains and losses. These decisions play an important part in the management and direction of our continuing operations.

Record net income for the second consecutive year of $412.4 million in 1985 compared with $411 million in 1984. Because of additional shares issued under the dividend reinvestment program, per share earnings of $3.84 were down from $3.87 a year ago.

However, as a result of laying foundations for the future, 1985 income of $301.3 million from continuing operations compared with $360.9 million in 1984.

Reflected in the 1985 results were outlays of $45.8 million for voluntary separation of employees required by our modernization programs, and the conversion of our Tyler, Texas, plant to radial tire production, both designed to strengthen our position as a low-cost producer. In addition, we closed the noncompetitive foundry and machining facilities of Motor Wheel Corporation at Lansing, Michigan.

In contrast to these outlays were the results of an adjustment in our energy-related activities. As the outlook for natural gas production and transmission became less favorable, we took advantage of an opportunity to sell off the gas pipeline operations and certain related assets of our Celeron subsidiary. We sold these operations last July at a profit of $103 million after they had generated $80 million in income since the acquisition of Celeron in June of 1983. The proceeds were applied to the purchase of substantial proven and potential oil and gas reserves and oil-producing properties in California, not far from our new West–East crude oil pipeline.

Construction of the new pipeline is well underway, and we expect it to become operational in January of 1987. Since the pipeline is designed to be the lowest-cost means of transporting crude oil from the West Coast to Gulf Coast refineries, its outlook remains bright despite the current fall in crude oil prices.

In improving our global sales and marketing abilities and competitive position, we undertook joint ventures and production agreements in the Far East to produce part of our requirements in earthmover tires, rubber products, and footwear products, providing a better opportunity for competitive operations in that part of the world.

In the United States we are significantly increasing our retail tire distribution system through acquisitions of several multi-outlet dealers. We also acquired two leading suppliers of retread materials and machinery to add to our growth in the tire retreading industry.

All of these moves will make our operations more responsive to world markets and strengthen our position as the most efficient manufacturer and premier marketer in the world.

Our aerospace business continued its very encouraging growth pattern in 1985, bringing it to the point where it is quite significant to the results of our worldwide operations. Accordingly, we are reporting our aerospace business as a separate segment for the first time, with 1985 sales of $707.5 million and operating income of $73 million.

As our horizons expanded in 1985, our capital expenditures reached $1.7 billion. Favorable rates in U.S. and foreign money markets enabled us to finance these expenditures in a prudent fashion. This year, we expect to make capital expenditures of $1.5 billion, with this investment in our future growth extending to virtually all segments of the corporation.

We increased our commitment to research and development in 1985 to $299 million. This year, the R&D expenditure may exceed $300 million to once again provide the innovation that separates us from the competition.

While the merit of these steps is obvious in any appraisal of Goodyear's commitment to the future, demonstrating our continuing social responsibility in the case of South Africa was much more difficult.

While it would have been easy to accede to the loud but short-sighted demands for disinvestment, we did not back away from our conviction that we can best serve the people of South Africa by providing jobs, education, and economic opportunity. We continued to oppose apartheid while stating our belief that the presence of U.S. companies can effect improvements in the social structure in that nation without destroying its economy.

During the past year we made encouraging progress in building an atmosphere in which our employees are aware of the global competition taking place in our markets and the need to meet it in terms of both quality and competitive costs.

The strategic refinements to our businesses in 1985 should bode well for Goodyear in the remainder of 1986. We expect tire market share increases in the United States

continued

EXHIBIT 3 (concluded)

and Europe; Latin American operations will continue to show resilience to economic problems; the Asia–Pacific region should benefit from our newest ventures there as well as plant modernizations.

Our aerospace business will maintain its steady growth, while recent investments in Celeron will begin to generate earnings.

In 1986 we must continue our concern with the portions of the U.S. tax reform proposal that would discourage investment and technology leadership by U.S. manufacturers. Passage of such impediments would assure that imported tires and other products would keep rolling into the United States in ever-increasing numbers.

Our success in changing the composition and thrust of the company, in concert with markets and operating conditions, reflect the quality and dedication of our employees.

Robert E. Mercer
Chairman of the Board
and Chief Executive Officer

Tom H. Barrett
President and
Chief Operating Officer

Goodyear's Diversification

Goodyear had been in the chemical and plastic business as an extension of its work with synthetic rubber. And the company had been in aerospace as an outgrowth of its experimentation with blimps. By 1985, 80 percent of Goodyear's sales were in tires and related transportation products, 11.5 percent of its sales were in chemicals, and 7.5 percent were from aerospace products.

The company had been actively looking at other diversification moves since 1982 to "flatten out the cyclical nature of the company's tire business." The company's chairman, Robert Mercer, said sarcastically that some analysts "think we should do such snappy things as buying back our own stock." However, Goodyear resolved to use the substantial cash flow from its tire business to expand the company. Mercer also said that "in 1981 or 1982, I said that we were not going to go out and buy some oil wells. Oil was the last thing on my mind." The suggestion from his staff, that the company explore a diversification into oil and gas, struck Mercer initially as "off the wall."

Nonetheless, a careful staff study did recommend diversification into oil and gas, and the acquisition of The Celeron Corporation was completed in late 1983 through an exchange of 24.6 million shares of stock valued at $860 million. At that time, Goodyear's total assets were about $7 billion, so the acquisition represented a 14 percent expansion in the business.

An expansion into oil made sense in that there are seven gallons of oil in every tire, and oil is the largest raw material component of tire production. With its own investment in oil reserves, it seemed logical to think that Goodyear might be able to smooth out the effects of fluctuations in the world price for oil. In 1985, Goodyear spun off Celeron's gas operations and invested the proceeds in additional oil reserves. Mercer announced that the company's goal was to have 50 percent of its sales from tires and the rest divided equally between aerospace and oil. The stock market was not pleased with the acquisition, evidently worrying that Goodyear didn't know enough about the energy business. The stock dropped $3.50 after the acquisition and for some time fluctuated around $30.

Well before Goodyear acquired it, Celeron had begun the construction of a pipeline across California into Texas. The California offshore oil fields (the site of some of Celeron's reserves) were coming on stream in volume, but because of environmental pressures little refinery capacity had been built in the area. There was plenty of refinery capacity in Texas, but getting it there from the California coast involved shipping it around Mexico through the Panama Canal. Transportation by pipeline would not only be less expensive, it would be safer.

It was expected that the pipeline could break even at 100,000 barrels a day, and it was estimated that the California fields had the potential for 500,000 to 1,000,000 barrels a day. Those fields were productive when oil prices were around $20: Prices in 1984–1985 had been as high as $27 and were at $24.75 by the end of 1985. Mercer said, "We're not in trouble at $20 a barrel; I'd get concerned at $15 a barrel." Other analyst estimates concluded that the pipeline would be able to attract business and cover its costs with oil at $12 a barrel. By December 31, 1985, the company had invested $500 million in the pipeline with another $500 million to go. Goodyear decided to construct the pipeline on its own rather than through a joint venture so that the approval process and the rate-setting process would be simplified.

Goodyear and Wall Street

On May 6, 1985, Donaldson, Lufkin & Jenrette (DL&J) issued a buy recommendation on Goodyear when the stock was about $25. The opening and closing segments of that report were as follows:[2]

> We recommend purchase of Goodyear because we believe that its long-term profitability is being shifted upward — from an ROE of 10 percent to 12 percent or more — by the advent of the Celeron pipeline and by Goodyear's increasing share of the premium segment of the tire market. Judging from Goodyear's very low multiple, the market appears to be treating the company's earnings and current ROE (12–13 percent) as cyclically inflated. By contrast, we view a 12 percent ROE as being the new floor under Goodyear's profitability. Together with our assumption that Goodyear can sustain growth at a 7.2 percent rate, which we consider conservative, that level of profitability calls for a multiple discount of 19 percent, not the current 35 percent, according to our valuation model. Moreover, we expect that Goodyear's profitability will continue to rise over the longer term. Over the past decade, the company has reinvested heavily in the tire industry in research, and by constructing plants that rank as global low-cost sources of premium tires, while other tire companies disengaged. Goodyear's investments are beginning to allow it to peel away from the pack as the company increases share of the faster-growing, technically advanced, higher-profit tire segments. The real payoff, however, will occur when industry overcapacity is reduced through the elimination of inefficient plants, which will increase profitability for the entire industry and especially for the dominant competitor, Goodyear. The potential that Goodyear could break out of the industry's competitive gridlock would produce large investment rewards, but those are not factored into our current recommendation. Ironically, it is the potential of a huge investment in a part of Goodyear that has disappointed investors — Celeron — that precipitates our current enthusiasm. The crude oil pipeline, which has nothing to do with Celeron's depressed gas transmission business, should begin pumping profits into Goodyear in 1987.
>
> Goodyear has been "down and out" for so long that it is not hard to conceive that such important changes have gone unappreciated. Goodyear has been a "story" stock for so long that perhaps a more quantitative approach is appropriate for determining the value that is developing at the company. Change is a process of consummate interest on Wall Street, and unperceived change is the nirvana of security analysts and investors alike. How can so much change, and yet perceptions remain the same?

Also, the report included an interesting table, supporting DL&J's suggested target price of $33 for the stock. That table is reproduced in Exhibit 4.

[2]Portions of the DL&J May 6, 1985 report reprinted with permission.

EXHIBIT 4

Valuation Schedule for Goodyear Tire and Rubber Company from the May 6, 1985, Donaldson, Lufkin & Jenrette Analysis

Key market assumptions:
1. Discount rate for the S&P 400 = 12.9% (DLJ estimate)
2. Terminal market/book for the S&P 400 = 1.5054 (DLJ estimate)

Goodyear-specific assumptions:
1. Book value = $30.07
2. Normalized earnings using a 12% ROE = $3.61
3. Normalized dividend at 40% payout = $1.44
4. Internal equity growth of 7.2% (ROE * 60%)

Year	Dividend	Book	
1985	$1.44	$ 30.07	
1986	1.60	32.24	
1987	1.72	34.56	
1988	1.84	37.04	
1989	1.97	39.71	
1990	2.12	42.57	
1991	2.27	45.64	
1992	2.43	48.92	
1993	2.61	52.44	
1994	2.81	56.22	
1995	3.00	60.27	
1996	3.21	64.61	
1997	3.44	68.26	
1998	3.69	74.24	
1999	3.96	79.59	
2000	4.24	85.32	
2001	4.55	91.46	
2002	4.88	96.05	
2003	5.23	105.11	
2004	5.60	112.68	
2005	6.01	120.78	$129.49 (year-end book)

Present value of dividends	$17.92
Present value of terminal book	15.25
Suggested value	33.17

Later in 1985, Mr. Mercer was given the gold award by the *Wall Street Transcript* as the best CEO in the tire and rubber industry. The *Transcript* had this to say:

> Mercer receives the gold award because industry analysts, virtually without exception, laud his performance in maintaining and augmenting Goodyear's worldwide industry leadership and in maintaining the company's profitability in a difficult market and in a difficult time.
>
> Goodyear has done a super job in their tire business, and they have really been able to take the lead on a worldwide basis in terms of quality performance tires. They have established a very good name for themselves, they're going in the right direction modernizing plants, and they seem to be able to identify strategies for both segments of the markets, both the high performance and also the more cost conscious, in terms of being able to bring in tires from lower-cost facilities in Brazil and Mexico and places like that; and they're beginning to earmark some of the Pacific areas as well.

EXHIBIT 5

Goodyear Tire and Rubber Company

Common Stock — Monthly Trading Ranges

		High	Low
1985	January	28	25
	February	29	27
	March	28	26
	April	28	25
	May	29	25
	June	30	28
	July	30	27
	August	29	27
	September	28	26
	October	27	25
	November	29	26
	December	31	28
1986	January	33	30
	February	35	32
	March	36	33
	April	35	31
	May	32	29
	June	33	29
	July	33	30
	August	34	30
	September	35	31
	October	49	33
	November	47	41
	December	43	41

> The oil pipeline should be a very cost competitive transportation source for crude oil into the Texas Gulf area, and that should bring eventually a great deal of earnings and cash flow to the company in about two or three years.[3]

In a February 1986 research report, Butcher and Singer recommended the stock when it was at $34. Although the company had just reported rather flat results for 1985 (EPS of $3.84, down slightly from $3.87 in 1984), B&S estimated 1986 earnings at $3.50–$3.60 and argued that the resulting multiple of 9.6 was — unjustifiably — 15 percent below the Dow Jones Industrial average. The B&S report concluded with these words:

> On balance, it is fair to say that GT was an unrewarding investment during the 1970s and 1980s. We now believe management has taken definitive steps to address the competitive situation facing them over the next 15 years. If they are successful in maintaining their dominant position in the industry (which we expect), the dynamics of this mature business should work in their favor. Consequently, the next 15 years should provide shareholders with a much better total return on investment. In fact, we would not be surprised to see GT trading in the mid-$40s over the next 12 months and in the $60 area by 1988.

Exhibit 5 provides the monthly highs and lows for the company's stock price through 1985 and 1986.

[3]"An Analyst Roundtable on the Tire Industry — The Summary Section," *Wall Street Transcript* (November 18, 1985).

EXHIBIT 6

Goodyear Tire and Rubber Company

Average Prices of Crude Oil at the Well, 1984 through June 1986

1984	January	$26.79
	February	$26.79
	March	$26.79
	April	$26.72
	May	$26.72
	June	$26.70
	July	$26.67
	August	$26.61
	September	$26.59
	October	$26.56
	November	$26.00
	December	$25.75
1985	January	$25.03
	February	$24.39
	March	$24.40
	April	$24.49
	May	$24.62
	June	$24.59
	July	$24.54
	August	$24.35
	September	$24.39
	October	$24.52
	November	$24.64
	December	$24.75
1986	January	$24.51
	February	$19.39
	March	$14.00
	April	$11.92
	May	$11.62
	June	$11.93

Source: "Business Statistics," The U. S. Department of Commerce.

The First Quarter of 1986

The accounting profession has been unable to settle on one best way to account for investments in oil and gas properties. In the face of that GAAP confusion, the SEC has required companies to spell out in detail the recorded costs and the market values of their oil and gas reserves, and has insisted that any capitalized costs in excess of market be written down. In early 1986, the market for crude oil dropped dramatically from $24 in January to $11 in early April. (Exhibit 6 provides the average well head price for crude oil through 1984, 1985, and the first six months of 1986.) No one expected that the market price would stay that low because of actions that were under consideration by OPEC. It was suggested that the SEC allow the oil companies to apply the lower-of-cost or market test for their oil properties using the market prices that were expected to prevail at the end of 1986. After hearing some testimony as to the efficiency of the stock market (that the market will react the same whether the shortfall was recorded as a write-down or simply made apparent in the footnotes), the SEC commissioners decided that there was no reason to make an exception to their own ruling and voted to require the application of the lower-of-cost or market rule using prices in effect at the end of each quarter.

EXHIBIT 7

Goodyear Quarterly Report for the Period Ended June 30, 1986

SECURITIES AND EXCHANGE COMMISSION
Washington, D.C. 20549

FORM 10-Q

QUARTERLY REPORT UNDER SECTION 13 OR 15 (d)
OF THE SECURITIES EXCHANGE ACT OF 1934

For Quarter Ended June 30, 1986

Commission File Number: 1-1927

THE GOODYEAR TIRE & RUBBER COMPANY
(Exact name of registrant as specified in its charter)

OHIO (State or other jurisdiction of incorporation or organization)	34-0253240 (I.R.S. Employer Identification No.)
1144 East Market Street, Akron, Ohio (Address of principal executive offices)	44316-0001 (Zip Code)

(216) 796-2121
(Registrant's telephone number, including area code)

Indicate by check mark whether the registrant (1) has filed all reports required to be filed by Section 13 or 15 (d) of the Securities Exchange Act of 1934 during the preceding 12 months, and (2) has been subject to such filing requirements for the past 90 days.

Yes X No ___

Indicate the number of shares outstanding of each of the registrant's classes of common stock, as of the latest practicable date.

Number of Shares of Common Stock, Without Par Value, Outstanding at July 31, 1986: 109,008,881

TOTAL NUMBER OF SEQUENTIALLY NUMBERED PAGES: 43

THE INDEX OF EXHIBITS TO THIS QUARTERLY REPORT BEGINS AT SEQUENTIALLY NUMBERED PAGE: 14

continued

Because Goodyear had been acquiring oil reserves more recently than other companies, its recorded costs were relatively high. The company was forced to record a $110 million write-down in the first quarter of 1986, resulting in a $60 million loss. The following period reflected some upturn in operations, but the burden of that loss was significant. (A copy of Goodyear's quarterly report for the six months ended June 30, 1986, is attached as Exhibit 7.)

EXHIBIT 7 (continued)

The Goodyear Tire & Rubber Company
and Subsidiaries
Financial Statements
Consolidated Statement of Income and Retained Earnings

	Three Months Ended June 30,		Six Months Ended June 30,	
(Dollars in millions, except per share)	**1986**	**1985**	**1986**	**1985**
Net sales	$2,646.2	$2,450.2	$4,983.3	$4,745.0
Other income	30.8	21.8	61.7	47.3
	2,677.0	2,472.0	5,045.0	4,792.3
Cost and expenses:				
Cost of goods sold	2,062.3	1,939.5	3,935.7	3,749.4
Selling, administrative, and general expense	414.9	350.3	794.9	694.4
Interest and amortization of debt discount and expense	35.0	29.5	61.6	61.1
Asset write-down and sale of facilities	—	—	214.8	(10.6)
Foreign currency exchange	0.9	9.4	6.2	19.4
Minority interest in net income of subsidiaries	3.9	1.7	5.4	2.7
	2,517.0	2,330.4	5,018.6	4,516.4
Income from continuing operations before income taxes	160.0	141.6	26.4	275.9
United States and foreign taxes on income	58.7	60.6	(14.9)	114.6
Income from continuing operations	101.3	81.0	41.3	161.3
Discontinued operations	—	5.7	—	12.1
Net income for the period	$ 101.3	$ 86.7	41.3	173.4
Retained earnings at beginning of period			3,172.2	2,931.1
			3,213.5	3,104.5
Cash dividends on common stock			86.7	85.3
Retained earnings at end of period			$3,126.8	$3,019.2
Per share of common stock:				
Income from continuing operations			$0.38	$1.51
Discontinued operations			—	0.11
Net Income			$0.38	$1.62
Dividends per share			$0.80	$0.80

Unaudited.

The accompanying notes are an integral part of this financial statement.

continued

EXHIBIT 7 (continued)

The Goodyear Tire & Rubber Company
and Subsidiaries
Consolidated Balance Sheet

(Dollars in millions)	June 30, 1986	December 31, 1985
Assets		
Current assets:		
Cash and short-term securities	$ 147.4	$ 139.0
Accounts and notes receivable, less allowance 1986 — $37.8, 1985 — $36.5	1,130.4	957.4
Inventories		
Raw materials	416.4	431.9
Work in process	165.8	123.5
Finished product	977.3	823.1
	1,559.5	1,378.5
Prepaid expenses	90.1	83.3
Total current assets	2,927.4	2,558.2
Other assets:		
Investments and miscellaneous assets	462.4	338.7
Deferred charges	45.1	31.6
	507.5	370.3
Properties and plants, less accumulated depreciation and depletion 1986 — $3,087.9, 1985 — $2,894.4	4,477.1	4,025.0
	$7,912.0	$6,953.5
Liabilities and shareholders' equity		
Current liabilities:		
Accounts payable and accrued expenses	$1,308.5	$1,223.9
United States and foreign taxes	199.0	232.0
Notes payable to banks and overdrafts	160.1	116.3
Long-term debt due within one year	20.9	35.2
Total current liabilities	1,688.5	1,607.4
Long-term debt and capital leases	1,884.5	997.5
Other long-term liabilities	304.3	301.6
Deferred income taxes	427.9	475.3
Minority equity in subsidiaries	71.2	64.3
Shareholders' equity:		
Preferred stock, no par value: Authorized 50,000,000 shares Outstanding shares, none	—	—
Common stock, no par value: Authorized 150,000,000 shares Outstanding shares, 109,003,353 (108,110,085 in 1985) after deducting 1,271,751 treasury shares (1,320,729 in 1985)	95.0	94.1
Capital surplus	681.6	655.4
Retained earnings	3,126.8	3,172.2
	3,903.4	3,921.7
Foreign currency translation adjustment	(367.8)	(414.3)
Total shareholders' equity	3,535.6	3,507.4
	$7,912.0	$6,953.5

Unaudited.

The accompanying notes are an integral part of this financial statement.

continued

EXHIBIT 7 (continued)

The Goodyear Tire & Rubber Company
and Subsidiaries
Consolidated Statement of Changes in Financial Position

(Dollars in millions)	Six Months Ended June 30, 1986	1985
Funds (used for) provided from operations:		
Income from continuing operations	$ 41.3	$ 161.3
Noncash items — Depreciation and depletion	185.3	149.3
— Asset write-down	110.8	—
— Other	27.8	29.7
Accounts and notes receivable (increase) reduction	(173.0)	85.7
Long-term accounts and notes receivable (increase) decrease	(87.8)	5.9
Inventories increase	(181.0)	(112.4)
Other items	32.3	6.2
	(43.8)	325.7
Income from discontinued operations	—	12.1
	(43.8)	337.8
Funds provided from financing:		
Notes payable to banks and overdrafts increase	43.8	16.3
Long-term debt and capital lease reduction	(62.5)	(17.8)
Long-term debt and capital lease increase	935.2	133.8
Common stock issued and acquired	27.1	18.7
	943.6	151.0
Funds used for investment:		
Capital expenditures	(839.8)	(415.6)
Property and plant dispositions	11.6	11.3
Other transactions	(23.0)	2.7
	(851.2)	(401.6)
Dividends paid	(86.7)	(85.3)
Foreign currency translation adjustment reduction (increase)	46.5	(13.6)
Cash and short-term securities increase (reduction)	$ 8.4	$ (11.7)

Unaudited.

The accompanying notes are an integral part of this financial statement.

continued

EXHIBIT 7 (continued)

The Goodyear Tire & Rubber Company
and Subsidiaries
Notes to Consolidated Financial Statements

Adjustments

In the opinion of the company, all adjustments, consisting of normal recurring adjustments, necessary for a fair statement of the results of these unaudited interim periods have been included.

Asset Write-Down

As a result of substantial declines in oil prices during the first quarter, a charge of $214.8 million ($110.8 million after tax) associated with the write-down of the Celeron Oil and Gas subsidiary's proved oil and gas reserves was included in the 1986 first quarter.

Goodyear Financial Corporation

Interest expense for the six months ended June 30, is reduced by pretax earnings of Goodyear Financial Corporation of $12.3 million in 1986 and $7.7 million in 1985, thus offsetting interest charges from Goodyear Financial Corporation included therein.

Net Income per Share

Net income per share has been computed based on the average number of common shares outstanding, including for this purpose only those treasury shares allocated for distribution under the incentive profit sharing plan; and for 1986 and 1985 was 108,639,501 and 106,983,082, respectively.

continued

EXHIBIT 7 (continued)

The Goodyear Tire & Rubber Company
and Subsidiaries
Segment Information

	Three Months Ended June 30,		Six Months Ended June 30,	
(Dollars in millions, except per share)	1986	1985	1986	1985
Industry segments				
Sales to unaffiliated customers				
Tires	$1,724.2	$1,578.7	$3,210.8	$3,043.3
Related transportation products	440.8	402.2	839.2	783.1
Tires and related transportation products	2,165.0	1,980.9	4,050.0	3,826.4
Industrial rubber, chemical, and plastic products	295.3	287.3	571.4	547.7
Aerospace	162.0	156.1	306.8	313.3
Oil and gas	10.7	11.2	25.1	22.6
Other products and services	13.2	14.7	30.0	35.0
Net Sales	$2,646.2	$2,450.2	$4,983.3	$4,745.0
Income (loss)				
Tires and related transportation products	$ 156.4	$ 143.9	$ 238.6	$ 269.5
Industrial rubber, chemical, and plastic products	34.2	33.7	56.9	57.2
Aerospace	9.6	15.0	18.8	33.5
Oil and gas	(2.5)	2.5	(215.2)	5.1
Other products and services	3.2	0.9	10.2	10.1
Total operating income	200.9	196.0	109.3	375.4
Exclusions from operating income	(40.9)	(54.4)	(82.9)	(99.5)
Income from continuing operations before income taxes	$ 160.0	$ 141.6	$ 26.4	$ 275.9
Geographic information				
Sales to unaffiliated customers				
United States	$1,742.6	$1,662.5	$3,272.5	$3,212.2
Foreign	903.6	787.7	1,710.8	1,532.8
	$2,646.2	$2,450.2	$4,983.3	$4,745.0
Operating income				
United States	$ 153.3	$ 144.5	$ 12.5	$ 268.0
Foreign	47.6	51.5	96.8	107.4
	$ 200.9	$ 196.0	$ 109.3	$ 375.4

Unaudited.

continued

EXHIBIT 7 (concluded)

Management's Discussion and Analysis of Financial Condition and Results of Operations

Results of Operations

Worldwide sales of $4.98 billion for the six months ended June 30, 1986, exceeded the 1985 six months' sales of $4.75 billion by 5 percent. Net income for the 1986 six months was $41.3 million ($0.38 per share), down 76.2 percent from the $173.4 million ($1.62 per share) recorded in the 1985 period. The income for the first half of 1986 was affected by the first quarter $110.8 million aftertax write-down of the proved oil and gas reserves of the Celeron subsidiary and charges associated with the conversion of the Tyler, Texas, plant to radial tire production. The 1985 period also included income of $12.1 million from the discontinued Celeron operations, which were sold in the third quarter of 1985.

Sales in the United States of $3.27 billion for the first six months of 1986 compare with $3.22 billion in the 1985 period, an increase of 1.9 percent. The operating income of $12.5 million was down 95.3 percent from the 1985 six-month operating income of $268.0 million primarily due to the write-down and charges referred to above. Domestic tire unit sales remained relatively unchanged from 1985.

Foreign sales of $1.71 billion in the 1986 six months exceeded the 1985 period sales of $1.53 billion by 11.6 percent. Foreign operating income for the period of $96.8 million was 9.9 percent below the 1985 six-months operating income of $107.4 million, mainly due to reduced profits in Latin America, where Brazil and Mexico suffered from depressed economic conditions. Foreign tire units for the 1986 six months increased 4.9 percent over the same period in 1985.

Sales of tires and related transportation products were up 5.8 percent in the half while operating income for that business fell 11.5 percent below last year's level.

Sales of industrial rubber, chemical, and plastic products were up 4.3 percent for the half while operating income for that segment of the business was slightly below last year for the half.

Worldwide sales in the second quarter of 1986 of $2.64 billion were up 8.0 percent from the $2.46 billion recorded in the 1985 second period. Income from continuing operations of $101.3 million ($0.93 per share) in the 1986 second quarter increased 24.9 percent from the $81.0 million ($0.76 per share) in the 1985 quarter.

Sales in the U.S. of $1.74 billion in the second quarter were up 4.8 percent from the year ago period with operating income up 6.1 percent to $153.3 million. Tire unit sales increased slightly from the year ago period.

Foreign sales of $903.6 million in the 1986 second quarter increased 14.7 percent from 1985's second quarter, however, foreign operating income was down 7.5 percent to $47.6 million compared to a year ago due to reduced operating income in the Latin America region. Foreign tire unit sales increased 8.2 percent in the 1986 second quarter compared to the 1985 period.

Sales of tires and related transportation products were up 9.3 percent in the quarter, and the operating income of this segment increased 8.7 percent for the quarter. Overall, North American auto tire operations showed increases in both sales and profits in the second quarter. Reflected in this performance was increased demand for the Eagle line of tires and a slight increase in private brand auto tire replacement units in the United States. Worldwide sales of truck tire units were up slightly in the second quarter.

Sales of industrial rubber, chemical, and plastic products were up 2.8 percent for the quarter while operating income for that segment of the business increased 1.5 percent for the quarter. Operating income from chemical operations in the quarter was up mainly due to improved margins. Roofing products continued to gain in both sales and profitability.

Second quarter sales increases in the wheel and brake and defense systems areas were bright spots in aerospace results. However, this segment's operating income for the quarter was below last year generally because of competitive pressures and the cancellation of the centrifuge program in mid-1985.

In the oil and gas segment, production levels from recently purchased properties continue to exceed expectations. Depressed oil prices, however, have negatively impacted the operating results of Celeron, more than offsetting increased production.

Liquidity and Capital Resources

During the first six months of 1986, funds generated from operations were less than sufficient to satisfy the company's requirements.

Consolidated debt, including capital lease obligations, increased from $1,149.0 million at December 31, 1985 to $2,065.5 million at June 30, 1986, an increase of $916.5 million. The debt of Goodyear Financial Corporation decreased from $580.6 million at December 31, 1985, to $407.3 million at June 30, 1986, a decrease of $173.3 million. Consolidated and Goodyear Financial Corporation debt increased $743.2 million during the first half of 1986 and, at June 30, 1986, was 41.2 percent of total debt and shareholders' equity.

The increase in debt was primarily from the drawdown of $530.0 million on the $650.0 million credit facility available to the Celeron Pipeline Company for the crude oil pipeline project.

Long-term debt associated with Yen and Swiss Franc bond issues increased by $84.3 million during the first half of the year as a result of revaluations of these currencies. Receivables from hedge contracts provide protection against this increase.

During the second quarter, the company negotiated interest rate swap agreements for an additional $230.0 million of Celeron Pipeline Company debt. The effect of these and similar contracts entered into during the first six months of the year was to convert floating interest cost on $435.0 million of long-term debt to fixed-rate obligations with various maturities beginning in 1987.

Nonetheless, in a research report dated April 22, 1986, McDonald and Co. recommended the stock as a "buy" at $32½, saying:

> The market has reacted extremely negatively to Goodyear's announcement of the possible write-off of $110 million after taxes, for Celeron's oil and gas reserves, and the indication of disappointing earnings. As we have indicated earlier, the write-off is noncash charge and will not impact on future earning power. We also expect the write-off to be more than offset by a $150–200 million aftertax gain on the reversion of a pension fund. More importantly, we anticipate greatly strengthened operating profits on both an absolute and a relative basis for the rest of the year.

The report concluded with an estimate of $3.50 EPS for 1986 and suggested that the P/E multiple should be 11.5, which would in turn indicate a market value of $40 for the stock.

On May 13, 1986, McDonald and Co. continued its recommendation of the stock, which was still at $32½. The analysts's report commented that the depressed oil prices should shave 5 percent off of the cost of a tire and should more than compensate for any softness in tire prices. They repeated their estimate that the company would earn between $3.25 and $3.50 a share for 1986, concluding as follows:

> If our estimates prove close to the mark, Goodyear is now realizing a rate of return on equity that is about 85 percent of the average manufacturing company's, and yet it is selling at about two-thirds of a market multiple. The value of its well above-average 5.2 percent yield should be enhanced if the proposed tax bill is passed, and the earnings outlook appears quite attractive over the next two to three years. At current prices we therefore believe the stock offers excellent fundamental value and recommend purchase in total rate of return accounts.

DL&J issued a report on June 18, 1986, recommending the stock at the current price of $31½. The report said the following:[4]

> We also look to Goodyear for a more proactive position toward shareholder value, and we note that the company appears to have several options available to improve shareholder returns and to close the growing gap between Goodyear's "private" value (which we estimate at $45), and its current market value. Strong cash flow and prospects for a continuing improvement in GT's return on shareholders' equity suggest that GT's 35 percent discount to the market (on the basis of our 1987) estimate is too severe. On the basis of our projection that GT's long-term level of return on equity should be at lease 12 percent, a 10 percent discount appears to be more appropriate and suggests that GT's shares have the potential for significant appreciation.
>
> *Goodyear's improving prospects imply that the stock is undervalued, but we do note that management will play a key role in any real improvement in shareholder returns.* Goodyear has historically been a company that has fallen short of investors' hopes, and past management actions (especially with regard to acquisitions) have often proved to be a powerful antidote to cases of investor optimism. An unanswered question is the degree to which Goodyear's management will assume a proactive role in boosting shareholder returns by trimming inefficient capacity, curtailing research and development expenses with diminishing returns, and aggressively exploiting other opportunities to lower overhead expenses. The company's powerful operating cash flow implies a potential private market value of at least $45 per share, and it also suggests that a significant stock repurchase at current prices would have very favorable implications for shareholders. The company has historically resisted

[4]Portions of the DL&J June 18, 1986 report reprinted with permission.

suggestions that it repurchase its stock and has indicated that it favors a policy of continued acquisitions. Perhaps the company's experiences in the oil patch, which have only underscored the risks of diversification into the unknown, will refocus management's attention on the exciting potential that they have within their very own company, a realization that would prove to be valuable for shareholders.

The Hostile Takeover Bid

It is not clear whether Sir James Goldsmith saw these analyst recommendations or whether he discovered the opportunity at Goodyear on his own. In any event, in October 1986 the Goldsmith interests announced that they had accumulated a 11.5 percent stake in the company (that investment could well have cost $425 million) and said that they were "considering various actions, including taking control of the company." After a series of board meetings and negotiations, Goodyear agreed to purchase the shares of the Goldsmith interests at $49.50 a share and to tender for up to 40 million of its own shares on the market at $50 a share. Under the agreement with the Goldsmith group, the company agreed to reimburse certain legal and other expenses the group had incurred, and the members of the group agreed that they would not acquire any Goodyear shares for a future period.

To fund the purchase of the Goldsmith shares and the purchase of the shares from the market, the company borrowed more than $2.5 billion. To reduce that debt to normal levels, the company was forced to put its oil properties (including the in-process pipeline) and the aerospace division up for sale. The management discussion and analysis accompanying the 1986 financials concluded, "After completion of the restructuring program, the company expects to remain a global leader in those areas representing its core business."

Required:

Re-read the comments from the June 18, 1986 DL&J report on Goodyear. Why would the stock trade at $31.50 if the "private value" was estimated at $45? Should management of the company have been concerned about that spread? If so, what should they have done?

C16.2 Cummins Engine Co., Inc. It was easy to believe in capitalism as it was practiced by Cummins Engine, at least during the 1970s and early 1980s. Everything seemed to work — the shareholders had good returns; the customers had reliable, high quality products; the workers were well paid and had stable employment; and the communities where Cummins located its facilities had a good corporate citizen as a neighbor. In retrospect, 1984 was a highpoint year for the Company, with sales of $2.3 billion and earnings of $189 million ($19.76 a share). However, the five year period, 1986–1990, provided a serious test of the Company's philosophy and those shareholders who were of faint heart lost out. The Company suffered a series of losses as it invested in its markets and products, and the share price fluctuated dramatically, as the annual highs and lows for its stocks depicted below illustrate: (All of these numbers are adjusted for the stock split in 1993)

	Annual	
	High	Low
1984	$44	$31
1985	44	29
1986	39	26
1987	47	20
1988	34	22
1989	36	24
1990	27	15
1991	27	16
1992	40	27
1993	54	38
1994	58	36

A truly long term investor could look back from the end of 1994 and feel vindicated, but that was easy to say only in hindsight. Cummins' road to 1994 had been full of potholes and detours.

The History and Culture of Cummins Engine

Cummins Engine Co., Inc. is the world's largest builder of diesel engines over 150 horsepower. The Company was founded in 1919 by Clessie Cummins, the chauffeur for Mr. Will G. Irwin, a wealthy industrialist and philanthropist in Columbus, Indiana. Mr. Cummins was a valued employee because he was the only one who could keep the Irwins' 1909 Packard working. But, when Mr. Cummins asked for a pay hike to $85 a month, Mr. Irwin balked. They eventually compromised with a lower salary payment but with an agreement that the Irwin garage would be equipped with enough equipment and tools such that Mr. Cummins could begin an engine repair business.

Mr. Cummins was intrigued with the promise presented by the newly invented Diesel engine, and with the challenge of making the existing engines — which were smelly and noisy — more suitable for transportation applications. When Sears Roebuck & Co. announced that they were intending to buy three horsepower diesel engines for use in farm tractors, Mr. Cummins convinced Mr. Irwin to help him negotiate that contract — and that was the beginning of today's Cummins Engine Co., Inc.[1] It has been reported that Mr. Cummins pledged to "make good engines first and eventually make a profit" . . . and that it took 18 years before the first profits came.[2] From the earliest years, Mr. Cummins and his new company had financial support from the Irwin family: the Irwins put $10,000 into the Company when the engine Cummins built for Sears ran into problems, and over the following start-up years the family invested another $2,500,000 into the new firm.

As a foreshadow of events to come, Mr. Cummins focused his energy on development of the fuel injectors and the ignition system for his diesels, so that the engines would be more powerful, more efficient and cleaner running. Others who were experimenting with diesels worked toward those goals by installing complicated devices on their basic engines, but Cummins worked toward simplification. The fuel injector he finally perfected was reported to be "as simple as a fountain pen." To demonstrate the reliability and the economy of his creation, he installed one of his engines in a Packard and drove it from Columbus, Indiana, to New York on $1.88 of heating oil.

Clessie Cummins was an inventor, an engineer, and an entrepreneur but was not much of a salesperson. He could not convince truck manufacturers to use his engines: they insisted on using gasoline engines while trying to develop their own diesels. Mr. Irwin came to Cummins' rescue once again by asking the truckers who supplied his chain of grocery stores to use the new Cummins engine. Those truckers liked the power and efficiency of the new engine and, as they shared their experience with their colleagues, Cummins' business began to grow.

But to succeed, the firm needed an organized marketing plan and more effective production procedures. Mr. Irwin's grandnephew, J. Irwin Miller took over as head of the firm in 1934, and developed what he called "the backdoor approach" to marketing the engines. During the depression, he urged cash-starved truckers to specify Cummins engines in the trucks they purchased, arguing that they would save money on their operations through reduced fuel costs, less down time and lower repair bills. From that initial appeal grew the unique Cummins approach to marketing engines — selling engines to truck makers based on the requirements of trucking companies.

---

[1] This discussion of Cummins' early years is taken from the *International Directory of Company Histories* (Chicago: St. James Press, 1988).

[2] R. Johnson, "With Its Spirit Shaken But Unbent, Cummins Shows Decade's Scars," *The Wall Street Journal* (December 13, 1989), p. A1.

Over time, the market for trucks and truck engines developed in a very unique way, reflecting both push and pull effects. Cummins continued to improve its engines making entry into the field difficult for any but the most dedicated truck manufacturers. Most of the major truck makers (Kenmore, White, PACCAR) were content to build the chassis and the body of the trucks they sold and to stay out of the more intense engine business. Although General Motors, Mack and International Harvester all produced diesel engines for the trucks they sold, even they were prepared to install Cummins diesels if the customer specified. And more and more customers did that. In addition to the Cummins engines' reputation for quality and endurance, the Company had stressed after-sale service, establishing a network of repair and service facilities across the country. The key to keeping trucks on the road — and productive — is simple maintenance and prompt repair, particularly of the engines. Truckers found that their maintenance and service problems were greatly eased by focusing on one line of engine, and most often the engine of choice came from Cummins. By the 1950s, the Company owned 60 percent of the market for engines in heavy duty trucks.

That market grew dramatically during the Second World War, and even more so as the country developed the interstate highway system in the 1950s and 1960s, encouraging the trucking industry to compete aggressively with the railroads for long distance freight hauling. The Company grew along with that market and, in the late 1950s, sales had reached $100 million. Twenty years later, by 1979, sales had grown to $1.8 billion.

Mr. Irwin led the Company through the Second World War and the expansion of the 1950s and 1960s. In 1969, Henry Schacht, graduate of Harvard's MBA program — class of 1962 — was appointed President. Mr. Schacht became Chairman of the Board and Chief Executive Officer in 1977 when James Henderson, another Harvard MBA, became President and Chief Operating Officer. Henderson described the company's growth explosion:

> "The name of the game in the 1970s was capacity. We couldn't build plants fast enough to keep up with demand, so we went on a plant buying spree. Of course, we tried to reduce costs, but still basically thought of them as a pass-through. We figured out our costs, added a profit margin, and that was our price, and the customer was only too glad to pay. Our problem was adding the capacity to keep up with demand."[3]

Even as that expansion was under way, Cummins realized that the big engine market (10 liter and up) was only about 10 percent of the total diesel market, and began a $1 billion investment in the development of medium and small diesel engines. That expansion in the product line was successful (although somewhat costly) and sales reached $2.4 billion in 1984. With all of that expansion, the Company's reputation for quality continued to grow. The owner of an Ohio steel hauling company, with 140 trucks, said: "We don't expect any major work on a Cummins engine until 600,000 miles, or about 100,000 more than most other brands." The company took great pride in its production quality, reporting that only about 1 percent of the engines that come off the line has to be reworked, fully one-third the rejection rate of the industry average.[4]

As a manufacturer of capital goods, the Company was subject to the ebb and flow of the economy, and there had been good years and not so good years. Still, Cummins had managed to turn in a remarkable history of profitability, and the $58 million profit earned in 1979 gave the Company 43 straight years in the black. Those profits were not wrung out of the workers or the community. On the contrary, Cummins was seen as an extraordinary place to work, and the company/worker relationship inspired a great deal of loyalty to the company and pride in the

---

[3]Charles R. Morris, *The Coming Global Boom.* (Bantam Books: NY, 1990), p. 48.

[4]Both citations from Johnson, "With Its Spirit Shaken."

product. The Company repeatedly invested in the communities where it had factories. Perhaps the best known of those programs was the agreement the Company made with its home city: It was understood that the Company would pay the architects' fees for any municipal project or church or other nonprofit building venture in the community. Over time, the Company invested over $9 million in the city's buildings in this way and, as a result, Columbus, Indiana, is a living museum of some of the finest public architecture in the country.

Earnings fluctuated in the early 1980s, as the Company worked on the expansion of its product lines and suffered through the "stagflation" of the Carter administration. The Company registered a small loss in 1980, a profit of $99.9 million in 1981 and broke even in 1982 and 1983. Earnings in 1984 were back on track with a record profit of $188 million, or $19.76 a share.

Attacks and Counter Attacks

The company's market dominance was daunting to many competitors; however in 1984 Cummins heard that some long time customers were going to be testing mid-sized engines from Japanese manufacturers and that those engines were reportedly to be priced from 10 percent to 40 percent lower than comparable Cummins' engines.

Henry Schacht reacted quickly: He said, "We were going to lose 20–30 percent of our business. With the Board's full backing, overnight, we decided to lower prices 20 percent to 40 percent."[5] He explained, "If you don't give the Japanese a price advantage, they can't get in. Besides, if we didn't lower prices, our truck manufacturing customer couldn't compete either. So not only would we lose share of market from him, he would lose share of market from the now-deregulated truckers. We would get a double hit."[6]

To confront this threat to its market position, the Company adopted a strategy that might almost be described as Japanese: It established pricing and service levels that were designed to protect market share as a first priority, and then went about restructuring its operations to reduce costs. And, the company continued to invest heavily in R&D (over $100 million a year). Those R&D programs had three major objectives:

- First, to improve the fuel economy of the entire line, which was sure to be important to truck buyers as diesel fuel caught up with gasoline in per gallon cost;
- Second, to improve emission controls, which were sure to be important as a competitive advantage as air quality regulations, here and abroad, became more stringent.
- Third, to reduce manufacturing costs by 30 percent while maintaining the facilities in Columbus.

As to the cost objective, Henderson explained, "What we found was that the Japanese had approximately a 30 percent cost advantage on us, even absorbing the costs of exporting."[7] He also observed "One of the things that nobody's cost system tracks is overhead. A lot of production costs, like producing for inventory or just the cost of moving a product around unnecessarily end up being buried in overhead."[8] The Company had been proud of its efficient operations, and originally saw the cost difference as insurmountable. Nonetheless, they set out to reduce overhead (adopting flexible manufacturing techniques and just-in-time inventory programs), material costs (changing from an adversarial relationship with its suppliers to a long-term, jointly-engineered, single source program) and personnel costs.

---

[5]"Mr. Rust Belt," *BusinessWeek*, October 17, 1988, p. 72.

[6]G. Smith, "The Yankee Samurai," *Forbes*, July 14, 1986, p. 82.

[7]"People as a Competitive Advantage," presentation by J.A. Henderson at the Silver Bay Management Conference, July 11, 1990.

[8]Smith, "The Yankee Samurai."

Through consolidation, layoffs, and plant reorganization, the Company reduced factory space by 25 percent and reduced the labor force by 30 percent. Those employee layoffs were traumatic for the Company, for the city and for Mr. Schacht personally. He told a reporter that he was saddened [when he passed by the unemployment office] to know that many of those people were put there by him. He said, "It would be easier if they ranted and raved. But they make it hard by saying 'I wish things could be different.' I wish I could help."[9] Product costs did come down 22 percent, an impressive achievement but short of the announced goal of 30 percent.

During the later half of the 1980s, Cummins' sales continued to grow, but margins shrank and R&D costs doubled. Reported results ranged from disappointing to frightening. But Schacht pressed on. In the 1987 annual report to stockholders the company summarized its strategy as follows:

> We have pursued a four-pronged strategy which is changing what we do and how we do it. The four major elements are:
>
> 1. Lower prices of our new products to be world competitive, before we achieve targeted cost levels.
> 2. Redesign for higher output, longer life, and greater efficiency the heavy-duty diesel engine, and simultaneously enter the medium- and light-duty diesel engine markets.
> 3. Change our concepts of cost, quality, and delivery to become more responsive to our customers.
> 4. Restructure the company into four business groups: Engine Business, Components, Power Systems, and Information and Services.

The strategy worked, at least as far as the company's market position was concerned. The Japanese manufacturers did not gain any significant foothold in the diesel truck market in the U.S. The slippage of the dollar may have helped somewhat, but it seems reasonable to conclude that customer loyalty helped a great deal, given Cummins' long history of good service and top quality, and the new competitive prices. Further, Cummins' new computer-controlled emission management system was clearly a world leader. That system meant that trucks with the Company's engines could meet the 1988 EPA standards, even though the federal government had been pressed (by other manufacturers) into delaying the effectiveness of those standards until 1990. Also, the Company's smaller engines, which had been under development during this time, were introduced in 1992 and those engines were said to be capable of meeting the 1997 emission standards for light trucks. Similar emission control accomplishments were announced for buses and for off-the-road construction equipment.

Financial Results Deteriorate

Unfortunately, the Company's counterattack carried considerable cost to the shareholders. Results were beginning to recover from the recession of the early 1980s when the defensive battle began. Cummins earned $188 million in 1984, but lost money or broke even in all of the years 1985 to 1990. In 1986, losses were $107 million and, in 1990, losses were $165 million. The stock price went from $44 in 1984 and 1985, to $15 and $16 in 1990 and 1991. Exhibit 1 summarizes operating results and stock prices for the years 1982 to 1994. And, in its 1989 story on the company, the *Wall Street Journal* provided this chart:

[9]Johnson, "With Its Spirit Shaken."

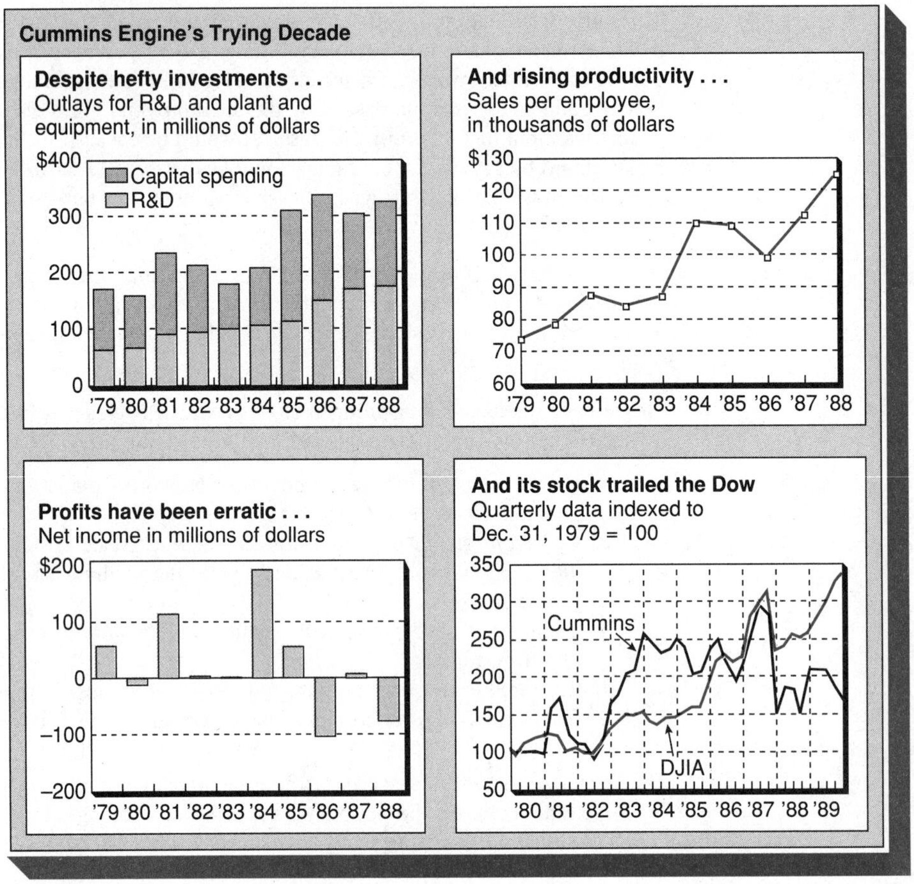

Source: Reprinted by permission of *The Wall Street Journal,* © 1989 Dow Jones & Company, Inc. All Rights Reserved Worldwide.

The five-year period, 1986 to 1990, was extraordinarily difficult for the Company. In addition to carrying the cost of the pricing conflict and the development efforts which were designed to protect its market position, those years reflected the impact of several peaks and valleys in the economy. Worse, the Company made several management errors which were reflected in the results.

- The new pollution-control system, which had consumed so much R&D effort, was a true technological breakthrough and paved the way for later successes. However, the introduction of that system, on engines sold in 1988, was probably hurried. To cover the normal and extended warranty costs required on those engines, the Company took charges of $220 million and $160 million against earnings in 1989 and 1990, respectively.
- Also, orders surged in 1987 and 1988, just as the company was implementing its restructuring program, laying off workers and closing older, less efficient plants. Cummins apparently had misread the early signs of that surge and was not prepared for the depth of the demand. Rather than turn orders away to the competition, the Company ran its plants on overtime, weakening already battered margins.
- While the Company was concentrating on the threat from the Japanese, G.M. sold a controlling interest in its subsidiary, Detroit Diesel, to the Penske interests. That newly revitalized company capitalized on Cummins' distractions and captured a significant piece of the diesel market.

- Finally, in 1990, just as the Company was digesting the costs of its restructuring, the economy went into a tail spin and orders fell off again. There was one six month period at the end of 1989 and the beginning of 1990 where the Company's newly streamlined operations were able to capitalize on the demands of an ordinary market and show how effective the Company could be. But it was a short spring. Exhibit 2 details sales, operating income, and net income for the quarters of 1988, 1989, and 1990.

The Company's Attempts to Communicate its Program

The business press was generally complimentary toward the company's efforts to beat the international competition at its own game. Schacht took the lead in selling the Company's story to the street. *Business Week* described the Company's campaign saying, "Bearing stacks of statistics and flip charts to support their strategy, Schacht and his lieutenants regularly huddle with analysts and investors."[10]

Schacht also went on the lecture circuit urging Wall Street to maintain a longer range perspective. *Forbes* quotes Schacht as saying, "We built this country on long-term money not on quarterly returns. The demands of being globally competitive mean the pay back is over years, not months."[11] The Company was a member of the Council on Competitiveness which sponsored research into ways to make American industry more competitive in the world economy. One of the Council's projects was summarized in a *Harvard Business Review* article which pointed out that institutional investors now accounted for 60 percent of the ownership of all stocks and that they were increasingly short-term holders. The average holding period for common stocks had slipped from seven years in 1970 to two years in the early 1990's. The explosive interest in indexing investment portfolios exacerbated the short-term problem.[12] As to the application of those issues specifically to Cummins, Schacht said, "We'll live with the short term pressures because we're determined to be builders."[13]

That same "building" theme was carried over to the annual report to shareholders. The following comments are from the Presidents' letters, in each of the respective years:

> **1987**
> We continue to believe we are on the right track. Progress is substantial and sustainable . . . We want to go faster and hope to do so, but it will probably take us a bit longer than we thought at this time last year — not too surprising given the size and the scope of the undertaking.
>
> **1988**
> While it has taken longer to achieve than we had hoped, we believe we now have completed the essential elements of our program . . . Now is the time to capitalize on these efforts and to begin to earn our targeted return on the investments put in place . . . 1989 should be a much improved year.
>
> **1989**
> The 1980s were turbulent and challenging. We implemented our long-term strategy during this period. We believed then and believe now that this is the best way to maximize long-term value for the shareholder and all constituent groups of the company . . . the company is well positioned for the decade of the 1990s.

---

[10]"Mr. Rust Belt," p. 72.

[11]"A Very Japanese Solution," *Forbes*, August 6, 1990, pp. 38–39.

[12]The research sponsored by the Council was summarized in Michael E. Porter, "Capital Disadvantage: America's Failing Capital Investment System," *Harvard Business Review*, September–October, 1992, p. 65.

[13]"Mr. Rust Belt," p. 72.

EXHIBIT 1

Cummins Engine Co., Inc.
Twelve-Year Statistical History

(in thousands except per share data)	1982	1983	1984	1985	1986	1987	1988	1989	1990	1991	1992	1993	1994
Net sales	$1,588	$1,605	$2,326	$2,146	$2,304	$2,767	$3,310	$3,520	$3,462	$3,406	$3,749	$4,247	$4,737
Gross profit	429	439	730	569	546	696	640	661	605	629	843	1,037	1,187
R&D expenses	78	78	87	93	125	149	125	140	144	148	180	210	238
Other expenses	372	364	399	415	578	513	562	500	603	527	587	622	656
Pretax income	(21)	(3)	244	61	(157)	34	(47)	21	(142)	46	76	205	293
After tax income (before extraordinary items)	$8	$5	$188	$50	($107)	$14	($63)	($6)	($165)	$(66)	$67	$183	$253
Per share:*													
Earnings (before extraordinary items)	$0.11	$0.18	$9.88	$2.64	($5.23)	$0.28	($3.36)	($0.76)	($7.24)	($2.48)	$1.77	$4.95	$6.11
Dividends	1.00	1.00	1.03	1.10	1.10	1.10	1.10	1.10	1.10	0.35	0.10	0.20	0.625
Book value	29.09	26.69	34.41	37.15	30.95	32.50	27.52	19.89	18.69	17.14	11.21	18.40	25.79
PP&E additions	$123	$76	$109	$198	$213	$133	$151	$138	$147	$124	$139	$174	$238
No. of employees	18.9	18.6	21.0	19.6	23.4	24.5	26.1	25.1	24.9	22.9	23.4	23.6	25.6
Share price:													
High	$25	$41	$44	$44	$39	$47	$34	$36	$27	$27	$40	$54	$57
Low	13	24	31	29	26	20	22	24	15	16	27	38	36

*Per Share data reflects the 2 for 1 split in 1993

EXHIBIT 2

Cummins Engine Co., Inc.
Twelve Quarters, 1988–1990

(in thousands except per share data)	1988				1989				1990			
	1st	2nd	3rd	4th	1st	2nd	3rd	4th	1st	2nd	3rd	4th
Net sales	$798	$834	$808	$869	$919	$928	$807	$856	$861	$871	$830	$899
Gross Margin	194	199	174	189	221	225	153	190	171	178	119	136
After Tax Income (before extraordinary items)	$8	$2	($18)	($55)	$20	$24	($40)	($10)	$9	$6	($56)	($124)
Share Price:												
High	$30	$31	$28	$34	$34	$36	$33	$29	$26	$28	$27	$20
Low	22	25	23	24	30	32	28	24	22	23	17	16

Unfortunately, the Company's deteriorating results began to wear away at the Company's (and Mr. Schacht's) credibility. In a 1986 *Barron's* article, Schacht claimed that the restructuring efforts would begin to pay off by late 1987 or 1988. The Company earned $14 million on sales of $2.7 billion in 1987 and lost $63 million on sales of $3.3 billion in 1988. Later, he pointed to 1989 as the year when all of the work would begin to bear fruit, but the Company barely broke even. As a final blow, the economic downturn of 1990 pushed the Company into a loss of $165 million. A quick comparison of the forecast-type statements contained in the President's letters from the Cummins' annual reports for a period of years to the comments on results achieved in the following year, can be summarized as:

Forecast	Results
1984 "strong performance"	"record sales and profits"
1985 "more of the same"	"market declined sharply"
1986 "increasing improvement"	"short of future profits"
1987 "beginning to restore profit"	"accepted lower profit"
1988 "forecasting not reliable"	[net loss of $63 million]
1989 "much improved year"	[net loss of $6 million]

Indeed, the analyst community began to express its impatience. A Prudential Bache analyst had this to say:

> "Cummins has been in a long-term mode 10 years . . . Schacht sounds great but at some point there has to be a payout for all of this spending."[14]

And, an analyst at Deutsche Bank said:

> "I've been hearing they're going to have things under control on a quarter by quarter basis for a long time. The target seems to recede into the future."

Regardless of the losses, the company continued its investment in R&D and its support of charities. Employment went from 19,600 in 1985 to a high of 26,100 in 1989 with a modest decline to 23,900 in 1991. Perhaps reflecting some of the frustration of the financial community, one astute observer noted "Cummins is one big, social slush fund . . . an incredibly naive

[14]Johnston, "With Its Spirit Shaken."

attitude exists at the company, and I think a lot of people involved with it are going to get their hearts broken."[15]

The Raiders Attack

In 1990, when the stock was trading at $32 ($8 below book value) Nomura Securities calculated that Cummins might be worth $180 a share to a European truck manufacturer such as Volvo or Renault. It seemed clear that the stock was undervalued, but given Cummins' recent history, no one was blaming the market.

All of this controversy and the depressed stock price attracted the international raiders. In 1989 Hanson Plc purchased a 9.8 percent interest in the company. The Irwin Miller family, held a 2 percent stake in Cummins, subsequently purchased the Hanson stake, paying a $5 million premium over the then-current price — a transaction described as "greenmail with a twist." The Company reacquired those shares from the family, exchanging 10 percent convertible preferred stock in return.

Later in 1989, Brierly Investments purchased a 14.9 percent interest in the Company. Brierly, a New Zealand investment company, was known for its skill in extracting greenmail. This time however, Cummins fought back. The Company sued under the takeover statutes, arguing that Brierly had fraudulently stated their purpose for buying the stock. Also, 1989 third quarter results were a disaster, and the stock fell dramatically putting financial pressure on Brierly. A standoff was reached in which Brierly reduced its holdings to 8 percent and was forced to stand by and hope for some recovery from its investment.

Patient Capital Arrives

In the face of the market's impatience, the Company went in search of an alternative. In 1990, 4 million new shares were issued in a private placement: Tenneco (owner of J.I. Case) and Ford each purchased a 10.8 percent interest in the company, and Kubota purchased a 5.4 percent interest. Those shares were sold at $62.50 at a time when the quoted market price was $51.25. Each investor-company promised to hold their shares for six years and — in that period — vote for the designated slate of directors. The 1990 annual report to stockholders cited this stock sale as the most important accomplishment of the year, with these words:

> This investment was made at a premium to the market price of the stock and reduced our debt-to-capital ratio, increased our book value, provided three long-term investors in Cummins whose presence lends stability to our shareholder base and reassured constituents who had grown apprehensive about our ability to continue our commitment to and investments in the business.
>
> The importance of this investment by these knowledgeable, worldwide companies cannot be overstated. Their vote of confidence at a time of considerable stress and turmoil means more than any company statement of competitive advantage and makes this event much more significant than the impact of the money involved.

McDonald and Company, described the stock sale as creating a "long term partnership" and suggested some implications of that partnership, with the following conclusions:

> SHORT TERM: 1) It virtually eliminates the possibility of a takeover of Cummins and thus investors' focus gets reverted to fundamental value versus the break-up valuation. 2) The number of shares increases to 14.9 million. 3) The financials of the company improve dramatically. The debt-to-total capital ratio drops from the

[15] Johnson, "With Its Spirit Shaken."

mid-40's to 27 percent, the book value increases to $46.75, and even during the current tight cashflow conditions, the dividend appears assured. 4) After months of worrying about the extrinsic concerns, management finally is able to focus on its core business and attempt to prove once and for all whether they are truly capable of ever realizing Cummins potential.

LONG TERM: 1) Reaffirming its confidence in the abilities of its new partner, Ford announced that it will source its medium-duty truck engines from Cummins. Currently, Ford sources these engines internally. The timing and size of the business has not been finalized, but considering that Ford sells over 40,000 medium trucks, the contract could amount to over $200 million. Cummins will source these engines through its CDC plant after incurring minimum capital investment and has the potential of significantly improving the profitability of its mid-range products. 2) The relationship with Tenneco gets strengthened. Cummins and Tenneco jointly own the CDC plant that manufactures the mid-range engines. The benefits of Tenneco's capital infusion are difficult to quantify and may reflect its concerns about insuring against any disruption in the supply of engines for its farm equipment. 3) The infusion of capital from Kubota is geared towards enhancing the breadth of the engine offering and improves business opportunities in Europe. Cummins is undoubtedly the world leader in heavy duty engines while Kubota is a leading producer of small engines. The relationship will also extend to a possible joint venture in Europe involving the manufacture of engines at a Cummins' plant in the U.K. Again, the financial benefits are yet to be quantified.[16]

Epilogue

The Company lost $65 million in 1991 on flat sales, but earned $67 million in 1992 as sales moved up 10 percent. All four quarters of 1992 produced positive operating earnings, culminating with fourth quarter earnings of $29.5 million on sales of $1 billion. In 1993 — the Company's 75th anniversary year — sales increased 13 percent while earnings jumped dramatically to $177 million, or almost $10.00 a share. The stock began trading in the $90s and, in October, 1993, the stock was split two-for-one. In 1994 sales grew again by almost 12 percent and earnings jumped to $252 million, or $6.11 a share, post split.

Results were better than satisfactory through the first half of 1995, but faltered in the third quarter: Sales continued to grow but margins were stressed as the market for heavy duty engines came under pressure. In October, 1995, the Company announced that it was considering the consolidation of certain assets and was evaluating plans to reduce its world wide work force by approximately 2,000 people. The Company earned $5.64 a share in 1995, after a charge for that consolidation, and the stock closed the year at $37. However, S.G. Warburg initiated coverage of the Company in early 1996, and concluded that the stock could be at $67 by late 1997. The Warburg report said,

> Cummins has made great strides in rationalizing assets and expenses, comparable to Caterpillar, Inc. . . . acknowledged as one of the world's best manufacturing companies. Cummins has made substantial improvements in terms of SG&A as a percentage of sales, working capital as a percentage of sales, total capital employed per dollar of sales, fixed asset utilization, relative sales growth and stability of profitability. These positive changes are not widely recognized in the financial markets, which capitalizes Cummins with a deep cyclical P/E.[17]

[16]Research report by Gurudutt M. Baliga, published by McDonald & Company (Cleveland, OH), August 30, 1990. Reprinted with permission.

[17]Research report by Barry B. Bannister, CFA published by S.G. Warburg & Co. Inc. February 16, 1996.

After the Warburg report was published, the stock moved up once again, to trade in the lower $40s, closing February, 1996 at $42.

In early 1995, in accordance with a previously announced succession plan, Henry Schacht retired as Chairman of the Board and was succeeded by his long term associate, Jim Henderson. J. Irwin Miller paid tribute to Mr. Schacht, saying "He has offered on every occasion a personal example of the highest commitment and selfless leadership." And, Mr. Miller also observed, "He understands that the effort is never ending, a race with no finish line."[18]

Required:

Put yourself in the position of Cummin's chief financial officer and prepare the arguments you would make to convince Ford, Tenneco, and Kubota to purchase the newly issued stock which you will offer them. How would you justify a premium for those stock purchases in excess of the then current market price?

---

[18]Quoted in the Company's 1st Quarter Report to Shareholders, 1995.

GLOSSARY

Accelerated Cost Recovery System (ACRS) A method to depreciate tangible assets placed in service between 1981 and 1986 for U.S. income tax purposes.

Accelerated depreciation A cost allocation method in which depreciation deductions are largest in an asset's earlier years but decrease over time.

Account (T-account) An accounting information file usually associated with the general ledger, which appears as follows:

Account

Debit side	Credit side

Accounting A language used by businesspeople to communicate the financial status of their enterprise to interested parties.

Accounting cycle The process of analyzing a transaction and then journalizing it, followed by posting it to the ledger accounts, and then preparing a trial balance, any necessary adjusting entries, financial statements, and closing entries.

Accounting equation Assets = Equities; Assets = Liabilities + Owners' equity. An equation depicting the balance sheet or statement of financial position.

Accounting exposure (risk) The hazard of recognizing and reporting foreign exchange gains (losses) in the income statement for a given period.

Accounting period The time period, usually a quarter or one year, to which accounting reports are related.

Accounting policies The specific accounting principles and practices adopted by a company to report its financial results.

Accounting Principles Board (APB) An organization of the AICPA that established GAAP during the 1957–1973 period; some of the APB's opinions remain in force today.

Accounting Standards Committee (ASC) The principal accounting standards-setting organization in the United Kingdom until 1990; issued statements of standard accounting practice or SSAPs.

Accounts payable (trade payable) Amounts owed to suppliers for merchandise purchased on credit but not yet paid for; normally classified as a current liability.

Accounts receivable (trade receivable) Amounts due to a company from customers who purchased goods or services on credit; payment is normally expected in 30, 60, or 90 days.

Accounts receivable turnover ratio A measure of the effectiveness of receivable management calculated as net credit sales for the period divided by the average balance in accounts receivable.

Accrual method (accrual basis of accounting) An accounting measurement system that records the financial effects of transactions when a business transaction occurs without regard to the timing of the cash effects of the transaction.

Accumulated depreciation (allowance for depreciation) A contra asset account deducted from the acquisition cost of property, plant, and equipment that represents the portion of the original cost of an asset that has been allocated to prior accounting periods.

Active investment An intercorporate investment by an investor-company that allows the investor to exercise influence or control over the operations of the investee-company.

Additional paid-in-capital Amounts paid by shareholders in excess of the minimum amount required for the shares to be fully paid (that is, par or stated value); also known as *paid-in capital in excess of par value* and *share premium reserve*.

Adjusting entries Journal entries recorded to update or correct the accounts in the general ledger.

Administrative expense A general operating expense, such as depreciation on a company's headquarters building, associated with the overall management of the company; a period expense.

Advance Corporation Tax (ACT) A British tax set at 25 percent in 1995 and paid by corporations based on the level of dividends expected to be distributed to shareholders.

Affiliated company A company in which an investor-company holds an equity investment in excess of 20 percent of the voting capital stock.

Aging of accounts receivables A method of accounting for uncollectible trade receivables in which an estimate of the bad debts expense is determined by classifying the specific receivable balances into age categories and then applying probability estimates of noncollection.

Aktiebolag (AB) A limited liability company in Sweden.

Aktiengesellschaft (AG) A publicly held corporation in Germany.

All-current method A method of translating foreign financial statements by which all assets and liabilities are translated at the current (that is, as of the statement preparation date) exchange rate; also called *current method.*

Allocation principle An accounting principle that permits the financial effects of business transactions to be assigned to or spread over multiple accounting periods.

Allowance for Decline in Value of Inventory A contra asset account deducted from the cost basis of ending inventory to reflect the write-down of inventory to its replacement value under the lower-of-cost-or-market method.

Allowance for Change in Value of Marketable Securities A contra asset (addendum) account deducted from (added to) the cost basis of marketable securities; represents the unrealized change in a portfolio of securities resulting from the application of the mark-to-market method.

Allowance for Uncollectible Accounts (allowance for bad debts) A contra asset account deducted from accounts or notes receivable; represents the portion of the outstanding receivables balance whose collection is doubtful.

American depositary receipt (ADR) A security issued by a bank or other recognized trustee representing an actual shareholding in a foreign company; these beneficial ownership shares are issued to avoid problems relating to the collection of dividends denominated in a foreign currency and to facilitate rapid ownership transfer; also referred to as *stock depositary receipts.*

American Institute of Certified Public Accountants (AICPA) The national professional association of certified public accountants (CPAs) in the United States.

Amortization A cost allocation process that spreads the cost of an intangible asset over the asset's expected useful life.

Annual report The report prepared by a company at year end for its stockholders and other interested parties. It frequently includes a letter to the shareholders from the chairperson of the board, management's discussion and analysis of financial performance, and a variety of financial highlights in addition to the basic financial statements. It also includes the auditor's report in which the independent accountants express an opinion as to the fairness of the financial data presented in the financial statements.

Annuity A payment, or a receipt, occurring every period for a set number of periods (for example, interest expense or interest income on a debt instrument).

Antidilutive security A security that, if converted or assumed to be converted into common stock, causes the level of earnings per share to increase.

Asset management The effective utilization of a company's revenue-producing assets; a measure of management's ability to effectively utilize a company's assets to produce income.

Asset turnover The rate at which sales (or revenues) are generated from a given level of assets; a measure of a company's effectiveness in generating revenues from the assets at its disposal, calculated as net sales divided by average total assets.

Assets Tangible and intangible resources of an enterprise that are expected to provide it future economic benefits.

Associated company One that is not a legal subsidiary of another company (control is less than 50+ percent) but in which the other company exercises significant influence (presumably at least a 20 percent shareholding).

Audit A process of investigating the adequacy of a company's system of internal controls, the company's consistent use of generally accepted accounting principles, and the presence of material errors or mistakes in the company's accounting data.

Auditor's opinion A report to a company's shareholders and the board of directors issued by an independent auditor summarizing his or her findings with regard to the company's financial statements. The four types of opinions that may be issued are clean or unqualified, qualified, adverse, and disclaimer.
Authorized shares The total number of shares of capital stock that are authorized to be sold under a company's charter of incorporation.
Available-for-sale investments Securities owned by a company where management's intent is not to trade them on a frequent basis but to sell if and when they deem best.
Average cost method An inventory cost-flow method that assigns the average cost of available finished goods to units sold and, thus, to cost of goods sold.
Average days'-inventory-on-hand ratio A measure of the effectiveness of inventory management calculated as 365 days divided by the inventory turnover ratio; a measure of the appropriateness of current inventory levels given current sales volume.
Average receivable collection period A measure of the effectiveness of accounts receivable management calculated by dividing the receivable turnover ratio into 365 days.
Bad debt An account receivable considered to be uncollectible.
Bad debt expense An estimate (under the allowance method) of the dollar amount of accounts receivable that will eventually prove to be uncollectible; the actual bad debts that are written off if the direct write-off method is used.
Balance The difference between the total left-side (debit) entries and the total right-side (credit) entries made in an account.
Balance sheet (statement of financial position) An accounting statement describing, as of a specific date, the assets, liabilities, and owners' equity of an enterprise.
Betterment An expenditure that extends the useful life or productive capability of an asset and that is capitalized to the balance sheet as an asset.
Blocked funds risk The hazard that a government will restrict the flow of funds either into or out of a given locale.
Board of directors A group of individuals elected by a company's shareholders to oversee the overall management of the company (that is, a board of advisers for the company's managers).
Bond (debenture) An interest-bearing obligation issued by a company to various creditors, usually in amounts of $1,000 or $5,000 and payable at some future maturity date.
Bond discount The amount by which the net proceeds of a bond issue are less than the amount of the principal that must be repaid at maturity date. The amount of the bond discount must be amortized over the life of the bond, thereby making the bond's effective rate of interest greater than its coupon rate of interest.
Bond indenture The document in which the details associated with a bond issue are specified.
Bond payable A financial instrument sold in the capital markets, carrying a specified rate of interest (coupon rate) and a specified repayment date (maturity date); usually classified as a long-term liability.
Bond premium The amount by which the net proceeds of a bond issue exceed the amount of the bond principal that must be repaid at maturity date. The amount of the bond premium that must be amortized over the life of the bond, thereby making its effective rate of interest less than its coupon rate of interest.
Book value (per share) The dollar amount of the net assets of a company on a per share of common stock basis; calculated as (total assets minus total liabilities) divided by the number of outstanding shares of class A common stock.
Book value (of an asset) The original cost of an asset less any accumulated depreciation (depletion or amortization) taken to date; also known as *carrying value*.
Borsa Valori di Milano The Italian stock exchange in Milan, Italy.
Bovespa The São Paulo stock exchange, the largest stock exchange in Brazil (Bolsa de Valores de São Paulo).
Brazilian commercial code A principal source of accounting and auditing standards in Brazil along with income tax laws and the CVM.
Business combination When one or more businesses are brought together into one accounting entity but not necessarily into one legal entity.

Callable debt Bonds or other obligations that may be legally retired before maturity at the discretion of the debtor-company.
Capital Another term for owners' equity; also used to mean the total assets of an organization.
Capital budgeting The process of proposing and selecting from among a variety of investment proposals or certain long-lived assets to be acquired. This process frequently considers the net present value of projected cash flows for proposed investments.
Capital expenditure An expenditure for the purchase of a noncurrent asset, usually property, plant, or equipment.
Capital intensity ratio A measure of a company's operating leverage, calculated as fixed assets divided by total assets.
Capitalization (of an expenditure) The process of assigning value to a balance sheet account— for example a capitalized asset (that is, a leased asset) or a capitalized liability (such as a lease liability).
Capitalization (of a company) The composition of a company's long-term financing, specifically, owners' equity and long-term debt.
Capital lease A noncancelable lease obligation accounted for as a liability on the balance sheet; a lease agreement in which the risks and rewards of asset ownership are passed (either formally or informally) to the lessee.
Capital stock A certificate representing an ownership interest in an enterprise. See also *common stock* and *preferred stock*.
Cash A current asset account representing the amount of money on hand or in the bank.
Cash basis of accounting An accounting measurement system that records the financial effects of business transactions when the underlying event has a cash effect.
Cash discount An amount, usually 2 percent of the gross purchase price, that a buyer may deduct from the final price of an asset if cash is remitted within the discount period, usually 10 days of purchase.
Cash dividend payout A measure of the cash return to common shareholders, calculated as the cash dividend per common share divided by the basic earnings per share.
Cash dividend yield A measure of the cash return to common shareholders, calculated as the cash dividend per common share divided by the average market price per common share.
Cash equivalents Bank deposits, usually in the form of certificates of deposit, whose withdrawal may be restricted but whose maturity is expected in the current accounting period.
Cash flow adequacy ratio A cash flow ratio calculated as the cash flow from operations divided by the sum of capital expenditures, dividends paid, and long-term debt repayment; indicates the extent to which cash flows from operations are sufficient to cover asset replacement and capital carrying costs.
Cash flow from operations (CFFO) A measure of the net cash flows from transactions involving sales of goods or services and the acquisition of inputs used to provide the goods or services sold; the excess of cash receipts over cash disbursements relating to the operations of a company for a given period; net income calculated on a cash basis.
CFFO to current liabilities ratio A measure of firm liquidity, calculated as the cash flow from operations (CFFO) divided by average current liabilities; reflects the short-term debt coverage provided by current cash flows from operations.
CFFO to interest charges ratio A measure of solvency, calculated as the cash flow from operations divided by interest charges; reflects the extent to which interest charges are covered by current cash flows from operations.
CFFO to total liabilities ratio A measure of solvency, calculated as the cash flow from operations divided by average total liabilities; reflects the extent to which current cash flow from operations is sufficient to satisfy both long-term and short-term obligations.
Certified public accountant (CPA) An accountant who has passed the Uniform CPA Examination prepared by the American Institute of CPAs and who has met prescribed requirements of the state issuing the CPA certificate.
Chaebol Korean business conglomerates (similar to Japan's *keiretsu*), numbering approximately 30, that dominate that country's economy (such as Samsung, Hyundai, Lucky Goldstar, and Daewoo).
Chartered accountant (CA) A certified public accountant in the U.K.

Charter of incorporation A legal document creating a corporate entity; specifies (among other things) the number and type of shares of capital stock that the corporate entity can sell.
Chart of accounts A list of the general ledger accounts used by an enterprise in its accounting system.
Chusik Hoesa A Korean joint-stock company formed by seven or more investors with a minimum capitalization of W50 million (approximately $62,000).
Class B common stock A form of common stock that usually carries a lower voting power and lower dividend return than Class A common stock.
Classified balance sheet A balance sheet that delineates the assets and liabilities as current and noncurrent.
Closing entries Accounting data entries prepared at the end of an accounting period; designed to close or set equal to zero the temporary accounts.
Collateral The value of various assets used as security for various debts, usually bank borrowings, that will be transferred to a creditor if the obligation is not fully paid.
Comissao de Valores Mobiliários (CVM) The securities and exchange commission of Brazil.
Commercial Code of Japan Dates to 1899; provides general rules for the valuation of assets and liabilities, provision of reserves, and the accounting for legal and capital reserves.
Commissione Nazionale per le Societa e la Borsa (CONSOB) The Italian equivalent of the U.S. Securities and Exchange Commission; regulates listing requirements and accounting disclosures for publicly held Italian companies.
Commitment A type of contingent liability in which the value of the future obligation is known but that is not currently an obligation because various future events or conditions have not transpired or are currently satisfied.
Common equity share of operating earnings (CSOE) A measure of the proportion of a company's operating earnings allocable to common shareholders.
Common shareholders' capital structure leverage ratio (CSL) A measure of a company's financial leverage, calculated as average total assets divided by average common equity.
Common-size balance sheet A balance sheet in which all account balances are expressed as a percentage of total assets or total equities.
Common-size financial statement Financial statements in which the dollar amounts are expressed as a percentage of some common statement item (for example, a common-size income statement might express all items as a percentage of sales).
Common-size income statements An income statement in which all revenue and expense items are expressed as a percentage of net sales.
Common stock A form of capital stock that usually carries the right to vote on corporate issues; a senior equity security.
Common stock equivalent A security that is not a common stock but that contains provisions to enable its holder to become a common stockholder.
Companies Act of 1985 Current British regulation governing the formation of corporations in that country.
Compensating balances The percentage of a line of credit or of a loan that a bank requires a borrower to keep on deposit at the bank. Its amount has the effect of increasing the effective interest rate of any amount borrowed.
Completed contract A revenue recognition method in which project or contract revenues are unrecognized until the project or contract is substantially completed.
Compound interest A method of calculating interest by which interest is figured on both the principal of a loan and any interest previously earned but not distributed.
Conservatism principle An accounting principle that stipulates that when there is a choice between two approaches to record an economic event, the one that produces the least favorable yet realistic effect on net income or assets should be adopted.
Consignment Inventory placed with a retailer for sale to a final consumer but not sold to the retailer; title to the inventory is retained by the manufacturer until a final sale occurs.
Consistency principle An accounting principle underlying the preparation of financial statements that stipulates that an enterprise should, when possible, use the same set of GAAP from one accounting period to the next.

Consolidated financial statements Financial statements prepared to reflect the operations and financial condition of a parent company and its wholly or majority-owned subsidiaries.
Consolidated reporting A reporting approach in which the financial statements of the parent and subsidiary companies are combined to form one set of financial statements.
Contingent asset An asset that may arise in the future if certain events occur.
Contingent liability A liability that may arise in the future if certain events occur.
Contra account (contra asset, contra liability, contra owners' equity) An account that is subtracted from a related account; for example, accumulated depreciation is subtracted from the Building or Equipment account; other examples include the Allowance for Uncollectible accounts, the Bond Discount account, and the Treasury Stock account.
Contributed capital The sum of the capital stock accounts and the capital in excess of par (or stated) value accounts. Also called *paid-in capital*.
Convenience statement A set of foreign financial statements translated into the language and the currency of another country.
Convenience translation A set of foreign financial statements translated into the language (not currency) of another country.
Conversion The exchange of convertible bonds or convertible preferred stock for a predetermined quantity of common stock.
Conversion ratio The exchange ratio used to determine the number of common shares that will be issued on conversion of a convertible bond or a convertible preferred stock.
Convertible debt (bond) An obligation or debt security exchangeable, or convertible, into the common stock of a company at a prespecified conversion (or exchange) rate.
Convertible preferred stock A preferred stock that is exchangeable or convertible into the common stock of a company at a prespecified conversion (or exchange) rate.
Corporation A business enterprise owned by one or more owners, called *stockholders*, that has a legal identity separate and distinct from that of its owners.
Correçao monetaria A system of monetary correction in Brazil designed to reflect the hyperinflationary effects of that country in reported financial statements.
Cost The total acquisition value of an asset; the value of resources given up to acquire an asset.
Cost of goods manufactured The total cost of goods manufactured in an accounting period; the sum of all product costs (such as direct materials, direct labor, and manufacturing overhead).
Cost of goods sold The value assigned to inventory units actually sold in a given accounting period.
Coupon interest rate (face rate) The rate of interest stated on the face of a debt instrument.
Countertrade A trade practice equivalent to barter or the exchange of goods and/or services for other goods and services (that is, no currency is exchanged); typically occurs as a consequence of restrictive currency laws.
Country risk analysis A process of identifying the various types of risks associated with investing or doing business in a given country.
Credit An entry on the right side of an account; credits increase liability, owners' equity, and revenue accounts but decrease asset and expense accounts.
Creditor An individual or company that loans cash or other assets to another person or company.
Cross-sectional analysis A process of analyzing financial data between or among firms in the same industry, or between a firm and industry averages, to identify comparative financial strengths and weaknesses.
Cruzada Plan Instituted in 1986; an attempt to rectify the hyperinflationary environment of Brazil. The heavily devalued cruzeiro was replaced by the cruzado as the primary monetary unit of Brazil.
Cumulative preferred stock A preferred stock in which any unpaid prior dividends accumulate year to year (called *dividends in arrears*) and must be paid in full before any current period dividends may be paid to either preferred or common shareholders.
Currency risk See *foreign exchange risk*.
Current asset Those resources of an enterprise, such as cash, inventory, or prepaid expenses,

whose consumption or use is expected to occur within the current operating cycle.

Current cost accounting A method of accounting in which financial data are expressed in terms of current rather than historical cost.

Current liability An obligation of an enterprise whose settlement requires the use of current assets or the creation of other current liabilities and occurs within one year.

Current maturity of long-term debt That portion of a long-term obligation that is payable within the next operating cycle or one year.

Current rate method A method of restating foreign financial statements using the current exchange rate.

Current ratio A measure of liquidity and short-term solvency calculated as current assets divided by current liabilities.

Date of declaration The calendar date on which the payment of a cash or stock dividend is officially declared by a company's board of directors.

Date of payment The calendar date on which a cash or stock dividend is actually paid or distributed.

Date of record The calendar date on which a shareholder must own a company's stock to be entitled to receive a declared dividend.

Debenture A general obligation bond of a company.

Debit An entry on the left side of an account; debits increase asset and expense accounts but decrease liability, owners' equity, and revenue accounts.

Debt-to-equity ratio A measure of solvency, calculated as long-term debt divided by total shareholders' equity.

Debt-to-total assets ratio A measure of solvency or long-term liquidity calculated as total debt divided by total assets.

Debt-to-total capitalization ratio A measure of solvency, calculated as long-term debt divided by the sum of total shareholders' equity and long-term debt.

Debtors An alternative designation for accounts and notes receivables, principally used in the financial statements of Great Britain and other Commonwealth companies.

Declining balance method A method to depreciate the cost of a tangible asset in which the allocated cost is greater in the early periods of the asset's life (that is, an accelerated method).

Default risk The probability (or risk) that a company will be unable to meet its short-term or long-term obligations.

Defeasance A method of early retirement of debt in which U.S. Treasury notes are purchased and then placed in a trust account to be used to retire the outstanding debt at its maturity.

Deferral A postponement in the recognition of an expense (such as Prepaid Insurance) or a revenue (such as Unearned Rent) account.

Deferred charge An asset that represents an expenditure whose related expense will not be recognized in the income statement until a future period. Prepaid rent is an example.

Deferred income taxes The portion of a company's income tax expense not currently payable that is postponed because of differences in the accounting policies adopted for financial statement purposes versus those policies used for tax reporting purposes.

Deferred revenue Revenue received as cash but not yet earned.

Deficit An accumulated loss in the retained earnings account; a debit balance in retained earnings.

Defined benefit plan A pension plan in which an employer promises to pay certain levels of future benefits to employees on their retirement from the company.

Defined contribution plan A pension plan in which an employer promises to make periodic payments to the plan on behalf of its employees.

Demand deposit A bank account that may be drawn against on demand.

Depletion A cost allocation method for natural resources.

Depreciation A systematic allocation process that allocates the acquisition cost of a long-lived asset over the expected productive life of the asset.

Devaluation A material downward adjustment of the exchange rate between two currencies.

Direct-financing-type lease A capital lease in which the lessor receives income only from financing the "purchase" of the leased asset.

Direct write-off method A method of accounting for uncollectible trade receivables in which no bad debt expense is recorded until specific receivables prove to be uncollectible.
Discount A reduction in the price paid for a security or a debt instrument below the security's face value.
Discount rate The rate of interest used to discount a future cash flow stream when calculating its present value.
Discounted cash flows The present value of a future stream of cash flows.
Discounting receivables The process of selling accounts or notes receivables to a bank or other financial company at a discount from the maturity value of the account or note.
Discretionary cash flows A measure of a company's cash flows from operations that are available to finance such discretionary corporate activities as the acquisition of another company, the early retirement of debt or equity, or some form of capital asset expansion; also referred to as *free cash flows*.
Dividend A distribution of the earned income of an enterprise to its owners.
Dividend payout ratio A measure of the percentage of net income (or cash flows from operations) paid out to shareholders as dividends; calculated as cash dividends divided by net income (or cash dividends divided by the cash flow from operations).
Dividends in arrears The dividends on a cumulative preferred stock that have been neither declared nor paid; not a legal liability of a company until declared.
Dividend yield A measure of the level of cash actually distributed to common stockholders, calculated as the cash divided per common share divided by the market price per common share.
Donated capital The increase in owners' equity resulting from a donation of an asset to a company.
Double-declining-balance depreciation A method of calculating depreciation by which a percentage equal to twice the straight-line percentage is multiplied by the declining book value to determine the depreciation expense for the period. Salvage value is ignored when calculating it.
Double-entry system An accounting record-keeping system that records all financial transactions in the accounting system using (at least) two data entries.
Double taxation The taxation of income at the company level plus the taxation of dividends declared and paid to investors from the company earnings.
Doubtful account An account receivable thought to be uncollectible.
Du Pont formula An overall indicator of corporate performance obtained by multiplying a company's asset turnover by its profit margin; equivalent to ROA or ROI.
Early retirement The process of prepaying, or retiring, outstanding debt before its stated maturity.
Earned surplus A term synonymous with *retained earnings*.
Earnings Income or profit.
Earnings per share A standardized measure of performance calculated as net income divided by the weighted-average number of common shares outstanding during an accounting period.
Economic exposure (risk) The risk of experiencing a real gain (loss) in purchasing power as a consequence of foreign exchange rate fluctuations.
Economic income The excess or additional resources of an enterprise resulting from its primary business activity and measured relative to the beginning level of resources.
Effective interest method A method to amortize a discount or a premium on a debt instrument based on the time value of money.
Effective interest rate The real rate of interest paid (or earned) on a debt instrument.
Efficient market hypothesis A theory to explain the functioning of capital markets in which stock and bond prices always reflect all publicly available information, and any new information is quickly impounded in security prices.
Emerging Issues Task Force (EITF) An affiliate organization of the FASB whose purpose is to address new accounting and reporting issues before divergent practice can become widely adopted.
Employee Retirement Income and Security Act (ERISA) Legislation passed by the U.S. Congress

in 1974 to govern the funding of private pension plans.

Entity principle An accounting convention that views a corporate enterprise as separate and distinct from its owners; thus, the financial statements of the corporation describe only the financial condition of the enterprise itself, not that of its shareholders.

Equity A claim against the assets of a company by creditors or the owners.

Equity in earnings of investee An income statement account representing an investor-company's percentage ownership of an investee's (or subsidiary's) net earnings.

Equity method A method to value intercorporate equity investments by adjusting the investor's cost basis for the percentage ownership in the investee's earnings (or losses) and for any dividends paid by the investee.

European currency unit (ECU) A currency intended to be used by all European Union members in conducting trade.

European exchange rate mechanism (ERM) A system created by the EU to stabilize the rate of exchange of currency between EU member nations.

European Union (EU) An organization of politically independent European nations (currently numbering 15), united to act as a single economic (trading) entity (or bloc); includes three cooperative alliances intended to improve the efficiency and competitive ability of its member nations: the European Coal and Steel Community, the European Atomic Energy Commission, and the European Economic Community.

Exchange Currency or legal tender used to facilitate trade between parties.

Exchange rate The rate at which one unit of currency may be purchased by another unit of currency.

Ex-dividend A condition of capital stock if sold (or purchased) after the date of record; that is, the purchaser of an ex-dividend stock is not entitled to receive the most recently declared dividend.

Executory contracts A category of legal agreements requiring some type of future performance.

Expenditure An outflow of cash, usually representing the acquisition of an asset or the incurring of an expense.

Expense An outflow of assets, an increase in liabilities, or both, from transactions involving an enterprise's principal business activity (such as sales of products or services).

Expropriation exposure (risk) The likelihood that a company's assets located in a foreign domain will be involuntarily appropriated by the local government, with or without compensation.

External reporting Financial reporting to stockholders and others outside an enterprise.

Extraordinary item A loss or gain that is both unusual in nature and infrequent in occurrence.

Face amount (maturity value) The value of a security as stated on the instrument itself.

Factor A financial corporation, bank, or other financial institution that buys accounts and notes receivables from companies; receivables may be purchased with or without recourse.

Factory overhead Another name for manufacturing overhead. For inventory valuation purposes, it is allocated to units of production by some type of rational systematic method.

Federal income tax The tax levied by the federal government on corporate and individual earnings.

Financial accounting The accounting rules and conventions used in preparing external accounting reports.

Financial Accounting Standards Board (FASB) An independent, private sector organization responsible for establishing generally accepted accounting principles.

Financial Reporting Council (FRC) An accounting standard-setting organization in the United Kingdom founded in 1990 that succeeded the Accounting Standards Committee; issues financial reporting standards.

Financial reporting standard (FRS) An official accounting pronouncement issued by the Financial Reporting Council of the United Kingdom.

Financial statements The basic accounting reports issued by a company, including the balance sheet, the income statement, and the statement of cash flows.

Financial statement analysis The process of reviewing, analyzing, and interpreting the basic financial statements to assess a company's operating performance and/or financial health.
Finished goods Inventory having completed the manufacturing process and ready for sale.
Finished goods inventory Fully assembled or manufactured goods available for sale and classified as a current asset on the balance sheet.
First-in, first-out (FIFO) An inventory cost-flow method that assigns the first cost value in finished goods inventory to the first unit sold and thus to cost of goods sold.
Fiscal year Any continuous 12-month period, usually beginning after a natural business peak.
Fixed assets A subcategory of noncurrent assets; usually represented by property, plant, and equipment.
FOB Free-on-board, some location. Examples are FOB shipping point and FOB destination. The location denotes the point at which title passes from the seller to the buyer.
Footnotes Written information by management designed to supplement the numerical data presented in a company's financial statement.
Foreign currency option contract A contract providing the right to buy or sell a set quantity of foreign currency at a present exchange rate within a specified future time frame; typically used to hedge foreign exchange risk exposure, and often thought of as *currency insurance*.
Foreign currency translation adjustment An owners' equity account measuring the change in value of a company's net assets held in a foreign country, attributable to changes in the exchange rate of a foreign currency as compared to the U.S. dollar.
Foreign exchange Any currency other than the one in which a company prepares its basic financial statements.
Foreign exchange risk The risk associated with changes in exchange rates between the U.S. dollar and foreign currencies when a company maintains operations in a foreign country.
Form 8-K A special SEC filing required when a material event or transaction occurs between Form 10-Q filing dates. Events that usually necessitate the filing of Form 8-K include a change in control or ownership of an enterprise, the acquisition or disposition of a significant amount of assets, a bankruptcy declaration, the resignation of an executive or director of an enterprise, or a change in the independent external auditor.
Form 10-K The annual financial report filing with the SEC required of all publicly held enterprises.
Form 10-Q The quarterly financial report filing with the SEC required of all publicly held enterprises; it is filed only for the first three quarters of a fiscal year.
Form 20-F The annual financial report filing with the SEC required of all foreign companies whose debt or equity capital is available for purchase/sale on a U.S. exchange.
Forward exchange contract A contract providing for the payment (receipt) of a foreign currency at a future date at a specified exchange rate; typically used to hedge foreign exchange risk exposure.
Forward exchange rate An exchange rate between two currencies quoted for 30, 60, 90, or 180 days in the future; a rate quoted currently for the exchange of currency at some future specified date.
Fourth Directive A European Union agreement, adopted in 1978, to (1) eliminate legal and bureaucratic obstacles to economic activity between EU member nations and (2) establish the basic reporting requirements and financial statement formats (that is, comparability) for companies operating in EU member nations.
Free cash flows See *discretionary cash flows*.
Freight-in Freight costs associated with the purchase and receipt of inventory.
Freight-out Freight costs associated with the sale and delivery of inventory.
Front-end loading An accounting process by which revenues (expenses) are recognized for income statement purposes before they have been earned (incurred).
Fully diluted earnings per share A standardized measure of performance calculated as net income applicable to common stock divided by the weighted-average number of common shares outstanding plus common stock equivalents and any other potentially dilutive securities.

Functional currency The currency of the primary business environment (country) of a company's operations.
Gain An increase in asset values, usually involving a sale (realized) or revaluation (unrealized), unrelated to the principal revenue-producing activity of a business.
General journal An accounting data file containing a chronological listing of financial transactions affecting an enterprise.
General ledger An accounting data file containing aggregate account information for all accounts listed in an enterprise's chart of accounts.
Generally accepted accounting principles (GAAP) Those methods identified by authoritative bodies (APB, FASB, SEC) as being acceptable for use in the preparation of external accounting reports.
Generally accepted auditing standards (GAAS) Those auditing practices and procedures established by the AICPA that are used by CPAs to evaluate a company's accounting system and financial results.
Gesellschaft mit beschränkter Haftung (GmbH) A privately held corporation in Germany.
Going-concern concept An accounting concept underlying the preparation of financial statements that assumes that the enterprise will continue its operations for the foreseeable future.
Goodwill An intangible asset representing the excess of the purchase price of acquired net assets over their fair market value.
Gross profit (gross margin) A measure of a company's profit on sales calculated as net sales minus the cost of goods or services sold.
Gross profit margin ratio A measure of profitability that assesses the percentage of each sales dollar that is recognized as gross profit (after deducting the cost of goods sold) and that is available to cover other operating expenses (such as selling, administrative, interest, and taxes).
Harmonization The attempt by various organizations (such as the IASC, the EU, and IOSCO) to establish a common set of international accounting and reporting standards.
Hedge A process of buying or selling commodities, forward contracts, or options for the explicit purpose of reducing or eliminating foreign exchange risk.
Hedged items Those accounts (assets, liabilities, revenues) or contracts for which an artificial or natural hedge exists.
Hedging instrument A forward exchange contract or option contract acquired to hedge some type of exposure (such as currency risk, expropriation risk, political risk).
Highest-in, first-out (HIFO) An inventory cost-flow method that assigns the highest cost value available in finished goods inventory to the first unit sold and thus cost of goods sold.
Historical cost principle An accounting principle that stipulates that all economic transactions should be recorded using the dollar value incurred at the time of the transaction.
Hold-to-maturity investments Securities, usually debt securities, owned by a company where management's intent is to hold them until the securities' stipulated maturity date.
Holding company (parent company) A company that owns a majority of the voting capital stock of another company.
Impairment A temporary or permanent reduction in asset value; usually necessitates a write-down in the asset's balance sheet value.
Income A generic term that may be used to indicate revenue from miscellaneous sources (such as interest income or rent income) or the excess of revenue over expenses for product sales or services.
Income and Loss Summary A temporary account used to transfer the net income or loss of an enterprise from the income statement to the retained earnings account on the balance sheet.
Income smoothing An accounting practice that implicitly or explicitly attempts to present a stable (but growing) measure of net income (such as straight-line depreciation).
Income statement (statement of earnings) An accounting statement describing the revenues earned and expenses incurred by an enterprise for a given period.
Independent auditor A professionally trained individual whose responsibilities include the objective review of a company's financial statements prepared for external distribution.
Inflation A phenomenon of generally rising prices.

Initial public offering (IPO) The first or initial sale of voting stock to the general market by a previously privately held concern.
Insolvent (bankrupt) A condition in which a company is unable to pay its current obligations as they come due.
Installment basis A method of recognizing revenue that parallels the receipt of cash.
Installment sale A credit sale in which the buyer agrees to make periodic payments, or installments, on the amount owed.
Instituto Brasileiro de Contadores (IBC) The professional society of certified public accountants in Brazil.
Intangible assets Those resources of an enterprise, such as goodwill, trademarks, or tradenames, that lack an identifiable physical presence.
Intercompany profit The profit resulting when one related company sells to another related company; intercompany profits are removed from the financial statements when consolidated financial statements are prepared.
Intercorporate investments Investments in the stocks and bonds of one company by another.
Interest coverage ratio See *times-interest-earned ratio.*
Interest expense The cost of borrowing funds.
Interim financial statements Financial statements prepared on a monthly or quarterly basis; usually unaudited.
Internal control structure The policies and procedures implemented by management to safeguard a company's assets and its accounting system against misapplication or misuse.
International accounting standards (IAS) The accounting and reporting standards adopted and promulgated by the IASC.
International Accounting Standards Committee (IASC) An association of professional accounting bodies formed in 1973 to develop and issue international accounting and reporting standards.
International Federation of Accountants (IFAC) An association of professional accounting organizations from more than 70 nations founded in 1977; largely concerned with developing international guidelines for the accounting profession in the areas of auditing, ethics, and education.
International Organization of Securities Commissions and Similar Organizations (IOSCO) An organization of securities regulatory agencies representing various member countries, whose goal is to assist in the creation and regulation of orderly international capital markets.
International Stock Exchange (ISE) The largest securities exchange in the United Kingdom.
Interperiod tax allocation The process of allocating the actual taxes paid by a company over the periods in which the taxes are recognized for accounting purposes.
Inventory The aggregate cost of salable goods and merchandise available to meet customer sales.
Inventory turnover A measure of the rate of inventory sales.
Inventory turnover ratio A measure of the effectiveness of inventory management calculated as the cost of goods sold for a period divided by the average inventory held during that period.
Investment ratio A cash flow ratio calculated as capital expenditures divided by the sum of depreciation and proceeds from the sale of assets; indicates the relative change in a company's investment in productive assets.
Investment tax credit A reduction in the current income taxes payable earned through the purchase of various applicable assets.
Investor company A company that holds an equity investment in another company (the investee company).
Issued shares The number of authorized shares of capital stock sold to shareholders less any shares repurchased and retired.
Japanese Securities and Exchange Law of 1948 Based largely on the U.S. securities laws of 1933 and 1934; requires companies issuing securities to the public to file financial statements (*zaimushohyo*) audited by an independent auditor with the Ministry of Finance; also known as *shokentorihikiho.*
Journal A chronological record of events and transactions affecting the accounts of a company recorded by means of debits and credits; a financial diary of a company.
Journal entry A data entry into a company's journal system.

Journalize The process of recording data in the journal system of a company by means of debits and credits.
Keiretsu An association of Japanese companies with interlocking shareholdings that provide economic support to one another; literally interpreted as "headless combines."
Last-in, first-out (LIFO) An inventory cost-flow method that assigns the last cost value in finished goods inventory to the first unit sold and thus to cost of goods sold.
Lease An agreement to buy or rent an asset.
Leasehold improvement Expenditures made by a lessee to improve or change a leased asset.
Lessee An individual or company who leases an asset.
Lessor The maker of a lease agreement; an individual or company who leases an asset to another individual or company.
Leverage The extent to which a company's long-term capital structure includes debt financing; a measure of a company's dependency on debt. A company with large quantities of debt is said to be highly leveraged.
Liabilities The dollar value of an enterprise's obligations to repay monies loaned to it, to pay for goods or services received by it, or to fulfill commitments made by it.
LIFO liquidation The sale of inventory units acquired or manufactured in a prior period at a lower cost; results when the level of LIFO inventory is reduced below its beginning-of-period level.
LIFO reserve An amount presented in the footnotes to the financial statements of companies employing the LIFO method of inventory valuation; calculated as the current cost of ending inventory minus the LIFO cost of ending inventory.
Limited company (Ltd) A limited liability but privately held company in the United Kingdom having no minimum capital requirement.
Limited liability The concept that shareholders in a corporation are not held personally liable for its losses and debts.
Limited partnership A partnership composed of at least one general partner and at least one limited partner, in which the general partner(s) assumes responsibility for all debts and losses of the partnership.
Line of credit An agreement with a bank by which an organization obtains authorization for short-term borrowings up to a specified amount.
Liquid assets Those current assets, such as cash, cash equivalents, or short-term investments, that either are in cash form or can be readily converted to cash.
Liquidating dividend A cash dividend representing a return of invested capital and, hence, a liquidation of a previous investment.
Liquidation The process of selling off the assets of a business, paying any outstanding debts, and then distributing any remaining cash to the owners.
Liquidity The short-term debt repayment ability of a company; a measure of a company's cash position relative to currently maturing obligations.
Listed company A company whose shares or bonds have been accepted for trading on a recognized securities exchange (such as the NYSE).
Long-term liabilities (noncurrent liabilities) The obligations of a company payable after more than one year.
Loss The excess of expenses over revenues for a single transaction.
Lower of cost or market A method to value inventories; the lower of an asset's cost basis or current market value is used to value the asset account for balance sheet purposes.
Machine-hour method A method to depreciate the cost of a machine or other equipment based on its actual usage.
Maintenance expenditure An expenditure to maintain the original productive capacity of an asset; deducted as an expense.
Managerial accounting The accounting rules and conventions used in the preparation of internal accounting reports.
Manufacturing overhead The factory-related costs indirectly associated with the manufacture or production of a good; for example, the costs of production-line supervision, maintenance of the production equipment, and depreciation of the factory building.
Market price The current fair value of an asset as established by an arm's length transaction between a buyer and a seller.

Marketable securities Short- or long-term investments in the stocks or bonds of other corporations.
Mark-to-market A method to value investments in trading or available-for-sale securities wherein they are reported on corporate balance sheets at their fair market value, not at cost.
Matching principle An accounting principle that stipulates that when revenues are reported, the expenses incurred to generate those revenues should be reported in the same accounting period.
Materiality principle An accounting principle underlying the preparation of financial statements; stipulates that only those transactions that might influence the decisions of a reasonable person should be disclosed in detail in the financial statements; all other information may be presented in summary format.
Maturity date The principal repayment date for a bond or debenture, specified as part of the indenture agreement.
Maturity value (face amount) The amount of cash required to satisfy an obligation at the date of its maturity.
Merger A combination of one or more companies into a single corporate entity.
Minority interest The percentage ownership in the net assets of a subsidiary held by investors other than the parent company.
Modified Accelerated Cost Recovery System (MACRS) A method to depreciate tangible assets placed in service after 1986 for U.S. income tax purposes.
Monetary assets Resources of an enterprise, such as cash and marketable securities, whose principal characteristic is monetary denomination.
Mortgage An agreement in which a lender (the mortgagee) agrees to loan money to a borrower (the mortgagor) to be repaid over a specified period of time and at a specified rate of interest.
Mortgage bond A bond secured or collateralized by a company's noncurrent assets, usually its property, plant, and equipment.
Multinational corporation (MNC) A for-profit organization with operations in two or more countries.
Multinational enterprise (MNE) A for-profit or not-for-profit organization with operations in two or more countries (such as a multinational corporation).
Multiple reporting Reporting by a company that requires the preparation of multiple sets of financial statements in the language and currency of another country.
Natural hedge A hedging instrument that exists as a consequence of the normal course of business.
Natural resources Noncurrent, nonrenewable resources such as oil and gas, coal, ore, and uranium.
Negative goodwill The excess of the net book value of an acquired company over the consideration paid for it.
Negotiable instruments Receivables, payables, or securities that can be bought and sold (that is, negotiated) between companies.
Net assets Total assets minus total liabilities; equal total owners' equity.
Net current assets Current assets minus current liabilities; working capital.
Net income (net earnings) The difference between the aggregate revenues and aggregate expenses of an enterprise for a given accounting period; when aggregate expenses exceed aggregate revenues, the term *net loss* is used.
Net realizable value The amount of funds expected to be received upon the sale or liquidation of an asset.
Net sales Total sales less sales returns and allowances and sales discounts.
Net worth (of an enterprise) Total assets minus total liabilities, or the value of owners' equity; also known as the *book value* of an enterprise.
Nonclassified balance sheet A balance sheet in which the assets and liabilities are not classified as current or noncurrent; in nonclassified balance sheets, assets and liabilities are considered to be noncurrent.
Noncurrent assets The long-lived resources of an enterprise, such as property, plant, and equipment, whose consumption or use is *not* expected to be completed within the current operating cycle.
Noncurrent asset turnover ratio A measure of the effectiveness of noncurrent asset management calculated as net sales for the period divided by the average balance of noncurrent assets.
Noncurrent liability An obligation of an enterprise whose settlement is not expected within one year.

Nondiversifiable risk Unique, nonsystematic risk associated with an investment that cannot be effectively hedged (through, for example, portfolio diversification).

Nonmonetary assets Those resources of an enterprise, such as inventory or equipment, whose principal characteristic is other than its monetary denomination or value.

Notes payable An obligation to repay money or other assets in the future evidenced by a signed contractual agreement or note.

Notes receivable Amounts due a company from customers who purchased goods or services on credit; the obligation is evidenced by a legal document called a *note*.

Off-balance-sheet debt Economic obligations that are not reported on the face of the balance sheet (such as operating leases).

Operating cycle The average length of time between the investment in inventory and the subsequent collection of cash from the sale of that inventory.

Operating expenses Expenses incurred in carrying out the operations of a business, for example, selling expenses.

Operating funds index A cash flow ratio calculated as net income divided by cash flow from operations that indicates the portion of operating cash flow provided by net income.

Operating lease A lease agreement in which the risks and rewards of asset ownership are retained by the lessor.

Operating leverage The extent to which a company operates with a high proportion of fixed costs.

Operational risk The probability that unforeseen or unexpected events will occur and consequently reduce or impair the revenue, earnings, and cash flow streams of a company.

Option A contract in which a buyer receives the right to buy inventory or stock in the future at a prespecified price.

Option contract Usually used for hedging purposes to grant one party the right to choose whether (and sometimes when) a currency exchange will actually take place.

Organization costs The expenditures associated with starting a new business venture, including legal fees and incorporation fees; frequently accounted for as an intangible asset of a company.

Outstanding shares The number of authorized shares of capital stock that have been sold to shareholders and are currently in the possession of shareholders; the number of issued shares less the shares held in treasury.

Owners' equity (shareholders' equity) The dollar value of the owners' (or shareholders') investment in an enterprise; may take two forms — the purchase of shares of stock or the retention of earnings in the enterprise for future use.

Paid-in-Capital in Excess of Par Value (Contributed Capital in Excess of Par Value) An owners' equity account reflecting the proceeds from the sale of capital stock in excess of the par value (or stated value) of the capital stock.

Participating preferred stock A preferred stock that entitles shareholders to share in any "excess dividend payments" (that is, after the common shareholders have received a fair dividend return).

Partnership A business enterprise jointly owned by two or more persons.

Par value A legal value assigned to a share of capital stock that must be considered in recording the proceeds received from the sale of the stock. See also *stated value*.

Passive investment An intercorporate investment in which the investor cannot (or does not) attempt to influence the operations of the investee-company.

Past service cost The cost of committed pension benefits earned by employees for periods of work prior to the adoption of a formal pension plan.

Payback period The period of time required to recover the cash outlay for an asset or other investment.

Pension A retirement plan for employees that will provide income to the employee upon retirement.

Percentage of completion A revenue recognition method in which total project or contract revenues are allocated between several accounting periods on the basis of the actual work completed in those periods.

Percentage of credit sales method A method of accounting for uncollectible trade receivables in which an estimate of the bad debts expense is recorded each period on the basis of the credit sales for the period.

Period costs Costs, such as administrative and selling expenses, associated with the accounting period in which they were incurred.

Periodic inventory system An inventory record-keeping system that determines the quantity of inventory on hand by a physical count.

Permanent accounts Those accounts, principally the balance sheet accounts, that are not closed at the end of an accounting period and that carry accounting information forward from one period to the next.

Permanent difference A difference in reported income or expenses between a company's tax return and its financial statements that will never reverse (that is, the difference is permanent).

Permanent earnings (cash flows) The recurring earnings (cash flows) of a company; earnings (cash flows) expected to recur in future periods.

Perpetual inventory system An inventory record-keeping system that continuously (or perpetually) updates the quantity of inventory on hand on the basis of units purchased, manufactured, and sold.

Pledging When assets are used as collateral for a bank loan, the assets are said to have been pledged.

Political exposure (risk) The degree of stability (or lack thereof) among political groups and the established government in a given country.

Pooling-of-interests A consolidation method that combines the financial results of a parent company and its subsidiary on the basis of existing book values.

Posting An accounting process involving the transfer of financial data from the general journal to the general ledger.

Preemptive right The privilege of a shareholder to maintain his or her proportionate ownership in a corporation by being able to purchase an equivalent percentage of all new capital stock offered for sale.

Preferred stock A (usually) nonvoting form of capital stock whose claims to the dividends and assets of a company precede those of common stockholders.

Premium An amount paid in excess of the face value of a security or debt instrument.

Prepaid expenses A current asset that represents prior expenditures and whose consumption is expected to occur in the next accounting period.

Present value The value today of a future stream of cash flows calculated by discounting the cash flows at a given rate of interest.

Price-earnings (P/E) ratio A market-based measure of the investment potential of a security, calculated as the market price per share divided by the earnings per share; also known as *P/E multiple*.

Price-level-adjusted financial statements Financial statements in which the account balances have been restated to reflect changes in price levels due to inflation.

Primary earnings per share A standardized measure of performance calculated as net income applicable to common stock (that is, net income minus preferred stock dividends) divided by the weighted-average number of common shares outstanding plus common stock equivalents.

Prime rate The interest rate charged by banks on borrowings by preferred customers.

Principal The remaining balance of an outstanding obligation to be paid in the future.

Prior period adjustment An accounting event or transaction that does not affect the current period's earnings but instead is reflected as an adjustment to retained earnings.

Private placement The sale, or "placement," of a significant number of stocks or bonds to a limited group of buyers; the securities are not offered for sale to the general marketplace.

Privatization The sale of all or part of a previously state-controlled entity to the general public.

Product cost A cost directly related to the production of a good or service — for example, the cost of goods sold.

Productivity index A cash flow ratio calculated as the cash flow from operations divided by the capital investment; indicates the relative cash productivity of a company's capital investments.

Profit The excess of revenues over expenses for a single transaction.

Profit and loss reserve The amount of retained earnings of a company; see *retained earnings*.

Profit margin The excess (or insufficiency) of operating revenues over operating expenses; a measure of a company's ability to generate profits from a given level of revenues; calculated as net income after tax divided by net sales; also known as the *return on sales ratio*.

Profitability The relative success of a company's operations; a measure of the extent to which accomplishment exceeded effort.

Pro forma (financial statement) A forecast or projected financial statement for a future accounting period.

Promissory note A written promise to pay a specific sum of money at a specific date; a liability.

Property, plant, and equipment The noncurrent assets of a company, principally used in the revenue-producing operations of the enterprise.

Proportionate consolidation A method of consolidating the financial results of a parent company and its subsidiary, in which only the proportion of net assets owned by the parent are consolidated; as a consequence there is no need for a minority interest account.

Proprietary company A label used in some countries to describe a privately held (or nonpublic) company.

Prospectus A document describing the nature of a business and its recent financial history, usually prepared in conjunction with an offer to sell capital stock or bonds by a company.

Proxy A legal document granting another person or company the right to vote for a shareholder on matters involving a shareholder vote.

Prudence The criterion used under German GAAP to establish the appropriateness and necessity of recognizing a loss contingency.

Public company One whose voting shares are listed for trading on a recognized securities exchange or are otherwise available for purchase (sale) by public investors.

Public limited company (Plc) A limited liability publicly held company in the United Kingdom; must have share capital of at least £50,000.

Purchase accounting A consolidation method in which the financial results of a parent-company and its subsidiary are combined using the fair market value of the subsidiary's net worth.

Purchase discount A cash discount (usually 2 percent) given to a buyer if the buyer pays for the purchases within the discount period (usually 10 days after purchase).

Purchase Discounts Lost An expense account representing the finance or interest costs incurred as a consequence of not paying for goods purchased on credit on a timely basis (such as 2/10, net 30).

Purchases Goods or inventory acquired for sale or manufacture.

Qualified opinion An opinion issued by an independent auditor indicating that the financial statements of a company are fairly presented on a consistent basis and use generally accepted accounting principles, but for which some concern or exception has been noted.

Quick assets Highly liquid, short-term assets such as cash, cash equivalents, short-term investments, and receivables.

Quick ratio (acid test ratio) A measure of liquidity and short-term solvency calculated as quick assets divided by current liabilities.

Ratio A financial indicator (such as the current ratio) formed by comparing two account balances (such as current assets and current liabilities).

Ratio analysis The process of analyzing and interpreting the ratios formed from two or more financial statement numbers.

Raw (basic) earnings per share (EPS) A measure of EPS, calculated as net income after taxes minus preferred dividends, divided by the weighted average number of common (or ordinary) shares outstanding.

Raw material inventory Materials and purchased parts awaiting assembly or manufacture; classified as a current asset on the balance sheet.

Realized loss (gain) A loss (gain) that is recognized in the financial statements, usually due to the sale of an asset.

Rear-end loading An accounting process by which expenses (revenues) are deferred for income statement purposes despite being incurred (earned).

Receivable turnover A measure of the rate of collections on sales.

Receivable turnover ratio A measure of the rate of collections on sales, calculated as net sales divided by the average receivable balance: the rate at which a company's receivables are converted to cash.

Recognition principle An accounting principle that stipulates that revenues should not be recorded in the accounting records until earned and that expenses should not be recorded until incurred.

Reconciliation report A statement or report reconciling the financial statements of a foreign entity to the accepted or prevailing accounting practice of another country.

Redeemable (callable) preferred stock A preferred stock that may be retired (redeemed or called) at the discretion of the issuing company, usually after a specified date and usually at a premium above the stated (or par) value of the preferred stock.

Redemption The retirement of preferred stock or bonds before a specified maturity date.

Registrar An independent agent, normally a bank or a trust company, that maintains a record of the number of shares of capital stock of a company that have been issued and to whom.

Relevance principle An accounting principle used to select which accounting information should be presented in a company's financial statements.

Reliability principle An accounting principle that stipulates that accounting information, and hence accounting reports, must be reliable to be useful to financial statement users.

Reorganization (quasi-reorganization) A process of changing the ownership structure of a company, usually as a direct result of a deficit in retained earnings.

Replacement cost The cost to reproduce or repurchase a given asset (such as a unit of inventory).

Reporting currency The currency used to measure and report a company's net assets (that is, the "local" currency).

Reserve An owners' equity account including the profit and loss reserve (retained earnings), revaluation reserve, capital reserve or share premium reserve (paid-in-capital in excess of par value), and legal reserves (those mandated by a given country's laws of incorporation).

Retained earnings Those earnings of an enterprise that have been retained in the enterprise (have not been paid out as dividends) for future corporate use.

Retained earnings — appropriated The amount of total retained earnings that has been allocated for specific corporate objectives, such as the redemption of debt or capital stock.

Retained earnings — restricted The amount of total retained earnings that is legally restricted from being paid out as dividends to shareholders; the restriction usually results from a borrowing agreement with a bank or other financial institution.

Return on common equity (ROCE) ratio A measure of profitability, calculated as the net income available to common shareholders divided by the average total common equity for the period.

Return on owners' equity (ROE) A measure of profitability; a measure of the relative effectiveness of a company in using the assets provided by the owners to generate net income; calculated as net income divided by average owners' equity.

Return on sales ratio (net profit margin ratio) A measure of profitability, calculated as the percentage of each sales dollar that is earned as net income; may be either retained in the company or paid out as a dividend.

Return on total assets (ROA) A measure of profitability that assesses the relative effectiveness of a company in using available resources to generate net income; also called the *return on investment*, or ROI; calculated as net income divided by average total assets.

Revaluation A material upward adjustment of the exchange rate between two currencies; an upward adjustment in asset value, usually undertaken to reflect the economic effects of inflation.

Revenue bond A bond secured or collateralized by a revenue stream from a particular group of assets.

Revenues The inflow of assets, the reduction in liabilities, or both, from transactions involving an enterprise's principal business activity (for example, sales of products or services).

Sale A legal term suggesting that the title to an asset has passed from a seller to a buyer.

Sale/Leaseback An accounting transaction in which an asset is first sold and then immediately leased back by the selling entity; a financing transaction.

Sales-type lease A capital lease that generates two income streams: (1) from the "sale" of the

asset and (2) from financing the "purchase" of the asset.
Salvage value (residual value) The amount that is expected to be recovered when an asset is retired, removed from active use, and sold.
Securities Act of 1933 A 1933 legislative act of the U.S. Congress that requires certain disclosures by enterprises issuing (or desiring to issue) shares of capital stock.
Securities and Exchange Commission (SEC) A government agency responsible for the oversight of U.S. securities markets; this agency also specifies the form and content of all financial reports by companies issuing securities to the public.
Securities Exchange Act of 1934 A 1934 legislative act of the U.S. Congress that created the Securities and Exchange Commission.
Self-sustaining foreign operation A foreign entity financially and operationally independent of its parent company.
Selling expense Expenses incurred directly as a consequence of selling and delivering a product to customers.
Sensitivity analysis A process by which the effect of a change in a given assumption is assessed (as in a pro forma analysis).
Seventh Directive A European Union agreement adopted in 1983, governing the preparation of consolidated financial statements for companies operating in EU member nations.
Sinking fund A trust account established in conjunction with the issuance of bonds into which funds are paid periodically to be used to retire the debt at maturity; an asset account.
Società a Responsibilità Limitada (S.r.l.) A closely held, limited liability entity in Italy.
Società per Azioni (S.p.A.) A publicly held (joint stock) company in Italy.
Sole proprietorship A business enterprise owned by one person.
Solvency The long-term debt repayment ability of a company; a measure of a company's long-term liquidity.
Special journal An accounting data file containing a chronological listing of special financial transactions (for example, cash purchases or cash receipts) affecting an enterprise.
Specific identification An inventory cost-flow method that assigns the actual cost of producing a specific unit to that unit; the only inventory method that matches exactly the cost flow and physical flow.
Spot rate The prevailing exchange rate between two currencies on a given date.
Standard product cost An inventory valuation method that uses estimated or projected costs of producing a product rather than actual costs.
Stated value The recorded accounting value of capital stock. See also *par value*.
Statement of cash flows An accounting statement describing the sources and uses of cash flows for an enterprise for a given period.
Statement of fund flows An accounting statement describing a company's inflows and outflows of funds over a given period; *funds* defined with reference to a company's cash, liquid assets, or working capital.
Statement of owners' equity (statement of shareholders' equity) An accounting statement describing the principal transactions affecting the owners' (or shareholders') interests in an enterprise for a given period.
Statement of retained earnings An accounting statement describing the beginning and ending balances in retained earnings and the major changes to the retained earnings account (for example, dividends and net income).
Statements of financial accounting standards (SFAS) The official pronouncements of the FASB.
Stewardship The management and supervision of enterprise resources.
Stock certificate A legal document evidencing the purchase of capital stock in a company.
Stock depositary receipt (SDR) A beneficial ownership share in a foreign entity held by a trustee (such as a bank or brokerage firm) on behalf of the investor; see *American depositary receipt*.
Stock dividend A distribution of additional shares of capital stock to a company's stockholders.
Stockholders' equity The owners' equity of a corporation; comprises paid-in capital and retained earnings.
Stock option A right issued by a company to its employees entitling an employee to buy a set

quantity of capital stock in the future at a prespecified price.

Stock split An increase (a forward split) or a decrease (a reverse split) in the number of shares issued by a company; equivalent to a large stock dividend.

Stock warrant (stock right) A certificate issued by a company that carries the right or privilege to buy a set quantity of capital stock in the future at a prespecified price.

Straight-line method A method to depreciate the cost of a tangible asset or to amortize the cost of an intangible asset in which the allocated cost is constant over the life of the asset.

Subchapter S corporation A small corporation that pays no corporate taxes; all earnings are divided among the owners and are taxed at the individual level.

Subsidiary A company in which an investor company (the parent) holds an equity investment in excess of 50 percent of the voting stock of the investee company.

Subsidiary ledger An accounting data file containing detailed account information to supplement or explain the aggregate account balance contained in the general ledger.

Sum-of-the-years' digits method A method to depreciate the cost of a tangible asset in which the allocated cost is greater in the early periods of the asset's life (that is, an accelerated method).

Take-or-pay contract An executory contract by which one party agrees to pay for certain inventory (or other products) regardless of whether the inventory is physically received or not.

Tangible asset Those resources of an enterprise, such as property, plant, and equipment, that possess physical characteristics or have a physical presence.

Temporal method A method of translating foreign financial statements in which cash, receivables, and payables are translated at the exchange rate in effect at the balance sheet date; other assets and liabilities translated at historical rates; revenues and expenses translated at the weighted-average rate for the period.

Temporary accounts Those accounts that are closed at the end of each accounting period — for example, the income statement accounts, dividends, and the income and loss summary.

Temporary difference A difference in reported income or expenses between a company's tax return and its financial statements that will reverse out in some future period.

Times-interest-earned ratio A measure of solvency and leverage calculated as net income plus interest and income taxes divided by interest charges; a measure of the extent to which current interest payments are covered by current earnings.

Time value of money Because money can always be invested at a bank to earn interest for the period it is on deposit, money is said to have a "time value."

Timing differences Differences in the timing of the reporting of certain revenues and expenses for tax purposes and for external financial reporting purposes.

Total asset turnover ratio A measure of asset management effectiveness reflecting the rate at which sales are generated from a company's investment in assets; calculated as net sales divided by average total assets.

Total debt-to-total assets ratio A measure of solvency or long-term liquidity, calculated as total debt divided by total assets.

Trade payables See *accounts payable* and *notes payable*.

Trade receivables See *accounts receivable*.

Trading investment A security owned by a company where management's intent is to sell it in the very near term.

Transaction exposure (risk) A source of foreign exchange risk resulting from exchange rate fluctuations between the date on which a contract is signed or goods delivered and the date of payment.

Transaction principle A concept underlying the preparation of financial statements that requires that the source of all accounting information be economic transactions affecting an enterprise and its resources.

Transfer agent An independent agent, usually a bank or a trust company, that maintains a record of, and executes all, capital stock transfers and sales, as well as the payment of dividends on those shares.

Transitory earnings (cash flows) The nonrecurring earnings (cash flows) of a company;

earnings (cash flows) that are not expected to reoccur in future periods.

Translation exposure (risk) A source of foreign exchange risk resulting from the restatement of foreign financial statements denominated in a foreign currency into U.S. dollar-equivalents; also known as *accounting exposure*.

Treasury stock Outstanding capital stock that has been repurchased but not retired and is usually held to be reissued at some future date.

Trend analysis The analysis of ratios or absolute account balances over one or more accounting periods to identify the direction or trend of a company's financial health.

Trial balance A listing of the preadjusted, preclosing account balances from the general ledger designed to verify that the sum of the accounts with debit balances equals the sum of the accounts with credit balances.

True and fair view The current standard of precision required of all audited financial data in the EU; analogous to the "fairly presented" standard used in the United States.

Turnover A measure of the rate of sales of goods or services; in the United Kingdom, a measure of net sales or net revenues.

Uncollectible account An account receivable that a company expects not to be able to collect.

Underwriter A brokerage house or investment banker hired by a company to help sell a bond or stock offering.

Unearned revenue Revenue that is received as cash but that has not yet been earned.

Unit-of-production method A method to depreciate the cost of a tangible asset or to deplete the cost of a natural resource; the allocated cost is based on the actual production by the asset.

Unleveraged ROA (UROA) A refinement of the return on assets (ROA) ratio, obtained by restating net income to include interest charges on an aftertax basis (that is, net income plus interest expense net of tax benefits).

Unrealized change in value of available-for-sale investment portfolio A contra owners' equity (addendum) account representing a write-down (write-up) in the available-for-sale portfolio for temporary market fluctuations, as a consequence of the mark-to-market method.

Unrealized loss (gain) A loss (gain) that is recognized in the financial statements but is not associated with an asset sale; usually involves a revaluation of an asset value.

Useful life The estimated productive life of a noncurrent asset.

Value-added statement A financial statement prepared by some foreign companies reflecting a measure of the wealth created by the operations of the company and the distribution of that wealth among its major constituents (for example, employees, investors, and the government).

Value-added tax A tax levied at each stage in the production and distribution chain on the basis of the value that is added to a product as it passes through a given stage.

Vendor A company selling goods or services.

Vested benefits Pension benefits owed to employees at retirement regardless of whether they continue to be employed by the company until they reach retirement age.

Warrant A legal document enabling the holder to buy a set number of shares of capital stock at a prespecified price within a set period of time.

Warranty obligation An obligation for future costs to maintain a product sold in good working condition.

Wasting assets Noncurrent assets, such as natural resources, that decrease in value as a result of depletion or consumption of the asset.

Weighted-average cost method An inventory cost-flow method that assigns the average cost of available finished goods, weighted by the number of units available at each price, to a unit sold and thus cost of goods sold, and to ending inventory.

Wirtschaftsprüfer (WP) A certified public accountant in Germany.

With (without) recourse Terms of the sale of an account or note receivable. A sale with recourse obligates the selling company to "make good" the receivable in the event that the factor is unable to collect on the receivable; a sale without recourse obligates the factor to assume all liability for noncollectibility.

Work in process inventory Partially completed goods or products; classified as a current asset on the balance sheet.

Working capital A measure of liquidity or short-term solvency, calculated as total current assets minus total current liabilities.

Working capital maintenance agreement An executory contract by which one entity guarantees to maintain the level of working capital of a second entity; usually arises as a consequence of a borrowing agreement by the second entity for which the first party becomes a guarantor.

World standards report A set of financial statements prepared according to IASC accounting standards.

Zaibatsu Japanese industrial conglomerates that existed prior to World War II but were disbanded and have been subsequently replaced by *keiretsu*.

INDEX

A

B

C

D

E

G

H

I

J

K

L

P

Q

R

S

U

V

W

Y

Z